CATALOGUE OF THE BOOKS OF THE DEAD AND OTHER RELIGIOUS TEXTS IN THE BRITISH MUSEUM

Volume IV

Books of Breathing and Related Texts

CATALOGUE OF THE BOOKS OF THE DEAD AND OTHER RELIGIOUS TEXTS
IN THE BRITISH MUSEUM

Volume IV

Books of Breathing and Related Texts

François-René Herbin

THE BRITISH MUSEUM PRESS

Published in 2008 by The British Museum Press
A division of The British Museum Company Ltd
38 Russell Square, London WC1B 3QQ
www.britishmuseum.org

A catalogue record for this book is available from the British Library

ISBN 978-0-7141-1968-7

Designed by Nigel Strudwick

Typeset in Meridian by Nigel Strudwick
using typeset hieroglyphs from the Cleo font designed by Cleo Huggins
Additional diacritical characters by Nigel Strudwick

Printed and bound in the UK by Cambridge Printing

Contents

List of papyri in numerical order	**vii**	
Preface	**viii**	
Foreword	**ix**	
Author's Note	**x**	
Abbreviations	**xi**	
Series and periodicals	xi	
Monographs	xii	
Introduction	**1**	
Appendix: A note on the Dossier Soter	4	
Ch. 1 Book of Breathing made by Isis for her brother Osiris	**11**	
P. BM EA 10048	11	Pls 1–14
P. BM EA 9995	37	Pls 15–24
P. BM EA 10260	45	Pls 25–8
Ch. 2 First Book of Breathing	**50**	
P. BM EA 10191	50	Pls 29–32
Abridged versions	**76**	
P. BM EA 10109	76	Pls 33–6
P. BM EA 10199	78	Pls 37–9
P. BM EA 10206	80	Pls 40–1
P. BM EA 10283	81	Pls 42–3
P. BM EA 10303	83	Pls 44–5
P. BM EA 10337	83	Pls 46–8
P. BM EA 10338	84	Pls 49–50
P. BM EA 10705 (part)	86	Pls 51–2
P. BM EA 71513B	87	Pls 53–4
P. BM EA 71513C	88	Pls 55–6
Ch. 3 Second Book of Breathing	**90**	
P. BM EA 10110+10111	90	Pls 57–9
P. BM EA 10304	100	Pls 60–1

Abridged Versions	**103**	
P. BM EA 9977	103	Pls 62–3
P. BM EA 10124	104	Pls 64–7
P. BM EA 10192	105	Pls 68–9
P. BM EA 10264	106	Pls 70–1
P. BM EA 10275	107	Pls 72–3
P. BM EA 10282	108	Pls 74–5
P. BM EA 10286	109	Pls 76–7
P. BM EA 10331	110	Pls 78–9
P. BM EA 71513D	111	Pls 80–1
Ch. 4 First and Second Book of Breathing	**112**	
P. BM EA 10125	112	Pls 82–5
P. BM EA 71513A	114	Pls 86–9
Ch. 5 Related and Original Texts	**117**	
P. BM EA 10108	117	Pls 90–3
P. BM EA 10112	123	Pls 94–7
P. BM EA 10115	125	Pls 98–9
P. BM EA 10116	126	Pls 100–3
P. BM EA 10123	132	Pls 104–7
P. BM EA 10194	134	Pls 108–9
P. BM EA 10201	135	Pls 110–13
P. BM EA 10254	140	Pls 114–17
P. BM EA 10256	141	Pls 118–19
P. BM EA 10261	142	Pl. 120
P. BM EA 10264A	142	Pls 121–2
P. BM EA 10285	143	Pls 123–6
P. BM EA 10290	144	Pls 127–8
P. BM EA 10340	146	Pls 129–30
P. BM EA 10343	147	Pls 131–4
P. BM EA 10344	148	Pls 135–6
P. BM EA 10718	149	Pls 137–40
Ch. 6 Book of Traversing Eternity	**151**	
P. BM EA 10091	151	Pls 141–2
P. BM EA 10114	153	Pls 143–4
P. BM EA 10262+10263	157	Pls 145–6
P. BM EA 10314	158	Pls 147–9
Ch. 7 Fragments	**160**	Pls 150–2
Index I: General Vocabulary	**163**	
Index II: Toponyms	**189**	
Index III: Names	**192**	
Divine names	192	
Personal names	196	
Titles	198	
List of Manuscripts Cited	**199**	
Plates	**210**	

List of papyri in numerical order

Papyrus	page no.	plate nos
P. BM EA 9977	103	Pls 62–3
P. BM EA 9995	37	Pls 15–24
P. BM EA 10048	11	Pls 1–14
P. BM EA 10091	151	Pls 141–2
P. BM EA 10108	117	Pls 90–3
P. BM EA 10109	76	Pls 33–6
P. BM EA 10110+10111	90	Pls 57–9
P. BM EA 10112	123	Pls 94–7
P. BM EA 10114	153	Pls 143–4
P. BM EA 10115	125	Pls 98–9
P. BM EA 10116	126	Pls 100–3
P. BM EA 10123	132	Pls 104–7
P. BM EA 10124	104	Pls 64–7
P. BM EA 10125	112	Pls 82–5
P. BM EA 10191	50	Pls 29–32
P. BM EA 10192	105	Pls 68–9
P. BM EA 10194	134	Pls 108–9
P. BM EA 10199	78	Pls 37–9
P. BM EA 10201	135	Pls 110–13
P. BM EA 10206	80	Pls 40–1
P. BM EA 10254	140	Pls 114–17
P. BM EA 10256	141	Pls 118–19
P. BM EA 10260	45	Pls 25–8
P. BM EA 10261	142	Pl. 120
P. BM EA 10262+10263	157	Pls 145–6

Papyrus	page no.	plate nos
P. BM EA 10264	106	Pls 70–1
P. BM EA 10264A	142	Pls 121–2
P. BM EA 10275	107	Pls 72–3
P. BM EA 10282	108	Pls 74–5
P. BM EA 10283	81	Pls 42–3
P. BM EA 10285	142	Pls 123–6
P. BM EA 10286	109	Pls 76–7
P. BM EA 10290	144	Pls 127–8
P. BM EA 10303	83	Pls 44–5
P. BM EA 10304	100	Pls 60–1
P. BM EA 10314	158	Pls 147–9
P. BM EA 10331	110	Pls 78–9
P. BM EA 10337	83	Pls 46–8
P. BM EA 10338	84	Pls 49–50
P. BM EA 10340	146	Pls 129–30
P. BM EA 10343	147	Pls 131–4
P. BM EA 10344	148	Pls 135–6
P. BM EA 10705 (part)	86	Pls 51–2
P. BM EA 10718	149	Pls 137–40
P. BM EA 71513A	114	Pls 86–9
P. BM EA 71513B	87	Pls 53–4
P. BM EA 71513C	88	Pls 55–6
P. BM EA 71513D	111	Pls 80–1
Fragments	160	Pls 150–2

Preface

This catalogue is the fourth in the British Museum series originally devoted solely to Books of the Dead but now extended to include similar religious documents. It publishes in full a large and important corpus of so-called Books of Breathing and related texts of the Graeco-Roman Period, each of which is reproduced in photograph, with transcription, translation and commentary. The majority of these papyri, almost fifty in total, are published here for the first time. Authored by Dr François Herbin of the Centre national de la recherche scientifique in Paris, a specialist in Late Egyptian religious texts, the volume represents a substantial contribution to new knowledge in an area of Egyptology which is now attracting increasing scholarly attention.

A vital adjunct to Dr Herbin's study has been the conservation and remounting of some of the papyri, expertly carried out by Bridget Leach of the Museum's Department of Conservation and Science. The photographs are the work of British Museum Photography and Imaging. The original French manuscript was translated into English by Dr Stephen Quirke, now of the Petrie Museum. Subsequent editorial assistance has been provided by Dr Nigel Strudwick and especially Dr Richard Parkinson of the Department of Ancient Egypt and Sudan. The catalogue has been guided through into its final form by Teresa Francis of the British Museum Press.

W.V. Davies
Keeper
Department of Ancient Egypt and Sudan
The British Museum

Foreword

The collection of the late hieratic religious papyri kept in the British Museum, especially of the Graeco-Roman Period, is no doubt one of the most important in the world not only because of the number of papyri, but also because of their diversity. Most of them bear funerary texts which were laid beside the deceased as guides in the underworld, although temple rituals, liturgies and texts of magical inspiration are also found. It is the whole corpus of these manuscripts, excepting the Books of the Dead, that I propose to publish in a sequence of three studies of late Egyptian religious texts.

This volume deals with Books of Breathing and related texts, i.e. about fifty papyri, all of the Ptolemaic or Roman Period. Although some of them were already known from older or more modern studies (e.g. Budge for P. BM EA 9995, Lieblein for P. BM EA 10108, 10109, 10110 and 10112, and Roccati for P. BM EA 10194 and 10201), it was of obvious interest to gather all the manuscripts of the British Museum collection into one edition. For that work, I am indebted to individuals and institutions whose help and cooperation were most useful. Here I would like to thank Mr W.V. Davies, Keeper of the Department of Ancient Egypt and Sudan, who entrusted me with the responsibility of publishing all the papyri and gave me complete liberty to pursue and fulfil the study of this prolific material. I am particularly grateful to Dr S. Quirke for translating the original French version of my work into English and for his friendly and constant assistance in the Egyptian Department of the British Museum. I express also my heartfelt gratitude to Dr R. Parkinson and Dr N. Strudwick, who took charge of revising the manuscript for publication. Because of the number of unpublished texts used in the commentary, I owe special thanks to the authorities of the Egyptian Department in the Louvre Museum for free consultation of its rich collection of Books of Breathing, and to those of the Bibliothèque Nationale de Paris, of the Kunsthistorisches Museum in Vienna and of the Ägyptisches Museum zu Berlin, who all provided me with photographs of documents.

F.R. Herbin
Université Paris IV
Centre de recherches égyptologiques de la Sorbonne
'Etat, religion et société dans l'Egypte ancienne et en Nubie'
CNRS, UMR 8152
1 rue Victor Cousin, 75005 Paris

Author's Note

It seems necessary to say here a few words on the method followed for the compilation of this catalogue, which aims to be both simple and practical. The classification of the documents has been made easier since the ancient Egyptians themselves distinguished several kinds of Books of Breathing, namely the First and the Second Book, and the Book of Breathing made by Isis for her brother Osiris. These categories are far from being exclusive, but make up the focus around which other texts of a less explicit, formal definition can all the same find a suitable place. Among them are the so-called original texts and the Book of Traversing Eternity. The catalogue entry for each papyrus therefore contains a general introduction, a translation and a commentary. The introduction includes a concise description of documents, comprising information about provenance and date, as well as names and titles of the owners.

The need to examine the papyri separately has led to the making of a complete translation for each text, rather than referring to a more or less representative model from which the parallel versions often digress. On the other hand, no translation is given for small fragments, for which only transliterations and references to main corresponding versions are provided.

The commentary requires some explanation. Following the method already used in my work on the Book of Traversing Eternity, each sequence of the papyri studied here is taken into account, not only the words or passages considered, rightly or wrongly, interesting. When a text is known through several copies, as is often the case in this catalogue, only the most important receives a detailed commentary in which variant readings found in other manuscripts from the British Museum and elsewhere are gathered. For that purpose all accessible publications on the matter have been consulted, as well as many unpublished texts, especially from the Louvre Museum. It goes without saying that the list of parallel versions and other citations mentioned in this catalogue is not exhaustive and is necessarily only a selection. Except for editions of the Book of the Dead, the published papyri are quoted without bibliographical references, which will be found at the end of the book in the complete list of all cited documents.

Abbreviations

Series and periodicals

ÄAT = Ägypten und Altes Testament. Studien zu Geschichte, Kultur und Religion Ägyptens und des Alten Testaments. Wiesbaden.

ADAIK = Abhandlungen des Deutschen Archäologischen Instituts Kairo. Glückstadt, Hamburg, New York, then Mainz.

AegTrev = Aegyptiaca Treverensia. Mainz.

ÄgAbh = Ägyptologische Abhandlungen. Wiesbaden.

ÄgFo = Ägyptologische Forschungen. Glückstadt, Hamburg and New York.

Ann. EPHE^{V} = Annuaire de l'Ecole Pratique des Hautes Etudes, Ve section. Paris.

ASAE = Annales du Service des Antiquités de l'Egypte. Cairo.

AV = Archäologische Veröffentlichungen des Deutschen Archäologischen Instituts, Abteilung Kairo. Berlin, then Mainz.

BiAe = Bibliotheca Aegyptiaca. Brussels.

BdE = Bibliothèque d'Étude. Cairo.

Bessarione = Bessarione. Pubblicazione periodica di studi orientali. Rome

BIE = Bulletin de l'Institut d'Egypte. Cairo.

BIFAO = Bulletin de l'Institut Français d'Archéologie Orientale. Cairo.

BiOr = Bibliotheca Orientalis. Leiden.

BMMA = Bulletin of the Metropolitan Museum of Art. New York.

CASAE = Cahiers des Annales du Service des Antiquités. Cairo.

CdE = Chronique d'Égypte. Brussels.

CGC = Catalogue Général du Musée du Caire. Cairo.

DemSt. = Demotische Studien. Leipzig and Sommerhausen.

Enchoria = Enchoria. Zeitschrift für Demotistik und Koptologie. Wiesbaden.

EPRO = Etudes préliminaires aux religions orientales dans l'empire romain. Leiden.

FIFAO = Fouilles de l'Institut Français d'Archéologie Orientale. Cairo.

GM = Göttinger Miszellen. Beiträge zur ägyptologischen Diskussion. Göttingen.

HPBM = Hieratic Papyri in the British Museum. London.

HTBM = Hieroglyphic Texts from Egyptian Stelae, etc. in the British Museum. London.

JAOS = Journal of the American Oriental Society. New Haven.

JARCE = Journal of the American Research Center in Egypt. Boston.

JEA = Journal of Egyptian Archaeology. London.

JEOL = Jaarbericht van het Vooraziatisch–Egyptisch Gezelschap/ Genootschap 'Ex Oriente Lux'. Leiden.

JNES = Journal of Near Eastern Studies. Chicago.

Kêmi = Kêmi. Revue de phologie et d'archéologie égyptiennes et coptes. Paris.

MÄS = Münchner ägyptologische Studien. Berlin.

MDAIK = Mitteilungen des Deutschen Archäologischen Instituts, Abteilung Kairo. Berlin and Wiesbaden, then Mainz.

MIO = Mitteilungen des Instituts für Orientforschung. Berlin.

MIFAO = Mémoires publiés par les membres de l'Institut Français d'Archéologie Orientale. Cairo.

MMAF = Mémoires publiés par les membres de la Mission archéologique Française au Caire. Paris and Cairo.

OA = Oriens Antiquus. Rome.

OBO = *Orbis Biblicus et Orientalis*. Freiburg and Göttingen.

OIP = Oriental Institute Publications. Chicago.

OLA = Orientalia Lovaniensia Analecta. Louvain.

OLP = *Orientalia Lovaniensia Periodica*. Louvain.

OLZ = *Orientalistische Literaturzeitung*. Leipzig.

OMRO = *Oudheidkundige Mededelingen uit het Rijksmuseum van Oudheden te Leiden*. Leiden.

Orientalia = *Orientalia*. Nova series, Rome.

PSBA = *Proceedings of the Society of Biblical Archaeology*. London.

RAPH = *Recherches d'archéologie, de philologie et d'histoire*. Cairo.

RdE = *Revue d'Égyptologie*. Paris, Cairo and Louvain.

RHR = Revue de l'histoire des religions. Paris.

RT = *Recueil de travaux relatifs à la philologie et à l'archéologie égyptiennes et assyriennes*. Paris.

SAOC = Studies in Ancient Oriental Civilization. Chicago.

SAK = *Studien zur altägyptischen Kultur*. Hamburg.

SDAIK = Sonderschriften des Deutschen Archäologischen Instituts, Anteilung Kairo. Mainz.

SEAP = Studi di Egittologia e di Antichità Puniche. Pisa.

SO = Sources Orientales, 8 vols. Paris.

UGAÄ = Untersuchungen zur Geschichte und Altertumskunde Ägyptens. Leipzig and Berlin.

ZÄS = *Zeitschrift für ägyptische Sprache und Altertumskunde*. Leipzig and Berlin.

WZKM = *Wiener Zeitschrift für die Kunde des Morgenlandes*. Vienna.

ZPE = *Zeitschrift für Papyrologie and Epigraphik*. Bonn.

Monographs

AeIB = G. Roeder, *Ägyptische Inschriften aus den Staatlichen Museen zu Berlin. 2 vols*. Leipzig 1901–24.

Allen, *Book of the Dead* = G. Allen, *The Book of the Dead or going forth by day. Ideas of ancient Egyptians concerning the Hereafter as expressed in their own Terms* (SAOC 37). Chicago 1974.

Allen, *Book of the Dead Documents* = T.G. Allen, *The Egyptian Book of the Dead Documents in the Oriental Institute Museum at the University of Chicago* (OIP 82). Chicago 1960.

Assmann, *Liturgische Lieder* = J. Assmann, *Liturgische Lieder an den Sonnengott. Untersuchungen zur altägptischen Hymnik* (*MÄS* 19). Berlin 1969.

Assmann, *Sonnenhymnen* = J. Assmann, *Sonnenhymnen in thebanischen Privatgräbern* (Theben 1). Mainz 1983.

BD, ed. Budge = E.A.W. Budge, *The Book of the Dead. The Chapters of coming forth by day. The Egyptian text in hieroglyphic edited from numerous papyri*. 3 vols. London 1898.

BD, ed. Lepsius = R. Lepsius, *Das Todtenbuch der Ägypter nach dem hieroglyphischen Papyrus in Turin*. Leipzig 1842.

BD, ed. Naville = E. Naville, *Das ägyptische Totenbuch der XVIII. bis XX. Dynastie*. 3 vols. Berlin 1886.

BD, ed. Pleyte = W. Pleyte, *Chapitres supplementaires du Livre des Morts 162 à 174*. 3 vols. Leiden 1881.

Bénédite, *Philae* = G. Bénédite, *Le temple de Philae* (*MMAF* 13). 2 fasc. Paris 1893–5.

Bierbrier (ed.), *Portraits and Masks* = M.L. Bierbrier (ed.), *Portraits and Masks: Burial Customs in Roman Egypt*. London 1997.

Boeser, *Beschreibung* = P.A.A. Boeser, *Beschreibung der Aegyptischen Sammlung der Niederländischen Reichsmuseums der Altertümer in Leiden* I–XIV. The Hague 1908–32.

Borchardt, *Statuen und Statuetten* = L. Borchardt, *Statuen und Statuetten von Königen und Privatleuten*. 5 vols (*CGC*). Cairo 1911–36.

Brugsch, *Thes.* = H. Brugsch, *Thesaurus inscriptionum Aegyptiacarum. Altaegyptische Inschriften. Gesammelt, verglichen, übertragen, erklärt und autographiert*. Leipzig 1883–91.

Burkard, *Die Papyrusfunde* = G. Burkard, *Die Papyrusfunde. Nach Vorarbeiten von D. Bidoli*. Grabung im Asasif 1963–1970, 3 (*AV* 22). Mainz 1986.

Caminos, *LEM* = R.A. Caminos, *Late Egyptian Miscellanies*. Oxford 1954.

Chassinat, *Khoiak* = E. Chassinat, *Le mystère d'Osiris au mois de Khoiak*. Cairo 1966–8.

CIG = A. Boeckh, *Corpus Inscriptionum Graecarum*. 4 vols. Berlin, 1828–77.

CT = A. De Buck, *The Egyptian Coffin Texts* I–VII (OIP 34, 49, 64, 67, 73, 81, 87). Chicago 1935–61.

Demot. Nb. = E. Lüddeckens, *Demotisches Namenbuch*. Wiesbaden 1980– .

Dendara = E. Chassinat and F. Daumas, *Le temple de Dendara* I–VIII. Cairo 1934–78; F. Daumas, *Le temple de Dendara* IX. Cairo 1987; S. Cauville, *Le temple de Dendara* X. *Les chapelles osiriennes*. Cairo 1997.

Devéria, *Catalogue* = T. Devéria, *Catalogue des manuscripts égyptiens écrits sur papyrus, toile, tablettes et ostraca en caractères hiéroglyphiques, hiératiques, démotiques, grecs, coptes, arabes et latins qui sont conservés au Musée égyptien du Louvre*. Paris 1872.

Dümichen, *HI* = J. Dümichen, *Historische Inschriften altägyptischer Denkmäler* I–IV. Leipzig 1866–85.

Edfou = E. de Rochemonteix and E. Chassinat, *Le Temple d'Edfou* I–XIV (MMAF 10–11 and 20–31); S. Cauville and D. Devauchelle, *Le Temple d'Edfou* XV (MMAF 32). Paris and Cairo 1897–1985.

Edwards, *HPBM IV* = I.E.S. Edwards, *Hieratic Papyri in the British Museum. Fourth Series. Oracular amuletic decrees of the late New Kingdom*. 2 vols. London 1960.

Egyptian Religion = S.A.B. Mercer (ed.), *Egyptian Religion* I–IV. New York.

Gardiner, *AEO* = Gardiner, *Ancient Egyptian Onomastica*. 3 vols. Oxford 1947.

Gardiner, *HPBM* III = A.H. Gardiner, *Hieratic Papyri in the British Museum*. Third Series. Chester-Beatty Gift. 2 vols. London 1935.

Gauthier, *Cercueils* I = H. Gauthier, *Cercueils anthropoïdes des prêtres de Montou* I (CGC). Cairo 1913.

GDG = H. Gauthier, *Dictionnaire des noms géographiques contenus dans les textes hiéroglyphiques* I–VII. Cairo 1925–31.

Golenischeff, *Pap. hiérat.* I = W. Golenischeff, *Papyrus hiératiques* I (CGC). Cairo 1927.

Goyon, *Les dieux gardiens* = J.C. Goyon, *Les dieux-gardiens et la genèse des temples (d'après les textes égyptiens de l'époque gréco-romaine). Les soixante d'Edfou et les soixante-dix-sept dieux de Pharbaethos*. 2 vols (*BdE* 93). Cairo 1985.

Goyon, *Rituels funéraires* = J.C. Goyon, *Rituels funéraires de l'ancienne Egypte*. Paris 1972.

Gutbub, *Textes fondamentaux* = A. Gutbub, *Textes fondamentaux de la théologie de Kom Ombo*. 2 vols (*BdE* 47). Cairo 1973.

Haikal, *Two Hier. Fun. Pap.* I–II = F. Haikal, *Two Hieratic Funerary Papyrus of Nesmin*. 2 vols (*BiAe* 14–15). Brussels 1970 and 1972.

Hermann, *Stelen* = A. Hermann, *Die Stelen der Thebanischen Felsgräber der 18. Dynastie* (*ÄgFo* 11). Glückstadt 1940.

Hibis III = N. de Garis Davies, *The Temple of Hibis in El Khargeh Oasis*, Part III: *The Decoration*. (Publ. of the Metropolitan Museum, Egyptian Expedition, vol. XVII). New York 1953.

Horrack, *Le Livre des Respirations* = P.S. de Horrack, *Le Livre des Respirations d'après les manuscrits du Musée du Louvre*. Paris 1887.

Hundred-Gated Thebes = S.P. Vleeming (ed.), *Hundred-Gated Thebes*. Acts of a Colloquium on Thebes and the Theban area in the Graeco-Roman Period (Papyrologica Lugduno-Batava 27). Leiden 1995.

Junker, *Die Stundenwachen* = H. Junker, *Die Stundenwachen in den Osirismysterien*. Vienna 1910.

Kamal, *Stèles* = A. Kamal, *Stèles hiéroglyphiques d'époque ptolémaïque et romaine* (*CGC*). Cairo 1905.

KO = J. de Morgan *et al.*, *Catalogue des monuments et inscriptions de l'Egypte antique*. Première série: *Haute Egypte*, II–III: *Kom Ombos*. Vienna, 1895–1909.

KRI = K.A. Kitchen, *Ramesside inscriptions historical and biographical*. 8 vols. Oxford 1975–90.

LÄ = W. Helck and E. Otto (eds), *Lexikon der Ägyptologie* I–VII. Wiesbaden 1975–92.

Lacau, *Sarcophages* = P. Lacau, *Sarcophages antérieurs au Nouvel Empire* (*CGC*). 2 vols. Cairo 1903–6.

Lange and Schäfer, *Grab- und Denksteine* = K. Lange and H. Schäfer, *Grab- und Denksteine des mittleren Reichs im Museum von Kairo* I–IV (*CGC*). Leipzig and Berlin 1902–25.

LD = K. Lepsius, *Denkmäler aus Ägypten und Äthiopien*. Berlin and Leipzig 1849–1913.

Lefebvre, *Grammaire* = G. Lefebvre, *Grammaire de l'Egyptien classique* (*BdE* 12). 2e éd. revue et corrigée avec la collaboration de S. Sauneron. Cairo 1955.

Lefebvre, *Petosiris* = G. Lefebvre, *Le tombeau de Petosiris*. 3 vols. Cairo 1923–4.

Lefebvre, *Tableau* = G. Lefebvre, *Tableau des parties du corps humain* (*CASAE* 17). Cairo 1952.

Legrain, *Statues et statuettes* = G. Legrain, *Statues et statuettes de rois et de particuliers* (*CGC*). 3 vols + index. Cairo 1906–25.

Leitz, *LGG* = Ch. Leitz (ed.), *Lexikon der ägyptischen Götter und Götterbezeichnungen*. 7 vols. Leuven 2002.

Lieblein, *Que mon nom fleurisse* = J. Lieblein, *Le Livre égyptien Que mon nom fleurisse*. Leipzig 1895.

LPE = F.R. Herbin, *Le Livre de parcourir l'éternité* (OLA 58). Louvain 1994.

Mariette, *Dendérah* = A. Mariette, *Dendérah. Description générale du grand temple de cette ville.* 5 vols. Paris 1870–5.

Maspero, *Sarcophages* I = G. Maspero, *Sarcophages des époques persane et ptolémaïque* I (*CGC*). Cairo 1914.

Maystre, *Les déclarations* = Ch. Maystre, *Les déclarations d'innocence. Livre de Morts, chapitre 125* (RAPH 8). Cairo 1937.

Meeks, *ALex* = D. Meeks, *Année lexicographique* I (1977), II (1978), III (1979). Paris 1980–2.

Möller, *Pal.* III = G. Möller, *Hieratische Palaeographie* III. Leipzig 1912.

Mond-Myers, *Temples of Armant* = R. Mond and O.H Myers, *Temples of Armant. A preliminary Survey.* 2 vols. London 1940.

Mond-Myers, *The Bucheum* = R. Mond and O.H Myers, *The Bucheum.* With the hieroglyphic inscriptions ed. by H.W. Fairman. 3 vols. London 1934.

Moret, *Sarcophages* I = A. Moret, *Sarcophages de l'époque bubastite à l'époque saïte* I (*CGC*). Cairo 1912.

Niwiński, *Seconde trouvaille* = A. Niwiński, *La seconde trouvaille de Deir el-Bahari* II (*CGC*). Cairo 1996.

Opet = C. de Wit, *Les inscriptions du temple d'Opet à Karnak I* (*BiAe* 11). Brussels 1958.

Piehl, *IH* = K. Piehl, *Inscriptions hiéroglyphiques recueillies en Europe et en Egypte* I–III. Stockholm and Leipzig 1886–1903.

Pierret, *Etudes égyptologiques* = P. Pierret, *Etudes égyptologiques comprenant le texte et la traduction d'une stèle éthiopienne inédite et de divers manuscrits religieux, avec un glossaire égyptien grec du décret de Canope*. Paris 1873.

Pierret, *Inscr. du Louvre* = P. Pierret, *Recueil d'inscriptions inédites du musée égyptien du Louvre*. 1ère–2e partie. Paris, 1874–8.

PM = B. Porter and R. Moss, *Topographical Bibliography of Ancient Egyptian Hieroglyphic Texts, Reliefs and Paintings*. 8 vols. Oxford, 1960–99.

ProsPtol = W. Peremans and E. Van 't Dack (eds), *Prosopographia Ptolemaica* I–IX (= Studia Hellenistica 6, 8, 11–13, 17, 20, 21, 25). Louvain 1950–81.

PT = K. Sethe, *Die altägyptischen Pyramidentexte*. Leipzig 1908–22.

Quirke, *Owners* = S.J. Quirke, *Owners of Funerary Papyri in the British Museum* (British Museum Occasional Paper 92). London 1993.

Ritual of Embalming = S. Sauneron, *Le rituel de l'embaumement*. Cairo 1952.

Ritual of the Opening of the Mouth = E. Otto, *Das Ägyptische Mundöffnungsritual.* 2 vols (*ÄgAbh* 3). Wiesbaden 1960.

R*PN* = H. Ranke, *Die ägyptischen Personennamen* I–III. Glückstadt 1935–77.

SB = F. Preisigke, *Sammelbuch griechischer Urkunden aus Ägypten*. 5 vols. Strassburg 1915–38.

Seeber, *Untersuchungen* = *Untersuchungen zur Darstellung des Totengerichts im alten Ägypten* (*MÄS* 35, 1976). Munich 1976.

Sethe, *Amun* = K. Sethe, *Amun und die acht Urgötter von Hermopolis. Eine Untersuchung über Ursprung und Wesen des ägyptischen Götterkönigs*. Abhandlungen der preussischen Akademie der Wissenschaften, Jahrgang 1929. Phil.-hist. Klasse, 4. Berlin 1929.

Smith, *Liturgy* = M. Smith, *The Liturgy of Opening the Mouth for Breathing*. Oxford 1993.

Smith, *Mortuary Texts* = M. Smith, *The Mortuary Texts of Papyrus BM 10507*. London 1987.

Urk. IV = *Urkunden der 18. Dynastie*. Berlin 1927–58.

Wb. = A. Erman and H. Grapow, *Wörterbuch der aegyptischen Sprache*. 7 vols and 5 vols *Belegstellen*. Leipzig and Berlin 1926–63.

Wilson, *A Ptolemaic Lexikon* = P. Wilson, *A Ptolemaic Lexikon. A Lexicographical Study of the Texts in the Temple of Edfu* (*OLA* 78). Louvain 1997.

Introduction

Books of Breathing

The group of texts called Books of Breathing have been known since the beginnings of the study of Egyptology[1] and occupy an important place in funerary literature of the Ptolemaic and Roman periods. The concept of this kind of texts appears to have been developed only in the Theban area,[2] where gradually they took the place of the old Book of the Dead, from which they are partly inspired, without ever totally replacing it. The manuscripts are of variable dimensions;[3] sometimes they are illustrated, and most frequently they are written in hieratic. Since they were private documents they were placed on the mummy which they protected in the hereafter with their efficacious formulae.[4]

The title Book of Breathing,[5] *tꜣ šꜥt n snsn*, originally underlining the importance of breathing for the dead,[6] has long been used by scholars to describe a type of document that corresponded to certain formal criteria. Very soon a classification into First Book and Second Book was formulated,[7] which permitted rapid and practical identification. Later a number of sub-groups were added with a view to accommodating all manuscripts, known or not yet known. Manuscripts that did not meet these criteria were left aside.[8] However, with the growing interest in late funerary texts and the diversity of manuscripts published under this title from museum collections, scholars were led gradually to reconsider the formal definition of these manuscripts, which are, in fact, less stereotypical than they would seem at first sight. Nowadays there is a consensus that the title *tꜣ šꜥt n snsn* designates a wide range of texts comprising not only the famous First Book and Second Book, but also documents written in hieratic, demotic or even in hieroglyphics, the contents of which vary from simple funerary formulae to elaborate, sometimes original, texts.[9]

The traditional main classification into First Book and Second Book has stayed in use so long because it was easy to operate,[10] but it was based on some fixed ideas and a partial knowledge of the papyri. Some recent studies of the *šꜥt n snsn mḥ 1* and *šꜥt n snsn mḥ 2* have seriously questioned its relevance.[11]

Only some of the papyri classified as the Second Book of Breathing actually bear the title *tꜣ šꜥt n snsn mḥ 2*,[12] and on this basis all similar manuscripts have been placed in this category.[13] Since the existence of a Second Book implies that of a First Book, the text introduced with the title 'Beginning of the Book of Breathing made by Isis for her brother Osiris' (*ḥꜣty-ꜥ m šꜥt n snsn ir.n Ꞽst n sn.s Wsir*), which is attested in about thirty manuscripts[14] and considered a separate entity

1. J.F. Champollion, *Notice descriptive des monuments égyptiens du musée Charles X* (Paris 1827), pp. 154–6; id. in F. Caillaud, *Voyage à Méroé ...* IV (Paris 1827), p. 28.
2. One large manuscript coming from Esna (P. OIC 25389) bears several kinds of texts: Book of the Dead, Books of Breathing, Book of Traversing Eternity. See *LPE*, pp. 13–18.
3. Almost all are papyri. In two instances, the text is written on linen: F.R. Herbin, *BIFAO* 84 (1984), p. 254, n. 4, with pls LV–LVI; another similar document, unpublished, was recently acquired by the British Museum (auction catalogue, Christie's, New York, June 14, 1996, p. 26, no. 26).
4. On Books of Breathing: Goyon, *Rituels funéraires*, pp. 189–211; M. Coenen, *OLP* 26 (1995), pp. 29–38
5. *šꜥt n snsn*, 'Book' or 'document of Breathing', depending on whether it is considered to be a textual category or a material manuscript accompanying the mummy.
6. Goyon, *Rituels funéraires*, p. 206.
7. See n. 1. In his *Catalogue*, Devéria classifies and describes these papyrus in two different chapters: 1) Le Livre des Respirations; 2) Textes imités du Livre de sortir du jour et du Livre des Respirations.
8. See e.g. Goyon, *Rituels funéraires*, p. 190, n. 2.
9. See *infra*, pp. 3–4: Original Texts, and *LPE*, p. 328; Smith, *Liturgy*, p. 14.
10. Goyon, *Rituels funéraires*, p. 191; id., *LÄ* I, 524–6; Herbin, *BIFAO* 84 (1984), p. 249; *LPE*, pp. 326–7.
11. J. Quaegebeur, in J. Duquesne (ed.), *Hermes Aegyptiacus. Discussion in Egyptology*, Special Number 3 (Fs. Stricker) (Oxford 1995), pp. 157–81; Coenen, *OLP* 26 (1995), pp. 35–6.
12. On the verso: P. BM EA 10110 + 10111 (dem.); P. Cairo CG 58007, where the title *mḥ 2.t* concerns only cols III–V of the manuscript; P. Louvre N 3157 rt.
13. See e.g. E. Chassinat, *RHR* 23 (1895), p. 314. The list includes also the short versions.
14. List in M. Coenen, *CdE* 79 (2004), pp. 61–2, and 72. The title introducing the version of P. Louvre N 3083 is *rꜣ n snsn ꜥnḫ m ṯꜣw m ẖrt-nṯr ḏd mdw ḥꜣ Wsir N*, 'Formula for breathing alive on the air in the god's domain'. See F.R. Herbin, *RdE* 50 (1999), p. 155.

because its structure and contents differ from the Second Book, naturally came to be held as the First Book. This title is a purely conventional construction made by Egyptologists and unknown by the Egyptians themselves to describe this kind of text.[15]

And yet, even if the title *šꜥt n snsn mḥ 1* is never found in manuscripts containing 'The Book of Breathing made by Isis for her brother Osiris', the existence of a First Book is explicitly mentioned in some documents[16] in the form *tꜣ šꜥt n snsn mḥ 1.t nty ỉw.w ḫꜣꜥ.s ẖr ḏꜣḏꜣ n p(ꜣ) nṯr*, 'The first Book of Breathing which is placed under the head of the god (= the deified deceased)'. This mention of a First Book has never gained acceptance, no doubt because it was unexpected in a text considered as a Second Book and so was misinterpreted by scholars, and could even be considered erroneous. For example, P. Louvre N 3148, III, x + 12,[17] which has largely contributed to the confusion in the past,[18] is entitled *tꜣ šꜥt n snsn* , a group of signs wrongly transcribed by Pierret,[19] instead of as was written in demotic. Another illustration of this tenacious confusion is provided by P. Florence 3662, I, 1 where is written normally but was misread by Pellegrini, then followed by other scholars.[20] The version found in the unpublished P. Vienna 3870 is unambiguous, since *mḥ 1.t* is written . In all cases the title is followed by the words *ḏd mdw*, 'to be recited', and then the classic formula *ḫr.f n Wsir N*, 'Thus speaks the Osiris N', which begins the identification of the dead with the rising and setting sun in the form *ỉnk Rꜥ m ḫꜥ.f ỉnk Ỉtm m ḥtp.f*.[21] The very numerous texts beginning with these words should be considered copies of the First Book of Breathing, whether they contain a long or a short version.

Complete mentions of the Second Book are equally rare. The full title *tꜣ šꜥ.t n snsn mḥ 2.t nty ỉw=w r ḫꜣꜥ=s ỉ.ỉr rd.wy.t*, 'Second Book of Breathing, to be placed at the feet' are read only in P. BM EA 10110 + 10111 (written on the verso and in demotic) and P. Louvre N 3157, I, 1 (in hieratic). The simplified title *tꜣ šꜥt n snsn mḥ 2* is also found on the verso of this manuscript, but *mḥ 2.t* is found above col. III in P. Cairo CG 58007. On the verso of P. BM EA 10282 we even find *2.t*. These papyri continue with the litany *mỉ rwḏ rn*. Therefore, all texts showing this litany are formally to be identified as the Second Book of Breathing.

The developed titles found in the manuscripts state explicitly that the First Book was placed under the head and the Second Book at the feet of the mummy. One may wonder whether this was a general rule. First, let us examine the various ways in which the placing is expressed. Corresponding to the titles *tꜣ šꜥt n snsn mḥ 1.t nty ỉw.w ḫꜣꜥ.s ẖr ḏꜣḏꜣ n p(ꜣ) nṯr* and *tꜣ šꜥt n snsn mḥ 2.t nty ỉw.w r ḫꜣꜥ.s ỉ.ỉr rd.wy.t Wsỉr N*, we find, in two manuscripts belonging to the same person, P. BM EA 10191 and 10304, the demotic formulation *tꜣ šꜥt n snsn nty šm ẖr ḏꜣḏꜣ=f* and *tꜣ šꜥt n snsn nty šm ẖr rṱ=f*, 'The Book of Breathing which proceeds under his head (under his feet)'.[22] These must correspond to the First Book and the Second Book according to the criteria set out above. In most cases the words *ḏꜣḏꜣ*, 'head', and *rd(wy)*, 'legs', are spelled in full, or simply with the image of a head or a leg drawn on the back of the document. More rarely the indication is written in Greek.[23]

Nevertheless, the presence on the back of the papyrus of a head or a leg does not constitute indisputable proof that the manuscript contains the First or the Second Book of Breathing. A study of the papyri leads to the conclusion that a head on the verso mostly corresponds to the First Book on the recto, and a leg to the Second Book,[24] but there are exceptions. Several manuscripts which show a head on the verso do not have the expected First Book on the recto, but an original text (see below).[25] Two of them even have the Second Book on the recto.[26] On the other hand, no First Book is accompanied by an indication of legs in any form. When the papyri were placed in pairs on the same mummy, it happens that instead of both,[27] only one of the papyri could have an indication,[28] or

15. Coenen, *OLP* 26 (1995), p. 34.
16. Coenen, *OLP* 26 (1995), p. 35. Add to the cited documents P. Vienna 3870. P. Berlin 3028 and P. BN 151 give only the title *tꜣ šꜥt n snsn nty ỉw.w ḫꜣꜥ.s ẖr ḏꜣḏꜣ n p(ꜣ) nṯr*, written on the recto, line 1, without specifying *mḥ 1*.
17. The preceding text contains a hymn to Mut, on which cf. Goyon, *Rituels funéraires*, p. 241.
18. Goyon, *Rituels funéraires*, p. 246 and n. 3. Contrary to what this author writes, the title does not figure on P. Louvre E 3865.
19. Pierret, *Etudes égyptologiques*, p. 47.
20. A. Pellegrini, *Bessarione*, serie 2, vol. 5 (1904), p. 49, n. 2, and pl. 1. The transcription by S. Schott, *Bücher und Bibliotheken im alten Ägypten* (Wiesbaden 1990), p. 367, no. 1614, is wrong.
21. The words *ḫr.f n Wsir N* also introduce the litany *mi rwḏ rn* in P. BM EA 10110 + 10111, I, 1; P. BM EA 10116, 1; P. BM EA 10282; P. BM EA 10304, 1; P. Cairo CG 58007, III; P. Cairo CG 58013, 1; P. Cairo CG 58018, I, 1; P. Louvre N 3148, VIII, 1; P. Louvre N 3174, I, 1; P. Louvre N 3177 A; and exceptionally an original text: P. BM EA 10123, 5, as well as a copy of the Book of Traversing Eternity: P. BM EA 10114.
22. Cf. also the title of P. Turin N.766 (M.A. Stadler, *Enchoria* 25 [1999], p. 85): ⌈*tꜣ šꜥ.t*⌉ *n snsn nt iy ẖr ḏꜣḏꜣ* [*n N*].
23. P. BM EA 10123 vs.: πρὸς κεφαλῇ; P. Louvre N 3289 vs. (ὑπὸ τὴν κεφαλήν); P. Louvre N 3176 A (κεφαλῇ); see also Devéria, *Catalogue*, p. 164 (V, 49).
24. Head / First Book: P. BM EA 10109; P. Cairo CG 58014; P. Louvre N 3176 A. Head / Second Book: P. Cairo CG 58017; P. Louvre N 3289. Feet / Second Book: P. BM EA 10108; P. BM EA 10116; P. BM EA 10282; P. Cairo CG 58013; P. Cairo CG 58018; P. Cairo CG 58022; P. Louvre N 3246; P. Turin 1861 B.
25. P. BM EA 10123; P. BM EA 10254; P. BM EA 10340; P. Moscow 4651.
26. P. Cairo CG 58017; P. Louvre N 3289.
27. P. BM EA 10109 (head, First Book) and P. BM EA 10108 (feet, Second Book); P. Cairo CG 58014 (head, First Book) and P. Cairo CG 58013 (feet, Second Book); P. BM EA 10340 (head, First Book) and P. Louvre N 3246 (feet, Second Book); P. Turin 1861 C (head, First Book) and P. Turin 1861 B (feet, Second Book).
28. P. BM EA 10123 (head, original text) and P. BM EA 10124 (without indication, Second Book); P. BM EA 10191 (without indication, First Book) and P. BM EA 10304 (feet, Second Book); P. BM EA 10283 (without indication, First Book) and P. BM EA 10282 (feet, Second Book); P. Berlin 3030 (without indication ?, First Book) and P. Cairo CG 58018 (feet, Second Book, long version); P. Louvre N 3156 (without indication, original text) and P. Louvre N 3289 (head, Second Book).

even that neither had it.[29] One may find the same book copied twice for the same mummy.[30] This distribution may be found, not only for the First and the Second Book of Breathing, but also for one or other of the two and an original text,[31] or for two original texts.[32] We must note that in a few instances both books are written on the same document;[33] in this case no indication of placement is given on the verso. These indications do not exclude the presence of a general title different from the official *šʿt n snsn*. On the verso of many of the papyri studied here we read what could be termed 'annexed formulae' which sum up the purpose of the manuscript. The most common is certainly *smꜣ-tꜣ nfr(t)*, 'good burial', which is nearly always followed by a short sentence for the protection of the deceased's bones and limbs,[34] and a mention of Amentet, the Goddess of the West,[35] who 'extends her arms' to receive him. This is also found in the Book of Traversing Eternity.[36] Another title, although not found in the papyri of the British Museum, sometimes defines this kind of document as 'Book for entering the god's domain and hastening into the Hall of the two Maats' (*mḏꜣt nt ʿḳ r ẖrt-nṯr wnšnš m wsḫt Mꜣʿty*).[37]

Original texts

As we have already seen, apart from the Book of Breathing made by Isis, the First and Second Book of Breathing, which together form the major part of *šʿt n snsn*, there exists a certain number of documents that may be attached to the same series, either because they explicitly bear the title, or because their contents are similar. For the sake of convenience, all those which do not follow the official version of these three kinds of Books of Breathing will be considered original texts. These fairly numerous manuscripts are mostly written in hieratic, but also in demotic[38] and sometimes in hieroglyphics.[39] Their length varies from a few lines to several pages or columns. When found in combination with one of the three larger categories,[40] they may as readily begin[41] as end[42] the main text, or even be inserted into it.[43] Many of them occupy a whole papyrus and are thus independent texts, eventually given a title.[44]

On account of their diversity, it is difficult and probably illusory to establish a systematic classification of these original texts which mostly seem not to follow any special model. As a rule, themes dealt with in most of these texts do not differ much from those found in the First and the Second Book of Breathing, or the Book of Breathing made by Isis, where it is not uncommon to find entire sentences taken from these later compositions. More often, the same ideas are expressed but with a distinct formulation. These ideas concern chiefly the modes of being of the deceased in the netherworld, his connection with gods of the Osirian realm, the forms he may assume by travelling, his participation in various festivals, and the many activities of his ba, without omitting the rituals of offering, libation and fumigation, by which the deceased is assured of a perpetual revivication.

Among the twenty original texts kept in the British Museum, the majority are adapted from one of the Books of Breathing,[45] four are made up of short funerary formulae,[46] and a few can be considered as forming rather homogeneous groups because of a close likeness among them.[47] In that category must be ranged the text known under the title of Book of Traversing Eternity (see below).

It happens also that original texts deal with more specific matters initially foreign to official Books of Breathing; they are taken from various rituals whose more or less extensive

29. P. BM EA 10114 (without indication, original text) and P. BM EA 10115 (without indication, beginning of First Book + *BD*); P. BM EA 10285 (without indication, original text) and P. BM EA 10286 (without indication, Second Book).
30. P. Cairo CG 58015 (without indication, First Book) and P. Cairo CG 58016 (without indication, First Book); P. Florence 3669 (head, original text + Second Book) and P. Florence 3670 (feet, original text + Second Book).
31. P. BM EA 10340 (head, original text) and P. Louvre N 3246 (feet, Second Book).
32. P. Moscow 4651 (head, original text) and P. Berlin 3164 + P. Moscow 4661 (feet, original text).
33. P. BM EA 10125; P. BM EA 71513A–C; P. Berlin 3052; P. Cairo CG 58007; P. Cairo CG 58009; P. Louvre E 3865; P. Louvre N 3148; P. Louvre N 3159 + 3194.
34. P. BM EA 10108, 10112, 10115, 10123, 10256, 10283, 10286, 10291 (= frag. 1), 10303, 10340. Some variants are checked by Goyon, *Le Papyrus du Louvre N 3279* (*BdE* 42, 1966), pp. 83–4.
35. One can also find here the name of a necropolis, such as *sṯꜣt*: P. BM EA 10109 vs.; see also P. BM EA 10108, **line 5**.
36. P. BM EA 10114.
37. P. Cairo CG 58009 vs.; P. Louvre E 3865 vs.; P. Parma 183 vs. Note the wording *ʿḳ.t r ẖrt-nṯr* in P. BM EA 10124 vs., *ʿḳ r Ἰmntt* […] in P. BM EA 10194 vs., and *ʿḳ šm m ẖrt-nṯr* in P. BM EA 10192 vs.
38. Some examples: M.A. Stadler, *Enchoria* 25 (1999), pp. 76–110; W. Brunsch, in *Studien zu Sprache und Religion Ägyptens* I (Fs. Westendorf) (Göttingen 1984), pp. 455–60; J. Quaegebeur, in *Studies in Egyptology Presented to Miriam Lichtheim* (1990), pp. 781–6.
39. B.A. Touraiev, in *Mémoires du Musée des Beaux-Arts de l'Empereur Alexandre III à Moscou* (Moscow 1912) (in Russian), pp. 23–9; F.R. Herbin, *BIFAO* 84 (1984), p. 254.
40. They are more rarely found on manuscripts of Book of the Dead; cf. e.g. P. Louvre N 3125, P. Tübingen 2012 (E. Brunner-Traut and H. Brunner, *Die Ägyptische Sammlung der Universität Tübingen* [Mainz 1981], pl. 151).
41. P. BM EA 10260, I, x + 1–16.
42. P. BM EA 9995, IV; P. BM EA 10110 + 10111, II, 22–31; P. BM EA 10116, 19–34; P. Cairo CG 58009, V.
43. P. Berlin 3030, VI, 17–IX, 6); P. Louvre N 3148, VII, 7–25 (Herbin, *BIFAO* 84 [1984], pp. 251–2); P. Louvre N 3083, N 3121, N 3166 (id., *RdE* 50 [1999], pp. 149–60).
44. Here they are P. BM EA 10108 (*smꜣ-tꜣ nfrt*), 10112 (*smꜣ-tꜣ nfrt*), 10115 (*smꜣ-tꜣ nfrt*), 10123 (*smꜣ-tꜣ nfrt*), 10194 (*ʿḳ r Ἰmntt*), 10201 (*tꜣ šʿt n snsn*), 10254, 10256, 10261, 10264A, 10285, 10290, 10340 (*smꜣ-tꜣ nfrt*), 10343, 10344, 10718. Also P. Cairo CG 58010; P. Louvre N 3236; Mss. Golenischeff 517–20; P. Beck; P. Berlin 3164 + Moscow 4661; P. Moscow 4651 and 4659 (Touraiev, op. cit.); P. Parma 183; P. Turin 766 (dem.); P. Vatican Inv. 38599, and many others.
45. Add to the seventeen papyri registered in the related section (pp. 282 ff.) the original texts recorded in P. BM EA 9995, IV and 10260, I (Book of Breathing made by Isis), and P. BM EA 10110 + 10111, II, 22–31 (Second Book of Breathing).
46. P. BM EA 10254, 10261, 10285, 10290.
47. P. BM EA 10108 and 10112, to be compared with P. Cairo CG 58009, IV, CG 58012, P. Toulouse 49–220 and P. Turin 1989; also P. BM EA 10718, to be compared in part with P. Parma 183 and P. OIC 25389, XXXIII. Note that the mentions of the theonyms Amenipet and Khonsu-Shu, which occur in various funerary texts of the Late Period, are not sufficient arguments to characterize a special group of the Book of Breathing, contrary to what Goyon has asserted in his *Rituels funéraires*, pp. 299–302.

sequences are copied out. In all cases, they are adapted to a private use, integrated or added to a funerary papyrus in favour of the deceased. If some are attested elsewhere in contemporary or even older documents, others now appear for the first time.[48]

Seven of these texts are represented in the present catalogue; they all precede or follow a version of Book of Breathing. Thus, the third sheet of P. BM EA 9995 shows two lines of a hieroglyphic inscription also known from Bucheum stela no. 14, 7–12, but written here for the benefit of the local bull that had recently died. In P. BM EA 10116, 19–33, the text introduced with the formula 'Pure offering that the king gives to Osiris', attested also in other manuscripts of Books of Breathing (partly in P. BM EA 10343) and on several offering tables, is also found in P. BM EA 10209, IV, 1–18 (extended version), as one of the chapters of a ritual dealing with the Festival of the Valley. In P. BM EA 10194, 10–12, are mentioned some rites performed in the same festival and at each decade, with some phrases of more common usage. P. BM EA 10256 shows an unusual text in which the deceased is placed under the protection of cow deities. In P. BM EA 10115, several masters of the offering table are presented as protectors of the deceased, a function unknown so far. Yet more unexpected are the invocations to parts of the body in P. BM EA 10201, followed by an unparalleled text inspired by Books of Breathing.

The association of such texts with Books of Breathing, the which title can be given to them, is not rare in the late funerary documentation. The multiplication of Osirian rituals in the Greco-Roman Period made it easier to insert them in private manuscripts accompanying the deceased in his tomb. It is not, therefore, surprising that the theological renewal observed in Thebes in that time, full of tradition but imbued with new ideas formed and developed in Houses of Life, should be attested in these local compositions called Books of Breathing, more open than the traditional Book of the Dead to contemporary beliefs and religious practices.

The Book of Traversing Eternity

Among original texts related to Books of Breathing, the Book of Traversing Eternity (*mḏ3t nt sb nḥḥ*) holds a place of special interest. Known in a score of versions, it is doubtless one of the most important compositions in the late funerary literature. The dates of the documents (principally papyri, but also two stelae and one sarcophagus)[49] are situated between the end of the first century BC and the second century AD. The evolution of this text, then, strictly parallels Books of Breathing and, like them, it is attested in extended and short versions. All these documents, except for three found in the Delta, Fayum and Abydos, are from Thebes and its surroundings.

The close connection between both books explains their frequent association in a single papyrus,[50] based especially on a common inspiration in the formulation of funerary topics.[51] Thus, the Book of Traversing Eternity (the title found on the verso of a papyrus in Berlin) may be considered an authentic Book of Breathing.[52]

Beyond the striking similarities with Books of Breathing, the originality of the Book of Traversing Eternity lies, at least according to the two known long versions,[53] in the extraordinary catalogue of festivals and rites in which the deceased participates from the beginning to the end of the year, drawn up at once in a chronological and cyclic order. The short versions leave out elements relative to the dates. This is the case for four manuscripts in the British Museum preserving that text. Beside the standard version (P. Leiden T 32), each of them shows, like all the other short versions, a preference for the beginning (P. BM EA 10114, 10314, 10262–63) or the end (P. BM EA 10091) of the Book of Traversing Eternity, where the resemblance to Books of Breathing is mostly apparent.

Appendix: a note on the Dossier Soter

The publication in this catalogue of a number of papyri that belonged either to the archon Soter or to his descendants provides an opportunity to look again at the members of this family who lived in Thebes during the first and the second centuries AD,[54] and whose fame is to a large extent due to the circumstances in which they were found in a collective tomb. In spite of the rich and varied finds of this tomb, it is difficult here to speak of an archive, because our knowledge of this family is based entirely on funerary objects and

48. Three texts of that kind, all in the Louvre Museum, have been recently published: P. Louvre N 3083, N 3121 and N 3166 (see n. 43). They contain respectively a ritual of the torch, a geographical text in which gods of Upper and Lower Egypt are invoked, and an offering ritual including some parts of a liturgy recited during the rites of the decade in Djeme.
49. For other manuscripts bearing some parts of the text: M. Coenen, *RdE* 52 (2001), p. 70, n. 8, and add P. Vatican Inv. 38580 (unpublished).
50. P. Louvre N 3166 and N 3284 (Book of Breathing made by Isis); P. Louvre N 3147 and P. Tübingen 2002 (Second Book of Breathing); P. OIC 25389 (Book of Breathing, version P. Parma 183).
51. *LPE*, pp. 326–8.
52. P. Berlin 3155. Note that the usual title, 'Book of Traversing Eternity', is read on col. IV, lines 5–6 of the recto. See *LPE*, p. 283.
53. P. Leiden T 32 and P. Vatican Inv. 38570.
54. The current dating of the Soter family only to the reigns of Trajan and Hadrian, established after the epitaphs found on the coffins of the children and grandchildren of the archon, must be revised. Not less than six generations of this family are known; inasmuch as Soter and Cleopatra Candace were certainly alive during the reigns of Domitian and Titus, it is likely that the first attested member of this family, Esoeris, mother of Cornelius Pollius and grandmother of Soter, was living in the reign of Tiberius.

because not a single civil document, be it commercial, administrative or judicial, mentions any of its members. Soter himself, in spite of his rather high position in the Theban hierarchy, seems to have been ignored completely by other contemporary sources.[55] Although gathered together in antiquity, probably in the reign of Antoninus Pius,[56] the funerary material discovered in the Soter tomb has nothing in common with family archives as they are known from Ptolemaic or Roman Egypt; it is more characteristic of a *dossier* than an archive *stricto sensu*.[57] Recognized early as original and important in the academic world,[58] this material, written in Greek and Egyptian (demotic, hieratic or hieroglyphics), has again of late excited scholarly curiosity concerning Soter and his descendants.[59]

In 1820 the Italian adventurer A. Lebolo, probably accompanied by the English traveller F. Henniker, who was also in the Theban region at this time,[60] laid hands on an extraordinary archaeological treasure from the Roman Period, consisting of many coffins with mummies and papyri, all found together in a collective tomb in Gurna.[61] The sheer quantity of these coffins might allow us to think that it was an older burial re-used later, but no details about the tomb itself are given by Lebolo.[62]

The location of the tomb, which remained doubtful until a few years ago, has now been established with near certainty through the work of the Hungarian archaeological team in TT 32, situated on the hill of El-Khokha, to the east of Gurna, and belonging to Djehutymes who lived at the time of Ramses II.[63] L. Kákosy has produced several convincing arguments on the subject.[64] Like so many others towards the end of the Ramesside Period, the tomb was pillaged, and was afterwards re-used several times, first in the Third Intermediate Period, then under the Ptolemies and, finally, under the Romans.

Shortly after its discovery, the material was dispersed by Lebolo and ended up, through Salt, Drovetti, Minutoli, Cailliaud, and Anastasi, in six European museums: London (British Museum), Turin (Museo Egizio), Berlin (Staatliche Museen), Paris (Musée du Louvre and Bibliothèque Nationale), and Leiden (Rijksmuseum).[65] In all probability no other collections contain objects found in this tomb.[66] The dispersal of the material into the European museums makes an important chapter of the history of the collections in the nineteenth century.

Since this first catalogue of *Late Egyptian Religious Texts* includes almost all the papyri from the Soter tomb, a few unpublished ones can now be added to the list of those already known:[67]

— P. BM EA 9977–9978 ((Cleopatra I) Candace) daughter of Sapaulis I, probably found in her coffin (now lost).[68]

— P. BM EA 10123–10124 (Senchonsis, alias Sapaulis II), probably found in her coffin (now lost).

— P. BM EA 10256[69] (Tphous, daughter of Sarapous), probably found in coffin BM EA 6708.

— P. BM EA 10282–10283 (Soter I, son of Pa-kerer (?) and Philous), found in coffin BM EA 6705.

— P. BM EA 10331 (Apollonides, son of Candace), probably found in his coffin (now lost).

With the help of these manuscripts we are now able to elaborate various details in the genealogy of the Soter family. In order to establish the genealogical table (p. 10), the following sources have been used:

55. This lack of information is probably to be connected in some part with the guerilla warfare which devastated the Thebaid for more than two years during the Jewish revolt, until the beginning of the reign of Hadrian, in AD 117. See N. Lewis, *Life in Egypt under Roman Rule* (Oxford 1983), pp. 30–1.
56. Senchonsis daughter of Tkauthi (nos **19** and **20**) was dead in AD 146.
57. On the question, see P.W. Pestman, in *Hundred-Gated Thebes*, pp. 91–2.
58. Kákosy, in *Hundred-Gated Thebes*, p. 64.
59. Recent bibliography: K. Van Landuyt, *Het Graf van Soter. Kroniek van een thebaans Groepsgraf uit de romeinse Periode* (unpublished dissertation, Leuven, 1990); id., in *Hundred-Gated Thebes*, pp. 69–82. L. Kákosy, in *Hundred-Gated Thebes*, pp. 61–7; F.R. Herbin, *Padiimenipet, fils de Sôter. Histoire d'une famille dans l'Egypte romaine* (Paris 2002) C. Riggs and M. Depauw, *RdE* 53 (2002), pp. 75–90 ; C. Nauerth, in H. Harrauer and R. Pintaudi (eds), *Gedenkschrift Ulrike Horak* II (Florence 2004), pp. 424–8.
60. On these individuals, see K. Van Landuyt, in *Hundred-Gated Thebes*, p. 69, n. 1. For Lebolo, add M. Dewachter, *BiOr* 33 (1980), p. 305.
61. The description of the tomb given by Henniker in his *Notes during a Visit to Egypt, Nubia, the Oasis, Mount Sinai and Jerusalem* (2nd. edn [1824), p. 139), repeated by Kákosy, in *Hundred-Gated Thebes*, pp. 63–4, gives anyway proof of his presence in the place where he would have seen fourteen coffins. Note that this important funerary material does not seem have belonged exclusively to the Soter family; see *infra*, n. 67.
62. C.G. di San Quintino, *Lezioni archeologiche intorno ad alcuni monumenti del regio muso egiziano di Torino* (Turin 1824), p. 6 (and not 108 as mentioned by Kákosy, in *Hundred-Gated Thebes*, pp. 64–5, n. 12).
63. On this tomb: Kákosy, in *Hundred-Gated Thebes*, pp. 61–7; id., in *Egyptian Archaeology* 8 (1996), pp. 34–6.
64. Kákosy, in *Hundred-Gated Thebes*, p. 67.
65. Kákosy, in *Hundred-Gated Thebes*, p. 63; van Landuyt, in *Hundred-Gated Thebes*, p. 69. Distribution: Salt, auction 1823: British Museum; auction 1826: Louvre Museum; Drovetti, auction 1824: Turin Museum; auction 1827: Louvre Museum; Minutoli, auction 1823: Berlin Museum; Cailliaud, auction 1823: Paris, Bibliothèque Nationale; Anastasi, auction 1828: Leiden Museum.
66. Van Landuyt adds elsewhere (*Hundred-Gated Thebes*, p. 82, n. 61) that Lebolo was in touch with American dealers of antiquities (cf. also J.J. Fiechter, *La moisson des dieux* [Paris 1994], p. 223); it cannot therefore be excluded that some documents related to the Soter family still remain to be discovered. Existence of a shroud belonging to a certain Cornelius, now in the North Carolina Museum of Art, and whose style recalls closely that of Soter material, is not formally connected to the family of the archon (Van Landuyt, in *Hundred-Gated Thebes*, p. 82, o).
67. Van Landuyt, in *Hundred-Gated Thebes*, p. 81. On the papyri of the Soter family, see now Quirke, *Owners*, p. 24. It is more than likely that some of the manuscripts coming from the tomb of Soter do not belong to members of his family (cf. Van Landuyt, in *Hundred-Gated Thebes*, p. 82, n. 62). Owners of P. BM EA 10108, 10109, 10110 + 10111, 10112 and 10116 seem never have had any direct relationship with the known descendants of Soter. However, attribution of these documents to the Ptolemaic Period must be reconsidered not only on account of palaeographical arguments, but also because in four papyri the designation of 'Hathor' is applied to female owners. Only P. BM EA 10110 + 10111 belongs to a man.
68. Contrary to what is said in PM I, p. 676, no. 13, coffin BM EA 6706, in which was found P. BM EA 10114 and 10115, and its mummy BM EA 6707 do not belong to Cleopatra Candace, but to Cleopatra daughter of Candace. See document **11**.
69. P. BM EA 10259, belonging like P. BM EA 10256 to *Tꜣ-ḥfꜣt*, shows texts unconnected with the Books of Breathing; it will be published in the third volume of the *Catalogue of Late Egyptian Religious Texts*.

1 Base board and cover of coffin BM EA 6950 + 6950 A, belonging to *Ḳwrnrys* (Cornelius). E.A.W. Budge, *A Guide to the First, Second and Third Egyptian Rooms* (London 1924), p. 138.

2 P. Louvre N 3290, probably found in **1**, belonging to *Ḳȝrnyr* (hier.), *[Ḳ]rnwylyw* (dem.) (Cornelius), son of *Ỉst-wrt* (Esoeris).

3 Coffin BM EA 6705 + shroud 6705 A, belonging to *Sȝwtr* (Soter I), son of *P(ȝ)y-mt* (Philous) = List PM no. 4.

4 P. BM EA 10282 and 10283, found in **3**, belonging to *Swtr* (Soter I), son of (?) *Pȝ-krr* and *Pylt* (Philous).

5 Coffin Louvre E 13048 + E 13016, belonging to *Pȝ-di-Ỉmn-Ỉpt* (Petemenophis I) son of *Grwptr* (Cleopatra I).

Greek inscription, mentioning Petemenophis, alias Ammonios, son of Soter son of Cornelius Pollius, whose mother is Cleopatra daughter of Ammonios. *CIG* III, 4824.

Shroud Louvre E 13382 CM 365, belonging to *Pȝ-di-Ỉmn-Ỉpt* (Petemenophis I), son of Cleopatra I.

6 P. BN 152, found in **5**, belonging to *Pȝ-di-Ỉmn-Ỉpt* (Petemenophis I), son of Cleopatra I.

7 Coffin Leiden M 75, belonging to Sensaos I, daughter of Soter I and Cleopatra I. *CIG* III, 4823 = *SB* V, 8366. List PM no. 9.

8 P. Leiden T 33, probably found in **7**, belonging to *Tȝ-šrỉt-Ḏd-Ḥr* (Sensaos I), daughter of Cleopatra I Candace: Stricker, *OMRO* 23 (1942), pp. 36–47.

9 Coffin BM EA 6706 (mummy: 6707), belonging to Cleopatra II, daughter of (Cleopatra I) Candace. List PM no. 13, with error of attribution.

10 P. BM EA 10114 and 10115, probably found in **9**, belonging to Cleopatra II daughter of (Cleopatra I) Candace.

11 P. BM EA 9977 (coffin lost), belonging to *Ḳndgȝy*, var. *Ḳndgy* (Cleopatra I) Candace, also written in Greek on the verso), daughter of *Ṯȝpȝr* (Sapaulis I).[70]

12 Coffin Berlin 505 (with 2 mummies), belonging to Sensaos II and Tkauthi II, daughters of Cleopatra I (Candace) = List PM no. 10.

13 P. Berlin 3068 (lost, found in **12**), belonging to *Tȝ-šrt-Ḏd-Ḥr* (Sensaos II) daughter of Cleopatra I (Candace), cf. U. Kaplony-Heckel, *Ägyptische Handschriften* III (Stuttgart 1986), p. 33, no. 48.

14 P. Berlin 3069 (lost, found in **12**), belonging to *Tȝ-ḳȝw-ḏȝ* (Tkauthi II), daughter of Cleopatra I Candace, cf. ibid., no. 49.

15 Coffin Berlin 504 (with mummy), belonging to Phaminis, son of Heracleios. *CIG* III, 4830 = *SB* V, 8373. List PM no. 11.

Demotic inscription mentioning *P[ȝỉ]-mnỉ* (Phaminis), son of *Tȝ-rw(ȝ)rw* alias *Tȝ-šrỉ.t-Sȝwȝtr*.

16 P. Berlin 3041, found in **15**, belonging to *Pȝ-Mnw*, son of *Tȝ-šrt-p(ȝ)n-Sȝw<tr>*. Van Landuyt, in *Hundred-Gated Thebes*, p. 78.

17 Coffin Turin 2230, belonging to *P(ȝ)-di-Ỉmn-Ỉpt* (Petemenophis II), son of *Tȝ-kwyḏȝ* (Tkauthi I). List PM no. 5.

Greek Inscription, mentioning Petemenophis, son of Pebos. *CIG* I, 4825 = *SB* V, 8368 and SB I, 3931.

18 P. Turin 1861 b and 1861 c, probably found in **17**, belonging to *Pȝ-di-Ỉmn-Ỉpt* (Petemenophis II), son of *Tȝ-kȝꜥȝṯȝ* (Tkauthi I).

19 Coffin (lost), of Senchonsis alias Sapaulis II, elder daughter of Pikos. *CIG* III, 4827 = *SB* V, 8370.

20 P. BM EA 10123 and 10124, probably found in **19**, belonging to *Tȝ-šrỉt-Ḫnsw* (Senchonsis) alias *Ṯȝp(w)r* (Sapaulis II), daughter of *Tȝḳḏȝ* (Tkauthi I).

21 P. Louvre N 3156 and N 3289 (coffin lost), belonging to Soter II (*Sȝwtr*, also written in Greek on the verso), son of *Ḏȝpwr* (Sapaulis II). Photograph of P. Louvre N 3156 in *Naissance de l'écriture* (catalogue Grand Palais, Paris, 1982), p. 161). See Goyon, *Rituels funéraires*, pp. 292–3.

22 Coffin BM EA 6708, belonging to *Tȝ-ḥfȝt* (Tphous), daughter of Heracleios, son of Soter I, and of *Srpw* (Sarapous). *CIG* III, 4826 + add., p. 12 = *SB* V, 8369.

23 P. BM EA 10256 and 10259, probably found in **22**, belonging to *Tȝ-ḥfȝt* (Tphous), daughter of *Srpw* (Sarapous).

24 P. Louvre N 3161 (coffin lost), belonging to *Pꜥtrꜥny* (Petronius), son of *Ḳndꜥgys* ((Cleopatra I) Candace). See Goyon, *Rituels funéraires*, pp. 293–4.

25 P. BM EA 10331 (coffin lost), belonging to *ȝprtynyds* (Apollonides), son of *Ḳndȝwgy* ((Cleopatra I) Candace).

26 Mummy label (lost), belonging to Apollonides, son of Soter I son of Cornelius. *SB* I, 3930.

List of the members of the Soter family

The numbers written in bold are those of the documents cited above. The roman numerals that follow some of the personal names are only to distinguish them and do not imply any knowledge of their respective ages, at least as far as the Soter children are concerned.

Ammonios I

— Father of Cleopatra I Candace. See under *Petemenophis I* and *Sensaos I*.

70. Another document, P. BM EA 9978, found with P. BM EA 9977, cannot be included here for study. Under a double iconographic register (adoration of Osiris and Isis by a ba-bird, and adoration of the deceased's mummy lying on a bier), are written five entirely illegible lines of fanciful hieroglyphs, followed by (line 6) a demotic subscription almost unintelligible because of the alteration of the signs, where would be read, according to M. Chauveau, the words *ḏd n=i pȝ mr* ... *Pȝ-Mnṯw*, 'the beloved told me ... Pa-Montu'. The presence of this name here is unexpected.

Ammonios II

See under Petemenophis I

Apollonides

— Son of Soter son of Cornelius.

Mummy label (lost, **26**), H. Hartleben, *Lettres de Champollion* I (Paris 1909), p. 92 = *SB* I, 3930:

Ἀπολλωνίδης Σωτῆρος Κορνηλίου, ἐβίωσεν ἔτη ἑξήκοντα ὀκτὼ μῆνας ἕνδεκα ἡμέρας εἴκοσι τρεῖς.

'Apollonides, son of Soter son of Cornelius, he lived for 68 years, 11 months and 23 days'.

— Son of *Ḳndꜣgy* (Candace)

P. BM EA 10331 (**25**), belonging to *ꜣprtynyds* (Apollonides), born of *Ḳndꜣwgy* (Candace).

Cleopatra I Candace

— Wife of Soter I.

— Daughter of Ammonios I. See under this name.

— Daughter of *Ḏꜣpwr* (Sapaulis I).

P. BM EA 9977 (**11**), belonging to *Ḳndgy* (Greek *ΚΑΝΔΑΚ*[*Η*]), born of *Ṯꜣpꜣr* (Sapaulis).

— Mother of Ammonios II. See under *Petemenophis I*.

— Mother of Ammonios II, Apollonides, Cleopatra II, Petronius, Sensaos I, Sensaos II, Tkauthi II. See under these names.

— Probably, mother of Heracleios and Tkauthi I.

Cleopatra II

— Daughter of Cleopatra I Candace. See under this name.

Coffin BM EA 6706 (**9**), belonging to *Grwptr* (Cleopatra) born of *Ḳndgy* (Candace); P. BM EA 10114 and 10115 (**10**), belonging to *Grꜣwꜣpꜣtr* (Cleopatra), born of *Ḳnt* [...] (Cand[ace]).

Cornelius Pollius = Pa-kerer?

— Son of *Ꞽst-wrt* (Esoeris).

P. Louvre N 3290 (**2**), belonging to *Ḳꜣrnyr* (Cornelius), born of *Ꞽst-wrt* (Esoeris); P. BN 152 vs., in a demotic subscription (**6**).

— Father of Soter I and grandfather of Apollonides. See under these names.

— Grandfather of *Tꜣ-šrît-Ḏd-Ḥr* (Sensaos I). See under this name.

Coffin BM EA 6950 + 6950 A (**1**), belonging to *Ḳwrnlys* (Cornelius): no filiation stated.

Esoeris (Ꞽst-wrt)

— Mother of Cornelius Pollius. See under this name.

Heracleios

— Probably son of Cleopatra I Candace.

— Son of Soter. See under *Tphous*.

— Husband of *Tꜣ-šrt-n-Sꜣwtr* (Sensoter), alias *Tꜣ-rw(ꜣ)rw* (Tlelous), alias *Srpw* / *Srpḏ* (Sarapous).

— Father of *Pꜣ-Mnw* (Phaminis). See under this name.

— Father of *Tꜣ-ḥfꜣt* (Tphous). See under this name.

Pa-kerer (Pꜣ-krr), to be identified to Cornelius?

— Husband of Philous?

— Father of Soter I?

P. BM EA 10282 and 10283, belonging to *Swtr* (Soter) son of (?) *Pꜣ-krr*, born of *Pylt* (Philous).

Pebos

Probably identical with *Pikos* (confusion between the Greek letters *K* and *B*?).[71]

— Husband of Tkauthi I (*Tꜣ-ḳꜣw-ḏꜣ*). See under this name.

— Father of Petemenophis II (*Pꜣ-di-Ꞽmn-Ꞽpt*). See under this name.

Petemenophis I (Pꜣ-di-Ꞽmn-Ꞽpt), alias Ammonios II (January 11, AD *95–June 2,* AD *116).*

— Son of Soter I, son of Cornelius Pollius, and of Cleopatra I, daughter of Ammonios I.

Coffin Louvre E 13048 + E 13016 (**5**). List PM no. 1. *CIG* III, 4824 = *SB* V, 8367:

Πετεμενῶφις ὁ καὶ Ἀμμώνιος Σωτῆρο[ς] Κορνηλίου Πολλίου, μητρὸς Κλεοπάτρας Ἀμμωνίου, ἐτῶν εἴκοσι ἑνός, μηνῶν δʹ καὶ ἡμερῶν εἴκοσι δύο, ἐτελεύ[τη]σε ιθ (ἔτους) Τραιανοῦ τοῦ κυρίου, Παῦνι ηʹ.

'Petemenophis, also called Ammonios, son of Soter son of Cornelius Pollius, whose mother is Cleopatra daughter of Ammonios; he lived for 21 years, 4 months and 22 days. He died in the year 19 of Trajan, the lord, on the 8th of Payni.'

P. BN 152 (**6**), belonging to *Pꜣ-di-Ꞽmn-Ꞽpt* (Petemenophis I) son of *Gꜣrwꜣptr* (Cleopatra I), also called *Ḳntiꜣgy* (Candace). On the verso, demotic subscription mentioning *Pꜣ-di-Ꞽmn-Ꞽpy* son of *Swtr*.

Shroud Louvre E 13382 CM 365 (**5**), belonging to *Pꜣ-di-Ꞽmn-Ꞽpt* (Petemenophis I), son of *Grwpdr* (Cleopatra I).

— Brother of *Tꜣ-šrt-Ḏd-Ḥr* (Sensaos I or II), see under this name.

71. Van Landuyt, in *Hundred-Gated Thebes*, p. 80.

Petemenophis II (Pꜣ-di-Ỉmn-Ỉpt) (December 20, AD 118–August 27, AD 123)

— Son of *Tꜣ-kꜣw-ḏꜣ* (Tkauthi I) and Pebos.

Coffin Turin 2230 (+ mummy) (**17**). List PM no. 5. *SB* I, 3931 and V, 8368. Revised by P.J. Sijpesteijn, *ZPE* 112 (1996), p. 178:[72]

Ταφὴ Πετεμενώφιος υἱοῦ Πεβῶτος ἐγεννήθη γ̄ (ἔτους) Ἁδριανοῦ τοῦ κυρίου, Χοίακ κ̄δ̄, ἐτελεύτα ζ (ἔτους) ἐπαγομένων δ̄, ὥστε ἐβίωσεν ἔτη δ̄, μῆνας η̄, ἡμέρας ῑ. Εὐψύχει.

'Coffin of Petemenophis, son of Pebos. He was born in (year) 3 of Hadrian, the Lord, on the 24th of Khoiak, and died in (the year) 7, on the 4th of the epagomenal days, so that he lived for 4 years, 8 months and 10 days.[73] Farewell!'

Coffin Turin 2230, hieroglyphic inscription:

Wsir Pꜣ-di-Ỉmn-Ỉpt mꜣʿ-ḫrw ms n Tꜣ-kꜣw-ḏꜣ s[nb] ʿḥʿ.f n ʿnḫ rnpt 4 ỉbd 8 hrw 10

'The Osiris *Pꜣ-di-Ỉmn-Ỉpt*, justified, born of *Tꜣ-kꜣw-ḏꜣ*, healthy. His lifetime was 4 years, 8 months and 10 days.'

P. Turin 14964 = 1861 B (**18**), belonging to *[Pꜣ-di]-Ỉmn-Ỉpt* (Petemenophis II), born of *Tꜣ-kꜣ-ʿꜣṯꜣ* (Tkauthi I).

P. Turin 14965 = 1861 C (**18**), belonging to *Pꜣ-di-Ỉmn-Ỉpt* (Petemenophis II), born of *Tꜣ-*[...] (T[kauthi] I).

Petronius

— Son of (Cleopatra I) Candace.

P. Louvre N 3161 (**24**), belonging to *Pʿtrʿny* (Petronius), born of *Ḳntʿgys* (Candace).

Phaminis (Pꜣ-Mnw)

— Son of *Tꜣ-šrỉt-(pn)-Sꜣwtr* (Sensoter).

P. Berlin 3041 (**16**), belonging to *Pꜣ-Mnw* (Phaminis), son of *Tꜣ-šrt-n-sꜣwtr* (Sensoter).

— Son of Heracleios and *Tꜣ-rw(ꜣ)rw* also called *Tꜣ-šrỉ.t-*[*n*-]*Sꜣwtr*.

Coffin Berlin 504 (+ mummy) (**15**). List PM no. 11. *CIG* III, 4830 = *SB* V, 8373:

Φαμῖνις Ηρακλείου (ἐτων) β

'Phaminis son of Heracleios, (he lived for) 2 (years).'

Demotic inscription (van Landuyt, in *Hundred-Gated Thebes*, p. 78):

ʿnḫ pꜣj=k bj nḥḥ rnpj=f ḏ.t Wsir P[ꜣj]-Mnj ms n Tꜣ-rw(ꜣ)rw ntj ỉw ḏd n.s Tꜣ-šrỉ.t-[n-]Sꜣwtr ʿḥʿ.f n ʿnḫ rnp.t 2 ỉbd 10 hrw 18 (?)

'May your ba live forever, (O) Osiris *P[ꜣj]-Mnj*, born of *Tꜣ-rw(ꜣ)rw* also called *Tꜣ-šrỉ.t-*[*n*-]*Sꜣwtr*! His lifetime was 2 years, 10 months and 18 days (?).'

Philous (Pylt, Pymt)[74]

— Wife of Cornelius Pollius and mother of Soter I.

Coffin BM EA 6705 (**3**). See under *Soter I*.

P. BM EA 10282 and 10283 (**4**). See under *Soter I*.

Pikos (probably identical with Pebos).

— Father of Senchonsis (*Tꜣ-šrt-Ḫnsw*) also called Sapaulis (II). See under this name.

Sapaulis I (Ṯꜣpwr)

— Wife of Ammonios and mother of Cleopatra I Candace. See under these names.

P. BM EA 9977 (**11**), belonging to *Ḳn[dg]ꜣy* (Candace), born of *Ṯꜣpwr* (Sapaulis).

Sapaulis II (Ḏꜣpwr, Ṯꜣpwr),[75] *alias Senchonsis (Tꜣ-šrỉt-Ḫnsw) (May 12, AD 101–March 11, AD 146).* See under this last name.

— Mother of Soter II. See under this name.

— Daughter of Pikos and *Tꜣḳḏꜣ* (Tkauthi I).

Greek inscription on her coffin (lost) (**19**). *CIG* III, 4827 = *SB* V, 8370:

Σενχῶνσις ἡ καὶ Σαπαῦλις πρεσβυτέρα Πικῶτος γεννηθεῖσα τῷ δ̄ (ἔτει) θεοῦ Τραιανοῦ, Παχὼν ι̅ζ̅ ἐτελεύτ[η]σεν τῷ θ̄ (ἔτει) Ἀντωνίνου Καίσαρος κυρίου Φαμενὼθ ι̅ε̅ ὥστε ἐβίωσεν ἔτη μ̅δ̅, μῆνας δέκα. Θάρσει.

'Senchonsis, alias Sapaulis, elder (daughter) of Pikos. She was born in year 4 of god Trajan, on the 17th of Pachons. She died in year 9 of Antoninus Caesar, the lord, on the 15th of Phamenoth, so that she lived for 44 years and 10 months. Be of good cheer!'

P. BM EA 10123 and 10124 (**20**), belonging to *Tꜣ-šrt-Ḫnsw* (Senchonsis) also called *Ḏꜣpwr* (Sapaulis II), born of *Tꜣḳḏꜣ* (Tkauthi I).

Sarapous (Srpw, Srpḏ).

— Wife of Heracleios.

— Mother of *Pꜣ-Mnw* (Phaminis). See under this name.

— Mother of *Tꜣ-ḥfꜣt* (Tphous). See under this name.

Senchonsis

See under *Sapaulis II*.

Sensaos I (Tꜣ-šrỉt-Ḏd-Ḥr) (May 7, AD 93–July 15, AD 109)

— Daughter of Soter I, son of Cornelius.

72. I thank H. Cuvigny for this reference.

73. This number 10 (ῑ), also attested in the demotic text of the coffin, would be the result of a wrongly copied number 8 (η̄), according to Sijpesteijn.

74. Van Landuyt, in *Hundred-Gated Thebes*, pp. 71–2, n. 10.

75. One must definitely exclude the equivalence *Ṯꜣpwr*–Zephora stated by Devéria, *Catalogue*, p. 163, n. 1, and still accepted by Goyon, *Rituels funéraires*, p. 292. No Greek inscription in the Dossier Soter mentions this anthroponym.

— Daughter of Cleopatra I, also called Candace.

Coffin Leiden M 75 (**7**). List PM no. 9. *CIG* III, 4823:

Σενσαὼς Σωτῆρος Κορνηλίου, μητρὸς Κλεοπάτρας τῆς καὶ Κανδάκης Ἀμμωνίου, παρθένος ἐτῶν ις, μηνῶν δύο, ἡμερῶν ἐννέα, ἐτελεύτησεν ιβ (ἔτους) Τραιανοῦ τοῦ κυρίου, Ἐπεὶφ κα.

'Sensaos, daughter of Soter, son of Cornelius and of (her) mother Cleopatra also called Candace (and) daughter of Ammonios. She died as a maiden of 16 years, 2 months and 9 days, in year 12 of Trajan, the lord, on the 21th of Epeiph.'

P. Leiden T 33 (**8**), belonging to *Tȝ-šrit-Ḏd-Ḥr* (Sensaos I), born of *Gȝrwȝptrʿ* (Cleopatra) also called *Ḳntigy* (Candace).

— Sister of *Pȝ-di-Imn-Ipy* (Petemenophis I): P. BN 152 vs., in a demotic subscription.[76]

Sensaos II (Tȝ-šrit-Ḏd-Ḥr)

— Daughter of Cleopatra I (Candace).

— Sister of Tkauthi II.

Coffin Berlin 505[77] (**12**). List PM no. 10. *CIG* III, 4828 = *SB* V, 8371:

Σενσαὼς καὶ Τκαῦθι ἀδελφή.

'Sensaos and Tkauthi, (her) sister.'

Hieroglyphic inscription:

Ḥwt-Ḥr Tȝ-šrit-Ḏd-Ḥr <*mȝʿ*->*ḫrw ms n Grwpȝdrʿ*

'The Hathor *Tȝ-šrit-Ḏd-Ḥr*, justified, born of Cleopatra.'

P. Berlin 3068 (**13**), now lost, belonging to *Tȝ-šrt-Ḏd-Ḥr* (Sensaos II).[78]

Sensoter (Tȝ-šri.t-[n-]Sȝwtr), alias Tlelous (Tȝ-lw(ȝ)lw).

— Mother of Phaminis (*Pȝ-Mnw*). See under this name.

Soter I

— Son of Cornelius Pollius and *Pymt* (Philous).

Title: Archon of Thebes.[79]

Coffin BM EA 6705 (**3**). List PM no. 4. *CIG* III, 4822 = *OGIS* II, 698:

Σωτὴρ Κορνηλίου Πολλίου, μητρὸς Φιλοῦτος, ἄρχων Θηβῶν.

'Soter, son of Cornelius Pollius and of (his) mother Philous, archon of Thebes.'

Hieroglyphic inscriptions:

Hȝ Wsir Sȝwȝḏr mȝʿ-ḫrw ms n Ḥwt-Ḥr Pymt

'Hail Osiris *Sȝwȝḏr*, justified, born of the Hathor *Pymt*.'

Wsir Sȝwyṯr bwȝ wr m niwt.f ms n Ḥwt-Ḥr Pymt

'The Osiris *Sȝwyṯr*, the great magistrate of his town, born of the Hathor *Pymt*.'

Shroud BM EA 6705 A (filiation and titles only):

Hȝ Wsir Sȝwtr ms n Ḥwt-Ḥr Pymt ... sr m niwt.f bwȝ ʿȝ n spȝt.f Wȝst.

'Hail Osiris *Sȝwȝḏr* born of *Pymt* ... the noble in his town, the great magistrate of his nome Thebes.'

P. BM EA 10282 and 10283 (**4**), found in the coffin BM EA 6705, and belonging to *Swtr*, born of *Pȝ-krr* (?) and *Pylt* (Philous).

— Father of Apollonides, Petemenophis I, Sensaos I. See under these names.

Soter II

— Son of *Ḏȝpwr* (Sapaulis II).

P. Louvre N 3156 and P. Louvre N 3289 (21), both belonging to *Swtr* (Soter II), born of *Ḏȝpwr* (Sapaulis II). His lifetime is indicated twice in P. Louvre N 3289, in hieratic (rt. 6–7) and in Greek on the verso: 4 years, 5 months and 2 days.

Tkauthi I[80] *(Tȝ-ḳȝw-ḏȝ)*

— Probably, daughter of Cleopatra I Candace.

— Wife of Pebos = (?) Pikos, and mother of *Pȝ-di-Imn-Ipt* II. See under this last name.

— Mother of Senchonsis (*Tȝ-šrit-Ḫnsw*), alias Sapaulis II (*Ḏȝpwr*). See under *Sapaulis II*.

Tkauthi II (Tȝ-ḳȝw-ḏȝ)

— Daughter of Cleopatra I Candace.

— Sister of *Tȝ-šrit-Ḏd-Ḥr* (Sensaos II). See under this name.

Coffin Berlin 505 (**12**). See under *Sensaos II*; P. Berlin 3069 (**14**), now lost, belonging to *Tȝ-ḳȝw-ḏȝ* (Tkauthi II).[81]

Tlelous (Tȝ-lw(ȝ)lw)

See under *Sensoter*.

Tphous (Tȝ-ḥfȝt) (October 29, AD 120–January 15, AD 127. Buried on November 9 AD, 127.[82]

— Daughter of Heracleios and of Sarapous (*Srpw*).

Coffin BM EA 6708 **(22)**. List PM no. 2. *CIG* III, 4826 + add., p. 12 = *SB* V, 8369, text revised by P.J. Sijpesteijn in *ZPE* 112 (1996), p. 178:

Ταφὴ Τφοῦτος Ἡρακλείου Σωτῆρος, μητρὸς Σαραποῦτος ἐγεν<*ν*>*ήθη τῶι ε (ἔτει) Ἁδριανοῦ τοῦ κυρίου, Ἀθὺρ* <*ι*>*β, καὶ*

76. In this subscription, the sequence *tȝy.f snt Tȝ- šrit-Ḏd-Ḥr* could be also a reference to Sensaos II.

77. Two children's mummies were found inside the coffin. See van Landuyt, in *Hundred-Gated Thebes*, p. 75, n. 26.

78. U. Kaplony-Heckel, *Ägyptische Handschriften* III (Stuttgart 1986), p. 33, no. 48.

79. Van Landuyt, in *Hundred-Gated Thebes*, p. 71. On the archon, see P. Jouguet, in *Précis de l'histoire d'Egypte par divers historiens et archéologues* I (Cairo 1932), pp. 346 and 379–80.

80. For this name: Van Landuyt, in *Hundred- Gated Thebes*, pp. 76–7.

81. U. Kaplony-Heckel, *Ägyptische Handschriften* III (Stuttgart 1986), no. 49.

82. For the delay, sometimes important, observed between the death and the burying, see van Landuyt, in *Hundred-Gated Thebes*, p. 77, n. 35.

ἐτελεύτησεν τῶι ια (ἔτει) μ̣η̣ν̣ὶ̣ Τ̣ῦ̣β̣ι̣ κ̄, [. .] ἐτῶν ἕξ, μηνῶν δύο, ἡμερῶν η̄ καὶ ἐταφη τῶι ιβ (ἔτει), μηνὶ Ἀθὺρ ι̅β̅.

'Coffin of Tphous daughter of Heracleios son of Soter, (and) of (his) mother Sarapous. She was born in (year) 5 of Hadrian, the lord, on the 12th of Athyr, and died in (the year) 11, on the 20th of Tybi. (She lived for) 6 years, 2 months and 8 days. She was buried in year 12, on the 12th of the month Athyr.'

Hieroglyphic inscription:
rnpt.s n ꜥnḫ 6 ꜣbd 3 (?) *Ḥwt-Ḥr ḥwnt Tꜣ-ḥfꜣt ms n Srpw*

'Her lifetime was 6 years, 3 (?) months. The Hathor, the maiden *Tꜣ-ḥfꜣt*, born of *Srpw*.'

P. BM EA 10256 and 10259 (**23**), belonging to *Tꜣ-ḥfꜣt* (Tphous), born of *Srpw* (Sarapous).

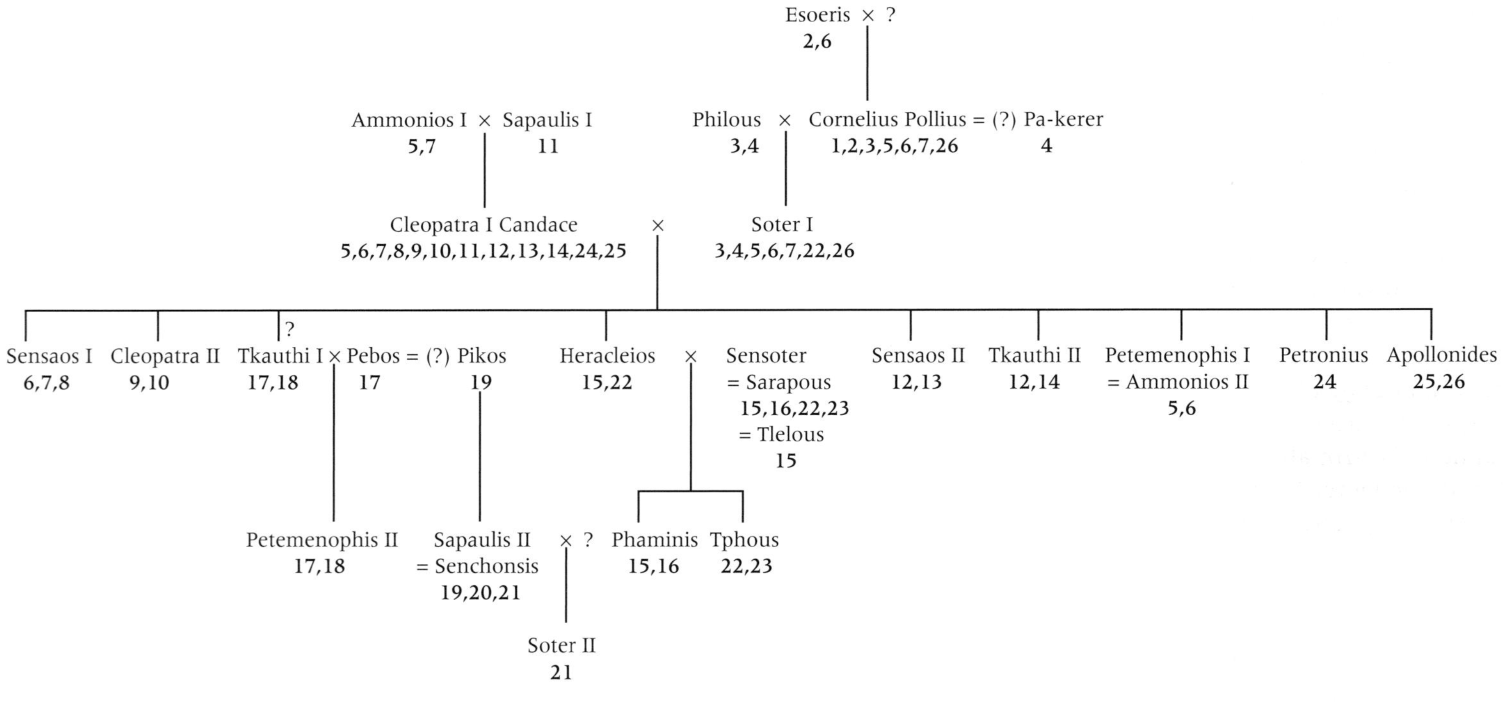

The Soter Family
Numbers in bold refer to the documents where the anthroponyms are cited. See the list on p. 6.

1. Book of Breathing made by Isis for her brother Osiris

P. BM EA 10048 (pls 1–14)

Sams Collection 42.
Unpublished.
Quirke, *Owners*, no. 186.
Provenance: Thebes.
Date: Ptolemaic Period.
Owner of the papyrus: *Pꜣ-ỉỉ-n-Ḥr* (Pinuris).
Titles: *ỉt-nṯr ḥm-nṯr n ỉmn-Rꜥ nsw nṯrw*, 'god's father and prophet of Amun-Re, king of the gods'.
Mother of the owner: *Tꜣ-ḫy-bỉꜣ* (Chibois).

Contents: Book of Breathing made by Isis for her brother Osiris

This *Pꜣ-ỉỉ-n-Ḥr*, son of *Tꜣ-ḫy-bỉꜣt*, is probably to be identified with the owner of P. BM EA 10033 and perhaps of P. Munich BSB cod. hier. 1. Since the father's name is not mentioned in P. BM EA 10048, the identification of *Pꜣ-ỉỉ-n-Ḥr* with the son of *Ḥr* and *Tꜣ-ḫy-bỉꜣ* (*ProsPtol* IX, no. 5775 j) remains uncertain despite a partial resemblance between their titles. On the name *Pꜣ-ỉỉ-n-Ḥr*, also written *Pꜣ-ỉw-n-Ḥr* in the manuscript: H. De Meulenaere, *BiOr* 34 (1977), p. 254; R. El Sayed, *MDAIK* 40 (1984), p. 255, n. p.

Manuscript of seven columns of text, now mounted in two glass frames (cols I–IV: 72 × 9 cm; cols V–VII: 68.5 × 9 cm). Although in a relatively good state of conservation, it bears stains from the bituminous or resinous matter which, over a broad area of col. I and the upper part of the rest of the papyrus, affects the legibility of the text. These columns, of broadly similar dimensions (apart from III and particularly VII, of greater length), each contain from seven to eleven lines. No text appears on the verso.

Translation

I (1) Beginning of the Book of Breathing made by Isis for her brother Osiris, in order to make his ba live, to rejuvenate his corpse, (2) to make live again each of his limbs; that he may join the horizon with his father Re, and cause his ba to appear in the sky as the disk of the moon; (3) that he may shine as Orion in the womb of Nut, and to cause that the same happen (for) the Osiris *Pꜣ-ỉỉ-n-Ḥr*, justified.

(4) To be recited: Hail Osiris, god's father and prophet of Amun-Re king of the gods *Pꜣ-ỉỉ-n-Ḥr*, justified, born of *Tꜣ-ḫy-bỉꜣ*: (5) you are pure, your *ḥꜣty*-heart is pure, your fore is pure, your rear is pure, your middle (is purified) with *bd*-natron and *ḥsmn*-natron (6) and there is no limb in you in a state of evil. The Osiris *Pꜣ-ỉỉ-n-Ḥr*, justified, born of *Tꜣ-ḫy-bỉꜣ*, is pure (7) in this pool of the Field of offerings, to the north of the Field of locusts. Wadjyt (8) and Nekhbet purify you in the fourth hour of the night and in the eighth hour of the day. Come then, Osiris *Pꜣ-ỉỉ-n-Ḥr*, justified! (9) You enter the hall of the two Maats, (for) you are pure from any fault and any crime! 'Stone of Maat' is your name.

II (1) Hail Osiris *Pꜣ-ỉỉ-n-Ḥr*, justified, born of *Tꜣ-ḫy-bỉꜣ*, you enter the Duat (2) in great purity. The two Maats purify you in the great hall, and purification is made for you in the hall of Geb. Your limbs (3) are purified in the hall of light, and you see Re when he sets, Atum in the evening. Amun is with you, (4) giving you breath. Ptah fashions your limbs. You arrive at the horizon with Re. Your ba is received (5) on board the *nšmt*-bark with Osiris. Your ba is divinized in the House of Geb, and you are justified for ever and eternally.

(6) Hail Osiris *Pꜣ-ỉỉ-n-Ḥr*, justified, born of *Tꜣ-ḫy-bỉꜣ*, your name is established, your corpse stable, (7) your mummy firm, (so that) you will not be turned back in the sky or on earth. Your mummy is illuminated before Re, your ba lives before Amun, your corpse (8) is renewed before Osiris, and you breathe for ever and eternally!

The son of your brother performs for you an invocation offering of bread, beer, oxen and fowl, with (9) libation and censing, every day. You come at his voice according to your form upon earth. You drink with your throat and eat with your mouth. You receive (10) *snw*-loaves with the bas of the gods. Anubis protects you and makes your protection (so that) you will not be turned back from the entrances of the Duat, the West of Thebes.

III (1) Thoth the twice great, lord of Hermopolis, comes to you; he writes for you a Book of Breathing, with his own fingers, and your ba breathes for ever. You repeat the form which was yours upon earth as a living man. (2) You are divine with the bas of the gods. Your heart is the heart of Re, your limbs are the limbs of the great god.

Hail Osiris *Pꜣ-ỉỉ-n-Ḥr*, justified, born of *Tꜣ-ḫy-biꜣ*, (3) Amun is with you every day, and Re renews you alive.Wepwawet opens for you a good way. You see with your eyes, hear with your ears, speak with your mouth, walk with your legs. Your (4) ba is divine in the Duat, assuming any form you desire, receiving the freshness (?) of the noble balanites-tree of Osiris. You are awakened every day and you see the rays of Re (or: of the disk). (5) The lord of the gods, Amun, comes to you, full of the breath of life. He causes you to breathe within the coffin. You go out upon earth every day (*bis*). The Book of Breathing of Thoth is your protection; you breathe (6) by it every day, like Re. Your eyes see the rays of the disk. 'Maat' is said concerning you in the presence of Osiris, and 'justified' is written on your tongue. Horus of Behedet protects your body; (7) he divinizes your ba like (that of) every god. The Ba of Re makes your ba live, and the Ba of Shu joins your nostrils.

Hail Osiris *Pꜣ-ỉỉ-n-Ḥr*, justified, born of *Tꜣ-*(8)*ḫy-biꜣ*, your ba breathes in every place you desire. You are Osiris, and 'Osiris foremost of the West' is your name. Hapy the great comes to you from Elephantine; he fills your offering-tables (9) with food. Osiris *Pꜣ-ỉỉ-n-Ḥr*, justified, the gods of Upper and Lower Egypt come to you, guiding you towards Areq-heh. Your ba lives, and you follow Osiris. (10) You breathe in Ro-setau, and Hapounnebes protects you together with the great god. Your corpse lives in Busiris and Ta-wer. Your ba lives in the sky every day. (11) Osiris N, Sekhmet controls those who plot against you. Horus the great makes your protection, and Horus of Behedet protects your heart.

IV (1) Hor-merty guards your body, and you are stable in life, prosperity and health; you are established on your throne, in the sacred land. Come then, Osiris (2) *Pꜣ-ỉỉ-n-Ḥr*, justified, born of *Tꜣ-ḫy-biꜣ*, you are great in your forms, equipped in your character, complete in your ornaments. You spend the night (3) in life, you spend the day in health. You walk, breathing in every place, and Re shines over you as (over) Osiris. You breathe, you live on (4) his rays. Amun-Re, he makes your ka live and he praises you by the Book of Breathing. You unite with Shu, the son of Re. You enter the Duat, and your enemies (5) exist no more. You are a divine ba in Busiris. Your heart belongs to you and will not be far from you; your eyes belong to you, open every day.

To be recited by the gods (6) who are in the retinue of Osiris, for the Osiris N: you follow Re, you follow Osiris, and your ba is alive for ever and eternally.

(7) To be recited by Osiris foremost of the West, to the gods who are in the Duat, (on behalf of) the Osiris, god's father and god's servant *Pꜣ-ỉỉ-n-Ḥr*, justified, born of *Tꜣ-ḫy-biꜣ*, (8) that there may be may be opened for him the gates of the Duat: May his corpse be received in the god's domain! May his ba live for ever! May he build a portal (9) in the god's domain! May his ka praise his god, (for) he has received a Book of Breathing. May he indeed breathe!

Offering that the king gives (10) to Osiris foremost of the West, the great god, lord of Abydos, that he may grant an invocation offering of bread, beer, cattle, fowl, wine, milk, *ḥtpw*-offerings and food, all things good (11) and pure, for the ka of the Osiris N. Your ba is alive, your corpse is firm by the decree of Re himself, (12) without destruction or decay, like Re, for ever and eternally.

V (1) O Far-strider, who came forth from Heliopolis, the Osiris *Pꜣ-ỉỉ-n-Ḥr*, justified, born of *Tꜣ-ḫy-biꜣ*, has done no evil.

(2) O Open-mouthed, who came forth from Kher-Aha, the Osiris *Pꜣ-ỉỉ-n-Ḥr*, justified, born of *Tꜣ-ḫy-biꜣ*, has committed no theft.

(3) O Beaked one, who came forth from Hermopolis, the Osiris *Pꜣ-ỉỉ-n-Ḥr*, justified, born of *Tꜣ-ḫy-biꜣ*, has created no harm.

(4) O Swallower of the Eye, who came forth from the two caverns, the Osiris *Pꜣ-ỉỉ-n-Ḥr*, justified, born of *Tꜣ-ḫy-biꜣ*, has taken no goods by stealth.

(5) O Nehaher who came forth from Ro-setau, the Osiris *Pꜣ-ỉỉ-n-Ḥr*, justified, born of *Tꜣ-ḫy-biꜣ*, has spread no rumours.

(6) O Ruty who came forth from the sky, the Osiris *Pꜣ-ỉỉ-n-Ḥr*, justified, born of *Tꜣ-ḫy-biꜣ*, has done no evil by (falsifying) the plummet (of the balance) (?).

(7) O He whose eye is a flame, who came forth from Letopolis, the Osiris *Pꜣ-ỉỉ-n-Ḥr*, justified, born of *Tꜣ-ḫy-biꜣ*, has not taken property of a god.

(8) O Fiery-faced, who came out backwards, the Osiris *Pꜣ-ỉỉ-n-Ḥr*, justified, born of *Tꜣ-ḫy-biꜣ*, has not aroused the anger of a god.

(9) O Breaker of bones, who came forth from Letopolis, the Osiris *Pꜣ-ỉỉ-n-Ḥr*, justified, born of *Tꜣ-ḫy-biꜣ*, has not taken the goods of another.

(10) O Savage-faced, who came forth from Bubastis, the Osiris *Pꜣ-ỉỉ-n-Ḥr*, justified, born of *Tꜣ-ḫy-biꜣ*, has not caused his eye to weep over sickness.

VI (1) O Repeller of the fighter, who came forth from Unu, the Osiris *Pꜣ-ỉỉ-n-Ḥr*, justified, born of *Tꜣ-ḫy-biꜣ*, has made no seditious combat.

(2) O He whose head is behind him, who came forth from Tepehet-djat, the Osiris *Pꜣ-ỉỉ-n-Ḥr*, justified, born of *Tꜣ-ḫy-biꜣ*, has not fornicated.

(3) O He who feeds on blood, who came forth from the

slaughterhouse, the Osiris *Pꜣ-ỉỉ-n-Ḥr*, justified, born of *Tꜣ-ḫy-bỉꜣ*, has not committed injury against the divine herd.

(4) O Wamenty who came forth from the place of execution, the Osiris *Pꜣ-ỉỉ-n-Ḥr*, justified, born of *Tꜣ-ḫy-bỉꜣ*, has not fornicated with a married woman.

(5) O Strong of voice, who came forth from the *wryt*-sanctuary, the Osiris *Pꜣ-ỉỉ-n-Ḥr*, justified, born of *Tꜣ-ḫy-bỉꜣ*, has not raised his voice.

(6) O Aged one, who came forth from Heqa-andj, the Osiris *Pꜣ-ỉỉ-n-Ḥr*, justified, born of *Tꜣ-ḫy-bỉꜣ*, has not aroused hatred.

(7) O He <whose head> is reversed, who came forth from Tenu, the Osiris *Pꜣ-ỉỉ-n-Ḥr*, justified, born of *Tꜣ-ḫy-bỉꜣ*, has not destroyed a burial.

(8) O Nefertum, who came forth from the Domain of the ka of Ptah, the Osiris *Pꜣ-ỉỉ-n-Ḥr*, justified, born of *Tꜣ-ḫy-bỉꜣ*, has not blasphemed against god.

(9) O Lord of the winds who gives to whom he wishes, the Osiris *Pꜣ-ỉỉ-n-Ḥr*, justified, born of *Tꜣ-ḫy-bỉꜣ*, has not blasphemed against the king.

(10) O Ihy, who came forth from Nun, the Osiris *Pꜣ-ỉỉ-n-Ḥr*, justified, born of *Tꜣ-ḫy-bỉꜣ*, has not vilified of his mother.

VII (1) O Nehebka foremost of Thebes, the Osiris *Pꜣ-ỉỉ-n-Ḥr*, justified, born of *Tꜣ-ḫy-bỉꜣ*, has not raised his voice.

(2) O gods who are in the Duat, hear the voice of the Osiris *Pꜣ-ỉỉ-n-Ḥr*, justified, born of *Tꜣ-ḫy-bỉꜣ*! He is come before you with no evil in him, and no iniquity about him, nor any witness standing against him. (3) He lives on Maat, and feeds on Maat, and the gods are pleased with all that he has done. He has given bread to the hungry, water to the thirsty, clothing to the naked; he has given *ḥtpw*-offerings to the gods and invocation offerings (4) to the spirits. No report has been made against him in the presence of any god. May he enter the Duat without being turned back! May he follow Osiris with the gods of the caverns, for he is praised (5) among the praised ones, divine among the excellent ones! May he live, may his heart live, (for) <he has> received his Book of Breathing. May he breathe indeed with the great bas (6) of the Duat, and may he assume any form at his wish like the Westerners. May his ba go wherever he desires (7) and he will be alive according to the living form as he was when alive upon earth, for ever (*bis*) and eternally (*bis*).

Commentary

I, 1–3

The opening of the papyrus (§ 1 of de Horrack's classification)[1] presents the title and the general programme of the text, both lost in P. Louvre N 3158,[2] omitted in P. BM EA 9995 = P. Louvre N 3126,[3] and partly in lacuna in P. Florence 3665 + P. Vienna 3850, I. The title is that found in most manuscripts of the Book of Breathing made by Isis, namely: *ḥꜣt-ꜥ m šꜥt (n) snsn ỉrt.n Ỉst n*[4] *sn.s Wsỉr* (P. Berlin 3154, I, 1 = P. Lausanne 3391, I, 1 = P. Louvre N 3121, I, 1 = P. Louvre N 3154, I, 1 = P. Louvre N 3291, 1). Variants concern the relative form *ỉrt.n* and are minor (masculine *ỉr.n*, P. Berlin 3135, I, 1 = P. BN 179–81, I, 1 = P. Denon, I, 1 = P. Louvre N 3167 + 3222, I, 1 = P. Louvre N 3284, I, 1 = P. Louvre N 3285, I, 1 = P. Tübingen 2016, II, 1 = P. Vienna 3863, I, 1, or simply *ỉr*, P. Louvre E 11079, I, 1[5] = P. Vienna 3931, I, 1). P. Joseph Smith, II, 1–4 is too lacunose to be considered.[6] On the ambiguity of the verb *ỉr* which can mean either 'do' (i.e. in this context 'write') or 'recite', see Smith, *Mortuary Texts*, p. 56 (I, 1, b). As in the present text, it is again Isis who is cited in the first composition drawn up in favour of Osiris in P. BM EA 10507 (dem.), as author or reciter of the text (*mḏꜣ ỉr.n ꜣst r Wsỉr ḫnt Ỉmnt*, 'Book written (recited ?) by Isis for Osiris foremost of the West').[7]

Comparison of the introductory passage of the text with other versions reveals some minimal divergences.

r sꜥnḫ bꜣ.f r srnp ẖꜣt.f. Same reading in P. Louvre N 3154, I, 1–2. Sequence in lacuna in P. Joseph Smith, II, 1 = P. Florence 3665 + P. Vienna 3850, I. Var. P. Lausanne 3391, I, 2: *r ꜥnḫ ẖꜣt.f*; P. Louvre N 3291, 1: *r snḫn ẖꜣt.f*; P. Berlin 3135, I, 2 = P. Berlin 3154, I, 1 = P. BN 179–81, I, 2 = P. Denon, I, 1 = P. Louvre E 11079, I, 2 = P. Louvre N 3121, I, 1–2 = P. Louvre N 3167 + 3222, I, 1–2 = P. Louvre N 3284, I, 1–2 = P. Louvre N 3285, I, 1 = P. Tübingen 2016, II, 2 = P. Vienna 3863, I, 2 = P. Vienna 3931, I, 1: *r sꜥnḫ ẖꜣt.f*. For the rejuvenation of the corpse, see *infra*, **II, 7–8**; P. BM EA 10314, I, 2: [*ꜥnḫ bꜣ.k m pt*] *ḫr Rꜥ rnp ẖꜣt.k m Dwꜣt ḫr Wsỉr*; P. Tübingen 2016, I, 13–14: *ꜥnḫ bꜣ.k r nḥḥ rnp ẖꜣt.k ḏt*; E. von Bergmann, *Der Sarkophag des Panehemisis* II (Vienna 1884), p. 15, n. 3: *srnp ẖꜣt.k m ẖrt-nṯr*; J.J. Clère, *OA* 12 (1973), p. 99: *ꜥnḫ bꜣ.k r<np> ẖꜣt.k rwḏ rn.k*; Maspero, *Sarcophages* I, p. 9, lines 15–16: *rnp ẖꜣt.f m Ỉmntt*; ibid., p. 22: *rnp ẖꜣt.k*; ibid., p. 56: *rnp ẖꜣt.k mỉ Ỉꜥḥ*.

r sꜥnḫ ḥꜥw.f nb m wḥm. Same reading in P. Louvre N 3154, I, 2. Sequence almost wholly in lacuna in P. Florence 3665 + P. Vienna 3850, I (only part of the word *wḥm* subsists in I, x + 1) = P. Joseph Smith, II, [1]–2 (same remark). Var. P. Berlin 3135, I, 2 = P. Berlin 3154, I, 1 = P. BN 179–81, I, 2–3 = P. Denon, I, 1–2 = P. Lausanne 3391, I, 2 = P. Louvre E 11079, I, 2–3 = P. Louvre N 3121, I, 2 = P. Louvre N 3167 + 3222, I, 2 = P. Louvre N 3284, I, 2 = P. Louvre N 3285, I, 2 = P. Louvre N 3291, 1 = P. Tübingen 2016, II, 2 = P. Vienna 3863, I, 2 = P. Vienna 3931, I, 2: *r srnp (ỉ)ḥꜥw.f*[8] *nb m wḥm*.

r ẖnm.f ꜣḫt ḥnꜥ ỉt.f Rꜥ. Same reading in P. BN 179–81, I, 3 = P. Denon, I, 2 = P. Louvre E 11079, I, 3 = P. Louvre N 3121, I, 2 = P. Louvre N 3154, I,

1. De Horrack, *Le Livre des Respirations*, pp. 1–2 and pls I–V. In fact, that classification, used here for sake of convenience, is initially due to Brugsch who divided the work into fourteen paragraphs (*Sai an sinsin* [Berlin 1851], pp. 25–32). Subsequently it was kept by Devéria (*Catalogue*, p. 130 ff.) and by De Horrack, who merely separated § 14 into § 14 a and § 14 b. See M. Coenen, *RdE* 49 (1998), p. 43.
2. The beginning of P. Louvre N 3158, II, corresponds to P. BM EA 10048, II, 2–3.
3. In P. Louvre N 3126, whose beginning corresponds to P. BM EA 10048, I, 4, probably the missing part showed some illustration, maybe that given as page 5 by Devéria (*Catalogue*, p. 136 [IV, 6]). See for comparison P. BM EA 9995.
4. *n* omitted in P. Lausanne 3391, I, 1 = P. Louvre N 3285, I, 1.
5. Among the copies of the Book of Breathing made by Isis, P. Louvre E 11079 is surely the least conventional. More than simple variants, it shows so many differences with the other versions (misplacing of sequences, large omissions, inversions of sequences and additions of new ones) that it cannot be considered in its largest part as a parallel version of P. BM EA 10048. Therefore references to it will not be made systematically.
6. Col. I of P. Joseph Smith is exceptionally preceded with § 14 b of de Horrack's classification which is usually found at the end of the Book of Breathing made by Isis.
7. Smith, *Mortuary Texts*, p. 21.
8. Note the form of *.f* in P. Berlin 3154, I, 1.

2–3 = P. Louvre N 3284, I, 2 = P. Louvre N 3285, I, 2 = P. Louvre N 3291, 1–2 = P. Tübingen 2016, II, 2 = P. Vienna 3863, I, 2 = P. Vienna 3931, I, 2. Sequence wholly in lacuna in P. Florence 3665 + P. Vienna 3850, I, x + 1, and partly in P. Joseph Smith, II, 2 = P. Louvre N 3167 + 3222, I, 2. Var. P. Berlin 3154, I, 2: *ḫnm.n.f*; P. Berlin 3135, I, 2: *ȝḫt.f*; P. Lausanne 3391, I, 3: *it.f Wsir*.

r sḫʿ bȝ.f m pt m itn n Iʿḥ. Same version in P. Denon, I, 2 = P. Louvre N 3121, I, 2–3 = P. Louvre N 3167 + 3222, 2–3 = P. Louvre N 3284, I, 2–3 = P. Louvre N 3291, 2 = P. Tübingen 2016, II, 3 = P. Vienna 3863, I, 3. Sequence wholly in lacuna in P. Joseph Smith, II, 2, and partly in P. Florence 3665 + P. Vienna 3850, I, x + 1–2. Var. P. Berlin 3135, I, 3 = P. Lausanne 3391, I, 3 = P. Louvre E 11079, I, 3–4 = P. Louvre N 3285, I, 3: *n pt* (equivalence of *n* and *m*); P. Louvre N 3154, I, 3: *r ḫʿ bȝ.f m pt*; omission of *r* in P. Vienna 3931, I, 2; of *n* before *Iʿḥ* in P. BN 179–81, I, 4 = P. Berlin 3154, I, 2.

r psḏ.f n Sȝḥ m ẖt Nnt (*Nwt*). Sequence wholly in lacuna in P. Joseph Smith, II, 2, and partly in P. Florence 3665 + P. Vienna 3850, I, x + 2. Var. P. Louvre N 3154, I, 3: *m Sȝḥ*; P. Berlin 3135, I, 3–4 = P. Berlin 3154, I, 2 = P. BN 179–81, I, 4–5 = P. Denon, I, 2–3 = P. Lausanne 3391, I, 3–4 = P. Louvre E 11079, I, 4 = P. Louvre N 3121, I, 3 = P. Louvre N 3167 + 3222, I, 3 = P. Louvre N 3284, I, 3 = P. Louvre N 3285, I, 3 = P. Louvre N 3291, 2 = P. Tübingen 2016, II, 3 = P. Vienna 3863, I, 3 = P. Vienna 3931, I, 3: *r psḏ ḥȝt.f m Sȝḥ*. On Osiris as 'Orion in the womb of Nenet (Nut)', see *LPE*, p. 276 (3).

[*r*] *rdit ḫpr mitt nn n Wsir N*. Same reading in P. Berlin 3135, I, 3–4 = P. BN 179–81, I, 5–9 = P. Denon, I, 3–6 = P. Florence 3665 + P. Vienna 3850, I, x + 3–4 = P. Louvre E 11079, I, 5 = P. Louvre N 3121, I, 3–4 = P. Louvre N 3284, I, 4–6 = P. Louvre N 3291, 2–5 = P. Tübingen 2016, II, 4–10. Sequence partly in lacuna in P. Joseph Smith, II, 2–3. Var. P. Louvre N 3154, I, 4–5: *r rdit ḫpr mitt nn Wsir N*; P. Vienna 3863, I, 4–6: *r rdit ḫpr mi nn n Wsir N*; P. Louvre N 3167 + 3222, I, 3–5 = P. Lausanne 3391, I, 4–5 = P. Vienna 3931, I, 3–4: *r rdit ḫpr mi nn Wsir N*; P. Louvre N 3285, I, 3–5: *r ir mitt nn Wsir N*; P. Berlin 3154, I, 2–4: *r rdit ḫpr mitt n-m* ( ) *Wsir* [9] *N*. Incorrect addition of *mitt ḥḥ n sp*, 'likewise, a million times', in P. Louvre E 11079, I, 7 (see *infra*, **I, 4–6**).

Some documents bear a different introduction:
P. Louvre N 3083, V, 1–2 (after *BD* ch. 54 [var.], 57 [var.], 58 [var.]:

rȝ n snsn ʿnḫ m ṯȝw m ẖrt-nṯr	'Formula for breathing alive on the air in the god's domain.
ḏd mdw hȝy Wsir N	To be recited: Hail Osiris N!'

The following phrases correspond to P. BM EA 10048, I, 5 ff. This is also the point where P. BM EA 9995 begins.
P. Louvre N 3166, I, 1–4:

ky rȝ n pr m hrw	'Another formula for going forth by day,
tm rdit wnm.f ḥsw m ẖrt-nṯr	to cause him not to eat excrement in the god's domain,
swr n Mȝʿt wnm n Mȝʿt	(but) to drink Maat, to eat Maat,[10]
ir ḫprw nb mr.f	to assume any form he desires,
sʿnḫ bȝ.f srnp ẖt.f	to make his ba live, to rejuvenate his body,[11]
sʿnḫ ḥʿw.f nb m wḥm	to make all his limbs live again,
rdit ḫnmf ȝḫt ḥnʿ it.f Rʿ	to cause him to join the horizon with his father Re,
rdi ḫʿ bȝ.f m pt m itn n Iʿḥ	to cause his ba to appear in the sky as the disk of the moon,
rdi psḏ.f n Sȝḥ m ẖt Nnt	to cause him to shine as Orion in the womb of Nenet
rdi ḫpr.f mi wnn.f ḫnt (?)	and cause him to become as he was before.'

On the manifestation of the Ba of Osiris as the moon, see the Ritual of bringing Sokar out of the *šṯyt*-shrine, P. Louvre I 3079, CXIII, 8 (J.C. Goyon, *RdE* 20 [1968] p. 67) = G. Burkard, *Spätzeitliche Osiris-Liturgien* (*ÄAT* 31, 1995), p. 231:

I Bȝ ʿnḫ n Wsir ḫʿ.f n Iʿḥ	'O living Ba of Osiris (when) he appears as the moon!'

For the well known connection between Osiris and the moon, see Ph. Derchain, in *La Lune, mythes et rites* (*SO* 5, 1962), pp. 44–6; R.K. Ritner, *JEA* 71 (1985), p. 152; F.R. Herbin, *BIFAO* 82 (1982), pp. 261–2, n. 6; Smith, *Mortuary Texts*, p. 60 (I, 12).

In a funerary context, this relation serves to model the rejuvenation of the god – and thus of the deceased person identified with him – on the lunar cycle; see e.g. P. Parma 183, 5–6:

ʿnḫ bȝ.k m pt ḫr Rʿ	'Your ba lives in the sky before Re,
rnp rn.k r nḥḥ ḥnʿ ḏt	your name is young for ever and eternally
wnn Iʿḥ ḥr psḏ m grḥ	(when) the moon shines during the night.'

Ritual of Embalming, IV, 4 (ed. Sauneron, p. 11):

mȝȝ bȝ.k ḥr ḫȝt.k ḏt	'Your ba remains upon your corpse, eternally,[12]
iw.k wḥm rnp mi Iʿḥ	and you renew youth like the moon.'

P. BM EA 10209, III, 3 (Haikal, *Two Hier. Fun. Pap.* I, p. 36):

dit ʿḳ.k m irt iȝbt	'(I) cause you to enter into the left eye
ḫpr.k m Iʿḥ	and (cause you to) become the moon.'

I, 4–6

ḏd mdw hȝy Wsir N iw.k wʿb ḥȝty.k wʿb ḫȝt.k m ʿb pḥ.k m twr ḥr(t)-ib.k m bd ḥsmn nn ʿt im.k m isft. Beginning of § 2 of de Horrack's classification. Same reading in P. Florence 3665 + P. Vienna 3850, II, 1–4 = P. Lausanne 3391, I, 7–9 = P. Louvre N 3121, I, 4–6 = P. Louvre N 3284, I, 8–11 = P. Louvre N 3285, I, 6–9 = P. Louvre N 3291, 6–7 = P. Vienna 3863, I, 7–11 = P. Vienna 3931, I, 6–8 (small lacunae). Sequence partly in lacuna in P. Joseph Smith, II, 5–6 = P. Louvre N 3167 + 3222, I, 7–9. Omission of *ḏd mdw* in P. BN 179–81, I, 11 = P. BM EA 9995, I, 1 = P. Berlin 3135, I, 8 = P. Berlin 3154, I, 5 = P. Louvre N 3166, I, 4 = P. Louvre N 3167 + 3222, I, 7 = P. Tübingen 2016, II, 11; of *ḥȝty.k wʿb* and of *m* after *ḫȝt.k* in P. Denon, I, 8. Speech in the third person in P. Louvre N 3166, I, 4–6 (*m bd.f ḥsmn.f* (?), *m isft.f*). Var. P. Louvre E 11079, I, 7–8: *ḏd mdw in Wsir Ḥwt-Ḥr N*; P. Louvre N 3083, V, 2 = P. Louvre N 3167 + 3222, I, 7: *twk* (*twt*) *wʿb*; P. BM EA 9995, I, 1 = P. Berlin 3154, I, 5: *iw.k wʿb.ti*; P. Louvre E 11079, I, 10: *m ʿt.t im.t*.

Many manuscripts place before this section a parenthetical set of clauses concerning the simultaneously secret and beneficial character of the text. P. Berlin 3135, I, 7–8 = P. Berlin 3154, I, 4–5 = P. BN 179–81, I, 9–11 = P. Denon, I, 6–7 = P. Florence 3665 + P. Vienna 3850, II, 4–5 = P. Joseph Smith, II, 3–4 (partly in lacuna) = P. Lausanne 3391, I, 5–6 = P. Louvre N 3167 + 3222, I, 5–6 = P. Louvre N 3284, I, 6–7 = P. Louvre N 3285, I, 5–6 = P. Louvre N 3291, 5–6 = P. Tübingen 2016, II, 10–11 = P. Vienna 3863, I, 6–7 = P. Vienna 3931, I, 5–6:

9. Written .
10. See P. BM EA 10048, **VII, 3**.
11. Or 'his corpse', if *ẖt* is considered to be a writing of *ḫȝt*: *LPE*, p. 83, n. 1.
12. On the spelling *mȝȝ* of the verb *mn*, 'remain': *LPE*, p. 249 (VIII, 3–4).

ḥꜣp sp 2	'This is a secret (*bis*)!
im.k[13] *rdit ꜥš s(w) s*[14] *nb*	Do not allow anyone to recite it.
ꜣḫ s(w) n[15] *s m ḫrt-nṯr*	It is useful to a man in the god's domain,
ꜥnḫ.f[16] *m wḥm*	(such that) he lives again,
m[17] *šs mꜣꜥt ḥḥ n sp*	truly, a million times.'

Except P. BM EA 9995, all texts including this passage introduce the elaboration of the theme of bodily purity with the words *ḏd mdw hꜣy (Wsir) N*, introducing § 2 of de Horrack's classification. This new sequence finds its roots in the Book of the Dead where it occurs in two formulae:

BD ch. 125 (ed. Budge, p. 262, 8–11):

iw.i wꜥb.kwi	'I am purified,
ḥꜣt.i m ꜥb	my fore is pure,
pḥwy.i twr	my rear is pure,
ḥr(t)-ib.i m šdyt Mꜣꜥt	my middle is in the pool of Maat.
nn ꜥt im.i šwt m Mꜣꜥt	There is no limb in me empty of Maat.'

BD ch. 125 (ed. Lepsius, pl. 48, 44–5):

iw.f wꜥb	'He is pure,
iw ḥꜣty.f wꜥb	his *ḥꜣty*-heart is pure,
ḥꜣt.f m ꜥb	his fore is pure,
pḥ.f m twr	his rear is pure,
ḥr(t)-ib.f m šdyt Mꜣꜥt	his middle is in the pool of Maat,
nn ꜥt im.f m isft	and there is no limb in him in evil.'

BD ch. 169 (ed. Budge, pp. 436, 15–437, 1):

iw.k wꜥb.ti sp 2	'You are purified (*bis*),
ḥꜣt.k m ꜥb	your fore is pure,
pḥwy.k m twr	your rear is pure,
m bd ḥsmn	with *bd*-natron and *ḥsmn*-natron.'

P. Rhind I, 6, 13 (ed. Möller, p. 32):

iw.k wꜥb ḥꜣty.k wꜥb	'You are pure, your *ḥꜣty*-heart is pure,
ꜥwt.k nb twr	all your limbs are pure.'

Book of Breathing, version P. Parma 183, 12–13 (G. Botti, in *Atti della 'Societa Colombaria Fiorentina'* (Florence 1939), pl. II:

iw ḥꜣt.k m wꜥb	'Your fore is pure,
pḥy.k m twr	your rear is pure,
ḥr(t)-ib.k m bd ḥsmn	your middle (is purified) with *bd*-natron and *ḥsmn*-natron.
iw Mꜣꜥt m ib.k	Maat is in your heart
nn isft m ꜥwt.k	and there is no evil in your limbs.'

A partial duplicate of this latter manuscript occurs in P. OIC 25389, XXXIII, 13–XXXIV, 2 (omission of *m* before *wꜥb*, *m twr ḥsmn* for *m bd ḥsmn*, *ibw* for *ib*, and different text after *isft*. See *LPE*, pp. 75 and 270; also P. BM EA 10718, **lines 6–8**.

On the distinction between the *ib*-heart and the *ḥꜣty*-heart: Smith, *Mortuary Texts*, p. 68 (II, 12); Th. Bardinet, *Les papyrus médicaux de l'Egypte pharaonique* (Paris 1995), pp. 68–81.

For these two kinds of natron, *bd* and *ḥsmn*: J.R. Harris, *Lexicographical Studies in Ancient Egyptian Minerals* (Berlin 1961), pp. 191–3; N. Guillou, *La vieillesse des dieux* (Montpellier 1989), p. 45. In P. Rhind I, 6, 3, the hieratic *ḥwt Ḥwt-Ḥr* translates demotic *ḥsmn*.

I, 6–7

wꜥb Wsir N m šdyt twy nt sḫwt[18] *ḥtpt ḥr mḥtt n sḫwt*[19] *sꜣnḥm*.[20] Same reading in P. BM EA 9995, I, 2–4 = P. Berlin 3135, I, 11–13 = P. Berlin 3154, I, 6–7 = P. BN 179–81, I, 17–20 = P. Denon, I, 9–11 = P. Florence 3665 + P. Vienna 3850, II, 4–6 = P. Louvre N 3121, I, 7–8 = P. Louvre N 3126, I, 4–5 = P. Louvre N 3166, I, 6–8 = P. Louvre N 3284, I, 11–13 = P. Louvre N 3291, 7–8 = P. Tübingen 2016, II, 15–17. Sequence omitted in P. Louvre E 11079, I; partly in lacuna in P. Joseph Smith, II, 6–7 = P. Louvre N 3167 + 3222, I, 9–10. Omission of *Wsir* before the deceased's name in P. Louvre N 154, I, 9; of the genitival *n* before *sḫt sꜣnḥmw* in P. Louvre N 3285, I, 12. Var. P. Vienna 3931, I, 9: *m šdšd* (?) *twy*; P. Lausanne 3391, I, 11 = P. Vienna 3863, I, 11–13: *ḥr mḥtt (n) sꜣnḥmw*; P. Vienna 3931, I, 10: *ḥr mḥtt nty ḥmw*.

Cf. also P. Louvre N 3083, V, 4–6:

i Ḥwt-Ḥr ḫnt Imntt	'O Hathor mistress of the West,
Nḫbt nbt Nḫb	Nekhbet lady of Nekheb,
mi wꜥb Wsir N m šdyt twy nt sḫwt ḥtpt	may the Osiris N be purified in this pool of the Field of offerings
ḥr mḥtt n sḫwt sꜣnḥmw	to the north of the Field of locusts!'

Cf. *BD* ch. 125, ed. Budge, p. 262, 11–12:

wꜥb.n.i m šdyt rsyt	'I am purified in the southern pool,
ḥtp.n.i m niwt mḥtt	I have rested in the northern town
m sḫt sꜣnḥmw	in the Field of locusts.'

BD ch. 125 (var.), ed. Naville, I, pl. 137, 19–20:

wꜥb.n.i m šdyt rsyt	'I am purified in the southern pool,
ḥtp.n.i m Ḥmt mḥt	I have rested in the northern *Ḥmt*,[21]
m sḫt sꜣnḥmw	in the Field of locusts.'

BD ch. 125 (ed. Lepsius, pl. 48, 45):

wꜥb Wsir N m šdyt twy	'The Osiris N is purified in this pool
rsy ḥtpt mḥtt sḫt sꜣnḥmw	south of *Ḥtpt* and north of the Field of locusts.'

For this sequence, cf. J. Vandier, *RdE* 16 (1964), pp. 61–3. If the toponym *Ḥmt* quoted in the upper citations is to be identified to *Ḥtpt*, by graphic confusion between the two words, as Vandier justly pointed out (p. 62), the var.  observed in P. Vienna 3931, mentioned after *sḫwt ḥtpt*, can only be an abbreviated and faulty form of <*sḫwt sꜣn*>*ḥm(w)*. For the *šdyt*-pool (*GDG* V, p. 150), also designated the southern pool (*šdyt rsyt*), cf. the statue base Cairo JE 46918, published by R. Engelbach, *ASAE* 21 (1921), p. 72, and quoted by Vandier, *RdE* 16 (1964), p. 63:

Wsir pr bꜣ.k r sḫt Iꜣrw	'(O) Osiris, your ba comes forth in the Field of reeds,
swꜥb.tw.k m mw nṯr šd m Ḥtpt	and you are purified in the divine water that is dug in Hetepet.'

13. Var. P. BN 179–81 = P. Lausanne 3391: *im sk*.
14. Var. P. Denon, I, 6 = P. Tübingen 2016, II, 10: *rmṯ*.
15. *n* omitted in P. Lausanne 3391 = P. Tübingen 2016.
16. Group of signs illegible instead of *ꜥnḫ.f* expected, in P. Denon, I, 7.
17. *m* omitted in P. BN 179–81.
18. On the use of the plural *sḫwt* and confusion of *ḥtp* and *ḥtpt*: A.H. Gardiner, *RdE* 11 (1957), p. 51, n. 1.
19. *sḫt* in P. Louvre N 3154, I, 10 = P. Louvre N 3291, 8.
20. Plural *sꜣnḥmw* in P. Berlin 3135 = P. Berlin 3154 = P. BN 170–81 = P. Denon = P. Louvre N 3121 = P. Louvre N 3126 = P. Louvre N 3284 = P. Louvre N 3285 = P. Tübingen 2016.
21. On this word: Allen, *Book of the Dead Documents*, p. 206, n. et.

On the Field of offerings (*sḫt ḥtp*): P. Vernus, *Athribis* (*BdE* 74, 1978), p. 430, n. 3.

I, 7–8

swꜥb twk Wꜣḏyt Nḫbt m wnwt 4.t nt grḥ m wnwt 8.t nt hrw. Var. P. Louvre N 3167 + 3222, I, 10 = P. Louvre N 3285, I, 12 = P. Vienna 3931, I, 10–11 = P. Vienna 3863, I, 13: *swꜥb tw*; P. Louvre N 3166, I, 8: *swꜥb twf*. Inversion fo the names *Wꜣḏyt* and *Nḫbt* in P. Louvre E 11079, I, 11. Var. P. Berlin 3154, I, 8 = P. BN 179–81, I, 20–1 = P. BM EA 9995, I, 4 = P. Denon, I, 11 = P. Florence 3665 + P. Vienna 3850, II, 6 = P. Lausanne 3391, I, 11–12 = P. Louvre N 3126, I, 5 = P. Louvre N 3167 + 3222, I, 10–11 = P. Louvre N 3284, I, 13 = P. Louvre N 3285, I, 13 = P. Louvre N 3291, 8–9 = P. Tübingen 2016, II, 17 = P. Vienna 3863, I, 14 = P. Vienna 3931, I, 11: *m wnwt 8.t nt grḥ*; P. Berlin 3135, I, 13: *m wnwt 9.t nt grḥ m wnwt 9.nt hrw*; P. Louvre E 11079, I, 11: *m wnwt 8.t nt grḥ m wnwt 9.t nt hrw*; P. Joseph Smith, II, 8: *m wnwt 3.t nt grḥ* (lacuna follows in the text). Lacuna after *grḥ* in P. Louvre N 3167 + 3222, I, 11. Omission of *8.t* before *nt hrw* in P. BM EA 9995, I, 4; of *m* before *wnwt 8.t nt hrw* in P. Louvre N 3121, I, 8–9 = P. Louvre N 3126, I, 5 = P. Louvre N 3154, I, 10–11 = P. Louvre N 3166, I, 8; of *m* before *wnwt 10.t* (?) *nt hrw* in P. Louvre N 3083, V, 6–7.

BD ch. 125 (ed. Lepsius, pl. 48, 45–6):

wꜥb Wꜣḏyt ỉm.s	'Wadjyt purifies herself there
m wnwt twy 4.t nt grḥ	at that 4th hour of the night,
8.nt hrw	and (at the) 8th (hour) of the day.'

On the purification of the deceased by Wadjyt and Nekhbet, cf. P. Louvre N 3083, V, 4–6, cited above, where Hathor mistress of the West and Nekhbet lady of Nekheb are invoked to assure the purification of the deceased; cf. too *Ritual of Embalming*, VI, 11; VII, 22–3; 16–17; *Ritual for the Opening of the Mouth*, scene VII. For the rite performed by Nekhbet only, cf. P. Louvre N 3121, IV, 8–9: *ỉ Nḫbt nbt Nḫb swꜥb.t Ḥwt-Ḥr N*, 'O Nekhbet lady of Nekheb, may you purify the Hathor N!'

I, 8–9

mỉ ỉr.k Wsỉr N ꜥḳ.k r wsḫt Mꜣꜥty ỉw.k wꜥb.tỉ r ḫw nb btꜣ nb. Same reading in P. Florence 3665 + P. Vienna 3850, II, 8–9 = P. Lausanne 3391, I, 12–14 = P. Louvre N 3121, I, 9–10 = P. Louvre N 3126, I, 6–7 = P. Louvre N 3285, I, 13–15 = P. Vienna 3863, I, 14–17. Sequence omitted in P. Louvre E 11079, I; partly in lacuna in P. Joseph Smith, II, 8–9 = P. Louvre N 3167 + 3222, I, 11–12. Omission of the flexional ending *.tỉ* after *wꜥb* in P. BN 179–81, I, 23; of *btꜣ nb* in P. Louvre N 3083, V, 9; of *ỉw.k wꜥb.tỉ* in P. Louvre N 3154, I, 12. Erroneous repetition of *r ḫw nb* in P. Denon, I, 12–13. Var. P. Berlin 3135, I, 15 = P. BN 179–81, I, 21 = P. Louvre N 3154, I, 11–12[22] = P. Louvre N 3284, I, 14–15: *mỉ r.k Wsỉr N*; P. Louvre N 3166, I, 9: *mỉ ỉr.k n N*; P. BM EA 9995, I, 4–5 = P. Berlin 3154, I, 8: *mỉ ỉr.k r Wsỉr N*; P. Tübingen 2016, II, 18: *mỉ r.k r Wsỉr N*; P. Vienna 3931, I, 11–12: *mỉ.t ỉr.t Wsỉr N*. P. Berlin 3154, I, 9 = P. Louvre N 3291, 9: *ḫw nb ḏw btꜣ nb*. Indistinct word, instead of *btꜣ*, in P. Vienna 3931, I, 13. Corrupt passage after *ḫw nb* in P. Louvre N 3166, I, 10. P. Louvre N 3154, I, 12–13: *sꜣw nb btꜣ*. P. Louvre N 3083, V, 9–11, gives a different reading:

rꜣ n[23] *ꜥḳ r wsḫt Mꜣꜥty*	'Formula for entering the hall of the two Maats.
ḏd mdw hꜣ Wsỉr N	To be recited: Hail Osiris N,
ꜥḳ.t r wsḫt Mꜣꜥty	you enter the hall of the two Maats
ỉw.t wꜥb.tỉ r ḏw nb	being pure of all evil.'

On the need for the deceased to be in a state of purity, see *infra*, **II, 1–2**. For the rites of purification preceding the entry of the deceased into the hall of the two Maats, see *LPE*, p. 14, n. 28.

I, 9

ỉnr n Mꜣꜥt rn.k. Same reading in P. BM EA 9995 = P. Berlin 3135, I, 17 = P. Berlin 3154, I, 9 = P. BN 179–81, I, 24 = P. Denon, I, 13 = P. Florence 3665 + P. Vienna 3850, II, 9 = P. Louvre E 11079, IV, 8 (misplaced sequence) = P. Louvre N 3121, I, 11 = P. Louvre N 3126, I, 8 = P. Louvre N 3166, I, 10 = P. Louvre N 3167 + 3222, I, 12 = P. Louvre N 3284, I, 16 = P. Louvre N 3285, I, 13 = P. Louvre N 3291, 10 = P. Tübingen 2016, II, 19–20 = P. Vienna 3863, I, 17 = P. Vienna 3931, I, 13. Sequence omitted in P. Louvre N 3083, V; in lacuna in P. Joseph Smith, II, 9. Omission of the genitival *n* in P. Lausanne 3391, I, 14. Var. P. Louvre N 3154, I, 13: *ṯḫ*, 'plummet', instead of *ỉnr*. The word *ỉnr*, usually written 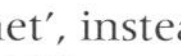, is rendered by  in P. Louvre N 3291, 10, and  in P. BN 179–81, I, 24 = P. Louvre N 3291, 10.

Applied to the deceased, the designation *ỉnr n Mꜣꜥt* seems not to be attested outside the Book of Breathing made by Isis (cf. A.M. Blackman, *PSBA* 40 [1918], p. 62, and id., *RT* 39 [1920], p. 52). For the various meanings of *ỉnr*: L. Christophe, *Mél. Maspero* I/4 (*MIFAO* 66, 1961), p. 18. According to Goyon, *Rituels funéraires*, p. 217, n. 2, it could refer to the base upon which Maat stands in most depictions.

II, 1–2

hꜣy Wsỉr N ꜥḳ.k r Dwꜣt m ꜥb wr. Beginning of § 3 of de Horrack's classification. Same reading in P. BM EA 9995, I, 6–7 = P. BM EA 10260, II, x + [1]–2 = P. Berlin 3135, I, 17–18 = P. Berlin 3154, I, 9–10 = P. BN 179–81, I, 24–6 = P. Denon, I, 13–14 = P. Florence 3665 + P. Vienna 3850, II, 9–10 = P. Louvre N 3121, I, 11 = P. Louvre N 3126, I, 8–9 = P. Louvre N 3154, I, 13–14 = P. Louvre N 3284, I, 16–18 = P. Louvre N 3285, I, 16–17 = P. Louvre N 3291, 10 = P. Tübingen 2016, II, 20–1 = P. Vienna 3863, I, 17–19 = P. Vienna 3931, I, 13–14. Sequence omitted in P. Louvre E 11079, I = P. Louvre N 3083, V, 11; partly in lacuna in P. Joseph Smith, II, 9–10 = P. Louvre N 3167 + 3222, I, 13–14. Var. P. Louvre N 3166, I, 10–11: *ỉ Wsỉr N*; P. Lausanne 3391, I, 14–15: *hꜣy ỉn Wsỉr N*.

On access of the deceased to the Duat, cf. P. BM EA 9995, IV, 1: *hꜣy Wsỉr N ꜥḳ.k r Dwꜣt wꜥb.tỉ r ḏw*. On the need to be purified before entering into the presence of Osiris, see A.M. Blackman, in J. Hastings, *Encyclopaedia of Religion and Ethics* 10 (1918), pp. 478–9. For *m ꜥb(w) wr*: F. Daumas, *ASAE* 51 (1951), p. 386, n. 2.

II, 2

swꜥb twk Mꜣꜥty m wsḫt ꜥꜣt. Same reading in P. BM EA 9995, I, 7 = P. BM EA 10260, II, x + 2 = P. Berlin 3135, I, 18–19 = P. Berlin 3154, I, 10 = P. BN 179–81, I, 26–7 = P. Denon, I, 14 = P. Florence 3665 + P. Vienna 3850, II, 10–11 = P. Louvre N 3083, V, 11–12 = P. Louvre N 3121, I, 11–12 = P. Louvre N 3126, I, 9–10 = P. Louvre N 3154, I, 14 = P. Louvre N 3284, I, 18–19 = P. Louvre N 3285, I, 17–18 = P. Louvre N 3291, 10 = P. Tübingen 2016, II, 21 = P. Vienna 3863, I, 19. Sequence omitted in P. Louvre N 3166, I; partly in lacuna in P. Joseph Smith, II, 10. Addition of the article *nꜣ* before *Mꜣꜥty*, and of *m wsḫt šw* after *wsḫt ꜥꜣt* in P. Louvre E 11079, I, 13 (cf. *infra*, **II, 2–3**). Var. P. Lausanne 3391, I, 16: *swꜥb.k Mꜣꜥty*; P. Louvre N 3167 + 3222, I, 14 = P. Louvre N 3285, I, 17: *swꜥb tw*; P. Vienna 3931, I, 14: *swꜥb.t*[24] (for *swꜥb tn*) *Mꜣꜥty*.

The presence of the two Maats in the great hall (*wsḫt ꜥꜣt*) may be compared to that of the 'just gods in the great hall' (*nṯrw mꜣꜥtyw m wsḫt ꜥꜣt*) mentioned in P. Rhind I, 9, 7.[25]

22. Omission of *Wsỉr* in this manuscript.
23. The scribe seems to have written originally *ky ḏd* instead of *rꜣ n*.
24. With the *t* written .
25. 'Gemeint sind die beiden Wahrheitsgottheiten' (G. Möller, *Die beiden Totenpapyrus Rhind* [*DemSt.* 6], Leipzig 1913, p. 90, n. 155).

ir.tw[26] *n.k ꜥb m wsḫt Gb*. Same reading in P. BM EA 9995, I, 7 = P. BM EA 10260, II, x + 2–3 = P. Berlin 3135, I, 19 = P. Berlin 3154, I, 10–11 = P. BN 179–81, I, 27–8 = P. Denon, I, 14–15 = P. Florence 3665 + P. Vienna 3850, II, 11 = P. Lausanne 3391, I, 17 = P. Louvre N 3083, V, 12 = P. Louvre N 3121, I, 12 = P. Louvre N 3154, I, 15 = P. Louvre N 3166, I, 10 = P. Louvre N 3284, I, 19 = P. Louvre N 3285, I, 18 = P. Louvre N 3291, 10 = P. Tübingen 2016, II, 21–2 = P. Vienna 3863, I, 19–20 = P. Vienna 3931, I, 15. Sequence omitted in P. Louvre E 11079, I; in lacuna in P. Joseph Smith, II, 10.

The hall of Geb (*wsḫt Gb*), as the place of purification of the deceased, is also known, outside the Book of Breathing made by Isis, from P. OIC 25389, XXXIV, 14, in an almost identical formulation (*LPE*, pp. 76 and 272). Chapter 185 of the *BD*, in the version provided by stela Louvre C 286 (Allen, *Book of the Dead*, p. 204), refers to this hall in several contexts. It is the place where Isis introduces Horus after his contestings with Seth (line 16), where the kingship of Osiris is granted to his son (lines 18, 24), and where Thoth draws up an *imt-pr* for Horus 'before the sole lord' (J.J. Clère, *ZÄS* 84 [1959], p. 92). The *wsḫt Gb* figures in the funerary literature above all as the setting for the judgement of the deceased; cf. e.g. the Middle Kingdom stelae Cairo CG 20089 and 20149 (Lange and Schäfer, *Grab- und Denksteine* I, pp. 109 and 176), and also, for the Late Period, in:

P. Cairo CG 58012, 9–10:

ir.k st.k r-gs Mꜣꜥty	'You take your place beside the two Maats,
dwn.n.k gst m wsḫt Gb	and you hasten in the hall of Geb.'

P. Louvre E 10263, 8:

wn.t nšnš (for *wnšnš.t*) *m wsḫt Gb*	'You hasten in the hall of Geb.'

Ritual of Embalming, IV, 19–20 (ed. Sauneron, p. 13):

mꜣꜥ-ḫrw.f m wsḫt Gb	'He is justified in the hall of Geb
m-bꜣḥ nṯr ꜥꜣ nb Ỉmntt	in the presence of the great god lord of the West.'

BD ch. 168 A (ed. Budge, p. 425):

Ỉmn di.f wsr Wsir m wsḫt Gb	'The Hidden One, may he grant that the Osiris (N) be powerful in the hall of Geb.'

For other references to the hall of Geb as location of activity by the deceased: Winlock, *BMMA* 2 (1907), p. 41; *Ritual of Embalming*, II, 3 and III, 2 (ed. Sauneron, pp. 2 and 6).

With reference perhaps to the offering ordered for Osiris by his father (stela Louvre C 286, 6), the hall of Geb is also identified as a place where the deceased receives offerings: statue Cairo JE 37866 (J. Leclant, *Enquêtes sur les sacerdoces et les sanctuaires égyptiens* [*BdE* 17, 1954], p. 8, and id., *JNES* 13 [1954], pp. 163–4) = statue Cairo CG 1219 (Borchardt, *Statuen und Statuetten* IV, p. 114): *di.f šsp.t snw m wsḫt Gb m-bꜣḥ nbw Ỉwnw*, 'He grants that you receive *snw*-loaves in the hall of Geb in the presence of the lords of Heliopolis'; statue T 36 of North Karnak (Leclant, op. cit., p. 76 and id., *Orientalia* 20 [1951], pl. 60): *di.f* (...) *šsp.i snw m ḫrt-hrw ḥr wḏḥw n nbw Ỉwnw ḥtp m wsḫt Gb ḥnꜥ šmsw n nb nḥḥ*, 'He grants (...) that I receive *snw*-loaves daily on the altar of the lords of Heliopolis and *ḥtpw*-offerings in the hall of Geb with the retinue of the lord of eternity (Osiris)'.[27]

II, 2–3

swꜥb ḥꜥw.k[28] *m wsḫt šw*. Same reading in P. BM EA 9995, I, 7–8 = P. BM EA 10260, II, x + 2–3 = P. Berlin 3135, I, 19 = P. Berlin 3154, I, 4 = P. BN 179–81, I, 28 = P. Denon, I, 15 = P. Lausanne 3391, I, 17 = P. Louvre N 3083, V, 12 = P. Louvre N 3121, I, 12 = P. Louvre N 3126, I, 10 = P. Louvre N 3154, I, 15 = P. Louvre N 3284, I, 19–20 = P. Louvre N 3285, I, 18 = P. Louvre N 3291, 11 = P. Vienna 3863, I, 20 = P. Vienna 3931, I, 15–16. Sequence omitted in P. Tübingen 2016, II, 22; wholly in lacuna in P. Joseph Smith, II, 10–11, and partly in P. Florence 3665 + P. Vienna 3850, II, 12 = P. Louvre N 3158, [I, ult.–]II, 1 = P. Louvre N 3167 + 3222, I, 15. Var. P. Louvre N 3166, I, 12: *iw.f wꜥb ḥꜥw.t* (*sic*) *m wsḫt šw*; P. Louvre N 3083, V, 12–13: *swꜥb ḳsw.t m wsḫt šw*, 'Your bones are purified in the hall of light'. For the mention of *wsḫt šw* in P. Louvre E 11079 (different context), cf. *supra*, **II, 2**. This *wsḫt šw* seems not to be otherwise attested.

II, 3

iw.k ḥr mꜣꜣ Rꜥ m ḥtp.f Ỉtm[29] *m mšrw*. Same reading in P. BM EA 9995, I, 8 = P. BM EA 10260, II, x + 3 = P. Berlin 3135, I, 20 = P. Berlin 3154, I, 11 = P. BN 179–81, II, 1 = P. Denon, I, 15 = P. Florence 3665 + P. Vienna 3850, II, 12 = P. Lausanne 3391, I, 17–18 = P. Louvre N 3121, I, 13 = P. Louvre N 3126, I, 10–11 = P. Louvre N 3154, I, 16 = P. Louvre N 3158, II, 1 = P. Louvre N 3284, I, 20 = P. Louvre N 3285, I, 18–19 = P. Louvre N 3291, 11 = P. Tübingen 2016, II, 22 = P. Vienna 3863, I, 20–1. Sequence omitted in P. Louvre E 11079, II; partly in lacuna in P. Joseph Smith, II, 11 = P. Louvre N 3167 + 3222, I, 15 = P. Vienna 3931, I, 16. Omission of *m* before *mšrw* in P. Vienna 3931, I, 16. Speech in the third person in P. Louvre N 3166, I, 12. Var. P. Louvre N 3083, V, 13:

mꜣꜣ tw Rꜥ m wbn	'Re sees you in (his) rising,
Ỉtm m mšrw	and Atum in the evening.'

Regular motif of sun hymns. On the relation of Atum to the *mšrw*, see Assmann, *Liturgische Lieder*, p. 234.

II, 3–4

Ỉmn irm.k ḥr dit n.k ṯꜣw. Same reading in P. BM EA 9995, I, 8 = P. BM EA 10260, II, x + 3–4 = P. Berlin 3135, I, 20 = P. Berlin 3154, I, 11 = P. BN 179–81, II, 1–2 = P. Denon, II, 1 = P. Lausanne 3391, I, 18–19 = P. Louvre N 3121, I, 13 = P. Louvre N 3126, I, 11 = P. Louvre N 3154, I, 16–17 = P. Louvre N 3158, II, 1–2 = P. Louvre N 3284, I, 20–1 = P. Louvre N 3285, I, 19 = P. Louvre N 3291, 11. Sequence omitted in P. Louvre E 11079, II; wholly in lacuna in P. Joseph Smith, II, 11 = P. Louvre N 3167 + 3222, I, 16, and partly in P. Florence 3665 + P. Vienna 3850, II, 12–13 = P. Tübingen 2016, III, 1 = P. Vienna 3863, I, 21 = P. Vienna 3931, I, 16–17. Omission of *irm.k* in P. Louvre N 3166, I, 13. Var. P. Louvre N 3083, V, 13–14: *Ỉmn im.t ḥr rdi n.t ṯꜣw*, 'Amun is in you, giving you breath'. Cf. *infra*, **III, 2–3**: *hꜣy Wsir N Ỉmn irm.k rꜥ nb*.

On Amun and breath, see *infra*, **III, 5**; Smith, *Mortuary Texts*, pp. 73 (III, 5), and 105 (VIII, 8); *LPE*, p. 87 (I, 5–6); F.R. Herbin, *RdE* 50 (1999), p. 199 (II, 17); id., *RdE* 54 (2003), p. 111.

II, 4

Ptḥ ḥr nbi ꜥwt.k. Same reading in P. Louvre N 3154, I, 17 = P. Louvre N 3158, II, 2. Sequence omitted in P. Louvre E 11079, II; wholly in lacuna in P. Joseph Smith, II, 11–12, and partly in P. Louvre N 3167 + 3222, I, 16 = P. Vienna 3863, I, 21. Omission of *ḥr* before *nbi* in P. Berlin 3135, I, 21. Var. P. BM EA 9995, I, 9 = P. BM EA 10260, II, x + 4 = P. Berlin 3135, I, 21 = P. Berlin 3154, I, 12 = P. Denon, II, 1–2 = P. Florence 3665 + P. Vienna 3850, II, 13 = P. Lausanne 3391, I, 19 = P. Louvre N 3121, I, 13–14 = P. Louvre N 3126, I, 12 = P. Louvre N 3166, I, 13 = P. Louvre N

26. Note the writing 𓏲 of the passive *.tw* in P. Vienna 3931, I, 15.
27. Parallel text in Moret, *Sarcophages* I , p. 303, bottom.
28. Written in the singular in P. BM EA 10260. P. Louvre N 3158 begins with this word (col. I is lost, cf. *supra*, n. 2).
29. Written *Tm* in P. BM EA 9995.

3284, I, 21 = P. Louvre N 3285, I, 19 = P. Louvre N 3291, 11 = P. Vienna 3931, I, 17: *(i)ḥʿw.k /.t* [30] (note the ambiguous spelling in P. BN 179–81, II, 2 = P. Tübingen 2016, III, 1, which can be read either *ʿwt* or *ḥʿw*); P. Louvre N 3083, V, 14: *ʿwt.i* (*sic*); P. Louvre N 3291, 11: *Ỉ*, 'Thoth', or *nṯr*, 'the god', in contrast to the usual version *Ptḥ*.

For the equivalence of *ʿwt* and *ḥʿw*: Haikal, *Two Hier. Fun. Pap.* II, p. 59, n. 16; E. Brunner-Traut, *ZÄS* 115 (1988), pp. 8–14.

On Ptah fashioning the limbs of the deceased: Smith, *Mortuary Texts*, p. 104 (VIII, 7, b); F.R. Herbin, *BIFAO* 84 (1984), p. 292, n. 68.

II, 4–5

ʿḳ.k r ȝḫt ḥnʿ Rʿ šsp.w bȝ.k r nšmt ḥnʿ Wsir. Same reading in P. BM EA 9995, I, 9 = P. BM EA 10260, II, x + 4–5 = P. BN 179–81, II, 2–3 = P. Denon, II, 2 = P. Lausanne 3391, I, 19–20 = P. Louvre N 3121, I, 14 = P. Louvre N 3154, I, 17–18 = P. Louvre N 3158, II, 2–3 = P. Louvre N 3284, I, 21–2 = P. Louvre N 3285, I, 20 = P. Louvre N 3291, 11–12 = P. Tübingen 2016, III, 1–2. Sequence omitted in P. Louvre E 11079, II; wholly in lacuna in P. Vienna 3863, I, 22, and partly in P. Florence 3665 + P. Vienna 3850, II, 14 = P. Joseph Smith, II, 12 = P. Louvre N 3126, I, 13 = P. Louvre N 3167 + 3222, I, 16–17. Var. P. Berlin 3135, I, 21 = P. Vienna 3931, I, 18: *šsp bȝ.k*; P. Berlin 3154, I, 12 = P. Louvre N 3166, I, 13–14: *iṯ.w bȝ.k*; P. Louvre N 3083, V, 14–15: *nšmt wrt*.

For the construction *šsp r*, cf. P. BM EA 10123, 5; P. Florence 3669, 10–11; P. Louvre N 3176 (J), 4.

II, 5

nṯr.w bȝ.k m pr[31] *Gb iw.k n*[32] *mȝʿ-ḫrw r nḥḥ ḏt*. Same reading in P. BM EA 10260, II, x + 5 = P. Berlin 3135, I, 22 = P. Berlin 3154, I, 12–13 = P. BN 179–81, II, 3–4 = P. Denon, II, 2–3 = P. Louvre N 3126, I, 13 = P. Louvre N 3158, II, 3 = P. Louvre N 3166, I, 14 = P. Louvre N 3284, I, 22 = P. Louvre N 3291, 12 = P. Tübingen 2016, III, 2 = P. Vienna 3931, I, 18–19 (small lacuna). Sequence omitted in P. Louvre E 11079, II; wholly in lacuna in P. Joseph Smith, III, 1 = P. Vienna 3863, I, 22, and partly in P. Florence 3665 + P. Vienna 3850, II, 14–15 = P. Louvre N 3167 + 3222, I, 17. Omission of suffix *.k* after *iw* in P. BM EA 9995, I, 10; of *n* (*m*) after *iw.k* in P. Lausanne 3391, I, 20 = P. Louvre N 3285, I, 21. Var. P. Lausanne 3391, I, 20: *nṯr.tw*; P. Louvre N 3083, V, 15 = P. Louvre N 3154, I, 18: *ib* instead of *bȝ*. On that substitution, cf. *infra*, **III, 1**: *snsn bȝ.k r nḥḥ*, compared to the var. *snsn ib.k r nḥḥ* in P. BM EA 9995, I, 16–17; also *infra*, **VII, 5**: *mi ʿnḫ ib.f*, rather than *mi ʿnḫ bȝ.f* in several parallel versions; Maspero, *Sarcophages* I, p. 38: *ʿpy ib.k r wiȝ n Rʿ*, rather than *ʿpy bȝ.k m-ḫt Rʿ*, ibid., p. 145; the confusion might be explained by writings of *ib* with the ba bird; cf. e.g. P. Leiden T 32, I, 9: *ib.k* ( ) *pn mn ḥr st.f*, instead of the writing of several parallel versions (*LPE*, p. 393).

The other differences are purely orthographical: P. Louvre N 3154, I, 18–19 (*m mȝʿ-ḫrw*); P. Louvre N 3083, V, 15 (*n pr Gb*; *m mȝʿ-ḫrw*); P. Louvre N 3121, I, 15 (*n nḥḥ ḏt*).

On the causative meaning of *nṯr* and the divinization of the ba (cf. P. BM EA 10116, 24: *nṯr.w bȝ.k m ḫrt-nṯr*), see M. Smith, *Enchoria* 15 (1987), p. 73); id., *Liturgy*, p. 40 (I, 18); Haikal, *Two hier. fun. Pap.* II, p. 43 with n. 149; G. Vittmann, *ZÄS* 117 (1990), p. 87 (line 23); J. Assmann, *JEA* 65 (1979), p. 61 with n. 65; *Urk.* IV, 1843, 12; Lefebvre, *Petosiris* II, p. 26, no. 53, 4; *Ritual of Embalming*, V, 23 (ed. Sauneron, p. 18). See also *infra*, **III, 3–4** for the divination of the ba in the Duat.

pr Gb (*GDG* II, p. 137) is very little attested in funerary texts outside the Book of Breathing made by Isis.[33] One occurrence is known from *CT* VII, 20, sp. 820,[34] where the deceased declares concerning the god Nu: 'I am his son created by Isis, born of Nut in the secrecy of the House of Geb.' The opinion of P. Kaplony (*MIO* 11 [1965], pp. 148–9, n. 54), seeing the *pr Gb* as a designation of the tomb, is not convincing. As in P. BM EA 10048 and parallel versions, both of these mentions are likely references to a Heliopolitan sanctuary.

II, 6–7

ḥȝy Wsir N mn rn.k ḏd ḫȝt.k rwḏ sʿḥ.k nn šnʿ.tw.k m pt tȝ. Beginning of § 4 of de Horrack's classification. Same reading in P. Denon, II, 3–5. Sequence omitted in P. Louvre E 11079, II; wholly in lacuna in P. Vienna 3863, I, almost wholly in P. Florence 3665 + P. Vienna 3850, II, 16–17, and partly in P. Joseph Smith, III, 1–2 = P. Louvre N 3167 + 3222, I, 18. Omission of *ḥȝy* in P. BM EA 9995, I, 10 = P. BM EA 10260, II, x + 5 = P. Berlin 3154, I, 13 = P. BN 179–81, II, 4 = P. Lausanne 3391, I, 21 = P. Louvre E 8079 + 11080, II, 1 = P. Louvre N 3083, V, 16 = P. Louvre N 3126, I, 14 = P. Louvre N 3154, I, 19 = P. Louvre N 3158, II, 3 = P. Louvre N 3166, I, 15 = P. Louvre N 3284, II, 1 = P. Louvre N 3285, I, 22 = P. Vienna 3931, I, 19. P. Louvre N 3291, 12: *ḏd mdw Wsir N*; P. Tübingen 2016, III, 2–3: *ḏd mdw ḥȝy Wsir N*. P. Louvre N 3083, V, 16–17 = P. Louvre N 3154, I, I, 19–20: *mn rn.k* (*/.t*) *ḫȝt.k* (*/.t*) *rwḏ*, 'Your name is established, your corpse endures'; P. Louvre N 3121, I, 15: *mn rn.t rwḏ ḫȝt.t ḏd sʿḥ.t*, 'Your name is established, your corpse endures, and your mummy is stable'. P. Louvre N 3166, I, 16: *rwḏ ḫprw.k*; P. Berlin 3135, I, 24 = P. Lausanne 3391, I, 22 = P. Louvre N 3083, V, 17 = P. Louvre N 3121, I, 16 = P. Louvre N 3166, I, 16 = P. Louvre N 3284, 3: *nn šnʿ.k* (*/.t*, */.f*);[35] P. BM EA 9995, I, 11: *m pt m tȝ*; P. Berlin 3135, I, 24: [36] *pt tȝ*.

mn rn.k ḏd ḫȝt.k rwḏ sʿḥ.k recalls certain wishes concerning elements of the human body frequently expressed, with many variants, in Books of Breathing: cf. P. BM EA 10108, 1–3. On the use of the verb *rwḏ* in relation to the mummy (*sʿḥ*): *Wb.* II, 411, 11 (*Belegst.*); Pierret, *Inscr. du Louvre* II, p. 23 (Coffin Louvre D 6); R. Mond, *ASAE* 6 (1905), p. 84; Hermann, *Stelen*, p. 48*, 9–10.

II, 7–8

sḥḏ sʿḥ.k ḥr Rʿ ʿnḫ bȝ.k ḥr Ỉmn rnp ḫȝt.k ḥr Wsir. Except in P. Louvre E 11079, II, where this sequence is omitted, all other consulted documents of the Book of Breathing made by Isis give *ḥr.k* (*/.t*) instead of *sʿḥ.k*: P. BM EA 9995, I, 11–12 = P. BM EA 10260, II, x + 6–7 = P. Berlin 3135, I, 24–5 = P. Berlin 3154, I, 14[37]= P. Denon, II, 5–6 = P. Lausanne 3391, I, 23 = P. Louvre E 8079 + 11080, II, 2 = P. Louvre N 3083, V, 17–18 = P. Louvre N 3121, I, 16 = P. Louvre 3126, I, 15–16 = P. Louvre N 3154, I, 20–1 = P. Louvre N 3158, II, 4–5 = P. Louvre N 3166, I, 16–17 = P. Louvre N 3284, II, 3–4 = P. Louvre N 3285, I, 24 = P. Louvre N 3291, 13 = P. Tübingen 2016, III, 4–5. Sequence wholly in lacuna in P. Vienna 3863, I; almost wholly in P. Florence 3665 + P. Vienna 3850, II, 18, and partly in P. Joseph Smith, III, 2 = P. Louvre N 3167 + 3222, I, 18–19 = P. Vienna 3931, I, 22. Var. P. BN 179–81, II, 7: *ḥnʿ Rʿ*.

On the illumination of the face of the deceased (*sḥḏ ḥr*), see *Ritual of Embalming*, III, 19 (ed. Sauneron, p. 9): *nwb* (...) *sḥḏ.f ḥr.k m-ḫnw Dwȝt snsn.k m nwb*, 'Gold (...) illuminates your face within the Duat, you breathe by gold'. This illumination of the face is generally the work of Re (or an assimilated god) in the 'paths of darkness' (*wȝwt kkw*): cf.

30. Written *iḥʿ* in P. Lausanne 3391.
31. P. Berlin 3135, I, 22, wrongly gives the sign here instead of , probably influenced by *wsḫt Gb*. For the regular writing of *pr* in the manuscript, see ibid., II, 18.
32. Note the writing in P. Louvre N 3166.
33. For mentions of this place in other contexts, cf. *Urk.* VIII § 103, a.; *Opet* 29.
34. M. Münster, *Untersuchungen zur Göttin Isis* (*MÄS* 11, 1968), p. 88.
35. *nn šnʿ.tw.k* only in P. Louvre N 3166.
36. For this hieratic group, see also P. BM EA 10191, **II, 7–8**.
37. Note the spelling of the name of Osiris in this manuscript.

Maspero, *Sarcophages* I, pp. 159, 160, 207; A. Szczudłowska, *ZÄS* 98 (1972), pp. 63 and 78 = G. Maspero, *ASAE* 1 (1900), p. 174; Metternich stela, line 17 (C.E. Sander-Hansen, *Die Texte der Metternichstele* [Copenhagen 1956], p. 22).[38] On the mummy illuminated by the sun, see *LPE*, p. 86 (I, 5–6), with references; also P. Skrine, Text 2, 53–4 (A.M. Blackman, *JEA* 4 [1917], pl. 27): *di.tn wꜣwꜣt n-im ḥr sꜥḥ.i n ḥtm n is.i psḏ stwt itn ḥr šnbt.i*,'Grant light on my mummy, without destruction for my tomb; may the rays of the disk shine on my breast!'; P. Vatican Inv. 38608, 22 (F.R. Herbin, *RdE* 54 [2003], pp. 107–8): *ptr.k ḥḏḏw ḥꜣy Rꜥ di.f s(w) ḥr šnbt.k wbn.f n.k m ḏww n Bꜣḫ smꜣ stwt.f n sꜥḥ.k* 'You see the rays of the light of Re; he places himself on your breast [39] when he shines for you in the mountain of the East that his rays may unite with your mummy'; T.G. Allen, *Egyptian Stelae in Field Museum of Natural History* (Chicago 1936), p. 54: *iꜣbḫ mꜣw.f m sꜥḥ.k*, 'His rays join to your mummy'; E. Ledrain, *Les monuments égyptiens de la Bibliothèque Nationale* (Paris 1879), p. vi (= Louvre E 13048): *imꜣ stwt.f n sꜥḥ.k*, 'His rays unite with your mummy'; *Dendara* X, 260, 7: *smꜣ stwt.f m sꜥḥ.k*, 'His rays unite with your mummy'.

ꜥnḫ bꜣ … rnp ḫꜣt.[40] For the rejuvenation of the corpse (*rnp ḫꜣt*),[41] see *supra*, **I, 1–3**.

II, 8

snsn.k r nḥḥ ḏt. Same reading in P. BM EA 9995, I, 12 = P. BM EA 10260, II, x + 7 = P. Berlin 3135, I, 25 = P. Berlin 3154, I, 14 = P. BN 179–81, II, 7–8 = P. Denon, II, 6 = P. Florence 3665 + P. Vienna 3850, II, 19 = P. Lausanne 3391, I, 24 = P. Louvre E 8079 + 11080, II, 2 = P. Louvre N 3083, V, 18 = P. Louvre N 3121, I, 17 = P. Louvre N 3126, I, 16 = P. Louvre N 3154, I, 22 = P. Louvre N 3158, II, 5 = P. Louvre N 3284, II, 4 = P. Louvre N 3285, I, 25 = P. Louvre N 3291, 13–14 = P. Tübingen 2016, III, 5 = P. Vienna 3931, I, 22. Sequence omitted in P. Louvre E 11079, II; wholly in lacuna in P. Vienna 3863, I; and partly in P. Joseph Smith, III, 2 = P. Louvre N 3167 + 3222, I, 19. Var. P. Louvre N 3154, I, 22 (*snsn bꜣ.k r nḥḥ ḏt*) = P. Louvre N 3166, I, 17 (*ir.k snsn r nḥḥ ḏt*); see also *infra*, **III, 1**: *snsn bꜣ.k r nḥḥ*, and cf. P. BM EA 10344, 15–16 (funerary formulae inspired from the Book of Breathing): […].*t snsn r nḥḥ ḥnꜥ ḏt*.

II, 8–9

ir n.k sꜣ n sn.k prt-ḫrw tꜣ ḥnkt kꜣw ꜣpdw m ḳbḥ sntr ḫrt-hrw. Beginning of § 5 of de Horrack's classification. The version *sꜣ n sn.k* is attested only in P. BM EA 10048. Abandoning the textual tradition whereby the son performs the invocation offering – at least in this passage of the Book of Breathing made by Isis – the compiler of this manuscript seems to refer here to the existence of an actual nephew of the deceased.

The predominant version may be cited from P. Louvre N 3284, II, 4–5:

ir n.k sꜣ.k prt-ḫrw	'Your son performs for you an invocation offering
m tꜣ ḥnḳt kꜣw ꜣpdw	consisting of bread, beer, oxen and fowl,
m ḳbḥ sntr m ḫrt-hrw	and libation and censing in the course
nt rꜥ nb	of every day.'

This version is found in P. BM EA 9995, I, 12–13 = P. BM EA 10260, II, x + 7–8 = P. Berlin 3135, II, 1 = P. Berlin 3154, I, 14–15 = P. Florence 3665 + P. Vienna 3850, II, 19–20 = P. Lausanne 3391, I, 24–5 = P. Louvre N 3126, II, 16–17 = P. Louvre N 3126, I, 16–17 and, with some variants, in P. Denon, II, 6–7 = P. Louvre N 3166, I, 17–18 (*bꜣ.k* instead of *sꜣ.k*, *ḫrt-hrw* only) = P. Louvre N 3291, 14 (omission of *m* before *ḳbḥ*) = P. Louvre N 3121, I, 17 (*bꜣ.k* instead of *sꜣ.k*, *m ḳbḥ n.t* and omission of *sntr*) = P. Vienna 3931, I, 23–4 (partly in lacuna) = P. Vienna 3863, I, ult.–II, 1 (lacuna at lower part of col. I, affecting the words preceding *m ḫrt-hrw nty rꜥ nb*) = P. Louvre E 8079 + 11080, II, 3 (omission of *m* before *ḳbḥ*) = P. Louvre N 3154, I, 22–II, 1 (*n* for *m* after *prt-ḫrw*, omission of *m ḫrt-hrw nt rꜥ nb*) = P. Louvre N 3285, I, 25–6 (omission of *m* before *tꜣ*) = P. Louvre N 3158, II, 6 (omission of *m* before *tꜣ*, *n* for *m* before *ḫrt-hrw*) = P. Tübingen 2016, III, 6 (omission of *m* before *ḳbḥ*). P. Louvre N 3083, V, 18–19: *ir twt prt-ḫrw*, with omission of *m* before *ḳbḥ*; P. BN 179–81, II, 9: *wꜥb* instead of *ḳbḥ*, not preceded with *m*. Sequence omitted in P. Louvre E 11079, II; wholly in lacuna in P. Joseph Smith, III, 3, and almost wholly in P. Louvre N 3167 + 3222, I, 20.

II, 9

iw.k ḥr ḫrw.f mi irw.k ḥr-tp tꜣ. Same reading in P. Louvre N 3158, II, 6. Sequence partly in lacuna in P. Joseph Smith, III, 3. Omission of *ḥr* before *ḫrw* in P. Louvre N 3166, I, 18. Var. P. Joseph Smith, III, 3 = P. Louvre N 3083, V, 19 = P. Louvre N 3154, II, 1: *mi ḳy.k* (*/.t*); P. Louvre N 3166, I, 18: *mi ḳd.k;* P. BM EA 9995, I, 12–14 = P. Berlin 3154, I, 15: *ii.k ḥr ḫrw.f ḥꜥw.k ḥr ḳsw.k mi irww.k ḥr-tp tꜣ*.

Var. P. BM EA 10260, II, x + 8 = P. Louvre N 3121, I, 18 = P. Louvre N 3126, II, 17–18 = P. Louvre N 3284, II, 5–6:

ḥꜥw.k ḥr ḳsw.k	'Your flesh is on your bones
mi irw.k ḥr-tp-tꜣ	according to your form upon earth.'

This is found, with some variants, in P. Berlin 3135, II, 1–2[42] = P. Denon 179–81, II, 9 = P. Florence 3665 + P. Vienna 3850, II, 20–1 = P. Lausanne 3391, I, 25 = P. Louvre N 3285, I, 26 = P. Vienna 3863, II, 1: *ḳs.k /.t;*[43] P. Denon 179–81, II, 9 = P. Louvre E 8079 + 11080, II, 3 = P. Tübingen 2016, III, 6: *mi ḳd.k* = P. Louvre N 3291, 14: *mi ḳy.k*. Sequence omitted in P. Louvre E 11079, II; partly in lacuna in P. Louvre N 3167 + 3222, I, 21 = P. Vienna 3931, I, 24.

In P. BM EA 9995, I, 13–14 = P. Berlin 3154, 15, the two sequences are juxtaposed:

ii.k (var.: *iw.k*) *ḥr ḫrw.f*	'You come at his voice,
ḥꜥw.k ḥr ḳsw.k	and your flesh is on your bones
mi irw.k ḥr-tp tꜣ	according to your form upon earth.'

On the recovery by the deceased of his original form, see also *infra*, **III, 1**.

II, 9–10

swr.k m šnbt.k wnm.k m rꜣ.k šsp.k snw ḥnꜥ bꜣw nṯrw. Same reading in P. BM EA 9995, I, 14–15 = P. BM EA 10260, II, x + 8–9 = P. Berlin 3135, II, 2–3 = P. BN 179–81, II, 10–11 = P. Denon, II, 8–9 = P. Florence 3665 + P. Vienna 3850, II, 21–2 = P. Louvre E 8079 + 11080, II, 3–4 = P. Louvre N 3083, V, 19–20 = P. Louvre N 3126, I, 18–19 (*nṯrw* in lacuna) = P. Louvre N 3154, II, 1–2 = P. Louvre N 3158, II, 6–7 = P. Louvre N 3284, II, 6–7 = P. Louvre N 3285, I, 26–7 = P. Louvre N 3291, 14–15 = P. Tübingen 2016, III, 6–7 = P. Vienna 3863, II, 1–2 = P. Vienna 3931, I, 24–5 (small lacuna). In P. Louvre E 11079, the sequence is quoted with variants in two places, first in II, 15–III, 1: *swr<.t> m rꜣ.t <wn>m.t m šnbt.t*, then in IV, 2–3: *mi šsp.s snw ḥnꜥ bꜣw nṯrw m ḫrt-hrw nt rꜥ nb*.

38. In the same context, the expression is often used *wbꜣ ḥr*, lit.: 'open the face' in *wbꜣ ḥr m wꜣ(w)t kkw*: cf. e.g. Cairo CG 41044 (Gauthier, *Cercueils* I, p. 43; Hermann, *Stelen*, p. 47*; Assmann, *Sonnenhymnen*, p. 100, Text 67; *Ritual of Embalming*, VI, 9 (ed. Sauneron, p. 20); Cairo CG 41003 and 41025 (Moret, *Sarcophages* I, pp. 64 and 245); *Urk*. IV, 1436, 10; Seeber, *Untersuchungen*, p. 114, n. 463.
39. Solar rays on the breast: Assmann, *Liturgische Lieder*, pp. 286–7.
40. *ḫꜣwt* in P. Louvre N 3166, I, 17.
41. *Wb*. II, 432, 19, cites as an example only this passage of the Book of Breathing.
42. *ḥꜥw* written with a prothetic *i*.
43. For the singular *ḳs*, denoting the collective bones of the skeleton: M. Smith, *Enchoria* 15 (1987), p. 73; id., *Mortuary Texts*, p. 69, n. (d).

Sequence partly in lacuna in P. Joseph Smith, III, 3 = P. Louvre N 3167 + 3222, I, 21. Var. P. Lausanne 3391, I, 26: *šnꜥ.k* (*Wb.* IV, 506, 15, written here), instead of *šnbt.k*; P. Berlin 3154, I, 16 = P. Louvre N 3166, I, 19: *ỉt.k snw*; omission of *bꜣw* in P. Louvre N 3121, I, 19; P. Lausanne 3391, I, 26: *bꜣ nṯrw*.

For this passage: *LPE*, pp. 252–3 (VIII, 6), and Mond–Myers, *The Bucheum* III, no. 33:

swr.k m šnbt.k wnm.k m rꜣ.k	'You drink with your throat and eat with your mouth;
šsp.k snw ḥr-ꜥwy Pꜣwtyw	you receive *snw*-loaves from the hands of the primordial gods
prt-ḫrw tꜣ sntr ḥnḳt rꜥ nb	and invocation offerings of bread, incense and beer, every day.'

On the *snw*-loaves: S. Sauneron, *BIFAO* 63 (1965), p. 81, n. (w).

II, 10

ḫw twk[44] *Ỉnpw ỉr.f sꜣ.k*. Same reading in P. BM EA 9995, I, 15 = P. BM EA 10260, II, x + 9 = P. Berlin 3135, II, 3 = P. Berlin 3154, I, 16 = P. Denon, II, 9 = P. Lausanne 3391, I, 26–7 = P. Louvre E 8079 + 11080, II, 4 = P. Louvre N 3083, V, 20–1 = P. Louvre N 3121, I, 19 = P. Louvre N 3126, I, 19 = P. Louvre N 3154, II, 2–3 = P. Louvre N 3166, I, 19–20 = P. Louvre N 3284, II, 7 = P. Louvre N 3285, I, 27 = P. Louvre N 3291, 15 = P. Florence 3665 + P. Vienna 3850, II, 22 = P. Vienna 3863, II, 2 = P. Vienna 3931, I, 26 (small lacuna). Sequence omitted in P. Louvre E 11079; wholly in lacuna in P. Louvre N 3167 + 3222, I, 21, and partly in P. Joseph Smith, III, 4. Omission of suffix *.f* in P. BN 179–81, II, 11. Var. P. Louvre N 3158, II, 7: *ḫw tw Ỉnpw*; P. Tübingen 2016, III, 7: *ḫw.k Ỉnpw*, by error.

On the protection of the deceased by Anubis: Haikal, *Two Hier. Fun. Pap. II*, p. 58, n. 12; *CT* I, 74 (sp. 24): *Ỉnpw ḥr.k m sꜣ.k*, 'Anubis is over you, as your protection'.

nn šnꜥ.tw.k m rꜣw nw Dwꜣt Ỉmntt Wꜣst. Sequence omitted in P. Louvre E 11079; wholly in lacuna in P. Louvre N 3167 + 3222, I, 21, and partly in P. Joseph Smith, III, 4–5. *Ỉmnt Wꜣst* is omitted in all other manuscripts used here of the Book of Breathing made by Isis: P. BM EA 9995, I, 15 = P. BM EA 10260, II, x + 9 = P. Berlin 3135, II, 3–4 = P. Berlin 3154, I, 16 = P. Denon, II, 9–10 = P. Florence 3665 + P. Vienna 3850, II, 22–3 = P. Lausanne 3391, I, 27 = P. Louvre E 8079 + 11080, II, 4–5 = P. Louvre N 3083, V, 21 (*nn šnꜥ.t*) = P. Louvre N 3121, I, 19 = P. Louvre N 3154, II, 3 (*nn šnꜥ.f twk*) = P. Louvre N 3158, II, 8 = P. Louvre N 3166, I, 20 = P. Louvre N 3284, II, 8 = P. Louvre N 3285, I, 27–8 = P. Louvre N 3291, 15 = P. Tübingen 2016, III, 8 = P. Vienna 3863, II, 2 = P. Vienna 3931, I, 26 (text partly rubbed out).

Besides P. BM EA 10048, several documents connect the Duat to the West of Thebes: cf. e.g. P. Berlin 3162, VI, 2: *ꜥḳ.k m Dwꜣt m Ỉmntt Wꜣst*, 'You enter the Duat, in the West of Thebes'; ibid., VIII, 4–5: *ỉw.k mn.tỉ m-ḫnw Dwꜣt nfrt ḥr Ỉmntt Wꜣst*, 'You are established in the beautiful Duat, on the West of Thebes'; Seeber, *Untersuchungen*, p. 115, n. 464.

On the gates of the Duat: F.R. Herbin, *BIFAO* 84 (1984), p. 290, n. 49. *Rꜣ*, 'entry', is the equivalent of the noun *sbꜣ* more often employed in this context; see e.g. Vernus, *Athribis*, p. 33, n. (c); also stela BM EA 165 (G. Martin, *The Tomb-Chapels of Paser and Ra'ia at Saqqara* (London 1985), pl. 9; stela BM EA 480 (*HTBM* V, pl. 39); N. de G. Davies, *Seven Private Tombs* (London 1948), pl. 20 (left); Kamal, *Stèles*, p. 63, 13–14. On the wish not to be turned back from the gates of the Duat, cf. P. BM EA 10260, I, x + 4–5, and J. Zandee, *Death as an Enemy* (2nd edn, New York 1977), pp. 120 and 124–5; G. Vittmann, in *Zwischen den beiden Ewigkeiten* (Fs. G. Thausing, Vienna 1994), p. 245, n. (v); etc.

III, 1

ỉw n.k Ỉ[45] *ꜥꜣ ꜥꜣ nb Ḫmnw sš.f n.k šꜥt n snsn m ḏbꜥw.f ḏs.f*. Same reading in P. Berlin 3135, II, 4–5 = P. Berlin 3154, I, 16–17 = P. Florence 3665 + P. Vienna 3850, II, 23–4 = P. Louvre E 8079 + 11080, II, 5 = P. Louvre N 3121, I, 19–20 = P. Louvre N 3291, 15–16. Sequence partly in lacuna in P. Joseph Smith, III, 5 = P. Louvre N 3167 + 3222, 22–3 = P. Vienna 3931, I, 27–8. Small lacuna between *ỉw n.k* and *nb Ḫmnw* in P. Louvre N 3126, I, 20. Var. P. BM EA 9995, I, 15 = P. BN 179–81, II, 12 = P. Denon, II, 10 = P. Louvre N 3166, I, 20 = P. Louvre N 3284, II, 8: *ỉỉ n.k*; P. BM EA 10260, II, x + 9–10: *Ỉ ꜥꜣ sp 2 nb Ḫmnw*; P. BN 179–81, II, 12: *ꜥꜣ ꜥꜣ*; P. Louvre E 11079, III, 5: *ỉỉ sp 2 n.t Ỉ ꜥꜣ ꜥꜣ ꜥꜣ*. Addition of (*m*) *nṯr* after *Ỉ* in P. Louvre N 3083, V, 21 = P. Louvre N 3154, II, 3. Omission of *šꜥt n* in P. Louvre N 3083, V, 22; of *n* before *snsn* in P. Lausanne 3391, I, 28 = P. Louvre N 3158, II, 8 = P. Louvre N 3285, I, 28 = P. Tübingen 2016, III, 8 = P. Vienna 3863, II, 3.

On Thoth as author of the Book of Breathing: *LPE*, p. 255 (VIII, 9); J. Quaegebeur, in *Studies in Egyptology Presented to Miriam Lichtheim* II (Jerusalem 1990), pp. 792–3; id., in M. Bierbrier (ed.), *Portraits and Masks: Burial Customs in Roman Egypt* (London 1997), p. 72. See also *infra*, **III, 5–6**, where this compilation written by Thoth guarantees the protection of the deceased.

snsn bꜣ.k r nḥḥ. Same reading in P. BM EA 10260, II, x + 10 = P. Berlin 3135, II, 5 = P. BN 179–81, I, 13 = P. Denon, II, 11 = P. Florence 3665 + P. Vienna 3850, II, 24 = P. Lausanne 3391, II, 1 = P. Louvre E 8079 + 11080, II, 5–6 = P. Louvre N 3126, I, 20–1 (*bꜣ.k* in lacuna) = P. Louvre N 3158, II, 9 = P. Louvre N 3166, I, 21 = P. Louvre N 3284, II, 9 = P. Louvre N 3285, I, 29 = P. Louvre N 3291, 16 = P. Tübingen 2016, III, 9 = P. Vienna 3863, II, 3–4 = P. Vienna 3931, I, 28. Addition of *ḏt* after *nḥḥ* in P. Louvre N 3154, II, 4. Sequence omitted in P. Louvre E 11079, III, 6; partly in lacuna in P. Joseph Smith, III, 5–6 = P. Louvre N 3167 + 3222, I, 23. See *supra*, **II, 8**. P. Louvre N 3121, II, 1, introduces before this sequence the invocation *hꜣy Ḥwt-Ḥr N*, 'Hail Hathor N'. Var. P. Berlin 3154, I, 17 = P. Louvre N 3083, V, 22 = P. Louvre N 3154, II, 4: *r nḥḥ ḏt*. Note the variant of P. BM EA 9995, I, 16: *snsn ỉb.k r nḥḥ*, 'your heart breathes for ever'; see *supra*, **II, 5**.

wḥm.k ḳy.k ḥr-tp tꜣ m ꜥnḫ. Same reading in P. BM EA 9995, I, 17 = P. Berlin 3154, I, 16–17 = P. Louvre N 3158, II, 9. Sequence partly in lacuna P. Joseph Smith, III, 6 = P. Louvre N 3167 + 3222, I, 24. Omission of *m ꜥnḫ* in P. Vienna 3931, I, 28; of suffix after *wḥm* in P. BN 179–81, II, 13, after *ḳy* in P. Louvre N 3121, II, 1. Var. P. Louvre N 3166, I, 21–2: *wḥm.w ḳd.k*; P. Louvre N 3291, 16: *wḥm.k ḳd.k* (...) *m-m ꜥnḫw*; P. Louvre N 3083, V, 22–VI, 1 = P. Louvre N 3154, II, 5: *wḥm.t* (*/.k*) *ḳyt.t* (*/.k*) *m ꜥnḫ ḥr-tp tꜣ*. P. Berlin 3135, II, 5 = P. Denon, II, 12 = P. Florence 3665 + P. Vienna 3850, II, 25 = P. Joseph Smith, III, 6 = P. Lausanne 3391, II, 1 = P. Louvre E 8079 + 11080, II, 6 = P. Louvre N 3121, II, 2 = P. Louvre N 3126, I, 21 = P. Louvre N 3284, II, 10 = P. Louvre N 3285, I, 29 = P. Tübingen 2016, III, 9 = P. Vienna 3863, II, 4: *m ꜥnḫw*, 'among the living'; P. BM EA 10260, II, x + 11: *n-m ꜥnḫw*; P. BN 179–81, II, 14: *n ꜥnḫw*. P. Louvre E 11079, III, 1–2 (misplaced and probably corrupt passage): ... (?)*m ḳy.t mỉ ỉr.t ḥr-tp tꜣ m ꜥnḫw*, '... (?) your form as you did upon earth among the living'. See *infra*, **VII, 6–7**.

44. Note the writing in P. Lausanne 3391, I, 26.

45. Written with the sign of the ibis (*Ḏḥwty*) in P. Berlin 3154, I, 17 = P. Denon, II, 10.

III, 1–2
ỉw.k nṯr ḥnꜥ bꜣw nṯrw. Same reading in P. BM EA 9995, I, 17 = P. Berlin 3135, II, 6 = P. Berlin 3154, I, 18 = P. BN 179–81, II, 14 = P. Denon, II, 12 = P. Florence 3665 + P. Vienna 3850, II, 25 = P. Louvre E 8079 + 11080, II, 6 = P. Louvre N 3121, II, 2 = P. Louvre N 3126, I, 21 = P. Louvre N 3154, II, 5 = P. Louvre N 3158, II, 9–III, 1 = P. Louvre N 3166, I, 22 = P. Louvre N 3284, II, 10 = P. Louvre N 3285, I, 29–30 = P. Louvre N 3291, 16 = P. Tübingen 2016, III, 9–10 = P. Vienna 3863, II, 4 = P. Vienna 3931, I, 29. Sequence omitted in P. Louvre E 11079; in lacuna in P. Louvre N 3167 + 3222, I, 24. Var. P. BM EA 10260, II, x + 11: *bꜣ.k nṯr*; P. Louvre N 3083, VI, 1: *nṯr.w bꜣ.k*; P. Lausanne 3391, II, 2: *ḥnꜥ bꜣ nṯrw*. Corrupt passage in P. Joseph Smith, III, 6. For another reference to the *bꜣw nṯrw*, see *supra*, **II, 10**.

On the divinization of the ba, see *supra*, **II, 5**.

III, 2
ib.k ib n Rꜥ ḥꜥw.k ḥꜥw n nṯr[46] *ꜥꜣ*. Same reading in P. BM EA 9995, I, 17–18 = P. BM EA 10260, II, x + 11–12 = P. Berlin 3135, II, 6 = P. Berlin 3154, I, 18 = P. BN 179–81, II, 14–15 = P. Denon, II, 10–11 = P. Florence 3665 + P. Vienna 3850, II, 25 = P. Louvre E 8079 + 11080, II, 6–7 = P. Louvre N 3083, VI, 1–2 = P. Louvre N 3121, II, 2 = P. Louvre N 3126, I, 22 (*ib.k* in lacuna) = P. Louvre N 3154, II, 5–6 = P. Louvre N 3158, III, 1 = P. Louvre N 3166, I, 22 = P. Louvre N 3284, II, 10–11 = P. Louvre N 3285, I, 30 = P. Louvre N 3291, 16 = P. Tübingen 2016, III, 10 = P. Vienna 3863, II, 4–5 = P. Vienna 3931, I, 29–30. Sequence omitted in P. Louvre E 11079; partly in lacuna P. Joseph Smith, III, 7 = P. Louvre N 3167 + 3222, 24. Var. P. Lausanne 3391, II, 2: *ib.k ib n Wsỉr*. P. Denon, II, 13, adds: *ꜥnḫ.k r nḥḥ ḥnꜥ ḏt*, 'You live for ever and eternally'.

For a relation between the heart of the deceased and Re, cf. P. Vatican Inv. 38596, 18–19 (F.R. Herbin, *RdE* 54 [2003], p. 83) = Maspero, *Sarcophages* I, p. 4: *ib.f n.f mi Rꜥ ḥꜣty.f n.f mi Ḫpri* (Glorifications of Osiris); H.D. Schneider, in *Hommages à Jean Leclant* IV (*BdE* 106, 1994), p. 359.

III, 2–3
hꜣy Wsỉr N Ỉmn ỉrm.k rꜥ nb Rꜥ ḥr wḥm.k ꜥnḫ. Beginning of § 6 of de Horrack's classification. Same reading in P. BN 179–81, II, 15–16 = P. Denon, II, 13–III, 1 = P. Florence 3665 + P. Vienna 3850, III, 1–3 = P. Louvre E 8079 + 11080, II, 7–8 = P. Louvre N 3126, II, 1–3 = P. Louvre N 3158, III, 1–2 = P. Louvre N 3291, 17 = P. Tübingen 2016, III, 10–11. Sequence omitted in P. Louvre E 11079; partly in lacuna in P. Joseph Smith, III, 7 = P. Vienna 3931, I, 30–1. Var. P. Louvre N 3166, I, 22–3 = P. Louvre N 3291, 17: *ỉ Wsỉr N*. Omission of the interjection (*hꜣy* or *ỉ*) before *Wsỉr N* in P. Lausanne 3391, II, 3 = P. Vienna 3863, II, 5 = P. Vienna 3931, I, 30. Omission of *ḥr* before *wḥm* in P. Louvre N 3154, II, 7 = P. Louvre N 3166, I, 23. Addition of *bꜣ*[*.k*] (?) *m pr Rꜥ*, '[Your] ba (?) is in the House of Re', after *rꜥ nb*, in P. Joseph Smith, III, 7, which shows then: *wḥm.k ꜥnḫ*, 'You renew life'. Indistinct sign after *rꜥ nb* in P. Louvre N 3121, II, 3.

Certain versions, omitting the name of Re, make *Ỉmn* the subject of *ḥr wḥm*: P. Berlin 3135, II, 7–8 = P. Vienna 3863, II, 5–6 = P. Louvre N 3126, II, 2–3 = P. Louvre N 3167 + 3222, II, 1–2:

(*hꜣy*) *Wsỉr N*	'(Hail) Osiris N!
Ỉmn ỉrm.k /*.t rꜥ nb*	Amun is with you, every day,
ḥr wḥm.k /*.t ꜥnḫ*	renewing you alive.'

In this latter group, omission of *rꜥ nb* in P. BM EA 9995, I, 18 = P. Berlin 3154, I, 19; of *ḥr* before *wḥm.k* in P. Louvre N 3284, II, 13–14.

P. BM EA 10260, II, x + 12 presents here a version corresponding to P. BM EA 10048, II, 3–4:

hꜣy Wsỉr N	'Hail Osiris N!
Ỉmn ỉrm.k rꜥ nb	Amun is with you, every day,
ḥr di n.k ṯꜣw	giving you breath.'

P. Louvre N 3083, VI, 2–3:

hꜣy Wsỉr N	'Hail Osiris N!
Ỉmn m sꜣ.k rꜥ nb	Amun is your protection, every day,
Rꜥ ḥr wḥm.k ꜥnḫ.	and Re renews you alive.'

III, 3
wp n.k Wp-wꜣwt wꜣt nfr(t). Same reading in P. BM EA 9995, I, 19 = P. BM EA 10260, II, x + 12 = P. Berlin 3135, II, 8 = P. Berlin 3154, I, 19 = P. Denon, III, 1–2 = P. Florence 3665 + P. Vienna 3850, III, 3 = P. Joseph Smith, III, 7–8 (partly rubbed out with small lacuna) = P. Lausanne 3391, II, 4 = P. Louvre E 8079 + 11080, II, 8 = P. Louvre N 3083, VI, 3 = P. Louvre N 3121, II, 3 = P. Louvre N 3126, II, 2 = P. Louvre N 3154, II, 7 = P. Louvre N 3158, III, 2 = P. Louvre N 3166, I, 24 = P. Louvre N 3167 + 3222, II, 2 = P. Louvre N 3284, II, 14 = P. Louvre N 3291, 17 = P. Tübingen 2016, III, 12 = P. Vienna 3863, II, 6–7. Sequence omitted in P. Louvre E 11079; partly rubbed out in P. Vienna 3931, I, 31. Omission of *n* before suffix *.k* in P. BN 179–81, II, 17. Var. P. Louvre N 3285, II, 3: *wꜣwt nfr*[*wt*]; P. Tübingen 2016, III, 12: *wꜣwt nfr(w)t*.

This function of 'opener of ways' (*wp wꜣwt*), the fundamental, but not exclusive[47] characteristic of Wepwawet, is already present in *PT* § 1090 a; it recurs in *CT* I, 34, sp. 10; 74, sp. 24; VII, 49, sp. 845, and in *BD* ch. 182 (ed. Budge, p. 484, 2–3). The late religious literature adopts the motif (e.g. Mariette, *Dendérah* I, 9: *Wp-wꜣwt mꜣꜥ n.f*[48] *mṯn*; P. Rhind, I, 8, 5: *Wp-wꜣwt ḥr mꜣꜥ n.k mṯn*; II, 8, 5: *Wp-wꜣwt ḥr wpt n.t mṯn*; G. Daressy, *ASAE* 20 [1920], p. 176: *wn n.k Wp-wꜣwt* (...) *wꜣwt nfrw(t)*); etc. Opening of the ways is intended to protect the deceased from his enemies or permit him to act against them[49] (*CT* I, 193, sp. 45; *Ritual for the opening of the mouth*, scene 55; P. Berlin 3055, XXXII, 6), at the same time as guaranteeing him freedom of movement at the gates of the Duat and in any place he might wish (P. Louvre N 3121, V, 2–3; Maspero, *Sarcophages* I, p. 46: *Wp-wꜣwt šmꜥw* (...) *wp.f n.k wꜣwt nfrwt pr.k ꜥḳ.k r mr.k*) for these are the ways of the West (*CT* IV, 376, sp. 345; 377, sp. 346), var.: of the sacred land, P. Parma 183, 11). In *CT* IV, 378, sp. 346, Wepwawet is said to 'guide' (*sšm*) the deceased toward the ways of the West;[50] cf. also Maspero, *Sarcophages* I, pp. 65 and 69: *Wp-wꜣwt sšm.f tw r bw nb mr.k* (var.: *mr kꜣ.k*).

Assimilated to Wepwawet, the deceased is empowered to open a way (*CT* II, 168, sp. 953), notably for the gods (*CT* I, 312, sp. 74); as such, he exercises his power (*bꜣw*) against his enemies (*CT* I, 313, sp. 74).

mꜣꜣ.k m ỉrty.k sḏm.k m ꜥnḫwy.k mdw.k[51] *m rꜣ.k šm.k m rdwy.k*. Same reading

46. Note the spelling of *nṯr* in P. Berlin 3154, I, 18, the first sign being hieroglyphic, the other hieratic. See also *infra*, n. 139.
47. *Wp wꜣwt* is also an epithet of Neith (*PT* § 643 a) and Anubis (*Wb.* I, 300, 15). In *BD* ch. 128, 6–7 (ed. Lepsius, pl. 51, 6–7), the ka of Osiris comes to him and opens the ways for him 'in this his name of *Wp-wꜣwt*'.
48. Suffix *.f* refers back to the king.
49. It is stated in *CT* IV, 376, sp. 345 that these enemies reside in heaven as well as on earth and in the underworld.
50. This function of Wepwawet accounts for his appearance on standards born before the king at time of battle. On the expression *sšm wꜣ(w)t*, cf. P. BM EA 10201, **II, 13–14**.
51. On this writing of the verb *mdw*, written as if the noun: M. Smith, *Enchoria* 15 (1987), p. 74.

in P. BM EA 9995, I, 19–20 = P. Berlin 3154, I, 19–20 = P. Lausanne 3391, II, 5 = P. Louvre N 3083, VI, 3–4 = P. Louvre N 3121, II, 3–4 = P. Louvre N 3291, 17–18 = P. Vienna 3863, II, 7. Inversion of the phrases *sḏm.k m ʿnḫwy.k* and *mdw.k m rꜣ.k* in P. BN 179–81, II, 17–18. Sequence omitted in P. Louvre E 11079; partly in lacuna in P. Joseph Smith, III, 8 = P. Vienna 3931, I, 32–II, 1. Omission of suffix after *irty* in P. Louvre N 3154, II, 7. Var. P. BM EA 10260, II, x + 13 = P. Berlin 3135, II, 9 = P. BN 179–81, II, 17 = P. Denon, III, 2 = P. Florence 3665 + P. Vienna 3850, III, 3 = P. Louvre E 8079 + 11080, II, 8 = P. Louvre N 3126, II, 3 = P. Louvre N 3158, III, 2 = P. Louvre N 3167 + 3222, II, 2 = P. Louvre N 3284, II, 14 = P. Louvre N 3285, II, 3–4 = P. Tübingen 2016, III, 12: *mꜣꜣ.k /.t* [52] *m irt.k /.t*;[53] P. Louvre N 3154, II, 7–8 (*m m* by error before *ʿnḫwy.k*); P. Berlin 3135, II, 9 = P. Joseph Smith, III, 8 = P. Louvre N 3158, III, 3 = P. Louvre N 3166, I, 24: *šm.k /.t m rd.k /.t*; 53 P. BN 179–81, II, 18: *šm.k m ib.k ky ḏd ibw.k*; P. Denon, III, 2–3: *šm.k m ib.k ky ḏd rd.k*.

On this evocation of the physical faculties of the deceased, see *LPE*, pp. 249–51 (VIII, 4) and Vernus, *RdE* 30 (1978), p. 142 with n. 165; cf. also *infra*, **III, 6**, and *LPE*, p. 250, n. 101.

Cf. P. Vatican Inv. 38608, 3 (F.R. Herbin, *RdE* 54 [2003], p. 83): *rꜣ.k n.k mdw.k im.f*; mummy label BM EA 36502, 1: *iw n.i rꜣ.i mdw.i im.f* (G. Vittmann, in *Zwischen den beiden Ewigkeiten* [Fs. G. Thausing, Vienna 1994], p. 267).

III, 3–4

iw bꜣ.k nṯr m Dwꜣt ḫr ir ḫprw nb mr.k. Sequence omitted in P. Louvre E 11079; partly in lacuna in P. Joseph Smith, III, 9. Var. P. Denon, III, 3: *iw bꜣ.k nṯr m pt*; P. Louvre N 3083, VI, 4: *nṯr.tw bꜣ.k m Dwꜣt*; P. Louvre N 3154, II, 9: *i-mr.f* (?); P. Louvre N 3158, III, 3: *i-mr.t*; P. Louvre N 3291, 18: *r ir ḫprw nb mr.f*; P. BM EA 10260, II, x + 13–14 = P. Berlin 3135, II, 10 = P. Berlin 3154, I, 20 = P. BN 179–81, II, 18–19 = P. Denon, III, 3 = P. Lausanne 3391, II, 6 = P. Louvre E 8079 + 11080, II, 9 = P. Louvre N 3154, II, 8–9 = P. Louvre N 3284, II, 15 = P. Louvre N 3285, II, 4 = P. Tübingen 2016, III, 13: *r ir ḫpr(w) nb i-mr.f (/.k)*;[54] P. BM EA 9995, I, 20 = P. Florence 3665 + P. Vienna 3850, III, 4–5 = P. Louvre N 3121, II, 4 = P. Vienna 3931, II, 1: *r ir ḫpr(w) nb i-mr.k (/.t)*; P. Louvre N 3126, II, 4 = P. Louvre N 3167 + 3222, II, 3 = P. Vienna 3863, II, 8: *r ir ḫpr(w) nb i-mrwt.f /.t*, 'to assume any form according to his (your) desire'; same version (var. *ḫr ir*) in P. Louvre N 3083, VI, 4–5.

III, 4

ir nꜣ šršr n p(ꜣ) išd šps n Wsir. Sequence partly in lacuna in P. Joseph Smith, III, 9. Compared with the predominant number of versions giving *ir.k nꜣ šršr*: P. BM EA 9995, I, 20 = P. BM EA 10260, II, x + 14 = P. Berlin 3135, II, 10 = P. Berlin 3154, I, 20 = P. BN 179–81, II, 19 = P. Denon, III, 3 = P. Florence 3665 + P. Vienna 3850, III, 5 = P. Lausanne 3391, II, 6–7 = P. Louvre E 8079 + 11080, II, 9 = P. Louvre E 11079, II, 10 = P. Louvre N 3121, II, 4–5 = P. Louvre N 3126, II, 4 = P. Louvre N 3284, II, 16 = P. Louvre N 3285, II, 4–5 = P. Louvre N 3291, 18 = P. Tübingen 2016, III, 13 = P. Vienna 3863, II, 8, the variant *ir nꜣ šršr* is attested outside P. BM EA 10048 only in P. Louvre N 3083, VI, 5 = P. Louvre N 3154, II, 9 = P. Louvre N 3158, III, 3 = P. Louvre N 3167 + 3222, II, 3. Two explanations may be suggested: either this is a case of simple omission, or the absence of suffix is intentional, in which case *ir* is to be considered an infinitive, dependent on *ḫr* as in the preceding instance of the same verb in *ḫr ir ḫprw*. Two other variants are supplied by P. Louvre N 3166, I, 25: *ir.n.k nꜣ šršr*, and by P. Vienna 3931, II, 2: *iw n.k nꜣ šršr*, 'Freshness (?) comes to you'.

šršr. This word, of which no other attestation is known outside the Book of Breathing made by Isis,[55] seems to have presented several compilers of the text with problems. It is always preceded by the plural definite article *nꜣ*. In most cases, it is written (note , P. Louvre N 3284, II, 16) or, like here, , to be compared with the rarer , found in P. Joseph Smith, III, 9 = (?) P. Louvre N 3154, II, 9 = P. Vienna 3931, II, 2. It occurs also once in the form in P. Louvre N 3083, VI, 5. The expected meaning, to judge from the determinative , would be 'breath'[56] or rather, in this context, 'fresh air', 'coolness', tied to the presence of leaves as suggested by the determinatives and .[57]

n p(ꜣ) išd šps n Wsir. The version with *Wsir*, compared with *Iwnw* in most of other manuscripts used here, seems faulty and probably derives from confusion of the hieratic writings of the toponym and of the god's name, exacerbated by the well established connection between the balanites and Osiris. Text partly rubbed out in P. Joseph Smith, III, 9. Var. P. BM EA 9995, I, 20–1 = P. BM EA 10260, II, x + 14 = P. BN 179–81, II, 19–20 = P. Louvre E 8079 + 11080, II, 9 = P. Louvre N 3121, II, 5 = P. Louvre N 3126, III, 4–5 = P. Louvre N 3158, III, 4 = P. Louvre N 3166, I, 25–6 = P. Louvre N 3285, II, 5 = P. Louvre N 3291, 18: *n p(ꜣ) išd šps n Iwnw*; P. Louvre N 3154, II, 9: *n p(ꜣ) išd n Iwnw*; P. Berlin 3154, I, 20 = P. Denon, III, 3–4 = P. Florence 3665 + P. Vienna 3850, III, 5–6 = P. Louvre N 3284, II, 16: *n p(ꜣ) išd šps m Iwnw*; P. Louvre N 3167 + 3222, II, 3–4: *m pꜣ išd šps m Iwnw*; P. Louvre N 3083, VI, 5: *n p(ꜣ) išd*; P. Lausanne 3391, II, 7 = P. Vienna 3863, II, 8 = P. Vienna 3931, II, 2: *pꜣ išd šps m Iwnw*; P. Berlin 3135, II, 11: *pꜣ išd šps n Iwnw*; P. Tübingen 2016, III, 13–14: *n pꜣ išd* [...] *Iwnw*; P. Louvre E 11079, II, 10–11: *n p(ꜣ) išd nty m Ḥwt Bnbn m Iwnw*, 'of the noble balanites tree which is in the Mansion of the obelisk in Heliopolis'.

III, 4–5

nhs.tw.k rʿ nb mꜣꜣ.k nꜣ stwt n p(ꜣ) Rʿ (or: *p(ꜣ) itn*). Nearly the whole of the manuscripts: P. BM EA 9995, I, 21 = P. BM EA 10260, II, x + 14 = P. Berlin 3135, II, 11 = P. Berlin 3154, I, 20 = P. BN 179–81, II, 20 = P. Denon, III, 4 = P. Florence 3665 + P. Vienna 3850, III, 6 = P. Lausanne 3391, II, 7 = P. Louvre E 8079 + 11080, II, 9–10 = P. Louvre N 3083, VI, 5 = P. Louvre N 3126, II, 5 = P. Louvre N 3167 + 3222, II, 4 = P. Louvre N 3284, II, 16–17 = P. Louvre N 3285, II, 5 = P. Louvre N 3291, 18 = P. Tübingen 2016, III, 14 = P. Vienna 3863, II, 9, gives here *nhs.k /.t rʿ nb*. The passive *nhs.tw.k /.t* also occurs in P. Louvre N 3154, II, 10, P. Louvre N 3158, III, 4, and a pronominal form *nḥs.k tw rʿ nb* is attested in P. Joseph Smith, III, 9 = P. Louvre N 3166, I, 26. Sequence omitted in P. Louvre E 11079; partly in lacuna in P. Joseph Smith, III, 10; rubbed out between *nh*[*s*] and *mꜣꜣ.k /.t* in P. Louvre N 3121, II, 5 = P. Vienna 3931, II, 2. Redundant suffix *.k* after *stwt* in P. Berlin 3135, II, 11. Omission of *n* before *p(ꜣ) Rʿ* in P. Louvre N 3285, II, 6 = P. Vienna 3863, II, 9 = P. Vienna 3931, II, 3. Var. P. Louvre N 3158, III, 4 = P. Louvre N 3166, I, 26: *mꜣꜣ.n.k /.t*; P. Louvre N 3083, VI, 5: *mꜣꜣ.k stwt itn*.

On the daily awakening of the deceased, cf. P. dem. Berlin 8351, II,

52. *mꜣꜣ.t* in lacuna in P. Louvre N 3158, III, 2.
53. See *infra*, n. 60.
54. Suffix *.f* refers back to the word *bꜣ*, suffix *.k* to the deceased. The ba of the deceased is considered as his full person.
55. *Wb*. IV, 529, 7 gives as source only this passage of the Book of Breathing. No other word *šršr* is cited. The example referring to P. Anastasi I, V, 4 (G. Posener, *Mél. Maspero* I/1 [*MIFAO* 66, 1934], p. 329 and *Catalogue des Ostraca hiér. litt. de Deir el Médineh* II [Cairo 1951], no. 1178, 1) is without relevance to the present instance.
56. The connection proposed by Budge (*Egyptian Hier. Dict.*, p. 750) with the verb *snsn*, cannot be retained, despite the existence of the expression *ir snsn*. None of the versions of the Book of Breathing made by Isis provides a variant *snsn* which might allow such a comparison.
57. For the meaning, see P. Leiden T 32, II, 1 (*LPE*, p. 118): 'You are seated beneath the branches of the noble balanites, and take shade (*iṯ.k šbt*) by its foliage'.

2: *nhs=k mw Rʿ ir rʿ nby*, 'You awake like Re, each day'; see Smith, *Liturgy*, pp. 24 and 41; ibid., V, 14: *nhs=k m hrw m sꜣt ir rʿ nby*, 'You awake by day in jubilation, each day'. For the sense of *nhs*, see ibid., p. 35 (I, 2, b). On the wish to see the rays of the sun, see *infra*, **III, 6**; P. BM EA 10110 + 10111, II, 14–15 = P. BM EA 10199, 27: *i Rʿ mi n.i stwt.k mi mꜣꜣ.i twk m ḫrt-rʿ nt rʿ nb*, 'O Re, may I see your rays, may I see you every day'; Maspero, *Sarcophages* I, p. 24: *di.k mꜣꜣ(.i) itn.k nn šnʿ.tw(.i) r mꜣꜣ stwt.k*, 'Grant that (I) may see your disk, and not be prevented from seeing your rays'. This vision enables the ba to live (ibid., p. 29: *ʿnḫ bꜣ.f m stwt itn*; p. 22: *ʿnḫ bꜣ.k m mꜣꜣ stwt.f*; pp. 24 and 36: *ʿnḫ.k m stwt itn*).

III, 5

iw n.k nb nṯrw Imn ḫr ṯꜣw n ʿnḫ. Omission of *nb nṯrw* in all other versions. Otherwise, same reading in P. BM EA 10260, II, x + 15 = P. Berlin 3135, II, 11–12 = P. Berlin 3154, I, 21 = P. Louvre N 3083, VI, 5–6 = P. Louvre N 3121, II, 5 = P. Louvre N 3158, III, 4–5 = P. Louvre N 3166, I, 26–7 = P. Louvre N 3167 + 3222, II, 4 = P. Vienna 3931, II, 3. Sequence partly in lacuna in P. Joseph Smith, III, 10. Var. P. Lausanne 3391, II, 8: *iw.f n.k*; P. BM EA 9995, I, 21 = P. BN 179–81, II, 20 = P. Denon, III, 4 = P. Florence 3665 + P. Vienna 3850, III, 6 = P. Louvre E 8079 + 11080, II, 10 = P. Louvre N 3126, II, 5 = P. Louvre N 3284, II, 17 = P. Louvre N 3285, II, 6 = P. Tübingen 2016, III, 14: *ii n.k*; P. Louvre E 11079, II, 9: *Ḥwt-Ḥr N ii sp 2 n.t Imn*; P. Louvre N 3291, 19: *m ṯꜣw n ʿnḫ*. P. Louvre N 3083, VI, 6, places after *iw n.t Imn ḫr ṯꜣw n ʿnḫ* a reference to the Osiris N.

For Amun as provider of breath, see *supra*, **II, 3–4**. For the breath of life (Greek πνεῦμα): F. Daumas, *Les Mammisis des temples égyptiens* (Paris 1958), p. 401 with nn. 2–3.

di.f ir.k snsn m-ḫnw ḏbꜣt. Omission of suffix after *ir* in P. Louvre E 11089, II, 10 = P. Louvre N 3083, VI, 7. The version *m-ḫnw ḏbꜣt* is attested only in P. Louvre N 3083, VI, 7 = P. Louvre N 3158, III, 5 = P. Louvre N 3166, I, 27. P. Louvre E 11079, II, 10 = P. Louvre N 3083, VI, 7 = P. Louvre N 3154, II, 11: *m-ḫnw ḏbꜣt.k /.t*. Most of the other sources give *m ḏbꜣt.k /.t*: P. BM EA 9995, I, 22 = P. BM EA 10260, II, x + 15 = P. Berlin 3135, II, 12 = P. Berlin 3154, I, 21 = P. BN 179–81, II, 21 = P. Denon, III, 5 = P. Lausanne 3391, II, 9 = P. Louvre E 8079 + 11080, II, 10 = P. Louvre N 3121, II, 6 = P. Louvre N 3126, II, 6 = P. Louvre N 3167 + 3222, II, 5 = P. Louvre N 3284, II, 18 = P. Louvre N 3285, II, 6 = P. Louvre N 3291, 19 = P. Tübingen 2016, III, 15 = P. Vienna 3863, II, 10 = P. Vienna 3931, II, 3–4. P. Florence 3665 + P. Vienna 3850, III, 7: *m ḏbꜣt*. P. Joseph Smith, III, 10: [...] *ḏbꜣt.k*.[58]

On the *ḏbꜣt*: J. Zandee, *JEOL* 27 (1981–2), pp. 12–13.

pr.k r tꜣ rʿ nb sp 2. Same reading in P. Louvre N 3083, VI, 7 = P. Louvre N 3154, II, 11 = P. Louvre N 3158, III, 5 = P. Louvre N 3166, I, 27. Sequence omitted in P. Louvre E 11079. Omission of *sp 2* in P. BM EA 9995, I, 22 = P. BM EA 10260, II, x + 15 = P. Berlin 3135, II, 12 = P. Berlin 3154, I, 21 = P. BN 179–81, II, 21 = P. Denon, III, 5 = P. Florence 3665 + P. Vienna 3850, III, 7 = P. Joseph Smith, III, 10 = P. Lausanne 3391, II, 9 = P. Louvre E 8079 + 11080, II, 10 = P. Louvre N 3121, II, 6 = P. Louvre N 3126, II, 6 = P. Louvre N 3167 + 3222, II, 5 = P. Louvre N 3284, II, 18 = P. Louvre N 3285, II, 7 = P. Louvre N 3291, 19 = P. Tübingen 2016, III, 15 = P. Vienna 3863, II, 10 = P. Vienna 3931, II, 4.

For *sp 2*, see Smith, *Mortuary Texts*, p. 74 (III, 7).

III, 5–6

šʿt n snsn n I m sꜣ.k snsn.k im.s rʿ nb mi Rʿ. Sequence omitted in P. Louvre E 11079; partly in lacuna in P. Joseph Smith, III, 11. Omission of *n* before *snsn* and *I* in P. Louvre N 3285, II, 7 = P. Tübingen 2016, III, 15; of *rʿ nb mi Rʿ* in P. Berlin 3154, I, 22; of *rʿ nb* in P. BN 179–81, II, 22 = P. Denon, III, 6 = P. Louvre E 8079 + 11080, II, 11 = P. Louvre N 3158, III, 6 = P. Louvre N 3166, I, 28[59] = P. Louvre N 3167 + 3222, II, 5 = P. Louvre N 3291, 20 = P. Tübingen 2016, III, 16. Omission of *mi Rʿ* in P. BM EA 9995, I, 23 = P. BM EA 10260, II, x + 16 = P. Berlin 3135, II, 13 = P. Florence 3665 + P. Vienna 3850, III, 8 = P. Joseph Smith, III, 11 = P. Lausanne 3391, II, 10 = P. Louvre N 3121, II, 7 = P. Louvre N 3126, II, 7 = P. Louvre N 3284, II, 19 = P. Louvre N 3285, II, 7 = P. Vienna 3863, II, 11 = P. Vienna 3931, II, 5. Var. P. Louvre N 3154, II, 11: *I m sꜣ.k*, 'Thoth is your protection'. P. Louvre N 3166, I, 28: *snsn.k im.k* by error. The phrase *šʿt n snsn n I m sꜣ.k*, is replaced in P. Louvre N 3083, VI, 7 by *pr m hrw m sꜣ.t*, 'going out by day is your protection'.

On the Book of Breathing of Thoth as a protection for the deceased, see *LPE*, p. 255 (VIII, 9). For the expression *snsn mi Rʿ*, cf. P. BM EA 10264A, x + 3.

III, 6

mꜣꜣ irt.k[60] *stwt itn*. Same reading in P. BN 179–81, II, 22–3 = P. Denon, III, 6–7 = P. Joseph Smith, III, 11 = P. Louvre E 8079 + 11080, II, 11 = P. Louvre N 3158, III, 6 = P. Louvre N 3167 + 3222, II, 5–6 = P. Louvre N 3284, II, 19 = P. Vienna 3931, II, 5. Sequence omitted in P. Louvre E 11079 = P. Louvre N 3083, VI, 7. Var. P. BM EA 9995, I, 23 = P. Berlin 3135, II, 13 = P. Berlin 3154, I, 22 = P. Florence 3665 + P. Vienna 3850, III, 8 = P. Lausanne 3391, II, 10 = P. Louvre N 3121, II, 7 = P. Louvre N 3126, II, 7 = P. Louvre N 3154, II, 11 = P. Louvre N 3166, I, 28 = P. Louvre N 3285, II, 8 = P. Louvre N 3291, 20 = P. Vienna 3863, II, 1: *irty.k /.t*. Var. P. BM EA 10260, II, x + 16 = P. Louvre N 3154, II, 12 = P. Tübingen 2016, III, 16 = P. Vienna 3863, II, 11: *stwt n itn*.

For the deceased viewing the solar disk, see *supra*, **III, 4–5** and P. BM EA 10260, **II, x + 15–16**. P. Skrine I, Text I, 5 (A.M. Blackman, *JEA* 4 [1917], pl. 26): *mꜣꜣ.k Rʿ m pr.f Tm m ḥtp.f*, 'You see Re at his emergence, Atum at his setting'; ibid., Text I, 7–8: *mꜣꜣ.k itn wbḫ.f ḥr ḏww stwt.f tkꜣ.s(n) ḳrr.k ḫpr.f ḥr šnbt.k*, 'You see the disk when it shines on the mountains, that its rays may light up your cave and that it may appear upon your breast'; ibid., Text II, 56–60 (Blackman, op. cit., pl. 27): *psḏ stwt itn ḥr šnbt.i tkꜣ sktt.f* (?) *ḳrrt.i m wsḫt Mꜣʿty*, 'The rays of the disk shine on my breast, and its rays light up my cave in the hall of the two Maats'. Below it is said of the deceased (IV, 3–4) that he lives and breathes thanks to the rays of Re.

ḏd.w Mꜣʿt r.k m-bꜣḥ Wsir. Same reading in P. BM EA 9995, I, 24 = P. BM EA 10260, II, x + 16 = P. Berlin 3154, I, 22 = P. BN 179–81, II, 23 = P. Denon, III, 7 = P. Florence 3665 + P. Vienna 3850, III, 9 = P. Louvre E 8079 + 11080, II, 11–12 = P. Louvre N 3083, VI, 7–8 = P. Louvre N 3121, II, 7 = P. Louvre N 3126, II, 7 = P. Louvre N 3154, II, 12 = P. Louvre N 3166, I, 28–9 = P. Louvre N 3167 + 3222, II, 6 = P. Louvre N 3284, II, 19 = P. Louvre N 3291, 20 = P. Tübingen 2016, III, 16. P. Louvre E 11079, IV, 8: *ḏd Mꜣʿt r.t* (misplaced), with omission of *m-bꜣḥ Wsir*. Sequence partly in lacuna in P. Joseph Smith, III, 12 = P. Louvre N 3158, III, 6. Omission of *r.t*[61] in P. Vienna 3931, II, 5; var. P. Lausanne 3391, II, 10 = P. Louvre N 3285, II, 8 = P. Vienna 3863, II, 11: *ir.k*. P. Berlin 3135, II, 14: *rn.k* instead of *r.k*. Omission of *m* before *bꜣḥ* in P. Lausanne 3391, II, 10. Omission of *Wsir* in P. Louvre N 3121, II, 8.

sš.w mꜣʿ-ḫrw ḥr ns.k. Same reading in P. Berlin 3135, II, 14 = P. Berlin

58. A little fragment seems have been laid out wrongly in this part of the text, and the size of the lacuna between [*sn*]*sn* and *ḏbꜣt*, usually separated by some signs only, seems to show that line 10 has not been written completely.

59. This manuscript incorrectly gives *im.k* for *im.s*.

60. For the use of singular in place of the expected dual to name parts of the body occurring in pairs (eyes, legs, feet, etc.), see *LPE*, p. 250, n. 101.

61. The possessor of the papyrus is a woman.

3154, I, 22 = P. Florence 3665 + P. Vienna 3850, III, 9–10 = P. Lausanne 3391, II, 10–11 = P. Louvre E 8079 + 11080, II, 12 = P. Louvre N 3121, II, 7–8 [62] = P. Louvre N 3126, II, 7–8 = P. Louvre N 3154, II, 12 = P. Louvre N 3158, III, 6–7 = P. Louvre N 3166, I, 29 = P. Louvre N 3167 + 3222, II, 6 = P. Louvre N 3284, II, 19–20 = P. Louvre N 3285 = P. Louvre N 3291, 20 = P. Vienna 3863, II, 11 = P. Vienna 3931, II, 6. Sequence omitted in P. Louvre E 11079, IV; partly in lacuna in P. BM EA 10260, II, x + 16–III, [1] = P. BN 179–81, II, 23–4 = P. Tübingen 2016, III, 17. After an initial lacuna, some signs of uncertain reading occur in P. Joseph Smith, III, 12.[63] Var. P. BM EA 9995, I, 24: *sš.w Mꜣʿt ḥr ns.k;* omission of the pronoun *.w* after *sš* in P. Denon, III, 7. P. Louvre N 3083, VI, 8: *sš I* [64] *mꜣʿ-ḫrw ḥr ns.t,* 'Thoth writes "justified" on your tongue'.

Cf. P. Berlin 3154, vignette, above Thoth (Seeber, *Untersuchungen,* fig. 27): *Ḏḥwty nb Ḫmnw nb mdw nṯr smꜣʿ-ḫrw.k N di.k Mꜣʿt ḥr ns.f dr.k isft r.f m ẖrt-nṯr,* '(O) Thoth lord of Hermopolis, lord of the divine words, vindicate N! May you place Maat on his tongue and chase evil from him in the god's domain!' Describing the conditions required of a man for reciting certain words, the Book of the Heavenly Cow (78, version Seti I) states that 'Maat is drawn upon his tongue with the white pigment of the painter' (*sš Mꜣʿt ḥr ns.f m ryt ḥḏt n sš*); cf. E. Hornung, *Der ägyptische Mythos von der Himmelskuh* (*OBO* 46, 1982), p. 46 (v. 259–60) = N. Guilhou, *La vieillesse des dieux* (Montpellier 1989), p. 21. Note here the frequent confusion among editors of the Book of Breathing made by Isis between *ḏt.k* and *ns.k,* due to the similarity between the hieratic forms of and ;[65] cf. e.g. Brugsch, in the transcription of P. Berlin 3135, I, 22; Pellegrini, in that of P. Florence 3665; Vallogia, in that of P. Lausanne 3391, II, 11; also Goyon, *Rituels funéraires,* p. 220. The facsimile and translation given by de Horrack for the word *ns* in P. Louvre N 3284, II, 20 (*Le Livre des Respirations,* pl. 2) are also inexact. Confusion of the terms might have extended to the ancient compilers; cf. P. BM EA 9995, II, 8–9.

III, 6–7

Ḥr Bḥdty ḫw.f ḏt.k nṯr.f bꜣ.k mi[66] *nṯrw nb(w).* Same reading in P. Louvre N 3158, III, 7 = P. Louvre N 3154, II, 13 = P. Louvre N 3166, I, 29–30. Sequence omitted in P. Louvre E 11079; in lacuna in P. BM EA 10260, III. Var. P. BM EA 9995, I, 24 = P. Berlin 3135, II, 14 = P. Berlin 3154, I, 23 = P. Denon, III, 7–8 = P. Florence 3665 + P. Vienna 3850, III, 10 = P. Louvre E 8079 + 11080, II, 12 = P. Louvre N 3284, II, 20 = P. Louvre N 3291, 20: *Ḥr-nḏ-it.f;* P. BN 179–81, II, 24 = P. Lausanne 3391, II, 11 = P. Louvre N 3121, II, 8 = P. Louvre N 3126, II, 8 = P. Louvre N 3167 + 3222, II, 6 = P. Louvre N 3285, II, 9 = P. Tübingen 2016, III, 17 = P. Vienna 3863, II, 12 = P. Vienna 3931, II, 6: *Ḥr-nḏ-ḥr-it(.f).* P. Tübingen 2016 gives a somewhat different version here: *nṯr.f bꜣ.k ḫw.f kꜣ.k mi nṯrw nbw,* 'He divinizes your ba and protects your ka like (that) all the gods'. P. Joseph Smith, III, 12: *mi ir nṯrw nb,* 'like all the other gods do (?)'. Omission of suffix *.f* after *ḫw* in P. Louvre N 3291, 21, of suffix *.k* after *bꜣ* in P. Lausanne 3391, II, 11. P. BN 179–81, II, 24–5 = P. Louvre E 8079 + 11080, II, 12–13 = P. Louvre N 3083, VI, 8–9 = P. Louvre N 3121, II, 8 = P. Louvre N 3126, II, 8 = P. Louvre N 3284, II, 20 = P. Louvre N 3291, 21: *nṯrw nbw.*

For the divinization of the ba, see *supra,* **II, 5**.

III, 7

Bꜣ n Rʿ ḥr sʿnḫ bꜣ.k Bꜣ n Šw ḥr ḫnm msty.k. Same reading in P. Berlin 3135, II, 15–16 = P. Berlin 3154, I, 23 = P. BN 179–81, II, 25 = P. Florence 3665 + P. Vienna 3850, III, 11 = P. Lausanne 3391, II, 12 = P. Louvre E 8079 + 11080, II, 13 = P. Louvre N 3121, II, 8–9 = P. Louvre N 3158, III, 7–8 (*n Rʿ ḥr* in lacuna) = P. Louvre N 3167 + 3222, II, 7 = P. Louvre N 3284, II, 20–1 = P. Tübingen 2016, III, 18 = P. Vienna 3931, II, 7–8. Sequence omitted in P. Louvre E 11079; wholly in lacuna in P. BM EA 10260, III, and partly in P. Joseph Smith, III, 13 = P. Louvre N 3291, 21. Var. P. BM EA 9995, I, 24–II, 1 = P. Denon, III, 8–9: *Bꜣw Rʿ, Bꜣw n Šw;* P. Louvre N 3285, II, 10 = P. Vienna 3863, II, 12–13: *Bꜣ Rʿ, Bꜣ Šw;* P. Louvre N 3166, I, 30: *Bꜣw n Šw;* P. Louvre N 3126, II, 9: *bꜣw.k;* P. Louvre N 3083, VI, 9: *ḥr ḫnm šrty.t;* P. Louvre N 3154, II, 14: *ḥr ḫnm snsn.ty.k.*[67] The same text is inscribed on stelae nos. 13 and 14 from the Bucheum; see *LPE,* pp. 86–7 (I, 6).

Bꜣ n Rʿ: designation of several divinities (L.V. Žabkar, *A Study of the Ba Concept* [*SAOC* 34, 1968], pp. 12–14), but also of Re himself (ibid., p. 9 and cf. p. 99, n. 64). The association of these two Bas is with the two vital elements, sun and air.

P. Louvre N 3166, I, 30–1, adds a sequence omitted in the other versions:

Wsir N	'Osiris N,
iṯ.k (*sic*) *bꜣ.k ḳbḥ ipn*	your ba receives this libation
[*ḥ*]*nʿ nꜣ nṯrw nty di ṯꜣw*	with the gods who give breath.'

Following upon this text, col. II of P. Louvre N 3166 inserts a series of various texts into the Book of Breathing made by Isis. On its contents: *LPE,* p. 18 and F.R. Herbin, *RdE* 50 (1999), pp. 158–60.

III, 7–8

hꜣy Wsir N snsn bꜣ.k r bw nb[68] *mr.k.* Beginning of § 7 of de Horrack's classification. Same reading in P. Louvre E 8079 + 11080, II, 14 = P. Louvre N 3158, III, 8–9 = P. Vienna 3931, II, 8–9. Omission of *hꜣy* in P. Vienna 3863, II, 17.[69] Sequence wholly in lacuna in P. BM EA 10260, III, and partly in P. Joseph Smith, III, 13–IV, 1. Var. P. BN 179–81, II, 26: *hꜣy n;* P. BM EA 9995, II, 2 = P. Berlin 3135, II, 17–18 = P. Berlin 3154, I, 24 = P. Denon, III, 10 = P. Florence 3665 + P. Vienna 3850, III, 13 = P. Lausanne 3391, II, 17[70] = P. Louvre N 3121, II, 10 = P. Louvre N 3126, II, 11 = P. Louvre N 3284, III, 2–3 = P. Louvre N 3285, II, 12 = P. Louvre N 3291, 22 = P. Tübingen 2016, III, 20 = P. Vienna 3863, II, 19: *r bw mr.k /.t;* P. Louvre N 3083, VI, 10–11 = P. Louvre N 3167 + 3222, II, 9: *r bw nb mrwt.t,* 'to every place of your desire'; omission of *mr.k* in P. Louvre N 3154, II, 15. Cf. P. BM EA 10048, IV, 3: *šm.k m snsn r bw nb.* Cf. also P. Louvre E 11079, II, 11–12 (different context): *snsn.t r bw nb mr.t m ḫrt-hrw nt rʿ nb,* 'May you breathe in every place you desire in the course of every day!'.

P. Louvre N 3166, III, 1–3, places before this passage an original sequence:[71]

hꜣy Wsir N	'Hail Osiris N,
pr bꜣ.k m hrw	your ba goes forth by day,
ḫnm.f itn	it unites with the disk
nn ḥr.f r.k rʿ nb	without being far from you, every day.

62. That manuscript adds in error *m-bꜣḥ* after *ns.t.* We cannot link this preposition to the following *Ḥr-nḏ-ḥr-it.f;* see *infra,* **III, 6–7**.
63. The first of these signs is surely the determinative of *mꜣʿ-ḫrw,* followed by what seems to be . Read *r* for *ḥr* ? The expected word *ns* cannot be identified in the remaining traces.
64. *I* rather than *nṯr.*
65. The presence of the piece of flesh which determines the word *ns,* and is invariably absent from writings of *ḏt,* removes any possible doubt.
66. Written *m-m* in P. Berlin 3154 = P. Louvre N 3291, 21.
67. Written: . The word does not seem to be attested elsewhere.
68. *nbw* in P. BN 179–81, II, 27.
69. This phrase and the next are staggered in the manuscript after *bꜣ.k ʿnḫ m pt rʿ nb* (= P. BM EA 10048, III, 10).
70. The position of this sequence in the Lausanne papyrus is different from that on the other manuscripts: there it follows phrases which occur in P. BM EA 10048, III, 10.
71. On that sequence: F.R. Herbin, *RdE* 50 (1999), p. 200 (III, 2–3).

štꜣt wr wn ḫr.k	The great tomb which contains you,
štꜣ sp 2 nn rḫ s(t)	it is a great secret which cannot be known,
nn tḫn (st) rḫyt m ḏrw nṯrw	which people cannot find out, as long as the gods endure,
kkw.ti ḫḫ.ti mḏ.ti sp 2	being very dark, forgotten, deep,
nn wn rḫ s(t) ḥꜣw-mr	and there is no layman who knows it;
ỉr.k snsn ỉm.s r bw nb mr.k	you breathe in it in every place you wish.'

ỉw.k m Wsỉr Wsỉr ḫnty Ỉmntt rn.k. Same reading in P. BM EA 9995, II, 2 = P. Berlin 3135, II, 18 = P. Berlin 3154, I, 24 = P. BN 179–81, II, 27 = P. Florence 3665 + P. Vienna 3850, III, 13–14 = P. Lausanne 3391, II, 17–18 = P. Louvre N 3126, II, 11 = P. Louvre N 3158, III, 9 (small lacuna) = P. Louvre N 3166, III, 3 = P. Louvre N 3285, II, 13 = P. Louvre N 3291, 22 = P. Vienna 3931, II, 9–10. Sequence omitted in P. Louvre E 11079 = P. Louvre N 3121, II; wholly in lacuna in P. BM EA 10260, III = P. Joseph Smith, IV, 1, and partly in P. Vienna 3863, II, 19. Omission of *ḫnty Ỉmntt* in P. Louvre N 3083, VI, 11 = P. Louvre N 3154, II, 15. Addition of *n* between the two mentions of Osiris in P. Louvre N 3284, III, 3.[72] P. Louvre E 8079 + 11080, II, 14–15 = P. Louvre N 3166, III, 3 = P. Louvre N 3167 + 3222, II, 9: *Wsỉr ḫnty Ỉmntyw rn.k*;[73] P. Tübingen 2016, III, 20: *ỉw.k m-sꜣ* (?) *Wsỉr*. Minor corruption in P. Denon, III, 11, which reads: *ỉw.k m st Wsỉr Ḫnty Ỉmntt rn.k*, 'You are in the place of Osiris; Foremost of the West is your name'.

Wsỉr ḫnty Ỉmntt rn.k: same designation of the deceased in the First Book of Breathing: cf. P. BM EA 10191, I, 50. In another passage of the same text, attested in only two manuscripts, the deceased is called 'Foremost of the West' (*ḫnty Ỉmntt rn.k*); see F.R. Herbin, *BIFAO* 84 (1984), p. 256.

III, 8–9

Ḥꜥpy wr ỉw n.k m ꜣbw mḥ.f ḥtpw.k m ḏfꜣw. Same reading in P. BN 179–81, II, 28 = P. Louvre E 8079 + 11080, II, 15 = P. Louvre N 3154, II, 15–16 = P. Louvre N 3158, III, 9–IV, 1 = P. Vienna 3931, II, 10–11. Sequence omitted in P. Louvre E 11079; in lacuna in P. BM EA 10260, III = P. Joseph Smith, IV. Var. P. BM EA 9995, II, 3 = P. Denon, III, 11: *ỉỉ n.k*; P. Louvre N 3167 + 3222, II, 9: *ỉỉ.w n.t*; P. BM EA 9995, II, 3 = P. Berlin 3135, II, 19 = P. Berlin 3154, I, 25 = P. Florence 3665 + P. Vienna 3850, III, 15 = P. Lausanne 3391, II, 18 = P. Louvre N 3126, II, 12 = P. Louvre N 3166, III, 4 = P. Louvre N 3167 + 3222, II, 9–10 = P. Louvre N 3284, III, 4 = P. Louvre N 3285, II, 13–14 = P. Louvre N 3291, 22 = P. Vienna 3863, II, 20: *ḥtp.k* / *.t*. P. Louvre N 3121, II, 10: *mḥ.f n.t*, 'He fills for you'; P. Louvre N 3083, VI, 11: *mḥ.f ḏfꜣw* (*sic*) *m ḏfꜣw.f*. P. Tübingen 2016, III, 21: *m ḏfꜣw* ... (?)

On the coming of Hapy to the deceased: *LPE*, p. 253 (VIII, 6–7); also P. BM EA 10209, II, 23–4: *ỉw n.k Ḥꜥpy m ṯpḥt.f ṯḥb.f n.k ꜣḫwt pꜣ wtyw*; dem. P. Oxford Bod. MS Egypt. a. 3 (P), I, 3: *ỉw n=k Ḥꜥpy m tpḥ=f*; Louvre Inv. 908 (Pierret, *Inscr. du Louvre* II, p. 117): *ỉw n.k Ḥꜥpy wr r tr.f ꜥwy.f ḫr mw n rnp*; P. Varsovie 147822, I, 2–3 (K. Michalowski, *Sztuka Starozytna* [Warsaw 1955], p. 19, fig. 6): *ỉw n.k Ḥꜥpy šmꜥy ḫr ḳbḥ*; Lefebvre, *Petosiris* II, p. 30, no. 58, 24: *ỉỉ n.k Ḥꜥpy r ḫ<r>t ỉb.k*.

On the use of the verb *ỉỉ* / *ỉw* for Hapy: A. de Buck, in *Orientalia Neerlandica* (Leiden 1948), p. 15; D. van der Plas, *L'hymne à la crue du Nil* (Leiden 1986), p. 60; M. Vallogia, *RdE* 40 (1989), p. 138 with fig. 4.

For Hapy as provider of offerings: Meeks, in *Génies, anges et démons* (*SO* 8, 1971), p. 24; van der Plas, op. cit., pp. 81–2.

III, 9

Wsỉr N ỉw n.k nṯrw nw Šmꜥ Mḥw sšm twk r ꜥrḳ-ḥḥ. Beginning of § 8 of de Horrack's classification. Same reading in P. Berlin 3135, II, 19–20 = P. Florence 3665 + P. Vienna 3850, III, 16–17[74] = P. Louvre N 3126, II, 13–14 = P. Louvre N 3154, II, 16–17 = P. Louvre N 3158, IV, 1–2. Sequence omitted in P. Louvre E 11079 = P. Vienna 3931, II; in lacuna in P. BM EA 10260, III = P. Joseph Smith, IV. Omission of *r ꜥrḳ* in P. BN 179–81, III, 1. Var. P. Denon, III, 12[75] = P. Lausanne 3391, II, 12–13 = P. Louvre N 3083, VI, 12 = P. Louvre N 3154, II, 16–18 = P. Vienna 3863, II, 13: *hꜣy Wsỉr* (*Ḥwt-Ḥr*) *N*; P. BM EA 9995, II, 4 = P. BN 179–81, II, 29 = P. Denon, III, 13 = P. Louvre N 3167 + 3222, II, 11 = P. Louvre N 3284, III, 5 = P. Louvre N 3285, II, 16 = P. Tübingen 2016, III, 22: *ỉỉ n.k* / *.t*; P. Louvre N 3154, II, 17 = P. Louvre N 3166, III, 4 = P. Louvre N 3167 + 3222, II, 11 = P. Louvre N 3284, III, 5: *nꜣ nṯrw*; P. BM EA 9995, II, 4 = P. Berlin 3154, I, 26 = P. Lausanne 3391, II, 14 = P. Louvre E 8079 + 11080, II, 16 = P. Louvre N 3121, II, 12 = P. Louvre N 3166, III, 5[76] = P. Louvre N 3284, III, 5 = P. Tübingen 2016, III, 22 = P. Vienna 3863, II, 15[77]: *sšm.w twk* / *twt*; P. Louvre N 3291, 23: *sšm.tw.w twk* (*sic*); P. Denon, III, 13: *sšm.sn* (?) *tw*; P. Louvre N 3083, VI, 13: *ḥr sšm bꜣ.t r ꜥrḳ-ḥḥ*, 'to guide your ba to Areq-heh'.

The nature of these gods of Upper and Lower Egypt is presented at length in P. Louvre N 3121, IV, 4–VII, 3, where a long text introduced by the words *ỉ nṯrw ỉmyw Šmꜥ Mḥw* enumerates from south to north the divinities of the 42 nomes of the land. See *infra*, **VII, 4**. Also F.R. Herbin, *BIFAO* 84 (1984), pp. 257 and 278–9, n. 2:

hꜣy Wsỉr N	'Hail Osiris N,
ỉw n.k nṯrw n Šmꜥ Mḥw	the gods of Upper and Lower Egypt come to you
ḥr sšm štꜣt.k m ẖrt-nṯr	to guide your mystery in the god's domain.'

On Areq-heh, a name of the Abydos necropolis: *LPE*, p. 103 (I, 18–19).

ꜥnḫ bꜣ.k šms.k Wsỉr. Same reading in P. Berlin 3135, II, 21 = P. Denon, IV, 1 = P. Lausanne 3391, II, 14 = P. Louvre E 8079 + 11080, II, 17 = P. Louvre N 3083, VI, 13 = P. Louvre N 3121, II, 12 = P. Louvre N 3126, II, 14 = P. Louvre N 3154, II, 17–18 = P. Louvre N 3158, IV, 2 = P. Louvre N 3167 + 3222, II, 11 = P. Louvre N 3284, III, 6 = P. Louvre N 3285, II, 17 = P. Louvre 3291, 23–4 = P. Tübingen 2016, IV, 1 = P. Vienna 3863, II, 16. Sequence omitted in P. Louvre E 11079 = P. Vienna 3931, II; damaged in P. Florence 3665 + P. Vienna 3850, III, 17 (cf. n. 74), and partly in lacuna in P. Joseph Smith, IV, 2–3. Var. P. Louvre N 3284, III, 6: *ḥnꜥ bꜣ.k*, 'together with your ba', to be connected to the preceding phrase, or mistake for *ꜥnḫ bꜣ.k*.

III, 10

snsn.k ḫnt rꜣ-stꜣw mk twk Ḥꜣp-n-nb.s ḥnꜥ nṯr ꜥꜣ. Same reading in P. BM EA 9995, II, 5 = P. Berlin 3135, II, 21–2 = P. Berlin 3154, I, 26–7 = P. BN 179–81, III, 2 = P. Denon, IV, 1–2 = P. Lausanne 3391, II, 14–15 = P. Louvre E 8079 + 11080, II, 17–III, 1 = P. Louvre N 3083, VI, 13–14 = P. Louvre N 3121, II, 12–13 = P. Louvre N 3126, II, 14–15 = P. Louvre N 3154, II, 18–19 = P. Louvre N 3158, IV, 2–3 = P. Louvre N 3284, III, 6–7 = P. Louvre N 3285, II, 17–18 = P. Louvre N 3291, 24 = P. Vienna 3863, II, 16–17. Sequence omitted in P. Louvre E 11079 = P. Vienna 3931, II;

72. An excessive extension of the base of the sign  does not seem possible.
73. On confusion between *ḫnty Ỉmntt* and *ḫnty Ỉmntyw*, see Smith, *Mortuary Texts*, p. 56 (I, 1, c).
74. All line 17, which starts with the words [*m*] *ꜥrḳ-ḥḥ*, is damaged because of the breaking of the document. Traces are visible on P. Florence 3665, more on P. Vienna 3850.
75. The writer of P. Denon had originally started the phrase with *Wsỉr*, in the continuation of the word *ḏfꜣw* of the former sequence; then he continued his text, after leaving a blank space, with the words *hꜣy Wsỉr*.
76. Note the writing  in P. Louvre N 3166.
77. Note in P. Lausanne 3391 and P. Vienna 3863 the writing  of *ꜥrḳ-ḥḥ*;  in P. BN 179–81.

wholly in lacuna in P. BM EA 10260, III, and partly in P. Florence 3665 + P. Vienna 3850, III, 17 = P. Joseph Smith, IV, 3. Omission of *rꜣ* before *stꜣw* in P. Tübingen 2016, IV, 1–2. Var. P. Louvre N 3167 + 3222, II, 12: *mk tw*; P. Louvre N 3166, III, 6: *Ḥꜣp-n-nb.f*.

A part of this text recurs, with insignificant variants, in Books of Breathing (P. Louvre N 3148, VII, 18–19 = P. Louvre N 3236, III, 6–7 = Ms. Golenischeff 517–18, 43): *šsp.f ḳbḥ m-ḫnw rꜣ-stꜣw mkt.f* (var. *mk sw*) *Ḥꜣp-n-nb.s ḥnꜥ nṯr ꜥꜣ m Imntt*; see Herbin, op. cit., pp. 278 and 295, n. 83. For *rꜣ-stꜣw*: G. Vittmann, *SAK* 22 (1995), p. 317, n. 157.

ḫꜣt.k ꜥnḫ m Ḏdw Tꜣ-wr[78] *bꜣ.k ꜥnḫ m pt rꜥ nb*. Same reading in P. BM EA 9995, II, 6 = P. Berlin 3154, I, 27 = P. BN 179–81, III, 2–3 = P. Denon, IV, 2–3 = P. Florence 3665 + P. Vienna 3850, III, 19 = P. Lausanne 3391, II, 15–16 = P. Louvre E 8079 + 11080, III, 1 = P. Louvre N 3121, II, 13–14 = P. Louvre N 3126, II, 15 = P. Louvre N 3158, IV, 3–4 = P. Louvre N 3166, III, 6–7 = P. Louvre N 3167 + 3222, II, 12–13 = P. Louvre N 3284, III, 7–8 = P. Louvre N 3285, II, 18–19 = P. Louvre N 3291, 24 = P. Tübingen 2016, IV, 2 = P. Vienna 3863, II, 17. Sequence omitted in P. Louvre E 11079 = P. Vienna 3931, II; wholly in lacuna in P. BM EA 10260, III, and partly in P. Joseph Smith, IV, 3. Omission of suffix *.k* after *bꜣ* in P. Louvre N 3285, II, 19. Var. P. Louvre N 3083, VI, 14 = P. Louvre N 3154, II, 19: *ḫꜣt.k /.t mn*; P. Berlin 3135, II, 22: *n pt*; see Herbin, op. cit., pp. 268 (A, VIII, 19) and 295, n. 83 (*ḫꜣt.f mn m-ḫnw Ḏdw*).

III, 11

Wsir N sḫm Sḫmt m wꜣw im.k. Beginning of § 9 of of de Horrack's classification. Same reading in P. BM EA 9995, II, 7 = P. Berlin 3135, II, 23–4 = P. Berlin 3154, II, 1 = P. Denon, IV, 3–4 = P. Florence 3665 + P. Vienna 3850, III, 19–20 = P. Louvre E 8079 + 11080, III, 2 = P. Louvre N 3121, II, 14–15 = P. Louvre N 3126, II, 16 = P. Louvre N 3154, II, 19–20 = P. Louvre N 3158, IV, 4–5 = P. Louvre N 3167 + 3222, II, 13–14 = P. Louvre N 3284, 8–9 = P. Louvre N 3291, 24–5. Sequence omitted in P. Louvre E 11079 = P. Louvre N 3166, III; in lacuna in P. BM EA 10260, III = P. Joseph Smith, IV = P. Vienna 3863, II. Var. P. Louvre N 3083, VI, 15: *hꜣy Wsir N*; P. Vienna 3931, II, 12: *sḫm Sḫmt ḫww.t*; P. Lausanne 3391, II, 19 = P. Louvre N 3285, II, 21: *sḫm Sḫmt ḫww im.k*; P. BN 179–81, III, 4 = P. Tübingen 2016, IV, 3–4: *sḫm Sḫmt wꜣw im.k*.

For this well-attested function of Sekhmet: Herbin, op. cit., p. 298, n. 96.

Ḥr ꜥꜣ ḥr ir mkt.k. Same reading in P. Louvre N 3083, VI, 16. Sequence omitted in P. Louvre E 11079 = P. Louvre N 3166, III; in lacuna in P. BM EA 10260, III = P. Vienna 3863, II. Omission of *ir* after *ḥr* in P. Vienna 3931, II, 12; of suffix after *mkt* in P. Joseph Smith, IV, 5. Var. P. BN 179–81, III, 4 = P. Denon, IV, 4 = P. Joseph Smith, IV, [4]–5 = P. Lausanne 3391, II, 20 = P. Louvre E 8079 + 11080, III, 2[79] = P. Louvre N 3154, II, 20[80] = P. Louvre N 3158, IV, 5 = P. Louvre N 3167 + 3222, II, 14 = P. Louvre N 3285, II, 21 = P. Louvre N 3291, 25 = P. Tübingen 2016, IV, 4 = P. Vienna 3931, II, 12: *Ḥr ꜥꜣ ib*; P. BM EA 9995, II, 7–8 = P. Berlin 3135, II, 24 = P. Berlin 3154, II, 1 = P. Florence 3665 + P. Vienna 3850, III, 20 = P. Louvre N 3121, II, 15 = P. Louvre N 3126, III, 17 = P. Louvre N 3284, III, 10: *Ḥr ꜥꜣ ibw*.

For Horus 'great of heart' (magnanimous), see Herbin, op. cit., p. 299, n. 98.

Ḥr Bḥdty ḥr ḫw ib.k (same reading in P. Louvre N 3083, VI, 17 = P. Louvre N 3154, II, 20, partly in lacuna in P. Joseph Smith, IV, 5) is replaced in P. BM EA 9995, II, 7–8 = P. BN 179–81, III, 5 = P. Louvre N 3291, 25 = P. Tübingen 2016, IV, 4 by *Ḥr Bḥdty ḥr ir n ib.k*, 'Horus of Behedet carries out your wish'. Var. P. Louvre N 3158, IV, 5 = P. Louvre N 3284, III, 10: *Ḥr Bḥdty ḥr ir ib.t*; P. BM EA 9995, II, 8 = P. Berlin 3154, II, 1 = P. Florence 3665 + P. Vienna 3850, III, 21 = P. Lausanne 3391, II, 20 = P. Louvre E 8079 + 11080, III, 3 = P. Louvre N 3121, II, 15 = P. Louvre N 3167 + 3222, II, 14 = P. Louvre N 3285, II, 22: *Ḥr Šdty ḥr ir n ib.k /.t*; P. Berlin 3135, II, 25 = P. Denon, IV, 4 = P. Louvre N 3126, III, 17 = P. Louvre N 3284, III, 10 = P. Vienna 3931, II, 13: *Ḥr Šdty ḥr ir ib.k /.t*, 'Horus of Shedet carries out your wish'. P. Louvre E 8079 + 11080, III, 3: *mk twk Ḥr Šdty ḥr ir n ib.k*, 'Horus of Shedet protects you, carrying out your wish'.

IV, 1

Ḥr Mrty ḥr sꜣ ḏt.k ḏd.k[81] *m ꜥnḫ wḏꜣ snb*. Same reading in P. Berlin 3135, II, 25–6 = P. Berlin 3154, II, 2 = P. Denon, IV, 4–5 = P. Florence 3665 + P. Vienna 3850, III, 21–2 = P. Louvre N 3167 + 3222, II, 15 = P. Louvre N 3291, 25–6 = P. Tübingen 2016, IV, 4–5. Sequence omitted in P. Louvre E 11079 = P. Louvre N 3166, III; wholly in lacuna in P. BM EA 10260, III = P. Vienna 3863, II, and partly in P. Joseph Smith, IV, 5. Var. P. Lausanne 3391, II, 20–1 = P. Louvre N 3154, II, 21 = P. Louvre N 3158, IV, 5–6: *ḥr sꜣ.k /.t*[82]; P. Louvre N 3126, III, 17 = P. Louvre N 3285, II, 22: *ḥr sꜣ.k ḏt.k* (*sic*); P. Vienna 3931, II, 13–14: *ḥr sꜣ.t iw.t ḏd.ti m ꜥnḫ ḏd wꜣs*; P. BN 179–81, III, 5–6: *ḥr ḫw ḏt.k*; P. Louvre N 3083, VI, 17: *ḥr ḫw.t*; P. Louvre N 3121, II, 16: *ḏd.ti*; P. Louvre N 3284, III, 10–11: *ḥr sꜣ ns.k*; addition of *ky ḏd ns.k*, 'otherwise said: your tongue', after *ḏt.k*, in P. BM EA 9995, II, 8–9. See *supra*, **III, 6**, for the confusion between the two terms. For P. Louvre E 8079 + 11080, see n. 79.

On this function of Hor-merty: J.C. Goyon, *Les dieux-gardiens* (*BdE* 93, 1985), p. 164.

iw.k mn.ti ḥr nst.k m tꜣ ḏsr. Same reading in P. Berlin 3154, II, 2 = P. Joseph Smith, IV, 6 = P. Louvre N 3083, VI, 18 = P. Louvre N 3158, IV, 6 = P. Tübingen 2016, IV, 5. Sequence omitted in P. Louvre E 11079 = P. Louvre N 3166, III = P. Louvre N 3167 + 3222, II; in lacuna in P. BM EA 10260, III = P. Vienna 3863, II. Omission of the ending *.ti* in P. BM EA 9995, II, 9 = P. Berlin 3135, II, 26 = P. BN 179–81, III, 6 = P. Florence 3665 + P. Vienna 3850, III, 22 = P. Lausanne 3391, II, 21 = P. Louvre E 8079 + 11080, III, 3 = P. Louvre N 3121, II, 16 = P. Louvre N 3126, II, 18 = P. Louvre N 3154, III, 1 = P. Louvre N 3284, III, 11 = P. Louvre N 3285, II, 23 = P. Louvre N 3291, 26; of suffix after *nst* in P. Vienna 3931, II, 14. For P. Louvre E 8079 + 11080, see n. 79.

On *tꜣ ḏsr*: G. Vittmann, *SAK* 22 (1995), p. 316, n. 156.

IV, 1–2

mi ir.k[83] *Wsir N*. Same reading in P. BM EA 9995, II, 9–10 = P. Berlin 3135, II, 26–III, 1 = P. Berlin 3154, II, 2–3 = P. BN 179–81, III, 6–7 =

78. Note the form in P. Louvre N 3083, VI, 15 and in P. Louvre N 3167 + 3222, II, 12–13; see also H.W. Fairman, *BIFAO* 43 (1945), p. 78, n. 3.

79. The arrangement of the text in P. Louvre E 8079 + 11080 is defective and presents an apparent misalignment in the order of the sequences. One reads: (2)... *Ḥr ꜥꜣ ib ḥr ir ḏd.k m ꜥnḫ wḏꜣ* **s** (3) *mk twk Ḥr Šdty ḥr ir ib.k Ḥr mrty ḥr sꜣ ib.k* **nb** *iw.k mn ḥr nst.k m tꜣ ḏsr*. The lines in this part of the text should read as follows. The reading of line 2 should be interrupted after *ḥr ir* and resumed at the beginning of line 3. After *sꜣ ḏt.k*, in line 3, it is necessary to return to line 2 to read *ḏd.k m ꜥnḫ wḏꜣ s*, and return to the last third of line 3 for the continuation of the text: *nb iw.k mn ḥr nst.k m tꜣ ḏsr*.

80. On *mkt.k* written *mkt twk* in this manuscript (as also in P. Louvre E 8079 + 11080, III, 3), cf. also P. Louvre N 3154, III, 9; P. Rhind II, 5, 1 (*ḥꜣt.t* written *ḥꜣt twt*); Haikal, *Two Hier. Fun. Pap.* II, p. 31, n. 53.

81. Written in P. Lausanne 3391, II, 21.

82. Written in P. Lausanne 3391, II, 21.

83. Note the form 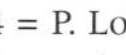 in P. Berlin 3135 = P. Denon = P. Louvre E 8079 + 11080 = P. Louvre N 3154 = P. Louvre N 3284 = P. Tübingen 2016. In P. Denon, IV, 6, the preposition *n* follows *r.k*.

P. Denon, IV, 5–6 = P. Florence 3665 + P. Vienna 3850, III, 22–3 = P. Louvre E 8079 + 11080, III, 4 = P. Louvre N 3083, VI, 18–19 = P. Louvre N 3121, II, 16–17 = P. Louvre N 3126, II, 18–19 = P. Louvre N 3154, III, 1–2 = P. Louvre N 3158, IV, 6–7 = P. Louvre N 3167 + 3222, II, 15–16 = P. Louvre N 3184, III, 11–12 = P. Louvre N 3285, II, 23–4 = P. Louvre N 3291, 26 = P. Tübingen 2016, IV, 5 = P. Vienna 3931, II, 14–15. Sequence omitted in P. Louvre E 11079 = P. Louvre N 3166, III; in lacuna in P. BM EA 10260, III = P. Joseph Smith, IV, 6 = P. Vienna 3863, II.

iw.k wr.ti m irww.k ˁpr.ti m ḳd.k twt m ḫkrw.k. Sequence omitted in P. Louvre E 11079 = P. Louvre N 3166, III; wholly in lacuna in P. BM EA 10260, III = P. Vienna 3863, II, and partly in P. Joseph Smith, IV, 6. Omission of *iw.k* in P. Louvre N 3154, III, 2 (var. *twt.ti*) = P. Louvre N 3158, IV, 7. Var. P. Louvre N 3083, VI, 19: *wr.ti m irw.t ˁpr.ti m ḳy.t*, with omission of *twt m ḫkrw.t*. P. BM EA 9995, II, 9–10 = P. Berlin 3135, III, 2 = P. Berlin 3154, II, 3 = P. BN 179–81, III, 7–8 = P. Denon, IV, 6–7 = P. Lausanne 3391, II, 22–3 = P. Louvre E 8079 + 11080, III, 4–5 = P. Louvre N 3121, II, 17 = P. Louvre N 3126, II, 19 = P. Louvre N 3167 + 3222, II, 16 = P. Louvre N 3284, III, 11–13 = P. Louvre N 3285, II, 24–5 = P. Louvre N 3291, 26–7 = P. Tübingen 2016, IV, 6–7 = P. Florence 3665 + P. Vienna 3850, III, 23–4 = P. Vienna 3931, II, 15–16:

iw.k /.t ḫˁ.ti [84] *m ḳy.k /.t*	'You are arisen in your forms,
twt.ti [85] *m ḫkrw.k /.t* [86]	complete with your ornaments.'

Cf. also P. Rhind I, 3, 11, concerning the deceased: *iw.k ˁpr.ti m ḫkr(w).k nb*, 'You are equipped with all your ornaments', and P. Rhind II, 4, 6: *iw.t ˁpr.ti m ḫkr(w).t m smn.t n Ḥwt-Ḥr ḥnwt Imntt*, 'You are equipped with your ornaments in your form of Hathor mistress of the West'.

Possession of these ornaments thus implies assimilation to the deity. Osiris is a god 'supplied with his ornaments'; cf. *BD* ch. 142, 22 (ed. Lepsius, pl. 59): *Wsir m ḫkrw.f nbw*.

IV, 2–3

sḏr.k m ˁnḫ wrš.k m snb šm.k m snsn r bw nb.[87] Same reading in P. Louvre N 3083, VI, 19–20 = P. Louvre N 3158, IV, 7–8. Sequence omitted in P. Louvre E 11079 = P. Louvre N 3166, III; wholly in lacuna in P. BM EA 10260, III = P. Vienna 3863, II, and partly in P. Joseph Smith, IV, 7. Omission of the preposition *m* before *ˁnḫ* in P. Louvre N 3291, 27; of suffix *.k* after *šm* in P. Louvre N 3154, III, 3. Var. P. Louvre N 3285, II, 25–6: *šm.k n snsn*; P. BM EA 9995, II, 11: *snsn.k*; P. Vienna 3931, 17: *šm.t r bw nb*; P. Berlin 3135, III, 3 = P. Berlin 3154, II, 3 = P. BN 179–81, III, 8–9 = P. Denon, IV, 7 = P. Florence 3665 + P. Vienna 3850, III, 24 = P. Louvre E 8079 + 11080, III, 5 = P. Louvre N 3121, II, 18 = P. Louvre N 3126, III, 20 = P. Louvre N 3167 + 3222, II, 17 = P. Louvre N 3284, III, 13–14 = P. Tübingen 2016, IV, 7: *šm.k /.t snsn.k /.t*; P. Louvre N 3291, 27: *šm.k snsn.k r bw nb mr.k*; P. Lausanne 3391, II, 23–4: *šm.k r bw nb* 'You go towards every place'. See *supra*, **III, 7–8**.

IV, 3

wbn Rˁ ḥr-tp.k mi Wsir. Same reading in P. Joseph Smith, IV, 8 = P. Louvre N 3158, IV, 8. Sequence omitted in P. Louvre N 3166, III; in lacuna in P. BM EA 10260, III = P. Vienna 3863, II. Var. P. BM EA 9995, II, 11 = P. Berlin 3154, II, 4: *ḥr ḥwt.k*; P. Vienna 3931, II, 17: *wbn ḥr ḥwt n Wsir*, with omission of *Rˁ*; P. Berlin 3135, III, 3 = P. BN 179–81, III, 9 = P. Florence 3665 + P. Vienna 3850, III, 25 = P. Denon, IV, 8 = P. Louvre E 8079 + 11080, III, 5 = P. Louvre N 3126, III, 20 = P. Louvre N 3167 + 3222, II, 17 = P. Louvre N 3284, III, 14 = P. Louvre N 3285, II, 26: *wbn Rˁ ḥr ḥwt.k /.t Wsir*, 'Re shines on your mansion, Osiris'; P. Louvre N 3291, 27 = P. Lausanne 3391, II, 24: *wbn ḥr ḥwt.k Wsir*, with omission of *Rˁ*; P. Louvre N 3121, II, 18–19: *wbn Rˁ ḥr-tp ḥwt.t*; P. Tübingen 2016, IV, 7–8: *wbn Rˁ tp ḥwt.k Wsir*; P. Louvre N 3083, VI, 20 = P. Louvre N 3154, III, 3–4: *wbn Rˁ ḥr ḏbꜣt.k /<.t> mi Wsir*, 'Re shines over your sarcophagus as (over) Osiris'; P. Louvre E 11089, II, 11: *wbn Rˁ ḥr ḥwt.t m ḫrt-hrw nt rˁ nb*, 'Re shines over your mansion in the course of every day'.

IV, 3–4

snsn.k ˁnḫ.k m stwt.f. Same reading in P. BM EA 9995, II, 11–12 = P. Berlin 3135, III, 3–4 = P. Berlin 3154, II, 4 = P. BN 179–81, III, 9–10 = P. Denon, IV, 8 = P. Florence 3665 + P. Vienna 3850, III, 25 = P. Lausanne 3391, II, 24 = P. Louvre E 8079 + 11080, III, 6 = P. Louvre N 3083, VI, 20–1 = P. Louvre N 3121, II, 18–19 = P. Louvre N 3126, II, 20 = P. Louvre N 3167 + 3222, II, 17 = P. Louvre N 3284, III, 14–15 = P. Louvre N 3285, II, 26 = P. Tübingen 2016, IV, 8 = P. Vienna 3931, II, 17–18. Sequence omitted in P. Louvre E 11079 = P. Louvre N 3166, III; wholly in lacuna in P. BM EA 10260, III = P. Vienna 3863, II, and partly in P. Joseph Smith, IV, 8. Omission of suffix after *ˁnḫ* in P. Louvre N 3083, VI, 21 = P. Louvre N 3154, III, 4. Var. P. Louvre N 3291, 27: *snsn.k stwt.f*; P. Louvre N 3158, IV, 8: *ˁnḫ.t snsn.t*.

On the deceased living on the rays of the sun: Maspero, *Sarcophages* I, pp. 9 and 56: *ˁnḫ bꜣ.f /.k m stwt itn*, 'His / your ba lives on the rays of the disk'; see also *supra*, **II, 7–8**.

IV, 4

Imn-Rˁ sˁnḫ.f kꜣ.k. Same reading in P. Berlin 3135, III, 4 = P. BN 179–81, III, 10 = P. Denon, IV, 8–9 = P. Florence 3665 + P. Vienna 3850, IV, 1 = P. Lausanne 3391, II, 24–5 = P. Louvre E 8079 + 11080, III, 6 = P. Louvre N 3083, VI, 21 = P. Louvre N 3121, II, 19 = P. Louvre N 3126, II, 21 = P. Louvre N 3154, III, 4 = P. Louvre N 3158, IV, 9 = P. Louvre N 3167 + 3222, II, 18 = P. Louvre N 3284, III, 15 = P. Louvre N 3285, II, 27 = P. Louvre N 3291, 28 = P. Tübingen 2016, IV, 8. Sequence omitted in P. Louvre E 11079 = P. Louvre N 3166, III; wholly in lacuna in P. BM EA 10260, III = P. Vienna 3863, II, and partly in P. Joseph Smith, IV, 8. Var. P. BM EA 9995, II, 12: *Imn-Rˁ-Ḥr-ꜣḫty*; P. Vienna 3931, II, 18: *sḥb.f* instead of *sˁnḫ.f*; P. Berlin 3154, II, 4: *bꜣ.k* instead of *kꜣ.k*.

ḥs.f twk m šˁt n snsn. Sequence omitted in P. Louvre E 11079 = P. Louvre N 3154, III = P. Louvre N 3166, III; in lacuna in P. BM EA 10260, III = P. Vienna 3863, II. Var. P. Louvre N 3167 + 3222, II, 18: *n šˁt n snsn*; P. Joseph Smith, IV, 8: *ḥs twk m šˁt snsn*; P. Louvre N 3083, VI, 21: *ḥs.f twt m ṯꜣw.f n snsn*, 'he praises you by the air of his breathing'; P. Louvre N 3158, IV, 9: *ḥs ...* (?) *m šˁt n snsn*; P. BM EA 9995, II, 12 = P. Louvre E 8079 + 11080, III, 6–7 = P. Louvre N 3121, II, 19 = P. Louvre N 3291, 28: *swꜣḏ.f twk* (*twt*) *n šˁt n snsn*, and the minor variant of P. Berlin 3154, II, 4: *m šˁt n snsn*. P. BN 179–81, III, 10–11: *swꜣḏ.f ṯꜣy.k* [88] *šˁt n snsn*; P. Denon, IV, 9: *swꜣḏ.f twk šˁt n snsn*; P. Tübingen 2016, IV, 9 = P. Vienna 3931, II, 18–19: *swꜣḏ ...* (?) *twk* (*twt*) *m šˁt* (*n*) *snsn*; P. Berlin 3135, III, 4 = P. Louvre N 3284, III, 15 = P. Louvre N 3285, II, 27: *swꜣḏ twk šˁt snsn* 'The Book of Breathing makes you prosper'; P. Florence 3665 + P. Vienna 3850, IV, 1 = P. Lausanne 3391, II, 25 = P. Louvre N 3126, II, 21: *swꜣḏ twk m* (*n*) [89] *šˁt m* (*n*) *snsn* confuse the two versions; either they omit suffix *.f* after *swꜣḏ* (the subject being Amun), or the *m* (*n*) before *šˁt n snsn* is superfluous (subject *šˁt*). The same is true of P. Joseph Smith, IV, 8, cited *supra* (var. *ḥs*). See also *infra*, **IV, 9**.

84. Ending *.ti* not observed in P. Berlin 3154, II, 3.
85. Ending *.ti* not observed in P. Berlin 3154, II, 3 = P. Louvre E 8079 + 11080, III, 4 = P. Louvre N 3291, 27.
86. Suffix omitted in P. Florence 3665 + P. Vienna 3850.
87. *nbw* in P. BN 179–81, III, 9.
88. Written . Corrupt word for *twk* ?
89. *n* omitted in the transcription by Pellegrini of P. Florence 3665.

IV, 4–5

ḫnm.k m Šw sꜣ Rꜥ ꜥḳ.k r Dwꜣt nn wnn ḫftyw.k. Beginning with variant of § 10 of de Horrack's classification. Preceding this sequence, the other documents of the Book of Breathing made by Isis contain a passage which does not appear here, and for which see P. BM EA 9995, II, 13 to II, 14–15. It seems probable that the mention of the *šꜥt n snsn*, which ends the preceding passage in every instance, gave rise to confusion and thus to the omission of an important elaboration. The following text, which constitutes a new paragraph, resumes the text of P. BM EA 10048, with some notable variants:

P. Louvre N 3083, VII, 1–3:

hꜣy Wsir N	'Hail Osiris N,
ꜥnḫ bꜣ.t m ṯꜣw n snsn	your ba lives on the air of breathing,
ḫnm.t m Šw sꜣ Rꜥ	and you unite with Shu son of Re;
ꜥḳ.t r Dwꜣt	you enter the Duat,
nn wn ḫftyw.t	and your enemies exist no more.'

P. Louvre N 3166, III, 7–8:

Wsir N	'Osiris N,
ꜥnḫ bꜣ.k m šꜥt n snsn	your ba lives by the Book of Breathing,
ḫnm.k m Šw sꜣ Rꜥ	and you unite with Shu son of Re;
ꜥḳ.k r Dwꜣt	you enter the Duat
nn wn ḫftyw.k	and your enemies exist no more.'

P. Louvre N 3158, V, 3–4:

hꜣy Wsir N	'Hail Osiris N,
ꜥnḫ bꜣ.t m šꜥt n snsn	your ba lives by the Book of Breathing,
ḫnm.t m Šw sꜣ Rꜥ	and you unite with Shu son of Re;
ꜥḳ.t r Dwꜣt	you enter the Duat,
nn wn ḫftyw.t	and your enemies exist no more.'

P. Louvre N 3154, III, 7–8:

hy Wsir N	'Hail Osiris N,
ꜥnḫ bꜣ.k	your ba lives,
ḫnm.k Šw sꜣ Rꜥ	and you unite with Shu son of Re;
ꜥḳ.k r Dwꜣt	you enter the Duat,
nn wn ḫfty.k	and your enemy exists no more.'

Sequence omitted in P. Louvre E 11079; partly in lacuna in P. Joseph Smith, IV, 12.

P. BM EA 9995, II, 15–17 = P. BM EA 10260, III, x + 1–2 (partly in lacuna) = P. Berlin 3135, III, 8–10 = P. Berlin 3154, II, 6–7 = P. Florence 3665 + P. Vienna 3850, IV, 7–8 = P. Louvre E 8079 + 11080, III, 9–11 = P. Louvre N 3121, III, 4 = P. Louvre N 3126, III, 24–5 = P. Louvre N 3167 + 3222, II, 21–2 = P. Louvre N 3285, III, 1–4 = P. Louvre N 3291, 30–1 = P. Tübingen 2016, IV, 12–14:

hꜣy Wsir (Ḥwt-Ḥr) N	'Hail Osiris (Hathor) N,
ꜥnḫ bꜣ.k /.t m šꜥt (n) snsn	your ba lives by the Book of Breathing,
ḫnm.k /.t m šꜥt (n) snsn	and you unite with the Book of Breathing;
ꜥḳ.k /.t r Dwꜣt	You enter the Duat,
nn wn ḫfty(w).k /.t	and your enemy(/ies) exist no more.'

P. Louvre N 3284, III, 19–21:

hꜣy Wsir N	'Hail Osiris N,
ꜥnḫ bꜣ.k m šꜥt n snsn	your ba lives by the Book of Breathing,
ḫnm.k m mitt <m šꜥt n snsn>	likewise you unite <with the Book of Breathing>;
ꜥḳ.k r Dwꜣt	you enter the Duat,
nn wn ḫftyw.k	and your enemies exist no more.'

P. BN 179–81, III, 16–17 = P. Lausanne 3391, III, 1–4 = P. Vienna 3863, III, 2–5 = P. Vienna 3931, II, 23–5:

hꜣy Wsir N	'O Osiris N,
ꜥnḫ bꜣ.k /.t m šꜥt snsn	your ba lives by the Book of Breathing,
snsn.k /.t m šꜥt snsn	and you breathe by the Book of Breathing;
ꜥḳ.k /.t r Dwꜣt	you enter the Duat,
nn wn ḫfty(w).k /.t	and your enemy(/ies) exist no more.'

P. Denon, IV, 11:[90]

hꜣy Wsir N	'Hail Osiris N,
ꜥnḫ bꜣ.k ḏt	your ba lives for ever.'

IV, 5

iw.k m bꜣ nṯr m Ḏdw. Same reading in P. BM EA 10260, III, x + 2 = P. Berlin 3135, III, 10 = P. Florence 3665 + P. Vienna 3850, IV, 8 = P. Joseph Smith, IV, 13 (partly in lacuna)[91] = P. Lausanne 3391, III, 4 = P. Louvre E 8079 + 11080, III, 11 = P. Louvre N 3083, VII, 3 = P. Louvre N 3121, III, 4–5 = P. Louvre N 3126, II, 25 = P. Louvre N 3154, III, 9 = P. Louvre N 3166, III, 8 = P. Louvre N 3284, III, 21 = P. Louvre N 3285, III, 4–5 = P. Louvre N 3291, 31 = P. Tübingen 2016, IV, 14 = P. Vienna 3863, III, 5–6 = P. Vienna 3931, II, 26. Sequence omitted in P. Denon, IV = P. Louvre E 11079. Var. P. BM EA 9995, II, 17 = P. Berlin 3154, II, 7–8 = P. Louvre N 3158, V, 4–5: *iw.k m bꜣ ꜥnḫ m Ḏdw*, 'You are a living ba in Busiris'; P. Louvre N 3167 + 3222, II, 22–3: *iw bꜣ.t nṯr m* [*Ḏdw*], 'Your ba is divine in [Busiris]'; P. BN 179–81, III, 18: *iw.k m* 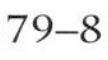 *nṯr*. On this passage: J. Assmann, *JEA* 65 (1979), p. 61 with n. 64.

ib.k n.k nn ḥr.f r.k irty.k r.k wn rꜥ nb. Sequence omitted in P. Denon, IV = P. Louvre E 11079. Omission of *r.k* (or *n.k*) after *irty.k* in P. Louvre N 3083, VII, 4 = P. Louvre N 3166, III, 9; of suffix *.f* after *ḥr* in P. Louvre N 3284, III, 21. Var. P. Louvre N 3285, III, 5 = P. Vienna 3863, III, 6: *nn ḥr.f ir.k*; P. Vienna 3931, II, 26–7: *ib.t ir.k nn ḥr.f ir.k*; P. BM EA 9995, II, 18 = P. Berlin 3154, II, 8 = P. Louvre N 3126, II, 26 = P. Louvre N 3158, V, 5 = P. Louvre N 3284, III, 22: *irty.k /.t n.k /.t*; P. Louvre N 3154, III, 9: *irty twk* (*sic*); P. BM EA 10260, III, x + 2 = P. BN 179–81, III, 19 = P. Berlin 3135, III, 11 = P. Florence 3665 + P. Vienna 3850, IV, 9 = P. Lausanne 3391, III, 4–5 = P. Louvre E 8079 + 11080, III, 11–12 = P. Louvre N 3121, III, 5 = P. Louvre N 3126, II, 26 = P. Louvre N 3167 + 3222, II, 23 = P. Louvre N 3285, III, 5 = P. Louvre N 3291, 31 = P. Tübingen 2016, IV, 14–15 = P. Vienna 3863, III, 6 = P. Vienna 3931, II, 27: *irt.k /.t n.k /.t*. For the singular *irt*, see *supra*, p. 23, n. 60.

P. BN 179–81, III, 18–19:

ib.k ib n Rꜥ ḥꜥw.k ḥꜥw n nṯr ꜥꜣ	'Your heart is the heart of Re, your limbs are the limbs of the great god (see *supra*, **III, 2**);
ib.k n.k nn ḥr.f r.k	your heart belongs to you and will not be far from you;
irt.k n.k wn rꜥ nb	your eyes belong to you, open every day.'

IV, 5–6

ḏd mdw n[92] *nṯrw imyw-ḫt Wsir*[93] *n Wsir N*. Beginning of § 11 of de Hor-

90. For the sequel of the text, see *infra*, p. 31 (P. BM EA 10048, **V, 1**).
91. The following text is lost in this manuscript.
92. Written *in* in all other manuscripts quoted here, except P. Louvre E 8079 + 11080, III, 12.
93. Written  in P. Berlin 3154, II, 8.

rack's classification. Same reading in P. BM EA 9995, II, 18–19 = P. Berlin 3135, III, 11–12 = P. Berlin 3154, II, 8 = P. Florence 3665 + P. Vienna 3850, IV, 10–11= P. Lausanne 3391, III, 6–7 = P. Louvre E 8079 + 11080, III, 12 = P. Louvre N 3126, III, 1 = P. Louvre N 3285, III, 6–8 = P. Louvre N 3291, 31–2 = P. Tübingen 2016, IV, 15–16. Sequence omitted in P. BM EA 10260, III = P. BN 179–81, III = P. Denon, IV = P. Louvre E 11079 = P. Louvre N 3166, III; partly in lacuna in P. Louvre N 3167 + 3222, II, 23–4. Omission of *n* before *nṯrw* in P. Louvre N 3158, V, 5 = P. Vienna 3931, III, 1; of *n* before *Wsir N* in P. Louvre N 3284, IV, 1; of *ḫt* after *imyw* in P. Louvre N 3121, III, 5. Garbled text in P. Louvre N 3083, VII, 4–5: *ḏd mdw n Wsir imy-ḫt Wsir n Wsir N*; P. Louvre N 3154, III, 10: *nꜣ nṯrw*.

Several documents, including the First Book of Breathing, invoke the 'gods of piercing sight' said to be 'in the retinue of Osiris'; see P. BM EA 10191, **I, 4**. In the tomb chapel of Petosiris,[94] the deceased addresses nine cynocephalous figures labelled as 'these gods who are in the retinue of Osiris and ensure his protection' (*nṯrw ipn imyw-ḫt Wsir ir sꜣ.f*). In the vignette illustrating col. IX of P. Rhind I (ed. Möller, p. 40), it is precisely the Ennead of Osiris which bears that designation. On a naos fragment now kept in the Museo Archeologico at Verona, these 'gods who are in the retinue of Osiris' are represented mummiform beside the sons of Horus, the Just ones (*Mꜣꜥtyw*), the Bas […] and obscure guardian demons (*iryw-ꜥꜣwy ds* ?); cf. J.J. Clère, *OA* 12 (1973), p. 103. On the function of the gods *imyw-ḫt Wsir*, see also Zandee, *Death as an Enemy* (2nd edn, New York 1977), pp. 40 and 212.

IV, 6

šms.k Rꜥ šms.k Wsir bꜣ.k ꜥnḫ r nḥḥ. Sequence omitted in P. BM EA 10260, III = P. Denon, IV = P. BN 179–81, III. Omission of suffix *.k* after *šms* (second mention) in P. Berlin 3135, III, 12; of *r nḥḥ* in P. Vienna 3931, III, 2. Var. P. BM EA 9995, II, 19 = P. Berlin 3135, III, 13 = P. Florence 3665 + P. Vienna 3850, IV, 12 = P. Lausanne 3391, III, 8 = P. Louvre E 8079 + 11080, III, 13 = P. Louvre N 3083, VII, 6 = P. Louvre N 3121, III, 7 = P. Louvre N 3126, III, 2 = P. Louvre 3154, III, 11 = P. Louvre N 3158, V, 7 = P. Louvre N 3166, III, 10 = P. Louvre N 3284, IV, 4 = P. Louvre N 3285, III, 9 = P. Louvre N 3291, 32 = P. Tübingen 2016, IV, 17 = P. Vienna 3863, 10: *r nḥḥ ḏt*; P. Louvre N 3154, III, 11: *ꜥnḫ bꜣ.k r nḥḥ ḏt*; P. Louvre N 3167 + 3222, II, 25: […] *r nḥḥ ḏt*. This sequence, written in the correct place in P. Louvre N 3167 + 3222, II, 24–5 (partly in lacuna), is repeated by error in that manuscript at III, 1–2. P. Berlin 3154, II, 9: group *iw.k* crossed out after *Wsir*.

P. Louvre E 11079, II, 2:

šms.t Rꜥ šms.t Wsir	'You follow Re, you follow Osiris,
r nḥḥ r nḥḥ ḏt ḏt	for ever, for ever and eternally, eternally,
mꜣꜣ.t Wsir m ḥb Wꜣg	and you see Osiris at the *Wꜣg*-festival.'[95]

ibid., IV, 9–10:

šms.t Rꜥ šms.t Wsir	'You follow Re, you follow Osiris,
r nḥḥ ḥnꜥ ḏt	for ever and eternally.'

šms.k Wsir: note the writing  for the name of the god, also attested in P. Louvre N 3158, V, 7, and on which see F.R. Herbin, *BIFAO* 84 (1984), p. 255, n. 2.

IV, 7–8

ḏd mdw n[96] *Wsir ḫnty Imntt n nṯrw imyw Dwꜣt Wsir N r wn n.f m sbꜣw nw Dwꜣt*. Sequence omitted in P. Denon, IV = P. Louvre E 11079; partly in lacuna in P. Florence 3665 + P. Vienna 3850, IV, 13 (the line corresponds to the junction of the two fragments). The omission of *n* before *Wsir N* is probably erroneous here, as indicated by the numerous variants for the phrase; nevertheless, it is attested in other manuscripts:

P. Louvre N 3083, VII, 6–8 = P. Louvre N 3154, III, 11–13:

ḏd mdw n Wsir ḫnty Imntt	'To be recited by Osiris foremost of the West
n nṯrw imyw Dwꜣt	to the gods who are in the Duat,
<*n*> *Wsir N*	<for> the Osiris N,
r wn n.s sbꜣw nw Dwꜣt	that the gates of the Duat be opened for him.'

P. Louvre N 3166, III, 10–11, presents the same peculiarity, but the ensuing phrase *iw mi wn n.f*, replacing the usual version *r wn n.f*, permits another interpretation:

ḏd mdw in Wsir ḫnty Imntt	'To be recited by Osiris foremost of the West
n nṯrw imyw Dwꜣt	to the gods who are in the Duat:
Wsir N	the Osiris N,
iw mi wn n.f sbꜣw nw Dwꜣt	may there be opened for him the gates of the Duat! '

P. Louvre N 3158, V, 8, provides a version identical to that of P. BM EA 10048, with the omission of *r* before *wn* followed by *n.t* 'for you', simply corrected by the addition of *s* ('for her').

Other versions include certain divergent passages:

P. Tübingen 2016, IV, 17–V, 2:

ḏd mdw in nṯrw imyw-ḫt Wsir	'To be recited by the gods who are in the retinue of Osiris;
ḏd mdw in nṯrw imyw Dwꜣt	to be recited by the gods who are in the Duat,
n Wsir ḫnty Imntt	to Osiris foremost of the West,
n Wsir N	for the Osiris N,
r wn n.f m sbꜣw nw Dwꜣt	that there be opened for him the gates of the Duat.'

P. Berlin 3154, II, 9–10 = P. Lausanne 3391, III, 8–10 = P. Vienna 3931, III, 3–5:

ḏd mdw in nṯrw imyw-ḫt Wsir ḫnty Imntt	'To be recited by the gods who are in the retinue of Osiris foremost of the West
n Wsir N	for the Osiris N,
r[97] *wn n.s m sbꜣw*[98] *nw Dwꜣt*	that there be opened for him the gates of the Duat.'

P. Vienna 3863, III, 10–11 gives a similar version, with *imyw n* (*sic*) *Wsir*, a mistake for *imyw-ḫt Wsir*.

P. BM EA 9995, II, 19–21 = P. BM EA 10260, III, x + 3 = P. Berlin 3135, III, 15 = P. BN 179–81, III, 21–4 = P. Florence 3665 + P. Vienna 3850, IV, 13–14 (partly in lacuna) = P. Louvre E 8079 + 11080, III, 13–14 = P. Louvre N 3121, III, 7–8 = P. Louvre N 3284, IV, 4–6 = P. Louvre N 3285, III, 10–13:

94. Lefebvre, *Petosiris* II, p. 172, no. 70, 2–3.
95. Cf. P. BM EA 9995, II, 14: *mꜣꜣ.k Ḫnty Imntt m ḥb Wꜣg*.
96. Written *in* in P. Lausanne 3391, III, 8 = P. Louvre N 3291, 38.
97. Omission of *r* in P. Berlin 3154.
98. The faulty writing 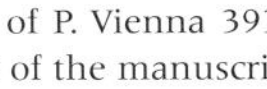 in P. Lausanne 3391, also found in P. Vienna 3863, III, 11, is based on confusion with *Dwꜣt*. Starting from this point, all the ends of lines in col. III of P. Vienna 3931 show a shift owing to the bad junction of the whole left edge of the manuscript which must be raised by one line to restore the original text.

ḏd mdw in nṯrw imyw Dwȝt	'To be recited by the gods who are in the Duat
n Wsir ḫnty Imntt[99]	to Osiris foremost of the West
n Wsir (Ḥwt-Ḥr) N	for the Osiris (the Hathor) N,
r[100] *wn n.f / .s m*[101] *sbȝw*[102] *nw Dwȝt*	that there be opened for him / her the gates of the Duat.'

Some manuscripts closely resemble these versions: P. Louvre N 3126, III, 2–3 (omission of the two *n* before *Wsir* and of *m* before *sbȝw*); P. Louvre N 3291, 32–3 (omission of *n Wsir ḫnty Imntt*) and P. Louvre N 3167 + 3222, II, 25–III, 2 (mistaken insertion after *n Wsir N* of the sequence *šms.t Rʿ šms.t Wsir bȝ.t ʿnḫ r nḥḥ ḏt*, on which see *supra*, **IV, 6**).

IV, 8

šsp ḫȝt.f m ḫrt-nṯr mi ʿnḫ bȝ.f r nḥḥ. Same reading in P. Louvre N 3158, V, 9. Sequence omitted in P. Denon, IV = P. Louvre E 11079. Var. P. Louvre N 3166, III, 11–12: *iṯ ḫȝt.f*; P. Vienna 3931, III, 5–6: *šsp bȝ.s*, 'Her ba is received' (*m ḫr-nṯr mi* in lacuna); P. Lausanne 3391, III, 11: *šsp bȝ.k*, 'Your ba is received'; P. BM EA 10260, III, x + 4 = P. Louvre E 8079 + 11080, III, 14–15 = P. Louvre N 3285, III, 13 = P. Tübingen 2016, V, 3: *šsp.f twk*, 'He receives you'; P. BM EA 9995, II, 21–2 = P. Berlin 3154, II, 10: *iṯ.f twk*, 'He receives you'; P. Vienna 3863, III, 11–12: *sšp.w twk*,[103] 'One receives you'; P. Berlin 3135, III, 15–16 = P. BN 179–81, III, 24 = P. Louvre N 3126, IV, 3 = P. Florence 3665 + P. Vienna 3850, IV, 15: *šsp.tw.k / .t*, 'You are received'; P. Louvre N 3121, III, 8–9: *šsp.w s(t)*, 'One receives her'; P. Louvre N 3291, 33: *šsp.s*, 'She is received'; P. Louvre N 3284, IV, 6: *sšp.k*, 'You are received';[104] P. Louvre N 3083, VII, 8–9 = P. Louvre N 3154, III, 13–14 = P. Louvre N 3291, 33: *r ḫrt-nṯr*; P. Louvre N 3083, VII, 8–9 = P. Louvre N 3291, 33–4: *r nḥḥ ḏt*.

IV, 8–9

ḳd.f sbḫt m ḫrt-nṯr.[105] Same reading in P. Lausanne 3391, III, 11 = P. Louvre N 3158, V, 9 = P. Louvre N 3285, III, 14 = P. Tübingen 2016, V, 3–4 = P. Vienna 3863, III, 12. Sequence omitted in P. BM EA 10260, III, x + 4 = P. Denon, IV = P. Louvre E 11079. Var. P. Louvre N 3154, III, 14: *ḳd sbḫt*; P. Louvre N 3291, 34 = P. Vienna 3931, III, 6: *ḳd.f / .s sbḫt.f / .s*; P. BM EA 9995, II, 21 = P. Berlin 3135, III, 16 = P. Berlin 3154, II, 11 = P. Florence 3665 + P. Vienna 3850, IV, 16 = P. Louvre E 8079 + 11080, III, 15 = P. Louvre N 3121, III, 9 = P. Louvre N 3126, IV, 4 = P. Louvre N 3167 + 3222, III, 3 = P. Louvre N 3284, IV, 7: *sbḫwt*; P. Louvre N 3166, III, 12: *ḳd sbḫwt.f*; P. BN 179–81, III, 24–5: *ḳd.n.f*; P. Louvre N 3083, VII, 8–9: *ḳd.n.s sbḫt m wsḫt Mȝʿty*; P. Berlin 3135, III, 16: *m igrt*. For *ḳd sbḫwt*, cf. *BD* ch. 188, title.

IV, 9

ḥs kȝ.f nṯr.f šsp.n.f šʿt n snsn mi ir.f snsn. Same reading in P. BM EA 9995, II, 22–3 = P. Florence 3665 + P. Vienna 3850, IV, 16–17 = P. Louvre E 8079 + 11080, III, 15–16 = P. Louvre N 3126, III, 4–5 = P. Louvre N 3284, IV, 8–9 = P. Louvre N 3291, 34 = P. Tübingen 2016, V, 4–5. Sequence omitted in P. Denon, IV = P. Louvre E 11079; partly rubbed out in P. Louvre N 3154, III, 14. Omission of *ḥs kȝ.f nṯr.f* in P. BM EA 10260, III, x + 4; of *nṯr.f* in P. Berlin 3135, III, 16. Var. P. Berlin 3154, II, 11: *iṯ.n.f*; P. Vienna 3863, III, 13: *šsp.f šʿt snsn*; *mi ir.f snsn* ... (?); P. Lausanne 3391, III, 12 = P. Vienna 3931, III, 7: *šsp.s* (?) *šʿt snsn*;[106] P. BN 179–81, III, 25–6: *šsp tȝy.f šʿt n snsn*; P. BM EA 10260, III, 4 = P. Louvre N 3121, III, 10 = P. Louvre N 3167 + 3222, III, 4 = P. Louvre N 3285, III, 16 (?): *mi ir.f / .s snsn n* (*sic*). Phrase in the 2nd person in P. Louvre N 3158, VI, 1 (*ḥs kȝ.t nṯr.t, šsp.n.t, mi ir.t*).

P. Louvre N 3166, III, 12–14:

ḥs kȝ.k (*sic*) *nṯr.k* (*sic*)	'Your ka praises your god;
iṯ.k (*sic*) *šʿt snsn*	you receive the Book of Breathing,
mi ir.f snsn r-dit ib.f	may he breathe indeed as he desires!
iṯ.k (*sic*) *s(t) r Imntt m ḥtp*	You carry it to the West, in peace,
ḏr-nty nn bwt n it	for there is no abomination for (your) father,
nn šmʿw n mwt	no malevolence for (your) mother,
nn wn is wnyw n nṯr niwt[107]	nor conspirators (?) of the local god.'

P. Louvre N 3083, VII, 9–10:

ḥs kȝ.s ḥs nṯr.s	'His ka is praised, his god is praised;
mi ir bȝ.s snsn ḥnʿ bȝw.tn	May his ba then breathe with your bas
m pt tȝ Dwȝt	in the sky, (on) earth and (in) the Duat.'

IV, 9–10

ḥtp di nsw[108] *n Wsir ḫnty Imntt*[109] *nṯr ʿȝ nb ȝbḏw*. Beginning of § 12 of de Horrack's classification. Same reading in P. BM EA 9995, II, 23 = P. BM EA 10260, III, x + 4–5 = P. Berlin 3135, III, 17–18 = P. Berlin 3154, II, 11–12 = P. BN 179–81, III, 26–7 = P. Florence 3665 + P. Vienna 3850, IV, 17–18 = P. Lausanne 3391, III, 12–13 = P. Louvre E 8079 + 11080, III, 16–IV, 1 = P. Louvre N 3121, III, 10 = P. Louvre N 3154, III, 15 = P. Louvre N 3158, VI, 1–2 = P. Louvre N 3167 + 3222, III, 4 = P. Louvre N 3284, IV, 9 = P. Louvre N 3285, III, 16–17 = P. Louvre N 3291, 34–5 = P. Vienna 3931, III, 8–9. Sequence omitted in P. Denon, IV = P. Louvre E 11079 = P. Louvre N 3166, III. Omission of *ḥtp di nsw* in P. Tübingen 2016, V, 5; of *n* before *Wsir* in P. Louvre N 3126, IV, 5; of *nṯr ʿȝ nb ȝbḏw* in P. Louvre N 3083, VII, 11; of *ʿȝ* after *nṯr* in P. Vienna 3863, III, 14.

IV, 10–11

di.f prt-ḫrw tȝ ḥnḳt kȝw ȝpdw irp[110] *irṯt ḥtpw ḏfȝw ḫt nbt nfrt wʿbt n kȝ n Wsir N*. Same reading in P. Louvre N 3154, III, 15–17 = P. Louvre N 3158, VI, 2–4. Sequence omitted in P. Denon, IV = P. Louvre E 11079 = P. Louvre N 3166, III. Addition of *m* (var. *n*) after *prt-ḫrw* in P. BM EA 9995, II, 23 = P. BM EA 10260, III, x + 5 = P. Berlin 3154, II, 12 = P. BN 179–81, III, 27 = P. Louvre E 8079 + 11080, IV, 1 = P. Louvre N 3121, III, 10 = P. Louvre N 3126, III, 5 = P. Louvre N 3291, 35. Omission of *wʿbt* in P. BM EA 9995, II, 23 = P. BM EA 10260, III, x + 5 = P. Berlin 3135, III, 19 = P. Berlin 3154, II, 12 = P. BN 179–81, III, 28 = P. Florence 3665 + P. Vienna 3850, IV, 19 = P. Lausanne 3391, III, 14 = P. Louvre E 8079 + 11080, IV, 1 = P. Louvre N 3121, III, 11 = P. Louvre N 3126, III, 6 = P. Louvre N 3167 + 3222, III, 5 = P. Louvre N 3284, IV, 11 = P. Louvre N

99. *Imntyw* in Louvre E 8079 + 11080. On confusion between the two terms, see *supra*, n. 73.
100. Omission of *r* in P. BM EA 9995.
101. Omission of *m* in P. Louvre N 3285.
102. Written [hieroglyphs] in P. Berlin 3135. Cf. *supra*, n. 98.
103. On the writing [hieroglyphs], cf. P. Vienna 3863, II, 15 and P. Lausanne 3391, II, 14, cited *supra*, **III, 9**.
104. In these two latter examples, the forms *šsp.s* (P. Louvre N 3291, 33) and *šsp.k* (P. Louvre N 3284, IV, 6) are to be understood as passive *sḏm.f* forms, or as corruptions from *šsp⟨.tw⟩s* and *šsp⟨.tw⟩f*.
105. In P. Louvre E 8079 + 11080, III, 15, an inexplicable horizontal sign intervenes between the *.f* of *ḳd.f* (?) and the *s* of *sbḫt*.
106. *snsn* in lacuna in P. Vienna 3931.
107. *LPE*, pp. 270–1; cf. too R. El Sayed, *ASAE* 69 (1983), p. 225: *bn ws n it.s mwt.s*, 'There is no fault with her father or her mother'.
108. In P. BM EA 10260 = P. Louvre N 3121 = probably P. Vienna 3863, this group is preceded by a horizontal sign similar to *n*; see F.R. Herbin, *RdE* 50 (1999), p. 223 (P. Louvre N 3121, III, 10).
109. In P. Vienna 3931, III, 9, the epithet *ḫnty Imntt*, omitted after the name of Osiris, has been appended at the end of the line.
110. *irp*, omitted by the scribe of P. Vienna 3931, III, 10, has been added at the line end.

3285, III, 18 = P. Louvre N 3291, 35 = P. Tübingen 2016, V, 6 = P. Vienna 3863, III, 15 = P. Vienna 3931, III, 10. Omission of *irṯt* in P. Louvre N 3121, III, 11; of *irp irṯt* and of *wꜥbt* in P. Louvre N 3291, 35.

P. Louvre N 3083, VII, 11–13:

ḥtp di nsw n Wsir ḫnty Imntt	'Offering that the king gives to Osiris foremost of the West,
di.f prt-ḫrw tꜣ ḥnḳt kꜣw ꜣpdw	that he may grant invocation offering of bread, beer, oxen and fowl,
ḳbḥ snṯr ḥtpw ḏfꜣw	libation and censing, *ḥtpw*-offerings and food,
ḫt nbt nfrt wꜥbt bnrt	all things good, pure and sweet,
n kꜣ n Wsir N	for the ka of the Osiris N.'

IV, 11

bꜣ.k ꜥnḫ ḫꜣt.k rwḏ m wḏwt n Rꜥ ḏs.f. Same reading in P. Berlin 3154, II, 13 = P. BN 179–81, IV, 1 = P. Louvre E 8079 + 11080, IV, 2 = P. Louvre N 3083, VII, 13–14 = P. Louvre N 3154, III, 17 = P. Louvre N 3158, VI, 4 = P. Louvre N 3167 + 3222, III, 6 = P. Louvre N 3291, 36 = P. Tübingen 2016, V, 8. Sequence omitted in P. Denon, IV. Omission of *n* before *Rꜥ* in P. Lausanne 3391, III, 15 = P. Vienna 3863, III, 17. Var. P. BM EA 9995, II, 25 = P. BM EA 10260, III, x + 6 = P. Florence 3665 + P. Vienna 3850, IV, 21 = P. Lausanne 3391, III, 15 (?) = P. Louvre N 3121, III, 12 = P. Louvre N 3126, IV, 7 = P. Louvre N 3284, IV, 12 = P. Louvre N 3285, III, 21 = P. Vienna 3863, III, 17 = P. Vienna 3931, III, 12: *ḫꜣt.k /.t rwḏ.ti.* P. Louvre N 3166, III, 14: *rwḏ.k* by error; P. Berlin 3135, III, 21: *bꜣ.f, ḫꜣt.f.* P. Louvre E 11079, IV, 9: *ꜥnḫ bꜣ.t r nḥḥ m wḏwt n Rꜥ ḏs.f.*

bꜣ.k ꜥnḫ ḫꜣt.k rwḏ is attested above all in the form *ꜥnḫ bꜣ / rwḏ ḫꜣt*:[111] *KRI* I, 328, 7; III, 1, 10; 349, 9; 594, 3; 601, 8; 607, 8; 704, 2; 793, 7; G. Daressy, *RT* 14 (1893), p. 172 (LXVI); Bruyère, *La Tombe n° 1 de Sennedjem* (*MIFAO* 88, 1959), p. 68; N. de G. Davies, *The Tomb of Nefer-hotep* (1933), pl. 35, left, col. 3; pl. 38, right, col. 3; E. Drioton, *RdE* 1 (1933), p. 28; B. Bruyère, *Deir el Médineh 1923–24* (*FIFAO* 2/2, 1925), p. 45; R. Mond, *ASAE* 6 (1905), p. 84; Mond-Myers, *Temples of Armant*, pl. 105; etc.

On the expression *rwḏ ḫꜣt*: *Wb.* II, 411, 11 (*Belegst.*); Lefebvre, *Petosiris* II, p. 172, no. 70, 8; *BD* ch. 168 (ed. Budge, p. 425, 15); Borchardt, *Statuen und Statuetten* II, p. 110: *rwḏ ḫt*; also *infra*, p. 129 n. 43.

IV, 12

nn sk nn mrḥ mi Rꜥ ḏt nḥḥ. Same reading in P. BM EA 9995, II, 25–III, 1 = P. BM EA 10260, III, x + 6 = P. Berlin 3135, III, 21 = P. Berlin 3154, II, 13–14 = P. BN 179–81, IV, 1–2 = P. Florence 3665 + P. Vienna 3850, IV, 22 = P. Lausanne 3391, III, 15 = P. Louvre E 8079 + 11080, IV, 2–3 = P. Louvre N 3121, III, 12–13 = P. Louvre N 3126, III, 7 = P. Louvre N 3158, VI, 4 = P. Louvre N 3167 + 3222, III, 7 = P. Louvre N 3284, 12–13 = P. Louvre N 3285, III, 21–2 = P. Louvre N 3291, 36 = P. Vienna 3863, III, 17. Sequence omitted in P. Denon, IV = P. Louvre E 11079; partly rubbed out in P. Vienna 3931, III, 13. Omission of *nḥḥ* in P. Tübingen 2016, V, 8. Var. P. Louvre N 3083, VII, 14 = P. Louvre N 3154, III, 18: *nn sk ḏt*; P. Louvre N 3166, III, 15: *mi Rꜥ m pt.*

V, 1

i Wsḫ-nmtt pr m Iwnw nn ir Wsir[112] *N isft.* Beginning of § 13 of de Horrack's classification.[113] Same reading in P. BM EA 9995, III, 1 = P. BM EA 10260, III, x + 6–7 = P. Berlin 3135, III, 22–3 = P. Berlin 3154, II, 14 = P. BN 179–81, IV, 2–3 = P. Denon, IV, 11–13 = P. Florence 3665 + P. Vienna 3850, V, 1–2 = P. Lausanne 3391, III, 16 = P. Louvre E 8079 + 11080, IV, 4 = P. Louvre N 3083, VII, 14–15 = P. Louvre N 3121, III, 13–14 = P. Louvre N 3126, III, 8 = P. Louvre N 3154, III, 18–19 = P. Louvre N 3158, VI, 5–6 = P. Louvre N 3166, III, 15–16 = P. Louvre N 3167 + 3222, III, 8 = P. Louvre N 3284, IV, 14–15 = P. Louvre N 3285, III, 22–3 = P. Louvre N 3291, 37 = P. Tübingen 2016, V, 9–10 = P. Vienna 3863, III, 18–19 = P. Vienna 3931, III, 14.

As epithet, *wsḫ-nmtt* is applied to various divinities: H. de Meulenaere, in *Ägyptologische Studien* (Fs. Grapow), Berlin 1954, p. 229, n. 5; A. Massart, *MDAIK* 15 (1957), p. 175, n. 6; Leitz, *LGG* II, pp. 586–87. As designation of a deity, it evidently refers, in the present context, to the sun-god.

Identical version in *BD*[114] ch. 125, 14; cf. Maystre, *Les déclarations*, p. 66.

V, 2

i Ptḥ-rꜣ pr m Ḫr-ꜥḥꜣ nn ir Wsir N ꜥwꜣy.[115] Same reading in P. Louvre N 3083, VII, 15–17 = P. Louvre N 3158, VI, 6–7 = P. Louvre N 3167 + 3222, III, 9. Var. P. Louvre N 3154, III, 19: *i Ptḥ-ꜣḫt*, 'O he who opens the horizon'; P. Berlin 3135, III, 23 = P. BN 179–81, IV, 3[116] = P. Denon, IV, 13 = P. Florence 3665 + P. Vienna 3850, V, 3 = P. Lausanne 3391, III, 17 = P. Louvre N 3126, III, 9 = P. Louvre N 3285, III, 23 = P. Tübingen 2016, V, 10 = P. Vienna 3863, III, 19 = P. Vienna 3931, III, 15 (?): *i Swꜣ-ꜣt*, 'O he who passes the moment ';[117] P. BM EA 9995, III, 2 = P. BM EA 10260, III, x + 7 = P. Berlin 3154, II, 14 [118] = P. Louvre E 8079 + 11080, IV, 5 = P. Louvre N 3121, III, 14 = P. Louvre N 3284, IV, 16: *i Wr-ꜣt*, 'O great of power'; P. Louvre N 3284, IV, 16 = P. Louvre N 3291, 38: *i wr šfyt*, 'O great of dignity'; P. Louvre N 3166, III, 16: *i Wsr-rꜣ pr m ẖrt-nṯr*, 'O mighty of word (lit.: of mouth), who came forth from the god's domain'.

BD ch. 125, 15: *i Ptḥ-rꜣ pr m Ḫr-ꜥḥꜣ nn ꜥwꜣ.i.* The earlier versions supply the variant *Ḥpt-sḏt* 'He who embraces the flame'; cf. Maystre, *Les déclarations*, pp. 66–7.

On the word *ꜥwꜣy*: P. Vernus, *Athribis* (*BdE* 74, 1978), p. 277, n. (d).

Ḫr-ꜥḥꜣ denotes a town of the XIIIth nome of Lower Egypt, corresponding to the Babylon of the Greek texts, on the site of what is now Old Cairo: Gardiner, *AEO* II, pp. 131*–44*, § 397 A; F. Gomaà, *Die Besiedlung Ägyptens* II (Wiesbaden 1987), pp. 200–3; H. de Meulenaere, *LÄ* I, 592.

V, 3

I Fndy pr m Ḫmnw nn ir Wsir N ḳmꜣ dḥrt. Omission of *ḳmꜣ* in P. Louvre N 3166, III, 18. Among the other sources the version *nn ir Wsir N ḳmꜣ dḥrt* occurs only, besides in P. BM EA 10048, in P. Louvre N 3083, VII, 17–18 = P. Louvre N 3166, III, 17–18 = P. Louvre N 3154, III, 20–1. Var. P. Louvre N 3158, VI, 8: *dḥrt.* The bulk of the manuscripts: P. BM EA 9995, III, 4–5 = P. BM EA 10260, III, x + 8 = P. Berlin 3135, IV, 2 = P. Berlin 3154, II, 16 = P. BN 179–81, IV, 7 = P. Denon, V, 1 = P. Florence 3665 + P. Vienna 3850, V, 6 = P. Lausanne 3391, III, 18 = P. Louvre E 8079 + 11080, IV, 6 = P. Louvre N 3121, III, 16 = P. Louvre N 3126, III,

111. The arrangement *rwḏ ḫꜣt ... ꜥnḫ bꜣ* seems far less frequent; cf. e.g. S. Sharpe, *Egyptian Inscriptions from the British Museum* II (London 1855), pl. 79.
112. Here as in the following invocations, the title 'Osiris' is consistently omitted in P. Vienna 3931.
113. The invocations to the divinities in P. Louvre E 11079 are too different from the other versions to be taken into consideration in the commentary.
114. Cited from the Lepsius edition, if not otherwise indicated.
115. In P. Tübingen 2016 this point marks the close of the invocations to the assessors of Osiris.
116. The word has been rubbed out in this manuscript, but the visible traces support a reading *swꜣ ꜣt*.
117. On the meaning of *ꜣt*, see A.H. Gardiner, *JEA* 34 (1948), pp. 13–15, especially p. 15 for the ambiguity between 'moment' and 'power'.
118. In that manuscript, *wr ꜣt* is preceded by another word, perhaps *swꜣ*.

10 = P. Louvre N 3167 + 3222, III, 10 = P. Louvre N 3284, IV, 19 = P. Louvre N 3285, III, 26 = P. Louvre N 3291, 39 = P. Vienna 3863, III, 21[119] = P. Vienna 3931, III, 16, give *ḳmꜣ ꜥš*.

BD ch. 125, 16: *nn ꜥwn ỉb.ỉ*, 'My heart is not rapacious'. For the earlier versions, see Maystre, *Les déclarations*, p. 67.

Fnḏy: P. Boylan, *Thot, the Hermes of Egypt* (Oxford 1922), p. 78 with n. 2; A. Zivie, *LÄ* III, 117 with n. 40; C. Leitz, *LGG* III, pp. 193–4.

V, 4

ỉ ꜥm-ỉrt pr m ḳrty nn ỉr Wsỉr N ỉṯ ḫwt m ṯꜣw. Same reading in P. BM EA 9995, III, 5–6 = P. BM EA 10260, III, x + 8 = P. BN 179–81, IV, 7–9 = P. Denon, V, 1–3 = P. Florence 3665 + P. Vienna 3850, V, 7–8 = P. Lausanne 3391, III, 19 = P. Louvre E 8079 + 11080, IV, 7 = P. Louvre N 3121, III, 16–18 = P. Louvre N 3126, III, 11 = P. Louvre N 3154, IV, 1–2 = P. Louvre N 3158, VI, 8–9 = P. Louvre N 3167 + 3222, III, 11 = P. Louvre N 3284, IV, 20–1 = P. Vienna 3931, III, 17. Sequence partly in lacuna in P. Vienna 3863, III, 22. Omission of *ỉṯ ḫwt m ṯꜣw* in P. Berlin 3135, IV, 4. Var. P. Berlin 3154, II, 16 = P. Louvre N 3285, III, 26 = P. Louvre N 3291, 40: *ỉrt.f*, 'his eye';[120] P. Louvre N 3166, III, 18–19: *nn ỉr Wsỉr N ỉṯ ḫwt n ky*, 'The Osiris N has not stolen the goods of another'. P. Louvre N 3083, VII, 18–20: *ỉ ꜥm[121]-ḥḥ pr m ꜥḥ nn ỉr N ỉṯ ḫwt m ḥtpw-nṯr*, 'O Swallower of eternity, who came forth from the palace, the Osiris N has committed no theft from among the divine offerings!' *BD* ch. 125, 17: *ỉ ꜥm-šwwt pr m ḳrty nn ṯꜣw.ỉ*. Var. Maspero, *Sarcophages* I, p. 50: *ỉ ꜥm-nṯrw pr m ḳrty nn ṯꜣw.ỉ*. Cf. Maystre, *Les déclarations*, p. 68.

On the expression *ꜥm ỉrt*: J.F. Borghouts, in *Studien zur Sprache und Religion Ägyptens* II (Fs. Westendorff), Göttingen 1984, p. 704, n. 5.

V, 5

ỉ Nhꜣ-ḥr pr m Rꜣ-sṯꜣw nn ỉr Wsỉr N sḫwn. Same reading in P. BM EA 9995, III, 6–8 = P. BM EA 10260, III, x + 8–9 = P. Berlin 3135, IV, 5–6 = P. BN 179–81, IV, 7–11 = P. Florence 3665 + P. Vienna 3850, V, 9–10 = P. Louvre E 8079 + 11080, IV, 8 = P. Louvre N 3083, VII, 20–2 = P. Louvre N 3121, III, 18–19 = P. Louvre N 3126, III, 12 = P. Louvre N 3154, IV, 2–3 = P. Louvre N 3167 + 3222, III, 12 = P. Louvre N 3284, V, 1 = P. Louvre N 3285, IV, 1–2. Sequence omitted in P. Louvre N 3166, III; partly in lacuna in P. Vienna 3863, III, 22–3; misplaced in P. Berlin 3154, I, 18, with omission of what follows *Rꜣ-sṯꜣw*. Var. P. Lausanne 3391, III, 20 = P. Louvre N 3158, VII, 1 = P. Louvre N 3291, 41 = P. Vienna 3931, III, 18: *ỉ Ḥꜣ-ḥr*, 'He whose face is reversed'. P. Denon, V, 4–5: *nn ỉr Wsỉr N ỉsft m-ḫt tẖ* (?) (conflation with the following phrase, see **V, 6**).

Var. *BD* ch. 125, 18: *nn smꜣ.ỉ rmṯ m grg*, 'I have not killed people unlawfully'. See Maystre, *Les déclarations*, p. 69.

Nhꜣ-ḥr ('He whose face is fearsome'): El Sayed, *Bulletin du Centenaire* (suppl. au *BIFAO* 81, 1981), pp. 120–40.

On the word *sḫwn*, 'rumours' (not in *Wb.*): Meeks, *ALex* 77.3791.

V, 6

ỉ Rwty pr m pt nn ỉr Wsỉr N ỉsft m tẖ (?). Same version in P. Louvre N 3154, IV, 3–4 = P. Louvre N 3158, VII, 2–3. Sequence omitted in P. Louvre N 3166, III; disturbed in P. Denon, V (see *supra*, **V, 5**); partly in lacuna in P. Vienna 3863, III, 24–5; partly rubbed out in P. Louvre N 3285, IV, 2–3.

The spelling of *tẖ* (?), found in only three manuscripts, seems to be unattested outside the Book of Breathing made by Isis.[122] Var. P. BN 179–81, IV, 13 = P. Louvre E 8079 + 11080, IV, 9 = P. Louvre N 3291, 42[123] = (?) P. Vienna 3931, III, 19:[124]; P. BM EA 9995, III, 9 = P. Berlin 3135, IV, 8 = P. Berlin 3154, II, 18 = P. Denon, V, 4 = P. Florence 3665 + P. Vienna 3850, V, 12 = P. Louvre N 3121, III, 20 = P. Louvre N 3126, III, 13 = P. Louvre N 3167 + 3222, III, 13:[125]; P. BM EA 10260, III, x + 10: ; P. Lausanne 3391, III, 21 and P. Louvre N 3284, V, 2 show respectively and . All these versions include the presence of the sign which can be the result of a confusion between the hieratic forms of the plummet (Gardiner sign-list U 41, not in Möller, *Pal.* III) and of the heart (F 34), leading in some cases to the determinative . The reading of the variants remains uncertain, and one could therefore suggest with reservation the existence of a word beginning with *ḫt*, such as *ḫt-ỉb* or *ḫt-ỉb-ḫt*, but the lack of any other known attestation lends little support to this hypothesis.

P. Louvre N 3083, VII, 22–3: *nn ỉr N ṯꜣ nkn n nṯr*, 'N has not stolen the goods of a god' (conflation with the following phrase, see **V, 7**); P. Berlin 3154, II, 17: *nn ỉr Wsỉr N sḫwn*, by conflation with the former phrase, then correction (II, 18): *nn ỉr Wsỉr N ỉsft m-ḫt tẖ* (?).

BD ch. 125, 18: *ỉ Rwty pr m pt nn ḥḏ.ỉ dbḥw*, 'O Ruty who came forth from the sky, I have not damaged the measure'; Maystre, *Les déclarations*, pp. 69–70.

On the lion-god Ruty: C. de Wit, *Le rôle et le sens du lion dans l'Egypte ancienne* (Leiden 1951), pp. 123–37; M. Heerma van Voss, *LÄ* V, 321; G. Vittmann, in *Zwischen den beiden Ewigkeiten* (Fs. G. Thausing, Vienna 1994), p. 252; Leitz, *LGG* IV, pp. 654–6.

V, 7

ỉ Ỉrt.f-m-sḏt pr m Ḫm nn ỉr Wsỉr N ṯꜣ nky n nṯr. Sequence omitted in P. Louvre N 3083 = P. Louvre N 3166; partly in lacuna in P. Vienna 3863, 26;[126] partly rubbed out in P. Louvre N 3285, IV, 3–4. Omission of *pr* in P. Louvre N 3158, VII, 3. Var. P. BM EA 10260, III, x + 10 = P. BN 179–81, IV, 13 = P. Denon, V, 5 = P. Florence 3665 + P. Vienna 3850, V, 13 = P. Lausanne 3391, III, 22 = P. Louvre E 8079 + 11080, IV, 10 = P. Louvre N 3121, III, 20–1 = P. Louvre N 3126, III, 14 = P. Louvre N 3167 + 3222, III, 14 = P. Louvre N 3284, V, 3 = P. Louvre N 3291, 41 = P. Vienna 3931, III, 20: *ỉ Ỉrt.f-m-ḫt*, 'O he whose eye is of fire'; P. BM EA 9995, III, 9–11 = P. Berlin 3154, II, 19: *ỉ Ỉrty.f-m-ḫt*.

nky (same version in P. Louvre N 3158, VII, 4) is here a graphic variant for *nkt*, 'goods', 'possessions', also written *nkn* (P. Louvre N 3083, VII, 23, cited *supra*, **V, 6**), and, in the parallel version to the present phrase, P. Louvre N 3154, IV, 6: *nn ỉr Wsỉr N ṯꜣ nkn n nṯr ꜥꜣ*, 'The Osiris N has not stolen the goods of the great god'.

Most of the manuscripts give *nn ỉr* (*Wsỉr / Ḥwt-Ḥr*) *N sꜣt*, 'The Osiris (the Hathor) N has committed no calumny': P. BM EA 9995, III, 9–11 = P. BM EA 10260, III, x + 10 = P. Berlin 3135, IV, 10 = P. Berlin 3154, II, 19 = P. BN 179–81, IV, 14–15 = P. Denon, V, 4–5 = P. Florence 3665 + P. Vienna 3850, V, 14 = P. Lausanne 3391, III, 22 = P. Louvre E 8079 + 11080, IV, 10 = P. Louvre N 3121, III, 20–1 = P. Louvre N 3126, III, 14 = P. Louvre N 3167 + 3222, III, 14 = P. Louvre N 3284, V, 3 = P. Louvre N 3285, IV, 3–4 = P. Louvre N 3291, 43 = P. Vienna 3931, III, 20.[127]

BD ch. 125, 20: *ỉ Ỉrty.fy-m-ds pr m ḫm n ỉr N ḫbt*, 'O he whose eyes are of flint, who came forth from the *ḫm*-shrine (var.: Letopolis), the Osiris N has committed no crime'; cf. Maystre, *Les déclarations*, pp. 70–1.

119. Note in this latter manuscript the writing for *ꜥš*.
120. *ỉrt* for *ỉrty*: see *supra*, **III, 6**.
121. Written .
122. Cf. the spelling in P. Louvre N 3154, I, 13, cited *supra*, **I, 9**.
123. Addition of the adjective *nb* 'every'.
124. Indistinct sign after .
125. Written with an abusive suffix pronoun *.k*.
126. In P. Vienna 3863, this point marks the close of the invocations to the assessors of Osiris.
127. In these manuscripts the invocations to the assessors of Osiris come to an end at this point.

Maspero, *Sarcophages* I, p. 50: *i Irty.f-m-sḏt pr m Ḫm nn ir.i ḫbt*, 'O he whose eyes are a flame, who came from Letopolis, I have committed no crime'. The word *ḫbt* is here a writing of *ḫꜣbt*, well attested in several manuscripts for this passage in *BD*.

V, 8

I Nbi-ḥr pr m ḫtḫt nn ir Wsir N bꜣw n nṯr. Same reading in P. Louvre N 3083, VII, 23–VIII, 2 = P. Louvre N 3154, IV, 6–7. Sequence omitted in P. Louvre N 3166. Omission of *n* before *nṯr* in P. Louvre N 3158, VII, 5.

BD ch. 125, 21: *i Nbi-ḥr pr m ḫtḫt pr m Iwnw nn ṯꜣ.i ḫwt n nṯr*; cf. Maystre, *Les déclarations*, pp. 71–2. Maspero, op. cit., p. 50: *i Nbi-ḥr pr m ḫ(ꜣ)ḫ pr m Iwnw nn ḫb.i ḫwt nṯr*, 'O he whose face is of fire, who comes in haste, who came from Heliopolis, I have not levied from the goods of a god'.

Note the existence of a deity *ꜣsb-ḥr* ('Fiery-faced') *pr m ḫtḫt*, P. Greenfield, p. 12.

ḫtḫt is in certain cases determined by the town sign, but this toponym appears not to be otherwise attested.

Word *bꜣw*: M.A. Green, *Glimpses of Ancient Egypt. Studies in Honour of H.W. Fairman* (Warminster 1979), pp. 107–15; J.F. Borghouts, in R.J. Demarée and J.J. Janssen (eds), *Gleanings from Deir el-Medîna* (Leiden 1982), pp. 1–70.

Two translations of the expression *ir bꜣw n nṯr* are possible here: 'arouse the anger of a god',[128] or 'arouse the hatred of a god', assuming an equivalence of the words *bꜣw* and *bwt*; see Smith, *Mortuary Texts*, p. 119 (X, 21). See also *supra*, **IV, 9**, on the passage P. Louvre N 3166, III, 13–14, and *LPE*, pp. 270–1.

V, 9

I Sd-ḳsw pr m Ḫm nn ir Wsir N ṯꜣ ḫwt n ky. Sequence omitted in P. Louvre N 3166 (but cf. *supra*, **V, 4**); partly in lacuna in P. Louvre N 3158, VII, 5–6. P. Louvre N 3083, VIII, 2: *i Sꜣw-ḳs*, 'O he who guards bones'. P. Louvre N 3083, VIII, 2–3 = P. Louvre N 3154, IV, 8–9: *nn ir* (*Wsir*) *N ṯꜣ ḫrt*, '(The Osiris) N has not stolen any goods'.

BD ch. 125, 22: *i Sd-ḳsw pr m Nn-nsw nn ḏd.i grg*, 'O Breaker of bones who came forth from Heracleopolis, I have spoken no falsehood'; cf. Maystre, *Les déclarations*, pp. 72–3.

V, 10

I Ḥsꜣ-ḥr pr m Bꜣst nn ir Wsir N rm irt.f r dḥr. Sequence partly in lacuna in P. Louvre N 3158, VII, 7–8. Omission of suffix *.f* after *irt* in P. Louvre N 3166, III, 20; P. Louvre N 3083, VIII, 3–5: *i …* (?)*-m-sḏt pr m Bꜣst nn ir N rm irty.s r dḥr*. P. Louvre N 3154, IV, 9–10: *i Ḫnm-sḏt* (?) *pr m Bꜣst nn ir Wsir N rm irt.f*.

None of the versions of this phrase preserved in the Book of Breathing made by Isis follows the ancient tradition. *BD* ch. 125, 23: *i Ṯꜣw.f-m-sḏt pr m Ḥwt-kꜣ-Ptḥ nn <n> ḥm.i wnmt*, 'O he whose breath is a flame, who came forth from the Domain of the ka of Ptah, I have seized no food'; cf. Maystre, *Les déclarations*, p. 73. Cf. also *BD* ch. 125, 24: *i Bꜣsty pr m šṯyt nn rm.i*, 'O Bubastite, who came forth from the sanctuary, I have not wept'.

Ḥsꜣ-ḥr: cf. also *BD* ch. 163, 4 and 164, 8.

VI, 1

I Dr-ꜥḥꜣ pr m Wnw nn ir Wsir N ꜥḥꜣ ḫnn. This sequence, omitted in P. Louvre N 3083, VIII, is very rarely present in the manuscripts of the Book of Breathing made by Isis. Among the other sources, only three may be cited: P. Louvre N 3158, VII, 8–9, and P. Louvre N 3166, III, 20–1. P. Louvre N 3154, IV, 10–11, substitutes *Dwꜣt(y)*, 'He of the Duat' for *Dr-ꜥḥꜣ*.

VI, 2

I Tp.f-ḥꜣ.f pr m Ṯpḥt-ḏꜣt nn ir Wsir N nknk. Sequence omitted in P. Louvre N 3083, VIII. Var. P. Louvre N 3154, IV, 11 = P. Louvre N 3158, VII, 9 = P. Louvre N 3166, III, 21: *i ḥr.f ḥꜣ.f*; P. Louvre N 3158, VII, 9–VIII, 1 = P. Louvre N 3166, III, 22: *nn ir Wsir N nk ky*, 'Osiris N has not fornicated with another man'.

BD ch. 125, 25: *i Ḥr.f-ḥꜣ.f pr m Ṯpḥt-ḏꜣt nn nwḥ.i*, 'O he whose face is behind him, who came forth from Tepehet-djat, I have had no homosexual intercourse'; cf. Maystre, *Les déclarations*, pp. 88–9.

Ḥr.f-ḥꜣ.f: A.M. Blackman, *JEA* 5 (1918), p. 28 with n. 7; Meeks, *ALex* 78.2750.

VI, 3

I Wnm-snf pr m nmt nn ir Wsir N ḳn r ꜥwt-nṯr. Same version in P. Louvre N 3158, VIII, 1–2 (partly in lacuna). Var. P. Louvre N 3083, VIII, 6: *ꜥwt n nṯr*; P. Louvre N 3154, IV, 14 = P. Louvre N 3166, III, 23: *ꜥwt*.

BD ch. 125, 29: *i Wnm-snf pr m nmt nn smꜣ.i ꜥwt nṯr*, 'O consumer of blood, who came forth from the slaughterblock, I have not slain the livestock of a god'; cf. Maystre, *Les déclarations*, p. 75.

For *wnm snf*, cf. the expression *sꜥm snf*, P. BM EA 10115, 11.

VI, 4

I Wꜣmmty pr m ḫbt nn ir Wsir N nk ḥmt ṯꜣ. Sequence partly in lacuna in P. Louvre N 3158, VIII, 3–4, and omitted in P. Louvre N 3166, III. Var. P. Louvre N 3154, IV, 14–15: *nn ir Wsir N nk št(ꜣ) ṯꜣ* (?). 'The Osiris N has not fornicated with a male (?) child'; P. Louvre N 3083, VIII, 6–8: *i wꜣmmti pr m Ḥwt ḥr-ib nn ir N ḏd wꜥꜣ r nṯr*, 'O Wamemty who came forth from Athribis,[129] the Osiris N has not blasphemed against god' (cf. *infra*, **VI, 8**).

BD ch. 125, 14: *i Wꜣmmty pr m ḫbt nn nk.i ḥmt ṯꜣ*, 'O Wamemty who came forth from the slaughterblock, I have not fornicated with a married woman'; cf. Maystre, *Les déclarations*, p. 81. For the god Wamemty: Leitz, *LGG* II, p. 245.

For the word *nk*, 'fornicate', in the sense of 'committing adultery': J.J. Janssen, in R.J. Demarée and J.J. Janssen (eds), *Gleanings from Deir el-Medina* (Leiden 1982), p. 127, n. 38.

VI, 5

I Šd-ḫrw pr m wryt nn ir Wsir N ꜥꜣ rꜣ. Sequence partly in lacuna in P. Louvre N 3158, VIII, 4–5, and omitted in P. Louvre N 3166, III = P. Louvre N 3083, VIII. Among the parallels only P. Louvre N 3154, IV, 15–16 presents the passage in full.

BD ch. 125, 18: *i Šd-ḫrw pr m wryt nn tꜣ rꜣ.i*, 'O *Šd-ḫrw* who came forth from the *wryt*-sanctuary, I have not been hot-tempered'; cf. Maystre, *Les déclarations*, pp. 85–6. On the *wryt*-sanctuary, see *LPE*, p. 179–80 (IV, 10).

Šd-ḫrw: Meeks, *ALex* 77.4336.

VI, 6

I Nḫḫ pr m Ḥḳꜣ-ꜥnḏ nn ir Wsir N mst. Sequence partly in lacuna in P. Louvre N 3158, VIII, 5–6, and omitted in P. Louvre N 3166, III. Var. P. Louvre N 3083, VIII, 8–10: *nn ir N ḫrḫr rꜣw-prw*, 'N has not destroyed sanctuaries'; P. Louvre N 3154, IV, 17–18: *nn ir Wsir mr*, 'The Osiris N has caused no suffering'.

BD ch. 125, 19; cf. Maystre, *Les déclarations*, p. 86.

128. Strictly this denotes a 'manifestation' but from the negative context it may be rendered here as 'wrath'.

129. Sole known reference to a connection between this god and Athribis.

VI, 7

Ỉ Sḥd pr m Tnw nn ir Wsir N ḫrḫr ḳrs. Sequence omitted in P. Louvre N 3083, VIII = P. Louvre N 3154, IV = P. Louvre N 3166, III, and partly in lacuna in P. Louvre N 3158, VIII, 6–7. Note, however, that in P. Louvre N 3083, VIII, 10, the preceding phrase (VI, 6) is followed by the words *ꜥn ḳrs*, not attested in any other manuscript.

No corresponding passage in *BD* ch. 125.

For *Sḥd*, probable abbreviation of *Sḥd-ḥr*, see Meeks, *Alex* 78.3786; J. Assmann, *Das Grab der Mutirdis* (*AV* 13, 1977), p. 94, n. 94.

VI, 8

Ỉ Nfr-tm pr m Ḥwt-kꜣ-Ptḥ nn ir Wsir N wꜥ(ꜣ) ḥr nṯr. Same reading in P. Louvre N 3154, IV, 18–19. Sequence partly in lacuna in P. Louvre N 3158, VIII, 7–8. 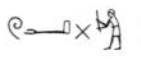 is a writing of the verb *wꜥꜣ* (*Wb.* I, 279, 14–17; Meeks, *ALex* 77.0855), found as here with the preposition *ḥr*. It is the same verb in the form  in P. Louvre N 3166, III, 24. Var. P. Louvre N 3083, VIII, 10–11: *nn ir N ṯꜣ irt n ky*, 'N has not stolen the eye of another', but cf. ibid., VIII, 7–8, cited *supra*, **VI, 4**: *nn ir N ḏd wꜥꜣ r nṯr*.

BD ch. 125, 26: *i Nfr-tm pr m Ḥwt-kꜣ-Ptḥ nn iw.i nn ir.i mn bin*, 'O Nefertum who came forth from the Mansion of the ka of Ptah (Memphis), I am without fault, I have caused no suffering or evil'; cf. Maystre, *Les déclarations*, p. 94.

VI, 9

Ỉ Nb-ṯꜣw di n mr.f nn ir Wsir N wꜥ(ꜣ) n ḥr nsw. Omission of *n* before *ḥr* in P. Louvre N 3166, III, 25 (writing  of *wꜥꜣ*) = P. Louvre N 3154, IV, 19–20 (writing 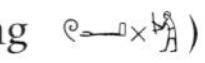) = P. Louvre N 3158, VIII, 8 (writing 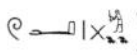). P. Louvre N 3083, VIII, 12–13: *nn ir N ḫtb* 'N has carried out no slaughter'.

BD ch. 125, 27: *Ỉ Tm-sp pr m Ḏdw nn šnt.i ḥr nsw*, 'O Tem-sep who came forth from Busiris, I have not conjured against the king'; cf. Maystre, *Les déclarations*, p. 95.

Nb-ṯꜣw: a designation of Osiris according to *BD*, ch. 125, 42, but also of Amun: F.R. Herbin, *RdE* 50 (1999), p. 175 (IV, 17–18).

VI, 10

Ỉ Ỉhy pr m Nwn nn ir Wsir N sḥwr mwt.f. Same sequence in P. Louvre N 3154, IV, 20–1.[130] Var. P. Louvre N 3083, VIII, 13–14 = P. Louvre N 3158, VIII, 9 = P. Louvre N 3166, III, 25–6: *nn ir (Wsir) N sḥwr* [131] *it.f / .s mwt.f / .s*, '(The Osiris) N has not vilified his / her father or mother'.

BD ch. 125, 29: *Ỉ Ỉhy pr m Nwn nn ir.i kꜣ n ḫrw*, 'O Ihy who came forth from Nun, I have not raised my voice'; cf. Maystre, *Les déclarations*, p. 96.

VII, 1

Ỉ Nḥb-kꜣ ḫnty Wꜣst nn ir Wsir N kꜣ n ḫrw. Same reading in P. Louvre N 3158, IX, 1–2 = P. Louvre N 3166, III, 26–7.[132] Omission of *n* before *ḫrw* in P. Louvre N 3083, VIII, 16.

BD ch. 125, 32: *i Nḥb-kꜣw pr m tpḥt.f nn ir.i sḫrw.f (sic) nn ir.i stnw.f (sic) nn ḥd.i* 'O Nehebkau who came forth from his cavern, I have not made plans for myself, I have not made distinction for myself, I have not harmed (another)'; cf. Maystre, *Les déclarations*, pp. 99–100 where a variant is given by the invocation *Nḥb-kꜣw pr m niwt*, 'Nehebkau who came forth from the City' (= Thebes).

VII, 2

Ỉ nṯrw imyw Dwꜣt sḏm ḫrw Wsir N. Beginning of § 14 of de Horrack's classification. Same reading in P. BM EA 9995, III, 11–12 = P. BM EA 10260, III, x + 10–11 = P. Berlin 3135, IV, 11–12 = P. Berlin 3154, II, 19–20 = P. Denon, V, 7–8 = P. Florence 3665 + P. Vienna 3850, V, 15–16 = P. Louvre N 3121, IV, 1 = P. Louvre N 3158, IX, 2 = P. Louvre N 3166, III, 27–8 = P. Louvre N 3167 + 3222, III, 15 = P. Louvre N 3284, V, 4 = P. Louvre N 3291, 44–5. Sequence partly in lacuna in P. Vienna 3863, III, 26–[7]; partly rubbed out, with omissions, in P. Louvre N 3285, IV, 5. Omission of *Wsir* in P. Louvre E 8079 + 11080, IV, 12 = P. Louvre N 3126, III, 15 = P. Tübingen 2016, V, 12. Var. P. Lausanne 3391, III, 23 = P. Vienna 3931, III, 21: *sḏm ḫrw ir.f / .s*; P. BN 179–81, IV, 15: *sḏm.tn*; P. Louvre E 11079, III, 3: *mi sḏm.tn*.[133]

P. Louvre N 3083, VIII, 16–18:

Ỉ nṯrw imyw Dwꜣt	'O gods who are in the Duat,
nṯrw sꜣww wsḫt Mꜣꜥty	guardian deities of the hall of the two Maats,
sḏm ḫrw Wsir ḫnty Ỉmntyw	hear the voice of Osiris foremost of the Westerners,
Wsir N	of the Osiris N.'

iw ḥr.tn iw nn ḏw nb ḥr.f iw nn isft nbt r.f. Same reading in P. Louvre N 3158, IX, 2–3. Sequence omitted in P. Louvre E 11079, III. In P. Lausanne 3391, III, 23 = P. Louvre N 3285, IV, 5 (partly rubbed out) = P. Vienna 3931, III, 21–2 = P. Vienna 3863, IV, 2–3, this sequence is not omitted but relayed, in whole or in part, after *nn ir.tw smi nb r.f m-bꜣḥ nṯrw (nbw)* and var., for which see *infra*, **VII, 4**). Whereas P. Vienna 3863, IV, 2–3 provides the complete phrase in the form *iw.f iw ḥr.tn nn ḏw nb ḥr.f nn isft nbt ḥr.f*, P. Lausanne 3391, III, 26 = P. Vienna 3931, III, 25 omit the section corresponding to *iw nn ḏw nb ḥr.f iw nn isft nb r.f*. The manuscripts contain minor but relatively frequent variants. P. Berlin 3135, IV, 12 = P. BN 179–81, IV, 16–17 = P. Lausanne 3391, III, 26 = P. Louvre N 3121, IV, 2 = P. Louvre N 3126, IV, 15 = P. Louvre N 3167 + 3222, III, 16 = P. Louvre N 3284, V, 4 give the variant *i(w).f / .s ii ḥr.tn* instead of *iw ḥr.tn*, also attested in P. Louvre N 3083, VIII, 18. P. Denon, V, 8 = P. Louvre E 8079 + 11080, IV, 14 = Vienna 3931, III, 25: *iw.f / .s iw ḥr.tn*; P. Louvre N 3291, 45–6: *iw.f iw.tw ḥr.tn*; P. BM EA 10260, III, x + 11: *iw ir.f ii ḥr.tn*; P. Tübingen 2016, V, 13: *iw.f ii ḥr.tn*; P. BM EA 9995, III, 12: *iw ir ii ḥr.tn*; P. Berlin 3154, II, 20: *ir ii ḥr.tn*; P. Louvre N 3166, III, 28: *iw.f ḥr.tn im*; P. Florence 3665 + P. Vienna 3850, V, 16: *ii.s ḥr.tn*. Lacunae make it impossible to identify securely the version selected in P. Louvre N 3285, IV, 9.

iw nn ḏw nb ḥr.f iw nn isft nb r.f. Sequence omitted in P. Louvre E 11079, III. Double omission of *iw* before *nn ḏw* and *nn isft* in P. BM EA 9995, III, 12 = P. BM EA 10260, III, x + 11 = P. Berlin 3135, IV, 12–13 = P. Berlin 3154, II, 20 = P. Florence 3665 + P. Vienna 3850, V, 16–[17] (partly in lacuna)[134] = P. Louvre N 3083, VIII, 18 = P. Louvre N 3121, IV, 2 = P. Louvre N 3126, III, 15 = P. Louvre N 3166, III, 28 = P. Louvre N 3167 + 3222, III, 16 = P. Louvre N 3284, V, 5 = P. Louvre N 3285, IV, 9–10 = P. Vienna 3863, IV, 2–3; before *nn isft* alone in P. BN 179–81, IV, 17 = P. Louvre E 8079 + 11080, IV, 15 = P. Louvre N 3291, 46 = P. Tübingen 2016, V, 14; omission of *nb r.f* after *isft* in P. Berlin 3135, IV, 13; of *nb* after *ḏw* in P. Berlin 3154, II, 20. Substitution of *m-ḫt.f* for *r.f* in P. BN 179–81, IV, 17; of *ḥr.f* for *r.f* after *isft nbt* in P. BM EA 9995, III, 13 = P. Berlin 3154, II, 20 = P. Louvre E 8079 + 11080, IV, 15 = P. Louvre N 3158, IX, 3 (?)[135] = P. Louvre N 3167 + 3222, III, 16 = P. Louvre N 3285, IV, 10 = P. Vienna 3863, IV, 2–3.

130. This manuscript terminates at this point.
131. *sḥwr.f* by mistake in P. Louvre N 3166.
132. In these two manuscripts the invocations to the Osiris tribunal come to an end at this point.
133. In this version the sequence is exceptionally placed *before* the invocation to divinities.
134. Line 17 is lost.
135. The scribe seems to have hesitated here between the variants *r* and *ḥr*.

nn mtr ꜥḥꜥ r.f. Same reading in P. BM EA 9995, III, 13 = P. BM EA 10260, III, x + 11 = P. Berlin 3135, IV, 13 = P. Berlin 3154, II, 20–1 = P. BN 179–81, IV, 18 = P. Denon, V, 9 = P. Louvre E 8079 + 11080, IV, 15–16 = P. Louvre N 3083, VIII, 18–19 = P. Louvre N 3121, IV, 2 = P. Louvre N 3126, III, 16 = P. Louvre N 3158, IX, 3 = P. Louvre N 3167 + 3222, III, 16 = P. Louvre N 3284, V, 5 = P. Louvre N 3285, IV, 5. Sequence omitted in P. Louvre E 11079, III = P. Louvre N 3166, III, 29 = P. Tübingen 2016, V, 14 = P. Vienna 3863, IV, 3; in lacuna in P. Florence 3665 + Vienna 3850, V, [17]. Var. P. Lausanne 3391, III, 23 = P. Vienna 3931, III, 22: *nn mtr ꜥḥꜥ ir.s*; P. Louvre N 3291, 46–7: *nn mtr nb r.f*.

For the expression *mtr r*, 'testify concerning' (but not necessarily 'against'): A.H. Gardiner, *Egyptian Hieratic Texts* (Leiden 1911), p. 22*, n. 17; B. van de Walle, *CdE* 83 (1967), p. 23.[136] For *ꜥḥꜥ* + preposition: Smith, *Mortuary Texts*, p. 127 (XII, 15, b). This witness might perhaps be the heart of the deceased (*BD* ch. 30 B [ed. Budge, p. 96, 2]):

ib.i n mwt.i sp 2	'O my *ib*-heart of my mother (*bis*),
ḥꜣty.i n ḫprw.i	my *ḥꜣty*-heart of my existence,
m ꜥḥꜥ r.i m mtr	do not stand against me as witness,
m ḫsf r.i m ḏꜣḏꜣ	do not oppose me in the tribunal,
m irt rky.k r.i	do not make yourself tilt (the balance) against me,
m-bꜣḥ iry mḫꜣt	in the presence of the keeper of the balance.'

The witness might also be the ba of the deceased (*BD*, ed. Budge, p. 16, 1–2 [no chapter specified]). Thoth says:

iw wḏꜥ.n.i ib n Wsir	'I have judged the heart of Osiris.
iw bꜣ.f ꜥḥꜥ m mtr r.f	His ba stands for him as witness,
sp.f mꜣꜥ ḥr mḫꜣt wr	his conduct is just on the great balance.
n gm.n.tw btꜣ.f nb	No fault has been found in him.'[137]

VII, 3

ꜥnḫ.f m Mꜣꜥt sꜥm.f m Mꜣꜥt. Same reading in P. BM EA 9995, III, 13 = P. BM EA 10260, III, x + 11–12 = P. Berlin 3154, II, 21 = P. Lausanne 3391, III, 23–4 = P. Louvre N 3083, VIII, 19 = P. Louvre N 3121, IV, 2 = P. Louvre N 3126, III, 16 = P. Louvre N 3158, IX, 3 = P. Louvre N 3167 + 3222, III, 16–17 = P. Louvre N 3284, V, 5 = P. Louvre N 3291, 47 = P. Tübingen 2016, V, 14. Sequence omitted in P. Louvre E 11079, III; wholly in lacuna in P. Vienna 3863, III, and partly in P. Florence 3665 + P. Vienna 3850, V, 17; partly rubbed out in P. Vienna 3931, III, 22 = P. Louvre N 3285, IV, 6. Var. P. Berlin 3135, IV, 13: *n Mꜣꜥt* (twice); P. BN 179–81, IV, 18 = P. Louvre E 8079 + 11080, IV, 17; *sꜥm.f n Mꜣꜥt*. Cf. also the title of P. Louvre N 3166, cited *supra*, **I, 1–3**.

For the expression *sꜥm m Mꜣꜥt*, cf. *BD* ch. 126, 2 (ed. Lepsius); Seeber, *Untersuchungen*, p. 139. On the nourishing function (*sꜥm, snm*) of Maat, see J. Zandee, *JEOL* 27 (1981–2), p. 15; Assmann, *Sonnenhymnen*, p. 249, line 12; F. Labrique, *Stylistique et théologie à Edfou* (*OLA* 51, 1992), p. 205; cf. also *nkꜣ m Mꜣꜥt*, *BD* ch. 85 (ed. Budge, p. 184, 5–6), cited in the commentary of P. BM EA 10114, **lines 6–7**. For the association *ꜥnḫ / sꜥm* (*snm*) *Mꜣꜥt*, cf. Maspero, *Sarcophages* I, p. 39: *inḏ-ḥr.tn nṯrw* (...)*ꜥnḫw m Mꜣꜥt m Iwnw sꜥmw m Mꜣꜥt m-bꜣḥ-ꜥ n nṯr imy itn.f*, 'Hail to you, gods (...) who live on Maat in Heliopolis, feed on Maat in the presence of the god who is in his disk'.

ḥr nṯrw ḥr ir.n.f nb. Same reading in P. BM EA 9995, III, 13–14 = P. BM EA 10260, III, x + 12 = P. Berlin 3135, IV, 14 = P. Berlin 3154, II, 21 = P. BN 179–81, IV, 19 (*nbw*) = P. Denon, V, 9–10 = P. Florence 3665 + P. Vienna 3850, V, 18 = P. Louvre E 8079 + 11080, IV, 17–18 = P. Louvre N 3083, VIII, 19 = P. Louvre N 3121, IV, 3 = P. Louvre N 3126, III, 16 = P. Louvre N 3158, IX, 3–4 = P. Louvre N 3167 + 3222, III, 17 = P. Louvre N 3284, V, 5 = P. Louvre N 3291, 47–8. Sequence omitted in P. Louvre E 11079, III = P. Tübingen 2016, V, 14; in lacuna in P. Vienna 3863, III, partly rubbed out in P. Louvre N 3285, IV, 6. P. Lausanne 3391, III, 24 = P. Vienna 3931, III, 23: *ḥr nṯrw ḥr ir.s nb*.

In the tomb chapel of Petosiris (no. 70, 4–5, cited *supra*, **VII, 2**), the absence of fault in the deceased and of accusation against him leads to the contentment of the gods (*ḥr nṯrw ḥr.s ꜥn*). That phrase, like the following, is excerpted from *BD* ch. 125; cf. also A. Varille, *BIFAO* 30 (1930), p. 503: *iw ir.n.i ḥsst rmṯ hrr nṯrw ḥr.s*, 'I have done what people praise and all that the gods rejoice in it', and H. Ranke, *ZÄS* 44 (1907), p. 43, n. 1.

VII, 3–4

ir.n.f tꜣ n ḥkr mw n ib ḥbs n ḥꜣy. Same reading in P. BM EA 10260, III, x + 12 = P. BN 179–81, IV, 19–20 = P. Lausanne 3391, III, 24–5 = P. Louvre E 8079 + 11080, IV, 18 = P. Louvre N 3083, VIII, 19–20 = P. Louvre N 3121, IV, 3 = P. Vienna 3931, III, 23–4. Sequence omitted in P. Louvre E 11079, III = P. Tübingen 2016, V; partly in lacuna in P. Vienna 3863, III, ult.–IV, 1; partly rubbed out in P. Louvre N 3285, IV, 7; corrupt in P. Denon, V, 10. Var. P. BM EA 9995, III, 14 = P. Berlin 3135, IV, 14 = P. Berlin 3154, II, 21 = P. Florence 3665 + P. Vienna 3850, V, 18 = P. Louvre N 3126, III, 16 = P. Louvre N 3158, IX, 4 = P. Louvre N 3167 + 3222, III, 17 = P. Louvre N 3284, V, 6 = P. Louvre N 3285, IV, 7 = P. Louvre N 3291, 48: *rdi.n.f /.s tꜣ*; P. Louvre N 3166, III, 29: (*r*)*di.f tꜣ*.

On this cliché, often attested in autobiographies, see J.M.A. Janssen, *De Traditioneele egyptische Autobiographie vóór het Nieuwe Rijk* I (Leiden 1946), pp. 78–80.

ir.f ḥtpw n nṯrw prt-ḫrw n ꜣḫw. Sequence omitted in P. Louvre E 11079, III = P. Tübingen 2016, V; corrupt in P. Denon, V, 10. Var. P. Louvre N 3158, IX, 4–5 = P. Louvre N 3166, III, 30: *ir.n.f /.s ḥtpw n nṯrw prt-ḫrw n ꜣḫw*; P. Louvre N 3083, VIII, 19–20 = P. Louvre N 3126, III, 17: *ir.n.f /.s ḥtpw n nṯrw prt-ḫrw n nꜣ ꜣḫw*; P. Lausanne 3391, III, 25 = P. Louvre N 3285, IV, 8[138] = P. Vienna 3931, III, 24: *di.f /.s ḥtpw nṯrw prt-ḫrw n nꜣ ꜣḫw*; P. BN 179–81, IV, 20–1 = P. Florence 3665 + P. Vienna 3850, V, 19–20 = P. Louvre E 8079 + 11080, IV, 18–19 = P. Louvre N 3167 + 3222, III, 18 = P. Louvre N 3284, V, 6 = P. Vienna 3863, IV, 1: *di.f /.s ḥtpw n nṯrw*[139] *prt-ḫrw n nꜣ ꜣḫw*; P. Berlin 3154, II, 22 = P. Louvre N 3291, 49–50: *di.f ḥtpw n nṯrw prt-ḫrw n ꜣḫw*; P. BM EA 10260, III, x + 12–13: *di.f ḥtpw n nꜣ nṯrw prt-ḫrw n nꜣ ꜣḫw*; P. BM EA 9995, III, 15 = P. Louvre N 3121, IV, 3–4: *di.f /.s ḥtpw n nꜣ nṯrw prt-ḫrw n ꜣḫw*; P. Berlin 3135, IV, 15–16: *di.f tꜣ* <*n*> *nꜣ nṯrw prt-ḫrw n nꜣ ꜣḫw*.

For this phrase, see *LPE*, p. 272; J. Assmann, *Der König als Sonnenpriester* (Glückstadt 1970), pp. 19 and 36, §§ 22–3.

The mythological papyrus Louvre N 3292 (Third Intermediate Period), gives a similar version, in a context identical to that of P. BM EA 10048: G. Nagel, *BIFAO* 29 (1929), p. 87 (S, 3–4):

136. A good illustration of this expression in Lefebvre, *Petosiris* II, p. 45, no. 70, 4: *nn ḏw r.i nn mtr r.i*, 'There is no evil against me, there is no witness against me'; ibid., p. 75, no. 102, 4–6: *i ḥmw-nṯr wꜥbw n Ḏḥwty* (...) *ink s n dm rn.f irt nfr irt n.f ḏw mitt Ḏḥwty m mtr r.tn* 'O prophets and *wꜥb*-priests of Thoth (...), I am a man whose name is uttered; he who acts well (towards me), will be treated (well); he who acts ill (towards me), (will be treated) likewise, and Thoth will be a witness against you.'

137. On the ba standing (as witness) in favour of the deceased, see also A.W. Shorter, *JEA* 23 (1937), p. 35; Seeber, *Untersuchungen*, p. 107, with n. 406.

138. Passage rubbed out after *nṯrw*, but probable traces of *nꜣ* before [*ꜣḫw*].

139. Note the writing 𓊹𓊹𓊹𓊹 of *nṯrw* in P. Berlin 3154, the first three being hieroglyphic, the last one hieratic; see *supra*, n. 46.

ỉw rdỉ.f tꜣ n ḥkr ḥbs n ḥꜣw	'He has given bread to the hungry, clothing to the naked,
rdỉ.f prt-ḫrw n ꜣḫw	he has given invocation offerings to the spirits,
srwḏ.f ḥtpw-nṯr n nṯrw	and has secured the divine *ḥtpw*-offerings for the gods.'

VII, 4

nn ỉr.tw smỉ nb r.f m-bꜣḥ nṯrw nbw. Same reading in P. BM EA 9995, III, 15–16 = P. BM EA 10260, III, x + 13 = P. Berlin 3135, IV, 16 (*nṯrw nb*) = P. Berlin 3154, II, 22 = P. BN 179–81, IV, 21 = P. Florence 3665 + P. Vienna 3850, V, 20 = P. Louvre E 8079 + 11080, IV, 19 = P. Louvre N 3083, VIII, 21 = P. Louvre N 3121, IV, 4 (*nṯrw nb*) = P. Louvre N 3126, III, 17 = P. Louvre N 3158, IX, 5 = P. Louvre N 3167 + 3222, III, 18 = P. Louvre N 3284, V, 6–7. Sequence omitted in P. Denon, V = P. Louvre E 11079, III = P. Louvre N 3166, III = P. Tübingen 2016, V. Var. P. BN 179–81, IV, 21 = P. Louvre N 3291, 50: *nn ỉr.tw smỉ r.f.* Omission of *nbw* in P. BN 179–81, IV, 21 = P. Lausanne 3391, III, 26 = P. Vienna 3931, III, 25. P. Louvre N 3285, IV, 9 = P. Vienna 3863, IV, 2: *ỉr.f* for *r.f.* Addition of *ỉw.f ỉw ḫr.tn nn ḏw nb ḫr.f nn ỉsft nb ḫr.f* in P. Vienna 3863, IV, 2–3; of *ỉ(w).s ỉỉ* (var.: *ỉw*) *ḫr.tn* in P. Lausanne 3391, III, 26 = P. Louvre N 3285, IV, 9 = P. Vienna 3931, III, 25; see *supra,* **VII, 2**.

Following this phrase, P. Louvre N 3121 appends a substantial, unparalleled passage (IV, 4–VII, 3), with invocations to the gods of Egypt in geographical order (from south to north).[140]

mỉ ʿḳ.f r Dwꜣt nn šnʿ.tw.f mỉ šms.f Wsỉr ḥnʿ nṯrw ḳrtyw. Same reading in P. BM EA 9995, III, 16–17 = P. BM EA 10260, III, x + 13–14 = P. Berlin 3135, IV, 17–18 = P. Denon, V, 10–12 = P. Florence 3665 + P. Vienna 3850, V, 21–2 = P. Lausanne 3391, III, 26–7 = P. Louvre E 8079 + 11080, IV, 19–20 = P. Louvre N 3126, III, 17–18 = P. Louvre N 3284, V, 7–8 = P. Vienna 3863, IV, 3–4. Sequence omitted in P. Tübingen 2016, V. Omission of *mỉ šms.f Wsỉr ḥnʿ nṯrw ḳrtyw* from P. Louvre N 3166, III. Var. P. Louvre N 3083, VIII, 21–2 = P. Louvre N 3158, IX, 6 = P. Louvre N 3166, III, 30 = P. Vienna 3931, III, 26: *nn šnʿ.f /.s*; P. Berlin 3154, II, 23 = P. BN 179–81, IV, 23 = P. Louvre N 3083, VIII, 22 = P. Louvre N 3167 + 3222, III, 19 = P. Louvre N 3285, IV, 11: *ḳrty*; P. Louvre N 3291, 51: *mỉ sḏr.f ḥnʿ Wsỉr ḥnʿ nṯrw ḳrtyw*, 'May he spend the night with Osiris, with the gods of the caverns'. P. Louvre E 11079, III, 4–5: *mỉ ʿḳ.s ...* (?) *mỉ šms<.s> Wsỉr ḫnty Ỉmntt*, 'May she enter ... (?) may she follow Osiris foremost of the West'.

For gods of caverns as guides: *LPE*, p. 106 (I, 21).

VII, 4–5

ỉw.f ḥs.tw m-m ḥs(y)w nṯr.tw m-m ỉḳrw. Same reading in P. Louvre N 3158, IX, 6–7.[141] Sequence omitted in P. Louvre E 11079, III = P. Louvre N 3083, VIII = P. Louvre N 3166, III = P. Tübingen 2016, V. Omission of *.tw* after *nṯr* in P. Denon, V, 12. Var. P. BM EA 9995, III, 17–18 = P. BM EA 10260, III, x + 14 = P. Berlin 3135, IV, 18–19 = P. Berlin 3154, II, 23 = P. Florence 3665 + P. Vienna 3850, V, 22 = P. Lausanne 3391, III, 27–8 = P. Louvre E 8079 + 11080, IV, 12 = P. Louvre N 3167 + 3222, III, 20 = P. Louvre N 3284, V, 8 = P. Louvre N 3285, IV, 11–12 = P. Vienna 3863, IV, 4–5 = P. Vienna 3931, III, 27–8: *ỉw.f /.s ḥs, ỉw.f /.s nṯr*; omission of *ỉw.f* before *nṯr* in P. BN 179–81, IV, 24 = P. Louvre E 8079 + 11080, IV, 20. P. BN 179–81, IV, 23–4 = P. Florence 3665 + P. Vienna 3850, V, 22 = P. Louvre N 3126, III, 18 = P. Louvre N 3291, 51 = P. Vienna 3863, IV, 5: *m-ʿ ḥs(y)w*; P. Louvre N 3285, IV, 12: *mỉ ḥs(y)w*; P. Louvre N 3284, V, 8: *m-ʿ*[142] *ʿnḫw, m-ʿ ỉḳrw*; P. Vienna 3931, III, 28: *mỉ nṯrw*[143] for *ỉḳrw*; P. Vienna 3863, IV, 5: *mỉ <ỉ>ḳrw*; P. Lausanne 3391, III, 28: *mỉ ỉḳrw*; P. BN 179–81, IV, 24: *n-m* (written ) *ỉḳrw.*

For the *ḥsyw*: R. El-Sayed, *BIFAO* 79 (1979), p. 185, n. (be), and P. BM EA 10260, I, x + 4–5, for the relation between the *ḥsyw* and the excellent ones.

VII, 5

mỉ ʿnḫ.f mỉ ʿnḫ ỉb.f. Same version in P. Louvre N 3083, VIII, 22–3. Sequence omitted in P. Louvre N 3166, III = P. Tübingen 2016, V. Var. P. BM EA 9995, III, 18 = P. BM EA 10260, III, x + 14 = P. Berlin 3135, IV, 19 = P. Berlin 3154, II, 23–4 = P. BN 179–81, IV, 24 = P. Denon, V, 13 = P. Florence 3665 + P. Vienna 3850, V, 23 (with omission of the second *ʿnḫ*) = P. Lausanne 3391, III, 28 = P. Louvre E 8079 + 11080, IV, 21 = P. Louvre E 11079, III, 6 = P. Louvre N 3126, III, 19 = P. Louvre N 3158, IX, 7 = P. Louvre N 3284, V, 8 = P. Louvre N 3285, IV, 12–13 = P. Louvre N 3291, 52 = P. Vienna 3863, IV, 5–6 = P. Vienna 3931, III, 29: *mỉ ʿnḫ.f / .s mỉ ʿnḫ bꜣ.f /.s*, 'May he live, may his ba live'; P. Louvre N 3167 + 3222, III, 20: *mỉ ʿnḫ bꜣ.s mỉ ʿnḫ.s m wḥm*, 'May his ba live, may she live again'. P. Tübingen 2016, V, 14: *mỉ ʿnḫ bꜣ.f r nḥḥ ḏt*, 'May his ba live for ever and eternally'.

On the variant *bꜣ* instead of *ỉb*, see *supra,* **II, 5**.

Most of the manuscripts cited here place after this sequence a short phrase omitted in P. BM EA 10048, as well as P. Louvre E 11079, III, P. Louvre N 3083, VIII and P. Louvre N 3158, IX: *šsp* (var.: *ỉṯ*) *bꜣ.f /.s r bw nb*[144] *mr.f /.s* (var.: *mrwt.f /.s*), 'His ba is received wheresoever he wishes', attested in P. BM EA 9995, III, 18–19 = P. BM EA 10260, III, x + 14–15 = P. Berlin 3135, IV, 20 = P. Berlin 3154, II, 24 = P. BN 179–81, IV, 25 = P. Florence 3665 + P. Vienna 3850, V, 23–4 = P. Lausanne 3391, III, 28 = P. Louvre E 8079 + 11080, IV, 21 = P. Louvre N 3126, III, 19 = P. Louvre N 3167 + 3222, III, 21 = P. Louvre N 3284, V, 8–9 = P. Louvre N 3285, IV, 13 = P. Louvre N 3291, 52 = P. Vienna 3863, IV, 6 = P. Vienna 3931, III, 29–30.

šsp tꜣy.f šʿt n snsn. Same reading in P. BM EA 10260, III, x + 15 = P. BN 179–81, 25–6 = P. Denon, V, 14 = P. Florence 3665 + P. Vienna 3850, V, 24 = P. Louvre E 8079 + 11080, IV, 21–2 = P. Louvre N 3126, III, 19 = P. Louvre N 3158, IX, 7–8 = P. Louvre N 3167 + 3222, III, 21 = P. Louvre N 3284, V, 9 = P. Louvre N 3291, 52 = P. Vienna 3931, III, 30. Sequence omitted in P. Louvre N 3166, III = P. Tübingen 2016, V. Omission of *n* before *snsn* in P. Louvre N 3285, IV, 14 = P. Vienna 3863, IV, 7; of *n snsn* in P. Lausanne 3391, III, 29. Var. P. BM EA 9995, III, 19: *šsp tꜣ šʿt n snsn*; P. Berlin 3154, II, 24: *ỉṯ* instead of *šsp*; P. Louvre N 3083, VIII, 23: *šsp.n.s ʿnḫ m wḏwt n Rʿ*, 'She has received life by order of Re'; P. Berlin 3135, IV, 20–1: *šsp ḫꜣtyw.f*[145] *šʿt n snsn*, 'His *ḫꜣtyw*-demons (*sic*) have received the Book of Breathing'.

VII, 5–6

mỉ ỉr.f snsn ḥnʿ bꜣw ʿꜣw nw Dwꜣt. Same version in P. Louvre N 3158, IX, 8. Sequence omitted in P. Louvre E 11079, IV = P. Louvre E 11079, IV = P. Louvre N 3166, III = P. Tübingen 2016, V. Var. P. BM EA 9995, III, 20: *ḥnʿ bꜣ.f pwy n Dwꜣt*; P. BM EA 10260, III, x + 15 = P. Berlin 3135, IV, 21–2 = P. Berlin 3154, II, 24 = P. BN 179–81, IV, 26 = P. Denon, V, 15 =

140. F.R. Herbin, *BIFAO* 84 (1984), p. 250, n. 3, and id., *RdE* 50 (1999), pp. 150–4.
141. Note the writing 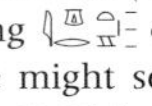 of *ỉḳrw.*
142. Otherwise one might see here a faulty version of ; cf. P. Florence 3665 + P. Vienna 3850, V, 23 in *m-m ỉḳrw.*
143. At first the scribe wrote the of *ỉḳrw,* which he then rubbed out. Its replacement by  is not certain, but the following signs:  leave no doubt as to the word to be read, despite the rather extraordinary writing of *nṯrw.*
144. Omission of *nb* in P. Berlin 3135.
145. Written . See A.M. Blackman and H.W. Fairman, *JEA* 29 (1943), p. 22.

P. Florence 3665 + P. Vienna 3850, V, 25 = P. Lausanne 3391, III, 29 = P. Louvre E 8079 + 11080, IV, 22 = P. Louvre N 3126, III, 20 = P. Louvre N 3284, V, 9–10 = P. Louvre N 3285, IV, 14–15 = P. Louvre N 3291, 53 = P. Vienna 3863, IV, 8: *ḥnꜥ bꜣ.f pfy n Dwꜣt*; P. Louvre N 3167 + 3222, III, 22: *ḥnꜥ bꜣ pfy n Dwꜣt*, 'with this ba of the Duat' (or erroneous omission of suffix *.s* after *bꜣ* ?); P. Vienna 3931, 30–1: *mi ir.f* [*snsn m*][146] *m Dwꜣt*; P. Louvre N 3083, VIII, 23: *mi ir.s snsn ḥnꜥ.tn*.

VII, 6

ḥnꜥ ir ḫpr nb r-dit ib.f mi Ỉmntyw. Same version in P. BN 179–81, IV, 27 (*ḫprw nbw*) = P. Denon, VI, 1 = P. Louvre E 8079 + 11080, IV, 22–3 (*ḫprw nb*) = P. Louvre E 8079 + 11080, IV, 15–16 = P. Louvre N 3158, IX, 8–9 = P. Louvre N 3291, 53. Sequence omitted in P. Louvre E 11079, IV = P. Louvre N 3083, VIII = P. Tübingen 2016, V, and partly rubbed out in P. Vienna 3931, III, 31–2; partly in lacuna in P. Louvre N 3285, IV, 16. Var. P. Louvre N 3167 + 3222, III, 22: *r mrwt ib.s*, 'according to the wish of his heart'. P. Louvre N 3166, III, 31: *mi ir.f ḫpr r-dit ib.f*; P. BM EA 9995, III, 21 = P. BM EA 10260, III, x + 16 = P. Berlin 3135, IV, 22 = P. Berlin 3154, II, 25 = P. Florence 3665 + P. Vienna 3850, V, 26 = P. Lausanne 3391, III, 30 = P. Louvre N 3126, III, 20 = P. Louvre N 3167 + 3222, III, 22 = P. Louvre N 3284, V, 10 = P. Vienna 3863, IV, 9: *ḥnꜥ Ỉmntyw*.

VII, 6–7

mi šm bꜣ.f r bw nb mrwt.f iw wnn.f ꜥnḫ mi ḳy ꜥnḫ ḥr-tp tꜣ r nḥḥ sp 2 ḏt sp 2. Same version in P. Louvre N 3158, IX, 9. Sequence omitted in P. Louvre E 11079, IV; almost wholly destroyed in P. Vienna 3931, III, 32–3. Omission of *mrwt.f* (ou *mr.f*) in P. BM EA 9995, III, 21 = P. BM EA 10260, III, x + 16 = P. Berlin 3154, II, 25. Var. P. Berlin 3135, IV, 23 = P. Tübingen V, 15: *r bw nb mr.f*. P. Denon, VI, 2: *r mrwt.f*. P. Louvre N 3166, III, 31–2: *iw wn.f mi ḳy.f ꜥnḫ ḥr-tp tꜣ iṯ nn ir n.k Wsir N r nḥḥ sp 2 ḏt sp 2*, 'That he may be as in his form in life on earth. Receive what has been made for you, Osiris N, for ever (*bis*) and eternally (*bis*)'. P. Berlin 3135, IV, 23–4 = P. Florence 3665 + P. Vienna 3850, V, 26–7 = P. Louvre N 3126, III, 21 = P. Louvre N 3284, V, 10–11:[147] *mi wn(n).f ꜥnḫ.tw ḥr-tp tꜣ r nḥḥ sp 2 ḏt sp 2*,[148] 'As he was when alive on earth for ever (*bis*) and eternally (*bis*)'. P. BM EA 9995, III, 21–2 = P. Berlin 3154, II, 25 = P. BN 179–81, IV, 28 = P. Denon, VI, 2–3 = P. Lausanne 3391, III, 30 = P. Louvre E 8079 + 11080, IV, 23 = P. Louvre N 3291, 46–7[149] = P. Vienna 3863, IV, 9–10: *iw wn.f* / *.s ꜥnḫ*[150] *ḥr-tp tꜣ r nḥḥ sp 2 ḏt sp 2*. Same version, without the initial *iw*, in P. BM EA 10260, III, x + 16 = P. Louvre N 3167 + 3222, III, 23: *wn.f ꜥnḫ ḥr-tp tꜣ r nḥḥ sp 2 ḏt sp 2*. P. Louvre N 3285, IV, 18: [...] *r nḥḥ sp 2 r ḏt sp 2*. *P.* Tübingen 2016, V, 15: *wn m ꜥnḫ ḥr-tp tꜣ r nḥḥ sp 2 ḏt sp 2*; P. Louvre N 3083, IX, 1: *iw wnn.s ꜥnḫ mi ḳy.s ḥr-tp tꜣ r nḥḥ ḏt*.[151]

For *mi ḳy ꜥnḫ ḥr-tp tꜣ*, exact equivalent of *mi wnn.f ꜥnḫ.tw ḥr-tp tꜣ* (P. Louvre N 3284, V, 10–11), see *supra*, **III, 1**: *wḥm.k ḳy.k ḥr-tp tꜣ m ꜥnḫ*, and *LPE*, p. 248 (VIII, 3).

146. The lack of space in the lacuna permits no other restoration. For the idea, cf. N. de G. Davies and A.H. Gardiner, *The Tomb of Antefoḳer* (1920), pl. 35, no. 15: *snsn m-m Dwꜣt*.
147. Note the writing  of *mi* in P. Louvre N 3284.
148. Written *ḏt ḏt* in P. Berlin 3154, which adds (II, 26–8) § 14 *bis* of de Horrack's classification.
149. This sequence is followed by the final formula *iw.f pw nfr n tꜣ šꜥt n snsn n N*.
150. All the documents cited, except P. Vienna 3863, present a flexional ending .
151. This text is followed by an extract of a ritual of the torch, on which see F.R. Herbin, *BIFAO* 84 (1984), pp. 249–50, with n. 3, and id., *RdE* 50 (1999), pp. 156–7.

P. BM EA 9995 (pls 15–24)

Clot Collection.

Quirke, *Owners*, no. 102.

Budge, *Book of the Dead. Facsimiles of the Papyri of Hunefer, Anhai, Kerasher and Netchemet* (London 1899), pp. 39–43 and pls I–III.

Provenance: Thebes.

Date: Reign of Augustus.[152]

Owner of the papyrus: *Gr-šr* (, ) (Kalasiris).[153]

Title: *rpꜥ-ḥꜣt-p-ꜥ*, 'nomarch'.[154]

Mother of the owner: *Tꜣ-snt-snty* (Tsonesontis),[155] everywhere written  except  in IV, 1 and final vignette.

Contents: Book of Breathing made by Isis for her brother Osiris

Gr-šr is also known from a demotic graffito in Medinet Habu (H.J. Thissen, *Die demotischen Graffiti von Medinet Habu* [*DemSt* 10, 1989], no. 43,[156] and from the stela from the Bucheum no. 13 (= Copenhagen ÆIN 1681), which gives his father's name: *Pꜣ-Mnṯw-pꜣ-ryn* (Pamonthes-Plenis). According to Thissen (*ZPE* 27 [1977], p. 188), he may be identified with 'Kalasiris son of Pamonthes, strategus', known on the demotic ostracon Medinet Habu 1769 (M. Lichtheim, *Demotic Ostraca from Medinet Habu* [Chicago 1957], no. 125).

Large manuscript divided into four sheets, written in hieratic, except for the legends accompanying the vignettes, and the two lines of text of the third sheet, written in hieroglyphs. There is no text on the verso.

Sheet 1 (70 × 23.5 cm): introduction of the deceased to Osiris. The picture is surmounted by a double painting of the winged disc, one above the other. A legend, repeated either side of the smaller of them, describes it as , 'He of Behedet, the great god, the many-coloured of plumage, he who comes forth from the horizon'.

In the left part of the vignette, and facing a bunch of lotus flowers, Osiris and Isis are depicted within a shrine whose

152. J. Quaegebeur, *GM* 119 (1990), p. 86 with n. 82.
153. On this name: M. Müller, *ZÄS* 26 (1888), p. 83.
154. P. BM EA 9995, IV, 1. This title occurs again in the legend of the deceased at the end of the manuscript (*infra*, p. 40), written . Everywhere else, the name *Gr-šr* is only preceded by the designation 'Osiris'. See J. Quaegebeur, in *Aspekte spätägyptischer Kultur* (Fs. Erich Winter) (*AegTrev* 7, 1994), p. 215.
155. J. Quaegebeur, *CdE* 91 (1971), pp. 158–72.
156. See also M. Chauveau, *RdE* 46 (1995), p. 252.

cornice is decorated with a frieze of uraei. The god, enthroned, is wrapped in a large cloak. He wears the *ꜣtf*-crown and, with his hands clasped over his chest, holds the *ḥḳꜣ*-sceptre and the flail. His name and titles are given in a legend written in three columns: ??, 'Osiris, god (?) of Djeme, king of the gods, great god lord of Heliopolis ...(?)'.[157]

Standing behind Osiris, her head covered by the symbol , Isis stretches out her left arm, while her right hand hangs along her body, holding the cross ☥. The legend reads: ?? , 'Isis the great, mother of the god, foremost of the West ...(?) Djeme'.

In front of the two divinities is a large bouquet of lotus. Outside the shrine, the four sons of Horus, Amset, Hapi, Duamutef and Qebehsenuf appear, standing on a lotus-flower. Their names are inscribed in four columns above them. Two pedestal tables separate them from the shrine of Osiris; behind them, a richly provided table of offerings is pictured.

The right half of the vignette shows the deceased, clothed with a loose white garment knotted at chest level, between Anubis bearing the *pschent*, qualified as , 'Embalmer, lord of the sacred land', and a cow-headed goddess with a human body – probably Hathor[158] – whose legend is practically illegible.[159] Preceding these three figures, Thoth, ibis-headed and wearing an elaborated *ꜣtf*-crown, raises his right arm in salutation to Osiris and Isis. Between Thoth and Anubis two columns of text containing the general title of the picture are to be read as an invocation to the deceased:  'Come! Enter the place where your father is;[160] he has placed you at the head of[161] the praised ones'.[162]

Sheet 2 (54 × 23.5 cm) bears three pages of hieratic text (respectively 24, 25 and 22 lines) and containing a version of the Book of Breathing made by Isis.

Translation

I (1) Hail Osiris *Gr-šr* born of *Tꜣ-snt-snty*, you are pure, your *ḥꜣty*-heart is pure, your *ib*-heart is pure, your fore is pure, (2) your rear is pure, your middle (is purified) with *bd*-natron and *ḥsmn*-natron, and there is no limb in you in a state of evil.

The Osiris *Gr*-(3)*šr* born of *Tꜣ-snt-snty*, is pure in this pool of the Field of offerings, to the north of the Field of (4) locusts. Wadjyt and Nekhbet purify you in the eighth hour of the night and in the <eighth> hour of the day. Come then, Osiris, (5) *Gr-šr* born of *Tꜣ-snt-snty*! You enter the hall of the two Maats, (for) you are pure from any fault and any crime! (6) 'Stone of Maat' is your name.

Hail Osiris *Gr-šr* born of *Tꜣ-snt-snty*, you enter the Duat in great purity. (7) The two Maats purify you in the great hall, and purification is made for you in the hall of Geb. Your limbs are purified (8) in the hall of light, and you see Re when he sets, Atum in the evening. Amun is with you, giving you breath. (9) Ptah fashions your limbs. You enter the horizon with Re. Your ba is received on board the *nšmt*-bark with Osiris. (10) Your ba is divinized in the House of Geb, and <you> are justified for ever and eternally.

(O) Osiris *Gr-šr* born of *Tꜣ-snt-snty*, (11) your name is established, your corpse stable, your mummy firm, (so that) you will not be turned back in the sky or on earth. Your face is illuminated before (12) Re, your ba lives before Amun, your corpse is renewed before Osiris, and you breathe for ever and eternally.

Your son performs for you an invocation offering (13) of bread, beer, cattle and fowl, with libation and censing, in the course of every day. You come at his voice and your flesh is on your bones (14) according to your form upon earth. You drink with your throat and you eat with your mouth. You receive *snw*-loaves with the bas (15) of the gods. Anubis protects you and makes your protection, (so that) will not be turned back from the entrances of the Duat.

Thoth the twice (16) great, lord of Hermopolis, comes to you; he writes for you a Book of Breathing, with his own fingers, and your heart breathes for(17)ever. You repeat the form which was yours upon earth as a living man. You are divine with the bas of the gods. Your heart is the heart of Re, your (18) limbs are the limbs of the great god.

Hail Osiris *Gr-šr* born of *Tꜣ-snt-snty*, Amun is with you, (19) renewing you alive. Wepwawet opens for you a good way. You see with your eyes, hear with your ears, speak with your mouth, (20) walk with your legs. Your ba is divine in the Duat, assuming any form you desire. You receive the freshness of (21) the noble balanites-tree in Heliopolis. You are awakened every day and you see the rays of Re (or: of the disk). Amun comes to you, (22) full of the breath of life. He causes you to breathe within the coffin. You go out upon earth every day. The Book of Breathing of (23) Thoth is your protection; you breathe by it every day. Your eyes see the rays of the disc. 'Maat' is said concerning you in the presence of Osiris, (24) and Maat is written on your tongue. Harendotes protects your body; he divinizes your ba like (that of)

157. One expects here: *Iwnw šmʿ*, 'Heliopolis of the South' = Karnak.
158. On this iconography: J. Berlandini, *BIFAO* 81 (1981), p. 15 with n. 4.
159. Like above in the legends of Osiris and Isis, the dark green shade of some columns has damaged the black ink of the inscriptions, making their reading uncertain or impossible.
160. *it.f*, by mistake for *it.k*.
161. Rather than *m-ḫnw* (Budge, op. cit.,p. 34. For *m tp n ḥsyw*, see *infra*, **IV, 2**.
162. See *infra*, **IV, 2**.

every god. The Ba of II (1) Re makes your ba live, and the Ba of Shu joins your nostrils.

Hail Osiris *Gr-šr* (2) born of *Tꜣ-snt-snty*, your ba breathes in every place you desire. You are Osiris, and 'Osiris foremost of the West' is your name. (3) Hapy the great comes to you from Elephantine; he fills your offering-table with food. Osiris *Gr-*(4)*šr* born of *Tꜣ-snt-snty*, the gods of Upper and Lower Egypt come to you, guiding you towards (5) Areqheh. Your ba lives, and you follow Osiris. You breathe in Rosetau, (6) and Hapounnebes protects you together with the great god. Your corpse lives in Busiris and Ta-wer. Your ba lives in (7) the sky every day. Osiris *Gr-šr* born of *Tꜣ-snt-snty*, Sekhmet controls those who plot against you. Horus great-(8)-of-hearts (i.e. magnanimous) makes your protection, and Horus of Shedet carries out your wish. Hor-merty guards your body – otherwise said: (9) your tongue –, and you are stable in life, prosperity and health; you are established on your throne, in the sacred land. Come then, Osiris *Gr-šr* (10) born of *Tꜣ-snt-snty*: you are arisen in your forms, complete with your ornaments. You spend the night in life, you spend the day (11) in health. You walk, breathing in every place, and Re shines over your domain as (over) Osiris. You breathe, (12) you live on his rays. Amun-Re-Horakhty, he makes your ka live and makes you flourish by the Book of Breathing. (13) You follow Horus, lord of the *ḥnw*-bark; you are the great god among the gods; your face is living, your births are good, your name (14) endures, every day. You enter the very large god's booth in Busiris, you see Khenty-menty at the *wꜣg*-festival. Your odour (15) is sweet among the praised ones, and your name is great among the mummies.

Hail Osiris *Gr-šr* born of (16) *Tꜣ-snt-snty*, your ba lives by the Book of Breathing, you unite with the Book of Breathing. (17) You enter the Duat, and your enemies exist no more. You are a living ba in Busiris. Your heart belongs to you and will not be far from you. Your eyes (18) belong to you, open every day.

To be recited by the gods who are in the retinue of Osiris, for the Osiris *Gr-šr* born of *Tꜣ-*(19)*snt-snty*: you follow Re, you follow Osiris, and your ba is alive for ever and eternally.

To be recited by the gods who are in the Duat (20) to Osiris foremost of the West, for the Osiris *Gr-šr* born of *Tꜣ-snt-snty* , <so that> there may be opened for him the gates of (21) the Duat! May he receive you (*sic*) in the god's domain! May his ba live for ever! May he build portals (22) in the god's domain! May his ka praise his god, (for) he has received a Book of Breathing. May he indeed (23) breathe!

Offering that the king gives to Osiris foremost of the West, the great god, lord of Abydos, that he may grant an invocation offering of bread, (24) beer, oxen, fowl, wine, milk, *ḥtpw*-offerings and food, all things good, for the ka of the Osiris *Gr-šr* (25) born of *Tꜣ-snt-snty*. Your ba is alive, your corpse is firm by the decree of Re himself, without destruction or decay III (1) like Re, for ever and eternally.

O Far-strider, who came forth from Heliopolis, the Osiris *Gr-šr* born of (2) *Tꜣ-snt-snty* has done no evil.

O Great of power, who came forth from Kher-Aha, (3) the Osiris *Gr-šr* born of *Tꜣ-snt-snty* has committed no theft.

O Beaked one, (4) who came forth from Hermopolis, the Osiris *Gr-šr* born of *Tꜣ-snt-snty* has created no (5) harm.

O Swallower of the Eye, who came forth from the two caverns, the Osiris *Gr-šr* (6) born of *Tꜣ-snt-snty* has taken no goods by stealth.

O Nehahor (7) who came forth from Ro-setau, the Osiris *Gr-šr* born of *Tꜣ-snt-snty* has spread no (8) rumours.

O Routy who came forth from the sky, the Osiris *Gr-šr* (9) born of *Tꜣ-snt-snty* has done no evil near the plummet (of the balance) (?)

O He whose eyes are (10) a flame, who came forth from Letopolis, the Osiris *Gr-šr* born of *Tꜣ-snt-snty* has commited no (11) calumny.

O gods who are in the Duat, hear the voice of the Osiris *Gr-šr* (12) born of *Tꜣ-snt-snty*! He is come before you with no evil in him, and no iniquity (13) in him, nor any witness standing against him. He lives on Maat, feeds on Maat, and the gods are pleased with (14) all that he has done. He has given bread to the hungry, water to the thirsty, clothing (15) to the naked; he has given *ḥtpw*-offerings to the gods and invocation offerings to the spirits. No re(16)port has been made against him in the presence of any god. May he enter the Duat without being turned back! (17)May he follow Osiris with the gods of the caverns, for he is praised among the praised (18) ones, divine among the excellent ones. May he live, may his heart live, for his (19) ba is received wherever he desires, and <he has> received <his> Book of Breathing. (20) May he breathe indeed with this ba of the Duat, and may he assume (21) any form at his wish together with the Westerners! May his ba go where(22)ever as he was when alive on earth, for ever (*bis*) and eternally (*bis*).

Sheet 3 (82.2 × 23.4 cm): two vignettes and a hieroglyphic text covering all of page IV. In the upper part, the deceased, depicted as a mummy, lies in a coffin laid out on a bark towed by priests. On both sides of the coffin, Isis and Nephthys make a gesture of worship. This illustration is in close connection with iconography of *BD* ch. 1.[163] On the left of this picture, a libation is depicted before the deceased, 'the Osiris *Gr-šr*', followed by Anubis in a posture of protection. On the left-hand side of the page, Re-Horakhty is depicted sitting down.

The lower register presents to the right part a funerary

163. See also J. Osing, in A. Fakhry, *Denkmäler der Oase Dachla* (*AV* 28, 1982), p. 62, n. 275.

bed flanked on both sides by kneeling representations of Isis and Nephthys as mourners. On the bed, under which one can see an unguent jar, lies the deceased as a mummy. Bent over him, Anubis performs funeral rite. The remaining part of the vignette derives directly from *BD* ch. 146. It shows twelve doorkeepers, seated and holding a knife. Each of them guards a numbered portal of the underworld (*sbḫt*).

1st portal *Nb(t)-snḏ*, 'Lady of fear' (lion-headed).[164]

2nd portal *Nb(t)-pt-ḥnt-tꜣwy*, 'Lady of the sky, mistress of the Two Lands' (monkey-headed ?).[165]

3d portal *Nb(t)-ḫꜣwt-<ꜥꜣt>-ꜥꜣbt*, 'Lady of the altar, <great> of offerings-*ꜥꜣbt* (bull-headed).[166]

4th portal *Sḫm(t)-ds-ḥnwt-tꜣwy*, 'Mighty of knives, mistress of the Two Lands' (hawk-headed).[167]

5th portal *Ḫt-nbt-tꜣw*, 'Fire, lady of the wind' (monkey-headed).[168]

6th portal *Nbt-sty-ꜥꜣ-hmhm*, 'Lady of darkness, loud-roaring' (cat-headed).[169]

7th portal *Ỉggy(t)* (written *Ỉkꜣikꜣ*) *ḥbs bꜣg*, 'Igegit, veiler of the Weary One' (human-headed).

8th portal *Rkḥ-bs-ꜥḫm-ḏꜣf*, 'Kindler of flames, Quencher of Embers' (snake-headed).[170]

9th portal *Ỉmy(t)-ḥꜣt-nb(t)-wsr*, 'Foremost One, possessor of power' (vulture-headed).[171]

10th portal *Tꜣ-ḳꜣt-ḫrw-nhs-dnw*, 'Loud-voiced, awaker of outcries' (ram-headed).[172]

11th portal *Wḥm(t)-ds-wbd(t)-sbi*, 'She who cuts repeatedly, who burns rebels' (human-headed).[173]

12th portal *Nis-tꜣwy.s-ssk-ii-nhp*, 'She whom her Two Lands invoke, who annihilates those that come at dawn' (cat-headed).[174]

Between these two registers, run two lines of a hieroglyphic text:

IV (1) Hail Osiris, the nomarch *Gr-šr*, justified, born of *Tꜣ-snt-snty*, you enter the Duat, being purified from each evil and without calumny in your limbs. Anubis the Embalmer makes pleasant your bones; He-who-is-on-his-hill, he unites your limbs, his arms (being raised) to you with the divine wrapping loosed from the body of the great god. You go forth to the *nšmt*-bark, you embark on the divine bark in that day of Sokar's rowing. You come forth (2) by day without being repulsed; you alight in (any) place at your heart's desire; your step is broad in the Mound of Djeme, being praised by the gods who are in it. Isis receives you in the Hall of the two Maats, and you unite yourself with the excellent Bas. Urtu, the great in Karnak, you receive cool water from his hands. Nephthys goes with you to the place where her brother is; he sets you at the head of the praised ones of Khenemet-ankh. You live therein, without any destruction, eternally.

Sheet 4 (88 × 23 cm): Psychostasis.[175] In a shrine supported by papyriform columns, Osiris is depicted with Isis standing behind him, enthroned, with the same attributes than in sheet 1. He is described as 'Osiris foremost of the West, the great god lord of Abydos, dwelling in the Mound of Djeme, king of the gods'. The legend of the goddess reads: 'Isis the great, mother of the god'. Both are witnessing the weighing of the deceased's heart.

All the rest of the picture is surmounted by a procession of 43 (instead of 42) assessors of Osiris, generally named as 'the gods of the hall of the two Maats'. On the right is pictured a goddess with an ostrich feather in place of a head; her legend is 'Maat-Hathor dwelling in the West'. Here she introduces the deceased, depicted twice,[176] with the same legend, , 'The Osiris *Gr-šr*'. Before him, Horus, helped by Anubis, checks the accuracy of the balance. Thoth stands before them, waiting to write down the result of the weighing. He is described as 'Thoth the twice great, lord of Hermopolis, master of Heseret, giving judgment for the Ennead'.[177] He is preceded by the monster perching on a shrine-shaped plinth, usually qualified as 'the Devouress of the dead', but here exceptionally called *'Tm-išr*, who is in the West',[178] a designation the meaning of which is unclear.

Facing a richly provided table of offerings and a pedestal table, the deceased raises his arms in salutation to Osiris and Isis. Legend: ? , 'Hail, Osiris, the nomarch *Krꜥšr*, justified (?), born of *Tꜣ-snt-snty*'.

164. Crocodile-headed in Lepsius' edition.
165. Human-headed with uraeus in Lepsius' edition.
166. Lion-headed in Lepsius' edition.
167. Bull-headed in Lepsius' edition.
168. Ibis-headed in Lepsius' edition.
169. Snake-headed in Lepsius' edition.
170. Human-headed in Lepsius' edition.
171. Feline-headed (?) with separated ears in Lepsius' edition.
172. Human-headed with *ꜣtf*-crown in Lepsius' edition.
173. Monkey-headed in Lepsius' edition.
174. Vulture-headed (?) in Lepsius' edition.
175. Curiously, the fourth sheet of the papyrus is not considered in the Budge edition. He seems not to have known of the existence of this sheet; cf. Budge, op. cit., p. 34: 'It will be noted that the Judgment Scene, which appears in the Book of the Dead, is here omitted.'
176. On this goddess, see P. BM EA 10191, **I, 5–6**, and Seeber, *Untersuchungen*, p. 144 with n. 641. The same scene, with double representation of the deceased, occurs also in P. BM EA 10479 (R.O. Faulkner, *The Ancient Egyptian Book of the Dead* [London 1985], p. 31).
177. For this title: P. Boylan, *Thot, the Hermes of Egypt* (Oxford 1922), pp. 54–5.
178. On this monster: Seeber, *Untersuchungen*, pp. 163–84; S. Sauneron, *Le Papyrus magique illustré de Brooklyn* (New York 1970), pp. 7–8.

Commentary

I, 1
ḥ3y Wsir N. Alone in its category, P. BM EA 9995 starts with this invocation, instead of the expected title *ḥ3t-ʿ m šʿt (n) snsn ir.t n.Ꞽst*, followed by the general programme of the text (§1 of de Horrack's classification). In the other documents, *ḥ3y Wsir* is preceded by the formula *ḏd mdw*. See P. BM EA 10048, **I, 1–3** and **4–6**.

I, 1–2
iw.k wʿb.ti ḥ3ty.k wʿb ḥ3t.k m ʿb pḥ.k m twr ḥr-ib.k m bd ḥsmn nn ʿt im.k m isft. See P. BM EA 10048, **I, 4–6**.

I, 2–4
wʿb Wsir N m šdyt twy nt sḫwt ḥtp ḥr mḥtt n sḫwt snḥm. On the different variants, see P. BM EA 10048, **I, 6–7**.

I, 4
swʿb twk W3ḏyt Nḫbt m wnwt 8.t nt grḥ m wnwt nt hrw. The number of the hour is omitted before *hrw*. See P. BM EA 10048, **I, 7–8**.

I, 4–6
mi ir.k r Wsir N ʿḳ.k wsḫt M3ʿty iw.k wʿb.ti r ḫw nb bt3 nb. Since this text is here addressed to the deceased, the invitation to him to come is unexpected. This singularity is found again in other manuscripts. The preposition *r* is wrong, because all the versions consider *Wsir* as the title of the deceased, and so it is right to translate: 'come then, Osiris N'. See P. BM EA 10048, **I, 8–9**.

I, 6
inr n M3ʿt rn.k. See P. BM EA 10048, **I, 9**.

I, 6–7
ḥ3y Wsir N ʿḳ.k r Dw3t m ʿb wr. See P. BM EA 10048, **II, 1–2**.

I, 7
swʿb twk M3ʿty m wsḫt ʿ3t. See P. BM EA 10048, **II, 2**.

ir.tw n.k ʿb m wsḫt Gb. See P. BM EA 10048, **II, 2**.

I, 7–8
swʿb ḥʿw.k m wsḫt Šw. See P. BM EA 10048, **II, 2–3**.

I, 8
iw.k ḥr m33 Rʿ m ḥtp.f Tm m mšrw. See P. BM EA 10048, **II, 3**.

I, 8–9
Ꞽmn irm.k ḥr di(t) n.k ṯ3w. See P. BM EA 10048, **II, 3–4**.

I, 9
Ptḥ ḥr nbi ḥʿw.k. Some manuscripts give the var. *ʿwt.k*. The two terms are equivalent. See P. BM EA 10048, **II, 4**.

ʿḳ.k r 3ḫt ḥnʿ Rʿ šsp.w b3.k r nšmt ḥnʿ Wsir. See P. BM EA 10048, **II, 4–5**.

I, 10
nṯr.w b3.k m pr Gb iw <.k> n m3ʿ-ḫrw r nḥḥ ḏt. See P. BM EA 10048, **II, 5**.

I, 10–11
Wsir N mn rn.k ḏd ḫ3t.k rwḏ sʿḥ.k nn šnʿ.tw.k m pt m t3. Some variants occur in the manuscripts. See P. BM EA 10048, **II, 6–7**.

I, 11–12
sḥḏ ḥr.k ḫr Rʿ ʿnḫ b3.k ḫr Ꞽmn rnp ḫ3t.k ḫr Wsir. Standard version. Among the documents consulted, only P. BM EA 10048, 7 gives the var. *sḥḏ sʿḥ.k*. See P. BM EA 10048, **II, 7–8**.

I, 12
snsn.k r nḥḥ ḏt. See P. BM EA 10048, **II, 8**.

I, 12–13
ir n.k s3.k prt-ḫrw m t3 ḥnḳt k3w 3pdw m ḳbḥ snṯr m ḫrt-hrw nt rʿ nb. Some noteworthy variants are provided by P. BM EA 10048, which gives here *s3 n sn.k*, 'the son of your brother', and by other manuscripts mentionning *b3.k* instead of *s3.k* as a result of a hieratic spelling confusion. For other minor divergences, see P. BM EA 10048, **II, 8–9**.

I, 13–14
ii.k ḥr ḫrw.f ḥʿw.k ḥr ḳsw.k mi irw.k ḥr-tp t3. See P. BM EA 10048, **II, 9**.

I, 14–15
swr.k m šnbt.k wnm.k m r3.k šsp.k snw ḥnʿ b3w nṯrw. See P. BM EA 10048, **II, 9–10**.

I, 15
ḫw twk Ꞽnpw ir.f s3.k. See P. BM EA 10048, **II, 10**.

nn šnʿ.tw.k m r3w nw Dw3t. See P. BM EA 10048, **II, 10**.

I, 15–16
ii n.k Ꞽ ʿ3 ʿ3 nb Ḫmnw sš.f n.k šʿt n snsn m ḏbʿw.f ḏs.f. See P. BM EA 10048, **III, 1**.

I, 16–17
snsn ib.k r nḥḥ. On the reading *ib.k*, in front of *b3.k* of the other versions, see P. BM EA 10048, **III, 1**.

I, 17
wḥm.k ḳy.k ḥr-tp t3 m ʿnḫ. See P. BM EA 10048, **III, 1**.

iw.k nṯr ḥnʿ b3w nṯrw. See P. BM EA 10048, **III, 1–2**.

I, 17–18
ib.k ib n Rʿ ḥʿw.k ḥʿw n nṯr ʿ3. See P. BM EA 10048, **III, 2**.

I, 18–19
ḥ3y Wsir N Ꞽmn irm.k ḫr wḥm.k ʿnḫ. See P. BM EA 10048, **III, 2–3**.

I, 19
wp n.k Wp-w3wt w3t nfrt. See P. BM EA 10048, **III, 3**.

I, 19–20
m33.k m irty.k sḏm.k m ʿnḫwy.k mdw.k m r3.k šm.k m rdwy.k. See P. BM EA 10048, **III, 3**.

I, 20
iw b3.k nṯr m Dw3t r ir ḫprw.k r mr.k. See P. BM EA 10048, **III, 3–4**.

I, 20–1
ir.k n3 šršr n p(3) išd šps n Ꞽwnw. See P. BM EA 10048, **III, 4**.

I, 21
nhs.k rʿ nb m33.k n3 stwt n p(3) Rʿ. See P. BM EA 10048, **III, 4–5**.

I, 21–2
ii n.k Ỉmn ḥr ṯꜣw n ꜥnḫ. See P. BM EA 10048, **III, 5**.

I, 22
di.f ir.k snsn m ḏbꜣt.k. See P. BM EA 10048, **III, 5**.

pr.k r tꜣ rꜥ nb. See P. BM EA 10048, **III, 5**.

I, 22–3
šꜥt n snsn n Ỉ m sꜣ.k snsn.k im.s rꜥ nb. See P. BM EA 10048, **III, 5–6**.

I, 23
mꜣꜣ irty.k stwt itn. See P. BM EA 10048, **III, 6**.

ḏd.w Mꜣꜥt r.k m-bꜣḥ Wsir. See P. BM EA 10048, **III, 6**.

I, 23–4
sš.w Mꜣꜥt ḥr ns.k. All other manuscripts give *mꜣꜥ-ḫrw* instead of *Mꜣꜥt*. See P. BM EA 10048, **III, 6**.

I, 24
Ḥr-nḏ-it.f ḫw.f ḏt.k nṯr.f bꜣ.k mi nṯrw nb. See P. BM EA 10048, **III, 6–7**.

I, 24–II, 1
Bꜣw n Rꜥ ḥr sꜥnḫ bꜣ.k Bꜣw n Šw ḥr ḫnm msty.k. See P. BM EA 10048, **III, 7**.

II, 1–2
hꜣy Wsir N snsn bꜣ.k r bw mr.k. See P. BM EA 10048, **III, 7–8**.

II, 2
iw.k m Wsir Wsir ḫnty Ỉmntt rn.k. See P. BM EA 10048, **III, 7–8**.

II, 3
Ḥꜥpy wr ii n.k m ꜣbw mḥ.f ḥtp.k m ḏfꜣw. See P. BM EA 10048, **III, 8–9**.

II, 3–5
Wsir N ii n.k nṯrw nw Šmꜥ Mḥw sšm.w twk r ꜥrḳ-ḥḥ. See P. BM EA 10048, **III, 9**.

II, 5
ꜥnḫ bꜣ.k šms.k Wsir. See P. BM EA 10048, **III, 9**.

II, 5–6
snsn.k ḫnt rꜣ-sṯꜣw mk twk Ḥꜣp-n-nb.s ḥnꜥ nṯr ꜥꜣ. See P. BM EA 10048, **III, 10**.

II, 6–7
ẖꜣt.k ꜥnḫ m Ḏdw Tꜣ-wr bꜣ.k ꜥnḫ m pt rꜥ nb. See P. BM EA 10048, **III, 10**.

II, 7
Wsir N sḫm Sḫmt m wꜣ im.k. See P. BM EA 10048, **III, 11**.

II, 7–8
Ḥr ꜥꜣ ibw ḥr ir mkt.k Ḥr Bḥdty ḥr ir n ib.k. See P. BM EA 10048, **III, 11**.

II, 8–9
Ḥr Mrty ḥr sꜣ ḏt.k ky ḏd ns.k ḏd.k m ꜥnḫ wḏꜣ s(nb). Note the addition *ky ḏd ns.k*, not found in any other manuscript. See P. BM EA 10048, **IV, 1**.

II, 9
iw.k mn ḥr nst.k m tꜣ ḏsr. See P. BM EA 10048, **IV, 1**.

II, 9–10
mi ir.k Wsir N. See P. BM EA 10048, **IV, 1–2**.

II, 10
iw.k ḥꜥ.ti m kꜣy.k twt.ti m ḫkrw.k. See P. BM EA 10048, **IV, 1–2**.

II, 10–11
sḏr.k m ꜥnḫ wrš.k m snb šm.k snsn.k r bw nb. See P. BM EA 10048, **IV, 2–3**.

II, 11
wbn Rꜥ ḥr ḥwt.k mi Wsir. See P. BM EA 10048, **IV, 3**.

II, 11–12
snsn.k ꜥnḫ.k m stwt.f. See P. BM EA 10048, **IV, 3–4**.

II, 12
Ỉmn-Rꜥ-Ḥr-ꜣḫty sꜥnḫ.f kꜣ.k. The other versions give *Ỉmn-Rꜥ*. See P. BM EA 10048, **IV, 4**.

swꜣḏ.f twk n šꜥt n snsn. See P. BM EA 10048, **IV, 4**.

II, 13
šms.k Wsir Ḥr nb ḥnw iw.k m nṯr ꜥꜣ ḫnt nṯrw. Same reading in P. Berlin 3135, III, 5 = P. Berlin 3154, II, 4–5 = P. Florence 3665 + P. Vienna 3850, IV, 2 = P. Louvre E 8079 + 11080, III, 7 = P. Louvre N 3083, VI, 22 = P. Louvre N 3121, II, 19–20 = P. Louvre N 3126, II, 21–2 = P. Louvre N 3154, III, 5 = P. Louvre N 3158, IV, 9–V, 1 = P. Louvre N 3167 + 3222, II, 18–19 = P. Louvre N 3284, III, 16 = P. Louvre N 3285, II, 27–8 = P. Louvre N 3291, 28 = P. Tübingen 2016, IV, 9–10 = P. Vienna 3931, II, 19–20. Sequence omitted in P. BM EA 10048, IV; wholly in lacuna in P. Vienna 3863, II, and partly in P. Joseph Smith, IV, 9–10. Var. P. Lausanne 3391, II, 25 = P. Louvre N 3121, II, 19: *šms twk (twt)*;[179] P. Denon, III, 9: *šms.k Wsir m Ḏdw*, 'You follow Osiris in Busiris'.

II, 13–14
ꜥnḫ ḥr.k nfr msw.k rn.k rwḏ.tw rꜥ nb. Same reading in P. Berlin 3154, II, 5 = P. Louvre N 3083, VI, 22–3 = P. Louvre N 3126, II, 22 = P. Louvre N 3167 + 3222, II, 19 (small lacuna) = P. Louvre N 3285, II, 28 = P. Louvre N 3291, 28–9 = P. Joseph Smith, IV, 10 = P. Vienna 3863, III, 1 (partly in lacuna) = P. Vienna 3931, II, 20–1. Sequence omitted in P. BM EA 10048, IV = P. Denon, III, 9. Omission of suffix *.k* after *msw* in P. Louvre N 3284, III, 17. Var. P. Berlin 3135, III, 6 = P. Florence 3665 + P. Vienna 3850, IV, 3 = P. Lausanne 3391, II, 26 = P. Louvre E 8079 + 11080, III, 7–8 = P. Louvre N 3121, II, 20 = P. Louvre N 3154, III, 5–6 = P. Louvre N 3158, V, 1 = P. Louvre N 3291, 28–9 = P. Tübingen 2016, IV, 10: *rn.k rwḏ*; P. Louvre N 3284, III, 17: *rn.k rwḏ.f*.

II, 14
ꜥḳ.k r sḥ-nṯr wr sp 2 m Ḏdw mꜣꜣ.k Ḫnty Ỉmntt m ḥb Wꜣg. Same reading in P. Berlin 3135, III, 6–7 = P. Florence 3665 + P. Vienna 3850, IV, 3–4 = P. Louvre E 8079 + 11080, III, 8 = P. Louvre N 3083, VI, 23 = P. Louvre N 3158, V, 1–2 = P. Louvre N 3167 + 3222, II, 19–20 = P. Louvre N 3285, II, 29 = P. Louvre N 3291, 29 = P. Tübingen 2016, IV, 10–11. P. Louvre N 3121, III, 1–2, mentions before that sentence the invocation

179. Respectively written  and .

hꜣy Ḥwt-Ḥr N. Sequence omitted in P. BM EA 10048, IV; partly in lacuna in P. Joseph Smith, IV, 10–11. Omission of *ꜥḳ.k r sḫ-nṯr wr sp 2 m Ḏdw* in P. Denon, III, 9; of *r* and *nṯr* in P. Vienna 3863, III, 1 = P. Lausanne 3391, II, 26; of *sp 2* in P. Berlin 3154, II, 5 = P. Louvre N 3154, III, 6; of suffix *.k* after *mꜣꜣ* in P. Louvre N 3126, II, 22. Var. P. Louvre N 3284, III, 17: *mi.k r sḫ-nṯr*; P. Vienna 3931, 21: *ḥr mꜣꜣ*.

In the vignette of P. Louvre N 3207, an unpublished copy of the Book of the Dead, the same text is addressed to the deceased, with the variant *m ḥb.f nfr n* (*sic*), 'in his beautiful festival of (*sic*)'.

II, 14–15
nḏm sty.k mi imꜣḫw [180] *ꜥꜣ rn.k m sꜥḥw*. Same reading in P. Berlin 3135, III, 7–8 = P. Denon, III, 1–2 = P. Florence 3665 + P. Vienna 3850, IV, 4–5 = P. Louvre E 8079 + 11080, III, 8–9 = P. Louvre N 3121, III, 2–3 = P. Louvre N 3126, II, 23 = P. Louvre N 3167 + 3222, II, 20 (small lacuna) = P. Louvre N 3284, III, 18 = P. Vienna 3863, III, 1–2 = P. Vienna 3931, II, 22–3. Sequence omitted in P. BM EA 10048, IV; partly in lacuna in P. Joseph Smith, IV, 11–12. Var. P. Berlin 3154, II, 6 = P. Louvre N 3083, VI, 23–VII, 1 = P. Louvre N 3154, III, 7 = P. Louvre N 3158, V, 2 = P. Tübingen 2016, IV, 11: *m-m imꜣḫw*; P. Lausanne 3391, III, 1 = P. Louvre N 3158, V, 3 = P. Louvre N 3291, 29 = P. Joseph Smith, IV, 11–12: *m sꜥḥ šps*; P. Louvre N 3083, VII, 2: *m-m sꜥḥw*.

Cf. also P. Louvre N 3207, vignette, continuation of the preceding text (cf. **II, 14**): *nḏm sty.k n-ḫnw Dwꜣt štꜣt ꜥꜣ* (?) *rn.k n sꜥḥ(w) šps(w) n* (?) *pr Wsir*, 'Your odour is sweet within the secret Duat, and your name is great (?) among the noble mummies in (?) the House of Osiris'. Here the parallel with P. BM EA 9995 stops.

For the odour (*sty*) of the deceased, cf. *Ritual of Embalment*, II, 2–3 (ed. Sauneron, p. 2):

ꜥntyw r.k pr m Pwnt	'Myrrh is for you, coming forth from Punt,
r snfr sty.k m sty nṯr (...)	to make beautiful your odour as the odour of a god (...);
rḏw r.k pr m Rꜥ	efflux is for you, coming forth from Re,
r snfr [...] *m wsḫt Mꜣꜥty*	to make beautiful [...] in the hall of the two Maats;
[...] *tw sty.k m wsḫt Gb*	your odour is [...] in the hall of Geb.
ḫnmt nṯr ꜥꜣ kꜣp.k	Fragrance of the great god perfumes you (?);
ḫnm nfr nn wn šbyt.f	the good fragrance, it is not mixed.'

II, 15–16
hꜣy Wsir N ꜥnḫ bꜣ.k m šꜥt n snsn ḫnm.k m šꜥt n snsn. See P. BM EA 10048, **IV, 4**.

II, 17
ꜥḳ.k r Dwꜣt nn wn ḫftyw.k. See P. BM EA 10048, **IV, 4–5**.

iw.k m bꜣ ꜥnḫ m Ḏdw. See P. BM EA 10048, **IV, 5**.

II, 17–18
ib.k n.k nn ḥr.f r.k irty.k n.k wn rꜥ nb. See P. BM EA 10048, **IV, 5**.

II, 18–19
ḏd mdw in nṯrw imyw-ḫt Wsir n Wsir N. See P. BM EA 10048, **IV, 5–6**.

II, 19
šms.k Rꜥ šms.k Wsir bꜣ.k ꜥnḫ r nḥḥ ḏt. See P. BM EA 10048, **IV, 6**.

II, 19–21
ḏd mdw in nṯrw imyw Dwꜣt n Wsir ḫnty Ỉmntt n Wsir N wn n.f m sbꜣw nw Dwꜣt. See P. BM EA 10048, **IV, 7–8**.

II, 21
iṯ.f twk m ẖrt-nṯr mi ꜥnḫ bꜣ.f r nḥḥ. See P. BM EA 10048, **IV, 8–9**.

II, 21–2
ḳd.f sbḫwt m ẖrt-nṯr. See P. BM EA 10048, **IV, 8–9**.

II, 22–3
ḥs kꜣ.f nṯr.f šsp.n.f šꜥt n snsn mi ir.f snsn. See P. BM EA 10048, **IV, 9**.

II, 23
ḥtp di nsw n Wsir ḫnty Ỉmntt nṯr ꜥꜣ nb ꜣbḏw. See P. BM EA 10048, **IV, 9–10**.

II, 23–5
di.f prt-ḫrw n tꜣ ḥnḳt kꜣw ꜣpdw irp irṯt ḥtpw ḏfꜣw ḫwt nbt nfrt n kꜣ n Wsir N. See P. BM EA 10048, **IV, 10–11**.

II, 25
bꜣ.k ꜥnḫ ẖꜣt.k rwḏ.ti m wḏt n Rꜥ ḏs.f. See P. BM EA 10048, **IV, 11**.

II, 25–III, 1
nn sk nn mrḫ mi Rꜥ ḏt nḥḥ. See P. BM EA 10048, **IV, 11**.

III, 1–2
i Wsḫ-nmtt pr m Ỉwnw nn ir Wsir N isft. See P. BM EA 10048, **V, 1**.

III, 2–3
i Wr-ꜣt pr m Ḫr-ꜥḥꜣ nn ir Wsir N ꜥwꜣy. See P. BM EA 10048, **V, 2**.

III, 3–5
i Fnḏy pr m Ḫmnw nn ir Wsir N ḳmꜣ-ꜥš. See P. BM EA 10048, **V, 3**.

III, 5–6
i ꜥm-irt pr m ḳrty nn ir Wsir N iṯ ḫwt m tꜣwy. See P. BM EA 10048, **V, 4**.

III, 6–8
i Nḥꜣ-ḥr pr m rꜣ-stꜣw nn ir Wsir N sḫwn. See P. BM EA 10048, **V, 5**.

III, 8–9
i Rwty pr m pt nn ir Wsir N isft m-ḫt tḫ (?). See P. BM EA 10048, **V, 6**.

III, 9–11
i Ỉrty.f-m-ḫt pr m Ḫm nn ir Wsir N sꜣt. See P. BM EA 10048, **V, 7**.

III, 11–12
i nṯrw imyw Dwꜣt sḏm ḫrw Wsir N. See P. BM EA 10048, **VII, 2**.

III, 12–13
iw ir ii ḫr.tn nn ḏw nb ḥr.f nn isft nbt ḥr.f. The variant *iw ir ii ḫr.tn* is attested in no other manuscript of the Book of Breathing. Restore here: *iw<.f> ir ii ḫr.tn*. See P. BM EA 10048, **VII, 2**.

III, 13
nn mtr ꜥḥꜥ r.f. See P. BM EA 10048, **VII, 2**.

180. Misled by the determinative  of *imꜣḫw*, the writers of P. Vienna 3863 (III, 2), P. Vienna 3931 (II, 22), and P. Lausanne 3391, II, 27 have added behind it the sign , as if it were the word *šps*. The presence of the plural in  (P. Vienna 3863) confirms this error. On the other hand, P. Louvre N 3285, II, 30 gives a rendering which could well be read *imꜣḫw špsw*.

ꜥnḫ.f m mꜣꜥt sꜥm.f m mꜣꜥt. See P. BM EA 10048, **VII, 3**.

III, 13–14
hr nṯrw ḥr ỉr.n.f nb. See P. BM EA 10048, **VII, 3**.

III, 14–15
rdỉ.n.f tꜣ n ḥkr mw n ỉb ḥbs n ḥꜣy. See P. BM EA 10048, **VII, 3–4**.

III, 15
dỉ.f ḥtpw n nꜣ nṯrw prt-ḫrw n ꜣḫw. See P. BM EA 10048, **VII, 3–4**.

III, 15–16
nn ỉr.tw smỉ nb r.f m-bꜣḥ nṯrw nb. See P. BM EA 10048, **VII, 4**.

III, 16–17
mỉ ꜥḳ.f r Dwꜣt nn šnꜥ.tw.f mỉ šms.f Wsỉr ḥnꜥ nṯrw ḳrtyw. See P. BM EA 10048, **VII, 4**.

III, 17–18
ỉw.f ḥs m-m ḥsyw ỉw.f nṯr m-m ỉḳrw. See P. BM EA 10048, **VII, 4–5**.

III, 18
mỉ ꜥnḫ.f mỉ ꜥnḫ bꜣ.f. See P. BM EA 10048, **VII, 5**.

III, 18–19
šsp bꜣ.f r bw nb mr.f. See P. BM EA 10048, **VII, 5**.

III, 19
šsp tꜣ šꜥt n snsn. See P. BM EA 10048, **VII, 5**.

III, 20
mỉ ỉr.f snsn ḥnꜥ bꜣ.f pwy n Dwꜣt. See P. BM EA 10048, **VII, 5–6**.

III, 20–1
ḥnꜥ ỉr ḫpr nb r-dỉt ỉb.f ḥnꜥ Ỉmntyw. See P. BM EA 10048, **VII, 6**.

III, 21
mỉ šm bꜣ.f r bw nb ỉw wn.f ꜥnḫ.tw ḥr-tp tꜣ r nḥḥ sp 2 ḏt sp 2. See P. BM EA 10048, **VII, 6–7**.

IV, 1
hꜣy Wsỉr N ꜥḳ.k r Dwꜣt wꜥb.tỉ r ḏw n sꜣt m ḥꜥw.k. On access to the Duat in condition of purity, cf. P. BM EA 10048, **II, 1–2**.

Ỉnpw ỉmy wt snḏm.n.f ḳsw.k Tpy-ḏw.f ỉꜥb.f ḥꜥw.k. Same sequence in stela Bucheum no. 14, 7–8 (cf. *LPE*, p. 248 [VIII, 3]); also canopy Edinburgh 559: M.A. Murray, *Catalogue of Egyptian Antiquities ... Edinburgh* (Edinburgh 1900), p. 38, and A.H. Rhind, *Thebes, its Tombs and their Tenants* (London 1862), frontispiece and pp. 111–12.

ꜥwy.f r.k m nṯr sfḫ m ḏt n nṯr ꜥꜣ. Same sequence in stela Bucheum no. 14, 8. For that role of Anubis, cf. J. Osing, in A. Fakhry, *Denkmäler der Oase Dachla* (*AV* 28, 1982), p. 68, Text D, 3–4 and corresponding remarks. For *nṯr*-wrapping, see *LPE*, p. 198 (V, 8–9). The inscription of canopy Edinburgh 559 (cf. *supra*) gives the var. *ỉỉ.f n.k ẖr ḏꜣr-nṯr sfḫ m ḏt n nṯr ꜥꜣ*, 'He is coming to you, bearing the divine *ḏꜣr*-wrapping loosed from the body of the great god'. The expression (*nṯr*) *sfḫ m ḏt n nṯr ꜥꜣ* can be compared with the construction *m sfḫ n nṯr ꜥꜣ* (and var.), 'as loosed from the great god', on which see *LPE*, pp. 178–9 (IV, 9–10) and p. 198 (V, 8–9). Add papyrus from private collection (Dublin), 3: *m sfḫ (n) Wsỉr ḫnty Ỉmntt*.[181]

pr.k r nšmt šsp.k dpt-nṯr hrw pfy n ḫn Skr. Same sequence in stela Bucheum no. 14, 9. On that phrase, see also Osing, in Fakhry, op. cit., p. 65, n. 297.

IV, 1–2
pr.k m hrw n ḫsf.tw.k ḫn.k r bw ḏr ỉb.k. Var. stela Bucheum no. 14, 10: *r-ḏr ỉb.k*. Note in both documents the writing of *ḫn*, on which see *Wb*. III, 287, 6.

IV, 2
wsṯn nmtt.k m Ỉꜣt Ḏꜣmt ḥs.tỉ[182] *ḫr nṯrw ỉmy(w).s*. Var. stela Bucheum no. 14, 10: *wsṯn.k*, 'you walk about freely', and *Ḥwt Ỉtm* instead of *Ỉꜣt Ḏꜣmt*, the 'House of Atum' being a designation of the Bucheum; see Fairman, in Mond–Myers, *The Bucheum* II, p. 7.[183] On gods in (the mound of) Djeme, see P. BM EA 10116, **lines 27–30**.

šsp twk Ỉst r wsḫt Mꜣꜥty. The reception of the deceased by Isis in the Hall of the two Maats seems not to be attested elsewhere in the funerary literature.

smꜣ.k m bꜣw ỉḳrw. For the union with the excellent bas, cf. e.g. P. Anastasi I, 3, 3 (*šbn.k bꜣw ỉḳrw*); P. Harris, I, 22, 2 (*šbn bꜣw ỉḳrw*); Boeser, *Beschreibung* X, p. 7 (*smꜣ n(.ỉ) bꜣw ỉḳrw*); F. Hassanein, *ASAE* 68 (1982), p. 42 (*ḫnm.k m bꜣw ỉḳrw*); H.P. Blok, *Acta Orientalia* 8 (1930), p. 177 (*smꜣ.k ḥnꜥ bꜣw ỉḳrw*); A.M. Blackman, *JEA* 4 (1917), pl. 27, cols 62–3 (*ḫnm.ỉ n bꜣw ỉḳrw*); ibid., pl. 28, cols 12–13 (*dmḏ.k m bꜣw ỉḳrw*); P. Montet, *La nécropole royale de Tanis* III (Paris 1960), p. 82 and pl. 46 (*ḫnm m bꜣw ỉḳrw*); also:

J. Bonomi and S. Sharpe, *The Triple Mummy Case of Aroeris-Ao* (London 1858), pl. 6, fig. 15, lines 55–7:

pr bꜣ.k r ḫnm.k m bꜣw ỉḳrw	'Your ba goes forth in order that you may join the excellent bas,
ỉḳr ḫꜣt.k m Dwꜣt Wsỉr N	and your corpse is excellent in the Duat, Osiris N.'

V. Schmidt, *Sarkofager, Mumierkister, og Mumiehylstre i det gamle Aegypten. Typologisk Atlas* (Copenhagen 1919), p. 140, no. 714:

(...) *dỉ.sn ḥtp.f r-gs.sn*	'(...) so that they may cause that he rest beside them,
ỉr.sn n.f st m ẖrt-nṯr	that they give him a place in the god's domain;
šbn.f[184] *bꜣw ỉḳrw*	he joins the excellent bas.'

Boeser, *Beschreibung* X, p. 10:

ḫnm.k sbꜣw n pt	'You join the stars of the sky
smꜣ.k bꜣw ỉḳrw	and you unite yourself with the excellent bas.'

181. I thank S. Quirke who informed me about that manuscript.
182. The sign , graphic variant of , must be read *ḥs* (so further in the same line). This value is found again in P. Rhind I, 6, 6; I, 8, 12; II, 8, 8; A. Rowe, *ASAE* 40 (1940), pp. 14, 17, 19, 22, 23, etc. See A. Moret, *RT* 17 (1895), p. 85. H. de Meulenaere, *BIFAO* 53 (1953), p. 110 with n. 10.
183. On the offering table Bucheum 36 (Mond-Myers, *The Bucheum* III, pl. 51), this *ḥwt Ỉtm* is said to be to the south of the Mound of Djeme (*ḥr rsyt n Ỉꜣt Ḏꜣm*).
184. Written .

Wrtw wr m Iwnw šmʿ šsp.k ḳbḥ.k m ʿwy.f. Var. stela Bucheum no. 14, 11–12: *Wrtw wr m Iwnw šmʿ swr.f ḏt.k šsp.k ḳbḥ m ʿwy.f,* 'Urtu, the great in Karnak, he magnifies your body; you receive cool water from his hands'. Urtu is a rare designation of Montu with the epithet 'the great in Karnak'. As a libationer, see P. BM EA 10254, 4–5:

Wrtw wr ii m Iwnw šmʿ	'Urtu the great is come from Karnak;
ḳbḥ.f n.t ḥnʿ it itw	he makes for you a libation together with the father of his fathers.'

On the god Urtu: Leitz, *LGG* II, p. 511.

šm Nbt-ḥwt ḥnʿ.k r bw ḫr sn.s. rdi.f (sic) tw m-tp ḥs(y)w Ḫnmt-ʿnḫ ʿnḫ.k im.s nn sk m-ḫnt.s ḏt. The preposition *ḫr* is here for *ḥr*. On the 'praised ones' (*ḥsyw*), see E. Drioton, *BIE* 33 (1952), pp. 257–8; J. Quaegebeur, *OLP* 8 (1977), pp. 129–43.

P. BM EA 10260 (pls 25–8)

Salt Collection 1, 2, 3, 16.
Unpublished.
Quirke, *Owners*, no. 63.
Provenance: probably Thebes.
Date: Ptolemaic Period.
Owner of the papyrus: *Gȝprn* [hieroglyphs] (I, x + 6, 12), [hieroglyphs] (II, x + 5), [hieroglyphs] (II, x + 12; III, x + 3), [hieroglyphs] (III, x + 7, 8, 10, 11). This name would correspond to Greek Kephalon.[185] Note the existence of a *Tȝ-šrit-Gpryn* in P. BM EA 10343.
Mother of the owner: *Tȝ-nȝ-kȝw* [hieroglyphs] (II, x + 5), [hieroglyphs] I, x + 12); [hieroglyphs] (I, x + 6). Absent from R*PN*. For the personal names formed with *Tȝ-nȝ-...*, see Smith, *Mortuary Texts*, p. 131. The masculine form **Pȝ-nȝ-kȝw* does not seem to be attested.

Contents: Book of Breathing made by Isis for her brother Osiris

Manuscript mounted in two sheets (61.4 × 20 cm and 62.7 × 19.7 cm), the entire upper part of which is kept in the Bodleian Library, Oxford.[186] Almost one half of its length is occupied with a polychrome vignette which, preceding col. I, shows the classical picture representing the introduction of the deceased before Osiris. The heads of the six persons depicted are absent in the London part. On the right, a priest – or Anubis – leads by the hand the deceased clothed with a long tunic. Both are facing Osiris, represented enthroned, and behind him are pictured a masculine deity (probably Horus) and two feminine ones (certainly Isis and Nephthys). The anomalies in the graphic treating of this vignette, obviously drawn hastily, derive from several retouches or new definitions of the contours. They can be observed along the arms of the deceased, on the forearm of the priest (or of Anubis), above the thigh of Osiris, and on a level with the buttocks and the abdomen of the goddess to the left edge of the vignette.

Col. I (x + 1–16) contains an incomplete text (name and filiation of the deceased are expected in the Oxford part) which does not belong to the usual version of the Book of Breathing made by Isis. In its present condition, it is not paralleled by any other manuscript. On the evidence of the end of text of col. II and the first line of col. III, one may estimate that ten or so lines are missing in col. III and therefore as many in col. II. No text occurs on the verso.

Translation

I (x + 1) Isis, the great, mother of the god, has come to you; she gives you a great, beautiful and ... (?) burial. (x + 2) Anubis the Embalmer, he makes beautiful your *wȝḏ*-cloth; he perfects you with his wrappings. (x + 3) Nephthys, sister of the god, the efficacious one, may you receive the libation from her hands. Osiris, foremost of (x + 4) the West, receives you; he causes you to enter the hall of the two Maats without being turned back (x + 5) from the gates of the Duat, for you are praised among the excellent ones. O (x + 6) Osiris *Gȝprn* born of *Tȝ-nȝ-kȝw*, justified, (x + 7) your ba goes forth to the firmament, he follows Re; you tread on the earth to the road you desire. Your father Geb (x + 8) praises you and Maat is by you in every place and there is no evil (x + 9) beside you. May you receive *snw*-bread and the libation from the hands of the two Sisters, the invocation-offering (x + 10) from the hand of the son of Isis. May you enter the hall of the two Maats. (x + 11) Those who are in the Duat receive you in joy. Your ba descends on your corpse in the length of eternity, (x + 12) (that) you will not be destroyed forever. (O) Osiris *Gȝprn* born of *Tȝ-nȝ-kȝw*, (x + 13) justified, may you come to Osiris, the great god in the West. He grants you become (one) among his praised ones, every day. May your ba be received (x + 14) in the sky, and your corpse be divinized in the Duat, that you breathe with (x + 15) the bas of the gods, for you are one of the praised ones, noble in the god's domain. (x + 16) May your ba (?) be praised on earth, eternally.

II (x + 1) [... ... Osiris] (x + 2) *Gȝ<p>rn*, you enter the Duat in great purity. The two Maats purify you in the great hall, and purification is made for you (x + 3) in the hall of Geb. Your limbs are purified in the hall of light, and you see Re when he sets, Atum in the evening. (x + 4) Amun is with you, giving you breath. Ptah fashions your limbs. You arrive at the horizon with Re. Your ba is received on board the *nšmt*-bark with (x + 5) Osiris. Your ba is divinized in the House of Geb, and you are justified for ever and eternally.

185. *Demot. Nb.*, p. 1021.

186. MS Egypt. a. 4 (P); see M. Coenen, *JEA* 86 (2000), pp. 93–6.

(O) Osiris *Gꜣ<p>rn* born of *Tꜣ-nꜣ-kꜣw*, justified, (x + 6) your name is established, your corpse stable, your mummy firm, (so that) you will not be turned back in the sky or on earth. Your face is illuminated before Re, your ba lives before (x + 7) Amun, your corpse is renewed before Osiris, and you breathe for ever and eternally. Your son performs for you an invocation offering of bread, beer, oxen and fowl, with libation (x + 8) and censing, in the course of every day. Your flesh is on your bones according to your form upon earth. You drink with your throat and eat with your mouth. You receive (x + 9) *snw*-loaves with the bas of the gods. Anubis protects you and makes your protection, (so that) you will not be turned back from the entrances of the Duat.

Thoth (x + 10) the twice great, lord of Hermopolis, comes to you; he writes for you a Book of Breathing, with his own fingers, and your ba breathes for ever. You repeat (x + 11) the form which was yours upon earth among the living. Your ba is divine with the bas of the gods. Your heart is the heart of Re, your limbs are the limbs of the (x + 12) great god.

Hail Osiris *Gꜣprn*, justified, Amun is with you every day, giving you breath. Wepwawet opens for you a good way. (x + 13) You see with your eyes, hear with your ears, speak with your mouth, walk with your legs. Your ba is divine in the Duat, assuming (x + 14) any form it desires. You receive the freshness (?) of the noble balanites-tree in Heliopolis. You awake every day and you see the rays of (x + 15) Re (or: of the disk). Amun comes to you, full of the breath of life; he causes you to breathe within your coffin. You go out upon earth every day. The Book of Breathing of (x + 16) Thoth is your protection. You breathe by it every day. Your eyes see the rays of the disk. One says: 'Maat' concerning you in the presence of Osiris, and ['justified'] is written [III (1) on your tongue ...]

[Hail Osiris] *Gꜣprn*, justified, your ba lives on the Book of Breathing; (x + 2) you unite with the Book of Breathing. [You enter] the Duat, and your enemies exist no more. You are a divine ba in Busiris. Your heart belongs to you and will not be far from you; your eyes belong to you, (x + 3) open every day.

Words to be recited by the gods who are in the Duat to Osiris foremost of the West, on behalf of the Osiris *Gꜣprn*, so that the gates of the Duat may be opened for him: (x + 4) May he receive you in the god's domain! May his ba live for ever, (for) he has received a Book of Breathing. May he indeed breathe!

Offering that the king gives to Osiris (x + 5) foremost of the West, the great god, lord of Abydos, that he may grant an invocation offering of bread, beer, oxen, fowl, wine, milk, *ḥtpw*-offerings and food, all things good and pure, for the ka of the Osiris *Gꜣprn*. (x + 6) Your ba is alive, your corpse is firm by the decree of Re himself, without destruction or decay, like Re, for ever and eternally.

O Far-strider, who came forth from Heliopolis, the Osiris *Gꜣprn* (x + 7) has done no evil.

O Great of power, who came forth from Kher-Aha, the Osiris *Gꜣprn* has committed no theft.

O Beaked One, who came forth from Hermopolis, the Osiris *Gꜣprn* (x + 8) has created no harm.

O Swallower of the Eye, who came forth from the two caverns, the Osiris *Gꜣ<p>rn* has not stolen goods by stealth.

O Nehaher (x + 9) who came forth from Ro-setau, the Osiris *Gꜣprn* has spread no rumours.

O Ruty who came forth from the sky, the Osiris *Gꜣprn* (x + 10) has done no evil near the plummet (of the balance) (?)

O He whose eye is a flame, who came forth from Letopolis, the Osiris *Gꜣprn* has committed no calumny.

O gods who are in the Duat, (x + 11) hear the voice of the Osiris *Gꜣprn*! He is come before you with no evil in him, and no iniquity about him, nor any witness standing against him. He lives on (x + 12) Maat, feeds on Maat, and the gods are pleased with all that he has done; he has given bread to the hungry, water to the thirsty, clothing to the naked; he has given *ḥtpw*-offerings to the (x + 13) gods and invocation offering to the spirits. No report has been made against him in the presence of any god. May he enter the Duat without being turned back! May he (x + 14) follow Osiris with the gods of the caverns, for he is praised among the praised ones, divine among the excellent ones. May he live, may his ba live, (x + 15) may his ba be received in any place he desires, (for) <he has> received his Book of Breathing. May he indeed breathe with this his ba of the Duat, and may he assume any form (x + 16) at his heart's desire with the Westerners! May his ba go wherever as he was when alive upon earth, for ever (*bis*) and eternally!

Commentary

I, x + 1

ỉw n.k Ỉst wrt mwt-nṯr dỉ.s n.k ḳrst ꜥꜣt nfrt ... (?).[187] Cf. P. Tübingen 2012, XII, 12: *ỉw n.k Ỉst wrt mwt-nṯr dỉ.s n.k ḳrst nfrt*; P. Tübingen 2016, vignette, legend of Isis: *dỉ(.ỉ) n.k ḳrst ꜥꜣt nfrt*; P. BM EA 10194, 13: *dỉ n.k Ỉst wrt mwt-nṯr ḳ(r)st ꜥꜣt nfrt mnḫt*; P. BM EA 10343, 6: *dỉ n.ỉ Ỉst wrt mwt-nṯr ḳrst ꜥꜣt nfrt mnḫt*; P. BM EA 10344, 1–2: *dỉ n.k Ỉst wrt* [...] *ḳrst ꜥꜣt nfrt*; ibid., 9–10: *dỉ n.t* (?) *Ỉst wrt ḳ(r)st* [...] *mnḫt*; P. Louvre E 11079, II, 4–5: *ỉw sp 2 n.t Ỉst wrt mwt-nṯr dỉ.s n.t ḳ(r)st ꜥꜣt nfrt mnḫt ḥnꜥ bꜣw ꜥꜣw nw Dwꜣt*; P. Vatican Inv. 38608, 1: *dỉ n.k Ỉst wrt mwt-nṯr ḳrst nfrt ḥr st ḳḥḳḥ*; shroud from private collection (K. Parlasca, in *Ägypten–Dauer und Wandel* [*SDAIK* 18, 1985], p. 99 and pl. 4: *dỉ n.k Ỉst wrt mwt*[*-nṯr*] *ḳrst nfrt ḥr Ỉmntt Wꜣst*); another shroud, id., *Mumienporträts und verwandte Denkmäler* (Wiesbaden 1966), p. 158, fig. 8, left = D. Kurth, *Der Sarg der Teüris* (*AegTrev* 6, 1990), pp. 26–7: *dỉ n.k Ỉst ḳrst nfrt ḥr Ỉmntt* [...]; P. Leiden T 11, 2–3: [*ỉw*] *n.t* [*mwt*]-*nṯr dỉ.s n.t ḳrst nfrt ꜥꜣt m Ỉmntt m Wꜣst*; too P. BM EA 10314, I, 5–6. This

187. The edge of the frame partly conceals the word following *nfrt*.

function of Isis is to be compared with her title 'mistress of the burial', on which see G. Vittmann, *ZÄS* 117 (1990), p. 85 (lines 12–13, b). It also appears among the functions of Hathor, see Bodl. Eg. Inscr. 1374 a + b, 3–4 (M. Smith, *Enchoria* 19–20 [1992–3], p. 134: *šms=k Ḥ.t-Ḥr nb Ỉmnt tw=s n=k ḳse.t ꜥꜣ mnḫ*, 'You will follow Hathor, lady of the West. She will give you a rich and efficacious mummification'.

I, x + 2

Ỉnpw imy wt snfr.n.f wꜣḏwt.k smnḫ.f tw m mnḫw.f. On *imy wt*, both a name and an epithet of Anubis, see Grenier, *Anubis alexandrin et romain* (*EPRO* 57, 1977), pp. 8–9; M. Smith, *The Demotic Mortuary Papyrus Louvre E 3452* (1979, unpublished dissertation), pp. 116–17.

For another connection between the verb *snfr* and clothes, see G. Legrain, *RT* 14 (1893), p. 64:

ḏd mdw in Nbt-ḥwt	'To be recited by Nephthys:
ii.n.i ḥr.k ḥr mnḫt	I have come to you bearing wrappings
r snfr ḥꜥw.k ḏt nḥḥ	to make beautiful your body eternally and for ever,
iw.k m nṯr	so that you are a god.'

On Anubis taking care of the wrappings of the deceased, cf. P. OIC 25389, XXXII, 3 (*LPE*, p. 503):

Ỉnpw snḏm.f wtyw.k	'Anubis, he makes pleasant your wrappings;
Tpy-ḏw.f swḏꜣ.f ḥꜥw.k	He-who-is-on-his-hill, he makes healthy your body.'

Maspero, *Sarcophages* I, p. 56:

ꜥwy Tꜣyt r iwf.k	'The arms of Tayt are on your flesh,
Ỉnpw srwḏ.f wtyw.k	Anubis, he makes firm your wrappings,
snsnty m sšm.k	and the two Sisters are your guide (?)'[188]

Ibid., p. 153, bottom:

iw.i m Ỉnpw ḥr srwḏ wtyw.k	'I am Anubis who makes firm your wrappings
ḫnm n ḏt.k	united to your body.'

Ibid., p. 9:

Ỉnpw ḥr srwḏ wtyw.f	Anubis makes firm his wrappings.'

BD ch. 167 (ed. Pleyte, pl. 136):

i Wsir N ṯs twk	'O Osiris N, raise yourself!
Ỉnpw tp ḏw.f r-ḥnꜥ.f	Anubis-who-is-on-his-hill is with him (*sic*)
srwḏ.f wtyw.k	and he makes firm your wrappings.'

BD ch. 170 (ed. Budge, p. 441, 6–8):

hꜣy Wsir N sṯs tw	'Hail Osiris N, raise yourself!
Ỉnpw tp(y)-ḏw.f srwḏ.f tw ḥbsw.k	Anubis-who-is-on-his-hill makes firm you and your clothes.'

P. Rhind I, 11, 13 (ed. Möller, p. 52):

Ỉnpw ḥry sštꜣ ḥr wsḫ wtyw.k	'Anubis, overseer of the mystery, broadens your wrappings,
šm.k m rdwy.k ḥr rdwy m ḫrt-nṯr	(that) you may walk with your legs – on (your) legs – in the god's domain.'

Cf. P. BM EA 9995, **IV, 1**; P. BM EA 10091, **I, 4**. P. Rhind II, 5–6 (ed. Möller, p. 56): *snfr.f iwf.t*, to which the demotic *di=f nꜣ-nfr nꜣy=t iwf* [*.w*] corresponds. See H. de Meulenaere, *CdE* 95 (1973), p. 58, n. b.

I, x + 3

Nbt-ḥwt snt-nṯr mnḫt šsp.k ḳbḥ m ꜥwy.s. For the libation from the hands of Nephthys, see P. Vienna 3865, 5 (F.R. Herbin, *RdE* 35 [1984], p. 124): *Nbt-ḥwt ḥr wꜣḥ mw n.k*, 'Nephthys pours out water for you'. More often, the libation is performed by Isis and Nephthys; see *infra*, **I, x + 9**.

I, x + 3–4

Wsir ḫnty Ỉmntt šsp.f twk. Cf. P. Leiden T 32, VIII, 3–4 (*LPE*, pp. 248–9):

Ḫnty Ỉmntt rš n mꜣꜣ.k	'Khentymenty rejoices seeing you;
šsp.f twk m wꜥ m mꜣꜥtyw.f	he receives you as one of his Just ones.'

I, x + 4–5

di.f ꜥḳ.k m-ꜥ wsḫt Mꜣꜥty nn šnꜥ.tw.k r sbꜣw n Dwꜣt iw.k ḥs.ti m-m iḳrw. On the free access to the gates of the Duat, see P. BM EA 10048, **II, 10**.

For the relation between this access and the deceased as a praised one (*iw.k ḥs.ti m-m iḳrw*), see P. BM EA 10048, VII, 4–5 and commentary:

mi ꜥḳ.f r Dwꜣt nn šnꜥ.tw.f	'May he enter the Duat without being turned back!
mi šms.f Wsir ḥnꜥ nṯrw ḳrtyw	May he follow Osiris with the gods of the caverns,
iw.f ḥs.tw m-m ḥs(y)w	(for) he is praised among the praised ones,
nṯr.tw m-m iḳrw	divine among the excellent ones!'

I, x + 5–7

hꜣy Wsir N pr bꜣ.k r ḥrt sšm.f Rꜥ. The going forth of the ba, which usually succeeds the 'going forth by day', precedes the union with the solar disk, and forms a well-attested thema in the funerary literature; see *LPE*, pp. 85 (I, 5–6) and 258 (VIII, 12–13). *sšm.f* is for *šms.f*, see n. 188; P. BM EA 10191, **I, 30** and Smith, *Mortuary Texts*, p. 71 (II, 17).

I, x + 7

ḫnd.k ḥr tꜣ r wꜣt mr.k. Cf. P. Leiden T 32, I, 15 (*LPE*, p. 98 [I, 14–15]): *ḫn.k r wꜣt n mr.n.k*; P. BM EA 10314, **II, 2**.

I, x + 8

ḥs twk it.k Gb. On Geb as father of the deceased, see P. 10191, **I, 50**.

I, x + 8–9

Mꜣꜥt ḥr.k m bw nbw nn isft nbt r-gs.k. For this idea: *LPE*, p. 252 (VIII, 5).

I, x + 9

šsp.k snw ḳbḥ m-ꜥwy snsnty prt-ḫrw m-ꜥ sꜣ Ỉst. On the libation performed by the two Sisters: *LPE*, p. 247 (VIII, 2); also situla ex-Meux collection (E.A.W. Budge, *Some Account of the Collection of Egyptian Antiquities in the Possession of Lady Meux* [London 1896], p. 153 and pl. 20) = offering table Chicago OIM 10496 (E. Graefe, *Studien zu den Göttern und Kulten im 12. und 10. oberägyptischen Gau* [Freiburg 1980], p. 33) = N. de G. Davies, *The Tomb of Rekh-mi-Rē' at Thebes* II (New York 1943), pl. 78: *mn n.k ḳbḥ.k ipn in n.k Ỉst ḥnꜥ Nbt-ḥwt*, 'take for you this your libation which Isis and Nephthys bring to you'; situla Louvre N 908 C, Pierret, *Inscr. du Louvre* II, p. 121 and F. von Bissing, *RT* 23 (1901), p. 42: *in.n n.k Ỉst ḥnꜥ Nbt-ḥwt ḳbḥ ipn*; stela Cairo CG 22120 (Kamal, *Stèles*, p. 104): *šsp.k mw m ḏrt* (?) *n snsnty.k tp ssw 10*, 'You receive water from the hand of your two Sisters at the beginning of (each) decade'; P. Cairo 979 (A. Piankoff, *The Litany of Re* [New York 1964], pp. 66 and 134): *ḳbḥ n.k Ỉst Nbt-ḥwt hrw pḫr Ỉnb-ḥḏ*, 'Isis and Nephthys perform a libation for you, the day of going around the White Wall'. For the libation performed by Nephthys only, see *supra*, **I, x + 3**.

188. Or: are in your retinue ? (*sšm* for *šms*). For this metathesis, see *infra*, **I, x + 5–7**.

I, x + 10–11
ʿḳ.k r wsḫt nt Mȝʿty šsp tw imyw Dwȝt m ḥʿʿ. On the reception of the deceased in a context of joy, see P. BM EA 10201, **I, 2**.

I, x + 11–12
hȝ bȝ.k ḥr ḫȝt.k m ȝw n nḥḥ nn wšr.k ḫnt ḏt. For the traditional theme of the ba on the corpse, see *LPE*, p. 147 (III, 3)

I, x + 12–13
Wsir N spr.k r Wsir nṯr ʿȝ m Imntt di.f ḫpr.k m ḥs(y)w.f rʿ nb. The access of the deceased to Osiris, here expressed with the verb *spr*, is more usually conveyed by the expressions *ii ḫr* (e.g. N. de G. Davies and A.H. Gardiner, *Seven Private Tombs at Qurnah* [London 1948], pl. 22); P. Leiden T 32, VIII, 19 [*LPE*, p. 260]); *ʿḳ ḫr* (Maspero, *Sarcophages* I, p. 17).

For the deceased described as a 'praised one' of Osiris, see P. BM EA 10048, **VII, 4–5**; also P. Leiden T 32, VIII, 4–5 (*LPE*, p. 251):

di.f ir.k ḫprw nb r-ḏr ib.k	'He causes you assume any form at your heart's desire,
iw.k m ḥsyw.f rʿ nb	(for) you are one of his praised ones, every day.'

Cf. also P. BM EA 10091, **I, 7** and P. BM EA 10264A, **x + 5–6**; P. dem. Berlin 8351, I, 15 (Smith, *Liturgy*, pp. 25 and 31: *ḏ=w n=k Wsir ḫnt Imnty.w mtw=k wʿ n nȝy=f ḥsy.w*, 'You will be told as for Osiris the foremost of the Westerners, you are one of his favoured ones'. For the *ḥsyw*, see also P. BM EA 10048, **VII, 4–5**.

I, x + 13–15
šsp bȝ.k r pt nṯr.w ḫt.k m Dwȝt r snsn.k ḥnʿ bȝw nṯrw. On *nṯr*, with the causative meaning of *snṯr*, see M. Smith, *Enchoria* 15 (1987), p. 79. For other activities of the deceased in relation with the bas of the gods, see P. BM EA 10048, **II, 9–10**; P. BM EA 10191, **I, 11**.

I, x + 15
iw.k m wʿ m ḥsyw šps(w) m ḫrt-nṯr. See P. BM EA 10264A, **x + 5–6**.

I, x + 15–16
iw bȝ.k (?) *ḥs ḥr-tp tȝ ḏt.* The sign read *bȝ* seems retouched. No exact parallel has been found.

II, x + 1–2
[... *hȝy Wsir N*] *ʿḳ.k r Dwȝt m ʿb wr.* As the first column of the manuscript bears an original text unknown in parallel documents, it seems unlikely that the missing lines at the beginning of col. II would have shown integrally the initial development corresponding to P. BM EA 10048, I, 1–9, and usually attested in the other versions of the Book of Breathing. See P. BM EA 10048, **II, 1–2**.

II, x + 2
swʿb twk Mȝʿty m wsḫt ʿȝt. See P. BM EA 10048, **II, 2**.

II, x + 2–3
ir.tw n.k wʿb m wsḫt Gb. See P. BM EA 10048, **II, 2**.

II, x + 3
swʿb ḥʿw.k m wsḫt šw. See P. BM EA 10048, **II, 2–3**.

iw.k ḥr mȝȝ Rʿ m ḥtp.f Itm m mšrw. See P. BM EA 10048, **II, 3**.

II, x + 3–4
Imn irm.k ḥr rdi n.k ṯȝw. See P. BM EA 10048, **II, 3–4**.

II, x + 4
Ptḥ ḥr nb ḥʿw.k. Other manuscripts give *ʿwt.k*. See P. BM EA 10048, **II, 4**.

II, x + 4–5
ʿḳ.k r ȝḫt ḥnʿ Rʿ šsp.w bȝ.k r nšmt ḥnʿ Wsir. See P. BM EA 10048, **II, 5**.

II, x + 5
nṯr.w bȝ.k m pr Gb iw.k n mȝʿ-ḫrw r nḥḥ ḏt. See P. BM EA 10048, **II, 5**.

II, x + 5–6
Wsir N mn rn.k ḏd ḫȝt.k rwḏ sʿḥ.k nn šnʿ.k m pt tȝ. See P. BM EA 10048, **II, 6–7**.

II, x + 6–7
sḥḏ ḥr.k ḥr Rʿ ʿnḫ bȝ.k ḥr Imn rnp ḫȝt.k ḥr Wsir. See P. BM EA 10048, **II, 7–8**.

II, x + 7
snsn.k r nḥḥ ḏt. See P. BM EA 10048, **II, 8**.

II, x + 7–8
ir n.k sȝ.k prt-ḫrw m tȝ ḥnḳt kȝw ȝpdw m ḳbḥ snṯr m ḫrt-hrw nt rʿ nb. See P. BM EA 10048, **II, 8–9**.

II, x–8
iwf.k ḥr ḳsw.k mi irw.k ḥr-tp tȝ. See P. BM EA 10048, **II, 9**.

II, x + 8–9
swr.k m šnbt.k wnm.k m rȝ.k šsp.k snw ḥnʿ bȝw nṯrw. See P. BM EA 10048, **II, 9–10**.

II, x + 9
ḫw twk Inpw ir.f sȝ.k. See P. BM EA 10048, **II, 10**.

nn šnʿ.tw.k m rȝw nw Dwȝt. See *supra*, **I, x + 4–5**, and see P. BM EA 10048, **II, 10**.

II, x + 9–10
iw n.k 1 ʿȝ sp 2 nb Ḫmnw sš.f n.k šʿt n snsn m ḏbʿw.f ḏs.f. See P. BM EA 10048, **III, 1**.

II, x + 10
snsn bȝ.k r nḥḥ. See P. BM EA 10048, **III, 1**.

II, x + 10–11
wḥm.k kȝy.k ḥr-tp tȝ n-m ʿnḫw. See P. BM EA 10048, **III, 1**.

II, x + 11
bȝ.k nṯr ḥnʿ bȝw nṯrw. See P. BM EA 10048, **III, 1–2**.

II, x + 11–12
ib.k ib n Rʿ ḥʿw.k ḥʿw n nṯr ʿȝ. See P. BM EA 10048, **III, 2**.

II, x + 12
hȝy Wsir N Imn irm.k rʿ nb ḥr di n.k ṯȝw. See P. BM EA 10048, **III, 3**.

wp n.k Wp-wȝwt wȝt nfr. See P. BM EA 10048, **III, 3**.

II, x + 13
mȝȝ.k m irt.k sḏm.k m ʿnḫwy.k mdw.k m rȝ.k šm.k m rdwy.k. See P. BM EA 10048, **III, 3**.

II, x + 13–14
iw bȝ.k nṯr m Dwȝt r ir ḫprw nb r mr.f. See P. BM EA 10048, **III, 3–4**.

II, x + 14
ir.k nȝ šršr n p(ȝ) išd šps n Iwnw. See P. BM EA 10048, **III, 4**.

II, x + 14–15
nhs.k rʿ nb mȝȝ.k nȝ stwt n p(ȝ) Rʿ (?). See P. BM EA 10048, **III, 4–5**.

II, x + 15
iw n.k Imn ḥr tȝw n ʿnḫ. See P. BM EA 10048, **III, 5**.

di.f ir.k ir.k snsn m ḏbȝt.k. See P. BM EA 10048, **III, 5**.

pr.k r tȝ rʿ nb. See P. BM EA 10048, **III, 5**.

II, x + 15–16
šʿt n snsn n I m sȝ.k snsn.k im.s rʿ nb. See P. BM EA 10048, **III, 5–6**.

II, x + 16
mȝȝ irt.k stwt n itn. See P. BM EA 10048, **III, 6**.

ḏd.w Mȝʿt r.k m-bȝḥ Wsir. See P. BM EA 10048, **III, 6**.

II, x + 16–III, [1]
sš.w [...]. Restore either *mȝʿ-ḫrw ḥr ns.k* or *Mȝʿt ḥr ns.k*. See P. BM EA 10048, **III, 6**.

III, x + 1–2
[... *hȝy Wsir*] *N ʿnḫ bȝ.k m šʿt n snsn ḫnm.k m šʿt n snsn*. For the different variants found in this passage, see P. BM EA 10048, **IV, 4** and **4–5**.

III, x + 2
[*ʿḳ.k r Dwȝ*]*t nn wn* [*ḫfty(w)*]*.k*. See P. BM EA 10048, **IV, 4–5**.

[*iw*]*.k m bȝ nṯr m Ḏdw*. See P. BM EA 10048, **IV, 5**.

III, x + 2–3
ib.k n.k nn ḥr.f r.k irt.k n.k wn rʿ nb. See P. BM EA 10048, **IV, 5**.

III, x + 3
ḏd mdw in nṯrw imyw Dwȝt n Wsir ḫnty Imntt n Wsir N. After a section omitted by the writer of the manuscript, and corresponding to P. BM EA 10048, **IV, 5–6**, the parallel resumes here. On the different variants, see P. BM EA 10048, **IV, 7–8**.

III, x + 4
šsp.f twk m ḫrt-nṯr mi nḥ bȝ.f r nḥḥ. See P. BM EA 10048, **IV, 8–9**.

šsp.f šʿt n snsn mi ir.f snsn. See P. BM EA 10048, **IV, 9**.

III, x + 4–5
ḥtp di nsw n Wsir ḫnty Imntt nṯr ʿȝ nb ȝbḏw. See P. BM EA 10048, **IV, 9–10**.

III, x + 5
di.f prt-ḫrw n tȝ ḥnḳt kȝw ȝpdw irp irtt ḥtpw ḏfȝw ḫwt nbt nfr(wt) n kȝ n Wsir N. See P. BM EA 10048, **IV, 10–11**.

III, x + 6
bȝ.k ʿnḫ ḫȝt.k rwḏ.ti m wḏt n Rʿ ḏs.f. See P. BM EA 10048, **IV, 11**.

nn sk nn mrḥ mi Rʿ ḏt nḥḥ. See P. BM EA 10048, **IV, 11**.

III, x + 6–7
i Wsḫ-nmtt pr m Iwnw nn ir Wsir N isft. See P. BM EA 10048, **V, 1**.

III, x + 7
i Wr-ȝt pr m Ḫr-ʿḥȝ nn ir Wsir N ʿwȝy. See P. BM EA 10048, **V, 2**.

III, x + 7–8
i Fnḏy pr m Ḫmnw nn ir Wsir N ḳmȝ ʿš. See P. BM EA 10048, **V, 3**.

III, x + 8
i ʿm-irt pr m ḳrty nn ir Wsir N iṯ ḫwt m tȝw. See P. BM EA 10048, **V, 8**.

III, x + 8–9
i Nḥȝ-ḥr pr m Rȝ-stȝw nn ir Wsir N sḫwn. See P. BM EA 10048, **V, 5**.

III, x + 9–10
i Rwty pr m pt nn ir Wsir N isft m ḥt-ib (?). See P. BM EA 10048, **V, 6**.

III, x + 10
i Irt.f-m-ḫt pr m Ḫm nn ir Wsir N sȝt. See P. BM EA 10048, **V, 7**.

III, x + 10–11
i nṯrw imyw Dwȝt sḏm ḫrw Wsir N. See P. BM EA 10048, **VII, 2**.

III, x + 11
iw ir.f ii ḥr.tn nn ḏw nb ḥr.f nn isft nb r.f. See P. BM EA 10048, **VII, 2**.

nn mtr ʿḥʿ r.f. See P. BM EA 10048, **VII, 2**.

III, x + 11–12
ʿnḫ.f m Mȝʿt sʿm.f m Mȝʿt. See P. BM EA 10048, **VII, 3**.

III, x + 12
hr nṯrw ḥr ir.n.f nb. See P. BM EA 10048, **VII, 3**.

ir.n.f tȝ n ḥkr mw n ib ḥbs n ḥȝy. See P. BM EA 10048, **VII, 3–4**.

III, x + 12–13
di.f ḥtpw n nȝ nṯrw prt-ḫrw n nȝ ȝḫw. See P. BM EA 10048, **VII, 3–4**.

III, x + 13
nn ir.tw smi nb r.f m-bȝḥ nṯrw nbw. See P. BM EA 10048, **VII, 4**.

III, x + 13–14
mi ʿḳ.f r Dwȝt nn šnʿ.tw.f mi šms.f Wsir ḥnʿ nṯrw ḳrtyw. See P. BM EA 10048, **VII, 4**.

III, x + 14
iw.f ḥs m-ʿ ḥs(y)w iw.f nṯr m-m iḳrw. See P. BM EA 10048, **VII, 4–5**.

mi ʿnḫ.f mi ʿnḫ bȝ.f. See P. BM EA 10048, **VII, 5**.

III, x + 14–15
iṯ bȝ.f r bw nb mr.f. See P. BM EA 10048, **VII, 5**.

III, x + 15
šsp tȝ(y).f šʿt n snsn. See P. BM EA 10048, **VII, 5**.

mi ir.f snsn ḥnʿ bȝ.f pfy n Dwȝt. See P. BM EA 10048, **VII, 5–6**.

III, x + 15–16
ḥnʿ ir ḫprw nb r-dit ib.f ḥnʿ Imntyw. See P. BM EA 10048, **VII, 6**.

III, x + 16
mi šm bȝ.f r bw nb wn.f ʿnḫ.tw ḥr-tp tȝ r nḥḥ ḏt sp 2. See P. BM EA 10048, **VII, 6–7**.

2. First Book of Breathing

P. BM EA 10191 (pls 29–32)

Hay Collection.
Unpublished.
Quirke, *Owners*, no. 181.
Provenance: probably Thebes.
Date: first to second century AD.
Owner of the papyrus: *P(ꜣ)-di-wr-i͗ꜣbt* (Peteporegebthis). He is also the owner of P. BM EA 10304. For the name, see *Pꜣ-wr-i͗ꜣbt*, R*PN* I, 104, 5 and *Demot. Nb.*, p. 178.
Mother of the owner: *Tꜣ-šryt-hry* (Senerieus, not recorded in R*PN*). Cf. the masculine form *Pꜣ-šr-hrj=w*, *Demot. Nb.*, p. 253.

Contents: First Book of Breathing, long version.

Manuscript of one sheet (30.7 × 24.1 cm), in good condition, bearing two columns of text (respectively 53 and 34 lines).

Demotic text on the verso: The Book of Breathing which proceeds (*šm*) under his head.[1]

Translation

Recto

I (1) Thus speaks the Osiris *P(ꜣ)-di-wr-i͗ꜣbt*, justified, born of *Tꜣ-šri͗t-hry*, justified:

I am Re (2) at his rising, I am Atum at his setting, I am Osiris foremost of the West during the night.

Turn towards me, doorkeepers of (3) the West, guardians of the Duat, doorkeepers of the House of Henu! Turn towards me, Anubis son of Osiris, (4) dependable doorkeeper of the Duat! Turn towards me, gods of piercing gaze who are in the retinue of Osiris, gods (5) who are in the hall of the two Maats, gods who are in the hall <of the Field> of reeds! Turn towards me, Hathor mistress <of the West>, (6) Maat to whom the West has been entrusted!

Turn towards me, all gods of the Duat, gods who watch over Osiris! (7) I am your father Re-Hor-akhty from whom you came forth at the first time; I am Horus son of Isis, son of Osiris, who is upon his throne, eternally. (8) I am Haroeris, lord of Upper Egypt, who causes the body of Re to be perfect, setting Horus upon the throne of his father. I am Hor-merty lord (9) of the battle, who causes all the gods to be strong. I am Horus lord of Letopolis, lord of Per-iit, who repels the enemies (10) from Heliopolis. I am Thoth lord of the god's words, who makes the discourse of all the gods.

Turn towards me, guardians of the Duat, (11) chase away for me the void of the hours of the night. May my ba go forth to heaven with the bas of the great gods! May I (12) receive offerings before Atum! May there be made for me a libation of water in the Mansion of the Prince, as (is done for) the great Prince who is in Heliopolis! (13) May I proceed to Heliopolis on the night of the festival of offerings on the altar and on the festival of the sixth day, with all the gods and goddesses of Upper and Lower Egypt, (for) I am one (14) of them. May I enter before Osiris foremost of the West, with the noble gods, on the night of the Henu-festival. Divine is my (15) ba, every day. May I come, may I go, (for) I am one of them.

O Thoth, turn towards me, vindicate me (16) against my enemies as you vindicated Osiris against his enemies before the great Council which is in Heliopolis, on that night of bat(17)tle to overthrow those enemies and annihilate the enemy of the Lord of All therein.

O Thoth, turn towards me, vindicate me against my enemies (18), as you vindicated Osiris against his enemies before the great Council which is in Letopolis, on that night of the festival of offerings on the altar in Leto(19)polis.

1. On this formulation, see *supra*, p. 2.

O Thoth, turn towards me, vindicate me against my enemies, as you vindicated Osiris against his enemies before the great Council which is in (20) Busiris, on that night of raising the *ḏd*-pillar in Busiris.

O Thoth, turn towards me, vindicate me against my enemies, as you vindicated (21) Osiris against his enemies before the great Council which is in Pe and Dep, on that night when Horus received the domicile of the gods, (22) and when there is confirmed the inheritance to Horus, namely the possessions of his father Osiris.

O Thoth, turn towards me, vindicate me against my enemies, as you vindicated Osiris against (23) his enemies, before the great Council which is in Idebu-rekhty, on that night which Isis spent awake, mourning for her brother (24) Osiris.

O Thoth, turn towards me, vindicate me against my enemies, as you vindicated Osiris against his enemies, before the great Council (25) which is in the road of the dead, on that night of taking stock of the nobodies.

O Thoth, turn towards me, vindicate me against my enemies, as you vindi(26)cated Osiris against his enemies, before the great Council which is in Naref, on that night of secreting the stately of form in Heracleopolis.

(27) O Thoth, turn towards me, vindicate me against my enemies, before the great Council which is in Busiris, on that night of the great earth-ploughing (28) in Busiris.

O Thoth, turn towards me, vindicate me against my enemies, before the great Council which is in Ro-setau, (29) on that night when Anubis put his hands over the relics (?), behind his father Osiris.

O Lord of the light, foremost of the Great Mansion, turn towards me! Grant me my mouth (30), that I may speak therewith! Guide for me my heart at the moment of the Evil. Make (?) for me my mouth, that I may speak therewith before the great god, lord of the Duat, without being turned back (31) [from] the sky and the earth, before the Council of all god and all goddess. I am the ba of Horus who causes fire to be quenched when it broke out.

O Ptah, father of the gods, (32)[turn towards me!] Open for me my mouth, open for me my eyes, as it was done for Sokar-Osiris in the Mansion of Gold in Memphis. My mouth has been open for me with the iron *mḏꜣt*-chisel (33) with which you opened the mouths of the gods. I am the ba of Sekhmet who sits at the West of the sky. Make my name to endure (34) [like that of Osiris] foremost of the West; promote me among (?) the primordial gods. Make for me my *ỉb*-heart in the House of *ỉb*-hearts, and my *ḥꜣty*-heart in the House of *ḥꜣty*-hearts! (35) [Make for me] my *ỉb*-heart rest in its place, and my *ḥꜣty*-heart be established in its right place! Grant me my mouth to speak, my legs to walk, my arms (36) [to] overthrow my enemies. May the double doors in the sky be opened <for me> as you do for the gods and the goddesses! May Anubis open for me the portals of the Duat! May I (37) be one of the retinue of Osiris! A decree is written within the Mansion of the ka of Ptah, to cause that my steps be not turned back in the god's domain, that I may do what my ka (38) desires in the sky and (on) earth, and that my ba may alight on earth <according to> my heart's desire. I am your lord, and you are not far from me, every day, by the decree of Tanen (39) the old. Obey me, my own heart, (for) you are in my body, and you are not far from me, (for) I am he before whom a decree is made in the Mansion of the ka of Ptah that he may be obeyed (40) in the god's domain. My heart is not taken away from me by the fighters in Heliopolis. I am he before whom Atum writes annals under the noble (41) balanites-tree in Heliopolis, by the writing of Thoth himself. I make light within my eyes to walk by night and by day <to see> his rays, every day. (O) my *ỉb*-heart (42) of my mother (bis), my *ḥꜣty*-heart is established at its right place; Atum tells me his perfection, and he commends me to Nehebka. He causes me to reach the earth in (43) the horizon of the sky, without causing me to die in the god's domain; he divinizes my ba, he glorifies my corpse, he makes my body live again. Atum sets me (44) in the bark of Re; he causes me to assume any form I desire. He grants me my mouth, that I speak therewith; he causes me to repeat life like Re, every day. If I prosper, he prospers, and vice-versa. (45) My hair is (that of) Noun; my face is (that of Re; my eyes are (those of) Hathor; (my) ears are (those of) Wepwawet; my nose is (that of) Khenty-Khem; (46) my lips are (those of) Anubis; my teeth are (those) of Serqet; my neck is (that of) Isis and Nephthys; my arms are (those of) Banebdjed; my chest is (that of) Neith, the lady of Saïs; (47) my back is (that of) the Lords of Kher-Aha; my belly is (that of) Sekhmet; my thighs are (those of) the Eye of Horus; my calves are (those of) Nut; my legs are (those of) Ptah; (48) my toes are (those of) live uraeus. None of (my) limbs is without a god, and Thoth is the protection of my body. My flesh is full of life, every day; I shall not be grasped (49) by my arms; I shall not be seized by my hands. 'He who is established for millions of years' is my name. My ba treads in the sky and on the earth, and fear of me is in the body of the gods. (50) Geb is my father, and Nut is my mother. 'Osiris foremost of the West' is my name. I am Horus presiding over millions of jubilees, ruler of his throne in each country; I am the old, son of (51) the old, the great son of the great; I am Horus, the heir of Re, I am the image of his father Osiris, I am the male child of Shu and Tefnut, I am the child of Geb (52) and Nut, I am the noble ba in Thebes, and Amun is my name. I am Thoth in each country, and I am risen as king of the gods, without dying again in the god's domain.

(53) O all gods and all goddess, turn towards me! I am your father; I am in the retinue of Osiris. I have traversed the sky, I have opened the earth, I have travelled the earth II (1) in the steps of the noble spirits, (for) I am equipped with millions (of magic spells), and Re-Horakhty is my name. I am

(2) the god lord of the Duat. I have ascended from the horizon against my enemy, and he cannot be rescued from me; I am triumphant as lord of the *wr(3)rt*-crown; I have stretched out my legs, continually (?) I rise and my enemy is overthrown, every day; I (4) sit in the sky. I am strong as Thoth, I am mighty as Atum; I walk with my feet, I speak with my (5) mouth, I see with my eyes, I hear with my ears; I am the lord of life, repeating life, and 'He who lives on rites' is my name. I am the Lion, I am Ruty, I am the first-born of Re-Atum. (7) I stand at the prow of the bark of Re; I seize the prow rope in the *sktt*-bark. O Amun, give me the sweet (8) breath to my nose; I am your noble ba, truly. I am this egg of the great Cackler; (9) I guard this great egg that Geb separated from the earth. If I live, it lives, and vice versa; if it (10) becomes old, I become old, and vice versa; if it breathes (air), I breathe (air), and vice versa. 'He who is judged pure' is my name. (11) Be on your guard against me, (gods) who are in the Duat, (for) I am he who is in his nest as the noble ibis; (12) Thoth is my name. O Amun, give a sweet breath to my nose! I am your noble ba who came forth from you; may (13) I live, may I breathe your air! I am the noble ibis within your nest; (14) I am a possessor of honour before Re. O Hapy, great one of the sky, turn towards me, do not be far from me! (15) I am the ba of the great gods; grant <me> a libation consisting in water of rejuvenation, every day; refresh my heart in <your> over(16)flow. I control water like Sekhmet; grant me that I attain old age like Osiris in Thebes. My throne (17) is Heliopolis; I reside in the Memphis; (my) house is Unu and Bah; my place is each nome being under my command. (18) Give (me) water in front of the gods; I am he who raised at the first time; I am the South, I am the North, I am the West, (19) I am the East. Does one of my appearance exist, except you? Hapy the great, give me water (20) and the breath which comes forth from you! I am he who occupies the place in the middle of the eye of Re. If you prosper, I prosper, and vice versa; if you live, (21) I live, and vice versa. Give me water, (that) I receive your libation therewith; Hapy the great, may I (22) quench my thirst in your overflow! I am one who stands and sits down as Hapy the great; I control him at my heart's desire. (23) Grant that I control this your water, fresh and abundant, as a sweet libation. I am the Lord of All, I am Atum, I am (24) Khepri, I am the first-born of Re, I am a noble ibis, I am Hapy, the first ba of Osiris, (25) I am he who came forth from Nun, I am Re, I am he who raised the sky, I am Ptah, I am he who ascended to (26) heaven. I walk on earth, I am immersed in Nun, and I proceed in the bark (27) of Re, Sekhmet having conceived me and Nut having given birth to me. I am Thoth who fills the *wḏꜣt*-eye, I am the ibis (28) who comes forth from Ptah. May the sky be open for me, may the earth be open for me! I control my *ỉb*-heart, I con(29)trol my *ḥꜣty*-heart, I control my arms, I control my mouth, I control (30) my whole limbs, I control the invocation offering, I control water of the overflow, I control my eyes (31) on earth, I control my eyes in the god's domain. I live on the bread of Geb, I am healthy thanks to the water (32) of Hapy, I rise by the beer, I drink milk, I consume wine (33) and *šdḥ*-brew. I receive the breath by means of kyphi and incense. I am the great god coming forth from the <(great) god>. (34) The rays of Re, the breath of Amun, the water of Hapy, that belongs to me, eternally!

Commentary

I, 1

ḫr.f n Wsỉr N. On this construction, see A. Erman, *Neuägyptische Grammatik* (Leipzig 1933), § 715; J. Černý and S.I. Groll, *A Late Egyptian Grammar* (third edn, Rome 1984), p. 157 (10.3.2). The suffix following *ḫr* designates the deceased, and the example of P. BM EA 10123, 5: *ḫr.f n Ḥwt-Ḥr N* arises from a mistake. Variants are rare, cf. e.g. P. Louvre SN, 1: *ḫr.f r Wsỉr N*; P. Cairo CG 58015, 1 and P. Cairo CG 58007, III, 1: *ḫr.s*[2] *Ḥwt-Ḥr N*. Note, however, the example of P. BM EA 10194, 2, beginning with the formula *ḏd mdw ḫr ỉt.f Wsỉr ḫnty Ỉmntt*, 'To be recited to his father foremost of the West', where Osiris is explicitly defined as the one to whom the recitation is addressed.

Some manuscripts, like P. Berlin 3028, I, 1 = P. BN 151, 1 = P. Florence 3662, I, I = P. Louvre N 3148, III, x + 12 = P. Vienna 3870, I, 1, place before this sequence the extensive title *tꜣ šꜥt n snsn (mḥ 1.t) nty ỉw.w ḫꜣꜥ.s ẖr ḏꜣḏꜣt n p(ꜣ) nṯr ḏd mdw*, '(First) Book of Breathing one lays out under the god's head.[3] To be recited'. See *supra*, p. 2.

I, 1–2

ỉnk Rꜥ m ḫꜥ.f ỉnk Ỉtm m ḥtp.f ỉnk Wsỉr ḫnty Ỉmntt m grḥ. Same reading in P. BM EA 10109, 1–2 = P. BM EA 10125, 2–3 = P. Berlin 3028, I, 6 = P. Berlin 3030, I, 6 = P. Leiden T 33, 2 = P. Louvre N 3176 G, 2–3. Sequence partly in lacuna in P. BM EA 10283, 1–2 = P. BM EA 10343, 3 = P. BM EA 71513C, 2 = P. Louvre N 3176 E, 2. Var. P. BM EA 10194, 2–3: *Rꜥ-Ḥr-ꜣḫty*, with omission of *ỉnk* before *Ỉtm*. P. BM EA 10337, 2 = P. BM EA 71513A, 2 = P. BM EA 71513B, 1 (partly in lacuna) = P. BM EA 71513C, 2–3 (?)[4] = P. Berlin 3028, I, 6 = P. Berlin 3030, I, 6 = P. Berlin 3052, 1–2 = P. BN 151, 3 = P. Florence 3662, I, 3 = P. Louvre N 3148, I, 13–14 = P. Louvre N 3176 E, 2 = P. Turin 1861 C, 1–2 = P. Vienna 3870, 3: *m grḥ m hrw*; P. BM EA 10199, 2–3 = P. Cairo CG 58009, I, 3–4 = P. Cairo CG 58014, 2–3 = P. Louvre E 3865, I, 5–6 = P. Louvre SN, 1–2: *m grḥ m hrw m nw nb nty rꜥ nb*; P. Louvre N 3176 A, 1–2: *ỉnk Wsỉr ḫnty Ỉmntt nṯr ꜥꜣ nb ꜣbḏw m grḥ m hrw*; P. BM EA 10115, 2–3 = P. BM EA 10194, 2–3 = P. BM EA 10303, 3–4 = P. Cairo CG 58015, 2–3 = P. Cairo CG 58019, 2 = P. Turin 1990, 2–3: *ỉnk Wsỉr ḫnty Ỉmntt nṯr ꜥꜣ nb ꜣbḏw* with omission of *m grḥ* and var. Corrupt and lacuna-ridden text in P. Cairo CG 58007, 1.

P. Vatican Inv. 38599, 2–3 shows here a triple invocation: *ỉ Rꜥ m ḫꜥ.f ỉ Ỉtm m ḥtp.f ỉ Wsỉr ḫnty Ỉmntt nb ꜣbḏw*, 'O Re at his rising, O Atum at his setting, O Osiris foremost of the West, the lord of Abydos!'.

P. Cairo CG 58009, I, 4–6 adds:

ỉnk hb km tp ḥḏ ẖt	'I am an ibis whose head is black, whose belly is white,

2. Note the spelling *st* in P. Florence 3662, I, 1.
3. The deceased identified with Osiris.

4. One reads in this manuscript: *m grḥ m hrw* [...].

ḥsbḏ psḏ	whose back is blue;
ỉnk pꜣ ỉr.w šꜥt ḥꜣt.f	I am he before whom a decree is made
m-bꜣḥ nꜣ nbw Ỉwnw	before the lords of Heliopolis.'

The same adjunction is found in P. BM EA 10109, 2–3, with the variant:

ỉnk pꜣ ỉr.w wḏwt ḥꜣt.f m Ỉwnw	'I am he before whom a decree is made in Heliopolis.'

Note that this passage relative to the identification with the ibis occurs again, in another context, in P. BM EA 10125, 13–14. See P. BM EA 10109, **line 2**.

I, 2–3

ḥr.tn r.ỉ nꜣ ỉryw-ꜥꜣ n Ỉmntt nꜣ sꜣwtyw n tꜣ Dwꜣt nꜣ ỉryw-ꜥꜣ n pr Ḥnw. Same reading in P. BM EA 10199, 3–4 (lacunae) = P. BM EA 10337, 2–3 (lacunae) = P. BM EA 71513A, 2–3 (lacunae) = P. BM EA 71513B, 1–2 (lacunae) = P. Berlin 3028, I, 6–7 = P. Berlin 3030, I, 6–8 = P. BN 151, 3–4 = P. Florence 3662, I, 3–4 = P. Leiden T 33, 2–3 = P. Louvre N 3148, III, x + 14[5] = P. Louvre N 3176 E, 2–3 (lacunae) = P. Louvre N 3290, 3–4. Omission of *nꜣ ỉryw-ꜥꜣ n pr Ḥnw* in P. BM EA 10109, 3–4 = P. BM EA 10125, 3–4 = P. Cairo CG 58009, I, 6–7; of *n pr Ḥnw* in P. Turin 1861 C, 2.

P. BM EA 10283, 2–3 = P. Berlin 3052, I, 2 = P. Louvre N 3176 F, [1]–2:[6]

ḥr.tn r.ỉ nꜣ ỉryw-ꜥꜣ n[7] *tꜣ Dwꜣt*	'Turn towards me, doorkeepers of the Duat,
nꜣ sꜣwtyw n[8] *Ỉmntt*	guardians of the West,
nꜣ ỉryw-ꜥꜣ n pr Ḥnw	doorkeepers of the House of Henu.'

Same reading, with omission of *nꜣ ỉryw-ꜥꜣ n pr Ḥnw*, in P. BM EA 10303, 4–5 = P. Louvre N 3176 G, 3–5.

P. BM EA 10343, 3–4:

[*ḥr*]*.tn r.ỉ nꜣ sꜣwtyw n tꜣ Dwꜣt*	'[Tu]rn towards me, guardians of the Duat,
nꜣ ỉryw-ꜥꜣ n Ỉmntt	doorkeepers of the West.'

P. BM EA 10194, 5–6 = P. BM EA 10340, 2:

ỉ nꜣ ỉryw-ꜥꜣ n tꜣ Dwꜣt	'O doorkeepers of the Duat,
nꜣ sꜣwtyw n Ỉmntt	guardians of the West.'

P. BM EA 10115, 2:

nꜣ ỉryw-ꜥꜣ n tꜣ ḏsr	'(O) doorkeepers of the sacred land,
nꜣ sꜣ<wtyw ... >	guard<ians ...> [*sic*].'

P. BM EA 71513C, 3:

[...]*Ỉmnt*[*t*]	'[...] of the West.'

After this sequence P. Cairo CG 58009, I, 7–8, shows a phrase corresponding in fact to P. BM EA 10191, I, 15:

mỉ ꜥḳ.ỉ mỉ pr.ỉ	'May I come, may I go,
mỉ ỉr.ỉ wꜥ n-ỉm.tn	may I be one of you!'

Some documents substitute *sꜣ.tn r.ỉ*, 'Be on your guard against me', for *ḥr.tn r.ỉ*, 'Turn towards me', e.g. P. Cairo CG 58015, 3–4 = P. Cairo CG 58016, 4–5 = P. Cairo CG 58019, 2–4:

sꜣ.tn r.ỉ nꜣ sꜣww n Dwꜣt	'Be on your guard against me, guardians of the Duat,
ỉw wn n.ỉ nꜣ sꜣww n pr Ḥnw	(for) the guardians of the House of Henu have open to me.'

See too *infra*, **I, 4** and **10–11**.

ḥr.tn r.ỉ: a very common expression in the manuscripts of the First Book of Breathing; it is an abridged form of *mỉ ḥr.tn r.ỉ*, meaning literally: 'give your face towards me'. For *rdỉ ḥr* + prep. *m* / *n* / *ḥr*, see *Wb*. III, 126, 10–12. Var. P. BM EA 10123, 1: *ḥr.tn ỉr n.ỉ*; P. BM EA 10125, 23 = P. BM EA 10199, 11–12: *mỉ ḥr.k r.ỉ; P. BM ꜥꜣ* 10343, 4: *mỉ n.ỉ ḥr.k r.ỉ*; P. dem BM EA 10507, I, 15: *my ḥr=k r-ḥr=y*.

On doorkeepers (here, the doorkeepers of the West, *ỉryw-ꜥꜣ n Ỉmntt*): J. Zandee, *Death as an Enemy* (2nd edn, New York 1977), pp. 114–15. 'Doorkeepers of the Duat (*ỉryw-ꜥꜣw Dwꜣt*) are mentioned in *BD* ch. 127 A (ed. Budge, p. 271, 2); they are probably to be identified with the 'doorkeepers of the gates of the Duat (*ỉryw-ꜥꜣw (n) sbꜣw Dwꜣt*) in *BD* ch.127 B (ed. Budge, p. 274, 3); ch. 141–2 (ibid., p. 320, 2–3).

Pr Ḥnw: not here a geographical term, but a designation of the netherworld or of a part of it: J. Yoyotte, *RdE* 13 (1961), p. 93, n. 1. Except for its mention in the First Book of Breathing, it is found only in the text known as the 'great decree issued to the *ỉgrt*-necropolis', in the long version provided by P. MMA 35.9.21, V, 3.

I, 3–4

ḥr.k n.ỉ Ỉnpw sꜣ Wsỉr pꜣ ỉry-ꜥꜣ mtr n tꜣ Dwꜣt. Same reading in P. BM EA 10109, 7–8 = P. BM EA 10125, 8 = P. BM EA 71513A, 3–4 = P. Berlin 3028, I, 7–8 = P. BN 151, 4 = P. Florence 3662, I, 4–5 (small initial lacuna) = P. Louvre N 3176 A, 2–3 = P. Louvre N 3176 G, 6–8 = P. Vienna 3870, 4. Sequence omitted in P. Louvre N 3176 F = P. BM EA 10283 = P. BM EA 10303; partly in lacuna in P. BM EA 10199, 4–5 = P. BM EA 10337, 3 = P. BM EA 71513D, 2 = P. BM EA 71513C, 3 = P. Louvre N 3176 E, 4. Omission of the article *tꜣ* (*Dwꜣt*) in P. Cairo CG 58007, I, 3 and P. Louvre SN, 3; of *ḥr.k n.ỉ* and *pꜣ ỉry-ꜥꜣ mtr n tꜣ Dwꜣt* in P. BM EA 10340, 2. Var. *ḥr.k r.ỉ* in P. Berlin 3030, I, 8 = P. Berlin 3052, I, 3 = P. BN 152, 3 = P. Leiden T 33, 3 = P. Louvre N 3290, 3 = P. Turin 1861 C, 3; P. BM EA 10340, 2–3: *p(ꜣ) sꜣ Wsỉr*.

On Anubis son of Osiris: A. Erman, *La Religion des Egyptiens* (Paris 1952), p. 100 with n. 1; G. Vittmann, *ZÄS* 117 (1990), p. 80, n. 9; J. Vandier, *Le Papyrus Jumilhac* (Paris 1961), p. 155, n. 130; D. Kurth, *Der Sarg der Teüris* (*AegTrev* 6, 1990), p. 24, n. 304.

I, 4

ḥr.tn r.ỉ nṯrw mdsw-ỉrty ỉmyw-ḫt Wsỉr. Same reading in P. Louvre N 3173 A, 3. Sequence omitted in P. BM EA 10283 = P. BM EA 10303 = P. BM EA 71513B. Var. P. BM EA 10109, 4 = P. BM EA 10199, 5 = P. Berlin 3028, I, 8 = P. Berlin 3030, I, 9 = P. BN 151, 4 = P. BN 152, 4 = P. Cairo CG 58007, I, 4 = P. Florence 3662, I, 5 = P. Leiden T 33, 4 = P. Louvre E 3865, II, 1 (different context)[9] = P. Louvre N 3176 E, 4 = P. Louvre N 3290, 3 = P. Vienna 3870, 5: *nꜣ nṯrw*. P. Berlin 3052, I, 3–4, substitutes for that sequence a first mention of the double invocation *ḥr.tn r.ỉ Ḥwt-Ḥr ḫnt Ỉmntt Mꜣꜥt ḥn.w n.s Ỉmntt*, which will be repeated at line 5 of the manuscript; see *infra*, **I, 5–6**.

P. BM EA 10125, 6:

[*ḥr.tn r.ỉ nꜣ*] *nṯrw n tꜣ Dwꜣt ḏr.w*	'[Turn towards me], all the gods of the Duat,

5. A long lacuna occurs after this sequence. Parallelism with P. BM EA 10191 resumes in I, 15.
6. Note, in P. Louvre N 3148, the spelling  of *ỉryw-ꜥꜣ*, showing a conflation of the words *sꜣwtyw* and *ỉryw-ꜥꜣ*.
7. *n* omitted in P. Berlin 3052.
8. Written *nꜣ* erroneously in P. BM EA 10283.
9. Here begins, in P. Louvre E 3865, parallel with P. BM EA 10191.

nṯrw mdsw-ỉrty ỉmyw-ḫt Wsỉr	gods of piercing eyes who are in the retinue of Osiris.'

P. BM EA 10337, 4 = P. BM EA 71513A, 4–5 (lacunae) = P. Louvre SN, 4 = P. Louvre N 3176 F, 3 = P. Turin 1861 C, 3:

ḥr.tn r.ỉ nꜣ nṯrw mdsw	'Turn towards me, gods of piercing <gaze>,
nṯrwt ỉmyw-ḫt Wsỉr	goddesses who are in the retinue of Osiris.'

P. Cairo CG 58008, I, 4;

[*ḥr.tn r.ỉ (nꜣ) nṯrw*] *ỉmyw-ḫr*[10] *Wsỉr*	'[Turn towards me, gods] who are in the retinue of Osiris.'

P. BM EA 71513C, 4:

[...] *nṯrw* [*m*]*ds(w)*	'[...] gods of piercing <gaze>,
nꜣ nṯr[*wt* ...]	god[desses ...].'

On *mdsw-ỉrty*-gods: *LPE*, p. 220 (VI, 9–10); Maspero, *Sarcophages des ép. pers. et ptol.* I (*CGC*), pp. 34 and 35; E. von Bergmann, *Der Sarkophag des Panehemisis* I (Vienna 1882), p. 6; Junker, *Stundenwachen*, p. 4. For the *nṯrw ỉmyw-ḫt Wsỉr*, see P. BM EA 10048, **IV, 5–6**.

I, 4–5

nꜣ nṯrw ỉmyw tꜣ wsḫt Mꜣꜥty nꜣ nṯrw ỉmyw tꜣ wsḫt <*sḫwt*>[11] *ỉꜣrw*. Same reading in P. Cairo 58007, 4–5. Sequence omitted in P. BM EA 10283 and P. BM EA 10303; partly in lacuna in P. BM EA 71513A, 5 = P. BM EA 71513B, 3 = P. BM EA 71513C, 5 = P. Cairo CG 58008, 4. Omission of *nꜣ nṯrw ỉmyw tꜣ wsḫt sḫwt ỉꜣrw* in P. BM EA 10199, 6; of *nꜣ* before *nṯrw ỉmyw tꜣ wsḫt Mꜣꜥty* in P. BM EA 10209, 5; of *tꜣ* before *wsḫt* (twice) in P. Vienna 3870, 5–6; of *ỉmyw* before *tꜣ wsḫt sḫwt ỉꜣrw* in P. Turin 1861 C, 4. P. Berlin 3030, I, 9 = P. BN 152, 4–5 = P. Leiden T 33, 4 = P. Louvre N 3290, 4 tie *ỉmyw tꜣ wsḫt Mꜣꜥty* to the former sequence and consider it as an epithet of the *nṯrw mdsw-ỉrty*. They then show the expected text *nꜣ nṯrw ỉmyw tꜣ wsḫt sḫwt ỉꜣrw*.

P. BM EA 10125, 7 = P. Louvre E 3865, II, 1–2 = P. Louvre N 3176 A, 3–4:

(*nꜣ*) *nṯrw n tꜣ wsḫt Mꜣꜥty*	'The gods of the hall of the two Maats,
(*nꜣ*) *nṯrw n tꜣ wsḫt sḫwt ỉꜣrw*	the gods of the hall of the Field of reeds.'

P. Berlin 3052, I, 4:

ḥr.tn n.ỉ	'Turn towards me,
nꜣ nṯrw ỉmyw tꜣ wsḫt sḫwt ỉꜣrw	gods who are in the hall of the Field of reeds.'

P. BM EA 10337, 4–5 = P. Berlin 3028, I, 9–10 = P. BN 151, 4–5 = P. Florence 3662, I, 6–7 = P. Louvre SN, 4–5 = P. Louvre N 3176 E, 4–5 (lacunae):

nꜣ nṯrw ỉmyw tꜣ wsḫt Mꜣꜥty	'The gods who are in the hall of the two Maats,
nꜣ nṯrw n tꜣ wsḫt sḫwt ỉꜣrw	the gods of the hall of the Field of reeds.'

P. Cairo CG 58009, I, 9–11, substitutes a different text (cf. P. BM EA 10108, **5–6** and **6**):

mỉ ꜥḳ.ỉ r wsḫt ww Mꜣꜥt	'May I enter the hall of the region of Maat,
mỉ ỉr.ỉ wꜥ m šms Skr	may I be in the retinue of Sokar,
ỉw.ỉ m wꜥ n-ỉm.sn	(for) I am one of them.
ḥtp di nsw	A boon which the king gives.
wꜥb.kwỉ	I am pure.'

I, 5–6

ḥr.t r.ỉ Ḥwt-Ḥr ḫnt <*ỉmntt*> *Mꜣꜥt ḥn.w n.s ỉmntt*. Completed with the word *ỉmntt*, this sequence is found in P. BM EA 10109, 6–7 = P. BM EA 10125, 5 = P. BM EA 10199, 6–7 = P. BM EA 10283, 5–6 = P. BM EA 10337, 5 = P. Berlin 3028, I, 10–11 = P. Berlin 3030, I, 10–11 = P. BN 152, 5–6 = P. Cairo CG 58007, I, 5–6 = P. Cairo CG 58008, 5 = P. Cairo CG 58009, II, 1 = P. Cairo CG 58011, 5 (lacunae) = P. Cairo CG 58014, 10–11 = P. Florence 3662, I, 7 = P. Leiden T 33, 5–6 = P. Louvre N 3176 A, 4 = P. Louvre N 3290, 4–5 = P. Vienna 3870, 6. Sequence omitted in P. BM EA 10303 = P. BN 151; in lacuna or omitted in P. BM EA 71513B = P. BM EA 71513C = P. Louvre N 3176 E, 6; partly in lacuna in P. BM EA 71513A, 6. Omission of suffix *.w* after *ḥn* in P. BM EA 10283, 6 = P. BM EA 71513A, 6 = P. Cairo CG 58014, 11 = P. Louvre N 3176 A, 4. Var.[12] P. Berlin 3052, I, 3–4 and 5[13] = P. Louvre SN, 5: *ḥr.tn n.ỉ*. P. Turin 1861 C, 4–5: *ḥr.tn r.ỉ Ḥwt-Ḥr ḫnt ỉmnt Mꜣꜥt ḥn.w n.s(n)*[14] *ỉmntt*, 'Turn towards me, Hathor lady of the West, Maat to whom the West has been entrusted'.

The presence of suffix *.w* renders the verb *ḥn* transitive. For *ḥn* 'to entrust', cf. *Wb.* III, 101, 12–15. In some instances this suffix, pointed out on occasion with the common mark of plural (P. Vienna 3870, 6), is not noted (cf. *supra*). One might then wonder whether the verb *ḥn* could not therefore have the meaning of 'to hurry' (*Wb.* III, 103, 11), taking into account the frequent confusion between *ỉmntt*, 'West', and *ỉmntyw*, 'Westerners' (cf. P. BM EA 10048, **III, 7–8**, with n. 73).

A very close sequence reads in P. dem. Louvre E 10607, 8: *ḥs t=t Ḥwt-Ḥr* <*r*> *ḥn=w n=s ỉmnt*, 'Hathor, to whom the West has been entrusted, will favour you', facing the parallel version of P. dem. Berlin 8351, I, 9 (M. Smith, *Enchoria* 15 [1987], pp. 66 and 75 = id., *Liturgy*, pp. 30 and 37: *ḥs=f t=k Wsỉr ḫnt ỉmnty.w nṯr ꜥꜣ nb ꜣbt*, 'He will favour you, Osiris the foremost of the Westerners, the great god and lord of Abydos'; also P. dem. Berlin 8351, IV, 22 = P. dem. Bodl. MS Egypt. c.9 + P. dem. Louvre E 10605, III, 16–17 (M. Smith, *Enchoria* 16 [1988], p. 59) = id., *Liturgy*, p. 28 (IV, 22, b): *ḥs t=k tꜣy ḥry.t Pyt Ḥ.t-Ḥr (r-)ḥn=w n=s (yw)*, 'This mistress of Libya will favour you, Hathor to whom the West (var.: the Westerners) have been entrusted'; mummy board BM EA 35464, 26–8 (G. Vittmann, *ZÄS* 117 [1990], pp. 82 and 87–8): *ḏd=f pꜣy=t ḥs m-bꜣḥ tꜣ Pyt.t Ḥ.t-Ḥr r-ḥn=w n=s ỉmnt.t*, 'He will say your praise before the Libyan, Hathor to whom the West has been entrusted'.

Except for P. Louvre SN, 5, and P. Berlin 3052, I, 3–4, 5, which separate the names of Hathor and Maat, all the other listed documents combine them in one deity. For Maat mistress of the West, often associated for that reason with Hathor, see W. Helck, *LÄ* III, 1112 and 1118, n. 12; Seeber, *Untersuchungen*, p. 143; also P. Cairo CG 58010, 4 and 6–7: *mỉ rwḏ.ỉ ḫnꜥ Mꜣꜥt ḥnwt ỉmntt* (or *ỉmntyw*); P. BM EA 9995, last vignette, right: figure of Maat-Hathor 'dwelling in the West'.

I, 6

ḥr.tn r.ỉ nꜣ nṯrw n tꜣ Dwꜣt ḏr.w nꜣ nṯrw nty rs r Wsỉr. Same reading in P. BM. 10283, 6–7 = P. BM EA 10337, 6 = P. BM EA 71513A, 6–7 (lacunae) = P. BN 151, 5 = P. BN 152, 6–7 = P. Berlin 3052, I, 5–6 = P. Cairo CG 58008, 5–6 = P. Cairo CG 58014, 7–8 = P. Florence 3662, I, 7–8 = P. Leiden T 33, 6 = P. Louvre N 3176 A, 4–5 = P. Louvre N 3290, 5–6 = P. Turin 1861 C, 5 (lacunae) = P. Vienna 3870, I, 6–7. Sequence omitted

10. For *ỉmyw-ḫt* see P. BM EA 10254, **line 3**.
11. Restoration after the parallels. Anyway, a 'hall of reeds' (*wsḫt ỉꜣrw*) does not seem attested elsewere in the funerary documentation.
12. Variant based on a different spelling of the verb *ḥn*, implying a new meaning.
13. The sequence is written twice, separated one from the other by *ḥr.tn r.ỉ nꜣ nṯrw ỉmyw tꜣ wsḫt sḫwt ỉꜣrw* (see *supra*, **I, 4–5**).
14. *n.sn* in P. Louvre SN, 5.

in P. Cairo 58009, I; partly in lacuna in P. BM EA 71513B, 4 = P. BM EA 71513C, 6 = P. Berlin 3028, I, 12 = P. Louvre N 3176 E, 7. Omission of *ḥr.tn r.i nꜣ nṯrw n tꜣ Dwꜣt ḏr.w* in P. BM EA 10199, 7; of *n tꜣ Dwꜣt ḏr.w nꜣ nṯrw* in P. BM EA 10303, 6–7 (but cf. **I, 2–3**);[15] of *n tꜣ Dwꜣt* in P. Louvre SN, 6; of *ḏr.w* in P. Berlin 3030, I, 11; of the article *nꜣ* before *nṯrw n tꜣ Dwꜣt ḏr.w* in P. Louvre N 3176 A, 4 = P. Cairo CG 58007, I, 6; of *nꜣ nṯrw nty rs r Wsir* in P. BM EA 10109, 5–6 = P. Louvre N 3176 G, 6. Addition of *ḥr.tn r.i* before *nꜣ nṯrw nty rs r Wsir* in P. Louvre E 3865, II, 3.

P. BM EA 10125, 6, quoted *supra*, **I, 4**:

[*ḥr.tn r.i nꜣ*] *nṯrw n tꜣ Dwꜣt ḏr.w*	'[Turn towards me], all the gods of the Duat,
nṯrw mdsw-irty imyw-ḫt Wsir	gods of piercing eyes who are in the retinue of Osiris.'

P. BM EA 10123, 1, which does not follow the classical version, mentions the 'doorkeepers of the Duat, the guardians of the West, the gods of the West, the gods who watch over Osiris'. The 'gods who watch over Osiris' (*nṯrw rs r Wsir*) are also quoted in the vignette of page VII of P. Rhind.

P. Louvre N 3176 G, 8–13, gives the following text here:

iw mi <nṯr> p(ꜣy.i) bꜣ m ḫrt-hrw	'May my ba be < divinized> every day,[16]
iw mi ꜥḳ.i mi pr.i	may I come, may I go,
mi wꜥ n-im.w	like somebody who is one of them!
iw mi sḳbḥ.w mw m ḥwt sr	May there be made for me a libation of water in the Mansion of the Prince[17]
[... ...]	[... ...]'

I, 7

ink it.tn Rꜥ-Ḥr-ꜣḫty i-[18]*pr.tn im.f m sp tpy*. Same reading in P. BM EA 10283, 3–4 = P. BM EA 10337, 6–7 = P. Berlin 3030, I, 12 = P. Berlin 3052, I, 6 = P. BN 151, 5–6 = P. Cairo CG 58008, 6–7 (lacunae) = P. Cairo CG 58011, 5–6 (lacunae) = P. Florence 3662, I, 7–8 = P. Leiden T 33, 6–7 = P. Louvre N 3176 A, 5 = P. Louvre N 3176 E, 8 (small lacuna) = P. Louvre N 3290, 6 = P. Turin 1861 C, 6 = P. Vienna 3870, 7–8. Sequence omitted in P. BM EA 10109 = P. BM EA 10125 = P. BM EA 10199 = P. Cairo CG 58007, I = P. Cairo 58009, I = P. Louvre N 3176 F; almost wholly in lacuna in P. Berlin 3028, I, 12–13, and partly in P. BM EA 71513A, 7–8 = P. BM EA 71513C, 6–7. Omission of *it* in P. Louvre SN, 6; of *iw pr.tn im.f* in P. BM EA 71513B, 4. Addition of *nṯr ꜥꜣ* after *Rꜥ-Ḥr-ꜣḫty* in P. BM EA 71513A, 7 = P. BM EA 71513B, 4. Var. P. Berlin 3052, I, 6: *Ḥr-ꜣḫty*, 'Horakhty'.

P. Cairo CG 58014, 3–5:

ḥr.tn r.i nꜣ iryw-ꜥꜣ n tꜣ Dwꜣt	'Turn towards me, doorkeepers of the Duat,
nꜣ sꜣwtyw n tꜣ Imntt	guardians of the West,
ink it.tn Rꜥ-Ḥr-ꜣḫty	I am your father Re-Horakhty
iw pr.tn im.f m sp tpy	from whom you came forth at the first time.'

Var. P. Louvre E 3865, II, 3–4:

ink hb pr m sp tpy	'I am the ibis which came forth at the first time.'

ink Ḥr sꜣ Ist sꜣ Wsir nt(y) ḥr nst.f ḏt. Same reading in P. BM EA 10283, 4 = P. BM EA 10337, 7 = P. BM EA 71513A, 8 = P. Berlin 3030, I, 12–13 = P. BN 151, 6 = P. BN 152, 7–8 = P. Cairo 58008, 7 = P. Cairo CG 58014, 5 = P. Florence 3662, I, 9 = P. Louvre N 3176 A, 5–6 = P. Louvre SN, 7 = P. Louvre N 3290, 6–7 = P. Turin 1861 C, 6 = P. Vienna 3870, 8. Sequence omitted in P. BM EA 10109 = P. BM EA 10125 = P. BM EA 10199 = P. Cairo 58009, I; partly in lacuna in P. BM EA 71513C, 7 = P. Berlin 3028, I, 13–14 = P. Louvre N 3176 E, 8. Var. P. Berlin 3052, I, 7 = P. Leiden T 33, 7: *ḥr nst r ḏt*; P. Louvre E 3865, II, 4: *ḥr nst it.f* 'on the throne of his father'.[19]

I, 8

ink Ḥr-wr nb Šmꜥ ir di(t) nfr ḥꜥw n Rꜥ iw.f di Ḥr ḥr nst it.f. Same reading in P. Berlin 3030, I, 13–14 = P. Leiden T 33, 7–8. Sequence omitted in P. BM EA 10109 = P. BM EA 10125 = P. BM EA 10199 = P. Cairo CG 58007, I = P. Cairo 58009, I; partly in lacuna in P. BM EA 71513B, 5 = P. BM EA 71513C, 8 = P. Louvre N 3176 E, 9. Var. P. BM EA 10283, 5 = P. BM EA 10337, 7 = P. BM EA 71513C, 8 (?) = P. BN 152, 8 = P. Cairo CG 58008, 7 = P. Cairo CG 58011, 7 = P. Louvre N 3176 E, 8 = P. Louvre N 3176 F, 5 = P. Louvre N 3290, 7 = P. Louvre SN, 7 = P. Turin 1861 C, 7 = P. Vienna 3870, 8: *nb tꜣ šmꜥ*; P. Berlin 3052, I, 7 = P. Cairo CG 58008, 7–8: *ir dit nḏm ḥꜥw-nṯr*[20] *n Rꜥ*; P. BM EA 10337, 8: *ir di* [... *nṯr-ḥ*]*ꜥw n Rꜥ*; P. BN 151, 6: *i-*( )*ir dit nḏm ḥꜥw n Rꜥ*; P. Florence 3662, I, 10: *iw(.f) ir dit nḏm iḥꜥw n Rꜥ*; P. Louvre N 3176 F, 5: *ir snḏm ḥꜥw-nṯr* [...]; P. BM EA 71513A, 9: *ir snḏm ḥꜥw n Rꜥ*; P. Berlin 3028, II, 1: *i-*( ) *ir dit nḏm iḥꜥw n Rꜥ*; P. BM EA 71513C, 8: [*ir*] *snḏm ḥꜥ*[*w* ...];[21] P. Louvre SN, 7–8 = P. Turin 1861 C, 7: *ir dit nḏm ḥꜥw n Rꜥ*; P. BM EA 10337, 8 = P. BM EA 71513A, 9 = P. BM EA 71513B, 5 = P. Louvre SN, 8 = P. Turin 1861 C, 7: *it.f Wsir*; P. Vienna 3870, 9: *iw ir dit Ḥr ḥr nst it.f*; P. BN 151, 6: *ḥr nst wr n it.f*.

Note too P. BM EA 10194, 4–5:

ink Iꜥꜣ nb Ḫmnw	'I am Thoth the great, lord of Hermopolis,
ir di Ḥr ḥr nst.f (*sic*) *it.f*	who causes Horus to be upon the throne of his father,
ink Ḥr-wr swnw	I am Haroeris the physician,
ir di nfr ḥꜥw-nṯr n it.f Rꜥ	who causes the divine body of his father Re to be perfect.'

P. Louvre E 3865, II, 4:

ink Ḥr-wr nb Ḫm	'I am Haroeris lord of Letopolis;
iw.f dit Ḥr ḥr nst it.f	he causes Horus to be upon the throne of his father.'

ir dit nfr ḥꜥw n Rꜥ. Var. P. BM EA 10194, 5: *ꜥwt-nṯr* instead of *ḥꜥw-nṯr*. On the meaning of *nfr*, see P. BM EA 10260, **I, 2**. Allusion to the healing function of Haroeris of Letopolis: E. Jelínková-Reymond, *Les inscriptions de la statue guérisseuse de Djed-Her-le-Sauveur* (*BdE* 23, 1956), p. 19, n. 8; H. Altenmüller, *LÄ* III, 42.

On Haroeris lord of Upper Egypt (designation of the god of Qus): H. Junker, *Der sehende und blinde Gott* (Munich 1942), pp. 58–9; Gutbub, *Textes fondamentaux*, pp. 118–19, n. (be).

I, 8–9

ink Ḥr mrty nb rꜣ-ꜥ-ḫt ir nḫt nꜣ nṯrw ḏr.w. Same reading in P. Berlin 3028,

15. In this manuscript, parallel with P. BM EA 10191 stops here, and resumes further on (cf. P. BM EA 10191, **I, 15**).
16. See *infra*, **I, 14–15**.
17. See *infra*, **I, 12**.
18. Prothetic *i* before a relative form, written here , and in P. Louvre N 3176 A, 5.
19. On a possible confusion between *nst.f* and *nst it.f*, see Smith, *Mortuary Texts*, p. 58 with n. 186.
20. A reading *iḥꜥw*, with a prothetic *i* confused with the sign *nṯr*, is also possible. For the phrase, see e.g. H. de Meulenaere, *CdE* 95 (1973), p. 57, lines 2–3, and p. 58, n. b: *Inpw ḫnty sḥ-nṯr snfr ḥꜥw-nṯr n Dmḏ-ꜥwt*.
21. The sequel of this manuscript is lost.

II, 2–3 = P. Berlin 3052, I, 8 = P. BN 152, 9 = P. Leiden T 33, 8 = P. Louvre N 3290, 8. Sequence omitted in P. BM EA 10109 = P. BM EA 10125 = P. BM EA 10199 = P. BM EA 10283 = P. Cairo CG 58007, I = P. Cairo 58009, I; partly in lacuna in P. BM EA 10337, 8[22] = P. BM EA 71513A, 9–10 = P. BM EA 71513B, 5–6 = P. Louvre N 3176 E, 10. Omission of *Ḥr* in P. Berlin 3030, I, 14; of *nꜣ* in P. Berlin 3030, I, 14 = P. Louvre N 3176 A, 6 = P. Louvre SN, 9 = P. Turin 1861 C, 8; of *nḫt* in P. Louvre E 3865, II, 5;[23] P. BN 151, 7 = P. Florence 3662, I, 11: *iw ir nḫt nṯrw ḏr.w*. In a different context, P. Cairo CG 58014, 11 presents a corrupt variant *ink Ḥr-mrty nb ir ḫt*, and adds: *nty ꜥmḏ sby<w> r*[24] *Iwnw*, 'who repels enemies from Heliopolis', a phrase tied to the following one in all other manuscripts.

In Edfu temple, the title 'lord of the battle' (*nb rꜣ-ꜥ-ḫt*) qualifies Hormerty, god of Chedenu, associated on the occasion to Thoth of Baqlieh; cf. *Edfou* III, 251, 4–5; J.C. Goyon, *Les dieux gardiens* (*BdE* 93 / 1, 1985), p. 162. At Kom Ombo, it is borne by Haroeris, god of Qus; Gutbub, *Textes fondamentaux*, p. 6, n. (l).

I, 9–10

ink Ḥr nb Ḫm nb pr iit nty ꜥmḏ sbiw r Iwnw. Same reading in P. Berlin 3028, II, 3–4 = P. Berlin 3030, I, 14–15 = P. Berlin 3052, I, 8–9 = P. BN 152, 9–10 = P. Florence 3662, I, 11–12 = P. Leiden T 33, 9 = P. Louvre E 3865, II, 5 = P. Louvre N 3290, 8–9[25] = P. Turin 1861 C, 8 = P. Vienna 3870, 10. Sequence omitted in P. BM EA 10109 = P. BM EA 10125 = P. BM EA 10199 = P. Cairo CG 58007, I = P. Cairo 58009, I; partly in lacuna in P. BM EA 71513A, 10–11 = P. BM EA 71513B, 6–7 = P. Louvre N 3176 E, 10–11. Var. P. BN 151, 7 = P. Louvre N 3176 A, 6–7: *nb iit*.

P. BM EA 10283, 4–5:

ink Ḥr-wr nb tꜣ Šmꜥ nb pr iit	'I am Haroeris, lord of Upper Egypt, lord of Per-iit,
nty ꜥmḏ sbi r Iwnw	who repels the enemy from Heliopolis.'

The verb is a writing of *ꜥmḏ*, 'repel', variously written according to the manuscripts: (P. Louvre N 3290, 9; P. Florence 3662, I, 11; P. Leiden T 33, 9; P. Berlin 3030, I, 15); (P. Vienna 3870, 10); (P. Louvre E 3865, II, 5); (P. BM EA 10283, 5); (P. Cairo CG 58008, 9); (P. Louvre SN, 10); (P. BN 151, 7); (P. Berlin 3028, II, 3); (P. Cairo CG 58014, 12). On this verb, see P. Vernus, *BIFAO* 75 (1975), p. 45, n. (aak).

pr iit, 'house of the sword' if one follows the spellings of the toponym including the determinative of the sword (here: ; in P. Leiden T 33, I, 9, P. Berlin 3030, I, 15 and P. Louvre N 3290, 9; but note the writing in P. Louvre SN, 9), is a sanctuary of Letopolis; see Gutbub, *Textes fondamentaux*, pp. 110–11, n. (n); D. Devauchelle, in *Egyptian Religion: The Last Thousand Years (Studies Dedicated to the Memory of Jan Quaegebeur)* (*OLA* 84, 1998), p. 602, n. 54.

I, 10

ink Ỉ nb mdw-nṯr nt(y) di smdwt n nṯrw nb. Sequence omitted in P. BM EA 10109 = P. BM EA 10125 = P. BM EA 10199 = P. BM EA 10283 = P. Cairo CG 58007, I = P. Cairo 58009, I, and probably P. BM EA 71513B; partly in lacuna in P. Louvre N 3176 E, 11. Var. P. Louvre E 3865, II, 6: *smdy*; P. Berlin 3030, I, 16 = P. BN 152, 10–11 = P. Leiden T 33, 9 = P. Louvre N 3290, 9–10: *smdt n nꜣ nṯrw nb(w)*; P. BM EA 71513A, 11 = P. Berlin 3052, I, 10 = P. Louvre N 3176 F, 7: *smdt n nṯr nb*; P. Florence 3662, I, 12 = P. Vienna 3870, 10–11: *smdt n nṯrw nb(w)*; P. Louvre N 3176 E, 11 = P. Turin 1861 C, 9: *n nṯr nb*; P. Berlin 3028, II, 4: *smdwt n nṯr nbw*.

P. Cairo CG 58008, 10:

ink Ỉ nb Ḫmnw	'I am Thoth, lord of Hermopolis,
ir di smdt n nṯrw nbw	who causes to be made the discourse of all the gods.'

P. Louvre N 3176 A, 7:

ink Ỉ ꜥꜣ ꜥꜣ nb Ḫmnw	'I am Thoth the twice great, lord of Hermopolis,
ir smdt n nṯrw nbw	who makes the discourse of all the gods;
ky ḏd nṯr nbw … (?)	otherwise said: all the gods … (?).'

On the word *smdt*, omitted in *Wb.* but mentioned in P. Anastasi I (*di smdt*), see S. Schott, *Bücher und Bibliotheken im alten Ägypten* (Wiesbaden 1990), p. 349, no. 1561. So expressed, this activity of Thoth seems unknown elsewhere. A comparison with the title *wḏ mdw m nṯrw* (Ph. Derchain, *CdE* 59 [1955], p. 249) remains possible.

I, 10–11

ḥr.tn r.i nꜣ sꜣwtyw n tꜣ Dwꜣt ḫꜣꜥ n.i wšr nꜣ wnwwt n grḥ. Sequence omitted in P. BM EA 10109 = P. BM EA 10125 = P. BM EA 10283 = P. Cairo 58009, I; mostly in lacuna in P. BM EA 71513A, 11–12 = P. BM EA 71513B, 7–8 = P. Louvre N 3176 E, 12–13.[26] Omission of *ḥr.tn r.i nꜣ sꜣwtyw n tꜣ Dwꜣt* in P. BM EA 10199, 7–8 and P. Cairo CG 58014, 8; of the article *tꜣ* (*Dwꜣt*) in P. Cairo CG 58007, I, 7. Addition of *ḏrw* after *Dwꜣt* in P. Louvre SN, 11 = P. Louvre N 3176 E, 12 = P. Turin 1861 C, 9. Var. P. BM EA 10199, 7–8 = P. Berlin 3028, II, 5–6 = P. Berlin 3052, I, 10 = P. BN 151, 8 = P. Cairo CG 58007, 7–8 = P. Florence 3662, I, 13 = P. Vienna 3870, 11–12: *wš n nꜣ wnwt*; P. Berlin 3030, I, 16–17 = P. BN 152, 11 = P. Leiden T 33, 10 = P. Louvre N 3290, 11: *wšr n nꜣ wnwt*; P. Turin 1861 C, 9–10: *wš n wnwt*; P. Cairo CG 58014, 8: *nbḏ* (cf. *infra*, **I, 30**), whereas the other versions give *ws(r)*; P. Florence 3662, I, 13: *n p(ꜣ) grḥ*; P. BM EA 10199, 8: *n p(ꜣ) hrw*, 'of the day'.

P. Cairo CG 58008, 10–11 = P. Louvre N 3176 A, 8:

ḥr.tn r.i nṯrw n tꜣ Dwꜣt	'Turn towards me, gods of the Duat,
ḫꜣꜥ n.i (p(ꜣ))wš nꜣ wnwwt n p(ꜣ) grḥ	repel for me the void of the hours of the night.'

Sꜣwtyw n tꜣ Dwꜣt: see *supra*, **I, 2–3**.

I, 11

mi pr p(ꜣy).i bꜣ r ḥrt ḥnꜥ nꜣ bꜣw n nṯrw wrw. Same reading in P. BM EA 10199, 8 = P. Berlin 3028, II, 6–7. Sequence mostly in lacuna in P. BM EA 71513A, 12–13,[27] and partly in P. BM EA 71513B, 8–9. Omission of *nꜣ* before *bꜣw* in P. Louvre N 3176 A, 8. Var. P. Berlin 3030, I, 17: *mi pr bꜣ(.i)*; P. Louvre SN, 12: *mi iw pr*; P. Cairo CG 58008, 11–12 = P. Florence 3662, I, 13–14 = P. Leiden T 33, 11 = P. Vienna 3870, 12: *ḥnꜥ nꜣ bꜣw n nꜣ nṯrw wrw*; P. Turin 1861 C, 10: *ḥnꜥ nꜣ bꜣw nꜣ nṯrw wrw*; P. Louvre SN, 12: *ḥnꜥ bꜣw n nꜣ nṯrw wrw*; P. BN 151, 8: *ḥnꜥ nꜣ bꜣw n nꜣ nṯrw*; P. Louvre N 3176 F, 8: *mi pꜣ(y)* *bꜣ*[…].

P. BM EA 10109, 7:

22. The text following the word *nḫ* is lost.
23. Unless one understands here *ir nṯrw ḏr.w*, 'he who makes all the gods', but the context does not support this hypothesis so well.
24. The transcription by Golenischeff (*Pap. hiérat.* I, p. 67) is erroneous.
25. The word *nb* before *Ḫm* is repeated by mistake in the beginning of line 9.
26. The following text is lost in this latter manuscript.
27. Line 13 of fragment A corresponds to line 2 of the fragment B.

mỉ ˁḳ.ỉ mỉ pr.ỉ mỉ pꜣy<.ỉ>	'May I go, may I come, may <I> fly
r ḥrt	to heaven
ḥnˁ bꜣw nw nṯrw nṯrwt	with the bas of the gods and the goddesses!'

P. BM EA 10283, 7:

mỉ pr pꜣy(.ỉ) bꜣ r ḥrt	'May my ba go forth to heaven
ḥnˁ nꜣ bꜣw nty šms Wsỉr	with the bas who follow Osiris
ỉnk wˁ n-ỉm.tn	(for) I am one of you.'

P. Louvre E 3865, II, 6–7:

mỉ pꜣy bꜣ(.ỉ) r ḥrt	'May my ba fly up to heaven
ḥnˁ nꜣ bꜣw n nṯrw wrw	with the bas of the great gods.'

P. Louvre N 3290, 11–12:

mỉ pꜣy bꜣ.ỉ r ḥrt	'May my ba fly up to heaven
ḥnˁ nꜣ bꜣw n nꜣ nṯrw wrw	with the bas of the great gods.'

P. Berlin 3052, I, 11:

mỉ pꜣ[y pꜣ]y.ỉ bꜣ r ḥrt	'May m[y] ba fl[y] up to heaven
ḥnˁ nꜣ bꜣw n nṯrw wrw	with the bas of the great gods.'

P. Cairo CG 58009, II, 1–3:

mỉ pꜣy pꜣy.ỉ bꜣ r ḥrt	'May my ba fly up to heaven
m-ˁb bꜣw nw nṯrw wrw	with the bas of the great gods.'

P. BM EA 10125, 10–11:

mỉ pꜣy pꜣy.ỉ bꜣ r ḥrt	'May my ba fly up to heaven
m-ˁb bꜣw	with the bas.'

P. BN 152, 12:

mỉ pꜣy pꜣy.ỉ bꜣ r ḥrt	'May my ba fly up to heaven
ḥnˁ nꜣ bꜣw n nꜣ nṯrw wrw	with the bas of the great gods.'

P. Cairo CG 58014, 8–10:[28]

ỉ nṯrw ỉmyw tꜣ wsḫt Mꜣˁty	'O gods who are in the hall of the two Maats,
mỉ pr pꜣ(.y) bꜣ r ḥrt	may my ba go forth to heaven
ḥnˁ nꜣ bꜣw nꜣ nṯrw wrw	with the bas of the great gods.'

On this thema, and on the var. *pꜣy* in front of *pr*, see also P. BM EA 10108, **lines 6–7**.

I, 11–12

mỉ smꜣ.ỉ ḫwt[29] *ḥnˁ Ỉtm*. Same reading in P. BM EA 10199, 9 = P. Berlin 3028, II, 7 = P. Berlin 3030, I, 17–18 = P. Berlin 3052, I, 13 = P. Cairo CG 58007, I, 9 = P. Cairo CG 58008, 12 = P. Florence 3662, I, 14 = P. Leiden T 33, 11 = P. Louvre E 3865, II, 7 = P. Louvre N 3176 A, 9 (?) = P. Louvre N 3290, 12. Sequence omitted in P. BM EA 10109 = P. BM EA 10125 = P. BM EA 10283 = P. Cairo CG 58009, II; in lacuna in P. BM EA 71513A, 13 = P. BM EA 71513B, 9. Omission of suffix *.ỉ* in P. Vienna 3870, 13. Var. P. Louvre SN, 13 = P. Turin 1861 C, 10–11: *ḥnˁ Ỉ* or *nṯr*, 'with Thoth' or 'with the god'; P. BN 151, 8–9: *mỉ ˁḳ.ỉ ḥnˁ Ỉtm*, 'May I go with Atum!'.

Cf. P. BM EA 10110 + 10111, II, 11: *sˁm.ỉ ḫwt ḥnˁ Ỉtm*. Too P. Louvre N 3148, IX, 2–3 (F.R. Herbin, *BIFAO* 84 [1984], pp. 269 and 297–8, n. 92):[30]

smꜣ bꜣ.f ḫwt m-ḫnw Ṯkw	'His ba receives offerings in Tjeku,
wnm.f ḥnˁ Ỉtm	and he eats with Atum.'

For use of the verb *smꜣ* with a name of offering, see R.A. Caminos, *A Tale of Woe* (Oxford 1977), p. 23, n. 9.

I, 12

mỉ ḳbḥ.w n.ỉ mw m ḥwt sr mỉ pꜣ sr wr nty m Ỉwnw. Same reading in P. Leiden T 33, 11–12. Sequence omitted in P. BM EA 10283; mostly in lacuna in P. BM EA 71513A, 14= P. BM EA 71513B, 9–10, and partly in P. Berlin 3028, II, 7–8. Omission of *mw* in P. Louvre N 3176 A, 9; of *nty* in P. BM EA 10109, 9 = P. BM EA 10125, 12 = P. BM EA 10199, 10 = P. Berlin 3030, I, 19 = P. Berlin 3052, I, 13 = P. Cairo CG 58007, I, 10 = P. Cairo CG 58008, 12 = P. Cairo 58009, II, 4 = P. Louvre N 3176 A, 9 = P. Louvre SN, 13 = P. Turin 1861 C, 11. Var. P. Vienna 3870, 13: *mỉ ḳbḥ n.ỉ*; P. BN 151, 9: *mỉ ḳbḥ<.w n>.ỉ m ḥwt sr wr nty m Ỉwnw*, 'May I be granted a libation in the Mansion of the great Prince who is in Heliopolis!'; P. Vienna 3870, 13–14: *m Ḥwt-kꜣ-Ptḥ ky ḏd nty m Ỉwnw* 'in the Mansion of the ka of Ptah, otherwise said: who is in Heliopolis'. Cf. also P. Louvre N 3176 G, 11–12, quoted *supra*, **I, 6**.

In a different context, this sequence reads in other manuscripts; see P. BM EA 10123, **line 2** and P. BM EA 10108, **line 12**.

On the 'great prince in Heliopolis' (*sr wr m Ỉwnw*): Edwards, *HPBM* IV (1960), p. 5, n. 35; P. Kaplony, in *Fs. zum 150 Jährigen Bestehen des Berliner ägyptischen Museums* (Berlin 1974), pp. 136–7.

I, 13–14

mỉ ˁḳ.ỉ r Ỉwnw n grḥ n [ḥwt ḫꜣ]wt snwt ḥnˁ nṯrw nṯrwt nb[31] *n Šmˁ Mḥw ỉw.ỉ m wˁ ỉm.sn*. Restoration *ḥwt ḫꜣwt* without *ḥr* before *ḫꜣwt* for lack of room (cf. *infra*). With *ḥr*, parallels are found in P. BN 152, 14 = P. Leiden T 33, 12–13 = P. Louvre N 3290, 13–14 = P. Turin 1861 C, 12. Sequence omitted in P. BM EA 10109 = P. BM EA 10125 = P. BM EA 10283 = P. Cairo 58009, II; mostly in lacuna in P. BM EA 71513A, 15–16 = P. BM EA 71513B, 10,[32] and partly in P. Berlin 3028, II, 8–9. Omission of *snwt* in P. Berlin 3052, I, 13. Var. P. BM EA 10199, 10–11: *n grḥ n ḥwt ḫꜣwt n snwt*; P. Cairo CG 58021, 7 = P. Florence 3662, I, 15 = P. Vienna 3870, 14–15: *m grḥ n ḥwt ḥr ḫ(ꜣ)wt n snwt*; P. Louvre E 3865, II, 8–9: *grḥ ḥr ḫꜣwt n snwt*; P. Cairo CG 58007, I, 10–11: *n grḥ n ḫꜣwt* ... (?);[33] P. BN 151, 9: *mỉ ˁḳ.ỉ r Ỉwnw m ḥwt ḫꜣwt n snwt*; P. Berlin 3030, I, 19 = P. BN 152, 14 = P. Louvre N 3176 A, 9–10 = P. Cairo CG 58008, 13 = P. Turin 1861 C, 12: *n snwt*; P. Cairo CG 58008, 13: *r* (?) *grḥ*; P. Berlin 3052, I, 13–14 = P. Vienna 3870, 14–15: *nꜣ nṯrw nṯrwt nb(w)*; P. Cairo CG 58007, I, 10–11: *ḥnˁ nꜣ nṯrw*; P. BM EA 10199, 11 = P. BN 152, 14–15 = P. Louvre E 3865, II, 8–9 = P. Louvre N 3290, 14: *n-ỉm.sn*; P. Louvre N 3176 A, 9–10: *m-ỉm.tn*; P. Louvre SN, 14: end of the text after *grḥ*.

On the night of the festival of offerings on the altar, cf. P. BM EA 10108, **lines 9–10**. It is an other designation of the festival of the fifth day, during which the deceased goes to Heliopolis; cf. P. BM EA 10201, **II, 4**. On his travelling in the capital of the XIIIth nome of Upper Egypt, cf. P. BM EA 10124, 9: *mỉ šm.ỉ r Ỉwnw*, 'May I proceed to Heliopolis!'; also P. BM EA 10123, 5: *mỉ šsp.w tw(ỉ) r Ỉwnw n grḥ*, 'May I be received in Heliopolis in the night!'

On the festival of the sixth day, see W. Barta, *ZÄS* 95 (1969), pp. 73–80; E. Winter, *ZÄS* 96 (1970), pp. 151–2; Smith, *Liturgy*, p. 54 (III, 16, b). For access to Heliopolis at that time, see also P. BM EA 10108, **lines 9–10**.

28. The passage is corrupt at certain points:  for *mỉ* (same writing in P. BM EA 10283, 7),  for *pꜣy.ỉ*,  for *bꜣ.ỉ*.
29. Written with a prothetic *ỉ* in P. Berlin 3028 and P. Florence 3662.
30. The reference to P. Louvre N 2131 here must be corrected to P. Louvre N 3121.
31. *nbw* in P. Berlin 3028, II, 10 = P. Leiden T 33, 13 = P. Louvre N 3290, 14.
32. This manuscript stops here.
33. On the inexplicable group which follows the word *ḫꜣwt* (I, 11), see Golenischeff, *Pap. hiérat.* I, p. 27, n. 24. One expects the word *snwt*.

I, 14
mi ꜥḳ.i r Wsir ḫnty Imntt ḥnꜥ nṯrw špsw m grḥ n ḥb Ḥnw. Same reading in P. Berlin 3030, I, 20–1. Sequence omitted in P. BM EA 10109 = P. BM EA 10125 = P. BM EA 10199 = P. BN 151 = P. Cairo 58009, II; wholly in lacuna in P. BM EA 71513A, 17, and partly in P. Berlin 3028, II, 10–11. Omission of *r* before *Wsir* in P. Berlin 3052, I, 14 = P. Cairo CG 58007, I, 12 = P. Florence 3662, II, 2 = P. Vienna 3870, 15. Var. P. Louvre N 3176 A, 11: *mi ꜥḳ.i r-m* (𓂋𓏤𓅓) *Wsir*; P. Cairo CG 58008, 14–15: *mi ꜥḳ.i n-m* (𓈖𓅓)[34] *Wsir*; P. Berlin 3052, I, 15 = P. BN 152, 15–16 = P. Cairo CG 58007, I, 12 = P. Leiden T 33, 13–14 = P. Louvre 3290, 15: *ḥnꜥ nꜣ nṯrw špsw*; P. Turin 1861 C, 13: *ḥnꜥ nṯrw nṯrwt*; P. Cairo CG 58007, I, 12 = P. Louvre N 3176 A, 11: *n grḥ n ḥb Ḥnw*.

Henu is a designation of Sokar, and the Henu-festival must then be another name, apparently rarely mentioned outside our text, for the festival of Sokar.

I, 14–15
nṯr p(ꜣy).i bꜣ m ḫrt-hrw. Same reading in P. Berlin 3028, II, 12 = P. Louvre N 3176 A, 11–12. Sequence omitted in P. BM EA 10109 = P. BM EA 10125 = P. BM EA 10199 = P. BN 151 = P. Cairo 58009, II; in lacuna in P. BM EA 71513A, 17–18. Omission of *bꜣ* in P. Louvre E 3865, II, 10. Text preceding *m ḫrt-hrw* lost in P. Louvre N 3148, IV. Var. P. Vienna 3870, 16: *pꜣ(y.i)*; P. Berlin 3052, I, 15: *mi pꜣy pꜣy.i bꜣ mi ḫrt-hrw*; P. Berlin 3030, I, 21 = P. BN 152, 16 = P. Louvre N 3290, 16: *m ḫrt-nṯr*; P. Leiden T 33, 14: *mi nṯr pꜣ(y.i) bꜣ m ḫrt-nṯr*; P. Cairo CG 58007, I, 13: *nṯr.i*; P. Cairo CG 58008, 15: *nṯr.w*. P. Turin 1861 C, 14: *nṯr.w p(ꜣy).i m ḫrt-nṯr m ḫrt-hrw*. Cf. also P. Louvre N 3176 G, 8–13, quoted *supra*, **I, 6**.

On the divinization of the ba, see P. BM EA 10048, **II, 5**.

I, 15
mi ꜥḳ.i mi pr.i iw.i m wꜥ im.sn. Same reading in P. Berlin 3030, I, 22 = P. Cairo CG 58007, I, 13–14 = P. Florence 3662, II, 3–4 = P. Leiden T 33, 14–15 = P. Louvre 3290, 16–17 = P. Vienna 3870, 17. Sequence omitted in P. BM EA 10109 = P. BM EA 10125 = P. BM EA 10199 = P. BN 151; partly in lacuna in P. BM EA 71513A, 18 = P. Berlin 3028, II, 12–13 = P. Louvre N 3148, IV, x + 1. Omission of *iw.i* in P. Cairo CG 58008, 16 = P. Louvre N 3176 A, 12. Var. P. Berlin 3052, I, 16: *pꜣy.i* instead of *pr.i*; P. BN 152, 17 = P. Louvre E 3865, II, 10: *n-im.sn*; P. Louvre N 3176 A, 12: *m-im.tn* (*sic*). P. Turin 1861 C, 14: *iw* striked out and omission of suffix *.i*. Addition of *mi snsn.i*, 'may I breathe', after *mi pr.i* in P. BM EA 10303, 7.

In a different context, that sequence reads again in P. Cairo CG 58009, I, 7–8; see *supra*, **I, 3–4**.

I, 15–29
With some variants and abridged texts, this section occurs again in P. BM EA 10109, 10–14 = P. BM EA 10125, 15–21 = P. BM EA 10199, 11–15 = P. BM EA 10206A + B, 1–4 = P. BM EA 10303, 9–13 = P. BM EA 10705, 1–5 = P. BM EA 71513A, 19–36 = P. Berlin 3028, III, 1–16 = P. Berlin 3030, I, 22–II, 11 = P. Berlin 3052, I, 16–II, 13 = P. BN 151, 9–18 = P. BN 152, 17–26 = P. Cairo CG 58007, I, 14–16 = P. Cairo CG 58008, 16–28 = P. Cairo CG 58009, II, 4–III, 3 = P. Florence 3662, II, 4–15 = P. Leiden T 33, 15–19 = P. Louvre E 10284, II, 1–III, 3 = P. Louvre N 3176 A, 12–13 = P. Louvre N 3290, 17–19 = P. Vienna 3870, 17–32. Omitted in P. Turin 1861 C.

I, 15–17
Preceded by the invocation *i Ỉ mi ḥr.k r.i* (omission of *mi* in P. BM EA 10303, 9), this section shows a litany *smꜣꜥ-ḫrw.k ḫrw.i r ḫftyw.i mi smꜣꜥ-ḫrw.k ḫrw Wsir r ḫftyw.f*, which recurs in P. BM EA 10303, 10–11 = P. Berlin 3028, III, 1 = P. BN 152, 17–18 = P. Florence 3662, II, 4–5 = P. Leiden T 33, 15 = P. Louvre N 3290, 17–18 = P. Vienna 3870, 17–18. Sequence wholly in lacuna in P. BM EA 10705, and partly in P. BM EA 71513A, 19. Var. P. BM EA 10303, 9–10: *mi smꜣꜥ-ḫrw.k Wsir r ḫftyw.f*; P. Berlin 3030, I, 23 = P. Cairo CG 58009, II, 5: *mi smꜣꜥ.k ḫrw Wsir r ḫftyw.f*; P. Cairo CG 58008, 16–17 = P. Louvre N 3176 A, 12–13: *mi smꜣꜥ-ḫrw.k ḫrw.k r ḫftyw.k*; P. BM EA 10125, 15 = P. BM EA 10199, 11 = P. BM EA 10206A + B, 1 (lacunae) = P. BN 151, 11, 12, 13, 14, etc.[35] = P. Louvre E 3865, II, 11: *smꜣꜥ.k ḫrw.i r ḫftyw.i mi smꜣꜥ.k ḫrw Wsir r ḫftyw.f*; P. BM EA 10109, 10: *smꜣꜥ.k ḫrw.i r ḫftyw.i mi smꜣꜥ.k ḫrw Wsir* (*sic*); P. Berlin 3052, I, 16–17 = P. Cairo CG 58007, I, 14–15: *smꜣꜥ ḫrw.i r ḫftyw(.i)*[36] *mi smꜣꜥ-ḫrw Wsir r ḫftyw(.f)*.[37]

I, 16–17
m-bꜣḥ ḏꜣḏꜣt ꜥꜣt imyw Iwnw. Same reading in P. BM EA 10109, 10 = P. BM EA 10125, 16 = P. BM EA 10199, 12–13 = P. BM EA 71513A, 20 = P. Berlin 3028, III, 2 = P. Berlin 3030, I, 23–4 = P. Berlin 3052, I, 17 = P. BN 151, 10 = P. BN 152, 18 = P. Cairo CG 58007, I, 15 = P. Cairo CG 58008, 18–19 = P. Cairo CG 58009, II, 5–6 = P. Florence 3662, II, 5 = P. Leiden T 33, right col. = P. Louvre N 3148, IV, x + 2 = P. Louvre N 3290, 18 = P. Vienna 3870, 18–19. Sequence omitted in P. BM EA 10303; partly in lacuna in P. BM EA 10705, 1. Omission of *ꜥꜣt* in P. Louvre E 3865, II, 11.

grḥ pfy n ꜥḥꜣ-ꜥ r sḥr sbiw pfy. Same reading in P. BM EA 10705, 1 (lacunae) = P. Berlin 3030, I, 24 = P. Berlin 3052, I, 16–17 = P. BM EA 151, 10 = P. BN 152, 18 = P. Leiden T 33, 16 = P. Louvre E 3865, II, 11 = P. Louvre N 3290, 18–19. Sequence omitted in P. BM EA 10303; partly in lacuna in P. BM EA 71513A, 20–21. Omission of *r* in P. Vienna 3870, 19; of *ꜥ* in *ꜥḥꜣ-ꜥ* in P. Cairo CG 58007, I, 15; of *sḥr* in P. Cairo CG 58008, 19 = P. Louvre N 3176 A, 13; of *pfy* in P. BM EA 10199, 13. Var. P. Florence 3662, II, 5 = P. Louvre N 3148, IV, x + 2: *m grḥ pfy*; P. Louvre E 10284, II, 1–2: *sbiw pwy* (partly in lacuna); P. Berlin 3028, II, 3: *sbiw.f pfy*; P. Cairo CG 58009, II, 6: *grḥ pfy n wḏꜥ snm*, 'on that night of cutting the hair'; P. BM EA 10109, 10–11: *grḥ pfy n snwt n* <*ꜥn*>*p*, 'on that night of the festival of the sixth day, of the *ꜥnp*-festival'. As a result of a confusion, P. BM EA 10125, 18–19 ties *grḥ pfy n ꜥḥꜣ-ꜥ r sḥr sbiw pfy* to the victory of the deceased before the Council of Abydos, while 'that night of the festival of offerings upon the altar at Heliopolis' (*grḥ pfy n ḥwt ḫr ḫꜣwt m Iwnw*) is substituted in this manuscript for the mention of the Council of Heliopolis expected here.

sḥtm ḫfty n Nb-ḏr[38] *im.f*. Sequence omitted in P. BM EA 10109 = P. BM EA 10125 = P. BM EA 10199 = P. BM EA 10303 = P. Cairo CG 58009, II. Omission of *im.f* in P. Berlin 3030, I, 25 = P. Louvre N 3176 A, 14 = P. Vienna 3870, 19. Var. P. Louvre N 3290, 18–19:[39] *n sḥtm*; P. Berlin 3028, III, 3 = P. Berlin 3030, I, 23–4: *ḫftyw*; P. Cairo CG 58008, 19: *hrw n sḥtm ḫfty*; P. BM EA 71513A, 21: *hrw pfy n ḥtm ḫfty*; P. Louvre N 3176 A, 13–14: *hrw pfy n sḥtm ḫfty*; P. BN 151, 10–11 = P. Louvre N 3148, IV, x + 3: *m hrw pfy n sḥtm ḫftyw n nb-r-ḏr im.f*; P. Louvre E 3865, II, 12: *m hrw pfy n sḥtm*; P. Cairo CG 58007, I, 16: *n hrw pfy n sḥtm ḫftyw*; P. BN 152, 18–19: *hrw pfy n sḥtm ḫftyw*; P. Leiden T 33, 16: *hrw pfy sḥtm*;

34. Same preposition, written 𓈖𓅓, in P. BM EA 10338, x + 6.
35. Main reading in this manuscript, where this litany is repeated before each invocation to Thoth. Note the variant (line 10): *mi smꜣꜥ-ḫrw.k Wsir r ḫfty.f*.
36. Suffix omitted in P. Cairo CG 58007.
37. Suffix omitted in P. Cairo CG 58007.
38. Written *Nb-r-ḏr* in P. Berlin 3030, I, 25 = P. BN 152, 18–19 = P. Louvre N 3290, 18–19 = P. Leiden T 33, 16 = P. Cairo CG 58007, I, 16 = P. Cairo CG 58008, 19 = P. Vienna 3870, 19.
39. The invocation to Thoth stops here in this manuscript.

P. Berlin 3052, II, 1 = P. Florence 3662, II, 6 = P. Vienna 3870, 19: *hrw pfy sḥtm ḫftyw*.

The whole of this passage is directly inspired by *BD* ch. 18, 19 and 20, quoted here from the Lepsius edition.

BD ch. 18, 1–3:

i Ḏḥwty smꜣꜥ ḫrw Wsir r ḫftyw.f	'O Thoth, who vindicated Osiris against his enemies,
smꜣꜥ.k ḫrw Wsir N r ḫftyw.f	vindicate the Osiris N against his enemies,
mi smꜣꜥ.k ḫrw Wsir r ḫftyw.f	as you vindicate(d) Osiris against his enemies
m-bꜣḥ ḏꜣḏꜣt ꜥꜣt imyw Rꜥ	before the great Council in which is Re,
m-bꜣḥ ḏꜣḏꜣt ꜥꜣt imyw Wsir	before the great Council in which is Osiris
m-bꜣḥ ḏꜣḏꜣt ꜥꜣt imyw Ỉwnw	before the great Council which is in Heliopolis,
grḥ pfy n ḫwt ḥr ḫꜣwwt	on that night of the offerings upon the altars,
hrw pfy n ꜥḥꜣ-ꜥ ir r sꜣw sbiw	on that day of battle to defeat the enemies,
hrw pfy n sḥtm ḫftyw n nb-ḏr im.f	on that day of annihilating the enemies of the Lord of All therein.'

In *BD* ch. 19, 5–6 (*rꜣ n mꜣḥw n mꜣꜥ-ḫrw*), the victories of Horus son of Osiris, and those of the deceased, are again proclaimed,

hrw pfy n smꜣꜥ ḫrw.f r Stš ḥnꜥ smꜣyw.f	'on that day of vindicating him against Seth and his gang
m-bꜣḥ ḏꜣḏꜣt ꜥꜣt imyw Ỉwnw	before the great Council which is in Heliopolis,
grḥ <*pfy*> *n ꜥḥꜣ-ꜥ sḫr sbi pfy*	on <that> night of battle and of overthrowing that enemy.'

BD ch. 20, 1 (*ky rꜣ n mꜣḥw n mꜣꜥ-ḫrw*):

i Ḏḥwty smꜣꜥ.k ḫrw Wsir N r ḫftyw.f	'O Thoth, vindicate the Osiris N against his enemies
m-bꜣḥ ḏꜣḏꜣt ꜥꜣt imyw Ỉwnw	before the great Council which is in Heliopolis,
grḥ pfy n ꜥḥꜣ-ꜥ sḫr sbiw	on that night of battle and of overthrowing the enemies.'

I, 18–19

m-bꜣḥ ḏꜣḏꜣt ꜥꜣt imyw Ḫm grḥ pfy ḫwt ḫꜣwt m Ḫm. Sequence omitted in P. BM EA 10109 = P. BM EA 10125 = P. BM EA 10199 = P. BM EA 71513A = P. Cairo 58009, II; partly in lacuna in P. BM EA 10705, 3. Omission of *m-bꜣḥ ḏꜣḏꜣt ꜥꜣt imyw Ḫm* in P. BM EA 10303, 11–12. Var. P. Berlin 3028, III, 5[40] = P. Berlin 3030, II, 3 = P. Berlin 3052, II, 4 = P. Cairo CG 58008, 21 = P. Leiden T 33, 18 = P. Louvre E 3865, II, 14 = P. Vienna 3870, 23: *n ḫwt*[41] *ḥr ḫꜣwt*; P. BN 152, 22: *n ḫwt ḫꜣwt*; P. BN 151, 12: *m grḥ pfy n ḫwt ḫꜣwt*; P. Florence 3662, II, 8 = P. Louvre N 3148, IV, x + 5–6: *m grḥ pfy n ḫwt ḥr ḫꜣwt*; P. Vienna 3870, 23: *n Ḫm*; P. Louvre E 10284, II, 6–7: *grḥ pwy n ḫwt ḥr ḫꜣwt*; P. BM EA 10303, 12–13: *grḥ pfy n ḫwt ḥr ḫꜣwt*.[42]

BD ch. 18, 18 = ch. 19, 2 = ch. 20, 3:

m-bꜣḥ ḏꜣḏꜣt ꜥꜣt imyw Ḫm	'before the great Council which is in Letopolis,
grḥ pfy n ḫwt ḥr ḫꜣwwt m Ḫm	on that night of offerings on the altars in Letopolis.'

Like *BD*, and contrary to P. BM EA 10191, all these versions show this sequence after that relating to Busiris.

I, 19–20

m-bꜣḥ ḏꜣḏꜣt ꜥꜣt imyw Ḏdw grḥ pfy [*n*] *sꜥḥꜥ ḏd m Ḏdw*. Same reading in P. BM EA 10109, 11 = P. BM. 10125, 17 = P. BM EA 10199, 14 = P. BM EA 10705, 2 = P. Berlin 3028, III, 4–5 = P. Berlin 3030, II, 2 = P. Berlin 3052, II, 2–3 = P. BN 152, 21 = P. Cairo CG 58008, 20 = P. Cairo CG 58009, II, 7–8 = P. Florence 3662, II, 6–7 = P. Leiden T 33, 17 = P. Louvre E 3865, II, 12 = P. Vienna 3870, 21. Sequence partly in lacuna in P. BM EA 10705, 2 = P. BM EA 71513A, 22–23.[43] Var. P. BN 151, 11 = P. Louvre N 3148, IV, x + 4: *m grḥ pfy n*; P. Louvre E 10284, II, 4–5: *grḥ pwy n*.

BD ch. 18, 10 = ch. 19, 7–8 = ch. 20, 2:

m-bꜣḥ ḏꜣḏꜣt ꜥꜣt imyw Ḏdw	'before the great Council which is in Busiris,
grḥ pfy n sꜥḥꜥ ḏd imy Ḏdw	in that night of raising the *ḏd*-pillar which is in Busiris.'

I, 21–2

m-bꜣḥ ḏꜣḏꜣt ꜥꜣt imyw P Dp grḥ pfy n šsp Ḥr msḫnt nṯrw smn iwꜥ n Ḥr m ḫwt[44] *it.f Wsir*. Same reading in P. BM EA 10705, 4 (lacunae) = P. Berlin 3028, III, 6–8 = P. Berlin 3052, II, 5–6 = P. Vienna 3870, 24–5. Sequence omitted in P. BM EA 10199 = P. Leiden T 33; partly in lacuna in P. BM EA 10705, 4. Omission of *smn iwꜥ n Ḥr m ḫwt it.f Wsir* in P. BM EA 10109, 13 (after *nṯrw*: *iw wḥm.n.Ḥr ḥknw sp 4*); of *n* after *iwꜥ* in P. Louvre N 3148, IV, x + 8. Var. P. BN 151, 13 = P. Florence 3662, II, 10 = P. Louvre N 3148, IV, x + 7: *m grḥ pfy*; P. Berlin 3030, II, 4 = P. Louvre E 10284, II, 9: *grḥ pwy n*; P. BN 152, 23 = P. Louvre E 3865, II, 15: *iṯ* instead of *šsp*; P. BN 151, 13: *msḫnt n nṯrw*; P. Cairo CG 58008, 22: *msḫnt n nꜣ nṯrw, smn Ḥr*; P. Cairo CG 58009, II, 8: *m-bꜣḥ ḏꜣḏꜣt ꜥꜣt imyw ꜣbḏw*. The next sequence (10–11) evokes *ḏꜣḏꜣt ꜥꜣt imyw P Dp*, but in relation to *grḥ pfy n mꜣꜥ ḫrw Ḥr sꜣ Ỉst sꜣ Wsir r ḫftyw.f*; P. BM EA 10125, 20–1: *grḥ pfy n smꜣꜥ-ḫrw Ḥr r ḫftyw.f* (follows: *iw wḥm.n Ḥr ḥknw sp 4*).

BD ch. 18, 25–6:

m-bꜣḥ ḏꜣḏꜣt ꜥꜣt imyw P Dp	'before the great Council which is in Pe and Dep,
grḥ pfy n sꜥḥꜥ snwt Ḥr	on that night of erecting the sanctuary of Horus
smn iwꜥ n Ḥr	and confirming the inheritance of Horus,
m ḫwt it.f Wsir	namely the possessions of his father Osiris.'

BD ch. 19, 9–10 = ch. 20, 4, 5 (var.):

m-bꜣḥ ḏꜣḏꜣt ꜥꜣt imyw P Dp	'before the great Council which is in Pe and Dep,
grḥ pfy n smn iwꜥ n Ḥr	on that night of confirming the inheritance of Horus,
m ḫwt it.f Wsir	namely the possessions of his father Osiris
(...)	(...)
m-bꜣḥ ḏꜣḏꜣt ꜥꜣt imyw Nꜣrrf ḥr st.f	before the great Council which is in Naref from his seat,
grḥ pfy n šsp Ḥr msḫnt nṯrw	on that night when Horus received the domicile of the gods.'

I, 23–4

m-bꜣḥ ḏꜣḏꜣt ꜥꜣt imyw Ỉdbw-rḫty grḥ pfy n sḏr Ỉst rs ḥr i(ꜣ)kb ḥr sn.s Wsir. Same reading in P. Berlin 3052, II, 7–8. Sequence omitted in P. BM EA 10199 = P. BN 152 = P. Cairo 58009, II = P. Leiden T 33; partly in lacuna in P. BM EA 10705, 5. Omission of *ḥr i(ꜣ)kb* in P. Berlin 3030, II, 7[45] =

40. This sequence follows in this manuscript the one relative to the Council of Busiris.
41. Written *iḫwt* in P. Berlin 3028.
42. This phrase, followed by the formula *ḥḥ sp 2 ḏt sp 2*, ends the manuscript
43. The parallel with P. BM EA 10191 ends here in this manuscript.
44. Written with a prothetic *.i* in P. Berlin 3028.
45. Note in this manuscript the presence of a cross in the end of line 6, probably to draw attention to the omission. The same omission is found again in P. Louvre E 3865, II, 17, but it has been corrected in the upper margin of the line.

P. Vienna 3870, 28. Var. P. Florence 3662, II, 10: *m grḥ pfy sḏr Ỉst*; P. BN 151, 14–15 = P. Louvre N 3148, IV, x + 9: *m grḥ pfy n sḏr Ỉst*; P. Louvre E 3865, II, 17: *grḥ pfy n sḏr n Ỉst*; P. Louvre E 10284, 12–13: *grḥ pwy n*; P. BM EA 10109, 12 = P. BM EA 10125, 19–20: *grḥ pfy n ḥb ḥkr*; P. Cairo CG 58008, 24: *grḥ pfy n ḳrs Ỉst* (orthographic confusion between *ḳrs* and *sḏr*, cf. P. Cairo CG 58008, 28); P. Berlin 3028, III, 9: *sḏr pfy n sḏr Ỉst* by confusion.

BD ch. 18, 33–4:

m-bꜣḥ ḏꜣḏꜣt ꜥꜣt imyw Ỉdbw-rḫty	'before the great Council which is in Idebu-rekhty,[46]
grḥ pf n sḏr Ỉst rs.ti	on that night which Isis spent awake,
ḥr ir i(ꜣ)kb ḥr sn.s Wsir	mourning over his brother Osiris.'

Var. *BD* ch. 20, 6: *grḥ pfy n i(ꜣ)kb Ỉst ḥr sn.s Wsir*, 'on that night when Isis was mourning over her brother Osiris'.

I, 24–5

m-bꜣḥ ḏꜣḏꜣt ꜥꜣt imyw wꜣwt mtw grḥ pfy n ir sip m iwty(w)-sn. Same reading in P. Berlin 3030, II, 8 = P. Louvre E 3865, II, 19–21. Sequence omitted in P. BM EA 10109 = P. BM EA 10125 = P. BM EA 10199 = P. Berlin 3052 = P. BN 152 = P. Cairo 58009, II = P. Leiden T 33. Var. P. Berlin 3028, III, 10–11 = P. BN 151, 15–16 = P. Florence 3662, II, 12 = P. Louvre N 3148, IV, x + 11: *m grḥ pfy*; P. Louvre E 10284, II, 15: *grḥ pwy n*; P. Vienna 3870, 29: *grḥ pfy n iw sip m iwty-sn*; P. Cairo CG 58008, 25: *grḥ pfy n sip*.

BD ch. 18, 14–15:

m-bꜣḥ ḏꜣḏꜣt ꜥꜣt imyw wꜣwt mtw	'before the great Council which is in the roads of the dead,
grḥ pfy n irt sip[47] *m iwtyw.sn*	on that night of taking stock of the nobodies.'

I, 26

m bꜣḥ ḏꜣḏꜣt ꜥꜣt imyw Nꜣrrf grḥ pfy n štꜣ ꜥꜣ irw m Ḥwt nn-nsw. Same reading in P. Berlin 3030, II, 9. Sequence omitted in P. BM EA 10109 = P. BM EA 10125 = P. BM EA 10199 = P. BN 152 = P. Cairo 58009, II = P. Leiden T 33. Omission of *n* before *štꜣ* in P. Berlin 3028, III, 12 = P. BN 151, 16 = P. Louvre N 3148, IV, x + 13; of *ꜥꜣ* before *irw* in P. Cairo CG 58008, 26. Addition of *ḥr st.f* after *Nꜣrrf* (cf. *supra*, **I, 21–2**, quotation of *BD* ch. 19, 9–10 = ch. 20, 4, 5 (var.) in P. Cairo CG 58008, 26). Var. P. Berlin 3052, II, 9–10 = P. Florence 3662, II, 12 = P. Louvre E 3865, III, 1 = P. Vienna 3870, 30: *m grḥ pfy n*; P. Louvre E 10284, II, 17: *grḥ pwy n*; P. BN 151, 17: *nsw* () instead of *Ḥwt nn-nsw*.

BD ch. 18, 29:

m-bꜣḥ ḏꜣḏꜣt ꜥꜣt imyw Nꜣrrf	'before the great Council which is in Naref,
grḥ pfy n štꜣ ꜥꜣ irw	on that night of secreting the stately of form.'

Note, in *BD* ch. 20, 5, the probably erroneous relationship between the 'great Council which is in Naref' and the reception by Horus of the domicile of the gods (cf. *supra*, **I, 21**).

I, 27–8

m-bꜣḥ ḏꜣḏꜣt ꜥꜣt imyw Ḏdw grḥ pfy n ḫbs-tꜣ ꜥꜣ m Ḏdw. Same reading in P. Berlin 3030, II, 10 = P. Louvre E 3865, III, 3 = P. Louvre N 3148, IV, x + 14.[48] Sequence omitted in P. BM EA 10109 = P. BM EA 10125 = P. BM EA 10199 = P. BN 152 = P. Leiden T 33. Var. P. Louvre E 10284, II, 20: *grḥ pwy* [...]; P. Berlin 3052, II, 11: *m grḥ pfy m ḫbs ꜥꜣ*;[49] P. BN 151, 17 = P. Cairo CG 58008, 27: *m grḥ pfy n*; P. Berlin 3028, III, 13 = P. Florence 3662, II, 14 = P. Vienna 3870, 31: *m grḥ pfy m*; P. BM EA 10206A + B, 2: *m grḥ* [...].

P. Cairo CG 58009, II, 11–III, 1:[50]

m-bꜣḥ ḏꜣḏꜣt ꜥꜣt imyw ḫbs-tꜣ ꜥꜣ m ꜣbḏw	'before the great Council which is at the great earth-ploughing in Abydos,
grḥ pfy n ḥb Hkr	on that night of the festival of Haker.'

BD ch. 18, 21:

m-bꜣḥ ḏꜣḏꜣt ꜥꜣt imyw ḫbs-tꜣ ꜥꜣt m Ḏdw	'before the great Council which is at the great earth-ploughing in Busiris,
grḥ pfy n ḫbs tꜣ m snf.sn	on that night of ploughing the earth with their (of the enemies) blood.'

BD ch. 19, 9–10:

m-bꜣḥ ḏꜣḏꜣt ꜥꜣt imyw ḫbs-tꜣ ꜥꜣt	'before the great Council which is at the great earth-ploughing
imy Ḏdw ky ḏd ꜣbḏw	which is in Busiris (otherwise said: Abydos),
grḥ pfy n wḏꜥ mdw	on that night of the judgement.'

BD ch. 20, 3:

m-bꜣḥ ḏꜣḏꜣt ꜥꜣt imyw ḫbs-tꜣ m Ḏdw	'before the great Council which is at the earth-ploughing in Busiris,
grḥ pfy ḥtp ḥr.s.	on that night to be content therewith.'

I, 28–9

m-bꜣḥ ḏꜣḏꜣt ꜥꜣt imyw Rꜣ-stꜣw grḥ pfy n Ỉnpw ꜥwy.f ḥr ḫwt ḥꜣ it.f Wsir. Sequence omitted in P. BM EA 10109 = P. BM EA 10125; partly in lacuna in P. BM EA 10705, 6 (end of the text). Omission of *ḥꜣ it.f Wsir* in P. Berlin 3028, III, 15;[51] of *it.f* in P. BM EA 10206A + B, 4 = P. Berlin 3030, II, 11 = P. BN 152, 26 = P. Leiden T 33, 19. Var. P. Louvre E 10284, III, 2–3: *grḥ pwy n rdi.n Ỉnpw* [*ꜥwy*]*.f ḥr ḫwt ḥꜣ it.f Wsir.*

Another version is given in P. Florence 3662, 15:

m-bꜣḥ ḏꜣḏꜣt ꜥꜣt imyw Rꜣ-stꜣw	'before the great Council which is in Rosetau,
m grḥ pfy sḏr Ỉnpw	on that night which Anubis spent
ꜥwy.f ḥr iḫwt ḥꜣ Wsir	his hands over the relics (?) behind Osiris.'

Related to this version are P. BM EA 10199, 15 = P. Berlin 3052, II, 13 = P. Cairo CG 58008, 28: (*m*) *grḥ pfy n sḏr Ỉnpw ꜥwy.f ḥr ḫwt ḥꜣ Wsir*; omission of *n* before *sḏr* in P. Vienna 3870, 32; of *ꜥwy.f* before *ḥr* in P. Louvre E 3865, III, 4; P. BN 151, 18: *ḥꜣ it.f Wsir.*

BD ch. 18, 36:

m-bꜣḥ ḏꜣḏꜣt ꜥꜣt imyw Rꜣ-stꜣw	'before the great Council which is in Rosetau,
grḥ pfy n rdit Ỉnpw ꜥwy.f ḥr ḫwt ḥꜣ Wsir	on that night when Anubis put his hands over the relics (?) behind Osiris.'

46. *Ỉdbw-rḫty* (*GDG* I, 127): an unidentified town in the Delta.
47. Var. *BD* ch. 19, 8: *grḥ pfy n sip*.
48. A long lacuna occurs after this sequence. The parallelism with P. BM EA 10191 resumes in I, 37–8.
49. Same omission of *tꜣ* in P. Louvre N 3079, CX, 17 and P. BM EA 10208, I, 17; cf. Haikal, *Two Hier. Fun. Pap.* I, p. 52.
50. This passage is followed by a final formula which ends the First Book of Breathing. Afterwards the Second Book begins.
51. The disposition of these words in the very beginning of col. IV, now rubbed out, seems improbable because of the lack of available space. On the other hand, a restoration *ḥꜣ Wsir* is not impossible.

I, 29–30
i Nb-šsp[52] *ḫnty Ḥwt-ꜥꜣt ḥr.k r.i di.k n.i rꜣ.i mdw.i im.f.* Same reading in P. BM EA 10199, 15–16 = P. Berlin 3052, II, 13–14 = P. BN 151, 18–19 = P. BN 152, 27–8 = P. Leiden T 33, 20 = P. Louvre E 3865, III, 4–5 = P. Louvre E 10284, III, 3–4 = P. Louvre N 3279, I, 1–2 = P. Vienna 3870, 34. Sequence omitted in P. BM EA 10109 = P. BM EA 10125; partly in lacuna in P. BM EA 10206A + B, 4, and partly rubbed out in P. Florence 3662, II, 15–16. Omission of *n.i* in P. Berlin 3030, II, 12; of *mdw.i* in P. Berlin 3028, IV, 1; of suffix *.i* after *mdw* in P. Cairo CG 58008, 29. Var. P. Cairo CG 58008, 29: *n-im.f.*

Passage adapted from *BD* ch. 21, 1–2 (Lepsius), following *CT* IV, 386–8 (sp. 351):

ind ḥr.k Wsir nb šsp	'Hail to you, Osiris, lord of light,
ḫnty Ḥwt-ꜥꜣt	presiding over the Great Mansion,
ḥry-ib[53] *kkw-smꜣw*	dwelling in darkness!
ii.n.i ḫr.k ꜣḫ wꜥb	I have come to you, blessed and pure,
ꜥwy.i ḥꜣ.k	my arms behind you;
iw.i ir.k iry-ꜥꜣ.k tp(y)w.k (?)[54]	I have (come) to you, your doorkeeper and your chiefs.
di.f n.f rꜣ.f mdw.f im.f	May he give him his mouth, that he may speak therewith.'

BD ch. 21 (ed. Budge, p. 85):

ind ḥr.k Nb-šsp	'Hail to you, Lord of light,
ḫnty ḥwt-ꜥꜣt	presiding over the Great Mansion,
ḥr-tp kkw-smꜣw	master of darkness!
ii.n.i ḫr.k ꜣḫ.ti wꜥb.ti	I have come to you, (you being) blessed and pure,
ꜥwy.k ḥꜣ.k	your arms behind you,
dniw.k tpw n.k	your bowls upon your head (?).
di.k n.i rꜣ.i mdw.i im.f	May you give me my mouth, that I may speak therewith.'

BD ch. 21 (E.A.W. Budge, *The Greenfield Papyrus in the British Museum*, London 1912, pl. 23, 9–10):

ind ḥr.k Nb-šsp	'Hail to you, Lord of light,
ḫnty ḥwt-ꜥꜣt	presiding over the Great Mansion,
ḥr-tp kkw-smꜣw	master of darkness!
ii.n.i ḫr.k ꜣḫ.ti wꜥb.ti	I have come to you, (you being) blessed and pure,
ꜥwy.k ḥꜣ.k	your arms behind you
… di.k n.i rꜣ.i mdw.i im.f	… May you give me my mouth, that I may speak therewith.'

Var. P. Vatican inv. 38581, VII, 1–2:

ind ḥr.k Nb-šsp	'Hail to you, Lord of light,
ḫnty ḥwt-ꜥꜣt	presiding over the Great Mansion,
ḥry-ib kkw-smꜣw	dwelling in darkness!
ii.n. Wsir N ꜣḫ wꜥb	The Osiris N has come blessed and pure,
ꜥwy.k ḥꜣ.k	your arms behind you
(… …)	(… …)
di.k n.f rꜣ.f mdw.f im.f	May you give him his mouth, that he may speak therewith! '

nb šsp as an epithet of Re: *BD* ch. 85 (ed. Budge, p. 184, 9). Cf. too P. Berlin 3162, II, 3–4: *Nb-išsp ḥr dr sty* (?); *Urk.* IV, 2101, 8.

I, 30
sšm.k n.i ib.i m ꜣt nt nbd. Same reading in P. BM EA 10199, 16 = P. Berlin 3028, IV, 1–2 = P. Berlin 3030, II, 12–13 = P. Berlin 3052, II, 14 = P. BN 151, 19 = P. BN 152, 28 = P. Cairo CG 58008, 30 = P. Florence 3662, II, 16 = P. Leiden T 33, 20 = P. Louvre E 10284, III, 4–5 = P. Louvre N 3279, I, 2 = P. Vienna 3870, 34–5. Sequence omitted in P. BM EA 10109 = P. BM EA 10125; partly in lacuna in P. BM EA 10206A + B, 5. Var. P. Louvre E 3865, III, 5: *sndm.k* instead of *sšm.k.*

BD ch. 21, 2:

šms ib.f r wnwt.f nbd grḥ	'guiding his heart at his evil hour, at night.'

Var. P. Ryerson, XII, 11–12 (Allen, *Book of the Dead Documents*, pl. 17 and p. 107): *sšm.k ib.f r / wnwt.f n nbd grḥ*. On the metathesis *sšm / šms*, see P. BM EA 10260, **I, x + 5–7**.

ꜣt nt nbd: on *nbd*, cf. H. Kees, *ZÄS* 59 (1924), pp. 69–70; Smith, *Mortuary Texts*, p. 57 (I, 4); *LPE*, pp. 215–16 (VI, 1).

I, 30–1
ir.k n.i rꜣ.i mdw.i im.f m-bꜣḥ nṯr ꜥꜣ nb Dwꜣt nn šnꜥ[.tw.i m] pt tꜣ m-bꜣḥ ḏꜣḏꜣt nt nṯr nb nṯrt nb(t). Same reading in P. Berlin 3052, II, 15–16 = P. Cairo CG 58008, 30 = P. Florence 3662, II, 16 = P. Vienna 3870, 34–5. Sequence omitted in P. BM EA 10109 = P. BM EA 10125 = P. BM EA 10199; partly in lacuna in P. BM EA 10206A + B, 5–6. Omission of *m-bꜣḥ ḏꜣḏꜣt nt nṯr nb nṯrt nb(t)* in P. Louvre N 3279. Var. P. Vienna 3870, 35: *nb Imntt* instead of *nb Dwꜣt*; P. Berlin 3028, IV, 2–3 = P. Berlin 3030, II, 14 = P. BN 152, 30 = P. Leiden T 33, 21 = P. Louvre E 3865, III, 6 = P. Louvre E 10284, III, 6 = P. Vienna 3870, 35: *nn šnꜥ.tw(i)*; P. Cairo CG 58008, 30–1 = P. Louvre E 3865, III, 6: *m pt m tꜣ*; P. Louvre E 10284, III, 6: *m štꜣ (sic)*;[55] P. Leiden T 33, 21: *nṯrt nbw (sic)*; P. Berlin 3028, IV, 3: *nṯrw nb nṯrwt nb*; P. BN 151, 20: *nṯrwt nbt.*

BD ch. 22, 1:

iw rdi.t(w) n.i rꜣ.i	'My mouth has been given me
mdt.n.i im	(that) I may speak therewith
iw.i m-bꜣḥ ḏꜣḏꜣt ꜥꜣt	when I am before the great Council,
m-bꜣḥ nṯr ꜥꜣ nb Dwꜣt	before the great god lord of the Duat,
<*nn*> *ḫsf ꜥ*	<without> being kept away
m ḏꜣḏꜣt nt nṯr nb nṯrt nbt	from the Council of every god and every goddess.'

On this passage, see also *infra*, **I, 35**.

P. Vatican Inv. 38608, 3 (F.R. Herbin, *RdE* 54 [2003] p. 83):

rꜣ.k n.k mdw.k im.f	'Your mouth belongs to you, (that) you may speak therewith.'

I, 31
ink bꜣ n Ḥr ir ꜥḥm ḫt m pr.s. Same reading in P. Berlin 3028, IV, 3–4 = P. Louvre E 10284, III, 6–7. Sequence omitted in P. BM EA 10109 = P. BM EA 10125 = P. BM EA 10199; partly in lacuna in P. BM EA 10206A + B, 6. Omission of *n* before *Ḥr* in P. Florence 3662, III, 1. Var. P. Cairo CG 58008, 31–2 = P. Louvre N 3279, I, 4: *ink Ḥr wr*;[56] P. Berlin 3052, II, 16: *ink Ḥr*; P. Vienna 3870, 35: *iw ir*; P. Berlin 3030, II, 15 = P. BN 151, 20 = P. BN 152, 31 = P. Leiden T 33, 22:[57] *i-ir*; P. Louvre E 3865, III, 7: *ꜥḥm sḏt.*

BD ch. 22, 2–3:

52. Written with a prothetic *i* in P. Florence 3662, II, 15.
53. Instead of *ḥry-ib*, other versions give *ḥr(y)-tp*, 'master', following the reading of *CT.*
54. Same reading in P. OIC 9787, XII, 9–10 (Allen, *Book of the Dead Documents*, pl. 17, and p. 107). This passage contains many variants and corruptions.
55. A confusion between the hieratic groups and is possible here.
56. *wr* is in lacuna in P. Louvre N 3279, but the restoration is probable.
57. For the continuation of the text, see P. BM EA 10191, **II, 34**.

ii.n.i ir.i mr ib.i	'I have come, having accomplished my heart's desire,
m hrw nsrt	on the day of the flame;
ꜥḫm.i sḏt m pr.s	I quench fire when it broke out.'

Var. ed. Naville, pl. 33: *ir.n.i mrt ib.i m iw nsrsr*, 'I have come, having accomplished my heart's desire in the Isle of Flame'.

On this sequence, see J.C. Goyon, *Le Papyrus du Louvre N 3279* (*BdE* 42, 1966), p. 31, n. 3; Y. Koenig, *Le Papyrus Boulaq 6* (*BdE* 87, 1981), p. 31, n. (o). Cf. too P. Ebers 499 and 500, where Isis is said to quench fire (*ꜥḫm ḫt*) following the burning of her son Horus in the desert.

I, 31–2

i Ptḥ it nṯrw [*ḫr.k r.i*]. Same reading in P. BM EA 10199, 16–17 = P. BM EA 10338, x + 1 (small initial lacuna) = P. Berlin 3028, IV, 4 = P. Berlin 3030, II, 15–16 = P. Berlin 3052, II, 16 = P. BN 151, 20 = P. Cairo CG 58007, I, 17 = P. Cairo CG 58008, 32 = P. Florence 3662, III, 1–2 = P. Louvre E 3865, III, 7 = P. Vienna 3870, 36–7. Sequence omitted in P. BM EA 10109 = P. BM EA 10125; mostly in lacuna in P. BM EA 10206A + B, 7. Omission of the interjection *i* before *Ptḥ* in P. Louvre N 3279, I, 5; of *ḫr.k r.i* in P. Louvre E 10284, III, 7.

I, 32

wn n.i r3.i wp n.i irty.i mi ir.t n Skr-Wsir m ḥwt-nwb m Inb-ḥḏ. Sequence omitted in P. BM EA 10109 = P. BM EA 10125; wholly in lacuna in P. BM EA 10338, x + 1, and partly in P. BM EA 10206A + B, 7. Omission of *mi ir.t n Skr-Wsir m ḥwt-nwb m Inb-ḥḏ* in P. BM EA 10199, 17; of suffix *.i* after *r3* in P. Vienna 3870, 37. Var. P. Berlin 3030, II, 16 = P. BN 152, 33: *irt.i*;[58] P. Berlin 3052, III, 1: *wp.k n.i sw*; P. BM EA 10199, 16–17 = P. Cairo CG 58008, 32–3 = P. Louvre N 3279, I, 5–6: *wn.k n.i*, *wp.k n.i*; P. Louvre E 10284, III, 7–8: *wp.k n.i*, *wp.k n.i irt.i*, *mi ir.k*; P. Cairo CG 58007, I, 18[59] = P. Cairo CG 58008, 33 = P. Berlin 3028, IV, 4 = P. Berlin 3030, II, 16 = P. Berlin 3052, III, 1 = P. BN 151, 21 = P. BN 152, 33 = P. Florence 3662, III, 2 = P. Louvre E 3865, III, 7 = P. Louvre E 10284, III, 8 = P. Louvre N 3279, I, 6 = P. Vienna 3870, 37: *mi ir.k*; P. Vienna 3870, 38: *n Inb-ḥḏ*.

BD ch. 23, 1:

wn r3.i in Ptḥ	'My mouth has been opened by Ptah.'

I, 32–3

i-wn n.i r3.i m mḏ3t [*nt*] *bi3 i-wp.k* [60] *r3 n nṯrw im.s*. Same reading in P. BN 151, 21 = P. BN 152, 34 = P. Berlin 3028, IV, 5–6 = P. Berlin 3030, II, 17–18 = P. Cairo CG 58007, I, 18–19 = P. Florence 3662, III, 3–4 = P. Louvre N 3279, I, 7. Sequence omitted in P. BM EA 10109 = P. BM EA 10125 = P. BM EA 10199 = P. Berlin 3052; partly in lacuna in P. BM EA 10206A + B, 8 and P. BM EA 10338, x + 2. Omission of the prothetic *i-* before *wn* in P. Louvre E 3865, III, 8; before *wp* in P. Cairo CG 58008, 34; of *n.i* after *wn* in P. Cairo CG 58008, 33. Var. P. BM EA 10338, x + 2 = P. Cairo CG 58007, I, 18 = P. Cairo CG 58008, 34 = P. Louvre N 3279, I, 7: *im.f*; P. Vienna 3870, 37–8: *im.sn*; P. Louvre E 3865, III, 8: *r3w.i* (*sic*); P. BM EA 10338, x + 2: *m-m mḏ3t*; addition of *twy* after *mḏ3t* in P. Louvre E 10284, III, 9.

In contrast to the writing  of the prothetic *i-* before the imperative *wn* and the relative form *wp*, present in P. BN 151, 21 = P. BN 152, 34 = P. Florence 3662, III, 3–4, note the forms  *wn n.i* ... *wp.k* in P. Louvre N 3279, I, 7; *wn n.i* ...  *wp.k* in P. Berlin 3028, IV, 5–6 = P. Cairo CG 58007, I, 18–19;  *wn n.i* ... *wp.k* in P. Berlin 3030, II, 17; *wn n.i* ... *wp.k* in P. Vienna 3870, 38 = P. Florence 3662, III, 3. On the prothetic *i-*, see Lefebvre, *Grammaire*, §§ 232 and 338; A. Erman, *Neuägyptische Grammatik* §§ 348–51 and 393; J. Černý and S.I. Groll, A *Late Egyptian Grammar* (3rd edn, Rome 1984), pp. 463–5.

BD ch. 23, 2–3:

wn r3.i in Ptḥ m mḏ3t.f twy nt	'My mouth has been opened by Ptah with this metal *bi3* chisel of his,
wp r3 n nṯrw im.s	with which the mouths of the gods were open.'

Lefebvre, *Petosiris* II, p. 62, no. 82, lines 69–72:

wn r3.k in Ptḥ	'Your mouth has been opened by Ptah,
wp r3.k in Skr	your mouth has been opened by Sokar
m mḏ3t twy n bi3	with this metal chisel,
wp.f r3 n nṯrw im.s	with which he opened the mouths of the gods.'

I, 33

ink b3 n Sḫmt nt(y) ḥms ḥr imy-wrt nt pt. Same reading in P. Berlin 3030, II, 18–19 = P. BN 151, 21 = P. BN 152, 34–5 = P. Louvre E 3865, III, 9. Sequence omitted in P. BM EA 10109 = P. BM EA 10125 = P. BM EA 10199; partly in lacuna in P. BM EA 10206A + B, 8–9 = P. BM EA 10338, x + 2–3. Omission of *n* before *Sḫmt* in P. Berlin 3028, IV, 6; of *nt pt* in P. Louvre N 3279, I, 9. Var. P. Louvre N 3279, I, 8: *ink Nfr-tm s3 Sḫmt*, 'I am Nefertum, son of Sekhmet'; P. Berlin 3052, III, 1 = P. Cairo CG 58007, I, 19 = P. Cairo CG 58008, 34 = P. Florence 3662, III, 4 = P. Vienna 3870, 39: *ink s3(t) Sḫmt*, 'I am the son (the daughter) of Sekhmet'; P. BM EA 10206A + B, 8: *ink b3* or *s3* (sign partly in lacuna); P. Louvre E 10284, III, 10: *nty ḥms.tw*.

BD ch. 23, 3:

ink Sḫmt	'I am Sekhmet
ḥms ḥr-gs imy-wrt ꜥ3t nt pt	who sits at the great West of the sky.'

For other cases of confusion between *s3* and *b3*, cf. *infra*, **II, 7–8**; P. BM EA 10109, **line 2**, n. 3; P. BM EA 10110 + 10111, **I, 2**; Goyon, *Rituels funéraires*, p. 218, n. d. On *Imy-wrt*, see G. Vittmann, *SAK* 22 (1995), p. 315, n. 137.

I, 33–4

srwḏ.k rn.i [*mi Wsir*] *ḫnty Imntt ṯnw.k wi ḫnt nṯrw p3wtyw*. Sequence omitted in P. BM EA 10109 = P. BM EA 10125 = P. BM EA 10199; partly in lacuna in P. BM EA 10338, 3. Omission of suffix *.i* after *rn* in P. BN 151, 22; of *Wsir* in P. Louvre E 3865, III, 9; of *ḫnty Imntt* in P. Berlin 3028, IV, 7. Var. P. Louvre E 3865, III, 9 = P. Vienna 3870, 39: *srwḏ twk* (*sic*). Apart from P. BM EA 10191, the variant *ṯnw.k wi* is only known in P. Cairo CG 58008, 35 and P. Cairo CG 58023 B, x + 1. P. BM EA 10338, x + 3 = P. Florence 3662, III, 5 = P. Louvre E 10284, III, 11 = P. Vienna 3870, 40: *ṯnw.k twi*,[61] the pronoun *twi* being written *tw* [62] in P. BM EA 10338, 3 = P. Berlin 3030, II, 19 = P. BN 152, 36 = P. Louvre N 3279, I, 10; P. Berlin 3028, IV, 7 = P. Berlin 3052, III, 2 = P. Cairo CG 58007, II, 1–2: *ṯnw.i twk*; P. Cairo CG 58008, 35: *ṯnw tw nṯrw p3wtyw*, 'the primordial gods promote

58. On the singular *irt.i*, see P. BM EA 10048, **III, 6**, with n. 60.
59. The transcription by Golenischeff is here to be corrected. Read in line 17: 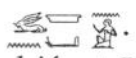.
60. Read  and not  ? in P. Cairo CG 58007, I, 19 (Golenischeff, *Pap. hiérat.* I, p. 25).
61. Written  in P. Florence.
62. See *LPE*, p. 263 (VIII, 23–4).

you'; P. BN 151, 22: *ṯnw.tw.k*, 'you are promoted'; P. BM EA 10206A + B, 9 = P. Louvre E 3865, III, 9–10: major lacuna, and *ṯnw.tw.k*.[63]

I, 34
ỉr.k n.ỉ ỉb.ỉ m pr ỉbw ḥꜣty.ỉ m pr ḥꜣtyw. Same reading in P. Berlin 3028, IV, 8 = P. Berlin 3030, II, 20 = P. Berlin 3052, III, 2–3 = P. BN 151, 22 = P. BN 152, 36 = P. Cairo CG 58007, II, 2–3 = P. Cairo CG 58008, 35–6 = P. Florence 3662, III, 5–6 = P. Louvre E 3865, III, 10 = P. Louvre E 10284, III, 12 = P. Vienna 3870, 40–1. Sequence omitted in P. BM EA 10109 = P. BM EA 10125 = P. BM EA 10199; wholly in lacuna in P. BM EA 10206A + B, 10, and partly in P. BM EA 10338, 3–4. Var. P. BM EA 10338, x + 4: *n pr ỉbw*; P. BM EA 10338, 4 = P. Louvre N 3279, I, 11: *n pr ḥꜣtyw*.

BD ch. 26, 1:

ỉb.ỉ n.ỉ m pr ỉbw	'My *ỉb*-heart belongs to me in the House of *ỉb*-hearts,
ḥꜣty.ỉ n.ỉ m pr ḥꜣtyw	my *ḥꜣty*-heart belongs to me in the House of *ḥꜣty*-hearts.
ỉw rdỉ.t(w) n.ỉ ỉb.ỉ ḥtp.f ỉm.ỉ	May my heart be given me, may it be content with me.'

For the distinction between the *ỉb*-heart and the *ḥꜣty*-heart, see P. BM EA 10048, **I, 4–6**.

I, 35
[*ỉr.k n.ỉ*] *ỉb.ỉ ḥtp ḥr st.f ḥꜣty.ỉ smn ḥr mkt.f*. Same reading in P. BM EA 10199, 17–18 = P. Berlin 3028, IV, 8–9 = P. Berlin 3030, II, 21 = P. Berlin 3052, III, 3 = P. BN 151, 22–3 = P. BN 152, 36–7 = P. Cairo CG 58007, II, 3–4 = P. Florence 3662, III, 6 = P. Louvre E 3865, III, 10–11 = P. Louvre E 10284, III, 12–13. Sequence omitted in P. BM EA 10109 = P. BM EA 10125; partly in lacuna in P. BM EA 10206A + B, 10-[11][64] and P. BM EA 10338, x + 4. Omission of suffix *.ỉ* after *ỉb* and *ḥꜣty* in P. Vienna 3870. Var. P. Cairo CG 58008, 37 = P. Louvre N 3279, I, 12 = P. Vienna 3870, 41: *ḥtp* instead of *smn*; P. Louvre N 3279, I, 12: *mn* instead of *ḥtp*; P. Cairo CG 58023, x + 2: *ḥꜣty.ỉ smn.f* (*sic*) *ḥr mkt n ꜥnḫ.f*.

On this sequence, cf. also *infra*, **I, 41 2;** *LPE*, pp. 90–1 (I, 9). For the right place of the heart, cf. Th. Bardinet, *Les papyrus médicaux de l'Egypte pharaonique* (Paris 1995), pp. 106–7.

I, 35–6
dỉ.k n.ỉ rꜣ.ỉ r mdw rdwy.ỉ r šm ꜥwy.ỉ [*r s*]*ḫr ḫftyw.ỉ*. Same reading in P. BM EA 10199, 18–19 = P. BN 151, 23 = P. BN 152, 37–8 = P. Cairo CG 58007, II, 4 = P. Louvre E 10284, III, 13–14. Sequence omitted in P. BM EA 10109 = P. BM EA 10125; partly in lacuna in P. BM EA 10338, x + 4–5. Omission of suffix *.ỉ* after *rꜣ*, *rdwy* and *ꜥwy* in P. Vienna 3870, 41–2; after *rdwy* in P. Berlin 3028, IV, 9; after *ꜥwy* in P. Cairo CG 58007, II, 4. Var. P. Louvre N 3279, I, 14: *ỉw n.ỉ ꜥwy.ỉ*, 'my arms belong to me'; addition of *nb* after *ḫftyw*, and of *ḏt* <*mỉ*> *Rꜥ*, 'eternally, <like> Re'; P. Berlin 3052, III, 4 = P. Cairo CG 58007, II, 4 = P. Louvre E 3865, III, 11: *mšꜥ* instead of *šm*;[65] P. Berlin 3030, II, 22 = P. Cairo CG 58008, 37 = P. Florence 3662, III, 7: *rd* instead of *rdwy*;[66] P. Cairo CG 58008, 38: *ḥw* instead of *sḫr*.

BD ch. 26, 2–3:

ỉw rdỉ.t(w) rꜣ.ỉ r mdt	'My mouth has been given me to speak,
rdwy.ỉ r šm	my legs to walk;
ỉw rdỉ.t(w) n.ỉ ꜥwy.ỉ	my arms have been given me
r sḫr ḫftyw.ỉ	to overthrow my enemies.'

r sḫr ḫftyw.ỉ: P. Louvre N 3279, 14: *r sḫr ḫftyw.ỉ nb* <*mỉ*> *Rꜥ ḏt*, 'to overthrow all my enemies, <like> Re, eternally.'

I, 36
ỉ-wn <*n.ỉ*>*ꜥꜣwy m pt mỉ ỉr.k n nṯrw nṯrwt*. Restoration after most parallels. Sequence omitted in P. BM EA 10109 = P. BM EA 10125 = P. BM EA 10199; partly in lacuna in P. BM EA 10338, x + 5. Omission of *ỉw* before *wn* in P. Cairo CG 58007, II, 5. Var. P. Louvre N 3279, II, 2–3: *ỉ wn*; P. Cairo CG 58023, x + 3 = P. Vienna 3870, 43: <*n*> *nꜣ nṯrw nṯrwt*. Addition of *n.ỉ*, 'for me', in P. Berlin 3030, II, 22 = P. Berlin 3052, III, 4 = P. BN 152, 38 = P. Cairo CG 58007, II, 5 = P. Cairo CG 58008, 38 = P. Louvre E 3865, III, 12; P. Louvre E 10284, III, 14 = P. Louvre N 3279, II, 3;[67] of *m tꜣ* after *m pt* in P. Berlin 3052, III, 4 = P. Cairo CG 58007, II, 5 = P. Cairo CG 58008, 38 = P. Florence 3662, III, 7 = P. Louvre E 3865, III, 12 = P. Vienna 3870, 42; of *tꜣ* after *m pt* in P. Berlin 3028, IV, 10 = P. BN 151, 24; of *nb* after *nṯrw ntrwt* in P. Louvre N 3279, II, 3. P. Cairo CG 58023, x + 3 = P. Louvre E 10284, III, 15: *n* instead of *m* before *pt*.

Alone among manuscripts consulted, P. Louvre N 3279 is preceded by an introductory sequence:

ḏd mdw ỉn Ḥwt-Ḥr N	'To be recited by the Hathor N,
ms n NN	born of NN,
ỉ nb Ỉwnw ỉr ḥḏ-tꜣ	O lord of Heliopolis who makes dawn,
ḥr.k r.ỉ	turn towards me.'

On the prothetic *ỉ* before the imperative *wn*, see *supra*, **I, 32–3**.

BD ch. 26, 3–4:

wn n.ỉ ꜥꜣwy pt	'The double doors of the sky are open for me;
sš n.ỉ Gb rpꜥ nṯrw ꜥrty.ỉ	Geb, the hereditary prince of the gods, opens for me my jaws;
wn.f n.ỉ ỉrty.ỉ šp	he opens for me my eyes (which were) closed;
dwn.f ꜥwy.ỉ ḳrf	he straightens my arms (which were) crooked.'

I, 36–7
mỉ wn[68] *n.ỉ Ỉnpw nꜣ sbḫwt n tꜣ Dwꜣt mỉ ỉr.ỉ wꜥ m šms Wsỉr*. Same reading in P. BM EA 10199, 19–20 = P. Berlin 3028, IV, 10–12 = P. Berlin 3052, III, 5 = P. Florence 3662, III, 8–9. Sequence omitted in P. BM EA 10109 = P. BM EA 10125; partly in lacuna in P. BM EA 10338, 6. Omission de *Wsỉr* in P. Vienna 3870, 44. Var. P. Cairo CG 58008, 39: *nꜣ sbꜣw* [69] *n nꜣ* (*sic*) *Dwꜣt*; P. Louvre E 10284, III, 16: *mỉ ỉr.ỉ wꜥ ḥnꜥ šms Wsỉr*; P. BN 151, 24 = P. Cairo CG 58007, II, 6 = P. Cairo CG 58008, 39 = P. Louvre N 3279, II, 4–5: *mỉ ỉr.ỉ wꜥ m šmsw Wsỉr*; P. Louvre E 3865, III, 13: *m šms Wsỉr*; P. Berlin 3030, III, 1 = P. BN 152, 39: *n šms Wsỉr*; P. BM EA 10338, x + 6: *n-m nꜣ šms*[*w Wsỉr*].

On the *sbḫt*-gate (funerary context): A.M. Blackman, *JEA* 4 (1917), p. 125 (Text II, col. 25).

63. Rather than *ṯnw twk*, the presence of the preposition *ḫnt* is an obstacle to seeing in *twk* the second person singular masculine dependant pronoun, equivalent to *tw* of P. Cairo CG 58008, 35.
64. Here ends the text of P. BM EA 10206A + B. The sequel (P. BM EA 10206C) corresponds to P. BM EA 10191, II, 21–2.
65. On the equivalence of these two terms, see *LPE*, p. 249 (VIII, 4).
66. On this use of the singular, see P. BM EA 10048, **III, 6**, with n. 60.
67. The sign read [sign] by J.C. Goyon (*Le Papyrus du Louvre N 3279*, *BdE* 42, 1966, p. 36) is actually the stretched base of the suffix *.ỉ*. Cf. the form of this sign at the beginning of line 4 in this papyrus.
68. Written [hieroglyphs] in P. Berlin 3028, IV, 11.
69. On the confusion between *sbꜣ* and *sbḫt*, see *LPE*, pp. 102–3 (I, 18–19).

I, 37
sš wḏwt m-ḫnw Ḥwt-kꜣ-Ptḥ r tm šnꜥ nmt.ỉ m ẖrt-nṯr. Same reading in P. Florence 3662, III, 9[70] = P. Louvre E 3865, III, 13–14 = P. Louvre E 10284, 17–18 = P. Vienna 3870, 44. Sequence omitted in P. BM EA 10109 = P. BM EA 10125; partly in lacuna in P. BM EA 10338, x + 6–7 and P. Berlin 3028, IV, 12. Omission of *r tm šnꜥ nmtt.ỉ m ẖrt-nṯr* in P. Berlin 3052, III, 6; of suffix *.ỉ* after *nmtt* in P. Berlin 3028, IV, 12. Var. P. Louvre N 3279, II, 5: *sš.k*; P. BM EA 10199, 20: *sš.k n.ỉ*; P. BN 151, 24: *sš n.ỉ*; P. Berlin 3052, III, 5–6 = P. Cairo CG 58007, II, 7 = P. Cairo CG 58008, 40: *sš.k wḏwt.ỉ*; P. Berlin 3030, III, 1: *wḏwt.ỉ*; P. BM EA 10338, 6–7: [...] *wḏwt.ỉ m-bꜣḥ ḫnw Ḥwt-kꜣ-Ptḥ*; P. Cairo CG 58007, II, 7 = P. Cairo CG 58008, 40: *nn šnꜥ nmtt.ỉ*.

On *ẖrt-nṯr*: M. Smith, *Enchoria* 15 (1987), pp. 79–80.

I, 37–8
r dỉ(t) ỉr.ỉ mr kꜣ.ỉ m pt tꜣ. Same reading in P. Berlin 3030, III, 2–3 = P. BN 151, 25 = P. Louvre E 10284, 18 = P. Florence 3662, III, 10 = P. Cairo CG 58023, x + 5. Sequence omitted in P. BM EA 10109 = P. BM EA 10125; partly in lacuna in P. Berlin 3028, IV, 13. Text preceding *m pt tꜣ* lost in P. Louvre N 3148, V. Omission of suffix *.ỉ* after *ỉr* in P. Cairo CG 58007, II, 8. Var. P. BM EA 10338, x + 7: *r dỉt ỉr.ỉ mr.ỉ hꜣ m* (?) [*pt tꜣ* (?)]; P. BM EA 10199, 22 = P. Cairo CG 58007, II, 8 = P. Cairo CG 58008, 41 = P. Louvre E 3865, III, 14 = P. Vienna 3870, 45: *m pt m tꜣ*.

P. Louvre N 3279, II, 6–7:

r rdỉt ỉr.ỉ mr.ỉ	'to cause that I may do what I desire,
r dỉt ỉr.ỉ mr kꜣ.ỉ	to cause that I may do what my ka desires
m pt m tꜣ	in the sky and on the earth.'

P. Berlin 3052, III, 6:

kꜣ.ỉ m pt m tꜣ	'My ka is in the sky and on earth.'

I, 38
r dỉ(t) ḫn bꜣ.ỉ ḥr-tp tꜣ mr ỉb.ỉ. Sequence omitted in P. BM EA 10109 = P. BM EA 10125. Omission of suffix *.ỉ* after *bꜣ* in P. Vienna 3870, 45. P. Cairo CG 58023, x + 5–6: *dỉ.tw ḫn bꜣ.ỉ* [...]; passage partly corrupt after *ḫn* in P. Berlin 3052, III, 6.

P. BM EA 10199, 21–2 = P. BM EA 10338, x + 7–8 = P. Berlin 3028, IV, 13 = P. Berlin 3030, III, 3 = P. BN 151, 25 = P. Cairo CG 58007, II, 8–9 = P. Cairo CG 58008, 41 = P. Florence 3662, III, 10 = P. Louvre E 3865, III, 14 = P. Louvre E 10284, 19 = P. Louvre N 3148, V, x + 1 = P. Louvre N 3279, II, 6–7 = P. Vienna 3870, 45:

r dỉ(t) ḫn bꜣ.ỉ[71] *ḥr ẖꜣt.ỉ*[72]	'to cause my ba to alight on my corpse.'

BD ch. 26, 5:

wn n.ỉ pt	'The sky is open for me,
ỉr.ỉ wḏwt m ḥwt-kꜣ-Ptḥ	I make a decree in the Mansion of the ka of Ptah;
rḫ.ỉ m ỉb.ỉ	I know with my heart.'

For the meaning of this sequence, cf. *BD* ch. 29 B (ed. Naville, pl. 41):

ỉnk Bnw bꜣ n Rꜥ	'I am the Phoenix, the Ba of Re,
sšm ꜣḫw <r> Dwꜣt	who leads the Spirits <to> the Duat,
rdỉ pr Wsỉr tp tꜣ	who causes Osiris to come forth on earth
r ỉrt mrr kꜣ.f	to do what his ka desires,
rdỉ pr Wsỉr N tp tꜣ	who causes (also) the Osiris N to come forth on earth
r ỉr mrr kꜣw.f	to do what his kas desire.'

I, 38–9
ỉnk nb.k nn wꜣ.k r.ỉ rꜥ nb m wḏwt n Tꜣ-nn wr. Sequence omitted in P. BM EA 10109 = P. BM EA 10125 = P. BM EA 10199; partly in lacuna in P. BM EA 10338, x + 8 = P. Louvre E 10284, III, 19–IV, 1. Omission of *ỉnk nb.k nn wꜣ.k r.ỉ rꜥ nb* in P. Cairo CG 58008, which ties *m wḏwt n Tꜣ-nn wr* to the next sequence (cf. **I, 39**).

Var. P. Berlin 3028, IV, 13–14 = P. Berlin 3030, III, 3–4 = P. BN 151, 25 = P. BN 152, 41 = P. Florence 3662, III, 10–11 = P. Louvre E 3865, III, 14 = P. Louvre N 3148, V, x + 1 = P. Louvre N 3279, II, 8–9 = P. Vienna 3870, 45–6:

ỉ ỉb.ỉ[73] *ỉnk nb.k*	'O my heart, I am your lord.'

P. Berlin 3052, III, 6 = P. Cairo CG 58007, II, 9:

nnk ỉb.ỉ[74] *ỉnk nb.k*	'My heart belongs to me! I am your lord.'

P. Cairo CG 58008, 41–2:

sḏm.k n.ỉ ỉb.ỉ ḏs.ỉ	'Obey me, my own heart,
m wḏwt n Tꜣ-nn wr	according to the decree of Tanen the old.'

I, 39
sḏm n.ỉ ỉb.ỉ ḏs.ỉ ỉw.k[75] *m ẖt.ỉ nn wꜣ.k r.ỉ*. Sequence omitted in P. BM EA 10109 = P. BM EA 10125 = P. BM EA 10199. Same omission of suffix *.k* after *sḏm* in P. Berlin 3030, III, 4 = P. BN 152, 42 = P. Cairo CG 58023, x + 6 = P. Florence 3662, III, 11 = P. Louvre E 10284, IV, 1 = P. Louvre N 3148, V, x + 1 = P. Vienna 3870, 46. Omission of *ḏs.ỉ* and *ỉw.k m ẖt.ỉ* in P. BN 151, 26. Var. P. BM EA 10338, x + 8 = P. Cairo CG 58007, II, 10 = P. Cairo CG 58008, 41 = P. Louvre N 3279, II, 10: *sḏm.k n.ỉ*; P. Berlin 3052, III, 7: *ỉr.k n.ỉ*, 'Act for me'; P. Cairo CG 58007, II, 10: *ẖt.k*; P. Louvre E 3865, III, 15: *ẖꜣt.ỉ* instead of *ẖt.ỉ*;[76] P. Cairo CG 58023, x + 6–7: *ỉw.ỉ m ẖt.ỉ nn rḳꜣ.ỉ* [...]; P. BM EA 10338, x + 8 = P. Berlin 3028, V, 1 = P. Berlin 3030, III, 5 = P. BN 151, 25 = P. BN 152, 42 = P. Cairo CG 58007, II, 10–11 = P. Florence 3662, III, 11–12 = P. Louvre E 3865, III, 15 (writing ) = P. Louvre N 3148, V, x + 2 = P. Louvre N 3279, II, 10–11 = P. Vienna 3870, 47: *nn rḳꜣ.k r.ỉ*; P. Louvre E 10284, IV, 1–2: *nn rḳꜣ.k m r.ỉ*; P. Cairo CG 58023, x + 6–7: *nn rḳꜣ.ỉ* (*sic*) [...]; P. Cairo CG 58008, 42, substitutes for *m wḏwt n Tꜣ-nn*, 'according to the decree of Tanen', *ỉw.k m ẖt.ỉ nn wꜣ.k r.ỉ* (see *supra*, **I, 38–9**).

BD ch. 27, 4–5:

ỉb.ỉ n.ỉ sḫm.ỉ ỉm.f ḏt	'My heart belongs to me and I control it, eternally;
ỉnk nb.k ỉw.k m ẖt.ỉ	I am your lord for you are in my body,
nn rḳꜣ.k r.ỉ	and you shall not oppose me.'

I, 39–40
ỉnk pfy ỉr.w wḏwt ḥꜣt.f m Ḥwt-kꜣ-Ptḥ ỉw.w sḏm n.f m ẖrt-nṯr. Same reading in P. Berlin 3030, III, 5–6 = P. BN 152, 42–3 = P. Louvre N 3148, V, x + 2–3. Sequence omitted in P. BM EA 10199. Omission of *ḥꜣt.f* in P. Louvre E 3865, III, 16; of *m Ḥwt-kꜣ-Ptḥ* in P. BM EA 10338, x + 9 = P. Cairo CG 58008, 42; of *ỉw.w* before *sḏm n.f* in P. Louvre E 10284, IV, 2; of suffix *.w* after *ỉw* in P. BN 151, 26 (or writing  for *r*). Var. P. Cairo CG 58008, 42

70. The transcription of this passage is wrong in Pellegrini's edition.
71. *bꜣw.ỉ* in P. Louvre N 3279. P. Florence 3662: *ḫn.ỉ bꜣ* by error.
72. *ẖꜣwt.ỉ* in P. Louvre N 3279. On this variant, cf. . *ẖt.ỉ* in P. BM EA 10338 and P. Cairo CG 58008; P. Louvre E 10284 adds: *ky ḏd* ... (?), 'otherwise said: ...' (?).
73. *ỉb.ỉ* in lacuna in P. Louvre N 3279.
74. *ỉbw* in P. Berlin 3052, III, 6.
75. *ỉw.k* repeated by error in P. Berlin 3028, IV, 14, probably because of the shift to a new page.
76. See *infra*, n. 86.

= P. Louvre N 3279, II, 11: *ink p(ꜣ)y*; P. Cairo CG 58007, II, 11: *Inb-ḥḏ* instead of *Ḥwt-kꜣ-Ptḥ*; P. Berlin 3028, V, 1–2 = P. Berlin 3052, III, 8 = P. Cairo CG 58007, II, 11 = P. Louvre N 3279, II, 11 = P. Vienna 3870, 47: *r di(t) sḏm.w n.f*; P. Cairo CG 58008, 42–3: *r dit sḏm.w rn.i* (*sic*); P. Florence 3662, III, 12: *r dit sḏm n.f*; P. BM EA 10338, x + 9: *r dit sḏm* [...].

P. BM EA 10109, 2–3:

ink pꜣ(y) ir.w wḏwt ḥꜣt.f m Iwnw	'I am he before whom a decree is made in Heliopolis,
r sḏm ḫrw.f m Imn-sḫrw	that his voice be heard in the *Imn-sḫrw*-necropolis.'

P. BM EA 10125, 12–13:

ink pꜣ(y) ir.w wḏwt ḥꜣt.f m Iwnw	'I am he before whom a decree is made in Heliopolis,
r sḏm ḫrw.f m Ḥwt-ꜥꜣt	that his voice be heard in the Great Mansion.'

BD ch. 27, 5:

ink wḏwt sḏm.k n.f m ẖrt-nṯr	'I am he who commands that you obey him in the god's domain.'

Ibid., ed. Budge, p. 91:

ink wḏd sḏm.k n.i <*m*> *ẖrt-nṯr*	'I am he who commands that you obey me <in> the god's domain.'

I, 40

nn iṯ.tw ib.i m-ꜥ.i in ꜥḥꜣw m Iwnw. Same reading in P. Berlin 3028, V, 2 = P. Berlin 3030, III, 6 = P. Berlin 3052, III, 8 = P. BN 152, 43–4[77] = P. Cairo CG 58007, II, 12 = P. Cairo CG 58008, 43 = P. Florence 3662, III, 13 = P. Louvre E 3865, III, 16–17 = P. Louvre E 10284, IV, 3 = P. Louvre N 3148, V, x + 3 = P. Louvre N 3279, II, 12 = P. Vienna 3870, 48. Sequence omitted in P. BM EA 10109 = P. BM EA 10125 = P. BM EA 10199. Sequence partly in lacuna in P. BM EA 10338, x + 9. Var. P. Cairo CG 58023, x + 7: *ꜥḥꜣ*. Omission of *m* before *Iwnw* in P. BN 151, 26.

BD ch. 28, 1 (cf. *CT* VI, 344–5, sp. 388, and also *CT* V, 59, sp. 389):

nn iṯ ib.i m-ꜥ iꜣkw m Iwnw	'My heart shall not be taken away by the Fighters in Heliopolis.'

I, 40–1

ink pfy ir Itm gnwt ḥꜣt.f ḥr pꜣ išd šps m Iwnw m sš n I ḏs.f. Same reading in P. Berlin 3030, III, 7–8 = P. Cairo CG 58007, II, 13–14[78] = P. Florence 3662, III, 13–14 = P. Louvre N 3148, V, x + 3–4. Sequence omitted in P. BM EA 10109 = P. BM EA 10125 = P. BM EA 10199. Omission of *m Iwnw* in P. Vienna 3870, 49. Var. P. Vienna 3870, 48: *ink pw*; P. BM EA 10338, x + 9 = P. Berlin 3028, V, 2 = P. Berlin 3052, III, 8 = P. Cairo CG 58008, 43 = P. Louvre N 3279, II, 11–12: *ink p(ꜣ)y / p(ꜣy)*; P. Cairo CG 58008, 43: *ir.w*; *P.* Louvre E 10284, IV, 4: *m gnwt*; *ḥr p(ꜣ) inb.f* (?) *šps*; P. Louvre E 3865, III, 17: *n ḥꜣt.f*; P. BN 151, 27 = P. Louvre E 3865, IV, 1: *n Iwnw*.

For this function of Atum, see J.C. Goyon, *Le Papyrus du Louvre N 3279* (*BdE* 42, 1966), p. 42 with n. 4.

I, 41

iw ir.i wnny m-ẖnw irt.i[79] *r šm m grḥ m hrw iw n.i* (*sic*) *stwt.f rꜥ nb*. Sequence omitted in P. BM EA 10109 = P. BM EA 10125 = P. BM EA 10199. Var. P. Berlin 3028, V, 3–4 = P. Berlin 3030, III, 8 = P. Berlin 3052, III, 9 = P. Cairo CG 58008, 44–5[80] = P. Cairo CG 58023, x + 8 = P. Florence 3662, III, 14 = P. Louvre E 3865, IV, 1 = P. Louvre E 10284, IV, 5 = P. Louvre N 3148, V, x + 4 = P. Louvre N 3279, II, 13 = P. Vienna 3870, 49: *r rdit wny(ny) m-ẖnw irt(y).i*, 'to cause light within my eyes'; P. BM EA 10338, x + 10: *r rdit wnyny m* [...]. P. BN 151, 27: *ḥꜣt.i*[81] instead of *m-ẖnw irt(y).i*. The variant *iw n.i* (*stwt.f*) is corrupt; all other manuscripts give: *r mꜣꜣ*. P. BN 151, 27 = P. Louvre N 3148, V, x + 4–5: *r mꜣꜣ.f stwt.f*.

I, 41–2

ib.i mwt.i sp 2 ḥꜣty.i smn ḥr mkt.f. Same reading in P. Berlin 3028, V, 4–5 = P. Berlin 3030, III, 9 = P. Louvre E 3865, IV, 2 = P. Louvre N 3148, V, x + 5; P. Vienna 3870, 50–1 (text partly rubbed out). Sequence omitted in P. BM EA 10109 = P. BM EA 10125 = P. BM EA 10199; partly in lacuna in P. BM EA 10338, x + 11. Omission of *ib.i mwt.i sp 2* in P. Berlin 3052, III, 10; of suffix *.i* after *mwt* in P. BN 151, 26 = P. Louvre E 10284, IV, 6;[82] of *smn* in P. Florence 3662, III, 15.

On this sequence, see also *supra*, **I, 35**. For the expression *smn ib*, see Smith, *Mortuary Texts*, p. 103 (VIII, 6, b).

BD ch. 30, 1:

ib.i n mwt(.i)	'(O) my *ib*-heart of my mother,
ḥꜣty.i n wnn.i ḥr-tp tꜣ	my *ḥꜣty*-heart that I had on earth. '

I, 42

ḏd n.i Itm nfrw.f swḏ.f tw(i) n Nḥb-kꜣ. Same reading in P. Berlin 3030, III, 10 = P. Louvre N 3148, V, x + 5–6. Sequence omitted in P. BM EA 10109 = P. BM EA 10125 = P. BM EA 10199 = P. BN 151, 28 = P. Louvre E 10284, IV, 6–7 = P. Louvre N 3279. Var. P. Cairo CG 58023, x + 9: *swḏ twi*; P. Louvre E 3865, II, 2–3: *swḏ tw(i)* .

Var. P. Berlin 3028, V, 5 = P. Berlin 3052, III, 10–11 = P. Florence 3662, III, 15–16:

ḏd n.i Itm nfr iḥꜥw.i m wḥm	'Atum tells me that my body is perfect again,
swḏ.tw.f n Nḥb-kꜣ	and that it is commended to Nehebka.'

Related to this version: P. BM EA 10338, x + 11 (partly in lacuna, var. *swḏ.f n Nḥb-kꜣ*); P. Vienna 3870, 50 (partly in lacuna, and end of the manuscript).

BD ch. 30 A (ed. Budge, p. 95):

inḏ ḥr.k ib.i inḏ ḥr.k ḥꜣty.i	'Hail to you, my *ib*-heart, hail to you, my *ḥꜣty*-heart,
inḏ ḥr.k bsk.i	hail to you, my *bsk*-heart,
inḏ ḥr.tn nṯrw ipw ḫntyw ḥnkstyw	hail to you, these gods who preside over the tressed ones,
ḏsrw ḥr ḏꜥmw.sn	and grip your sceptres,[83]
ḏd.tn nfrw(.i) n Rꜥ	tell (my) perfection to Re,
swḏ.tn wi n Nḥb-kꜣw	commend me to Nehebka.'

77. The parallel with P. BM EA 10191 ends here, and resumes only in **II, 27–8**.
78. The parallel with P. BM EA 10191 ends here, and resumes only in **II, 31**.
79. On the use of singular *irt* instead of the expected dual *irty*, see P. BM EA 10048, **III, 6**, and *supra*, n. 58.
80. The manuscript ends here.
81. For *r-ḥꜣt.i*.
82. On the spelling  in P. Louvre E 3865, IV, 2, to be read perhaps *mwt.i*, see *infra*, n. 98.
83. Lit.: 'on their sceptres'. On this use of *ḏsr*: J.K. Hoffmeier, Sacred *in the Vocabulary of Ancient Egypt* (*OBO* 59, 1985), pp. 34 ff. and 64–5.

On this function of Nehebka, see Barta, *LÄ* IV, 389 with n. 14. For the spelling *tw* of the pronoun *twi*, see *LPE*, p. 263 (VIII, 23–4).

I, 42–3
di.f sꜣḫ.i tꜣ m ꜣḫt nt pt nn di.f mt.i m ḫrt-nṯr. Same reading in P. Berlin 3028, V, 5–6 = P. Berlin 3030, III, 10–11 = P. Florence 3662, II, 16 = P. Louvre N 3148, V, x + 6 = P. Louvre N 3279, II, 15–16. Sequence omitted in P. BM EA 10109 = P. BM EA 10125 = P. BM EA 10199. Omission of suffix *.i* after *mt* in P. BM EA 10338, x + 12 = P. Louvre E 10284, IV, 8. Var. P. Louvre E 10284, IV, 7: *di.f sꜣḫ.k*; P. BM EA 10338, x + 12: *dit šms.i tꜣ m* [...]; P. Louvre E 3865, IV, 3: *nn mt.i*; P. Louvre E 10284, IV, 8: *nn di.f mt*; P. Berlin 3052, III, 11: *n ḫrt-nṯr*; P. Louvre N 3279, II, 16, adds after *ḫrt-nṯr*: *ḥr ir mr.i im ḏt*, 'doing there what I desire, eternally'; P. BN 151, 28: *nn ḫm.f wi m ḫrt-nṯr*, 'he will not repel me in the god's domain'.

BD ch. 30, 3–4:[84]

isk smꜣ.n.i tꜣ imy-wrt ꜥꜣt nt pt	'Though I have been buried (at) the great west side of the sky,
wꜣḥ.i tp tꜣ	may I continue on earth,
tm mt m Imntt	that I not die in the West.'

I, 43
nṯr.f bꜣ.i sꜣḫ.f ḫꜣt.i sꜥnḫ.f ḥꜥw.i[85] *m wḥm*. Same reading in P. Berlin 3030, III, 11–12 = P. Berlin 3052, III, 11–12 = P. BN 151, 28–9 = P. Louvre E 3865, IV, 3–4 = P. Louvre E 10284, IV, 8–9 = P. Louvre N 3148, V, x + 6–7. Sequence omitted in P. BM EA 10109 = P. BM EA 10125 = P. BM EA 10199 = P. Louvre N 3279; partly in lacuna in P. BM EA 10338, x + 12–13. Omission of suffix *.i* in P. Berlin 3028, V, 5–6 = P. Florence 3662, IV, 1 (after *bꜣ*, *ḫꜣt*); var. P. Cairo CG 58023, x + 10: *ḫt.i* instead of *ḫꜣt.i*.[86]

BD ch. 30, 4:

ꜣḫ.i im.s ḥr nḥḥ	'I am a blessed one therein for ever.'

I, 43–4
dd (w)i Itm r wiꜣ n Rꜥ di.f ir.i ḫprw nb mr.i. Sequence omitted in P. BM EA 10109 = P. BM EA 10125 = P. BM EA 10199 = P. Louvre N 3279; partly in lacuna in P. BM EA 10338, x + 13. Var. P. Berlin 3028, V, 7 = P. Florence 3662, IV, 1–2 = P. Louvre N 3148, V, x + 7: *ḥr wiꜣ n Rꜥ*; P. Louvre E 10284, IV, 9: *m wiꜣ n Rꜥ*; P. Berlin 3052, III, 12 = P. BN 151, 29 = P. Louvre E 3865, IV, 4: *di tw(i) Itm ḥr wiꜣ*[87] *n Rꜥ*; P. Berlin 3030, III, 12: *di twi Itm r wiꜣ n Rꜥ*; P. Louvre E 10284, IV, 9–10: *di.f ir.i di.f* (*sic*) *ḫprw nb mr.i*; P. BN 151, 29: *di.f ir.i ḫprw r mr.i*.

For another mention of the bark of Re in the First Book of Breathing (different context), see *infra*, **II, 7** and **26–7**.

Cf. also Maspero, *Sarcophages* I, p. 9:

ḫn bꜣ.f r wiꜣ n Rꜥ	'His ba alights on the bark of Re,
iw.f m wꜥ m šms Wsir	he is one of the retinue of Osiris.'

Ibid., p. 49:

pr bꜣ.f r wiꜣ n Rꜥ	'May his ba go forth in the bark of Re,
šms.f nṯr nfr m ḫrt-nṯr	may he follow the perfect god in the god's domain!'

Ibid., p. 28:

ꜥpy ib.k (*sic*)[88] *r wiꜣ n Rꜥ*	'May his ba fly in the bark of Re!'

Ibid., p. 46:

ꜥḳ-pr.k m-m ḥsyw	'May you come and go among the praised ones
r bw nb mr ib.k	in every place your heart desires,
n šnꜥ.tw r wiꜣ n Rꜥ	without being repulsed from the bark of Re!'

Ibid., p. 67:

ꜥḳ.k r wiꜣ n Rꜥ	'May you go in the bark of Re,
šms.k nṯr ꜥꜣ m ḫrt-nṯr	may you follow the great god in the god's domain,
n ḫsf rdwy.k m pt tꜣ	without your legs being repulsed from the sky and the earth!'

I, 44
di.f n.i rꜣ.i mdw.i im.f di.f wḥm.i ꜥnḫ mi Rꜥ rꜥ nb. Same reading in P. Berlin 3028, V, 7–8 = P. Berlin 3030, III, 13 = P. BN 151, 29–30 = P. Louvre E 3865, IV, 4–5 = P. Louvre N 3148, V, x + 7–8. Sequence omitted in P. BM EA 10109 = P. BM EA 10125 = P. BM EA 10199 = P. Louvre N 3279; partly in lacuna in P. BM EA 10338, x + 13–14. Omission of *di.f* after *im.f* in P. Louvre E 10284, IV, 10; of *n.i* after *di.f* in P. Florence 3662, IV, 2; of *ꜥnḫ* after *wḥm.i* in P. Berlin 3052, III, 13. Var. P. Cairo CG 58023, x + 11: *di.f wḥm ꜥnḫ.i*; P. BM EA 10338, x + 13: *di.f ꜥnḫ.i*. See too *supra*, **I, 30–1**.

On the giving of the mouth to the deceased so that he may speak to the gods of the netherworld, cf. *BD* ch. 21 and 22.

I, 44–5
wḏꜣ.i wḏꜣ Rꜥ ṯs pḫr. Same reading in P. BM EA 10338, x + 14 = P. Berlin 3028, V, 8 = P. Berlin 3052, III, 13 = P. BN 151, 30 = P. Cairo CG 58023, x + 11 (*ṯs-pḫr* in lacuna) = P. Florence 3662, IV, 3 = P. Louvre E 3865, IV, 5 = P. Louvre E 10284, IV, 11 = P. Louvre N 3148, V, x + 8. Sequence omitted in P. BM EA 10109 = P. BM EA 10125 = P. BM EA 10199 = P. Louvre N 3279. Var. P. Berlin 3030, III, 14: *wḏꜣ Rꜥ wḏꜣ.i* instead of *ṯs pḫr*.

Same reading in *BD* ch. 42, 3.

I, 45
iw šnw.i m Nwn iw ḥr.i m Rꜥ iw irty.i m Ḥwt-Ḥr iw msḏrwy(.i) m Wp-wꜣwt. Same reading in P. Berlin 3030, III, 14–15 = P. Berlin 3052, III, 13–14 = P. BN 151, 30 = P. Louvre E 3865, IV, 5–6 = P. Louvre N 3148, V, x + 8–9. Sequence omitted in P. BM EA 10109 = P. BM EA 10125 = P. BM EA 10199 = P. Louvre N 3279; partly in lacuna in P. BM EA 10338, x + 14–15. Omission of suffix *.i* after *šnw* in P. Berlin 3028, V, 8 = P. Florence 3662, IV, 3. Var. P. Louvre E 10284, IV, 12: *n Ḥwt-Ḥr*.

BD ch. 42 (ed. Budge, p. 112):

šnw.i m Nwn ḥr.i m itn	'My hair is (that of) Nun, my face is (that of) the sun-disk;
iw irty.i m Ḥwt-Ḥr iw msḏrwy.i	my eyes are (those of) Hathor, my ears are
m Wp-wꜣwt	(those of) Wepwawet.'

In the Lepsius edition, all identifications of parts of the body with deities (42, 4–10) are introduced by *iw*, and suffix *.i* is regularly omitted. Note here the variant *Rꜥ* instead of *itn* (42, 3). On the association hair/Nun, face/Re, eyes/Hathor, ears/Wepwawet, see A. Massart, in *Studia Biblica et Orientalia* III (= *Analecta Biblica* 12, 1959), respectively pp. 237,

84. Same reading in P. Ryerson, XX, 17–20 (Allen, *Book of the Dead Documents*, pl. 18 and p. 115). This text is also found in ch. 30 A (ed. Budge, p. 95), in the third person and with the effective presence of the preposition *r* and the omission of *wrt*.
85. Note the spelling 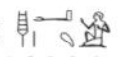 in P. Berlin 3030, III, 12. Prothetic *i* in P. Berlin 3052, III, 12 = P. Louvre E 10284, IV, 9 = P. Florence 3662, IV, 1 = P. Louvre E 3865, IV, 4.
86. See *supra*, **I, 39**, and *LPE*, p. 83, n. 1.
87. Written  in P. Berlin 3052; see *LPE*, p. 135 (II, 19), and *infra*, n. 133.
88. For *bꜣ.k*; see P. BM EA 10048, **II, 5** and **III, 1**.

no. 69; 235, no. 51; 231, no. 11; 233, no. 37; T. DuQuesne, in Y. Koenig (ed.), *La magie en Egypte: à la recherche d'une définition* (Paris 2002), p. 254.

I, 45–6

iw fnḏ.i m Ḫnty-ḫm iw spt.i m Ꞽnpw iw ibḥw.i m Srḳt iw nḥbt.i m Ꞽst Nbt-ḥwt. Sequence omitted in P. BM EA 10109 = P. BM EA 10125 = P. BM EA 10199 = P. Louvre N 3279; partly in lacuna in P. BM EA 10338, x + 15. Omission of *Ḫnty* before *ḫm* in P. Louvre E 10284, IV, 13; of suffix *.i* after *ibḥw* in P. Berlin 3052, III, 14. Var. P. Berlin 3028, V, 10 = P. Berlin 3030, III, 16 = P. Berlin 3052, III, 14 = P. BN 151, 31 = P. Florence 3662, IV, 5 = P. Louvre E 3865, IV, 6 = P. Louvre E 10284, IV, 13 = P. Louvre N 3148, V, x + 9: *spty.i*; P. Berlin 3052, III, 14–15: *iw ẖꜣt.i ḥtp ḥr st.s,*[89] 'my corpse rests in its place', instead of *iw nḥbt.i m Ꞽst Nbt-ḥwt.*

BD ch. 42 (ed. Budge, p. 112):

fnḏ.i m Ḫntt Ḫꜣs	'My nose is (that of) Khentet-Khas,[90]
iw spty.i m Ꞽnpw	my lips are (those of) Anubis,
iw ibḥw m Srḳt	my teeth are (those of) Serqet,
nḥḏwt.i m Ꞽst nṯrt	my canines are (those of) the divine Isis.'[91]

Var. Lepsius: *Ḫnty-ḫm* instead of *Ḫntt Ḫꜣs* (42, 8); *nḥbt.i* instead of *nḥḏwt.i* (42, 4). On the association nose/Khenty-khem, lips/Anubis, teeth/Serqet, neck/Isis and Nephthys, see Massart, op. cit., pp. 233, no. 27; 236, no. 63; 230, no. 5; 234, no. 40 (omission of Nephthys).

I, 46–7

iw ꜥwy.i m Bꜣ-nb-Ḏd iw šnbt.i [*m Nt nbt*] *Sꜣw*[92] *iw psḏ.i m nꜣ Nbw-Ḫr-ꜥḥꜣ* [*iw ẖt.i*] *n Sḫmt.* Same reading in P. BN 151, 31–2 = P. Louvre N 3148, V, x + 10–11. Sequence omitted in P. BM EA 10109 = P. BM EA 10125 = P. BM EA 10199 = P. Louvre N 3279; partly in lacuna in P. BM EA 10338, x + 16. Var. P. Berlin 3028, V, 11–12 = P. Berlin 3030, III, 17: *n Nt*; P. Berlin 3030, III, 18 = P. Berlin 3052, III, 15 = P. Florence 3662, IV, 6 = P. Louvre E 3865, IV, 8: *n nꜣ nbw Ḫr-ꜥḥꜣ*; P. BM EA 10338, x + 16: *n nb Ḫr-ꜥḥꜣ* and *n Sḫmt*; P. Louvre E 10284, IV, 15: , a conflation of *ẖrt-nṯr* and *Ḫr-ꜥḥꜣ*.

BD ch. 42 (ed. Budge, p. 112–13):

ꜥwy.i m Bꜣ-nb-Ḏdt	'My arms are (those of) Banebdjed,
šnꜥ.i m Nt nbt Sꜣw	my breast is (that) of Neith, the lady of Saïs,
psḏ.i m Swty	my back is (that of) Seth,
ḥnn.i m Wsir	my phallus is (that of) Osiris,
iwf.i m nbw Ḫr-ꜥḥꜣ	my flesh is (that of) the Lords of Kher-Aha,
šnbt.i m ꜥꜣ šfyt	my breast is (that of) the Great of Dignity,
iw ẖt.i iꜣt.i m Sḫmt	my belly and my backbone are (those of) Sekhmet.'

Var. Lepsius: *iw šnbt(.i) m nb Ḫr-ꜥḥꜣ*, 'my breast is (that of) the Lord of Kher-Aha' (42, 7); *iw ẖt(.i) (i)ꜣt(.i) m Stš ky ḏd Ḏḥwty*, 'my belly and my backbone are (those of) Seth – otherwise said: of Thoth –' (42, 8); *iw psḏ(.i) m Sḫmt*, 'my back is (that of) Sekhmet' (42, 9); *iw ꜥwy(.i) m Ḥry-šf*, 'my arms are (those of) Herishef' (42, 8). On the association arms/Banebdjed, breast/Neith lady of Saïs, back/lords of Kher-Aha, belly/Sekhmet, see Massart, op. cit., pp. 231, no. 13; 237, no. 71; 236, no. 57. No reference to the relationship of back/lords of Kher-Aha occurs in Massart. As to the arms, see too J.F. Borghouts, *The Magical Texts of Papyrus Leiden I 348* (*OMRO* 51, 1971), p. 91, n. 153. On the gods of Kher-Aha, see L.P. Cesaretti, *SEAP* 1 (1987), pp. 31–45.

I, 47–8

iw ḫpšw.i m irt Ḥr iw mnty.i m Nwt iw rdwy.i m Ptḥ iw sꜣḥw.i m iꜥrwt ꜥnḫw. Same reading in P. Louvre E 10284, IV, 16–17 = P. Berlin 3030, III, 18–20. Sequence omitted in P. BM EA 10109 = P. BM EA 10125 = P. BM EA 10199 = P. Louvre N 3279; partly in lacuna in P. BM EA 10338, x + 17, with possible omission of text. P. Florence 3662, IV, 3 = P. Louvre N 3148, V, x + 11: *ḫpš.i*. P. Berlin 3028, V, 12: *iw ḫpšwy.i m Sḫmt m irt Ḥr*; P. BN 151, 32: *ḫpšwy.i*. P. Berlin 3052, III, 16: *inḥwy.i* (?), 'my eyebrows' (?) instead of *ḫpšw.i*; P. Cairo CG 58023, x + 15: *iꜥrty nb ꜥnḫ.*[93]

BD ch. 42 (ed. Budge, p. 113):

iw ḫpd.i m irt Ḥr	'My buttocks are (those of) the eye of Horus,
iw mnty.i sstwy.i m Nwt	my thighs and my calves are (those of) Nut,
iw rdwy.i m Ptḥ	my legs are (those of) Ptah,
iw sꜣḥw.i mbikw ꜥnḫw	my toes are (those of) live falcons.'

Var. Lepsius: *iw mnty(.i) m Nwt*, 'my thighs are (those of) Nut' (42, 6); *iw ḏbꜥw(.i) ḳsw(.i) m iꜥrwt ꜥnḫw(t)*, 'my fingers and my bones are (those of) the live uraeus' (42, 9).

Cf. too *BD* ch. 169 (ed. Pleyte, pl. 160):

sꜣḥw.k n bik ꜥnḫ	'Your toes are (those of) the live falcon;
sšm.sn tw r wꜣt nṯr sp 2	they guide you on the divine road (*bis*).'

On the association arms/Eye of Horus, thighs/Nut, legs/Ptah, toes/live falcons, see Massart, op. cit., pp. 233, no. 30; 235, no. 46; 236, no. 61. Massart does not discuss the relationship of arms/Eye of Horus.

I, 48

nn ꜥt im[*.i*] *šw m nṯr Ꞽ m sꜣ n ḥꜥw.i*[94] *iwf.i tm n ꜥnḫ rꜥ nb.* Same reading in P. Berlin 3028, V, 13–14 = P. Berlin 3030, III, 20 = P. BN 151, 32–3 = P. Florence 3662, IV, 8–9 = P. Louvre E 3865, IV, 10 = P. Louvre E 10284, IV, 17–18 = P. Louvre N 3148, V, x + 12. Sequence omitted in P. BM EA 10109 = P. BM EA 10125 = P. BM EA 10199 = P. Louvre N 3279; partly in lacuna in P. BM EA 10338, x + 17. Omission of suffix *.i* after *im*, and of *rꜥ nb*, in P. Berlin 3052, IV, 1.[95] Addition of *nb* after *ḥꜥw.i* and of *iw* before *iwf.i* in P. BM EA 10338, x + 17.

BD ch. 42, 10 (there follows the identification of the parts of the body with deities):

nn ꜥt im.f šw m nṯr	'None of his members is without a god;
Ḏḥwty m sꜣ iwf.f tm	Thoth is the protection of his whole flesh
m hrw nb	every day.'

For the construction, cf. P. Leiden T 32, VIII, 26–7 (*LPE*, pp. 72 and 264): *nn ꜥt im.i šw m bs wꜥb*, 'None of my limbs is without protection (?) and purity'. On the expression *tm n ꜥnḫ*, speaking of limbs, see J.C. Goyon, *BIFAO* 74 (1974), pp. 76–7.

89. This variant raises the question whether the determinative in the word  (P. Cairo CG 58023, x + 13) is to be considered a misspelling.
90. On *Ḫntt-ḫꜣs*, designation or epithet of Sekhmet in connection with the second nome of Upper Egypt: S. Sauneron, *Kêmi* 11 (1950), pp. 120–2; S.E. Hoenes, *Untersuchungen zu Wesen und Kult der Göttin Sachmet* (Bonn 1976), pp. 108–9; see Leitz, *LGG* V, p. 923. The var. *Ḫntt Ḫm* pointed out by Sauneron, p. 121, n. 3, in reference to several versions of *BD* ch. 42, is actually to be read *Ḫnty Ḫm*, the determinatives proving in these documents the masculine nature of the deity.
91. On this evocation of the teeth: Th. Bardinet, *Dents et mâchoires dans les représentations religieuses et la pratique médicale de l'Egypte ancienne* (Rome 1990), pp. 27 ff., especially pp. 40–1.
92. Note the spelling  of *Sꜣw* in P. Louvre E 3865, IV, 8. The toponym is partly erased in P. Berlin 3028, V, 11.
93. According to the transcription by Golenischeff (no published photograph).
94. Written with a prothetic *i* in P. Berlin 3028, V, 13.
95. The parallel with P. BM EA 10191 stops here, and resumes only in **II, 27**.

I, 48–9
nn ḫfꜥ.tw(.ỉ) ḥr ꜥwy.ỉ nn ꜣm.tw(.ỉ)[96] *ḥr ḏrt.ỉ.*[97] Same reading in P. Berlin 3028, V, 14 = P. Berlin 3030, III, 21 = P. BN 151, 33 = P. Cairo CG 58023, x + 16 (initial lacuna) = P. Florence 3662, IV, 9 = P. Louvre E 3865, IV, 10–11 = P. Louvre E 10284, IV, 18–V, 1 = P. Louvre N 3148, V, x + 12–13. Sequence omitted in P. BM EA 10109 = P. BM EA 10125 = P. BM EA 10199 = P. Berlin 3052 = P. Louvre N 3279. Omission of that follows *ꜥwy.ỉ* in P. BM EA 10338, x + 17.

BD ch. 42, 10–11:

nn ḫfꜥ.tw.f ḥr ꜥwy.f	'He will not be grasped by his arms,
nn ꜣm.f ḥr ḏrty.f	he will not be seized by his hands.'

I, 49
smn n ḥḥ n rnpwt rn.ỉ. Sequence omitted in P. BM EA 10109 = P. BM EA 10125 = P. BM EA 10199 = P. Berlin 3052 = P. Louvre N 3279. Var. P. Berlin 3030, III, 21–2 = P. Cairo CG 58023, x + 16 = P. Florence 3662, IV, 9–10 = P. Louvre E 3865, III, 11: *mn n ḥḥ n rnp(w)t rn.ỉ*; P. Louvre E 10284, V, 1: *mn nb ḥḥ n rnpwt rn.ỉ*; P. Berlin 3028, V, 14 = P. BN 151, 33 = P. Louvre N 3148, V, x + 13: *mn ḥḥ n rnpwt rn.ỉ*, *mn* being a spelling of *mꜣꜣ*; cf. with this meaning the variant *BD* ch. 42, 12:

mꜣꜣ ḥḥ n rnpwt rn.f	'He who sees millions of years is his name.'

On the variant *mꜣꜣ* in front of *mn*, see P. BM EA 10048, **I, 1–3**, n. 12.

ḫnd.ỉ m pt m tꜣ iw snḏ.ỉ m ḫt n nꜣ nṯrw. Sequence omitted in P. BM EA 10109 = P. BM EA 10125 = P. BM EA 10199 = P. Berlin 3052 = P. Louvre N 3279. Omission of *m* before *tꜣ* in P. Berlin 3028, V, 15 = P. Berlin 3030, III, 22 = P. Florence 3662, IV, 10; of *n nꜣ* before *nṯrw* in P. BN 151, 34; of *nꜣ* before *nṯrw* in P. Berlin 3028, V, 15 = P. Louvre E 3865, IV, 12 = P. Louvre N 3148, V, x + 14. Var. P. Louvre E 10284, V, 1: *ḫnd bꜣ.ỉ*.

I, 50
ỉt(.ỉ) pw Gb mwt(.ỉ)[98] *pw Nwt.* Same reading in P. Berlin 3028, V, 15 (*ỉt.ỉ* rubbed out) = P. BN 151, 34 = P. Florence 3662, IV, 10–11; P. Cairo CG 58023, x + 7 (partly in lacuna) = P. Louvre E 10284, V, 2 = P. Louvre N 3148, V, x + 14 = P. Louvre N 3279, III, 1–2.[99] Sequence omitted in P. BM EA 10109 = P. BM EA 10125 = P. BM EA 10199 = P. Berlin 3052. Omission of suffix *.ỉ* after *ỉt* in P. Berlin 3030, III, 22; after *mwt* in P. Cairo CG 58023, x + 17. Cf. J.C. Goyon, *Le Papyrus du Louvre N 3279* (*BdE* 42, 1966), p. 77, n. 2.

Cf. *BD* ch. 31, 5 = ch. 69, 4 (different context): *ỉt.ỉ pw Gb mwt.ỉ pw Nwt*; *CT* III, p. 261, sp. 227 = *BD* ch. 34, 5 = 69, 4): *ỉt.ỉ/.f pw Gb mwt.ỉ/.f pw Nwt*, text adapted in the Late Period in a formula entitled: *rꜣ n wn n-gs Wsỉr*;[100] G. Maspero, *ASAE* 1 (1900), p. 257: *ỉt.ỉ pw Gb mwt.ỉ pw Nwt*; Cairo CG 38368 (G. Daressy, *Statues et statuettes de divinités* I [*CGC*], Cairo 1905, p. 100), and J. Yoyotte, *BIFAO* 77 (1977), p. 146, on Osiris: *ỉt.f pw Gb mwt.f pw Nwt*; P. Carlsberg 228, x + v[101] (former context lost): [...] *Gb mwt.f Nwt*.

Wsỉr ḫnty Ỉmntt rn.ỉ. Same reading in P. Berlin 3028, V, 16 = P. Berlin 3030, IV, 1 = P. BN 151, 34 = P. Cairo CG 58023, x + 17 = P. Florence 3662, IV, 10 = P. Louvre E 3865, IV, 12 = P. Louvre E 10284, V, 2–3 = P. Louvre N 3279, III, 3. Sequence omitted in P. BM EA 10109 = P. BM EA 10199 = P. Berlin 3052. Var. P. Louvre E 10284, V, 3: *ỉr.n.ỉ* instead of *rn.ỉ*, erroneously.

Same designation of the deceased in the Book of Breathing made by Isis; cf. P. BM EA 10048, **III, 8**. Also P. dem. Berlin 8351, I, 15 (Smith, *Liturgy*, pp. 25 and 31: *ḏ=w n=k Wsỉr ḫnt Ỉmnty.w mtw=k wꜥ n nꜣy=f ḥsy.w*, 'You will be called Osiris the foremost of the Westerners, you are one of his favoured ones'.

ink Ḥr ḫnty ḥḥ n ḥb-sd ḥkꜣ nst.f n tꜣ nb. Same reading in P. Berlin 3028, V, 16–17 = P. BN 151, 34.[102] = P. Louvre N 3148, V, x + 14–VI, 1. Sequence omitted in P. BM EA 10109 = P. BM EA 10125 = P. BM EA 10199 = P. Berlin 3052. Omission of *ḫnty* in P. Louvre N 3279, III, 3. Var. Florence 3662, IV, 12: *ḥkꜣ nst ỉt.f*;[103] P. Berlin 3030, IV, 1 = P. Florence 3662, IV, 12 = P. Louvre E 3865, IV, 12 = P. Louvre E 10284, V, 3: *m tꜣ nb*.

BD ch. 42, 13–14:

ntf Ḥr ḫnty ḥḥ ky ḏd ḫnd	'He is Horus presiding over millions, otherwise said treading (on millions);
wḏ <n.>f nst.f ḥkꜣ.f sw	his throne has been assigned <to> him, that he may rule it.'

BD ch. 19, 13:

iw wḥm.n Ḥr sꜣ Ỉst sꜣ Wsỉr ḥḥ n ḥb-sd	'Horus, son of Isis, son of Osiris, has repeated millions of *sd*-festivals,
iw ḫftyw.f nb ḫr sḫr bḫn	that all his enemies are fallen, overthrown, slain.'

I, 50–1
ink wr bꜣ (*sic*) *wr ꜥꜣ bꜣ* (*sic*) *ꜥꜣ ink Ḥr iwꜥ n Rꜥ.* Same reading in P. Berlin 3030, IV, 2 = P. Louvre E 3865, IV, 13–14 = P. Louvre N 3279, III, 4. Sequence omitted in P. BM EA 10109 = P. BM EA 10125 = P. BM EA 10199 = P. Berlin 3052. Var. P. Berlin 3028, V, 17 = P. BN 151, 35 = P. Louvre N 3148, VI, 1: *sꜣ wr*; P. Louvre E 10284, V, 4: *Ḥr ꜥꜣ*;[104] P. Florence 3662, IV, 12: *sꜣ n Rꜥ*.

Considering some parallel versions, the readings *ink bꜣ wr* and *ꜥꜣ bꜣ ꜥꜣ* seem wrong, and can probably be ascribed to a confusion between the hieratic signs *bꜣ* and *sꜣ*.

I, 51–2
ink sḫm n ỉt.f Wsỉr ink ṯꜣ w n Šw ḥnꜥ Tfnwt ink ms n Gb ḥnꜥ Nwt. Same reading in P. Berlin 3030, IV, 2–3 = P. Cairo CG 58023, x + 18–19 (partly in lacuna) = P. Louvre E 10284, V, 4–5. Sequence omitted in P. BM EA 10109 = P. BM EA 10125 = P. BM EA 10199 = P. Berlin 3052. Omission of *ḥnꜥ* after *Šw* and *Gb* in P. Louvre N 3279, III, 5. Var. P. Berlin 3028, V, 17 = P. BN 151, 35 = P. Florence 3662, IV, 13 = P. Louvre E 3865, III, 14 = P. Louvre N 3148, VI, 1 = P. Louvre N 3279, III, 5: *ỉt.f Rꜥ*.

On the deceased as the image (*sḫm*) of Osiris, cf. P. BM EA 10110 + 10111, I, 3; II, 1; P. BM EA 10116, 2; P. BM EA 10304, 2, 35; P. BM EA 71513D, x + 2.

I, 52
ink bꜣ šps m Wꜣst Ỉmn rn.ỉ ink Ỉ (or *nṯr* ?) *m tꜣ nb.* Same reading in P. Berlin 3028, V, 18–19 = P. Berlin 3030, IV, 4 = P. BN 151, 35–6 = P. Florence

96. Note the spelling 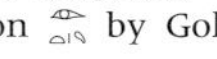 in P. Florence 3662, IV, 9.
97. The transcription  by Golenischeff (P. Cairo CG 58023, x + 16) is probably erroneous.
98. On the spelling 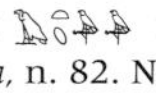 in P. BN 151, 34, P. Louvre N 3279 and P. Louvre E 3865, IV, 12, see *supra*, n. 82. Note too *ỉt.ỉ* written  in P. BN 151, 34.
99. This latter manuscript shows, as at the beginning of each column (cf. **I, 36**): *ḏd mdw in Ḥwt-Ḥr N*, 'To be recited by the Hathor N'.
100. Title of *BD* ch. 184 (*n-gs* for *r-gs*).
101. To be published by A. von Lieven in the series *The Carlsberg Papyri*, 8.
102. In this latter manuscript, the sequence is preceded with *ink wr sꜣ ꜥꜣ*, 'I am the great, son of the great'; see *infra*, **I, 50–1**.
103. On the confusion between *nst.f* and *nst ỉt.f*, see *supra*, n. 19.
104. The word *iwꜥ* has been added in the upper margin of the line above *ꜥꜣ*.

3662, IV, 13–14 = P. Louvre E 3865, V, 1 = P. Louvre E 10284, 5–6 = P. Louvre N 3148, VI, 1–2. Sequence omitted in P. BM EA 10109 = P. BM EA 10125 = P. BM EA 10199 = P. Berlin 3052; partly in lacuna in P. Cairo CG 58023, x + 19. Var. P. Louvre N 3279, III, 6: *nṯr* instead of *Ỉ*; P. Louvre E 3865, V, 1: *Ỉ* rather than *nṯr*. P. Louvre E 3865, V, 1: *tꜣ w nb*.

ḫꜥ.ỉ m nsw nṯrw[105] *nn mt.ỉ m wḥm m ẖrt-nṯr*. Same reading in P. Berlin 3030, IV, 4–5 = P. Florence 3662, IV, 14–15 = P. Louvre E 3865, V, 1–2 = P. Louvre E 10284, V, 6–7. Sequence omitted in P. BM EA 10109 = P. BM EA 10199 = P. Berlin 3052; partly rubbed out in P. Berlin 3028, V, 19. Var. P. Louvre N 3279, III, 7: *ḫꜥ.tw(ỉ)*. P. Cairo CG 58023, x + 19–20: text partly in lacuna, with probable corruption. P. BN 151, 36: *ḫꜥ.ỉ m nṯr nsw nṯrw*; P. Louvre N 3148, VI, 3: *ḫꜥ nṯr m nsw nṯrw*.

On the second death (mentioned also in P. BM EA 10290, x + 4), see *LPE*, p. 276 (**N**, 3); J. Zandee, *JEOL* 24 (1975–6), p. 5, § 8b; P.A. Bochi, *GM* 171 (1999), pp. 76–8.

BD ch. 44 (ed. Budge, p. 120), following *CT* VI, 415 (sp. 787):

ḫꜥ.kwỉ m nsw <nṯrw>[106]	'I am risen as king <of the gods>;
nn mt.ỉ m wḥm m ẖrt-nṯr	I shall not die again in the god's domain.'

I, 53

ỉ nṯr nb nṯrt nb(t) ḥr.tn r.ỉ ink ỉt.tn wnn.ỉ m šmsw Wsỉr. Sequence omitted in P. BM EA 10109 = P. BM EA 10125 = P. BM EA 10199 = P. Berlin 3052. Omission of *nṯrt nbt* in P. Berlin 3030, IV, 5. Var. P. Florence 3662: *ỉ nṯrw nb nṯrwt nb(w)*; P. Louvre E 10284, V, 8 = P. Berlin 3030, IV, 5: *m šms Wsỉr*.

Var. P. Louvre N 3279, III, 8:

ỉ nṯr nb nṯrt nb(t) ḥr.tn r.ỉ	'O every god and every goddess, turn towards me!
ink nb.tn ink nb.tn sꜣ nb.tn	I am your lord, I am your lord, son of your lord!
mỉ n.ỉ	Come to me!
ink ỉt.tn wnn.ỉ m šmsw Wsỉr	I am your father, I am in the retinue of Osiris.'

P. BN 151, 36–7 = P. Florence 3662, IV, 15–16 = P. Louvre E 3865, V, 2–3 = P. Louvre N 3148, VI, 3–5:

ỉ nṯr nb nṯrt nb(t)[107] *ḥr.tn r.ỉ*	'O every god and every goddess, turn towards me!
ink nb.tn	I am your lord.
mỉ n.ỉ m šms.ỉ	come to me, in my retinue!
ink nb.tn sꜣ nb.tn	I am your lord, son of your lord!
ḥr.tn r.ỉ	Turn towards me!
ink ỉt.tn wnn.ỉ m šms Wsỉr	I am your father, I am in the retinue of Osiris.'

To this latter version is related P. Berlin 3028, V, 19–21, partly rubbed out. The continuation of the text corresponds to P. BM EA 10191, II, 28.

BD ch. 47, 1–2:

Ḏd mdw ỉn Wsỉr N mꜣꜥ-ḫrw	'To be recited by the Osiris N, justified:
st(.ỉ) nst(.ỉ)	My place and my throne,
mỉ n.ỉ ky ḏd mỉ rdỉ n.ỉ pḫr n.ỉ	come to me (otherwise said: given to me, serve me)!
ink nb.tn nṯrw	I am your lord, (o) gods!
mỉ.tn n.ỉ m šmsw.ỉ	Come to me as my followers!
ink sꜣ nb.tn ỉw.tn n.ỉ	I am the son of your lord, and you belong to me
in ỉt.ỉ rdỉ tn n.ỉ	(for) it is my father who gave you to me
wnn.ỉ m šmsw Ḥwt-Ḥr	while I was in the retinue of Hathor.'

I, 53–II, 1

nmt.n.ỉ m pt wbꜣ.n.ỉ m tꜣ šꜣỉs.n.ỉ tꜣ r nmt ꜣḫw špsw. Sequence omitted in P. BM EA 10109 = P. BM EA 10125 = P. BM EA 10199 = P. Berlin 3052. Omission of *tꜣ* after *šꜣỉs.n.ỉ* in P. Louvre E 10284, V, 9; of *m* after *wbꜣ.n.ỉ* in P. BN 151, 37 = P. Louvre E 3865, V, 3 = P. Louvre N 3148, VI, 5. Var. P. Cairo CG 58023, x + 20: *nmt.ỉ*; P. Berlin 3030, IV, 6: *šꜣỉs.n.ỉ m tꜣ*; P. Louvre N 3279, III, 10: *šꜣỉs.n.ỉ m Dwꜣt*, 'I have travelled the Duat'; P. Louvre E 3865, V, 3–4: *šꜣỉs.n.ỉ n Dwꜣt r nmt ꜣḫw*,[108] 'I have travelled the Duat in the steps of the spirits'; P. BN 151, 37: *šꜣỉs.ỉ tꜣ m ẖrt-nṯr rꜥ nb*, 'I travel the earth in the god's domain, every day'; P. Louvre N 3279, III, 10–11: *ỉw nmt.n.ỉ m ꜣḫ šps*, 'I have travelled as a noble spirit'. Words of uncertain reading after *šꜣỉs.n.ỉ*.

BD ch. 48, 1–2 (some var. in ch. 10, 2–3):

ꜥḏ.n.ỉ m pt wbꜣ.n.ỉ tꜣ	'I have hacked up the sky, I have opened the earth,
šꜣỉs.n.ỉ tꜣ r nmt ꜣḫw smsw	I have travelled the earth in the steps of the elder spirits.'

CT VI, 183–4 (sp. 574):

ꜥḏ.n.ỉ pt wbꜣ.n.ỉ ꜣḫt	'I have hacked up the sky, I have opened the horizon,
šꜣs.n.ỉ ỉꜣḫw šꜣs.n.ỉ nmtt.f	I have travelled the sunshine, I have travelled its movements,
ỉṯ.n.ỉ ꜣḫw smsw r.ỉ	I have seized the power of those who were older than I,
n-ntt ink ỉs ꜣḫ ꜥpr ḥḥ.f	for I am indeed a spirit equipped with his millions (of magical spells).'

II, 1–2

ink ꜥpr ḥḥ Rꜥ-Ḥr-ꜣḫty rn.ỉ ink nṯr nb Dwꜣt. Same reading in P. Berlin 3030, IV, 6–7 = P. BN 151, 38 = P. Louvre E 10284, V, 9–10 (corrupt spelling of *Rꜥ-Ḥr-ꜣḫty*) = P. Louvre N 3148, VI, 6 = P. Louvre N 3279, III, 11–12. P. Florence 3662, IV, 17, ends with *rn.ỉ*. Sequence omitted in P. BM EA 10109 = P. BM EA 10125 = P. BM EA 10199 = P. Berlin 3052. Var. P. Louvre E 3865, V, 4: *nṯr ꜥꜣ*.

BD ch. 48, 2–3:

(… …)	'(… …)
ḥr-ntt ink ꜥpr ḥḥ m ḥkꜣw.f	for I am one who is equipped with millions of his magical spells;
wnm.ỉ m rꜣ.ỉ	I eat with my mouth,
fgn.ỉ m ꜥrt.ỉ	I excrete with my anus,
ink ỉs nṯr nb Dwꜣt	I am indeed the god lord of the Duat.'

CT VI, 184 (sp. 574):

(… …)	'(… …)
n-ntt ink ỉs ꜣḫ ꜥpr ḥḥ.f	for I am indeed a spirit equipped with his millions (of magical spells);
wnm.ỉ m rꜣ.ỉ	I eat with my mouth,

105. Different passage, probably corrupt, in P. Cairo CG 58023, x + 19.
106. *nṯrw* omitted in the Lepsius edition.
107. Var. P. Florence 3662 and P. Louvre N 3148, VI, 3: *ỉ nṯrw nb nṯrwt nb(t)*.
108. The absence of *špsw* can be explained by a confusion created by the presence of the determinative [hieroglyph] in *ꜣḫw*.

fgn.ỉ m pḥ.ỉ	I excrete with my anus,
n-ntt ỉnk ỉs nṯr nb Dwꜣt	for I am indeed the god lord of the Duat.’

II, 2

pr.ỉ m ꜣḫt r ḫftyw.ỉ nn nḥm.f m-ꜥ.ỉ. Sequence omitted in P. BM EA 10109 = P. BM EA 10125 = P. BM EA 10199 = P. Berlin 3052. Omission of *r ḫftyw.ỉ nn nḥm.f m-ꜥ.ỉ* in P. Louvre N 3279, III, 12. Addition of *ỉnk Rꜥ* before *pr.ỉ* in P. Berlin 3030, IV, 7 = P. Cairo CG 58023, x + 21 = P. Louvre E 3865, V, 4 = P. Louvre E 10284, V, 10 = P. Louvre N 3148, VI, 6 = P. Louvre N 3279, III, 12; P. BN 151, 38: *ỉnk Rꜥ pr m ꜣḫt*, ‘I am Re coming forth from the horizon’.

BD ch. 49, 1–2 = *BD* ch. 11, 2–3:

ỉnk Rꜥ pr.n.ỉ m ꜣḫt r ḫftyw.ỉ	‘I am Re, and I have gone forth from the horizon against my enemy,
nn nḥm.f[109] *m-ꜥ.ỉ*	he shall not be rescued from me.’

The Budge edition, p. 32, 6, gives after *ḫftyw.ỉ*: *ỉw.f rdỉ n.ỉ nn nḥm.f m-ꜥ.ỉ*, ‘he is given to me and he shall not be rescued from me’.

II, 2–3

mꜣꜥ-ḫrw.ỉ mỉ[110] *nb wrrt twn.ỉ rdwy.ỉ m dwn*. Same reading in P. Berlin 3030, IV, 8 = P. Louvre E 10284, V, 11 = P. Louvre N 3279, III, 12–13. Sequence omitted in P. BM EA 10109 = P. BM EA 10125 = P. BM EA 10199 = P. Berlin 3052. Omission of suffix *.ỉ* after *mꜣꜥ-ḫrw* in P. Louvre E 3865, V, 5; of *mꜣꜥ-ḫrw mỉ* in P. BN 151, 38. Var. P. Louvre E 3865, V, 5: *mꜣꜥ-ḫrw mỉ nb wrrt*; P. Louvre N 3148, VI, 7: *m* instead of *mỉ*; P. Cairo CG 58023, x + 22: [... *rdwy*].*ỉ m wn*.

BD ch. 11 (ed. Budge, p. 32, 7–8):

mꜣꜥ.n.ỉ ꜥ.ỉ m nb wrrt	‘I have extended my arm as lord of the *wrrt*-crown,
dwn.n.ỉ rdwy.ỉ m wn ḫꜥw	I have stretched out my legs as one who is in glory.’

CT VI, 166 (sp. 567):

mꜣꜥ.n <.ỉ> ꜥ.f m nb wr	‘I have extended his (*sic*) arm as the great lord,
dwn.n.ỉ rdwy.ỉ m wnn ḫꜥ	I have stretched out my legs as one who is in glory.’

m dwn: J. Capart, A.H. Gardiner and B. van de Walle, *JEA* 22 (1936), pp. 175–6 (ii).

II, 3–4

ḫꜥ.ỉ sḫr ḫftyw.ỉ rꜥ nb ḥms.ỉ m pt. Same reading in P. Louvre E 10284, V, 11–12. Sequence omitted in P. BM EA 10109 = P. BM EA 10125 = P. BM EA 10199 = P. Berlin 3052. Omission of suffix *.ỉ* after *ḫftyw* in P. Cairo CG 58023, x + 22. Var. P. Berlin 3030, IV, 8 = P. BN 151, 39 = P. Louvre E 3865, V, 6 = P. Louvre N 3148, VI, 7: *sḫr.ỉ*; P. Cairo CG 58023, x + 22: *sḫr.n.ỉ*.

BD ch. 11 (ed. Budge, p. 32, 8–11):

nn rdỉ.n.ỉ ḫrt m-ꜥ.ỉ	‘Do I not cause one to be overthrown by my hand ?
ḫftyw.ỉ pw	They are my enemies (*sic*);
ỉw.f rdỉ n.ỉ	he is given to me
n nḥm.f m-ꜥ.ỉ	and he cannot be rescued from me.
ꜥḥꜥ.n.ỉ m Ḥr	I have stood as Horus,
ḥms.n.ỉ m Ptḥ	I have sat as Ptah.’

II, 4–5

nḫt.ỉ m Ỉ wsr.ỉ[111] *m Ỉtm šm.ỉ m rdwy.ỉ mdw.ỉ m rꜣ.ỉ mꜣꜣ.ỉ m ỉrty.ỉ sḏm.ỉ m ꜥnḫwy.ỉ*.[112] Same reading in P. BN 151, 39 = P. Louvre N 3148, VI, 8–9. Sequence omitted in P. BM EA 10109 = P. BM EA 10125 = P. BM EA 10199 = P. Berlin 3052. Var. P. Berlin 3030, IV, 9 = P. Louvre E 3865, V, 6: *nḫt.ỉ m nṯr*; P. Louvre N 3279, III, 14: *nḫt.n.ỉ m nṯr*; *wsr.n.ỉ*; *sḏm.n.ỉ*; P. Louvre E 10284, V, 12–13: *nḫt.ỉ ỉw wsr.ỉ m Ỉtm*.

BD ch. 11 (ed. Budge, p. 32, 11–15):

nḫt.n.ỉ m Ḏḥwty	‘I have grown strong as Thoth,
wsr.n.ỉ m Tm[113]	I have grown powerful as Atum;
šm.ỉ m rdwy.ỉ	I walk with my feet,
mdw.ỉ m rꜣ.ỉ	I speak with my mouth,
r ḥḥ ḫftyw.ỉ	to seek my enemy;
ỉw.f rdỉ n.ỉ	(for) he is given to me,
nn nḥm.tw.f m-ꜥ.ỉ	and he cannot be rescued from me.’

II, 5–6

ỉnk nb ꜥnḫ wḥm ꜥnḫ ꜥnḫ ỉrw rn.ỉ. Same reading in P. Berlin 3030, IV, 10–11 = P. Louvre E 3865, V, 7–8 = P. Louvre N 3148, VI, 9. Sequence omitted in P. BM EA 10109 = P. BM EA 10125 = P. BM EA 10199 = P. Berlin 3052. Omission of *ꜥnḫ* before *ỉrw* in P. BN 151, 40. Var. P. Louvre E 10284, V, 14: *ꜥnḫ ỉrw nb rn.ỉ*; P. Louvre N 3279, III, 15: *ỉnk nb ꜥnḫ wḥm ꜥnḫ ḏt*, ‘I am the lord of life, who repeats life, eternally’. The continuation of this text corresponds to P. BM EA 10191, II, 14.

On the designation *nb ꜥnḫ* for Osiris, see F.R. Herbin, *BIFAO* 84 (1984), p. 289, n. 44. For *ꜥnḫ ỉrw*, see *LPE*, pp. 115–16 (I, 29–30); Leitz, *LGG* II, p. 137.

II, 6

ỉnk rw ỉnk rwty ỉnk smsw n Rꜥ-Ỉtm. Same reading in P. Berlin 3030, IV, 11. Sequence omitted in P. BM EA 10109 = P. BM EA 10125 = P. BM EA 10199 = P. Berlin 3052; partly in lacuna in P. Cairo CG 58023, x + 24. Omission of *ỉnk* before *smsw* in P. BN 151, 40 = P. Louvre E 3865, V, 8 = P. Louvre N 3148, VI, 9. Var. P. Louvre E 10284, V, 14: *ỉnk nb* instead of *ỉnk rw*.

BD ch. 38, 1:

ỉnk Rwty	‘I am Ruty,
smsw n Rꜥ-Tm m ꜣḫ-bỉt	the first-born of Re-Atum in Khemmis.’

On the identification of the deceased with Ruty, see G. Vittmann, in *Zwischen den beiden Ewigkeiten* (Fs. G. Thausing, Vienna 1994), p. 252, n. kk.

II, 7

ꜥḥꜥ.ỉ ḥr ḥꜣt n wỉꜣ n Rꜥ šsp.ỉ ḥꜣtt m sktt. Same reading in P. Berlin 3030, IV, 11–12 = P. BN 151, 40 = P. Louvre N 3148, VI, 10. Sequence omitted in P. BM EA 10109 = P. BM EA 10125 = P. BM EA 10199 = P. Berlin 3052. Omission of suffix *.ỉ* behind *šsp* in P. Louvre E 3865, V, 9. Var. P. Louvre E 10284, V, 15: *ḫnms* (otherwise an unknown word, written) instead of *wỉꜣ*. Passage partly in lacuna in P. Cairo CG 58023, x + 24–5.

109. All the manuscripts consulted give the singular suffix *.f*, while *ḫftyw* is regularly in the plural.

110. Written in P. Berlin 3030, IV, 8 and in P. Louvre E 3865, V, 5.

111. The suffix is written in P. Louvre N 3148.

112. Written in P. Louvre E 3865, V, 7.

113. P. Ryerson, XXXV, 16–17 (ch. 49 = ch.11) gives here the variant *Nfr-tm* instead of *Ỉtm* (Allen, *Book of the Dead Documents*, pl. 22 and p. 130).

BD ch. 38, 2:

ꜥḥꜥ.ỉ ḥr bgꜣsw n wỉꜣ n Rꜥ	'I stand on the deck (?)[114] of the bark of Re.'

On the deceased in the bark of Re, see *supra*, **I, 43–4**.

II, 7–8

ỉ Ỉmn mỉ ṯꜣw nḏm r fnḏ.ỉ ỉnk sꜣ.k šps n mꜣꜥt. Sequence omitted in P. BM EA 10109 = P. BM EA 10125 = P. BM EA 10199[115] = P. Berlin 3052, IV. Omission of suffix *.k* after *sꜣ* in P. Louvre E 3865, V, 9. Var. P. Cairo CG 58023, x + 25 = P. Louvre E 10284, V, 16 = P. Louvre N 3148, VI, 11: *bꜣ.k* instead of *sꜣ.k* (cf. *supra*, **I, 33**); P. Louvre E 10284, V, 16 = P. Louvre 3148, VI, 11 = P. BN 151, 41 = P. Cairo CG 58023, x + 25 = P. Louvre E 10284, V, 16: *m mꜣꜥt*; P. Berlin 3030, IV, 12–13: [116] *mꜣꜥt*. On this sequence, see *infra*, **II, 12–13**.

BD ch. 54, 1:

ỉ Tm ỉmy n.ỉ ṯꜣw nḏm	'O Atum, give me the sweet breath
ỉmy šrty.k	which is in your nostrils.'

BD ch. 56, 1:

ỉ Tm dỉ.k n.ỉ ṯꜣw nḏm	'O Atum, give me the sweet breath
m šrty.k	(which is) in your nostrils.'

II, 8–9

ỉnk swḥt twy nt ngg wr sꜣ.ỉ swḥt twy ꜥꜣt wp.n Gb r tꜣ.[117] Same reading in P. BN 151, 41. Sequence omitted in P. BM EA 10109 = P. BM EA 10125 = P. BM EA 10199 = P. Berlin 3052, IV; partly in lacuna in P. Cairo CG 58023, x + 25–6 = P. Louvre N 3148, VI, 12. Omission of *swḥt* after *sꜣ.ỉ* in P. Berlin 3030, IV, 13. Var. P. Louvre E 10284, V, 17 = P. Berlin 3030, IV, 13: *wp Gb*.

BD ch. 54 (ed. Lepsius):

ỉnk swḥt twy nt ngg wr	'I am this egg of the great Cackler;
ỉw sꜣ.n.ỉ swḥt twy ꜥꜣt	I guard this great egg
wp(t) Gb r tꜣ	that Geb separated from the earth.'

A part of this sequence reads too, with some little variants, in ch. 56 and 59 of *BD* (ed. Budge, p. 127, 10–11 and p. 131, 1–2):
(*ỉw*) *sꜣ.n.ỉ swḥt twy nt Ngg wr* 'I guard this egg of the great Cackler.'

CT III, 209 (sp. 223):

ỉnk swḥt ỉmyt Ngng wr	'I am the egg that was in the great Cackler,
m sꜣ sḫnt[118] *twy ꜥꜣt*	as the protection of this great prop
wpt tꜣ r Nwt	that separated the earth from Nut.'

II, 9–10

ꜥnḫ.ỉ ꜥnḫ.s ṯs-pẖr nḫḫ.s nḫḫ.ỉ ṯs-pẖr snsn.s snsn.ỉ ṯs-pẖr. Same reading in P. Louvre E 10284, V, 17–18. Sequence omitted in P. BM EA 10109 = P. BM EA 10125 = P. BM EA 10199 = P. Berlin 3052, IV; partly in lacuna in P. Cairo CG 58023, x + 26. Omission of *nḫḫ.s nḫḫ.ỉ* in P. BN 151, 42 = P. Louvre N 3148, VI, 12. Var. P. Louvre E 3865, V, 11: *snsn.ỉ snsn.s*; P. Berlin 3030, IV, 14: *ꜥnḫ.s ꜥnḫ.ỉ* instead of *ṯs-pẖr*.

BD ch. 54, 2 (ed. Lepsius):

rwḏ.ỉ rwḏ.s ṯs-pẖr	'If I prosper, it prospers, and vice versa;
ꜥnḫ.ỉ ꜥnḫ.s ṯs-pẖr	If I live, he lives, and vice versa;
nḫḫ(.ỉ) sn(.ỉ) ṯꜣw	(I) grow old and I breathe air.'

BD ch. 56, 2 (ed. Lepsius):

rwḏ.s rwḏ.ỉ ṯs-pẖr	'If it prospers, I prosper, and vice versa;
ꜥnḫ.s ꜥnḫ.ỉ ṯs-pẖr	If it lives, I live, and vice versa;
snsn.s ṯꜣw snsn.ỉ ṯꜣw ṯs pẖr	if it breathes air, I breathe air, and vice versa.'

BD ch. 59, 2 (ed. Lepsius):

rwḏ.ỉ rwḏ.s ṯs-pẖr	'If I prosper, it prospers, and vice versa;
ꜥnḫ.ỉ ꜥnḫ.s ṯs-pẖr	If I live, it lives, and vice versa;
snsn.ỉ ṯꜣw snsn.s ṯꜣw	If I breathe air, it breathes air.'

II, 10

wḏꜥ ꜥb rn.ỉ. Same reading in P. Berlin 3030, IV, 15 = P. BN 151, 42 = P. Louvre E 10284, V, 18–19 = P. Louvre N 3148, VI, 12. Sequence omitted in P. BM EA 10109 = P. BM EA 10125 = P. BM EA 10199 = P. Berlin 3052, IV. Omission of *wḏꜥ* in P. Louvre E 3865, V, 11.

BD ch. 54, 2–3 (ed. Lepsius):

ỉnk wḏꜥ ꜥb rn.f	'I am he whose name is He-who-is-judged-pure.
<pḫ>r.n.f ḥꜣ swḥwt.f	<He has cir>cled around his eggs (*sic*);
bkꜣw.f n ꜣt	his morrow (comes) in (due) time.
wr pḥty Swtḫ	Great is the strength of Seth.'

BD ch. 54, ed. Budge, p. 126, 8–10:

ỉnk wḏꜥ ꜣꜥb	'I am judge of the reconstituted One (?);
pḫr.n.ỉ ḥꜣ swḥt.f	I have circled around his egg;
bkꜣ.ỉ n ꜣt	my morrow (comes) in (due) time.
wr pḥty Swty	Great is the strength of Seth.'

II, 11–12

sꜣw.tn sꜣw r.ỉ ỉmyw Dwꜣt ỉnk ỉmy sš.f m hb šps Ỉ rn.ỉ. Same reading in P. Berlin 3030, IV, 15–16 = P. Louvre N 3148, VI, 13. Sequence omitted in P. BM EA 10109 = P. BM EA 10125 = P. BM EA 10199 = P. Berlin 3052, IV. Omission of *sꜣw.tn* in P. Louvre E 10284, V, 19. Var. P. BN 151, 42: *n.ỉ* instead of *r.ỉ*; P. Louvre E 3865, V, 11–12: *ỉnk pr m sš.f m hb šps*, 'I am he who comes forth from his nest as a noble ibis'; P. Cairo CG 58023, x + 27: *m sš rn.ỉ*,[119] 'by writing my name (?)'.

On the first part of this sequence, cf. P. Cairo CG 58015, 3–4 = P. Cairo CG 58016, 4 = P. Cairo CG 58019, 2–3:

sꜣw.tn r.ỉ	'Be on your guard against me,
nꜣ sꜣwtyw n (tꜣ) Dwꜣt	guardians of the Duat.'

BD ch. 54, 3 (ed. Lepsius):

sꜣw.tn r ỉmy sš.f nḫn	'Be on your guard against him who is in his nest, the child,
pr.f r.tn	when he goes forth against you.'

On the identification of the deceased with an ibis, see P. BM EA 10109, **line 2**.

II, 12–13

ỉ Ỉmn dỉ.k ṯꜣw nḏm r fnḏ.ỉ ỉnk bꜣ.k šps pr ỉm.k mỉ ꜥnḫ.ỉ mỉ snsn.ỉ ṯꜣw.k.[120]

114. D. Jones, *A Glossary of Ancient Egyptian Nautical Titles and Terms* (London 1988), p. 163.
115. The first part of this invocation is found in this last manuscript, line 26 (different context).
116. On this hieratic group, see P. BM EA 10048, **II, 6–7**, with n. 36.
117. The expected sign — is written like —.
118. Better than the variant *ḫprt*.
119. Following the transcription by Golenischeff, unverifiable because of the lack of a photograph. The meaning is not clear.
120. P. Cairo CG 58023, x + 27, incorrectly adds *ṯꜣw.ỉ* after *ṯꜣw.k*.

Sequence omitted in P. BM EA 10109 = P. BM EA 10125 = P. BM EA 10199[121] = P. Berlin 3052, IV. Omission of what follows *fnḏ.i* in P. BN 151, 43; of suffix *.k* after *bꜣ* in P. Berlin 3030, IV, 17 = P. Louvre E 3865, V, 12 = P. Louvre E 10284, V, 20 = P. Louvre N 3148, VI, 14.

P. Cairo CG 58014, 12:

i Ỉmn di.k n.i ṯꜣw nḏm r fnḏ.i	'O Amun, give me sweet breath to my nose,
ink bꜣ šps pr im.k	(for) I am the noble ba who came forth from you' .

For the first part of the sequence, see *supra*, **II, 7–8**.

P. BM EA 10110 + 10111, II, 13:

i Ỉmn mi n.i ṯꜣw nḏm	'O Amun, give me a sweet breath
ink sꜣ.k mr.k	(for) I am your son whom you love.'

BD ch. 56, 1 (ed. Lepsius):

i Tm di.k n.i ṯꜣw nḏm m šrty.k	'O Atum, may you give me the sweet breath (which is) in[122] your nostrils;
ink im smsw wr ḥr-ib Wnw	I am the first-born, the eldest, dwelling in Unu.'

BD ch. 56, ed. Budge, p. 127, 8–10:[123]

i Tm di.k n.i ṯꜣw nḏm imy šrt.k	'O Atum, may you give me the sweet breath which is in your nostrils;
ink sḫn st ṯwy ḥr(y)t-ib Wnw	it is I who occupy this place in the middle of Unu.'

II, 13–14

ink hb[124] *šps m-ḫnw sš.k ink nb imꜣḫ ḫr Rꜥ*. Same reading in P. Berlin 3030, IV, 17–18 = P. Louvre E 10284, VI, 1–2 = P. Louvre N 3148, VI, 15. Sequence omitted in P. BM EA 10109 = P. BM EA 10125 = P. BM EA 10199 = P. Berlin 3052, IV; partly in lacuna in P. Cairo CG 58023, x + 28–9. Var. P. Louvre E 3865, V, 14: *imꜣḫ wr*; P. BN 151, 43: *imꜣḫ šps*.

On the deceased as an ibis, cf. *supra*, **II, 11–12**.

II, 14

i Ḥꜥpy wr n pt ḥr.k r.i nn wꜣ.k r.i. Same reading in P. BN 151, 43 = P. Cairo CG 58023, x + 29 = P. Louvre E 10284, VI, 2–3 = P. Louvre N 3148, VI, 15–16. Sequence omitted in P. BM EA 10109 = P. BM EA 10125 = P. BM EA 10199 = P. Berlin 3052, IV. Omission of *nn wꜣ.k r.i* in P. Louvre E 3865, V, 14 = P. Louvre N 3279, IV, 2. Var. P. Louvre N 3279, IV, 2: *it nṯrw* substituted for *wr n pt*; P. Berlin 3030, IV, 18 = P. Louvre E 3865, V, 14: *m pt*.

BD ch. 57, 1 (ed. Lepsius):

i Ḥꜥpy wr n pt	'O Hapy, great one of the sky,
m rn.k n ꜥḏ pt	in your name of Hacker of the sky.'

II, 15–16

ink bꜣ n nṯrw wrw mi ḳbḥ m mw n rnp rꜥ nb ḳbḥ.k ib.i m ḥbbt. Sequence omitted in P. BM EA 10109 = P. BM EA 10125 = P. BM EA 10199 = P. Berlin 3052, IV. Var. P. Cairo CG 58023, x + 29–30: *sꜣ* instead of *bꜣ* (according to the transcription by Golenischeff);[125] P. Berlin 3030, IV, 19 = P. Louvre E 3865, V, 14 = P. Louvre N 3148, VI, 16 = P. Louvre N 3279, IV, 3: *n nꜣ nṯrw wrw*; P. Louvre E 10284, VI, 3: *ink bꜣ.k nꜣ nṯrw* (*sic*) *wrw*; P. Louvre E 3865, VI, 1:[126] *mi sḳbḥ ib.i m ḳbḥ*; P. BN 151, 44 = P. Louvre N 3279, IV, 3–4: *sḳbḥ.k*; P. Berlin 3030, IV, 19 = P. BN 151, 44 = P. Louvre E 10284, VI, 3 = P. Louvre N 3148, VI, 16 = P. Louvre N 3279, IV, 3: *mi n.i iw.k m mw*[127] *n rnp rꜥ nb*, 'Come to me! You are the water of rejuvenation, every day'.

mw n rnp: G. Foucart, *BIFAO* 24 (1924), pp. 34–5; M. Smith, *Enchoria* 15 (1987), pp. 80–1; id., *Liturgy*, p. 41 (II, 2); R. El Sayed, *BIFAO* 80 (1980), p. 239, n. (l).

II, 16

di.k sḫm.i m mw mi Sḫmt di.k iꜣw.i mi Wsir m Wꜣst. Same reading in P. Berlin 3030, IV, 20–1 = P. Louvre E 10284, VI, 4. Sequence introduced in P. Louvre E 3865, I, 6–7, with *ḥr.k r.i Wsir ḫnty Ỉmntyw*, 'Turn towards me, Osiris the foremost of the Westerners'; omitted in P. BM EA 10109 = P. BM EA 10125 = P. BM EA 10199 = P. Berlin 3052, IV. Var. P. BN 151, 44 = P. Louvre E 3865, I, 7 = P. Louvre N 3148, VI, 17: *mw.k*, 'your water'; P. Louvre N 3279, IV, 5: addition of *m Dwꜣt* after *iꜣw.i*; P. Cairo CG 58023, x + 30: *di.i iꜣw.i* (according to Golenischeff); P. Louvre N 3148, VI, 17: *n Wꜣst*.

BD ch. 57, 1 (ed. Lepsius):

di.k sḫm Wsir N m mw mi Sḫmt	'May you let the Osiris N control water like Sekhmet
ꜥwꜣ Wsir N grḥ pwy n nšny ꜥꜣ	who snatched away the Osiris N on that night of the great storm.'

sḫm m mw: J. Zandee, *JEOL* 24 (1975–6), pp. 4–5.

II, 16–17

nst.i n Ỉwnw ḥms.i m Ỉnb-ḥḏ pr(.i) n Wnw Bꜥḥ st.i spꜣt nbt ḫr wḏt.i. Sequence omitted in P. BM EA 10109 = P. BM EA 10125 = P. BM EA 10199 = P. Berlin 3052, IV. Omission of *n* (*m*) before *Ỉwnw* and *Ỉnb-ḥḏ* in P. Berlin 3030, IV, 21 = P. Louvre E 3865, I, 7–8 = P. Louvre E 10284, VI, 5 = P. Louvre N 3148, VI, 18 = P. Louvre N 3279, IV, 5; before *Ỉwnw*: P. BN 151, 45; before *Wnw Bꜥḥ* in P. Berlin 3030, IV, 21 = P. BN 151, 45 = P. Louvre E 3865, I, 8 = P. Louvre N 3148, VI, 18 = P. Louvre N 3279, IV, 5. Omission of suffix *.i* after *wḏt* in P. BN 151, 45. Var. P. BN 151, 45 = P. Louvre E 10284, VI, 5 = P. Louvre N 3148, VI, 18 = P. Louvre N 3279, IV, 6: *spꜣwt*.

II, 18

mi mw r-ḥꜣt nṯrw ink ḫpr m sp tpy. Sequence omitted in P. BM EA 10109 = P. BM EA 10125 = P. BM EA 10199 = P. Berlin 3052, IV. Var. P. Berlin 3030, IV, 22 = P. BN 151, 45 = P. Cairo CG 58023, x + 31 = P. Louvre E 3865, I, 8 = P. Louvre E 10284, VI, 6 = P. Louvre N 3148, VI, 18 = P. Louvre N 3279, IV, 6: *mi n.i mw*.

P. Louvre E 10284, VI, 6–7:

mi n.i mw ṯꜣw im.k	'Give me water and the breath (which comes forth) from you,
ink sḫn st	I am he who occupies the place;
ink ḫpr m sp tpy	I am he who arose in the first time.'

On this variant, see *infra*, **II, 19–20**.

121. See however, *supra*, **II, 7–8**, for a comparable invocation in this manuscript.
122. Or: '(which comes forth) from your nostrils'; but cf. *BD* ch. 54, 1, quoted *supra* (**II, 7–8**): *ṯꜣw nḏm imy šrty.k*.
123. Cf. P. Louvre E 10284, VI, 6–7, quoted *infra*, **II, 18**.
124. Written  in P. BN 151, 43.
125. On the confusion between *sꜣ* and *bꜣ*, see *supra*, **I, 33** and **II, 7–8**.
126. From here, this manuscript diverges from the others. The immediate continuation of P. Louvre E 3865 corresponds to P. BM EA 10191, II, 29 ff., while the principal reading expected here is found in I, 7 ff.
127. Uncertain word here in P. Louvre E 10284.

II, 18–19
ink rsyt ink mḥtt ink imntt ink iꜣbtt. Same reading in P. Berlin 3030, IV, 22–3 = P. BN 151, 45–6 = P. Louvre E 10284, VI, 6 = P. Louvre N 3148, VI, 19. Sequence omitted in P. BM EA 10109 = P. BM EA 10125 = P. BM EA 10199 = P. Berlin 3052, IV = P. Louvre N 3279. Var. P. Louvre E 3865, I, 9: *ink Iꜣbtt ink Imntt*.

II, 19
nm irw [128] *mi ḳ(ꜣ)y.i wpw-ḥr.k*. Same reading in P. BN 151, 46 = P. Louvre E 10284, VI, 7–8 = P. Louvre N 3148, VI, 19–20. Sequence omitted in P. BM EA 10109 = P. BM EA 10125 = P. BM EA 10199 = P. Berlin 3052, IV. Var. P. Cairo CG 58023, x + 32: *ḳꜣyw.i*; P. Louvre N 3279, IV, 7: *ḳꜣyw.k*; P. Berlin 3030, IV, 23 = P. Louvre E 3865, I, 10: *ḳd.i* and *wpw r ḥr.k*.

II, 19–20
Ḥꜥpy wr mi n.i mw ṯꜣw im.k ink sḫn st ḥr-ib irt Rꜥ. Same reading in P. Berlin 3030, IV, 23–V, 1 = P. Louvre E 10284, VI, 8–9. Sequence omitted in P. BM EA 10109 = P. BM EA 10125 = P. BM EA 10199 = P. Berlin 3052, IV. Var. P. Louvre N 3279, IV, 8: *mi ṯꜣw nḏm im.k*, 'give (me) the sweet breath which is in you'; P. BN 151, 47 = P. Louvre E 3865, 11 = P. Louvre N 3148, VI, 20 = P. Louvre N 3279, IV, 8: *Ḫmnw*, 'Hermopolis', instead of *irt Rꜥ*.

BD ch. 59, 1 (ed. Lepsius):

i nht twy nt Nwt	'O this sycomore of Nut,
rdi n.i mw imy.t	give me water which is in you,
ink sḫn st twy ḥr-ib Wnwt	I am he who occupies this place in the middle of Unut.'

II, 20–1
rwḏ.k rwḏ.i ṯs-pẖr ꜥnḫ.k ꜥnḫ.i ṯs-pẖr. Same reading in P. Berlin 3030, V, 1–2 = P. BN 151, 47 = P. Louvre E 10284, VI, 9–10 = P. Louvre N 3148, VI, 20–1. Sequence omitted in P. BM EA 10109 = P. BM EA 10125 = P. BM EA 10199 = P. Berlin 3052, IV. Omission of *ṯs-pẖr* after *rwḏ.i* in P. Cairo CG 58023, x + 33; of *ꜥnḫ.k ꜥnḫ.i ṯs-pẖr* in P. Louvre E 3865, I, 11 = P. Louvre N 3279, IV, 9.

P. Cairo CG 58023, x + 33–4:

rwḏ.k rwḏ.i	'If you prosper, I prosper,
sḫm.i im.f	I control it
r-dit ib.i	at my heart's desire'
di.k […]	see **II, 22–3**.

II, 21
di.k n.i mw snsn.i ḳbḥ.k im. Same reading in P. Berlin 3030, V, 2. Sequence omitted in P. BM EA 10109 = P. BM EA 10125 = P. BM EA 10199 = P. Berlin 3052, IV = P. Cairo CG 58023 = P. Louvre N 3279. Omission of suffix *.i* after *snsn* in P. Louvre N 3148, VI, 21. Var. P. BN 151, 47: *snsn.i m ṯꜣw.k*; P. BM EA 10206C, 1 = P. Louvre E 3865, I, 11 = P. Louvre E 10284, VI, 10 = P. Louvre N 3148, VI, 21: *im.i*.

On the meaning of *snsn* in this context, see *LPE*, p. 254 (VIII, 7).

II, 21–2
Ḥꜥpy wr mi sꜣ.i m ḥbbt.k ink ꜥḥꜥ ḥms m Ḥꜥpy wr. Same reading in P. Berlin 3030, V, 2–3 = P. Louvre E 3865, I, 11–12 = P. Louvre N 3148, VI, 21–2. Sequence omitted in P. BM EA 10109 = P. BM EA 10125 = P. BM EA 10199 = P. Berlin 3052, IV; partly in lacuna in P. BM EA 10206C, 1. Omission of *ꜥḥꜥ* in P. Louvre E 10284, VI, 11; of *m* before the second mention of *Ḥꜥpy wr* in P. BN 151, 48. Var. P. BN 151, 47 = P. Louvre N 3279, IV, 9: *i Ḥꜥpy wr*.

ꜥḥꜥ ḥms: J. Zandee, *ZÄS* 101 (1974), p. 71 (33 g).

II, 22–3
sḫm.i im.f r-dit ib.i di.k sḫm.i m ḳbḥ.k ipw wrw m ḳbḥ nḏm. Same reading in P. BN 151, 48 = P. Louvre E 10284, VI, 11–12 = P. Louvre N 3148, VI, 22–3. Sequence omitted in P. BM EA 10109 = P. BM EA 10125 = P. BM EA 10199 = P. Berlin 3052, IV; partly in lacuna in P. BM EA 10206C, 2 = P. Cairo CG 58023, x + 33[129] Var. P. Berlin 3030, V, 4: *r-ḏr ib.i*; P. Louvre E 3865, I, 12: *di.t(w) sḫm.i*; P. Louvre N 3279, IV, 10: *ipn* instead of *ipw*.

II, 23–4
ink Nb-ḏr[130] *ink Itm ink* [*Ḫpr*]*i*[131] *ink smsw n Rꜥ*. Same reading in P. Berlin 3030, V, 4–5 = P. BN 151, 48–9 = P. Louvre E 3865, I, 13 = P. Louvre E 10284, VI, 12–13 = P. Louvre N 3148, VI, 23 = P. Louvre N 3279, IV, 11. Sequence omitted in P. BM EA 10109 = P. BM EA 10125 = P. BM EA 10199 = P. Berlin 3052, IV; partly in lacuna in P. BM EA 10206C, 2–3 = P. Cairo CG 58023, x + 34.

II, 24
ink hb šps ink Ḥꜥpy bꜣ tpy n Wsir. Same reading in P. Berlin 3030, V, 5–6 = P. Louvre E 10284, VI, 13–14 = P. Louvre N 3148, VI, 23–4. Sequence omitted in P. BM EA 10109 = P. BM EA 10125 = P. BM EA 10199 = P. Berlin 3052, IV; wholly in lacuna in P. BM EA 10206C, and partly in P. Cairo CG 58023, x + 34–5. Omission of *ink Ḥꜥpy* in P. Louvre E 3865, I, 14. Var. P. BN 151, 49 = P. Louvre N 3279, IV, 12: *sꜣ* instead of *bꜣ*.

On the identification of the deceased with an ibis, see P. BM EA 10109, **line 2**.

II, 25–6
ink pr m Nwn ink Rꜥ ink ꜥḥ pt ink ḫy r nnt. Sequence omitted in P. BM EA 10109 = P. BM EA 10125 = P. BM EA 10199 = P. Berlin 3052, IV. Var. P. BM EA 10206, C, 4: *ḥnꜥ Rꜥ*, 'with Re' (following text in lacuna). Addition of *ink Ptḥ*, 'I am Ptah', after *ink ꜥḥ pt* in P. Berlin 3030, V, 6–7 = P. BN 151, 49 = P. Louvre E 10284, VI, 15. P. Cairo CG 58023, x + 35: *ink Ptḥ ḫy nnt*, 'I am Ptah who raises heaven'. The transcription *ink*  in this latter document, as Golenischeff admits himself, is doubtful, and could mask the expected reading *ink ꜥḥ pt*. In the absence of a photograph, this cannot be verified.

P. Louvre E 3865, I, 14–15 = P. Louvre N 3148, VI, 24–5:

ink pr m Nwn ḥnꜥ Rꜥ	'I am he who came forth from Nun with Re,
ink ꜥḥ pt ḥnꜥ Ptḥ	I am he who raised the sky with Ptah,
ink ḫy r nnt	I am he who ascended to heaven.'

P. Louvre N 3279, IV, 12–14:

ink pr m Nwn ḥnꜥ Rꜥ	'I am he who came forth from Nun with Re,
ink ꜥḥ pt ḥnꜥ Ptḥ	I am he who raised the sky with Ptah,
ink I mḥ wḏꜣt	I am Thoth who filled the *wḏꜣt*-eye,
ink hb pr m Ḥwt-kꜣ-Ptḥ	I am the ibis who came forth from the Mansion of the ka of Ptah.'[132]

128. For the writing: Lefebvre, *Petosiris* I (1924), p. 116 with n. 1; M. Smith, *RdE* 57 (2006), p. 228 with n. 75.
129. The transcription by Golenischeff: *ḥr.i* instead of *ib.i* is probably erroneous.
130. Written *Nb-r-ḏr* in P. Berlin 3030, V, 4 = P. BN 151, 48 = P. Louvre E 3865, I, 13 = P. Louvre N 3148, VI, 23 = P. Louvre N 3279, IV, 11.
131. A reading  is unlikely, taking the parallels into account. The sign  is erased in the end of line 23, as is the determinative  in the name *Wsir* which ends line 24.
132. On the relation between Thoth (here, the ibis) and Ptah: J.C. Goyon, *Le Papyrus du Louvre N 3279* (*BdE* 42, 1966), p. 59, n. 1.

II, 26–7
šm.i ḥr tꜣ hrp.i m Nwn šm.n.i m wiꜣ n Rꜥ. Sequence omitted in P. BM EA 10109 = P. BM EA 10125 = P. BM EA 10199 = P. Berlin 3052, IV = P. Louvre N 3279; mostly in lacuna in P. BM EA 10206C, 5 = P. Cairo CG 58023, x + 35–6. Omission of suffix *.i* after *hrp* in P. BM EA 10206, C, 5 = P. Louvre E 3865, I, 15 = P. Louvre N 3148, VI, 25. Var. P. Berlin 3052, IV, 1[133] = P. Louvre E 3865, I, 15: *pr.n.i* instead of *šm.n.i*; P. Berlin 3030, V, 8 = P. BN 151, 50 = P. Louvre E 10284, VI, 16 = P. Louvre N 3148, VI, 26: *pr.i*; P. BM EA 10206, C, 5: *pr*[...].

hrp: Edwards, *HPBM* IV, p. 7, n. 43; Assmann, *Liturgische Lieder*, p. 200, n. 23. Cf. P. Edwin Smith, II, 8, quoted in *Wb.* II, 320, 19. On the deceased in the bark of Re, see *supra*, **I, 43–4** and **II, 7**.

II, 27
iwr tw(i) Sḫmt ms tw(i) Nwt. Same reading in P. Louvre E 10284, VI, 16. Sequence omitted in P. BM EA 10109 = P. BM EA 10125 = P. BM EA 10199 = P. Louvre N 3279; partly in lacuna in P. BM EA 10206C, 6. Var. P. Berlin 3030, V, 8 = P. BN 151, 50 = P. Cairo CG 58023, x + 36 = P. Louvre E 3865, I, 15 = P. Louvre E 10284, VI, 16 = P. Louvre N 3148, VI, 26: *Nt* instead of *Nwt*; the full form *twi* is read before *Nwt* in P. Berlin 3052, IV, 2.

BD ch. 66, 1 (title: *rꜣ n pr m hrw*):

iw rḫ.kwi iwr.kwi in Sḫmt	'I know that I was conceived by Sekhmet,
ms.n (?) *wi in Nt*	and born of Neith.'

BD ch. 174[134] (ed. Budge, p. 456):

pr.n.i imytw mnty Psḏt	'I came forth from between the thighs of the Ennead,
iwr.i in Sḫmt	I was conceived by Sekhmet;
in Šsmtt mst wi	it was Shesemtet who bore me.'

II, 27–8
ink I[135] *mḥ wḏꜣt ink hb pr m Ptḥ*. Same reading in P. Berlin 3030, V, 8–9 = P. BN 151, 50–1 = P. Louvre E 3865, I, 15 = P. Louvre N 3148, VI, 26–VII, 1. Sequence omitted in P. BM EA 10109 = P. BM EA 10125 = P. BM EA 10199; partly in lacuna in P. BM EA 10206C, 6 and P. Cairo CG 58023, x + 36–7. Var. P. Louvre E 10284, VI, 17: *pr.i m Ptḥ*, 'I come forth from Ptah'; P. Berlin 3052, IV, 3 = P. Louvre N 3279, IV, 14: *Ḥwt-kꜣ-Ptḥ* instead of *Ptḥ*.

On the deceased as an ibis, see *supra*, **II, 11–12**.

II, 28
i-[136]*wn n.i pt iw wn n.i tꜣ*. Same reading in P. BM EA 10109 = P. BM EA 10125 = P. BM EA 10199, 22 (after a long interruption, see *supra*, **I, 38**) = P. Berlin 3030, V, 9 = P. Berlin 3052, IV, 3 = P. Louvre E 10284, VI, 17. Lacuna in P. BM EA 10206C. Omission of both prothetics *i-* in P. Louvre E 3865, I, 16; of the second only in P. Louvre N 3148, VII, 1; of *n.i* in P. BN 151, 51. Sequence partly rubbed out in P. Berlin 3028, V, 21 which resumes the text after an interval (see *supra*, **I, 53**). Var. P. Louvre N 3279, IV, 14: [hieroglyphs] *wn n.i tꜣ*.

Cf. *supra*, I, 36: *iw wn* <*n.i* > *ꜥꜣwy m pt*.

BD ch. 68 (ed. Budge, p. 150, 6):

wn n.i ꜥꜣwy pt	'The double doors of the sky are open for me,
wn n.i ꜥꜣwy tꜣ	the double doors of the earth are open for me.'[137]

II, 28–9
sḫm.i m ib.i sḫm.i m ḥꜣty.i[138] *sḫm.i m ꜥwy.i sḫm.i m rꜣ.i*. Same reading in P. BM EA 10199, 22–3 = P. Berlin 3030, V, 10 = P. BN 151, 51 = P. Louvre E 3865, II, 1 = P. Louvre N 3148, VII, 1–2. Sequence omitted in P. BM EA 10109 = P. BM EA 10125 = P. Louvre N 3279; partly in lacuna in P. BM EA 10206, C, 7. This latter manuscript interrupts the text here with the word *rꜣ.i*. There then follows the sequence *ḥr.tn r.i nꜣ nṯrw mdsw-irty*, corresponding to P. BM EA 10191, I, 4. Sequence partly rubbed out in P. Berlin 3028, V, 22. Omission of *sḫm.i m ḥꜣty.i* in P. Louvre E 10284, VI, 18. P. Berlin 3052, IV, 4, inserts *sḫm.i m iḥꜥw.i*, 'I control my limbs', before *sḫm.i m ḥꜣty.i*.

BD ch. 68 (ed. Budge, p. 150, 12–15):

sḫm.i m ib.i sḫm.i m ḥꜣty.i	'I control my *ib*-heart, I control my *ḥꜣty*-heart,
sḫm.i m ꜥwy.i sḫm.i m rdwy.i	I control my hands, control my legs,
sḫm.i m rꜣ.i	I control my mouth.'

BD ch. 68, 3 (ed. Lepsius):

iw sḫm.f m ḥꜣty.f	'He controls his *ḥꜣty*-heart.'

II, 29–30
sḫm.i m ꜥwt.i irw sḫm.i m prt-ḫrw sḫm.i m mw m ḥbbt. Same reading in P. BM EA 10199, 23–4. Sequence omitted in P. BM EA 10109 = P. BM EA 10125 = P. Louvre N 3279. Omission of suffix *.i* after *ꜥwt* in P. Berlin 3052, IV, 5; of *sḫm.i m mw m ḥbbt* in P. Louvre E 3865, VI, 2 and P. Louvre E 10284, VI, 19. Var. P. Louvre E 3865, VI, 1 = P. Louvre E 10284, VI, 18: *ꜥwy.i* instead of *ꜥwt.i*;[139] P. BM EA 10206, C, 8 (partly in lacuna) = P. Berlin 3028, V, 22 = P. Berlin 3030, V, 11 = P. Berlin 3052, IV, 5 = P. BN 151, 51 = P. Louvre E 3865, VI, 1–2[140] = P. Louvre E 10284, VI, 19 = P. Louvre N 3148, VII, 2: addition of (*m*) *tꜣ ḥnḳt iḥw ꜣpdw*, '(namely) bread, beer, oxen and fowl', after *prt-ḫrw*; P. Berlin 3030, V, 11: *ḥbbt.k*.

BD ch. 68 (ed. Budge, pp. 150, 15–151, 3):

sḫm.i m ꜥwt.i sḫm.i m prt r ḫrw	'I control my limbs, I control the invocation offering,
sḫm.i m mw sḫm.i m ṯꜣw	I control water, I control the breath,
sḫm.i m nw sḫm.i m itrw	I control the flood, I control the river,
sḫm.i m wḏbw	I control the shores.'

Ibid.(ed. Budge, pp. 151, 15–152, 2):

sḫm.i m ꜥwy.i sḫm.i m mw	'I control my hands, I control water,
sḫm.i m nw sḫm.i m itrw	I control the flood, I control the river,
sḫm.i m wḏbw	I control the shores.'

BD ch. 68, 3–4 (ed. Lepsius):

sḫm.f m ꜥwt.f tm	'He controls all his limbs,

133. The transcription given by Lieblein (*Que mon nom fleurisse*, p. lviii), and accepted by Goyon in the translation of this passage (*Rituels funéraires*, p. 261, n. 5), is erroneous. [hieroglyphs] is to be read *wiꜣ* here, with a writing attested in other documents (cf. *supra*, n. 87). The two signs which follow *n Rꜥ*, at the very left of the line, must be considered as ordinary spelling corrections.
134. Adapted from *PT* § 262.
135. Written [hieroglyphs] in P. BN 151, 50.
136. Written [hieroglyph] in P. BN 151, 51 = P. Louvre N 3148, VII, 1.
137. There follows a development omitted in the First Book of Breathing.
138. The transliteration [hieroglyphs] by Golenischeff for the version of P. Cairo CG 58023, x + 37, is surely erroneous (read [hieroglyphs], determinative of *ḥꜣty*).
139. In the case of P. Louvre E 3865, one may wonder whether the word [hieroglyphs], already mentioned in the same phrase in II, 1, is not simply a spelling of *ꜥwt*; see *LPE*, p. 92 and n. 5 [I,10]).
140. After an interruption (see *supra*, **II, 28–9**), the parallel of P. Louvre E 3865 with P. BM EA 10191 resumes at this point.

sḫm.f m prt-ḫrw	he controls the invocation offering,
sḫm.f m mw sḫm.f m nw	he controls water, he controls the flood,
sḫm.f m wḏbw	he controls the shores.'

II, 30–1

sḫm.i m irt.i m tꜣ sḫm.i m irt.i m ḫrt-nṯr. Sequence omitted in P. BM EA 10109 = P. BM EA 10125 = P. Louvre N 3279; in lacuna in P. BM EA 10206C; almost entirely rubbed out in P. Berlin 3028, V, 23. Omission of *irt.i* before *m ḫrt-nṯr* in P. Louvre E 10284, VI, 20; of *sḫm.i m irt.i m ḫrt-nṯr* in P. BM EA 10199, 24. Var. P. BN 151, 52: *irty.i*; P. Louvre E 3865, VI, 2: *imy mꜣꜣ.n.i m irty.i m tꜣ*, 'May I see with my eyes on earth'; P. BM EA 10199, 24 = P. Berlin 3052, IV, 6 = P. Louvre E 3865, VI, 2: *irty.i* (twice); P. Berlin 3030, V, 12, and perhaps P. Louvre N 3148, VII, 3:[141] *ḏrt.i* instead of *irt.i*, by confusion in the hieratic spellings of and .[142]

P. Cairo CG 58007, II, 14: *sḫm.i m irty.i m ḫrt-nṯr* (only sequence, different context).

BD ch. 68 (ed. Budge, p. 151, 4–6 = p. 152, 2–4).

sḫm.i m iryw r.i	'I control those who act against me,
sḫm.i m irywt r.i m ḫrt-nṯr	I control those who act against me in the god's domain,
sḫm.i m wḏw irt r.i tp tꜣ	I control those who commanded to act against me on earth.'

BD ch. 68, 4 (ed. Lepsius):

sḫm.f m iryw r.f m ḫrt-nṯr	'He controls those who act against him in the god's domain,
sḫm.f m wḏt ir n.f ḥr-tp tꜣ	he controls what is commanded against him on earth.'

II, 31–3

ꜥnḫ.i m tꜣ m Gb snb.i m mw m Ḥꜥpy ꜥḥꜥ.i m ḥnḳt sꜥm.i m irṯt wšꜥ.i m irp šdḥ. Same reading in P. BN 151, 52–3 = P. Louvre E 3865, VI, 3–4. Sequence omitted in P. BM EA 10109 = P. BM EA 10125; partly rubbed out in P. Berlin 3028, V, 24. Var. P. BM EA 10206C, 9 = P. Berlin 3028, V, 23 = P. Louvre N 3148, VII, 3 = P. Louvre N 3279, IV, 15: *tꜣ n Gb*; P. Berlin 3028, V, 24: *mw n Ḥꜥpy*; P. BM EA 10199, 25 = P. Louvre N 3279, IV, 16: *ḥms.i* instead of *sꜥm.i*; P. Cairo CG 58023, x + 39: *sꜥm.i m irp.f* (*sic*); P. Louvre E 10284, VI, 20:[143] *ssnb.n.i*.

P. BM EA 10338, x + 18:

ḥms.k m tꜣ wšꜥ.k m ḥnḳt	'You sit down by the bread, you consume beer,
wn[m.k m ḫt (?)] nb(t) nfr(t)	and e[at ? ...] every good [thing].'

P. Berlin 3030, V, 12–13:

ꜥnḫ.n.i m tꜣ n Gb	'I live on the bread of Geb,
snb.n.i m mw[144] *m Ḥꜥpy*	I am healthy by the water of Hapy,
swr.n.i m ḥnḳt	I drink beer,
sꜥm.n.i m irṯt	I drink milk,
wšꜥ.n.i irp šdḥ	I consume wine and *šdḥ*-brew.'

P. Berlin 3052, IV, 6–7:

ꜥnḫ.i m tꜣ	'I live on bread,
sḳbḥ(.i) m mw m Ḥꜥpy	(I) refresh myself with water of Hapy,
ꜥḥꜥ.i m tꜣ	I rise by the bread,
ḥms.i m irṯt	I sit down by the milk,
wšꜥ.i m irp	I consume wine.'

P. Cairo CG 58007, II, 15–16:

ꜥnḫ.i m irty.i	'I live with my eyes,
sḳbḥ.i m mw m Ḥꜥpy	I refresh myself with water of Hapy,
ꜥḥꜥ.i m tꜣ	I rise by the bread,
ḥms.i m irṯt	I sit down by the milk,
wšꜥ.i m irp	I consume wine.'

BD ch. 68, 4–5, states an opposite proposition:

iwms mi ḏd.tw Wsir N	'One says of the Osiris N mistakenly:
ꜥnḫ.f is m tꜣ n Gb	he lives indeed on the bread of Geb;
bwt.f ḫf (?) wnm.f s(w)	(it is) his abomination; he will not eat it.
ꜥnḫ.f m tꜣ n bdt dšr nt Ḥꜥpy	He lives on bread of red wheat of Hapy
m bw wꜥb	in the pure place.'

BD ch. 68 (ed. Budge, p. 151, 6–10):

iwms ḏd.tn r.i	'You say of me mistakenly:
ꜥnḫ.f is m tꜣ n Gb	he lives indeed on the bread of Geb.
bwt.i nn wnm.i sw	(it is) my abomination; I shall not eat it;
ꜥnḫ.i m tꜣ n bdt ḥḏ	I live on bread of white wheat
ḥnḳt.i m it dšr n Ḥꜥpy	and my beer is of red barley of Hapy
m bw wꜥb	in the pure place.'

Bread of Geb: A. Roccati, in *Atti del 1° Convegno italiano sul Vicino Oriente Antico* (Rome 1978), pp. 101–8. For the *šdḥ*-brew (a variety of wine), see Smith, *Mortuary Texts*, p. 99 (VII, 5, a); P. Tallet, *BIFAO* 95 (1995), pp. 459–89.

II, 33

šsp.i snsn m kꜣp snṯr ink nṯr ꜥꜣ pr m <nṯr (ꜥꜣ)>. Sequence omitted in P. BM EA 10109 = P. BM EA 10125 = P. BM EA 10206C; partly rubbed out in P. Berlin 3028, V, 25. Omission of *šsp.i snsn m kꜣp snṯr* in P. Cairo CG 58007, 16; of *snsn* in P. Louvre E 3865, VI, 4; of both *ꜥꜣ* in P. Cairo CG 58007, II, 16 (different context); of the second only in P. BN 151, 53 = P. Cairo CG 58014, 13 (different context) = P. Cairo CG 58023, x + 40 = P. Louvre N 3148, VII, 5 = P. Louvre N 3279, first marginal line. Var. P. Louvre N 3279, first marginal line: *šsp.n.i snsn.i*; P. BM EA 10199, 26: *iṯ.i snsn*;[145] P. Berlin 3052, IV, 8: *ḳmꜣ.i šsp.i snsn m Rpwwt* (?); P. Berlin 3028, V, 25: *šsp.i snw* ( ); P. BN 151, 53: *šsp.i snw* ( ); P. Louvre E 3865, VI, 4: *ink nṯrt ꜥꜣt pr m nṯr ꜥꜣ*, 'I am the great goddess coming forth from the great god'; P. Berlin 3030, V, 14: *pr m tꜣ*, 'coming forth from the earth'; P. Berlin 3052, IV, 8: *pr m ḫrt-nṯr*, 'coming forth from the god's domain'.

The version of P. BM EA 10199 interrupts with the word *snṯr* the parallel with P. BM EA 10191, and includes, up to the end of the manuscript (lines 26–9), some phrases extracted from other passages of the First Book of Breathing.

II, 34

stwt n Rꜥ ṯꜣw n Imn mw n Ḥꜥpy nnk[146] *st ḏt*. Same reading in P. Berlin 3028, V, 25–6 = P. Berlin 3030, V, 15 = P. Leiden T 33, 22 = P. Louvre E 3865, VI, 4–5 = P. Louvre N 3148, VII, 5–6. Partly in lacuna in P. BM EA 10206C, 11.[147] P. Cairo CG 58023, x + 40, ends abruptly with the name

141. The word is partly in lacuna.

142. Cf., for instance, the form of the eye P. Berlin 3030, III, 5, 7, 8, and see Möller, *Pal.* III, nos 82 and 115.

143. The last known column of this manuscript ends with *ꜥḥꜥ.i*. The sequel, if it ever existed, is now lost.

144. *m mw* repeated twice by mistake.

145. On the equivalence between *iṯ* and *šsp*, see *LPE*, p. 247 (VIII, 2).

146. On *nnk*: M. Gilula, *RdE* 20 (1968), pp. 55–61.

147. End of the text in this manuscript.

Imn. Omission of *mw n Ḥ*ᶜ*py* in P. Berlin 3052, IV, 9. Var. P. BM EA 10125, 28: *stwt n Šw*, and inversion of the places of *ṯ*ꜣ*w n Imn* and of *mw n Ḥ*ᶜ*py*; P. BM EA 10340, 6: *šw n R*ᶜ; P. BN 151, 53: *ḥwt n Ḥ*ᶜ*py*, 'the flow of Hapy'; P. BM EA 10282, 27[148] = P. BM EA 10283, 10 = P. Cairo CG 58014, 14: *sn* instead of *st*; P. BM EA 10109, 14 = P. BM EA 10125, 28: *ḏr.w* instead of *ḏt*; P. Cairo CG 58007, 17: *n ḏt*; P. Louvre N 3279, second marginal line: *r* ꜣ*w ḏt*.

Abridged Versions

P. BM EA 10109 (pls 33–6)

Hay Collection.
Quirke, *Owners*, no. 263.
Lieblein, *Que mon nom fleurisse*, pp. iv–vi and 5–6.
E.A.W. Budge, *A Guide to the Fourth, Fifth and Sixth Egyptian Rooms* (London 1922), pp. 297–8, no. 21.
B.H. Stricker, *OMRO* 23 (1942), p. 32.

Provenance: Thebes. Possibly from the tomb of the archon Soter, but apparently without relation with his family.[149]
Date: first to second century AD.[150]
Owner of the papyrus: *T*ꜣ*-nt-Ḏ*ꜣ*m* (Tasemis).[151] She is also owner of P. BM EA 10108.
Mother of the owner: *T*ꜣ*-(nt)-k*ꜣ (Tikos).

Contents: First Book of Breathing, abridged version.

Manuscript of one sheet (26.2 × 16.5 cm), in very good condition, bearing fourteen lines of writing.

Text on the verso: The necropolis extends [her arms to receive you]. The Book [of Brea]thing of Thoth is your protection, (O) Hathor *T*ꜣ*-nt-Ḏ*ꜣ*m*, justified, born of *T*ꜣ*-(nt)-k*ꜣ, justified.
(*In demotic*): (at) her head.

Translation

Recto

(1) Thus speaks the Hathor *T*ꜣ*-nt-Ḏ*ꜣ*m*, justified, born of *T*ꜣ*-(nt)-k*ꜣ, justified:
I am Re at his rising, I am Atum at his setting, (2) I am Osiris foremost of the West during the night. I am an ibis with black head, white breast, and blue back. I am (3) he before whom a decree is made in Heliopolis, that his voice be heard in the *Imn-sḫrw*-necropolis. Turn towards me, doorkeepers of (4) the West, guardians of the Duat! May I come, may I go! Turn towards me, gods of piercing gaze who are in (5) the retinue of Osiris, gods who are in the hall of the two Maats, gods who are in the hall of the Field of reeds! Turn towards me, all gods of the (6) Duat! May I go, may my ba go! Turn towards me, Hathor mistress of the West, to whom the West has been entrusted! (7) May I come, may I go, may <I> fly to heaven with the bas of the gods and the goddesses! Turn towards me, (8) Anubis son of Osiris, dependable doorkeeper of the Duat! May I enter the hall of the region of Maat! May I be one of the (9) crew of Osiris, (of) these excellent ones who follow the satisfied bull! May there be made for me a libation of water in the Mansion of the Prince as (is done for the) great Prince (who is) in Heliopolis!

(10) O Thoth, turn towards me! Vindicate me against my enemies as you vindicated Osiris before the great Council which is in Heliopolis, on that night (11) of the festival of the sixth day, at the festival ... (?) before the Council which is in Busiris, on that night of raising the *ḏd*-pillar in Busiris before the great Council which is in (12) Abydos, on that night of the festival of raising the sky before the great Council which is in Idebu-rekhty, on that night of the Haker-festival before the great Council (13) which is in Pe and Dep, on that night when Horus received the domicile of the gods. Horus has repeated the praises, four times. The rays of (14) Re, the breath of Amon, the water of Hapy, all that belongs to me.

Commentary

Lines 1–2
*ink R*ᶜ *ḫ*ᶜ*.f ink Itm m ḥtp.f ink Wsir ḫnty Imntt m grḥ*. On this sequence, extremely common among copies of the First Book of Breathing, see P. BM EA 10191, **I, 1–2**.

Line 2
ink hb km tp ḥḏ ḥt ḫsbḏ psḏ. Same reading in P. BM EA 10125, 13–14 = P. Cairo CG 58009, I, 4–5.

This description of the ibis (black head, blue back, and white breast) evokes that of an amulet and seems otherwise unknown. The correspondence between those colours and some minerals used in the production of amulets is implicitly formulated (see J.R. Harris, *Lexicographical Studies in Ancient Egyptian Minerals*, Berlin 1961, pp. 127 [*ḫsbḏ*] and 42–3 [*ḥḏ*]). Assimilation of the deceased to the ibis is already found in *CT* VII, 75 k-l (sp. 871), entitled *ḫpr m hb*, 'to take the form of an ibis'. Also present in Late Period texts, it recurs in section IV of P. dem. Louvre E 3452, IV, under the title 'To make the transformation into an ibis by the Osiris N' (M. Smith, *The Demotic Mortuary Papyrus Louvre E. 3452* [unpublished dissertation, 1979], pp. 87–8, col. IV, 5–10), and above all in the First Book of Breathing, with varying formulations.

148. A version of the Second Book of Breathing. See p. 108 ff.
149. See *supra*, p. 5, n. 67.
150. P. BM EA 10108 and 10109 belong to a group of five documents usually attributed to the Ptolemaic Period, but the only mention of the deceased as a Hathor makes this dating not quite trustworthy; see *supra*, p. 5, n. 67 and *LPE*, p. 12 with n. 25.
151. For personal names on the model *P*ꜣ */ T*ꜣ *n* + toponym, see G. Vittmann, *ZÄS* 109 (1982), pp. 169–70.

P. BM EA 10110 + 10111, II, 8–9:

ḫꜥ.ỉ m mwt.ỉ m Ḥr nfr n nwb	'I appear from my mother as the beautiful Horus of gold,
m hb km ḥꜣt pḥw	as the ibis of black fore and rear.'

P. BM EA 10304, 40–1 = P. Cairo CG 58018, III, 6–8:

ḫꜥ.ỉ n mwt.ỉ m Ḥr nfr n nwb	'I appear from my mother as the beautiful Horus of gold,
m hb km pḥ	as the ibis of black rear.'

On the appearance of the deceased in the guise of a falcon, and the association of falcon and ibis in the transformations of the deceased, see M. Smith, *Enchoria* 19–20 (1992–3), p. 137, n. (f).

P. BM EA 10110 + 10111, II, 1 = P. BM EA 10304, 35 = P. Cairo CG 58007, V, 1 = P. Cairo CG 58018, II, 18–19:

dỉ.ỉ ḫꜥ.kwỉ m hb ꜥꜣ	'I cause that I appear as the great ibis
pr m ẖt n mwt.ỉ	come forth from the womb of my mother.'

More readily, this relation with the ibis is underlined by explicit identification with Thoth:

P. BM EA 10110 + 10111, II, 2–3 = P. BM EA 10304, 36 = P. Cairo CG 58007, V, 2–3 = P. Cairo CG 58018, II, 20–1:

Ỉ ḥr.tw (var.: *kꜣ.tw*) *r rn.ỉ*	'Thoth is said (var. is uttered) as my name
iw.ỉ m hb m mḥ 5	(for) I am an ibis of five cubits
(*iw*) *psḏ.ỉ m wꜣḏ šmꜥw* .	and my back is of malachite of Upper Egypt.'[152]

P. BM EA 10110 + 10111, II, 20–1 = P. BM EA 10304, 48–9 = P. Cairo CG 58013, 21 = P. Cairo CG 58018, III, 23–4:

ink hb wḥm ꜥnḫ	'I am an ibis who repeats life
Ỉ (var.: *Ḏḥwty*) *kꜣ.tw m* (var.: *r*) *rn.ỉ*	Thoth is uttered as my name.'

P. BM EA 10191, II, 11–12 = P. Cairo CG 58023, x + 27:

ink imy sš.f m hb šps	'I am he who is in his nest as the noble ibis;
Ỉ rn.ỉ	Thoth is my name.'

Var. P. Louvre E 3865, V, 11–12:

ink bꜣ pr m sš.f m hb šps	'I am the ba[153] who comes forth from his nest as the noble ibis.
Ỉ rn.ỉ	Thoth is my name.'

P. BM EA 10191, II, 27–8 = P. Louvre E 3865, I, 16 = P. Louvre N 3148, VI, 26–VII, 1:

ink Ỉ mḥ wḏꜣt	'I am Thoth who fills the *wḏꜣt*-eye,
ink hb pr m Ptḥ .	I am the ibis who came forth from Ptah.'

P. Cairo CG 58023, x + 36–[7] = P. Louvre N 3279, IV, 13–14:[154]

ink ꜥḥ pt ḥnꜥ Ptḥ	'I am he who raises the sky with Ptah,
ink Ỉ mḥ wḏꜣ	I am Thoth who fills the *wḏꜣt*-eye,
ink hb pr m Ḥwt-kꜣ-Ptḥ	I am the ibis who came forth from the Mansion of the ka of Ptah.'

P. BM EA 10191, II, 13:

ink hb šps m-ẖnw sš.k (*sic*)	'I am the noble ibis within your (*sic*) nest.'

P. BM EA 10191, II, 24 = P. Cairo CG 58023, x + 34–[5] = P. Louvre E 3865, I, 13–14:

ink smsw n Rꜥ ink hb šps	'I am the eldest of Re, I am the noble ibis,
ink Ḥꜥpy sꜣ tpy n Wsir .	I am Hapy, the first son[155] of Osiris.'

Lines 2–3

ink pꜣw ir.w wḏt ḥꜣt.f m Ỉwnw r sḏm ḫrw.f m Ỉmn-sḫrw. Some variants refer to *Ḥwt-kꜣ-Ptḥ*, *Ỉnb-ḥḏ*, *Ḥwt-ꜥꜣt* instead of *Ỉwnw*. The mention of *Ỉmn-sḫrw*, a designation of the theban necropolis,[156] is unique in that context; all other versions give here *ẖrt-nṯr*. See P. BM EA 10191, **I, 39–40**.

P. Cairo CG 58009, I, 5–6:

ink pꜣ i-ir.w šꜥt ḥꜣt.f	'I am he before whom a document is made
m-bꜣḥ nꜣ nbw Ỉwnw	before the lords of Heliopolis.'

Lines 3–4

ḥr.tn r.ỉ nꜣ iryw-ꜥꜣ n Ỉmntt nꜣ sꜣwtyw n tꜣ Dwꜣt. Same reading in P. BM EA 10125, 3–4. The parallel sequences mention thereafter: *nꜣ iryw-ꜥꜣ n pr Ḥnw*, 'the doorkeepers of the House of Henu'. See P. BM EA 10191, **I, 2–3**.

Line 4

mi ꜥḳ.ỉ mi pr.ỉ. Same sequence line 7. On the expression *ꜥḳ/pr* conveying the freedom of the deceased, see J. Assmann, *MDAIK* 28 (1972), p. 119, n. 22. This wish, in P. BM EA 10191, I, 15, is formulated in a more detailed context:

mi ꜥḳ.ỉ r Wsir ḫnty Ỉmntt ḥnꜥ nṯrw špsw	'May I enter before Osiris foremost of the West with the noble gods,
m grḥ n ḥb Ḥnw	on the night of the festival of Henu;
nṯr p(ꜣy).ỉ bꜣ m ẖrt-rꜥ	divine is my ba, every day;
mi ꜥḳ.ỉ mi pr.ỉ	May I come, may I go,
iw.ỉ m wꜥ im.sn	(for) I am one of them.'

P. BM EA 10303, 6–7:

ḥr.tn r.ỉ nꜣ nṯrw nty rs r Wsir	'Turn towards me, gods who watch over Osiris!
mi ꜥḳ.ỉ mi pr.ỉ mi snsn.ỉ	may I come, may I go, may I breathe,
iw.ỉ m wꜥ im.sn	(for) I am one of them.'

P. BM EA 10110 + 10111, II, 6–7 = P. BM EA 10304, 39:

ꜥḳ.ỉ ḥs.tw pr.ỉ mr.tw	'I come praised and go beloved
m Dwꜣt nt ḥwt Bnbn	in the Duat of the Mansion of the Obelisk.'

Lines 4–5

ḥr.tn r.ỉ nꜣ nṯrw mdsw-irty imyw-ḫt Wsir. See P. BM EA 10191, **I, 4**.

Line 5

nṯrw imyw tꜣ wsḫt Mꜣꜥty nꜣ nṯrw imyw tꜣ wsḫt sḫwt iꜣrw. See P. BM EA 10191, **I, 4–5**.

Lines 5–6

ḥr.tn r.ỉ nꜣ nṯrw n tꜣ Dwꜣt ḏrw mi ꜥḳ.ỉ mi ꜥḳ pꜣy.ỉ bꜣ. The parallel versions replace *mi ꜥḳ.ỉ mi ꜥḳ pꜣy.ỉ bꜣ* with the invocation to the 'gods who watch over Osiris'. See P. BM EA 10191, **I, 6**.

152. On *wꜣḏ Šmꜥ* in relation with the parts of the body: Harris, op. cit., p. 103.

153. Read *ink bꜣ* for *ink pꜣ*, 'I am he who'?

154. J.C. Goyon, *Le Papyrus du Louvre N 3279* (*BdE* 42, 1966), p. 59, n. 1.

155. Var. P. Louvre E 3865: *ink bꜣ tpy n Wsir*, 'I am the first ba of Osiris'. Probable confusion of *bꜣ* with *sꜣ*, 'son'; see P. BM EA 10191, **I, 33** and **II, 7–8**.

156. C. de Wit, *Les inscriptions du temple d'Opet à Karnak* III (*BiAe* 13, 1968), p. 139, n. 425; Gutbub, *Textes fondamentaux*, p. 151, n. (c).

Lines 6–7
ḥr.t r.i Ḥwt-Ḥr ḥnwt Imntt ḥn.w n.s Imntt. See P. BM EA 10191, **I, 5–6**.

Line 7
mi ꜥḳ.i mi pr.i mi pꜣy<.i> r ḥrt ḥnꜥ bꜣw nw nṯrw nṯrwt. On the different variants attested with this sequence, see P. BM EA 10191, **I, 11**.

Lines 7–8
ḥr.k r.i Inpw sꜣ Wsir pꜣ iry-ꜥꜣ mtr n tꜣ Dwꜣt. See P. BM EA 10191, **I, 3**.

Line 8
mi ꜥḳ.i r wsḫt ww Mꜣꜥt. See P. BM EA 10108, **lines 5–6**.

Lines 8–9
mi ir.i wꜥt m ist Wsir iḳrw nn šms Kꜣ-ḥtp. See P. BM EA 10108, **line 6**.

Kꜣ-ḥtp, 'satisfied bull', is a possible reinterpretation of a name of Osiris with the original meaning 'satisfied ka' (*PT* § 582 d), a tradition continued down to *BD* ch. 128 (ed. Lepsius, pl. 52, 6); cf. too G. Maspero, *ASAE* 1 (1900), p. 256: *ink kꜣ ḥtp*, in a text entitled *rꜣ n rdit tꜣ m Iwnw*, 'Spell for giving bread in Heliopolis'.[157] In the other examples consulted, the image of the bull in this designation is beyond doubt; cf. *Edfou* V, 293, 11–12, where the name 'satisfied bull' is juxtaposed with 'bull of sharp horns';[158] also *LD* IV, 61 f; *Dendara* VIII, 21, 17; P. Skrine I, Text II, 51–3 (A.M. Blackman, *JEA* 4 [1917], p. 126 and pl. 27): *šms.i Kꜣ-ḥtp* ( ) *m ḫprw.f.* Other references: S. Cauville, *Dendara. Les chapelles osiriennes* III (*BdE* 119, 1997), p. 584; Leitz, *LGG* VII, pp. 268–9.

Line 9
mi ḳbḥ.w n.i mw m ḥwt sr mi p(ꜣ) sr wr m Iwnw. See P. BM EA 10191, **I, 12**.

Lines 10–13
On this series of invocations to Thoth, adapted from *BD* ch. 18, 19 and 20, see P. BM EA 10191, **I, 15–29**, with the references to the different versions. The text here is severely abridged.

Line 13
iw wḥm.n Ḥr ḥknw sp 4. This phrase also closes the invocations to Thoth in P. BM EA 10125, 21; a more developed form occurs in P. Cairo CG 58009, III, 1–2:

iw wḥm.n Ḥr ḥknw sp 4	'Horus has repeated the praises, four times,
iw wḥm.n Wsir ḫnty Imntyw	Osiris foremost of the Westerners,
Wn-nfr mꜣꜥ-ḫrw	Wennefer justified,
<ḥknw> sp 4	has repeated <the praises>, four times;
iw wḥm.n ḥm ḥknw sp 4	the servant has repeated the praises, four times.'

BD ch. 19, 12–13 (ed. Lepsius):

iw wḥm.n Ḥr ḥknw sp 4	'Horus has repeated the praises, four times,
iw ḫftyw.f nb ḫr sḫr bḥn	(for) all his enemies are fallen, overthrown, slain.
iw wḥm.n Wsir N ḥknw sp 4	The Osiris N has repeated the praises, four times,
iw ḫftyw.f nb ḫr sḫr bḥn	(for) all his enemies are fallen, overthrown, slain.
iw wḥm.n Ḥr sꜣ Ist sꜣ Wsir ḥḥ n ḥb-sd	Horus the son of Isis, son of Osiris, has repeated millions of *sd*-festivals
iw ḫftyw.f nb ḫr sḫr bḥn	(for) all his enemies are fallen, overthrown, slain.'

Lines 13–14
stwt n Rꜥ tꜣw n Imn mw n Ḥꜥpy nnk st ḏrw. On this sequence, which closes a number of copies of the First Book of Breathing, see P. BM EA 10191, **II, 33–4**.

P. BM EA 10199 (pls 37–9)

Hay Collection.
Unpublished.
Quirke, *Owners*, no. 36.
Provenance: probably Thebes.
Date: first to second century AD.
Owner of the papyrus: *Ist-wrt* (Esoeris).
Mother of the owner: *Tꜣ-ḫrt-(nt-)Mnw* (Tchormenis ?).

Contents: First Book of Breathing, abridged version.

Manuscript of one sheet (37.5 × 22 cm), including at several points tears which affect in particular line 3 and the right edge of the document. The text is partly effaced in the second half of line 2. On the recto are written 29 lines of text.

Text on the verso: The Book of Breathing of the Hathor *Ist-wrt*, justified, born of *Tꜣ-ḫrt-(nt)-Mnw*.

Translation

Recto

(1) Thus speaks the Hathor *Ist-wrt*, justified, born of *Tꜣ-ḫrt-(nt-)Mnw*, justified:

(2) I am Re at his rising, I am Atum at [his] setting, I am Osiris [foremost of the West] (3) during the night, during the day, at every moment of each day. [Turn towards me, doorkeepers of the West,] (4) guardians of the Duat, doorkeepers of the house of Henou. Turn towards me, Anubis son (5)[of Osiris], dependable doorkeeper of the Duat. Turn towards me, gods of piercing gaze who are in the (6) retinue of Osiris, gods who are in the hall of the two Maats! Turn towards me, Hathor mistress of the West, (7) Maat to whom the West has been entrusted! <Turn towards me>, gods who watch over Osiris, chase away for me the void (8) of the hours of the day. May my ba go forth to heaven with the bas of the great gods! (9) May I receive offerings with Atum! May there be made for me a libation of water in the Mansion of the Prince as (10) (is done for) the great Prince who is in Heliopolis! May I proceed to Heliopolis on the night of the festival of offerings on the altar, (11) and on the festival of the sixth day, with all the gods and goddesses of Upper and Lower Egypt, (for) I am one of them. O Thoth, turn (12) towards

157. On the different texts bearing this title, see S. Schott, *Bücher und Bibliotheken im alten Ägypten* (Wiesbaden 1990), p. 191, no. 668 a–c.

158. This epithet occurs also in sp. 218 of *CT* (III, 195), entitled: *rdit tꜣ m Iwnw*.

me! Vindicate me against my enemies as you vindicated Osiris against his enemies before the great Council (13) which is in Heliopolis, on this night of battle to overthrow (his) enemies, before the great Council which is in (14) Busiris, on this night of raising the *ḏd*-pillar in Busiris, before the great Council which is in Ro-setau, (15) on that night when Anubis put his hands over the relics (?), behind Osiris.

O Lord of the light, foremost of the Great Mansion, turn towards me! (16) Grant me my mouth, that I may speak therewith! Guide for me my heart at the moment of the Evil! O Ptah, father of the gods, turn (17) towards me! Open for me my mouth, open for me my eyes! Make for me my *ib*-heart rest in its place, and my *ḥꜣty*-heart (18) be established in its right place. Grant me my mouth to speak, my legs to walk, my arms to overthrow (19) my enemies! May Anubis open for me the portals of the Duat! May I (20) be one of the retinue of Osiris! You write a decree in my favour within the Mansion of the ka of Ptah, (21) to cause that my steps be not turned back in the god's domain, that I may do what my ka desires in the sky and on earth, and that my ba may alight (22) on my corpse. May the sky be open for me, may the earth be open for me, I control my *ib*-heart, I control (23) my *ḥꜣty*-heart, I control my arms, I control my mouth, I control my whole limbs, I control (24) the invocation offering, I control the water of the overflow, I control my eyes on earth. I live on the bread of Geb, I am healthy (25) thanks to the water of Hapy, I rise by the beer, and sit down by the milk, I consume wine and *šdḥ*-brew. (26) I receive the breath by means of kyphi and incense. O Amun, give sweet air to my nose! (27) O Re, give me your rays! May I see you in the course of every day! O Hapy, (28), give me libation, Nepyt, give me bread, Menqet, give me beer! My arms (29) are raised to receive invocation offerings, unendingly, for ever and eternally.

Commentary

Line 1

ḫr.s n Ḥwt-Ḥr N. See P. BM EA 10191, **I, 1**.

Lines 2–3

ỉnk Rꜥ m ḫꜥw.f ỉnk Ỉtm m ḥtp.f ỉnk Wsỉr [ḫnty Ỉmntt] m grḥ m hrw m nw nb nty rꜥ nb. This sequence, attested complete in P. Cairo CG 58009, I, 2–4 = P. Cairo CG 58014, 1–3 = P. Louvre SN, 1–2 = P. Louvre E 3865, I, 5–6, but often abridged in the second half, opens most surviving copies of the First Book of Breathing. See P. BM EA 10191, **I, 1–2**.

Lines 3–4

[ḥr.tn r.ỉ nꜣ ỉryw-ꜥꜣ n Ỉmntt] nꜣ sꜣwtyw n tꜣ Dwꜣt nꜣ ỉryw-ꜥꜣ n pr Ḥnw. See P. BM EA 10191, **I, 2–3**.

Lines 4–5

ḥr.k n.ỉ Ỉnpw sꜣ [Wsỉr pꜣ ỉry-]ꜥꜣ mtr n tꜣ Dwꜣt. See P. BM EA 10191, **I, 3–4**.

Lines 5–6

ḥr.tn r.ỉ nꜣ nṯrw mdsw-ỉrty ỉmyw-ḫt Wsỉr. See P. BM EA 10191, **I, 4**.

Line 6

nꜣ nṯrw ỉmyw tꜣ wsḫt Mꜣꜥty. The parallels add here: *nꜣ nṯrw ỉmyw tꜣ wsḫt sḫt ỉꜣrw*, 'the gods who are in the hall of the Field of reeds'. On this passage and its variants, see P. BM EA 10191, **I, 4–5**.

Lines 6–7

ḥr.t n.ỉ Ḥwt-Ḥr ḫnt Ỉmntt Mꜣꜥt ḥn.w n.s Ỉmntt. See P. BM EA 10191, **I, 5–6**.

Line 7

nꜣ nṯrw nty rs r Wsỉr. The complete versions insert before this sequence the invocation *ḥr.tn r.ỉ nꜣ nṯrw n tꜣ Dwꜣt ḏr.w*, 'Turn towards me, all gods of the Duat'. See P. BM EA 10191, **I, 6**.

Lines 7–8

ḫꜣꜥ n.ỉ wš n nꜣ wnwwt n p(ꜣ) hrw. With a single exception, all versions consulted which include this phrase place before it a sequence invoking the guardians (var. the gods) of the Duat. However it seems unlikely that the text here is corrupt, and a parallel for the omission may be found in P. Cairo CG 58014, 7–8:

ḥr.tn r.ỉ nꜣ nṯrw n tꜣ Dwꜣt ḏr.w	'Turn towards me, all gods of the Duat,
nꜣ nṯrw nty rs r Wsỉr	gods who watch over Osiris,
ḫꜣꜥ n.ỉ nbḏ n nꜣ[159] *wnwwt n grḥ*	chase away for me the Evil of the hours of the night'.

P. BM EA 10199 is also the only known version to replace *grḥ* with the word *hrw*, 'day'. The predominant version, represented by numerous manuscripts, gives the following text:

ḥr.tn r.ỉ nꜣ sꜣwtyw[160] *n (tꜣ) Dwꜣt*	'Turn towards me, guardians of the Duat,
ḫꜣꜥ n.ỉ wš(r) n[161] *nꜣ wnwwt n (pꜣ) grḥ*	chase away for me the void of the hours of the night.'

Line 8

mỉ pr p(ꜣ)y.ỉ bꜣ r ḥrt ḥnꜥ nꜣ bꜣw n nṯrw wrw. See P. BM EA 10191, **I, 11** and P. BM EA 10108, **lines 6–7**.

Line 9

mỉ smꜣ.ỉ ḫwt ḥnꜥ Ỉtm. See P. BM EA 10191, **I, 11–12**.

Lines 9–10

mỉ ḳbḥ.w n.ỉ mw m ḥwt-sr mỉ p(ꜣ) sr wr m Ỉwnw. See P. BM EA 10123, **line 2** and P. BM EA 10191, **I, 12**.

Lines 10–11

mỉ ꜥḳ.ỉ r Ỉwnw n grḥ n ḫwt ḫꜣwt n snwt ḥnꜥ nṯrw nṯrwt nw Šmꜥ Mḥw ỉw.ỉ m wꜥ ỉm.sn. See P. BM EA 10191, **I, 13–14**.

Lines 11–15

On this litany addressed to Thoth, see P. BM EA 10191, **I, 15–29** (long version).

159.  is a miswriting of *nꜣ*; cf. in the preceding line *nꜣ nṯrw*, and P. BM EA 10283, **lines 2–3**.

160. Var. P. Cairo CG 58008, 10: *nꜣ nṯrw*.

161. *n* omitted in P. Cairo CG 58008, I, 11.

Lines 12–13
m-bꜣḥ ḏꜣḏꜣt nsw ꜥꜣt imyw Ỉwnw grḥ pfy n ꜥḥꜣ-ꜥ r sḫr sbiw. P. BM EA 10125 here substitutes *ꜣbḏw* for *Ỉwnw*. Most parallels give a more extended version at this juncture. See P. BM EA 10191, **I, 16–17**.

Lines 13–14
m-bꜣḥ ḏꜣḏꜣt nsw ꜥꜣt imyw Ḏdw grḥ pfy n sꜥḥꜥ ḏd m Ḏdw. See P. BM EA 10191, **I, 19–20**.

Lines 14–15
m-bꜣḥ ḏꜣḏꜣt nsw ꜥꜣt imyw Rꜣ-stꜣw grḥ pfy n sḏr Ỉnpw ꜥwy.f ḥr ḫwt ḥꜣ Wsir. See P. BM EA 10191, **I, 28–9.**

Lines 15–16
i Nb-šsp ḫnty ḥwt-ꜥꜣt ḥr.k r.i di.k n.i rꜣ.i mdw.i im.f. See P. BM EA 10191, **I, 29–30**.

Line 16
sšm.k n.i ib.i m ꜣt nt nbḏ. The extended versions add:

ir.k n.i rꜣ.i mdw.i im.f	'Make for me my mouth, that I may speak by it,
m-bꜣḥ nṯr ꜥꜣ nb Dwꜣt	before the great god, lord of the Duat,
nn šnꜥ.tw(.i) m pt tꜣ	without being turned back from the sky or the earth,
m-bꜣḥ ḏꜣḏꜣt nt nṯr nb nṯrt nbt	before the Council of all god and all goddess.
ink bꜣ n Ḥr ir ꜥḫm ḫt m pr.s	I am the ba of Horus who causes fire to be quenched when it breaks out.'

On this passage and its variants, see P. BM EA 10191, **I, 30–31**.

Lines 16–17
i Ptḥ it nṯrw ḥr.k r.i wn.k n.i rꜣ.i wp.k n.i irty.i. Some versions add: *mi ir.t* (var.: *ir.k*) *n Skr-Wsir m ḥwt-nwb m Ỉnb-ḥḏ*, 'as it was done (var.: as you did) for Sokar-Osiris in the Mansion of Gold in the White-Wall'. See P. BM EA 10191, **I, 31–2**.

Lines 17–18
ir.k n.i ib.i ḥtp ḥr st.f ḥ(ꜣ)ty.i smn ḥr mkt.f. For this sequence, see P. BM EA 10191, **I, 35**, and *LPE*, pp. 90–1 (I, 9).

Lines 18–19
di.k n.i rꜣ.i r mdw rdwy.i r šm ꜥwy.i r sḫr ḫftyw.i. See P. BM EA 10191, **I, 35–6**.

Line 19
mi wn n.i Ỉnpw nꜣ sbḫwt n tꜣ Dwꜣt. See P. BM EA 10191, **I, 36**.

Lines 19–20
mi ir.i wꜥ m šms(w) Wsir. See P. BM EA 10191, **I, 36–7**.

Lines 20–2
sš.k n.i wḏt.i m-ḫnw Ḥwt-kꜣ-Ptḥ r tm šnꜥ nmtt.i m ẖrt-nṯr r dit ir.i mr kꜣ.i m pt m tꜣ r di(t) ḫn bꜣ.i ḥr ḫꜣt.i. On this sequence and its variants, see P. BM EA 10191, **I, 37** and **37–8**.

Line 22
iw wn n.i pt iw wn n.i tꜣ. In the extended manuscripts of the First Book of Breathing, this passage follows a prolonged elaboration of the motif absent from P. BM EA 10199. See P. BM EA 10191, **II, 28**. This long interruption might be explained by confusion with the corresponding sequence in P. BM EA 10191, **I, 36**: *iw wn ꜥꜣwy m pt* or its variant in P. Cairo CG 58008, 38: *iw wn n.i ꜥꜣwy m pt m tꜣ*.

Lines 22–4
sḫm.i m ib.i sḫm.i m ḥ(ꜣ)ty.i sḫm.i m ꜥwy.i sḫm.i m rꜣ.i sḫm.i m ꜥwt.i irw sḫm.i m prt-ḫrw sḫm.i m mw m ḥbbt sḫm.i m irty.i m tꜣ. Omission, after *tꜣ*, of *sḫm.i m irt.i m ẖrt-nṯr*, 'I control my eyes in the god's domain'. See P. BM EA 10191, **II, 28–31**.

Lines 24–5
ꜥnḫ.i m tꜣ m Gb snb.i m mw m Ḥꜥpy. See P. BM EA 10191, **II, 31–3**.

Line 25
ꜥḥꜥ.i m ḥnḳt ḥms.i m irtt wšꜥ.i m irp šdḥ. On this sequence, and the variant *ḥms* as compared with the more commonly attested *sꜥm*, see P. BM EA 10191, **II, 32–3**.

Line 26
iṯ.i snsn m kꜣp snṯr. Numerous variants and additions are attested in the parallel sources. See P. BM EA 10191, **II, 33**.

i Ỉmn mi ṯꜣw nḏm r fnḏ.i. P. BM EA 10110 + 10111, II, 13 replaces *r fnḏ.i* by *ink sꜣ.k mr.k* ', (for) I am your son beloved'. On Amun and the wind, see P. BM EA 10110 + 10111, **II, 13–14**.

Line 27
i Rꜥ mi n.i stwt.k mi mꜣꜣ<.i> twk m ẖrt-hrw nt rꜥ nb. See P. BM EA 10110 + 10111, **II, 14–15**.

i Ḥꜥpy mi n.i ḳbḥ. See P. BM EA 10110 + 10111, **II, 15–16**.

Line 28
Npyt mi n.i tꜣ. Other versions place before the name of the deity the interjection *i*, and give the masculine form *Npri*. See P. BM EA 10110 + 10111, **II, 16**.

Mnḳt mi n.i ḥnḳt. See P. BM EA 10110 + 10111, **II, 17**.

Lines 28–9
ꜥwy.i fꜣ.w r iṯ prt-ḫrw nn ws r nḥḥ ḥnꜥ ḏt. The formula *nn ws r nḥḥ ḥnꜥ ḏt*, closing the manuscript, is absent from the other versions, which add different clauses. See P. BM EA 10110 + 10111, **II, 18**.

P. BM EA 10206 (pls 40–1)

Unpublished.
Provenance: probably Thebes.
Date: first to second century AD
Owner of the papyrus: name lost.

Contents: First Book of Breathing, fragmentary version.

This manuscript covers four fragments of which one, on the photograph at the right and inverted, is written in a different hand and presumably therefore derives from a separate manuscript. The other three (A, B, C), although probably all part of the same document, are certainly not from a single column. Between A (7.1 × 2.4 cm) and B (5.8 × 2.7 cm) about 4.5 cm of text are missing. It is impossible to determine which exact words opened and closed each line, but the missing text, whether at the beginning or at the end, would

have taken in total between 4.5 and 5 cm. Thus, the line of writing of this column can be estimated to within about 10 cm. Numbering of the lines in the translation is that of the fragments, and not, of course, of the original papyrus. Fragment C (8.6 × 4.3 cm), preserving eleven lines of text between apparent blank margins, gives a precise idea of the height of the text on each column. The verso bears no visible trace of text.

Translation

Recto

A + B

(1) [... O Thoth] turn towards me, vindicate [me against my enemies, as you vindicated] Osiris against his enemies [before the great Council which is in Bu](2)siris, on [that] night [of raising the *ḏd*-pillar in Busiris]. O Thoth, turn towards me, vindicate me [against my enemies, as you vindi](3)cated Osiris against [his] enemies [before the great Council which is in] Ro-setau, on [that] night [when Anubis put his hands over the relics (?) (4) be]hind Osiris.

O Lord of the li[ght, foremost of the Great Mansion, turn towards me!] Grant me my mouth, that [I] may speak [therewith! Guide for me my heart] (5) at the moment of the Evil. [Make (?) for me my mouth, that I may speak therewith before] the great god lord of the Dua[t, without being turned back from the sky and the earth] (6), before the Council of all god and all goddess. I am the ba] of Horus who causes fire to be quenched [when it breaks out.

O Ptah, father of the gods, turn] (7) towards me! Open [for me my mouth, open for me my eyes, as is was done] for Sokar-Osiris in the Man[sion of Gold in the White-Wall. My mouth has been open for me with the iron *mḏꜣt*-chisel with which you opened the mouths] (8) of the gods. I am the ba [of Sekhmet who sits at the West of the sky. Make my name to endure like that of Osiris foremost of the West]; (9) you are promoted among [the primordial gods. Make for me my *ib*-heart in the House of the *ib*-hearts, and my *ḥꜣty*-heart in the House of the *ḥꜣty*-hearts! Make for me my *ib*-heart] (10) rest in its place, [and my *ḥꜣty*-heart be established in its proper place ...]

C

(1) [... i]n me. Hapy the great, may I que[nch my thirst in your overflow! I am one who stands and sits down as Hapy the great; I control] (2) him at my heart's desire. Grant that I control [this your water, fresh and abundant, as a sweet libation. I am the Lord of All, I am Atum, I am] Khepr(3)i, I am the first-born of Re, I am [a noble ibis, I am Hapy, the first ba of Osiris. I am he who] (4) emerged from Nun with Re, I [am he who raised the sky, I am Ptah, I am he who ascends to heaven. I walk] (5) on earth, I am immersed in Nun, and I pro[ceed in the bark of Re, Sekhmet having conceived me and Nut having given birth to me. I am Thoth who fi](6)lls the *wḏꜣt*-eye, I am the ibis who comes forth [from Ptah. May the sky be open for me, may the earth be open for me! I control my *ib*-heart], (7) I control my *ḥꜣty*-heart], I control my arms, [I control my mouth, I control my whole limbs, I control the invocation offering], (8) [(namely) bread, beer], oxen and fowl, I control water of the over[flow, I control my eyes on earth, I control my eyes in the god's domain. I live on (9)] the bread of Geb, I am healthy [thanks to the water of Hapy, I rise by the beer, I drink] milk, I consume (10)] wine and *šdḥ*-brew. [I] receive [the breath by means of kyphi and incense. I am the great god coming forth from the great god. The rays (11)] of Re, the breath of Amun, [the water of Hapy, that belongs to me, eternally!]

Commentary

The three fragments **A + B**, **C** give a text corresponding to P. BM EA 10191, I, 25–35 (**A + B**), and II, 21–34 (**C**), to which the reader is referred for the detailed commentary. Generally, the two manuscripts show no striking divergence, although the following variants may be noted:

A + B:
Line 2: *m grḥ*. See P. BM EA 10191, **I, 27–8**.
Line 4: *ḥꜣ Wsir*. See P. BM EA 10191, **I, 28–9**.
Line 8: *ink sꜣ* [*n Sḫmt*]. See P. BM EA 10191, **I, 33**.
Line 9: *ṯn twk*. See P. BM EA 10191, **I, 33–4**.

C:
Line 1: [*i*]*m.i*. See P. BM EA 10191, **II, 21**.
Line 4: [*ink p*]*r m Nwn ḥnꜥ Rꜥ*. See P. BM EA 10191, **II, 25–6**.
Line 5: *hrp*. See P. BM EA 10191, **II, 26–7**.
Line 8: *kꜣw ꜣpdw*. See P. BM EA 10191, **II, 29–30**.

P. BM EA 10283 (pls 42–3)

Salt Collection 1, 133.
Unpublished.
Quirke, *Owners*, no. 229.
Provenance: Thebes. Found with P. BM EA 10282 on the mummy inside coffin BM EA 6705 in the collective tomb of the archon Soter.[162]
Date: End of the first to beginning of the second century AD.
Owner of the papyrus: *Swtr* (Soter). He is also owner of P. BM EA 10282.
Father of the owner (?): *Pꜣ-krr*.

162. See *supra*, p. 6, no. **4**, and p. 9.

Mother of the owner: *Pylt*[163] (Philous).

Contents: First Book of Breathing, abridged version.

Manuscript of one sheet (36.3 × 19.2 cm), bearing eleven lines of text of which the second is almost entirely effaced. Minor break in line 10.
Text on the verso: A good burial. May it be stable over your bones, may it remain over your flesh, without destruction for you ... eternally.
(*In demotic*): (at) his head.

Translation

Recto

(1) Thus speaks the Osiris *Swtr*, justified, (son of) *Pꜣ-krr* (?), justified, born of *Pylt*, justified:

I am Re at his rising, (2) I am Atum at his setting, [I am Osiris foremost of the West during the night ... (?). [Turn] (3) towards me, doorkeepers of the Duat, guardians of the West, doorkeepers of the House of Henu! I am (4) your father Re-Horakhty from whom you emerged at the first time. I am Horus, son of Isis, son of Osiris, who is upon his throne, eternally. I am Har-(5)oeris lord of Upper Egypt, lord of Per-Iit, who repels the enemy from Heliopolis. Turn towards me, Hathor mistress of the West, (6) Maat to whom the West has been entrusted! Turn towards me, all gods of the Duat, gods who watch (7) over Osiris! May my ba go forth to heaven with the bas who follow Osiris, (for) I am one of you. O gods who (8) are in heaven! O gods who are on earth! O gods who are in the South, the North, the West and the East, may my ba go forth (9) to heaven with the bas who are in the retinue of Osiris! O Re, I am your beloved! O Thoth, I am your heir, in truth! O Re-Horakhty, I am your image! (10) The rays of Re, the breath of Amun, the water of Hapy, that belongs to me, eternally. May your ba live for (11) ever, may it be renewed eternally!

Commentary

Line 1
ḥr.f n Wsỉr. See P. BM EA 10191, **I, 1**.

On the form , see P. BM EA 10282, **line 1**.

Lines 1–2
ỉnk Rꜥ m ḫꜥ.f ỉnk ỉtm m ḥtp.f [...]. Other than a few signs, virtually the entire line is effaced. For the expected restoration and the possible variants, see P. BM EA 10191, **I, 1–2**.

Lines 2–3
[*ḥr*]*.tn r.ỉ nꜣ ỉryw-ꜥꜣ n tꜣ Dwꜣt nꜣ sꜣwtyw n ỉmntt nꜣ ỉryw-ꜥꜣ n pr Ḥnw*. Other versions give *ỉryw-ꜥꜣ n ỉmntt* and *sꜣwtyw n tꜣ Dwꜣt*. For the variants, see P. BM EA 10191, **I, 2–3**. The writings of the articles are confused:  for *nꜣ* (again lines 6, 7, and cf. *supra*, n. 158),  for *n*.

Lines 3–4
ỉnk ỉt.tn Rꜥ-Ḥr-ꜣḫty ỉw pr.tn ỉm.f m sp tpy. In other versions, this sequence is addressed to 'all gods of the Duat, the gods who watch over Osiris'. See P. BM EA 10191, **I, 7**.

Line 4
ỉnk Ḥr sꜣ ỉst sꜣ Wsỉr nty ḥr nst.f ḏt. See P. BM EA 10191, **I, 7**.

Lines 4–5
ỉnk Ḥr wr nb tꜣ šmꜥ nb pr ỉỉt nty ꜥmḏ sbỉ r ỉwnw. This sequence condenses two normally independent passages:

ỉnk Ḥr wr nb Šmꜥ	'I am Haroeris, lord of Upper Egypt,
ỉr dỉ nfr ḥꜥw n Rꜥ	who causes the body of Re to be regenerated,
ỉw.f dỉ Ḥr ḥr nst ỉt.f	placing Horus on the throne of his father'
and	
ỉnk Ḥr nb Ḥm nb pr ỉỉt	'I am Horus lord of Per-iit,
nty ꜥmḏ sbỉw r ỉwnw	who repels the enemies from Heliopolis.'

See P. BM EA 10191, **I, 8** and **9–10**.

Lines 5–6
ḥr.t r.ỉ Ḥwt-Ḥr ḥnwt ỉmntt Mꜣꜥt ḥn n.s ỉmntt. In contrast to the usual version *ḥn.w n.s*, the writing  suggests two possible interpretations. Either this would be a faulty writing of *ḥn*, 'offer', omitting the suffix *.w* (hypothesis adopted in the translation), or this would be the verb *ḥn*, 'to move', with subject *ỉmntt*. See P. BM EA 10191, **I, 5–6**.

Lines 6–7
ḥr.tn r.ỉ nꜣ nṯrw n tꜣ Dwꜣt ḏr.w nꜣ nṯrw nty rs r Wsỉr. See P. BM EA 10191, **I, 6**.

Line 7
mỉ pr pꜣy(.ỉ) bꜣ r ḥrt ḥnꜥ nꜣ bꜣw nty šms[164] *Wsỉr ỉnk wꜥ n-ỉm.tn*. P. BM EA 10191, I, 11, substitutes *nꜣ bꜣw n nṯrw wrw*, 'the bas of the great gods' for *nꜣ bꜣw nty šms Wsỉr ỉnk wꜥ n-ỉm.tn*; see commentary. A similar wish is expressed again in lines 8–9 of P. BM EA 10283. On the flight to heaven by the ba of the deceased, see P. BM EA 10108, **lines 6–7**.

Lines 7–8
ỉ nṯrw ỉmy(w) pt ỉ nṯrw ỉmy(w) tꜣ ỉ nṯrw ỉmy(w) rsyt mḥtt ỉmntt ỉꜣbtt. See P. BM EA 10282, **lines 2–3**.

Lines 8–9
mỉ pr bꜣ(.ỉ) r ḥrt ḥnꜥ nꜣ bꜣw ỉmyw-ḫt Wsỉr. See *supra*, **line 7**.

Line 10
stwt n Rꜥ ṯꜣw n ỉmn mw n Ḥꜥpy nnk sn ḏt. See P. BM EA 10191, **II, 33–4**.

Lines 10–11
ꜥnḫ p(ꜣy).k bꜣ r nḥḥ rnp.f r ḏt. See P. BM EA 10282, **line 26**.

163. The sign □ is written in demotic.

164. The word *šms* is written in demotic.

P. BM EA 10303 (pls 44–5)

Salt Collection 1, 167.
Unpublished.
Quirke, *Owners*, no. 282.
Provenance: probably Thebes.
Date: first to second century AD.
Owner of the papyrus: name lost. Probably a man as indicated by the reference in the text on the verso to 'your corpse' in the masculine (*ḫ3t.k*).[165] The text of the recto, written in the first person, does not distinguish the sex of the deceased.
Mother of the owner: [...-] (?) *t3-šrit* (R*PN* I, 368, 5). It does not seem possible to restore as a compound name of the type *X-t3-šrit*, the beginning of which would have been lost in the lacuna of line 1.

Contents: First Book of Breathing, abridged version.

Manuscript of one sheet (14.6 × 27.4 cm), lacking the first line of text, and bearing, in its present state, thirteen lines with large and widely spaced signs. Between the eleventh and the twelfth line is drawn the image of a recumbent mummy.

Text on the verso: A good [bur]ial. May it endure over your corpse by the word of Hathor mistress of the West!

Translation

Recto

(1) [... ... born] of [... ?]-(2)*t3-šrit*, justified.

I am Re at his rising, I am Atum (3) at his setting, I am Osiris foremost of the West, the great god lord (4) of Abydos. Turn towards me, guardians (5) of the Duat, guardians of the West. (6) Turn towards me, gods who watch (7) over Osiris! May I come, may I (8) go, may I breathe, (9) (for) I am one of them! O Thoth, turn (10) towards me! vindicate me against my enemies as (11) you vindicated Osiris against his enemies, (12) on that night of the festival of offerings on (13) the altar in Letopolis (14) for ever (*bis*) and eternally (*bis*).

Commentary

Lines 2–4
ink Rʿ m ḫʿ.f ink Itm m ḥtp.f ink Wsir ḫnty Imntt nṯr ʿ3 nb 3bḏw. On the different variants of this introductory sequence, see P. BM EA 10191, **I, 1–2**.

Lines 4–5
ḥr.tn r.i n3 iryw-ʿ3 n t3 Dw3t n3 s3wtyw n Imntt. See P. BM EA 10191, **I, 2–3**.

Lines 6–7
ḥr.tn r.i n3 nṯrw nty rs r Wsir. See P. BM EA 10191, **I, 6**.

Lines 7–9
mi ʿḳ.i mi pr.i mi snsn.i iw.i m wʿ im.sn. Omission of *mi snsn.i* in other versions. See P. BM EA 10191, **I, 15**.

Lines 9–13
Highly abridged version of a litany addressed to Thoth and adapted from *BD* ch. 18–20. It is followed by the ending formula *nḥḥ sp 2 ḏt sp 2*. See P. BM EA 10191, **I, 15–29**, and especially **18–19**.

P. BM EA 10337 (pls 46–8)

Anastasi Collection 3, 1069.
Unpublished.
Quirke, *Owners*, no. 173.
Provenance: probably Thebes.
Date: first to second century AD (?).
Owner of the papyrus: *P3-di-Ḫnsw* (Petechonsis).
Mother of the owner: *T3*-[...] (erased name).

Contents: First Book of Breathing, incomplete version.

Manuscript of one sheet (34 × 14.7 cm), in poor condition, bearing eight lines of text of which the first three are partially effaced, and darkened by black liquid stains across parts of lines 2 to 7. The unusually sharp break, except on the left-hand side, would seem to indicate that the papyrus has been cut in modern times. On the verso the title is written in hieratic, as well as a Greek text; cf. F. Lenormant, *Catalogue d'une collection égyptienne (M. D'Anastasi)* (Paris 1857), no. 1069, where this document is identified as a 'manuscrit grec ptolémaïque opisthographe, portant au revers les restes d'un texte hiératique de basse époque'.

Text on the verso: A good [burial]. May it endure over your bones, may it re[main over your flesh] with neither destruction nor decay, for ever!

Translation

Recto

(1) Thus speaks the Osiris *P3-di-Ḫnsw*, born of *T3* ..., justfied:

I am Re at his rising, [I am Atum at his setting], (2) I am [Osiris foremost of] the West during the night and during the day.

165. Caution is required here because many manuscripts written for women give in error the masculine pronoun.

[Turn] towards me, door[keepers] of the West, guar[dians of the Duat, (3) doorkeepers of the] House of the Henu! Turn [towards me, Anubis son] of Osiris, [dependable door]keeper [of the Duat]! (4) Turn towards me, gods of piercing <gaze>, goddesses who are in the retinue of Osiris, gods who are in the hall of the two Maats, (5) gods of the hall of the Field of reeds! Turn towards me, Hathor mistress of the West, Maat to whom the West has been entrusted! (6) Turn towards me, all gods of the Duat, gods who watch over Osiris! I am your father Re-Horakhty from whom you came forth (7) at the first time; I am Horus son of Isis, son of Osiris, who is upon his throne, eternally. I am Haroeris, lord of Upper Egypt, (8) who causes the [divine] body of Re to be perfect (or: comforted), setting Horus upon the throne of his father Osiris. I am Hor-merty lord of the battle, who causes [all the gods ...] to be strong ...

Commentary

Line 1
ḥr.f n Wsir N. See P. BM EA 10191, **I, 1**.

Lines 1–2
ink Rꜥ m ḫꜥ.f ink [*Ỉtm m ḥtp.f*] *in*[*k Wsir ḫnty*] *Ỉmntyw m grḥ m hrw.* See P. BM EA 10191, **I, 1–2**.

Lines 2–3
[*ḥr.tn*] *r.i nꜣ iry*[*w-ꜥꜣ*] *n Ỉmntt nꜣ sꜣ*[*wtyw n tꜣ Dwꜣt nꜣ iryw-ꜥꜣ n*] *pr Ḥnw.* The presence of the  after  in the word *iryw-ꜥꜣ* derives from confusion between the signs *sꜣ* and *iry;* see Golenischeff, *Pap. hiérat.* I, p. 68, n. 4). See P. BM EA 10191, **I, 2–3**.

Line 3
ḥr[*.k r.i Inpw sꜣ*] *Wsir* [*pꜣ iry-*]*ꜥꜣ* [*mtr n tꜣ Dwꜣt*]. See P. BM EA 10191, **I, 3–4**.

Line 4
ḥr.tn r.i nꜣ nṯrw mds nꜣ nṯrwt imyw-ḫt Wsir. Mention of the feminine *nṯrwt*, however exceptional it appears, is also found in one other manuscript, P. Louvre SN, 4: *ḥr.tn r.i nꜣ nṯrw mds nṯrwt* [*imyw-ḫt*] *Wsir.* The omission of *irty* in both cases is remarkable. See P. BM EA 10191, **I, 4**.

Lines 4–5
nṯrw imyw tꜣ wsḫt Mꜣꜥty nꜣ nṯrw n tꜣ wsḫt sḫwt iꜣrw. See P. BM EA 10191, **I, 4–5**.

Line 5
ḥr.t r.i Ḥwt-Ḥr ḥnwt Ỉmntt Mꜣꜥt ḥn.w n.s Ỉmntt. See P. BM EA 10191, **I, 5–6**.

Line 6
ḥr.tn r.i nꜣ nṯrw n tꜣ Dwꜣt ḏr.w nꜣ nṯrw nty rs r Wsir. See P. BM EA 10191, **I, 6**.

Lines 6–7
ink it.tn Rꜥ-Ḥr-ꜣḫty iw pr[*.tn*] *im.f m sp tpy.* See P. BM EA 10191, **I, 7**.

Line 7
ink Ḥr sꜣ Ỉst sꜣ Wsir nty ḥr nst.f ḏt. See P. BM EA 10191, **I, 7**.

Lines 7–8
ink Ḥr wr nb Tꜣ Šmꜥ ir di [*... ḥ*]*ꜥw-*[*nṯr*] *n Rꜥ iw.f dit Ḥr ḥr nst it.f Wsir.* Restore in the lacuna either *nḏm* or *nfr*. Some manuscripts give *ḥꜥw n Rꜥ*, *ḥꜥw-nṯr n it.f Rꜥ*. See P. BM EA 10191, **I, 8**.

Line 8
ink Ḥr mrty nb rꜣ-ꜥ-ḫt ir nḫt [*nꜣ nṯrw ḏr.w*]. The part in lacuna, restored after the parallels, is lost with the remainder of the text. See P. BM EA 10191, **I, 8–9**.

P. BM EA 10338 (pls 49–50)

Unpublished.
Provenance: Thebes probably.
Date: first to second century AD.
Owner of the papyrus: name lost.

Contents: First Book of Breathing, incomplete version.

This manuscript, in very poor condition, at present comprises fragments which may be reassembled only to restore the lower part of one page, the upper being lost. The correspondence with P. BM EA 10191, I, 31–49, which offers a complete version of the First Book of Breathing, gives an idea of the amount of text missing before and after this page. The total number of written columns in the whole papyrus is difficult to establish as the height of each of them remains uncertain. All that can be determined is the approximate length of the lines (± 30 cm), after restoration of the gaps and rearrangement of the small fragments on the left of the document. There is no text on the verso.

Translation

(x + 1) [... O Pt]ah, father of the gods, turn towards me! [Open for me my mouth, open for me my eyes, as it was done for Sokar-Osiris in the Mansion of Gold in Memphis. (x + 2) My mouth has been open for me with the [iron] *mḏꜣt*-chisel with which you opened the mouths of the gods. I am [the ba of Sekhmet (x + 3) who sits at the West] of the sky. Make my name to endure like [that of Osiris foremost of the West]; promote me among (?) the pri[mordial] gods. [Make for me] (x + 4) my *ib*-heart in the House of *ib*-hearts, and my *ḥꜣty*-heart in the House of *ḥꜣty*-hearts! [Make for me] my [*ib*-heart] rest in its place and my *ḥꜣty*-heart be esta[blished in its right place! Grant me] (x + 5) my mouth to speak, my legs to walk, [my] arms [to overthrow] my [enemies. May the double doors in the sky be open for me [as you do for the gods and the goddesses!] (x + 6) May Anubis open for me the [portals of the Duat!] May I be one of the retinue [of Osiris! You write (?)] my [de]cree (x + 7) within the Mansion of the ka of Ptah [to cause that my steps be not turned back in the god's do]main, that I may do what I desire and travel (?) [in the sky and (on) earth (?), and that] my ba may alight (x + 8) on my corpse. (O) my *ib*-heart, I am <your> lord, and [you] are not far [from me, every day, by the decree of]

Tanen the old. Obey me, my own heart, (for) you [are in my body], and you are not far from me, (x + 9) (for) I am he before whom a decree is made that [he] may be obeyed [in the god's domain]. My heart is not taken away from me by the fighters [in Heliopolis. I am] he before whom Atum writes (x + 10) annals under the noble balanites-tree [in Heliopolis, by the wri]ting of Thoth himself, to cause light with[in my eyes, to walk by night] and by day, (x + 11), to see his rays, every day. (O) my *ib*-heart of [my] mother [(bis), my *ḥꜣty*-heart] is established in its right place; Atum tells me that [my body is perfect again, and he commends (x + 12) to Nehebka to cause that I reach the earth in [the horizon of the sky, without causing me] to die in the god's domain; he divinizes my ba, [he glorifies my corpse] (x + 13)[... (?) he makes my] body to live again. [Atum] sets [me] (?) [in the bark of] Re; he causes me to assume any form I desire. [He grants me my mouth, that I speak] therewith; he causes me to live (x + 14) like Re, every day. I prosper like Re prospers, and vice versa. [My hair is (that of) N]un; my face is (that of) Re; my eyes are (those of) [Hathor; my [ea]rs (x + 15) are (those of) Wepwawet; my nose is (that of) Khenty-Khem; [my lips are (those of) Anu]bis; my teeth are (those of) Serqet; [my neck is (that of)] Isis and Nephthys; (x + 16) my arms are (those of) Banebdjed; my chest [is (that of) Neith, the lady of Saïs; my back is (that of) the Lord of Kher-Aha; [my belly is] (that of) Sekhmet; (x + 17) my thighs are (those of) the Eye of Horus; my calves (?) ... (?), [and Thoth is the protection of] all my body. My flesh is full of life, [every day; I shall not be grasped] by my arms. (x + 18) You sit down by the bread, you consume beer, and e[at? ...] every good [thing].

Commentary

Line x + 1
[i͗ Pt]ḥ i͗t nṯrw ḥr.k r.i͗. The sequel of this line is lost. For the known variants of the text, see P. BM EA 10191, **I, 31–2** and **32**.

Line x + 2
[wn] n.i͗ rꜣ.i͗ m-m mḏꜣt [nt bi͗ꜣ i͗]w wp.k rꜣ n nṯrw i͗m.f. See P. BM EA 10191, **I, 32–3**.

Lines x + 2–3
i͗nk [bꜣ ? n Sḫmt nty ḥms ḥr i͗my-wrt] nt pt. Restoration after the parallels. See P. BM EA 10191, **I, 33**.

Line x + 3
srwḏ.k rn[.i͗] mi͗ [Wsi͗r ḫnty] I͗mntt ṯnw.k tw(.i͗) ḫnt nṯrw pꜣ[wtyw]. Restoration after the parallels. See P. BM EA 10191, **I, 33–4**.

Lines x + 3–4
[i͗r.k n.i͗] i͗b.i͗ n pr i͗bw ḥꜣty.i͗ n pr ḥꜣtyw. Restoration after the parallels. See P. BM EA 10191, **I, 34**.

Line x + 4
[i͗r.k n.i͗ i͗b].i͗ ḥtp ḥr st.f ḥꜣty.i͗ smn [ḥr mkt.f]. Restoration after the parallels. See P. BM EA 10191, **I, 35**.

Lines x + 4–5
[di͗.k n.i͗] rꜣ.i͗ r mdw rdwy.i͗ r šm ꜥwy[.i͗ r sḫr ḫfty]w.i͗. Restoration after the parallels. See P. BM EA 10191, **I, 35–6**.

Line x + 5
i͗w wn n.i͗ ꜥwy m pt [mi͗ i͗r.k n nṯrw nṯrwt]. On the different variants of this sequence, see P. BM EA 10191, **I, 36**.

Line x + 6
mi͗ wn n.i͗ I͗npw nꜣ sbḫ[w]t [n tꜣ Dwꜣt] mi͗ i͗r.i͗ wꜥ n-m nꜣ šms[w Wsi͗r]. On the different variants of this sequence, see P. BM EA 10191, **I, 36–7**. Note here the spelling  of the preposition *n-m*, attested also in P. Cairo CG 58008, 15; see P. BM EA 10191, **I, 14**.

Lines x + 6–7
[sš.k] wḏwt.i͗ m-bꜣḥ ḫnw Ḥwt-kꜣ-Ptḥ [r tm šnꜥ nmt.i͗ m ẖr]t[-nṯr]. Restoration *[sš]* is also possible. On the different variants of this sequence, see P. BM EA 10191, **I, 37**.

Lines x + 7
r di͗t i͗r.i͗ mr.i͗ hꜣ m (?) [pt tꜣ (?)]. In that place, the word *hꜣ* is omitted in all the other listed versions, which all read: *r di͗(t) i͗r.i͗ mr kꜣ.i͗ m pt (m) tꜣ.* Because of the length of the lacuna, the proposed restoration is probable. See P. BM EA 10191, **I, 37–8**.

Lines x + 7–8
[r di͗t] ḫn bꜣ.i͗ ḥr ẖ(ꜣ)t.i͗. Restoration after the parallels. See P. BM EA 10191, **I, 38**.

Line x + 8
i͗b.i͗ i͗nk nb<.k> nn wꜣ[.k r.i͗ rꜥ nb m wḏwt n] Tꜣ-nn wr. Restoration after the parallels. See P. BM EA 10191, **I, 38–9**.

sḏm.k n.i͗ i͗b.i͗ ḏs.i͗ i͗[w.k m ẖt.i͗] nn rḳꜣ.k r.i͗. Restoration after the parallels. See P. BM EA 10191, **I, 39**.

Line x + 9
i͗nk pfy i͗r.w wḏwt ḥꜣt.f r di͗t sḏm[.w n.f m ẖrt-nṯr]. Restoration after the parallels. Most of the versions add after *ḥꜣt.f*: *m Ḥwt-kꜣ-Ptḥ*, 'in the Mansion of the ka of Ptah', with the variant *Mn-nfr*, 'Memphis', or *I͗wnw*, 'Heliopolis'. See P. BM EA 10191, **I, 39–40**.

nn i͗ṯ.w i͗b.i͗ m-ꜥ.i͗ i͗n ꜥḥꜣw [m I͗wnw]. Restoration after the parallels. See P. BM EA 10191, **I, 40**.

Lines x + 9–10
[i͗nk] pw i͗r I͗tm gnwt ḥꜣt.f ḥr pꜣ i͗šd šps [m I͗wnw m s]š n I͗ ḏs.f. Restoration after the parallels. A variant reading gives *n I͗wnw*, and another version omits this Heliopolitan reference. See P. BM EA 10191, **I, 40–1**.

Lines x + 10–11
r di͗t wnyny m-[ḫnw i͗rty.i͗ r šm m grḥ] m hrw r mꜣꜣ stwt.f rꜥ nb. Restoration after the parallels. Some manuscripts give the variant *i͗rt.i͗*. See P. BM EA 10191, **I, 41**.

Line x + 11
i͗b.i͗ mwt[.i͗ sp 2 ḥꜣty.i͗] smn ḥr mkt.f. Restoration after the parallels. See P. BM EA 10191, **I, 41–2**.

Lines x + 11–12
ḏd n.i͗ I͗tm [nfrw.f] swḏ.f n Nḥb-kꜣ di͗t šms.i͗ tꜣ m [ꜣḫt nt pt nn di͗.f] mt<.i͗> m ẖrt-nṯr. Restoration after the parallels. Var. everywhere else: *sꜣḥ.i͗* instead of *šms.i͗*. The absence of the pronoun *twi͗* here, attested in all other ver-

sions after *swḏ.f*, is not a mistake. In that context, *dit* (in front of *di.f* given in the other manuscripts) directly depends on the verb *swḏ*. See P. BM EA 10191, **I, 42** and **42–3**.

Lines x + 12–13
nṯr.f bꜣ.i [...] ... (?) [...]. The expected reading, as seen in the parallel versions, is *nṯr bꜣ.i sꜣḫ.f ẖꜣt.i sꜥnḫ.f ḥꜥw.i m wḥm*. However, the illegible traces which remain in the end of line x + 12, and the major lacuna which, in line x + 13, precedes the fragments of signs where one can guess the words *ḥꜥw* and, farther along, *wḥm*, allow one to think that the version of P. BM EA 10338 originally presented noticeable variants apparently unattested elsewhere. See P. BM EA 10191, **I, 43**.

Line x + 13
di [*twi Ỉtm r wiꜣ n*] *Rꜥ di.f ir.i ḫpr nb mr.i*. For the different variants of this sequence, see P. BM EA 10191, **I, 43–4**.

Lines x + 13–14
[*di.f n.i rꜣ.i mdw*]*.i im.f di.f ꜥnḫ.i mi Rꜥ rꜥ nb*. Restoration after the parallels. The other versions give *di.f wḥm.i ꜥnḫ*, *di.f wḥm ꜥnḫ.i*. See P. BM EA 10191, **I, 44**.

Line x + 14
wḏꜣ.i mi wḏꜣ Rꜥ ṯs-pḫr. The other versions omit *mi*. See P. BM EA 10191, **I, 44–5**.

Lines x + 14–15
[*iw šnw.i m*] *Nwn iw ḥr.i m Rꜥ iw irty.i m* [*Ḥwt-Ḥr iw m*]*sḏrwy.i m Wp-wꜣwt*. Restoration after the parallels. See P. BM EA 10191, **I, 45**.

Line x + 15
iw fnḏ.i m Ḫnty-ḫm [*iw spty.i m Ỉ*]*npw iw ibḥw.i m Sḫkt iw* [*nḥbt.i*] *n Ỉst Nbt-ḥwt*. Restoration after the parallels. Several versions give *spt.i*. See P. BM EA 10191, **I, 45–6**.

Line x + 16
iw ꜥwy.i m Bꜣ-nb-Ḏd iw šnbt.i [*m Nt nbt Sꜣ*]*w iw psḏ.i n Nb-Ḫr-ꜥḥꜣ* [*iw ẖt.i*] *n Sḫmt*. Restoration after the parallels. See P. BM EA 10191, **I, 46–7**.

Line x + 17
iw ḫpšw.i m irt Ḥr iw mnty.i (?) ... (?) [...]. The visible traces after *iw* are not readily identifiable with the words *mnty.i m Nwt* expected here in accord with all parallel documents. The limited length of the lacuna, which should contain the beginning of the next sequence, does not allow the two identifications present in the other manuscripts (legs/ Ptah and toes/live uraeus). See P. BM EA 10191, **I, 47–8**.

[... *Ỉ m sꜣw n*] *ḥꜥw.i nb iwf.i tm n ꜥnḫ* [*rꜥ nb*]. Restoration after the parallels. See P. BM EA 10191, **I, 48**.

Lines x + 17–18
[*nn ḫfꜥ*] *tw(.i) ḥr ꜥwy.i*. Restoration after the parallels, all of which add: *nn ꜣm.tw(.i) ḥr ḏrt*, 'I shall not be seized by my hands'. See P. BM EA 10191, **I, 48–9**.

Line x + 18
ḥms.k m tꜣ wšꜥ.k m ḥnkt wn[*m.k m ḫt* (?)] *nb(t) nfr(t)*. Sequence without any known parallel in the First Book of Breathing, but see P. BM EA 10191, **II, 31–3**.

P. BM EA 10705 (part) (pls 51–2)

Formerly O.C. 1457.
Unpublished.
Provenance: Thebes.
Date: first to second century AD.
Owner of the papyrus: name lost.

Contents: Fragment of the First Book of Breathing.

One of several fragments of different texts grouped as a whole under a same classification number.[166] Fragment of a manuscript in very poor condition (12.5 × 6.7 cm), from which more than half the upper fibres have lifted. The upper part contains vignette with two figures in thick, rough lines. The first represents a lion-headed goddess wearing a disk flanked with an uraeus, and holding before her what appears to be a papyriform sceptre; the second, of which there remains only an indefinite contour and the top of a white crown, is probably to be identified as Osiris. The traces before and behind suggest that they were preceded and followed by other deities.

In the lower part are six lines of thick writing. The repetition of the words *grḥ pfy n* at the start of the lines gives an idea of the original structure of the document, which probably included an initial invocation to Thoth. There is no text on the verso.

Translation

[O Thoth, turn) towards me, vindicate me against my enemies as you vindicated Osiris before the great Council which is in]

(1) [Heliopolis], on that [night] of battle to overthrow [those enemies...] (?)

(2) [Busiris], on that [ni]ght of raising the *ḏd*-pillar in Busiris,

(3) [Letopolis], on that [ni]ght of the festival of offerings on the altar [in Letopolis],

(4) [Pe and] Dep, on that night when Horus received the domicile [of the gods] ... (?)

(5) [Idebu-rekhty (?)], on [that] night [which Isis spent ...] ... (?)

(6) [Ro-setau, on that night when Anubis put his hands] over the relics (?) <behind> his father [Osiris].

Commentary

For the initial restoration of the invocation to Thoth, see P. BM EA 10191, **15–17**.

166. Quirke, *Owners*, nos 22 and 239.

Line 1
[*Iwnw grḥ*] *pfy n ꜥḥꜣ r sḫr* [*sbiw pfy*]. See P. BM EA 10191, **16–17**.

Line 2
[*Ḏdw grḥ*] *pfy n sꜥḥꜥ ḏd m Ḏdw*. See P. BM EA 10191, **19–20**.

Line 3
[*Ḫm grḥ*] *pfy n ḫwt* [*ḥr*] *ḫꜣwt* [*m Ḫm*]. See P. BM EA 10191, **18–19**.

Line 4
[*P*] *Dp grḥ pfy n šsp Ḥr ms*[*ḫnt nṯrw nṯrwt*]. See P. BM EA 10191, **21–2**.

Line 5
[*Ỉdbw-rḫty* (?)] *grḥ* [*pfy n sḏr Ỉst* …] … (?). If the absent toponym is correctly to be identified with *Ỉdbw-rḫty*, the parallel versions show some variants at this point, and thus the restoration of the text is not certain. See P. BM EA 10191, **I, 23–4**.

Line 6
[*Rꜣ-stꜣw grḥ pfy n Ỉnpw ꜥwy.f*] *ḥr ḫwt* <*ḥꜣ*> *it.f* [*Wsir*]. The presence in this place of the words *ḥr ḫwt* <*ḥꜣ*> *it.f* shows that the writer has obviously omitted several sequences, as happens in other manuscripts. See P. BM EA 10191, **I, 28–9**.

P. BM EA 71513B (pls 53–4)

Unpublished.
Provenance: probably Thebes.
Date: first to second century AD.
Owner of the papyrus: name lost.

Contents: First Book of Breathing, incomplete version.

Manuscript in poor condition, comprised of two large fragments (16.7 × 4.9 cm and 17.6 × 7.6 cm). The whole of the right side is missing. The recto bears ten lines of text, written in a hand growing bigger from one line to the next.

Text on the verso: [The Book of Breathing of Thoth is your protection, (so that) you] will [not be turned back] from the hall of Osiris. May you […].[167]

Translation

(1) [… I am Re at his rising], I am Atum at his setting, I am [Osiris foremost of the West, during the night] and during the day.

Turn (2) [towards me … … turn] towards me, Anubis son of Osiris, de[pendable] doorkeeper [of] the Duat! (3) [Turn towards me, gods of piercing gaze who are in the retinue of Osiris …], gods who are in the hall of the Field of ree[ds]! Turn towards me (4) [Hathor mistress of the West, Maat to whom the West has been entrusted! Turn towards me, all gods of the Duat, gods who] watch over Osiris! I am your father Re[-Horakhty], the great [god] from whom <you came forth> at the first time; (5) [I am Horus son of Isis, son of Osiris, who is upon his throne, eternally. I am Haroeris lord of Upper Egypt, who causes the body of] Re [to be perfect], setting Horus upon [the throne of] his [father] Osiris. I am (6) [Hor-merty lord of the battle, who causes all the gods to be strong. I am Horus lord of Letopolis, lord of Per]-Iit, who repe[ls the ene]mies (7) [from Heliopolis … … Turn towards me, guar]dians of the Duat, [cha]se away (8)[for me the void of the hours of the night. May my ba go forth] to heaven with the bas of the (9) [great gods! … …] May there be made for me a libation in the Mansion [of the great Prince! (…?). May] there be laid down (10) [for me … on the night of the festival of offerings] on the altar [and of ?] the festival [of the sixth day]!

Commentary

Line 1
[*ḫr.f n Wsir N ink Rꜥ m ḫꜥ.f*] *ink Ỉtm m ḥtp.f ink* [*Wsir ḫnty Ỉmntt m grḥ*] *m hrw*. The restoration of the beginning can be considered as certain, according to the reading provided by most of the manuscripts establishing in the first person the identification of the deceased with Re and Atum. The rare attested exceptions are not relevant as they concern texts whose structure and contents are original. Those are P. BM EA 10115 and 10194, which start with the invocation *hꜣy* (respectively *hꜣy Ḥwt-Ḥr N* and *hꜣy Wsir N ḏd mdw ḫr it.f Wsir ḫnty Ỉmntyw*). See P. BM EA 10191, **I, 1–2**.

Lines 1–2
ḥr.tn [*r.i* …]. The existence of several readings makes any restoration uncertain. The different possibilities are following:

a) *nꜣ iryw-ꜥꜣ n Ỉmntt nꜣ sꜣwtyw n tꜣ Dwꜣt nꜣ iryw-ꜥꜣ n pr ḥnw*
b) *nꜣ sꜣwtyw n Ỉmntt nꜣ iryw-ꜥꜣ n tꜣ Dwꜣt nꜣ iryw-ꜥꜣ n pr ḥnw*
c) *nꜣ iryw-ꜥꜣ n tꜣ Dwꜣt nꜣ sꜣwtyw n Ỉmntt nꜣ iryw-ꜥꜣ n pr ḥnw*
d) the same combinations without *nꜣ iryw-ꜥꜣ n pr ḥnw*. See P. BM EA 10191, **I, 2–3**

Line 2
[*ḥr.k*] *n.i Ỉnpw sꜣ Wsir p(ꜣ) iry-ꜥꜣ* [*mtr n*] *tꜣ Dwꜣt*. See P. BM EA 10191, **I, 3–4**.

Line 3
[…]. The second part of the expected invocation being partly preserved (cf. *infra*), the only certainty here is the existence, at the beginning of the line, of the first one, whose most common formulation is: *ḥr.tn r.i nṯrw mdsw-irty imyw-ḫt Wsir*. On the different known variants, see P. BM EA 10191, **I, 4**.

[… *nꜣ*] *nṯrw imyw tꜣ wsḫt sḫwt iꜣ*[*rw*]. A restoration *nꜣ nṯrw imyw tꜣ wsḫt Mꜣꜥty* in the first part of this sequence remains the most likely. See P. BM EA 71513C, **lines 4–5**.

167. Restoration after P. Parma 183 vs. cf. also P. BM EA 10124 vs., and see *LPE*, p. 255 (VIII, 9).

Lines 3–4
ḥr.t r.i [*Ḥwt-Ḥr ḫnt Ỉmntt Mꜣꜥt ḥn(.w) n.s Ỉmntt*]. See P. BM EA 10191, **I, 5–6**.

Line 4
[…] *rs r Wsir*. The principal reading invites the restoration in the lacuna of [*ḥr.tn r.i nꜣ nṯrw n tꜣ Dwꜣt ḏrw nꜣ nṯrw nty*], but many omissions and variants attested in the parallel versions make it hypothetical. See P. BM EA 10191, **I, 6**.

ink it.tn Rꜥ[*-Ḥr-ꜣḫty nṯr*] *ꜥꜣ im* (*sic*) *m sp tpy*. The usual reading is here, after *Rꜥ-Ḥr-ꜣḫty*: *iw pr.tn im.f m sp tpy*. The epithet *nṯr ꜥꜣ* is also mentioned, in this context, in P. BM EA 71513A, 7. See P. BM EA 10191, **I, 7**.

Line 5
[…]. Like line 3 above, the expected clause *ink Ḥr sꜣ Ỉst sꜣ wsir nty ḥr nst.f ḏt*] is entirely lost, but this restoration is probable, given the parallels. See P. BM EA 10191, **I, 7**.

[*ink Ḥr wr nb* (*tꜣ*) *šmꜥ ir … ḥꜥw*] *n Rꜥ iw.f di Ḥr ḥr* [*nst it.f*] *Wsir*. The differences recorded in the various readings concern especially the words following *Šmꜥ* (or *tꜣ šmꜥ*). Most often one reads: *ir di nfr ḥꜥw n Rꜥ*, but one finds too *ir di nḏm ḥꜥw-nṯr n Rꜥ*, *ir di nḏm ḥꜥw n Rꜥ*, *iw(.f) ir di nḏm iḥꜥw n Rꜥ*, which are only possible variants here. See P. BM EA 10191, **I, 8**.

Lines 5–6
ink [*Ḥr Mrty nb rꜣ-ꜥ-ḫt ir nḫt nꜣ nṯrw ḏr.w*]. See P. BM EA 10191, **I, 8–9**.

Lines 6–7
[*ink Ḥr nb Ḫm nb pr i*]*it nty ꜥm*[*ḏ sb*]*iw* [*r Ỉwnw* …]. See P. BM EA 10191, **I, 9–10**.

Lines 7–8
[… *ḥr.tn r.i nꜣ sꜣwty*]*w n tꜣ Dwꜣt* [*ḫ*]*ꜣꜥ* [*n.i nꜣ wnwt n grḥ*]. See P. BM EA 10191, **I, 10–11**.

Lines 8–9
[*mi pr pꜣy.i bꜣ*] *r ḥrt ḥnꜥ bꜣw n nꜣ* [*nṯrw wrw*]. See P. BM EA 10191, **I, 11**.

Lines 9–10
[… *m*]*i ḳbḥ.w n.i m ḥwt* [*sr* … (?) *mi*] *wꜣḥw* [*n.i* …] *ḥr ḫꜣwy* [*n snwt*]. Restorations after the parallels. The signs preceding *ḳbḥ.w* belong to the optative particle *mi* whose spelling , although rare, is nevertheless well attested (e.g. P. Louvre N 3176 A, 8, 9, 11). In comparison with P. BM EA 10191, the text is here noticeably abridged. After the word *ḥwt*, the gap is too short to contain the expected sequence *m ḥwt* [*sr mi pꜣ wr nty m Ỉwnw*]; see P. BM EA 10191, **I, 12**. Neither does the next phrase, introduced with [*mi*], follow the traditional version.

P. BM EA 71513C (pls 55–6)

Unpublished.
Provenance: probably Thebes.
Date: first to second century AD.
Owner of the papyrus: […]-*ḥtp*.

Contents: First Book of Breathing, incomplete version.

Manuscript of one sheet, in poor condition, comprised of two fragments of similar dimensions (± 18 × 6 cm), torn at their right and left sides. It is therefore impossible to determine with precision the beginning and the end of each line, except for the beginning of the first one, where it seems that the right missing part of the document is much smaller than the left. Another argument in favour of this hypothesis is the presence of the title on the verso of the manuscript, the beginning of which (corresponding consequently with the left part of the recto) is missing.

In its present condition, the papyrus bears eight lines of a text showing considerable variations in writing.

Text of the verso: [A good burial. May it be stable over] your bones, [may it remain over your flesh], without decay![168]

Translation

Recto

(1) Thus speaks the Osiris […]-*ḥtp*, born [of … I am Re at his rising, I am Atum at] (2) his setting, I am Osi[ris foremost of the We]st during the night, during the day. [… (?) Turn towards me, doorkeepers of the Duat, guar](3)dians of the West (?). [Turn] towards me, Anubis son [of Osiris, dependable doorkeeper of the Duat! Turn towards me], (4) go[ds] of piercing <gaze>, god[desses (?) who are in the retinue of Osiris, gods who are in the hall of the two Maats], (5) gods who are in [the hall of the Field] of reeds! [Turn towards me, Hathor mistress of the West, Maat to whom the West has been entrusted! Turn towards me], (6) all gods of the Duat, gods who [watch over Osiris! I am your father Re-Horakhty from whom you came forth] (7) at the first time; [I am Horus] son of Isis, son of O[siris, who is upon his throne, eternally. I am Haroeris, lord of] (8) Upper Egypt, who comforts the body [of Re …].

Commentary

Line 1
ḥr <.f n > Wsir [*N*]. See P. BM EA 10191, **I, 1**.

Lines 1–2
[*ink Rꜥ m ḫꜥ.f ink Ỉtm m*] *ḥtp.f ink Wsir m grḥ m hrw*. See P. BM EA 10191, **I, 1–2**.

Lines 2–3
[*ḥr.tn r.i nꜣ … n tꜣ Dwꜣt nꜣ* …] *n Ỉmntt*. It is impossible to know whether this passage referred to the doorkeepers (*iryw-ꜥꜣ*) of the Duat and of the guardians (*sꜣwtyw*) of the West, or the guardians of the Duat and the doorkeepers of the West, both versions being attested in the parallel documents. The signs , line 3, can end the word *iryw-ꜥꜣ* as well as *sꜣwtyw*. See P. BM EA 10191, **I, 2–3**.

168. See *supra*, p. 3 with n. 34.

Line 3

[*ḥr.k*] *r.i͗ I͗npw* [*sꜣ Wsi͗r* ...]. The expected restoration after *Wsi͗r*: *pꜣ i͗ry-ꜥꜣ mtr n tꜣ Dwꜣt*, in the parallel manuscripts, is uncertain because of the variants attested for this sequence. See P. BM EA 10191, **I, 4**.

Lines 3–4

[*ḥr.tn r.i͗ nꜣ* (?)] *nṯrw mds nꜣ nṯr*[*wt i͗myw-ḫt Wsi͗r*]. The absence of the word *i͗rty* (in the epithet *mds i͗rty* attested in most documents) and the image of the cow preceded by the article *nꜣ* invite us to see in this animal, alone or in combination, a spelling of the word *nṯrt*, 'goddess'. See P. BM EA 10191, **I, 4**.

Lines 4–5

[... *nꜣ*] *nṯrw i͗myw wsḫt sḫwt i͗ꜣrw*. One can restore in the lacuna either *nꜣ nṯrw i͗myw tꜣ wsḫt Mꜣꜥty*, 'the gods who are in the hall of the two Maats', or simply *i͗myw tꜣ wsḫt Mꜣꜥty*, making *i͗myw tꜣ* an epithet of *nṯrw mdsw nṯrwt i͗myw-ḫt Wsi͗r*. See P. BM EA 10191, **I, 4–5**.

Lines 5–6

[*ḥr.tn r.i͗*] *nꜣ nṯrw n tꜣ Dwꜣt ḏr.w nꜣ nṯrw nt*[*y rs r Wsi͗r*]. Before this sequence all the versions show the invocation *ḥr.t r.i͗ Ḥwt-Ḥr ḫnt I͗mntt Mꜣꜥt ḥn.w n.s I͗mntt*, with some occasionnal variants; the absence of any trace of this sequence render doubtful its presence in this text. See P. BM EA 10191, **I, 6**.

Lines 6–7

[*i͗nk i͗t.tn Rꜥ-Ḥr-ꜣḫty i͗w pr.tn*] *i͗m<.f> m sp tpy*. Reading attested in most of documents with only minor variants. Restoration probable after the parallel versions. See P. BM EA 10191, **I, 7**.

Lines 7–8

[*i͗nk Ḥr*] *sꜣ I͗st sꜣ Ws*[*i͗r nty ḥr nst.f ḏt*]. See P. BM EA 10191, **I, 7**.

Lines 8–9

[*i͗nk Ḥr wr nb*] *tꜣ* ... (?) [*i͗r*] *snḏm ḥꜥw* [*n Rꜥ* ...]. The reading of the eye  (*Bꜣḳt*?) is problematic. One expects to read here *tꜣ šmꜥ*, 'Upper Egypt', as in most of the documents. See P. BM EA 10191, **I, 8**.

3. Second Book of Breathing

P. BM EA 10110 + 10111 (pls 57–9)

Hay Collection nos 493 and 509.
Quirke, *Owners,* no. 200.
P. BM EA 10110: unpublished. E.A.W. Budge, *A Guide to the Fourth, Fifth and Sixth Egyptian Rooms* (London 1922), p. 296, no. 9; B.H. Stricker, *OMRO* 23 (1942), p. 33.
P. BM EA 10111: S. Birch, *PSBA* 7 (1885), pp. 207–8 and pl.; Lieblein, *Que mon nom fleurisse*, pp. xxxi–xxxiii.
Provenance: Thebes. Possibly from the tomb of the archon Soter, but apparently unconnected with his family.[1]
Date: first to second century AD (?).
Owner of the papyrus: *P(ꜣ)y.f-ṯꜣw-ꜥwy-Mnṯw.* Personal name not recorded in R*PN*, but attested in *Demot. Nb.* I, p. 447, citing the sole example of O. Leiden 145, x + 8.
Titles:
— *sꜣwty pr-ḥḏ n pr Ỉmn*, 'guardian of the Treasury of the House of Amun' [2]
— *ḥm-nṯr n ḥwt-nwb Ỉmn*, 'Prophet of the Mansion of gold [3] of Amun'.
Mother of the owner: *Ns-wrt* (Esoeris): R*PN* I, 174, 11.

Contents: Second Book of Breathing, followed by an original text.

Manuscript of one sheet (29.4 × 56 cm) arranged in two columns with respectively 36 and 31 lines of text, and in fairly good condition. The document was cut into two portions of about equal size, and the break affects only one line of text in both parts. The upper left section of the document contains some lacunae.

Demotic text on the verso: Second Book of Breathing, to be placed at the feet of (?) the Osiris, guardian [of the Treasury] of the House of Amun and of his temples, great scholar in ... (?).

Translation

Recto

I (1) Thus speaks the Osiris, guardian of the Treasury of the Amun domain, prophet of the Mansion of gold of Amun, (I, 2) *P(ꜣ)y.f-ṯꜣw-ꜥwy-Mnṯw,* justified, born of *Ns-wrt*, justified:

O Re, I am your son! (3) O Thoth, I am your beloved! O Osiris, I am your image! O Lord of Hermopolis, I am your heir, in (4) truth! O Horakhty, O great Ennead, O lesser Ennead! May my name endure (5) within the nomes for ever and eternally!

(6) (*In one column*):

May my name endure within Thebes and within the nomes for ever and eternally,

(7) as the name of Atum lord of Heliopolis endures in Heliopolis,

(8) as the name of Shu endures in the upper Menset in Heliopolis,

(9) as the name of Tefnut endures in the lower Menset in Heliopolis,

(10) as the name of Geb endures in the place of the foreigners,

(11) as the name of Nut endures in the Mansion of *šnw,*

(12) as the name of Osiris foremost of the West endures in Abydos,

(13) as the name of Isis endures in Ta-wer,

1. See *supra*, p. 5, n. 67.
2. *sꜣwty pr-ḥḏ n pr Ỉmn*: see S.S. Eichler, *Die Verwaltung des 'Hauses des Amun' in der 18. Dynastie* (Hamburg 2000), pp. 137–8. In the Roman Period, the title is also borne by *Pꜣy.f-kꜣ* son of *Ỉst-wrt*, P. Berlin 3164 + Moscow 4661, 1 and P. Moscow 4651, 6; see B.A. Touraiev, in *Mémoires du Musée des Beaux-Arts de l'Empereur Alexandre III à Moscou* (1912–13), p. 27 (in Russian); also J. Quaegebeur, in *Hundred-Gated Thebes* (1995), pp. 158–60.
3. *ḥwt* is written in demotic.

(14) as the name of Horus endures in Pe,

(15) as the name of Wadjyt endures in Dep,

(16) as the name of Nephthys endures in Heliopolis,

(17) as the name of Banebdjed endures in the House of Banebdjed,

(18) as the name of Thoth endures in Hermopolis,

(19) as the name of the four Montus endures in their town,

(20) as the name of Khnum endures in Elephantine,

(21) as the name of Haroeris endures in Ombos,

(22) as the name of Horus-Behedety endures in Djeba,

(23) as the name of Nekhbet endures in Nekheb,

(24) as the name of all the gods endures in Thebes,

(25) as the name of Haroeris lord of Upper Egypt endures within Kus,

(26) as the name of Isis endures in Neter-shema,

(27) as the name of Hathor endures in Iq,

(28) as the name of Neferhotep endures in Diospolis Parva,

(29) as the name of Min endures in Ipu,

(30) as the name of Nemty endures in Wadjet,

(31) as the name of Wepwawet endures in Siut,

(32) as the name of Hathor endures in Cusae,

(33) as the name of Horus endures in Hebenu,

(34) as the name of Anubis endures in Hardai,

(35) as the name of Harsaphes endures in Heracleopolis,

(36) as the name of Sobek endures in Merwer,

(37) as the name of Ptah, of Sekhmet and of Nefertum endures within Memphis.

II (1) I cause that I appear as the great ibis come forth from the womb of my mother, for I am the image (2) of Osiris-Wennefer, justified. Thoth is said as my name, for I am an ibis of five cubits. (3) My back is of malachite of Upper Egypt. I am the great god come forth from the *sktt*-bark, I am the silver (4) come forth from the mountain of the East. I enter the *sktt*-bark and tread the *mꜥnḏt*-bark; I am (5) the second of Re-Horakhty. They grant me adoration, those who are in the bark, and the land is embraced (6) by the crew of Re. I come praised and go beloved in the Duat of the Mansion (7) of the obelisk. I am told: Stand up! May your heart be glad! My step is broad (8) in the secret sanctuary. I appear from my mother as the beautiful Horus of gold, as the ibis (9), black in fore and rear. I reach Osiris, he hears my words when I come forth from (10) the womb with him. He grants me greatness and power in him. I am lord of faces, numerous of (11) forms. I consume offerings with Atum, and I sit down for the *nnw*-loaves (?) of (12) Shu. I receive libation with Osiris, and I am transfigured with him, more than any god. The lords of libation (13) make libation for me, (their) arms full of offerings, in the course of every day.

O (14) Amun, give me sweet air, (for) I am your son beloved. O Re, give me (15) your rays, that I may see you in the course of every day! O (16) Hapy, give me libation! Nepri, give me bread! (17) Menqet, give me beer! Akhet, give me milk! (18) My arms are raised to receive invocation offering of bread, beer, oxen and fowl. (19) I am he who comes forth from the womb with Osiris, and I am not far from him in the god's domain. (20) Give me life, lords of life, (for) I am an ibis whose life is renewed. (21) Thoth is uttered as my name, and all gods live by pronouncing my name for ever and eternally.

(22) The activity in your favour is that of your beloved son; his sustenance is at the place carrying your ka, (23) sweet (?) at its entrance to place them in your presence, so great is the greatness of your efficacy, as is done by (24) a father for children to make them live by what he gives them. How great what (25) is engraved through his own fingers, namely: 'be in peace'. Your heart is glad in righteousness (26) because there is no end to your sustenance in your house. <Your> step is broad in the region of Maat (27) thanks to your staff (?). You are transfigured in the streets with he who is perfect in your ka (??), without ill for (28) your name, by the decree … (?). Equipped is (29) your burial, hidden are your plans. Rejoice! (?) The opening of your mouth is performed at the best moment, that (30) of hearing invocations. The king of the gods, ruler of the land of the blessed receives you among his praised ones. (31) You speak with your mouth and at your voice is made a meat offering (?) for his ka while you collect the revenues.

Commentary

I, 2–5

ỉ Rꜥ ỉnk sꜣ.k ỉ Ỉ ỉnk mr.k ỉ Wsỉr ỉnk sḫm.k ỉ nb Ḫmnw ỉnk ỉwꜥ.k m mꜣꜥt ỉ Ḥr-ꜣḫty ỉ Psḏt ꜥꜣt ỉ Psḏt nḏst. This invocation to the gods is attested in several other documents, with some variants: P. BM EA 10116, 2–3 = P. BM EA 10304, 2–4 = P. BM EA 71513D, 1–4 = P. Berlin 3052, IV, 10–11 = P. Cairo CG 58007, III, 2–5 = P. Cairo CG 58013, 2–4 = P. Cairo CG 58018, I, 3–6 = P. Louvre N 3148, VIII, 2–3 = P. Louvre N 3157, 3 = P. Louvre N 3162, 1–3 = P. Louvre N 3174, 1–2 = P. Louvre N 3177 A, 2–3 = P. Turin 1861 B, 1–3. See following notes for details.

I, 2

ỉ Rꜥ ỉnk sꜣ.k. Same reading in P. BM EA 71513D, 1 = P. Berlin 3052, IV, 10 = P. Cairo CG 58007, III, 2 = P. Cairo CG 58018, I, 3 = P. Louvre N 3148, VIII, 2 = P. Louvre N 3157, 3 = P. Louvre N 3162, 1. Sequence wholly in lacuna in P. Louvre N 3177 A, 2, and partly in P. BM EA 10304, 2. Var. P. Cairo CG 58013, 2 = P. Turin 1861 B, 1: *ỉnk bꜣ.k* by spelling confusion (cf. P. BM EA 10191, **I, 33**); P. BM EA 10116, 2: *ỉnk sꜣ.k ỉnk mr.k*.

ỉ Ỉ ỉnk mr.k. Same reading in P. BM EA 10304, 2 = P. BM EA 71513D, 1–2 = P. Berlin 3052, IV, 10 = P. Cairo CG 58007, III, 2 = P. Cairo CG 58018, I, 4 = P. Louvre N 3148, VIII, 2 = P. Louvre N 3157, 3 = P. Louvre N 3162, 1 = P. Louvre N 3174, 1 = P. Louvre N 3177 A, 2. Sequence partly in lacuna in P. Cairo CG 58013, 2 = P. Turin 1861 B, 1–2. The omission of this phrase in P. BM EA 10116, 2 is probably due to the occurrence of *mr.k* in the preceding invocation to Osiris, unless one restores <*ỉ Ỉ*>.

I, 3

i Wsir ink sḫm.k. Same reading in P. BM EA 10116, 2 = P. BM EA 10304, 2 = P. BM EA 71513D, 2 = P. Cairo CG 58013, 2 = P. Cairo CG 58018, I, 4 = P. Louvre N 3157, 3 = P. Louvre N 3162, 2 = P. Louvre N 3174, 1. Sequence partly in lacuna in P. Turin 1861 B, 2. Omission of *i* in P. Louvre N 3177 A, 2. Var. P. Berlin 3052, IV, 10 = P. Louvre N 3148, VIII, 2 = P. Cairo CG 58007, III, 2: *sḫmw.k*. P. Cairo CG 58023, x + 18–19: *ink sḫm n it.f Wsir ink ṯ3wy n Šw ḥnꜥ* [*Tfnwt*], 'I am the image of his father Osiris, I am the nestling of Shu and [Tefnut]'.

I, 3–4

i [*nb*]-*Ḫmnw ink iwꜥ.k m m3ꜥt*. Same reading in P. Cairo CG 58018, I, 4–5 = P. Louvre N 3174, 1. Sequence wholly in lacuna in P. Louvre N 3177 A, 2–3, and partly in P. BM EA 10304, 3. Var. P. BM EA 10116, 2 = P. BM EA 71513D, 3 = P. Berlin 3052, IV, 11 = P. Cairo CG 58007, III, 2–3[4] = P. Louvre N 3148, VIII, 2 = P. Louvre N 3157, 3: *n m3ꜥt*; P. Louvre N 3162, 2 = P. Turin 1861 B, 2 = P. Cairo CG 58013, 3: *iwꜥ n M3ꜥt*, 'the heir of Maat'.

I, 4

i Ḥr-3ḫty. Sequence wholly in lacuna in P. BM EA 71513D, 3 = P. Louvre N 3177 A, 3 = P. Turin 1861 B, and partly in P. BM EA 10304, 3 = P. Cairo CG 58013, 3. Var. P. BM EA 10116, 2 = P. Cairo CG 58007, III, 3 = P. Cairo CG 58018, I, 5 = P. Louvre N 3157, 3 = P. Louvre N 3162, 2 = P. Louvre N 3174, 2: *ỉ Rꜥ-Ḥr-3ḫty*; P. Berlin 3052, IV, 11: *i Ḥr*.

i Psḏt ꜥ3t i Psḏt nḏst. Same reading in P. BM EA 10116, 2–3 = P. BM EA 10304, 3 = P. Berlin 3052, IV, 11 = P. Cairo CG 58007, III, 3 = P. Cairo CG 58013, 3–4 = P. Cairo CG 58018, I, 5–6 = P. Louvre N 3148, VIII, 2 = P. Louvre N 3157, 3 = P. Louvre N 3162, 2–3 = P. Louvre N 3174, 2–3 = P. Louvre N 3177 A, 3 = P. Turin 1861 B, 2–3. Sequence partly in lacuna in P. BM EA 71513D, 4.

Cf. also, in another context, P. BM EA 10283, 9–10:

i Rꜥ ink mr.k	'O Re, I am your beloved,
i Ỉ ink iwꜥ.k n m3ꜥt	O Thoth, I am your heir, in truth,
i Rꜥ-Ḥr-3ḫty ink sḫm.k	O Re-Horakhty, I am your image.'

A different list is given before the same text of *mi rwḏ rn* in P. BM EA 10282, 2–3:

i nṯrw imy(w) pt	'O gods who are in the sky,
i nṯrw imy(w) t3	O gods who are on earth,
i nṯrw imy(w) rsyt	O gods who are in the South,
i nṯrw imy(w) mḥtt imntt i3btt	O gods who are in the North, West and East.'

Another listing again is supplied by P. Louvre N 3176 J, 1–2:

i Wsir ḫnty Ỉmntyw	'O Osiris foremost of the Westerners,
nṯr ꜥ3 nb 3bḏw	great god lord of Abydos,
i Ỉst wrt mwt-nṯr	O Isis the great, mother of the god,
i Ḥr s3 Ỉst s3 Wsir	O Horus son of Isis, son of Osiris,
i Nbt-ḥwt mwt-nṯr	O Nephthys, mother of the god,
i Ỉnpw s3 Wsir	O Anubis son of Osiris,
i p(3) rs nty rs r t3 Dw3t	O watchman who watches over the Duat.'

In P. Cairo CG 58022, 1, the text before the litany reads:

i nṯrw imyw wsḫt M3ꜥty	'O gods who are in the hall of the two Maats,
n3 iryw-ꜥ3 [...]	doorkeepers [...].'

P. Louvre N 3147, V, 2 (*LPE*, p. 264 [VIII, 27]):

i nṯr pn šps it nṯrw nṯrwt	'O this noble god, father of the gods and goddesses.'

I, 4–5, 6

mi rwḏ rn.i m-ḫnw sp3wt r nḥḥ ḏt. This phrase, closing the preceding passage, is repeated in a vertical column (6) alongside the right edge of lines 7–37 in an almost identical formulation (addition of *m-ḫnw W3st* after *rn.i*). Same reading in P. Louvre N 3148, VIII, 3. This same formulation, with the addition *m-ḫnw W3st* and the variant *sp3t(.i)*, is also found in P. BM EA 10125, 22 = P. BM EA 10282, 3 = P. Cairo CG 58007, III, 3–4 = P. Cairo 58009, III, 3–4 [5] = P. Cairo CG 58013, 4 = P. Cairo CG 58018, I, 6–7 = P. Louvre N 3157, 3–4[6] = P. Louvre N 3162, 3 = P. Turin 1861 B, 3 = P. Louvre N 3174, 2: *mi rwḏ rn(.i) m-ḫnw W3st m-ḫnw sp3t(.i)*[7] *r nḥḥ* (*ḏt*).[8] P. Berlin 3052, IV, 11, gives the less expansive version: *mi rwḏ rn.i m-ḫnw W3st*. Sequence wholly in lacuna in P. Louvre N 3159, 1, and partly in P. BM EA 10304, 4 = P. Louvre N 3177 A, 3.

For another introduction, cf. P. Florence 3669, 9–12:

im3ḫw ꜥ3w nw Ỉmntt	'The great revered ones of the West,
šsp.sn ḫ3t.t r Dw3t m ḥtp	they receive your corpse in the Duat, in peace,
srwḏ rn.t m-ḫnw Dw3t ḏsrt	making your name endure inside the sacred Duat,
mi rwḏ rn n Ỉtm nb Ỉwnw m Ỉwnw	as the name of Atum lord of Heliopolis endures in Heliopolis (...)'

The nomes (*sp3wt*) of the deceased are probably those of Osiris with whom he is identified; cf. *Ritual of Embalming*, X, 12 (ed. Sauneron, p. 41): *wr rn.k m sp3wt n Wsir m r3w-prw*, 'Your name is great in the nomes of Osiris and in the temples'. In the singular, *sp3t* denotes the Theban nome, where the deceased lived.

I, 7–37

Considerably elaborated in the Second Book of Breathing, the development of the litany *mi rwḏ rn* dates back to the earliest periods of pharaonic history, as demonstrated by its occurrence in *PT* (§§ 1660–71, **A**). The context, unsurprisingly, is different.

The same text was adapted over the millennia to different rituals, abbreviated to a greater or lesser extent:

— Ritual of the torch, attested on a naos from Dahshur (**B**, Middle Kingdom),[9] the tomb of *Ṯ3y* (**C**, TT 23, Merneptah),[10] that of *Nfr-ḥtp* (**D** and **D'**, TT 50, Horemheb),[11] the hypostyle hall at Karnak[12] (**E**) and P. Louvre N 3083 (Ptolemaic Period, **F**).[13]

— Offering Ritual, in a 'spell for making the divine *ḥtpw*-offerings

4. The transcription of this passage by Golenischeff, *Pap. hiérat.* I, p. 31, is to be amended. Read: 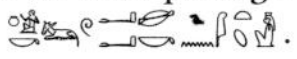.
5. Text preceded by the words *i Ỉ mi ḥr.k r.i*, 'O Thoth, turn towards me!'
6. With some additions, the formula is repeated twice in this manuscript on two columns, preceding the names of the gods: *mi rwḏ rn.i m-ḫnw W3st m-ḫnw sp3t.i r nḥḥ ḏt mi rwḏ rn n.*
7. *sp3wt* in P. BM EA 10116, 3, 4, 18 = P. BM EA 10304, 4 = P. Cairo CG 58018, I, 7. This sequence is found again in P. Louvre N 3174, 6 (= first column on the right of the manuscript), with the variant *sp3wt*.
8. Only in P. Cairo CG 58018, I, 7 and P. Louvre N 3174.
9. A. Fakhry, *The Monuments of Sneferu at Dahshur* II/2 (Cairo 1961), p. 63, fig. 385.
10. F. Haikal, *Mélanges Gamal Eddin Mokhtar* I (*BdE* 97/1, 1985), pp. 366–7 with pls 1–2.
11. The litany is inscribed twice on the east wall of the tomb corridor; see R. Hari, *La tombe thébaine du père divin Neferhotep (TT 50)* (Geneva 1985), pp. 42 and 55, with pls 28 and 41. For the disposition of the texts, see G. Bénédite, *Le tombeau de Neferhotpou* (*MMAF* V/3, 1894), pl. III.
12. H.H. Nelson, *JNES* 8 (1949), pp. 337–9 (ep. 53) = H.H. Nelson and W.J. Murnane, *The Great Hypostyle Hall at Karnak* I/1 (Chicago 1981), pl. 211.
13. F.R. Herbin, *BIFAO* 84 (1984), pp. 249–50, n. 3; id., *RdE* 50 (1999), pp. 156–7. In a similar context, the litany occurs in P. BM EA 10818 (Eighteenth Dynasty), to be published by T.G.H. James.

endure' (*rꜣ n srwḏ ḥtpw-nṯr*), inscribed at Karnak (**G**)[14] and incorporated into the Ritual of Amenhotep I: P. Cairo CG 58030 + Turin CG 58042 (**H**),[15] and P. BM EA 10689 = P. Chester-Beatty IX, rt., 8, 3–21 (**I**).[16]

I, 7

mỉ rwḏ rn n Ỉtm nb Ỉwnw m Ỉwnw. Same reading in P. BM EA 9977, 2–3 = P. BM EA 10116, 5[17] = P. BM EA 10125, 23 = P. BM EA 10282, 5 = P. BM EA 10331, 1 = P. Berlin 3052, IV, 12 = P. BM EA 10304, 4 = P. Cairo CG 58007, III, 5 = P. Cairo 58009, III, 4–5 = P. Cairo CG 58013, 6 = P. Cairo CG 58017, 2 = P. Cairo CG 58018, I, 7–8 = P. Florence 3669, 12[18] = P. Louvre E 3865, VI, 10 = P. Louvre N 3148, VIII, 3 = P. Louvre N 3157, 7 = P. Louvre N 3161, 3–4 = P. Louvre N 3162, 5 = P. Louvre N 3174, 2 = P. Louvre N 3177 A, 5. Sequence probably omitted or in lacuna in P. Turin 1861 B; wholly in lacuna in P. Louvre N 3159, and partly in P. BM EA 10275, 6 = P. BM EA 71513, A, 25 = P. Cairo CG 58020, 5 = P. Cairo CG 58022, 3 = P. Lieblein, 21. Omission of *nb Ỉwnw* in P. BM EA 10286, 3. Var. P. BM EA 10124, 1: *ỉt*, 'father', for *Ỉtm* (spelling confusion); P. Louvre N 3289, 7–8: *mỉ rwḏ rn Ỉtm nbw* (*sic*) *Ỉwnw m Ỉwnw mỉ Ỉtm nty m Ỉwnw.*

Former sources: **A**, § 1660 c: *mỉ rwḏ rn Tm ḫnty Psḏt ꜥꜣt*; **B**, 13–14: *mỉ rwḏ rn n Tm* [*nb*] *Ỉwnw*; **C**, 13: *mỉ* [*rwḏ rn n Tm*] *nb* [*Ỉwnw*] *m Ỉwnw*; **D**, 18: *Tm nb tꜣwy Ỉwnw m Ỉwnw*; **D'**, 260: [*Tm nb Tꜣwy Ỉwnw*] *m Ỉwnw*; **E**, 5: *mỉ rwḏ rn n Tm nb tꜣwy Ỉwnw*; **F**, IX, 3–4: *mỉ rwḏ rn n Ỉtm nb Ỉwnw m Ỉwnw*; **G**, 6: *rwḏ rn n Tm nb tꜣwy m Ỉwnw*; **H**, IX, 15: *rwḏ rn n Tm nb tꜣwy Ỉwnw*; **I**, 4–5: *rwḏ sp 2 rn n Tm nb tꜣwy Ỉwnw m Ỉwnw.*

I, 8

Šw m Mnst ḥrt m Ỉwnw. Same reading in P. BM EA 10116, 6 = P. BM EA 10125, 23–4 = P. BM EA 10304, 6 = P. Cairo CG 58007, III, 6 = P. Cairo 58009, III, 5 = P. Cairo CG 58017, 2–3 = P. Cairo CG 58018, I, 10 = P. Florence 3669, 14[19] = P. Louvre E 3865, VI, 11 = P. Louvre N 3157, 8 = P. Louvre N 3161, 5 = P. Louvre N 3162, 6 = P. Louvre N 3177 A, 6. Sequence omitted in P. BM EA 10286; wholly in lacuna in P. Lieblein, 22 = P. Louvre N 3159, and partly in P. BM EA 10264, 3 = P. BM EA 10275, 7–8 = P. BM EA 71513, A, 26 = P. Cairo CG 58022, 3 = P. Turin 1861 B, 5;[20] omitted in P. Louvre N 3289; omitted or in lacuna in P. Cairo CG 58020, 7. Omission of *m* before *Mnst* in P. BM EA 10331, 2. Var. P. BM EA 9977, 4 = P. Berlin 3052, IV, 12: *n* instead of *m* before *Mnst*; P. BM EA 10124, 2 = P. BM EA 10275, 8 = P. BM EA 10282, 6 = P. Cairo CG 58013, 7 = P. Louvre N 3148, VIII, 6 = P. Louvre N 3174, 7: *st ḥrt*.

Former sources: **A**, § 1661 a**:** *Šw nb Mnst ḥrt m Ỉwnw*; **B**, 14–15**:** *Šw m Mn*[*st*] *ḥrt m Ỉwnw*; **C**, 14: *Šw <m> Mnst ḥr(t) m* [*Ỉwnw*]; **D**, 18: *Šw <m> Mnst ḥr(t) m Ỉwnw*; **D'**, 260–1: *Šw <m> Mnst ḥr(t)* [*m Ỉwnw*]; **E**, 5: *Šw m Mnst ḥrt m Ỉwnw*; **F**, IX, 5: *Šw m Mnst ḥr(t) m Ỉwnw*; **G**, 7: *Šw m Mnst ḥrt m Ỉwnw*; **H**, X, 1: *Šw mn ḥr st ḥrt m Ỉwnw*; **I**, 7: *Šw mn m st ḥrt m Ỉwnw.*

Mnst ḥrt, *Mnst ẖrt*: on these two quarters of Heliopolis, cf. G*DG* III, 41–2; P. Montet, *Géographie de l'Egypte ancienne* I (Paris 1957), p. 168; F. Gomaà, *Die Besiedlung Ägyptens* II (Wiesbaden 1987), pp. 187–8, and especially J. Vandier, *RdE* 17 (1962), pp. 152–6.

I, 9

Tfnwt m Mnst[21] *ẖrt m Ỉwnw.* Same reading in P. BM EA 10116, 7 = P. BM EA 10125, 24 = P. BM EA 10304, 7 = P. Berlin 3052, IV, 13 = P. Cairo CG 58007, III, 7 = P. Cairo 58009, III, 7 = P. Cairo CG 58017, 3–4 = P. Cairo CG 58018, I, 11 = P. Florence 3669, 15–16[22] = P. Lieblein, 22 = P. Louvre E 3865, VI, 11 = P. Louvre N 3148, VIII, 7 = P. Louvre N 3161, 6. Sequence omitted in P. BM EA 10286 = P. Cairo CG 58013 = P. Louvre N 3162 = P. Louvre N 3289; partly in lacuna in P. BM EA 10264, 3–4 = P. BM EA 10275, 8–9[23] = P. BM EA 71513, A, 27 = P. Cairo CG 58020, 7 = P. Cairo CG 58022, 3 = P. Louvre N 3159, 2 = P. Turin 1861 B, 6. Omission of *m* before *Mnst* in P. BM EA 9977, 5 (?) = P. BM EA 10331, 3. Var. P. BM EA 10124, 2 = P. BM EA 10275, [9] = P. BM EA 10282, 8 (misplaced) = P. Louvre N 3157, 9 = P. Louvre N 3174, 8 = P. Louvre N 3177 A, 7: *st ẖrt*, 'lower place'.

Former sources: **A**, § 1662 a: *Tfnwt nbt Mnst ẖrt m Ỉwnw*; **B**, 15–7: *Tfnwt* [...]*Mnst ẖrt* [*m Ỉwnw*]; **C**, 15: *Tfnwt <m> Mnst ẖrt m Ỉwnw*; **D**, 19: [...] *Mnst ẖrt m Ỉwnw*; **D'**, 261: [...]*st ẖrt m Ỉwnw*; **E**, 6: *Tfnwt m Mnst ẖrt m Ỉwnw*; **F**, IX, 5–6: *Tfnwt m Mnst ẖrt m Ỉwnw*; **G**, 8: *Tfnwt m Mnst ḥrt* (*sic*) *m Ỉwnw*; **H**, X, 2: *Ḥr m P* (*sic*); [24] **I**, 8: *Tfnwt mn m st ẖrt m Ỉwnw.*

I, 10

Gb m bw šmꜣw. Same reading in P. BM EA 9977, 6 = P. BM EA 10116, 8 = P. BM EA 10124, 2–3 = P. BM EA 10125, 24 = P. BM EA 10282, 7 = P. BM EA 10304, 8 = P. BM EA 10331, 4 = P. Cairo CG 58007, III, 8 = P. Cairo 58009, III, 8 = P. Cairo CG 58013, 8 = P. Cairo CG 58017, 4 = P. Cairo CG 58018, I, 12 = P. Florence 3669, 17[25] = P. Louvre E 3865, VI, 12 = P. Louvre N 3148, VIII, 8 = P. Louvre N 3157, 10 = P. Louvre N 3161, 7 = P. Louvre N 3162, 7 = P. Louvre N 3174, 9 = P. Louvre N 3177 A, 8. Sequence omitted in P. BM EA 10286 = P. Louvre N 3289; wholly in lacuna in P. Lieblein, 23 = P. Louvre N 3159, 1, and partly in P. BM EA 10264, 4 = P. BM EA 71513, A, 28 = P. Cairo CG 58022, 4 = P. Turin 1861 B, 7. Var. P. Berlin 3052, IV, 13 = P. Cairo CG 58020, 7:[26] *n* instead of *m*. Note the writing of *bw* in P. BM EA 9977, 6 = P. BM EA 10116, 8 = P. BM EA 10264, 4 = P. BM EA 10282, 7 = P. BM EA 10331, 4 = P. Berlin 3052, IV, 13 = P. Cairo CG 58013, 8. Cf. also P. BM EA 10254, **7**.

Former sources: **A**, § 1663, a: *Gb ỉr bꜣ tꜣ*; **B**, 17–18**:** insignificant traces; **C**, 15–16: *Gb bꜣ* [*tꜣ m*] *Ỉwnw*; **D**, 19–20: *Gb* [...]; **D'**, 262: *Gb bꜣ* [...]; **E**, 6: *Gb bꜣ tꜣ m Ỉwnw*; **F**, IX, 6–7: *Gb m bw* (written *bꜣ*) *šmꜣw m Ỉwnw*; **G**, 9: *Gb m bꜣ tꜣ m Ỉwnw*; **H**, X, 4: *Gb ỉr bꜣ-tꜣ m Ỉwnw*; **I**, 9: *Gb bꜣ m tꜣ m Ỉwnw.*

Bw šmꜣw: locality in the Heliopolitan nome (G*DG* II, 19), also attested in R.O. Faulkner, An *Ancient Egyptian Book of Hours* (Oxford 1958), p. 32* (20, 14), and *Edfou* I, 504, 45, where it is cited in relation to Geb within the same context of the litany *mỉ rwḏ rn*.

14. H.H. Nelson, op. cit., pp. 324–7 (ep. 32) = H.H. Nelson and W.J. Murnane, op. cit., pl. 202.
15. Golenischeff, *Pap. Hiérat.* I, p. 149 and pl. 26; E. Bacchi, *Il rituale di Amenhotpe I* (Turin 1942), pp. 49–50 and pl. 20. The two segments are part of the same papyrus; the litany *mỉ rwḏ rn* is preserved entirely on both sections of the manuscript.
16. Gardiner, *HPBM* III, p. 91 with pl. 53.
17. Supply before the name of the god *mỉ rwḏ rn (n)*, 'as the name of … endures'.
18. Before (lines 11–12): *srwḏ rn.t m-ẖnw Dwꜣt ḏsrt mỉ rwḏ*, 'making your name endure inside the sacred Duat, as the name of … endures'. See *supra*, **I, 4–5, 6**.
19. Before (line 13): *sḏd ẖꜣt.t m-ẖnw Ỉmntt mỉ rwḏ rn n,* 'making your corpse be stable within the West, as the name of … endures'.
20. The line 4, now lost, probably consisted of a vertical text preceding lines 5–16.
21. Written <> in P. Louvre N 3161, 6. On this writing, see M. Smith, in *Grammata Demotika* (Fs. Lüddeckens, Würzburg 1984), pp. 193–210.
22. Before (lines 14–15): *rwḏ rn.t m-ẖnw pr.t mỉ rwḏ rn n*, 'may your name endure within your house, as the name of … endures'.
23. The following lines of the text (lines 10–13) are too lacunose to be taken into consideration.
24. Bacchi, op. cit., p. 49: *Tfnwt nbt Mnst ẖrt m Ỉwnw,* although no trace of this sequence is to be found on the Cairo portion which alone contains the litany *mỉ rwḏ rn*. The reference to Horus of Pe recurs below in the expected place, at **F,** X, 6.
25. Before (line 16): *sḏḏ ẖꜣt.t m-ẖnw šṯyt.t mỉ rwḏ rn n*, 'making your corpse be stable within your tomb, as the name of … endures'.
26. The two last lines of this manuscript are too lacunose to be intelligible.

I, 11

Nwt m Ḥwt šnw. Same reading in P. BM EA 10116, 9 = P. BM EA 10124, 4 = P. BM EA 10125, 25 = P. BM EA 10282, 8 = P. BM EA 10304, 9 = P. Cairo CG 58007, III, 9 = P. Cairo CG 58013, 9 = P. Lieblein, 23 = P. Louvre E 3865, VI, 12 = P. Louvre N 3159, 3 = P. Louvre N 3162, 8 = P. Louvre N 3174, 10. Sequence omitted in P. BM EA 10286 = P. Cairo 58009, III; partly in lacuna in P. BM EA 10264, 4 = P. BM EA 71513, A, 29 = P. Louvre N 3177 A, 9 = P. Turin 1861 B, 8; omitted or in lacuna in P. Cairo CG 58022, 4. Var. P. Cairo CG 58017, 5 = P. Cairo CG 58018, I, 13: *Ḥwt šns*. P. Florence 3669, 18[27](end of the litany) = P. Louvre N 3148, VIII, 9: *Ḥwt šnis*; P. BM EA 9977, 7 = P. BM EA 10331, 5 = P. Berlin 3052, IV, 14 = P. Louvre N 3157, 11 = P. Louvre N 3161, 8: *Ḥwt šnws*; P. Louvre N 3289, 11: *Nwt m P Dp mi Wꜣḏt m Dp*.

Former sources: **A**, § 1664, a: *Nwt m Ḥwt šnw m Ỉwnw*; **B**, 18: *Nwt* (*sic* and end); **C**, 16: *Nwt m Ḥwt-bꜣ m Ỉwnw*;[28] **D**: in lacuna; **D′**: in lacuna; **E**, 7: *Nwt m Ḥwt šnw*; **F**, IX, 8–9: *Nwt m Ḥwt šnw m Ỉwnw*; **G**, 9–10: *Nwt m Ḥwt šnm* (*sic*) *m Ỉwnw*; **H**, X, 5: *Nwt m Ḥwt šnyt m Ỉwnw*; **I**, 10: *Nwt <m Ḥwt> šnyt m Ỉwnw*.

On *Ḥwt šnw*, a sanctuary in the Heliopolitan nome: Gomaà, op. cit., p. 74; D. Kurth, *LÄ* IV, 540, n. 78; Leitz, *LGG* III, p. 539.

I, 12

Wsir ḫnty Ỉmntt m ꜣbḏw. Same reading in P. BM EA 9977, 10 = P. BM EA 10116, 10 = P. BM EA 10124, 5 = P. BM EA 10125, 25 = P. BM EA 10282, 12 (misplaced) = P. BM EA 10286, 4 = P. BM EA 10304, 10 = P. BM EA 10331, 6 = P. Berlin 3052, IV, 14 = P. Cairo CG 58007, III, 10 = P. Cairo 58009, III, 9 = P. Cairo CG 58013, 10 = P. Cairo CG 58017, 5–6 = P. Cairo CG 58018, I, 14 = P. Cairo CG 58022, 5 = P. Louvre E 3865, VI, 12–13 = P. Louvre N 3148, VIII, 10 = P. Louvre N 3159, 4 = P. Louvre N 3161, 9 = P. Louvre N 3174, 11. Sequence wholly in lacuna in P. BM EA 71513, A, 30 = P. Lieblein, 24, and partly in P. BM EA 10264, 4 = P. Louvre N 3157, 12 = P. Louvre N 3162, 9 = P. Louvre N 3177 A, 10 = P. Turin 1861 B, 9. Var. P. Louvre N 3289, 12–13: *Wsir ḫnty Ỉmntt nṯr ꜥꜣ nbw* (*sic*) *ꜣbḏw mi Wsir nty m Dwꜣt*, 'Osiris foremost of the West, great god lord of Abydos, like Osiris who is in the Duat'; P. Louvre N 3156, 10–11 (end of the litany): *Wsir ḫnty Ỉmntt nṯr ꜥꜣ nbw* (*sic*) *ꜣbḏw m ꜣw n ḏt nḥḥ*, 'Osiris foremost of the West, great god lord of Abydos, in the length of eternity and perpetuity'.

Former sources: **A**, § 1665, a: *Wsir m Tꜣ-wr* (or: *ꜣbḏw*); § 1666, a: *Wsir m ḫnty Ỉmntt*; **C**: sequence omitted; **D**, 20: *Wsir m Tꜣ-wr*; **D′**, 262: *Wsir m Tꜣ-wr* (or: *ꜣbḏw*); **E**, 7: *Wsir ḫnty Ỉmntt m ꜣbḏw*; **F**, IX, 10–11: *Wsir ḫnty Ỉmntt* (?) *m ꜣbḏw*; **G**, 10–11: *Wsir ḫnty Ỉmntt m ꜣbḏw*; **H**, X, 3: *Wsir ḫnty Ỉmntt* (?) *m ꜣbḏw*; **I**, 11: *Wsir ḫnty Ỉmntt m ꜣbḏw*.

I, 13

Ỉst m Tꜣ-wr. Same reading in P. BM EA 9977, 8 = P. BM EA 10116, 11 = P. BM EA 10124, 5 = P. BM EA 10125, 25–6 = P. BM EA 10282, 10 = P. BM EA 10286, 5 = P. BM EA 10304, 11 = P. BM EA 10331, 7 = P. Berlin 3052, IV, 15 = P. Cairo CG 58007, III, 11 = P. Cairo 58009, III, 9–10 = P. Cairo CG 58013, 11 = P. Cairo CG 58017, 6 = P. Cairo CG 58018, I, 15 = P. Lieblein, 24 = P. Louvre N 3148, VIII, 11 = P. Louvre N 3157, 13 = P. Louvre N 3161, 10 = P. Louvre N 3174, 12 = P. Louvre N 3177 A, 11. P. BM EA 10125, 26, adds: *mitt Wsir m ꜥnḏ*, 'likewise Osiris in Andj', and P. Cairo 58009, III, 10–11: *mi rwḏ Wsir nb Ḏdw m nṯr ꜥꜣ nb ꜥnḏ nṯr niwwt ḥkꜣ spꜣwt*, 'as the name of Osiris lord of Busiris endures as great god lord of Andj, god of the towns, ruler of the nomes'. Sequence omitted in P. Louvre E 3865, VI; wholly in lacuna in P. BM EA 71513, A, 31 = P. Louvre N 3159, 4–5, and partly in P. BM EA 10264, 5 = P. Louvre N 3162, 10 = P. Turin 1861 B, 10; omitted or in lacuna in P. Cairo CG 58022, 5.

Former sources: **A:** sequence omitted; **C**, 17: *Ỉst m Nṯrw*; **D**, 19–20: *Ỉst* [...]; **D′**, 263: *Ỉst m nṯrw.s*, 'her *nṯrw*-lake'; **E**, 8: *Ỉst m Nṯri*; **F**, IX, 12: *Ỉst m Tꜣ-wr*;[29] **G**, 12: *Ỉst m Nṯr*; **H**, X, 4: *Ỉst m nṯr* (or *itrw*); **I**, 12: *Ỉst m itrw*.

This phrase produces confusion in the sources between *Nṯrw* and *itrw* in part explicable on orthographic grounds.

I, 14

Ḥr m P. Same reading in P. BM EA 10116, 12 = P. BM EA 10282, 14 (misplaced) = P. BM EA 10286, 6 = P. BM EA 10304, 12 = P. Berlin 3052, IV, 15 = P. Cairo CG 58007, III, 12 = P. Cairo 58009, III, 11 = P. Cairo CG 58013, 13 = P. Cairo CG 58018, I, 16 = P. Cairo CG 58022, 6 = P. Louvre N 3148, VIII, 12 = P. Louvre N 3157, 14 = P. Louvre N 3159, 5 = P. Louvre N 3174, 13 = P. Louvre N 3177 A, 12. Sequence omitted in P. BM EA 9977 = P. BM EA 10125 = P. Louvre E 3865, VI = P. Louvre N 3161; wholly in lacuna in P. Lieblein, 25 = P. Turin 1861 B, 11, and partly in P. BM EA 71513, A, 32 = P. Cairo CG 58017, 7 = P. Louvre N 3162, 11. Var. P. BM EA 10331, 8: *n* instead of *m* (?); P. BM EA 10264, 5: *Ḥwt-ꜥꜣt* (?) instead of P.

Former sources: **A:** sequence omitted; **C**, 18: *Ḥr m P*; **D**, 20: in lacuna; **D′**, 263: *Ḥr m P*; **E**, 9: *Ḥr m P*; **F**, IX: sequence omitted; **G**: sequence omitted; **H**, X, 6: *Ḥr m P*; **I**, 13: *Ḥr m P*.

I, 15

Wꜣḏyt m Dp. Same reading in P. BM EA 10116, 13 = P. BM EA 10282, 15 = P. BM EA 10304, 13 = P. BM EA 10331, 9 = P. Berlin 3052, IV, 15–16 = P. Cairo 58009, III, 12 = P. Cairo CG 58013, 14 = P. Cairo CG 58017, 7–8 = P. Cairo CG 58018, I, 17 = P. Lieblein, 25 = P. Louvre N 3148, VIII, 12 = P. Louvre N 3157, 15 = P. Louvre N 3162, 13 = P. Louvre N 3177 A, 13. Sequence omitted in P. BM EA 9977 = P. BM EA 10124 = P. BM EA 10125 = P. Louvre N 3161; omitted or in lacuna in P. BM EA 10264, 5 = P. Cairo CG 58022, 6 = P. Louvre N 3159, 6. Var. P. BM EA 71513, A, 33 = P. Cairo CG 58007, III, 13 = P. Louvre E 3865, VI, 14 = P. Louvre N 3174, 14 = P. Turin 1861 B, 12:[30] *Wꜣḏyt m P Dp*; P. BM EA 10286, 6: *Nbt-ḥwt m Dp* (end of the litany).

Former sources: **A**, § 1671, a: *Wꜣḏyt m Dp* (end of the litany); **C**, 19: *Wꜣḏyt m Dp*; **D**, 20: in lacuna; **D′**, 264: *Wꜣḏyt m Dp*; **E**, 10: *Wꜣḏyt m Dp*; **F**, IX, 16: *Nbt-ḥwt Wꜣḏyt m Dp*; **G**: sequence omitted; **H**: sequence omitted; **I**: sequence omitted.

I, 16

Nbt-ḥwt m Ỉwnw. Same reading in P. BM EA 9977, 9 = P. BM EA 10116, 14 = P. BM EA 10125, 26 = P. BM EA 10282, 16 = P. BM EA 10304, 14 = P. BM EA 10331, 10 = P. BM EA 71513, A, 34 = P. Berlin 3052, IV, 16 (end of the litany)[31] = P. Cairo CG 58007, III, 14 = P. Cairo 58009, III, 12 = P. Cairo CG 58013, 15 = P. Cairo CG 58017, 8 = P. Cairo CG 58018, I, 18 = P. Louvre N 3148, VIII, 13 = P. Louvre N 3157, 16 = P. Louvre N 3159, 6 = P. Louvre N 3161, 11 = P. Louvre N 3162, 14 = P. Louvre N 3174, 15 = P. Louvre N 3177 A, 14. P. Cairo CG 58009, III, 13, adds: *mi rwḏ rn n Ỉst m spꜣwt nb*(*t*), 'as the name of Isis endures in all nomes.' Sequence omitted in P. Louvre E 3865, VI; wholly in lacuna in P. Lieblein, 26, and partly in P. BM EA 10264, 6 = P. Turin 1861 B, 13; omitted or in lacuna in P. Cairo CG 58022, 6. Var. P. BM EA 10124, 7: *m*

27. Tied to the former sequence by the preposition *ḥnꜥ*, 'together with'.
28. Haikal, op. cit., p. 371, n. (v), takes this as probable error for *Ḥwt šnw*.
29. Cf. the title of Isis: *ḥry(t)-ib ꜣbḏw*, 'dwelling in Abydos'; Ch.F. Nims, *JEA* 38 (1952), p. 42.
30. *Wꜣḏyt* in lacuna in P. Turin 1861 B.
31. It is followed by a final wish (IV, 16–17): *mi pꜣy p(ꜣ) bꜣ n Wsir N snsn r nḥḥ ḥnꜥ ḏt*, 'may the ba of the Osiris N fly up and breathe for ever and eternally!'

Ḥwt šnw; P. BM EA 10286, 5: *m Dp*. P. 10286, 6: conflation with the preceding sequence, see *supra*, **I, 15**.

Former sources: **C**, 18: *Nbt-ḥwt m Ỉwnw*; **D**: in lacuna; **D′**, 264: sequence omitted; **E**, 8: *Nbt-ḥwt m* [...]; **F**, IX, 16: *Nbt-ḥwt m Ỉwnw*; **G**, 14: *Nbt-ḥwt m Ḥwt m Ỉwnw*; **H**, X, 7: *Nbt-ḥwt m Ḥwt m Ỉwnw*; **I**, 15: *Nbt-ḥwt m Ỉwnw*.

On Nephthys in Heliopolis: E. Graefe, *LÄ* IV, 459 with n. 32, citing only this passage of the Second Book of Breathing.

I, 17

Bꜣ-nb-Ḏdt m pr Bꜣ-nb-Ḏdt. Same reading in P. BM EA 10304, 15 = P. Cairo CG 58018, I, 19 = P. Louvre N 3148, VIII, 14 = P. Louvre N 3159, 7 = P. Louvre N 3174, 16. Sequence omitted in P. BM EA 9977 = P. BM EA 10125 = P. Louvre E 3865, VI = P. Louvre N 3161; wholly in lacuna in P. Louvre N 3177 A, 15, and partly in P. BM EA 10264, 6 = P. Turin 1861 B, 14. Omission of *m pr Bꜣ-nb-Ḏdt* in P. BM EA 10116, 15 = P. BM EA 10282, 17 = P. BM EA 10331, 11 (or in lacuna ?) = P. BM EA 71513, A, 35 = P. Cairo CG 58009, III, 13–14 = P. Cairo CG 58013, 16 = P. Cairo CG 58017, 9 (or in lacuna ?) = P. Cairo CG 58022, 7 (end of the litany ?) = P. Lieblein, 26 = P. Louvre N 3162, 15. Var. P. Cairo CG 58007, IV, 1: *Nb Ḏdt m pr Ḏdt*; P. BM EA 10116, 14: *Bꜣ-nb-Ḏdw*; *n* for *m* in P. Louvre N 3157, 17.

Former sources: **C**, 20: [...] *m Ḏd(t)*; **D**: in lacuna; **D′**, 264: *Bꜣ-nb-Ḏdt* [...] (?); **E**, 10: *Bꜣ m Ḏdw* (*sic*);[32] **F**, IX, 18: *Bꜣ-nb-Ḏdt*; **G**, 15: *Bꜣ m Ḏdw* (*sic*); **H**, X, 8: *Bꜣ-nb-Ḏdt m Ḏdt*; **I**, 16: *Bꜣ-nb-Ḏdw m Ḏdt*.

For Banebdjed: H. de Meulenaere, *LÄ* IV, 44. On the Bas of Mendes: Gardiner, *HPBM* III, p. 73 with n. 10 (plural).

I, 18

Ỉ m Ḫmnw. Same reading in P. BM EA 10116, 16 = P. BM EA 10304, 16 = P. Cairo CG 58007, IV, 2 = P. Cairo CG 58018, I, 20 = P. Louvre N 3148, VIII, 15 = P. Louvre N 3157, 18 = P. Louvre N 3174, 17. Sequence omitted in P. BM EA 10125; wholly in lacuna in P. BM EA 10264, 6–7 (end of the litany) = P. Lieblein, 27 (end of the litany) = P. Louvre N 3159, 8 = P. Louvre N 3177 A, 16, and partly in P. BM EA 71513, A, 36[33] = P. Turin 1861 B, 15. Var. P. Louvre N 3157, 18: *Ḏḥwty* instead of *Ỉ*; P. Cairo CG 58013, 17 = P. Louvre N 3161, 12: *Ỉ ꜥꜣ nb Ḫmnw*; P. BM EA 9977, 9 (end of the litany) = P. BM EA 10331, 12 (text rubbed out, end of the litany ?): *Ỉ ꜥꜣ wr nb Ḫmnw*; P. Louvre E 3865, VI, 14 (end of the litany) = P. Louvre N 3162, 16: *Ỉ ꜥꜣ sp 2 nb Ḫmnw*; P. Cairo CG 58009, III, 14: *Ỉ ꜥꜣ ꜥꜣ wr nb Ḫmnw* (end of the litany); P. Cairo CG 58017, 9: *Ỉ ꜥꜣ ꜥꜣ ꜥꜣ nb Ḫmnw*; P. BM EA 10282, 19: *Ỉ ꜥꜣ ꜥꜣ ꜥꜣ wr nb Ḫmnw*. See J. Quaegebeur, in *Hommages à François Daumas* II (Montpellier 1986), pp. 525–44.

Former sources: **C**, 20–1: *Ḏḥwty m Ḫmnw* (end of the litany); **D**: in lacuna, and probable end of the litany; **D′**: in lacuna, and probable end of the litany; **E**, 11: *Ḏḥwty m Ḫmnw* (end of the litany); **F**, IX, 20: *Ỉ ꜥꜣ ꜥꜣ nb Ḫmnw* (end of the litany); **G**, 15–16: *Ḏḥwty m Ḫmnw* (end of the litany); **H**, X, 8: *Ḏḥwty m Ḫmnw* (end of the litany); **I**, 17: *Ḏḥwty m Ḫmnw* (end of the litany).

I, 19

Mnṯw 4 m-ḫnw niwt.sn.[34] Same reading in P. Cairo CG 58007, IV, 3 = P. Cairo CG 58013, 18 = P. Louvre N 3157, 19 = P. Louvre N 3162, 17 = P. Louvre N 3174, 18. Sequence omitted in P. BM EA 10125 = P. Louvre N 3161; wholly in lacuna in P. Louvre N 3177 A, 17, and partly in P. Turin 1861 B, 16. Var. P. BM EA 10116, 17 (end of the litany) = P. BM EA 10304, 17 = P. Cairo CG 58018, I, 21 = P. Louvre N 3148, VIII, 16 = P. Louvre N 3159, 8: *niwwt.sn*.

On the four Montus: Leitz, *LGG* III, p. 323. The singular *niwt* refers back to Thebes, while the plural refers to the Theban sanctuaries of Armant, Medamud and Tod.

I, 20

Ḫnmw m ꜣbw. Same reading in P. BM EA 10304, 18 = P. Cairo CG 58007, IV, 4[35] = P. Cairo CG 58013, 19[36] = P. Cairo CG 58018, I, 22 = P. Louvre N 3148, VIII, 17 = P. Louvre N 3162, 18 = P. Louvre N 3174, 19 = P. Turin 1861 B, 18. Sequence omitted in P. BM EA 10125 = P. Louvre N 3161; in lacuna in P. Louvre N 3159, 9 = P. Louvre N 3177 A, 18. Var. P. Louvre N 3157, 20: *m-ḫnw* instead of *m*.

Gardiner, *AEO* II, p. 4, no. 315.

I, 21

Ḥr wr m Nwbt (Ombos). Same reading in P. BM EA 10304, 19 = P. Cairo CG 58018, I, 23 = P. Louvre N 3162, 21 (misplaced) = P. Louvre N 3174, 20 = P. Louvre N 3177 A, 19. Sequence omitted in P. BM EA 10125 = P. Cairo CG 58007 = P. Louvre N 3148 = P. Louvre N 3161 = P. Turin 1861 B. Sequence omitted in P. BM EA 10125 = P. Louvre N 3157; partly in lacuna in P. Louvre N 3159, 9.

Former sources: **A**, § 1667, a: *Stš m Nwbt*; **E**, 8: *Stš nb Nwbt*; **G**, 13: *Stš nb Nwbt*; **H**, X, 6: *Stš m Nwbt*; **I**: *Stš m Nwbt*.[37]

Gardiner, *AEO* II, pp. 5*–6*, no. 316.

I, 22

Ḥr Bḥdty m Ḏbꜣ (Edfu). Same reading in P. BM EA 10304, 20 = P. Cairo CG 58007, IV, 5 = P. Cairo CG 58018, II, 2 = P. Louvre N 3148, VIII, 18 = P. Louvre N 3157, 21 = P. Louvre N 3162, 19 (misplaced) = P. Louvre N 3174, 21 = P. Louvre N 3177 A, 20 = P. Turin 1861 B, 19. Sequence omitted in P. BM EA 10125 = P. Louvre N 3161; in lacuna in P. Louvre N 3159, 10.

Former source: **A**, § 1668, a: *Ḥr m Ḏbꜣt*.

Gardiner, *AEO* II, p. 6*, no. 318.

I, 23

Nḫbt m Nḫb (Elkab).[38] Same reading in P. BM EA 10304, 21 = P. Cairo CG 58007, IV, 6 = P. Cairo CG 58018, II, 3 = P. Louvre N 3148, VIII, 19 = P. Louvre N 3174, 22 = P. Louvre N 3177 A, 21 = P. Turin 1861 B, 20. Sequence omitted in P. BM EA 10125 = P. Louvre N 3161; almost wholly in lacuna in P. Louvre N 3157, 22; in lacuna (or omitted ?) in P. Louvre N 3159, 10 = P. Louvre N 3162, 20.

Gardiner, *AEO* II, p. 8*, no. 321.

I, 24

nꜣ nṯrw nbw m Wꜣst. Same reading in P. Louvre N 3177 A, 22. Sequence omitted in P. BM EA 10125 = P. Louvre N 3161; in lacuna (or omitted ?) in P. Louvre N 3159, 10–11 = P. Louvre N 3162, 21 = P. Louvre N 3174, 23. Omission of *nꜣ* in P. BM EA 10304, 22 = P. Cairo CG 58018, II, 4;[39]

32. For confusion between *Ḏdw* and *Ḏdt*: D. Meeks, *RdE* 25 (1973), p. 212, n. 3.
33. The rest of this manuscript is lost.
34. P. BM EA 10282, 20, gives here another text: *Ḥr sꜣ Ỉst sꜣ Wsỉr*, 'Horus son of Isis, son of Isis', then (21–22): *Ḥwt-Ḥr ḫnt Ỉmntt Mꜣꜥt ḫn.w* (written *ḫnt* by confusion with the preceding epithet of Hathor), 'Hathor mistress of the West, Maat to whom the West has been entrusted', on which see P. BM EA 10191, **I, 5–6**.
35. Amend the transcription by Golenischeff at this point. Read: .
36. After interruption the common version of P. Cairo CG 58013 and P. BM EA 10110 + 10111 resumes only in II, 20–4.
37. Noted between Horus of Pe and Nephthys in Heliopolis.
38. Amend the transcription by Golenischeff for P. Cairo CG 58018, II, 3 (in place of).
39. Amend the transcription by Golenischeff at this point (in place of). For another similar error, see *infra*, n. 49.

of *m* in P. Cairo CG 58007, IV, 7 = P. Louvre N 3148, VIII, 20 = P. Louvre N 3157, 25 = P. Turin 1861 B, 21.

I, 25

Ḥr wr nb Šmꜥ m-ḫnw Gsỉ. Same reading in P. Louvre N 3148, VIII, 21 = P. Louvre N 3157, 26 = P. Louvre N 3177 A, 23. Sequence omitted in P. BM EA 10125 = P. Louvre N 3161; partly in lacuna in P. Louvre N 3162, 23. Omission of *m-ḫnw Gsy* in P. BM EA 10282, 12 = P. Cairo CG 58007, IV, 8 = P. Turin 1861 B, 22; of *nb Šmꜥ* in P. BM EA 10304, 23 = P. Cairo CG 58018, II, 5 = P. Louvre N 3159, 11 = P. Louvre N 3174, 24; of *wr* in P. Louvre N 3148, VIII, 19.

For *Gsỉ* and the cult of Haroeris, attested since the Old Kingdom: Gardiner, *AEO* II, pp. 27*-8*, no. 339; Gomaà, op. cit., pp. 161–2.

I, 26

Ỉst m Nṯr-šmꜥ. Same reading in P. BM EA 10125, 26 (misplaced) = P. BM EA 10304, 24 = P.Cairo CG 58007, IV, 9[40] = P. Cairo CG 58018, II, 6 = P. Louvre N 3148, VIII, 20 = P. Louvre N 3157, 27 = P. Louvre N 3159, 12[41] = P. Louvre N 3162, 22 = P. Louvre N 3174, 25 = P. Louvre N 3177 A, 24 = P. Turin 1861 B, 23. Sequence omitted in P. Louvre N 3161.

For *Nṯr-šmꜥ*, a Late Period designation of Coptos (*GDG* III, 109): C. Traunecker, *Coptos* (*OLA* 43, 1992), pp. 311–91.

I, 27

Ḥwt-Ḥr m Ỉḳ. Same reading in P. BM EA 10304, 25 = P. Cairo CG 58018, II, 7 = P. Louvre N 3148, VIII, 23 = P. Louvre N 3157, 28 = P. Louvre N 3162, 23 = P. Louvre N 3174, 26 = P. Louvre N 3177 A, 25 = P. Turin 1861 B, 24. Sequence omitted in P. BM EA 10125 = P. Louvre N 3161; in lacuna in P. Louvre N 3159, 13. Var. P. Cairo CG 58007, IV, 10: *Ḥwt-Ḥr m Wꜣḏt*, by confusion between the signs  and .

Ỉḳ: Gomaà, op. cit., pp. 168–9.

I, 28

Nfr-ḥtp m Ḥwt-sḫmw. Same reading in P. BM EA 10304, 26 = P. Cairo CG 58007, IV, 11[42] = P. Cairo CG 58018, II, 8 = P. Louvre N 3148, VIII, 24 = P. Louvre N 3157, 29 = P. Louvre N 3159, 13 = P. Louvre N 3174, 27 = P. Turin 1861 B, 25. Sequence omitted in P. BM EA 10125 = P. Louvre N 3161; partly in lacuna in P. Louvre N 3162, 24 = P. Louvre N 3177 A, 26. Var. P. Louvre N 3174, 27: *Ḥwt sḫmwy*.

On the cult of Neferhotep in *Ḥwt-sḫmw* (Hu, Diospolis Parva): J.C. Goyon and C. Traunecker, *Cahiers de Karnak* VII (Paris 1982), p. 300; Ph. Collombert, *RdE* 48 (1997), pp. 64–9.

I, 29

Mnw m Ỉpw. Same reading in P. BM EA 10304, 27 = P. Cairo CG 58018, II, 9 = P. Louvre N 3148, VIII, 25 = P. Louvre N 3157, 30 = P. Louvre N 3159, 14 = P. Louvre N 3174, 28. Sequence omitted in P. BM EA 10125 = P. Louvre N 3161; in lacuna in P. Louvre N 3177 A, 27. Var. P. Cairo CG 58007, IV, 12[43] = P. Louvre N 3162, 25 = P. Turin 1861 B, 26: *Mnw nb Ỉpw*.

I, 30

Nmty m Wꜣḏt. Same reading in P. BM EA 10304, 28 = P. Cairo CG 58018, II, 10 = P. Louvre N 3148, VIII, 26 = P. Louvre N 3157, 31 = P. Louvre N 3162, 26 = P. Louvre N 3174, 29 = P. Turin 1861 B, 27. Sequence omitted in P. BM EA 10125 = P. Louvre N 3161; wholly in lacuna in P. Louvre N 3159, 15, and partly in P. Louvre N 3177 A, 28.

On the cult of Nemty (written *Nṯrwy*) in Wadjet, capital of the Xth nome of Upper Egypt: P. Montet, *Géographie de l'Egypte ancienne* II (Paris 1961), pp. 118–19; Gardiner, *AEO* II, pp. 50*-2*, and 55*-62*, no. 362, and in particular the monograph by E. Graefe, *Studien zu den Göttern und Kulten im 12. und 10. oberägyptischen Gau* (Freiburg 1980), pp. 16–17 with n. 104.

I, 31

Wp-wꜣwt m Sꜣw. Same reading in P. BM EA 10304, 29 = P. Cairo CG 58018, II, 11 = P. Louvre N 3148, VIII, 28 = P. Louvre N 3157, 32 = P. Louvre N 3159, 15 = P. Louvre N 3174, 30 = P. Turin 1861 B, 28. Sequence omitted in P. BM EA 10125 = P. Louvre N 3161; in lacuna in P. Louvre N 3162, 27[44] = P. Louvre N 3177 A, 29.

I, 32

Ḥwt-Ḥr m Ḳs. Same reading in P. Cairo CG 58018, II, 12 = P. Louvre N 3148, VIII, 29 = P. Louvre N 3157, 33 = P. Louvre N 3159, 16 = P. Louvre N 3174, 32 = P. Turin 1861 B, 29. Sequence omitted in P. BM EA 10125 = P. Louvre N 3161; in lacuna in P. BM EA 10304, 30 = P. Louvre N 3177 A, 30.

On Cusae (capital of the XIVth nome of Upper Egypt): Gardiner, *AEO* II, p. 77*, no. 374.

I, 33

Ḥr m Ḥbnw. Same reading in P. Cairo CG 58018, II, 13 = P. Louvre N 3148, VIII, 30 = P. Louvre N 3157, 34 = P. Louvre N 3174, 33 = P. Turin 1861 B, 30. Var. P. BM EA 10304, 31: *Ḥwt-Ḥr*. Sequence omitted in P. BM EA 10125 = P. Louvre N 3161; in lacuna in P. Louvre N 3159, 17 = P. Louvre N 3177 A, 31.

I, 34

Ỉnpw m Ḥr-dy. Same reading in P. BM EA 10125, 27 = P. BM EA 10304, 32 = P. Cairo CG 58018, II, 14 = P. Louvre N 3148, VIII, 31 = P. Louvre N 3157, 35 = P. Louvre N 3174, 34 = P. Turin 1861 B, 32. Sequence omitted in P. Louvre N 3161; in lacuna in P. Louvre N 3159, 17 = P. Louvre N 3177 A, 32.

On Hardai (capital of the XVIIIth nome of Upper Egyptian): J. Vandier, *Le Papyrus Jumilhac* (Paris 1961), pp. 38–9.

I, 35

Ḥr-šfy m Ḥwt-nn-nsw. Same reading in P. BM EA 10304, 33 = P. Cairo CG 58018, II, 15 = P. Louvre N 3148, VIII, 33 = P. Louvre N 3157, 36 = P. Louvre N 3159, 17 = P. Louvre N 3174, 35 = P. Turin 1861 B, 33. Sequence partly in lacuna in P. Louvre N 3177 A, 33. Var. P. BM EA 10125, 27 (end of the litany): *Ḥr*;[45] P. Louvre N 3161, 13: *Nsw-tꜣwy* instead of *Ḥwt-nn-nsw*.[46]

I, 36

Sbk m Mr-wr. Same reading in P. BM EA 10304, 34 = P. Cairo CG 58018, II, 16 = P. Louvre N 3148, VIII, 33 = P. Louvre N 3157, 37 = P. Louvre N 3159, 18 = P. Louvre N 3174, 36 = P. Turin 1861 B, 34. Sequence partly in lacuna in P. Louvre N 3177 A, 34.

40. Between Haroeris lord of *Šmꜥ*, and Hathor in *Wꜣḏt*.
41. Preceding clause in lacuna, and close of a first section involving the litany *mi rwḏ rn*, followed by another lacuna.
42. Read probably: 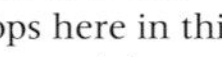.
43. The litany stops here in this manuscript.
44. The following text is lost.
45. In this manuscript, the litany is followed (28) by a final formula belonging to the First Book of Breathing, and on which see P. BM EA 10191, **II, 34**.
46. The last line of text (14) in this manuscript is partly in lacuna and shows the name of a goddess in connection with a place named *Ḥwt nsw tꜣwy*. One reads then a concluding formula: *rnp rn.f r ḏt*, 'May his name be renewed for ever!'

On Sobek in Merwer (Gurob, at the entrance to the Fayum): Gardiner, *AEO* II, pp. 115*–16*, no. 392; W. Rübsam, *Götter und Kulte im Faijum* (Bonn 1974), p. 123.

I, 37

Ptḥ Sḫmt Nfr-tm m-ḫnw Ỉnb-ḥḏ. Same reading in P. Cairo CG 58018, II, 17 = P. Louvre N 3148, VIII, 34–5 = P. Louvre N 3157, 38–9 = P. Louvre N 3174, 37 = P. Turin 1861 B, 35. Var. P. BM EA 10304, 35: *Mn-nfr* instead of *Ỉnb-ḥḏ*. Sequence wholly in lacuna in P. Louvre N 3159, 19,[47] and partly in P. Louvre N 3177 A, 35.[48]

II, 1

di.ỉ ḫꜥ.kwỉ m hb ꜥꜣ pr m ḫt n mwt.ỉ.[49] Same reading in P. BM EA 10304, 36 = P. Cairo CG 58018, II, 18–19 = P. Louvre N 3157, 40. Sequence omitted in P. Turin 1861 B, in lacuna in P. Louvre N 3159, 20. Var. P. Cairo CG 58007, V, 1 = P. Louvre N 3174, 38: *twỉ ḫꜥ.kwỉ*. P. Louvre N 3148, VIII, 36: *di.k ḫꜥ.n.ỉ*. On the manifestation of the deceased as an ibis, see P. BM EA 10109, **line 2**.

II, 1–2

ỉw.ỉ m sḫm n Wsỉr Wn-nfr mꜣꜥ-ḫrw. Same reading in P. Cairo CG 58007, V, 1–2 = P. Cairo CG 58018, II, 19–20 = P. Louvre N 3148, VIII, 38–40 = P. Louvre N 3157, 41. Sequence truncated in P. Turin 1861 B, 36 (only *Wn-nfr mꜣꜥ-ḫrw* may be read); partly in lacuna in P. Louvre N 3159, 20. Omission of *mꜣꜥ-ḫrw* in P. BM EA 10304, 36; P. Louvre N 3174, 40: *ꜥnḫ wḏꜣ snb* instead of *mꜣꜥ-ḫrw*.

On the deceased as the *sḫm* of a deity, see *supra*, **I, 3**.

II, 2–3

Ỉ ḫr.tw r rn.ỉ. ỉw.ỉ m hb m mḥ 5 ỉw psḏ.ỉ m wꜣḏ Šmꜥ. Same reading in P. Cairo CG 58018, II, 20–2 = P. Louvre N 3148, VIII, 40–3 = P. Louvre N 3174, 41–3 = P. Turin 1861 B, 36–8. Sequence partly in lacuna in P. Louvre N 3159, 20. Var. P. BM EA 10304, 37: *kꜣ.tw* instead of *ḫr.tw*; P. Louvre N 3159, 20 = P. Cairo CG 58007, V, 2: *Ỉ ḫr.tw rn.ỉ*; P. Louvre N 3157, 41–2: *Ḏḥwty, m rn.ỉ*. P. Cairo CG 58007, V, 3: *n mḥ 5*. Cf. also *infra*, **II, 20–1**: *Ỉ kꜣ.tw m rn.ỉ*.

On the assimilation of the deceased to an ibis, see *supra*, **II, 1**.

II, 3

ỉw.ỉ m nṯr wr pr m sktt. Same reading in P. BM EA 10304, 37–8 = P. Cairo CG 58007, V, 3 = P. Cairo CG 58018, II, 22 = P. Louvre N 3148, VIII, 43–4 = P. Louvre N 3157, 43 = P. Louvre N 3174, 43–4 = P. Turin 1861 B, 39. Sequence in lacuna in P. Louvre N 3159, 21. This 'great god' is Osiris (*BD* ch. 142, 2, Lepsius), or Re, both often designated *nṯr ꜥꜣ*.

II, 3–4

ỉw.ỉ m ḥḏ pr ḫr ḏw ỉꜣbtt. Same reading in P. BM EA 10304, 38 = P. Cairo CG 58007, V, 4 = P. Cairo CG 58018, II, 23 = P. Louvre N 3148, VIII, 44–5 = P. Louvre N 3157, 44 = P. Louvre N 3174, 44–5 = P. Turin 1861 B, 40–1. Sequence partly in lacuna in P. Louvre N 3159, 21.

The 'Mountain of the East' is a rarely attested designation (cf. *GDG* VI, 116) of the Arabian chain. On the various provenances of silver, see J.R. Harris, *Lexical Studies in Ancient Egyptian Minerals* (Berlin 1961), p. 42, without reference to the present example. An original passage of the Book of Breathing, known only from P. Louvre N 3174, 71–2, and N 3220 A, 8–9,[50] evokes 'the silver which comes from the desert' (*ḥḏ pr m ḫꜣswt*).

II, 4–5

ꜥḳ.ỉ sktt ḫnd.ỉ mꜥnḏt ỉw.ỉ m snw n Rꜥ-Ḥr-ꜣḫty. Same reading in P. BM EA 10304, 38–9 = P. Cairo CG 58007, V, 4–5 = P. Cairo CG 58018, III, 1–2 = P. Louvre N 3148, VIII, 46–7 = P. Turin 1861 B, 43. Var. P. Louvre N 3157, 44: *ꜥḳ.n.ỉ*; P. Louvre N 3159, 21:[51] *r sktt*. P. Louvre N 3174, 46: *ỉw.ỉ m-ḫnw Rꜥ-Ḥr-ꜣḫty*, by confusion between the hieratic forms of  and . Cf. too P. Cairo CG 58007, V, 5 and, for the activity of the deceased in the *mꜥnḏt*- and *sktt*-barks, P. BM EA 10201, **II, 5–6**.

II, 5–6

di.w n.ỉ ỉꜣw ỉmyw wỉꜣ sn tꜣ ỉn ỉst Rꜥ. Same reading in P. BM EA 10304, 39–40 = P. Cairo CG 58018, III, 2–3[52] = P. Louvre N 3148, VIII, 47–IX, 1. Sequence partly in lacuna in P. Louvre N 3159, 22. Var. P. Louvre N 3157, 46: *di.w n.ỉ ỉꜣw ỉn ỉmyw wỉꜣ*. P. Cairo CG 58007, V, 5 = P. Louvre N 3174, 46–7: *di.w n.ỉ ỉꜣw ỉn ỉmyw sktt*; P. Turin 1861 B, 43–4: *di.tw n.ỉ ỉꜣw ỉn ỉmyw sktt*.[53]

On the correlation of *di ỉꜣw* and (*ỉr*) *sn tꜣ*, cf. e.g. *BD* ch. 110 (ed. Budge, p. 223, 3). For this concept, cf. *BD* ch. 15 (ed. Budge, p. 44, 6–7) = *Urk.* IV, 1819, 4–5 = M. Vallogia, *RdE* 40 (1989), p. 140:

ỉr.tw n.k ḥknw m wỉꜣ	'Praises are addressed to you in the *wỉꜣ*-bark[54]
nis.tw.k m mꜥnḏt	and you are summoned in the *mꜥnḏt*-bark.'

II, 6–7

ꜥḳ.ỉ ḥs.tw pr.ỉ mr.tw m Dwꜣt nt Ḥwt Bnbn. Same reading in P. BM EA 10304, 40 = P. Cairo CG 58018, III, 4–5 = P. Louvre N 3157, 47–9 = P. Louvre N 3159, 22. Sequence omitted in P. Turin 1861 B. Var. P. Cairo CG 58007, V, 6: *ꜥḳ.ỉ ḥs mr.tw pr.ỉ mr.tw*; P. Louvre N 3148, IX, 1: *ꜥḳ.ỉ ḥs.ỉ pr.ỉ mr.tw*. P. Louvre N 3174, 47–8: *ꜥḳ.n.ỉ ḥs.tw mr.tw pr.ỉ mr.tw*.

On the pairing *ꜥḳ ḥs / pr mr*, see *LPE*, pp. 145–6 (III, 1).

The 'crypt of the Mansion of the obelisk' seems to be not otherwise known, but for the existence of a Duat in Heliopolis, see P. BM EA 10116, **line 24**. Cf. too P. BM EA 10201, **II, 5**, on the movements of the deceased in the Mansion of the obelisk.

II, 7

ḏd.w n.ỉ dwn twk nḏm ỉb.k. Same reading in P. Louvre N 3157, 49–50. Sequence in lacuna in P. Louvre N 3159, 23. Var. P. BM EA 10304, 41 = P. Cairo CG 58018, III, 5[55] = P. Louvre N 3148, IX, 2: *dwn.k*; P. Cairo CG 58007, V, 7: *dwn.ỉ*. P. Louvre N 3148, IX, 2 = P. Louvre N 3174, 49 = P. Cairo CG 58007, V, 7: *ỉb.ỉ*.

The verb *dwn* is used in these versions either intransitively (P. BM EA 10304, P. Cairo CG 58007, P. Cairo CG 58018), or, as here, with the independent pronoun with pronominal force. The sense here is proba-

47. After this sequence, this manuscript ends the litany with the phrase [*mỉ*] *rwḏ rn.ỉ m-ḫnw Ỉꜣt Ḏꜣm m-bꜣḥ nꜣ nṯrw pꜣwtyw r nḥḥ ḏt mỉ rwḏ rn.sn* [...], 'May my name endure in the Mound of Djeme before the primordial gods for ever and eternally'. Amend here the transcription of this passage by Lieblein, *Que mon nom fleurisse*, p. lxiv.
48. Last line of this manuscript.
49. The form  in P. BM EA 10304, 36 = P. Cairo CG 58018, III, 7 = P. Louvre N 3148, VIII, 38 = P. Louvre N 3174, 40 seems to require the reading *mwt.ỉ*. The transcription by Golenischeff (*Pap. Hiérat.* I, p. 79) should be amended accordingly. See also *supra*, p. 65, n. 82, p. 68, n. 98 and p. 95, n. 39.
50. P. Louvre N 3220 A belongs actually to P. Louvre N 3148; it constitutes a segment of it which has previously been considered lost (Goyon, *Rituels funéraires*, p. 236, n. 2).
51. The sign *m* before *mꜥnḏt* should be removed in the transcription by Lieblein, *Que mon nom fleurisse*, p. lxiv.
52. The transcription 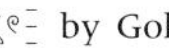 by Golenischeff, *Pap. hiérat.* I, p. 79, is erroneous. Read: .
53. The parallel with P. BM EA 10110 + 10111 stops here, and resumes only in II, 20.
54. The reference is to the bark of Re, cf. A. Piankoff, *Mythological Papyri* (New York 1957), p. 158, and Niwiński, *Seconde trouvaille*, p. 125: *ỉr.tw n.k ḥknw m wỉꜣ n Rꜥ*.
55. The verb *nḏm* was read wrongly as *sḫm* by Golenischeff, *Pap. hiérat.* I, p. 78.

bly 'extend (one's step)' (cf. the expression *dwn gst*, *Wb.* V, 431, 15), in parallel with *wsṯn*, occurring shortly afterwards.

A similar phrase is found in P. BM EA 10209, II, 31 (Haikal, *Two Hier. Fun. Pap.* I, pp. 34–5): *ḏd.w n.k dwn tw ꜥnḫ ib.k*.

II, 7–8

wsṯn nmtt.i m kꜣr štꜣ. Same reading in P. Louvre N 3148, IX, 2 = P. Louvre N 3159, 23.[56] Var. P. BM EA 10304, 41: *wsṯn.i* (*sic*); P. Louvre N 3174, 49: *nmtt.k*; P. Cairo CG 58018, III, 5–6 = P. Louvre N 3157, 50 tie, with variant, this sequence to the foregoing (*ḏd.w n.i dwn.k nḏm ib.k*) *m sḫn nmt.i m kꜣr štꜣ*; P. Cairo CG 58007, V, 7–8: *wsṯn.i m Wsir* (cf. *infra*, **II, 9**). For *wsṯn nmtt*, cf. Meeks, *ALex* 78.1106.

II, 8

ḫꜥ.i m mwt.i m Ḥr nfr n nwb. Same reading in P. Louvre N 3148, IX, 2–3 = P. Louvre N 3159, 23. Sequence omitted in P. Cairo CG 58007. Var. P. BM EA 10304, 41 = P. Cairo CG 58018, III, 6:[57] *n mwt.i*. P. Louvre N 3174, 50: *mwt.s*; P. Louvre N 3157, 51: *m-ḫnw mwt.i*.[58]

A transformation of the deceased into a golden falcon is evoked in the *Ritual of Embalming*, III, 20 (ed. Sauneron, p. 9).

II, 8–9

m hb km ḥꜣt pḥ. Sequence omitted in P. Cairo CG 58007; partly in lacuna in P. Louvre N 3159, 23–4. Omission of *ḥꜣt* in P. BM EA 10304, 42 = P. Cairo CG 58018, III, 8 = P. Louvre N 3148, IX, 3 = P. Louvre N 3157, 52 = P. Louvre N 3174, 51.

II, 9

ꜥḳ.i r Wsir. Same reading in P. Cairo CG 58018, III, 8 = P. Louvre N 3148, IX, 3. Sequence in lacuna in P. Louvre N 3159, 24. Omission of suffix *.i* in P. Louvre N 3174; 51. P. Cairo CG 58007, 7–8 (cf. *supra*, **II, 7–8**) adds without interruption *wsṯn.i* to *m Wsir*. Var. P. Louvre N 3157, 52: *ꜥḳ.n.i i-ir Wsir*.

sḏm.f mdw.i m pr.i m ẖt ḥnꜥ.f. Sequence partly in lacuna in P. Louvre N 3159, 24. Omission of *m* before *pr.i* in P. BM EA 10304, 42 = P. BM EA 58007, V, 8 = P. Cairo CG 58018, III, 8 = P. Louvre N 3148, IX, 3 = P. Louvre N 3157, 53 = P. Louvre N 3174, 51. Var. P. Cairo CG 58007, 8: *pr.i n.i* (*sic*) *m ẖt ḥnꜥ.f*; P. Louvre N 3157, 53 = P. Louvre N 3174, 19: *pr.n.i*.

pr m ẖt: 'come forth from the womb', i.e. 'be born'. See also *infra*, **II, 19**.

II, 10

di.f n.i ꜥꜣ wsr im.f. Same reading in P. Louvre N 3159, 24.[59] Var. P. BM EA 10304, 43 = P. Louvre N 3148, IX, 3–4 = P. Louvre N 3174, 52: *wsr.i*. P. Louvre N 3157, 53: *ꜥꜣwy*; P. BM EA 58018, III, 9: *di.f n.i ꜥꜣwy* ( ) *wsṯn.i im.f*; P. Cairo CG 58007, V, 8–9: *di.f n.i ꜥ wsr.i* (?) *im.f*.[60]

II, 10–11

iw.i m nb hrw ꜥšꜣ ḫprw. Same reading in P. BM EA 10304, 43 = P. Cairo CG 58018, III, 9–10 = P. Louvre N 3157, 54 = P. Louvre N 3159, 24 = P. Louvre N 3174, 52. Var. P. Louvre N 3148, IX, 4: *m*, 'as', instead of *iw.i*.

For these epithets, characteristic of solar deities: Assmann, *Liturgische Lieder*, p. 205.

II, 11

sꜥm.i ḥwt ḥnꜥ Itm. Same reading in P. BM EA 10304, 43–4 = P. Cairo CG 58018, III, 10–11 = P. Louvre N 3157, 55 = P. Louvre N 3174, 53. Sequence in lacuna in P. Louvre N 3159, 25. Omission of suffix *.i* after *sꜥm* in P. Louvre N 3148, IX, 4.

On this sequence, see P. BM EA 10191, **I, 11–12**.

II, 11–12

ḥms.i ḥr nn nw Šw. Same reading in P. BM EA 10304, 44 = P. Cairo CG 58018, III, 11. Sequence partly in lacuna in P. Louvre N 3157, 55–6, P. Louvre N 3159, 25 and P. Louvre N 3174, 53. Var. P. Louvre N 3148, IX, 4: *ḥms.i ḥr ḫytyw* ? ( ) *ḥr* (*blank*) *n Šw*.

The verb *ḥms*, constructed with *ḥr* + name of offering, is apparently not known outside this text. From the context of sustenance already present in the preceding clause, the action here may be considered to have some relation to eating (cf. *ḥms m wḥꜥ*, *LPE*, p. 136 [II, 22]).

The word read here as *nn* (cf. Wilson, *A Ptolemaic Lexikon*, p. 523), clearly denoting a category of loaf or offering, is attested in connection with Shu only in this passage. Except in P. Cairo CG 58018, III, 11, which gives the form [61], and in P. Louvre N 3148, IX, 4 (*blank*), it is regularly written [61] (P. BM EA 10304, 44 = P. Louvre N 3174, 53). The word might perhaps be identified with the noun *nn* written (*Wb.* II, 275, 1, citing as sole example the onomasticon of Amenemope, 6, 15 = Gardiner, *AEO* II, p. 231*, no. 535).

II, 12

šsp.i ḳbḥ ḥnꜥ Wsir. Same reading in P. BM EA 10304, 44 = P. Cairo CG 58018, III, 12 = P. Louvre N 3148, IX, 5. Sequence partly in lacuna in P. Louvre N 3157, 56, and partly erased in P. Louvre N 3159, 25. Var. P. Louvre N 3174, 53–4: *šsp.n.i*. Cf. P. Cairo CG 58010, 7: *mi šsp.i ḳbḥ ḥnꜥ Wsir*, 'May I receive water with Osiris!'

ꜣḫ.i ḥnꜥ.f r nṯr nb. Same reading in P. BM EA 10304, 44 = P. Cairo CG 58018, III, 12–13. Sequence erased in P. Louvre N 3159, 25. Var. P. Louvre N 3174, 55: *ꜣḫ.n.i*, *nbw*; P. Louvre N 3148, IX, 5: *nṯrw nb*; P. Louvre N 3157, 56: *ḥnꜥ wr nṯr* ... (?)

II, 12–13

ḳbḥ n.i nꜣ nbw ḳbḥ ꜥwy ḥr ḥwt m ḫrt-hrw nt rꜥ nb. Same reading in P. BM EA 10304, 45 = P. Cairo CG 58018, III, 13–14 = P. Louvre N 3148, IX, 5–6. Sequence partly in lacuna in P. Louvre N 3157, 56–7 = P. Louvre N 3159, 25–6. Var. P. Louvre N 3174, 54–5: *nꜣ nbw Iwnw*, 'the lords of Heliopolis'.

II, 13–17

This whole passage, raising the various wishes of the deceased in the form of invocations to different deities, is found in a number of copies of the Second Book of Breathing: P. BM EA 10199, 26–9 = P. BM EA 10304, 44–7 = P. Cairo CG 58018, III, 14–21 = P. Louvre N 3148, IX, 6–8 = P. Louvre N 3157, 57–8[62] = P. Louvre N 3159, 26–8 = P. Louvre N 3174, 55–9. In inspiration, it recalls the gift of offerings on the part of

56. Amend here the transcription by Lieblein, *Que mon nom fleurisse*, p. lxiv. Read: .

57. The transcriptions ? and by Golenischeff, *Pap. hiérat.* I, p. 78, are erroneous. Read: and .

58. Note here the spelling of *ḫꜥ.i*: and *mwt.i*: ; see *supra*, p. 97, n. 49.

59. Amend here the transcription by Lieblein (*Que mon nom fleurisse*, p. lxv). Read: .

60. P. Cairo CG 58007 ends here.

61. Or .

62. The following part of this manuscript is lost.

certain specialized deities, variously formulated in a great number of sources;[63] cf. Assmann, *JEA* 65 (1979), p. 72 with n. 133. It may be compared with the standard phrasing *stwt n Rꜥ ṯꜣw n Ỉmn mw n Ḥꜥpy nnk st r ꜣw ḏt*, 'The rays of Re, the breath of Amun, the water of Hapy, this belongs to me for ever'; see P. BM EA 10191, **II, 33–4**.

II, 13–14

ỉ Ỉmn mi n.ỉ ṯꜣw nḏm ink sꜣ.k mr.k. Same reading in P. BM EA 10304, 44–5 = P. Louvre N 3148, IX, 6 = P. Louvre N 3159, 26. Var. P. Cairo CG 58018, III, 15: *mḥyt nḏm(t)*; Omission of *n.ỉ* in P. Louvre N 3174, 55. P. BM EA 10199, 26, substitutes for *ink sꜣ.k mr.k*: *r fnḏ.ỉ*, 'for my nose'. Cf. too P. Cairo CG 58014, 12–13:

ỉ Ỉmn di.k n.ỉ ṯꜣw nḏm r fnḏ.ỉ	'O Amun, give me sweet breath for my nose,
ink bꜣ šps pr im.k	(for) I am a noble ba that has come forth from you.'

For Amun as provider of breath, see P. BM EA 10048, **II, 3–4**; P. BM EA 10191, **II, 7–8** and **12–13**.

II, 14–15

ỉ Rꜥ mi n.ỉ stwt.k mi mꜣꜣ.ỉ twk m ḫrt-hrw nt rꜥ nb. Same reading in P. BM EA 10304, 46 = P. Louvre N 3148, IX, 6–7 = P. Louvre N 3174, 56–7. Sequence partly in lacuna in P. Louvre N 3159, 26–7. Omission of suffix *.ỉ* after *mꜣꜣ* in P. Cairo CG 58018, III, 16. The wish for daily sight of the rays of the sun is a common theme of solar hymns; see P. BM EA 10048, **III, 4–5** and **6**.

II, 15–16

ỉ Ḥꜥpy mi n.ỉ ḳbḥ. Same reading in P. BM EA 10304, 47 = P. Louvre N 3148, IX, 7. Sequence partly in lacuna in P. Louvre N 3159, 27. Omission of *n.ỉ* in P. Louvre N 3174, 57. For Hapy provider of the libation see *LPE*, p. 253 (VIII, 6–7).

II, 16

Npri mi n.ỉ tꜣ. Same reading in P. BM EA 10304, 47. Var. P. Cairo CG 58018, III, 17 = P. Louvre N 3148, IX, 7 = P. Louvre N 3159, 27: *Np(r)it*; P. Louvre N 3174, 58: *ỉ Npri*.
On Nepri, god of grain, see F.R. Herbin, *RdE* 35 (1984) p. 112, n. 23; for *Np(r)it*, see W. Guglielmi, *LÄ* IV, 981 with n. 47; Leitz, *LGG* IV, p. 202–4.

II, 17

Mnḳt mi n.ỉ ḥnḳt. Same reading in P. BM EA 10304, 47 = P. Cairo CG 58018, III, 18 = P. Louvre N 3148, IX, 7–8 = P. Louvre N 3159, 27 = P. Louvre N 3174, 58–9.

For Menqet and beer: F.R. Herbin, *RdE* 35 (1984), p. 114, n. 28; W. Guglielmi, in *Aspekte spätägyptischer Kultur* (Fs. Erich Winter) (*AegTrev* 7, 1994), pp. 113–32; Leitz, *LGG* III, p. 317–8.

ꜣḫt mi n.ỉ irṯt. Same reading in P. BM EA 10304, 48 = P. Cairo CG 58018, III, 19 = P. Louvre N 3148, IX, 8 = P. Louvre N 3174, 59. Sequence partly in lacuna in P. Louvre N 3159, 27–8.

On Akhet (the 'luminous cow'), a form of Hathor: *LPE*, p. 125 (II, 8–9); Leitz, *LGG* I, p. 48–9.

II, 18

ꜥwy.ỉ fꜣ.w r šsp prt-ḫrw tꜣ ḥnḳt kꜣw ꜣpdw. Sequence in lacuna in P. Louvre N 3159, 28. Var. P. Cairo CG 58018, III, 20–1: *r iṯ*; addition of: *ṯꜣw ḥr sḏt*, 'grains of incense on the flame'; omission of *tꜣ ḥnḳt kꜣw ꜣpdw* in P. BM EA 10199, 29 = P. BM EA 10304, 48 = P. Louvre N 3148, IX, 8 = P. Louvre N 3174, 60.

II, 19

ink pr m ḫt ḥnꜥ Wsir nn ḥr.ỉ r.f m ḫrt-nṯr. Same reading in P. BM EA 10304, 48–9 = P. Cairo CG 58018, III, 21–2 = P. Louvre N 3148, IX, 8–9 = P. Louvre N 3159, 28. Omission of suffix *.ỉ* after *ḥr* in P. Louvre N 3174, 61. P. BM EA 10199, 29, replaces this sequence with the words *nn ws r nḥḥ ḥnꜥ ḏt*.
For *pr m ḫt*, see *supra*, **II, 9**.

II, 20–1

mi n.ỉ ꜥnḫ nꜣ nbw ꜥnḫ ink hb wḥm ꜥnḫ Ỉ kꜣ.tw m rn.ỉ. Same reading in P. Cairo CG 58018, III, 22–4 = P. Louvre N 3148, IX, 9–10. Sequence partly in lacuna in P. Louvre N 3159, 28–9. Omission of *mi n.ỉ ꜥnḫ nꜣ nbw ꜥnḫ* in P. Cairo CG 58013, 21 = P. Turin 1861 B, 44;[64] of *n.ỉ* in P. Louvre N 3174, 61. Var. P. BM EA 10304, 50: *Ḏḥwty* instead of *Ỉ*; P. Louvre N 3174, 61: *nꜣ nbw ꜥnḫw* (); P. Cairo CG 58013, 21: *r rn.ỉ*.
On the identification of the deceased with an ibis, see *supra*, **II, 1** and P. BM EA 10109, **line 2**.
The 'lords of life': Leitz, *LGG* III, p. 806.

II, 21

ꜥnḫ nṯrw nbw[65] *m dm rn.ỉ r nḥḥ ḏt*. Same reading in P. BM EA 10304, 50[66] = P. Cairo CG 58018, III, 24 = P. Louvre N 3148, IX, 10.[67] = P. Turin 1861 B, 45–6.[68] Sequence partly in lacuna in P. Louvre N 3159, 29.[69] Var. P. Louvre N 3174, 63: *r nḥḥ ḥnꜥ ḏt*.

II, 22–31

This final section of the text is unparalleled among the documents consulted containing the Second Book of Breathing.

II, 22

rꜣ-ꜥwy r.k nty sꜣ.k mr.k kꜣw.f r bw ḫr kꜣ.k. On the word *rꜣ-ꜥwy*, cf. R. El Sayed, *BIFAO* 84 (1984), p. 145, n. (s). *Nty* is clearly not the relative, but a writing of the genitival adjective *n*, common in the Late Period (A. Erman, *Neuägyptische Grammatik* § 214). On insertion of the dative *r.k* before *nty*, see Lefebvre, *Grammaire* § 151.
kꜣw: not the kas of the deceased, which would make little sense in this context, but the food and drink given to the deceased. On this meaning of the word *kꜣ*, see J. Assmann, *JEA* 65 (1979), pp. 63–4, n. (k).

II, 23

nḏm (?) *m rꜣ.f r rdi(t) st m-bꜣḥ.k*. Passage of uncertain interpretation. The first problem is raised by the group 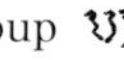, for which the transcription is

63. For the pairings Hapy/water, Nepri/bread, Hesat/milk, Hathor/beer, cf. e.g. Turin 125, G. Jourdain, *La tombe du scribe royal Amenemopet* (*MIFAO* 73, 1939), p. 42; Boeser, *Beschreibung* X, p. 4; G. Maspero, *RT* 36 (1914), pp. 144–5; W. Spiegelberg, *ZÄS* 50 (1912), pp. 41–2; offering-table Cairo CG 23127 (A. Kamal, *Tables d'offrandes* [*CGC*], 1906–9, p. 102).
64. See *supra*, n. 53.
65. *nb* in P. BM EA 10304 = P. Cairo CG 58013, 21 = P. Turin 1861 B.
66. The manuscript ends here.
67. Here ends the parallel with P. BM EA 10110 + 10111. The following of the text shows a copy of *BD* ch. 162.
68. The manuscript ends here.
69. The parallel with P. BM EA 10110 + 10111 ends here. The following text corresponds (lines 29–32) to a text unknown elsewhere, with a titulary of the deceased, and then (lines 33–42) to a text also known, with some variants, by P. Louvre N 3148, X, x + 8–XI, 11 and P. Beck, 1–13.

not sure. It is tempting to read *nḏm*, but palaeographical comparison with the clearly written form of the same word in line 25 reveals substantial difference. Another difficulty lies in the ambiguity of *m rꜣ.f*, which might denote equally either the mouth of the deceased or the entrance to the place (*bw*), both cited in line 22. The determinative of the word *rꜣ* argues in favour of the first hypothesis, but might be due to confusion in transmission.

ḥr ꜥꜣ wr n mnḫw.k. Cf. the expression *n ꜥꜣ n mnḫ.f*, Meeks, *ALex* 79.1233.

II, 23–4
mi ir it n ḥꜥꜣw r sꜥnḫ.sn m di.f n.sn. On the word *ḥꜥꜣw*, denoting children during the period of growth, see *LPE*, p. 163 (III, 21). For another reference to the relation between a *ḥꜥꜣ* and a parent, cf. D. Jankuhn, *Das Buch 'Schutz des Hauses'* (Bonn 1971), p. 68.

II, 24–5
wr.wy nn ḫt m ḏbꜥw.f r-nty wn m ḥtp. As suggested by the determinative, *wn m ḥtp* seems to be a designation of a book (cf. S. Schott, *Bücher und Bibliotheken*, Wiesbaden 1990, p. 156, nos 433–5 b).

II, 25–6
nḏm ib.k m bw mꜣꜥ ḥr nn ws n kꜣw.k m sꜣ.k. Cf. *P.* Cairo CG 58034, 6: *nn ws n ḏfꜣw.f*. Cf. stela Vienna 5857, 8 (G. Vittmann, *SAK* 22 [1995], pp. 289 and 320, n. 195: *nn wšr.n kꜣ.t*, 'dein Ka hat keinen Mangel').

sꜣ is here translated 'house' (*Wb.* IV, 13, 4), but, one cannot exclude *Wb.* IV, 13, 8: 'Speicher', 'Magazin'.

II, 26
wsṯn nmtt<.k> m-ḫnt ww Mꜣꜥt ḥr ṯt.k. For the reading *wsṯn nmtt* of , see *supra*, **II, 7–8**. The 'region of Maat' is otherwise attested only in the designation *wsḫt ww Mꜣꜥt*; see P. BM EA 10108, **line 5**.

II, 27–9
ꜣḫ.tw m mrwt ḥnꜥ nfr n kꜣ.k nn nfy n rn.k m wḏwt n ḫpr ḫnt m ꜥm ꜥḳw ḥr ḫpr r.k ḏbꜣ ḳrst.k imn sḫrw.k nhm r.k.

The translation of this passage remains uncertain. It is possible to recognize the phrase *m ꜥm ꜥḳw ḥr ḫpr r.k*, attested in several other documents (see P. BM EA 10108, **line 8**), but these provide no clear meaning.

II, 29–30
wpt rꜣ.k r nfr ꜣt r.s nty sḏm sprw. Lit.: 'The opening of your mouth (is performed) at the best moment for it, (that) of hearing petitions'. The construction of this phrase, if our interpretation is correct, seems somewhat over elaborate, but cf. line 22 of the papyrus: *rꜣ ꜥwy r.k nty sꜣ mr.k*.

II, 30
nsw nṯrw ḥḳꜣ imꜣḫt iṯ.f tw imytw ḥs(y)w.f. The 'king of the gods' is Osiris. Note the variant *ḥḳꜣ* for the designation of the god *ḥḳꜣ imꜣḫt* (*Wb.* I, 81, 24). For *imꜣḫt*, 'land of the blessed', cf. P. OIC 25389, XX, 9 (*pḥ.n.k*) and the earlier expression *st imꜣḫ*; Fischer, *ZÄS* 105 (1978), p. 43, n. 5. On the reception of the deceased among the praised ones of the god, see *LPE*, pp. 251–2 (VIII, 4–5).

II, 31
ḏd.k m rꜣ.k ir.w ḥr ḫrw.k ḫryt n kꜣ.f r ḥb.k inw. The determinative of *ḫryt* derives from confusion with (cf. Möller, *Pal.* III, nos 52 and 522). Here the word denotes a meat offering. For the expression *ir ḫryt*, see *Wb.* III, 322, 10. Another possible interpretation might be: 'one acts at your voice' if *ḫryt n kꜣ.f* is taken as a non-verbal phrase 'A meat offering is (made) for his ka'. For *ḥb inw*, see *Wb.* III, 252, 1–5; Meeks, *ALex* 782976.

P. BM EA 10304 (pls 60–1)

Salt Collection, 3, 1250.
Unpublished.
Quirke, *Owners*, no. 181.
E.A.W. Budge, *Guide to the Egyptian Collections in the British Museum* (1909), p. 63 (photograph).
Provenance: probably Thebes.
Date: first to second century AD.
Owner of the papyrus: *Pꜣ-di-wr-iꜣbt(t)* (Peteporegebthis). This person is also owner of P. BM EA 10191.
Mother of the owner: *Tꜣ-šrit-hry* (Senerieus).

Contents: Second Book of Breathing.

Manuscript of one sheet (c. 30.5 × 13.7 cm, allowing for break and part concealed by binding), broken horizontally at the level of line 29, with a tear in the upper right-hand section. The recto bears 49 lines in a small hand identical to that of the other papyrus of *Pꜣ-di-wr-iꜣbt(t)*.

Demotic text on the verso: The Book of Breathing which proceeds (*šm*) under his feet.[70]

Translation

Recto

(1) Thus speaks the Osiris [*Pꜣ-di-wr-*]*iꜣbt(t)*, justified, born of *Tꜣ-šrit-hry*, justified:

(2) O Re, [I am your son!] O Thoth, I am your beloved! O Osiris, I am your image! O Lord of Hermopolis, I am (3) your heir, [in truth! O Re-]Horakhty, O great Ennead, O lesser Ennead, may there endure (4) my name in [Thebes and] in the nomes for ever and eternally! May there endure the name of Atum lord of Heliopolis in Heliopolis!

(*Vertical column and incipit of lines 5–30*): (5) May my name endure within Thebes and within the nomes for ever and eternally, as the name endures of

(6) Shu in the upper Menset in Heliopolis,
(7) Tefnut in the lower Menset in Heliopolis,
(8) Geb in the place of the foreigners,
(9) Nut in the Mansion of *šnw*,
(10) Osiris foremost of the West in Abydos,

70. On this formulation, see *supra*, p. 2.

(11) Isis in Ta-wer,
(12) Horus in Pe,
(13) Wadjyt in Dep,
(14) Nephthys in Heliopolis,
(15) Banebdjed in the House of Banebdjed,
(16) Thoth in Hermopolis,
(17) the four Montus in their towns,
(18) Khnum in Elephantine,
(19) Haroeris in Ombos,
(20) Horus Behedety in Djeba,
(21) Nekhbet in Nekheb,
(22) all the gods in Thebes,
(23) Haroeris within Kus,
(24) Isis in Neter-shema,
(25) Hathor in Iq,
(26) Neferhotep in Diospolis Parva,
(27) Min in Ipu,
(28) Nemty in Wadjet,
(29) Wepwawet in Siut,
(30) [Hathor in Cusae],
(31) Hat[hor] in [He]benu,
(32) Anubis in Hardai,
(33) Harsaphes in Heracleopolis,
(34) Sobek in Merwer,
(35) Ptah, Sekhmet, Nefertum within Memphis.

(36) I cause that I appear as the great ibis come forth from the womb of my mother, for I am the image of Osiris-Wennefer (37). Thoth is said as my name, for I am an ibis of five cubits. My back is of malachite of Upper Egypt. I am the great god (38) come forth from the *sktt*-bark, I am the silver come forth from the mountain of the East. I enter the *sktt*-bark and tread (39) the *mꜥnḏt*-bark; I am the second of Re-Horakhty. They grant me adoration, those who are in the bark, and the land is embraced (40) by the crew of Re. I come praised and go beloved in the Duat of the Mansion of the obelisk. I am told: (41) stand up! May your heart be glad! My step is broad in the secret sanctuary. I appear from my mother (42) as the beautiful Horus of gold, as the ibis, black in rear. I reach Osiris, he hears my words when I come forth from the womb (43) with him. He causes that my might be great in him. I am lord of faces, numerous of forms. I consume offerings with (44) Atum, and I sit down for the *nnw*-loaves (?) of Shu. I receive libation with Osiris, and I am transfigured with him, more than any god. (45) The lords of libation make libation for me, (their) arms full of offerings, in the course of every day.

O Amun, grant me sweet air (46) (for) I am your son your beloved. O Re, give me your rays, may I see you in the course of every day! (47) O Hapy, give me libation! Nepri, give me bread! Menqet, give me beer! (48) Akhet, give me milk! My arms are raised to receive invocation offering. I am the one who comes forth (49) from the womb with Osiris, and I am not far from him in the god's domain. Give me life, lords of life, (for) I am an ibis (5) whose life is renewed. Thoth is uttered as my name, and all gods live pronouncing my name for ever and eternally.

Commentary

Line 1
ḫr.f n Wsỉr N. For this expression see P. BM EA 10191, **I, 1**.

Lines 2–3
ỉ Rꜥ [ỉnk sꜣ.k] ỉ Ỉ ỉnk mr.k ỉ Wsỉr ỉnk sḫm.k ỉ Nb-Ḫmnw ỉnk ỉwꜥ.k [n mꜣꜥt ỉ Rꜥ]-Ḥr-ꜣḫty ỉ Psḏt ꜥꜣt ỉ Psḏt nḏst. On this invocation, see P. BM EA 10110 + 10111, **I, 2–5**.

Lines 3–4
mỉ rwḏ rn.ỉ m-[ẖnw Wꜣst m-ẖ]nw spꜣwt r nḥḥ ḏt. See P. BM EA 10110 + 10111, **I, 4–5**.

Line 4
mỉ rwḏ rn n Ỉtm nb Ỉwnw m Ỉwnw. Note the original place of this sequence in the text. See P. BM EA 10110 + 10111, **I, 6**.

Lines 5–35
For the litany *mỉ rwḏ rn* and its attestations in sources prior to the Second Book of Breathing, see P. BM EA 10110 + 10111, **I, 7–37**.

Line 6
Šw m Mnst ḥrt m Ỉwnw. See P. BM EA 10110 + 10111, **I, 8**.

Line 7
Tfnwt m Mnst ẖrt m Ỉwnw. See P. BM EA 10110 + 10111, **I, 9**.

Line 8
Gb m bw šmꜣw. See P. BM EA 10110 + 10111, **I, 10**.

Line 9
Nwt m ḥwt šnw. See P. BM EA 10110 + 10111, **I, 11**.

Line 10
Wsỉr ḫnty Ỉmntt m ꜣbḏw. See P. BM EA 10110 + 10111, **I, 12**.

Line 11
Ỉst m Ṯꜣ-wr. See P. BM EA 10110 + 10111, **I, 13**.

Line 12
Ḥr m P. See P. BM EA 10110 + 10111, **I, 14**.

Line 13
Wꜣḏyt m Dp. See. P. BM EA 10110 + 10111, **I, 15**.

Line 14
Nbt-ḥwt m Ỉwnw. See P. BM EA 10110 + 10111, **I, 16**.

Line 15
Bꜣ-nb Ḏdw m pr Bꜣ-nb-Ḏdw. See P. BM EA 10110 + 10111, **I, 17** with n. 32 for the confusion between *Ḏdw* and *Ḏdt*.

Line 16
Ỉ m Ḫmnw. See P. BM EA 10110 + 10111, **I, 18**.

Line 17
Mnṯw 4 m-ẖnw nỉwwt.sn. See P. BM EA 10110 + 10111, **I, 19**.

Line 18
Ḫnmw m ꜣbw. See P. BM EA 10110 + 10111, **I, 20**.

Line 19
Ḥr-wr m Nwbt. See P. BM EA 10110 + 10111, **I, 21**.

Line 20
Ḥr Bḥdty m Ḏbꜣ. See P. BM EA 10110 + 10111, **I, 22**.

Line 21
Nḫbt m Nḫb. See P. BM EA 10110 + 10111, **I, 23**.

Line 22
nṯrw nbw m Wꜣst. See P. BM EA 10110 + 10111, **I, 24**.

Line 23
Ḥr-wr m-ḫnw Gsy. See P. BM EA 10110 + 10111, **I, 25**.

Line 24
Ỉst m Nṯr-šmꜥ. See P. BM EA 10110 + 10111, **I, 26**.

Line 25
Ḥwt-Ḥr m Ỉḳ. See P. BM EA 10110 + 10111, **I, 27**.

Line 26
Nfr-ḥtp m Ḥwt-sḫmw. See P. BM EA 10110 + 10111, **I, 28**.

Line 27
Mnw m Ỉpw. See P. BM EA 10110 + 10111, **I, 29**.

Line 28
Nmty m Wꜣḏt. See P. BM EA 10110 + 10111, **I, 30**.

Line 29
Wp-wꜣwt m Sꜣw. See P. BM EA 10110 + 10111, **I, 31**.

Line 30
Of this line, almost entirely obliterated by the break in the papyrus, only one trace remains, but the restoration *mi rwḏ rn n Ḥwt-Ḥr m Ḳs* is probable. See P. BM EA 10110 + 10111, **I, 32**.

Line 31
Ḥwt[*-Ḥr*] *m* [*Ḥ*]*bnw*. The name of the deity is partly in lacuna; one expects here the name of Horus, given in all other copies consulted, but the surviving traces indicate a different reading. See P. BM EA 10110 + 10111, **I, 33**.

Line 32
Ỉnpw m Ḥr-dy. See P. BM EA 10110 + 10111, **I, 34**.

Line 33
Ḥr-šfy m Ḥwt-nn-nsw. See P. BM EA 10110 + 10111, **I, 35**.

Line 34
Sbk m Mr-wr. See P. BM EA 10110 + 10111, **I, 36**.

Line 35
Ptḥ Sḫmt Nfr-tm m-ḫnw Mn-nfr. See P. BM EA 10110 + 10111, **I, 37**.

Line 36
di.i ḥꜥ.kwi m hb ꜥꜣ pr m ḫt n mwt.i. See P. BM EA 10110 + 10111, **II, 1**, with n. 49.

iw.i m sḫm n Wsir Wn-nfr. The usual version adds *mꜣꜥ-ḫrw* after *Wn-nfr*. See P. BM EA 10110 + 10111, **II, 1–2**.

Line 37
Ỉ kꜣ.tw r rn.i. Other sources: *ḫr.tw*. See P. BM EA 10110 + 10111, **II, 2**.

iw.i m hb m mḥ 5 psḏ.i m wꜣḏ Šmꜥ. See P. BM EA 10110 + 10111, **II, 2–3**.

Lines 37–8
iw.i m nṯr wr pr m sktt. See P. BM EA 10110 + 10111, **II, 3**.

Line 38
iw.i m ḥḏ pr m ḏw ỉꜣbtt. See P. BM EA 10110 + 10111, **II, 3–4**.

Lines 38–9
ꜥḳ.i sktt ḫnd.i mꜥnḏt iw.i m snw n Rꜥ-Ḥr-ꜣḫty. See P. BM EA 10110 + 10111, **II, 4–5**.

Line 39
di.w n.i ỉꜣw imyw wiꜣ. The sign 𓎛 legible before the word *ỉꜣw* is an error. The scribe, by a *lapsus calami*, began to write *wiꜣ*, and then corrected the determinative 𓊛 to 𓀢. See P. BM EA 10110 + 10111, **II, 5**.

Lines 39–40
sn tꜣ in ist Rꜥ. See P. BM EA 10110 + 10111, **II, 5–6**.

Line 40
ꜥḳ.i ḥs.tw pr.i mr.tw m Dwꜣt nt Ḥwt Bnbn. See P. BM EA 10110 + 10111, **II, 6–7**.

Lines 40–1
ḏdw<n>.i dwn.k nḏm ib.k. The omission of the *n* is probably due to the presence, at the beginning of line 39, of the word *in*, of which the *n* is placed immediately above the suffix *.i*. On this sequence, see P. BM EA 10110 + 10111, **II, 7**.

Line 41
wsṯn.i nmt.i m kꜣr štꜣ. On the different variants of this sequence, see P. BM EA 10110 + 10111, **II, 7–8**.

Lines 41–2
ḥꜥ.i n mwtt.i m Ḥr nfr n nwb m hb km pḥ. As in most versions, omission of *ḥꜣt* before *pḥ*. See P. BM EA 10110 + 10111, **II, 8–9**. On *mwt.i*, see *supra*, **line 36**.

Line 42
ꜥḳ.i r Wsir. See P. BM EA 10110 + 10111, **II, 9**.

Lines 42–3
sḏm.f mdw.i pr.i m ḫt ḥnꜥ.f. Other versions give *m* before *pr*. See P. BM EA 10110 + 10111, **II, 9**.

Line 43
di.f n.i ꜥꜣ wsr.i im.f. See P. BM EA 10110 + 10111, **II, 10**.

iw.i m nb ḫrw ꜥšꜣ ḫprw. See P. BM EA 10110 + 10111, **II, 10–11**.

Lines 43–4
sꜥm.i ḫwt ḥnꜥ Ỉtm. See P. BM EA 10110 + 10111, **II, 11**.

Line 44
ḥms.i ḥr nn nw Šw. See P. BM EA 10110 + 10111, **II, 11–12**.

šsp.i ḳbḥ ḫnꜥ Wsir ꜣḫ.i ḫnꜥ.f r nṯr nb. See P. BM EA 10110 + 10111, **II, 12**.

Line 45
ḳbḥ n.i nꜣ nbw ḳbḥ ꜥwy ḫr ḥwt m ẖrt-hrw nt rꜥ nb. See P. BM EA 10110 + 10111, **II, 12–13**.

Lines 45–8
For this passage, see P. BM EA 10110 + 10111, **II, 13–7**.

Lines 45–6
i Imn mi n.i ṯꜣw nḏm ink sꜣ.k mr.k. See P. BM EA 10110 + 10111, **II, 13–14**.

Line 46
i Rꜥ mi n.i stwt.k mi mꜣꜣ.i twk m ẖrt-hrw nt rꜥ nb. See P. BM EA 10110 + 10111, **II, 14–15**.

Line 47
i Ḥꜥpy mi n.i ḳbḥ. See P. BM EA 10110 + 10111, **II, 15–16**.

Npri mi n.i tꜣ. See P. BM EA 10110 + 10111, **II, 16**.

Mnḳt mi n.i ḥnḳt. See P. BM EA 10110 + 10111, **II, 17**.

Line 48
ꜣḫt mi n.i irṯt. See P. BM EA 10110 + 10111, **II, 17**.

ꜥwy.i fꜣ.w r šsp prt-ḫrw. The usual version adds *tꜣ ḥnḳt kꜣw ꜣpdw*. For the variants, see P. BM EA 10110 + 10111, **II, 18**.

Lines 48–9
ink pr m ḫt ḫnꜥ Wsir nn ḫr.i r.f m ẖrt-nṯr. See P. BM EA 10110 + 10111, **II, 19**.

Lines 49–50
mi n.i ꜥnḫ nꜣ nbw ꜥnḫ ink hb wḥm ꜥnḫ Ḏḥwty kꜣ.tw m rn.i. The other versions consulted here write *I* instead of *Ḏḥwty*. See P. BM EA 10110 + 10111, **II, 20–1**.

Line 50
ꜥnḫ nṯrw nb m dm rn.i r nḥḥ ḏt. See P. BM EA 10110 + 10111, **II, 21**.

Abridged Versions

P. BM EA 9977 (pls 62–3)

Salt Collection 1, 107.
Unpublished.
Quirke, *Owners*, no. 40.
Provenance: Thebes. Found with P. BM EA 9978 in the collective tomb of the archon Soter.[71]
Date: End of the first to beginning of the second century AD.
Owner of the papyrus: *Ḳn[dg]ꜣy*, *Ḳndgy*. Written also in Greek on the verso.
Mother of the owner: *Ṯꜣpꜣr* (Sapaulis).

Contents: Second Book of Breathing, abridged version.

Manuscript of one sheet (26.4 × 22.6 cm), broken on its whole width just below line 10 and on level with line 12, where only few signs are legible. The first line is written in hieroglyphs, all the others in hieratic.

Text on the verso: The Book of Breathing of the Hathor *Ḳndgy*, justified, born of [...]. (*Written below and in the opposite direction of the precedent line*): *KANΔAK[H]*.

Translation

(1) Hail Hathor mistress of the West of Djeme, great Ennead of the West,
(2) (*in a vertical column*): may the name endure of
(3) Atum, lord of Heliopolis in Heliopolis,
(4) Shu in the upper Menset in Heliopolis,
(5) Tefnut in the lower Menset in Heliopolis,
(6) Geb in the place of the foreigners,
(7) Nut in the Mansion of *šnws*,
(8) Isis in Ta-wer,
(9) Nephthys in Heliopolis,
(10) Osiris foremost of the West in Abydos,
(11) Thoth the very great, lord of Hermopolis.
(12) Come to the Hathor *Ḳn[dg]ꜣy* , justified,
(13) born of *Ṯꜣpꜣr*, for ever and eternally.

Commentary

Line 1
Ḥwt-Ḥr ḥnwt Imntt n[72] *Ḏꜣm*. On this rare epithet of Hathor, see W. Spiegelberg, *Demotica* II (Munich 1928), pp. 24–8; J.D. Ray, *GM* 45 (1981), pp. 57–8. It is also attested in P. dem. Louvre E 3452, I, 5–6[73] in which the owner of the manuscript bears among other titles that of *wꜥb n Ḥ.t-Ḥr ḥnwt Imnt n Ḏm*, 'priest of Hathor mistress of the West in Djeme'.

Psḏt ꜥꜣt Imntt. The great Ennead of the West (cf. *Psḏt ꜥꜣt ḫnt Imntt*; Boeser, *Beschreibung* X, p. 6) is probably to be identified here with that of Djeme; cf. P. BM EA 10116, **lines 27–30**.

Lines 2–11
Highly abridged version of the litany *mi rwḏ rn*, on which see P. BM EA 10110 + 10111, **I, 6–36**.

Line 3
Itm nb Iwnw m Iwnw. See P. BM EA 10110 + 10111, **I, 6**.

71. See *supra*, p. 6, no. **11** with n. 70, and p. 7. The coffin of Candace is lost.
72.  = *n* < *Nt*.

73. M. Smith, *The Demotic Mortuary Papyrus Louvre E. 3452* (unpublished dissertation, 1979), p. 14. The author sees in the mention of Djeme evidence for the place of origin of the owner of the manuscript.

Line 4
Šw n Mnst ḥrt m Ỉwnw. See P. BM EA 10110 + 10111, **I, 7**. For the writing  of *Mnst* (also attested in line 5), see supra, p. 93, n. 21.

Line 5
Tfnwt n Mnst ẖrt m Ỉwnw. See P. BM EA 10110 + 10111, **I, 8**.

Line 6
Gb n bw šmꜣw. See P. BM EA 10110 + 10111, **I, 9**. The current reading gives *m* instead of *n*.

Line 7
Nwt m Ḥwt šnws. See P. BM EA 10110 + 10111, **I, 10**.

Line 8
Ỉst m Ṯꜣ-wr. See P. BM EA 10110 + 10111, **I, 12**.

Line 9
Nbt-ḥwt m Ỉwnw. See P. BM EA 10110 + 10111, **I, 15**.

Line 10
Wsỉr ḫnty Ỉmntt m ꜣbḏw. See P. BM EA 10110 + 10111, **I, 11**.

Line 11
Ỉ ꜥꜣ wr nb Ḫmnw. See P. BM EA 10110 + 10111, **I, 17**.

Lines 12–13
mỉ n Ḥwt-Ḥr N ms n NN. The invocation is probably addressed either to Hathor, already mentioned in line 1, or to Hathor and the Ennead of the West (ibid.).

P. BM EA 10124 (pls 64–7)

Salt Collection 1, ?
Unpublished.
Quirke, *Owners*, no. 246.
Provenance: Thebes. Found with P. BM EA 10123 probably inside the now lost coffin of Senchonsis in the collective tomb of the archon Soter.[74]
Date: 146 AD.[75]
Owner of the papyrus: *Tꜣ-šrỉt-Ḫnsw* (Senchonsis) also called *Ṯꜣp(w)r* (Sapaulis). For the different variants in the writing of these names, see P. BM EA 10123.
Mother of the owner: *Ṯꜣḳḏꜣ* (Tkauthi).

Contents: Second Book of Breathing, abridged version, with some original elements.

Manuscript of one sheet (19.3 × 35.4 cm), in good condition, bearing ten lines in a hand identical to that of P. BM EA 10123.

Text on the verso: I enter the god's domain. The Book of Breathing of Thoth is my protection, (so that) I shall not be turned back from the god's domain ... (?) Field of reeds.

Translation

Recto

(1) You come and go in the god's domain. The Book of Breathing of Thoth is your protection. May the name endure of the father (*sic*) lord of Heliopolis in Heliopolis! May the names (*sic*) (2) endure of Shu in the upper place in Heliopolis! May the name endure of Tefnut in the lower place in Heliopolis! May the name endure of Geb in the place (3) of the foreigners! May the name endure of the Hathor *Tꜣ-šrỉt-Ḫnsw* also called *Ṯꜣp(w)r*, justified! May (4) the name endure of Nut in the mansion of *šnw*! May the name endure of the Hathor *Tꜣ-šrỉt-Ḫnsw* also called (5) *Ṯꜣp(w)r*, justified! May the names (*sic*) endure of Osiris foremost of the West in Abydos! May the names (*sic*) endure of Isis in Ta-wer! (6) May <the name endure> of Horus in Pe! May the names (*sic*) endure of the Hathor *Ṯꜣp(w)r* born of *Ṯꜣḳḏꜣ*! (7) May the names (*sic*) endure of Nephthys in the mansion of *šnw*! May I enter the Mansion of the Prince! May I assume any form (8) according to my *ỉb*-heart and my *ḥꜣty*-heart desire! May I enter upon the way of all gods in Thebes the victorious. May I adore (9) Osiris, the great of the Mound of Djeme! May I proceed to Heliopolis! May there <be> made <for me> a libation of water before Amenipet at the festival of the Valley!

Commentary

Line 1
ꜥḳ.ỉ šm.ỉ r ẖrt-nṯr. *ꜥḳ-šm* is the equivalent of the expressions *ꜥḳ-pr*, *šm-ỉỉ* and *hꜣ-pr*, more usually found (F.R. Herbin, *RdE* 50 [1999], p. 176, n. 51). The suffix pronoun is consistently written in this manuscript with the sign , which can convey either first or second person singular feminine. In line 8, the second person is observed in clear manner by a in *ꜥḳ.t*, whereas the pronoun *.ỉ*, written , occurs in line 8 in *ỉb.ỉ*, *ḥꜣty.ỉ* and *wš.ỉ*, and line 9 in *šm.ỉ*. The text of P. BM EA 10123, written for the same person, is in the first person, rendered either or (on verso).

šꜥt n snsn n Ỉ m sꜣ.ỉ Same phrase on the verso, and in P. BM EA 10125, 14 and P. BM EA 10048, III, 5. On the protection afforded by the Book of Breathing, drawn up by Thoth, see *LPE*, p. 255 (VIII, 9). The miswriting  for *šꜥt* also occurs on the verso.

mỉ rwḏ rn n ỉt (*sic*) *nb Ỉwnw m Ỉwnw*. Unexpected formulation of a wish usually expressed on the model 'May the name of N endure as the name of X divinity endures'. Here the model is inverted, evoking the name of the deceased three times (lines 3, 4 and 6), after the respective reference to the deities. Confusion affects the orthography of the optative particle *mỉ*, written normally  in lines 6, 7, 8 and 9, and  in lines 1, 2, 3, 5 and 7.

74. Cf. *supra*, p. 6, no. **20**, and p. 8.

75. After the Greek inscription of her coffin, see *supra*, p. 6, no. **19**.

 is, of course, an error for *Ỉtm*. See P. BM EA 10110 + 10111, **I, 7**.

Lines 1–2
mỉ rḏ rnw n. At several points in the manuscript, the scribe has written in error *rnw* instead of *rn*; cf. lines 4, 5 and 7.

Line 2
Šw m st ḥrt m Ỉwnw and *Tfnwt m st ḫrt m Ỉwnw*. The parallels give *Mnst ḥrt* or *Mnst ḫrt*. See P. BM EA 10110 + 10111, **I, 8** and **9**.

Lines 2–3
Gb m bw šmꜣw. See P. BM EA 10110 + 10111, **I, 10**.

Line 4
Nwt m Ḥwt šnw. See P. BM EA 10110 + 10111, **I, 11**.

Lines 4–5
mỉ rwḏ rnw n Ḥwt-Ḥr N. A translation 'as the name of the Hathor N endures', theoretically possible, remains problematic in view of the place of the phrase in the text, between mention of Nut of *Ḥwt-šnw* and of Osiris in Abydos, which usually follow in the sources. In line 6, the same sequence *mỉ rwḏ rnw n Ḥwt-Ḥr N*, is inserted between reference to Isis of Ta-wer and that to *Nbt-ḥwt* in *Ḥwt šnw*. The spelling , conveying either the optative or the adverb 'like', underscores the ambiguity (cf. *supra*, **line 1**).

Line 5
Wsỉr ḫnty Ỉmntt m ꜣbḏw. See P. BM EA 10110 + 10111, **I, 12**.

Ỉst m Tꜣ-wr. See P. BM EA 10110 + 10111, **I, 13**.

Line 6
Read: *mỉ <rwḏ rn> n Ḥr m P*. See P. BM EA 10110 + 10111, **I, 14**.

Line 7
Nbt-ḥwt m Ḥwt šnw. Before this sequence on Nephthys the scribe omits mention of Wadjyt in Dep, which regularly accompanies Horus of Pe. *Ḥwt šnw*, a sanctuary in the Heliopolitan nome encountered above in connection with Nut (cf. **line 4**), is not expected here; the toponym *Ỉwnw* is usually cited here; see P. BM EA 10110 + 10111, **I, 16**.

mỉ ꜥḳ.ỉ r ḥwt sr. On access of the deceased to the Mansion of the Prince, see P. BM EA 10201, **II, 4**.

Lines 7–8
mỉ ỉr.ỉ ḫpr nb r mr ỉb.ỉ ḥꜣty.ỉ. See P. BM EA 10123, **lines 7–8**.

Line 8
ꜥḳ.t ḥr wꜣt n nṯr nbw (*sic*) *m Wꜣst nḫt*. See P. BM EA 10123, **lines 6–7**.

Lines 8–9
mỉ wš.ỉ Wsỉr ꜥꜣ n Ỉꜣt Ḏꜣm. This title of Osiris occurs more often under the form *ꜥꜣ n Ḏꜣm* (*LPE*, p. 139 [II, 26]; P. dem. Louvre E 3452, II, 2). Another common designation is *Wsỉr ḥr-ỉb Ỉꜣt Ḏꜣm*.

Line 9
mỉ šm.ỉ r Ỉwnw. On access of the deceased into Heliopolis, see P. BM EA 10191, **I, 13–14**.

Lines 9–10
mỉ ḳbḥ mw m-bꜣḥ Ỉmn-Ỉpt n ḥb ỉnt. Read probably here *mỉ ḳbḥ<.w n.ỉ> mw*. The same omission occurs in P. BM EA 10123, 2, in the clause *mỉ ḳbḥ mw m ḥwt sr*, as compared with the usual version *mỉ ḳbḥ.w n.ỉ mw m ḥwt sr* (cf. P. BM EA 10191, **I, 12**).

The mention of Amenipet, generally evoked in the context of the rites of each decade in Djeme, instead of at the performance of a libation on the occasion of the festival of the Valley, reveals assimilation of two celebrations; see C. Traunecker, *La chapelle d'Achôris à Karnak* II (Paris 1981), pp. 136–7. P. BM EA 10124 provides one of the latest known attestations for the festival of the Valley (*LPE*, p. 134 ff.).

P. BM EA 10192 (pls 68–9)

Hay Collection.
Unpublished.
Provenance: probably Thebes.
Date: first to second century AD.
Owner of the papyrus: name lost.
Mother of the owner: *T(ꜣ)-ẖrd(t)-Mnw* (?).[76]

Contents: probably a part of the Second Book of Breathing, as suggested by a similar document, P. BM EA 10331.

Fragmentary manuscript (12.7 × 18.1 cm), only the end of which survives, bearing twelve incomplete lines of thick and clumsy writing.

Text on the verso: Come and go in the god's domain. Hathor causes your legs to go freely to [...].[77]

Translation

Recto

No funerary text remains on this fragment. Only the mother's name of the deceased is readable in each of the twelve lines of text, preceded by [*ms*] *n*, 'born of'. After P. BM EA 10331, one can restore their structure as follows: *mỉ rwḏ rn* + deity *ḫr N mꜣꜥ-ḫrw*, 'May the name endure of X-deity, by N, born of *T(ꜣ)-ẖrd-Mnw*, justified!'.

76. If this reading is correct, note the presence of *mꜣꜥ-ḫrw*, 'justified', before the sign of the god Min.

77. For the causative meaning of *wstn*, cf. *Ritual of Embalming*, V, 10 (ed. Sauneron, p. 16): (Hathor) *wstn.s rdwy.k m-ẖnw tꜣ ỉnt*, '(Hathor,) she causes your legs to go freely in the valley'.

P. BM EA 10264 (pls 70–1)

Unpublished.
Provenance: Thebes probably.
Date: first to second century AD
Owner of the papyrus: *Ἰst-wrt* (Esoeris).
Mother of the owner: name lost.

Contents: incomplete version of the Second Book of Breathing.

Two small fragments (8.6 × 7.4 cm and 8.6 × 5 cm) corresponding to each other, but between which a short part of text is missing, as line 3, which is attested in other documents, shows. The manuscript bears eight lines of a garbled text (mispellings and corrections) which is difficult to read at points. The beginning and the end of the lines are lost. Illegible traces on the verso.

Translation

(1)[...] *Ἰst-wrt*, born of [...] her lifetime is 6 years (?) [...] (2) [...] ... (?) Osiris ... (?) [...] Isis the great, mother of the god, the [great] goddess [...] (3) [...] May the name endure [of Shu in the] upper [Men]set in Heliopolis; may [the name] endure [of Tefnut in the lower Menset in Heliopolis]; [may the name endure of Geb] (4) in the place of forei[gners; may] the name endure of Nut in [the Mansion of the *šnw*-tree (?); [may the name endure of Osiris foremost of the West in] (5) Abydos; may [the name endure of Isis in] Ta-wer and Horus in the great Mansion (?) [Wadjyt in Dep...] (6) [may] the name [endure] of Nephthys in Heliopo[lis; may] the name [endure] of Banebdjed [... May the name endure of Thot in Hermopolis] (?) (7) [May] my *ḥtpw*-offerings be [laid down] (?) [... May] a libation [be poured out] (?) for me [...] (8) [...] ... (?)

Commentary

Line 1
ʿḥʿ.s n ʿnḫ rnpt 6 (?)[...]. References to the lifetime of the deceased are more usually found in autobiographies or on monuments consecrating the death of sacred animals than in funerary documents such as Books of Breathing where their presence is particularly rare (e.g. P. Cairo CG 58019, 10; P. dem. Munich ÄS 834 a, vs., 9–11; P. dem. Munich ÄS 834 b, vs., 9–12, both using the expression *rnp.t n ʿnḫ*), but note that the entire beginning of our text is atypical. For the expression *ʿḥʿ.f/.s n ʿnḫ*, see R. El Sayed, *BIFAO* 78 (1978), pp. 469–70, n. j.

Line 2
[...] *mi.s* (?) *Wsir r* (?) [...] *Ἰst wrt mwt-nṯr tꜣ nṯrt* [*ʿꜣt* ...]. The meaning of the first words causes some difficulties, and this phrase, which precedes a short and corrupt version of the litany *mi rwḏ rn*, does not occur in the other documents of the Second Book of Breathing consulted. On Isis designated as *tꜣ nṯrt ʿꜣt*, cf. P. BM EA 10282, 28, P. dem. Florence 3676, vs., 1–2, and P. Louvre E 3865, whose the owner bears, among many other titles,[78] that of (I, 1–2) *ḥm-nṯr n Ἰst wrt nṯrt ʿꜣt ḥr(t)-ib Gbtyw*, 'prophet of Isis the great, the great goddess dwelling in Coptos'.[79]

Line 3
[...] *mi rwḏ rn* [*Šw m* (*Mn*)]*st ḥrt m Ἰwnw*. See P. BM EA 10110 + 10111, **I, 8**.

Lines 3–4
mi rwḏ [*rn Tfnwt m* (*Mn*)*st ẖrt m Ἰwnw*]. See P. BM EA 10110 + 10111, **I, 9**.

Line 4
[*mi rwḏ rn Gb*] *m bw šmꜣw*. See P. BM EA 10110 + 10111, **I, 10**.

[*mi*] *rwḏ rn Nwt m* [*ḥwt šnw*]. See P. BM EA 10110 + 10111, **I, 11**.

Lines 4–5
[*mi rwḏ rn Wsir ḫnty Ἰmntt m*] *ꜣbḏw*. See P. BM EA 10110 + 10111, **I, 12**.

Line 5
mi [*rwḏ rn Ἰst m*] *Tꜣ-wr*. Note the corrupt writing of *Tꜣ-wr*, written  ??  . See P. BM EA 10110 + 10111, **I, 13**.

Ḥr m Ḥwt-ʿꜣt (?). All other versions give here the toponym Pe. See P. BM EA 10110 + 10111, **I, 14**.

[*Wꜣḏyt m Dp*]. The localization of this phrase in line 5 is not certain, but its presence somewhere within this text remains probable. See P. BM EA 10110 + 10111, **I, 15**.

Line 6
[*mi rwḏ*] *rn Nbt-ḥwt m Ἰwnw*. See P. BM EA 10110 + 10111, **I, 16**.

[*mi rwḏ*] *rn Bꜣ-nb-Ḏdt*. Despite the determinative 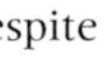 of *Bꜣ-nb-Ḏdt*, it certainly refers not to the toponym, but to the deity, as is shown by the mention of *rn*. The careless writing of the papyrus, and the frequent omission in the documents of *m pr Bꜣ-nb-Ḏdt*, have probably facilitated this confusion. See P. BM EA 10110 + 10111, **I, 17**.

Lines 6–7
[*mi rwḏ rn Ἰ m Ḫmnw*] (?). As above with Wadjyt, the existence of this phrase, if not certain, is nevertheless expected. It is this line that closes most documents of Book of Breathing bearing the litany *mi rwḏ rn*. See P. BM EA 10110 + 10111, **I, 18**.

Line 7
[*wꜣḥ* ?] *ḥtp.i* [*mi sti* ?].*w n.i ḳbḥ* [...]. The restoration of the verb lost in the second lacuna is not certain, and *sti* is proposed with some reservation, because of the determinative  which follows. For the idea, see P. BM EA 10191, **I, 12** and P. BM EA 10123, **line 2**.

Line 8
[...] *wꜣḥ ḥtpt*. One expects here the expression *wꜣḥ ḥtpw*, 'to lay down offerings' (cf. perhaps line 7, the mention of which could correspond with the above-named libation), but the spelling  seems to refer to the toponym *Ḥtpt*, inexplicable here.

78. Cf. G. Maspero, *RT* 37 (1915), p. 2.

79. On Isis of Coptos, see C. Traunecker, *Coptos. Hommes et dieux sur le parvis de Geb* (*OLA* 43, 1992), pp. 333–5.

P. BM EA 10275 (pls 72–3)

Hay Collection.
Unpublished.
Quirke, *Owners*, no. 253.
Provenance: probably Thebes.
Date: first to second century AD
Owner of the papyrus: *Tꜣ-šrἰt-(n-)p(ꜣ)* [...].
Mother of the owner: [*Ἰst*]-*wrt* (Esoeris). The name, partly in lacuna in line 3 of the recto, is written clearly on the verso.

Contents: Second Book of Breathing, abridged version.

Manuscript of one sheet (36 × 12.7 cm), broken at the left for its full height, bearing eighteen lines of text.

Text on the verso: The Book of Breathing [...] born of *Ἰst-wrt* [...].

Translation

Recto

(1) O Osiris foremost of the West, [great god lord of Abydos ... (?)] (2) this [...] from (?) the ba of *Tꜣ-šrἰt-p(ꜣ)* [... born of ... *Ἰst*]-(3)*wrt*, in good health. May [... ... I am] (4) loyal, I am preserved [from the ba ...] (5) come daily (?) [... at] (6) every moment of each day. [May the name endure of Atum] (7) lord of Heliopolis in Heliopolis! [May the name endure of Shu] (8) in the upper place [in Heliopolis! May] the name [endure] (9) of Tefnut in the [lower place in Heliopolis!] (10) May the name endure [of Geb in the place of the foreigners! (?)] (11) May the name endure [of Nut in the Mansion of the *šnw*-tree! (?)] (12) May endure [the name ... May] (13) the name endure [...] (14) in the temple of ... (?) [...] (15) during the night, during the day, at [every] moment [of each day, in] (16) the length of eternity and perpetuity [...] (17) upon earth of [...] (18) preserved (?) from the wrath of [...]

Commentary

Line 1
ἰ Wsἰr ḫnty Ἰmntt nṯr [*ꜥꜣ nb ꜣbḏw* ?]. This restoration, though expected (the base of the 𓊹 is visible), would fill the entire estimated length of the lacuna (a little more than the surviving width again, cf. lines 7–9, 15), excluding the possibility of the beginning of the sequence for which line 2 gives the necessary continuation. The absence of parallels prevents any certainty in restoring the text before the beginning of line 2 as *pfy r bꜣ n Tꜣ-šrἰt-(n-)p(ꜣ)* [...].

Lines 2–3
[...]-*wrt snb*. The name of the owner of the papyrus occurs in line 2, and the end of the name written at the beginning of line 3 presumably belongs to that of the mother, who survived her daughter, to judge from the designation *s*(*nb*); cf. R. El Sayed, *MDAIK* 40 (1984), p. 256, n. a.

Lines 3–4
[*ink*] *mnḫ ib iw.i wḏꜣ* [*r bꜣ* ...]. Cf. P. Louvre N 3156, 6–7 = P. Louvre N 3289, 5–6: *ink mnḫ ib iw.i wḏꜣ r bꜣ r mꜥn* (?) *ḫrr* () *n nṯr* (var.: *n nṯr nṯrt*). On the meaning of ba (determinative ), see J.F. Borghouts, *The Magical Texts of Papyrus Leiden I 348* (*OMRO* 51, 1971), pp. 178–9.

Line 5
mi m ḫr (?) ... (?). The text seems corrupt, and no parallel has beeen found elsewhere.

Lines 6–7
[*mi rwḏ rn n Ἰtm*] *nbw Ἰwnw m Ἰwnw*. Plural *nbw* by error, as often in this passage (cf. P. Louvre N 3156, 10; P. Louvre N 3289, 7, 13). See P. BM EA 10110 + 10111, **I, 7**.

Lines 7–8
[*mi rwḏ rn Šw*] *m st ḥrt m Ἰw*[*nw*]. See P. BM EA 10110 + 10111, **I, 8**.

Lines 8–9
[*mi rwḏ*] *rn Tfnwt m* [*st ḫrt m Ἰwnw*]. See P. BM EA 10110 + 10111, **I, 9**.

Lines 10–13
Each of these lines begins with the formula (*mi*) *rwḏ* [*rn*]. The absence of any trace of the name of a deity prevents absolute certainty in restoring the expected names of Geb (*m bw šmꜣw*), Nut (*m ḥwt šnw*), Osiris (*ḫnty Ἰmntt m Tꜣ-wr*) and perhaps (see *infra*, **lines 13–14**) Isis (*m Tꜣ-wr*) as in most of the surviving sources, since some documents contain inversions and omissions among the deities listed.

Lines 13–14
[...] *m ḥwt-nṯr nt* [...]. The lack of parallels precludes identification of the temple mentioned in line 13, but some relationship with the preceding phrase (12–13) seems highly probable. It is not necessary to posit a sequence of the type *mi rwḏ rn* (*n*) *N m ḥwt-nṯr nt* [...], for the name of this deity would of itself fill the entire second half of line 13.

Lines 14–16
[...] *m grḥ m hrw m nw* [*nb nty rꜥ nb m*] *ꜣw n ḏt nḥḥ*. From other sources, three types of restoration may be envisaged:
P. Louvre N 3289, 3–4:

mi rnp rn n Wsἰr N	'May the name of N be young,
m grḥ m hrw	during the night, during the day,
m nw nb nt(y) rꜥ nb	at every moment of each day,
m ꜣw n ḏt nḥḥ	in the length of eternity and perpetuity!'

P. BM EA 10194, 8–9:

mi ir.i ḫpr r mr ib.i	'May I assume (my) forms according to my heart's desire
m grḥ m hrw	during the night, during the day,
m nw nb nty rꜥ nb	at every moment of each day!'

P. BM EA 10199, 2–3 = P. Cairo CG 58009, I, 2–4 = P. Cairo CG 58014, 1–3 = P. Louvre E 3865, I, 5–6 = P. Louvre SN, 1–2:

ink Wsἰr ḫnty Ἰmntt	'I am Osiris foremost of the West,
m grḥ m hrw	during the night, during the day,
m nw nb nty rꜥ nb	at every moment of each day.'

Lines 16–17
[...] *ḥr-tp tꜣ n p(ꜣ)* (?)[...]. For want of a known parallel, no restoration can be suggested.

Line 18

ı͗w.w wḏꜣ r šni n [*nḥḥ ḏt*]. Cf. P. Louvre N 3289, 18–19: *ı͗w ı͗ḥꜥw(.ı͗) wḏꜣ r šny n nḥḥ nḥḥ ḏt*. The suffix *.w* might well, in this context, refer back to the word (*ı͗*)*ḥꜥw* in the lacuna of line 17.

P. BM EA 10282 (pls 74–5)

Salt Collection 1, 132.
Unpublished.
Quirke, *Owners*, no. 229 and p. 83.
Provenance: Thebes. Found with P. BM EA 10283 on the mummy inside coffin BM EA 6705 in the collective tomb of the archon Soter.[80]
Date: End of the first–beginning of the second century AD.
Owner of the papyrus: *Swtr* (Soter).
Father of the owner (?): *Pꜣ-krr*.
Mother of the owner: *Pylt*[81] (Philous).

Contents: Second Book of Breathing, abridged version.

Manuscript of one sheet (36.5 × 20.2 cm), with three horizontal lines of text above, introducing the litany *mi rwḏ rn* divided into three sections, each preceded by the same formula arranged in a vertical column.

Text on the verso: Second (Book). Giving the West by the decree of the mistress of the foundations of the earth.[82]
(*In demotic*): at his feet.

Translation

Recto

(1) Thus speaks the Osiris *Swtr*, justified, (son of ?) *P(ꜣ)krr*, justified, born of *Pylt*, justified ... (?)

(2) O gods who are in the sky, O gods who are on earth, O gods who are in the South, O gods who are (3) in the North, West and East, may my name endure within Thebes and within (my) nome, for ever and eternally,

(*in columns, repeated three times*):
(4) as the name endures of
(5) Atum, lord of Heliopolis in Heliopolis,
(6) Shu in the upper place in Heliopolis,
(7) Geb in the place of the foreigners,
(8) Nut in the Mansion of *šnw*,
(9) Tefnut in the lower place in Heliopolis,
(10) Isis in Ta-wer,
(11) (*Text of the second column, identical to that of line 4*).
(12) Haroeris lord of Upper Egypt,
(13) Osiris foremost of the West in Abydos,
(14) Horus in Pe,
(15) Wadjyt in Dep,
(16) Nephthys in Heliopolis,
(17) Banebdjed,
(18) (*Text of the third column, identical to that of line 4*).
(19) Thoth Trismegistus lord of Hermopolis,
(20) Horus son of Isis, son of Osiris,
(21) Hathor mistress of the West,
(22) Maat to whom the West has been entrusted,

(23–4) May there endure (25) (my) name within (my) nome, for ever!

(26) The rays of Re, the breath of Amun, (27) the water of Hapy, that belongs to me eternally!

(28) May your ba live for ever, may it be renewed eternally! Refresh yourself! Take for you water at the voice of Isis the great, mother of the god, the great goddess lady of ... (?)

Commentary

Line 1

ḫr.f n Wsir N. See *supra*, p. 2 with n. 21, and P. BM EA 10191, **I, 1**.

On the form [hieroglyphs] : M. Smith, *Enchoria* 19–20 (1992–3), p. 135, n. (f).

The reading for the signs [hieroglyphs] at the end of line 1 remains doubtful.

Lines 2–3

i nṯrw imy(w) pt i nṯrw imy(w) tꜣ i nṯrw imy(w) rsyt i nṯrw imy(w) mḥtt imntt iꜣbtt. This invocation to the gods of the universe, here preceding the formula for the preservation of the name, is one of the texts preceding the litany *mi rwḏ rn*; see P. BM EA 10110 + 10111, **I, 4**; it recurs in P. BM EA 10283 where it introduces the wish of the deceased for the exit of his ba. Note the exceptional writings of *imy* [hieroglyphs], [hieroglyphs] and [hieroglyphs]. A similar invocation is found in the Book for the protection of the king during the night, P. Cairo CG 58027, III, 4: *i nṯrw imyw pt i nṯrw imyw tꜣ i nṯrw imyw tꜣ rsyt i Psḏt ꜥꜣt i Psḏt nḏst i nbw Dwꜣt ꜥꜣw m pr mḏꜣt*. On the role of these gods: J.C. Goyon, *BIFAO* 75 (1975), p. 370 with n. 1. In the *Ritual of Embalming*, VI, 18 (ed. Sauneron, p. 21), they come to the deceased to offer him 'dignity in the West and to arouse fear at the gate of Ankhet'.

Line 3

mi rwḏ rn.i m-ḫnw Wꜣst m-ḫnw spꜣ(w)t r nḥḥ. See P. BM EA 10110 + 10111, **I, 4–5, 6**.

Line 4

mi rwḏ rn. Note the original spelling [hieroglyphs] for *mi*, 'as', and the abusive suffix [hieroglyphs] *.i* after *rn* (so in lines 11 and 18).

Line 5

Itm nb Iwnw m Iwnw. See P. BM EA 10110 + 10111, **I, 7**.

80. See *supra*, p. 6, no. **4** and p. 9.
81. The sign □ is written in demotic. So in P. BM EA 10283, 1.
82. Same text on the verso of P. Cairo CG 58013.

Line 6
Šw m st ḥr(t) m Ỉwnw. See P. BM EA 10110 + 10111, **I, 8**.

Line 7
Gb m bw šmꜣw. See P. BM EA 10110 + 10111, **I, 10**.

Line 8
Nwt m Ḥwt šnw. See P. BM EA 10110 + 10111, **I, 11**.

Line 9
Tfnwt m st ḥr(t) m Ỉwnw. See P. BM EA 10110 + 10111, **I, 9**.

Line 10
Ỉst m Tꜣ-wr. See P. BM EA 10110 + 10111, **I, 13**.

Line 12
Ḥr wr nb tꜣ šmꜥ. See P. BM EA 10110 + 10111, **I, 25**.

Line 13
Wsir ḫnty Ỉmntt m ꜣbḏw. See P. BM EA 10110 + 10111, **I, 12**.

Line 14
Ḥr m P. See P. BM EA 10110 + 10111, **I, 14**.

Line 15
Wꜣḏyt m Dp. See P. BM EA 10110 + 10111, **I, 15**.

Line 16
Nbt-ḥwt m Ỉwnw. See P. BM EA 10110 + 10111, **I, 16**.

Line 17
Bꜣ-nb-Ḏdt. See P. BM EA 10110 + 10111, **I, 17**.

Line 19
Ỉ ꜥꜣ ꜥꜣ ꜥꜣ wr nb Ḫmnw. See P. BM EA 10110 + 10111, **I, 18**.

Line 20
Ḥr sꜣ Ỉst sꜣ Wsir. This deity is not found in any other source with the text *mi rwḏ rn*.

Lines 21–2
Ḥwt-Ḥr ḥnwt Ỉmntt and *Mꜣꜥt ḥn.w n.s Ỉmntt*. Like Horus above, Hathor and Maat, here representing two aspects of the same goddess (cf. First Book of Breathing, P. BM EA 10191, **I, 5–6**), are not generally cited among the deities whose names are said to 'endure' like that of the deceased. Reference to them here is thus exceptional. Note the writing for the verb *ḥn*, influenced by the word *ḥnwt*, 'mistress', mentioned in line 21 (cf. *supra*, p. 95, n. 34).

Lines 23–5
mi rwḏ rn(.i) m-ḫnw sp(ꜣ)t(.i) r nḥḥ. See *supra*, **line 3**. The sign □, apparently incorrect, placed beneath the word *rn* (itself erroneously repeated), is problematic. One could interpret this as *p(ꜣy.i) rn*, but this construction is never employed by the scribes, who favour instead the classic expression *rn.i*. Equally it seems impossible to link the sign to the word *stwt* of line 26, never preceded by an article in this context (and one would expect the plural *nꜣ*). The curious arrangement of this phrase, embedded in lines 23 and 24 of the text, which give an exceptional order of reading, may explain the uncertainty.

Lines 26–7
stwt n Rꜥ ṯꜣw n Ỉmn mw n Ḥꜥpy nnk sn ḏt. This sequence, which generally concludes the First Book of Breathing, is unexpected here. See P. BM EA 10191, **II, 34**.

Line 28
ꜥnḫ p(ꜣy).k bꜣ r nḥḥ rnp.f r ḏt. Same formulation in P. BM EA 10283, 10–11 = P. BM EA 10343, 14–15 (which adds: *sp 2*) = P. Cairo CG 58016, 7–8. Cf. the var. *ꜥnḫ sp 2 nḥḥ bꜣ.k r nḥḥ r ḏt*, P. Cairo CG 58019, 13. The simplest expression is *ꜥnḫ bꜣ.k r nḥḥ ḏt*, P. BM EA 10194, 14; also P. BM EA 10344, 14: *ꜥnḫ bꜣ.t r nḥḥ ḥnꜥ ḏt*. Cf. too P. dem. Cairo CG 31172, 7–8 cited by M. Depauw, *SAK* 31 (2003), p. 97: *rpy pꜣy=f by šꜥ nḥḥ ḏt*. Note here the spelling of the verb *rnp*.

ḳbḥ ḏꜣ n.k mw r ḫrw Ỉst wrt mwt-nṯr nṯrt ꜥꜣt tꜣ nbt … (?). A close parallel for the first part of this sequence occurs in the demotic graffito no. 57 from Medinet Habu (H.J. Thissen, *Die demotischen Graffiti von Medinet Habu* [Sommerhausen 1989], p. 60), revised by M. Chauveau, *RdE* 46 (1995), p. 254:

ꜥnḫ pꜣy=t by (r) nḥḥ	'May your ba live for ever,
rpy=f r ḏt N	may it be renewed eternally, N!
ḳbḥ ṯꜣi n=t mw ḥr tꜣ ḥtp.t	Refresh yourself! Take for you water upon the altar
m-sꜣ Wsir …	behind Osiris …'[83]

On the libation to the deceased effected 'at the voice' of Isis, see P. BM EA 10285, **line 2**, and M. Smith, *Enchoria* 19–20 (1992–3), pp. 142–3 (line 7, c). For Isis as *nṯrt ꜥꜣt*, see P. BM EA 10264, **line 2**.

P. BM EA 10286 (pls 76–7)

Salt Collection 1, 154.1.
Unpublished.
Quirke, *Owners*, no. 25.
Provenance: probably Thebes.
Date: first to second century AD.
Owner of the papyrus: *ꜣpwltyty* (Apollodote).[84] She is also owner of P. BM EA 10285.
Mother of the owner: not mentioned here, but see P. BM EA 10285.

Contents: Second Book of Breathing, abridged version.

Manuscript of one sheet (19.2 × 12.3 cm), torn at the sides, with the same features of text as P. BM EA 10285.

83. One expects after *Wsir: r ḫrw Ỉst*, 'at the voice of Isis'.
84. This name in recorded neither in *RPN* nor in the *Demot. Nb.*, but the equivalence between the Egyptian and the Greek seems probable. H. Cuvigny informs me that the anthroponym Apollodote, feminine counterpart of the common Apollodotos, is extremely rare, and points out only two non-Egyptian attestations. The example recorded in P. BM EA 10285 and 10286 belonging to the same owner is the only known witness of this name in Egypt.

Text on the verso: A good burial. May it be stable over your bones.

Translation

Recto

(1) Hail Hathor Apollodote, born (2) of Hathor mistress of the foundations of the earth (*sic*). May (your) ba endure (3) every day as the name of Atum in Heliopolis endures, (4) as the name of Osiris foremost of the West endures in Abydos, (5) as the name of Isis endures in Ta-wer, as <the name of> (6) Horus endures in Pe, as <the name of> Nephthys endures in Dep, (7) for ever and eternally.

Commentary

Lines 1–2
In place of the expected name of the mother (Arsinoe), at the start of line 2, which would normally follow that of the daughter, owner of the papyrus (*N ms n NN*), the name of the goddess Hathor, qualified as *ḥnwt ndbwt*, is written. Clearly, the manuscript was compiled in haste and this error can only be explained as due to a monumental distraction of the scribe. Reference to the goddess and her title, frequently attested in copies of the Book of Breathing (cf. *LPE*, p. 267), cannot be justified in this passage.

Lines 2–3
mi͗ rwḏ p(ꜣy.t) bꜣ m ḫrt-hrw. Variant of the formula *mi͗ rwḏ rn*. The verb *rwḏ* is relatively little used in connection with the ba (*Wb.* II, 411, 12, *Belegst.*; S. Donadoni, *OA* 12 [1973], p. 49), whereas it is frequently attested qualifying certain other constituent elements of the person (*ẖt, sꜥḥ, šwt, ẖꜣt*) or simply the body, envisaged as a whole (*i͗wf, ḥꜥw*) or in its parts (*ḳsw, mtwt*, etc.).

Lines 3–7
See P. BM EA 10110 + 10111, **I, 7**, and **11–5**.

Line 3
mi͗ rwḏ rn n I͗tm m I͗wnw. See P. BM EA 10110 + 10111, **I, 7**.

Line 4
Wsi͗r ḫnty I͗mntt m ꜣbḏw. See P. BM EA 10110 + 10111, **I, 12**.

Line 5
I͗st m Ṯꜣ-wr. See P. BM EA 10110 + 10111, **I, 13**.

Line 6
Ḥr m P. See P. BM EA 10110 + 10111, **I, 14**.

Nbt-ḥwt m Dp. The usual version would be either *Wꜣḏyt m Dp* or *Nbt-ḥwt m I͗wnw*. See P. BM EA 10110 + 10111, **I, 15** and **16**.

P. BM EA 10331 (pls 78–9)

Salt Collection 1, 114.2.
Unpublished.
Quirke, *Owners*, no. 26
Provenance: Thebes, collective tomb of the archon Soter.[85]
Date: probably reign of Antoninus.[86]
Owner of the papyrus: *ꜣprtynyds* (Apollonides).
Mother of the owner: *Ḳndꜣwgy* (Candace).

Contents: Second Book of Breathing, abridged version.

Manuscript of one sheet (20.4 × 35.1 cm), bearing thirteen lines of text partly effaced from general wear.

Illegible text on the verso: only a few signs can be discerned.

Translation

Recto

(1) May the name endure of Atum lord of Heliopolis in Heliopolis, by the Osiris Apollonides born of Candace,

(2) May the name endure of Shu < in> the upper Menset in Heliopolis, by the Osiris Apollonides born of Candace,

(3) May the name endure of Tefnut <in> the lower Menset in Heliopolis, by the Osiris Apollonides born of Candace,

(4) May the name endure of Geb in the place of the foreigners, by the Osiris Apollonides born of Candace,

(5) May the name endure of Nut in the Mansion of *šnw* by the Osiris Apollonides born of Candace,

(6) May the name endure of Osiris foremost of the West in Abydos, by the Osiris Apollonides born of Candace,

(7) May the name endure of Isis in Ta-wer, by the Osiris Apollonides born of Candace,

(8) May the name endure of Horus of Pe, by the Osiris Apollonides born of Candace,

(9) May the name endure of Wadjyt in Dep, by the Osiris Apollonides born of Candace,

(10) May the name endure of Nephthys in Heliopolis, by the Osiris Apollonides born of Candace,

(11) May the name endure of Banebdjed in the House of Banebdjed, by the Osiris Apollonides born of Candace,

(12) May the name endure of Thoth the very great, lord of Hermopolis, [by the Osiris Apollonides born] of [Candace].

85. See *supra*, p. 6, no. **25**.

86. The owner, son of Candace, lived for little less than 69 years.

Commentary

Among the surviving versions of the litany on the endurance of the name, P. BM EA 10331 presents a particular structure of its own. Each line is comprised of two elements, the first giving the formula *mi rwḏ rn n* + deity, and the second recording the name and filiation of the deceased introduced by the preposition *ḫr*.

The litany *mi rwḏ rn* is here highly abbreviated. For a commentary, see P. BM EA 10110+ 10111, **I, 7–18**.

P. BM EA 71513D (pls 80–1)

Unpublished.
Provenance: probably Thebes.
Date: first to second century AD.
Owner of the papyrus: name lost.
Mother (?) of the owner: [...]-*p(ꜣ)-Mnṯw*. The sign , which here determines this truncated proper noun, can follow masculine anthroponyms as well as feminine ones. Except in very few manuscripts of Books of Breathing, where the names of both the father and the mother are mentioned, it is chiefly that of the mother which is found in the filiation of the deceased. In this case, the most probable restoration is *Tꜣ-šrit-(nt-)p(ꜣ)-Mnṯw* (R*PN* I, 368, 17). However, one clearly reads in line 1 *ink sꜣ.k*, 'I am your son', and not *ink sꜣt.k*, 'I am your daughter'. This contradiction is not so rare and it can happen that some papyri belonging to women are written as if for men (cf. for instance P. Cairo CG 8007, III, 2).

Contents: Fragment of the Second Book of Breathing.

In its present state, the document comprises five fragments bearing five lines of hieratic, in a large hand. The last two are particularly lacunose.

Text on the verso (two fragmentary lines written in opposite directions):
(1) [...] Book (?) [...]
(2) [... may it remain over] your [flesh], without decay!

Translation

[...](x+1)-*p(ꜣ)-Mnṯw*, [justified] (?): O Re, I am your son! O (x+2) Thoth, I am your beloved! O Osiris, I am your image! (x+3) O Lord of Hermopolis, I am your heir, in truth! [O Horakhty, (x+4) O great Ennead, O lesser Ennead [...].

Commentary

On this text, which appears in some other documents, see P. BM EA 10110 + 10111, **I, 2–5**.

4. First and Second Book of Breathing

P. BM EA 10125 (pls 82–5)

Unpublished.
Provenance: probably Thebes.
Date: first to second century AD.
Owner of the papyrus: name lost.
Titles:
— *iry-ꜥꜣ n pr-nwb n Ỉmn*, 'doorkeeper of the treasury of Amun'
— *ḥry mnḫt n pr Ỉmn-Rꜥ nsw nṯrw*, 'head of clothing of the estate of Amun-Re king of the gods'.[1]
Mother of the owner: *Ḫꜣꜥ.s(.t)-n-Ỉst* (*RPN* I, 262, 19; II, 380).

Contents: First and Second Book of Breathing, abridged version.

Manuscript of one sheet (47.7 × 22.1 cm), lacking the upper edge and the upper right corner for 7 lines (the papyrus contains 28). A resinous or bituminous matter has darkened the upper central area of the text, but this remains legible.

Text on the verso: (1) [A good burial. May it be stable] over your bones ... [without] decay! The beautiful Amentet extends her arms to receive you (2) by the decree of the lady of the foundations of the earth.

Translation

Recto

(1)[Thus speaks the Osiris ...], doorkeeper of the treasury of Amun, head of clothing of the estate of Amun-Re king of the gods, (2)[...] born of *Ḫꜣꜥ.s(.t)-n-Ỉst*, justified:

I am Re at his rising, I am Atum (3) [at his setting, I am] Osiris foremost of the West during the night.

Turn towards me, door (4)[keepers of the] West, guardians of the Duat. May I come, may I (5)[go! Turn] towards me, Hathor mistress of the West, Maat to whom the West has been entrusted! (6) [Turn towards me] all gods of the Duat, gods of piercing gaze who are in the retinue of Osiris, (7) [gods who are in] the hall of the two Maats, gods who are in the hall of the Field of reeds! (8) Turn towards me, Anubis son of Osiris, dependable doorkeeper of the Duat! May (9) I enter the hall of the region of Maat, may I be one of these excellent praised ones (10) who follow Sokar! May my ba fly up to (11) heaven with the bas, and alight likewise on my corpse in the necropolis! May (12) there be made for me a libation of water in the Mansion of the Prince (as is done for the) great Prince (who is) in Heliopolis. I am he (13) before whom decree is made in Heliopolis, that his voice be heard in the Great Mansion. I am an ibis with black head (14), white breast and blue back. The Book of Breathing of Thoth is my protection.

(15) O Thoth, turn towards me! Vindicate me against my enemies as you vindicated Osiris against his enemies (16) before the great Council which is in Heliopolis, on that night of the festival of offerings on the altar in Heliopolis, (17) before the great Council which is in Busiris, on that night of raising the *ḏd*-pillar in Busiris, (18) before the great Council which is in Abydos, on that night of battle to overthrow (19) those enemies, before the great Council which is in Idebu-rekhty, on that (20) night of the Haker-festival, before the great Council which is in Pe and Dep, on that (21) night of vindicating Horus against his enemies, (for) Horus has repeated praises, four times.

(22) O Thoth, turn towards me! May my name endure within Thebes, within my nome, for ever, (23) as the name of Atum, lord of Heliopolis endures in Heliopolis, as the

1. Cf. the title *ḥry mnḫt n Ỉmn* borne by the owner of P. BN 179-81. See also *ProsPtol* IX, p. xvii, and H. de Meulenaere, in *Egyptian Religion the last thousand years. Studies dedicated to the memory of Jan Quaegebeur* (*OLA* 85, 1998), pp. 1128–30, n. (d).

name of Shu endures in the upper Menset in (24) Heliopolis, as the name of Tefnut endures in the lower Menset in Heliopolis, likewise Geb in the place of the foreigners, likewise (25) Nut in the Mansion of *šnw*, likewise Osiris foremost of the West in Abydos, likewise Isis in (26) Ta-wer, likewise Osiris in Andj, likewise Isis in Neter-shema, likewise Nephthys in Heliopolis, (27) likewise Osiris in Ro-setau, likewise Anubis in Hardai, likewise Horus in Heracleopolis. (28) The rays of Shu, the water of Hapy, the breath of Amun, all that belongs to me.

Commentary

Lines 1–2
[*ẖr.f n Wsỉr*] *p*(*ꜣ*) *ỉry-ꜥꜣ n pr-nwb n Ỉmn ḥry mnḫt n pr Ỉmn-Rꜥ nsw nṯrw* [*N*]. Restoration of the beginning after the parallels.

Lines 2–3
ỉnk Rꜥ m ḫꜥ.f ỉnk Ỉtm [*m ḥtp.f ỉnk*] *Wsỉr ḫnty Ỉmntyw m grḥ*. See P. BM EA 10191, **I, 1–2**.

Lines 3–4
ḥr.tn r.ỉ nꜣ ỉry[*w-ꜥꜣ n*] *Ỉmntt nꜣ sꜣwtyw n tꜣ Dwꜣt*. On this sequence, parallel to P. BM EA 10109, 3–4, see P. BM EA 10191, **I, 2–3**.

Lines 4–5
mỉ ꜥḳ.ỉ mỉ [*pr.ỉ*]. See P. BM EA 10109, **line 4** and P. BM EA 10191, **I, 15**.

Line 5
[*ḥr.t*] *r.ỉ Ḥwt-Ḥr ḥnwt Ỉmntt Mꜣꜥt ḥn.w n.s Ỉmntt*. See P. BM EA 10191, **I, 5–6**.

Line 6
ḥr.tn r.ỉ nꜣ nṯrw n tꜣ Dwꜣt ḏrw nṯrw mdsw-ỉrty ỉmyw-ḫt Wsỉr. These two invocations are placed at two different points in P. BM EA 10191. See the commentary at **I, 6**, and **I, 4**.

Line 7
nṯrw ỉmyw tꜣ wsḫt Mꜣꜥty nṯrw ỉmyw tꜣ wsḫt sḫwt ỉꜣrwt. See P. BM EA 10191, **I, 4–5**.

Lines 8–9
ḥr.k r.ỉ Ỉnpw sꜣ Wsỉr pꜣ ỉry-ꜥꜣ mtr n tꜣ Dwꜣt mỉ ꜥḳ.ỉ r wsḫt ww Mꜣꜥt. On Anubis son of Osiris, and his role as 'doorkeeper of the Duat', see P. BM EA 10191, **I, 3–4**. In this part of First Book of Breathing, the order of clauses follows no fixed rule. Whereas P. BM EA 10191 inserts it in a series of addresses to various divinities (*ḥr.k /.tn r.ỉ*), here it introduces the wish of the deceased to enter the 'hall of the region of Maat' (*mỉ ꜥḳ.ỉ r wsḫt ww Mꜣꜥt*: P. BM EA 10109, 7–8 = P. Cairo CG 58009, I, 8–10). On that hall, see P. BM EA 10108, **lines 5–6**.

Lines 9–10
mỉ ỉr.ỉ wꜥ m ḥsyw ỉḳrw nn šms Skr. On this phrase and its variants, see P. BM EA 10108, **line 6**.

Lines 10–11
mỉ pꜣy pꜣy.ỉ bꜣ r ḥrt m-ꜥb bꜣw ḫn.f mỉtt ḥr ẖꜣt.ỉ m ỉgrt. See P. BM EA 10108, **lines 6–7**.

Lines 11–12
mỉ ḳbḥ.w n.ỉ mw m ḥwt sr mỉ p(*ꜣ*) *sr wr m Ỉwnw*. See P. BM EA 10191, **I, 12**. Note here the special writing  for *wr*.

Lines 12–13
ỉnk pꜣy ỉr.w wḏwt ḥꜣt.f m Ỉwnw r sḏm ḫrw.f m Ḥwt-ꜥꜣt. See P. BM EA 10109, **2–3** and 10191, **I, 39–40**.

Lines 13–14
ỉnk hb km tp ḥḏ ḫt ḫsbḏ psḏ. See P. BM EA 10109, **line 2**.

Line 14
šꜥt n snsn n Ỉ m sꜣ.ỉ. See P. BM EA 10124, **1** and P. BM EA 10048, **III, 1** and **5–6**; *LPE*, p. 255 (VIII, 9).

Lines 15–21
On the litany *smꜣꜥ.k ḫrw.ỉ r ḫftyw.ỉ* 'vindicate me against my enemies', addressed by the deceased to Thoth, and found – more or less abbreviated – in many copies of First Book of Breathing, see P. BM EA 10191, **I, 15–29**.

Line 16
m-bꜣḥ ḏꜣḏꜣt nsw ꜥꜣt ỉmyw Ỉwnw grḥ pfy n ḫwt n ḫꜣwt m Ỉwnw. For the variants in other sources, see P. BM EA 10191, **I, 16–17**.

Line 17
m-bꜣḥ ḏꜣḏꜣt nsw ꜥꜣt ỉmyw Ḏdw grḥ pfy n sꜥḥꜥ ḏd m Ḏdw. See P. BM EA 10191, **I, 19–20**.

Lines 18–19
m-bꜣḥ ḏꜣḏꜣt nsw ꜥꜣt ỉmyw ꜣbḏw grḥ pfy n ꜥḥꜣ-ꜥ r sḫr sbỉw pfy. See P. BM EA 10191, **I, 16–17**.

Lines 19–20
m-bꜣḥ ḏꜣḏꜣt nsw ꜥꜣt ỉmyw Ỉdbw-rḫty grḥ pfy n ḥb ḥkr. The other sources give different versions. See P. BM EA 10191, **I, 23–4**.

Lines 20–1
m-bꜣḥ ḏꜣḏꜣt nsw ꜥꜣt ỉmyw P Dp grḥ pfy n smꜣꜥ-ḫrw Ḥr r ḫftyw.f r wḥm. Same version in P. Cairo CG 58009, II, 10–11. Most other sources give a different text. See P. BM EA 10191, **I, 21–2**.

For the clause *ỉw wḥm.n Ḥr ḥknw sp 4* (line 21), see P. BM EA 10109, **line 13**.

Lines 22–7
New litany addressed to Thoth and concerning the preservation of the name. This version is abridged. The Second Book of Breathing starts here.

Line 22
ỉ Ỉ mỉ ḥr.k r.ỉ. For this unusual variant of *ḥr.k r.ỉ*, see P. BM EA 10191, **I, 2–3**.

mỉ rwḏ rn.ỉ m-ḫnw Wꜣst m-ḫnw spꜣt.ỉ r nḥḥ. On the known variants of this sequence, see P. BM EA 10110 + 10111, **I, 4–5, 6**.

Line 23
mỉ rwḏ rn n Ỉtm nb Ỉwnw m Ỉwnw. See P. BM EA 10110 + 10111, **I, 7**.

Lines 23–4
Šw m Mnst ḥrt m Ỉwnw. See P. BM EA 10110 + 10111, **I, 8**.

Line 24
Tfnwt m Mnst ḫrt m Ỉwnw. See P. BM EA 10110 + 10111, **I, 9**.

Gb m bw šmꜣw. From this point, the names of the deities are no longer preceded by the formula *mi rwḏ rn n*, 'May the name endure of', but simply by the preposition *mitt*, 'likewise'. On 'Geb in the place of the foreigners', see P. BM EA 10110 + 10111, **I, 10**.

Line 25
Nwt m Ḥwt šnw. See P. BM EA 10110 + 10111, **I, 11**.

Wsir ḫnty Ỉmntt m ꜣbḏw. See P. BM EA 10110 + 10111, **I, 12**.

Lines 25–6
Ỉst m Ṯꜣ-wr. See P. BM EA 10110 + 10111, **I, 13**.

Line 26
Wsir m ꜥnḏ. This reference to Osiris in Andj, preceding that of Isis in Neter-shema, is absent from the other British Musem manuscripts with the litany *mi rwḏ rn*. It may be compared with the version in P. Cairo CG 58009, III, 10–11, citing, after Isis in Ta-wer, 'Osiris lord of Busiris, the great god lord of Andj' (*Wsir nb Ḏdw nṯr ꜥꜣ nb ꜥnḏ*).[2]

Ỉst m Nṯr-šmꜥ. See P. BM EA 10110 + 10111, **I, 26**.

Nbt-ḥwt m Ỉwnw. See P. BM EA 10110 + 10111, **I, 16**.

Line 27
Wsir m Rꜣ-sṯꜣw. Apparently the sole known reference to this form in this litany.

Ỉnpw m Ḥr-dy. See P. BM EA 10110 + 10111, **I, 34**.

Ḥr m Ḥwt-nsw. The usual text gives *Ḥr-šfy m Ḥwt-nn-nsw.* See P. BM EA 10110 + 10111, **I, 35**.

Line 28
stwt n Šw mw n Ḥꜥpy ṯꜣw n Ỉmn nnk st ḏrw. Note here the var. *stwt n šw* (cf. K. Sethe, *ZÄS* 59 [1924], p. 11) instead of *šw n Rꜥ* (P. BM EA 10340, 6), as compared with the usual version *stwt n Rꜥ*. For this clause, see P. BM EA 10191, **II, 34**.

P. BM EA 71513A (pls 86–9)

Unpublished.
Provenance: probably Thebes.
Date: first to second century AD.
Owner: *Pꜣ-di-p*[...].
Mother of the owner: *Tꜣ-*[...]*yn*.

Contents: First and Second Book of Breathing, abridged version.

Although reconstructed from eighteen fragments, this papyrus, in its present condition, constitutes a very poorly preserved document. The lower part is missing, and it is difficult to tell whether one or several other pages followed this one originally. The papyrus, written in a hand that grows larger, shows some traces of erosion which affect the first eleven lines in places.

Text on the verso (in two lines): (1) A good burial. [May it be stable (?)] over [... ... The Book] of Breathing of Thoth is your protection., May you be not taken away [...] (2) the Osiris *Pꜣ-di-p*[..., justified, ...] born of *Tꜣ-*[...]*yn*, justified.

Translation

Recto

(1) Thus speaks the Osiris *P(ꜣ)-di-p*[..., born of ...], justified:

(2) I am Re at his rising, [I am Atum] at <his> setting, I am Osiris foremost of the West [during the night] and during the day.

Turn towards me, (3) doorkeepers of the West, guardians of the Duat, doorkeepers of the House of Henu! Turn towards me, (4) [Anubis son of Osir]is, dependable doorkeeper of the Duat! Turn towards me, gods of piercing <gaze>, goddesses who are in the (5)[retinue of Osiris, go]ds who are in the hall of the two Maats, gods who are in the hall [of the Field] of reeds! (6) Turn towards me], Hathor mistress of the West, Maat to whom the West has been entrusted!

Turn towards me, all gods of the (7) Duat, gods who watch over Osiris! I am your father Re-Horakhty, the great god (8) from <whom you emerged> at the first time; I am Horus son of Isis, son of Osiris, who is upon his throne, eternally. I am Haroeris (9) [lord of Upper Egypt], who comforts the body of Re, setting Horus upon the throne of his father Osiris. I am Hor-merty (10) [lord of the bat]tle, who causes all the gods to be strong. [I am Horus lord of Leto]polis, lord of Iit, who repe[ls (11) the ene]mies from Heliopolis. I am Thoth lord of the god's words, who makes the discourse of all the gods.

Turn towards me (12), [guardians of the Duat, chase away for me the void of the hours of the night]. May (13) [my ba] go forth [to heaven with the] bas of the [great] gods! [May I receive offerings before Atum! (14) May there be made for me a libation] of water in the Mansion of the Prince, as [(is done) for the great Prince who is in Heliopolis! May I proceed to Heliopolis (15) on the night of the festival]

2. The transcription by Golenischeff, *Pap. hiérat.* I, p. 49, should be amended at this point. Read: .

of offerings on the altar [and on the festival of the sixth day, (16) with all the gods and goddesses of Upper and Lower Egypt, (for) I] am one of them. [May I enter before Osiris foremost of the West, (17) with the noble gods], on the night of the Hen[u-festival. Divine (18) is my ba, every day (or: in the god's domain).] May I come, may I go, [(for) I am one of them].

(19) O [Thoth], vindicate me against my enemies as you vindi[cated Osiris against his enemies] (20) before the great Council which is in Heliopolis, on that night of bat[tle to] (21) overthrow those enemies, on that day of annihilating the enemy of the Lord of All therein.

O Thoth, turn towards me, vin[dicate me against my enemies, as you vin]dicated (22) Osiris against his enemies, before the <great> Council which is in Busiris, on that night of (23) raising the *ḏd*-pillar in Busiris.

O [Thoth], turn towards me! (24) May [my name] endure [as endure the name of] (?)

(25) Atum lord of Heliopolis [in Heliopolis],
(26) Shu in [the upper Menset in] Heliopolis,
(27) Tefnut [in the lower Menset] in Heliopolis,
(28) Geb [in the place of the forei]gners,
(29) Nut [in the Mansion of *šn*]*w* (?)
(30) [Osiris foremost of the West in Abydos],
(31) [Isis in Ta-wer ?],
(32) Horus in [Pe],
(33) Wadjyt in Pe and Dep,
(34) Nephthys in Heliopolis,
(35) Banebdjed,
(36) [Thoth ... (?)] lord of Hermopolis.

Commentary

Line 1
ḫr.f n Wsꞽr N. See P. BM EA 10191, **I, 1**. For *mꜣꜥ-ḫrw* written ⌇, see Golenischeff, *Pap. hiérat.* I, p. 71, n. 3 (line 2).

Line 2
ꞽnk Rꜥ m ḫꜥ[.f ꞽnk Ꞽtm m] ḥtp ꞽnk Wsꞽr ḫnty Ꞽmntt [m grḥ m] hrw. See P. BM EA 10191, **I, 1–2**.

Lines 2–3
ḥr.tn r.ꞽ [nꜣ] ꞽryw-ꜥꜣ n Ꞽmntt nꜣ sꜣwtyw n tꜣ Dwꜣt nꜣ [ꞽryw-ꜥꜣ n pr] Ḥnw. See P. BM EA 10191, **I, 2–3**.

Lines 3–4
ḥr.k r.ꞽ [Ꞽnpw sꜣ Ws]ꞽr p(ꜣ) ꞽry-ꜥꜣ mtr n tꜣ Dwꜣt. See P. BM EA 10191, **I, 3–4**.

Lines 4–5
ḥr.tn r.ꞽ nṯrw mds (sic) *nṯrwt ꞽmyw-[ḫt Wsꞽr]*. See P. BM EA 10191, **I, 4**.

Line 5
[nꜣ nṯr]w ꞽmyw tꜣ wsḫt Mꜣꜥty nꜣ nṯrw ꞽmyw tꜣ wsḫt [sḫwt] ꞽꜣrw. See P. BM EA 10191, **I, 4–5**.

Line 6
[ḥr.t r.ꞽ] Ḥwt-Ḥr ḥnwt Ꞽmntt Mꜣꜥt ḥn n.s Ꞽmntt. One may also understand: Maat to whom the Westerners move. See P. BM EA 10191, **I, 5–6**.

Lines 6–7
ḥr.tn r.ꞽ nꜣ nṯrw [n tꜣ Dwꜣt] ḏrw nꜣ nṯrw nty rs r Wsꞽr. See P. BM EA 10191, **I, 6**.

Lines 7–8
ꞽnk ꞽt.tn Rꜥ-Ḥr-ꜣḫty nṯr ꜥꜣ [ꞽw pr.tn ꞽm.f m sp] tpy. See P. BM EA 10191, **I, 7**.

Line 8
ꞽnk Ḥr sꜣ Ꞽst sꜣ Wsꞽr nty ḥr nst.f ḏt. See P. BM EA 10191, **I, 7**.

Lines 8–9
ꞽnk Ḥr wr [nb tꜣ (?) šmꜥ] ꞽr snḏm ḥꜥw n Rꜥ ꞽw.f dꞽt Ḥr ḥr nst ꞽt.f Wsꞽr. The word *tꜣ* before *šmꜥ*, though attested in most sources, cannot be restored with certainty. Other sources omit the name *Wsꞽr*. See P. BM EA 10191, **I, 8**.

Lines 9–10
ꞽnk Ḥr Mrty [nb rꜣ-n]ḫt ꞽr nḫt nṯrw ḏrw. See P. BM EA 10191, **I, 8–9**.

Lines 10–11
ꞽnk Ḥr nb Ḫm nb Ꞽꞽt nty ꜥm[ḏ sbꞽw] r Ꞽwnw. See P. BM EA 10191, **I, 9–10**.

Line 11
ꞽnk Ꞽ nb mdw-nṯr [nty dꞽ s]mdt <n> nṯr nb. See P. BM EA 10191, **I, 10**.

Lines 11–12
ḥr.tn r.ꞽ [nꜣ sꜣwtyw n tꜣ Dwꜣt ḫꜣꜥ n.ꞽ wšr nꜣ wnwt n grḥ]. See P. BM EA 10191, **I, 10–11**.

Lines 12–13
mꞽ pr [pꜣy.ꞽ bꜣ r ḥrt ḥnꜥ nꜣ] bꜣw n nꜣ [nṯrw wrw]. Restoration following the predominant version. The variant *mꞽ pr bꜣ.ꞽ* is also possible. See P. BM EA 10191, **I, 11**. The faint traces at the upper edge of fragment **B** (= **B**, 1) belong in part to line 12 of A and specifically to a word in the segment [*nꜣ sꜣwtyw n tꜣ Dwꜣt ḫꜣꜥ n.ꞽ wšr nꜣ wnwt n grḥ*].

Lines 13–14
The clause expected after [*nṯrw wrw*]: *mꞽ smꜣ.ꞽ ḫwt ḥnꜥ Ꞽtm* is lost, and its restoration here is not certain since some manuscripts omit it. See P. BM EA 10191, **I, 11–12**.

Line 14
[mꞽ ḳbḥ.w n.ꞽ] mw m ḥwt sr mꞽ [pꜣ sr wr (*nty*) *m Ꞽwnw]*. On this phrase and its variants, see P. BM EA 10191, **I, 12**.

Lines 14–16
[mꞽ ꜥḳ.ꞽ r Ꞽwnw n grḥ n] ḫwt ḥr ḫꜣwt [sꞽs-nt ḥnꜥ nṯrw nṯrwt nb n Šmꜥ Mḥw ꞽw].ꞽ m wꜥ ꞽm.s[n]. See P. BM EA 10191, **I, 13–14**.

Lines 16–17
*[mꞽ ꜥḳ.ꞽ r Wsꞽr ḫnty Ꞽmntt ḥnꜥ nṯrw šps*w] *m grḥ n ḥb Ḥ[nw]*. See P. BM EA 10191, **I, 14**.

Lines 17–18
[(*mꞽ*) *nṯr pꜣy.ꞽ bꜣ m ẖrt-hrw* (or *ẖrt-nṯr*)]. Sequence wholly in lacuna. On the possible variants, see P. BM EA 10191, **I, 14–15**.

Line 18
[mi] ꜥḳ.i mi pr[.i iw.i m wꜥ im.sn]. See P. BM EA 10191, **I, 15**.

Line 19
i Ỉ smꜣꜥ-ḫrw<.k> ḫrw.i r ḫftyw.i mi s[mꜣꜥ-ḫrw.k ḫrw Wsir r ḫftyw.f]. Despite a lacuna affecting in part the group *i Ỉ smꜣꜥ*, the surviving traces do not permit the reading as found in all other sources: *mi ḥr.k r.i*, var. *ḥr.k r.i*, 'turn towards me' (cf. in this document, **line 23**). The same omission is repeated below (cf. **line 21–22**). For the various variants of this sequence, see P. BM EA 10191, **I, 15–29**.

Line 20
m-bꜣḥ ḏꜣḏꜣt ꜥꜣt imyw Ỉwnw. See P. BM EA 10191, **I, 16**.

Line 20–21
grḥ pfy [n] ꜥḥꜣ-ꜥ [r] sḫr sbiw pfy. See P. BM EA 10191, **I, 16–17**.

Line 21
hrw pfy n ḥtm ḫfty n Nb-ḏr i[m.f]. See P. BM EA 10191, **I, 17**.

Lines 21–22
i Ỉ ḥr[.k r.i] smꜣꜥ[.k ḫrw] ḫrw Wsir r ḫftyw.f. Omitted by the scribe, the words *ḥr[.k r.i]* were added above *i smꜣꜥ[.k ḫrw]*. On this clause, see *supra*, **line 19**.

Lines 22–23
m-bꜣḥ ḏꜣḏꜣt ⟨ꜥꜣt⟩ imyw Ḏdw grḥ [pfy n] sꜥḥꜥ ḏd m Ḏdw. See P. BM EA 10191, **I, 19–20**.

Line 23
i [Ỉ] ḥr.k r.i. These words, closing line 6, here introduce a new phrase developed on the theme of the survival of the name. For a similar instance, cf. P. BM EA 10125, 22.

Line 24 (*in one column*)
mi rwḏ [rn...]. Several restorations are possible from the parallels. The most complete would be *mi rwḏ [rn.i m-ḫnw spꜣwt r nḥḥ ḏt mi rwḏ rn n]*, but it would extend markedly the restored height of the papyrus; it would also imply considerable loss to the text, which seems not to be the case because only two lines are missing (**lines 30** and **31**). A simple reading of **line 24**: *mi rwḏ [rn n]*, cannot be excluded, with as the writing of 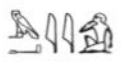, with omission of *mi rwḏ rn.i*, although such an omission appears not to be attested in any other manuscript source for the litany. See P. BM EA 10110 + 10111, **I, 4–5**, **6**.

Line 25
Ỉtm nb [Ỉwnw m Ỉw]nw. See P. BM EA 10110 + 10111, **I, 7**.

Line 26
Šw [m Mnst ḫrt m] Ỉwnw. See P. BM EA 10110 + 10111, **I, 8**.

Line 27
Tfnwt [m Mnst ḫrt] m Ỉwnw. See P. BM EA 10110 + 10111, **I, 9**.

Line 28
Gb [m bw šmꜣ]w. See P. BM EA 10110 + 10111, **I, 10**.

Line 29
Nwt [m Ḥwt šnw]. See P. BM EA 10110 + 10111, **11**.

Lines 30–31
Given the length of the missing portion in **line 24** and the mention of Horus of Pe on the left of the manuscript, it seems reasonable to suppose that the sequences on Osiris (**line 30**) and Isis (**line 31**) were placed below the phrase concerning Nut.

Line 32 (*aligned with* ***line 25***)
Ḥr m [P]. See P. BM EA 10110 + 10111, **I, 14**.

Line 33
Wꜣḏyt m P Dp. See P. BM EA 10110 + 10111, **I, 15**.

Line 34
Nbt-ḥwt m Ỉwnw. See P. BM EA 10110 + 10111, **I, 16**.

Line 35
Bꜣ-nb-Ḏdw. See P. BM EA 10110 + 10111, **I, 17**.

Line 36
[Ỉ ...] nb Ḫmnw. For the various possible reconstructions, see P. BM EA 10110 + 10111, **I, 18**.

5. Related and Original Texts

P. BM EA 10108 (pls 90–3)

Hay Collection, no. 502.
Quirke, *Owners*, no. 263.
Lieblein, *Que mon nom fleurisse*, pp. vii–ix.
E.A.W. Budge, *A Guide to the Fourth, Fifth and Sixth Egyptian Rooms*, pp. 297–8, no. 21.
B.H. Stricker, *OMRO* 23 (1942), p. 32.
Provenance: Thebes. Possibly from the tomb of the archon Soter, but apparently unconnected with his family.[1]
Date: first to second century AD (?).[2]
Owner of papyrus: *Tꜣ-nt-Ḏꜣm* (Tasemis). She is also owner of P. BM EA 10109.
Mother of the owner: *Tꜣ-(nt)-kꜣ* (?) (Tikos).

Contents: Original text adapted from the Book of Breathing.

Manuscript of one sheet (22 × 20.6 cm) broken along the entire right-hand side, bearing sixteen lines of text. The parallels indicate the extent of the lacuna in each line to be about two to three groups.

Text on the verso: A good burial. May it be stable over your bones, may it remain over your flesh, without decay! The beautiful Amentet extends her arms to receive you by the decree of [...].

Below are two notes in demotic: one gives the name *Ta-Ḏmꜣꜥ*, that of the owner of the papyrus, the other contains the indication 'at her feet', specifying where the document was to be placed. It may accordingly be assumed that the second manuscript of the same person (P. BM EA 10109) would have been placed at head level.[3]

Translation

Recto

(1) [Hail] Hathor *Tꜣ-nt-Ḏꜣm*, justified, born of *Tꜣ-(nt)-kꜣ* (?), justified, may your ba live in the sky before Re, (2)[may your ka be divine] among the gods, may your mummy be blessed at the head of the spirits, while your name is stable on earth before Geb, (3) [and your corpse is firm in the god's] domain! May your house be peopled with your children! Your spouse mourns you since the moment you left him after (4)[... ...] after that, there was made for you a great, beautiful and efficacious burial, and your Majesty is satisfied on the West of Thebes, opposite your children. (5)[...]. The beautiful Amentet extends her arms to receive you, and the mummies stand up at your approach. Anubis receives you in the hall [of the region of Maat]; (6) he causes you to be one of these excellent praised ones who follow Sokar and the crew of the bull of the West. Your ba flies up to heaven (7) [with the bas]; he alights also on your corpse in the necropolis. You hasten into Hebes-bag (when) the waters overflow (?) (8) [...] you walk on earth, you see what there is on it; you observe all the rules of your house, recognizing the evil which happens in you (?), and likewise for the Ba of Bas (?) (9)[(when) he goes forth ?] in procession from his house, on the days when he who is in the day of festival lives. You hear the crowd of *Ỉwntyw*-women on the days of acclaiming Sekhmet. You proceed (10) [towards Heliopolis upon the] festival of [offerings] on the altar, on that night of the festival of the sixth day, at the festival ... (?); you arrive in Ta-wer, the town of the scarab, on the day of the festival (*cross*) (11)[...] Sokar shining in the *ḥnw*-bark, Fenedjef-ankh in his reliquary. For you are performed all the ceremonies of the embalming house, all the rites of the

1. See *supra*, p. 5, n. 67.
2. See *supra*, p. 76, n. 149.
3. See *supra*, p. 2, n. 27.

festival of going forth by day. (12) [For you is made a libation] of water in the Mansion of the Prince as (for the) great Prince in Heliopolis. Your name endures within Thebes, within your nome for ever, as the name of the (13) [four Montus] endures [within] their town; your nostrils [breathe] the breath of air by the grace of Khonsu-Shu, great in Thebes, when he proceeds to the Mound of Djeme (14) [daily ?] to present the *mꜣꜥ*-offerings to the father of the fathers. You stand up in the Valley, with your arms in adoration of the great image master of all the gods. Re-Horakhty, (15)[he has illuminated your face] in this his moment of every day. Oblation is offered for your ka at the beginning of each decade, by the grace of the living image of Re in Thebes the victorious after he has proceeded to Khenemet-ankh (16) [laden with offerings for] his [mo]ment, to lay down the offerings for his fathers and mothers. <Your> lifetime is eternity, your kingship is everlastingness, and your time is the ignorance of destruction.

Commentary

Lines 1–3

[*hꜣy Ḥwt*]-*Ḥr N ꜥnḫ bꜣ.t m pt ḫr Rꜥ nṯr kꜣ.t ḫnt nṯrw ꜣḫ sꜥḥ.t m-ḫnty ꜣḫw rn.t ḏd m tꜣ ḫr Gb* [*ẖꜣt.t wꜣḥ.ti m*] *ẖrt*[-*nṯr*]. The restorations at the start of these lines follow the text of P. BM EA 10112, 2–5 and P. Toulouse 49–220, 2–5 (which adds *ḫr Wsir kꜣ nb Ỉmntt* after *m ẖrt-nṯr*). Cf. also P. Turin 1989, 4–5: *wꜣḥ ẖꜣt.t m Dwꜣt ḫr kꜣ Ỉmntt rn.t ḏd m tꜣ ḫr Gb kꜣ.t* [*n*]*fr tp rꜣ n wnyw*, 'May your corpse remain in the Duat before the bull of the West, while your name is stable before Geb and your ka (i.e.: your name) is good in the mouth of the people'. See too P. BM EA 10114, **lines 2–3**. On the fate of the various elements of the human being (here: ba, ka, mummy, name and corpse), which is widely cited in the funerary documents of the Late Period (with numerous variants), see *LPE*, pp. 81–3 (I, 3–4).

Line 3

pr.t grg ḫr msw.t (same reading in P. BM EA 10112, 5). On the theme of children in the house, see *LPE*, pp. 257–8 (VIII, 11).
Var. P. Toulouse 49–220, 6–7:

kꜣ.t mn.ti m pr.t nn ws	'Your ka is established in your house, without cease;
wnn.f grg.ti ḫr msw.t ṯꜣyw	it will be peopled with your male children.'

Lines 3-[4]

ṯꜣy.t ỉwỉw m-ḫt.t ḏr nš.n.t s(w) m-ḫt [...].
Var. P. BM EA 10112, 6–7:

ṯꜣy.t ỉmỉm m-ḫt.t	'Your spouse pines for you
ḏr nš.n.t s(w) ḥnꜥ msw.t	since you left him and your children.'

Cf. P. Cairo CG 58012, 5:

mwt.k ḳmd m-ḫt.k	'Your mother wails after you
ỉwỉw r-ḥnꜥ.k snw.k ỉrw	and all your brothers lament in your presence.'

P. Cairo CG 58009, IV, 6:

[...] *twk ḥr ḳmd m-ḫt.k*	'[...] you [...] to wail over you.'

In view of the version *ḥnꜥ msw.t* in P. BM EA 10112, 7, *m-ḫt* [...] presents some difficulty. Mention of the children in the lacuna seems excluded by their presence at the end of line 4.

nš: the sense 'leave', 'abandon', for a person who, passing from this life to the next, leaves his loved ones on the earth of the living, is not cited in the *Wb.* For the idea, cf. P. Parma 183, 15:

ꜥḳ.n.k ỉgrt	'You have entered the necropolis
ỉw nbt-pr.k m-ḫt.k	while your spouse is behind you,'

and the parallel of P. OIC 25389, XXXIV, 3–4:

ꜥḳ.n.k ỉgrt	'You have entered the necropolis
ỉw mwt.k ḥr-tp tꜣ	while your mother is on earth.'

On the mourning for the family, see W. Westendorf, *LÄ* VI, 744–5; *LPE*, p. 254 (VIII, 8–9).

Line 4

[*m-*]*ḫt nn ỉr.sn n.t smꜣ-tꜣ ꜥꜣt nfrt mnḫt*. The restoration of the beginning of the line is problematic in the absence of exact parallels. The closest version to this text, P. BM EA 10112, 7, gives a different phrasing here: *ỉswy n nn* 'the reward for this'. In all probability, *nn* depends here on the preposition [*m*]-*ḫt*, with the expected meaning of 'following that'.

Note here the variant *n.t*, compared with *n kꜣ.t* of P. BM EA 10112 and *n ḥm.k* in P. Cairo CG 58012.

In contrast to P. BM EA 10112 (also P. Turin 1989, 7–8), it is probably not to *msw* that the suffix *.sn* refers in *ỉr.sn n.t smꜣ-tꜣ*, even if elsewhere the descendants of the deceased assure his or her burial (cf. e.g. R. El Sayed, *BIFAO* 84 [1984], p. 143). Therefore the suffix may be understood here as indefinite 'one'; cf. P. Toulouse 49–220, 8–9:

ỉr.tw n.t tp-rd nb n wꜥbt	'There are performed for you all the ceremonies of the embalming house,
ỉrw nb n pr-nfr	all the rites of the *pr-nfr*,[4]
ỉr.sn n.t ỉsk smꜣ-tꜣ nfr	a beautiful burial is made for you likewise
m wḏt n ḥnt ndbwt	by decree of the mistress of the foundations of the earth.'

In this context, the epithet *mnḫt*, 'efficacious', applied to the burial (here *smꜣ-tꜣ*, *ḳrst* in P. BM EA 10194, 13; P. BM EA 10343, 6; P. BM EA 10344, 10) could be a reference to its protection against corruption, as suggests P. Skrine I, Text I, col. 44–9 (A.M. Blackman, *JEA* 4 [1917], pl. 27 and p. 126:

smnḫ.tn smꜣ-tꜣ r ỉmyw ḥꜥw.ỉ	'May you make efficacious (my) burial against those who are in my body,
sḥr.tn tm r ẖꜣt.ỉ	may you drive away the worm from my corpse.'

For another interpretation, see Smith, *Liturgy*, p. 40.

sḥtp.sn ḥm.t ḫr Ỉmntt Wꜣst m sty n mswt.t. On the meaning of the suffix *.sn*, see *supra*, **line 4**. The parallels diverge on certain points here. The version *m sty n mswt.t* is also attested in P. Lieblein, 8 (writing 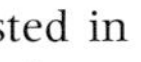 *sic*). P. Cairo CG 58009, IV, 11–12 and 58012, 7, have: *m sty n nỉwt.k*, 'facing your town', qualified in one instance by *ḥnwt nỉwwt*, 'mistress of towns' (*Wb.* III, 108, 18; A.H. Zayed, *ASAE* 57 [1962], p. 151), and in another by *ḥnwt rꜣw-prw*, 'mistress of temples'. A variant *m sty n ḥdbw(t).t* is provided by P. Turin 1989, 8–9 (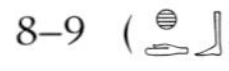),[5] P. Toulouse 49–220, 10

4. On the *pr-nfr*: W.C. Hayes, *The Burial Chamber of the Treasure Sobk-Mose from er-Rizeikat* (New York 1939), p. 13 with n. 62.

5. The transcription by Lieblein (*Que mon nom fleurisse*, p. xiv) is erroneous.

( )[6] and P. BM EA 10112, 8–9 ( ), with the epithet *ḥnwt niwwt*, 'mistress of towns', var.: *ḥnwt r3w-prw*, 'mistress of temples', qualifying Thebes, notably Karnak (*Ipt-swt*; R. El Sayed, *ASAE* 69 (1983), p. 277; Sethe, *Amun* § 2 and n. 1; J.C. Goyon, *JARCE* 20 (1983), p. 55, col. 6 and pp. 59–60, with n. 60, but also *W3st-nḫt* (G. Lefebvre, *Inscriptions concernant les grands prêtres d'Amon* [Paris 1929], p. 29, n. a; M. Abd el-Raziq, *Die Darstellungen und Texte des Sanktuars Alexanders des Grosses* (*AV* 16, 1984), p. 40).[7] For reasons of palaeography, a writing of *niwt* cannot be envisaged here (the sign is entirely different from in all versions), nor can a reading *Ipt-swt* (cf. the form of in P. Turin 1989, 2), even if the latter would be the most expected. In P. Turin 1989 and P. Toulouse 49–220, *ḫdbw(t)* is considered a mere substantive, not a place-name. As a substantive, the word is rarely attested (two examples in E. Drioton, *Fouilles de Médamoud 1925* [*FIFAO* 3/2, 1926], p. 46, no. 105, and p. 89, no. 146, where denotes a kind of land). Since *ḫdbw(t)*, written with the determinative or not, is always followed in the Book of Breathing by a suffix pronoun, it seems probable that there is a confusion over the text at this point.

For *ḥm* qualifying the deceased, see P. BM EA 10201, **I, 4**.

Line 5

di Imntt nfrt ꜥwy.s r šsp.t. Same reading in P. Toulouse 49–220, 11 = P. BM EA 10112, 9–10 = P. Cairo 58012, 8 = P. Lieblein, 11-[12]; also P. Parma 183, 20–1. Its presence with some occasional variants on the verso of a number of manuscripts seems to correspond to a sort of general programme (P. BM EA 10108, 10109, 10112, 10194 (?), 10283, Cairo CG 58012).[8] This act of the goddess of the West responds to a 'decree of the mistress of the foundations of the earth' (*m wḏt n ḥnwt ndbwt*).

The image of the arms extended towards the deceased[9] to welcome him is not new; under various guises, it dates back at least as far as the Middle Kingdom (L. Bull, *JAOS* 56 [1936], p. 168 and n. 17: *di smt ꜥwy.s r.k*), also P. BN 59, I, 11 [unpublished, Nineteenth Dynasty]: *ꜥḥ3-ḥr-nb.s ꜥwy.s r šsp.k*, but it is particularly in the Late Period and after that its usage becomes widespread: cf. e.g. *BD* ch. 148, 28 (ed. Lepsius): *Imntt nfrt ꜥwy.s r šsp.k*; P. Skrine, I, 8 (A.M. Blackman, *JEA* 4 [1917], p. 124 with pl. 26): *di t3 ꜥwy.f r šsp.k*; stela Cairo CG 22179 (Kamal, *Stèles*, p. 157) and Vernus, *Athribis*, p. 215: *sṯ3t nfrt di.s ꜥwy.s* [...]; S. Gabra and E. Drioton, *Rapport sur les fouilles d'Hermopolis ouest (Touna el Gebel)* (Cairo 1941), p. 18 = A.H. Zayed, *Egyptian Antiquities* (Cairo 1962), p. 47 and fig. 36, col. 2: (*t3*) *smt nfrt di.s ꜥwy.s r šsp.k*;[10] coffin Cairo 22.1.21.3–4, Piehl, *IH* III, pl. 69, col. 2: *di Imntt* ( ) *ꜥwy.s r ḥpt twk*; P. BN 171, scene 1, A. Piankoff, *Egyptian Religion* 4 (1936), p. 55: *Imntt* ( ) *di.s ꜥwy.s n Wsir N*; Maspero, *Sarcophages* I, p. 39, 6–7: *ḫnm.k nb Imntt rdi.n Ist ꜥwy.s r šsp.k*; in P. Rhind I, 6, 10–11 = II, 7, 3–4 (var.), it is Nut who receives the deceased, in her aspect of 'Hathor mistress of the West': *di Nwt ꜥwy.s r šsp.k m irw.s n Ḥwt-Ḥr ḥnwt Imntt*. Cf. also A. Rusch, *Die Entwicklung der Himmelsgöttin Nut zu einer Totengottheit* (Leipzig 1922), pp. 55–6.

ꜥḥꜥ sꜥḥw m ḫsf.t. Sequence attested only in P. Cairo CG 58012, 8, omitted in P. BM EA 10112. The compiler of the latter manuscript, after misinterpreting the word *ꜥḥꜥ* (line 10), passes to a new phrase not found in P. BM EA 10108.

The mummies (*sꜥḥw*) here designate collectively the dead, who welcome the newcomer by rising. Cf. R. Hari, *La tombe thébaine du père divin Neferhotep (TT 50)* (Geneva 1985), pl. XXVI, 15: *sꜥḥꜥ sꜥḥw.sn m-b3ḥ Rꜥ*.

Lines 5–6

šsp twt Inpw r wsḫt [*ww M3ꜥt*]. Restoration after P. BM EA 10112, 12 (var.: *šsp tn*). Cf. P. Toulouse 49–220, 12–13:

sꜥḳ twt Inpw r Ḥbs-b3g[11]	'Anubis causes you to enter Hebes-bag,
pr.t h3.t m wsḫt ww M3ꜥt	(such that) you come and go in the hall of the region of Maat.'

P. Lieblein, 10–11:

šsp twtn [*Inpw*] *r wsḫt ww M3ꜥt*	'[Anubis] receives you in the hall of the region of Maat.'

Ibid., 12:

[*šsp*] *twtn Inpw r wsḫt* [...]	'Anubis [receives] you in the hall [...].'

P. Cairo CG 58012, 9–10:

pr.k h3.k m wsḫt ww M3ꜥt	'You come and go in the hall of the region of Maat,
ir.k st.k r-gs M3ꜥty	and take your place beside the two Maats.'

For the idea, cf. P. BM EA 10125, 8–9 = P. BM EA 10109, 7–8 = P. Cairo CG 58009, I, 8–10:

ḥr.k r.i Inpw s3 Wsir	'Turn towards me, Anubis son of Osiris,
p3 iry-ꜥ mtr n t3 Dw3t	the dependable doorkeeper of the Duat!
mi ꜥḳ.i r wsḫt ww M3ꜥt	May I enter the hall of the region of Maat!'

P. Rhind II, 5, 1–2 (ed. Möller, p. 60):

Inpw imy wt nb t3 ḏsr	'Anubis the embalmer, lord of the sacred land,
sr.f w3t r ḥ3t.t r Ḥbs-b3g	he shows a way before you to Hebes-bag;
sphr.f n.t w3t w3t nfrw r wsḫt M3ꜥty	he opens for you every beautiful way to the hall of *M3ꜥty* the two Maats.'

Line 6

di.f wꜥ.t m ḥsyw iḳrw nn šms Skr ist n k3 Imntt. Omission of *ist n k3 Imntt* in P. BM EA 10112. The parallel manuscripts give the following variants:

P. BM EA 10125, 9–10:

mi ir.i wꜥ m ḥsyw iḳrw nn šms Skr	'May I be one of these excellent praised ones who follow Sokar!'

P. Cairo CG 58009, I, 10:

mi ir.i wꜥ m šms Skr	'May I be one of (those who) accompany Sokar,
iw.i m wꜥ n-im.sn	(for) I am one of them!'

P. Cairo CG 58012, 12:

ir.w n.k rd[12] *r-gs Wsir*	'A position is made for you beside Osiris,
mi wꜥ m šms ḥm.f	as (for) one of (those who) accompany His Majesty.'

6. The transcription by J.C. Goyon (in P. Ramond, *Notes sur le Papyrus 49–220* [Toulouse 1978], fig. 1a, 9) is erroneous.
7. For *ḥnwt niwwt* used absolutely, cf. E. Laskowska-Kuztal, *Le sanctuaire ptolémaique de Deir el-Bahari* III (Warsaw 1984), pp. 46–7 (inscription no. 49), and pp. 51–2 (inscription no. 63).
8. See *supra*, p. 3 with n. 35.
9. A comparable formulation may be seen in hymns to the sun to express the reception in the West of the star or an assimilated deity; cf. e.g. G. Vittmann, *WZKM* 72 (1980), p. 4 (2–8): *pḏ t3 ꜥwy.fy r šsp.k*; *CT* I, 270, f (sp. 62): *Nwt ꜥwy.s r.k*; etc.
10. In stela Cairo CG 22179 and the sarcophagus elements published by Gabra and Zayed, it is stated that the goddess grants that the ba of the deceased be excellent before the excellent bas, i.e. the blessed dead (*di.s iḳr b3.k ḫr b3w iḳrw*).
11. On *Ḥbs-b3g*, see *infra*, **line 7**.
12. On the meaning of *rd*: Smith, *Liturgy*, pp. 51–2 (III, 6, c).

P. Bodl. Eg. Inscr. 1374 a + b, 5–6 (M. Smith, *Enchoria* 19–20 [1992–3], p. 134):

tw=w n=k rt n ꜥḥꜥ	'They will give you a position
[*iwt nꜣ* (?)] *nt šms Skr-Wsir*	[among those (?) who follow Sokar-Osiris.'

P. Lieblein, 13:

[...] *ir.w n.t rd.t imytw iḳrw* [...]	'[...]Your place (?) is made for you among the excellent ones [...].'

P. Toulouse 49–220, 13:

ir.t wꜥt m šms Skr	'You are one of the retinue of Sokar.'

Cf. Bodl. Eg. Inscr. 1374 a + b, 5 (M. Smith, *Enchoria* 19–20 [1992–3], p. 134):

šms=k nꜣ by.w iḳrw	'You follow the excellent bas
nt šms Skr-Wsir	who follow Sokar-Osiris.'

Cf. too, in a different context, P. BM EA 10109, 8–9:

mi ir.i wꜥt m ist Wsir	'May I be one of the crew of Osiris,
iḳrw nn šms Kꜣ-ḥtp	(of) these excellent ones who follow the satisfied bull.'

Stela Cairo CG 22151 (Kamal, *Stèles*, p. 140, 5):

di.k wn.i m-m sꜥḥw iḳrw šmsw nṯr	'Grant that I be among the excellent mummies who follow the god.'

The 'excellent ones who follow Sokar' (*iḳrw nn šms Skr*) are mentioned again in P. Louvre N 3166, II, 26 (*LPE*, p. 89 [I, 7–8]); see too R.J. Demarée, *The ꜣḫ iḳr n Rꜥ-Stelae* (Leiden 1983), p. 274, n. 396, and K. Mysliwiec, *SAK* 6 (1978), p. 148, fig. 6: *di.f šms nṯr r štyt m-m iḳrw*. On the deceased following Sokar, see Smith, *Liturgy*, p. 57.

Lines 6–7

pr bꜣ.t r ḥrt [*m-ꜥb bꜣw*] *ḫn.f sk ḥr ẖꜣt.t m igrt*. Restoration after the parallels. P. BM EA 10112, 14–15 and P. Toulouse 49–220, 13–14 (in both cases with variant *pꜣy* rather than *pr*, the more often attested in this context; the two terms are equivalent; see M. Smith, *Enchoria* 15 (1987), p. 72 and n. 27; G. Vittmann, *ZÄS* 117 (1990), p. 88 (line 29)). For the ba of the deceased alighting on the corpse: L.V. Žabkar, *A Study of the Ba Concept* (*SAOC* 34, 1968), p. 133; *LPE*, p. 147 (III, 3).

P. BM EA 10112, 14–15:

pꜣy bꜣ.t r ḥrt m-ꜥb bꜣw	'Your ba flies up to heaven with the bas,
ḫn.f ḥr ẖꜣt.t m igrt	it alights on your corpse in the necropolis.'

P. Cairo CG 58012, 11–12 = P. Toulouse 49–220, 13–14:

pꜣy bꜣ.k (*/..t*) *r ḥrt m-ꜥb bꜣw*	'Your ba flies up to heaven with the bas,
ḫn.f mitt ḥr ẖꜣt.k (*/..t*)	it alights likewise on your corpse.'

P. Turin 1989, 6–7:

pꜣy pꜣy.t bꜣ r ḥrt m-ꜥb bꜣw	'Your ba flies up to heaven with the bas,
ḫn.f mitt ḥr ẖꜣt.t	it alights likewise on your corpse.'

P. BM EA 10125, 10–11:

mi pꜣy pꜣy.i bꜣ r ḥrt m-ꜥb bꜣw	'May my ba fly up to heaven with the bas,
ḫn.f mitt ḥr ẖꜣt.i m igrt	and alight likewise on my corpse in the necropolis!'

The example of P. Cairo CG 58009, II, 1–3 is particularly interesting:

mi pꜣy pꜣy.i bꜣ r ḥrt m-ꜥb	'May my ba fly up to heaven with the
bꜣw n nṯrw wrw	bas of the great gods,
ḫn.f sk ḥr ẖꜣt.i	and alight also on my corpse!'

Var. P. Louvre N 3290, 11–12:

mi pꜣy pꜣy.i bꜣ r ḥrt ḥnꜥ	'May my ba fly up to heaven with
nꜣ bꜣw n nꜣ nṯrw wrw	the bas of the great gods,
ḫn.f sk ḥr ẖꜣt.i	and alight also on my corpse!'

Because of the precision concerning the identity of the ba, it may be compared with the sequence P. BM EA 10191, 11, in whose commentary here many other parallels will be found. The variant *bꜣw n nṯrw* (*wrw*) seems preferable to the rather unexpected version *bꜣw*. The collective *bꜣw* is generally qualified by some adjective (*špsw, iḳrw*, etc.), and it would be justified to ask, in the light of two passages of P. Rhind, I, 9, 2 and II, 9, 2, if another interpretation should not be sought for the word *bꜣw*, consistently written 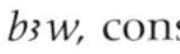 (P. BM EA 10112, 14; P. Toulouse 49–220, 14; P. Lieblein, 14; P. BM EA 10125, 11).

P. Rhind I, 9, 1–2:

s pw ib.f iḳr	'This man whose heart is excellent,
imy s(w) imytw ḥsyw	grant that he be among the praised ones,
imy pr bꜣ.f r pt ḥnꜥ bꜣw ()	that his ba go forth to the sky with the bas.'

P. Rhind II, 9, 1–2:

mt-ḥnt nfrt ib.s iḳr	'(This) beautiful woman whose heart is excellent,
imy s imytw špswt	grant that she be among the noblewomen,
m šms nb nḥḥ	in the retinue of the lord of eternity (Osiris),
imy pr bꜣ.s ḥnꜥ bꜣw ()	that her ba go forth with the bas.'

The demotic versions of the sequence concerning the passage of the ba are as follows:

mi šm pꜣy=f by r tꜣ p.t irm pꜣy=w by	'May his ba go forth to the sky together with their bas.'
mi rpy pꜣy=s by irm pꜣy=w by	'May her ba be renewed together with their bas.'

If then in these latter examples it is necessary to understand the ba of the deceased as appearing with those of the *ḥsyw* and the *špswt*, the interpretation should apply equally to our text evoking in line 6 the union of the deceased with the *ḥsyw iḳrw* (var. *iḳrw*) and the passage of his or her ba with theirs. If this reasoning is followed, the 'great gods' (*nṯrw wrw*, P. Cairo CG 58009 cited *supra*) ought to refer here collectively to the deified dead.[13] Note that the presence of a genitive after *bꜣw* is attested only in those sequences not preceded by the mention of the *ḥsyw* or an equivalent term (P. Berlin 3052, P. Louvre N 3176 A, P. BM EA 10109, P. Cairo 58008, 58014). The writing *bꜣw* thus probably conceals a singular *bꜣ* followed by the suffix *.w*.

Line 7

wn.t nšnš ḫnty Ḥbs-bꜣg ṯtf ꜥḥm [...]. *wn.t nšnš* is for *wnšnš.t*. This form is also attested in P. Louvre E 10263, 8, in the sequence *wn.t nšnš* () *m wsḫt Gb*. The verb *wnšnš*, relatively rare (*Wb*. I, 325, 10), takes various prepositions, such as *m* (P. Leiden T 32, II, 28; P. Parma 183, vs.; P. Cairo CG 58009, vs.); *m-ḫt* (P. Leiden T 32, V, 13);

13. J. Zandee, *Death as an Enemy* (2nd edn, New York 1977), pp. 199, 212 and n. 10; H. Goedicke, in Lipiński (ed), *State and Temple Economy in the Ancient Near East* (*OLA* 5, 1979), pp. 125–6.

ḫr (P. BM EA 10201, II, 10); and *ḫnt* (Cairo CG 42208, ed. Legrain, *Statues et statuettes* III, p. 21). It is probably this preposition which should be seen after the *ḫnty* of our document.

Ḥbs-bꜣg: originally the designation for the necropolis of Heracleopolis (*GDG* IV, 26). For mention of it in Theban texts: Haikal, *Two Hier. Fun. Pap.* II, pp. 30–1, n. 48. In P. Toulouse 49–220, 12, cited *supra*, **lines 5–6**, Anubis introduces the deceased to Hebes-bag. Another reference in P. Louvre E 10263, 9: *pr.t h[ꜣ].t ḫnt Ḥbs-bꜣg*, 'You come and go in Hebes-bag', equivalent to *wn.t nšnš ḫnty Ḥbs-bꜣg* in our text.[14] In P. Rhind I, 4, 13, and II, 5, 1, the hieratic *Ḥbs-bꜣg* is rendered in demotic as *tꜣ wsḫꜣ.t n tꜣ Dwꜣ.t*, 'the hall of the Duat'.

ṯtf ꜥḫm [...]: beginning of a sequence of which the end is lost in the lacuna of line 8. The expression is obscure and without known parallel in the other versions of the Book of Breathing. *ꜥḫm*, probable subject of *ṯtf*, causes some difficulty. As a noun, the water determinative suggests a comparison with the word read *ꜥḫw* by the *Wb.* (I, 224, 14 'Gewasser'), with as sole reference the onomasticon of Amenemope, 39. The other versions of the text offer a variant *ꜥḫmy(t)*, for which the translation suggested by Gardiner in *AEO* I, p. 8* ('river-bank' ?) and by myself in *BIFAO* 86 (1986), p. 193 ('rive') ought probably to be reconsidered. In the present instance, the presence of the legs sign as second determinative could allow interpretation of *ꜥḫm* as water in movement. Some connection with the rising waters of the inundation might be envisaged.

Line 8

šm.t ḥr tꜣ mꜣꜣ.t imyw.f ḫf.t sḫrw nb n pr.t. Var P. BM EA 10112, 15–16: *dgꜣ.t* instead of *ḫf.t*, and *sḫrw nb m pr.t.*

P. Turin 1989, 12–13:

pr.t r tꜣ mꜣꜣ.t sḫrw n pr.t	'You go forth upon earth and see the rules of your house,
hrw nhs bꜣ.t	on the day when your ba awakes.'

P. Cairo CG 58012, 12–13:

šm.k ḥr tꜣ mꜣꜣ.k imyw.f	'You go upon earth and see what it contains,
ḥnꜥ bꜣw n nṯrw	with the bas of the gods;
mꜣꜣ.k sḫrw nb n pr.k	you see all the rules of your house.'

P. Cairo CG 58018, vs.:

pr.k hꜣ.k ḥr tꜣ n Gb	'You come and go upon the earth of Geb,
dgꜣ.k sḫrw nb nty im	and behold all the rules which are there.'

m ꜥm ꜥky ḥr ḫpr mitt.sn n bꜣ bꜣw. Phrase of doubtful interpretation, for which several parallels are known, none of them facilitating understanding:

P. BM EA 10112, 16–17: *m ꜥm ꜥkw* ( ) *ḥr ḫpr im.t ḫpr mitt.sn n bꜣ bꜣw.*

P. BM EA 10110 + 10111, II, 28: *m ꜥm ꜥkw* ( ) *ḥr ḫpr r.k.*

P. Lieblein, 7: [...] *ḥr ḫpr* [*im.t*] *ḫpr*[*w*] *mitt* [...].

P. Cairo CG 58009, V, 5–6: *m ꜥm ꜥky* (?) *ḥr ḫpr im.k ḫpr mitt is n kꜣ ḫry.*

ꜥm has two possible senses: either 'swallow', 'devour' (*Wb.* I, 183–4), or 'know', 'understand' (*Wb.* I, 184). In both cases, the word read *ꜥkw/ꜥky* provides the complement as object, but its identification remains problematic.

The antecedent to the suffix *.sn* in *mitt.sn*, attested in P. BM EA 10108 and 10112, ought theoretically to be the plural *sḫrw*, but in the light of the other versions, this is open to doubt. It seems likely that some confusion has affected the compilers of the various manuscripts cited.

Bꜣ Bꜣw: On this divine designation in general, see G. Vittmann, *SAK* 22 (1995), pp. 296–7, n. 14. The context here, as in P. 10112, is unclear. The determinative and the mention of the *kꜣ ḫry* in the parallel passage of P. Cairo CG 58009, V, 6, make identification with an animal probable, and it is possible to envisage an identification with the name Baba (Bebon), written *Bꜣ Bꜣw*; cf. Ph. Derchain, *RdE* 9 (1952), p. 47. No other occurrence of this name so written seems attested elsewhere.

Line 9

[...] *r-hꜣ m pr.f hrww nw ꜥnḫ imy hrw ḥb*. Sequence absent from the other versions. On *r-hꜣ* conveying the idea of a procession, see *LPE*, p. 202 (V, 12). Restore along the lines of [*pr.f*] *r-hꜣ*, '(when) he goes out on procession', with *.f* probably referring back to *Bꜣ Bꜣw* in the preceding line.

sḏm.t nꜣ wpwt nt Iwntyw hrww nhm n Sḫmt. Sequence partly in lacuna in P. Lieblein, 17–18; P. Louvre E 10263, 3. Cf. also P. Leiden T 32, VI, 23–4 (*LPE*, pp. 229–30):

sḏm.k ḫrw wpwt nt Iwntyw	'You hear the voice of the crowd of *Iwntyw*-women
hrw nhm n Sḫmt	on the day of acclaiming Sekhmet.'

Lines 9–10

šm.t [*r Iwnw m ḫwt*] *ḥr ḫꜣwt grḥ pfy n snwt n p(ꜣ) ḥb* (?). On access to Heliopolis on the the festival of offerings on the altar (fifth day of the lunar month) and the festival of the sixth day, see P. BM EA 10191, **I, 13–14**, with numerous parallels.

The reading and the meaning of the word , so written in all the known manuscripts, are problematic. Apart from P. BM EA 10108, it is only found, always in the same context, in the following documents:

P. BM EA 10112, 18–19:

šm.t r Iwnw m ḫwt ḥr ḫꜣwt	'You proceed to Heliopolis at the festival of offerings on the altar,
grḥ pfy n snwt n	on that night of the festival of the sixth day and at the ...-festival.'

P. BM EA 10109, 10–11:

i I mi ḥr.k r.i	'O Thoth, turn towards me!
smꜣꜥ.k ḫrw.i r ḫftyw.i	Vindicate me against my enemies
mi smꜣꜥ.k ḫrw Wsir	as you vindicated Osiris,
m-bꜣḥ ḏꜣḏꜣt ꜥꜣt imyw Iwnw	before the great Council which is in Heliopolis,
grḥ pfy n snwt n	on that night of the festival of the sixth day and at the ...-festival.'

P. Cairo CG 58012, 13–14:

šm.k r Iwnw ḥnꜥ iryw Iwnw	'You proceed to Heliopolis with the guardians of Heliopolis,[15]
grḥ pfy n snwt n	on that night of the festival of the sixth day and of the ...-festival.'

Given the paucity of the variants, all found in the Book of Breathing, the possible readings of this word are limited. The readings *ꜥnp* and *np*, proposed first by Lieblein (*Que mon nom fleurisse*, pp. 6 and xxvii), then by Golenischeff (*Pap. hiérat.* I, p. 61 and pl. 12), on the basis of a faulty transcription of the word in P. Cairo 58012, 14, are to be excluded; it is also improbable that the writing corresponds to a

14. Cf. also the equivalence of *wnšnš* and *dwn gst*, *LPE*, p. 103 (I, 18–19).

15. Cf. P. Louvre E 10263, 1: *dhn.t tꜣ n iryw Iwnw*, 'You prostrate yourself before the guardians of Heliopolis'.

reading *np*[16] (one would rather expect a disposition), and a reading <>*np*, with reference to , the twentieth day of the lunar month (Brugsch, *Thes.*, p. 47), remains doubtful.[17] With reservation, it seems preferable to see in a writing of *n p(ꜣ)*, well attested in similar contexts indicating a 'night of the festival of X and of (*n pꜣ*) Y', but *p(ꜣ) ḥb* is not entirely convicing since, in all the examples, a new sequence begins afterwards, without any relation with the former one.

Lines 10–[11]
spr.k r Tꜣ-wr niwt nt ḫprr hrw ḥb [...]. The tenth line ends with the image of a cross, the significance of which is not clear.[18] The parallel versions diverge at this point:

P. BM EA 10112, 19–20:

ꜥḳ.k r Tꜣ-wr m ḥb rkḥ nḏs	'You enter Ta-wer at the festival of the small flame,
hrw ḥb ꜥḫ pt	on the day of the festival of raising the sky.'

P. Cairo CG 58012, 14:

ꜥḳ.k r Tꜣ-wr ḥnꜥ nṯrw šps w	'You enter Ta-wer with the noble gods,
m hrw ḥb ꜥḫ pt	on the day of the festival of raising the sky.'

P. Lieblein, 19:

šm.t r Tꜣ-wr	'You proceed to Ta-wer,
r tr n [...]	at the moment of [...].'

In view of these parallels, it is hardly possible to restore with confidence in P. BM EA 10108 the indication of the moment of the move to Ta-wer. For the festivals of the small flame and of the raising of heaven, see P. BM EA 10112, **lines 19–20**. On the 'town of the scarab', see *LPE*, p. 109, n. 23.

Line 11
[...] *Skr psḏ m ḥnw Fnḏ.f-ꜥnḫ m ꜣbd.f*. For lack of exact parallel, the words in lacuna preceding the mention of Sokar cannot be certainly restored. For Sokar *psḏ m ḥnw*: *LPE*, p. 157 (III, 14–15). Fenedj(ef)-ankh is an aspect of Osiris. On this divinity and his *ꜣbd*-reliquary, see ibid., pp. 109–10 (I, 23–4).

ir.w n.t tp-rd nb n wꜥbt irw nb n pr m hrw. Var. P. Toulouse 49–220, 8 (cited *supra*, **line 4**): *n pr-nfr* instead of *pr m hrw*.

This sequence may be compared with the passage P. Leiden T 32, V, 27–8 (*LPE*, p. 212):

ḫrp n.k tp-rd nb n wꜥbt	'Every rite of the embalming house is directed for you
hrww nw wn pr	on the days of opening the house.'

This text enables the performance of the rites to be placed within Khoiak (the 16th and 24th of this month), and it may be supposed that the rites for coming forth by day are to be located within the same month (as for the episode of Sokar in his bark). Without proposing a calendrical content, which cannot be justified here, it is worth pointing out in passing the frequency of passages taken from the rites of Khoiak in manuscripts of the Book of Breathing.

Line 12
[*ḳbḥ.w n.t*] *mw m ḥwt sr mi pꜣ sr wr m Iwnw*. The restoration seems probable after the parallels. In general, the wish for a libation is expressed in the first person, in the form *mi ḳbḥ.w n.i mw* (cf. e.g. P. BM EA 10199, 9–10). In the second person, *mi* is not used; cf. P. Cairo CG 58012, 15:

ḳbḥ.w n.k mw m rꜣ-stꜣw	'A libation of water is made for you in Ro-setau
mi pꜣ sr wr m Iwnw	as (for) the great prince in Heliopolis.'

For the general commentary, see P. BM EA 10191, **I, 12**.

rwḏ rn.t m-ḫnw Wꜣst m-ḫnw spt r nḥḥ. General formula outlining the endurance of the name of the deceased in the capital and in the provinces. See P. BM EA 10110 + 10111, **I, 4–5, 6**.

Lines 12–13
mi rwḏ rn n [*Mnṯw 4 m-ḫnw*] *niwt.sn*. Probable restoration after the parallels. See P. BM EA 10110 + 10111, **I, 19**.

Lines 13–14
[*nšp ḫ*]*nmty.t is-niw m-ꜥ Ḫnsw-Šw wr m Wꜣst ḫft*[19] *ꜥḳ.f Iꜣt Ḏꜣm* [*tp smin rꜥ nb*]. The restoration seems guaranteed by the parallels, notably P. Leiden T 32, I, 6 (*LPE*, p. 387), and especially P. Cairo CG 58009, V, 10–12 = P. Cairo CG 58012, 15–16:

nšp ḫnmty.k is-niw	'Your nostrils breathe the breath of air
m-ꜥ Ḫnsw-Šw wr m Wꜣst	by the grace of Khonsu-Shu, great in Thebes,
ḫft ḥfḥf Iꜣt Ḏꜣm (var.: *Ḫnmt-ꜥnḫ*)	upon crossing (the river) <towards> the Mound of Djeme (var.: Khenemet-ankh),[20]
tp smin rꜥ nb	daily (?).'[21]

P. Lieblein, 28–9:

[*is*]*-niw srḳ iḫty.t*	'The breath of] wind allows your throat to breathe
m-ꜥ Ḫnsw [*Šw wr m Wꜣst*	by the grace of Khonsu[-Shu, great in Thebes
ḫft ḥfḥf Ḫnm]*-ꜥnḫ*	upon crossing (the river) <towards> Khenem]-ankh,
tp smin rꜥ nb	daily (?).'

P. BM EA 10112, 21–2:

is-niw srḳ.n.f ḫtyt.t	'The breath of wind, it allows your throat to breathe
m-ꜥ Ḫnsw-Šw wr m Wꜣst	by the grace of Khonsu-Shu, great in Thebes.'

See too P. BM EA 10114, **line 5**.

On receiving breath (*is niw*) from Khonsu-Shu, and the function of this deity: *LPE*, pp. 88 (I, 6) and 146 (III, 1).

Line 14
r sꜥr mꜣꜥ n it itw. Same reading in P. Cairo CG 58012, 17. Sequence partly in lacuna in P. Lieblein, 30–1. Cf. too the variant of P. Cairo CG 58009, V, 13: *ḥr mꜣꜥ* () *snw n ḥtptyw*, 'bearer of *mꜣꜥ*-offerings and *snw*-loaves for those who rest' (*ḥtptyw*: M. Doresse, *RdE* 25 [1973], p. 97, n. 3, and *LPE*, pp. 106–7, 273–4).

16. So Chassinat, *RHR* 31 (1895), p. 318: 'en cette nuit de la *Fête des six* et de la *Fête napi*'.
17. The word is read *stp* by R.A. Parker, *The Calendars of Ancient Egypt* (*SAOC* 26, 1950), p. 11, but a list of the days of the lunar month at Edfou gives for the twentieth day: *hrw n Inpw* (pun between *ꜥnp* and *Inpw* ?), illustrated by a representation of the god (ibid., pl. V).
18. Cf. e.g. P. Berlin 3030, II, 4, 6; P. Berlin 3052, II, 5; P. BN 152, 25; P. Louvre E 3865, II, 16, 17; P. Vienne 3870, 25 and 26.
19. The scribe originally wrote *m ꜥḳ.f*. He then added, without correction, *ḫft* in the space above.
20. For the variant *Ḫnmt-ꜥnḫ* in place of *Iꜣt Ḏꜣm*: J. Quaegebeur, in *Studi in onore di E. Bresciani* (Pisa 1985), pp. 464–5. For *Ḫnmt-ꜥnḫ* in this context: M. Doresse, *RdE* 31 (1979), p. 62, n. 144.
21. *tp smin rꜥ nb*: rare expression not recorded in *Wb.*, but cf. III, 453.

On *ỉt ỉtw*, designation of Amun, see M. Doresse, *RdE* 25 (1973), p. 131, n. 3. For another designation, cf. P. BM EA 10254, 5.

ʿḥʿ.t ḥr ỉnt ʿwy.t m ỉꜣw n sḫm wr ḥr(y) nṯrw nbw. Same reading in P. Cairo CG 58009, V, 14–15 and 58012, 17–18. Sequence partly in lacuna in P. Louvre E 10263, 6 and P. Lieblein, 30.

On the 'great image master of all the gods', see M. Doresse, *RdE* 31 (1979), p. 63 and n. 152.

Lines 14–15

Rʿ-Ḥr-ꜣḫty [*sḥḏ.n.f ḥr.k*] *r tr.f* [*pfy n rʿ nb*]. Restoration after P. Cairo CG 58009, 13–14 and 58012, 18. Sequence in lacuna (or omitted ?) in P. Lieblein, 31. Among the two possible options to fill the lacuna following *tr.f*: *pfy n rʿ nb* (P. Cairo CG 58012), and *n rʿ nb* (P. Cairo CG 58009), only the first corresponds to the space available in this manuscript.

Line 15

sfsf ꜣw n kꜣ.t tp ssw 10 nb m-ʿ snn ʿnḫ n Rʿ m Wꜣst-nḫt. Sequence partly in lacuna in P. Lieblein, 31. Var. P. BM EA 10112, 22–3: *Wꜣst* P. Cairo CG 58012, 18 and P. Toulouse 49–220, 18: *Ỉwnw šmʿ* instead of *Wꜣst-nḫt*; P. Lieblein, 31: *Ỉpt-swt* instead of *Wꜣst-nḫt*. P. Cairo CG 58009, V, 8–9: *sfsf ꜣw n ḥm.k m-ʿ snn n Rʿ tp ssw 10 nbw*. Cf. the title of Amenipet *snn ʿnḫ n Rʿ m Ỉwnw šmʿ*, *Urk.* VIII, § 96b = P. Clère and C. Kuentz, *La porte d'Evergète à Karnak* (*MIFAO* 84, 1961), pl. 47, and the statue Cairo JE 37075, H.W. Fairman, *JEA* 20 (1934), p. 2 and pl. 1, left, col. 6. For the offering at the beginning of each decade: *LPE*, pp. 140–2.

Lines 15–16

m-ḫt šm.f <r> Ḫnmt-ʿnḫ [*ḫr ḫwt r*] *tr.f r wꜣḥ ḫwt n ỉtw.f mwwt.f*. Restoration after P. Cairo CG 58012, 19, which offers the variant: *ḫft ʿḳ.f Ỉꜣt Ḏꜣm*, 'when he has entered the Mound of Djeme' and (20): *r wꜣḥ ḥtpw*, 'to lay down *ḥtpw*-offerings'. Sequence partly in lacuna in P. Lieblein, 31–2. For the version *Ỉꜣt Ḏꜣm* in place of *Ḫnmt-ʿnḫ*, see *supra*, **lines 13–14**.

On the journey of Amenipet: *LPE*, pp. 140–2.

Line 16

ʿḥʿ.t nḥḥ nsyt.t ḏt ḥnty.t pw ḫm sk. For this clause, cf. P. BM EA 10314, II, 7 (var.) and *LPE*, pp. 246–7 (VII, 26).

P. BM EA 10112 (pls 94–7)

Hay Collection 506.
Quirke, *Owners*, no. 254.
S. Birch, *PSBA* 7 (1885), pp. 209–10 with pl.
Lieblein, *Que mon nom fleurisse*, pp. i–iii and 3–5.
B.H. Stricker, *OMRO* 23 (1942), p. 32.
Provenance: Thebes. Possibly from the tomb of the archon Soter, but apparently unconnected with his family.[22]
Date: first to second century AD (?).
Owner of the papyrus: *Tꜣ-šrỉt-pꜣ-wr-ỉꜣbt(t)* (Senporegebthis)
Mother of the owner: *Tꜣ-nt-nwb*.

Contents: Original text adapted from the Book of Breathing.

Manuscript of one sheet (25.6 × 14.2 cm), in good condition, bearing 24 lines of text.

Text on the verso: A good burial. May it be stable over your bones, may it remain over your flesh, without decay! The beautiful Amentet extends her arms to receive you by the decree of the Mistress of the foundations of the earth.

Translation

Recto

(1) Hail Hathor *Tꜣ-šrỉt-pꜣ-wr-ỉꜣbt(t)*, justified, (2) born of *Tꜣ-nt-nwb*, justified, may your ba live in the sky before <Re>, (3) may your ka be divine among the gods, may your mummy be blessed (4) at the head of the spirits, while your name is stable on earth before Geb, (5) and your corpse remains in the god's domain! May your house be peopled with your children! (6) Your spouse pines for you since you left him (7) and your children. The reward for this that they have done for your ka: a good and excellent burial (8); they satisfy your Majesty in the West of Thebes opposite … (?) mistress of temples. The good goddess of the West extends her arms (10) to receive you by the decree of the Mistress of the foundations of the earth. Your tomb (11) will not be upside down, your wrapping will not be trampled, and there will not be displacement of (12) your body for ever.

Anubis receives you in the hall of the region of Maat; (13) he causes you to be one of these excellent praised ones who follow Sokar. (14) Your ba flies up to heaven with the bas; (15) it alights on your corpse in the necropolis. You walk on earth, (16) and see what is on (lit.: in) it, you behold all the rules of your house, recognizing (17) the evil which survives in you, and likewise for the Ba of Bas (?). (18) You proceed to Heliopolis at the festival of offerings on the altar, on (19) that night of the festival of the sixth day, at the festival … (?). You enter Ta-wer at the festival of the small (20) flame, on the day of the festival of raising the sky, and you journey to Busiris at the Khoiak festival, (21) on the day of raising the *ḏd*-pillar. The breath of air, it allows your throat to breathe by the grace of Khonsu-Shu, (22) great in Thebes. Oblation is offered to your ka at the beginning of each decade, by the grace of the living image of Re (23) in Thebes. Your lifetime is eternity, your kingship is everlastingness, and your time is (24) the ignorance of destruction.

Commentary

Lines 2–5

ʿnḫ bꜣ.t m pt ḫr <Rʿ> nṯr kꜣ.t ḫnty nṯrw ꜣḫ sʿḥ.t m-ḫnt ꜣḫw rn.t ḏd m tꜣ ḫr Gb

22. See *supra*, p. 5, n. 67.

ẖꜣt.t wꜣḥ.ti m ẖrt-nṯr. For these formulae, frequently attested in the funerary documentation from the Late Period, see P. BM EA 10108, **lines 1–3**.

Line 5
pr.t grg ẖr msw.t. See P. BM EA 10108, **line 3**.

Lines 6–7
ṯꜣy.t i̓mi̓m m-ẖt.t ḏr nš.n.t s(w) ḥnꜥ msw.t. See P. BM EA 10108, **lines 3–[4]**.

Line 7
i̓swy n nn i̓r.sn n kꜣ.t smꜣ-tꜣ nfr i̓ḳrt. See P. BM EA 10108, **line 4**, giving a different version apparently, despite the lacuna at the beginning of the line, which omits reference to the reward (*i̓swy*).

On provision of a burial as a 'reward': R. El Sayed, *BIFAO* 84 (1984), pp. 143 and 145, n. (r); P. Rhind, I, IV, 10; P. Chester-Beatty IV (= P. BM EA 10684), VII, 4 = Gardiner, *HPBM* III, p. 32 and pl. 15.

Lines 8–9
sḥtp.sn ḥm.t ḥr I̓mntt Wꜣst m sty n ḫdbw.t (?) *ḥnwt rꜣw-prw.* See P. BM EA 10108, **line 4**.

Lines 9–10
di̓ I̓mntt nfrt ꜥwy.s r šsp.t m wḏ n ḥnwt ndbwt. See P. BM EA 10108, **line 5**. After *šsp*, the word *ꜥḥꜣ* occurs, bungled by the scribe, the remnant of a sequence attested in P. BM EA 10108, 5: *ꜥḥꜣ sꜥḥw m ḫsf.t*, 'the mummies stand up at your approach'.

On the 'mistress of the foundations of the earth' (*ḥnwt ndbwt*), see *LPE*, p. 267.

Lines 10–12
nn sḫd i̓s.k nn ptpt wtw.t nn mnmn n ḏt.k ḏt. None of the known parallels for this sequence provides the entire text:

P. Parma 183, 21–2: *nn sḫd i̓s.k nn ptpt wtyw.k.*

P. Turin 1989, 11–12: *nn sḫd i̓s.t nn ptpt wtyw.t nn mrḫ n ḏt.t r ḏt.*

P. Cairo CG 58009, IV, 13 = P. Cairo CG 58012, 8–9: *nn ptpt wtw.k nn mrḫ n ḏt.k (r) ḏt.*

nn sḫd i̓s.k. The meaning of *sḫd*, 'be upside down' with reference to a building, is not cited in *Wb.* (IV, 265–6).

ptpt, 'trample': Y. Koenig, *BIFAO* 82 (1982), pp. 289–90 (k).

For *nn mnmn n ḏt.k ḏt*, cf. the expressions *nn mnmn ẖꜣt.k* (P. MMA 35.9.21, XXIX, 10 and XXXII, 5) and *nn mnmn n sꜥḥ.k* (E. von Bergmann, *Der Sarkophag des Panehemisis* II [Vienna 1884], p. 18, n. 5 = Boeser, *Beschreibung* X, pp. 5 and 8); *nn mnmn n* [...] (P. Cairo CG 58034, 13), or again *(n)n mnmn* in the absolute (Bucheum stelae nos 17, 6; 18, 5; 19, 5). The word  gives an otherwise unattested writing of *mnmn*, with  *mn* < *rmn*; see Edwards, *HPBM* IV (1960), p. 53, n. 30; R.A. Caminos, *A Tale of Woe* (Oxford 1977), p. 26.

For the general sense, cf. *Edfou* I, 173, 13–14: *n wḥꜥ i̓s.sn n th ẖꜣt.sn*, 'Their tomb will not be defaced, their corpse will not be infringed'. See also Koenig, *BIFAO* 78 (1979), p. 109, n. (d).

Line 12
šsp tn I̓npw r wsḫt ww Mꜣꜥt. See P. BM EA 10108, **lines 5–6**.

Line 13
di̓.f wꜥ.t m ḥsyw i̓ḳrw nn šms Skr. See P. BM EA 10108, **line 6**.

Lines 14–15
pꜣy bꜣ.t r ḥrt m-ꜥb bꜣw ḥn.f ḥr ẖꜣt.t m i̓grt. See P. BM EA 10108, **lines 6–7**.

Lines 15–16
šm.t ḥr tꜣ mꜣꜣ.t i̓myw.f dgꜣ.t sḫrw nb m pr.t. See P. BM EA 10108, **line 8**.

Lines 16–17
m ꜥm ꜥḳw ḥr ḫpr i̓m.t ḫpr mi̓tt.sn n bꜣ bꜣw. See P. BM EA 10108, **line 8**.

Lines 18–19
šm.t r I̓wnw m ḥwt ḥr ḫꜣwt grḥ pfy n snwt n p(ꜣ) ḥb (?). See P. BM EA 10108, **lines 9–10**, and 10191, **I, 13–14**.

I̓wnw: the scribe originally wrote the word *Tꜣ-wr* which he garbled and rewrote in the space above the line.

Lines 19–20
ꜥḳ.k r Tꜣ-wr m ḥb rkḥ nḏs hrw ḥb ꜥḥ pt. For this sequence and its variants, see P. BM EA 10108, **10–[11]**.

On the 'festival of the small flame' (*rkḥ nḏs*): *Wb.* II, 459, 3–6; H. Altenmüller, *LÄ* II, 173 with n. 41; 177 with n. 111 (1st of Pharmouti). For a calendrical concordance between this festival and the festival of raising the sky, cf. *LPE*, p. 162 (III, 19–20). P. BM EA 10109, 11–12 provides an invocation addressed to Thoth 'that he may vindicate the deceased as he vindicated Osiris before the great Council which is in Abydos, on that night of the festival of raising the sky'.

Lines 20–1
wḏꜣ.t r Ḏdw m ḥb Kꜣ-ḥr-kꜣ hrw sꜥḥꜥ ḏd. Sequence without known parallel in the Book of Breathing. Structurally, this phrase, like the preceding, is interesting for siting the journey of the deceased simultaneously in the setting of a festival (here: *ḥb Kꜣ-ḥr-kꜣ*) and, in the subsequent specification, on a particular day (*hrw sꜥḥꜥ ḏd*).

The journey to Busiris, complementing that to Abydos mentioned before, is here undertaken 'on the day of raising the *ḏd*-pillar', i.e. the 30th of Khoiak (*LPE*, p. 227 [VI, 20]). Cf. P. BM EA 10344, 10–11:

i̓w (?)[...] *bꜣ.t r Ḏdw*	'Your ba [goes ?] to Busiris,
m grḥ sꜥḥꜥ ḏd m Ḏdw	on the night of erecting the *ḏd*-pillar in Busiris.'

Maspero, *Sarcophages* I, p. 32, 9–11:

ꜥḳ.k r Ḏdw hrw sꜥḥꜥ ḏd	'You enter Busiris (on) the day of raising the *ḏd*-pillar,
šms.k Wsi̓r m Tꜣ-wr	you follow Osiris in Ta-wer,
nn ḫsf.tw(.k) ḥr nšmt wrt	without being repulsed from the *nšmt*-bark;
pr bꜣ.k ḥnꜥ bꜣw nṯrw	your ba goes forth with the bas of the gods,
šms.k nb tꜣ ḏsr ḥnd.k Rꜣ-stꜣw	you follow the lord of the sacred land and tread Ro-setau,
ꜥḳ.k r Ḏdw ꜣbḏw	you enter Busiris and Abydos,
šms.k nṯr ꜥꜣ ḫnm.n.f i̓ꜣbt	you follow the great god when he has united with the left eye,
hrw mḥ wḏꜣt	on the day of filling the *wḏꜣt*-eye.'

Lines 21–2
i̓s-ni̓w srḳ.n.f ḥtyt.t m-ꜥ Ḫnsw-Šw wr m Wꜣst. See P. BM EA 10108, **lines 13–14**.

Lines 22–3
sfsf ꜣw n kꜣ.t tp ssw 10 nb m-ꜥ snn ꜥnḫ n Rꜥ m Wꜣst. See P. BM EA 10108, **line 15**.

Lines 23–4
ꜥḥꜥ.t nḥḥ nsyt.t ḏt ḥnty [*.t*] *pw ḫm sk*. See P. BM EA 10108, **line 16**.

P. BM EA 10115 (pls 98–9)

Salt Collection 1 (in coffin).
Unpublished.
Quirke, *Owners*, no. 41.
E.A.W. Budge, *A Guide to the Fourth, Fifth and Sixth Egyptian Rooms* (London 1922), p. 298, no. 24.
B.H. Stricker, *OMRO* 23 (1942), p. 32.
Provenance: Thebes. Found with P. BM EA 10114, probably on the mummy inside coffin BM EA 6706 in the collective tomb of the archon Soter.[23]
Date: End of the first to beginning of the second century AD.
Owner of the papyrus: *Grꜣỉwptr* (Cleopatra).
Mother of the owner: *Ḳnt* [...] (Candace).

Contents: Original text partly adapted from the First Book of Breathing and the Book of the Dead.

Manuscript of one sheet (24.5 × 23.2 cm), in fairly good condition except for the upper part, and bearing fourteen lines of text. The second line is written in hieroglyphs, all the others in hieratic. At three places (lines 1, 8 and 12), the ink has suffered from the erosion of the surface.

Text on the verso: A good burial. May it be stable [over your ...], may it remain [over your ...]. The beautiful Amentet extends [her arms ...].

Translation

Recto

(1) Hail Hathor Cleopatra, born of the Hathor Can[dace]!

(*In hieroglyphics*):

(2) I am Re at his rising, I am Atum at his setting, I am Osiris foremost of the West, the great god (3) lord of Abydos. (O) doorkeepers of the sacred land, guardians (?) (*sic*).

(*In hieratic*):

Offering that the king gives, of bread, beer, oxen and fowl (4), what heaven gives and earth creates. Access to the hall of the two Maats (is made) by the gods masters of the offering-tables of Re; (5) they turn towards you. I am Semawer, the likeness of Re, living image (6) of the Ba which crosses the sky, who multiplies the *ḥtpw*-offerings of the primordial gods, who provisions (7) the bight of the trap for the Sauensen-deities. Agebwer, likewise, is beside me (?) in the form of Foremost of the bed. He for his part is (8) multiplying the possessions of the two Maats in the Duat [...] invoking [...]

(9) Hail to you, righteous gods! Hail <to you>, great god, lord of the two Maats! I come to you, my lord, (10) having been led to see your perfection. I know <your> name and I know the names of the 42 gods who are with you in the hall of the two Maats (11), who live on the guardians (?) of evil and drink of their blood. Behold, lord<s> of the two Maats, I know you, (12) lords of the two Maats, I have brought to you the two Maats (*sic*) – otherwise said: Maat –, I have repelled evil for you; I have not [mal]treated (13) people, I have not committed an abomination in the Place of Truth, I have done no wrong to men, (14) I have not killed in wrong because I know their name, the lords of Heliopolis come forth from Heliopolis, living for ever.

Commentary

Lines 2–3
ỉnk Rꜥ m ḫꜥ.f ỉnk Ỉtm m ḥtp.f ỉnk Wsỉr ḫnty Ỉmntt nṯr ꜥꜣ nb ꜣbḏw. Usual opening of the First Book of Breathing. For the variants, see P. BM EA 10191, **I, 1–2**.

Line 3
nꜣ ỉryw-ꜥꜣ n tꜣ ḏsr nꜣ sꜣwtyw (?) (*sic*). The sequence ends abruptly, exactly at the point where the writing changes from hieroglyphic to hieratic. Omission at the start either of an interjection (*ỉ, hꜣy*), or, more probably, of *ḥr.tn r.ỉ*, 'turn towards me', which is expected here. In its wording, this sequence deviates from the predominant version *nꜣ ỉryw-ꜥꜣ n Ỉmntt nꜣ sꜣwtyw n tꜣ Dwꜣt*. See P. BM EA 10191, **I, 2–3**.

Lines 3–4
ḥtp dỉ nsw m tꜣ ḥnḳt ỉḥw ꜣpdw n dỉ.n pt ḳmꜣ.n tꜣ. The ancient offering formula, for which see W. Barta, *Aufbau und Bedeutung* (*ÄgFo* 24, 1968).

bs r wsḫt nt Mꜣꜥty. *Bs*, used to denote the introduction of the deceased before Osiris by a deity (Seeber, *Untersuchungen*, p. 160), is not the usual term to convey access to the hall of the two Maats. In that case it is more common to find the verbs *ꜥḳ*: *BD* ch. 125, title; stela Louvre C 117 (H. de Meulenaere, *OLP* 4 [1973], p. 78 and pl. 5, line 11); P. BM EA 9995, I, 5; *spr*: *BD* ch. 125 (ed. Budge, p. 249, 3, and see Seeber, op. cit., p. 64, n. 221); *hꜣy*: *BD* ch. 125, title; *wnšnš*: P. Parma 183, vs. (twice); *pḥrr*: P. Leiden T 32, I, 19; *ḫnd*: P. Rhind I, 4, 1–2; TT 157 (*Wb*. II, *Belegst.*, 21, 2); *ẖnm*: *Urk*. IV, 116, 9.

nṯrw ḥryw wḏḥw n Rꜥ: these divinities, also known as *nṯrw ḥryw wḏḥw*, are a generic designation of the offering-bearer deities: J.L. Simonet, *Le collège des dieux maîtres d'autel* (Montpellier 1994), p. 195 (index). Note that here this designation concerns only Semawer and Agebwer, cited in lines 5 and 7. Their access to the hall of the two Maats seems otherwise unattested.

Line 5
ḫrp.sn n.k m ḥr.sn. *Ḫrp m ḥr* is a synonymous expression, not recorded in the *Wb.*, for *rdỉ ḥr*, 'to turn (towards)' (lit.: to show one's face).

23. see *supra*, p. 6, no. **10**, and p. 7.

Lines 5–6

ink Smꜣ-wr snn n Rꜥ šsp ꜥnḫ n Bꜣ ḏꜣ pt. For Semawer ('the great slayer'), name of the Buchis bull, see F.R. Herbin, *RdE* 35 (1984), p. 119, n. 47, with references for his role as an offering-bearer; Simonet, op. cit., pp. 187–8.

The epithet *snn n Rꜥ* is known as a designation of Imenipet of Djeme: M. Doresse, *RdE* 25 (1973), p. 129, n. 13; H.W. Fairman, *JEA* 20 (1934), p. 2. No other attestation seems to be known in connection with Semawer, although the links of the latter with Re are well established (Mond-Myers, *The Bucheum* II, pp. 40–1).

šsp ꜥnḫ n Bꜣ ḏꜣ pt: this recalls the epithet of Buchis *šsp ꜥnḫ n Mnṯw* (Mond-Myers, *The Bucheum* II, pp. 12 [stela no. 13, line 8] and 41), suggesting an explicit identification with the enigmatic 'Ba who crosses the sky', identified with Amun by Sethe (*Amun*, § 232) on the basis of the determinative in one of the three attestations which he cites. See also K. Jansen-Winkeln, *Biographische und religiöse Inschriften der Spätzeit* (*ÄAT* 45, 2002), p. 152, n. 13. However, in the present context, *Bꜣ ḏꜣ pt* could be a designation of a solar deity, probably Re-Horakhty-Atum: see Leitz, *LGG* II, p. 709.

Line 6

swr ḥtpw n nꜣ nṯrw pꜣwtyw. Semawer is unknown elsewhere as supplier of the offering table of the primordial gods; however, this function is attested for the Mnevis bull (F.R. Herbin, *RdE* 35 [1984], p. 120, n. 51), and it may be supposed that deities of similar nature could assume identical or interchangeable functions, as the continuation of the text indicates.

Lines 6–7

sḏfꜣ ib n ibṯt n Sꜣw-n.sn. This clause, still referring to Semawer, specifies a previously unattested role. It should be noted that the relation of Semawer to the Sauensen-deities is not exclusive: while he is himself designated as the one who 'distributes the *snw*-loaves to the Sauensen-deities' (*dš snw n Sꜣw-n.sn*; *Dendara* VII, 34, 18), Agebwer, who is mentioned further on in the text, is said to 'stock the altar of the Sauensen-deities (*sḏfꜣ wḏḥw nty Sꜣw-n.sn*; *Edfou* I, 488, 9 = 519, 16), and 'offer (...) food-offerings <to the> Sauensen-deities' (*ꜥb (...) drpw <n> Sꜣw-n.sn*; *Dendara* VII, 74, 4).

These activities are normal and expected for offering deities, but the role given here in P. BM EA 10115 is different in character and raises certain problems of vocabulary. In may probably be recognized the word *ib* of *Wb.* I, 61, 17, 'Teil des Vogelnetze', with the sole example in *BD* ch. 153 A (ed. Budge, p. 390, 14). The rarity of the word probably accounts for the diversity in translation: 'carcasse' (P. Barguet, *Le Livre des Morts des anciens Egyptiens* [Paris 1967], p. 219), 'frame' (Allen, *Book of the Dead*, p. 151), 'anse' (Meeks, *ALex* 78.0257). In this passage of *BD*, the deceased, addressing the fishermen, says that he has escaped the part of the trap called used for snaring the dead (M. Alliot, *RdE* 5 [1946], pp. 113–14); the version preserved in sp. 474 of the *CT* (VI, 17 h) gives the form , also variously interpreted (R.O. Faulkner, *The Ancient Egyptian Coffin Texts* II [Warminster 1977], p. 112: 'bight' (?); P. Barguet, *Textes des Sarcophages du Moyen Empire* [Paris 1986], p. 306: 'piège'. The word occurs again, in the same spell and in an identical context, in *CT* VI, 21 l ( ).

On the word *ibṯt*, see D. Bidoli, *Die Sprüche der Fangnetze* (*ADAIK* 9, 1976), p. 75, n. (b). For the writing of the word in this text, Meeks, *ALex* 78.0270.

For the *Sꜣw-n.sn*: Leitz, *LGG* VI, pp. 126–7.

Line 7

ꜣgb-wr mitt r-gs.i (?) *m irw.f n Ḫnty nmt*. This phrase, identifying Agebwer with Osiris ('Foremost of the bed'), previously unattested, would more usually refer to Buchis, alias Semawer, as indicated by some of the titles attested on his stelae: *bꜣ ꜥnḫ n ḫnty nmi.f* (stelae from Bucheum nos 8, B and 9, 2), *dmḏ ḥr bꜣ ḫnty-ꜣtt*[*.f*] (stela no. 14, C), or, simpler still, *snn n Wn-nfr* (stela no. 13, 8); see Mond-Myers, *The Bucheum* III, pl. 40 and 43. On Agebwer, see F.R. Herbin, *RdE* 35 [1984], p. 119, n. 49; Simonet, op. cit., pp. 177–81.

Since the passage is in the first person (cf. line 5: *ink Smꜣ-wr*), a reading *r-gs.i* may be envisaged for .

Lines 7–8

wn.f ir.f ḥr swr ḫrt n Mꜣꜥty (?) *m Dwꜣt*. The expression *swr ḫrt* is comparable to *swr ḥtpw* in line 6 wih the same meaning. Cf. *KO* 700, 13: (*nṯrw ḥryw wḏḥw*) *swr.sn ḫrt.f*, '(the gods masters of the offering-table), they multiply his (of Pharaoh) possessions'. In this context, the reference to the two Maats (?) seems unattested elsewhere. The identification of the is problematic; these might be either the two Maats or the righteous gods (*mꜣꜥtyw*). On this ambiguity: *LPE*, p. 263 (VIII, 23–4).

The remainder of the text is too badly defaced to be intelligible.

Lines 9–14

Text inspired from *BD* ch. 125 (col. 1–5 of Lepsius ed.), with variants and notable omissions. For a general commentary, see Maystre, *Les déclarations*, pp. 13–26, 37, 115–18.

Line 9

inḏ <ḥr.k> nṯr ꜥꜣ nb . As above (line 8), confusion is possible between *Mꜣꜥty* and *mꜣꜥtyw*. The parallels suggest rather *Mꜣꜥty*, as also in lines 11 and 12.

Line 10

iw.i rḫ . *rn.k* would be expected. On the 42 gods, see Seeber, *Untersuchungen*, pp. 136–9.

Line 12

nn . Two restorations might be envisaged: or . Whichever reading is preferred, *ꜣ(i)r* or *mꜣr*, the meaning is the same.

Line 13

to be read *wnḏw* ? For a possible confusion between *wnḏw*, 'people', and *wnḏw*, 'short-horned cattle', see Maystre, *Les déclarations*, pp. 24–5.

Line 14

rn.sn, to be understood as the name of the gods of the two Maats mentioned above.

P. BM EA 10116 (pls 100–3)

Hay Collection.

Unpublished.

Quirke, *Owners*, no. 252.

E.A.W. Budge, *A Guide to the Fourth, Fifth and Sixth Egyptian Rooms* (London 1922), p. 298, no. 22.

B.H. Stricker, *OMRO* 23 (1942), p. 33.

Provenance: Thebes. Possibly from the tomb of the archon Soter, but apparently unconnected with his family.[24]

Date: first to second century AD (?).

Owner of the papyrus: *Tꜣ-šrỉt-Ns-Mnw* (Senesminis). The name is more common in the masculine form *Pꜣ-šr-Ns-Mnw*; cf. *Demot. Nb.* I, p. 253.

Mother of the owner: *Tꜣ-šrỉt-pꜣ-dỉ-H̱nsw-pꜣ-ẖrd* (Senpeṭeche-spochrates). For other examples of this name (not recorded in R*PN*), see P. BN 239, P. dem. Louvre N 3258 and H.J. Thissen, *Die demotischen Graffiti von Medinet Habu* (*DemSt.* 10, 1989), no. 121, 12.

Contents: Original text partly adapted from the Second Book of Breathing.

Manuscript of one sheet (22.6 × 21.4 cm), in fairly good condition apart from the damaged lower edge. The manuscript comprises three sections: arranged beneath three lines covering the entire breadth of the document are written two texts of inequal length, each preceded by a vertical line of text.

Text on the verso: A good burial. May it endure over your bones, may it remain over your flesh, without destruction nor decay, eternally!
(*In demotic*): (at) her feet.

General note.
For convenient reference, the numbering of the lines follows this order:
lines 1–3: the first three lines at the top.
line 4: vertical line at the right of the manuscript.
lines 5–17: text alongside the first vertical line.
line 18: second vertical line
lines 19–33: text alongside the second vertical line.
line 34: the lowermost line.

Translation

Recto

(1) Thus speaks the Hathor *Tꜣ-šrỉt-Ns-Mnw*, justified, born of *Tꜣ-šrỉt-pꜣ-dỉ-H̱nsw-pꜣ-ẖrd*, in good health:

(2) O Re, I am your son! I am your beloved! O Osiris, I am your image! O Lord of Hermopolis, I am your heir, in truth! O Re-Horakhty, O great Ennead, (3) O lesser Ennead! May my name endure within Thebes and within the nomes for ever as the name of Atum Lord of Heliopolis endures in Heliopolis.

(4) (*In one column*):

May (my) name endure within Thebes and within the nomes for ever (as endures the name)

(5) of Atum lord of Heliopolis in Heliopolis,
(6) of Shu in the upper Menset in Heliopolis,
(7) of Tefnut in the lower Menset in Heliopolis,
(8) of Geb in the place of the foreigners,
(9) of Nut in the Mansion of *šnw*,
(10) of Osiris foremost of the West in Abydos,
(11) of Isis in Ta-wer,
(12) of Horus in Pe,
(13) of Wadjyt in Dep,
(14) of Nephthys in Heliopolis,
(15) of Banebdjed,
(16) of Thoth in Hermopolis,
(17) of the four Montus in their towns.
(18) (*In one column*):

May (my) name be stable within Thebes and within the nomes for ever!

(19) Pure offering that the king gives to Osiris. I make for you a libation of water come forth (20) from Elephantine, and of milk (come forth) from Kem(-wer); I bring you the *nmst*-jug filled with *wdḥw*-water. You take (21) the libation in the House of Re, you receive the *ḥtpw*-offerings given by Tanen, the *snw*-loaves which come forth before. (22) Your ba goes forth to [follow] the god and you are not repelled from heaven or earth. Your ba lives, your (23) muscles are firm, and you are renewed as the ruler of the living. You are twice great and you are elevated in Busiris. (24) Your place is firm in Ta-wer, and libation is made for you before the offering-table (25) in the middle of the Mound of Djeme. Your heart rejoices and joy takes hold of you (26) within the noble balanite. Your ba becomes divine in the necropolis, and <you> receive libation with offerings; (27) your heart is happy (when) you reach Manu. Your father Shu begets Osiris (?) foremost of the West, (28) the god lord of Abydos, Osiris of Coptos foremost of the Mansion of Gold, Osiris-Sokar amid (29) the *štyt*-sanctuary, Osiris lord of Busiris, Wennefer justified, Amset, Hapy, Duamutef, (30) Qebehsenuf, the gods and goddesses who are in the Mound of Djeme, the gods and goddesses who are in the great place, the gods and goddesses (31) who are in the Mansion of Sokar, the gods and goddesses (32) who are in the Mansion of Gold, the most great and noble bull dwelling in Medamud, the Ogdoad (33) most great of the first primordial times, the Ennead … (?) Imhotep (34) …(?) [royal] scribe, scribe of recruits and leader, Amenhotep son of Hapu … (?) Receive what your ba receives (*sic*).

24. see *supra*, p. 5, n. 67.

Commentary

Line 1
ḫr.s n Ḥwt-Ḥr N snb. See P. BM EA 10191, **I, 1** and P. BM EA 10275, **lines 2–3** for *snb* after a personal name.

Lines 2–3
i Rʿ ink sꜣ.k ink mr.k i Wsir ink sḫm.k Ỉ Nb-Ḫmnw ink iwʿ.k n mꜣʿt i Rʿ-Ḥr-ꜣḫty i Psḏt ʿꜣt i Psḏt nḏst. For this invocation, here followed by the beginning of the litany *mi rwḏ rn* (line 3), see P. BM EA 10110 + 10111, **I, 2–5**.

Line 4 (= col. 1)
mi rwḏ rn(.i) m-ḫnw Wꜣst m-ḫnw spꜣwt r nḥḥ. See P. BM EA 10110 + 10111, **I, 4–5**.

Lines 5–17
Abridged version of the section of the Second Book of Breathing devoted to the litany *mi rwḏ rn*, for which see P. BM EA 10110 + 10111, **I, 7–37**.

Line 5
Ỉtm nb Ỉwnw m Ỉwnw. See P. BM EA 10110 + 10111, **I, 7**.

Line 6
Šw m Mnst ḫrt m Ỉwnw. See P. BM EA 10110 + 10111, **I, 8**.

Line 7
Tfnwt m Mnst ḫrt m Ỉwnw. See P. BM EA 10110 + 10111, **I, 9**.

Line 8
Gb m bw šmꜣw. See P. BM EA 10110 + 10111, **I, 10**.

Line 9
Nwt m Ḥwt šnw. See P. BM EA 10110 + 10111, **I, 11**.

Line 10
Wsir ḫnty Ỉmntt m ꜣbḏw. See P. BM EA 10110 + 10111, **I, 12**.

Line 11
Ỉst m Tꜣ-wr. See P. BM EA 10110 + 10111, **I, 13**.

Line 12
Ḥr m P. See P. BM EA 10110 + 10111, **I, 14**.

Line 13
Wꜣḏyt m Dp. See P. BM EA 10110 + 10111, **I, 15**.

Line 14
Nbt-ḥwt m Ỉwnw. See P. BM EA 10110 + 10111, **I, 16**.

Line 15
Bꜣ-nb-Ḏdw (*sic* for *Ḏdt*). The usual version adds: *m pr Bꜣ-nb-Ḏdt*. See P. BM EA 10110 + 10111, **I, 17**.

Line 16
Ỉ m Ḫmnw. See P. BM EA 10110 + 10111, **I, 18**.

Line 17
Mnṯw 4 m-ḫnw niwwt.sn. See P. BM EA 10110 + 10111, **I, 19**.

Line 18 (= col. 2)
Same text as line 4 (= col. 1)

Lines 19–33
Text known from twelve other more or less extended sources: P. BM EA 10209, IV, 1–18;[25] P. BN 239; P. Florence 3669 and 3670;[26] P. Brussels E 5298;[27] coffin Cairo CG 29301;[28] offering-tables Cairo CG 23119, 23127, 23169 and 23233;[29] stelae Cairo CG 22038 and 22150;[30] offering-table Hanover 1935.200.692.[31]

Line 19
ḥtp di nsw wʿb Wsir. The text introduced by reference to the royal offering is addressed, depending on the manuscript, either to Osiris as deity, or to the deceased identified with him. The first category includes, besides P. BM EA 10116, the version preserved on the offering-tables Cairo CG 23119, CG 23127 and CG 23233: *ḥtp di nsw wʿb.k Wsir*, 'offering that the king gives. You are pure, Osiris'. P. BM EA 10209, IV, 1: *ḥtp di nsw wʿb Wsir*, 'pure offering that the king gives to Osiris' (rather than: 'Pure offerings which the king gives. O Osiris ...' (Haikal). P. Brussels E 5298, 5: [*ḥtp di nsw*] *wʿb n Wsir* 'pure [offering that the king gives] to Osiris'; P. Cairo CG 58019, 11–12: *ḥtp di nsw wʿb n Wsir*; P. BN 239, 4: *ḥtp di nsw* [...], 'offering that the king gives [...]'.

The second category may be illustrated from the offering-table Cairo CG 23169: *ḥtp di nsw wʿb n.k Wsir N*, 'pure offering that the king gives to you, O Osiris N', and the stelae Cairo CG 22038: *ḥtp di nsw wʿb.k Wsir N*, and CG 22150: *ḥtp di nsw wʿb Wsir N*; offering-table Hanover 1935.200.692, 1: [...]*.k Wsir*. The truncated clause of P. Cairo CG 58009, I, 11: *ḥtp di nsw iw.i wʿb.kwi* (*sic*), requires separate consideration.

Other parallels for this text (coffin Cairo CG 29301 and P. Florence 3669) bear no introduction. That on the offering-table Louvre D 79 is introduced by a simple invocation: *hy Wsir N*, for which see Spiegelberg, *RT* 24 (1902), pp. 175–7.

Lines 19–20
ḳbḥ.i n.k mw pr m ꜣbw irṯt m Km. Same reading in P. BN 239, 5 = P. Brussels E 5298, 5. Var. offering-tables Cairo CG 23119 = CG 23127 = stela Cairo CG 22038 = offering- table Hanover 1935.200.692, 1: *ḳbḥ.w n.k*; P. Cairo CG 58019, 12 = offering-table Cairo CG 23169 = offering-table Louvre D 79: *ḳbḥ n.k*; offering-table Cairo CG 23233: *ḳbḥ*; P. Florence 3669, 2–3: *šsp n.t ḳbḥ*; coffin Cairo CG 22038: *di Rʿ n.k mw*; P. BM EA 10209, IV, 2: *Km-wr*. Addition of *m* before *pr* in stela Cairo CG 22038 = offering-table Cairo CG 23169 = offering-table Hanover 1935.200.692, 2; omission of *m ꜣbw* in offering-table Cairo CG 23233; *irṯt m Km* in lacuna in offering-table Hanover 1935.200.692, 2.

Cf. also P. Rhind I, 6, 3:

swʿb.n twk m mw pr m	'We purify you with the water come forth from Elephantine,
m ḫt Ḥr pr m Nḫb	with the offerings of Horus[32] come forth from Nekheb (Elkab),
m irṯt m Km(-wr)	with the milk come forth from Kem-our (Athribis).'

On this sequence, see also Vernus, *Athribis* (*BdE* 74, 1978), pp. 303–4.

25. Haikal, *Two Hier. Fun. Pap.* II, pp. 39–41.
26. A. Pellegrini, *Sphinx* 8 (1904), pp. 216–22.
27. L. Speleers, *RT* 39 (1921), pp. 25–43, pls I–II.
28. Maspero, *Sarcophages* I, pp. 62–3.
29. A. Kamal, *Tables d'offrandes* (*CGC*), 1906, pp. 97, 102, 127 and 156.
30. Kamal, *Stèles*, pp. 36 and 137–8; A. Awadalla, *GM* 181 (2001), pp. 9–14.
31. P. Munro, in *Städel Jahrbuch* NF Band 3 (1971), pp. 40–1, no. 43.
32. I.e. natron, as shown by the demotic version which gives here the word *ḥsmn*.

Lines 20–1

ỉn.ỉ n.k nmst ỉ(w).s mḥ.tỉ m wdḥw ỉṯ.k ḳbḥ n pr Rꜥ. Omission of *ỉw.s* in all other versions.

Var. P. BM EA 10209, IV, 2 = offering-table Cairo CG 23169:

ỉn.ỉ (*ỉn.n(.ỉ)*)*n.k nmst*	'I bring you the *nmst*-jug
mḥ m wdḥw	filled with the *wdḥw*-water
wdḥw ḳbḥ m pr Rꜥ	and the libation from the House of Re.'[33]

Offering-table Cairo CG 23233:

ỉn(.ỉ) n.k nmst mḥ … (?)[34]	'(I) bring you the *nmst*-jug filled … (?)
ḳbḥ <m> pr Rꜥ	and the libation <from> the House of Re.'

Offering-table Cairo CG 23119:

ỉn.w n.k nmst mḥ m wdḥw	'You are brought the *nmst*-jug filled with the *wdḥw*-water,
m ḳbḥ ḥnḳt	with fresh water (?) and beer.'

Stelae Cairo CG 22038, 3–4 and CG 22150, 4–5:

ỉn.w n.k nmst mḥ m wdḥw	'You are brought the *nmst*-jug filled with the *wdḥw*-water,
ḳbḥ m (var.: *n*) *pr Rꜥ*	and the libation from the House of Re.'

Offering-table Cairo CG 23127:

ỉn.w n.k nmst mḥ m wdḥw	'You are brought the *nmst*-jug filled with the *wdḥw*-water.'

P. Florence 3669, 4–5:

ỉn.w n.t nmst mḥ.tỉ m wdḥw	'You are brought the *nmst*-jug filled with the *wdḥw*-water,
šsp.t ḳbḥ m pr Rꜥ	and you receive the libation from the House of Re.'

P. Cairo CG 58019, 13:

ỉn n.k nmst n ꜥnḫ sp 2 r nḥḥ	'You are brought the *nmst*-jug of life (bis), for ever.'

Coffin Cairo CG 29301:

ỉỉ.tw[35] *n.k nmst mḥ.tỉ m ḳbḥ*	'You are brought (?) the *nmst*-jug filled with fresh water;
šsp.k ḳbḥ ḥtpw m dỉ	You receive the libation and the offerings given (*sic*).'

P. BN 239, 5–6:

ỉn […] *mḥ m wdḥw*	'You are brought […] filled with the *wdḥw*-water,
šsp.k ḳbḥ m pr Rꜥ	you receive the libation from the House of Re.'

P. Brussels E 5298, 6:

[… *nm*]*st mḥtỉ m wdḥw*	'[… *nm*]*st*-jug filled with the *wdḥw*-water,
šsp.k ḳbḥ n pr Rꜥ	and you receive the libation from the House of Re.'

Offering-table Hanover 1935.200.692, 2–4 is here very lacunose: [… *n*]*mst* […] *ḳbḥ Wsỉr N*.

On the *nmst*-jug: Assmann, *Sonnenhymnen*, p. 127, c.

Line 21

šsp.k ḥtpw dỉ.n Tꜣ-nn snw n pr m-bꜣḥ. The closest parallel is provided by P. BM EA 10209, IV, 3: *šsp.k ḥtpw dỉ Tꜣ-nn snw n pr bꜣḥ*, 'You receive the *ḥtpw*-offerings given by Tanen, the *snw*-loaves which come forth before (*n pr bꜣḥ*)'. There are numerous variants:

P. Florence 3669, 5–6: *šsp n.t ḥtpw ḥr-sꜣ ḫnw rꜥ nb sp 3 n hrw*, 'Receive the *ḥtpw*-offerings after the *ḫnw*-offerings, every day, three times a day'. The text following is different from P. BM EA 10116.

P. Brussels E 5298, 6–7: *šsp.k dỉt.n* […] *bꜣḥ* ([hieroglyphs]).

P. BN 239, 6–7: *šsp.k dỉ* […] *n pr bꜣḥ* ([hieroglyphs]).[36]

offering-table Cairo CG 23119: *šsp.k ḥtpw* [hieroglyphs] *Wsỉr N.*

offering-table Cairo CG 23169: *šsp.k ḥtpw tnw m …* (?) *pr bꜣḥ*.[37]

offering-table Cairo CG 23233: *šsp<.k> …*[38] *Tꜣ-Tnn prt-ḫrw n kꜣ ꜣpd*.

coffin Cairo CG 29301:[39] *šsp.k ḳbḥ ḥtpw m dỉ pt … snw m pr ḥḥ*.

Offering-table Hanover 1935.200.692, 5–6: [*šsp*]*.k ḥtpw Tꜣ-Tn* […].

Stelae Cairo CG 22038, 4 = CG 22150, 5–6:

šsp.k ḥtpw n (var.: *m*) *Tꜣ-Tnn*	'You receive the *ḥtpw*-offerings of Ta-Tenen
n pr bꜣḥ	which come forth before.'

On the gift of *ḥtpw*-offerings by Ta-Tenen, see H.A. Schlögl, *Der Gott Tatenen* (*OBO* 29, 1980), p. 13.

snw n pr m-bꜣḥ. Note the form [hieroglyphs], compared with P. BM EA 10209, IV, 3: [hieroglyphs]. On that formulation: Haikal, *Two Hier. Fun. Pap.* II, p. 28, n. 31, and O. Perdu, *RdE* 43 (1992), pp. 148–50, n. (b).

Line 22

pr bꜣ.k r šms nṯr nn nšny.tw(*.k*) *n pt m*[40] *tꜣ*. The word *šms*, almost entirely effaced by the writer, can nonetheless be detected in the surviving traces. The restoration is secure on the basis of the parallels. Var. P. BM EA 10209, IV, 4: *r swꜣš nṯr.k*, 'to adore your god'; *nn šnꜥ.tw*(*.k*) *m pt tꜣ*; P. BN 239, 7: *nn šnꜥ.n.tw*(*.k*) *m pt tꜣ*; offering-table Hanover 1935.200.692, 6–7: *nn šnꜥ.n*[*tw*]*.k m pt tꜣwy*; P. Brussels E 5298, 7: *bꜣw.k*[41]; offering-table CG 23169 = P. Brussels E 5298, 7: *nn šnꜥ.tw* (*.k*); coffin Cairo CG 29301: *n šnꜥ.tw.k m pt tꜣ Dwꜣt*. The signs read [hieroglyphs] by Kamal in the version CG 23169, ought probably to be taken as [hieroglyphs]. The entire clause is placed after *wr st.k m Tꜣ-wr* (see *infra*, **lines 23–4**) on stela Cairo CG 22038 = stela Cairo CG 22150: *nn šnꜥ.tw.k m pt tꜣwy* (*sic*).

nšny is written here for *šny*, which in turn is for *šnꜥ*; cf. Berlin 7281 (*AeIB* II, p. 163): *dỉ.sn pr ꜥḳ m ẖrt-nṯr nn šny* ([hieroglyphs]) *ḥr sbꜣw Dwꜣt*. On the verb *šnꜥ* in this context: *LPE*, p. 94 (I, 11–12); P. Vernus, *Athribis* (*BdE* 74, 1978), p. 33, n. (c).

Lines 22–3

ꜥnḫ bꜣ.k rwḏ mtwt.k. Same reading in P. BM EA 10209, IV, 4–5 = stela Cairo CG 22038, 6 = stela Cairo CG 22150, 7[42] = offering-table Hanover 1935.200.692, 7–8. Sequence partly in lacuna in P. BN 239, 7–8 = P. Brussels E 5298, 8. [hieroglyphs] is a corrupt writing of *mtwt*, written normally in the other versions. The phrase pairing, with many variants,[43]

33. Haikal, *Two Hier. Fun. Pap.* II, p. 21, translates this passage inaccurately: 'I have brought to thee the *nmst*-jars full of fresh alms from the estate of Re'.
34. Kamal: [hieroglyphs]. The text seems corrupt. Without a photograph or examination of the original it remains impossible to check this.
35. Probable confusion of [hieroglyphs] and [hieroglyphs], unless the passage is to be understood: 'one comes to you, <bearer> of the *nmst*-jar filled with fresh water'.
36. On the spellings of *bꜣḥ* in P. Brussels E 5298 and P. BN 239: S. Sauneron, in *Coptic Studies in Honor of W.E. Crum* (Washington 1950), pp. 155–7.
37. Kamal: [hieroglyphs].
38. Kamal: [hieroglyphs] for [hieroglyphs] ? Photograph is missing.
39. Maspero, *Sarcophages* I, p. 63.
40. One can hesitate here between the transcription [hieroglyphs] and [hieroglyphs].
41. On *bꜣw* for *bꜣ*, see Smith, *Liturgy*, p. 36 (I, 3, d).
42. Read [hieroglyphs] instead of [hieroglyphs] in the Kamal edition.
43. Cf. e.g. *ꜥnḫ bꜣ … rwḏ šwt*: L. Habachi, *Tavole d'offerta* (1977), pp. 34 and 53; *KRI* III, 633, 6; 711, 10; *ꜥnḫ bꜣ … rwḏ sꜥḥ*: Pierret, *Inscr. du Louvre* II, p. 23; *ꜥnḫ bꜣ … rwḏ ḫꜣt*,

assures the recovery of the physical faculties of the deceased: J. Assmann, *JEA* 65 (1979), p. 61, n. (f) and id., *Liturgische Lieder*, p. 191 (4). On the word *rwḏ* to qualify a part of the body, see ibid., and Goyon, *Le Papyrus Louvre N 3279* (*BdE* 42, 1966), p. 55, n. 4.

Cf. P. dem. Berlin 8351, I, 3–8 (M. Smith, *Enchoria* 15 [1987}, p. 66 = id., *Liturgy*, p. 23), on the recovery of the physical faculties of the deceased:

rpy=k rpy by.w=k	'May you be renewed and your bas be renewed.
rpy [b]y.w=k rpy=k	May your [b]as be renewed and you be renewed.
ꜥnḫ ḫe.(t)=k tme ḳs=k	May your body live and your bones be soundly knit,
rwṯ ꜥwy.w=k	and your limbs be firm.
rpy mty=k ꜥnḫ psḏ.t=k	May your muscles be reinvigorated, and your spine be enlivened.
nw n=k ir.ṭ=k	May your eyes see for you,
mš[ꜥ] n=k pt=k wn n=k ꜥnḫ	your feet g[o] for you, and your ears be open for you.
wpy n=k ls=k	May your tongue be open for you,
wp]y n=k šnb=k	and your throat [be op]en for you.
mt.t n=k spꜣ.ṭ=k	May your lips speak for you.
ḳmꜣ n=k ib=k [nfr.w]	May your heart create [perfection] for you
r-ḫr=n	similar to our own.'

Line 23

rnp.k m ḥḳ(ꜣ) ꜥnḫw. Same reading in P. BM EA 10209, IV, 5 = P. BN 239, 8 = stela Cairo CG 22038, 6–7 = offering-table Hanover 1935.200.692, 8. Addition of *r* (written) after *ḥḳꜣ* in P. Brussels E 5298, 8; omission of *m* in offering-table Cairo CG 23169. Var. stela Cairo CG 22150, 7–8: *rnp*  (*sic*) ⟷ *ꜥnḫw*. Coffin Cairo CG 29301 substitutes: *rnp ḫꜣt.k*, 'your corpse is renewed'.

On Osiris as 'ruler of the living' (i.e. of the deceased living in the nether world), see Seeber, *Untersuchungen*, p. 124, n. 510. Also P. Cairo CG 58034, 9: (Osiris) *iw.f ḫꜥ.tw ḥr nst m ḥḳꜣ ꜥnḫw*, 'he has appeared on the throne as ruler of the living'. Also Piehl, *IH* I, pl. 11, 4; 98, 6; 118, 1; 122, 1; A. Piankoff, *Mythological Papyri* (New York 1957), nos 8, 10, 11, 18, 25; Boeser, *Beschreibung* VI, pl. III; K. Kuhlmann and W. Schenkel, *Das Grab des Ibi, Obergutsverwalters der Gottesgemahlin des Amun* I (*AV* 15, 1983), pl. 69; G. Daressy, *Cercueils des cachettes royales* (*CGC*), 1909, pp. 79, 120, 128, 199, 204, 216; *Opet* 186 and 250, 6; N. de G. Davies, *The Tomb of Nefer-Hotep at Thebes* I (New York 1933), pl. 38, right, 1; etc. Note the variants *nb ꜥnḫw*: P. dem. Louvre E 3452, II, 4; *nsw ꜥnḫw*: Assmann, *Liturgische Lieder*, p. 240, n. 62; Ph. Virey, *RT* 20 (1898), p. 218; B. Bruyère, *Rapport préliminaire sur les fouilles de Deir el-Médineh (1928), FIFAO* 6/2, 1929, pp. 86, 92, 96; *KRI* III, 70, 1; O. Koefoed-Petersen, *Catalogue des sarcophages et cercueils égyptiens* (Copenhagen 1951), pl. 23; L. Habachi, *Tavole d'offerta* (1877), p. 33; etc. See Leitz, *LGG* V, p. 501.

Lines 23–4

ꜥꜣ.k ḥy.k m Ḏdw rwḏ st.k m Tꜣ-wr. The scribe wavered between two versions: *rwḏ st.k*, written in originally, and *wr st.k, wr*, added in the space above the line. Both versions are known from parallels: P. BM EA 10209, IV, 5: *ꜥꜣ.k ḥy.k*[44] *m Ḏdw wr st.k m Tꜣ-wr*; offering-table Hanover 1935.200.692, 8: *ꜥꜣ* [...] *Ḏdw wr st.k* <*m*> *Tꜣ-wr*; P. BN 239, 8–9: *ꜥꜣ.k ḥy.k* [...] *rwḏ st.k m Tꜣ-wr*; P. Brussels E 5298, 8–9: *ꜥꜣ.k ḥꜥ.k m Ḏdw rwḏ st.k* [...]; offering-table CG 23169: *mꜣꜥ-ḫrw.k m Ḏdw wr m st.k m Tꜣ-wr*; coffin Cairo CG 29301, stelae Cairo CG 22038 and CG 22150: *ꜥꜣ.k ḥy.k m Ḏdw wr st.k m Tꜣ-wr*.[45]

Lines 24–5

ir.tw n.k sꜣṯ m ḥꜣt wḏḥw ḥr-ib Ỉst Ḏꜣm. Same reading in P. BM EA 10209, IV, 6–7. Major lacuna before *Ḏꜣm* in P. BN 239; small lacuna in lacuna in P. Brussels E 5298, 9 and offering-table Hanover 1935.200.692, 10. In  may be recognized the word *sꜣṯ* usually read at this place in the parallels; stela Cairo CG 22038: *ir.tw n.k sꜣṯ* [...] *wꜥb* (?) *m ḥꜣt wḏḥw*  (Kamal). Corrupt text on offering-table CG 23169, omitting *ḥr-ib Ỉst Ḏꜣm*. The provenance of the latter two sources, Akhmim, probably accounts for these variants, showing the existence of the same rite in different places.

On the *wḏḥw*-altar and its role in Djeme: J.C. Goyon, *CdE* 90 (1970), p. 272, n. (c); J. Leclant, *Montouemhat* (*BdE* 35, 1961), p. 140; F.R. Herbin, *RdE* 35 (1984), p. 112, n. 19. Food offerings, and not simply libations, are made before this altar; cf. P. Cairo CG 58030, V, 1; Maspero, *Sarcophages* I, p. 43, 14.

On libation in relation with the Mound of Djeme, cf. E. von Bergmann, *ZÄS* 20 (1882), p. 42: *šsp n.k ḳbḥ pn pr m Ỉst Ḏꜣm*, 'Receive for you this libation come forth from the Mound of Djeme'.[46]

Lines 25–6

rš ib.k ḫnm n.k ꜣwt-ib m-ḫnw išd šps. Same reading in P. BM EA 10209, IV, 7–8 = offering table Hanover 1935.200.692, 11–12 (corrupt writing  of *rš*). Sequence partly in lacuna in P. Brussels E 5298, 10. Var. P. BN 239, 10 and P. Brussels E 5298, 9: *ḫnm.k*; stela Cairo CG 22038: *m-ḫnt n išd šps Wsir ḫnty Ỉmntt nṯr ꜥꜣ* (*sic*, and end of text). The expression *m-ḫnw pꜣ išd* may be compared with the well-known epithet of Osiris *ḥry-ib pꜣ išd*. The presence of the god in the tree is not often attested (J. Leclant, *Recherches sur les monuments thébains* [*BdE* 36, 1965], p. 278). Plutarch (*De Iside et Osiride*, 15) speaks of the ἐρείκη (= the *ꜥš*-tree of the Egyptian sources), which concealed the god within itself: J.G. Griffiths, *Plutarch's De Iside et Osiride* (Cardiff 1970), pp. 322–4. On this theme: P. Koemoth, *Osiris et les arbres* (Liège 1994), pp. 123ff.

Line 26

nṯr.w bꜣ.k m ẖrt-nṯr. Same reading in P. BM EA 10209, IV, 8 = P. BN 239, 11. Sequence omitted in offering-table Hanover 1935.200.692. P. Brussels E 5298, 10–11 replaces this sequence with: [...] *ḫnt.k r ꜣbḏw šsp.k mw r ḥtp n rs Dwꜣt m Ỉwnw ṯꜣw n Ỉmn mw n Ḥꜥpy nnk st ḏt*, '[...] you sail to Abydos, you receive water at the altar of the hall of vigil of the Duat[47] in Heliopolis. The breath of Amun, the water of Hapy, that belongs to me, eternally'.[48] For this latter phrase, see P. BM EA 10191, **II, 33–4**.

On the divinization of the ba, see P. BM EA 10048, **II, 5**.

šsp ḳbḥ m ḥwt. Var. P. BM EA 10209, IV, 9: *šsp n.k ḳbḥ m ḫt nbt*, 'Receive for yourself libation with all things'; P. BN 239, 11: *šsp.k ḳbḥ m ḫt nbt* [...].

KRI I, 328, 7–8; Mond-Myers, *Temples of Armant*, pl. 105; *ꜥnḫ bꜣ ... rwḏ ḥꜥw*: L. Habachi, *BIFAO* 71 (1972), p. 78, fig. 6. In a future study it is intended to investigate these expressions more fully.

44. The transcription of the verb *ḥy* given by Haikal should be amended.
45. Kamal (Cairo CG 22150): ⟨*m*⟩ *Tꜣ*⟨*-wr*⟩ *Wsir N*, and end of the text.
46. Another uncertain example in D. Wildung, *Imhotep und Amenhotep* (*MÄS* 36, 1977), p. 265.
47. Parallels with variants in P. Cairo CG 58015, 9–10; P. Cairo CG 58019, 7–8; P. Turin 1990, 10–11; on this 'hall of watch (*rs*) of the Duat', see Goyon, *Rituels funéraires*, p. 312, n. 3. For other attestations of the word *rs*: id., *BIFAO* 75 (1975), p. 396 with n. 2. Cf. the word *nhst*, P. BM EA 10209, II, 4, ed. Haikal, p. 31.
48. The manuscript ends here.

Line 27

nḏm ib.k ḫnm.n.k M3<n>w. Same reading in P. BM EA 10209, IV, 9. Sequence omitted in offering-table Hanover 1935.200.692.  is a corrupt writing of *M3nw*.[49] Var. P. BN 239, 11–12: [...] *ḫnm.k M3nw*.

On reaching Manu (here *ḫnm M3nw*), see also C. Robichon and A. Varille, *CdE* 23 (1937), p. 179, fig. 6; P. Berlin 3162, I, 3. It is differently expressed in the synonymous phrases *ḫnm ꜥwy M3nw, ḫnm t3 m/n M3nw, ḫnm mwt m M3nw*, for which see Assmann, *Liturgische Lieder*, pp. 231–2. On Manu: D. Kurth, *LÄ* III, 1185–6; Smith, *Mortuary Texts*, p. 120 (XI, 7, b).

Lines 27–8

wṯt it.k Šw n Wsir ḫnty Imntt nṯr ꜥ3 nb 3bḏw. Var. P. BM EA 10209, IV, 10: *dw3 tw it.k Šw Wsir ...*, 'your father Shu adores you, Osiris ...'; P. BN 239, 12: *twt tw it.k Šw Wsir ḫnty Imntt nṯr* [...]. Omission of *wṯt it.k Šw* in offering-table Hanover 1935.200. 692, 12.

In view of the parallels, the version in P. BM EA 10116 seems corrupt. For coherence, the speech beginning here can only be addressed to Osiris. The preposition *n* before the name of Osiris (*wṯt it.k Šw n Wsir*) is inexplicable, *wṯt* usually being transitive. The absence of the dependent pronoun should also be noted.

For another instance of variants giving *twt* or *dw3*: F.R. Herbin, *BIFAO* 84 (1984), pp. 265 and 291, n. 57.

it.k Šw. On the designation of Shu as 'father' of the god: F.R. Herbin, *BIFAO* 88 (1988), p. 109.

Line 28

Wsir Gbty ḫnty Ḥwt nwb. Same reading in P. BM EA 10209, IV, 11 = P. BN 239, 13 = offering-table Hanover 1935.200.692, 13 (corrupt writing  of *Gbty*). Cf. also stela Copenhague 740 (O. Koefoed-Petersen, *Recueil des inscriptions hiéroglyphiques* [*BiAe* 6, 1936], p. 68). On the title 'foremost of the Mansion of Gold' for Osiris of Coptos: J. Yoyotte, *Ann. EPHe*[V] 86 (1977–8), p. 168; Haikal, *Two Hier. Fun. Pap.* II, p. 44, n. 152; Leclant, *Recherches sur les monuments thébains* (*BdE* 36, 1965), p. 282, n. (a); H. de Meulenaere, *CdE* 135 (1993), pp. 51–2 (a); C. Traunecker, *Coptos* (*OLA* 43, 1992), p. 98, § 95, b. Other attestations: A. Rowe, *ASAE* 40 (1940), p. 12 with n. 1 and p. 292; H.W. Fairman, *JEA* 20 (1934), p. 3; P. Barguet, *Le Papyrus N 3176 (S) du Musée du Louvre* (*BdE* 37, 1962), p. 32, etc. See H. de Meulenaere, *CdE* 135 (1993), pp. 51–3, n. (a), and Leitz, *LGG* V, pp. 833–4.

Lines 28–9

Wsir-Skr ḥr(y)-ib štyt. Same reading in stela Copenhagen 740 (Koefoed-Petersen, op. cit.) = offering-table Hanover 1935.200.692, 12 which ends with the words *ꜥnḫ ḏt*, 'living for ever'. Text partly erased in P. BM EA 10209, IV, 11. P. BN 239, 13, interrupts the text with the word *štyt*. On this sanctuary: R. El Sayed, *BIFAO* 84 (1984), p. 135, n. (b); id., *ASAE* 69 (1983), p. 233, n. (a), and Leitz, *LGG* V, p. 348.

Line 29

Wsir nb Ḏdw Wn-nfr m3ꜥ-ḫrw. Var. P. BM EA 10209, IV, 12: *Wsir mryty ḥḳ3 ḏt*, 'Osiris the beloved,[50] ruler of eternity' in place of *m3ꜥ-ḫrw*; omission of *m3ꜥ-ḫrw* in stela Copenhagen 740 (Koefoed-Petersen, op. cit.).

Lines 29–32

Imst Ḥpy Dw3-mwt.f Ḳbḥ-snw.f nṯrw nṯrwt imyw I3t Ḏ3m nṯrw nṯrwt imyw t3 st ꜥ3t nṯrw nṯrwt imyw Ḥwt Skr nṯrw nṯrwt imyw Ḥwt nwb.

Parallel text in P. BM EA 10343, 13–14, omitting the names of the four sons of Horus.

P. BM EA 10209, IV, 13–15, presents a somewhat different order:

Imst Ḥpy Dw3-mwt.f Ḳbḥ-snw.f	'Amset, Hapy, Duamutef, Qebehsenuf,
nṯrw nṯrwt imyw I3t Ḏ3m	the gods and goddesses who are in the Mound of Djeme,
nṯrw nṯrwt imyw Ḥwt Skr	the gods and goddesses who are in the Mansion of Sokar,
nṯrw nṯrwt imyw Ḥwt nwb	the gods and goddesses who are in the Mansion of Gold,
nṯrw nṯrwt imyw st ꜥ3t	the gods and goddesses who are in the great place.'

Var. stela Copenhagen 740:

Imst Ḥꜥpy Dw3-mwt.f Ḳbḥ-snw.f	'Amset, Hapy, Duamutef, Qebehsenuf,
nṯrw nṯrwt imyw I3t Ḏ3m[51]	the gods and goddesses who are in the Mound of Djeme,
nṯrw nṯrwt imyw ... (?)	the gods and goddesses who are in ... (?)
nṯrw nṯrwt imy(w) Ḥwt Skr	the gods and goddesses who are in the Mansion of Sokar.'

Imst Ḥpy Dw3-mwt.f Ḳbḥ-snw.f. On the four sons of Horus as protectors of the deceased, see Haikal, *Two Hier. Fun. Pap.* II, p. 44, n. 155. Note here the remarkable writing  for *Ḳbḥ-snw.f*.

nṯrw nṯrwt imyw I3t Ḏ3m. Same formulation in G. Daressy, *RT* 20 (1898), p. 76, § CLIV (= statue Cairo CG 969); A.H. Zayed, *ASAE* 56 (1959), pp. 93–4;[52] P. Berlin 3041, 11, probably to be identified to the *n3 nṯrw imyw ḫrt-nṯr* (ibid., 11–12) and to the *nṯrw p3wtyw* mentioned in relation with the Mound of Djeme in P. Louvre N 3159, 19. The Ennead of the Mound of Djeme is variously identified as *nṯrw imyw I3t D3m* (P. BM EA 10123, 2; P. Louvre N 3293, part X, A. Piankoff, in *Egyptian Religion* 3 (1935), p. 146);[53] *nṯrw I3t Ḏ3m, nṯrw ntrwt* (?) *ḥr(yw)-ib I3t Ḏ3m, nṯrw nṯrwt* (?) *nbw I3t Ḏ3m* (Leclant, op. cit., pp. 309 and 347), *n3 nbw i3wt*[54] *Ḏ3m* (C. Traunecker, *La chapelle d'Achôris à Karnak* II [Paris 1981], p. 110, fig. 12), *nṯrw m I3t Ḏ3m* (Haikal, *Two Hier. Fun. Pap.* I, p. 72; J. Assmann, *Das Grab des Basa* [*AV* 6, 1973], p. 95, fig. 35, col. 1); *Psḏt n(t) I3t Ḏ3m* (R. El Sayed, *ASAE* 69 [1983], p. 232); *Psḏt ꜥ3t imyw I3t Ḏ3m* (id., *BIFAO* 80 [1980], pp. 235 and 236–7, n. (d); and *nṯrw n Ḏmꜥ* (P. dem. Cairo CG 31170, 7–8, ed. Spiegelberg, II, p. 281; R. Jasnow, *Grammata demotika* [Fs. E. Lüddeckens, Würzburg 1984], p. 93, F); see P. BM EA 9995, **IV, 2**. Perhaps to be identified with the 'righteous gods in the Mound of Djeme' (P. Rhind, II, 7, 6), and the *ḥtptyw*, dead deities residing in the Mound of Djeme, to whom Amenipet comes to make offerings at each decade, and who can be identified as the Hermopolitan Ogdoad (M. Doresse, *RdE* 25 [1973], pp. 97 and 132, n. 6). A title 'prophet of the gods of Djeme' is known (J. Quaegebeur, in *Hundred-Gated Thebes*, p. 156).

nṯrwt imyw t3 st ꜥ3t. The 'great place' (G*DG* V, p. 71) is a term for the royal tomb but also for the whole of the royal Theban necropolis, as attested above all in the New Kingdom sources: see E. Otto, *Topographie des thebanischen Gaues* (*UGAÄ* 16, 1952), p. 50; J. Černý, *A Community of*

49. P. BM EA 10209, IV, 9: ; cf. Bologna 1940, cited *Wb.* II, 29, 13 (G. Kminek-Szedlo, *Catalogo di Antichità Egizie* [Turin 1895], p. 209): *ḫnm tw mwt.k m* . Cf. also Boeser, *Beschreibung* X, pp. 4 and 8: .
50. On this epithet of Osiris: M. Doresse, *RdE* 25 (1973), p. 120, n. 5.
51. Read .
52. One of the versions of the decree of Osiris. See *LPE*, p. 261, adding L. Kákosy, *OLP* 23 (1992), pp. 311–28; P. BM EA 10259 (unpublished), and stela (number unknown) of the Naprstek Museum in Prague.
53. Note the mention of *nṯrw imyw Ḏ3m* (written ) in Niwiński, *Seconde trouvaille*, p. 129.
54. For the plural *I3wt* in this toponym: Sethe, *Amun*, § 103.

Workmen at Thebes (*BdE* 50, 1973), pp. 69–74, and especially P. Barguet, *Le Papyrus N 3176 (S) du Musée du Louvre* (*BdE* 37, 1962), pp. 31–2, where he proposes to site the *st ꜥꜣt* to the north of the temple of Osiris of Coptos at Karnak. However, it is not a specifically Theban feature, for other references to the 'great place' may be found in other places than Thebes; see, for instance, S. Sauneron, *Esna* V (Cairo 1962), pp. 62–3, where the *st ꜥꜣt* designates the necropolis of the dead gods.

nṯrw nṯrwt imyw Ḥwt Skr and *nṯrw nṯrwt imyw Ḥwt nwb*: see Haikal, *Two Hier. Fun. Pap.* II, p. 45, nn. 156 and 157.

Line 32

p(ꜣ) kꜣ ꜥꜣ wr šps ḥry-ib Mꜣdw. Var. P. BM EA 10209, IV, 16: *nty m Mꜣdw.*

On the bull of Medamud (Montu): C. Sambin, *BIFAO* 92 (1992), pp. 174–8.

Lines 32–3

nꜣ Ḫmnw ꜥꜣw wrw n pꜣwt tpy(t). Omission of *nꜣ* in P. BM EA 10209, IV, 16, which refers to *Wsir Ḥr ꜣst Nbt-ḥwt*, 'Osiris, Horus, Isis, Nephthys'. On that formulation, Sethe, *Amun*, § 90.

Line 33

Psḏt sn nṯr (?). P. BM EA 10209, IV, 17: *Psḏt sꜣw-nṯr* (?), 'the Ennead, the divine watches (?)' (Haikal, *Two Hier. Fun. Pap.* II, p. 21: 'the divine bodies').

Lines 33–4

Ii-m-ḥtp … (?)[*sš nsw*] (?) *sš nfrw ḥr-tp*[55] *Imn-ḥtp sꜣ Ḥpw.* Passage omitted in P. BM EA 10209, IV.

In this funerary context, Imhotep and Amenhotep son of Hapu are identified, to use the expression of L. Kákosy (*Studia Aegyptiaca* 7 [1981] p. 175), as veritable 'patrons of the dead'. On these individuals: D. Wildung, *Imhotep und Amenhotep* (*MÄS* 36, 1976), passim, and E. Laskowska-Kusztal, *Le sanctuaire ptolemaïque de Deir el-Bahari* III (Warsaw 1984), pp. 114–15.

The titles *sš nsw* and *sš nfr ḥr-tp* are frequently linked in the titulatury of Amenhotep, hence this restoration; see e.g. Laskowska-Kusztal, op. cit.., doc. 15, 16, 17, 33; A. Varille, *Inscriptions concernant l'architecte Amenhotep fils de Hapou* (*BdE* 44, 1968), texts nos 8, 3; 9, 1; 11, 2; 48; with var. *sš nsw ḥr-tp nfrw*: no. 13, 13; *Ritual of Embalming*, III, 24 (ed. Sauneron, p. 10).

šsp.tn iṯ bꜣ.tn. The manuscript ends with these words. P. BM EA 10209, IV, 18–20 and P. BM EA 10343, 10–11 supply the expected continuation of the text: (*šsp.tn šsp bꜣ.tn*) *šsp kꜣ.tn ḥtpw ḏfꜣw tꜣ*[56] *ḥnkt irp irṯt mw m ḥbbt ꜥnḫ nṯrw im.sn*, 'You receive, your ba receives, your ka receives *ḥtpw*-offerings and food, bread, beer, wine, milk and water of the inundation on which the gods live'. Cf. also P. BM EA 10209, I, 9–10: *šsp bꜣ.tn šsp kꜣ.tn ḥtpw ḏfꜣw tꜣ ḥnkt mw m ḥbbt ꜥnḫ nṯrw im irp irṯt snṯr ḳbḥ*, 'Your ba receives, your ka receives *ḥtpw*-offerings, bread, beer, and water of the inundation on which the gods live, wine, milk, incense and a libation'.

P. BM EA 10123 (pls 104–7)

Salt Collection 1, ?
Unpublished.
Quirke, *Owners*, no. 246.
Provenance: Thebes. Found with P. BM EA 10124 probably inside the coffin (now lost) of Senchonsis in the collective tomb of the archon Soter.[57]
Date: AD 146.[58]
Owner of the papyrus: *Tꜣ-šrit-Ḫnsw* called *Ṯꜣp(w)r*. The name *Tꜣ-šrit-Ḫnsw* (Senchonsis) is written in different ways in the two manuscripts: [hieroglyphs] (P. BM EA 10123, 5–6); [hieroglyphs] (P. BM EA 10124, 4);[59] [hieroglyphs] (P. BM EA 10124, 3). Once it is found abridged to [hieroglyphs] (P. BM EA 10123, 10). For the second name of *Tꜣ-šryt-Ḫnsw*: *Ṯꜣp(w)r* (Sapaulis), see K. van Landuyt, in *Hundred-Gated Thebes*, p. 80. Here it is written [hieroglyphs] (P. BM EA 10123, 6, 11), [hieroglyphs] (P. BM EA 10124, 5), [hieroglyphs] (P. BM EA 10124, 3), and [hieroglyphs] (P. 10124, 6). The name of this woman is also attested in P. Louvre N 3156 and N 3289[60] in the forms [hieroglyphs] and [hieroglyphs]. The same name is also found in P. BM EA 9977,[61] written [hieroglyphs], where it refers to another member of the Soter family.[62]
Mother of the owner:[63] *Tꜣḳḏꜣ* (Tkauthi). Written twice, in the forms [hieroglyphs] (P. BM EA 10123, 11) and [hieroglyphs] (P. BM EA 10124, 6). On this name, see K. van Landuyt, in *Hundred-Gated Thebes*, pp. 76–7, with n. 32.

Contents: Original text adapted from the First Book of Breathing.

Manuscript of one sheet (19 × 35.3 cm), in poor condition. Although the papyrus itself has suffered relatively little loss, with lacunae from insect holes at intervals, the ink is effaced at several points to the extent of leaving only virtually illegible traces. Eleven lines of text.

Text on the verso: A good burial. May it be stable over my body; may it remain over my flesh. The great Amentet (?) … (?)
(*in Greek*): πρὸς κεφαλῇ, 'at the head'.[64]

55. Written [hieroglyphs] in error.
56. *tꜣ* omitted in P. BM EA 10343.
57. See *supra*, p. 6, no. **20**, and p. 8.
58. After the Greek inscription of her coffin, see *supra*, p. 8.
59. This writing of *Ḫnsw*, without the *n*, is also found in the title *ḥm-nṯr n Ḫnsw-m-Wꜣst-Nfr-ḥtp*, borne by the owner of P. Louvre N 3175.
60. See *supra*, p. 6, no. **21**.
61. See *supra*, p. 6, no. **11**.
62. An older mention of this name, written [hieroglyphs] (masculine), is attested in P. Anastasi III, vs., 6, 1; cf. Caminos, *LEM*, p. 110, who compares, after Burchardt and Ranke, a semitic noun for 'bird'.
63. The Greek inscription written on the coffin (no. **19**) gives the name of the father: Pikos, absent from both manuscripts. Cf. *supra*, p. 8.
64. See *supra*, p. 2 with n. 23. P. BM EA 10124, which bears no such note concerning its localization on the mummy, was presumably placed at the feet; see *supra*, p. 2 with n. 28.

Translation

Recto

(1) Turn towards me, doorkeepers of the Duat, guardians of the West, gods of the West, gods who watch over Osiris, gods who are in the hall (2) of the two Maats, gods who are in the Mansion of the Prince, gods who are in the Mound of Djeme! May then be made <for me> a libation of water in the Mansion of the Prince! May …(?) (3) May offerings be laid down for me …(?) before Amenipet at each of his decades when he comes to the Mound of Djeme! May I seize the cord (4) of the great bark of Osiris, of which the name is the *nšmt*-bark! May …(?) the doorkeepers of Osiris …(?) (5) in the night of the festival of the pure bull in his fields! May I be received in Heliopolis in the night!

Thus speaks the Hathor *Tꜣ-šri͗t*(6)-*Ḫnsw*, justified, alias *Ṯꜣpwr*, justified …(?): I am a star of the sky, for my heart is upon the way of its god …(?) each day, and I recognize (?) (7) the gods who are within Thebes the victorious. May I be led before the spirits! (?) May I be received in the hall of the two Maats! May I (8) assume all the forms according to my heart's desire, to every place and every …(?). May I (…) Medamud (9) (…) go to Thebes the victorious, to the house of Amun (?) to see his (?) father …(?) festival …(?), Amun-Re. May …(?) (10) …(?) Amun lord of Thebes he proceed to the House of Amun (?) … (?) star of the sky for the Hathor <*Tꜣ-šri͗t*>-*Ḫnsw*, justifed, born of …(?) (11) *Ṯꜣpwr*, justifed, born of *Tꜣḳ(w)ḏꜣ* […] … (?) West in the <god's> domain (?), every day.

Commentary

Line 1

ḥr.tn ir n.i͗. One expects *ḥr.tn n.i͗*; for the different variants, see P. BM EA 10191, **I, 2–3**.

nꜣ iryw-ꜥꜣ n tꜣ Dwꜣt nꜣ sꜣww n I͗mntt. The texts more often evoke the doorkeepers of the West and the guardians of the Duat (*nꜣ iryw-ꜥꜣ n I͗mntt nꜣ sꜣwtyw n tꜣ Dwꜣt*). For the different variants attested, see P. BM EA 10191, **I, 2–3**.

nṯrw n I͗mntt nṯrw nty rs r Wsir. The usual version omits *n I͗mntt*. See P. BM EA 10191, **I, 6**.

Lines 1–2

nṯrw imyw tꜣ wsḫt Mꜣꜥty. On these gods, see P. BM EA 10191, **I, 4–5**. Note the writing for *Mꜣꜥty*, repeated in line 7.

Line 2

nṯrw imyw ḥwt sr. These gods, not mentioned elsewhere in the Books of Breathing, are perhaps to be identified with the 'gods in the Mansion of the Benben in Heliopolis' (*nṯrw m Ḥwt Bnbn m I͗wnw*) known from the Glorifications of Osiris.

nṯrw imyw I͗ꜣt Ḏꜣm. The invocation to the gods of Djeme more often takes the form *nṯrw nṯrwt imyw I͗ꜣt Ḏꜣm*; see P. BM EA 10116, **29–32**.

mi ḳbḥ mw m ḥwt-sr… (?). Beginning of a phrase of which the end is illegible. Restore probably *ḳbḥ<.w n.i͗>*. Same omission in P. BM EA 10124, 9: *mi ḳbḥ mw m-bꜣḥ I͗mn-I͗pt*. This recalls the sequence *mi ḳbḥ.w n.i͗ mw m ḥwt sr mi pꜣ sr wr m I͗wnw*, 'May there be made for me a libation in the Mansion of the Prince as (is done for the) great Prince (who is) in Heliopolis', well attested in several manuscripts of Books of Breathing: cf. P. BM EA 10108, 12 = P. BM EA 10109, 9 = P. BM EA 10125, 11–12 = P. BM EA 10191, I, 12 = P. Lieblein, 15 = P. Louvre N 3176 A, 9 = P. Cairo CG 58007, I, 9–10 = P. Cairo CG 58009, II, 4 = P. Cairo CG 58012, 15 (var.: *ḳbḥ.w n.k mw m Rꜣ-sṯꜣw*) = P. Berlin 3052, I, 12–13.

The problem arises here that the surviving traces in the second part of the phrase do not permit restoration of the sequence as a whole. The word *mi* () which introduces it cannot then be considered as a writing of the preposition denoting 'as' (cf. the form 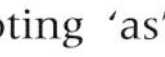 in the examples of P. Louvre N 3176 A, 9 and P. Cairo CG 58008, 12). Therefore it may be considered more plausibly as the start of another phrase.

Line 3

mi wꜣḥ.w n.i͗ ḥwt … (?) *m-bꜣḥ I͗mn-I͗pt n p(ꜣy).f ssw 10 nb n ii r I͗ꜣt Ḏꜣm*. The signs after *ḥwt* are indistinct. A reading *ḥtpw* remains doubtful.

On the rite *wꜣḥ ḥwt*: C. Favard-Meeks, *Le temple de Behbeit el-Hagara* (Hamburg 1991), pp. 401–33.

The construction *n pꜣy.f ssw 10 nb n ii r* is rarely used in this context; cf. e.g.:

P. BM EA 10344, 2–3:

i͗ṯ.k ḳbḥ n ḏrt n [*I͗mn-I͗pt*	'Take your libation from the hand of [Amenipet
n] *p(ꜣ)y.f ssw 10 nb ii r Ḏꜣm*	at] each of his decades when (he) comes to Djeme.'

P. Cairo CG 58019, 8–9:

mn ḳbḥ n ḏrt n I͗mn-I͗pt	' Take your libation from the hand of Amenipet
n p(ꜣ)y.f ssw 10 nb n ii [*r*] *int*	at each of his decades when (he) comes [to] the Valley.'

Also P. Louvre N 3176 M, 2: […]*I͗mn-I͗pt m p(ꜣy).f ssw 10 nb n ii r I͗ꜣt Ḏꜣm*, and perhaps P. Turin 1990, 7–9: *šsp.i͗ ḳbḥ n ḏrt I͗mn-I͗pt n p(ꜣ)y.f ssw 10 nb …* (?).

On the offering of each decade in the setting of the rites of Djeme, see *LPE*, pp. 143–5 (II, 30–1); P. BM EA 10194, **lines 10–11** and P. BM EA 10201, **II, 7**.

Lines 3–4

mi šsp.i͗ p(ꜣ) swꜣš n p(ꜣ) wiꜣ ꜥꜣ n Wsir nšmt rn.f. The noun *swꜣš* seems not to belong to the technical vocabulary of the elements of a boat. Its use here in the expression *šsp swꜣš*, comparable to that of the terms *ḥꜣtt*, *šsnw*, *sinw*, or *wꜣrt* (D. Jones, *A Glossary of Ancient Egyptian Nautical Titles and Terms* [London 1988], pp. 227–8), is not known to me elsewhere. It is therefore not possible to exclude the interpretation by the editors of the *Wb.* (IV, 64, 6), who took *swꜣš* to be the cord of the harpoon used to attack the enemies of the god in his bark. On this word: S. Sauneron, *BIFAO* 62 (1964), pp. 41–2, n. 6.

Line 4

mi … (?) *n.i͗ …* (?) *nꜣ iryw-ꜥꜣ n Wsir*. The text, badly erased here, does not allow us to understand the exact meaning of this short sequence. The *iryw-ꜥꜣ n Wsir* are defined in the Book of Caverns as 'these doorkeepers who do not come forth from their cavern to prevent the exit of those who are in it': A. Piankoff, *BIFAO* 42 (1944), p. 5 and pl. 12, col. 1.

Lines 4–5

… (?) *ꜥš ḥknw* (?) *n grḥ n ḥb ngꜣ wꜥb n sḫwt.f*. The expression *ꜥš ḥknw*, if

the reading is correct, seems unattested elsewhere. Probably it is synonymous with *nis ḥknw* (*Wb.* III, 189, 9). On the festival of the pure bull in his fields, corresponding to the birth of Osiris on the first epagomenal day, see *LPE*, p. 175 (IV, 5–6). For another reference to a *ngꜣ wꜥb m sḫwt.f*: F.R. Herbin, *RdE* 54 (2003), p. 98 (P. Vatican Inv. 38608, 15).

Line 5
mi šsp.w tw(i) r Ỉwnw n grḥ. See P. BM EA 10191, **I, 13–14**.

Lines 5–6
ḫr.s n Ḥwt-Ḥr N mꜣꜥ-ḫrw wn ... (?). This phrase opens a new passage introduced by a formula with which most copies of the First Book of Breathing begin: for *ḫr.s n N* (writing for), see P. BM EA 10191, **I, 1**.

Line 6
ink sbꜣ n pt. On the relation of the deceased to the stars: *LPE*, pp. 95–6 (I, 12–13).

Lines 6–7
iw ib.i ḥr wꜣt n nṯr.s rꜥ nb iw.i siꜣ (?) *nṯrw nty m-ḫnw Wꜣst-nḫt*. Cf. P. BM EA 10124, 8: *ꜥḳ.i ḥr wꜣt n nṯr nbw* (*sic*) *m Wꜣst nḫt*, 'I proceed upon the way of all the gods in Thebes the victorious'.

On the heart on the way of the god: G. Lefebvre, *Petosiris* II, p. 38, no. 62; G. Daressy, *Statues et statuettes de divinités* I (*CGC*), 1905, p. 303. For the way of the god (another attestation in P. BM EA 10718, 11): F. von Bissing, *ZÄS* 53 (1917), pp. 144–5; S. Sauneron, *Esna* V (Cairo 1962), p. 181, n. (ee); R. Anthes, in *Fs. zum 150 Jährigen Bestehen des Berliner ägyptischen Museums* (Berlin 1974), p. 36, bottom; R. El Sayed, *BIFAO* 84 (1984), p. 139, and id., *ASAE* 70 (1985), pp. 329 and 334, n. (iiii').

Line 7
mi in.w tw(i) r (?) *ꜣḫw mi šsp.tw.w* (?) *r tꜣ wsḫt Mꜣꜥty*. The groups (after *in*) and (after *šsp*) are probably to be read *.w tw(i)*, like *supra*, **line 5**, in *šsp.w tw(i)*. For the writing of *ꜣḫw*, cf. *Ritual of Embalming*, V, 3 (ed. Sauneron, p. 14).

Lines 7–8
mi ir.i ḫpr[*w* ... (?)] *nbw r mr ib.i r bw nb* ... (?) *nb*. Cf. P. BM EA 10124, 7–8: *mi ir.i ḫpr(w) nbw r mr ib.i ḥꜣty.i*, and see P. BM EA 10194, **lines 7–9**.

Lines 8–11
The last four lines of the text are interrupted by lacunae and effacing of the ink, rendering transcription and translation difficult and uncertain. Fragments of text apparently not attested elsewhere can occasionally be recognized.

P. BM EA 10194 (pls 108–9)

Hay Collection.

R.A. Caminos, in A. Roccati and A. Siliotti (eds), *La magia in Egitto ai Tempi dei Faraoni* (Verona 1987), pp. 147–51 with fig. 1; id., in *Ancient Egypt and Kush. In Memoriam M.A. Korostovtsev* (Moscow 1993), pp. 104–23 and pl. 11.

Quirke, *Owners*, no. 199.

Provenance: probably Thebes.

Date: first to second century AD.

Owner of the papyrus: *Pꜣ-wr-iꜣbtt* (Poregebthis and var.): *RPN* I, 104, 5, citing only one example, demotic; *Demot. Nb.* I, 178. Compare the name *Pꜣ-di-wr-iꜣbtt*, P. BM EA 10191 and 10304.

Mother of the owner: *Tꜣ-(nt)-nꜣ-mꜥꜣw* (?). The name seems not to be attested elsewhere. On the personal names on the model *Tꜣ-nꜣ* ..., see Smith, *Mortuary Texts*, p. 131.

Contents: Original text partly adapted from the First Book of Breathing.

Manuscript of one sheet (24.5 × 22 cm), fairly well preserved (lacunae affect the beginning of lines 7–9). The text is bordered by a double line, except on the left where at certain points it exceeds the preset area (lines 3, 5, 6, 11, 12).

Text on the verso: Enter the West according the decree (?) of the lady of the foundations of the earth.[65]

Translation

Recto

(1) Hail Osiris *Pꜣ-wr-iꜣbtt*, born of *Tꜣ-(nt)-nꜣ-mꜥꜣw* (?)!

(2) To be recited to his father Osiris foremost of the West: 'I am Re-Horakhty at his rising, (3) Atum at his setting, I am Osiris foremost of the West, the great god, lord of Abydos. (4) I am Thoth the great, lord of Hermopolis, who causes Horus to be upon the throne of his father; I am (5) Haroeris the physician who causes the divine body of his father Re to be perfect. O doorkeepers (6) of the Duat, guardians of the West, may my ba go (7) to the Duat with the excellent bas who are in the god's domain! May I (8) proceed wheresoever I desire, and assume (my) forms according to (9) my heart's desire during the night, during the day and at every moment of each day!

(10)You receive libation and censing from the hand of Amenipet of Djeme (11) at every moment of each decade! You receive bread, beer, oxen and fowl at the festival of the Valley. (12) You go to *Mꜥꜣt*-land (?) daily; you come and go wheresoever you desire. (13) Isis the great, mother of the god, grants you a great, beautiful and efficacious burial. May your ba live for ever and eternally!

Commentary

Line 2
ḏd mdw ḥr it.f Wsir ḫnty Ỉmntt. P. BM EA 10194 is the sole known manuscript to establish explicitly the person addressed in the following declaration, who is otherwise presented without introduction.

65. Cf. P. BM EA 10124, vs.

Lines 2–3
Ink Rꜥ-Ḥr-ꜣḫty m ḥꜥ.f Itm m ḥtp.f ink Wsir ḫnty Imntt nṯr ꜥꜣ nb ꜣbḏw. On this sequence, see P. BM EA 10191, **I, 1–2**. Note the exceptional reference to *Rꜥ-Ḥr-ꜣḫty* in place of *Rꜥ*, the version found in all other manuscripts, and the absence of the pronoun *ink* before *Itm*.

Line 4
ink I ꜥꜣ nb Ḫmnw ir di Ḥr ḥr nst.f it.f. The role attributed here to Thoth is usually that of Haroeris. See P. BM EA 10191, **I, 8**. The error *nst.f it.f* derives from combination of two traditions, present in the First Book of Breathing where the deceased asserts that he or she is 'Horus son of Isis, son of Osiris, who is upon his throne, eternally', with the variant 'who is upon the throne of his father'. See P. BM EA 10191, **I, 7**.

Lines 4–5
ink Ḥr-wr swnw ir di nfr ꜥwt-nṯr n it.f Rꜥ. On Haroeris as physician, see E. Jelinkova-Reymond, *Les inscriptions de la statue guérisseuse de Djed-her-le-Sauveur* (*BdE* 23, 1956), p. 19, n. 8; Caminos, op. cit., p. 120, n. 19. Note here the absence of the expected epithet 'lord of Upper Egypt' (*nb Šmꜥ*, *nb tꜣ šmꜥ*) or of Letopolis (*Ḫm*) given to the deity in this context. See P. BM EA 10191, **I, 8**.

Lines 5–6
i nꜣ iryw-ꜣꜥ n tꜣ Dwꜣt nꜣ sꜣwtyw n Imntt. For this invocation, see P. BM EA 10191, **I, 2–3**.

Lines 6–7
mi ꜥḳ pꜣ(y).i bꜣ.i (*sic*) *r tꜣ* <*Dw*>*ꜣt ḥnꜥ nꜣ bꜣw iḳrw nty m ẖrt-nṯr*. The *bꜣw iḳrw* denote the deceased collectively; see *LPE*, p. 142 (II, 30). They are said to 'rest' in the necropolis; cf. P. MMA 35.9.21, I, 9 and III, 3: *bꜣw iḳrw nty ḥtp m ẖrt-nṯr*. On the relationship of the deceased (or his ba) with the excellent bas: F.R. Herbin, *BIFAO* 84 (1984), pp. 277 and 283, n. 23; Maspero, *Sarcophages* I, p. 222: *pr.k ḥnꜥ Rꜥ r bw nb mrr.k ḥnꜥ bꜣw iḳrw*, 'You go forth with Re to each place you desire with the excellent bas'; ibid., p. 59: *di.tn pr.i ḥnꜥ bꜣw iḳrw r mꜣꜣ nṯr ꜥꜣ m ẖrt-nṯr*, 'Grant that I go forth with the the excellent bas to see the great god in the god's domain'; ibid., p. 30: *ꜥpy bꜣ.k ḥnꜥ bꜣw iḳrw r bw mr.k*, 'May your ba fly up with the excellent bas to the place you desire!'.

Cf. also Lefebvre, *Petosiris* II (1923), no. 82, 91: *pr bꜣ.k ḥnꜥ bꜣw iḳrw m ḥb nb niwt.k*, 'You go forth with the excellent bas at each festival of your town'.

Lines 7–9
iw mi šm.i r bw nb mr.i mi ir.i ḫpr r mr ib.i m grḥ m hrw m nw nb nty rꜥ nb. Cf. P. BM EA 10123, 7–8 = P. BM EA 10124, 7–8:

pr(w) nbw	'May I assume all the forms
r mr ib.i	according to my heart's desire.'[66]

On the forms assumed at will by the deceased, *LPE*, p. 245 (VII, 21–2).

Lines 10–11
šsp.k ḳbḥ snṯr m-ꜥ Imn-Ipt n Ḏꜣm r tr nb n ssw 10 nb. Same sequence, with inversion of the words *ḳbḥ* and *snṯr* and omission of *n Ḏꜣm*, in P. BM EA 10343, 7. P. BM EA 10344, 7–8:

šsp[*.k ḳbḥ*] *snṯr*	'[You] receive [libation] and censing
m-ꜥ Imn-Ipt [*n*] *Ḏꜣm*	from the hand of Amenipet [of] Djeme,
nṯr ꜥꜣ ꜥnḫ ḥry[*y nṯrw*]	the great god mas[ter of the gods],
r tr n ssw 10 nb	at the moment of each decade.'

For other examples of receiving fresh water and incense from Amenipet, see *LPE*, pp. 143–5 (II, 30–1), and add: P. Vatican 38599, 17–19; shroud, auction of Sotheby's, New York, 18 June 1991, no. 48. For a case of libation alone, cf. too P. Berlin 3162, III, 5:

šsp.k ḳbḥ m-ꜥ Imn-Ipt n Ḏꜣm	'You receive libation by the grace of Amenipet of Djeme
tp ssw 10 nb	at the moment of each decade.'

For similar rites, see P. BM EA 10123, **line 3**, and P. BM EA 10201, **II, 7.**

Line 11
šsp.k tꜣ ḥnḳt kꜣw ꜣpdw m ḥb int. For the deceased receiving offerings at the festival of the Valley, cf. P. Berlin 3162, III, 6–7:

di n.k Imn prt-ḫrw	'Amun grants you an invocation offering,
tꜣ ḥnḳt kꜣw ꜣpdw	bread, beer, oxen and fowl,
snṯr ḳbḥ irp irtt tpw	incense, libation, wine, milk, *tpw*-loaves
m tr.f n ḥb int	at his moment of the festival of the Valley.'

Stela Turin 1585, L. Habachi, *BIFAO* 71 (1972), p. 72, l. 2–3.

šsp.f snw m ḏsrw	'He receives *snw*-loaves in the sacred place,
m ḥb int	in the festival of the Valley
m bꜣḥ nbw nḥḥ	before the lords of eternity.'

On the relationship between the festival of the Valley and the previously mentioned rites of Djeme: C. Traunecker, *La chapelle d'Achôris à Karnak* II (Paris 1981), pp. 134–7. The offerings presented on that occasion concern both the gods and the dead (ibid., p. 125).

Line 12
ꜥḳ.k r Mꜥꜣt (?) *m ẖrt-hrw pr.k hꜣ.k r bw nb mr.k*. The word , probably corrupt, is difficult to explain. No other attestation, at least with this writing, is known. is a known writing for *pr*. On that basis it can only be for the verb *hꜣ* (couple *pr/hꜣ*) here.

Line 13
di n.k Ist wrt mwt-nṯr ḳrst ꜥꜣt nfrt mnḫt. On the grant of a burial by Isis, see P. BM EA 10260, **I, 1**.

Line 14
ꜥnḫ bꜣ.k r nḥḥ ḏt. For this clause, see P. BM EA 10282, **line 23**.

P. BM EA 10201 (pls 110–13)

Hay Collection.
Caminos, in A. Roccati and A. Siliotti (eds), *La magia in Egitto ai Tempi dei Faraoni* (Verona 1987), pp. 151–9 and fig. 2.
Quirke, *Owners*, no. 259.
Provenance: probably Thebes.
Date: first to second century AD.
Owner of the papyrus: *Tꜣ-(nt-)Ist* (Taesis, R*PN* I, 357, 20)
Mother: *Tꜣ-(nt-)Imn-Ipt* (Tamennopis, R*PN* I, 358, 5 and II, 395).

Contents: Original text with invocations to parts of the body and new funerary text.

66. P. BM EA 10124 adds here: *ḥꜣty.i*, 'and of my *ḥꜣty*-heart'.

This version of the Book of Breathing, written on one sheet, comprises two columns of different dimensions (maximum 57.3 × 21.5 cm). The entire lower area of the manuscript is unfortunately marred by major lacunae which detract from the understanding of the text. To date no parallel has been identified.

In its present condition, col. I contains twenty lines of text (the last now containing no more than a few signs). After a brief introduction (I, 1–2), begins a series of invocations to parts of the body, which continue as far as line 2 of col. II. This portion of the text is the most original. It is followed (II, 3–17) by a passage more in keeping with the motifs of other Books of Breathing, concerning the afterlife of the deceased.

Text on the verso: The Book of Breathing of *Tꜣ-(nt-)Ỉst* [...]

Translation

Recto

I (1) Hail Hathor *Tꜣ-(nt)-Ỉst* born of *Tꜣ-(nt)-Ỉmn-Ỉpt*, (2) you enter the great Duat in peace, and he who is there receives you in joy.

(3) Hail to your ka without equal. 'Hathor the great' they say of you.

(4) Hail to <your> limbs purified of sickness, ill health being removed far from your Majesty.

(5) Hail to your head, when it has ... (?) to earth ... (?)

(6) Hail to your face as it soothes the guardians without there being any fault of their Majesty before you.

(7) Hail to your eyes as they protect your body, and behold ... (?)

(8) Hail to your brow when you have touched the earth (with your brow) before the face of your lord in order to satisfy him.

(9) Hail to your nose as it breathes and inhales the offerings free of impurity.

(10) Hail to your gullet (?) provided with your good things; what is told to your ears, you hear it (?)

(11) Hail to your tongue which distinguishes your words, without its issue returning.

(12) Hail to your jaws [as they eat] the offerings with which you took from those altars.

(13) Hail to [your ...] as it [...] to vindicate [you against] your [enemies].

(14) Hail to [...] as it [...] to remove (?) [...] of your ka.

(15) Hail to your [... ...] as it [...] to satisfy [...].

(16) Hail to [... ...] this [...] come forth [from ... ...] excellent.

(17) Hail to [... ...] before him (?)

(18) Hail to [... ...]

(19) [Hail to ... ...]

(20) [Hail to ... ...]

II (1) Hail to your arms as they take the *snw*-loaves with the excellent mummies which are in the underworld.

Hail to your back, the great courtiers will not turn their backs on you in (2) the great Duat.

Hail to your legs as they walk quickly for you in the excellent place where offerings are given.

Hail to your limbs reunited with their place in which your flesh is joining your bones.

(3) Hail to your ka that you may come in peace with the great bas which are in the sacred Duat.

Receive for yourself a libation in the sacred place, at the moment of assembling (?) the divine offerings of the ruler of the necropolis. Take for yourself all the offerings (4) which come forth from the earth, and the dew of the sky above them. You come in peace to the Mansion of the Prince, and he who is there receives you in peace.

(O) Hathor *Tꜣ-(nt)-Ỉst*, born of *Tꜣ-(nt)-Ỉmn-Ỉpt*, (5) you are justified against the enemies of your Majesty (after) your ka has moved to the Mansion of the obelisk to eat food before their (*sic*) lord, while coming and going (are achieved) by your ba in the *sktt*-bark ...(?), his Majesty rests (6) upon your corpse in the evening. The *mꜥnḏt*-bark is for your ka in the place of promenade with the bas of the great mummies. All the guardians of the gates receive you without there being (7) any fault of their Majesty before you. Take for yourself a libation at the moment of each decade after the Ba of Amun the Elder has moved. Take for yourself these good things from the altars, bread and water (8), without there being any impurity. The breath of air enters your limbs, (while) coming and going (are achieved) by your ba. Your image has appeared to take the great offerings as the remainder of the divine offerings of the mummies.

(9) (O) Hathor *Tꜣ-(nt)-Ỉst*, justified, born of *Tꜣ-(nt-)Ỉmn-Ỉpt*, take for yourself the *ḥtpw*-offerings before Osiris the great; they enter your body; they fill your œsophagus (?), (so that) you are mighty against your enemies; (10) they fill your nostrils with the breath of air. Your ba hastens before the noble bas. You are indeed a noble lady, equipped with riches more than the great nobles (?) (11)[...] before the [...] ... (?) raised by your dignity which is among them. Your Majesty is magnified by the Embalmer, among the mummies who are in his retinue, giving (?) (12) [...] arms [...] your [...] to make [...] ... (?) [your ba] (?). Then the Ruler (?) made an incantation (?) by his magical spells, that your ba may approach (?) your corpse. Then the two Sisters (13)[...] ... (?) over [...] your (?) arms [...]. Then the excellent bas magnified [your] image, and <your> dignity is great in their heart. You are shown the ways (14)[fair ? in] the Duat [...] ... (?) heart [...](?) [...] in accordance with your desire at any moment you desire. Your ba comes (15) [...] it [...] [your] corpse [...] this ... (?) [... ... ...] hall of the two Maats [... ... ...] which are in (16) [... ...] evil (?) [... ... Du]at in (?) [...] to your face [...]. Then (?) your Majesty [...] ... (?)

the Mansion of the obelisk by the decree (17) [of … …] dig[nity …] noble mummies […] house … (?) Your heart is glad when your Majesty beholds what is in it entirely.

Commentary

I, 2
ꜥḳ.t m ḥtp r Dwꜣt wrt. Cf. *Ritual of Embalming*, II, 8 (ed. Sauneron, p. 3): *swḏꜣ.f twk m ḥtp r Dwꜣt wrt*, 'It (the *ibr*-unguent) causes you to go in peace to the great Duat'.

Same epithet *wrt* for the Duat in II, 2.

iṯ twtn[67] *imy.s m ḥꜥꜥ*. *Twtn* is problematic. Here it clearly cannot be the rare second person plural independent pronoun (A.H. Gardiner, *Eg. Gram.* § 43, obs. 2; A. Erman, *Neuägypt. Gramm.* § 76), first because the text is addressed to only one person, and then for reasons of orthography (there is no attestation of a writing). The second person singular feminine dependent pronoun *tn* would be expected here, since the text concerns a deceased woman. This pronoun is found (II, 6) in the phrase *šsp twtn sꜣwtyw*, 'the guardians receive you'. The same peculiarity is also found in other documents, all in favour of a woman:

P. Lieblein, 10–11:

šsp twtn […] *r wsḫt ww Mꜣꜥt*	'[…] receives you […] in the hall of the land of Maat.'

P. Lieblein, 12:

[*šsp*] *twtn Inpw r wsḫt* […]	'Anubis receives you in the hall […].'

Here the 'usual' versions employ either the dependent pronoun *tn* (*šsp tn Inpw r wsḫt Mꜣꜥty*, P. BM EA 10112, 12), or the independent pronoun *twt* (*šsp twt Inpw r wsḫt* [*Mꜣꜥty*], P. BM EA 10108, 5–6).

Imy.s (He who is in it, the previously cited Duat), in the clause *iṯ twtn imy.s m ḥꜥꜥ*, probably refers here to Osiris (cf. however *Imy Dwꜣt* denoting the sun according to K. Mysliwiec, *SAK* 6 [1978], p. 149, fig. 7).

On the deceased being received in the Duat in joy, cf. P. BM EA 10260, I, x + 10–11; also Maspero, *Sarcophages* I, pp. 97 and 129: *šsp s*(*w*) *imyw Dwꜣt m ḥꜥꜥ*; stela Moscow 4103 (ed. S. Hodjash and O. Berlev, *The Egyptian Reliefs and Stelae in the Pushkin Museum of Fine Arts, Moscow* [Leningrad 1982], no. 117) = stela Cairo 27/1/25/12, lines 7–8 (A.H. Zayed, *RdE* 20 [1968], pl. 15 B) = stela Cairo CG 22141, 8 (ed. Kamal, p. 123) = P. Bremner-Rhind, 16, 28 = P. BM EA 10260, I, x + 11: *šsp tw imyw Dwꜣt m ḥꜥꜥ*; Assmann, *Sonnenhymnen*, p. 179: *šsp.n tw imyw Dwꜣt m ḥꜥꜥ*; P. Berlin 3162, II, 7 = P. Louvre N 3125, V, 5–6: *šsp twk imyw Dwꜣt m ḥꜥꜥ*; W.J. Tait, *Papyri from Tebtunis in Egyptian and Greek* (London 1977), pl. 6, no. 25, fragm. 1, line 3: [… *i*]*m*[*yw*] *Dwꜣt m ḥꜥꜥ*; Bénédite, *Philae*, 134, 8–9: *šsp twk imyw Dwꜣt m ḥꜥꜥ*; 135, 3: *šsp k*(*w*) *imyw Dwꜣt m ḥꜥꜥ*.

I, 3
hꜣy n kꜣ.t iwty wḥm.ty.fy Ḥwt-Ḥr wrt ḥr.tw r.t. Applied to the ka, the expression *iwty wḥm.ty.fy* (*Wb.* I, 341, 1) does not seem otherwise attested.

I, 4
hy n ḥꜥw<.t> wꜥb.ti r st-ꜥ st-ḳsnt m ḥr r ḥm.t. On the word *st-ꜥ*: Assmann, *Sonnenhymnen*, p. 204, n. a; A.H. Gardiner, *PSBA* 34 (1912), p. 261, n. 14; R.J. Demarée, *The ꜣḫ iḳr n Rꜥ-Stelae* (Leiden 1983), p. 266, n. 361. On the formation of nouns with the prefix *st*: H. Grapow, *ZÄS* 79 (1954), pp. 91–4. For *ḳsn(t)*, see A. Ember, *ZÄS* 51 (1913), p. 117, no. 67. *Ḥm*, 'Majesty', to qualify the deceased (cf. *Wb.* IV, 92, 11) is found again II, 5, 11, 16; also P. BM EA 10108, 4; P. BM EA 10112, 8; P. BM EA 10114, 7.

I, 5
hy n tp.t … (?) *n.f r tꜣ nn ꜥnḏ ḏꜣis*[68] *n.f*. Phrase of uncertain interpretation. The idea seems to be that of a movement of the head towards the earth, but the exact meaning is not forthcoming.

I, 6
hy n ḥr.t ḥr swnwn sꜣwtyw nn sp n ḥm.sn ḥr.t. The phrase *nn sp n ḥm.sn ḥr.t* occurs again in II, 6–7. On the word *sp*, 'fault': J.J. Clère, *BIFAO* 30 (1930), p. 436, n. 5; J. Berlandini, *BIFAO* 79 (1979), p. 252.

I, 7
hy n ꜣḫty.t ḥr ḫw ḏt[*.t*] *ḥr dgꜣ r sš* … (?)*.n.t* (?). On *ꜣḫty* denoting the eyes: Lefebvre, *Tableau*, p. 16.

I, 8
hy n dhnt.t dhn.n.t tꜣ m ḥr n nb.t r sḥtp.f. The translation by Caminos, op. cit., p. 155, for this passage ('the land gleams or shines (*thn*) in front of your lord to propitiate him') seems inaccurate, *dhn.n.t* being probably a *sḏm.n.f* form. The construction *dhn tꜣ m*, 'to prostrate oneself before', is well attested. Note the pun between *dhn*, 'brow' (Lefebvre, op. cit., p. 12) and *dhn* 'touch (with the brow)'.

I, 9
hy n fnḏ.t ḥr snsn bhd m ḫwt ḥr.ti r isft. The word *ḫwt* here encompasses a wide scope, for it can denote either 'offerings' inhaled or sweet-smelling products such as incense.

I, 10
hy n ḥtmw-ntt.t ḥtm m nfrw.t ḏd n ꜥnḫwy.t (?) *sḏm.t sn*. The second part of this sequence remains doubful. The word *ḥtm-ntt*, written here in the plural, is attested elsewhere, so far as I know, only in *Edfou* IV, 65, 13: 'I grant you that your arms be held out to your throat and that your gullet (?) receive your offerings' (*di.i n.k ꜥwy.k ḥr dwn r nfrt.k ḥtm-ntt.k ḥr šsp inw.k*). The exact identification of *ḥtm-ntt* remains obscure, but since this word is cited in the text between mentions of the nose (I, 9) and of the tongue (I, 11), it refers probably to an inner and lower part of the neck near the throat. Note here the pun between *ḥtm-ntt* and *ḥtm*, 'be equipped'.

I, 11
hy n ns.t wp mdw nn ꜥn.n pr im.f. For the expression *wp mdw* with reference to the tongue: 'which distinguishes the words', see S. Sauneron, *Esna* V, pp. 221 and 222, n. (i).

nn ꜥn n pr im.f: cf. P. Leiden T 32, VII, 33 (*LPE*, p. 477): *nn fḫ.n ḏdw.f nn ꜥn.n pr m rꜣ.f*, 'without his words being undone, without the issue of his mouth being returned'; also Lefebvre, *Petosiris* II, p. 82, no. 115, line 2: *nn ḫm* (*sic*)*.n pr m rꜣ.k*, 'without the issue of your mouth being repelled'.

I, 12
hy n [*w*]*gyt.t sn*[*m*] (?) *m nn iṯ.n.t m ḥtpw iptn*. On the word *wgyt*, 'jaws' (from *wgi* 'to chew'), see Lefebvre, *Tableau*, p. 15, § 15; T. Bardinet, *Dents et mâchoires dans les représentations religieuses et la pratique médicale de l'Egypte ancienne* (Rome 1990), pp. 61–2. Two restorations, after *wgyt.t*,

67. The scribe has first written the pronoun *tn*, then added *tw* in the space above the line.
68. The word *ḏꜣis* has been crossed out except for the determinative .

are conceivable: whether *snm*, or *snw*, both attested in II, 1 and II, 5. In this context, and despite the determinative , one expects a verb, not a substantive. The preposition *ḥr* has probably been omitted here (cf. II, 1: *hꜣy n ꜥwy.t ḥr šsp snw*), so the restoration *snw* appears very hypothetical.

I, 13
From this line to the end of col. I (line 18), lacunae cover all the names for parts of the body, and most of the remainder of the text. In line 14, no restoration can be suggested, other than perhaps the hypothesis of a noun providing alliteration with the following verb *smꜣꜥ-ḫrw*, on the model adopted in other lines of this text. In this position after the tongue and jaws (lines 11 and 12), the word might be that for the temples (*mꜣꜥwy*, Lefebvre, *Tableau*, p. 14, § 13).

II, 1
hy n ꜥwy.t ḥr šsp snw ḥnꜥ sꜥḥw iḳrw imyw ꜥt imnt. On the share of the deceased in the offerings alongside the 'excellent mummies', cf. P. OIC 25389, XXXII, 5 (*LPE*, p. 503): *sfsf ꜣw n kꜣ.k ḥnꜥ sꜥḥw iḳrw*; the deceased wishes to join their number; cf. e.g. stela Cairo CG 22151, 17 (Kamal, *Stèles*, p. 140: *di.k wn.i m-m sꜥḥw iḳrw šmsw nṯr*, 'Grant that I may be among the excellent mummies who follow the god'; stela Cairo CG 34099, 5 (P. Lacau, *Stèles du Nouvel Empire*[*CGC*], Cairo 1909, p. 155): *wnn.i m-m sꜥḥw iḳr(w) ḫr ḥswt n nṯr ꜥꜣ*, 'I will be among the excellent mummies under the praises of the great god'.

ꜥt imnt: on the meaning 'underworld', see S. Schott, *ZÄS* 95 (1969), p. 64, n. 46; Chassinat, *Khoiak* II, p. 769; Meeks, *ALex* 77.0554.

II, 1–2
hy n psḏ.t nn psḏ.n.t in wrw ꜥꜣw ḫnt Dwꜣt wrt. For the verb *psḏ*, 'turn one's back' (*Wb.* I, 556, 12–13), see Meeks, *Alex* 77.1496, citing P. Lacau and H. Chevrier, *Une chapelle d'Hatshepsout à Karnak* (Cairo 1977), p. 378, § 665, n. (b). The verb is punning upon the substantive *psḏ*.[69] Note here the special construction of this verb, not previously observed (passive + *in*).

wrw ꜥꜣw ḫnt Dwꜣt wrt: apparently a rare designation; see Leitz, *LGG* II, p. 477, s.v. *Wrw-Dwꜣt*. may be interpreted here as the preposition 'in', rather than as the adjective *ḫnty*, 'foremost of'; cf. **II, 2** and **11**.

II, 2
hy n wꜥrwt.t ḥr wꜥr n.t ḫnt bw iḳr n rdit ḥwt. On the word *wꜥrt*, cf. Lefebvre, *Tableau*, pp. 52–4, § 60.

hy n ꜥwt.t dmḏ r st.sn imy iwf.t ḥr ꜣm ꜣḫꜣḫ.t. Note here the inverted sense of *imy*, on which see Meeks, *ALex* 78.0288. A translation with *imy iwf.t* as the subject of *ꜣm* seems improbable.

II, 3
h(ꜣ)y n kꜣ.t iw ii.t(i) m ḥtp ḥnꜥ bꜣw ꜥꜣw imyw Dwꜣt ḏsrt. On the great Bas, denoting the deities of the necropolis, see *LPE*, p. 240 (VII, 9–10). In P. Louvre 11079, II, 4–5, Isis is said to give 'a great, fine and efficient tomb to the deceased together with the great Bas of the Duat' (*di ḳrst ꜥꜣt nfrt mnḫt ḥnꜥ Bꜣw ꜥꜣw nw Dwꜣt*).

The 'sacred Duat' (P. BM EA 10344, 10; P. Florence 3669, 9, 11–12, 20–1; *Ritual of Embalming*, V, 3 (ed. Sauneron, p. 14); P. dem. Louvre E 3452, 14) is a designation of the necropolis: see M. Smith, *Enchoria* 15 (1987), pp. 77–8, n. 48; D. Kurth, *Der Sarg der Teüris* (*AegTrev* 6, 1990), p. 21, n. 226; *BD* ch. 17, 20 (ed. Lepsius); H.C. Schmidt, *SAK* 22 (1995), p. 246, n. 48: Sethe, *Amun*, § 104, 106: also P. Rhind I, 6, 1: *ꜥḳ.k r ḫrt-nṯr ky ḏd Dwꜣt ḏsrt*, 'You enter the god's domain, otherwise said the sacred Duat'. The demotic version gives simply *Dwꜣ.t tsr.t*. Farther in the text, the same demotic phrase conveys the expression *tꜣ ḏsr* (I, 9, 7); see G. Möller, *Die beiden Totenpapyrus Rhind* (*DemSt.* 6, 1913), p. 90, n. 154. This equation is not noted by J.K. Hoffmeier, *Sacred in the Vocabulary of Ancient Egypt* (*OBO* 59, 1985), p. 194. The possibility cannot be excluded that the identification of the sacred Duat varied from place to place: in Abydos, it seems to have local reference (Goyon, *Rituels funéraires*, p. 58, n. 4). In Thebes, the sacred Duat may perhaps be identified with the Duat of the sacred land, located on the Mound of Djeme; cf. Dümichen, *HI* II, pl. 36 a, ß, 5.

šsp n.t ḳbḥ m bw ḏsr m ṯs ḥtpw-nṯr (?) *n ḥḳꜣ igrt*. On the form for *šsp*, encountered again in line 4, see *LPE*, p. 247 (VIII, 2). For the region of the underworld called *bw ḏsr*: *LPE*, pp. 104–5 (I, 19); Hoffmeier, op. cit., p. 206. The word *ṯs* is written under the influence of the verb *ḏꜣis*; see R. Anthes, in *Fs. zum 150 Jährigen bestehen des Berliner ägyptischen Museums* (Berlin 1974), p. 23, n. k. *Ḥḳꜣ igrt* is a title and a designation of Osiris.

II, 3–4
iṯ n.t ḥwt nbt pr m tꜣ i(ꜣ)dt n(t) pt m ḥrw.sn. For *i(ꜣ)dt n(t) pt*, cf. *Wb.* I, 36, 1–2. In the context of an offering, cf. *Urk.* IV, 217, 8–10:

srwḏ.s pꜣwt.tn	'She strengthens your *pꜣt*-offerings,
swꜣḏ.s wḏḥw.tn [...]	she provisions your altars [...]
shꜣ i(ꜣ)dt imyt pt m hꜣw.s	causing the dew which is in heaven to descend in her vicinity.'

Also P. Louvre I 3292, K, 19–20 (G. Nagel, *BIFAO* 29 [1929], pp. 55 and 59, n. 19):

wnm.n.sn tꜣ	'We eat bread
sꜥm.n.n m i(ꜣ)dt.k	and feed on your dew.'

II, 4
ꜥḳ.k m ḥtp r ḥwt sr šsp tn imy.s m ḥtp. On the entry of the deceased into the Heliopolitan sanctuary *ḥwt sr* (*GDG* IV, 127), cf. P. BM EA 10124, 7: *mi ꜥḳ.i r ḥwt sr*; *Ritual of Embalming*, V, 23–6, 1 (ed. Sauneron, p. 18): *sꜥḳ.f twk r ḥwt sr*, 'He (Osiris) causes you to enter the Mansion of the Prince'; ibid., X, 19 (ed. Sauneron, pp. 43–4):

šm.k r ḥwt sr	'You go to the Mansion of the Prince
ḫns.k ḥwt Bnbn nḥḥ	and traverse the Mansion of the obelisk eternally,
m ḥb diw	on the day of the festival of the fifth day.'

Ritual of Embalming, V, 11 (ed. Sauneron, p. 16): *rdi.tw n.k st m-ḫnw ḥwt sr*, 'You are granted a place in the Mansion of the Prince'. There Isis and Nephthys weep and mourn the deceased (ibid., VIII, 7). The *Ritual of the Opening of the Mouth* (scenes 26 and 46, ed. Otto, I, pp. 66–7 and 108–9) explains how, once the deceased had his mouth opened by the *msḫtyw*-instrument, 'he walks of himself before the great Ennead in the Mansion of the Prince which is in Heliopolis, and there he receives the *wrrt*-crown before Horus lord of mankind'[70] (*šm.f mdw.f ḏt.f ḫr Psḏt ꜥꜣt m ḥwt sr wr imy Iwnw iṯ.f wrrt im ḫr Ḥr nb pꜥt*). There the deceased is also purified by incense (ibid., scene 62, ed. Otto, pp. 166–7), and receives a libation (see P. BM EA 10123, **line 2** and P. BM EA 10191, **I, 12**) or offerings (E. von Bergmann, *Der Sarkophag des Panehemisis* I [Vienna 1883], p. 11).

šsp tn imy.s m ḥtp: cf. P. BM EA 10290, x + 4–5: *šsp twk imyw Dwꜣt m ḥtp*, 'Those who are in the Duat receive you in peace'; J. Berlandini, *BIFAO* 85 (1985), p. 44, with reference to the West (*Imntt*): *šsp tw imy.s*

69. For another case of a pun on the word *psḏ*, 'back': Assmann, *Liturgische Lieder*, p. 268.
70. On the second part of this phrase, cf. ibid., scene 50 B (ed. Otto, I, pp. 126–7).

m ḥtp, 'He who is there receives you, in peace'. On this expression, cf. *supra*, **I, 2**: *šsp twtn imy.s m ḥꜥꜥ*.

Cf. also P. Florence 3669, 9–11:

imꜣḫw ꜥꜣw nw Imntt	'The great revered ones of the West,
šsp.sn ḫꜣt.t r Dwꜣt m ḥtp	they receive your corpse in the Duat, in peace.'

II, 4–5

Ḥwt-Ḥr N mꜣꜥ-ḫrw.t r sbiw ḥm.t. For *ḥm*, 'Majesty', to qualify the deceased, see *supra*, **I, 4**. Her justification here seems tied with her access to the Heliopolitan place evoked in the next sentence.

II, 5

ḫnd.n kꜣ.t r-ḫnt ḥwt Bnbn r sꜥm snm(t) ḥr nb.sn tm. *Ḥwt Bnbn*, as above *ḥwt sr*, is a shrine in Heliopolis, connected with Osiris. On the entry of the deceased into this place, cf. *Ritual of Embalming*, X, 19, cited *supra* (**II, 4**); also P. BM EA 10110 + 10111, **II, 6–7**. There his name is magnified; see F.R. Herbin, *BIFAO* 84 (1984), p. 278.

The word *tm* is problematic. It cannot be negation introducing the following phrase without undermining its fundamental meaning, but there is no other obvious sense in the present sequence.

II, 5–6

ꜥḳ pr (?) *in bꜣ.t ḥr sktt wrt ḫnm.n ḥm.f ḥr ḫꜣt.t m ssy*. Although the group *ꜥḳ pr* has been altered by the scribe, the surviving traces allow no other reading; cf. **II, 8**: *ꜥḳ pr in bꜣ.t*. *ꜥḳ*, like *pr*, can be constructed with the preposition *ḥr*. In spite of its rather unusual form (cf., however, line 7 in *bꜣ n Imn wr*), the transcription of the word read *bꜣ* seems probable, but I cannot account for the sign preceding it. Between the determinative of the name of the *sktt*-bark and the solar disk are two inexplicable signs. The passage seems garbled. Corruption of *sktt wrt* ?

For the meaning, cf. P. BM EA 10110 + 10111, II, 4: *ꜥḳ.i sktt ḫnd.i mꜥndt*, 'I enter the *sktt*-bark and tread the *mꜥndt*-bark'; P. BM EA 10191, II, 7: *ꜥḥꜥ.i ḥr ḥꜣt n wiꜣ n Rꜥ šsp.i ḥꜣtt m sktt*, 'I stand at the prow of the bark of Re; I seize the prow rope in the *sktt*-bark'. On the access of the deceased in the solar bark, see Assmann, *Liturgische Lieder* (*MÄS* 19, 1969), pp. 288–9.

ḫnm ḥr, 'to rest upon': Meeks, *Alex* 78.3214. From the context, the subject can scarcely be other than the word read *bꜣ* in line 5. On the ba resting on the corpse of the deceased, see P. BM EA 10108, **lines 6–7**.

II, 6

mꜥndt n kꜣ.k m st n swtwt ḥnꜥ bꜣw n sꜥḥw ꜥꜣw.[71] The correlation previously posited between the ba of the deceased and the *sktt*-bark paves the way for another between the ka and the *mꜥndt*-bark.

The bas of the great mummies are not otherwise known, but the reference is certainly to the dead. In a comparable context, cf. P. dem. Louvre E 10605, 9 = P. dem. Berlin 8351, III, 9 (M. Smith, *Enchoria* 16 [1988], pp. 58 and 67 = id., *Liturgy*, p. 26: *pr r-bnr-n tꜣ twꜣ.t r mr swtwt iwt nꜣ by.w ꜥy.w*, 'Go forth from the Duat for love of travelling about among the great bas'. For the *st swtwt* (*Wb.* IV, 5 and 78, 1), see Gardiner, *AEO* II, p. 216*, no. 461; F. Daumas, *Les mammisis des temples égyptiens* (Paris 1958), p. 304, n. 3; S. Sauneron, *BIFAO* 64 (1966), pp. 189–90; Smith, *Mortuary Texts*, p. 118 (X, 20).

II, 6–7

šsp twtn sꜣwtyw irw nw sbꜣw nn sp n ḥm.sn ḥr.t. On *twtn*, see *supra*, **I, 2**. For the clause *nn sp n ḥm.sn ḥr.t*, see *supra*, **I, 6**, also in connection with the *sꜣwtyw*. On the word *irw*: W. Golenischeff, *ZÄS* 15 (1877), pp. 59–63; Lefebvre, *Petosiris* III, p. 23 (index); G. Burkard, *Spätzeitliche Osiris-Liturgien* (*ÄAT* 31, 1995), p. 189, n. 84.

II, 7

ꜣm n.t ḳbḥ m tr n ssw 10 nb m-ḫt ḫnd.n Bꜣ n Imn wr. On the libation on each decade, see P. BM EA 10123, **line 3**, and P. BM EA 10194, **lines 10–11**. Its formulation here is unusual. Amun the Elder is a name of Montu (Sethe, *Amun*, § 6), but the designation *Bꜣ n Imn wr* is not otherwise known in the context of a rite of the decade.

II, 7–8

šsp n.t nfrw nn n ḥtpw tꜣ ḥnꜥ mw nn isft. The word *ḥtpw* occurs above in I, 12, with the same spelling and the probable meaning 'altars', suggested in both instances by the determinative, clearly distinct from the sign which closes *ḥtpw* in II, 8 and 9, in an unambiguous context.

II, 8

is n niw m ꜥḳ r ḥꜥw.t iw ꜥḳ pr in bꜣ.t. On the 'breath of air' (*is* (*n*) *niw*), *LPE*, p. 88 (I, 6–7). On the entry of air into the limbs, here permitting the ba to enter and leave, cf. J. Berlandini, *BIFAO* 85 (1985), p. 44:

ꜥḳ n.k ṯꜣw r tpḥt.k	'The wind enters for you in your chapel
sḳbb.f ḥꜥw.k n tꜣy.f	and refreshes your limbs (so that) they do not burn.'

ꜥḳ pr in bꜣ.t: see *supra*, **II, 5**.

II, 8–9

ḥꜥ.n sḫm.t ḥr it ḥtpw wrw m spy ḥtpw-nṯr n sꜥḥw. On the *sḫm* of an individual performing the act *ḥꜥ*, cf. *BD* ch. 140 (ed. Budge, p. 314, 14–15).

II, 9

Ḥwt-Ḥr N iṯ n.t ḥtpw ḥr Wsir wr ꜥḳ.sn r ḫt.t mḥ.sn šꜣw.t (?) *wsr.t r sbiw.t*. So written, is apparently a *hapax*, but may be identified with the word *šꜣt* of *Wb.* IV, 402, 4, 'ein innerer Körperteile des Menschen', where it is compared with *šsšꜣt*, on which see Lefebvre, *Tableau*, p. 22. It would denote the upper part of the œsophagus. The formulation of this phrase, as of the following, is somewhat unusual. The use of the verb *ꜥḳ* to convey absorption of food by the body seems to be unparalleled, and the connection with power over enemies of the deceased is otherwise unattested in Egyptian sources.

II, 10

bꜥḥ.sn ḫnmty.t (?) *m is n niw*. As above in *ꜥḳ.sn*, the subject of *bꜥḥ* can only be *ḥtpw*. If I have understood the text correctly, implausible though it may seem, it is the consumption of offerings which enables the nose to inhale the 'breath of air'. Garbled text ?

iw wnšnš.n bꜣ.t ḥr bꜣw špsw. For the verb *wnšnš*, see P. BM EA 10108, **line 7**. *Bꜣw špsw* is a designation of the collectivity of the dead, comparable with the *bꜣw iḳrw* more often attested.

II, 10–11

šps ir.t šps.ti r špsw ꜥꜣwy n (?) [...]. Sequence of uncertain reading and interpretation. The writing (cf. *Wb.* IV, 450, 16–451, 6: 'herrliche Dinge', 'dargebrachten Speisen') probably conceals the verb *šps* (*Wb.* IV, 448, 13–20): 'jem. vertsehen, ausstatten', with intransitive force not previously recorded. The meaning of *ꜥꜣwy* (false dual ?) at the end of the sequence is unclear, and the lacuna at the start of line 11 rules out any certainty.

71. This sequence is cited, without reference and with errors, by S. Birch, *ZÄS* 10 (1872), p. 120.

II, 11
[...]*w.t ḥr* [...]*w ꜣḫ* [...*k*]*ꜣ n šfy(t) imy(t).sn*. From this line, the increase in the lacunae and the absence of any parallel make consecutive translation difficult.

swr ḥm.t in Imy-wt ḫnt sꜥḥw wn m swꜣw.f. The mummies (*sꜥḥw*), created by the labour of Anubis on each dead person, make up the natural retinue of the god. The expression *swr ḥm* is not otherwise known, but for the meaning, see *infra*, **II, 13**. The retinue (*swꜣw*) of Anubis may be compared with his 'entourage' (*gs*), attested in *BD* ch. 125 (ed. Budge, p. 246, 16); see Allen, *Book of the Dead*, p. 101.

II, 11–12
rdi.n i[...] *ꜥwy* [...]*.t r ir* [...]*.tw n bꜣ.t* (?). Incomprehensible passage.

II, 12
wn.in Ḥḳ(ꜣ) (?)*ḥr šn m ḥkꜣw.f*. For the construction *wn.in* ... *ḥr* + infinitive, see P. Vernus, in *L'égyptologie en 1979. Axes prioritaires de recherches* I (Paris 1982), pp. 87–8. Caminos, op. cit., pp. 156–7, considers the signs following *wn.in* as the designation of a deity *Iḳr* ([hieroglyphs]) which he would like to identify with Osiris in view of the mummy determinative, generally not attested for the word *iḳr*, but found one line below in (*bꜣw*) *iḳrw*. In the latter instance, the presence of this determinative may be explained by the very nature of the *bꜣw iḳrw* denoting the dead collectively. For the writing of *iḳr* without *r*: R.J. Demarée, *The ꜣḫ iḳr n Rꜥ-Stelae* (Leiden 1983), p. 197, n. 44. The reading, on the purely palaeographical level, is not entirely convincing (hieratic form of [hieroglyph], total absence of other attestation of Osiris as *Iḳr*). The proposed reading *ḥḳ(ꜣ)* remains hypothetical and is subject to the same criticisms: the determinative [hieroglyph] is not encountered in any other example of the word.

For *Ḥḳꜣ*, here written *Ḥḳ*, as a designation of a deity: Leitz, *LGG* V, pp. 552–54; as god protecting Osiris: Meeks, *ALex*, 78.2832.

The entire phrase is rightly compared by Caminos (op. cit., p. 156) with a passage in P. Chester-Beatty I, rt., 4–5 where it is said of Isis: *wn.in.s ḥr šnt m ḥkꜣw.s*. On this passage, cf. too Borghouts, in A. Roccati and A. Siliotti (eds), *La magia in Egitto ai Tempi dei Faraoni* (Verona 1987), p. 40, in connection with *ḥkꜣw*.

r iꜥr (?) *bꜣ.t ḥr ḫꜣt.t*. Caminos, op. cit., p. 156, translates, transposing to the third person: '(...) so that Taaset's spirit (*bꜣ*) might join her dead body (*ḫꜣt*)'. He does not give a reading for the verb which he translates 'join', but clearly regards it as one of the expressions used in the funerary literature to convey the approach to the body by the ba, such as *ḫn*, *sḫn*, *ḥtp* and *wꜣḥ* (all constructed with the preposition *ḥr*).[72] The word read *(i)ꜥr* (?) seems to have been modified by the scribe; in the upper part are traces of an erasure.

II, 12–13
wn.in snsn[*ty* ... ?] *šd ḥr* [...] *ꜥwy* [*.sn* ?]. The uncertain context makes it impossible to know the meaning of *šd* – apparently a verb –, but the sequence seems to refer to a protection of the deceased by Isis and Nephthys (cf. e.g. P. Berlin 3162, I, 1: *ꜥwy snsnty m sꜣ.k*, 'The arms of the two Sisters are your protection').

II, 13
wn in bꜣw iḳrw ḥr sꜥꜣ wrm.t fꜣw<.t> wr m-ḫnt ib.sn. For *sꜥꜣ wrm*, cf. the similar expressions *sꜥꜣ ḳd* and *sꜥꜣ ḳyw* in F.R. Herbin, *BIFAO* 84 (1984), pp. 265 and 291, n. 60.

II, 13–14
sšm.tw n.t wꜣwt [*nfrwt m Dw*]*ꜣt*. The motif of ways revealed to the deceased is common in the funerary literature, under various formulations; cf. e.g. E. von Bergmann, *Der Sarkophag des Panehemisis* I (Vienna 1883), p. 11: *sšm.n.(i) n.k wꜣwt nfrwt m Dwꜣt*; Herbin, op. cit., pp. 257 and 279, n. 5: *šm.sn n.k wꜣt (nb) nfrt m-ḫnw Dwꜣt*; *Urk.* IV, 247, 6: *sšm.sn n.s wꜣwt nfrwt*. In other instances, the deceased is the one 'guided' on these ways: A. Kamal, *ASAE* 11 (1911), p. 21: *sšm.t(w).f ḥr wꜣwt ḏsrwt*. The ka of the deceased occasionally serve as guides: W. Barta, *Aufbau und Bedeutung* (*ÄgFo* 24, 1968), p. 40, B. 33 and 37; see also P. BM EA 10314, **II, 2**.

II, 14–17
Little comment can be made for the last part of the papyrus, which is particularly riddled with lacunae. In II, 17, may be noted a reference to the 'noble mummies' (*sꜥḥw špsw*, same reference as the *sꜥḥw iḳrw* of II, 1), and the final sequence [...] *pr.t* [...]*nḏm ib.t dgꜣ in ḥm.t imy.f tm*, for which cf. P. Cairo CG 58018 vs.:

ḥr ib.k pr.k hꜣ.k ḥr tꜣ Gb	'Your heart is satisfied, you come and go upon the earth of Geb
dgꜣ.k sḫrw nb nty im.f	and behold all the rules which are there.'

P. Cairo CG 58012, 12–13:

šm.k ḥr tꜣ mꜣꜣ.k imyw.f	'You go upon earth and see what it contains,
ḥnꜥ bꜣw n nṯrw	with the bas of the gods;
mꜣꜣ.k sḫrw nb n pr.k	you see all the rules of your house.'

P. BM EA 10254 (pls 114–17)

Chester Collection, 1876.
Unpublished.
Quirke, *Owners*, no. 238.
Provenance: probably Thebes.
Date: first to second century AD.
Owner of the papyrus: *Tꜣ-ḥtrt-nnt*. The name, not otherwise attested, is composed of the elements *Tꜣ-ḥtrt* (Thatres, *RPN* I, 366, 8) and *nnt* (designation of the sky ?). Cf. the names *Ḥtr* (Atres), W. Spiegelberg, *Aegyptische und griechische Eigennamen* (*DemSt.* 1, 1901), p. 12*, no. 78, and W. Clarysse, *CdE* 105 (1978), p. 233; *Tꜣ-šrit-pꜣ-ḥtr* (?), J. Quaegebeur, in *Studies in Egyptology presented to Miriam Lichtheim* II (1990), pp. 777 and 778, n. b.
Mother of the owner: *Tꜣ-ḥtrt...* (?)

Contents: Original text with some funerary formulae.

Manuscript of one sheet (25.8 × 13.5 cm) composed of nine fragments preserving seven lines in a rapid and clumsy hand. The left-hand fragments, apparently also containing seven lines, ought to be arranged in a different order. The fragment which is presented as the seventh line is in fact the upper

72. *ḫn*: Maspero, *Sarcophages* I, pp. 27, 39, 45, 56, 165; *sḫn*: ibid., p. 56; *ḥtp*: ibid., p. 23; *wꜣḥ*: P. BM EA 10340, 4.

part of what seems to be the fourth. Thus this left-hand group has not seven but six lines, and the last is missing. Illegible traces on the verso, with an image of a head indicating the place where the manuscript was to be deposited.

Translation

Recto

(1) O Hathor *Tꜣ-ḥtr-nnt* (?) born of *Tꜣ-ḥtrt* ... (?), [you enter] the Duat before (2) Osiris foremost of the West, Wennefer justified. You sail downstream to [Busiris], you sail upstream to (3) Abydos with those who are in the retinue of Osiris. Receive the libation [at the beginning of] each decade, at the (4) coming to the Mound of Djeme by Amenipet [...] Urtu the great (5) has come to Karnak; he makes a libation for you with the father of fathers. Your ba enters the (6) hall of the two Maats with those who are in the Duat ... (?) who are in you. (7) You come and go in every place [...]

Commentary

Lines 1–2

i Ḥwt-Ḥr N [*ꜥḳ.t*] *r Dwꜣt ḫr Wsir ḫnty Imntt Wn-nfr mꜣ-ḫrw*. Probable restoration from the parallels. *ꜥḳ* is the most common verb of motion for entry into the Duat: Herbin, *BIFAO* 84 (1984), p. 255 with n. 5.

Lines 2–3

ḫd.t r [*Ḏdw*] *ḫnt.t r ꜣbḏw ḥnꜥ imyw-ḫr Wsir*. On the restoration *ḫd.t r ḏdw ḫnt.t r ꜣbḏw*, see P. BM EA 10114, **lines 14–15**.
imyw-ḫr (for *imyw-ḫt*) is also found in P. Cairo CG 58008, 4. Note the inverse instance of *ḫt* for *ḫr* in P. BM EA 10344, 3.

Lines 3–4

šsp.k ḳbḥ [*tp*] *ssw 10 nb n p(ꜣ) ii r Iꜣt Ḏꜣm n Imn-Ipt*. This sequence recalls certain formulations of the offering ritual at the festival of the decade, when the deceased is said to receive a libation from Amenipet *n pꜣy.f ssw 10 nb n ii r Iꜣt Ḏꜣm*, 'in each of his decades when he comes to Djeme'; see P. BM EA 10123, **line 3**. For the libation received each decade, see P. BM EA 10194, **lines 10–11**.

Lines 4–5

Wrtw wr ii m Iwnw šmꜥ ḳbḥ.f n.t ḥnꜥ it itw. On *Wrtw wr*, designation of Montu, see P. BM EA 9995, **IV, 2**. *it itw* is here a designation of the bull Buchis: Sethe, *Amun*, p. 85, n. 1 and § 116. For another identification, see P. BM EA 10108, **line 14**.

Lines 5–6

ꜥḳ bꜣ.t r wsḫt Mꜣꜥty ḥnꜥ imyw Dwꜣt [...] *.t imyw.t*. For the relation between the hall of the two Maats and the Duat, cf. P. 10260, I, x + 10–11:

ꜥḳ.k r wsḫt nt Mꜣꜥty	'May you enter the hall of the two Maats;
šsp tw imyw Dwꜣt m ḥꜥꜥ	those who are in the Duat receive you in joy.'

Ibid., I, x + 4–5:

di.f ꜥḳ.k m-ꜥ wsḫt Mꜣꜥty	'He (Osiris) causes you to enter the hall of the two Maats
nn šnꜥ.tw.k r sbꜣw nw Dwꜣt	without being turned back from the gates of the Duat.'

Line 7

šm.t ꜥḳ.t r bw nbw [...]. Restore something like *r mr.t*, 'according to your desire'. For the pairing *šm*/*ꜥḳ* (or *ꜥḳ*/*šm*), see P. BM EA 10124, **line 1**. Note the unusual form of *bw*, written as *bꜣ*; see P. BM EA 10110 + 10111, **I, 10**.

P. BM EA 10256 (pls 118–19)

Salt Collection, 1, 22.
Unpublished.
Quirke, *Owners*, no. 236.
Provenance: Thebes. Found with P. BM EA 10259 probably inside the coffin BM EA 6708 in the collective tomb of the archon Soter.[73]
Date: AD 127.[74]
Owner of the papyrus: *Tꜣ-ḥfꜣt* (Tphous).
Mother of the owner: *Srpy* (Sarapous).

Contents: Original text with formulae of protection.

Manuscript of one sheet (12 × 22.7 cm), in rather good condition despite some gaps in the upper part, and bearing nine lines of text in a large and clumsy hand.

Text on the verso (some legible traces): (1) A good burial ... (?) (2) lady of the West ... (?)

Translation

Recto

(1) I am Hathor, the lady of the West, I am Isis the great, mother [of the god], I am the Hathor, the maiden (2) *Tꜣ-ḥfꜣt*, born of *Srpy* [...] Amunet the great, who hides herself (?) (3) within them in the *imntt*-necropolis; the four cows, they protect you. (4) Ahet the great, mother of Re, is the protection of your body full (5) of life. The efficient Nubet, she fashions your limbs gathered in the place they occupied (6) before. Akhet glorify you (?) ... (?) Mehet-(7)weret protects you, and your protection is the protection of this child (who is) between (8) the horns of his mother Ahet (?), the lady of the West, *Tꜣ-ḥfꜣt*, born of *Srpy*.

73. See *supra*, p. 6, no. **23**, and pp. 9–10.

74. After the Greek inscription of her coffin; see *supra*, p. 6, no. **22**, and pp. 9–10. The owner lived 6 years, 2 months, 8 days.

Commentary

Line 1

ḥwnt, known as an epithet of Hathor (Meeks, *ALex* 77.2633 and 78.2625; H. Kees, *ZÄS* 60 [1925], pp. 5–6), designates here the deceased, a young girl of six years. This designation occurs again in the inscription on her coffin (BM EA 6708). It is also found for a woman twenty years old (stela Hildesheim 6352; K. Jansen-Winkeln, *MDAIK* 53 [1997], pp. 91–100 and pl.)

Lines 2–3

Ỉmnt wrt ỉmn … (?) *m-ẖnw.sn*. For another pun on the name of the goddess, cf. *Hibis* III, pl. 33, col. 23. As the end of line 2 is erased, it is difficult to interpret the traces following the verb *ỉmn*.

Line 3

wšbt 4 wšb.sn ḥr.t. The determinative transcribed by the sign of the cow is different from lines 4, 5, 6 and 7. On the *wšbt*-cow: Meeks, *Alex* 78.1117; J.L. Simonet, *Le collège des dieux maîtres d'autel* (Montpellier 1994), p. 123, n. (e). For *wšb ḥr*, cf. *Wb.* I, 372, 5.

Lines 3–4

ꜣht wrt mwt nt Rꜥ. On this goddess: F.R. Herbin, *BIFAO* 84 (1984), p. 287, n. 37.

Line 5

Nwbt mnḫ(t) nb.s ḥꜥw.t. Pun on the name of the goddess and the verb *nb* (written with the sign [hieroglyph]), also attested in Mariette, *Dendérah* II, pl. II, 40 c, 1: *Nwbt ḥr nb ḥꜥw.k*; *Dendara* VIII, 150, 19: *Nwbt wrt ḥnt bnr nb ḥꜥw n Nbty*.

Lines 5–6

sꜣḳ.tw r wnn.f ḫnt. Cf. P. Louvre N 3166, I, 4: *rdỉt ḫpr.f mỉ wnn.f ḫnt* ([hieroglyph]). For the use of the singular *.f* (also in P. BM EA 10091, I, 4): G. Burkard, *Spätzeiliche Osiris-Liturgien im Corpus der Asasif-Papyri* (*ÄAT* 31, 1995), p. 251, n. 12.

Line 6

sꜣḫ twk (*sic*) *ꜣḫ twt ꜣḫ(t) štꜣ* … (?). This passage raises difficulties of reading and comprehension.

Lines 6–8

Mḥt-wrt ḥr swḏꜣ.t mkt.t mkt ḥy pfy ỉmytw ḥnwty n mwt.f ꜣht ḥnwt ḥnwt (*sic*) *Ỉmntt N*. Mehet-weret, mother of Re, is depicted as a cow bearing the young solar god between her horns: L. Kákosy, *LÄ* IV, 4, with n. 7; J.G. Griffiths, *Plutarch's De Iside et Osiride* (Cardiff 1970), p. 512; S. Gabra, *ASAE* 44 (1944), pp. 173–8; M. Heerma van Voss, *De oudste Versie van Dodenboek* (Leiden 1963), p. 72 with n. 256: J.C. Goyon, *JARCE* 20 (1983), p. 58 with n. 58.

P. BM EA 10261 (pl. 120)

Salt Collection 1, 30.
Unpublished.
Quirke, *Owners*, no. 278.
Provenance: Thebes probably.
Date: first to second century AD.
Owner of the papyrus: *Wrš-nfr* (Orsenouphis).
Mother of the owner: *Tꜣ-ḫy-bỉꜣ* (Chibois).

Contents: Original text with some funerary formulae.

Small fragmentary manuscript (6.8 × 11.6 cm) bearing five lines of large writing. Some traces above line x + 2 are still visible. Elsewhere the inscription seems complete. There is no text on the verso.

Translation

(x + 1) [… …] (x + 2) May your ba live, may your bones be stable, may your corpse rejoice (x + 2), (O) Osiris *Wrš-nfr* born of (x + 3) *Tꜣ-ḫy-bỉꜣ*. Your corpse (?) (x + 4) will not be destroyed in the god's domain, (x + 5) for ever and eternally.

Commentary

Line x + 2

ꜥnḫ bꜣ.k ḏd ḳsw.k ḥꜥ(ꜥ) ẖꜣt.k. Note here the writing 𓊽 of *ḏd*. The verb *ḥꜥꜥ* is very rare relating to the corpse, for which expressions such as *ꜥnḫ*,[75] *wḏꜣ*,[76] *nṯr*,[77] *rwḏ*,[78] *rnp*,[79] *ḥtp*[80] and *ḏd*[81] are more attested. A close parallel is found in W. Spiegelberg, *ZÄS* 50 (1912), p. 41 (mummy label in Strasbourg):

ꜥnḫ bꜣ.f ḏd ḳsw.f	'May his ba live, may his bones be stable,
ḥꜥꜥ ẖꜣt.f	may his corpse rejoice
r nḥḥ ḥnꜥ ḏt (?)	for ever and eternally (?).'

Cf. also P. Berlin 3164 + Moscow 4661, 6:

ꜥnḫ bꜣ.k ḫnt bꜣw	'May your ba live among the bas,
ḥꜥꜥ ẖꜣt.k	may your corpse rejoice,
ḏd ḳsw.k m-ḫt ỉwf.k	may your bones be stable near (?) your flesh!'

Line x + 5–6

nn sk ẖꜣt.k (?) *m ẖrt-nṯr ḏt nḥḥ*. Although uncertain (cf. the form of the sign, line x + 1), the word *ẖꜣt* is expected here. Cf. *BD* ch. 163, title (Lepsius): *rꜣ n tm rdỉt sk ẖꜣt n s m ẖrt-nṯr*.

P. BM EA 10264A (pls 121–2)

Salt Collection 1, 168.
Unpublished.
Provenance: unknown, but probably Thebes.
Date: first to second century AD.
Owner of the papyrus: name lost.

75. P. BM EA 9995, II, 25.
76. Assmann, *Sonnenhymnen*, p. 308 [Text 224]; *KRI* III, 383, 6; Boeser, *Beschreibung* X, p. 3.
77. *KRI* III, 38, 9.
78. P. BM EA 9995, II, 25; P. BM EA 10260, III, x + 6; *KRI* I, 328, 8; III, 1, 10; 349, 9.
79. P. BM EA 9995, I, 12; J.J. Clère, *OA* 12 (1973), p. 99; Maspero, *Sarcophages* I, pp. 9, 22, 56.
80. Boeser, *Beschreibung* X, p. 4.
81. P. BM EA 9995, I, 11; Maspero, *Sarcophages* I, pp. 9, 11, 45, 56; Kamal, *Stèles*, p. 140.

Contents: Original text adapted from the Book of Breathing.

Manuscript of one sheet (16.5 × 9 cm), in sad condition of preservation. Several tears, and the deplorable style of the writing, which is eroded in some places, make it particularly difficult to read the text. No parallel version seems to be known. There is no text on the verso.

Translation

(x + 1) [... ...] (x + 2) May [...] the doorkeeper [of] the Duat, the guardian of the West. (x + 3) May [...] ... (?) [May] I (?) breathe like <Re> every day. Come to me, Anubis (x + 4) son of Osiris, I have satisfied the hearts of the Westerners, satisfy for me my heart (?) (x + 5), every day; I have satisfied (?) your *wšb* (?) like one who is on earth (?), for ever. Count me (x + 6) among [your] praised ones (?) ... (?) like when (I) was on earth ... (?) like one who is (?) (x + 7) ... (?) (x + 8) I fly (?) every [day] (?) ... (?) to do ... (?) like he who is within the Mansion (9) of the West. May you make ... (?) on earth, eternally.

Commentary

Line x + 2
pꜣ iry-ꜥꜣ [*n*] *tꜣ Dwꜣt pꜣ sꜣwty n Ỉmntt*. In the beginning of the First Book of Breathing, the deceased usually invokes the 'doorkeepers of the West and the guardians of the Duat': *ḥr.tn r.i nꜣ iryw-ꜥꜣ n tꜣ Dwꜣt nꜣ sꜣwtyw n Ỉmntt* (see P. BM EA 10191, **I, 2–3**). This double designation is here expressed in the singular, and in a different context, for the sequence is introduced with the particle *mi*. The doorkeeper and the guardian are probably references to Osiris.

Line x + 3
mi [...] ... (?) [...] *snsn.i mi <Rꜥ> rꜥ nb*. Cf. P. BM EA 10048, III, 5–6: *snsn.k im.s rꜥ nb mi Rꜥ*, 'You breathe by it every day, like Re'.

Lines x + 3–4
mi n.i Ỉnpw sꜣ Wsir. On Anubis son of Osiris, see P. BM EA 10191, **I, 3–4**. This appeal to Anubis, extended in the next sequence, does not seem attested elsewhere.

Lines x + 4–5
[*s*]*ḥtp.n.i nꜣ ibw n Ỉmntyw sḥtp.k n.i ib.i rꜥ nb ḥtp n.i wšb.k n.i* (?) *mi nty ḥr-tp tꜣ* (?) *n ḏt*. This sequence, of uncertain reading in places, seems unknown in the funerary literature. For the expression *sḥtp ib*, cf. *BD* ch. 85 (ed. Budge, p. 184, 11).

Lines x + 5–6
ḥsb.k [*w*]*i mi ḥsyw* (?) ... (?)*.k* ... (?) Cf. P. Louvre N 3284, 2 = P. Turin 1848, V, 1–2 = statue Cairo JE 37075, quoted in *LPE*, p. 275 (2): *ḥsb.k* (*wi*) *r ꜣḫw iḳrw*, 'May you count me among the excellent spirits'. *mi* is a spelling either of *m* (Erman, *Neuäg. Gram.* § 606 and 621), or of *m-ꜥ*, 'among' (D. Kurth, *Der Sarg der Teüris* [*AegTrev* 6, 1990], p. 40, n. 546).

For the wish of the deceased to be set among the praised ones of a deity, cf. E.A.W. Budge, *The Chapters of coming forth by day* I (London 1898), p. 4, 15–16: *di.k wnn.i m-m* ( ) *ḥsyw.k*; ch. 30 B (ed. Budge, p. 17: *imy wn.i m-ꜥ* ( ) *ḥsyw nty imy-ḫt.k*; Smith, *Mortuary Texts*, p. 39 (IV, 14): *iw=k ẖn nꜣ ḥs.w n tꜣ ḥm.t-nswt tp.t ꜣst wry.t*; P. Leiden T 32, VIII, 5 (*LPE*, p. 251): *iw.k m ḥsyw.f rꜥ nb*; A. Piankoff, *Mythological Papyri* (New York 1957), p. 134 (no. 15, scene 3): *ꜥḳ.t m ḥsyw*; Maspero, *Sarcophages* I, p. 46, cited *supra* (P. 10191, **I, 43–4**); unpublished statue Cairo JE 36983, quoted by H. de Meulenaere, *CdE* 125 (1988), p. 240: 'May I come with the praised ones, may I go with the bas of the gods, by the decree of the great god'. See too P. BM EA 10260, **I, x + 12–13**.

Line x + 6
[...] *mi wn.i tp tꜣ*. All the beginning of this sequence is either lacunose or illegible. Wishes of similar formulation are read elsewhere: P. BM EA 10048, **II, 9** and **VII, 6–7**, on the terrestrial aspect of the deceased. See too *infra*, **line 9**, P. BM EA 10091, **I, 4** and P. BM EA 10718, **lines 3–4**.

Lines x + 6–9
Despite being apparently legible, this passage presents difficulties of all kinds, and only some scraps are identifiable. Line x + 6, end: after a damaged passage, the reading *mi nty* seems likely (cf. lines 5 and 8), in spite of the papyrus being worn beneath the *n* that would suggest the presence of an *aleph* (*nꜣ*). The last sign or word of this line is not identified.

Line x + 7
After the first word (*r* or *iw*), the erasing of roughly written signs allows only a few identifications. In the middle of the line, one could read [...] *ꜣḫ ḥr ḥw*, then a little farther: [...] *twk ꜥpy* (?) [...].

Lines 8–9
The first sign could be the suffix pronoun *.i* excessively lengthened; one reads then with reservations: *m-ḫrt-hrw* (?) ... (?) *ḥr ir* ... (?) ... (?) *twk mi nty m-ẖnw ḥwt* (written *ḫt*) (9) *Ỉmntt ir twk* (?) *n* (?) ... (?) *di.k nfr.i mi wn ḥr-tp.i*.

P. BM EA 10285 (pls 123–6)

Salt Collection 1, 154, 2.
Unpublished.
Quirke, *Owners*, no. 25.
Provenance: probably Thebes.
Date: first to second century AD.
Owner of the papyrus: *ꜣpwltyty* (Apollodote). She is also owner of P. BM EA 10286.
Mother of the owner: *ꜣrwꜣsyny* (Arsinoe).

Contents: Original text with some funerary formulae.

Manuscript of one sheet (12.8 × 18.8 cm), with tears on all sides, bottom right-hand corner missing and lacunae affecting in particular the beginning of line 2. It bears seven lines of text, with alternating hieratic and hieroglyphic signs.

Text on the verso: grant ... to the West according to the decree of the lady of the foundations of the earth.
(*In demotic*): (at) her feet.

Translation

(1) Hail Hathor Apollodote, born of Arsinoe, (2) [may there be] poured out for me water upon the altar behind Osiris, may (3) my ba live, may I see Osiris in the hall of the two Maats! O (4) Anubis the embalmer, Anubis lord of the sacred land! O (5) Anubis foremost of the god's booth, may there be poured out for me water upon the (6) altar! May my ba go forth to the place it desires! (7) [May I] follow Osiris in the hall of the two Maats for ever and eternally!

Commentary

Line 2
[*mi*] *wꜣḥ.w n.i mw ḥr tꜣ ḥtpt m-sꜣ Wsir*.
Cf. P. dem. Louvre N 2420 c, 2–3:

iw=w r ḳbḥ n=s mw ḥr tꜣ ḥtp.t	'Libation will be made for him upon the altar
m-sꜣ Ꞽs.t irm Wsir	behind Isis and Osiris.'

P. dem. Brussels E. 8258, 7–8:

mtw=f ṯꜣi mw ḥr(tꜣ) ḥtpt	'May he take water upon the altar
m-sꜣ Wsir n pꜣ šy m-sꜣ Wn-nfr	behind Osiris in the lake, behind Wennefer!'

P. dem. Cairo CG 31172, 4–6, cited by M. Depauw, *SAK* 31 (2003), p.97:

mtw=f ṯꜣi mw ḥr tꜣ ḥtp.t	'He receives water upon the altar
m-sꜣ Wsir n pꜣ š	behind Osiris of the lake,
m-sꜣ Wn-nfr	behind Wennefer!'

P. dem. Florence 3676, vs., 1–2:

ṯꜣi n=k mw ḥr tꜣ ḥtp.t	'Take for you water upon the altar
m-sꜣ Wsir	behind Osiris,
ḥr ḫrw Ꞽst tꜣ nṯr.t ꜥꜣ.t	at the voice of Isis, the great goddess.'

H.J. Thissen, *Die demotischen Graffiti von Medinet Habu* (1989), no. 57, and M. Chauveau, *RdE* 46 (1995), p. 254:

ṯꜣi n=k mw ḥr tꜣ ḥtp.t	'Take for you water upon the altar
m-sꜣ Wsir	behind Osiris,

Cf. P. dem. Berlin 8351, II, 1–3, M. Smith, *Enchoria* 15 (1987), p. 67 = id., *Liturgy*, p. 24:

šp=k mw n rpy m-sꜣ Wsir	'You receive the water of rejuvenation behind Osiris.
nhs=k mw Rꜥ in rꜥ nby	You awake like Re, every day.
Wsir n N sꜣ NN	(O) Osiris N son of NN,
šp sntr ḳbḥ ntm n-tr.ṯ=i	receive incense and sweet libation from my hand!
šp=k mw n rpy m-sꜣ Wsir	You receive water of rejuvenation behind Osiris,
šp=k ḳbḥ m-sꜣ pꜣ nb ntr.w	and receive libation behind the lord of the gods.'

For other references, cf. P. BM EA 10282, **line 28**; M. Chauveau, *RdE* 41 (1990), p. 4, n. 2; G. Botti, *Testi demotici* I (Florence 1941), p. 34, n. 2; G.R. Hughes, *Catalog of Demotic Texts in the Brooklyn Museum* (OIC 29, 2005), p. 9.

Lines 2–3
The expected reading of this passage is *mi ꜥnḫ p(ꜣy).i bꜣ*, although the fragmentary sign over the suffix 𓀀 seems closer to a 𓈖 than to a □. Cf. P. BM EA 10286, 2, where the base of the □ in *p(ꜣy.i) bꜣ* is very extended to the left. A wish *mi ꜥnḫ n.i bꜣ* would give no satisfactory sense.

Line 3
mi mꜣꜣ.i Wsir m wsḫt Mꜣꜥty. See P. BM EA 10115, 10, where the deceased enters the hall of the two Maats to see the perfection of Osiris, and cf. P. BM EA 10340, 3–4: *mi šms<.i> m wsḫt Mꜣꜥty*, 'May I follow Osiris in the hall of the two Maats'.

Lines 3–5
i Ꞽnpw imy wt Ꞽnpw nb tꜣ ḏsr i Ꞽnpw ḫnty sḥ-nṯr. These invocations are unparalleled in the present context. The relationship between Anubis and the libation upon the altar (line 6) seems to be unattested elsewhere.

Lines 5–6
mi wꜣḥw n.i mw ḥr tꜣ [...] (?) *ḥtpt*. For the libation upon the altar, see *supra*, **line 2**; also G. Vittmann, *ZÄS* 117 (1990), pp. 81 and 84 (lines 7–8).

Line 6
mi pr p(ꜣy.i) bꜣ r bw mr.f. Frequently expressed wish, cf. P. BM EA 10290, x + 6: *šm bꜣ.k r bw mr.k*; P. BM EA 9995, III, 18–19: *šsp bꜣ.f r bw nb mr.f*. See P. BM EA 10048, **VII, 5** and **6–7**.

Line 7
[...] *Wsir m wsḫt Mꜣꜥty r nḥḥ ḥnꜥ ḏt*. It seems unlikely that the same phrase would occur here as in line 3 and that one should therefore restore this as [*mi mꜣꜣ.i*]. Another possibility, suggested by P. BM EA 10340, 3, is to restore in the gap [*mi šms.i*], and to understand: 'May I follow] Osiris in the hall of the two Maats!', or something similar.

P. BM EA 10290 (pls 127–8)

Salt Collection 413.1.
Unpublished.
Provenance: probably Thebes, as stated in the 1835 auction catalogue.
Date: first to second century AD.
Owner of the papyrus: name lost.

Contents: Original text with some funerary formulae.

Manuscript of one sheet (25 × 17.1 cm), torn along its upper edge. Small traces of ink there indicate that at least one line of text is missing. The papyrus bears seven lines in a clumsy hand, interrupted at several places by lacunae.

Text on the verso: [... mistress] of the foundations of the earth.

Translation

Recto

(x + 2) [...] every day. The Embalmer ... (?) makes (x + 3) for you a tomb by order of the mistress of the foundations of the earth, a good burial on the West (x + 4) of Thebes, with-

out dying a second death. Those who are in the Duat receive you in (x + 5) peace. There is said to you [hail!], in peace, (for) you are a praised one before the (x + 6) lord of pra[ise] (?). Libation is made for your ka, consisting of wine, milk, *šdḥ*-brew, and malt, (x + 7). Your ba goes to the place you desire. You are justified beside the balance, (x + 8) being alive, enduring and powerful, and you are satisfied in your tomb, every day eternally.

Commentary

Line x + 2

Most of the text preceding the mention of *Ỉmy-wt* is illegible because of the lacunae. Only a few traces are identifiable.

Lines x + 2–4

Ỉmy-wt... (?) *ḥr ỉr n.k smꜣ-tꜣ m wḏt n ḫnwt ndbwt ḳ(r)st nfr(t) ḥr ỉmntt n Wꜣst*. Provision of a burial by Anubis proceeds naturally from his nature as god of the necropolis. In a 'formula for burial (*ḳrs*) in the West' (*CT* II, 125 c [sp. 111]), the god is invoked in his role of 'He who inters in the *ꜥnḏrrns*-necropolis (*smꜣ-tꜣ m ꜥnḏrrns*). One of this most common titles is 'lord of burial' (*nb ḳrst*), which he can have provided (e.g. I.E.S. Edwards, *HTBM* VIII [1939], pl. 21), or even make himself (*ḳrst nfrt ỉryt n Ỉnpw*, J.J. Clère and J. Vandier, *Textes de la Première Période Intermédiaire* [*BiAe* 10, 1948], p. 25). A 'good burial' is among the gifts granted the deceased by Anubis: coffin Cairo CG 28033 (ed. Lacau, p. 87); A. Wiedemann, *PSBA* 8 (1886), pp. 88–9, etc. However, this role is chiefly devoted to Anubis as embalmer (*ỉmy-wt*), as shown by the following examples:

B. Bruyère, *Tombes thébaines de Deir el-Médineh à décoration monochrome* (*MIFAO* 86, 1952), p. 82:

Ỉnpw ỉmy wt nṯr ꜥꜣ	'Anubis the embalmer, the great god,
dỉ.f ḳrst nfrt ḥr-ḫt ỉꜣw	may he grant a good burial after the old age,
smꜣ-tꜣ m smt ḥsyw	a burial in the necropolis of the praised ones
n kꜣ n N	for the ka of N.'

L. Gamwell and R. Wells (eds), *Sigmund Freud and Art* (1989), p. 74:

ỉw n.t Ỉnpw ỉmy wt nb tꜣ ḏsr	'Anubis the embalmer, lord of the sacred land, comes to you;
dỉ.f n.t ḳrst nfrt	he grants to you a good burial
ḥr ỉmntt m spꜣt nṯrwy	on the west of the nome of the two gods.'

Cartonnage Louvre N 2627:

ỉw n.k Ỉpw ỉmy wt ḫnty sḥ-nṯr	'Anubis the embalmer, foremost of the god's booth, comes to you;
dỉ.f n.k ḳrst	he grants to you a burial
m ỉmntt Wꜣst	on the west of Thebes.'

Cartonnage from tomb 403 in Armant (O.H. Myers and H.W. Fairman, *JEA* 17 [1931], p. 225 and pl. 55):

ỉw n.k Ỉnpw ḫnty sḥ-nṯr	'Anubis, foremost of the god's booth, the embalmer,
ỉmy wt nb tꜣ ḏsr	lord of the sacred land, comes to you;
dỉ.f n.k ḳrst nfrt mnḫt	he grants to you a good and excellent burial
m-m ḫrt-nṯr	in the god's domain.'

Cartonnage BM EA 6969 (ibid., p. 227 and pl. 55):

ỉw n.k Ỉnpw ỉmy wt nb tꜣ ḏsr	'Anubis, the embalmer, lord of the sacred land, comes to you;
dỉ.f n.k ḳrst nfrt	he grants to you a good burial
ḥr ỉmntt Wꜣst	on the west of Thebes.'

A similar text is found on cartonnages BM EA 6965 (ibid., pl. 57) and BM EA 6966 (ibid., p. 227, and E.A.W. Budge, *A Guide to the First, Second and Third Egyptian Rooms* [London 1924], p. 152).

Bucheum stela no. 15 (ed. Mond-Myers, *The Bucheum* III, pl. 44):

ỉỉ n.k Ỉnpw ỉmy wt nb tꜣ ḏsr	'Anubis the embalmer, lord of the sacred land, comes to you;
dỉ.f n.k ḳrst nfrt	he grants to you a good burial
ḥr ỉmntt Ỉwnw šmꜥ	on the west of Karnak.'

Offering-table Louvre E 18444 (A. Moret, *Catalogue du Musée Guimet* [Paris 1909], p. 130 and pl. 62):

ḥtp dỉ nsw Ỉnpw tpy ḏw.f	'Offering that the king gives to Anubis who is on his hill,
ỉmy wt nb tꜣ ḏsr	the embalmer, lord of the sacred land,
dỉ.f ḳrst nfrt	that he grants a good burial
m smt ỉmntt nt ꜣbḏw	in the western desert of Abydos.'

J. Bonomi and S. Sharpe, *The Triple Mummy Case of Aroeri-Ao* (London 1858), pl. 1 = V. Schmidt, *Sarkofager* (Copenhagen 1919), p. 177, no. 977:

ḥtp dỉ nsw n Ỉnpw ỉmy wt	'Offering that the king gives to Anubis the embalmer,
dỉ.f ḳrst nfrt m ḫrt-nṯr	that he grants a good burial in the god's domain
m smt ỉmntt Wꜣst	in the western desert of Thebes,
n kꜣ n Wsỉr N	for the ka of the Osiris N.'

J. Osing, in A. Fakhry, *Denkmäler der Oase Dachla* (*AV* 28, 1982), p. 68 (Text D) = p. 69 (Text F):

ỉnk Ỉnpw ỉmy wt nb tꜣ ḏsr	'I am Anubis the embalmer, lord of the sacred land,
dỉ.ỉ tw ḫt ꜥwy(.ỉ)	I place you under (?) my hands;
n<f>r.k n ḳrst ꜥꜣt nfrt mnḫt n ḏt	(so that) you are well for a great, good and excellent burial, for ever.'

He also comforts the deceased in his tomb; cf. e.g. P. Berlin 3162, III, 3:

šsp twk Ỉnpw ỉmy wt	'Anubis the embalmer,
ḫnty sḥ-nṯr	foremost of the god's booth,
nb tꜣ ḏsr	lord of the sacred land, receives you;
smn.f twk m-ḫnw ḳrst.k nfrt	he establishes you in your good burial
m-ḫnw Dwꜣt nfrt ỉmytw Wsỉr	in the Duat beside Osiris.'

ḫnwt ndbwt: on that designation, see P. BM EA 10112, **lines 9–10**; P. BM EA 10286, **lines 1–2**; Leitz, *LGG* V, p. 192.

ỉmntt n Wꜣst denotes the place in the necropolis where the tomb is constructed, but also the realm of the dead assimilated to the Duat; see P. BM EA 10048, **II, 10**.

Line x + 4

tm mt m mt n wḥm. On the second death, see P. BM EA 10191, **I, 52**.

Lines x + 4–5

šsp twk ỉmyw Dwꜣt m ḥtp. See P. BM EA 10201, **II, 4**.

Line x + 5

ḏd.w n.k ỉ[ꜣw].tw m ḥtp. See *LPE*, p. 259 (VIII, 13–14).

Lines x + 5–6

ỉw.k ḥs.tỉ m-bꜣḥ nb [*ḥs*... ?]. Note the unusual spelling of the verb *ḥs*, written like the word *ḥsꜣ* (*Wb*. III, 161). The lacuna probably covers a reference to Osiris, defined as lord of the praised (or: of praise ?); cf. *BD*

ch. 127, 5 (Lepsius): (Osiris) *ḥs.f tw m-bꜣḥ.f m tꜣ int*; for the deceased considered as a *ḥsy*, cf. also P. BM EA 10048, VII, 4–5: *iw.f ḥs.tw m-m ḥs(y)w*.

Line x + 6
ḳbḥ n kꜣ.k m irp irtt šdḥ mrsw. For the *šdḥ*-brew, see P. BM EA 10191, **II, 31–3**.

: faulty writing of the word *mrsw* denoting malt (*Wb*. II, 112, 15; E. Dévaud, *RT* 39 [1921], pp. 168–70; Meeks, *ALex* 77.1796 and 79.1280), and regularly used after *šdḥ*.

Line x + 7
šm bꜣ.k r bw mr.k. On the freedom of the ba to go where it wishes, see P. BM EA 10285, **line 6**.

mꜣꜥ-ḫrw.k r-gs tꜣ mḫꜣt. Cf. Berlin 12441 (cited in *Wb*. II, 130, 9, *Belegst*.): *ink smꜣꜥ ḫrw.tn r-gs mḫꜣt*, 'I am he who justifies you beside the balance'; P. OIC 25389, XI, 3: *ꜥḳ.k m wsḫt Mꜣꜥty mꜣꜥ-ḫrw.k r-gs tꜣ mḫꜣt*, 'You enter the hall of the two Maats and you are justified beside the balance'; again Maspero, *Sarcophages* I, p. 97: *n gm.tw wn.f r-gs mḫꜣt*, 'Fault has not been found in him beside the balance'; P. Moscow 4651, 8–9: *sꜥḳꜣ-ib r-gs mḫꜣt*, 'He-who-makes-the-heart-right is beside the balance'. On the function of this balance: Seeber, *Untersuchungen*, pp. 67–83.

Line x + 8
ꜥnḫ.ti ḏd.ti iw.k ḥtp.ti m štyt.k rꜥ nb ḏt. Ending formula without known parallel in Books of Breathing or the Book of the Dead.

P. BM EA 10340 (pls 129–30)

Anastasi Collection, 3, 14.
Unpublished.
Quirke, *Owners*, no. 245.
Provenance: probably Thebes.
Date: first to second century AD.
Owner of the papyrus: *Tꜣ-šrit-Inpw* (Senanoupis). She is also owner of P. Louvre N 3246 (Devéria, *Catalogue*, p. 139).
Mother of the owner: *Tꜣ-špst*.

Contents: Original text adapted from the First Book of Breathing.

Manuscript of one sheet (13.7 × 22.5 cm), in good condition apart from the tear along the fourth line, and bearing ten lines of text. One line of text on the verso, including the image of a head to indicate the place where the manuscript was to be deposited.[82]

Text on the verso: Her head. A good burial. May it be stable over your corpse, may it clothe (my) limbs.

Translation

Recto

(1) Hail Hathor *Tꜣ-šrit-Inpw* born of the Hathor *Tꜣ-špst*!

(2) O doorkeepers of the Duat, guardians of the West! O Anubis, son of (3) Osiris! May there be water poured out for <me> daily! May [I] follow Osiris [in] the hall of the (4) two Maats! May my ba go forth daily, and remain over my corpse! (5) May I have air for breathing for my nose! May I see Re (6) upon the *sktt*-bark, and Atum upon the *mꜥnḏt*-bark! The breath of Amun, the light of Re, (7) the water of Hapy, that belongs to me, eternally!

May *pꜥt*-offerings be laid down for me upon the altar! (8) I have done nothing evil; I am a (woman) praised (because) her voice is sweet at making libation (9) for Osiris (?), daily. May it happen that my house be established and healthy (10) together with (my) children, for ever and eternally!

Commentary

Line 2
i nꜣ iryw-ꜥꜣ n tꜣ Dwꜣt nꜣ sꜣwtyw n Imntt. Same sequence in P. BM EA 10194, 5–6. This is a variant, inverting the persons invoked, of one of the first phrases of the First Book of Breathing: *ḥr.tn r.i nꜣ iryw-ꜥꜣ n Imntt nꜣ sꜣwtyw n tꜣ Dwꜣt*. See P. BM EA 10191, **I, 2–3**.

Lines 2–3
Inpw p(ꜣ) sꜣ Wsir. The article *pꜣ* is generally omitted in this phrase. Omission of the title *pꜣ iry-ꜥꜣ mtr n tꜣ Dwꜣt*, 'dependable doorkeeper of the Duat'. On Anubis son of Osiris, see P. BM EA 10191, **I, 3–4**.

Line 3
mi wꜣḥ.w n<.i> mw m ḫrt-hrw. Cf. P. BM EA 10285, 2: [*mi*] *wꜣḥ.w n.i mw ḥr tꜣ ḥtpt m-sꜣ Wsir*.

Lines 3–4
mi šms<.i> Wsir [*m*] *wsḫt Mꜣꜥty*. On the relationship between the deceased and Osiris in the setting of the hall of the two Maats, see P. BM EA 10285, **lines 3** and **7**.

Line 4
mi pr p(ꜣy.i) bꜣ m ḫrt-hrw. For the daily journey of the ba: *LPE*, p. 147 (III, 3).

mi wꜣḥ.f ḥr ḫꜣt.i. See P. BM EA 10108, **lines 6–7**.

Line 5
mi n.i ṯꜣw n snsn r fnḏ.i. On the gift of breath to the nose of the deceased, generally accorded by Amun, see P. BM EA 10199, **line 26**.

Lines 5–6
mi mꜣꜣ.i Rꜥ ḥr sktt Itm ḥr mꜥnḏt. On the reversing of the role of these barks (*sktt* being here the morning bark, and *mꜥnḏt*, the evening bark): Smith, *Mortuary Texts*, p. 85 (IV, 11), with references.

82. Note that the text on the verso of P. Louvre N 3246 indicates that it was to be placed at the feet of the deceased. See *supra*, p. 2 with n. 27.

Lines 6–7
ṯꜣw n Ỉmn šw n Rꜥ mw n Ḥꜥpy nnk st ḏt. Note here the variant [hieroglyphs] as compared with the usual version *stwt n Rꜥ*, and cf. P. BM EA 10125, 28, the intermediate and faulty version *stwt n šw*. For this sequence, see P. BM EA 10191, **II, 34**.

Line 7
mi wꜣḥ.w n <.i> pꜥt ḥr ḥtpt. The offering of *pꜥt*-loaves (written [hieroglyphs]) to the deceased is not mentioned on any other surviving copy of the Book of Breathing. On these loaves (*Wb.* I, 503, 12): Caminos, *LEM*, p. 204.

Line 8
nn ir.i ḫt nbt bw ḏw. To be taken literally as 'anything of (or concerning) evil'? However, *bw ḏw* seems not to be considered as second object, *nn ir.i ḫt nbt* giving no clear sense. The phrase recalls the expected expression *ḫt nbt bint ḏwt*, a simpler and more widely attested formulation.

Lines 8–9
ink ḥs iw nḏm ḫrw.s r ḳbḥ n Wsir m ḫrt-hrw. The suffix *.s* can only refer back to the deceased as a 'woman praised'. This passage is reminiscent of the libation in favour of Osiris – or to the deceased assimilated to him – at the sound of the voice of Isis (*r ḫrw Ỉst*); see P. BM EA 10282, **line 23**.

Lines 9–10
mi ḫpr pr.i iw.f smn iw.f snb ḥnꜥ msw <.i> r nḥḥ ḏt. On the theme of the survival of the house of the deceased and of the children living there, see *LPE*, pp. 256–8 (VIII, 11). The word *pr*, 'house', has here more the meaning of 'abode'. Note the unusual construction *mi ḫpr* ... *iw* + suffix + verb, and cf. P. Louvre N 3156, 2–3: *mi ḫpr pr.i iw.f mn m-sꜣ.i iw pr.i nfr n iḫwt nb nfr*, 'May it happen that my house be established after me, that my abode be perfect with all good things'.

P. BM EA 10343 (pls 82–3)

Salt Collection 1, 168–9.
Unpublished.
Quirke, *Owners*, no. 244.
Provenance: Thebes.
Date: first to second century AD.
Owner of the papyrus: *Tꜣ-šrỉt-Gpryn*. This name is otherwise unattested, but cf. *Gꜣprn*, P. BM EA 10260.
Mother of the owner: *Hꜣyrn*.

Contents: Beginning with the First Book of Breathing, then original text.

Manuscript of one sheet (25.8 × 23.6 cm) lacking the upper right-hand corner. Two-thirds of the surface are darkened the full height of the papyrus, but not so much as to affect legibility. Fifteen lines of text on the recto, one on the verso.

Text on the verso: ... *Tꜣ-šrỉt-Gpryn*.

Translation

Recto

(1)[... ...] Hathor *Tꜣ-šrỉt-Gpryn* born of (2)[*Hꜣyrn*: I am Re at his rising, I] am Atum at his setting, I am Osiris (3) [foremost of the West ... Turn] towards me, guardians of the Duat, (4) doorkeepers of the West. Come to me! Turn towards me, Thoth the great, lord of Hermopolis, (for) I am (5) one of the retinue of Osiris; I am one of the hall of the two Maats. May I be one (6) of you! Isis the great, mother of the god, has given me a great, beautiful and efficacious burial. (7) You receive incense and libation from Amenipet at the moment of each decade; you smell the (8) odour ... (?) divine (?) *ḥtpw*-offerings in the course of every day.

May your ba live in the sky before (9) Re, may your corpse < remain> in the Duat before Osiris, may your ka be divine before the two Maats.

Receive (10) what your ba receives, what your ka receives, *ḥtpw*-offerings and food, bread (11) beer, wine milk, the water of the overflow on which the gods live. Take for yourselves the eye of Horus! [I] (12) offer you the water which is in him, the libation, (I who am) praised and beloved, *Tꜣ-šrỉt-Gpryn* born of (13) *Hꜣyrn*, (O) gods and goddesses who are in the Mound of Djeme, gods and goddesses who are in (14) the great place, gods and goddesses who are in the Mansion of Sokar, gods and goddesses who are in the Mansion of gold.

May your (15) ba live for ever, may it (?) be renewed eternally (bis).

Commentary

Lines 2–3
[*ink Rꜥ m ḫꜥ.f in*]*k Ỉtm m ḥtp.f ink Wsir* [*ḫnty Ỉmntt* ...]. For this sequence, see P. BM EA 10191, **I, 1–2**.

Lines 3–4
nꜣ sꜣwtyw n tꜣ Dwꜣt nꜣ iryw-ꜥꜣ n Ỉmntt. Most manuscripts refer here to *iryw-ꜥꜣ n tꜣ Dwꜣt* and *sꜣwtyw n Ỉmntt*. P. BM EA 10343 is, to my knowledge, the only manuscript to invert the two designations. See P. BM EA 10191, **I, 2–3**.

Line 4
mi n.i. This injunction in this position is not attested in any other manuscript of the Book of Breathing, and the text here seems faulty. In the present passage it refers to Thoth rather than to the guardians of the Duat and the doorkeepers of the West.

Lines 4–6
ḥr.k r.i Ỉ ꜥꜣ nb Ḫmnw ink wꜥt m šms Wsir ink wꜥt n tꜣ wsḫt Mꜣꜥty. The invocation to Thoth is unparalleled in this context. It occurs without its title in the litany 'vindicate me against my enemies' for which see P. BM EA 10191, **I, 15–17**. Whereas other sources frequently refer to the deceased as member of the retinue of Osiris (P. BM EA 10191, **I, 36–7**), there seems to be no other attestation of the deceased as member of the hall of the two Maats.

Line 6
di n.ỉ Ỉst wrt mwt-nṯr ḳ(r)st ꜥꜣt nfrt mnḫt. On the gift of a good burial by Isis, see P. BM EA 10260, I, **x + 1**. For the meaning of *mnḫt* in this context, see P. BM EA 10108, **line 4**.

Line 7
šsp.t snṯr ḳbḥ m-ꜥ Ỉmn-Ỉpt r tr tp ssw 10 nb. On receiving incense and libation from Amenipet, in the context of rites of the decade, see P. BM EA 10194, **lines 10–11**. For libation only, see also P. BM EA 10123, **line 3**.
m-ꜥ written *mi*: see P. BM EA 10264A, **lines x + 5–6**.

Lines 7–8
ḫnm.t p(ꜣ) sty ... (?) *ḥtpw-nṯr* (?) *m ẖrt-hrw nt rꜥ nb*. The signs after the word *sty* are of uncertain reading.

Lines 8–9
ꜥnḫ bꜣ.t m pt ḫr Rꜥ ḫꜣt.t m Dwꜣt ḫr Wsir nṯr kꜣ.t ḫr mꜣꜥtyw. Before (or after) *ḫꜣt.k*, one might expect a verb like *wꜣḥ*, *mn* or *wḏꜣ*. For this type of phrasing, see P. BM EA 10262 + 10263, **line 1** and **line 2**; *LPE*, pp. 81–3 (I, 3–4).

Lines 9–11
šsp.tn šsp bꜣ.tn šsp kꜣ.tn ḥtpw ḏfꜣw tꜣ ḥnḳt irp irṯt mw m ḥbbt ꜥnḫ nṯrw im.sn. At this point the manuscript shows, in fairly extended form, a development attested in other texts unrelated to the Book of Breathing. P. BM EA 10209, I, 9–10, omits *šsp.tn* and gives: *ḥtpw ḏfꜣw tꜣ ḥnḳt mw m ḥbbt ꜥnḫ nṯrw im irp irṯt snṯr ḳbḥ*. P. BM EA 10209, IV, 18–19 gives a version closer to our document. It is difficult to follow Haikal in the translation of these two passages (*Two Hier. Fun. Pap.* II, pp. 17 and 21): '(...) that your soul and your ka may receive the offerings ...' and 'may you receive, may your soul receive and may your ka receive offerings ...'. Cf. also P. BM EA 10116, 34: *šsp.tn iṯ bꜣ.tn*, 'receive what your ba receives'. Rather than a simple *sḏm.f*, both *šsp* (*bꜣ.tn*) and *šsp* (*kꜣ.tn*) may be interpreted as relative verbal forms.
Note the writing for *im*.

Lines 11–13
mi n.tn irt-Ḥr ꜥb[.i] n.tn mw imy.s ḳbḥ ḥs mr N. The same text reads in P. BM EA 10209, IV, 20–1 and V, 7–8 (ed. Haikal, pp. 41, 43–4) and in the chapel of Amenirdis, line 183 (ibid., pp. 43–4 = G. Daressy, *RT* 23 [1901], pp. 9–10). Text in the second person sing. masc. on stela Brooklyn 16.211, see Ph. Collombert, *RdE* 48 (1997), p. 19. Var. *iṯ n.tn* instead of *mi n.tn*, and omission of all that follows *mr*, see E. von Bergmann, *ZÄS* 20 (1882), p. 42. On the expression *ḥs mr* in this context: Ph. Collombert, *RdE* 48 (1997), p. 23, n. (n), who rather reads *ḥst-mrt* as a designation of the libation. For other instances of this expression, see E.A.W. Budge, *Some Account of the Collection of Egyptian Antiquities in the Possession of Lady Meux* (London 1896), p. 153; A. Wiedemann, *RT* 8 (1896), p. 64; Junker, *Stundenwachen*, p. 106.
Note here the form for *mi*, variant of *mn* (*Wb.* II, 36, 2).

Lines 13–14
On this passage, see P. BM EA 10116, **lines 29–32.** In P. BM EA 10209, IV, 13–14, it precedes the sequence on receiving offerings (*supra*, **lines 9–11** and **11–13**).

Lines 14–15
ꜥnḫ p(ꜣy).t bꜣ r nḥḥ rnp.f (?)*r ḏt sp 2*. The traces between *rnp* and *ḏt* are illegible, and the proposed restoration is founded on the formulation of other clauses, e.g. P. BM EA 10282, 23 = P. BM EA 10283, 10–11: *ꜥnḫ p(ꜣy).k bꜣ r nḥḥ rnp.f r ḏt*; P. Cairo CG 58016, 7–8: *ꜥnḫ p(ꜣy).ỉ bꜣ r nḥḥ rnp.f r ḏt*.

P. BM EA 10344 (pls 135–6)

Anastasi Collection, 3, ?
Unpublished.
Quirke, *Owners*, no 265.
Provenance: Thebes.
Date: first to second century AD.
Owner of the papyrus: *Tꜣ-(nt)-Ḫnsw* (Tachonsis).[83]
Mother of the owner: *Tꜣ-rmṯ-n-ip-ib* (?). This name, the reading of which seems probable at least in line 1 of the manuscript, seems not to be attested elsewhere. Nevertheless the type is that of a number of personal names on the model *Pꜣ* / *Tꜣ* + name of deity (or of place). It would thus mean 'the woman[84] of *Ỉp-ib*', a designation of Thoth and other gods (Leitz, *LGG* I, pp. 215–16).

Contents: Original text with funerary formulae.

Manuscript of one sheet (28.5 × 22 cm), broken the full height of the left side. The recto bears sixteen lines in a variable and markedly clumsy hand, the difficulties of reading which are exacerbated by the effacement of the text at several points on the papyrus.

Text on the verso (traces of two lines): [Book of Brea]thing of *Tꜣ-(nt)-Ḫnsw*, born of *Tꜣ-rmṯ-n-ip-ib* (?).

Translation

Recto

(1) Hail Osiris *Tꜣ-(nt)-Ḫnsw*, born of *Tꜣ-rmṯ-n-ip-ib*, Isis [the great, mother of the god (?)], gives you a great and beautiful (2) burial. She gathers your flesh, she strengthens your bones. You take the libation from the hand of [Amenipet at] each (3) of his decades when (he) comes to Djeme. Your ba lives in the sky before <Re>, the sky and the earth [...] (4) before those who are on earth. Your ba lives, your limbs are renewed when (?) Amun goes to [...] (5) you go among the guardians of the Duat who ... (?) the entrances of [...]

83. Originally the manuscript was written for a man named *Grꜣ...*, as indicated by the inital invocation *hꜣy Wsir*. His name was subsequently smudged and cancelled by a horizontal line. and replaced above the line by the name of a woman designated *Tꜣ-(nt)-Ḫnsw* with the title of 'Hathor' in lines 6 and 14 (see *LPE*, p. 12 with n. 25).

84. Woman in the sense of servant woman: D. Meeks, in *State and Temple Economy in the Ancient near East* (*OLA* 6, 1979), p. 45, n. 177.

(6) Hail Hathor *Tꜣ-(nt)-Ḫnsw*, born of *Tꜣ-rmṯ-n-ỉp*[*-ỉb*], (7) your ba (?) is renewed, your corpse breathes; [you] receive [libation] (8) and censing from the hand of Amenipet of Djeme, the great living god mas[ter of the gods] (9) at the moment of each decade. Isis the great gives you a burial gr[eat, beautiful (?)] (10) and efficacious.

O doorkeepers who are in the sacred Duat ... (?) [...] (11) your ba [sails downstream] to Busiris, on the night of raising the *ḏd*-pillar in Busiris; (12) you proceed towards Abydos at the Haker festival: you ... (?) [...] (13)... (?) Montu, lord of (?)... Karnak (?), the fourth month of Akhet [...] (14) May your ba live for ever and eternally.

The <Hat>hor *Tꜣ-(nt)-Ḫnsw*, [born of *Tꜣ-rmṯ-n-ỉp*]*-ỉb*, ... (?) [that...] breathes (16) for ever and eternally.

Commentary

Lines 1–2
dỉ n.k Ỉst wrt [*mwt-nṯr*] *ḳrst ꜥꜣt nfrt*. On the gift of a burial to the deceased by Isis, see P. BM EA 10260, **I, x+1**. Restoration of the epithet *mwt-nṯr* may be envisaged here, taking account of the supposed length of the lacuna; it does not figure among the epithets of the goddess in line 9.

Note the writing  for *ḳrst*.

Line 2
stwt.s m ỉwf.k srwḏ.s ḳs.k. So expressed, this function of Isis seems unrecorded elsewhere. She is said gather the bones (e.g. *ỉnḳ ḳsw*, Lacau, *Sarcophages* I, p. 79; Bénédite, *Philae*, p. 120, 3: *ỉnḳ.s n.k ḳsw.k dmḏ.s n.k ꜥt.k*); and, with Nephthys, joins together either the bones (*CT* I, 306 [sp. 74]; G. Steindorff, *ZÄS* 33 [1895], p. 85), or the limbs of the deceased (W.C. Hayes. *Royal Sarcophagi of the XVIII Dynasty* [Princeton 1935], text 17). The construction of *stwt* with the preposition *m* is exceptional. For the use of the singular *ḳs*, cf. Smith, *Liturgy*, p. 36 (I, 4).

Lines 2–3
ỉṯ.k ḳbḥ n ḏrt n [*Ỉmn-Ỉpt n*] *p(ꜣ)y.f ssw 10 nb n ỉt r Ḏꜣm*. See P. BM EA 10123, **line 3**.

Line 3
ꜥnḫ bꜣw.k n pt ḫt ⟨*Rꜥ*⟩. On the plural *bꜣw* used here in place of *bꜣ*: Smith, *Mortuary Texts*, p. 105 (VIII. 10). This sequence is intelligible only if  is read as a form of *ḫr* (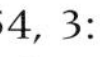 = *ḫr*, and cf. P. BM EA 10254, 3: *ỉmyw-ḫr* for *ỉmyw-ḫt*), and restoring *Rꜥ* after *pt*, as in the standard formulation *ꜥnḫ bꜣ.k n pt ḫr Rꜥ*: see P. BM EA 10343, **lines 8–9**.

Lines 3–4
...(?) *pt tꜣ* [...]. Passage unintelligible, for which no parallel seems to be known.

Line 4
ꜥnḫ bꜣ.k rnp ḥꜥw.k n ḏrt (?) *ꜥḳ Ỉmn r* [...]. Cf. Coffin BM EA 6705 (unpublished), left side: *ꜥnḫ bꜣ.k rnp ḥꜥw.k*; Turin 2444, L. Habachi, *BIFAO* 71 (1972), p. 78 and B. Bruyère, *Deir el Medineh 1948–51* (*FIFAO* 26, 1953), p. 38 : *ꜥnḫ bꜣ.k rwḏ ḥꜥw.k*: G. Daressy, *ASAE* 19 (1920), p. 143: *ꜥnḫ bꜣ.k twt ḳsw.k rnp ꜥwt.k*.

Line 5
ꜥḳ.k ⟨*m-*⟩*ḫnw nꜣ sꜣww n tꜣ Dwꜣt nty* ... (?) *n nꜣ rꜣw n* [...]. No known parallel. For the *sꜣww* (var. : *sꜣwtyw*) *n tꜣ Dwꜣt*, P. BM EA 10191, **I, 2–3**. The word following *nty* is not clear.

Line 7
rnp bꜣ.t (?) *snsn ẖꜣt.t*. No known parallel.

Lines 7–9
šsp[*.t ḳbḥ*] *snṯr m-ꜥ Ỉmn-Ỉpt* [*n*] *Ḏꜣm nṯr ꜥꜣ ꜥnḫ ḥr*[*y nṯrw*] *r tr n ssw 10 nb*. For the restoration, see P. BM EA 10194, **lines 10–1**, and M. Doresse, *RdE* 25 (1973), pp. 124–6 (doc. B, D, J).

Lines 9–10
dỉ [*n.t*] *Ỉst wrt ḳ(r)st* [*ꜥꜣt nfrt*] *mnḫt*. On this sequence, see supra, **lines 1–2**.

Line 10
ỉ nꜣ ỉryw-ꜥꜣ ỉmyw Dwꜣt ḏsrt ỉ[...]. On the doorkeepers of the Duat, see P. BM EA 10191, **I, 1–2**. For *Dwꜣt ḏsrt*, see P. BM EA 10201, **II, 3**.

Lines 10–11
[...] *bꜣ.t r Ḏdw m grḥ* [*n*] *sꜥḥꜥ ḏd m Ḏdw*. Restore probably *ḫd* in the lacuna. In the First Book of Breathing, the 'night of raising the *ḏd*-pillar in Busiris' is generally evoked in connection with the status of 'justified' attributed to the deceased by the local Council (cf. *BD* ch. 19): cf. P. BM EA 10109,11; 10125,17; 10191, I, 20. On the journey of the deceased to Busiris at that moment, see P. BM EA 10112, **lines 20–1**. For his aspect of ba on this occasion: *LPE*, p. 99, n. 9.

Line 12
šm.k r ꜣbḏw m ḥb Hkr ꜥḳ.k r (?) [...]. On the Haker festival and its relation to Abydos: J.G. Griffiths, *LÄ* II, 929–31; *LPE*, p. 236 (VII, 2–3).

Line 13
Of this line, practically illegible, virtually nothing can be read with certainty other than the mention of the period *ꜣbd 4 ꜣbd* (Khoiak), comparable to the 'festival of Khoiak' (*ḥb Kꜣ-ḥr-kꜣ*) during which the deceased is said, in P. BM EA 10112, 20–1, to go to Busiris, 'on the day of raising the *ḏd*-pillar'. Before that mention, traces of the names of Montu and Karnak (*Ỉwnw šmꜥ*) can be guessed.

Line 14
ꜥnḫ bꜣ.t r nḥḥ ḥnꜥ ḏt. For this formula, see P. BM EA 10282, **line 26**.

Lines 15–16
[...] *snsn* [...] *r nḥḥ ḥnꜥ ḏt*. See P. BM EA 10048, **II, 8**.

P. BM EA 10718 (pls 137–40)

Unpublished.
Provenance: probably Thebes.
Date: first to second century AD.
Owner of the papyrus: name illegible (line 8).
Mother of the owner: *Nfr* (?) [...]

Contents: Original text partly adapted from the Book of Breathing (Parma version).

Manuscript of one sheet (26 × 13.4 cm), broken the full height of the papyrus on the right side. On the basis of the known parallel to lines 6–7, the missing part amounts to about one third of the present width of the document. The hand, irregular and effaced at various points, poses

numerous problems in reading. Twelve lines of text are partly preserved. At the bottom, on the right, is part of a recumbent mummy.

Trace of a great cross on the verso, with text erased in great part: [Book of] Brea[thing] (?) of the Hathor [... ...]
[... ...] may it be stable] over [your] bones ... eternally.

Translation

Recto

(1) [...Book] of Breathing. You enter [the sacred land] and your voice (2) [is just ... ...] (3) [...] joy ... Anubis as [embalmer] preserves your flesh (4)[... He who is upon] his mountain rejuvenates your body in the form (5) [it had on earth (?)...] ... goes forth... without fail (6) [...] your fore is pure, [your] rear (7) [is pure, your middle (is pure) with *bd*-natron (?) and *ḥsmn*-natron, and Maat is in your heart, without evil (8) [...] the Hathor ... (?), justified, born of *Nfr* (?) (9)[... Osi]ris [fore]most of the Westerners ... (?) embrace the earth (10) [... ...]... (?) (11) which I wish (?), free of all fault. It is the way of the god which has arrived (?) (12) [... ...] every day. I am on earth and in the Duat, eternally.

Commentary

Line 1
[... *šꜥt*] *n snsn*. The restoration is probable. Here this is not the title of the manuscript (the preceding lacuna being too long), but a reference, within the body of the text, to the Book of Breathing.

Lines 1–2
ꜥḳ[*.t tꜣ ḏsr*] *iw ḫrw.t* [*mꜣꜥt*]. Probable restoration after P. Parma 183, 7 and P. OIC 25389, XXXIII, 10: *ꜥḳ.k tꜣ ḏsr iw ḫrw.k mꜣꜥt*; see *LPE*, p. 505.

Line 3
The traces visible before the word *hꜥꜥ* afford no certain reading. Some connection might be envisaged with P. Parma 183, 9–10 = P. OIC 25389, XXXIII, 12 (lacunae):

ḫnd.k pr Mꜣnw m hꜥꜥ	'You tread the House of Manu, in joy.'

Lines 3–4
Inpw m [*Imy-wt*] *ḥr swḏꜣ iwf.t*[85] [*Tpy-*]*ḏw.f ḥr srnp ḥꜥw.t m irw.f* [*ḥr-tp tꜣ*].

On the double aspect of Anubis *imy-wt* and *tpy-ḏw.f* in charge of the deceased, cf. P. BM EA 9995, IV, 1:

Inpw imy wt snḏm.n.f ḳsw.k	'Anubis the embalmer makes pleasant your bones;
Tpy-ḏw.f ꜥb.f iwf.k	He-who-is-on-his-hill, he unites your limbs.'

P. OIC 25389, XXXII, 3 (*LPE*, p. 503):

Inpw snḏm.f wt.k	'Anubis, he makes pleasant your wrappings;
Tpy-ḏw.f swḏꜣ.f ḥꜥw.k	He-who-is-on-his-ill, he preserves your body.'

Read *m irw.f* [*ḥr-tp tꜣ*]: probable reference to the original condition of the body on earth; cf. P. Leiden T 32, VIII, 3 (*LPE*, pp. 248 and 479) = P. BM EA 10091, I, 4:

Inpw imy wt smnḫ.n.f ḳsw.k	'Anubis the embalmer, he has perfected your bones,
ir.n.f ḥꜥw.k mi wnn.f	and has caused your limbs to be as they were.'

For the idea, cf. P. Rhind II, III, 5–6 (ed. Möller, p. 56):

(*Inpw imy wt nb ḏwꜣt ḏsrt*)	'(Anubis the embalmer, lord of the sacred Duat),
snfr.f iwf.t	he perfects your flesh,
di.f ꜥḏ inm.t	he causes your skin to be in good condition,
di.f mnḫ ḳsw.t	he causes your bones to be excellent,
di.f rnp ꜥwt.t nbt	he causes each of your limbs to be renewed.'

Again P. BM EA 9995, I, 13–14 (see P. BM EA 10048, **II, 9**):

ḥꜥw.k ḥr ḳsw.k	'Your flesh is on your bones
mi irw.k ḥr-tp tꜣ	according to your form upon earth.'

On the title and the designation *imy-wt*: J.C. Grenier, *Anubis alexandrin et romain* (*EPRO* 57, 1977), pp. 8–9; M. Smith, *The Demotic Papyrus Louvre E 3452* (unpublished dissertation, 1979), pp. 116–17.

Lines 6–8
iw ḥꜣt.t m wꜥb iw pḥ [*.t m twr ḥr-ib.t m bd* (?)] *ḥsmn iw Mꜣꜥt m ib.t nn isft* [...] (?). The mention of the word *bd* is not certain (it is omitted in the parallel version of P. OIC 25389), but a trace of the determinative seems discernible. Some versions close this sequence with *isft*, so a restoration in the lacuna, at the beginning of line 8, remains hypothetical; for additions after *isft*, cf. P. Parma 183, 12–13 and P. OIC 25389, XXXIV, 1–2 (*LPE*, p. 505). See P. BM EA 10048, **I, 4–6** and P. BM EA 10091, **I, 7–II, 1**.

Lines 8–11
Apparently a new development, almost completely erased, with an invocation (?) to the deceased whose name is illegible. No parallel to this has been found. Note in line 11 the mention of the way of the god (*wꜣt nṯr*), on which see P. BM EA 10123, **lines 6–7**.

85. Or: *ḥꜥw.t*.

6. Book of Traversing Eternity

P. BM EA 10091 (pls 141–2)

Salt Collection 1, 240–1.
Quirke, *Owners*, no. 62.
LPE, pp. 22–3 and pl. XXVI (doc. **L**).
Provenance: Thebes (mentioned in the owner's titulary).
Date: first to second century AD
Owner of the papyrus: *P(ꜣ)-fdw-Mnṯw*, *Fdw-Mnṯw* (Phtomontes and variants, see *LPE*, p. 8 with n. 10).
Title: '*ḫt-ꜥḥ* (?) *n Ỉꜣt Ḏꜣm tꜣ ḏsr m Wꜣst* '*ḫt-ꜥḥ* (?)[1] of the Mound of Djeme and of the sacred land in Thebes'.
Father of the owner: *P(ꜣ)y-Tm* (Patemis, see *LPE*, p. 23 with n. 66).
Title: *mỉ nn* (same rank as the son).
Mother of the owner: *Tꜣ-šri(t)-(n-)p(ꜣ)-šri-Mnṯw* (Senpsemonthes, see *LPE*, p. 23 with n. 67).
Title: *nbt pr*, 'housewife'.

Contents: Book of Traversing Eternity (short version).

Manuscript of one sheet (61 × 26 cm) composed of two large but low columns with series of vignettes above and each bearing seven lines of writing. The whole is enclosed in a double borderline. Rather than simple illustration, the vignettes, except for their purely iconographical elements, may themselves be considered as authentic texts. The first comprises two small scenes separated by a vertical double line. That on the right presents the deceased, with the name written above the figure, followed by a *wꜣḏ*-column, facing a tray of offerings; the group may be interpreted *wḏḥw Wsir P(ꜣ)-fdw-Mnṯw wꜣḏ*, 'the altar of the Osiris *P(ꜣ)-fdw-Mnṯw* is richly provided'.[2] The second scene is different in character, giving the hieroglyphic signs , to be read *Rꜥ-Ḥr-ꜣḫty wbn* (or *psḏ*)[3] *tꜣwy*, 'Re-Horakhty who shines on the Two Lands'.

In the vignette over column II of the text, to the right is another depiction of the deceased with his name, 'the Osiris *Fdw-Mnṯw*', standing before the image of a coffin followed by three ornamental hieroglyphs . The whole may be read *šṯyt Wsir Fdw-Mnṯw ỉm ḏd.ti*, 'The tomb of the Osiris *Fdw-Mnṯw* is there, stable'.[4] A similar disposition of text and vignettes recurs in P. BM EA 10314.

Text on the verso: The Osiris *P(ꜣ)-fdw-Mnṯw* born of *Tꜣ-šrit-p(ꜣ)-šri-Mnṯw*.

Translation

Recto

I (1) Hail, Osiris *ḫt-ꜥḥ* of the Mound of Djeme and of the sacred land in Thebes, *Fdw-Mnṯw*, (2) justified, son of the (priest) of the same rank *P(ꜣ)y-Tm*, justified, made by the lady of the house *Tꜣ-šri(t)-(n-)p(ꜣ)-šri-Mnṯw*!

Receive libation and censing, (3) in the course of every day, from the hands of Isis and Nephthys! Horus is satisfied with all your words and Thoth with your voice, (so that) Maat and Hathor (4) protect you. Anubis the embalmer, he has perfected your bones, and has caused your limbs to be as they were. Khenty (5) menty rejoices to see you and receives you as one of his just ones. He causes your eyes to (6) see, your ears to hear, your legs to walk, and all your limbs to perform their function. Assume all (7) forms according to your heart's desire, for you are among his praised ones, in his retinue. Your arms are pure, II (1) your legs are pure, and

1. *ProsPtol* IX, p. xvii. The title is translated 'He who is behind the palace', 'chamberlain', by P. Montet, *Kêmi* 8 (1946), p. 88. The examples given in *ProsPtol* have *ḫt-ꜥḥ* either without qualification or in relation to a divinity. No other source places it in direct relation to a toponym.

2. F. Hoffmann, *BiOr* 54 (1997), 657. For this meaning of *wꜣḏ*, *Wb*. I, 265, 21.
3. Both verbs can be used transitively.
4. Hoffmann, op. cit. His interpretation is preferable to that given in *LPE*, p. 23.

your *ḥ3ty*-heart is full of Maat, without evil. You eat with your mouth, drink with (2) your throat, and anoint your flesh in the rays of the disk. Hapy comes to you, and you live on his sweat. The breath (3) of air (comes) from Shu. Amenipet, you receive his libation, and Amun, you are healthy thanks to his water. His breath is for your nose without (4) being far from you. Your ba is on earth to assemble your flock. You are mourned by your housewife during the day, by your daughter (5) also during the night. The Book of Breathing of Thoth is your protection. Your burial is perfect and it ages by you, (6) without the worms taking up place beside you. You are a divine spirit who is beloved, and Osiris, he desires (7) to see you to be among his Just ones. Osiris *P3-fdw-Mnṯw*, you are stable, beloved … (?) until ever and eternally.

Commentary

This short version of the Book of Traversing Eternity corresponds, with some variants and omissions, to P. Leiden T 32, VIII, 2–12 (reference manuscript). The other documents bearing this text are P. Vatican Inv. 38570, IV, 4–15, P. Berlin 3155, I, 2–II, 6, P. Leiden T 22, 1–4, P. Louvre 3147, I, 4–II, 7, and P. dem. BN 149, I, 2–13. See *LPE*, pp. 247–58 for a detailed commentary.

I, 2–3
šsp n.k[5] *ḳbḥ sntr m ḫrt-hrw nt rʿ nb m-ʿ Ꞽst Nbt-ḥwt*. The parallel versions give as variant *m ḫrt-hrw*, and connect *Ꞽst* and *Nbt-ḥwt* by the conjunction *ḥnʿ*. P. BN 149, I, 2: *š(s)p=k sntr ḳbḥ m ḫr-hrw n-tr.ṯ Ꞽst irm Nb.t-ḥw.t*, 'You receive censing and libation, in the course of every day, from the hand of Isis and Nephthys'. See *LPE*, p. 247 (VIII, 2).

I, 3–4
ḥtp Ḥr ḥr ḏdw.k Ꞽ ḥr ḫrw.k M3ʿt Ḥwt-Ḥr ḥr ḫw twk. Same reading in P. Berlin 3155, I, 2–3 = P. Leiden T 32, VIII, 2 = P. Louvre N 3147, I, 5 = P. Vatican Inv. 38570, IV, 4–5. Sequence partly in lacuna in P. Leiden T 22, 2. P. BN 149, I, 3: *hr Ḥr ḥr n3y ḏ=k* (?) *Ḏḥwty ḥtp=f m ḫrw=k n m3ʿ(.t) Ḥw.t-Ḥr iḥ ḥwy.ṯ=k*, 'Horus is pleased with what you say (?), Thoth, he is satisfied with your just voice; Hathor protects you'. See *LPE*, pp. 247–8 (VIII, 2) and P. BM EA 10718, **lines 3–4**.

I, 4
Ꞽnpw imy-wt smnḫ.n.f ḳsw.k ir.n.f ḥʿw.k mi wnn.f. Same reading in P. Berlin 3155, I, 3–4 = P. Leiden T 22, 2 = P. Leiden T 32, VIII, 3 = P. Louvre N 3147, I, 5–6 = P. Vatican Inv. 38570, IV, 5–6. P. BN 149, I, 3–4: *Ꞽnpw wyt ti=f mnḫ n3y=k ḳs.w ir=f n3y=k iwf.w n p3y gy*, 'Anubis the embalmer, he perfects your bones, he causes your flesh to be as it was'. See *LPE*, p. 248 (VIII, 3); P. BM EA 10260, **I, x + 2** and P. BM EA 10718, **lines 3–4**. For the singular *.f* in *wnn.f*, see P. BM EA 10256, **lines 5–6**.

I, 4–5
Ḫnty Ꞽmntt rš n m33.k šsp.f twk mi wʿ m m3ʿtyw.f. Omission of the *n* after *rš* in P. Vatican Inv. 38570, IV, 6 = Berlin 3155, I, 4 = P. Louvre N 3147, I, 6. Sequence partly in lacuna in P. Leiden T 22, 3. Var. P. Berlin 3155, I, 4: *iṯ.f twk*; P. Berlin 3155, I, 4 = P. Leiden T 32, VIII, 3 = P. Louvre N 3147, I, 6 = P. Vatican Inv. 38570, IV, 6: *m wʿ*; P. BN 149, I, 4–5: *Wsir ḫnt Ꞽmnt ršy=f n mne=k š(s)p=f ṯ=k ḫn* [*n3 M3ʿ*]*ṭ.w*, 'Osiris foremost of the West, he rejoices at the sight of you and receives you among [the Just] ones'. See *LPE*, pp. 248–9 (VIII, 3–4).

I, 5–6
di.f irty.k ḥr m33 ʿnḫwy.k ḥr sḏm rdwy.k ḥr šm. Var. P. Leiden T 22, 3 = P. Vatican Inv. 38570, IV, 6 = P. Berlin 3155, I, 5: *di.f n.k* (*/.t*); P. Leiden T 22, 3 = P. Leiden T 32, VIII, 4 = P. Vatican Inv. 38570, IV, 7: *rdwy.k ḥr nmt r mr.k*; omission of *rdwy.t ḥr nmt* in P. Berlin 3155, I, 5; P. Louvre N 3147, I, 7: *ṯbty.k ḥr nmt r mr.k*. P. BN 149, I, 5: *ti=f ir.ṯ=k r nw iw n3y=k msḏʿ.w sḏm rṭ=k ḥr mšʿ r mr=k*, 'He causes your eyes to see, while your ears hear and your legs walk where you wish'. See *LPE*, pp. 249 (VIII, 4) and 92 (I, 10); also A. Awadalla, *BIFAO* 89 (1989), pp. 29–30.

I, 6
ʿwt.k nbw(t) ḥr ir k3t.sn. Sequence omitted in all other versions in this place, but cf. P. Leiden T 32, I, 10: *ʿwy.k nb ḥr ir k3t.sn*. See *LPE*, pp. 92–3 (I, 10) and 249–50 (VIII, 4).

I, 6–7
ir.n.k ḫprw nbw r-ḏr ib.k iw.k m ḥs(y)w.f wn ḥr šmsw.f. Sequence wholly in lacuna in P. Leiden T 22, 4. Var. P. Louvre N 3147, I, 7–8: *di.f ḫprw nb*; all other versions: *di.f ir.k*, 'he (Osiris) causes you to assume'; P. Vatican Inv. 38570, IV, 7= P. Berlin 3155, I, 6: *r dit* (var.: *dd*) *ib.k*. For *wn ḥr šmsw.f*, the other documents give *rʿ nb*, 'every day'. P. BN 149, I, 5–6: *ti=f ir=k ḫrb nb nt n ḥ3.ṯ=k iw-iw=k ḫn n3y=f ḥs(y).w n mne*, 'He causes you to assume any transformation according to your heart, for you are one of his favoured ones, daily'. See *LPE*, pp. 251–2 (VIII, 4–5) and J.F. Quack, *OLZ* 91 (1996), 155.

I, 7–II, 1
ʿwy.f wʿb rdwy.f m ʿb ḥ3ty.k ḥr M3ʿt nn isft. The suffix *.f* is an error for *.k*. So corrected, same reading in P. Berlin 3155, I, 6–7= P. Leiden T 32, VIII, 5[6]= P. Vatican Inv. 38570, IV, 8. Sequence partly in lacuna in P. Leiden T 22, 4.[7] Omission of the suffix *.k* after *ḥ(3)ty* in P. Louvre N 3147, I, 8. P. BN 149, I, 6–7: *iw ḏrṭ=k wʿb iw rṭ=k wʿb n ʿb iw ḥ3.ṯ=k ḫr M3ʿ.t iw mn mt.t n ʿḏ*, 'Your hands are pure, your legs are purified (?), and your heart is full of Maat, without fault'. See P. BM EA 10718, **lines 6–8**, and *LPE*, p. 252 (VIII, 5), adding Dümichen, *HI* II, pl. 44 e, 5–6: *ii n.k ib.i ḫr M3ʿt n isft m ḫt.i*, 'My heart comes to you, full of Maat, without evil in my body'.

II, 1–2
wnm.k m r3.k swr.k m šnbt.k wrḥ.k iwf.k m stwt itn. Same reading in P. Berlin 3155, I, 7–8 = P. Leiden T 32, VIII, 6 = P. Vatican Inv. 38570, IV, 9. Sequence partly in lacuna in P. Louvre N 3147. P. BN 149, I, 7: *wnm=k swr=k n t3y=k šnb.t tḥs n3 stw.w n p3 Rʿ n3y=k iwf.w*, 'You eat and drink with your throat, and the rays of Re anoint your flesh'. See *LPE*, pp. 252–3 (VIII, 6).

II, 2–3
ii n.k Ḥʿpy ʿnḫ.k m fdw.f is niw m-ʿ Šw. Same reading in P. Leiden T 32, VIII, 6–7. Var. P. Vatican Inv. 38570, IV, 9 = P. Berlin 3155, I, 8: *iw n.k*. Sequence partly in lacuna in P. Louvre N 3147, II, 2. P. BN 149, I, 8: [*iw*] *n=k Ḥʿpy ʿnḫ=k n t3y=f fty3.t* … (?) *snsn n-tr.ṯ Šw*, 'Hapy [comes] to you, and you live on his sweat … (?) the breath from Shu'. On the sweat of Hapy: D. van der Plas, *L'hymne à la crue du Nil* I (Leiden 1986), pp. 75–6. See *LPE*, pp. 253–4 (VIII, 6–7), and F. Hoffmann, *BiOr* 54 (1997), 658.

5. Not *šsp.n.k*, as wrongly written in *LPE*, p. 251.
6. *m ʿb* erased.
7. The rest of the text is lost.

II, 3
Ỉmn-Ỉpt snsn.k ḳbḥ.f Ỉmn snb.k mw.f. Same reading in P. Leiden T 32, VIII, 7 = P. Vatican Inv. 38570, IV, 10. Sequence omitted in P. BN 149; partly in lacuna in P. Louvre N 3147, II, 2. Var. P. Berlin 3155, I, 9: *sb.t mw.f* by error. See *LPE,* p. 254 (VIII, 7).

II, 3–4
ṯꜣw.f n fnḏ.k nn ḥr.f r.k bꜣw.k m tꜣ r ṯs wnḏw.k. Var. P. Leiden T 32, VIII, 7 = P. Vatican Inv. 38570, IV, 11 = P. Berlin 3155, I, 10: *m fnḏ.k. Bꜣw* is written with the seated man determinative, as if the word in question is *sꜣw,* which would be admissible in this context (the sons of the deceased remaining on earth). The other versions give *bꜣ.k.* Sequence omitted in P. BN 149. See *LPE,* p. 254 (VIII, 7–8).

II, 4–5
i(ꜣ)kb.tw n.k in nbt-pr.k m hrw sꜣt.k sk m grḥ. Var. P. Leiden T 32, VIII, 8–9: *sꜣt..k is m grḥ ky ḏd sn.k m grḥ,* 'your daughter also, during the night – otherwise said: your brother also during the night'; P. Berlin 3155, I, 11 = P. Vatican Inv. 38570, IV, 12: *sꜣt.t /.k is m grḥ ky ḏd snt.t/.k is m grḥ,* 'your daughter also, during the night – otherwise said: your sister also, during the night'. As in P. BM EA 10091, the addition *ky ḏd...* is omitted in P. Louvre N 3147, II, 4. P. BN 149, I, 8–9: *rym ṯ=k nꜣ ḥwṭ.w nhp ṯ=k nꜣ s-ḥm.w.t ẖr* [...] *n rn=k,* 'Men mourn you, women lament for you, bearing [...] of your name'. See *LPE,* pp. 254–5 (VIII, 8–9).

II, 5
šꜥt [*n snsn*] *n Ỉ m sꜣw.k.*[8] Same reading in P. Berlin 3155, I, 12 = P. Leiden T 32, VIII, 9 = P. Vatican Inv. 38570, IV, 12. Note here the omission, after *sꜣw.k,* of the sequence *nn ḥm.n.tw(.k /.t) m wsḫt Wsir,* 'and you will not be repelled from the hall of Osiris', present in all other versions. P. BN 149, I, 9–10: *šꜥ.t n snsn n Ḏḥwty m sꜣ=k nt sẖ n ḏbꜥ=f hꜥ=f ti=f nꜣ-nfr tꜣy=k mt.t m-bꜣḥ Wsir* [...]*=k r tꜣ wsḫꜣ.t Mꜣꜥṭ.w,* 'The Book of Breathing of Thoth is your protection, written with his own fingers; he causes your utterance to be good in the presence of Osiris [so that] you [may gain access] to the hall of the Just ones'. See *LPE,* p. 255 (VIII, 9).

smꜣ-tꜣ.k nfr.ti. Same reading in P. Berlin 3155, II, 2[9] = P. Leiden T 32, VIII, 9 = P. Vatican Inv. 38570, IV, 13. Sequence partly in lacuna in P. Louvre N 3147, II, 4. All these documents add: *ḏd.s ḥr* (var.: *m,* cf. *infra* in citation of P. BN 149, 10) *ḳsw.k wꜣḥ.s ḥr iwf.k nn mrḥ,* 'It (your burial) is firm over your bones, and remains over your flesh, without decay', phrase found in full on the verso of numerous examples of the Book of Breathing. P. BM EA 10314, I, 5–6, where starts a parallel with P. BM EA 10091, provides a new variant:

wḏ n.k Ỉst wrt mwt-nṯr irt Rꜥ	'Isis the great, mother of the god, eye of Re [...],
[... *smꜣ*]*-tꜣ.k*	orders for you [... ...] your [bu]rial
ḥr imn[*tt Wꜣst*]	on the We[st of Thebes].'[10]

P. BN 149, I, 10–11: *tꜣy=k ḳ(r)s.t nfr.t mne ẖn nꜣy=k ḳs.w iw=s mne ẖn* [*nꜣy=k iwf.w*] *ẖn pꜣy=k ḥnw* 'Your perfect burial is stable in (*sic*) your bones, it is stable in (*sic*) [your flesh] in your coffin'. See *LPE,* pp. 255–6 (VIII, 9–10) and J.F. Quack, *OLZ* 91 (1996), 155. Cf. also P. Louvre E 3865, VI, 7–8:

smꜣ-tꜣ.k nfrt ḏd.s ḥr ḳsw.k	'Your perfect burial, it is stable over your bones,
wꜣḥ.s ḥr iwf.k	it remains over your flesh;
nn mrḥ wty.k	your coffin will not decay,
mn.ti nn ws r nḥḥ	stable unendingly for ever.'

II, 5–6
iꜣw.s ẖr.k nn tmmw ir.sn r-gs.k. P. BN 149, 11: [...] (?) *iꜣwy=f ẖr-r=k* [*nn*] *ꜥl tꜣw ꜥyb ẖr*[*-r=k*] (so Quack) 'It grows old by you, and the breath of illness [will not] ascend before you'. Except for P. BM EA 10314 (cf. *supra*), all other versions set before this phrase: *mn.k* (*/.t*) *m wt.k,* 'You are established in your coffin' (var. P. BN 149, 10: ... *ẖn pꜣy=k ḥnw*), the suffix *.s* of *iꜣw.s* referring back to *wt.* In P. BM EA 10091 as also in P. BM EA 10304, this subject is *smꜣ-tꜣ.* P. Leiden T 32, VIII, 11 = P. Vatican Inv. 38570, IV, 14 = P. Berlin 3155, II, 6 give as var. *ir.sn* in place of *ir.f.* For *r-gs* all other versions give *m-ḫnt.k* (*/.t*). See *LPE,* p. 256 (VIII, 10–11) and Quack, op. cit.

II, 6–7
ntk ꜣḫ nṯr mry Wsir ỉsb.n.f mꜣꜣ.k r mꜣꜥtyw.f. In the other documents, this phrase is preceded by a short sequence omitted in P. Louvre N 3147, II, 6: *pr.k* (*/.t*) *mn msw.k* (*/.t*) *ꜣḫ.tw rn.k* (*/.t*) *m tꜣ nn ws.f,* 'Your house is established, your children are glorified, and your name is on earth, without cease', var. P. BN 149, I, 12: *nfr rn=k ḥr pꜣ tꜣ iw mn wš* 'Your name is perfect on earth, without stain'.

Var. P. Berlin 3155, II, 5: *mꜣꜣ.t ꜣḫ nṯr* 'you see the divine spirit'; P. Leiden T 32, VIII, 12 = P. Vatican Inv. 38570, IV, 15: *isb.f mꜣꜣ.k r mꜣꜥtyw;* P. BN 149, I, 12: *mtw=k iyḫ nṯr i-mr=w Wsir ti.f ꜥḳ=k ẖn* [*nꜣ mꜣꜥ.t.w*], 'You are a divine spirit who is beloved, and Osiris, he causes you to enter [among the Just ones]'. See *LPE,* p. 258 (VIII, 11–12) and Quack, op. cit.

II, 7
Wsir N ḏd.ti mr (?) *r-ꜥ nḥḥ ḏt.* Final sequence, in P. BM EA 10091 only. The spelling 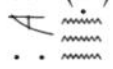 of *mr* is unexpected.

P. BM EA 10114 (pls 143–4)

Salt Collection 1 (in coffin).
LPE, p. 11 and pl. 18 (doc. **E**).
Quirke, *Owners,* no. 41.
Provenance: Thebes. Found with P. BM EA 10115, probably on the mummy inside coffin BM EA 6706 in the collective tomb of the archon Soter.[11]
Date: End of the first to the beginning of the second century AD.
Owner of the papyrus: *Grꜣwꜣpꜣtr* (Cleopatra).
Mother of the owner: *Ḳnt* [...] Canda[ce].

Contents: Book of Traversing Eternity (short version).

Manuscript of one sheet (25.3 × 23.4 cm), bearing sixteen lines of writing. The second half of line 1 is partly erased, and some gaps affect the text here and there.

8. *sꜣ.k* in P. Leiden T 32, VIII, 9 = P. Vatican Inv. 38570, IV, 12.
9. Phrase preceded in this manuscript by an invocation *hꜣy Ḥwt-Ḥr N,* 'Hail Hathor N!' (II, 1), as at the beginning of each column.
10. On the allotment of a tomb by Isis, see P. BM EA 10260, **I, x + 1**.
11. See *supra*, p. 6, no. **10**, and p. 7.

Text on the verso: A good burial. May <it> remain over your ... (?),[12] without destruction for you, eternally.

Translation

Recto

(1) Thus speaks the Hathor Cleopatra born of Can[dace].

(2) May your ba live in the sky before Re, may your ka be divine among the gods, may your corpse remain in the Duat before Osiris, may your mummy be blessed a(3)mong the living, may your heir endure on earth before Geb, (so that) he who is on your throne is among the living, while your name is stable in the mouth of the people (4) by this Book of Traversing Eternity!

You go forth by day, you unite with the disk, and its brightness illumines your face. Your nostrils (5) inhale the scent of Shu, and your nose breathes the north wind; the breath of air, it opens your throat (so that) life is united with <your> body. (6) <You> open your mouth, you speak to the gods, (so that) your words are efficacious among the living. You eat bread, you drink beer, (so that) (7) your Majesty goes forth as a living ba. You open your eyes, you open your ears, (so that) you see and hear by them. (8) This your *ib*-heart is stable in its place, and this *ḥꜣty*-heart is satisfied in its right place; your organs are in the place where they must be, (9) and the god's children are the protection of their body. Your hands seize, your feet walk, and each of your members makes (10) its work (?); you alight as a wind, you fly as a shadow, and assume (all) form at your [heart's] desire. (11) You ascend to heaven without your arm being restrained, and you go down in the Duat without being turned back; you walk (12) on the way of the gods of the horizon, and take your place by the Westerners. You travel round heaven, accompanying the stars. (13) You go as a messenger of the master of the horizon, and follow those who are in the god's domain; you are united with Neheh when (he) makes the circuit, and with Djet (14) when he enters the night. You pass by that earth as the wind's shape, and you go speedily to the way you [desire]; (15) [you] sail downstream to Busiris, you sail upstream to Ta-wer, (so that) the districts of the god are full of your image. You accede to the *nšmt*-bark (16) and [you ?] live [...].

Commentary

This version of the Book of Traversing Eternity corresponds to P. Leiden T 32, I, 3–16 = P. Vatican Inv. 38570, I, 3–16 = P. Vienna 3875, 5–29 = P. Berlin 3044, 2–13 = P. Berlin 3155, IV, 2–12 (partial text) = P. OIC 25389, XXVI–XXVII, 1–5 (partial text) = XXX, 5–XXXI, 1 (partial text) = P. Louvre N 3166, II, 19–28 (partial text) = stela Vatican 128 A, 1–9 = lid of coffin, Horniman Museum, 1–3 (partial text) = stela Cairo JE 44065, 3 (partial text) = P. BM EA 10262 + 10263, 2–7 (partial text) = P. Tübingen 2001, 2–11 (partial text).

Line 1

ḥr.s n Ḥwt-Ḥr N. Among manuscripts containing the Book of Traversing Eternity, only P. BM EA 10114 is introduced by these words on which see P. BM EA 10191, **I, 1**. See also *supra*, p. 2 with n. 21.

Lines 2–3

ꜥnḫ bꜣ.t m pt ḫr Rꜥ nṯr kꜣ.t ḫr nṯrw wꜣḥ ḫꜣt.t m Dwꜣt ḫr Wsir ꜣḫ sꜥḥ.t m-ḫnt ꜥnḫw. Sequence partly in lacuna in P. BM EA 10262 + 10263, 1–2. Var. P. Leiden T 32, I, 3 = P. Berlin 3044, 2 = P. Vienna 3875, 6 = P. Berlin 3155, IV, 2 = P. OIC 25389, XXVI–XXVII, 2 = XXX, 5 = P. Vatican Inv. 38570, I, 3–4 = stela Vatican 128 A, 1 = lid of coffin, Horniman, 2 = P. BM EA 10262 + 10263, 2: *ḫnt nṯrw*; P. Louvre N 3166, II, 19: *ḫr ḫnt nṯrw* (*sic*). P. Leiden T 32, I, 4: *ḫnty ꜥnḫw*; P. Vatican Inv. 38570, I, 4 = P. Berlin 3155, IV, 3: *m-ḫnty ꜥnḫw*; P. OIC 25389, XXVI–XXVII, 2 = XXX, 6: *ꜣḫ sꜥḥ.k m tꜣ ḫnt ꜥnḫw*; P. Louvre N 3166, II, 20 = stela Vatican 128 A, 2 = lid of coffin, Horniman, 2: *m-ḫnt ꜣḫw*.

P. BM EA 10314, I, 1–3, gives a somewhat different version:

[... ...] *N ḫr Ḥwt*[-*Ḥr*	'[... ...] N before Hat[hor
... ...] *ḫr Rꜥ*	... ...] before Re;
rnp ḫꜣt.k m Dwꜣt ḫr Wsir	may your corpse be renewed in the Duat before Osiris,
wꜣḥ rn.k [... ...]	may your name remain [... ...].'

See *LPE*, pp. 81–3 (I, 3–4) and 277; also J. Osing, in A. Fakhry, *Denkmäler der Oase Dachla* (*AV* 28, 1982), p. 66, Text C:

[...] *m Knmt N*	'[...] in Kenemet, N,
ꜥnḫ bꜣ.k m pt ḫr Rꜥ	May your ba live in the sky before Re,
iw.f m-m nṯrw (?)	for he is among the gods (?)
sb.n.k ꜥḥꜥw ꜥꜣ (?)	after you spent a long lifetime (?);
... (?) *ḫꜣt.k m Dwꜣt ḫr Wsir*	may your corpse ... (?) in the Duat before Osiris,
ꜣḫ sꜥḥ.k m-ḫnt ꜣḫw	may your mummy be blessed among the spirits!'

Osing, op. cit., p. 68, Text D, 7:

ꜥnḫ bꜣ.k m pt ḫr Rꜥ	'May your ba live in the sky before Re!'

A. Kamal, *ASAE* 14 (1914), p. 64:

ꜥnḫ bꜣ.k n pt ḫr Rꜥ	'May your ba live in the sky before Re,
rnp ḫt.k m tꜣ ḫr Gb	may your corpse be renewed on earth before Geb,
ꜥnḫ bꜣ.k ḫr nṯrw mꜣꜥtyw	may your ba live before the just gods!'

Coffin BM EA 6705, left side (unpublished):

ꜥnḫ bꜣ.k m pt ḫr Rꜥ	'May your ba live in the sky before Re,
nṯr rn.k m tꜣ ḫr Gb	may your name be divine on earth before Geb,
rnp ḫꜣt.k m Dwꜣt ḫr Wsir	may your corpse be renewed in the Duat before Osiris!'

See also P. BM EA 10108, **lines 1–3**.

Line 3

rwḏ iwꜥ.t m tꜣ ḫr Gb ḥry nst.t m-ḫnt ꜥnḫw. Sequence omitted in P. OIC 25389 (**G** and **G'**); partly in lacuna in P. BM EA 10262 + 10263, 2. Var. P. BM EA 10262 + 10263, 2: *m hrw* instead of *m tꜣ*; P. Leiden T 32, I, 4 =

12. Illegible group. Read *iwf* or *ḳs(w)*.

P. Berlin 3155, 4: *ḥry nsty.k /.t ḫnty ꜥnḫw*; P. Vatican Inv. 38570, I, 5 = P. Louvre N 3166, II, 20–1 = stela Vatican 128 A, 2 = lid of coffin, Horniman, 2: *ḫnt ꜥnḫw*; P. Vienna 3875, 7–8: *ḥry nsty.k ḫnt ꜥnḫw*.

P. Berlin 3044, 3:

mn pr.k m tꜣ ḫr Gb	'May your house be stable on earth before Geb,
imyw pr.k ḫnt ꜥnḫw	may those who are in your house be among the living!'

See *LPE*, pp. 83–4 (I, 4); also Osing, op. cit., line 6:

mn iwꜥ.k m tꜣ ḫr Gb	'May your heir be stable on earth before Geb!'

Osing, op. cit., p. 68, Text D, 8:

[*mn*] *rn.k m tꜣ ḫr Gb*	'May your name [be stable] on earth before Geb!'

Lines 3–4

rn.t ḏd[13] *tp rꜣ n wnyw ḥr mḏꜣt tn sb nḥḥ*. Same reading in P. Leiden T 32, I, 4–5 = P. Vatican Inv. 38570, I, 5–6. Omission of *ḥr mḏꜣt tn sb nḥḥ* in the lid of coffin, Horniman, 2. Sequence partly in lacuna in P. BM EA 10314, I, 3[14] and P. BM EA 10262 + 10263, 4. Var. P. Vienna 3875, 9: *mḏꜣt tn n sb nḥḥ*; P. Berlin 3155, IV, 5–6: *mḏꜣt tn ḥr* (*sic*) *sb nḥḥ*; P. Berlin 3044, 3–4: *mḏꜣt n sb nḥḥ*; stela Vatican 128 A, 2–3: *mḏꜣt tn n sb nḥḥ*. Substitution of *ḥr tꜣ* to *ḥr mḏꜣt tn sb nḥḥ* in P. OIC 25389, XXX, 7.

P. OIC 25389, XXVI–XXVII, 2 (*LPE*, p. 385):

rn.k ḏd tp rꜣ n wnyw	'Your name is stable in the mouth of the people,
sꜣḫw.k rwḏ m tꜣ pn	and your glorifications endure on that earth
<*ḥr*> *mḏꜣt nḥḥ sb ḏt*	<by> the Book of Eternity passing perenniality.'

P. Louvre N 3166, II, 21:

rn.k ḏd tp rꜣ n wnyw	'Your name is stable in the mouth of the people,
kꜣ.k mn m ḥwwt-nṯrww	and your ka is established in the temples.'

See *LPE*, p. 84 (I, 4–5); also Osing, op. cit., p. 66, Text C, 7:

rn.k rwḏ m-m ꜥnḫw	'Your name endures among the living.'

Line 4

pr.t m hrw ḫnm.t itn ḥꜣy ḥḏḏ<.f>n ḥr.t. Restoration of suffix *.f* after the parallels. Sequence partly in lacuna in P. BM EA 10262 + 10263, 5. Omission of suffix after *ḫnm*, and of *ḥḏḏ* in P. Berlin 3155, IV, 6. This sequence is also found in P. Turin 1848, V, 2–3. See *LPE*, pp. 84–6 (I, 5–6); also G. Legrain, *Collection Hoffmann. Catalogue des antiquités égyptiennes* (Paris 1894), p. 101, no. 326: [*pr.k*] *m hrw ḫnm.k itn ḥꜣy ḥḏḏ.f ḥr.k*.

Lines 4–5

nšp ḫnmty.t nwd[15] *m Šw snsn fnḏ.t mḥyt*. Same reading in P. Leiden T 32, I, 6 = P. Vatican Inv. 38570, I, 6–7 = P. Vienna 3875, 10–11 = P. Berlin 3044, 4–5 = P. OIC 25389, XXX, 7–8 = P. Louvre N 3166, II, 22–3 = lid of coffin, Horniman, 3. Sequence partly in lacuna in P. BM EA 10262 + 10263, 5. Omission of suffix *.k /.t* after *ḫnmty* in P. Berlin 3155, IV, 7; P. OIC 25389, XXVI–XXVII, 3: *n Šw*; *mḥyt nfrt*. See *LPE*, pp. 86–7 (I, 6); also Osing, op. cit., p. 66, Text C, 10: *nšp ḫnmty.k m nwd*.

Line 5

is srd.n.f ḥtyt.k ḫnm ꜥnḫ m ḏt<.k>. Restoration of suffix *.k* after the parallels. Sequence partly in lacuna in P. BM EA 10262 + 10263, 5. Apart from P. Berlin 3155, IV, 8, which also gives *is*, all other documents read *is-niw*, 'breath of air'. Everywhere else *srḳ* is substituted for *srd*, well attested in the expression *srḳ ḥtyt*; note *srḳ iḫtyt.k* in P. Berlin 3044, 5; *srḳ.f (i)ḫtyt.k* in P. Louvre N 3166, II, 23 = stela Vatican 128 A, 3–4. P. Vienna 3875, 12 = P. Berlin 3044, 5: *ḫnm.k ꜥnḫ*; P. OIC 25389, XXVI–XXVII, 3 and XXX, 9: *ḫnm.f ꜥnḫ*. See *LPE*, pp. 87–8 (I, 6–7); also P. Vatican Inv. 38608, 26–7: *nšp ḫnmty.k is-niw srḳ iḫty.k m ꜥnḫ*, 'Your nostrils breathe, and the breath of air causes your throat to breathe by the life'.

Lines 5–6

wp rꜣ.t mdw.t n nꜣ nṯrw wꜣḏ ḏdw.k[16] *m-ḫnt ꜥnḫw*. Sequence partly in lacuna in P. BM EA 10262 + 10263, 6. Var. P. Leiden T 32, I, 7 = P. Vatican Inv. 38570, I, 8 = P. Vienna 3875, 13 = P. Berlin 3044, 5 = P. Berlin 3155, IV, 8 = P. Louvre N 3166, II, 24 (?) = stela Vatican 128 A, 4 = lid of coffin, Horniman, 3: *wp.k /.t*. Opposite to the writing of *mdw* with the sign , attested also in P. OIC 25389, XXX, 9 = P. Louvre N 3166, II, 24 = stela Vatican 128 A, 4 = lid of coffin, Horniman, 3, all other versions: P. Leiden T 32, I, 7 = P. Vatican Inv. 38570, I, 8 = P. Vienna 3875, 13 = P. Berlin 3044, 6 = P. Berlin 3155, IV, 8 = P. OIC 25389, XXVI–XXVII, 3, give . P. Louvre N 3166, II, 24 = stela Vatican 128 A, 4 = lid of coffin, Horniman, 3: *n nṯrw*;[17] P. Louvre N 3166, II, 24: *wḏ.k mdw*; P. BM EA 10262 + 10263, 6: *wꜣḏ ḏd.k*.[18] P. Leiden T 32, I, 7 = P. Vienna 3875, 13 = P. Berlin 3155, IV, 9 = P. OIC 25389, XXVI–XXVII, 3 = P. BM EA 10262 + 10263, 6 (?): *n* (*m*)[19] *nṯrwy*; P. Vatican Inv. 38570, I, 8: 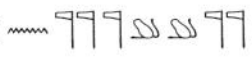; P. Berlin 3044, 6: *n nṯr*; P. OIC 25389, XXX, 9: *ḫnt nṯrw*. P. Leiden T 32, I, 7 = P. Vatican Inv. 38570, I, 8 = P. Vienna 3875, 13–14 = P. Berlin 3044, 6 = P. Berlin 3155, IV, 9 = P. Louvre N 3166, II, 24 = stela Vatican 128 A, 4: *m-ḫnt ꜣḫw*. See *LPE*, p. 88 (I, 7).

Lines 6–7

nkn.t m tꜣ sꜥm.t m ḥnḳt pr ḥm.t m bꜣ ꜥnḫ. Omission of the text after *ḥnḳt* in P. OIC 25389, XXVI–XXVII, 3; this passage is corrupt in XXX, 10: *ḥr tꜣ ḥm n bꜣ ꜥnḫ*. Given as a *hapax* in *LPE*, the word *nkn* is probably identical with the term *nkꜣ* attested in *BD* ch. 85 (ed. Budge, p. 184, 5–6), in the phrase *nkꜣ.i m Mꜣꜥt ꜥnḫ.i im.s*, 'I eat Maat and I live on her', to be compared with *ꜥnḫ.f m Mꜣꜥt sꜥm.f m Mꜣꜥt*, P. BM EA 10048, VII, 3.[20] Var. P. Vatican Inv. 38570, I, 9 = P. Berlin 3155, IV, 10 = P. Tübingen 2001, II, 2–3: *ḫn ḥm.k /.t m bꜣ ꜥnḫ*. All the parallels give the verb *wnm*. P. Louvre N 3166, II, 24–6, shows here an extensive variant:

ꜥḥ.k r pt ir.k st.k m ꜣḫt	'You fly to the sky, take your place in the horizon,
iṯ Nnt ḥm.k m ḥtp	and Nenet (the sky) receives your Majesty, in peace.

13. Illegible traces after *ḏd*. Whereas P. Leiden T 32 = P. Louvre N 3166 = P. OIC 25389 (**G** and **G'**) = lid of coffin in the Horniman Museum all give the reading *ḏd*, P. Vatican Inv. 38570 = P. Vienna 3875 = P. Berlin 3044 = P. Berlin 3155 = P. BM EA 10314 = stela Vatican 128 A, show an ending *ti*, written  or .
14. The text immediately following corresponds to P. Leiden T 32, I, 12.
15. Incorrect spelling  in P. OIC 25389, XXX, 8.
16. For *ḏdw.t*. The owner of the manuscript is a woman.
17. The version of the lid of the coffin in the Horniman Museum ends here.
18. Continuation of the text lost after *wꜣḏ ḏd.k m-ḫnt* [...].
19. *m* in P. OIC 25389.
20. The translators of this sequence usually consider *nkꜣ* as the verb of *Wb.* II, 345, 13–14 'überlegen, an etwas denken'; cf. Allen, *Book of the Dead*, p. 72: 'I ponder on truth'; P. Barguet, *Le Livre des Morts des anciens Egyptiens* (Paris 1967), p. 123: 'Je crois en Maât'; E. Hornung, *Das Totenbuch der Ägypter* (Zurich 1979), p. 173: 'Ich denke (stets) an *Maat*'.

wnm.k tꜣ ḥr ḫꜣwt n Rꜥ	You eat bread on the altar of Re,
smꜣ.k ḫwt m-ꜥb bꜣw nṯrw	you receive offerings with the bas of the gods,
di.tw n.k ꜣw m-ḳꜣb ḥtptyw	and *ꜣw*-offerings are given to you among the peaceful gods
in iḳrw nn šms Skr	by these excellent ones who follow Sokar.'

See *LPE,* pp. 88–90 (I, 7–8), and add *Dendara* X, 251, 3: *wnm.k m tꜣ ꜥm.k m ḥnḳt pr ḥm.k m bꜣ ꜥnḫ,* 'you eat bread, you drink beer, (so that) your Majesty goes forth as a living ba'.

Line 7
wn <n>.t irty.t wbꜣ n.t ꜥnḫwy.t mꜣꜣ.t sḏm.t im.sn. Restoration of *n* after P. Leiden T 32, I, 8 = P. Vatican Inv. 38570, I, 9 = P. Vienna 3875, 15 = P. Berlin 3044, 6 = P. Berlin 3155, IV, 10 = stela Vatican 128 1, 4 = P. Tübingen 2001, II, 3 = P. OIC 25389, XXVI–XXVII, 4. Sequence omitted in P. Louvre N 3166 = P. OIC 25389, XXX, 10. Var. P. OIC 25389, XXVI–XXVII, 4: *irt.k.*[21] Omission of suffix after *ꜥnḫwy* in P. OIC 25389, XXVI–XXVII, 4. P. Berlin 3044, 7: *m-im.sn.*

Cf. P. dem. Berlin 8351, I, 6 (M. Smith, *Enchoria* 15 [1987], p. 73 = id., *Liturgy,* p. 23): *wn n=k ꜥnḫ,* 'May your ears be open for you!'. See *LPE,* p. 90 (I, 8–9).

Line 8
ib.t pn mn.tw ḥr st.f ḥ(ꜣ)ty.t ḥtp ḥr mkt<.f>. Completed with suffix after *mkt,* the phrase occurs in P. Leiden T 32, I, 9 = P. Vatican Inv. 38570, I, 9–10 = P. Vienna 3875, 16–17 = P. Berlin 3044, 7[22] = P. Berlin 3155, IV, 11–12 = P. OIC 25389, XXX, 10–11 = stela Vatican 128 A, 5. Sequence omitted in P. Louvre N 3166. Omission of *pn* after *ib.k* in P. OIC 25389, XXVI–XXVII, 4. Var. P. Tübingen 2001, II, 4: *tp st.k.* See P. BM EA 10191, **I, 35.**

On the difference between *ib* and *ḥꜣty,* see P. BM EA 10048, **I, 4–6**.

Lines 8–9
imyw-ḫt.k r bw wnn.sn msw-nṯr m sꜣ ḏt.sn. Sequence omitted in P. Louvre N 3166. Var. P. Vatican Inv. 38570, I, 10 = P. Vienna 3875, 17 = P. Berlin 3044, 8 = P. Berlin 3155, IV, 12 = P. OIC 25389, XXVI–XXVII, 4 = stela Vatican 128 A, 5 = P. Tübingen 2001, II, 5: *wn.sn;* P. Leiden T 32, I, 10 = P. Vatican Inv. 38570, I, 10 = P. Vienna 3875, 18 = P. Berlin 3044, 8 = P. Berlin 3155, IV, 12 = P. Tübingen 2001, II, 6: *m sꜣ.sn;* P. OIC 25389, XXVI–XXVII, 4: *m iry.sn;* stela Vatican 128 A, 5: *ḥr sꜣ.sn.* See *LPE,* pp. 91–2 (I, 9–10), and J. Berlandini, *BIFAO* 85 (1985), p. 45, n. g.

Lines 9–10
ḏrty.t ḥr ḫfꜥ ṯbty.t <ḥr> nmt ꜥwt[.t] nbt ḥr ir … .sn (?). Sequence omitted in P. Louvre N 3166. One expects *kꜣt.sn* after *ir,* reading given by all other parallels, but the remaining traces do not confirm that restoration. Omission of *ḥr* after *ḏrty.k* in stela Vatican 128 A, 5; after *ḏrty* and *ṯbty.k* in P. Tübingen 2001, II, 6; after *ṯbty.k* in P. Leiden T 32, I, 10 and P. Vatican Inv. 38570, I, 11. Omission of *ir* after *ir* in P. Berlin 3044, 8. Var. P. OIC 25389, XXVI–XXVII, 4 and XXX, 11: *ḏrwt.k;* P. Leiden T 32, I, 10 = P. Vatican Inv. 38570, I, 11 = P. Vienna 3875, 18 = P. Berlin 3044, 8 = stela Vatican 128 A, 6: *ꜥwy.k;* P. Tübingen 2001, II, 6: *ꜥwy ꜥwt.t* (*sic*). See *LPE,* pp. 92–3 (I, 10); also J. Osing, in A. Fakhry, *Denkmäler der Oase Dachla* (*AV* 28, 1982), p. 66, Text C: *ꜥw(t).k nb ḥr irt kꜣt.sn.*

Line 10
ḫn.t m ḏꜥw ꜥḥ.t m šwt ir.t ḫprw [*nb*] *r-dit* [*ib*]*.t.* Restorations after the parallels. Sequence omitted in P. OIC 25389, XXX. Omission of *nb* in P. Leiden T 32, I, 11 = P. Vatican Inv. 38570, I, 12 = P. Louvre N 3166, II, 27 = stela Vatican 128 A, 6 = P. Tübingen 2001, II, 8. Var. stela Vatican 128 A, 6: *ꜥḫm* in front of *ꜥḥ;* P. Leiden T 32, I, 11 = P. Vatican Inv. 38570, I, 11 = P. Vienna 3875, 20 = P. Berlin 3044, 9 = P. Tübingen 2001, II, 7: *šbt* in front of *šwt;* P. Vatican Inv. 38570, I, 11 = P. Vienna 3875, 20 = P. Berlin 3044, 9 = P. Tübingen 2001, II, 8: *r-dd ib.k;* stela Vatican 128 A, 6: *r-ḏr ib.k.* See *LPE,* p. 93 (I, 10–11) and for the expression *ꜥḥ m šwt,* F.R. Herbin, *RdE* 54 (2003), pp. 116–17; Ch. Thiers and Y. Volokhine, *Ermant* I (*MIFAO* 124, 2005), pp. 30 and 51.

Line 11
šw.t r pt nn tn.tw ꜥ.t sḫr[.t] r Dwꜣt nn šnꜥ.t. Sequence omitted in P. Louvre N 3166. Var. P. Vienna 3875, 20 = P. OIC 25389, XXVI–XXVII, 5 and XXX, 12 = stela Vatican 128 A, 6: *ḥy.k r pt.*

For *sḫd*: L.V. Žabkar, *A Study of the Ba Concept* (*SAOC* 34, 1968), p. 105, n. 102; Smith, *Mortuary Texts,* p. 74 (III, 5). See *LPE,* p. 94 (I, 11–12).

Lines 11–12
šꜣis[*.t*] *ḥr wꜣt n nṯrw ꜣḫtyw ir.t st.t ḥr Imntyw.* Same reading in P. Leiden T 32, I, 12 = P. Vatican Inv. 38570, I, 12–13 = P. Vienna 3875, 22–3 = P. Berlin 3044, 10 = stela Vatican 128 A, 7. Sequence omitted in P. Louvre N 3166; partly in lacuna in P. BM EA 10314, I, 3–4. Var. P. OIC 25389, XXVI–XXVII, 5: *ir.tw st.k;* XXX, 14: *drp st.k ḥr Mꜣꜥtyw;* P. Tübingen 2001, II, 9: *tp wꜣt.* See *LPE,* pp. 94–5 (I, 12) and 277 (I, 3–4).

Line 12
dbn[*.t*] *ḥr*[*t*] *m-ḫt* [*ḫ*]*ꜣbsw.* Same reading in P. Leiden T 32, I, 12–13 = P. Vatican Inv. 38570, I, 13 = P. Vienna 3875, 23 = P. Berlin 3044, 10 = P. OIC 25389, XXX, 14 = P. Tübingen 2001, II, 10–11. Sequence omitted in P. OIC 25389, XXVI–XXVII. Var. P. Louvre N 3166, II, 27: *pḫr.k ḥrt m-ḳꜣb ḫꜣbsw;* stela Vatican 128 A, 7: *pḫr.k ḥrt.*

All other versions: P. Leiden T 32, I, 13 = P. Vatican Inv. 38570, I, 13–14 = P. Berlin 3044, 11 = stela Vatican 128 A, 7 = P. Tübingen 2001, II, 11, add the phrase *šn.k Nnt m-ꜥb siww.*[23] Var. P. Louvre N 3166, II, 27–8: *šn.k g(ꜣ)bt m-ꜥb sbꜣw;* P. OIC 25389, XXX, 14: *ḫn.k Nnt;* P. Vienna 3875, 24: *m-ꜥb siww.sn.* See *LPE,* pp. 95–6 (I, 12–13).

Line 13
šm.t m [*wpwty*] *n nb ꜣḫt šms.t imyw ḫrt<-nṯr>.* Restorations after the parallels. Sequence omitted in P. OIC 25389, XXVI–XXVII = P. Louvre N 3166, II. Var. P. OIC 25389, XXX, 15: *wp.k <wꜣt> m wp(w)t(y);* P. Leiden T 32, I, 13 = P. Vatican Inv. 38570, I, 14 = P. Berlin 3044, 11 = stela Vatican 128 A, 8: *nbw ꜣḫt;* P. Vienna 3875, 25: *nbw ꜣḫtyw.* See *LPE,* pp. 96–7 (I, 13).

Lines 13–14
ḫnm.n.t nḥḥ ḥft šn ḏt ḥft ꜥḳ m grḥ. Sequence omitted in P. OIC 25389, XXVI–XXVII = P. Louvre N 3166, II. Var. P. Leiden T 32, I, 14 = P. Vatican Inv. 38570, I, 14–15: *ḫnm.n.k nḥḥ ḥft wbn.f m hrw ḏt ḥft ꜥḳ.f m grḥ;* P. OIC 25389, XXX, 15–16: *mꜣꜣ.k Rꜥ ḥft šn m hrw;* P. Vienna 3875, 26 = P. Berlin 3044, 11 = stela Vatican 128 A, 8: *ḫnm.k.* See *LPE,* pp. 97–8 (I, 14).

Line 14
sš.n.t tꜣ pn m sꜥḥ [*n*] *ṯꜣw sḫn.n.t r wꜣt* [*mr*]*.n.t.* Restorations after the parallels. Sequence omitted in P. OIC 25389, XXVI–XXVII. All other versions give *ḫn.k* instead of *sḫn.k.* Var. P. Leiden T 32, I, 15: *wꜣt n mr.n.k;*

21. For use of the singular instead of the plural for designating some parts of the body, see P. BM EA 10048, **III, 6**.

22. Erroneous repetition in this manuscript of the preposition *ḥr* before *st.f.*

23. P. Tübingen 2001 ends here.

P. Louvre N 3166, II, 28 = P. OIC 25389, XXXI, 1: *mr.k.*[24] See *LPE*, p. 98 (I, 14–15).

Line 15

ḫd[*.t r Ḏ*]*dw ḫnt.t r Ṯ3-wr sp3wt<-nṯr> ḫr wrmw.t.* Restorations after the parallels. Sequence omitted in P. OIC 25389, XXVI–XXVII and P. Louvre N 3166, II; partly in lacuna in P. OIC 25389, XXXI, 1–2. Var. P. Leiden T 32, I, 15: *ḫr šsm.k;* P. Vatican Inv. 38570, I, 16 = P. Berlin 3044, 13: *ḫr šsm.f.* P. Vienna 3875, 29 erroneously juxtaposes both suffixes. See *LPE*, pp. 98–9 (I, 15). On the travel to Busiris and Ta-wer, also mentioned in P. BM EA 10254, 2–3, and P. BM EA 10344, 10–12: Smith, *Liturgy*, p. 63 (V, 6, f and V, 7, a); G. Vittmann, *ZÄS* 117 (1990), p. 81, lines 6–7, and p. 84 (This and Ta-wer).

Lines 15–16

h3.t r nšmt ʿnḫ [...]. The manuscript ends with these words. The writer has here abridged the official text, as the other versions show. Sequence omitted in P. OIC 25389, XXVI–XXVII, XXXI = P. Louvre N 3166, II. P. Leiden T 32, I, 16 = P. Vatican Inv. 38570, I, 16 = P. Vienna 3875, 29 = P. Berlin 3044, 13 = stela Cairo JE 44065, 3: *h3.k r nšmt ḥnʿ im3ḫw.* Var. stela Vatican 128 A, 9: *pr.k.* See *LPE*, p. 100 (I, 16).

P. BM EA 10262 + 10263 (pls 145–6)

Salt Collection 1, 36–7.
LPE, pp. 30–1 and pl. XXXIV (doc. **Q**).
Quirke, *Owners*, no. 174.
Provenance: probably Thebes.
Date: first to second century AD.
Owner of the papyrus: *P3-di-Ḫnsw-p3-ḫrd* (Petechenpocrates).

Contents: Book of Traversing Eternity (short version).

Two separately numbered fragments (10.7 × 6.8 cm, and 10.2 × 5.7 cm), together forming one highly fragmentary document.

The problem raised by this document concerns the joining of these two fragments. In our previous publication of the text (*LPE*, p. 519), the manuscript has been reconstructed as bearing seven lines of hieratic, the join coming at the level of line 5. Although that remains possible, two other possibilities can be envisaged. Because of our ignorance of the original measurements of the text (we can only restore with relative certitude the word *h3y* before the word Osiris in line 1) and of irregularity in the writing, it is not excluded that line 5 of the first fragment is to be placed at the level of line x + 2 of the second, or that the latter is to be placed below the first (the width of the two fragments is the same). So the length of the lacunae and the numbering of the lines – which does not correspond to their real beginning – are to be considered with reservations.

Text on the verso: A good burial. May [it] endure [over your bones ...]

Translation

(1) [Hail] Osiris *P3-di-Ḫnsw-p3-ḫrd*! [May your ba live in the sky before Re], (2) may your ka [be divine] among the god<s>, may your corpse remain in the Duat [before Osiris, may your mummy be blessed among the living], (3) may your heir [endure] by day before Geb, (so that) he who is on [your throne is among the living, while your name is stable in the mouth of] (4) the people by [this] Book [of Traversing Eternity]! [You go forth by day, you unite with the disk], and its [rays (5) illumine] your face. [Your nostrils] inhale [the scent of Shu], and your [nose breathes (6) the north wind]; the breath of air, [it opens your throat ... You open your mouth, speak] to (7) the two gods, and your words are efficacious among [the spirits ...].

Commentary

Line 1

[...] *Wsir N* [...]. Probably restore, in the lacuna preceding the title of Osiris, the invocation *h3*, as in most of the parallels. See *LPE*, p. 81 (I, 1); R.A. Caminos, in *Ancient Egypt and Kush. In Memoriam M.A. Korostovtsev* (Moscow 1993), p. 119, n. 14.

Line 2

[*nṯr*] *k3.k ḫnt nṯr<w> w3ḥ ḫ3t.k m Dw3t* [*ḫr Wsir*]. Part of a section devoted to the different components of the human personality (ba, ka, corpse and mummy), inspired by the Book of Breathing. Note the variants *nṯr k3.t ḫr m3ʿtyw,* P. BM EA 10343, 9; *rnp ḫ3t.k m Dw3t ḫr Wsir,* P. BM EA 10314, I, 2, and see *LPE*, pp. 81–3 (I, 3–4).

Line 3

[*rwḏ*] *iwʿ.k m hrw ḫr Gb ḥry* [*nst.k ḫnty ʿnḫw*]. The predominant version gives *m t3* rather than *m hrw.* For the variants on this phrase, see *LPE*, p. 83 (I, 4).

Line 4

[*rn.k ḏd tp r3 n*] *wnyw ḥr mḏ3t* [*tn (n) sb nḥḥ*]. See P. BM EA 10314, **I, 2**, and see *LPE*, p. 84 (I, 4–5).

Lines [4]–5

[*pr.k m hrw ḫnm.k itn ḥ3y ḥḏḏ*]*.f* [*n*] *ḥr.k.* One possible variant, though attested in only one document (P. Berlin 3155, IV, 6), gives: *ḥ3y.f n ḥr.k,* with *itn* as subject. See *LPE*, pp. 84–5 (I, 5–6).

Lines 5–6

nšp [*ḫnmty.k nwd m Šw snsn fnḏ*]*.k* [*mḥyt*] *is niw* [*srḳ.n.f ḫtyt.k* ...]. On the writing *sšp* for the word *nšp*, see *LPE*, p. 518, a. On the minor variants among the parallel, see ibid., p. 86 (I, 6 and 6–7).

Line 7

[*wp.k r3.k m ḏd.k n*] *nṯrwy w3ḏ ḏd.k m-ḫnt* [*3ḫw* ...]. For the different variants, see *LPE*, p. 88 (I, 7).

24. *mr* in lacuna in P. OIC 25389.

P. BM EA 10314 (pls 147–9)

Salt Collection 3, 413.2.
LPE, pp. 28–9 and pl. XXXII (doc. **O**).
Quirke, *Owners*, no. 280.
Provenance: probably Thebes.
Date: first to second century AD.
Owner of the papyrus: [...]-*Mnṯw*.
Mother of the owner: *Tꜣ-(nt)-pꜣ-iḥꜣy*.

Contents: Book of Traversing Eternity (short version).

In general layout and style, this manuscript (54.5 × 22.9 cm) is singularly close to P. BM EA 10091. Its upper part contains the image of a starry sky. Like P. BM EA 10091, it originally comprised two columns of seven lines each, of which about one third is missing at the right side of the first. Both are surmounted by what appears at first sight to be a vignette but which is in fact a full text written in large-scale hieroglyphs, similar to P. BM EA 10091. That of the first column is of uncertain interpretation; that of the second reads *šṯyt* <*Wsir* [...]-*Mnṯw*>[25] *ḏd.ti m Imntt*, 'The tomb <of the Osiris [...]-*Mnṯw*> is stable in the West'. On the verso, beneath the last two lines of col. 2 of the recto, may be seen a series of black ink smudges, but these, if they were ever signs, give no readable text.

Translation

Recto

I (1) [...]-*Mnṯw*, justified, born of the housewife *Tꜣ-(nt) pꜣ-iḥꜣy*, before Hat[(2)hor ... ... May your ba live in the sky] before Re, may your corpse be renewed in the Duat before Osiris, may your name remain (3)[... ...] be stable in the mouth of men by this Book of Traversing Eternity!

[You] walk (4)[upon the way of the gods of the hori]zon; you reach the House of he who lives on rites, in peace. You go in life (5)[... ...] (*bis*), without fail. Isis the great, mother of the god, eye of Re decrees for you (6)[... ...] your burial on the We[st of Thebes]; it grows old [... ...] your [...] your bones (7)[... ... without] the worms [taking place beside you ...] Anubis [... ...] ... (?) II (1) ... (?) like the gods who stand on this earth. The two mourners, the two kites, mourn you in their hearts. You eat bread, (2) drink beer, (so that) your heart rejoices until ever. You are given ways to every place which your ka desires; (3) your ba flies to the sky before Re, and his rays unite with your mummy. Hedjhotep comes (4) to you from the Mansion of the Bee, full of cloths the names of which are *ḥḏ*, *wꜣḏ*, *irtyw* and *id*(5)*mi*, to clothe your limbs, without soiling (?), in peace (?) (*bis*), (so that) your heart is satisfied in the sacred region (6) and (that) you become one of the Just ones. Your name is stable on this earth, everyday, as there the name (7) of the gods and goddesses who are in Upper and Lower Egypt endures. Your lifetime is eternity, your kingship is everlastingness, and it is [...] that you exist for ever.

Commentary

I, 1–2
[... ...] *N ḫr Ḥwt-*[*Ḥr* ...]. Restoration of the broken portions is difficult in the absence of parallels. At least one may observe the similarity with the formulation *ḫr Ḥwt-Ḥr* and *ḫr Rꜥ*, *ḫr Wsir* in the following clauses.

I, 2
[*ꜥnḫ bꜣ.k m pt*] *ḫr Rꜥ rnp ḫꜣt.k m Dwꜣt ḫr Wsir*. The restoration *ꜥnḫ bꜣ.k m pt* is based on the parallels in both the Book of Traversing Eternity (cf. in this volume P. BM EA 10114, **lines 2–3**), and in other Books of Breathing (P. BM EA 10112, 2; P. BM EA 10108, 1). The most commonly attested version in the parallels gives *wꜣḥ ḫꜣt.k m Dwꜣt ḫr Wsir*, 'May your corpse be firm in the Duat before Osiris!'. See P. BM EA 10048, **II, 7–8**, and *LPE*, pp. 81–3 (I, 3–4).

I, 2–3
wꜣḥ[26] *rn.k* [... ...] *ḏd tp rꜣ n wnyw ḫr mḏꜣt tn sb nḥḥ*. The divergence between P. BM EA 10314 and the parallels prevents certain restoration for the text in the lacuna. The other sources give the version *rn.k ḏd tp rꜣ n wnyw*. See *LPE*, pp. 84 (I, 4–5) and 277 (I, 1–3).

I, 3–4
šꜣ [... ...]*tyw* . All parallels (P. Leiden T 32, I, 12 = P. Vatican Inv. 38570, I, 13 = P. Vienna 3875, 22 = P. Berlin 3044, 10 = P. BM EA 10114, 11–12 = P. OIC 25389, XXVII, 5 = stela Vatican 128 A, 7) give the version *šꜣis.k ḥr wꜣt n nṯrw ꜣḫtyw*, 'You walk upon the way of the gods of the horizon', which would provide, if the parallel is exact, the precise length of the lacuna affecting the right-hand side of the papyrus. However, the nearby reference to the *Imntyw* in the clause *ir.k st.k ḫr Imntyw* invites caution. See *LPE*, pp. 94 (I, 12) and 277 (I, 3–4).

I, 4
hb.k pr ꜥnḫ irw m ḥtp. P. Louvre N 3284, 2, gives a variant on this phrase, formulated in the first person: *pḥ.i pr ꜥnḫ irw m ḥtp*, 'I reach the House of He who lives on rites, in peace'. See *LPE*, pp. 114–16 (I, 29–30).

I, 4–5
šm.k m ꜥnḫ (?) [...] *sp 2 nn ws*. Doubt remains over the transcription of the sign 𓋹, which could also be 𓎛. Cf. the words *ꜥnḫ* in *pr ꜥnḫ irw* (line 4) and *nḥḥ* (line 3). The phrase *šm.k m ꜥnḫ* is absent from the other sources for the Book of Traversing Eternity, and *šm.k m ḥꜥꜥ* occurs farther on in a passage of P. Leiden T 32 (III, 18), without parallel. See *LPE*, p. 277 (I, 4–5). The words *sp 2 nn ws* probably closed this phrase.

I, 5–6
wḏ n.k Ist wrt mwt-nṯr irt Rꜥ [... *smꜣ*]*-tꜣ.k ḫr Imntt Wꜣst*. On this passage, see P. BM EA 10091, **II, 5**, and *LPE*, pp. 278 (I, 5–7). For the provision of a burial by Isis, see P. BM EA 10260, **I, x + 1**.

25. Unlike in P. BM EA 10091, no name is written near the depiction of the deceased.

26. For the spelling for the verb *wꜣḥ*: *LPE*, p. 81 (I, 3–4); J. Yoyotte, *Biblica* 39 (1958), p. 208.

For burial on the West of Thebes, cf. P. Louvre N 3122, IV (?), 3: *ḳrst.t m-ẖnw ỉmntt Wꜣst*. On *imntt Wꜣst*, see P. BM EA 10048, **II, 10**.

I, 6–7

ỉꜣw.s [... ...]*.k ḥḏw.k* [... ... *nn t*]*mmw* [... ...]. Cf. P. BM EA 10091, II, 5: *smꜣ-tꜣ.k nfr ỉꜣw.s ẖr.k*. The first, fairly brief, lacuna, does not permit a complete restoration [*ẖr.s* (or *ẖr.s*) *ḏd.s ḥr iwf*] from the other versions, reading: 'it grows old with you, and endures over your bones and your flesh'. The available space would allow for a restoration [*ḥr iwf*] which, without following the parallels word for word, at least does not exceed the limits of the lacuna. P. BM EA 10314 and P. BM EA 10091 are the only versions of the Book of Traversing Eternity where the subject of *ỉꜣw* is *smꜣ-tꜣ*; the others place before this passage the phrase: *mn.k m wt.k*, 'you are stable in your coffin', with *wt* as subject of *ỉꜣw*. See *LPE*, pp. 255–6 (VIII, 9–10).

The lacuna after *tmmw* can be filled comfortably after the parallels, either *ir.sn st.sn r-gs.k* according to P. BM EA 10091, II, 6, or *ir.f st.f m-ḫnt.k*. See *LPE*, p. 256 (VIII, 10–11).

I, 7–II, 1

[...] (?)*Inpw* [... ...] *mi ꜥḥꜥw m tꜣ pn*. Unidentified sequence. Line 7 closes with the signs , attested as the determinatives for various words; one might suggest *ḳmꜣ* or *tnw*, but the traces a little before permit of no certain restoration. *ꜥḥꜥw*, literally 'those who are standing', might refer, despite the determinative , to the living who remain on earth (*m tꜣ pn*); cf. *Wb*. I, 221, 8.

II, 1

i(ꜣ)kb n.k Ḥꜣyty Ḏrty m ibw.sn. See *LPE*, pp. 203 (V, 13–14) and 278 (I, 7–II, 8). This lament could well have been set in the context of glorifications of the god realized by the two goddesses: Smith, *Mortuary Texts*, p. 21.

II, 1–2

wnm.k m tꜣ sꜥm.k m ḥnḳt. Despite its form, the word  must be read *sꜥm.k*. This unusual writing recurs in P. Leiden T 32, I, 8 = P. Vienna 3875, 14 = P. Berlin 3044 = P. BM EA 10114, 6. See *LPE*, pp. 88–9 (I, 7–8); 146 (III, 2), and 194 (V, 2–3).

For *m* used here with partitive sense: J.C. Goyon, *Le papyrus du Louvre N 3279* (*BdE* 42, 1966), p. 61, n. 5.

II, 2

ḫntš ib.k r-ꜥ nḥḥ. No parallel in the other sources for the Book of Traversing Eternity.

rdit(w) n.k wꜣwt r bw nb mr kꜣ.k. These ways are those of the West, of the necropolis or of the Duat. On the ka leading the deceased on the ways: C.M. Firth and B. Gunn, *Teti Pyramid Cemeteries* I (Cairo 1926), p. 122: *sšm sw kꜣw.f ḥr wꜣwt nfrwt nwt Imntt*; F. Petrie, *Deshasheh* (London 1898), pl. 28: *šms.tw.s in kꜣw.s ḥr wꜣwt nfr(w)t*; A.M. Blackman, *ZÄS* 47 (1910), p. 116: *šms.tw.s nfr in kꜣ.s r swt nfrwt*; A. Kamal, *ASAE* 11 (1911), p. 27: *šms.t(w).f in kꜣ(.f) nfr r swt nb(w)t nfr(w)t nt Imntt*, etc. See *LPE*, p. 278 (II, 2).

II, 3

pꜣy bꜣ.k r pt ḥr Rꜥ smꜣ mꜣw.f n sꜥḥ.k. For the flight of the ba to the sky and the union of the mummy with the rays of the sun, see P. BM EA 10048, **II, 7–8**.

II, 3–5

ii n.k Ḥḏ-ḥtp m Ḥwt-bit ḫr mnḫwt m rn.sn ḥḏ wꜣḏ irtyw idmi r stꜣm ḥꜥw.k nn iwms ḥtp sp 2. This entire sequence is unparalleled among the other sources for the Book of Traversing Eternity. In formulation, the first part recalls numerous passages of the *Ritual of Embalming* introduced by the formula *ii* (*iw*) *n.k* followed either by the name of a deity entrusted with bringing the deceased a particular product, or by direct mention of the product. See *LPE*, pp. 278–9 (II, 3–5).

II, 5–6

ḥtp ib.k m ḫꜣst ḏsrt. *Ḫꜣst ḏsrt*: probable equivalent of *tꜣ ḏsr*, denoting the necropolis.

II, 6

ir.k wꜥ ḫr mꜣꜥtyw. See *LPE*, p. 279 (II, 6).

II, 6–7

rn.k ḏd.ti m tꜣ pn rꜥ nb mi rwḏ rn n nṯrw nṯrwt imyw Šmꜥ Mḥw. One version of the Book of Traversing Eternity, P. Louvre N 3147, presents a very similar text in its final section (V, 3–5):

imy rwḏ rn.i m tꜣ pn	'May my name endure on this earth,
rꜥ nb nn šw	every day, without gap,
mi rwḏ rnw n Psḏt ꜥꜣt	as the names endure (of the members) of the great Ennead!
dm rn.sn	May their names be pronounced
mi rwḏ rnw n Psḏt nbt Wꜣst	as long as there endure the names of the Ennead of the lords of Thebes,
nṯrw nṯrwt nbw Šmꜥ Mḥw	of all the gods and goddesses of Upper and Lower Egypt'.

See *LPE*, p. 264 (VIII, 27).

II, 7

ꜥḥꜥ.k nḥḥ nsyt.k ḏt [...]*pw wnn.k ḏt*. On this clause, see P. BM EA 10108, **line 16**.

7. Fragments (pls 150–2)

Except for P. BM EA 10291 (= frag. 1), the twenty fragments presented here are laid out inside two frames (EA 76197), together with miscellaneous pieces belonging to different manuscripts, some of which are in demotic and apparently foreign to Books of Breathing or related texts.

Fragment 1 (= P. BM EA 10291)

12.9 × 18.3 cm. Of this papyrus only the title is known, written on the verso of a sheet: *smꜣ-tꜣ nfr wꜣḥ.s ḥr ḫt.t ḏd.s ḥr ḥr ḥꜥw.s*, 'A good burial. May it remain over your body; may it endure over its limbs'. After this text, the image of a leg is summarily drawn.[1]

Fragment 2

Upper left part of a manuscript. Part of EA 76197. 6.3 × 3.4 cm. Remains of three lines.

1 [… *ink Rꜥ m ḫꜥ*].*f ink Ỉtm m ḥtp.f*
2 [… *ḥr.tn r.i nꜣ iryw-ꜥꜣ*] *n tꜣ Ỉmntt nꜣ sꜣwtyw*
3 [… *ḥr.k n.i Ỉnpw sꜣ Wsir pꜣ iry-ꜥꜣ*] *mtr n tꜣ Dwꜣt*
= First Book of Breathing, P. BM EA 10191, I, 1–4.

Fragment 3

Upper left part of a manuscript. Part of EA 76197. 4.6 × 5.1 cm. Remains of five lines.

1 [… *N*] *ink Rꜥ m ḫꜥ.f*
2 [… *nꜣ sꜣwty*]*w n tꜣ Dwꜣt*
3 [… *ḥr.k n.i Ỉnpw sꜣ Wsir pꜣ iry-ꜥꜣ mtr n tꜣ Dw*]*ꜣt ḥr.tn r.i*
4 [… *tꜣ wsḫt Mꜣꜥty nꜣ nṯr*]*w n tꜣ wsḫt sḫwt*
5 [*iꜣrw … ḥr.tn*]*r.i nꜣ nṯrw*
= First Book of Breathing, P. BM EA 10191, I, 1–6.

Fragment 4 (two detached pieces joined together)

Upper part of a manuscript. Part of EA 76197. 6.7 × 5.0 cm. Remains of four lines.

1 […] *ḏd n.f* (?) *Pwr* … (?) *mꜣꜥ-ḫrw r-ms* […]
2 […] *nꜣ iryw-ꜥꜣ n tꜣ* […]
3 […] *ink it.tn Rꜥ-Ḥr-ꜣḫty i-pr.tn* […]
4 […] *ḥr.t r.i Ḥwt-Ḥr ḥnwt* […]
= First Book of Breathing, P. BM EA 10191, I, 2–3, 7, 5.

Fragment 5

Upper part of a manuscript. Part of EA 76197. 3.1 × 2.0 cm. Remains of one line.

[…] *m ḫꜥ.f*
= First Book of Breathing, P. BM EA 10191, I, 2.

Fragment 6 (two detached pieces joined together).

Part of EA 76197. 5.8 × 8.2 cm. Remains of four lines.

1 [… *m*]*s n Ḥwt-Ḥr* […]
2 [… *nꜣ iryw-ꜥꜣ* ?] *n* […]
3 [… *Ỉmnt*]*t nꜣ sꜣ*[*wtyw*] (?) […]
4 […] *tꜣ Dwꜣt* […]
= probably First Book of Breathing, or text adapted from this book; see P. BM EA 10191, **I, 2–3**.

1. See *supra*, pp. 2–3.

Fragment 7

Part of EA 76197. 4.8 × 5.0 cm. Remains of one line.
smꜣ-tꜣ nfr [...]
Title of one of the Books of Breathing (see *supra*, p. 3 with note 34).

Fragment 8

Part of EA 76197. 6.4 × 3.5 cm. Remains of one line.
smꜣ-tꜣ nfr [...]
Title of one of the Books of Breathing.

Fragment 9

Part of EA 76197. 4.1 × 2.0 cm. Remains of one line.
[*s*]*mꜣ-tꜣ nfr* [...]
Title of one of the Books of Breathing.

Fragment 10

Part of EA 76197. 4.3 × 7.1 cm. Beginning of the four first lines of a page.
1 *h(ꜣ)y* [...]
2 *hꜣ* [...]
3 *ḫprw* [...]
4 ... (?) [...]
Unidentified text.

Fragment 11

Part of EA 76197. 8.2 × 5.2 cm. Beginning of the three first lines of a page.
1 ... *t* (?) (end of a goddess's name)
2 *ms.n* [...]
3-*šrît-Mn*[*ṯw* ...] (end of a personal name).

Fragment 12

Part of EA 76197. 1.6 × 4.2 cm. Remains of five lines with some hieratic signs.
1 [...]*ꜣdt* [...]
2 [...]*w n mdw* [...]
3 [...] *r s*[...]
4 [...]*t s*[...]
5 [...] ... (?) *.sn m* [...]
Unidentified text.

Fragment 13

Upper part of a manuscript. Part of EA 76197. 2.8 × 6.4 cm. Remains of five lines.
1 *ỉrt Ḥr ꜥnḫ* [...]
2 *wꜥ m* [...]
3 *nỉs* [...]
4 *ỉ* [...]
5 *nb* [...]
Unidentified text.

Fragment 14

Part of EA 76197. 3.1 × 2.1 cm. Remains of three lines.
1 [...]
2 [... *nṯr*]*w dwꜣtyw* [...]
3 [...] *sḏrw* (?) *ḥr* [...]
Unidentified text.

Fragment 15

Part of EA 76197. 1.0 × 5.0 cm. Remains of six lines. This fragment is too narrow to allow a transliteration of the hieratic signs.
Unidentified text.

Fragment 16

Part of EA 76197. 1.7 × 5.2 cm. Remains of seven lines.
1 [...] *bꜣ* (?) [...]
2 [...] *Ḥr* [...]
3 [... *hꜣ*]*y* (?)
4 [...]*wt* (?)*Ỉmn*[*tt* ...]
5 [...]*p.n.t* ... [...]
6 [...*h*]*ꜣy* [...]
7 [...*ḏꜣḏꜣt* ?] *ꜥꜣt* [...]
Unidentified text.

Fragment 17

Part of EA 76197. 1.0 × 1.8 cm. Remains of two lines.
1 [...] ... (?)
2 [...] *Wꜣst*
Unidentified text.

Fragment 18

Part of EA 76197. 1.9 × 1.6 cm. Remains of two lines.

1 [...] *m* ... (?)

2 [...] *mt* (?) *m wḥm* [...]

Unidentified text, but cf. P. BM EA 10191, **I, 52**.

Fragment 19

Part of EA 76197. 3.7 × 2.1 cm. Traces on the right of the fragment, and on the left, name of Isis.

Fragment 20

Part of EA 76197. 2.0 × 3.2 cm. Remains of three first lines of a page.

1 [...] ... (?) *.sn* ... (?)

2[...] *šmꜥ* [...]

3 [...] ... (?)

Unidentified text.

Index I: General Vocabulary

Words preceded by an * asterisk are absent from *Wb.*

ꜣt — moment
P. 10110 + 10111, II, 29; **P. 10191**, I, 30; **P. 10199**, 16; **P. 10206A + B**, 5
see under *Wr ꜣt*, index III

ꜣw — length
P. 10260, I, x + 11; **P. 10275**, 16

ꜣw — offerings, oblation
see under *sfsf ꜣw*

ꜣb — desire (verb)
P. 10091, II, 6; **P. 10201**, II, 14

ꜣb — in *nn ꜣb*: without fail
P. 10718, 5

ꜣbd — (Abydenian) reliquary
P. 10108, 11

ꜣbd — month
P. 10344, 13

ꜣpdw — fowl
P. 9995, I, 13; II, 24; **P. 10048**, II, 8; IV, 10; **P. 10110 + 10111**, II, 18; **P. 10194,** 11; **P. 10206C**, 8; **P. 10260**, II, x + 7; III, x + 5

ꜣm — seize
P. 10191, I, 49; **P. 10201**, II, 7
join (verb)
P. 10201, II, 2

ꜣḥt — field
P. 10124 vs.

ꜣḫ — be transfigured, blessed
P. 10108, 2; **P. 10110 + 10111**, II, 12, 27; **P. 10112**, 3; **P. 10114**, 2; **P. 10256**, 6; **P. 10304**, 44

ꜣḫ — spirit
P. 9995, III, 15; **P. 10048**, VII, 4; **P. 10091**, II, 6; **P. 10108**, 2; **P. 10112**, 4; **P. 10123**, 7; **P. 10191**, II, 1; **P. 10260**, III, x + 13

ꜣḫꜣḫ — bones
P. 10201, II, 2

ꜣḫty — eyes
P. 10201, I, 7

ꜣḫt — akhet (first season)
P. 10344, 13

ꜣḫt — horizon
P. 9995, I, 9; **P. 10048**, I, 2; II, 2, 4; **P. 10191**, I, 43; II, 2; **P. 10264**, II, 4

ꜣḫty — he of the horizon
see under *Rʿ-Ḥr-ꜣḫty, Ḥr-ꜣḫty*, index III
in the plural *ꜣḫtyw*: gods of the horizon
P. 10114, 12; **P. 10314**, I, [4]; **P. 10115, 7** (?)

ỉ — O
P. 9995, III, 1, 2, 3, 5, 6, 8, 9, 11; **P. 10048**, V, 1–10; VI, 1–10; VII, 1; **P. 10109**, 10; **P. 10110 + 10111**, I, 2, 3, 4; II, 13, 14, 15; **P. 10116**, 2, 3; **P. 10125**, 15, 22; **P. 10191**, I, 15, 17, 19, 20, 22, 24, 25, 27, 31, 53; II, 7, 12, 14; **P. 10194**, 5; **P. 10199**, 11, 15, 16, 26, 27, 28, 29; **P. 10206A + B**, 2, 4; **P. 10254**, 1; **P. 10260**, III, x + 6, 7, 8, 9, 10; **P. 10275**, 1; **P. 10282**, 2; **P. 10283**, 7, 8, 9; **P. 10285**, 3, 4; **P. 10303**, 9; **P. 10304**, 2, 3, 45, 46, 47; **P. 10340**, 2; **P. 10344**, 10; **P. 71513A**, 19, 21, 23; **P. 71513D**, x + 1, 2, 3

ỉ — prothetic particle
before relative form
P. 10191, I, 33; **P. 10338**, x + 2; **P. 71513A**, [8] (?)
before imperative
P. 10338, x + 5; **P. 10191**, I, 32, 36

ỉt — father
P. 10048, I, 2; **P. 10108**, 14, 16; **P. 10110 + 10111**, II, 24; **P. 10123**, 9; **P. 10124**, 1; **P. 10191**, I, 7, 8, 22, 29, 31, 50, 51, 53; **P. 10194**, 2, 4, 5; **P. 10199**, 16; **P. 10254**, 5; **P. 10260**, I, x + 8; **P. 10283**, 4; **P. 10337**, 6, 8; **P. 10338**, x + 1; **P. 10705**, 6; **P. 71513A**, 7, 9; **P. 71513B**, 4, [5]; **frag. 4**, 3
see under *Ḥr-nḏ-ỉt.f*, index III

ỉꜣw — adoration
P. 10108, 14; **P. 10110 + 10111**, II, 5; **P. 10304**, 39

ỉꜣw — in *ỉꜣw.tw*: hail
P. 10290, x + 5

ỉꜣw — grow old
P. 10091, II, 5; **P. 10314**, I, 6

ỉꜣwt — old age
P. 10191, II, 16

ỉꜣbtt — East
P. 10110 + 10111, II, 4; **P. 10191**, II, 19; **P. 10282**, 3; **P. 10283**, 8; **P. 10304**, 38

ỉꜣrw — reeds
see under *wsḫt sḫt ỉꜣrw*, index II

i͗(ꜣ)kb — mourn
P. 10091, II, 4 (+ *n*); **P. 10191**, I, 23 (+ *ḥr*); **P. 10314**, II, 1 (+ *n*)

i͗ꜣt — mound
see under *I͗ꜣt Ḏꜣm*, index II

i͗(ꜣ)dt — dew
P. 10201, II, 4

i͗i͗ — go, come
P. 9995, I, 13, 15; II, 3, 4; III, 12; **P. 10091**, II, 2; **P. 10115**, 9 (+ *ḫr*); **P. 10123**, 3; **P. 10201**, II, 14; **P. 10254**, 4, 5; **P. 10260**, III, x + 11 (+ *ḫr*); **P. 10314**, II, 3–4; **P. 10344**, 3

i͗i͗t — see under *pr i͗i͗t*, index II

i͗ꜥb — unite
P. 9995, IV, 1

i͗ꜥr (?) — approach (+ *ḥr*)
P. 10201, II, 12

i͗ꜥrꜥt — uraeus
P. 10191, I, 48

i͗w — auxiliary
+ suffix
P. 9995, I, 1, 5, 8, 17; II, 2, 9, 10, 13, 17; III, 17, 18; **P. 10048**, I, 5, 9; II, 3, 5; III, 2, 8; IV, 1, 5; VII, 4; **P. 10091**, I, 7; **P. 10110 + 10111**, II, 1, 2, 4, 10; vs. (dem.); **P. 10115**, 10; **P. 10123**, 6, 10; **P. 10191**, I, 8, 13, 15, 39; **P. 10199**, 11; **P. 10260**, I, x + 5, 15; II, x + 3, 5; III, x + 2, 14; **P. 10275**, 18; **P. 10290**, x + 5, 8; **P. 10303**, 9; **P. 10304**, 36, 37, 39, 43; **P. 10337**, 8; **P. 10338**, x + 8; **P. 10340**, 9; **P. 10718**, 12; **P. 71513A**, 9, [16]; **P. 71513B**, 5
+ substantive
P. 9995, I, 20; **P. 10048**, III, 3; **P. 10110 + 10111**, II, 2; **P. 10191**, I, 45, 46, 47, 48, 49; **P. 10123**, 6; **P. 10260**, II, x + 13; **P. 10338**, x + 14, 15, 16, 17; **P. 10340**, 8 (?); **P. 10718**, 1, 6, 7
+ *sḏm.f*
P. 9995, III, 22; **P. 10048**, VII, 7; **P. 10109**, 13; **P. 10283**, 4; **P. 10337**, 6; **P. 10110 + 10111**, II, 31; **P. 10191**, I, 36, 41; II, 28; **P. 10199**, 22; **P. 10201**, II, 10
+ *sḏm.n.f*
P. 10338, x + 5; **P. 10125**, 21
+ infinitive
P. 10201, II, 8
+ *nn*
P. 10048, VII, 2

i͗w — go, come
P. 10048, II, 9; III, 1, 5, 8, 9; VII, 2; **P. 10260**, I, x + 1; II, x + 9, 15

i͗wty — negative adjective
in *i͗wty wḥm.tify*: without equal
P. 10201, I, 3

i͗wi͗w — mourn (+ *m-ḫt*)
P. 10108, 3

i͗wꜥ — inheritance
P. 10191, I, 22

i͗wꜥ — heir
P. 10110 + 10111, I, 3; **P. 10114**, 3; **P. 10116**, 2; **P. 10191**, I, 51; **P. 10262 + 10263**, 3; **P. 10283**, 9; **P. 10304**, 2; **P. 71513D**, x + 3

i͗wf — flesh
P. 10091, II, 2; **P. 10108** vs.; **P. 10112** vs.; **P. 10115** [vs.]; **P. 10116** vs.; **P. 10123** vs.; **P. 10191**, I, 48; **P. 10201**, II, 2; **P. 10260**, II, x + 8; **P. 10283** vs.; **P. 10337** vs; **P. 10338**, x + 17; **P. 10344**, 2; **P. 10718**, 3, 4

i͗wms — soiling (?)
in *nn i͗wms*
P. 10314, II, 5

I͗wntyw — *I͗wntyw*-women
P. 10108, 9

i͗wr — conceive
P. 10191, II, 27

i͗b — heart
P. 9995, I, 16, 17; II, 8, 17; **P. 10048**, III, 2, 11; IV, 5; VII, 5; **P. 10110 + 10111**, II, 7, 25; **P. 10114**, 8; **P. 10123**, 6; **P. 10124**, 8; **P. 10264A**, x + 4; **P. 10191**, I, 30, 34, 35, 38, 39, 40, 41; II, 15, 28; **P. 10194**, 9; **P. 10199**, 16, 17, 22; **P. 10201**, II, 13, 14, 17; **P. 10260**, II, x + 11; III, x + 2; **P. 10264A**, x + 4; **P. 10275**, 4; **P. 10304**, 41; **P. P. 10314**, II, 1, 2, 5; **P. 10338**, x + 4, 8, 9, 11; **P. 10718**, 7
r dit i͗b + suffix
as the heart desires
P. 9995, III, 21; **P. 10048**, VII, 6; **P. 10114**, 10; **P. 10191**, II, 22; **P. 10206C**, 2; **P. 10260**, III, x + 16
r-ḏr i͗b + suffix
P. 10091, I, 7
see under *pr i͗bw*, index II

i͗b — bight (?)
P. 10115, 6

i͗b — be thirsty
P. 9995, III, 14; **P. 10048**, VII, 3; **P. 10260**, III, x + 12

i͗bḥt — tooth
P. 10191, I, 46; **P. 10338**, x + 15

i͗bṯt — trap
P. 10115, 7

I͗pt — see under *I͗mn-I͗pt*, index III

i͗pw — demonstrative adjective
P. 10191, II, 23

i͗ptn — demonstrative adjective
P. 10201, I, 12

i͗m — therewith
P. 10191, II, 21

i͗mi͗m — pine (for: *m-ḫt*)
P. 10112, 6

i͗mꜣḫ — honour
P. 10191, II, 14

i͗mꜣḫw — praised ones
P. 9995, II, 15

i͗my (= *mi*) — proclitic particle
P. 10194, 7

i͗my — who (which) is in
P. 9995, II, 19; III, 11; IV, 2; **P. 10048**, IV, 8; VII, 2; **P. 10108**, 8, 9; **P. 10109**, 5, 10, 11, 12, 13; **P. 10110 + 10111**, II, 5, 30; **P. 10112**, 16; **P. 10114**, 8, 13; **P. 10115**, 13; **P. 10123**, 1, 2; **P. 10125**, 7, 16, 17, 18, 19, 20; **P. 10191**, I, 5, 16, 18, 19, 21, 23, 25, 26, 27, 28; II, 11; **P. 10199**, 6, 13, 14; **P. 10201**, I, 2; II, 1, 3, 4, 11, 15, 17; **P. 10254**, 6; **P. 10260**, I, x + 11; III, x + 3, 10; **P. 10282**, 2–3 (written ; **P. 10283**, 7–8, 8; **P. 10290**, x + 4; **P. 10304**, 39; **P. 10314**, II, 7; **P. 10337**, 4; **P. 10343**, 12, 13, 14; **P. 71513A**, 5, 20, 22; **P. 71513B**, 3; **P. 71513C**, 5, 6
inverse meaning (in which is/are)
P. 10201, II, 2

imy — writing of *m*
P. 10343, 11

imy-wrt — West
P. 10191, I, 33

imy-ḫt — in the retinue of
P. 9995, II, 18
in the plural (*imyw-ḫt*)
P. 10048, IV, 6; **P. 10109**, 4–5; **P. 10125**, 6; **P. 10191**, I, 4; **P. 10199**, 5–6; **P. 10283**, 9; **P. 10337**, 4; **P. 71513A**, 4–[5]; **P. 71513C**, [4]
written *imyw-ḫr*
P. 10254, 3

imyw-ḫt — organs
see under *ḫt*

imytw — between
P. 10256, 7

imn — be hidden
P. 10110 + 10111, II, 29; **P. 10256**, 2
see under *ꜥt imnt*

Imntyw — Westerners
P. 9995, III, 21; **P. 10048**, VII, 6; **P. 10114**, 12; **P. 10260**, III, x + 16; **P. 10264A**, x + 4; **P. 71513A**, 6

Imntt — West
P. 9977, 1; **P. 9995**, II, 2, 20, 23; **P. 10048**, II, 10; III, 8; IV, 7, 10; **P. 10091**, I, 5; **P. 10108**, 4, 5; **P. 10109**, 2, 4, 6, 7; **P. 10112**, 8, 9; **P. 10115**, 2; **P. 10116**, 29; **P. 10123**, 1, 11; **P. 10125**, 3, 4, 5; **P. 10191**, I, 2, 3, 6, 14, 34, 50; II, 18; **P. 10194** , 3, 6; vs.; **P. 10199**, [2], 6, 7; **P. 10254**, 2; **P. 10256**, 1, 8; vs.; **P. 10260**, I, x + 4, 13; III, x + 3, 5; **P. 10264A**, x + 2; **P. 10275**, 1; **P. 10282**, 3, 21, 22; vs.; **P. 10283**, 5, 6, 8; **P. 10285** vs.; **P. 10290**, x + 3; **P. 10303**, 3, 5; **P. 10337**, 2, 5; **P. 10338**, x + 3; **P. 10340**, 2; **P. 10343**, [2], 4; **P. 10718**, 9; **P. 71513A**, 2, 3, 6; **P. 71513B**, [1], [2], [4]; **P. 71513C**, 2, 3; **frag. 2**, 2; **frag. 6**, [3]
see under *Imntt*, *Wsir*, *Ḫnty Imntt*, index III

imntt — *imntt*-necropolis
P. 10256, 3

in — by
P. 9995, II, 18, 19; **P. 10091**, II, 4; **P. 10110 + 10111**, II, 6; **P. 10115**, 4; **P. 10191**, I, 40; **P. 10201**, II, 1, 5, 8, 11, 16, 17; **P. 10260**, III, x + 3; **P. 10304**, 40; **P. 10338**, x + 9
in *wn in … ḥr*: see under *wn*

int — valley
P. 10108, 14
see under *ḥb int*

in — bring
P. 10115, 10; **P. 10116**, 20

inw — tribute, products
P. 10110 + 10111, II, 31

inr — stone
in *inr n Mꜣꜥt*: stone of Maat
P. 9995, I, 6; **P. 10048**, I, 9

ink — first person singular independent pronoun
P. 10109, 1, 2, 14; **P. 10110 + 10111**, I, 2, 3; II, 3, 14, 19, 20; **P. 10115**, 2, 5; **P. 10116**, 2; **P. 10123**, 6; **P. 10125**, 2, [3], 12, 13; **P. 10191**, I, 1, 2, 7, 8, 9, 10, 31, 33, 38, 39, 40, 50, 51, 52, 53; II, 1, 5, 6, 8, 11, 12, 13, 14, 15, 18, 19, 20, 22, 23, 24, 25, 27, 33; **P. 10194**, 4; **P. 10199**, 2; **P. 10206A + B**, 8; **C**, 3, 4, 6; **P. 10256**, 1; **P. 10283**, 1, 2, 3, 4, 7, 9; **P. 10303**, 2, 3; **P. 10304**, 2, 45, 47, 48; **P. 10337**, 1, 2, 6, 7, 8; **P. 10338**, x + 2, 9; **P. 10340**, 8; **P. 10343**, [2], 4, 5; **P. 71513A**, 2, 7, 8, 9, 10, 11; **P. 71513B**, 1, 4, 5; **P. 71513C**, 2, [7]; **P. 71513D**, x + 1, 2, 3; **frag. 2**, 1; **frag. 3**, 1; **frag. 4**, 3
see under *nnk*

inḏ — see under *nḏ*

ir — give, grant
P. 9995, I, 7, 12, 15, 20, 21; II, 8, 22; III, 1, 2, 4, 5, 7, 8, 10, 12, 14, 15, 20; **P. 10048**, II, 2, 8, 10; III, 4, 5, 11; IV, 9; V, 1–10; VI, 1–10; VII, 1, 3, 4, 5, 6; **P. 10091**, I, 6; II, 6; **P. 10108**, 4, 11; **P. 10109**, 3, 8; **P. 10110 + 10111**, II, 23, 31; **P. 10112**, 7; **P. 10114**, 9; **P. 10115**, 13; **P. 10116**, 24; **P. 10123**, 1, 8; **P. 10124**, 7; **P. 10125**, 13; **P. 10191**, I, 8, 9, 25, 30, 32, 34, 36, 37, 39, 40, 41, 44; **P. 10194**, 8; **P. 10199**, 17, 21; **P. 10260**, II, x + 2, 7, 9, 13, 15; III, x + 4, 6, 7, 8, 9, 10, 11, 12, 13, 14, 15; **P. 10264A**, x + 8, 9; **P. 10290**, x + 2; **P. 10340**, 8; **P. 71513A**, [11]
do (a writing) = write, recite
P. 10048, I, 1
in *ir.n* + name of woman: born of
P. 10091, I, 2; **P. 10314**, I, 1
in *ir wꜥ*
P. 10125, 9; **P. 10191**, I, 37; **P. 10199**, 20; **P. 10314**, II, 6; **P. 10343**, 5; **P. 10718**, 10
in *ir rdi*
P. 10194, 4, 5; **P. 10337**, 7
in *ir ḫpr(w)*: assume the form(s)
P. 10048, III, 4; VII, 6
in *ir st*: take seat
P. 10114, 12
in *ir šršr*: receive the freshness (?)
see under *šršr*
cause (verb)
P. 10091, I, 4, 31; **P. 10206A + B**, 6; **P. 10337**, 8; **P. 71513A**, 9, 10; **P. 71513B**, [6]

iry-ꜥꜣ — doorkeeper
P. 10109, 3, 8; **P. 10115**, 3; **P. 10123**, 1, 4; **P. 10125**, 3–[4], 8; **P. 10191**, I, 2, 3, 4; **P. 10194**, 5; **P. 10199**, 4; **P. 10283**, 3; **P. 10303**, 4; **P. 10337**, 2 (?); **P. 10340**, 2; **P. 10343**, 4; **P. 10344**, 10; **P. 71513A**, 3, 4; **P. 71513B**, 2; **frag. 2**, [2, 3]; **frag. 3**, [3]; **frag. 4**, 2; **frag. 6**, [2]

ir(y)w — whole (adverbial use)
P. 10191, II, 30; **P. 10199**, 23
enclitic particle
P. 10191, II, 19

irw — form, appearance
P. 9995, I, 14; **P. 10048**, II, 9; IV, 2; **P. 10115**, 7; **P. 10191**, I, 26; **P. 10260**, II, x + 8.

irw — rite, ceremony
P. 10108, 11
see under *ꜥnḫ irw*, index III; *pr ꜥnḫ irw*, index II

irp — wine
P. 9995, II, 24; **P. 10048**, IV, 10; **P. 10191**, II, 32; **P. 10199**, 25; **P. 10206C**, 10; **P. 10260**, III, x + 5; **P. 10290**, x + 6; **P. 10343**, 11

irm — with
P. 9995, I, 8, 18; **P. 10048**, II, 3; III, 3; **P. 10110 + 10111** vs.; **P. 10260**, II, x + 4, 12

irt — eye
P. 10048, III, 6; V, 10; **P. 10191**, I, 41; II, 30, 31; **P. 10260**, II, x + 13, 16; III, x + 2
see under *ꜥm irt*, index III
dual *irty*
P. 9995, I, 19, 24; II, 17–18; **P. 10048**, III, 3; IV, 5; **P. 10091**, I, 5; **P. 10338**, x + 14

see under *mdsw-irty*, and *Irt(y).f-m-ḫt*, *ꜥm-irt*, index III

irt Ḥr Eye of Horus
P. 10191, I, 47; **P. 10338**, x + 17; **P. 10343**, 11; **frag. 13**, 1

irtyw *irtyw*-cloth
P. 10314, II, 4

irṯt milk
P. 9995, II, 24; **P. 10048**, IV, 10; **P. 10110 + 10111**, II, 17; **P. 10116**, 20; **P. 10191**, II, 32; **P. 10199**, 25; **P. 10260**, III, x + 5; **P. 10290**, x + 6; **P. 10304**, 48; **P. 10343**, 11

iḥw oxen
in *iḥw ꜣpdw*: oxen and fowl
P. 10115, 3

is tomb
P. 10112, 11

is in *is (n) niw*: breath of air
P. 10091, II, 2–3; **P. 10108**, 13; **P. 10112**, 21; **P. 10114**, 5; **P. 10201**, II, 8, 10; **P. 10262 + 10263**, 6

iswy reward
P. 10112, 7

isft evil, iniquity, impurity
P. 9995, I, 2; III, 2, 9, 12; **P. 10048**, I, 6; V, 1, 6; VII, 2; **P. 10091**, II, 1; **P. 10115**, 12; **P. 10201**, I, 9; II, 8; **P. 10260**, I, x + 8; III, x + 7, 10, 11; **P. 10718**, 7

ist crew
P. 10108, 6; **P. 10109**, 9; **P. 10110 + 10111**, II, 6; **P. 10304**, 40

išd balanites-tree
P. 9995, I, 21; **P. 10048**, III, 4; **P. 10191**, I, 40; **P. 10260**, II, x + 14; **P. 10338**, x + 10

iḳr excellent
P. 10108, 6; **P. 10112**, 8, 13; **P. 10125**, 10; **P. 10201**, I, 16; II, 2
in *bꜣw iḳrw*: excellent bas
P. 10194, 7; **P. 10201**, II, 13
in *sꜥḥw iḳrw*: excellent mummies
P. 10201, II, 1

iḳrw the excellent ones
P. 9995, III, 18; **P. 10048**, VII, 5; **P. 10109**, 9; **P. 10260**, I, x + 5; III, x + 14

igrt necropolis
P. 10108, 7; **P. 10112**, 15; **P. 10125**, 11; **P. 10201**, II, 3

itn disk (solar or lunar)
P. 9995, I, 23; **P. 10048**, I, 2; III, 6; **P. 10091**, II, 2; **P. 10114**, 4; **P. 10260**, II, x + 16

iṯ take, receive
P. 9995, II, 21; III, 6; **P. 10048**, V, 4, 9; **P. 10110 + 10111**, II, 30; **P. 10112** vs.; **P. 10116**, 20; **P. 10125** vs.; **P. 10191**, I, 40; **P. 10199**, 26, 29; **P. 10201**, I, 12; II, 3, 8, 9; **P. 10260**, III, x + 8, 14; **P. 10338**, x + 9; **P. 10344**, 2

idmi *idmi*-cloth
P. 10314, II, 4–5

ꜥ arm
P. 10114, 11
see under *m-ꜥ*
dual *ꜥwy*
P. 9995, IV, 1, 2; **P. 10091**, I, 7; **P. 10108**, 5, 14; vs.; **P. 10109** [vs.]; **P. 10110 + 10111**, II, 13, 18, 22; **P. 10112**, 9; vs.; **P. 10115** [vs.]; **P. 10125** vs.; **P. 10191**, I, 29, 35, 46, 49; II, 29; **P. 10199**, 15, 18, 23, 28; **P. 10201**, II, 1, 12, 13; **P. 10206C**, 7; **P. 10260**, I, x + 3; **P. 10338**, x + 5, 16, 17; **P. 10304**, 45, 48
in *rꜣ ꜥwy*: activity
P. 10110 + 10111, II, 22

ꜥt limb
P. 9995, I, 2; **P. 10048**, I, 6; II, 4; **P. 10091**, I, 6; **P. 10114**, 9; **P. 10191**, I, 48; II, 30; **P. 10199**, 23; **P. 10201**, II, 2; **P. 10256**, 4

ꜥwt-nṯr divine body
P. 10194, 5

ꜥt in *ꜥt imnt*: underworld
P. 10201, II, 1

ꜥꜣ be great
P. 10116, 23; **P. 10304**, 43

ꜥꜣ great
P. 9977, 1 (?), 10; **P. 9995**, I, 7, 15, 16, 17; II, 6, 13, 15, 17, 23; IV, 1; **P. 10048**, II, 2; III, 1, 2, 10, 11; IV, 10; VI, 5; VII, 5; **P. 10108**, 4; **P. 10109**, 10, 11, 13; **P. 10110 + 10111**, I, 4; II, 1; **P. 10115**, 2, 9, 10; **P. 10116**, 2, 33; **P. 10123**, 3; **P. 10124**, 9, 12, 13, 14; **P. 10125**, 16, 17, 18, 19, 20; **P. 10191**, I, 16, 18, 19, 21, 23, 24, 26, 27, 28, 51; II, 9, 33; **P. 10194**, 3, 13; **P. 10201**, II, 1, 3, 6, 10; **P. 10206A + B**, 5; **P. 10260**, I, x + 13; II, x + 2, 10, 12; III, x + 5; **P. 10303**, 3; **P. 10304**, 3, 36; **P. 10343**, [3], 4, 6, 14; **P. 10344**, 2, 8; **P. 71513A**, 7, 20; **P. 71513B**, 4; **P. 71513D**, [x + 4]; **frag. 16**, 7
in *wr ꜥꜣ ꜥꜣ*: Trismegistus
P. 10282, 19

ꜥꜣ greatness
P. 10110 + 10111, II, 23

ꜥꜣ door
dual *ꜥꜣwy*
P. 10191, I, 36; **P. 10338**, x + 5

ꜥwꜣy theft
P. 9995, III, 3; **P. 10048**, V, 2; **P. 10260**, III, x + 7

ꜥwt-nṯr divine herd
P. 10048, VI, 3

ꜥb (be) pure
P. 9995, I, 1–2; **P. 10091**, II, 1; **P. 10191**, II, 10

ꜥb offer
P. 10343, 11

ꜥb see under *m-ꜥb*

ꜥpy fly (?)
P. 10264A, x + 7

ꜥpr be equipped
P. 10048, IV, 2; **P. 10191**, II, 1

ꜥm recognize
in *ꜥm ꜥḳw (ꜥḳy)*: recognize the evil (?)
P. 10108, 8; **P. 10110 + 10111**, II, 28; **P. 10112**, 16

ꜥmḏ repel
in *ꜥmḏ sbiw*: repel the enemies
P. 10191, I, 9; **P. 10283**, 5 (written ); **P. 71513A**, 10; **P. 71513B**, 6

ꜥn return
P. 10201, I, 11

ꜥnḫ live
P. 9995, I, 12; II, 15, 6, 12, 13, 16, 19, 21, 25; III, 13, 18, 22; IV, 2; **P. 10048**, II, 7; III, 3, 9, 10; IV, 3, 6, 8, 11; VII, 3, 5, 7; **P. 10091**, II, 2; **P. 10108**, 1, 9, 15; **P. 10110 + 10111**, II, 21; **P. 10112**, 2, 22; **P. 10114**, 1, 2, 7, 16; **P. 10115**, 5, 11; **P. 10116**, 22; **P. 10191**, I, 48; II, 9, 13, 20, 21, 31; **P. 10194**, 14; **P. 10199**, 24; **P. 10260**, II, x + 6; III, x + 4, 6, 11, 14, 16; **P. 10261**, x + 2; **P. 10282**, 28; **P. 10283**, 10; **P. 10285**, 3; **P. 10290**, x + 8; **P. 10304**, 50;

P. 10343, 8, 11, 14; **P. 10344**, 3, 4, 8, 14
see under *Fnḏ.f-ꜥnḫ*, index III

ꜥnḫ life
P. 9995, I, 17, 19, 22; II, 10; **P. 10048**, III, 5; IV, 3; **P. 10110 + 10111**, II, 20; **P. 10114**, 5; **P. 10191**, I, 44, 48; II, 5; **P. 10260**, II, x + 15; **P. 10264**, 1; **P. 10304**, 49; **P. 10314**, I, 4; **P. 10338**, x + 17; **P. 10344**, 8 (?)
in *ꜥnḫ wḏꜣ snb*: life, prosperity and health
P. 9995, II, 9; **P. 10048**, IV, 1

ꜥnḫw the living
P. 10114, 3, 6; **P. 10116**, 23; **P. 10260**, II, x + 11

ꜥnḫwy ears
P. 9995, I, 19; **P. 10048**, III, 3; **P. 10091**, I, 6; **P. 10114**, 7; **P. 10191**, I, 45; II, 5; **P. 10260**, II, x + 13

ꜥnḏ uncertain meaning
P. 10201, I, 5

ꜥḥꜣ fighter
P. 10191, I, 40; **P. 10338**, x + 9
see *Dr ꜥḥꜣ*, index III

ꜥḥꜣ-ꜥ battle
P. 10125, 18; **P. 10191**, I, 16–17; **P. 10199**, 13; **P. 10705**, 1; **P. 71513A**, 20

ꜥḥꜥ lifetime
P. 10108, 16; **P. 10112**, 23; **P. 10264**, 1; **P. 10314**, II, 7

ꜥḥꜥ stand, stand up
P. 9995, III, 13; **P. 10048**, VII, 2; **P. 10108**, 5, 14; **P. 10112**, 10; **P. 10191**, II, 7, 32; **P. 10260**, III, x + 11
in the expression *ꜥḥꜥ … ḥms*: stand up and sit down
P. 10191, II, 22; **P. 10199**, 25

ꜥḥꜥw gods who stand
P. 10314, II, 1

ꜥḫ rise
in *ꜥḫ pt*: rise the sky
P. 10191, II, 25
see under *(ḥb) ꜥḫ pt*

ꜥḫ fly
P. 10114, 10

ꜥḫm quench
P. 10191, I, 31; **P. 10206A + B**, 6

ꜥḫm waters ?
P. 10108, 7

ꜥš invoke, appeal
P. 10123, 4

ꜥš harm
P. 9995, III, 5; **P. 10048**, V, 3; **P. 10260**, III, x + 8

ꜥšꜣ numerous
P. 10110 + 10111, II, [10]; **P. 10304**, 43

ꜥḳ go, enter
P. 9995, I, 5, 6, 9; II, 14, 17; III, 16; IV, 1; **P. 10048**, I, 9; II, 1, 4; IV, 4; VII, 4; **P. 10108**, 13; **P. 10109**, 6, 8; **P. 10110 + 10111**, II, 4, 6, 9; **P. 10112**, 19; **P. 10114**, 14; **P. 10124**, 7, 8; vs.; **P. 10125**, 9; **P. 10191**, I, 13, 14; **P. 10192** vs.; **P. 10194**, 6; vs.; **P. 10199**, 10; **P. 10201**, I, 2; II, 4, 9; **P. 10254**, 5; **P. 10260**, I, x + 4, 10; II, x + 2; III, x + 13; **P. 10304**, 38, 40, 42; **P. 10344**, 4, 5; **P. 10718**, 1
in *ꜥḳ … pr, pr … ꜥḳ*: come and go
P. 10109, 4, 7; **P. 10125**, 4–5; **P. 10191**, I, 15; **P. 10194**, 12; **P. 10201**, II, 8; **P. 10303**, 7–8; **P. 71513A**, 18
in *ꜥḳ … šm, šm … ꜥḳ*: come and go
P. 10124, 1; **P. 10254**, 7

ꜥḳy (ꜥḳw) evil
see under *ꜥm*

w third person plural suffix pronoun
P. 9995, I, 9, 10, 24; II, 4; **P. 10048**, II, 4, 5; III, 6; **P. 10108**, 11, [12]; **P. 10109**, 3, 6, 9, 14; **P. 10110 + 10111**, II, 5, 7; **P. 10123**, 5, 7; **P. 10125**, 6, 12, 13, 28; **P. 10191**, I, 6, 9, 12; **P. 10199**, 7, 9, 29; **P. 10260**, I, x + 14; II, x + 4, 5, 16; **P. 10275**, 18; **P. 10283**, 6; **P. 10290**, x + 5; **P. 10304**, 40: **P. 10337**, 6; **P. 71513A**, 7, 10; **P. 71513B**, [4 ?], [6 ?]; **P. 71513C**, 6

wꜣ be far (from: *r*)
P. 10191, I, 38, 39; **P. 10338**, x + 8

wꜣ plot (+ *m*)
P. 10048, III, 11; **P. 10338**, x + 8

wꜣw those who plot
P. 9995, II, 7

wꜣt way, road
P. 9995, I, 19; **P. 10048**, III, 3; **P. 10114**, 12, 14; **P. 10123**, 6; **P. 10124**, 8; **P. 10191**, I, 25; **P. 10201**, II, 13; **P. 10260**, I, x + 7; II, x + 12; **P. 10314**, II, 2; **P. 10718**, 11
see under *Wp-wꜣwt*, index III

wꜣḥ remain, be firm
P. 10108 vs.; **P. 10112**, 5; vs.; **P. 10114**, 2; vs.; **P. 10115** [vs.]; **P. 10116** vs.; **P. 10123** vs.; **P. 10262 + 10263**, 2; **P. 10283** vs.; **P. 10314**, I, 2; **P. 10340**, 4; **P. 71513C** vs.; **frag. 1**.

wꜣḥ lay down, pour out
in *wꜣḥ ḫwt*: lay down the offerings
P. 10108, 16; **P. 10123**, 3
in *wꜣḥ pꜥt*: lay down the *pꜥt* offerings
P. 10340, 7
in *wꜣḥ mw*: pour out water
P. 10285, 2, 5; **P. 10340**, 3
in *wꜣḥ ḥtpw* (?): lay down the *ḥtpw*-offerings (?)
P. 10264, 8

wꜣs be powerful
P. 10290, x + 8

wꜣg *wꜣg*-festival
P. 9995, II, 14

wꜣḏ be efficacious
P. 10114, 6; **P. 10262 + 10263**, 7

wꜣḏ malachite
P. 10110 + 10111, II, 3; **P. 10304**, 37

wꜣḏ(t) *wꜣḏ(t)*-cloth
P. 10260, I, x + 2; **P. 10314**, II, 4

wiꜣ bark
P. 10110 + 10111, II, 5; **P. 10123**, 4; **P. 10191**, I, 44; II, 7, 26; **P. 10304**, 39

wꜥ be one (of: *m*)
P. 10108, 6; **P. 10112**, 13; **frag. 13**, 2

wꜥ one
P. 10091, I, 5; **P. 10191**, I, 13, 15, 37; **P. 10199**, 11, 20; **P. 10260**, I, x + 15; **P. 10283**, 7; **P. 10303**, 9; **P. 10343**, 5; **P. 10718**, 10; **P. 71513A**, 16
in the expression *ir wꜥ*: be one (of: *m, n-m, ḫr*)
P. 10109, 8; **P. 10125**, 9; **P. 10314**, II, 6; **P. 10338**, x + 6

wꜥ blaspheme (against: *ḫr*)
P. 10048, VI, 8, 9

wꜥb (be) pure (from: *r*)
P. 9995, I, 1, 2, 5; IV, 1; **P. 10048**, I, 5, 6, 9; IV, 11; **P. 10123**, 5; **P. 10191**, II, 10; **P. 10201**, I, 4; **P. 10718**, 6

wꜥb purification
P. 9995, I, 7; **P. 10048**, II, 2; **P. 10260**, II, x + 2

wʿbt embalming house
P. 10108, 11

wʿr walk quickly
P. 10201, II, 2

wʿrt leg
P. 10201, II, 2

ww region
see under *ww Mꜣʿt, wsḫt ww Mꜣʿt*, index II

wbꜣ open
P. 10114, 7; **P. 10191**, I, 53

wbn shine
P. 9995, II, 11; **P. 10048**, IV, 3

wp open
P. 9995, I, 19; **P. 10048**, III, 3; **P. 10110 + 10111**, II, 29; **P. 10114**, 6; **P. 10191**, I, 32, 33; **P. 10199**, 17; **P. 10201**, I, 11; **P. 10260**, II, x + 12; **P. 10338**, x + 2
separate (from: *r*)
P. 10191, II, 9

wpwt crowd
P. 10108, 9

wpwty messenger
P. 10114, 13

wn be, exist
P. 9995, II, 17; **P. 10048**, IV, 5; **P. 10091**, I, 4, 7; **P. 10114**, 8; **P. 10115**, 7, 10; **P. 10123**, 6; **P. 10191**, 53; **P. 10201**, II, 11; **P. 10256**, 5; **P. 10260**, III, x + 2, 16; **P. 10264A**, x + 6, 9; **P. 10314**, II, 7
in the construction *wn in … ḥr*
P. 10201, II, 12, 13

wnyw men, people (lit.: those who exist)
P. 10114, 3; **P. 10262 + 10263**, 4; **P. 10314**, I, 3

wn open
P. 9995, II, 18, 20; **P. 10048**, IV, 5; **P. 10114**, 7; **P. 10191**, I, 32, 36; II, 28; **P. 10199**, 17, 19, 22; **P. 10206A + B**, 7; **P. 10260**, III, x + 3; **P. 10338**, x + 1, 2, 6

wn(y)ny light
P. 10191, I, 41; **P. 10338**, x + 10

wnwt hour
P. 9995, I, 4; **P. 10191**, I, 11; **P. 10199**, 8; **P. 71513A**, [12]; **P. 71513B**, [8]

wnm eat
P. 9995, I, 14; **P. 10048**, II, 9; **P. 10091**, II, 1; **P. 10260**, II, x + 8; **P. 10314**, II, 1

wnšnš hasten
P. 10108, 7; **P. 10201**, II, 10

wnḏw flock
P. 10091, II, 4

wr be great
P. 10048, IV, 2

wr great, old, abundant
P. 9995, I, 7; II, 3, 14; IV, 2; **P. 10048**, II, 2; III, 8; **P. 10108**, 12, 13, 14; **P. 10109**, 9; **P. 10110 + 10111**, II, 3, 24; **P. 10112**, 22, 23; **P. 10116**, 24; **P. 10123** vs.; **P. 10191**, I, 11, 12, 39, 50, 51; II, 8, 14, 15, 19, 21, 22, 23; **P. 10194**, 13; **P. 10199**, 8, 10; **P. 10201**, I, 2, 3; II, 1, 7, 8, 13; **P. 10256**, 2; **P. 10260**, I, x + 1; II, x + 2; **P. 10282**, 19, 28; **P. 10304**, 37; **P. 10314**, I, 5; **P. 10343**, 6; **P. 10344**, 1, 9; **P. 10338**, x + 8; **P. 71513B**, [9], [10]
after an adjective, with the meaning of 'very', 'most'
P. 9977, 11; **P. 10116**, 33
see under *Ḥr-wr*, index III

wryt *wryt*-sanctuary
P. 10048, VI, 5

wrm image
P. 10114, 15; **P. 10201**, II, 13

wrrt *wrrt*-crown
P. 10191, II, 2–3

wrḥ anoint
P. 10091, II, 2

wrš spend the day
P. 9995, II, 10; **P. 10048**, IV, 3

wḥm repeat, renew
P. 9995, I, 17, 19; **P. 10048**, III, 1, 3; **P. 10109**, 13; **P. 10110 + 10111**, II, 20; **P. 10125**, 21; **P. 10191**, I, 44; **P. 10260**, II, x + 10; **P. 10304**, 50
in *iwty wḥm.ti.fy*: without equal
P. 10201, I, 3

wḥm in *m wḥm*: again
P. 10048, I, 2; **P. 10191**, I, 43, 52; **P. 10290**, x + 4; **P. 10338**, x + 13; **frag. 18**, 2

ws end
P. 10110 + 10111, II, 26
in *nn ws*: unendingly
P. 10199, 29; **P. 10314**, I, 5

wsr be mighty, powerful
P. 10191, II, 4; **P. 10201**, II, 9

wsr might, power
P. 10110 + 10111, II, 10; **P. 10304**, 43

wsḫt hall
P. 9995, I, 7; **P. 10048**, II, 2; **P. 10260**, II, x + 2
see under *wsḫt iꜣrw, wsḫt ww Mꜣʿt, wsḫt (nt) Mꜣʿty, wsḫt Gb*, index II

wstn in *wstn nmt*: broad of step
P. 9995, IV, 2; **P. 10110 + 10111**, II, 7, 26; **P. 10304**, 41

wstn cause to go freely
P. 10192 vs.

ws in *nn ws*: unendingly
P. 10110 + 10111, II, 26; **P. 10199**, 29; **P. 10314**, I, 5

wš adore
P. 10124, 8

wšʿ consume
P. 10191, II, 32; **P. 10199**, 25; **P. 10338**, x + 18

wšb uncertain meaning
P. 10264A, x + 5

wšb protect (+ *ḥr*)
P. 10256, 3

wšbt *wšbt*-cow
P. 10256, 3

wš(r) void
P. 10191, I, 11; **P. 10199**, 7; **P. 10260**, I, x + 12

wgyt jaws
P. 10201, I, 12

wt wrappings
P. 10112, 11; **P. 10260**, I, x + 2
see under *Inpw*, index III

**wdḥw* *wdḥw*-water
P. 10116, 20

wḏ decree (verb)
P. 10314, I, 5

wḏt decree
P. 9995, II, 25; **P. 10048**, IV, 11; **P. 10109**, 3; **P. 10108** vs.; **P. 10110 + 10111**, II, 28; **P. 10112** vs.; **P. 10125**, 13; vs.; **P. 10191**, I, 37, 38, 39; II, 17; **P. 10199**, 20; **P. 10201**, II, 16; **P. 10260**, III, x + 6; **P. 10282** vs.; **P. 10285** vs.; **P. 10290**, x + 3; **P. 10338**, x + 6, 9

wḏꜣ prosper
P. 10191, I, 44; **P. 10338**, x + 14
see under *ꜥnḫ wḏꜣ snb*

wḏꜣ preserve (from: *r*)
P. 10275, 4, 18

wḏꜣ journey (verb)
P. 10112, 20

wḏꜣt *wḏꜣt*-eye
P. 10191, II, 27

wḏꜥ to be judged
in *wḏꜥ ꜥb rn.i*: 'He who is judged pure' is my name
P. 10191, II, 10

wḏḥw offering-table
P. 10115, 4; **P. 10116**, 24

bꜣ ba
P. 9995, I, 9, 10, 12, 20, 24; II, 1, 2, 5, 6, 16, 17, 19, 21, 25; III, 18, 19, 20, 21; **P. 10048**, I, 1, 2; II, 4, 5, 7; III, 1, 4, 7, 8, 9, 10; IV, 5, 6, 8, 11; VII, 5, 6; **P. 10091**, II, 4; **P. 10108**, 1, 6, [7], 8; **P. 10109**, 6, 7; **P. 10112**, 2, 14; **P. 10114**, 1, 2, 7; **P. 10116**, 22; **P. 10125**, 10; **P. 10191**, I, 11, 15, 31, 33, 38, 43, 52; II, 12, 15, 24; **P. 10194** (?), I, 6, 15; **P. 10199**, 8, 21; **P. 10194**, 6, 14; **P. 10201**, II, 8, 10, 12, 14; **P. 10254**, 5; **P. 10260**, I, x + 7, 14; II, x + 4, 5, 6, 10, 11, 13; III, x + 2, 4, 6, 14, 15, 16; **P. 10261**, x + 2; **P. 10275**, 2; **P. 10282**, 28; **P. 10283**, 7, 8, 10; **P. 10285**, 3, 6; **P. 10286**, 2; **P. 10290**, x + 7; **P. 10314**, II, 3; **P. 10338**, x + 7, 12; **P. 10340**, 4; **P. 10343**, 8, 10, 15; **P. 10344**, 3, 4, 7 (?), 11, 14; **P. 10338**, x + 7, 12; **P. 71513A**, [13]; **P. 71513B**, [8]; **frag. 16**, 1 (?)
See under *Bꜣ Bꜣw, Bꜣ n Rꜥ, Bꜣ n Šw, Bꜣ ḏꜣ pt*, index III
in the plural:
P. 10125, 11; **P. 10283**, 7
and in some designations:
bꜣw ỉḳrw: excellent bas
P. 9995, IV, 2; **P. 10194**, 7; **P. 10201**, II, 13
bꜣw ꜥꜣw: great bas
P. 10201, II, 3
bꜣw (n nꜣ) nṯrw: bas of the gods
P. 9995, I, 14–15, 17; **P. 10048**, II, 10; III, 2; **P. 10191**, I, 11; **P. 10199**, 8; **P. 10260**, I, x + 15; II, x + 9, 11; **P. 10283**, 7; **P. 71513A**, 13; **P. 71513B**, 8–[9]
bꜣw n sꜥḥw ꜥꜣw: bas of the great mummies
P. 10201, II, 6
bꜣw špsw: noble bas
P. 10201, II, 10

bꜣw anger
P. 10048, V, 8

bꜣg see under *Ḥbs-bꜣg*, index II

biꜣ iron
P. 10191, I, 33

bit bee
see under *Ḥwt bit*, index II

bꜥḥ fill
P. 10201, II, 10

bw place
P. 9995, II, 2, 11; III, 19, 21; IV, 2; **P. 10048**, III, 8; IV, 3; VII, 6; **P. 10110 + 10111**, II, 22; **P. 10123**, 8; **P. 10194**, 8, 12; **P. 10201**, II, 2, 3; **P. 10254**, 7 (written *bꜣ*); **P. 10260**, I, x + 8; III, x + 15, 16; **P. 10285**, 6; **P. 10290**, x + 7; **P. 10314**, II, 2; **P. 10331** vs.
in the formation of abstract expressions
bw mꜣꜥ: righteousness
P. 10110 + 10111, II, 25
bw ḏw: evil
P. 10340, 8
see under *bw šmꜣyw, bw ḏsr*, index II

bwt abomination
P. 10115, 13

bhd inhale
P. 10201, I, 9

bs access (to: *r*)
P. 10115, 4

btꜣ crime
P. 9995, I, 6; **P. 10048**, I, 9

bd natron
P. 9995, I, 2; **P. 10048**, I, 5; **P. 10718**, [7]

pt sky
P. 9995, I, 11; II, 7; III, 8; **P. 10048**, I, 2; II, 7; III, 10; V, 6; **P. 10108**, 1; **P. 10109**, 12; **P. 10112**, 2, 20; **P. 10114**, 1, 2, 11; **P. 10115**, 4, 6; **P. 10116**, 22; **P. 10123**, 6, 10; **P. 10191**, I, 31, 33, 36, 38, 43, 49, 53; II, 4, 14, 25, 28; **P. 10199**, 21, 22; **P. 10260**, I, x + 14; II, x + 6; III, x + 9; **P. 10282**, 2; **P. 10286**, 6; **P. 10314**, II, 3; **P. 10338**, x + 3, 5; **P. 10343**, 8; **P. 10344**, 3
see under *ꜥḥ*

p(ꜣ) masculine singular definite article
P. 9995, I, 21; **P. 10048**, III, 4; **P. 10108**, 10, 12; **P. 10109**, 8, 9, 11; **P. 10110 + 10111**; **P. 10112**, 19; **P. 10123**, 4; **P. 10125**, 8, 12; **P. 10191**, I, 4, 12, 40; **P. 10194**, 6; **P. 10199**, 8; **P. 10260**, II, x + 14, 15; **P. 10264A**, x + 2; **P. 10282**, 26; **P. 10285**, 6; **P. 10286**, 2; **P. 10338**, x + 10; **P. 10343**, 7; **P. 71513A**, 4; **P. 71513B**, 2, [10]; **frag. 2**, 3; **frag. 3**, [3]

pꜣy + suffix masculine singular possessive adjective
P. 10109, 6; **P. 10125**, 10; **P. 10191**, I, 11, 14; **P. 10282**, 28; **P. 10283**, 7, 10; **P. 10343**, 14; **P. 10344**, 3; **P. 71513B**, [8 ?]

pꜣy masculine singular demonstrative pronoun
P. 10109, 3; **P. 10125**, 12

pꜣy fly up
P. 10109, 7; **P. 10112**, 14; **P. 10125**, 10; **P. 10199**, 8; **P. 10314**, II, 3; **P. 71513B**, [8 ?]

pꜣwt primordial times
P. 10116, 33

pꜣwty primordial
P. 10115, 6; **P. 10191**, I, 34; **P. 10338**, x + 3

pꜥt *pꜥt*-offerings
P. 10340, 7

pw demonstrative pronoun
P. 10108, 16; **P. 10112**, 23; **P. 10191**, I, 50; **P. 10314**, II, 7; **P. 10338**, x + 9; **P. 10718**, 11

pwy masculine singular demonstrative adjective
P. 9995, III, 20

pfy masculine singular demonstrative adjective
P. 9995, IV, 1; **P. 10108**, 10, 15; **P. 10109**, 10, 11, 12, 13; **P. 10125**, 16, 17, 18, 19, 20, 21; **P. 10191**, I, 16, 17, 18, 20, 21, 23, 25, 26, 27, 29, 39, 40; **P. 10199**, 13, 14, 15; **P. 10260**, III, x + 15; **P. 10275**, 1; **P. 10705**, 1, 2, 3, 4; **P. 71513A**, 20, 21, 22
masculine singular demonstrative pronoun
P. 10338, x + 9

pn masculine singular demonstrative adjective
P. 10114, 8, 14; **P. 10314**, II, 1; II, 6

pr go out, come forth
P. 9995, I, 22; III, 1, 2, 4, 5, 7, 8, 10; IV, 1; **P. 10048**, III, 5; V, 1–10; VI, 1–10; **P. 10108**, 6; **P. 10109**, 4, 7; **P. 10110 + 10111**, II, 1, 3, 4, 6, 9, 19; **P. 10114**, 4, 7; **P. 10115**, 14; **P. 10116**, 19, 21; **P. 10125**, [5]; **P. 10191**, I, 7, 11, 15; II, 2, 12, 25, 28, 33; **P. 10194**, 12; **P. 10201**, I, 11, 16; II, 4, 8; **P. 10206C**, 4, 5, 6; **P. 10260**, I, x + 7; II, x + 15; III, x + 6, 7, 8, 9, 10; **P. 10283**, 4, 7, 8; **P. 10303**, 8; **P. 10285**, 6; **P. 10304**, 36, 38, 40, 42, 48; **P. 10337**, 6; **P. 10340**, 4; **P. 10718**, 5; **P. 71513A**, <8>, 18; **P. 71513B**, [8]; **P. 71513C**, [6]; **frag. 4**, 3

pr m hrw festival of going forth by day
P. 10108, 11

pr house
P. 10108, 8, 9; **P. 10112**, 5, 16; **P. 10191**, II, 17; **P. 10340**, 9

pr-ḥḏ Treasury
P. 10110 + 10111 vs.

prt-ḫrw invocation offering
P. 9995, I, 12–13; II, 23; III, 15; **P. 10048**, II, 8; IV, 10; VII, 3; **P. 10110 + 10111**, II, 18; **P. 10199**, 24, 29; **P. 10260**, I, x + 9; II, x + 7, 30; III, 5, 13; **P. 10304**, 48

pḥ rear
P. 9995, I, 2; **P. 10048**, I, 5; **P. 10110 + 10111**, II, 9; **P. 10304**, 42; **P. 10718**, 6

pḫr see under *ṯs-pḫr*

psḏ shine
P. 10048, I, 3; **P. 10108**, 11

psḏ turn one's back (+ *n*)
P. 10201, II, 1

psḏ back
P. 10109, 2; **P. 10110 + 10111**, II, 3; **P. 10125**, 14; **P. 10191**, I, 47; **P. 10201**, II, 1; **P. 10304**, 37; **P. 10338**, x + 16

Psḏt Ennead
Psḏt ꜥꜣt: great Ennead
P. 9977, 1; **P. 10110 + 10111**, 4; **P. 10116**, 2, 33; **P. 10304**, 3; **P. 71513D**, x + 4
Psḏt nḏst: lesser Ennead
P. 10110 + 10111, 4; **P. 10116**, 3; **P. 10304**, 3; **P. 71513D**, x + 4

ptpt trample
P. 10112, 11

fꜣy raise
P. 10110 + 10111, II, 18; **P. 10199**, 29; **P. 10304**, 48

fꜣw dignity
P. 10201, II, 13

fnḏ nose
P. 10091, II, 3; **P. 10114**, 5; **P. 10191**, I, 45; **P. 10199**, 26; **P. 10201**, I, 9; **P. 10338**, x + 15; **P. 10340**, 5
see under *Fnḏ.f-ꜥnḫ*, index III

fdw four
P. 10110 + 10111, I, 19; **P. 10116**, 17; **P. 10256**, 4; **P. 10304**, 17; **P. 10344**, 13

fdt sweat
P. 10091, II, 2

m preposition
1) in (a place, a state), written *im* before a suffix
P. 9977, 2, 3, 4, 6, 7, 8, 9; **P. 9995**, I, 2, 3, 7 (?), 7, 8, 10, 17, 20, 22, 24; II, 6, 9, 10, 11, 14, 15, 17, 20, 21, 22; IV, 1, 2; **P. 10048**, I, 2, 3, 6, 7, 8; II, 2, 3, 5; III, 4, 10; IV, 1, 3, 5, 8, 9; **P. 10091**, I, 7; II, 7; **P. 10108**, 1, 2, [3], 4, 7, 11, 12, 13, 14, 15, 22, 23; **P. 10109**, 3, 9, 10; **P. 10110 + 10111**, I, 7–18, 20–4, 26–37; II, 8, 10, 19, 23, 25, 27; vs.; **P. 10112**, 2, 4, 5, 6, 15, 16, 17, 22, 23; **P. 10114**, 1, 2, 3, 14; **P. 10115**, 7, 8, 10, 13; **P. 10116**, 3, 5, 6, 7, 8, 9, 10, 11, 12, 13, 14, 16, 22, 23; **P. 10123**, 5, 11; **P. 10124**, 1, 2, 4, 5, 6, 7, 8; **P. 10125**, 11, 12, 13, 23, 24, 25, 26, 27; **P. 10191**, I, 7, 12, 14, 15, 17, 20, 26, 28, 30, 32, 34, 37, 38, 39, 40, 41, 42, 43, 48, 49, 52, 53; II, 4, 7, 16, 18, 26, 31; **P. 10192** vs.; **P. 10194**, 7, 9, 11, 12; **P. 10199**, 3, 9, 10, 14, 16, 21, 24, 27; **P. 10201**, I, 2; II, 3, 4, 6, 11; **P. 10206A + B**, 7; **C**, 5; **P. 10260**, I, x + 8, 11, 13, 14, 15; II, x + 2, 3, 5, 13, 15; III, x + 2, 3, 4; **P. 10261**, x + 5; **P. 10262 + 10263**, 2; **P. 10264**, 3, 4, 5, 6; **P. 10275**, 8, 9, 14; **P. 10282**, 4, 5, 6, 7, 8, 9, 12, 13, 14; **P. 10285**, 3, 7; **P. 10286**, 3, 4, 5, 6; **P. 10290**, x + 4, 5, 8; **P. 10303**, 13; **P. 10304**, 4, 6–16, 18–22, 24–9, [30], 31, 32, 33, 40, 43, 49; **P. 10314**, I, 2, 4; II, 1, 5, 6; **P. 10331**, 1, 2 (?), 3 (?), 4–7, 9, 10; **P. 10338**, x + 5, 6, 12; **P. 10340**, [3]; **P. 10343**, 8, 9; **P. 10344**, 11; **P. 10705**, 2; **P. 10718**, 4, 7; **P. 71513A**, 3, 23, [25], 26, 27, [28], [29], [30], [31], 32, 33, 34; **P. 71513B**, [10]; **P. 71513C**, 7
2) in, during, on (a day, a night)
P. 9995, I, 4, 8; II, 14; IV, 1; **P. 10091**, II, 4, 5; **P. 10109**, 2; **P. 10112**, 18, 19, 20; **P. 10114**, 4; **P. 10125**, 2, 3; **P. 10191**, I, 2; **P. 10194**, 2; **P. 10199**, 2, 3; **P. 10201**, II, 6, 7, 14; **P. 10206A + B**, 2, 3, 5; **P. 10262 + 10263**, 3; **P. 10275**, 15; **P. 10283**, 4; **P. 10286**, 3; **P. 10337**, 2, 7; **P. 10338**, x + 10; **P. 10340**, 3, 4, 9; **P. 10344**, 11, 12, 13; **P. 71513A**, 2, [8], 17; **P. 71513B**, 1, 4; **P. 71513C**, 2, 7
3) as, namely, in a state of
P. 9995, I, 1, 2, 13, 24; II, 2, 9, 10, 13, 17; III, 9; **P. 10048**, I, 2, 5; III, 5, 8; IV, 5; **P. 10091**, II, 1, 5; **P. 10109** vs.; **P. 10110 + 10111**, II, 1, 2, 3, 5, 8, 10, 21; **P. 10114**, 7, 9, 10, 13, 14; **P. 10115**, 3; **P. 10116**, 23; **P. 10124**, 1; vs.; **P. 10125**, 14; **P. 10191**, I, 13, 15, 41 (?), 45, 46, 47, 48, 52; II, 4, 11, 17 (?), 22; **P. 10199**, 11, 20; **P. 10201**, I, 4; II, 8; **P. 10256**, 4; **P. 10260**, I, x + 13 (?), 15; II, x + 16; III, x + 2; **P. 10303**, 9; **P. 10304**, 36, 37, 38, 39, 42, 43, 50; **P. 10718**, 3, 6, [7]; **P. 71513A**, 5; vs.
4) with (*im* + suffix)
P. 9995, I, 2, 14, 16, 19, 20; II, 3, 10, 12, 16, 25; III, 6, 9 (?), 13; IV, 1; **P. 10048**, I, 5; II, 8, 9; III, 1, 3, 6, 9; IV, 2, 3, 4, 11; V, 6; VII, 3; **P. 10091**, II, 1, 2; **P. 10108** vs.; **P. 10112** vs.; **P. 10343**, 11 (written *imy*); **P. 10110 + 10111**, II, 25, 31; **P. 10114**, 7; **P. 10115**, 11; **P. 10116**, 20; **P. 10125** vs.; **P. 10191**, I, 22, 30, 32, 33, 38, 44; II, 4, 5, 15, 16, 22, 23, 28, 29, 30, 31; **P. 10199**, 16, 22, 23, 24, 25, 26; **P. 10201**, I, 10; II, 10, 12; **P. 10206A + B**, 8; **C**, 1; **P. 10260**, I, x + 2; II, x + 7, 8, 10, 13, 16; III, x + 6, 8, 11; **P. 10303** vs.; **P. 10314**, II, 1; **P. 10338**, x + 2, 13; **P. 10718**, [7]
5) = *n*
P. 10114, 5; **P. 10191**, I, 36; II, 30, 31, 32, 33; **P. 10199**, 24, 25; **P. 10206C**, 8; **P. 10343**, 11
6) partitive
P. 10115, 11; **P. 10125**, 9; **P. 10191**, II, 32; **P. 10199**, 25; **P. 10260**, III, 12; **P. 10303**, 9; **P. 10338**, x + 18; **P. 10314**, II, 2
in *wꜥ m*: **P. 10108**, 6; **P. 10112**, 13; **P. 10109**, 8; **P. 10343**, 5; **frag. 13**, 2
7) from, out of (*im* + suffix)

P. 9995, I, 11, 15; II, 3; III, 1, 2, 4, 5, 7, 8, 10; IV, 1, 2; **P. 10048**, II, 7, 10; III, 8; V, 1–10; VI, 1–10; **P. 10108**, 13; **P. 10110 + 10111**, II, 1, 4, 6, 9; **P. 10115**, 14; **P. 10116**, 20; **P. 10124** vs.; **P. 10191**, I, 7, 31, 40; II, 2, 12, 20, 25, 28, 33; **P. 10201**, I, 11; II, 4; **P. 10206C**, 5; **P. 10254**, 5 (?); **P. 10260**, I, x + 3; II, x + 6, 9; III, x + 6, 7, 8, 9, 10; **P. 10283**, 4; **P. 10304**, 36, 38, 41, 42, 49; **P. 10314**, II, 4; **P. 10337**, 7; **P. 71513A**, [8]; **P. 71513B**, 4; vs.
8) when
P. 10109, 1; **P. 10110 + 10111**, II, 9; **P. 10115**, 2; **P. 10125**, 2, [3]; **P. 10191**, I, 2, 31; **P. 10194**, 2, 3; **P. 10199**, 2; **P. 10283**, 1, 2; **P. 10303**, 2, 3; **P. 10337**, 1; **P. 10343**, 2; **P. 71513A**, 2; **P. 71513B**, 1; **P. 71513C**, [1]; **frag. 2**, 1; **frag. 3**, 1; **frag. 5**
9 + infinitive
P. 10108, 8; **P. 10110 + 10111**, II, 21; **P. 10112**, 16; **P. 10201**, II, 3, 8; **P. 10304**, 50
10) = *m-m*: among
P. 10260, I, 15
with verbs *wn*: **P. 10048**, IV, 8; *wšꜥ*: **P. 10191**, II, 32; **P. 10199**, 25; *bḥd*: *wꜣ*: **P. 10048**, III, 11; **P. 10201**, I, 9; *nkn*: **P. 10114**, 6; *ḥms*: **P. 10338**, x + 18; *ḫrp*: **P. 10115**, 5; *ẖnm*: **P. 9995**, II, 16; **P. 10048**, IV, 4; **P. 10260**, III, x + 2; *sꜥm*: **P. 9995**, III, 13; **P. 10048**, VII, 3; **P. 10114**, 6; **P. 10115**, 11; **P. 10191**, II, 32; **P. 10260**, III, x + 12; **P. 10314**, II, 2; *smꜣ*: **P. 9995**, IV, 2; *snm*: **P. 10201**, I, 12; *sḫm*: **P. 9995**, II, 7; **P. 10048**, III, 11; **P. 10206C**, 2; *stwt* (*m*): **P. 10344**, 2
uncertain meaning
P. 10314, II, 4
see under (*m*) *wḥm*, (*m*) *ḫsf*, (*m*) *grg*, *ḥꜣt-ꜥ* (*m*), *šw* (*m*)
by, according to
in *m wḏt* by the decree
P. 9995, II, 25; **P. 10048**, IV, 11; **P. 10108** vs.; **P. 10110 + 10111**, II, 28; **P. 10112**, 10; vs.; **P. 10125** vs.; **P. 10191**, I, 38; **P. 10201**, II, 16; **P. 10260**, III, x + 6; **P. 10285** vs.

m-ꜥ for *m*
P. 10260, I, x + 4
writing of *m* among
P. 10260, III, x + 14

m-ꜥ from, from the hand(s) of
P. 10091, I, 3; II, 3; **P. 10194**, 10; **P. 10338**, x + 9; **P. 10260**, I, x + 11; **P. 10344**, 8
by the grace of
P. 10108, 15; **P. 10112**, 21, 22; **P. 10191**, II, 2
at the dual *m-ꜥwy*: from the hands of
P. 10260, I, x + 9

m-ꜥb with
P. 10108, [7]; **P. 10112**, 14; **P. 10125**, 11

m-bꜣḥ in the presence of, before
P. 9995, I, 23; III, 16; **P. 10048**, III, 6; VII, 4; **P. 10109**, 10, 11, 12; **P. 10110 + 10111**, II, 23; **P. 10116**, 21; **P. 10123**, 1; **P. 10124**, 9, 12, 13, 14; **P. 10125**, 16, 17, 18, 19, 20; **P. 10191**, I, 16, 18, 19, 21, 23, 24, 26, 27, 28, 30, 31; **P. 10206A + B**, 5, 6; **P. 10260**, II, x + 16; III, x + 13; **P. 10290**, x + 5; **P. 10338**, x + 7; **P. 71513A**, 20, 22

m-m among
P. 9995, III, 17, 18; **P. 10048**, VII, 5; **P. 10091**, I, 5; **P. 10260**, I, x + 5; III, x + 14
with
P. 10338, x + 2

m-ḥꜣt before, in front of
P. 10116, 24

m-ḫt after (+ substantive)
P. 10108, 4; **P. 10201**, II, 7
after, when (+ verb)
P. 10108, 15
accompanying
P. 10114, 12
see under *iwiw*: mourn; *imim*: pine

m-ḫnt at the head of
P. 10108, 2; **P. 10112**, 4

m-ḫnt in, among
P. 9995, IV, 2; **P. 10110 + 10111**, II, 26; **P. 10114**, 2–3, 3, 6; **P. 10201**, II, 13; **P. 10262 + 10263**, 7

m-ẖnw in, within
P. 9995, IV, 2; **P. 10048**, III, 5; **P. 10108**, 12; **P. 10110 + 10111**, I, 5, 19, 25, 37; **P. 10116**, 3, 4, 17, 18; **P. 10123**, 7; **P. 10125**, 22; **P. 10191**, I, 37, 41; II, 13; **P. 10199**, 20; **P. 10256**, 2; **P. 10264A**, x + 8; **P. 10282**, 3, 23; **P. 10304**, 4, 5, 23, 35; **P. 10344**, 5 (without *m*)

m-sꜣ behind
P. 10285, 2

m-sty opposite (+ *n*)
P. 10108, 4; **P. 10112**, 8

mt die
P. 10191, I, 43, 52

mt death
P. 10191, I, 25

mꜣꜣ see
P. 9995, I, 8, 19, 21, 24; II, 14; **P. 10048**, II, 3; III, 3, 4, 6; **P. 10091**, I, 5, 6; II, 6; **P. 10108**, 8; **P. 10110 + 10111**, II, 15; **P. 10112**, 16; **P. 10114**, 7; **P. 10115**, 10; **P. 10123**, 9; **P. 10191**, II, 5; **P. 10260**, II, x + 3, 13, 14, 16; **P. 10285**, 3; **P. 10304**, 46; **P. 10338**, x + 11; **P. 10340**, 5

mꜣꜥ (be) just
P. 10718, [2]

mꜣꜥ in *bw mꜣꜥ*: righteousness
P. 10110 + 10111, II, 25

mꜣꜥ *mꜣꜥ*-offerings
P. 10108, 14

mꜣꜥt in *n mꜣꜥt*
in truth
P. 71513D, x + 3
see under *Mꜣꜥt*, index III

mꜣꜥ-ḫrw be justified, triumphant
P. 10191, II, 2; **P. 10201**, II, 5; **P. 10290**, x + 7
see under *Wn-nfr*, index III

mꜣꜥ-ḫrw justified
P. 10048, II, 5; III, 6
after a personal name: passim
written *ḫrw* in **P. 10282**, 1; **P. 10283**, 1

mꜣꜥty just
in *nṯrw mꜣꜥtyw*: righteous gods
see also under *Mꜣꜥtyw*, index III
P. 10115, 9

mꜣw rays
P. 10314, II, 3

mi writing of *mn*
P. 10343, 11

mi come
P. 9977, 12; **P. 9995**, I, 4; II, 9; **P. 10048**, I, 8; IV, 1; **P. 10264A**, x + 3; **P. 10275**, 5

mi enclitic particle + *sḏm.f*, to express wishes
P. 9977, 2; **P. 9995**, II, 21, 22; III, 16, 17, 18, 20, 21; **P. 10048**, IV, 8, 9; VII, 4, 5, 6; **P. 10110 + 10111**, I, 4, 5;

II, 15, 20; **P. 10109**, 4, 6, 7, 8 , 9; **P. 10116**, 3, 4, 18; **P. 10123**, 2, 3, 5; **P. 10124**, 1, 2, 3, 4, 5, 6, 7, 8–9, 9; **P. 10125**, 4, 8–9, 9, 10, 11, 22; **P. 10191**, I, 11, 12, 13, 14, 15, 36, 36–7; II, 12–13, 13, 21; **P. 10194**, 6, 8; **P. 10206C**, 1; **P. 10260**, III, x + 4, 13, 14, 15, 16; **P. 10264**, 3, 5; **P. 10264A**, x + 3; **P. 10275**, 3 (?), 10, 11, 12; **P. 10282**, 3, 23; **P. 10283**, 7 (?), 8 (?); **P. 10285**, 2, 3, 5, 6; **P. 10286**, 2; **P. 10303**, 7, 8; **P. 10304**, 3, 5, 46; **P. 10331**, 1–12 (? written); **P. 10338**, x + 6; **P. 10340**, 3, 4, 5, 7, 8, 9; **P. 10343**, 5; **P. 71513A**, 12, 18, 24 (written); **P. 71513B**, [8], [9]

mi — imperative form of *rdi*
P. 10110 + 10111, II, 14, 16, 17; **P. 10123**, 4, 7; **P. 10125**, 15, 22; **P. 10191**, I, 15; II, 7, 15 (?), 18, 19; **P. 10199**, 8, 9, 10, 11, 19, 26, 27, 28; **P. 10264A**, x + 2 (?), 3 (?); **P. 10304**, 45, 46, 47, 48, 49

mi — in *mi n.i*: may I have
P. 10340, 5

mi — as, like
P. 9995, I, 24; II, 15 (written); **P. 10048**, II, 9; III, 6, 7; IV, 3, 12; VII, 6, 7; **P. 10091**, I, 4, 5; **P. 10108**, 12; **P. 10109**, 9, 10; **P. 10110 + 10111**, I, 7–37; II, 23; **P. 10116**, 3; **P. 10125**, 12, 15, 23, 24; **P. 10191**, I, 12, 16, 18, 19, 20, 22, 24, 25, 32, 36, 44; II, 2, 16, 19; **P. 10199**, 9, 12; **P. 10260**, II, x + 8; III, x + 6; **P. 10264A**, x + 5, 6, 8, 9; **P. 10282**, 4, 11, 18; **P. 10286**, 3, 4, 5, 6; **P. 10303**, 10; **P. 10304**, 6–35; **P. 10314**, II, 1, 6; **P. 10338**, x + 3, 14; **P. 71513A**, 14, 19; **P. 71513B**, [10]

mi — writing of *m-ꜥ*
P. 10264A, x + 6

mitt — likewise
P. 10048, I, 3; **P. 10108**, 8; **P. 10112**, 17; **P. 10115**, 7; **P. 10125**, 11, 24, 25, 26, 27

mꜥnḏt — *mꜥnḏt*-bark
P. 10110 + 10111, II, 5; **P. 10201**, II, 6; **P. 10304**, 38; **P. 10340**, 6

mw — water
P. 9995, III, 14; **P.10048**, VII, 3; **P. 10091**, II, 3; **P. 10108**, 12; **P. 10109**, 9, 14; **P. 10116**, 19; **P. 10123**, 2; **P. 10124**, 9; **P. 10125**, 12, 28; **P. 10191**, I, 12; II, 15, 16, 18, 19, 21, 30, 31, 34; **P. 10199**, 9, 24, 25; **P. 10201**, II, 7; **P. 10206C**, 8; **P. 10254**, 5 (?); **P. 10260**, III, x + 12; **P. 10282**, 27, 28; **P. 10283**, 10; **P. 10285**, 2; **P. 10340**, 3, 7; **P. 10343**, 11, 12; **P. 71513B**, [10]
see under *rnp*, *ḳbḥ*

mwt — mother
P. 10048, VI, 10; **P. 10108**, 16; **P. 10110 + 10111**, II, 1, 8; **P. 10191**, I, 42, 50; **P. 10256**, 4, 8; **P. 10304**, 36, 41

mwt-nṯr — mother of the god (epithet of Isis)
see under *Ꜣst*, index III

mn — be established, stable
P. 9995, I, 11; II, 9; **P. 10048**, II, 6; IV, 1 (?); **P. 10114**, 8; **P. 10260**, II, x + 6

mn — in *mn n.tn*
take for yourselves (written)
P. 10343, 11

mnmn — displacement
P. 10112, 11

mnḫ — efficacious, efficient
P. 10108, 4; **P. 10194**, 13; **P. 10256**, 5; **P. 10260**, I, x + 3; **P. 10343**, 6; **P. 10344**, 10
in the expression *mnḫ ib*: loyal
P. 10275, 4

mnḫ — efficacy
P. 10110 + 10111, II, 23

mnḫt — wrapping, cloth
P. 10260, I, x + 2; **P. 10314**, II, 4

mndwy — thighs
P. 10191, I, 47

mr — desire
P. 9995, II, 2; III, 19; **P. 10048**, III, 4, 8; VI, 9; VII, 6; **P. 10091**, II, 6, 7 (?); **P. 10110 + 10111**, I, 3; II, 6, 14, 22; **P. 10114**, [14]; **P. 10116**, 2; **P. 10191**, I, 37–8, 38, 44; **P. 10194**, 8, 12; **P. 10199**, 21; **P. 10260**, I, x + 7; II, x + 14; III, x + 15; **P. 10283**, 9; **P. 10285**, 6; **P. 10290**, x + 7; **P. 10304**, 2, 40, 46; **P. 10314**, II, 2; **P. 10338**, x + 7, 13; **P. 10718**, 11; **P. 71513D**, x + 2
in *r mr ib* + suffix: according to one's heart desire
P. 10123, 8; **P. 10124**, 8
in *r mr.k*: according to your desire
P. 9995, I, 20

mrḥ — decay
in *nn mrḥ*
P. 9995, II, 25; **P. 10048**, IV, 12; **P. 10108** vs.; **P. 10112** vs.; **P. 10116** vs.; **P. 10125** vs.; **P. 10260**, III, x + 6; **P. 10337** vs; **P. 71513C** vs.; **P. 71513D** vs (?)

mrsw — malt
P. 10290, x + 6

mrt — street
P. 10110 + 10111, II, 27

mḥ — fill
P. 9995, II, 3; **P. 10048**, III, 8; **P. 10116**, 20; **P. 10191**, II, 27; **P. 10201**, II, 9

mḥ — in the formation of ordinal number
P. 10110 + 10111 vs. (dem.)

mḥ — cubit
P. 10110 + 10111, II, 2; **P. 10304**, 37

mḥyt — north wind
P. 10114, 5

mḥtt — north
P. 9995, I, 3; **P. 10048**, I, 7; **P. 10191**, II, 18; **P. 10282**, 3; **P. 10283**, 8

mḫꜣt — balance
P. 10290, x + 7

ms — give birth
P. 10191, II, 27

ms + n — born of
P. 9977, 13; vs.; **P. 9995**, I, 1, 3, 5, 6, 10, 18; II, 1, 4, 7, 10, 15, 18, 20, 25; III, 1–2, 3, 4, 6, 7, 9, 10, 12; IV, 1; **P. 10048**, III, 2; **P. 10091** vs.; **P. 10108**, 1; **P. 10109** vs.; **P. 10112**, 1; **P. 10115**, 1; **P. 10116**, 1; **P. 10123**, 10, 11; **P. 10124**, 6; **P. 10125**, 2; **P. 10191**, I, 1, 51; **P. 10192**, [1–12]; **P. 10194**, 1; **P. 10199**, 1; vs.; **P. 10201**, I, 1; II, 4, 9; **P. 10254**, 1; **P. 10256**, 2, 9; **P. 10261**, x + 3; **P. 10264**, 1; **P. 10275** vs.; **P. 10282**, 1 (*r-ms*); **P. 10283**, 1 (*r-ms*); **P. 10285**, 1; **P. 10304**, 1; **P. 10331**, 1–12; **P. 10337**, 1; **P. 10340**, 1; **P. 10343**, 1, 12; **P. 10344**, 1, 6; vs.; **P. 10718**, 8; **P. 71513A** vs.; **frag. 4**, 1 (*r-ms*); **frag. 6**, [1]; **frag. 11**, 2

ms — child
P. 10108, 3, 4; **P. 10112**, 7; **P. 10340**, 10

msw-nṯr — god's children
P. 10114, 9

ms(t) — birth
P. 9995, II, 13

msḫnt — domicile
P. 10109, 13; **P. 10191**, I, 21; **P. 10705**, [4]

msty — nostrils
P. 9995, II, 1; **P. 10048**, III, 7

msḏ — hatred
P. 10048, VI, 6

msḏr — ear
P. 10191, I, 45; **P. 10338**, x + 14

mšrw — evening
P. 9995, I, 8; **P. 10048**, II, 3; **P. 10260**, II, x + 3

mk — protect
P. 9995, II, 5; **P. 10048**, III, 10

mk — proclitic particle: behold
P. 10115, 11

mkt — protection
P. 9995, II, 8; **P. 10048**, III, 11; **P. 10256**, 7

mkt — right place
P. 10114, 8; **P. 10191**, I, 35, 42; **P. 10199**, 18; **P. 10338**, x + 11

mt — die
P. 10191, I, 43, 52; **P. 10290**, x + 4; **P. 10338**, x + 12; **frag. 18**, 2 (?)

mt — dead
P. 10191, I, 25

mtwt — muscles
P. 10116, 23 (written )

mtr — dependable
P. 10109, 8; **P. 10125**, 8; **P. 10191**, I, 4; **P. 10199**, 5; **P. 71513A**, 4; **P. 71513B**, [2]; **frag. 2**, 3; **frag. 3**, [3]

mtri — witness
P. 9995, III, 12; **P. 10048**, VII, 2; **P. 10260**, III, x + 11

mdw — speak
P. 9995, I, 19; **P. 10048**, III, 3; **P. 10114**, 6; **P. 10191**, I, 30, 35, 44; II, 4; **P. 10199**, 16, 18; **P. 10206A + B**, 4; **P. 10260**, II, x + 13

mdw — words
P. 10110 + 10111, II, 9; **P. 10201**, I, 11; **P. 10260**, III, x + 3; **P. 10304**, 42; **frag. 12**, 2
see under *ḏd mdw*

mdw-nṯr — god's words
P. 10191, I, 10; **P. 71513A**, 11

mdsw-irty — of piercing gaze
P. 10109, 4; **P. 10125**, 6; **P. 10191**, I, 4; **P. 10199**, 5; **P. 10337**, 4 (without *irty*); **P. 71513A**, 4 (without *irty*); **P. 71513C**, 4 (without *irty*)

mḏ — ten
P. 10108, 15; **P. 10112**, 22; **P. 10123**, 3; **P. 10194**, 11; **P. 10201**, II, 7; **P. 10254**, 3; **P. 10343**, 7; **P. 10344**, 3, 9

mḏꜣt — book
in *mḏꜣt tn sb nḥḥ*: this Book of Traversing Eternity
P. 10114, 4; **P. 10314**, I, 3; **P. 10262 + 10263**, 4

mḏꜣt — chisel
P. 10191, I, 32; **P. 10338**, x + 2

mḏt — unguent
P. 9995, IV, 1

n — genitival adjective
masculine
P. 9977, 2; vs.; **P. 9995**, I, 3, 15, 16, 17, 18, 20, 21 (for *m* ?), 21, 22, 24; II, 1, 4, 12, 16, 20, 22, 24, 25; III, 19, 20; IV, 1; **P. 10048**, I, 1, 2, 7, 9; II, 8, 10; III, 1, 2, 4, 5, 7, 9; IV, 4, 8, 9, 11; V, 9; VII, 5, 6; **P. 10091**, II, 5; **P. 10108**, 8, 9, 10, 11, 12, 14, 15; **P. 10109**, 3, 4, 5, 7, 8, 10, 11, 12, 13, 14; **P. 10110 + 10111**, I, 1, 7–37; II, 1, 2, 5, 8, 11, 31; **P. 10112**, 7, 9, 10, 19, 22; vs.; **P. 10114**, 3, 12, 13; **P. 10115**, 4, 5, 6, 7, 8, 10, 13; **P. 10116**, 21, 33; **P. 10123**, 1, 3, 4, 5, 6, 9, 10; **P. 10124**, 1, 2, 3, 8; vs.; **P. 10125**, 4, 6, 8, 14, 16, 17, 18, 20, 28; **P. 10191**, I, 2, 3, 6, 8, 10, 11, 13, 14, 17, 22, 26, 29, 31, 33, 36, 38, 41, 44, 48, 49, 50, 51; II, 6, 7, 14, 15, 24, 27, 34; vs. (dem.); **P. 10194**, 5, 6, 10, 11; **P. 10199**, 4, 5, 8, 11, 13, 14, 15, 19; vs.; **P. 10201**, I, 6, 8; II, 2, 3, 6, 7, 8; vs.; **P. 10206C**, 9; **P. 10260**, I, x + 5, 11; II, x + 9, 10, 11, 14, 15, 16; III, x + 2, 3, 4, 5, 6, 15; **P. 10264A**, x + 2, 4; **P. 10275**, 2, 16, 18; **P. 10282**, 26, 27; **P. 10283**, 3, 6, 10; **P. 10286**, 3, 4, 5; **P. 10303**, 5; 12; **P. 10304**, 4, 6–35, 36, 39, 42, 44; vs. (dem.); **P. 10314**, I, 3; II, 6; **P. 10331**, 1–12; **P. 10337**, 2, 5, 6, 8; **P. 10338**, x + 2, 10; **P. 10340**, 2, 5, 6; **P. 10344**, 5, 9; vs.; **P. 10705**, 1, 2, 3, 4; **P. 10718** vs.; **P. 71513A**, 3, 4, [7], 9, [11], [12], 13, 17, [20], 21, [22 ?]; vs; **P. 71513B**, [2], [4], [5], 7, 8; **P. 71513C**, 3, 6, [8]; **frag. 2**, 2, 3; **frag. 3**, 2, [3], 4; **frag. 4**, 2; **frag. 6**, 2
written *nty*
P. 10110 + 10111, II, 22 (?); **P. 10194**, 9; **P. 10275**, 6
feminine (*nt, nty*)
P. 9995, I, 3, 4; **P. 10048**, I, 7, 8; **P. 10108**, 6, 9, 10; **P. 10109** vs. (*n*); **P. 10110 + 10111**, II, 6, 29 (?); **P. 10191**, I, 30, 33, 43; II, 8; vs. (*n*, dem.); **P. 10199**, 16; **P. 10206A + B**, 5; **P. 10256**, 4; **P. 10275**, 14; **P. 10282** vs. (*n*); **P. 10285** vs. (*n*); **P. 10290**, x + 3, 4 (*n*); **P. 10304**, 40; vs. (*n*, dem.); **P. 10338**, x + 3; **P. 10343**, 3, 4, 5; **P. 10344**, 2; vs. (*n*); **P. 10718** vs.; **P. 71513A** vs. (*n*)

n — preposition
1) for, to
P. 9995, I, 7, 8, 12, 16, 19; II, 8 (?), 17, 18, 20, 23, 24; III, 14, 15; **P. 10048**, I, 1, 3; II, 2, 4, 8; III, 1, 3; IV, 5, 6, 7, 8, 10, 11; VI, 9; VII, 3, 4; **P. 10091**, I, 2; II, 3; **P. 10108**, 3 (?), 4, 8, 11, [12], 14, 15; **P. 10109**, 9; **P. 10110 + 10111**, II, 5, 7, 13, 14, 19, 24, 27; **P. 10112**, 6, 7, 11 (?), 17, 22; **P. 10206A + B**, 4; **P. 10114**, 4, 6, [14]; **P. 10115**, 5, 12, 13; **P. 10116**, 17, 18, 22; **P. 10123**, 3, 4, 6, 8, 10; **P. 10124**, 4; **P. 10125**, 12; **P. 10191**, I, 11, 12, 29, 30, 32, 33, 34, 35, 36, 39, 41 (?), 42, 44; II, 19, 21, 28; **P. 10194**, 13; **P. 10199**, 9, 16, 17, 18, 19, 20, 22, 27, 28; **P. 10201**, I, 3–11, [12–20]; II, 1, 2, 3, 6, 7, 13; **P. 10254**, 5; **P. 10260**, I, x + 1; II, x + 2, 7, 12; III, x + 2, 3, 4, 5, 12, 13; **P. 10282**, 22, 28; **P. 10285**, 2 (?), 3 (?), 5; **P. 10290**, x + 3, 5, 6; **P. 10304**, 39, 43, 45, 46, 47, 48; **P. 10314**, I, 25; II, 2; **P. 10338**, x + 2, 5, 8, 11, 12; **P. 10340**, 3 (?), 5, 7 (?), 9; **P. 10343**, 6, 11, 12; **P. 10344**, 1, 9; **P. 71513A**, [12]; **P. 71513B**, [8], [10]
2) for *m*
P. 9977, 4, 5, 6; **P. 9995**, I, 10 (?); II, 12, 23 (?); **P. 10048**, I, 3; II, 5; **P. 10109**, 1; **P. 10110 + 10111**, I, 1; **P. 10114**, 1; **P. 10116**, 21; **P. 10123**, 5; **P. 10124**, 9; **P. 10191**, I, 1, 50; II, 17; **P. 10199**, 1, 10; **P. 10260**, II, x + 5; III, x + 5, 15; **P. 10283**, 1; **P. 10304**, 41; **P. 10331**, 8; **P. 10338**, x + 4, 16; **P. 10344**, 2
3) in *sḏm.n.f*
P. 9995, II, 22; III, 14; IV, 1; **P. 10048**, I, 1; IV, 9; VII, 3; **P. 10091**, I, 4, 6; II, 6; **P. 10108**, [15]; **P. 10112**, 21; **P. 10114**, 7, 13, 14; **P. 10115**, 4, 13; **P. 10116**, 19; **P. 10123**, 8 (?); **P. 10125**, 21; **P. 10191**, II, 9; **P. 10201**, I, 11, 12; II, 5, 8, 10, 14, 15; **P. 10260**, III, x + 4, 12;

P. 10264A, x + 4, 5; **P. 10303** vs.; **P. 10343**, 4; **P. 71513A** vs.
4) towards (+ suffix)
P. 9995, I, 15, 21; II, 3, 4; **P. 10048**, III, 1, 5, 8, 9; **P. 10091**, II, 2; **P. 10109**, 7; **P. 10125**, 5; **P. 10191**, I, 3, 6; **P. 10199**, 4, 6, 7; **P. 10260**, I, x + 1; II, x + 9, 15; **P. 10264A**, x + 3; **P. 10283**, 6; **P. 10314**, II, 4; **P. 10337**, 5; **P. 10338**, x + 6
5) for *r*
P. 10191, I, 49; **P. 10264A**, x + 5
6) for *in*
P. 10048, IV, 5, 7
7) uncertain meaning
P. 10123, 4; **P. 10201**, I, 7; **P. 10254**, 4; **P. 10275**, 17; **P. 10343**, 12
8) after the verbs *i(ȝ)kb*: **P. 10091**, II, 4; **P. 10314**, II, 1, *psḏ*: **P. 10201**, II, 1, *rš*: **P. 10091**, I, 5, *smȝ*: **P. 10314**, II, 3

n-m among (*n-im* + suffix)
P. 10199, 11; **P. 10260**, II, x + 11; **P. 10283**, 7; **P. 10338**, x + 6; **P. 10343**, 6

nȝ plural definite article
P. 9995, I, 20, 21; III, 15; **P. 10048**, III, 4; **P. 10108**, 9; **P. 10109**, 3, 4, 5; **P. 10110 + 10111**, I, 24; II, 13, 20; **P. 10114**, 6; **P. 10115**, 3, 4; **P. 10116**, 32; **P. 10123**, 1, 4; **P. 10125**, 3, 4, [6]; **P. 10191**, I, 2, 3, 5, 6, 9, 10, 11, 36, 47, 49; **P. 10194**, 5, 6, 7; **P. 10199**, 4, 5, 6, 7, 8, 19; **P. 10260**, II, x + 14; III, x + 12, 13; **P. 10264A**, x + 4; **P. 10283**, 3, 6, 7, 9; **P. 10303**, 4, 5, 6; **P. 10304**, 45, 49; **P. 10337**, 2, 4, 6; **P. 10338**, x + 6; **P. 10340**, 2; **P. 10343**, 3, 4; **P. 10344**, 5, 9; **P. 71513A**, 3, 5, 7, [12], 13; **P. 71513B**, [2], [4], [7], 8; **P. 71513C**, 4, [5], 6; **frag. 2**, 2; **frag. 3**, [4], 5; **frag. 4**, 2; **frag. 6**, [2], 3

nȝy + suffix masculine plural possessive adjective
P. 10110 + 10111 vs.

niw see under *is (n) niw*

niwt town
P. 10108, 10; **P. 10110 + 10111**, I, 18; **P. 10116**, 17; **P. 10304**, 17

nis invoke
P. 10115, 8; **frag. 13**, 3

nw moment
P. 10194, 9; **P. 10201**, II, 14; **P. 10275**, 6, 15

nwb gold
P. 10110 + 10111, II, 8; **P. 10304**, 42
see under *Ḥwt nwb*, index II

nwd scent
P. 10114, 5

nb every, any
P. 9995, I, 5, 6, 25; II, 11, 24; III, 12, 14, 16, 19, 21, 22; **P. 10048**, I, 2, 9; III, 4, 7; IV, 3, 10; VII, 2, 3, 4, 6; **P. 10091**, I, 6, 7; **P. 10108**, 8, 11, 14, 15; **P. 10110 + 10111**, I, 24; II, 12, 21; **P. 10112**, 16, 22; **P. 10114**, [9], [10]; **P. 10115**, 13; **P. 10123**, 3, 8; **P. 10124**, 7, 8; **P. 10190**, I, 10; **P. 10191**, I, 13, 31, 44, 50, 52, 53; II, 17; **P. 10194**, 8, 9, 11, 12; **P. 10199**, 11; **P. 10201**, II, 3, 7, 14; **P. 10254**, 3, 7; **P. 10260**, I, x + 8; II, x + 14; III, x + 5, 11, 13, 15, 16; **P. 10275**, 6; **P. 10304**, 22, 44, 50; **P. 10338**, x + 13, 17, 18; **P. 10340**, 8; **P. 10343**, 7; **P. 10344**, 3, 9; **P. 10718**, 11; **P. 71513A**, 11

nb lord
P. 9977, 3, 11; **P. 9995**, I, 16; II, 13, 23; **P. 10048**, III, 1, 5; IV, 10; **P. 10110 + 10111**, I, [3], 7, 25; II, 10, 13, 20; **P. 10114**, 13; **P. 10115**, 3, 9, 11, 12, 14; **P. 10116**, 3, 4; **P. 10123**, 10; **P. 10124**, 1; **P. 10125**, 23; **P. 10191**, I, 8, 9, 10, 29, 30, 38, 46, 47; II, 2, 5, 14; **P. 10199**, 15; **P. 10194**, 3, 4; **P. 10201**, I, 8; II, 5; **P. 10206A + B**, 5; **P. 10260**, II, x + 10; III, x + 5; **P. 10275**, 7; **P. 10282**, 4, 10; **P. 10285**, 4; **P. 10290**, x + 6; **P. 10303**, 3; **P. 10304**, 2, 4, 42, 44, 48; **P. 10331**, 1, 11, 12; **P. 10337**, 8; **P. 10338**, x + 8; **P. 10343**, [3], 4; **P. 10344**, 13; **P. 71513A**, [9], 10, 11, 25, 36; **P. 71513B**, [5], [6]; **P. 71513C**, [8]

nbt-pr housewife
P. 10091, II, 4; **P. 10314**, I, 1

nb fashion
P. 9995, I, 9; **P. 10048**, II, 4; **P. 10256**, 5; **P. 10260**, II, x + 4

nbḏ evil
P. 10191, I, 30; **P. 10199**, 16

nfy in *nn nfy*: without ill (?)
P. 10110 + 10111, II, 27

nfr be beautiful, perfect
P. 10191, I, 8; **P. 10264A**, x + 9

nfr good, beautiful, perfect
P. 9995, I, 19; II, 13, 24; **P. 10048**, III, 3; IV, 10; **P. 10091**, II, 5; **P. 10108**, 4, 5; vs.; **P. 10110 + 10111**, II, 8, 27; **P. 10112**, 9; vs.; **P. 10114** vs.; **P. 10115** vs.; **P. 10116** vs.; **P. 10123** vs.; **P. 10194**, 13; **P. 10112**, 8; **P. 10256** vs.; **P. 10260**, I, x + 1; II, x + 12; III, x + 5; **P. 10262 + 10263** vs.; **P. 10283** vs.; **P. 10286** vs.; **P. 10290**, x + 3; **P. 10303** vs.; **P. 10304**, 42; **P. 10337** vs.; **P. 10338**, x + 18; **P. 10340** vs.; **P. 10343**, 6; **P. 10344**, 2; **P. 71513A** vs.; **frag. 1**; **frag. 7**; **frag. 8**; **frag. 9**
in *r nfr* + substantive
P. 10110 + 10111, II, 29

nfrw good things
P. 10201, II, 7
perfection
P. 10115, 10; **P. 10191**, I, 42; **P. 10201**, I, 10; **P. 10338**, x + 11

nm who ?
P. 10191, II, 19

nmt slaughterhouse
P. 10048, VI, 3

nmst *nmst*-jug
P. 10116, 20

nmt walk, travel
P. 10114, 9; **P. 10191**, I, 53; II, 1

nmtt step(s)
P. 9995, IV, 2; **P. 10191**, I, 37; **P. 10110 + 10111**, II, 7, 26; **P. 10199**, 21; **P. 10304**, 41
see under *Wsḫ nmtt*, index III

nmt bed, bier
see under *Ḫnty nmt*, index III

nn demonstrative adjective
P. 10108, 6; **P. 10109**, 9; **P. 10112**, 13; **P. 10125**, 10; **P. 10201**, I, 12; II, 7, 15

nn demonstrative pronoun
P. 10048, I, 3; **P. 10110 + 10111**, II, 24

n(n) negation
P. 9995, I, 2, 11; II, 17, 25; III, 1, 2, 4, 5, 7, 8, 10, 12, 15, 16; IV, 1, 2; **P. 10048**, I, 6; II, 7, 10; IV, 4, 5; V, 1–10; VI, 1–10; VII, 1, 2, 4; **P. 10091**, II, 1, 3, 6; **P. 10110 + 10111**, II, 19, 26; **P. 10112**, 10, 11; **P. 10114**, 11; **P. 10115**, 12, 13, 14; **P. 10116**, 22; **P. 10124** vs.; **P. 10191**, I, 30, 38, 39, 40, 43, 48, 49, 52; II, 2, 14; **P. 10201**, I, 5, 6, 11; II,

1, 6, 8; **P. 10260**, I, x + 4, 8, 12; II, x + 6, 9; III, x + 2, 7, 8, 9, 10, 11, 13; **P. 10304**, 49; **P. 10314**, II, 5; **P. 10338**, x + 8, 9; **P. 10340**, 8; **P. 71513A** vs.; **P. 71513B** vs.
in *nn ꜣb*, *nn iwms*, *nn ws*, *nn mrḥ*, *nn nfy*, *nn sk*, see the second element

nn child
see under *Ḥwt nn nsw*, index II

nnw *nnw*-loaves (?)
P. 10110 + 10111, II, 11

nnk first person singular independent pronoun, expressing possession
P. 10109, 14; **P. 10125**, 28; **P. 10191**, II, 34; **P. 10282**, 27; **P. 10283**, 10; **P. 10340**, 7

nnt (lower) heaven
see under *Nnt*, index III

nhm rejoice (?)
P. 10110 + 10111, II, 29

nhm acclaim (+ *n*)
P. 10108, 9

nhs awake
P. 9995, I, 21; **P. 10048**, III, 4; **P. 10260**, II, x + 14

nḥbt neck
P. 10191, I, 46

nḥm rescue (+ *m*)
P. 10191, II, 2
take away
P. 71513A vs.

nḥḥ eternity
P. 10108, 16; **P. 10112**, 23; **P. 10114**, 4; **P. 10314**, I, 3; II, 7
m ꜣw n nḥḥ: **P. 10260**, I, x + 11
[m] ꜣw n ḏt nḥḥ: **P. 10275**, [15]–16
n [nḥḥ ḏt]: **P. 10275**, [18]
r nḥḥ: **P. 9995**, I, 16–17; II, 21; **P. 10048**, III, 1; IV, 6, 8; **P. 10108**, 12; **P. 10116**, 3, 4, 18; **P. 10125**, 22; **P. 10260**, II, x + 10; III, x + 4; **P. 10282**, 3, 25, 28; **P. 10283**, 10–11; **P. 10343**, 15
r nḥḥ sp 2 ḏt sp 2: **P. 9995**, III, 22; **P. 10048**, VII, 7; **P. 10260**, III, x + 16
r nḥḥ ḏt: **P. 9995**, I, 10, 12; II, 19; **P. 10048**, II, 5, 8; **P. 10110 + 10111**, I, 5; II, 21; **P. 10194**, 14; **P. 10260**, II, x + 5, 7; **P. 10304**, 4, 5, 50; **P. 10340**, 10
r nḥḥ ḏt sp 2: **P. 10260**, III, x + 16
r nḥḥ ḥnꜥ ḏt: **P. 10199**, 29; **P. 10285**, 7; **P. 10286**, 7; **P. 10344**, 14, 16
r-ꜥ nḥḥ ḏt: **P. 10091**, II, 7; **P. 10314**, 2
see *Nḥḥ*, index III

nḥḥ (adverb) for ever
P. 9995, III, 1; **P. 10261**, 5; **P. 10303**, 14
in *ḏt nḥḥ*
P. 9995, III, 1; **P. 10048**, IV, 12; **P. 10260**, III, x + 6; **P. 10261**, x + 6
in *nḥḥ sp 2 ḏt sp 2*
P. 10303, 14

nḫt (be) strong
P. 10191, I, 9; II, 4; **P. 10337**, 8; **P. 71513A**, 10; **P. 71513B**, [6]

nḫḫ become old
P. 10191, II, 9, 10

ns tongue
P. 9995, I, 24; II, 9; **P. 10048**, III, 6; **P. 10201**, I, 11

nsyt kingship
P. 10108, 16; **P. 10112**, 23; **P. 10314**, II, 7

nsw king
P. 10048, VI, 9; **P. 10110 + 10111**, II, 30; **P. 10191**, I, 52
see under *ḥtp di nsw*

nst throne
P. 9995, II, 9; **P. 10048**, IV, 1; **P. 10114**, 3; **P. 10191**, I, 7, 8, 50; II, 16; **P. 10194**, 4; **P. 10283**, 4; **P. 10337**, 7, 8; **P. 71513A**, 8, 9; **P. 71513B**, [5]

nš leave
P. 10108, 3; **P. 10112**, 6

nšp breathe
P. 10108, [13]; **P. 10114**, 4; **P. 10262 + 10263**, 5

nšmt *nšmt*-bark
P. 9995, I, 9; IV, 1; **P. 10048**, II, 5; **P. 10114**, 15; **P. 10123**, 4; **P. 10260**, II, x + 4

nšny repel
P. 10116, 22

nk fornicate
P. 10048, VI, 4

nknk fornicate
P. 10048, VI, 2

**nkn* eat (+ *m*)
P. 10114, 6

ngꜣ bull
P. 10123, 5

ngꜣ cackler
P. 10191, II, 8

nty relative adjective
P. 10110 + 10111 vs. (dem.); **P. 10123**, 1, 6, 7; **P. 10124**, 4; **P. 10191**, I, 6, 7 (written *nt*), 9, 10 (written *nt*), 12, 33 (written *nt*); **P. 10191** vs. (dem.); **P. 10194**, 7; **P. 10264A**, x + 5, 8; **P. 10283**, 4, 5, 6, 7; **P. 10303**, 6; **P. 10304** vs. (dem.); **P. 10337**, 6, 7; **P. 71513A**, 7, 8, 10, [11]; **P. 71513B**, [4], [5], 6, [10]
writing of the genitival *n(t)*
P. 10260, I, x + 10

nṯr (be) divine
P. 9995, I, 17, 20; **P. 10048**, III, 2, 4; IV, 5; VII, 5; **P. 10091**, II, 6; **P. 10112**, 3; **P. 10114**, 2; **P. 10191**, I, 14; **P. 10260**, II, x + 11, 13; III, x + 2, 14; **P. 10343**, 9
divinize (transitive)
P. 9995, I, 10, 24; III, 18; **P. 10048**, II, 5; III, 7; **P. 10191**, I, 43; **P. 10260**, I, x + 14; II, x + 5; **P. 10338**, x + 12

nṯr god
P. 9977, 2; **P. 9995**, I, 17; II, 6, 13, 22, 23; IV, 1; **P. 10048**, III, 2, 10; IV, 9, 10; VI, 8; VII, 2, 3; **P. 10110 + 10111**, II, 3, 12; **P. 10115**, 2, 8, 10; **P. 10116**, 22; **P. 10123**, 6; **P. 10124**, 8; **P. 10191**, I, 10, 30, 31 (plural ?), 48, 53 (plural ?); II, 2, 33; **P. 10194**, 3; **P. 10206A + B**, 5; **P. 10260**, I, x + 13; II, x + 12; III, x + 5; **P. 10262 + 10263**, 2; **P. 10303**, 3; **P. 10304**, 37, 44; **P. 10343**, [3]; **P. 10718**, 11; **P. 71513A**, 7, 11; **P. 71513B**, [4]
in the plural:
P. 9995, I, 15, 17, 24; II, 4, 13, 18, 19; III, 14, 15, 16, 17; IV, 2; **P. 10048**, II, 10; III, 2, 5, 7, 9; IV, 5, 7; VII, 3, 4; **P. 10108**, 2, 14; **P. 10109**, 4, 5, 7, 13; **P. 10110 + 10111**, I, 24; II, 21, 30; **P. 10109**, 4; **P. 10112**, 3; **P. 10114**, 2, 6, 12; **P. 10115**, 4, 6, 9; **P. 10116**, 33; **P. 10123**, 1, 2, 7; **P. 10125**, 6, 7; **P. 10191**, I, 4, 5, 6, 9, 10, 11, 13, 14, 21, 31, 33, 34, 36, 49, 52; II, 15, 18; **P. 10199**, 5, 6, 7, 8, 11, 16; **P. 10206A + B**, 8; **P. 10260**, I, x + 15; II, x + 9, 11; III, x + 3, 10, 12, 13, 14; **P. 10282**, 2; **P. 10283**, 7, 8; **P. 10286**, 6; **P. 10303**, 6; **P. 10304**, 22, 50; **P. 10314**, II, 7; **P. 10337**, 4, 5, 6; **P. 10338**, x + 1, 2, 3; **P. 10343**, 11,

13, 14; **P. 10344**, 8; **P. 71513A**, 4, 5, 6, 7, 10. [13]; **P. 71513B**, 3, [4], [6], [9]; **P. 71513C**, 4; **frag. 3**, [4], 5; **frag. 14**, [2]
in the dual (?):
P. 10262 + 10263, 7
see also under the compounds *ꜥwt-nṯr, mwt-nṯr, msw-nṯr, ḥꜥw-nṯr, ẖrt-nṯr, dpt-nṯr*

nṯrt — goddess
P. 10264, 2; **P. 10282**, 28
in the plural: **P. 10109**, 12; **P. 10191**, I, 13, 31 (plural ?), 36, 53 (plural ?); **P. 10199**, 11; **P. 10314**, 7; **P. 10337**, 4; **P. 10343**, 13, 14; **P. 71513A**, 4; **P. 71513C**, 4

ndb(w)t — foundations of the earth
see under *Ḥwt-Ḥr, Ḥnwt ndb(w)t*, index III

nḏ — hail (+ *ḥr*)
P. 10115, 9

nḏ — see under *Ḥr-nḏ-it.f*, index III

nḏm — sweet, glad
P. 9995, II, 14–5; **P. 10110 + 10111**, II, 7, 14, 23, 25; **P. 10191**, II, 8, 12, 23; **P. 10199**, 26; **P. 10304**, 41, 46; **P. 10337**, [7 ?]; **P. 10340**, 8

nḏs — lesser
P. 10110 + 10111, 4; **P. 10112**, 20; **P. 10116**, 3; **P. 10304**, 3; **P. 71513D**, [x + 4]

r — to, upon (spatial and temporal) (*ir* + suffix)
P. 9995, I, 4, 6, 9, 10, 12, 16, 22; II, 2, 4, 9, 11, 14, 17, 19, 21; III, 16, 19, 21, 22; IV, 1, 2; **P. 10048**, I, 8, 9; II, 1, 4, 5, 8; III, 1, 5, 8, 9; IV, 1, 3, 4, 5 (?), 6, 8; VII, 4, 6, 7; **P. 10091**, II, 7; **P. 10108**, 5, 6, 10, 11 (?), 12; **P. 10109**, 3, 4, 5, 6, 7, 8, 10; **P. 10110 + 10111**, I, 5; II, 2, 9, 21, 22; **P. 10112**, 12, 14, 18, 19, 20; **P. 10114**, 8, 11, 11, 14, [15]; vs.; **P. 10115**, 4; **P. 10116**, 3, 4, 18; **P. 10123**, 1, 3, 5, 7, 8, 9; **P. 10124**, 1, 7; vs.; **P. 10125**, 3, 5, [6], 8, 9, 10, 15, 22; **P. 10191**, I, 2, 4, 5, 6, 10, 11, 13, 14, 15, 17, 19, 20, 22, 24, 25, 27, 28, 29, [32], 41, 44, 53; II, 1, 8, 12, 14, 25, 26; **P. 10192** vs.; **P. 10194**, 7, 8, 14; vs.; **P. 10199**, 5, 8, 10, 15, 17, 22, 26, 29; **P. 10201**, I, 2, 5; II, 4, 8, 9; **P. 10206A + B**, I, 2, 7; **P. 10254**, 2, 4, 5, 7; **P. 10260**, I, x + 7, 11, 14; II, x + 2, 4, 5, 7, 10, 14, 15; III, x + 4, 13, 15, 16; **P. 10282**, 3, 25; **P. 10283**, 3, 5, 6, 7, 9, 10, 11; vs.; **P. 10285**, 6, 7; vs.; **P. 10286**, 7; **P. 10290**, x + 7; **P. 10303**, 4, 6, 7, 10; **P. 10304**, 4, 5, 42, 50; **P. 10314**, II, 2, 3; **P. 10331** vs.; **P. 10337**, 2, 3, 4, 5, 6; **P. 10338**, x + 1; **P. 10340**, 5, 10; **P. 10343**, 3, 4, 15; **P. 10340** vs.; **P. 10344**, 3, 4, 11, 12, 14, 16; **P. 71513A**, 2, 3, 4, 6, 11, [13], [21], 23; **P. 71513B**, 1, 2, 3, [4], [7], 8; **P. 71513C**, 3; **frag. 2**, [2]; **frag. 3**, 3, 5; **frag. 4**, 4
in *r mr ib.f ḥꜣty.i*: according as my *ib*-heart and my *ḥꜣty*-heart desire
P. 10124, 8
in *r di ib.f*: at his heart's desire
P. 10260, III, x + 16
against
P. 9995, III, 13, 16; **P. 10048**, VII, 2, 4; **P. 10109**, 10; **P. 10125**, 15, 21; **P. 10191**, I, 16, 17, 18, 19, 20, 21, 22, 24, 25, 26, 27, 28, 38, 39; II, 2; **P. 10199**, 12; **P. 10201**, II, 5, 9; **P. 10206A + B**, 1, 3; **P. 10260**, III, x + 11, 13; **P. 10303**, 10, 11; **P. 71513A**, 19, 22
more than
P. 10110 + 10111, II, 12; **P. 10304**, 44
= *ḥr*
P. 9995, IV, 1; **P. 10110 + 10111** vs. (dem.); **P. 10256**, 5; **P. 10260**, I, x + 5; **P. 10282**, 23; **P. 10340**, 8 (?)
about, concerning (*(i)r* + suffix)
P. 9995, I, 24; **P. 10048**, III, 6; **P. 10115**, 7; **P. 10201**, I, 3; **P. 10260**, II, x + 16; III, x + 11; **P. 10304**, 37
from (after verbs *ꜥmḏ, wꜣ, wp, rḳꜣ, ḥri, sꜣw*)
P. 9995, II, 17; **P. 10048**, IV, 5; **P. 10091**, II, 4; **P. 10110 + 10111**, II, 19; **P. 10191**, I, 10; II, 9, 14; **P. 10201**, I, 4, 9; **P. 10260**, III, x + 2; **P. 10275**, 2 (?); **P. 10283**, 5; **P. 10304**, 49; **P. 10338**, x + 8; **P. 71513A**, 11; **P. 71513B**, [7]
after verbs *wꜥb, rs, dmḏ, dgꜣ*
before *tr*
P. 10343, 7; **P. 10344**, 9
after an imperative (*(i)r* + suffix):
P. 9995, I, 4; II, 9; **P. 10048**, I, 8; IV, 1
uncertain meaning
P. 10110 + 10111, II, 28; **P. 10275**, 2
to, in order to (+ infinitive)
P. 10048, I, [1], 2, 3; **P. 10091**, II, 4; **P. 10108**, 5, 15, 14; vs.; **P. 10109**, 3; **P. 10115**, 10; **P. 10110 + 10111**, II, 18, 23; **P. 10112**, 10; vs.; **P. 10116**, 22; **P. 10125**, 13, 18; vs.; **P. 10191**, I, 17, 35, [36], 41; **P. 10199**, 13, 18, 19, 29; **P. 10201**, I, 8; II, 12 (?); **P. 10260**, II, x + 13; **P. 10304**, 48; **P. 10338**, x + 5, 7, 9, 10, 11; **P. 10705**, 1; **P. 71513A**, [20]
(so) that (+ *sḏm.f*)
P. 10048, I, 3; IV, 8; **P. 10191**, I, 37; **P. 10199**, 21; **P. 10201**, II, 3, 12 (?); **P. 10260**, I, x + 14; III, x + 3; **P. 10314**, II, 5
in negative prop. (*r tm*)
P. 10191, I, 37; **P. 10199**, 21

r-ꜥ — until
P. 10091, II, 7; **P. 10314**, II, 2

r-nty — namely
P. 10110 + 10111, II, 25

r-ḥꜣ — in procession
P. 10108, 9

r-ḥꜣt — in front of
P. 10191, II, 18

r-ḫnty — to, as far as
P. 10201, II, 5

r-gs — beside
P. 10091, II, 6; **P. 10115**, 7; **P. 10260**, I, x + 9

r-ḏr — in *r-ḏr ib.k*: according to your heart's desire
P. 10091, I, 7

rꜣ — mouth
P. 9995, I, 8; **P. 10048**, II, 3, 9; III, 3; VI, 5; **P. 10091**, II, 1; **P. 10110 + 10111**, II, 23, 29 (?), 31; **P. 10114**, 3, 6; **P. 10191**, I, 29, 30, 32, 33, 35, 44; II, 4–5, 29; **P. 10199**, 16, 17, 18, 23; **P. 10206A + B**, 4; **P. 10260**, II, x + 4, 8, 12, 13; **P. 10314**, I, 3; **P. 10338**, x + 2, 5

rꜣ — entrance
P. 10048, II, 10; **P. 10260**, II, x + 9; **P. 10344**, 5

rꜣ-ꜥ-ḫt — battle
P. 10191, I, 9; **P. 10337**, 8; **P. 71513A**, 10; **P. 71513B**, [6]

rꜣ-ꜥwy — activity
P. 10110 + 10111, II, 22

rꜣ-pr — temple
P. 10112, 9

rꜥ — in *rꜥ nb*: every day
P. 10048, III, 3, 4, 5, 6, 10; IV, 5; **P. 10108**, [15]; **P. 10123**, 6, 11; **P. 10191**, I, 38, 41, 44, 48; II, 3, 15;

P. 10194, 9; **P. 10199**, 3; **P. 10260**, I, x + 13; II, x + 12, 14, 15, 16; III, x + 3; **P. 10264A**, x + 3 (?) 5; **P. 10275**, 6; **P. 10290**, x + 2, 8; **P. 10314**, II, 6; **P. 10338**, x + 11, 14; **P. 10718**, 12
in *m ẖrt-hrw nt rꜥ nb*; see under *ẖrt-hrw*
in *m hrw nty rꜥ nb*; see under *hrw*

rw (?) lion
P. 10191, II, 6

rwḏ endure, be firm, prosper
P. 9977, 2; **P. 9995**, I, 11; II, 14, 25; **P. 10048**, II, 7; IV, 11; **P. 10108**, 12; **P. 10110 + 10111**, I, 4, 6, 7–37; **P. 10114**, 3; **P. 10116**, 3, 4, 18, 22, 24; **P. 10124**, 1, 2, 3, 4, 5, 6; **P. 10125**, 22, 23, 24; **P. 10191**, II, 20; **P. 10260**, II, x + 6; III, x + 6; **P. 10262 + 10263**, 3; **P. 10264**, 3, 4, [5]; **P. 10275**, 10, 11, 12, 13; **P. 10282**, 3, 4, 11, 18, 23; **P. 10286**, 2, 3, 4, 5, 6; **P. 10304**, 3, 4, 5, 6–35; **P. 10314**, II, 6; **P. 10331**, 1–12; **P. 71513A**, 24

rpy temple
P. 10110 + 10111 vs. (dem.)

rm weep
P. 10048, V, 10

rmṯ men, people
P. 10115, 13

rn name
P. 9977, 2; **P. 9995**, I, 11; II, 2, 13, 15; **P. 10048**, I, 9; II, 6; III, 8; **P. 10108**, 2, 12; **P. 10110 + 10111**, I, 4, 6, 7–37; II, 2, 21, 28; **P. 10112**, 4; **P. 10114**, 3; **P. 10115**, 10, 14; **P. 10116**, 3, 4, 18; **P. 10123**, 4; **P. 10124**, 1, 2, 3; **P. 10125**, 22, 23, 24; **P. 10191**, I, 33, 49, 50, 52; II, 1, 6, 10, 12; **P. 10338**, x + 3; **P. 10260**, II, x + 6; **P. 10264**, 3, 4, 6; **P. 10275**, 9, 13; **P. 10282**, 3, 4, 11, 18, 20; **P. 10286**, 3, 4, 5; **P. 10304**, 4, 5, 6–35, 37, 50; **P. 10314**, I, 2; II, 4, 6; **P. 10331**, 1–12

rnp be renewed
P. 9995, I, 12; **P. 10048**, II, 7–8; **P. 10116**, 23; **P. 10260**, II, x + 7; **P. 10282**, 28; **P. 10283**, 11; **P. 10314**, I, 2; **P. 10343**, 15; **P. 10344**, 4, 7

rnp in *mw n rnp*: water of rejuvenation
P. 10191, II, 15

rnpt year
P. 10191, I, 49; **P. 10264**, 1

rḫ know
P. 10115, 10, 11, 14
in the title *rḫ ḫyt wr*: great scholar
P. 10110 + 10111 vs. (dem.)

rs watch (over: *r*)
P. 10123, 1; **P. 10191**, I, 6, 23 (+ *ḥr*); **P. 10199**, 7; **P. 10283**, 6; **P. 10303**, 6; **P. 10337**, 6; **P. 71513A**, 7; **P. 71513B**, 4; **P. 71513C**, [6]

rsyt the South
P. 10191, II, 18; **P. 10282**, 2; **P. 10283**, 8

rš rejoice
P. 10091, I, 5

rḳꜣ be far (from: *r*)
P. 10338, x + 8

rkḥ flame
P. 10112, 19

rd leg
P. 10192 vs.
at the dual *rdwy*
P. 10048, III, 3; **P. 10091**, I, 6; II, 1; **P. 10108** vs. (dem.); **P. 10110 + 10111** vs. (dem.); **P. 10191**, I, 35, 47; II, 3, 4; **P. 10199**, 18; **P. 10260**, II, x + 13; **P. 10282** vs.; **P. 10304** vs. (dem.); **P. 10338**, x + 5

(r)di give, grant, place, put
P. 9995, I, 2; IV, 2; **P. 10048**, II, 4; IV, 10; VI, 9; **P. 10108**, 5; vs.; **P. 10109** vs.; **P. 10110 + 10111**, II, 5, 24; **P. 10112**, 9, 13; vs.; **P. 10115**, 4; vs.; **P. 10116**, 19; **P. 10123** vs.; **P. 10125** vs.; **P. 10191**, I, 8, 10, 29, 35, 43; II, 12, 21; **P. 10194**, 4, 13; **P. 10199**, 16, 18; **P. 10201**, I, 5; II, 2, 11; **P. 10206A + B**, 4; **C**, 2; **P. 10260**, I, x + 1; II, x + 12; III, 5, 12; **P. 10282** vs.; **P. 10304**, 39; **P. 10314**, II, 2; **P. 10337**, 8; **P. 10343**, 6; **P. 10344**, 1, 9; **P. 71513A**, 9; **P. 71513B**, 5
see under *r di ib.f*, *ḥtp di nsw*
cause, grant (verb)
P. 10048, I, 3; III, 5; **P. 10091**, I, 5; **P. 10108**, 6; **P. 10110 + 10111**, II, 1, 10; **P. 10191**, I, 8, 37, 38, 42, 43, 44; II, 15, 23; **P. 10199**, 21; **P. 10260**, I, x + 4, 13, 15; **P. 10264A**, x + 9; **P. 10285** vs.; **P. 10304**, 36, 43; **P. 10338**, x + 7, 9, 10, 12, 13; **P. 71513A**, 11

hꜣ(y), hy hail
P. 9977, 1; **P. 9995**, I, 1, 6, 18; II, 1, 15; IV, 1; **P. 10048**, I, 4; II, 1, 6; III, 2, 7; **P. 10091**, I, 1; **P. 10108**, [1]; **P. 10112**, 1; **P. 10115**, 1; **P. 10194**, 1; **P. 10201**, I, 1, 3–18, [19–20]; II, 1, 2, 3; **P. 10260**, I, x + 5–6; II, x + 12; **P. 10285**, 1; **P. 10286**, 1; **P. 10340**, 1; **P. 10344**, 1 (+ *n* ?), 6; **frag. 10**, 1

hꜣy accede (to: *r*), descend
P. 10114, 15; **P. 10260**, I, x + 11 (+ *ḥr*); **P. 10338**, x + 7
in *pr hꜣ* (written *hr*): come and go
P. 10194, 12

hb proceed
P. 10314, I, 4

hb ibis
P. 10109, 2; **P. 10110 + 10111**, II, 1, 2, 8, 20; **P. 10125**, 13; **P. 10191**, II, 11, 13, 24, 27; **P. 10206C**, 6; **P. 10304**, 36, 37, 42, 49–50

hri be pleased (with: *ḥr*)
P. 9995, III, 13–14; **P. 10048**, VII, 3; **P. 10260**, III, x + 12

hrw day
P. 9995, I, 4; IV, 1, 2; **P. 10048**, I, 8; **P. 10091**, II, 4; **P. 10108**, 9, 10, 15; **P. 10112**, 20, 21, 22; **P. 10114**, 4; **P. 10191**, I, 41; **P. 10194**, 9; **P. 10199**, 3, 8; **P. 10201**, II, 7; **P. 10262 + 10263**, 3; **P. 10275**, 15; **P. 10337**, 2; **P. 10338**, x + 10; **P. 10343**, 7; **P. 71513A**, 2; **P. 71513B**, 1; **P. 71513C**, 2
m hrw nty rꜥ nb: every day
P. 10123, 11
m ẖrt-hrw nt rꜥ nb, see under *ẖrt-hrw*
see under *pr m hrw*

hrp be immersed
P. 10191, II, 26; **P. 10206C**, 5

ḥꜣ behind
P. 10191, I, 29; **P. 10199**, 15; **P. 10206A + B**, 4

ḥꜣy naked
P. 9995, III, 15; **P. 10048**, VII, 3; **P. 10260**, III, x + 12

ḥꜣy illumine (+ *n*)
P. 10114, 4

ḥꜣt fore
P. 9995, I, 1; **P. 10048**, I, 5; **P. 10110 + 10111**, II, 9; **P. 10718**, 6

ḥꜣt before
P. 10109, 3; **P. 10125**, 13 (?); **P. 10191**, I, 39, 40;

P. 10338, x + 9, 10
see under *r-ḥꜣt*, *ḥr-ḥꜣt*

ḥꜣt-ꜥ beginning (of: *m*)
P. 10048, I, 1

ḥ(ꜣ)ty *ḥ(ꜣ)ty*-heart
P. 9995, I, 1; **P. 10048**, I, 5; **P. 10091**, II, 1; **P. 10114**, 8; **P. 10124**, 8; **P. 10191**, I, 34, 35, 42; II, 29; **P. 10199**, 17, 23; **P. 10206C**, 7; **P. 10338**, x + 4

ḥꜣtt prow rope
P. 10191, II, 7

ḥꜥꜣ child
P. 10110 + 10111, II, 24

ḥꜥꜥ rejoice
P. 10261, x + 2

ḥꜥꜥ joy
P. 10201, I, 2; **P. 10260**, I, x + 11; **P. 10718**, 3

ḥꜥw body, limbs, flesh (rarely)
P. 9995, I, 7–8, 9, 14, 17, 17–18; IV, 1; **P. 10048**, I, 2; II, 3; III, 2; **P. 10091**, I, 4; **P. 10191**, I, 8, 43, 48; **P. 10201**, I, 4; II, 8; **P. 10256**, 5; **P. 10260**, II, x + 3, 4, 11; **P. 10314**, II, 5; **P. 10338**, x + 13, 17; **P. 10340** vs.; **P. 10344**, 4; **P. 71513A**, 9; **P. 71513B**, [5]; **P. 71513C**, 8; **frag. 1**.

ḥꜥw-nṯr divine body
P. 10194, 5; **P. 10337**, 8

ḥw uncertain meaning
P. 10264A, x + 7

ḥwt mansion, domain
P. 9995, II, 11

ḥwt-nṯr temple
P. 10275, 14

ḥwnt maiden
P. 10256, 1

ḥb feast, festival
P. 10108, 9, 10; **P. 10109**, 11; **P. 10112**, 19; **P. 10115**, 14

ḥb int festival of the Valley
P. 10124, 10; **P. 10194**, 11

ḥb ꜥḥ pt festival of raising the sky
P. 10109, 12; **P. 10112**, 20

ḥb ngꜣ wꜥb m sḫwt.f festival of the pure bull in his fields
P. 10123, 5

ḥb rkḥ nḏs festival of the small flame
P. 10112, 19–20

ḥb Hkr Haker-festival
P. 10109, 12; **P. 10344**, 12

ḥb Ḥnw Henu-festival
P. 10191, I, 14

ḥb-sd jubilee
P. 10191, I, 50

ḥb kꜣ-ḥr-kꜣ Khoiak festival
P. 10112, 20

ḥbbt overflow
P. 10191, II, 15–16, 22, 30; **P. 10199**, 24; **P. 10206C**, 8; **P. 10343**, 11

ḥbs clothing
P. 9995, III, 14; **P. 10048**, VII, 3; **P. 10260**, III, x + 12

ḥm Majesty
P. 10108, 4; **P. 10112**, 8; **P. 10114**, 7; **P. 10201**, I, 4, 6; II, 5, 6, 7, 11, 16

ḥm turn back
P. 71513B, [vs.]

ḥmt woman
P. 10048, VI, 4

ḥms sit, sit down
P. 10110 + 10111, II, 11; **P. 10191**, I, 33; II, 3; **P. 10304**, 44; **P. 10338**, x + 18
reside, live
P. 10191, II, 17
see under *ꜥḥꜥ … ḥms*

ḥn entrust
P. 10109, 6; **P. 10125**, 5; **P. 10191**, I, 6; **P. 10199**, 7; **P. 10282**, 22; **P. 10283**, 6, 7; **P. 10337**, 5; **P. 71513A**, 6; **P. 71513B**, [4]

ḥnꜥ (together) with
P. 9995, I, 9, 14, 17; II, 6; III, 17, 20, 21; IV, 2; **P. 10048**, I, 2; II, 4, 5, 10; III, 2, 10; VII, 4, 5, 6; **P. 10109**, 7; **P. 10110 + 10111**, II, 10, 11, 12, 19, 27; **P. 10112**, 7; **P. 10115**, 10; **P. 10191**, I, 11, 12, 13, 14, 51, 52; **P. 10194**, 7; **P. 10199**, 8, 9, 11, 29; **P. 10201**, II, 1, 3, 6, 7; **P. 10206C**, 4; **P. 10254**, 3, 5, 6; **P. 10260**, I, x + 14; II, x + 4, 9, 11; III, x + 14, 15, 16; **P. 10283**, 7, 9; **P. 10285**, 7; **P. 10286**, 7; **P. 10304**, 43, 44, 49; **P. 10340**, 10; **P. 10344**, 14, 16; **P. 10718**, 12; **P. 71513A**, [13]; **P. 71513B**, 8

ḥnw *ḥnw*-bark
P. 9995, II, 13; **P. 10108**, 11

ḥnwt mistress
P. 9977, 1; **P. 10109**, 6; **P. 10112**, 9, 10; vs.; **P. 10125**, 5; vs.; **P. 10191**, I, 5; **P. 10194** vs.; **P. 10199**, 6; **P. 10256**, 1, 8; vs.; **P. 10282**, 21; vs.; **P. 10283**, 5; **P. 10285** vs.; **P. 10286**, 2; **P. 10290**, x + 3; [vs.]; **P. 10303** vs.; **P. 10337**, 5; **P. 71513A**, 6; **P. 71513B**, [4]; **frag. 4**, [4]

ḥnḳt bier
P. 9995, I, 13; II, 24; **P. 10048**, II, 8, 10; **P. 10110 + 10111**, II, 17, 18; **P. 10114**, 6; **P. 10115**, 3; **P. 10191**, II, 32; **P. 10194**, 11; **P. 10199**, 25, 28; **P. 10260**, II, x + 7; **P. 10304**, 47; **P. 10314**, II, 2; **P. 10343**, 11

ḥnty time
P. 10108, 16; **P. 10112**, 23

ḥnty horns
P. 10256, 8

ḥr face
P. 9995, I, 11; II, 13; **P. 10108**, [15]; **P. 10109**, 3, 4, 5, 6, 7, 10; **P. 10110 + 10111**, II, [10]; **P. 10114**, 4; **P. 10115**, 5; **P. 10123**, 1; **P. 10125**, 3, [5], [6], 8, 15, 22; **P. 10191**, I, 2, 3, 4, 5, 6, 10, 15, 17, 19, 22, 24, 25, 27, 28, 29, [32], 45, 53; II, 14; **P. 10199**, 4, 5, 6, 15, 16; **P. 10201**, I, 6; II, 16; **P. 10206A + B**, 1, 2; **P. 10260**, II, x + 6; **P. 10262 + 10263**, 5; **P. 10283**, 5, 6; **P. 10303**, 4, 5, 6, 9; **P. 10304**, 43; **P. 10337**, 2, 3, 4, 5, 6; **P. 10338**, x + 1; **P. 10343**, [3], 4; **P. 71513A**, 2, 3, 4, 11, 21, 23; **P. 71513B**, 1, [2], 3, [4], [7]; **P. 71513C**, [3]; **frag. 2**, [2, 3]; **frag. 3**, 3, [5]; **frag. 4**, 4
in *m ḥr*: before
P. 10201, I, 8
see under *Nḥꜣ-ḥr*, *Ḥs-ḥr*, index III

ḥr preposition
1) at, on, upon, over
P. 9995, I, 3, 13, 24; II, 9, 11; **P. 10048**, I, 7; III, 6; IV, 1, 3; VI, 8, 9; **P. 10108**, 4, 7, 8, 14; vs.; **P. 10110 + 10111**, II, 27; **P. 10112**, 8, 15; vs.; **P. 10114**, 8, 12; vs.; **P. 10115** [vs.]; **P. 10116** vs.; **P. 10123**, 6; vs.; **P. 10124**, 8; **P. 10125**, 11; vs.; **P. 10191**, I, 7, 8, 23, 29, 33, 35, 42; **P. 10194**, 4; **P. 10199**, 15, 17, 18; **P. 10201**, II, 5, 6, 12, 13, 16 (?); **P. 10206A + B**, 10; **C**, 5; **P. 10260**, I, x + 7, 11; II, x + 8; **P. 10283**, 4; vs.; **P. 10285**, 2, 5; **P. 10286**

vs.; **P. 10290**, x + 3; **P. 10303** vs.; **P. 10314**, I, 6; **P. 10337**, 7, 8; vs.; **P. 10338**, x + 4, 8, 11; **P. 10340**, 4, 6, 7; vs.; **P. 10718** vs.; **P. 71513A**, 8, 9; **P. 71513B**, 5; **frag. 1**; **frag. 14**, 3
see under *ḥr-tp*
2) because of, by, for
P. 9995, III, 14; **P. 10048**, VII, 3; **P. 10091**, I, 3; **P. 10110 + 10111**, II, 23, 27; **P. 10114**, 4; **P. 10260**, III, x + 12; **P. 10262 + 10263**, 4; **P. 10314**, I, 3; **P. 10304**, 44
in the expressions
ꜣm ḥr ḏrt: seize by the hand
P. 10191, I, 49
wꜥ ḥr: blaspheme against
P. 10048, VI, 8, 9
hr ḥr: be pleased with
P. 9995, III, 13–14; **P. 10048**, VII, 3; **P. 10260**, III, x + 12
ḥr ḫrw at the voice
P. 9995, I, 13; **P. 10048**, II, 9; **P. 10110 + 10111**, II, 31
ḥtp ḥr be satisfied with
P. 10091, I, 3
ḫfꜥ ḥr ꜥwy grasp by the arms
P. 10191, I, 48–9; **P. 10338**, x + 17
3) from
P. 10110 + 10111, II, 4
because (?)
P. 10110 + 10111, II, 26, 28
4) + infinitive
P. 9995, I, 8, 9, 18; II, 1, 8; **P. 10048**, II, 3, 4; III, 3, 4, 7, 11; IV, 1; **P. 10091**, I, 4, 5, 6, 7; **P. 10108**, 8; **P. 10110 + 10111**, II, 24; **P. 10112**, 17; **P. 10114**, 9; **P. 10115**, 8; **P. 10201**, I, 6, 7, 9, 13, 14, 17; II, 1, 2, 8, 12, 13, 14; **P. 10256**, 7; **P. 10260**, II, x + 3, 4, 12; **P. 10264A**, x + 7, 8; **P. 10290**, x + 2; **P. 10718**, 3, 4

ḥr-ib — in the middle of
P. 10116, 25; **P. 10191**, II, 20

ḥr(t)-ib — middle
P. 9995, I, 2; **P. 10048**, I, 5; **P. 10718**, [7]

ḥr-ntt — because
P. 10115, 14

ḥr-ḥꜣt — at the prow of (a bark)
P. 10191, II, 7

ḥr-tp — on, upon
P. 9995, I, 14, 18; III, 22; **P. 10048**, II, 9; VII, 7; **P. 10191**, I, 38; **P. 10260**, I, x + 16; II, x + 8, 11; III, x + 16; **P. 10264A**, x + 5; **P. 10275**, 17; **P. 10718**, 12

ḥri — be far (from: *r*)
P. 9995, II, 17; **P. 10048**, IV, 5; **P. 10091**, II, 4; **P. 10110 + 10111**, II, 19; **P. 10201**, I, 4, 9; **P. 10260**, III, x + 2; **P. 10304**, 49

ḥry — master, who preside at
P. 10108, 14; **P. 10115**, 4
who is (up)on
P. 10114, 3; **P. 10262 + 10263**, 3; **P. 10344**, 4
upper, in toponyms; see under *Mnst*, *st*, index II

ḥr(y)-ib — dwelling
P. 10116, 32

ḥrw — top, upper part
in *m ḥrw*: above
P. 10201, II, 4

ḥrt — heaven
P. 10108, 6; **P. 10109**, 7; **P. 10112**, 14; **P. 10114**, 12; **P. 10125**, 11; **P. 10191**, I, 11; **P. 10199**, 8; **P. 10260**, I, x + 7; **P. 10283**, 7, 9; **P. 71513A**, [13]; **P. 71513B**, 8

ḥḥ — millions
P. 10191, I, 49, 50; II, 1

ḥs — praise, favour (verb)
P. 9995, II, 22; III, 17; IV, 2; **P. 10048**, IV, 4, 9; VII, 4; **P. 10110 + 10111**, II, 6; **P. 10260**, I, x + 5, 8, 16; III, x + 14; **P. 10290**, x + 5; **P. 10304**, 40

ḥsy — praised, favoured one
P. 9995, III, 17–18; **P. 10048**, VII, 5; **P. 10091**, I, 7; **P. 10108**, 6; **P. 10112**, 13; **P. 10125**, 9; **P. 10260**, I, x + 13 (?), 15; III, x + 14; **P. 10264A**, x + 6 (?); **P. 10290**, x + 6 (?); **P. 10340**, 8

ḥs-mr — praised and beloved
P. 10343, 12

ḥsb — count
P. 10264A, x + 5

ḥsmn — natron
P. 9995, I, 2; **P. 10048**, I, 5; **P. 10718**, 7

ḥḳꜣ — ruler
P. 9977, 1 (?); **P. 10110 + 10111**, II, 30; **P. 10116**, 23; **P. 10191**, I, 50; **P. 10201**, II, 3

ḥkꜣw — magical spells
P. 10201, II, 12

ḥḳr — hungry man
P. 9995, III, 14; **P. 10048**, VII, 3; **P. 10260**, III, x + 12

ḥknw — praises
P. 10109, 13; **P. 10123**, 4 (?); **P. 10125**, 21

ḥtp — set (verb)
P. 9995, I, 8; **P. 10048**, II, 3; **P. 10109**, 1; **P. 10114**, 8; **P. 10115**, 2; **P. 10125**, [3]; **P. 10191**, I, 2; **P. 10194**, 3; **P. 10199**, 2; **P. 10260**, II, x + 3; **P. 10283**, 2; **P. 10303**, 3; **P. 10337**, [2]; **P. 10343**, 2; **P. 71513A**, 2; **P. 71513B**, 1; **P. 71513C**, 2; **frag. 2**, 1
rest
P. 10191, I, 35; **P. 10199**, 17; **P. 10206A + B**, 10; **P. 10338**, x + 4
be satisfied (with: *ḥr*)
P. 10091, I, 3; **P. 10109**, 9; **P. 10114**, 8; **P. 10290**, x + 8; **P. 10314**, II, 5

ḥtp — peace
P. 10110 + 10111, II, 25; **P. 10201**, I, 2; II, 3, 4; **P. 10290**, x + 5; **P. 10314**, I, 4; II, 5 (?)

ḥtp — in the formula *ḥtp di nsw*: offering that the king gives
P. 9995, II, 23; **P. 10048**, IV, 9; **P. 10115**, 3; **P. 10116**, 19; **P. 10260**, III, x + 4

ḥtpw — *ḥtpw*-offerings
P. 9995, II, 24; III, 15; **P. 10048**, IV, 10; VII, 3; **P. 10115**, 6; **P. 10116**, 21; **P. 10201**, I, 12; II, 8, 9; **P. 10260**, III, x + 5, 12; **P. 10264**, 7, 8 (?); **P. 10343**, 8, 10

ḥtpw-nṯr — divine offerings
P. 10201, II, 3, 8

ḥtp — offering table
P. 9995, II, 3; **P. 10048**, III, 8; **P. 10201**, II, 7; **P. 10285**, 2, [6]

ḥtpt — offering table
P. 10340, 7

ḥtm — provide (with: *m*)
P. 10201, I, 10

ḥtm — annihilate
P. 71513A, 21

**ḥtm-ntt* — gullet
P. 10201, I, 10

ḥtyt — throat
P. 10112, 21; **P. 10114**, 5

ḥḏ white
P. 10109, 2; **P. 10125**, 14
see under *Ỉnb-ḥḏ*, index II

ḥḏ silver
P. 10110 + 10111, II, 3; **P. 10304**, 38

ḥḏ *ḥḏ*-cloth
P. 10314, II, 4

ḥḏw bones
P. 10314, I, 6

ḥḏdwt brightness
P. 10114, 4

ḫt thing
P. 9995, II, 24; III, 6; **P. 10048**, IV, 10; **P. 10260**, III, x + 5; **P. 10340**, 8
offerings
P. 10110 + 10111, II, 13; **P. 10191**, I, 13
in *wꜣḥ ḫwt*: lay down the offerings
P. 10108, 16; **P. 10123**, 3
in *ḫwt* (*ḥr*) *ḫꜣwt*: festival of offerings on the altar
P. 10108, 10; **P. 10112**, 18; **P. 10191**, I, 13, 18; **P. 10199**, 10; **P. 10303**, 12–13; **P. 10705**, 3; **P. 71513A**, 15; **P. 71513B**, [10]
in *sꜥm ḫwt*: consume offerings
P. 10110 + 10111, II, 11; **P. 10304,** 43
in *smꜣ ḫwt*: receive offerings
P. 10191, I, 12; **P. 10199**, 9
goods
in *ỉṯ ḫwt*: take goods
P. 9995, III, 6; **P. 10048**, V, 4, 9; **P. 10260**, III, x + 8
relics (?)
P. 10191, I, 29; **P. 10199**, 15; **P. 10705**, 6

ḫt fire
P. 10191, I, 31; **P. 10206A + B**, 6
see under *Ỉrt(y).f-m-ḫt*, index III

ḫt in *rꜣ-ꜥ-ḫt*
see under this word

ḫꜣꜥ chase away
P. 10191, I, 11; **P. 10199**, 7; **P. 71513B**, 7
put, place
P. 10110 + 10111 vs. (dem.)

ḫꜣwt altar
see under *ḫwt* (*ḥr*) *ḫꜣwt*

ḫꜣbsw stars
P. 10114, 12

ḫꜣst region
see under *ḫꜣst dšrt*, index II

ḫy be elevated, ascend (to: *r*)
P. 10116, 23; **P. 10191**, II, 25

ḫy child
P. 10256, 7

ḫꜥ rise (of sun), appear
P. 10109, 1; **P. 10110 + 10111**, II, 1, 8; **P. 10115**, 2; **P. 10125**, 2; **P. 10191**, I, 2, 52; II, 3; **P. 10194**, 2; **P. 10199**, 2; **P. 10201**, II, 8; **P. 10283**, 1; **P. 10303**, 2; **P. 10304**, 36, 41; **P. 10337**, 1; **P. 10343**, 2; **P. 71513A**, 2; **P. 71513B**, [1]; **P. 71513C**, [1]; **frag. 3**, 1

ḫw protect
P. 9995, I, 15, 24; **P. 10048**, II, 10; III, 6; **P. 10091**, I, 4; **P. 10201**, I, 7; **P. 10260**, II, x + 9

ḫw fault
P. 9995, I, 5; **P. 10048**, I, 9

ḫb collect
P. 10110 + 10111, II, 31

ḫbt place of execution
P. 10048, VI, 4

ḫbs plough
in *ḫbs-tꜣ ꜥꜣ*: great earth-ploughing
P. 10191, I, 27

ḫpr happen, exist, come into being
P. 10048, I, 3; **P. 10108**, 8; **P. 10110 + 10111**, II, 28; **P. 10112**, 17; **P. 10191**, II, 18; **P. 10260**, I, x + 13; **P. 10340**, 9; **P. 10718**, 11

ḫpr form, transformation
P. 9995, I, 20; III, 21; **P. 10048**, III, 4; VII, 6; **P. 10091**, I, 7; **P. 10110 + 10111**, II, 10–11; **P. 10114**, 10; **P. 10123**, 8; **P. 10124**, 7; **P. 10191**, I, 44; **P. 10194**, 8; **P. 10260**, II, x + 14; III, x + 15–16; **P. 10304**, 43; **P. 10338**, x + 13; **frag. 10**, 3

ḫpr scarab
P. 10108, 10

ḫpš thigh
P. 10191, I, 47; **P. 10338**, x + 17

ḫf observe
P. 10108, 8

ḫfꜥ seize
P. 10114, 9; **P. 10191**, I, 48

ḫft when
P. 10108, 13; **P. 10114**, 13, 14

ḫfty enemy
P. 9995, II, 17; **P. 10048**, IV, 5; **P. 10109**, 10; **P. 10125**, 15, 21; **P. 10191**, I, 16, 17, 18, 19, 20, 21, 22, 23, 24, 25, 26, 27, 28, 36; II, 2, 3; **P. 10199**, 12, 19; **P. 10206A + B**, 1, 3; **P. 10260**, III, x + 2; **P. 10303**, 10, 11; **P. 10338**, x + 5; **P. 71513A**, 19, 21, 22

ḫm ignorance
P. 10108, 16; **P. 10112**, 24

ḫmnw eight
P. 9995, I, 4; **P. 10048**, I, 8

ḫn alight (on: *ḥr*)
P. 9995, IV, 2; **P. 10108**, 7; **P. 10112**, 15; **P. 10114**, 10; **P. 10125**, 11; **P. 10191**, I, 38; **P. 10199**, 21; **P. 10338**, x + 7

ḫnm smell
P. 10201, I, 9; **P. 10343**, 7

ḫnt in
P. 9995, II, 5; **P. 10048**, III, 10; **P. 10201**, II, 2
among (?)
P. 9995, II, 13; **P. 10191**, I, 34; **P. 10201**, II, 11; **P. 10206A + B**, 9; **P. 10262 + 10263**, 2; **P. 10338**, x + 3
before
P. 10256, 6
in *ḫnt ḏt*, see under *ḏt*.

ḫnty spelling of *ḫnt*
in
P. 10108, 7

ḫnty foremost of
P. 9977, 10; **P. 9995**, II, 2, 20, 23; **P. 10048**, III, 8; IV, 7, 10; VII, 1; **P. 10109**, 2; **P. 10110 + 10111**, I, 12; **P. 10115**, 2; **P. 10116**, 10, 29; **P. 10124**, 5; **P. 10125**, 3, 25, 26; **P. 10191**, I, 2, 14, 29, 34, 50; **P. 10194**, 3; **P. 10199**, [2]; **P. 10201**, II, 1; **P. 10254**, 2; **P. 10260**, I, x + 3–4; III, 3, 5; **P. 10275**, 1; **P. 10282**, 13; **P. 10285**, 5; **P. 10286**, 4; **P. 10303**, 3; **P. 10304**, 10; **P. 10331**, 6; **P. 10337**, 2; **P. 10343**, [2]; **P. 10718**, 9; **P. 71513A**, 2;

P. 71513B, [1]; **P. 71513C**, [2]
see under *Wsir*, *Ḫnty Imntt*, index III

ḫnt sail upstream
P. 10114, 15; **P. 10254**, 2

ḫntš rejoice
P. 10314, II, 2

ḫnd tread, move
P. 10110 + 10111, II, 4; **P. 10191**, I, 49 (+ *m*); **P. 10260**, I, x + 7 (+ *ḥr*); **P. 10201**, II, 5 (+ *r-ḫnty*), 7; **P. 10304**, 38

ḫr say
P. 10110 + 10111, II, 2; **P. 10201**, I, 3
in *ḫr.f /.s n N*: Thus speaks N
P. 10109, 1; **P. 10110 + 10111**, I, 1; **P. 10114**, 1; **P. 10116**, 1; **P. 10123**, 5; **P. 10191**, I, 1; **P. 10199**, 1; **P. 10282**, 1; **P. 10283**, 1; **P. 10304**, 1; **P. 10337**, 1; **P. 71513A**, 1; **P. 71513C**, 1 (omission of *.f n*)
in *ḫr.s*: uncertain meaning
P. 10123, 10

ḫr before, in, by
P. 9995, I, 11, 12; III, 12, 13; IV, 2; **P. 10048**, II, 7, 8; VII, 2; **P. 10091**, II, 5; **P. 10108**, 1, 2; **P. 10112**, 2, 4; **P. 10114**, 1, 2, 3, 12; **P. 10191**, II, 14; **P. 10201**, I, 6; II, 5, 7, 9, 10, 11; **P. 10260**, I, x + 8; II, x + 6, 7; **P. 10262 + 10263**, 3; **P. 10314**, I, 2; II, 3; **P. 10331**, 1–12; **P. 10343**, 8, 9
in *ii ḫr*: come to
P. 10115, 9; **P. 10260**, III, x + 11
in *ir wꜥ ḫr Mꜣꜥtyw*: become one of the justified
P. 10314, II, 6
in *ḏd mdw ḫr*: to be recited to
P. 10194, 2

ḫr for *ẖr*; see under this word

ḫryt meat-offering ?
P. 10110 + 10111, II, 31

ḫrw voice
P. 9995, I, 14; III, 11; **P. 10048**, II, 9; VII, 1, 2; **P. 10109**, 3; **P. 10110 + 10111**, II, 31; **P. 10125**, 13; **P. 10191**, I, 15, 16, 17, 18, 19, 20, 22, 24, 25, 26, 27, 28; **P. 10199**, 12; **P. 10206A + B**, 3; **P. 10260**, III, x + 11; **P. 10282**, 23; **P. 10340**, 8; **P. 10718**, 1; **P. 71513A**, 19, 22
see under *mꜣꜥ-ḫrw*, *smꜣꜥ-ḫrw*

ḫrwy see under *Dr-ḫrwy*, index III

ḫrp in *ḫrp m ḥr*: turn (towards: *n*)
P. 10115, 5

ḫrḫr destroy
P. 10048, VI, 7

ḫsbd lapis-lazuli
P. 10109, 2; **P. 10125**, 14

ḫsf repulse
P. 9995, IV, 2

ḫsf in *m ḫsf*: at the approach of
P. 10108, 5

ḫt ... (?) plummet ?
P. 9995, III, 9; **P. 10260**, III, x + 10
see also under *tḫ*, and commentary of **P. 10048**, V, 6.

ḫt engrave
P. 10110 + 10111, II, 25

ḫtḫt backwards
P. 10048, V, 8

ḫd sail downstream
P. 10114, 15; **P. 10254**, 2

**ḫdb* meaning uncertain
P. 10112, 9

ẖt body
P. 10123 vs.; **P. 10191**, I, 39, 49; **P. 10201**, II, 9; **P. 10338**, x + 8; **frag. 1**.
womb
P. 10048, I, 3; **P. 10110 + 10111**, II, 1 (dem.), 10, 19; **P. 10304**, 36, 42, 49
breast
P. 10109, 2; **P. 10125**, 14
belly
P. 10191, I, 47
in *imyw-ẖt*, organs
P. 10114, 8
spelling for *ẖꜣt* 'corpse', see under this word

ẖꜣt corpse
P. 9995, I, 11, 12; II, 6, 25; **P. 10048**, I, 1; II, 6, 8; III, 10; IV, 8, 11; **P. 10108**, 7; **P. 10112**, 5, 15; **P. 10114**, 2; **P. 10125**, 11; **P. 10191**, I, 43; **P. 10199**, 22; **P. 10201**, II, 6, 12, 15; **P. 10260**, I, x + 11, 14 (written *ẖt*); II, x + 6, 7; III, x + 6; **P. 10261**, x + 2, 5 (?); **P. 10262 + 10263**, 2; **P. 10303** vs.; **P. 10314**, I, 2; **P. 10343**, 9; **P. 10340** vs.; **P. 10344**, 7

ẖn row
P. 9995, IV, 1

ẖnm join, unite
P. 9995, II, 1, 16 (+ *m*); **P. 10048**, I, 2; III, 7; IV, 4; **P. 10114**, 4, 5 (+ *m*), 13; **P. 10260**, III, x + 2
rest upon
P. 10201, II, 5

ẖnmty nostrils
P. 10108, 13; **P. 10201**, II, 10; **P. 10114**, 4

ẖr under
P. 10191, I, 40, 44; vs. (dem.); **P. 10304** vs. (dem.); **P. 10338**, x + 10
full of, carrying, being under
P. 9995, I, 22; IV, 2 (written *ḫr*); **P. 10048**, III, 5; **P. 10091**, II, 1; **P. 10108**, 3; **P. 10110 + 10111**, II, 13, 22; **P. 10112**, 5; **P. 10114**, 15; **P. 10191**, II, 17; **P. 10260**, II, x + 15; **P. 10314**, II, 4

ẖry lower
see under *Mnst ẖrt*, *st ẖrt*, index II

ẖrt possessions
P. 10115, 8

ẖrt-nṯr god's domain
P. 9995, II, 21, 22; **P. 10048**, IV, 8, 9; **P. 10108**, 3; **P. 10110 + 10111**, II, 19; **P. 10112**, 5; **P. 10124**, 1; vs.; **P. 10191**, I, 37, 40, 43, 52; II, 31; **P. 10192** vs.; **P. 10194**, 7; **P. 10199**, 21; **P. 10260**, I, x + 15; III, x + 4; **P. 10261**, x + 5; **P. 10304**, 49; **P. 10338**, x + 7, 12

ẖrt-hrw in (*m*) *ẖrt-hrw*: daily
P. 10048, II, 9; **P. 10194**, 12; **P. 10264A**, x + 8 (?); **P. 10286**, 3; **P. 10340**, 3, 4, 9
in *m ẖrt-hrw nt rꜥ nb*: in the course of every day
P. 9995, I, 13; **P. 10091**, I, 3; **P. 10110 + 10111**, II, 13, 15; **P. 10199**, 27; **P. 10260**, II, 8; **P. 10304**, 45, 46; **P. 10343**, 8

ẖkrw ornaments
P. 9995, II, 10; **P. 10048**, IV, 2

st that
P. 10109, 14; **P. 10125**, 28; **P. 10191**, II, 34

st third person plural dependent pronoun
P. 10110 + 10111, II, 23

st place
P. 10091, II, 6; **P. 10114**, 8, 12; **P. 10116**, 24; **P. 10191**, I, 35; II, 17, 20; **P. 10199**,17; **P. 10201**, II, 2; **P. 10343**, 14; **P. 10338**, x + 4
in the combinations
st swtwt: place of promenade
P. 10201, II, 6
see under *st ʿꜣt, st Mꜣʿt*, index II

st-ʿ sickness
P. 10201, I, 4

st-ḳsnt ill health
P. 10201, I, 4

sꜣ son
P. 9995, I, 12; **P. 10048**, II, 8; IV, 4; **P. 10109**, 8; **P. 10110 + 10111**, I, 2; II, 14, 22; **P. 10116**, 2; **P. 10125**, 8; **P. 10191**, I, 3, 7, 51; II, 8; **P. 10206A + B**, 8; **P. 10260**, I, x + 10, 16 (?); II, x + 7; **P. 10282**, 20; **P. 10283**, 4; **P. 10304**, [2], 46; **P. 10337**, 3, 7; **P. 10340**, 2; **P. 71513 A**, [4], 8; **P. 71513B**, 2, [5]; **P. 71513C**, 3; **P. 71513D**, x + 1

sꜣt daughter
P. 10091, II, 4

sꜣ (?) house (?)
P. 10110 + 10111, II, 26

sꜣw quench
P. 10191, II, 21–2; **P. 10206C**, 1

sꜣw guard
P. 9995, II, 8; **P. 10048**, IV, 1; **P. 10191**, II, 9
be on one's guard (against: *r*)
P. 10191, II, 11

sꜣw protection
P. 9995, I, 15, 24; **P. 10048**, II, 10; III, 5; **P. 10109** vs.; **P. 10114**, 9; **P. 10124**, 1; II, 9, 16; vs.; **P. 10125**, 14; **P. 10191**, I, 48; **P. 10256**, 4; **P. 71513A** vs.

sꜣw guardian
P. 10115, 3, 11; **P. 10123**, 1; **P. 10191**, II, 11 (?); **P. 10194**, 6

sꜣwty guardian
P. 10109, 4; **P. 10110 + 10111**, I, 1; vs. (*swꜣt*, dem.)**P. 10125**, 4; **P. 10191**, I, 3, 10; **P. 10199**, 4; **P. 10201**, I, 6; II, 6; **P. 10264A**, x + 2; **P. 10283**, 3; **P. 10303**, 5; **P. 10340**, 2; **P. 10344**, 5; **P. 10343**, 3; **P. 71513A**, 3, [12]; **P. 71513B**, [2]; **P. 71513C**, [3 ?]; **frag. 2**, 2; **frag. 3**, [2]; **frag. 6**, [3]

sꜣḥ reach
P. 10191, I, 42

sꜣḥ toe
P. 10191, I, 48

sꜣḫ glorify
P. 10191, I, 43; **P. 10256**, 6

sꜣḳ gather
P. 10256, 5

sꜣt calumny
P. 9995, III, 11; IV, 1 **P. 10260**, III, x + 10

sꜣṯ libation
P. 10116, 24

siꜣ recognize (?)
P. 10123, 6

sip take stock
P. 10191, I, 25

sisw (?) six (?)
P. 10264, 1

sʿꜣ magnify
P. 10201, II, 13

sʿm feed (on: *m*), consume
P. 9995, III, 13; **P. 10048**, VII, 3; **P. 10110 + 10111**, II, 11; **P. 10201**, II, 5; **P. 10260**, III, x + 12; **P. 10304**, 43
drink (bier, milk)
P. 10114, 6; **P. 10115**, 11; **P. 10191**, II, 32 (+ *m*); **P. 10314**, II, 2

sʿnḫ make live
P. 9995, II, 1, 12; **P. 10048**, I, 1, 2; III, 7; IV, 4; **P. 10191**, I, 43

sʿḥ mummy
P. 9995, I, 11; II, 15 (plural); **P. 10048**, II, 7; **P. 10108**, 2, 5; **P. 10112**, 3; **P. 10114**, 2; **P. 10201**, II, 8–9, 11; **P. 10260**, II, x + 6; **P. 10314**, II, 3
in the plural, in:
sʿḥw iḳrw: excellent mummies
P. 10201, II, 1
sʿḥw ʿꜣw: great mummies
P. 10201, II, 6
sʿḥw špsw: noble mummies
P. 10201, II, 17
shape
P. 10114, 14

sʿḥʿ raise
P. 10109, 11; **P. 10112**, 21; **P. 10191**, I, 20; **P. 10199**, 14; **P. 10344**, 11; **P. 10705**, 2; **P. 71513A**, 23

sw writing of the third person singular feminine suffix pronoun
P. 10123, 5, 6, 9, 10; vs.

swꜣš cord
P. 10123, 3

swꜣḏ make to flourish
P. 9995, II, 12

swʿb purify
P. 9995, I, 4, 7; **P. 10048**, I, 7; II, 2, 2–3; **P. 10260**, II, x + 2, 3

swꜣw retinue
P. 10201, II, 11

swnwn soothe
P. 10201, I, 6

swr drink
P. 9995, I, 14; **P. 10048**, II, 9; **P. 10091**, II, 1; **P. 10260**, II, x + 8

swr multiply
P. 10115, 6, 8
magnify
P. 10201, II, 11

swḥt egg
P. 10191, II, 8, 9

swtwt promenade
in *st n swtwt*: place of promenade
P. 10201, II, 6

swḏ commend
P. 10191, I, 42; **P. 10338**, x + 11

swḏꜣ preserve
P. 10256, 7; **P. 10718**, 3

sb traverse
P. 10114, 4; **P. 10314**, I, 3

sbꜣ star
P. 10123, 6, 10

sbꜣ gate
P. 9995, II, 20; **P. 10048**, IV, 8; **P. 10201**, II, 6; **P. 10260**,

I, x + 5; III, x + 3

sbi enemy
P. 10125, 19; **P. 10191**, I, 9, 17; **P. 10199**, 13; **P. 10201**, II, 5, 9; **P. 10283**, 5; **P. 10705**, [1]; **P. 71513A**, [11], 21; **P. 71513B**, 6

sbḫt gateway, portal
P. 9995, II, 21; **P. 10048**, IV, 8; **P. 10191**, I, 36; **P. 10199**, 19; **P. 10338**, x + 6

sp time
in *sp 2* twice = very (after an adjective)
P. 9995, II, 14; III, 22; **P. 10048**, III, 5; VII, 7; **P. 10191**, I, 42; **P. 10260**, II, x + 10; III, x + 16; **P. 10303**, 14; **P. 10314**, I, 5; II, 5; **P. 10343**, 15
in *sp 4*: four times
P. 10109, 13; **P. 10125**, 21
in *m sp tpy*: at the first time
P. 10191, I, 7; II, 18; **P. 10283**, 4; **P. 10337**, 7; **P. 71513A**, 8; **P. 71513B**, 4; **P. 71513C**, 7

sp fault
P. 10201, I, 6; II, 7; **P. 10718**, 11

sp remainder
P. 10201, II, 8

spꜣt nome
P. 10108, 12; **P. 10110 + 10111**, I, 5, 6; **P. 10114**, 15; **P. 10116**, 4, 18; **P. 10125**, 22; **P. 10191**, II, 17; **P. 10282**, 3, 20; **P. 10304**, 4, 5

spr arrive (at: + *r*), come (to: + *r*)
P. 10108, 10; **P. 10260**, I, x + 13

sprw invocations
P. 10110 + 10111, II, 30

spt lip
P. 10191, I, 46

sfḫ loose
in the expression *m sfḫ n*: loosed from the body of
P. 9995, IV, 1

sfsf offer
in *sfsf ꜣw*: offer oblation
P. 10108, 15; **P. 10112**, 22

smꜣ kill
P. 10115, 14

smꜣ unite
P. 9995, IV, 2 (+ *m*); **P. 10314**, II, 3 (+ *n*)

smꜣ receive
in *smꜣ ḫwt*: receive offerings
P. 10191, I, 12; **P. 10199**, 9

smꜣ-tꜣ burial
P. 10091, II, 5; **P. 10108**, 4; vs.; **P. 10112**, 7; vs.; **P. 10114** vs.; **P. 10115** vs.; **P. 10116** vs.; **P. 10123** vs.; **P. 10256** vs.; **P. 10262 + 10263** vs.; **P. 10283** vs.; **P. 10286** vs.; **P. 10290**, x + 3; **P. 10303** vs.; **P. 10314**, I, 5–6; **P. 10340** vs.; **P. 71513A** vs.; **frag. 1**; **frag. 7**; **frag. 8**; **frag. 9**

smꜣꜥ make just
in *smꜣꜥ ḫrw*: vindicate
P. 10109, 10; **P. 10125**, 15; **P. 10199**, 12; **P. 10206A + B**, 1, 2

smꜣꜥ-ḫrw vindicate
P. 10125, 21; **P. 10191**, I, 22; **P. 10201**, I, 13; **P. 10303**, 11
in *smꜣꜥ-ḫrw ḫrw* + suffix or noun (same meaning):
P. 10191, I, 15, 16, 17, 18, 19, 20, 22, 24, 25–6, 27, 28; **P. 10303**, 10; **P. 71513A**, 19 (?), 21, 22

smi report
P. 9995, III, 15–16; **P. 10048**, VII, 4; **P. 10260**, III, x + 13

smn establish , confirm
P. 10191, I, 22, 35, 42, 49; **P. 10199**, 18; **P. 10340**, 9; **P. 10338**, x + 4, 11

smnḫ perfect (verb)
P. 10091, I, 4; **P. 10260**, I, x + 2

smsw first-born
P. 10191, II, 6, 24; **P. 10206C**, 3

smdt discourse
in *rdi smdt*: make the discourse
P. 10191, I, 10; **P. 71513A**, 11

sn embrace, kiss
in *sn tꜣ* embrace the earth = prostate oneself
P. 10110 + 10111, II, 5; **P. 10304**, 39; **P. 10718**, 9

sn brother
P. 9995, IV, 2; **P. 10048**, I, 1; II, 8; **P. 10191**, I, 23

sn-nw second
P. 10110 + 10111, II, 5; **P. 10282** vs. (dem.); **P. 10304**, 39

snt-nṯr sister of the god, epithet of Nephthys
see under *Nbt-ḥwt*, index III

snw *snw*-loaves
P. 9995, I, 14; **P. 10048**, II, 10; **P. 10116**, 21; **P. 10201**, II, 1; **P. 10260**, I, x + 9; II, x + 9

snwt festival of the sixth day
P. 10108, 10; **P. 10112**, 19; **P. 10191**, I, 13; **P. 10199**, 11

snb be healthy, well
P. 10091, II, 3; **P. 10191**, II, 31; **P. 10199**, 24; **P. 10206C**, 9; **P. 10340**, 9

snb health
P. 9995, II, 11; **P. 10048**, IV, 3
see under *ꜥnḫ wḏꜣ snb*

snf blood
P. 10115, 11
see under *Wnm-snf*, index III

snfr make beautiful
P. 10260, I, x + 2

sn[*m*] (?) eat (+ *m*)
P. 10201, I, 12

snm food
P. 10201, II, 5

snn image
P. 10108, 15; **P. 10112**, 22; **P. 10115**, 5

snsn breathe
P. 9995, I, 12, 16, 24; II, 1, 5, 11; **P. 10048**, II, 8; III, 1, 5–6, 8, 10; IV, 3; **P. 10114**, 5; **P. 10191**, II, 13, 21 (?); **P. 10201**, I, 9; vs.; **P. 10260**, II, x + 7, 10, 16; **P. 10264A**, x + 3; **P. 10303**, 8; **P. 10344**, 7, 15

snsn join (something) = receive
P. 10091, II, 3

snsn breath, breathing
P. 9977 vs.; **P. 9995**, I, 16, 22; II, 12, 16, 22, 23; III, 19, 20; **P. 10048**, I, 1; III, 1, 5; IV, 4, 9; VII, 5; **P. 10091**, II, 5; **P. 10109**, [vs.]; **P. 10110 + 10111** vs. (dem.); **P. 10124**, 1; vs.; **P. 10125**, 14; **P. 10191**, II, 10, 33; vs. (dem.); **P. 10199**, 26; vs.; **P. 10260**, II, x + 10, 15; III, x + 2, 4, 15; **P. 10304** vs. (dem.); **P. 10340**, 5; **P. 71513A** vs.
see under *šꜥt* (*n snsn*)

snṯr censing
P. 9995, I, 13; **P. 10048**, II, 9; **P. 10091**, I, 2; **P. 10194**, 10; **P. 10260**, II, x + 8; **P. 10344**, 8

incense
P. 10191, II, 33; **P. 10199**, 26

snḏ fear
P. 10191, I, 49

snḏm make pleasant, comfort
P. 9995, IV, 1; **P. 71513A**, 9; **P. 71513C**, 8

sr Prince (a designation of Osiris)
P. 10108, 12; **P. 10109**, 9; **P. 10125**, 12; **P. 10191**, I, 12; **P. 10199**, 10; **P. 71513A**, 14; **P. 71513B**, [10]

srwḏ strengthen, make to endure
P. 10114, 5; **P. 10191**, I, 33; **P. 10338**, x + 3; **P. 10344**, 2

srnp rejuvenate
P. 10048, I, 1; **P. 10718**, 4

srḳ allow to breathe
P. 10112, 21

sḥ-nṯr god's booth
P. 9995, II, 14; **P. 10285**, 5

sḥwr vilify
P. 10048, VI, 10

sḥn for *ḥn* ?
go speedily
P. 10114, 14

sḥr remove, drive away
P. 10201, I, 14

sḥtp satisfy
P. 10108, 4; **P. 10112**, 8; **P. 10201**, I, 8, 15; **P. 10264A**, x + 4

sḥtm annihilate
P. 10191, I, 17; **P. 71513A**, 4

sḥḏ illuminate
P. 9995, I, 11; **P. 10048**, II, 7; **P. 10108**, [15]; **P. 10260**, II, x + 6

sḫt field
P. 10123, 5
see under *wsḫt sḫwt ỉꜣrw*, index II

sḫꜥ cause to appear
P. 10048, I, 2

**sḫwn* rumours
P. 9995, III, 8; **P. 10048**, V, 5; **P. 10260**, III, x + 9

sḫm control
P. 9995, II, 7; **P. 10048**, III, 11; **P. 10191**, II, 16, 22, 23, 28, 29, 30, 31; **P. 10199**, 22, 23, 24

sḫm image
P. 10108, 14; **P. 10110 + 10111**, I, 3; II, 1; **P. 10116**, 2; **P. 10191**, I, 51; **P. 10201**, II, 8; **P. 10206C**, 2, 7, 8; **P. 10283**, 9; **P. 10304**, 2, 36; **P. 71513D**, x + 2

sḫn in *sḫn st*: occupy the place
P. 10191, II, 20

sḫr overthrow
P. 10125, 18; **P. 10191**, I, 17, 36; II, 3; **P. 10199**, 13, 18; **P. 10338**, [x + 5]; **P. 10705**, [1]

sḫrw rules, plans
P. 10108, 8; **P. 10110 + 10111**, II, 29; **P. 10112**, 16
see under *Ỉmn-sḫrw*, index II

sḫd be upside down
P. 10112, 10

sḫd go down
P. 10114, 11

ssw day
P. 10123, 3; **P. 10194**, 11; **P. 10254**, 3; **P. 10344**, 3, 9

sš write
P. 9995, I, 16, 24; **P. 10048**, III, 1, 6; **P. 10191**, I, 37; **P. 10199**, 20; **P. 10260**, II, x + 10, 16

sš writing
P. 10191, I, 41; **P. 10338**, x + 10

sš pass by
P. 10114, 14

sš... (?) meaning uncertain
P. 10201, I, 7

sšyt evening
P. 10201, II, 6

sšm guide (verb)
P. 10048, III, 9; **P. 10191**, I, 30; **P. 10199**, 16
in *sšm wꜣt*: show the way
P. 10201, II, 13
for *šms*, follow
P. 10260, I, x + 7

sk enclitic particle
also
P. 10091, II, 5; **P. 10108**, 7

sk destruction
P. 10108, 16; **P. 10112**, 24
in *nn sk*
P. 9995, II, 25; IV, 2; **P. 10048**, IV, 12; **P. 10114** vs.; **P. 10116** vs.; **P. 10260**, III, x + 6; **P. 10261**, x + 5; **P. 10283** vs.; **P. 10337** vs.

sktt *sktt*-boat
P. 10110 + 10111, II, 3, 4; **P. 10191**, II, 7; **P. 10201**, II, 5; **P. 10304**, 38; **P. 10340**, 6

sty see under *m-sty*

sty odour, scent
P. 9995, II, 15; **P. 10343**, 8

stwt gather
P. 10344, 2 (+ *m*)

stwt rays
P. 9995, I, 21, 24; II, 12; **P. 10048**, III, 4, 6; IV, 4; **P. 10091**, II, 2; **P. 10109**, 13; **P. 10110 + 10111**, II, 15; **P. 10125**, 28; **P. 10191**, I, 41; II, 34; **P. 10199**, 27; **P. 10260**, II, x + 14, 16; **P. 10282**, 26; **P. 10283**, 10; **P. 10304**, 45; **P. 10191**, I, 41; II, 34; **P. 10338**, x + 11

sṯꜣm clothe
P. 10314, II, 5

sṯꜣt *sṯꜣt*-necropolis
P. 10109 vs.

sḏb wrong
P. 10115, 13

sḏfꜣ provision (verb)
P. 10115, 6

sḏm hear
P. 9995, I, 19; III, 11; **P. 10048**, III, 3; VII, 2; **P. 10091**, I, 6; **P. 10108**, 9; **P. 10109**, 3; **P. 10110 + 10111**, II, 9, 30; **P. 10114**, 7; **P. 10125**, 13; **P. 10191**, II, 5; **P. 10201**, I, 10; **P. 10260**, II, x + 13; III, x + 11; **P. 10304**, 42
obey (+ *n*)
P. 10191, I, 39; **P. 10338**, x + 8, 9

sḏr spend the night
P. 9995, II, 10; **P. 10048**, IV, 2; **P. 10191**, I, 23; **P. 10199**, 15; **P. 10705**, 5

sḏrw (?) sleepers
frag. 14, 3

šꜣw (?) œsophagus (?)
P. 10201, II, 9

šꜣỉs travel, walk (upon: *ḥr*)
P. 10114, 11; **P. 10191**, I, 53; **P. 10314**, I, 3–4

šꜥt book, document
in *šꜥt n snsn*: Book of Breathing
P. 9977 vs.; **P. 9995**, I, 16, 22; II, 12, 16, 22; III, 19; **P. 10048**, I, 1; III, 1, 5; IV, 4, 9; VII, 5; **P. 10091**, II, 5; **P. 10109** vs.; **P. 10110 + 10111** vs. (dem.); **P. 10124**, 1; vs.; **P. 10125**, 14; **P. 10191** vs (dem.); **P. 10199** vs.; **P. 10201** vs.; **P. 10260**, II, x + 10, 15; III, x + 2, 4, 15; **P. 10275** vs.; **P. 10304** vs. (dem.); **P. 10344** [vs].; **P. 10718**, 1; [vs.]; **P. 71513A** vs.; **P. 71513D** vs (?)

šw light
P. 10340, 6
see under *wsḫt šw*, index II

šw be without, be free (of: *m*)
P. 10191, I, 48; **P. 10718**, 11

šw ascend (to: *r*)
P. 10114, 11

šwt (*šbt*) shadow
P. 10114, 10

šps noble
P. 9995, I, 21; **P. 10048**, III, 4; **P. 10191**, I, 14, 41, 52; II, 1, 8, 11, 12, 13, 24; **P. 10201**, II, 10, 17; **P. 10260**, I, x + 15; II, x + 14; **P. 10338**, x + 10

šfy see under *Ḥr-šfy*, index III

šfyt dignity
P. 10201, II, 11, 17 (?)

šm walk, go, proceed (to, towards: *r*)
P. 9995, I, 20; II, 11; III, 21; IV, 2; **P. 10048**, III, 3; IV, 3; VII, 6; **P. 10091**, I, 6; **P. 10108**, 8, 9, 15; **P. 10112**, 15, 18; **P. 10114**, 13; **P. 10123**, 9; **P. 10191**, I, 35, 41; II, 4, 26; vs. (+ *ẖr*, dem.); **P. 10192** vs.; **P. 10194**, 8; **P. 10199**, 18; **P. 10260**, II, x + 13; III, x + 16; **P. 10290**, x + 7; **P. 10304** (+ *ẖr*, dem.); **P. 10314**, I, 4; **P. 10338**, x + 5; **P. 10344**, 12
in *šm* … *ꜥḳ*, *ꜥḳ* … *šm*: come and go
P. 10124, 1; **P. 10254**, 7

šmꜣyw see under *bw šmꜣyw*, index II

šms follow
P. 9995, II, 5, 13, 19; III, 17; **P. 10048**, III, 9; IV, 6; VII, 4; **P. 10091**, I, 7; **P. 10108**, 6; **P. 10109**, 9; **P. 10112**, 13; **P. 10114**, 13; **P. 10116**, [22]; **P. 10125**, 10; **P. 10191**, I, 37; **P. 10260**, I, x + 7 (written *sšm*); III, x + 14; **P. 10283**, 7 (dem.); **P. 10338**, x + 12 (for *sꜣḥ*); **P. 10340**, 3

šms(w) followers, retinue
P. 10191, I, 53; **P. 10199**, 20; **P. 10338**, x + 6; **P. 10343**, 5

šn make an incantation
P. 10201, II, 12

šn make the circuit
P. 10114, 13

šni wrath
P. 10275, 18

šnꜥ turn back, repulse
P. 9995, I, 11, 15; III, 16; **P. 10048**, II, 7, 10; VII, 4; **P. 10114**, 11; **P. 10124** vs.; **P. 10191**, I, 30, 37; **P. 10199**, 21; **P. 10260**, I, x + 4; II, x + 6, 9; III, x + 13

šnw hair
P.10191, I, 45

šnw uncertain meaning
see under *ḥwt šnw*, index II

šnbt throat
P. 9995, I, 14; **P. 10048**, II, 9; **P. 10091**, II, 2; **P. 10260**, II, x + 8
chest
P. 10191, I, 46; **P. 10338**, x + 16

šršr freshness
in *ir šršr*: receive the freshness (?)
P. 9995, I, 20; **P. 10048**, III, 4; **P. 10260**, II, x + 14

šrt (?) nose
P. 10191, I, 45; II, 8, 12

šs nest
P. 10191, II, 11, 13

šsp receive, seize
P. 9995, I, 9, 14; II, 22; III, 18–19; IV, 1 (?), 2; **P. 10048**, II, 4, 9–10; IV, 8, 9; VII, 5; **P. 10091**, I, 2, 5; **P. 10108**, 5; vs.; **P. 10109**, 13 vs.; **P. 10110 + 10111**, II, 12, 18; **P. 10112**, 12; **P. 10116**, 21, 26, 34; **P. 10123**, 3, 7; **P. 10191**, I, 21; II, 7, 33; **P. 10194**, 10, 11; **P. 10201**, II, 1, 3, 4, 6, 7, 14; **P. 10206C**, 10; **P. 10254**, 3; **P. 10260**, I, x + 3, 4, 9, 10, 14; II, x + 4, 8; III, x + 4, 15; **P. 10290**, x + 4; **P. 10304**, 44, 48; **P. 10343**, 7, 9, 10; **P. 10705**, 4

šsp light
see under *Nb-šsp*, index III.

šsp image
P. 10115, 5

štꜣ secret
P. 10110 + 10111, II, 8; **P. 10304**, 41

štꜣ secrete (verb) in *štꜣ ꜥꜣ irw*: secrete the stately of form
P. 10191, I, 26

štꜣ meaning uncertain
P. 10256, 6

šṯyt tomb
P. 10290, x + 8
sanctuary
see under *Wsir-Skr*, index III

šd meaning uncertain
P. 10201, II, 13

šdyt pool
P. 9995, I, 3; **P. 10048**, I, 7

šdḥ *šdḥ*-brew
P. 10191, II, 33; **P. 10199**, 25; **P. 10206C**, 10; **P. 10290**, x + 6

ḳꜣ raise
in the expression *ir ḳꜣn ḫrw*: raise one's voice
P. 10048, VII, 1

ḳy form, appearance
P. 9995, I, 17; II, 10; **P. 10048**, VII, 7; **P. 10260**, II, x + 11; **P. 10191**, II, 19

ḳbḥ intransitive verb: make libation
P. 10110 + 10111, II, 12; **P. 10191**, II, 15; **P. 10304**, 45; **P. 71513B**, 9
transitive verb, in *ḳbḥ mw*: make a libation of water
P. 10108, [12]; **P. 10109**, 9; **P. 10116**, 19; **P. 10123**, 2; **P. 10124**, 9; **P. 10125**, 12; **P. 10191**, I, 12; **P. 10199**, 9

ḳbḥ refresh oneself
P. 10282, 23

ḳbḥ libation
P. 9995, I, 13; IV, 2; **P. 10048**, II, 9; **P. 10091**, I, 2; II, 3; **P. 10110 + 10111**, II, 12, 13, 16; **P. 10116**, 21; **P. 10191**, II, 15, 21, 23; **P. 10194**, 10; **P. 10199**, 28; **P. 10201**, II, 3, 7; **P. 10254**, [3]; **P. 10260**, I, x + 3, 9; II, x + 7; **P. 10264**, 7; **P. 10290**, x + 6; **P. 10304**, 44, 45, 47; **P. 10343**, 7, 12; **P. 10344**, 2

ḳmꜣ create
P. 10115, 4; **P. 9995**, III, 4; **P. 10048**, V, 3; **P. 10260**, III, x + 8

ḳn injury, offence
P. 10048, VI, 3

ḳrst burial
P. 10048, VI, 7; **P. 10110 + 10111**, II, 29; **P. 10194**, 13; **P. 10260**, I, x + 1; **P. 10290**, x + 3; **P. 10343**, 6; **P. 10344**, 2 (written [hieroglyphs]), 9

ḳrty the two caverns
P. 9995, III, 5, 17; **P. 10048**, V, 4; **P. 10260**, III, x + 8

ḳrtyw gods of the caverns
P. 10048, VII, 4; **P. 10260**, III, x + 14

ḳs bone
P. 9995, I, 13–14; IV, 1; **P. 10091**, I, 4; **P. 10108** vs.; **P. 10112** vs.; **P. 10115** [vs.]; **P. 10116** vs.; **P. 10260**, II, x + 8; **P. 10261**, x + 2; **P. 10283** vs.; **P. 10337** vs; **P. 10344**, 2; **P. 10718** vs.; **P. 71513C** vs.
see under *Sd ḳsw*, index III

ḳsn see under *st-ḳsn*

ḳd form
P. 10048, IV, 2

ḳd build
P. 9995, II, 21; **P. 10048**, IV, 8

kꜣ ka
P. 9995, II, 12, 22, 24; **P. 10048**, IV, 4, 9, 11; **P. 10108**, 15; **P. 10110 + 10111**, II, 22, 27; **P. 10112**, 3, 7, 22; **P. 10191**, I, 38; **P. 10199**, 21; **P. 10201**, I, 3, 14; II, 3, 6; **P. 10262 + 10263**, 2; **P. 10290**, x + 6; **P. 10314**, II, 2; **P. 10343**, 9, 10

kꜣ-ḥr-kꜣ Khoiak
P. 10112, 20

kꜣ say, utter
P. 10110 + 10111, II, 21; **P. 10304**, 37, 50

kꜣ bull
P. 9995, I, 13; II, 24; **P. 10108**, 6; **P. 10109**, 9
see under *Kꜣ ḥtp*, index III
in the plural, in the *ḥtp di nsw* formula: oxen
P. 10048, II, 8; IV, 10; **P. 10110 + 10111**, II, 18; **P. 10194**, 11; **P. 10206C**, 8; **P. 10260**, II, x + 7; III, x + 5

kꜣw sustenance
P. 10110 + 10111, II, 22, 26

kꜣp kyphi
P. 10191, II, 33; **P. 10199**, 26

kꜣr sanctuary
P. 10110 + 10111, II, 8; **P. 10304**, 41

kꜣt function
P. 10091, I, 6

ky another
P. 10048, V, 9

ky other
in *ky ḏd*; otherwise said
P. 9995, II, 8

km black
P. 10109, 2; **P. 10110 + 10111**, II, 9; **P. 10125**, 13; **P. 10304**, 42

gnwt annals
P. 10191, I, 40; **P. 10338**, x + 10

grḥ night
P. 9995, I, 4; **P. 10048**, I, 8; **P. 10091**, II, 5; **P. 10109**, 2; **P. 10114**, 14; **P. 10123**, 5; **P. 10125**, 3; **P. 10191**, I, 2, 11, 41; **P. 10194**, 9; **P. 10199**, 3; **P. 10275**, 15; **P. 10337**, 2; **P. 10338**, x + 10; **P. 71513A**, 2, [12]; **P. 71513B**, [1], [8]; **P. 71513C**, 2

grḥ pfy n Ỉnpw ꜥwy.f ḥr ẖwt ḥꜣ it.f Wsir: that night when Anubis put his hands over the relics of his father Osiris
P. 10191, I, 29; **P. 10206A + B**, [4]
grḥ pfy n ir sip m iwty(w).sn: that night of tacking stock of the nobodies
P. 10191, I, 25
grḥ pfy n ꜥḥꜣ-ꜥ: that night of battle
P. 10125, 18; **P. 10191**, I, 16–17; **P. 10199**, 13; **P. 10705**, 1; **P. 71513A**, 20
grḥ pfy n ḥb ꜥḥ pt: that night of the festival of raising the sky
P. 10109, 12
grḥ n ḥb ngꜣ wꜥb n sḫwt.f: the night of the festival of the pure bull in his fields
P. 10123, 5
grḥ pfy n ḥb Hkr: that night of the Haker-festival
P. 10109, 12; **P. 10125**, 19–20
see also under *Hkr*, index III
grḥ n ḥb Ḥ[nw]: night of Henu-festival
P. 10191, I, 14; **P. 71513B**, 6
grḥ (pfy n) ḫwt (ḥr) ḫꜣwt: (that) night of the festival of offerings on the altar
P. 10125, 16; **P. 10191**, I, 13, 18; **P. 10199**, 10; **P. 10303**, 12–13; **P. 10705**, 3
grḥ pfy ḫbs tꜣ ꜥꜣ m Ḏdw: that night of the great earth-ploughing in Busiris
P. 10191, I, 27
grḥ pfy (n) sꜥḥꜥ ḏd m Ḏdw: that night of raising the *ḏd*-pillar in Busiris
P. 10109, 11; **P. 10125**, 17; **P. 10191**, I, 20; **P. 10199**, 14; **P. 10206A + B**, [2]; **P. 10344**, 11 (without *pfy*); **P. 10705**, 2; **P. 71513A**, 22, 23
grḥ pfy n snwt: that night of the festival of the sixth day
P. 10108, 10; **P. 10109**, 10–11; **P. 10112**, 18–19
grḥ pfy n smꜣꜥ ḫrw Ḥr r ḫftyw.f: that night of justifying Horus against his enemies
P. 10125, 20–1
grḥ pfy n sḏr Ỉnpw ꜥwy.f ḥr ẖwt ḥꜣ Wsir: that night when Anubis put his hands over the relics (?), behind Osiris
P. 10199, 15
grḥ pfy n sḏr Ỉst: that night which Isis spent
P. 10191, I, 23; **P. 10705**, 5
grḥ pfy(n) šsp Ḥr msḫnt nṯrw: that night when Horus received the domicile of the gods
P. 10109, 13; **P. 10191**, I, 21; **P. 10705**, 4
grḥ pfy n štꜣ ꜥꜣ irw m Ḥwt-nn-nsw: that night of secreting the stately of form in Heracleopolis
P. 10191, I, 26

grg people (a house) (with: *ḫr*)
P. 10108, 3; **P. 10112**, 5

grg (m—) in wrong
P. 10115, 14

tꜣ feminine singular definite article
P. 9977 vs.; **P. 9995**, III, 19; **P. 10109**, 4, 5, 8; **P. 10110 + 10111** vs. (dem.); **P. 10123**, 1, 7; **P. 10125**, 4, 6, 7, 8; **P. 10191**, I, 3, 4, 5, 6, 10, 36; II, 31; vs. (dem.); **P. 10194**, 6, 7; **P. 10199**, 4, 5, 6, 19, 21, 22; vs.; **P. 10201** vs.; **P. 10260**, III, x + 15; **P. 10264**, 2; **P. 10264A**, x + 2; **P. 10275** vs; **P. 10283**, 3, 6; **P. 10285**, 2, 5; **P. 10290**, x + 7; **P. 10303**, 5; **P. 10304** vs. (dem.); **P. 10337**, 4, 5, 6; **P. 10340**, 2; **P. 10343**, 3, 5, 14; **P. 10344**, 5; **P. 71513A**, 3, 4, [7], [12]; **P. 71513B**, 2,

[4], 7; **P. 71513C**, 6; **frag. 2**, 2, 3; **frag. 3**, 2, [3], 4; **frag. 4**, 2; **frag. 6**, 4

tȝy — element in the possessive article used before feminine singular substantive
P. 10048, VII, 5

tȝ — earth, land
P. 9995, I, 11, 14, 17, 22; III, 22; **P. 10048**, II, 7, 9; III, 5; VII, 7; **P. 10091**, II, 4; **P. 10108**, 2, 8; **P. 10110 + 10111**, II, 5; **P. 10112**, 4, 15; **P. 10114**, 3, 14; **P. 10115**, 4; **P. 10116**, 22; **P. 10191**, I, 27, 31, 38, 42, 49, 50, 52, 53; II, 26, 28; **P. 10199**, 24; **P. 10201**, I, 5, 8; II, 4; **P. 10206C**, 5; **P. 10260**, I, x + 7, 16; II, x + 6, 8, 11, 15; III, x + 16; **P. 10264A**, x + 5, 6, 9 (?); **P. 10275**, 17; **P. 10282**, 2; **P. 10283**, 8; **P. 10304**, 39; **P. 10314**, II, 1, 6; **P. 10344**, 3, 4; **P. 10718**, 9, 12
see under *ḥbs*, and *tȝ ḏsr*, index II

tȝ — bread
P. 9995, I, 13; II, 23; III, 14; **P. 10048**, II, 8; IV, 10; VII, 3; **P. 10110 + 10111**, II, 16, 18; **P. 10114**, 6; **P. 10115**, 3; **P. 10191**, II, 31; **P. 10194**, 11; **P. 10199**, 24, 28; **P. 10201**, II, 7; **P. 10206C**, 9; **P. 10260**, II, x + 7; III, x + 12; **P. 10314**, II, 1; **P. 10304**, 47; **P. 10343**, 10

tw — ending third person masculine singular
P. 10260, III, x + 16

tw — mark of passive, found either alone ('one'), or with suffix pronoun
P. 9995, I, 7, 11, 15; III, 16; **P. 10048**, II, 2, 7, 10; III, 4; VII, 4; **P. 10091**, II, 4; **P. 10110 + 10111**, II, 2; **P. 10114**, 11; **P.10116**, 24; **P. 10191**, I, [31], 40, 48, 49; **P. 10201**, II, 13; **P. 10260**, I, x + 5; II, x + 2, 6, 9; III, x + 13; **P. 10304**, 37, 50; **P. 71513A**, vs.

tw — indefinite pronoun in passive construction
P. 9995, III, 15; **P. 10048**, VII, 4; **P. 10201**, I, 3; **P. 10260**, III, x + 13

twi — first person singular dependent pronoun
P. 10115, 14; **P. 10338**, x + 3 (written *tw*), 17 (written *tw*); **P. 10123**, 5 (written *tw*); **P. 10191**, II, 27 (written *tw*)

twy — feminine singular demonstrative adjective
P. 9995, I, 3; **P. 10048**, I, 7; **P. 10191**, II, 8, 9

twr — (be) pure
P. 9995, I, 2; **P. 10048**, I, 5; **P. 10718**, [7]

twk — second person singular masculine dependent pronoun
P. 9995, I, 4, 7; IV, 2; **P. 10048**, I, 7; II, 2, 10; III, 9 (?), 10; IV, 4; **P. 10091**, I, 4, 5; **P. 10110 + 10111**, II, 7, 15; **P. 10199**, 27; **P. 10206A + B**, 9; **P. 10260**, I, x + 4, 8; II, x + 2, 9; III, x + 4; **P. 10290**, x + 4; **P. 10304**, 46

twt — be complete (with: *m*)
P. 9995, II, 10; **P. 10048**, IV, 2

twtn — second person singular feminine dependent pronoun
P. 10201, I, 2; II, 6

tp — at the beginning of
P. 10108, 15; **P. 10112**, 22; **P. 10340** vs.; **P. 10343**, 7

tp — on, upon
P. 10264A, x + 6, 9

tp — head
P. 10048, IV, 3; **P. 10109**, 2; **P. 10125**, 14; **P. 10201**, I, 5
in *tp rȝ n*: in the mouth of
P. 10114, 3; **P. 10314**, I, 3
see under *ḏȝḏȝ*

tp-rd — ceremony
P. 10108, 11

tpy — first
P. 10116, 33; **P. 10191**, I, 7; II, 18, 24; **P. 10283**, 4; **P. 10337**, 7; **P. 71513A**, 8; **P. 71513B**, 4; **P. 71513C**, 7

tm — entirely
P. 10201, II, 17

tm — negative verb
P. 10201, II, 5 (?); **P. 10290**, x + 4
see under *r tm*

tm — full
in *tm n ꜥnḫ*: full of life
P. 10191, I, 48; **P. 10256**, 4–5; **P. 10338**, x + 17

tmm — worm
P. 10091, II, 6; **P. 10314**, I, 7

tn — feminine singular demonstrative adjective
P. 10114, 4; **P. 10314**, I, 3

tr — moment
P. 10108, [15], 16; **P. 10194**, 11; **P. 10201**, II, 7; **P. 10343**, 7; **P. 10344**, 9

tḫ — plummet
P. 10048, V, 6
see under *ḫt-ib* (?)
P. 10260, III, x + 10.

ṯt — staff (?)
P. 10110 + 10111, II, 27

ṯȝy — male
in *ḥmt ṯȝ*: married woman
P. 10048, VI, 4
spouse
P. 10108, 3; **P. 10112**, 6

ṯȝwy — male child
P. 10191, I, 51

ṯȝw — stealth
in the expression *m ṯȝw*: by stealth
P. 9995, III, 6; **P. 10048**, V, 4; **P. 10260**, III, x + 8

ṯȝw — breath, air
P. 9995, I, 8, 22; **P. 10048**, II, 4; III, 5; **P. 10091**, II, 3; **P. 10109**, 14; **P. 10110 + 10111**, II, 14; **P. 10125**, 28; **P. 10191**, II, 7, 10, 12, 13, 20, 34; **P. 10199**, 26; **P. 10206C**, 11; **P. 10260**, II, x + 4, 12, 15; **P. 10282**, 26; **P. 10283**, 10; **P. 10304**, 45; **P. 10340**, 5, 6
see under *Nb ṯȝw*, index III

ṯbty — feet
P. 10114, 9

ṯni — promote
P. 10191, I, 34; **P. 10206A + B**, 9; **P. 10338**, x + 3

ṯs — assemble
P. 10091, II, 4; **P. 10201**, II, 3

ṯs-pẖr — vice-versa
P. 10191, I, 45; II, 9, 10, 20, 21; **P. 10338**, x + 14

ṯtf — overflow
P. 10108, 7

diw — five
P. 10110 + 10111, II, 2; **P. 10304**, 37

Dwȝt — Duat
P. 9995, I, 6, 15, 20; II, 17, 19–20, 20; III, 11, 16, 20; IV, 1; **P. 10048**, II, 1, 10; III, 4; IV, 4, 7, 8; VII, 2, 4, 6; **P. 10109**, 4, 6, 8; **P. 10110 + 10111**, II, 6; **P. 10114**, 2, 11; **P. 10115**, 8; **P. 10123**, 1; **P. 10125**, 4, 6, 8; **P. 10191**, I, 3, 4, 6, 10, 30, 36; II, 2, 11, 16; **P. 10194**, 6, 7 (?); **P. 10199**, 4, 5, 19; **P. 10206A + B**, 5; **P. 10254**, 1, 6;

P. 10260, I, x + 5, 11, 14; II, x + 2, 9, 13; III, x + 2, 3, 10, 13, 15; **P. 10262 + 10263**, 2 (written); **P. 10264A**, x + 2; **P. 10283**, 3, 6; **P. 10290**, x + 4; **P. 10303**, 5; **P. 10304**, 40; **P. 10337**, 6; **P. 10340**, 2; **P. 10343**, 3, 9; **P. 10718**, 12 (?); **P. 71513A**, 3, 4, [7], [12]; **P. 71513B**, [4], 7; **P. 71513C**, 6; **frag. 2**, 3; **frag. 3**, 2, [3]; **frag. 6**, 4
— *wrt*: **P. 10201**, I, 2; II, 2
— *ḏsrt*: **P. 10201**, II, 3; **P. 10344**, 10

dwꜣty dweller in the Duat
frag. 14, 2

dwn stretch out
P. 10191, II, 3
stand up (?)
P. 10110 + 10111, II, 7; **P. 10191**, II, 3; **P. 10304**, 41
in *m dwn*: continually
P. 10191, II, 3

dbn travel round
P. 10114, 12

dpt-nṯr divine bark
P. 9995, IV, 1

dm pronounce
P. 10110 + 10111, II, 21; **P. 10304**, 50

dmi clothe (+ *r*)
P. 10340 vs.

dmḏ reunite (with: *r*)
P. 10201, II, 2

dni restrain
P. 10114, 11

dr repel
P. 10115, 12

dhn touch (with one's brow)
P. 10201, I, 8

dhnt brow
P. 10201, I, 8

dḥr sickness
P. 10048, V, 10

dgꜣ behold
P. 10112, 16; **P. 10201**, I, 7 (+ *r*); II, 17

ḏt eternity
P. 10108, 16; **P. 10112**, 23; **P. 10314**, II, 7
in expressions where *nḥḥ* also occurs, see under *nḥḥ*
n ḏt: **P. 10264A**, x + 5
r ḏt: **P. 10282**, 28; **P. 10283**, 11
r ḏt sp 2: **P. 10343**, 15
ḫnt ḏt: **P. 10260**, I, x + 12
Djet (eternity divinized)
P. 10114, 13
eternally
P. 9995, IV, 2; **P. 10112**, 12; **P. 10114** vs.; **P. 10116** vs.; **P. 10191**, I, 7; II, 34; **P. 10260**, I, x + 16; **P. 10264A**, x + 9; **P. 10282**, 27; **P. 10283**, 4, 10; vs.; **P. 10290**, x + 8; **P. 10314**, II, 7; **P. 10337**, 7; vs.; **P. 10340**, 7; **P. 10718**, 12; vs.; **P. 71513A**, 8; **P. 71513B**, [5]

ḏt body
P. 9995, I, 24; II, 8; IV, 1; **P. 10048**, III, 6; IV, 1; **P. 10112**, 12; **P. 10114**, 5, 9; **P. 10201**, I, 7

ḏꜣ cross
P. 10115, 6

ḏꜣ spelling for *ṯꜣ* take
P. 10282, 28

ḏꜣḏꜣ head
P. 10109 vs. (dem.); **P. 10191** vs. (dem.); **P. 10283** vs. (dem.); **P. 10286** vs. (dem.); **P. 10340** vs.

ḏꜣḏꜣt Council
P. 10109, 10, 11, 12; **P. 10125**, 16, 17, 18, 19, 20; **P. 10191**, I, 16, 18, 19, 21, 23, 24, 26, 27, 28, 31; **P. 10199**, 12, 13, 14; **P. 10206A + B**, 6; **P. 71513A**, 20, 22; **frag. 16**, [7]

ḏꜥ wind
P. 10114, 10

ḏw evil
P. 10048, VII, 2; **P. 10115**, 11 (written); **P. 10260**, III, x + 11

ḏw mountain
P. 10110 + 10111, II, 4; **P. 10304**, 38
see under *Tpy ḏw.f*, index III

ḏbꜣ equip
P. 10110 + 10111, II, 28

ḏbꜣt coffin
P. 9995, I, 22; **P. 10048**, III, 5; **P. 10260**, II, x + 15

ḏbꜥ finger
P. 9995, I, 16; **P. 10048**, III, 1; **P. 10110 + 10111**, II, 25; **P. 10260**, II, x + 10

ḏfꜣw food, sustenance
P. 9995, II, 3, 24; **P. 10048**, III, 9; IV, 10; **P. 10260**, III, x + 5; **P. 10343**, 10

ḏr since
P. 10108, 3; **P. 10112**, 6

ḏr see under *Nb-r-ḏr*, index III

ḏrt hand
P. 9995, IV, 2 (?); **P. 10191**, I, 49; **P. 10344**, 2
in the dual:
P. 10114, 9

ḏr + suffix all
P. 10109, 6, 14; **P. 10125**, 6, 28; **P. 10191**, I, 6, 9; **P. 10283**, 6; **P. 10337**, 6; **P. 71513A**, 7, 10; **P. 71513B**, [4 ?], [6 ?]; **P. 71513C**, 6

ḏs own, himself
P. 9995, I, 16; II, 25; **P. 10048**, III, 1; IV, 11; **P. 10191**, I, 39, 41; **P. 10260**, II, x + 10; III, x + 6; **P. 10338**, x + 8, 10

ḏsr sacred
P. 10201, II, 3; **P. 10344**, 10
see under *bw ḏsr*, *ḫꜣst ḏsrt*, *tꜣ ḏsr*, index II

ḏd say, tell, speak
P. 9995, I, 23; **P. 10048**, III, 6; **P. 10110 + 10111**, II, 7, 30; **P. 10123**, 6; **P. 10124**, 4; **P. 10191**, I, 42; **P. 10201**, I, 10; **P. 10260**, II, x + 16; **P. 10290**, x + 5; **P. 10303** vs.; **P. 10304**, 40; **P. 10338**, x + 11

ḏd word
P. 9995, II, 8; **P. 10091**, I, 3; **P. 10114**, 6; **P. 10262 + 10263**, 7; **P. 10303** vs.
see under *ky ḏd*

ḏd mdw to be recited
P. 9995, II, 18, 19; **P. 10048**, I, 4; IV, 5, 7; **P. 10194**, 2; **P. 10260**, III, x + 3; **P. 71513A**, 2

ḏd be stable
P. 9995, I, 11; II, 9; **P. 10048**, II, 6; IV, 1; **P. 10091**, II, 7; **P. 10108**, 2; vs.; **P. 10112**, 4; vs.; **P. 10114**, 3; **P. 10115** vs.; **P. 10116** vs.; **P. 10123** vs.; **P. 10125** vs.; **P. 10260**, II, x + 6; **P. 10261**, x + 2; **P. 10262 + 10263** vs.; **P. 10283** vs.; **P. 10286** vs.; **P. 10290**, x + 8; **P. 10303** vs.; **P. 10314**, I, 3; II, 6; **P. 10337** vs; **P. 10340** vs.; **frag. 1**.

ḏd *ḏd*-pillar
P. 10109, 11; **P. 10112**, 21; **P. 10125**, 17; **P. 10191**, I, 20; **P. 10199**, 14; **P. 10344**, 11; **P. 10705**, 2; **P. 71513A**, 23

Index II: Toponyms

ꜣbw — Elephantine
P. 9995, II, 3; **P. 10048**, III, 8; **P. 10110 + 10111**, I, 20; **P. 10116**, 20; **P. 10304**, 18

ꜣbḏw — Abydos
P. 9977, 9; **P. 9995**, II, 23; **P. 10048**, IV, 10; **P. 10109**, 12; **P. 10110 + 10111**, I, 12; **P. 10115**, 3; **P. 10116**, 10, 28; **P. 10124**, 5; **P. 10125**, 18, 25; **P. 10194**, 3; **P. 10254**, 3; **P. 10260**, III, x + 5; **P. 10264**, 5; **P. 10282**, 11; **P. 10286**, 4; **P. 10303**, 4; **P. 10304**, 10; **P. 10331**, 6; **P. 10343**, [3]; **P. 10344**, 12
see under *Wsir*, index III

Ỉꜣt Ḏꜣm — Mound of Djeme
P. 9995, IV, 2; **P. 10108**, 13; **P. 10116**, 25, 30; **P. 10123**, 2, 3; **P. 10254**, 4; **P. 10343**, 13
see under *Ḏꜣm*

Ỉit — Iit
P. 71513A, 10
see under *pr ỉit*

Ỉwnw — Heliopolis
P. 9977, 2, 3, 4; **P. 9995**, I, 21; III, 1; **P. 10048**, V, 1; **P. 10108**, 12; **P. 10109**, 3, 9, 10; **P. 10110 + 10111**, I, 7, 8, 9, 16; **P. 10112**, 18; **P. 10115**, 14; **P. 10116**, 3, 5, 6, 7, 14; **P. 10123**, 5; **P. 10124**, 1, 2, 9, 10; **P. 10125**, 12, 13, 16, 23, 24, 26; **P. 10191**, I, 10, 12, 13, 16, 40, 41; II, 17; **P. 10199**, 13; **P. 10260**, II, x + 14; III, x + 6; **P. 10264**, 3, 6; **P. 10275**, 7; **P. 10282**, 5, 6, 9, 16; **P. 10283**, 5; **P. 10286**, 3; **P. 10304**, 4, 6, 7, 14; **P. 10331**, 1–3, 10; **P. 71513A**, 11, 20, 25, 26, 27, 34; **P. 10705**, [1]

Ỉwnw šmꜥ — Karnak
P. 9995, IV, 2; **P. 10254**, 5; **P. 10344**, 13

Ỉpt — see under *Ỉmn-Ỉpt*, index III

Ỉpw — Ipu (Panopolis-Akhmim)
P. 10110 + 10111, I, 29; **P. 10304**, 27

ỉmꜣḫt — land of the blessed
P. 10110 + 10111, II, 30

Ỉmn-sḫrw — *Ỉmn-sḫrw*-necropolis
P. 10109, 3

Ỉnb-ḥḏ — White Wall, designation of Memphis
P. 10110 + 10111, I, 37; **P. 10191**, I, 32; II, 17; **P. 10338**, x + 1

Ỉrt Rꜥ — Eye of Re, designation of Hermopolis
P. 10191, II, 20
See also index III

Ỉḳ — *Ỉḳ* (nome of Dendara)
P. 10110 + 10111, I, 27; **P. 10304**, 25

Ỉdbw-rḫty — Idebu-rekhty
P. 10109, 12; **P. 10125**, 19; **P. 10191**, I, 23; **P. 10705**, [5]

ꜥnḏ — Andj
P. 10125, 26

ꜥrḳ-ḥḥ — Areq-heh
P. 9995, II, 4–5; **P. 10048**, III, 9

Wꜣst — Thebes
P. 10048, II, 10; VII, 1; **P. 10108**, 13, 15; **P. 10108**, 4, 12; **P. 10110 + 10111**, I, 24; **P. 10112**, 8, 22, 23; **P. 10116**, 3, 4, 18; **P. 10123**, 10; **P. 10191**, I, 52; II, 16; **P. 10282**, 3; **P. 10290**, x + 4; **P. 10304**, [4], 5, 22; **frag. 17**, 2

Wꜣst-nḫt — Thebes the victorious
P. 10123, 7, 9; **P. 10124**, 8

Wꜣḏt — Wadjet
P. 10110 + 10111, I, 30; **P. 10304**, 28

ww Mꜣꜥt — region of Maat
P. 10110 + 10111, II, 26
see under *wsḫt ww Mꜣꜥt*

Wnw — Unu (= Hermopolis)
P. 10048, VI, 1; **P. 10191**, II, 17

wsḫt ỉꜣrw — hall <of the Fields> of reeds
P. 10191, I, 5

wsḫt ww Mꜣꜥt — hall of the region of Maat
P. 10108, [5]; **P. 10109**, 8; **P. 10112**, 12; **P. 10125**, 9

wsḫt Wsir — hall of Osiris
P. 71513B, vs.

wsḫt (nt)Mꜣꜥty — hall of the two Maats
P. 9995, I, 5; IV, 2; **P. 10048**, I, 9; **P. 10109**, 5; **P. 10115**, 4, 10; **P. 10123**, 1–2, 7; **P. 10125**, 7; **P. 10191**, I, 5; **P. 10199**, 6; **P. 10201**, II, 15; **P. 10254**, 6; **P. 10260**, I, x + 4, 11; **P. 10285**, 3, 7; **P. 10337**, 4; **P. 10340**, 3–4; **P. 10343**, 5; **P. 71513B**, [3]; **frag. 3**, [3]

wsḫt sḫwt ỉꜣrw — hall of the Field of reeds
P. 10109, 5; **P. 10125**, 7; **P. 10337**, 5; **P. 71513A**, 5; **P. 71513B**, 3; **P. 71513C**, 5; **frag. 3**, 4–[5]

wsḫt šw — hall of light
P. 9995, I, 8; **P. 10048**, II, 3; **P. 10260**, II, x + 3

wsḫt Gb hall of Geb
P. 9995, I, 7; **P. 10048**, II, 2; **P. 10260**, II, x + 3

Bꜣst Bubastis
P. 10048, V, 10
bꜣg see under *Ḫbs-bꜣg*
Bꜥḫw Bah
P. 10191, II, 17
bw šmꜣyw place of the foreigners
P. 9977, 6; **P. 10110 + 10111**, I, 10; **P. 10124**, 2–3; **P. 10116**, 8 (written *bꜣ*—); **P. 10124**, 2–3; **P. 10125**, 24; **P. 10264**, 4 (written *bꜣ*—); **P. 10282**, 7 (written *bꜣ* —); **P. 10304**, 8; **P. 10331**, 4 (written *bꜣ*—); **P. 71513A**, [28]
bw ḏsr sacred place
P. 10201, II, 3

P Pe
P. 10109, 13; **P. 10110 + 10111**, I, 14; **P. 10116**, 12; **P. 10124**, 6; **P. 10125**, 20; **P. 10191**, I, 21; **P. 10199**, 10; **P. 10264**, 5 (?); **P. 10282**, 14; **P. 10304**, 12; **P. 10331**, 8; **P. 10191**, I, 3; **P. 10199**, 4; **P. 10283**, 3; **P. 10705**, [4]; **P. 71513A**, [32], 33
see under *Dp*
pr ỉỉt Per-iit
P. 10191, I, 9; **P. 71513B**, 6
see under *Ỉỉt*
pr ỉbw House of *ỉb*-hearts
P. 10191, I, 34; **P. 10338**, x + 4
pr ꜥnḫ ỉrw House of he who lives on rites
P. 10314, I, 4
pr Bꜣ-nb-Ḏdt House of Banebdjed
P. 10110 + 10111, I, 17; **P. 10304**, 15
pr Rꜥ House of Re
P. 10116, 21
pr ḥ(ꜣ)tyw House of *ḥ(ꜣ)ty*-hearts
P. 10191, I, 34; **P. 10338**, x + 4
pr Ḥnw House of Henu
P. 10191, I, 3; **P. 10199**, 4; **P. 10283**, 3; **P. 71513A**, 3; **P. 71513B**, [2]
pr Gb House of Geb
P. 9995, I, 10; **P. 10048**, II, 5; **P. 10260**, II, x + 5
Mꜣnw Manu (written )
P. 10116, 27
Mꜣdw Medamoud
P. 10116, 32
Mꜥꜣt *Mꜥꜣt*-land (?)
P. 10194, 12
Mn-nfr Memphis
P. 10304, 35
Mnst Menset
in *Mnst ḥrt*: upper Menset
P. 9977, 3; **P. 10110 + 10111**, 8; **P. 10116**, 6; **P. 10125**, 23; **P. 10264**, 3; **P. 10304**, 6; **P. 10331**, 2; **P. 71513A**, [26] (?)
in *Mnst ẖrt*: upper Menset
P. 9977, 4; **P. 10110 + 10111**, 9; **P. 10116**, 7; **P. 10125**, 24; **P. 10304**, 7; **P. 10331**, 3; **P. 71513A**, 27 (?)
see under *st ḥrt, st ẖrt*
Mr-wr Merwer
P. 10110 + 10111, I, 36; **P. 10304**, 34

Mḥw North, Lower Egypt
P. 9995, II, 4; **P. 10048**, III, 9; **P. 10191**, I, 13; **P. 10199**, 11; **P. 10314**, II, 7

Nꜣrf Naref
P. 10191, I, 26
Nwbt Ombos
P. 10110 + 10111, I, 21; **P. 10304**, 19
Nḫb Nekheb
P. 10110 + 10111, I, 23; **P. 10304**, 21
Nṯr-šmꜥ Neter-shema (a name of Coptos)
P. 10110 + 10111, I, 26; **P. 10125**, 26; **P. 10304**, 24

Rꜣ-stꜣw Ro-setau
P. 9995, II, 5; III, 7; **P. 10048**, III, 10; V, 5; **P. 10109** vs.; **P. 10125**, 27; **P. 10191**, I, 28; **P. 10199**, 14; **P. 10206A + B**, 3; **P. 10260**, III, x + 9; **P. 10705**, [6]

Ḥꜣp-(n)-nb.s Hapounnebes
P. 9995, II, 6; **P. 10048**, III, 10
Ḥwt Ỉmntt Mansion of the West
P. 10264A, x + 8–9
Ḥwt-ꜥꜣt Great Mansion
P. 10125, 13; **P. 10191**, I, 29; **P. 10199**, 15
Ḥwt bỉt Mansion of the bee
P. 10314, II, 4
Ḥwt Bnbn Mansion of the obelisk
P. 10110 + 10111, II, 6–7; **P. 10201**, II, 5, 16; **P. 10304**, 40
Ḥwt nwb Mansion of Gold
P. 10116, 28, 32; **P. 10191**, I, 32; **P. 10206A + B**, [7]; **P. 10338**, x + 1; **P. 10343**, 14
see under *Wsỉr*, index III
Ḥwt nn-nsw Heracleopolis
P. 10110 + 10111, I, 35; **P. 10191**, I, 26; **P. 10304**, 33
Ḥwt-nsw Heracleopolis
P. 10125, 27
Ḥwt sr Mansion of the Prince
P. 10108, 12; **P. 10109**, 9; **P. 10123**, 2; **P. 10124**, 7; **P. 10125**, 12; **P. 10191**, I, 12; **P. 10199**, 9; **P. 10201**, II, 4; **P. 71513A**, 14; **P. 71513B**, 10
see under *sr*, index I
Ḥwt sḫmw Diospolis Parva
P. 10110 + 10111, I, 28; **P. 10304**, 26
Ḥwt Skr Mansion of Sokar
P. 10116, 31; **P. 10343**, 14
Ḥwt šnw Mansion of *šnw*
P. 10110 + 10111, I, 11; **P. 10116**, 9; **P. 10124**, 4, 7; **P. 10125**, 25; **P. 10282**, 8; **P. 10304**, 9; **P. 10331**, 5; **P. 71513A**, [29]
Ḥwt-kꜣ-Ptḥ Mansion of the ka of Ptah (Memphis)
P. 10048, VI, 8; **P. 10191**, I, 37, 39; **P. 10199**, 20; **P. 10338**, x + 7
Ḥbnw Hebenu
P. 10110 + 10111, I, 33; **P. 10304**, 31
Ḥbs-bꜣg Hebes-bag
P. 10108, 7
Ḥr-dy Hordaï
P. 10110 + 10111, I, 34; **P. 10125**, 27; **P. 10304**, 32
Ḥkꜣ ꜥnḏ Heqa-andj
P. 10048, VI, 6

ḫꜣst ḏsrt — sacred region
P. 10314, II, 5–6

Ḫm — Letopolis
P. 9995, III, 10; **P. 10048**, V, 7, 9; **P. 10191**, I, 9, 18, 18–19, 45; **P. 10260**, III, x + 10; **P. 10303**, 13; **P. 10338**, x + 15; **P. 10705**, [3]; **P. 71513A**, 10; **P. 71513B**, [6]

Ḫmnw — Hermopolis
P. 9977, 11; **P. 9995**, I, 16; III, 4; **P. 10048**, III, 1; **P. 10110 + 10111**, I, 3, 18; **P. 10116**, 2, 16; **P. 10194**, 4; **P. 10260**, II, x + 10; III, x + 7; **P. 10282**, 16; **P. 10304**, 2, 16; **P. 10331**, 12; **P. 10343**, 4; **P. 71513A**, 36; **P. 71513D**, x + 3
see under *I͗*, *Nb Ḫmnw*, index III

Ḫnmt-ꜥnḫ — Khenemet-ankh
P. 9995, IV, 2; **P. 10108**, 15

Ḫr-ꜥḥꜣ — Kher-Aha
P. 9995, III, 2; **P. 10048**, V, 2; **P. 10191**, I, 47; **P. 10260**, III, x + 7; **P. 10338**, x + 16
see under *Nb Ḫr-ꜥḥꜣ*, index III

st ꜥꜣt — great place
P. 10116, 31; **P. 10343**, 14

st Mꜣꜥt — Place of Truth
P. 10115, 13

st ḥrt — upper place
P. 10124, 2; **P. 10275**, 8; **P. 10282**, 6
see under *Mnst ḥrt*

st ẖrt — lower place
P. 10124, 2; **P. 10275**, [9]; **P. 10282**, 9
see under *Mnst ẖrt*

Sꜣw — Saïs
P. 10338, x + [16]; **P. 10191**, I, 46
see under *Nt*, index III

Sꜣw — Siout
P. 10110 + 10111, I, 31; **P. 10304**, 29
see under *Wp-wꜣwt*, index III

sḫwt i͗ꜣrw — Field of reeds
P. 10124 vs.
see under *wsḫt sḫwt i͗ꜣrw*

sḫwt ḥtp — Field of offerings
P. 9995, I, 3; **P. 10048**, I, 7

sḫwt snḥm — Field of locusts
P. 9995, I, 3–4; **P. 10048**, I, 7

Šmꜥ — Upper Egypt
P. 9995, II, 4; **P. 10048**, III, 9; **P. 10110 + 10111**, I, 25; II, 3; **P. 10191**, I, 8, 13; **P. 10199**, 11; **P. 10304**, 37; **P. 10314**, II, 7; **P. 10344**, 13; **frag. 20**, 2 (?)
see under *Nṯr-šmꜥ*, *tꜣ šmꜥ*

Ḳws — Cusae
P. 10110 + 10111, I, 32; **P. 10304**, [30]
see under *Ḥwt-Ḥr*, index III

Km(-wr) — Kem(-wer) (Athribis)
P. 10116, 20

Gbtyw — Coptos
P. 10116, 28
see under *Wsir*, index III

Gsy — Kus
P. 10110 + 10111, I, 25; **P. 10304**, 23
see under *Ḥr-wr*, index III

tꜣ šmꜥ — Upper Egypt
P. 10282, 12; **P. 71513A**, [9]; **P. 71513B**, [5 ?]; **P. 71513C**, 8 (?)
see under *Šmꜥ*

tꜣ ḏsr — sacred land
P. 9995, II, 9; **P. 10048**, IV, 1; **P. 10115**, 3; **P. 10718**, [1]; **P. 10285**, 4
see under *I͗npw*, index III

Tnw — This
P. 10048, VI, 7

Tꜣ-wr — Ta-wer
P. 9977, 8; **P. 9995**, II, 6; **P. 10048**, III, 10; **P. 10108**, 10; **P. 10110 + 10111**, I, 13; **P. 10112**, 19; **P. 10114**, 15; **P. 10116**, 11, 24; **P. 10124**, 5; **P. 10125**, 26; **P. 10264**, 5; **P. 10282**, 10; **P. 10286**, 5; **P. 10304**, 11; **P. 10331**, 7
see under *I͗st*, index III

Ṯpḥt-ḏꜣt — Tepehet-djat
P. 10048, VI, 2

Dp — Dep
P. 10109, 13; **P. 10110 + 10111**, I, 15; **P. 10116**, 13; **P. 10282**, 15; **P. 10304**, 13; **P. 10331**, 9
in the pairing *P Dp*
P. 10125, 20; **P. 10191**, I, 21; **P. 10705**, [4]; **P. 71513A**, 33
see under *Wꜣḏyt*, *Nbt-ḥwt*, index III

Ḏꜣm — Djeme
P. 9977, 1; **P. 10124**, 9; **P. 10194**, 10; **P. 10344**, 3, 8
see under *I͗ꜣt Ḏꜣm*, and *I͗mn-I͗pt*, *Ḥwt-Ḥr*, index III

Ḏbꜣ — Djeba (Edfu)
P. 10110 + 10111, I, 22; **P. 10304**, 20

Ḏdw — Busiris
P. 9995, II, 6, 14, 17; **P. 10048**, III, 10; IV, 5; **P. 10109**, 11; **P. 10112**, 20; **P. 10114**, 15; **P. 10116**, 15, 23, 29; **P. 10125**, 17; **P. 10191**, I, 20, 27, 28; **P. 10199**, 14; **P. 10206A + B**, 2; **P. 10254**, 2; **P. 10260**, III, x + 2; **P. 10344**, 11; **P. 10705**, 2; **P. 71513A**, 22, 23
see under *Wsir*, index III

Ḏdt — Mendes
see under *pr Bꜣ-nb-Ḏdt* and *Bꜣ-nb-Ḏdt*, index III

Index III: Names

Divine names

ꜣḥt Ahet
P. 10256, 8
— *wr(t) mwt nt Rꜥ*
P. 10256, 3–4

ꜣḫt Akhet
P. 10110 + 10111, II, 17; **P. 10114**, 13; **P. 10304**, 47

ꜣḫt Akhet (a cow)
P. 10256, 6

ꜣgb-wr Agebwer
P. 10115, 7

Ỉ name of Thoth
P. 9995, I, 23; **P. 10048**, III, 5; **P. 10091**, I, 3; II, 5; **P. 10109**, 10 vs.; **P. 10110 + 10111**, I, 3; II, 21; **P. 10124**, 1; vs.; **P. 10125**, 14, 15, 22; **P. 10191**, I, 15, 19, 22, 24, 25, 27, 28, 41, 48, 52; **P. 10191**, II, 4, 12, 24; **P. 10199**, 11; **P. 10260**, II, x + 16; **P. 10283**, 9; **P. 10303**, 9; **P. 10304**, 2, 36; **P. 10338**, x + 10; **P. 71513A**, 11, [19], 21, 23; vs.; **P. 71513D**, x + 2
— *ꜥꜣ ꜥꜣ ꜥꜣ wr nb Ḫmnw*: **P. 10282**, 16
— *ꜥꜣ ꜥꜣ nb Ḫmnw*: **P. 9995**, I, 15–16; **P. 10048**, III, 1; **P. 10260**, II, x + 10
— *ꜥꜣ nb Ḫmnw*: **P. 10194**, 4; **P. 10343**, 4
— *ꜥꜣ wr nb Ḫmnw*: **P. 9977**, 11; **P. 10331**, 12
— *m Ḫmnw*: **P. 10110 + 10111**, I, 18; **P. 10116**, 16; **P. 10304**, 16
— *mḥ wḏꜣt*: **P. 10191**, II, 27
— *nb mdw-nṯr*: **P. 10191**, I, 10; **P. 71513A**, 11
— *nb Ḫmnw*: **P. 10331**, 12; **P. 71513A**, 36
— *nty (r)dỉ smdwt n nṯrw nb*: **P. 10191**, I, 10
see under *Nb Ḫmnw* and *Ḏḥwty*

ỉt ỉtw father of fathers
P. 10108, 14; **P. 10254**, 5

Ỉỉ-m-ḥtp Imhotep
P. 10116, 33

Ỉꜥḥ Iah (the moon)
P. 10048, I, 2

Ỉmy-wt the Embalmer (epithet and designation of Anubis)
P. 10201, II, 11; **P. 10290**, x + 2
as epithet, see under *Ỉnpw*

Ỉmn Amun
P. 9995, I, 8, 12, 18, 21, 22; **P. 10048**, II, 3, 7; III, 3, 5; **P. 10091**, II, 3; **P. 10109**, 14; **P. 10110 + 10111**, II, 14; vs.; **P. 10125**, 28; **P. 10191**, I, 52; II, 7, 12, 34; **P. 10199**, 26; **P. 10206C**, 11; **P. 10260**, II, x + 3, 7, 12, 15; **P. 10282**, 26; **P. 10283**, 10; **P. 10304**, 44; **P. 10340**, 6; **P. 10344**, 4

Ỉmn-Ỉpt Amenipet
P. 10091, II, 3; **P. 10123**, 3; **P. 10124**, 9; **P. 10194**, 10; **P. 10254**, 4; **P. 10343**, 7; **P. 10344**, [2], 8

Ỉmn-Ỉpt n Ḏꜥm Amenipet of Djeme
— *nṯr ꜥꜣ ꜥnḫ ḥr[y nṯrw]*
P. 10344, 8

Ỉmn-wr Amun the Elder
see under *Bꜣ n Ỉmn-wr*

Ỉmn-Rꜥ Amun-Re
P. 10048, IV, 4; **P. 10123**, 9

Ỉmn-Rꜥ-Ḥr-ꜣḫty Amun-Re-Horakhty
P. 9995, II, 12

Ỉmn-ḥtp Amenhotep
— *sꜣ Ḥpw*: **P. 10116**, 34
— *sš [nsw] sš nfrw ḥr-tp*: **P. 10116**, 34

Ỉmnt Amunet
— *wrt*: **P. 10256**, 2

Ỉmntt Amentet (divinized necropolis)
— *wrt*: **P. 10123** vs.
— *nfrt*: **P. 10108**, 5, vs.; **P. 10112** vs.; **P. 10115** vs.; **P. 10125** vs. (?)

Ỉmst Amset
P. 10116, 29

Ỉnpw Anubis
P. 9995, I, 15; **P. 10048**, II, 10; **P. 10108**, 5; **P. 10112**, 12; **P. 10191**, I, 3, 29, 36, 46; **P. 10199**, 15, 19; **P. 10260**, II, x + 9; **P. 10314**, I, 7; **P. 10338**, x + 6, 15; **P. 10705**, [6]
— *(m) ỉmy wt*: **P. 9995**, IV, 1; **P. 10091**, I, 4; **P. 10260**, I, x + 2; **P. 10285**, 4
— *pꜣ ỉry-ꜥꜣ mtr n tꜣ Dwꜣt*: **P. 10109**, 8; **P. 10125**, 8; **P. 10191**, I, 4; **P. 10199**, 5; **P. 10337**, [3]; **P. 71513A**, 4; **P. 71513B**, 2; **P. 71513C**, 3; **frag. 2**, [3]
— *m Ḥr-dy*: **P. 10110 + 10111**, I, 34; **P. 10125**, 27; **P. 10304**, 32;
— *nb tꜣ ḏsr*: **P. 10285**, 4
— *ḫnty sḥ-nṯr*: **P. 10285**, 5
— *sꜣ Wsỉr*: **P. 10109**, 8; **P. 10125**, 8; **P. 10191**, I, 3; **P. 10199**, 4–[5]; **P. 10264A**, x + 4; **P. 10337**, 3;

P. 10340, 2; **P. 71513A**, [4]; **P. 71513B**, 2;
P. 71513C, 3; **frag. 2**, [3]; **frag. 3**, [3]
see under *Ỉmy-wt*

Ỉrt(y).f-m-ḫt He whose eye(s) is (are) fire
— *pr m Ḫm*: **P. 9995**, III, 9–10; **P. 10260**, III, x + 10

Ỉrt.f-m-sḏt He whose eye is a flame
— *pr m Ḫm*: **P. 10048**, V, 7

Ỉrt Rꜥ Eye of Re
as designation of Hermopolis, see index II
as designation of Isis
P. 10314, I, 5

Ỉḥy Ihy
— *pr m Nwn*: **P. 10048**, VI, 10

Ỉst Isis
P. 9995, IV, 2; **P. 10048**, I, 1; **P. 10091**, I, 3; **P. 10191**, I, 7, 23, 46; **P. 10260**, I, x + 10; **P. 10282**, 20; **P. 10283**, 4; **P. 10338**, x + 15; **P. 10705**, [5]; **P. 71513A**, 8; **P. 71513B**, [5]; **P. 71513C**, 7
— *irt Rꜥ*: **P. 10314**, I, 5
— *wrt*: **P. 10194**, 13; **P. 10256**, 1; **P. 10260**, I, x + 1; **P. 10264**, 2; **P. 10282**, 23; **P. 10343**, 6; **P. 10344**, 1, 9; **P. 10282**, 28; **P. 10314**, I, 5
— *m Nṯrw-šmꜥ*: **P. 10110 + 10111**, I, 26; **P. 10125**, 26; **P. 10304**, 24
— *m Tꜣ-wr*: **P. 9977**, 8; **P. 10110 + 10111**, I, 13; **P. 10116**, 11; **P. 10124**, 5; **P. 10125**, 25–6; **P. 10282**, 10; **P. 10286**, 5; **P. 10304**, 11; **P. 10331**, 7
— *mwt-nṯr*: **P. 10194**, 13; **P. 10256**, 1; **P. 10260**, I, x + 1; **P. 10264**, 2; **P. 10282**, 28; **P. 10314**, I, 5; **P. 10343**, 6
— *nṯrt* [...]: **P. 10264**, 2
— *nṯrt ꜥꜣt*: *P.* **10282**, 28
— *tꜣ nbt* ... (?): **P. 10282**, 28

(Ỉ)tm Atum
P. 9995, I, 8; **P. 10048**, II, 3; **P. 10109**, 1; **P. 10110 + 10111**, II, 11; **P. 10115**, 2; **P. 10191**, I, 2, 12, 40, 42, 43; II, 4, 23; **P. 10199**, 2, 9; **P. 10260**, II, x + 3; **P. 10283**, 2; **P. 10303**, 2; **P. 10304**, 44; **P. 10337**, [1]; **P. 10338**, x + 9, 11; **P. 10340**, 6; **P. 10343**, 2; **P. 71513A**, [2], 8; **P. 71513B**, 1; **frag. 2**, 1
— *m Ỉwnw*: **P. 10286**, 3
— *nb Ỉwnw m Ỉwnw*: **P. 9997**, 3; **P. 10110 + 10111**, I, 7; **P. 10116**, 5; **P. 10125**, 23; **P. 10282**, 5; **P. 10304**, 4; **P. 10331**, 1; **P. 71513A**, 25
see under *Rꜥ-Ỉtm*

ꜥm irt Swallower of the eye
P. 10048, V, 4; **P. 10260**, III, x + 8
— *pr m ḳr(r)ty*: **P. 9995**, III, 5; **P. 10048**, V, 4; **P. 10260**, III, x + 8

ꜥnḫ irw He who lives on rites
P. 10191, II, 5–6
see under *pr ꜥnḫ irw*, index II

Wꜣmmty Wamenty
— *pr m ḫbt*: **P. 10048**, VI, 4

Wꜣḏyt Wadjyt
P. 9995, I, 4; **P. 10048**, I, 7–8
— *m P Dp*: **P. 71513A**, 33
— *m Dp*: **P. 10110 + 10111**, I, 15; **P. 10116**, 13; **P. 10282**, 15; **P. 10304**, 13; **P. 10331**, 9

Wp-wꜣwt Wepwawet
P. 9995, I, 19; **P. 10048**, III, 3; **P. 10191**, I, 45; **P. 10260**, II, x + 12; **P. 10338**, x + 15
— *m Sꜣw*: **P. 10110 + 10111**, I, 31; **P. 10304**, 29

Wn-nfr Wennefer
— *mꜣꜥ-ḫrw*: **P. 10116**, 29
see under *Wsir*

Wnm-snf He who feeds on blood
— *pr m nmt*: **P. 10048**, VI, 3

Wr ꜣt Great of power
— *pr m Ḫr-ꜥḥꜣ*: **P. 9995**, III, 2; **P. 10260**, III, x + 7

Wrtw Urtu
— *wr*: **P. 10254**, 4
— *wr m Ỉwnw šmꜥ*: **P. 9995**, IV, 2

Wsir Osiris
1) as designation of the god
P. 9995, I, 9, 12, 24; II, 2, 5, 11, 13, 18, 19, 10, 23; III, 17; **P. 10048**, I, 1; II, 5; III, 4, 6, 8, 9; IV, 3, 6, 7, 10; VII, 4; **P. 10091**, II, 6; **P. 10109**, 5, 8, 9, 10; **P. 10110 + 10111**, I, 3; II, 9, 12, 19; **P. 10114**, 2; **P. 10115**, 2; **P. 10116**, 2, 19; **P. 10123**, 1, 4; **P. 10125**, 6, 8, 15; **P. 10191**, I, 3, 4, 6, 16, 18, 19, 21, 22, 24, 26, 29, 37, 51, 53; II, 24; **P. 10199**, 6, 7, 12, 15, 20; **P. 10206A + B**, 1, 3, 4; **P. 10254**, 3; **P. 10260**, II, x + 5, 7, 16; III, x + 4, 14; **P. 10264**, 2; **P. 10282**, 20; **P. 10283**, 4, 7, 9; **P. 10285**, 2, 3, 7; **P. 10286**, 4; **P. 10303**, 7, 11; **P. 10304**, 2, 42, 44, 49; **P. 10314**, I, 2; **P. 10337**, 3, 6, 8; **P. 10340**, 3, 9; **P. 10343**, 2, 5, 9; **P. 10705**, [6]; **P. 71513A**, 4, [5], 7, 8, 9, [19], 22; **P. 71513B**, 2, 4, 5; **P. 71513C**, [3], [4], [6], 7; **P. 71513D**, x + 2
— *ꜥꜣ n Ỉꜣt Ḏꜣm*: **P. 10124**, 9
— *Wn-nfr*: **P. 10304**, 35; **P. 10304**, 36
— *Wn-nfr mꜣꜥ-ḫrw*: **P. 10110 + 10111**, II, 2; **P. 10254**, 2
— *wr*: **P. 10201**, II, 9
— *m ꜥnḏ*: **P. 10125**, 26
— *m Wꜣst*: **P. 10191**, II, 16
— *m Rꜣ-stꜣw*: **P. 10125**, 27
— *nb ꜣbḏw*: **P. 9995**, II, 23; **P. 10048**, IV, 10: **P. 10115**, 3 (?); **P. 10194**, 3; **P. 10260**, III, x + 5; **P. 10303**, 3–4; **P. 10343**, [2]
— *nb Ḏdw*: **P. 10116**, 29
— *nṯr ꜥꜣ*: **P. 9995**, II, 23; **P. 10048**, IV, 10; **P. 10115**, 2; **P. 10194**, 3; **P. 10260**, III, x + 5; **P. 10303**, 3; **P. 10343**, [2]
— *nṯr ꜥꜣ m Ỉmntt*: **P. 10260**, I, x + 13
— *nṯr nb ꜣbḏw*: **P. 10116**, 28
— *ḫnty Ỉmntt*: **P. 9995**, II, 2, 20, 23; **P. 10048**, III, 8; IV, 7, 10; **P. 10109**, 2; **P. 10115**, 2; **P. 10116**, 29; **P. 10125**, 3; **P. 10191**, I, 2, 14, 34, 50; **P. 10194**, 3; **P. 10199**, [2]; **P. 10254**, 2; **P. 10260**, I, x + 3–4; III, x + 3, 5; **P. 10275**, 1; **P. 10303**, 3; **P. 10337**, 2; **P. 10343**, [2]; **P. 10718**, 9; **P. 71513A**, 2; **P. 71513B**, [1]; **P. 71513C**, 2
— *ḫnty Ỉmntt m ꜣbḏw*: **P. 9977**, 10; **P. 10110 + 10111**, I, 12; **P. 10116**, 10; **P. 10124**, 5; **P. 10125**, 25; **P. 10282**, 13; **P. 10286**, 4; **P. 10304**, 10; **P. 10331**, 6
— *Gbtyw ḫnty Ḥwt-nwb*: **P. 10116**, 28
see under *Ḫnty Ỉmntt*, *Skr*
2) as designation of the deceased
P. 9995, I, 1, 2, 4, 6, 10, 18; II, 1, 3, 7, 9, 15, 18, 20, 24; III, 1, 3, 4, 5, 7, 8, 10, 11; IV, 1; **P. 10048**, I, 3, 4, 6, 8; II, 1, 5; III, 2, 7, 9, 11; IV, 1, 6, 7, 11; V, 1–10; VI, 1–10; VII, 1, 2; **P. 10091**, II, 7; vs.; **P. 10110 + 10111**, I, 1; vs. (dem.); **P. 10191**, I, 1; **P. 10194**, 1; **P. 10260**, I, x + 6, 12; II, x + 5, 12; III, x + 3, 6, 7, 8, 9, 10;

P. 10262 + 10263, 1; **P. 10282**, 1; **P. 10283**, 1; **P. 10304**, 1; **P. 10331**, 1–12; **P. 10337**, 1; **P. 10344**, 1; **P. 71513A**, 1; vs.; **P. 71513C**, 1

Wsir-Skr Osiris-Sokar
— *ḥry-ib štyt*: **P. 10116**, 28–9

Wsḫ-nmtt Far-strider
— *pr m Iwnw*: **P. 9995**, III, 1; **P. 10048**, V, 1; **P. 10260**, III, x + 6

Bꜣ n Imn-wr Ba of Amun the Elder
P. 10201, II, 7

Bꜣ Bꜣw Ba of Bas
P. 10108, 8; **P. 10112**, 17

Bꜣ n Rꜥ Ba of Re
P. 9995, I, 24–II, 1; **P. 10048**, III, 7
in the plural *Bꜣw n Rꜥ*
P. 9995, II, 1

Bꜣ n Šw Ba of Shu
P. 9995, II, 1; **P. 10048**, III, 7

Bꜣ-nb-Ḏdt Banebdjed
P. 10116, 15; **P. 10191**, I, 46; **P. 10264**, 6; **P. 10282**, 17
— *m pr Bꜣ-nb-Ḏdt*: **P. 10110 + 10111**, I, 17; **P. 10304**, 15; **P. 10331**, 11 (?); **P. 10338**, x + 16; **P. 71513A**, 35
see under *pr Bꜣ-nb-Ḏd*, index II

Bꜣ ḏꜣ pt Ba which crosses the sky
P. 10115, 6

Bḥdty see under *Ḥr Bḥdty*

Ptḥ Ptah
P. 9995, I, 9; **P. 10048**, II, 4; **P. 10191**, I, 47; II, 25, 28; **P. 10260**, II, x + 4
— *it nṯrw*: **P. 10191**, I, 31; **P. 10199**, 16; **P. 10338**, x + 1
— *m-ḫnw Inb-ḥḏ*: **P. 10110 + 10111**, I, 37
— *m-ḫnw Mn-nfr*: **P. 10304**, 35

Ptḥ-rꜣ Open-mouthed
— *pr m Ḫr-ꜥḥꜣ*: **P. 10048**, V, 2

Fnḏ.f-ꜥnḫ Fenedjef-ankh
— *m ꜣbd.f*: **P. 10108**, 11

Fnḏy Beaked One
— *pr m Ḫmnw*: **P. 9995**, III, 3–4; **P. 10048**, V, 3; **P. 10260**, III, x + 7

Mꜣꜥt Maat
P. 9995, I, 24, 25; III, 13; **P. 10048**, III, 6; VII, 3; **P. 10091**, I, 3; II, 1; **P. 10115**, 13; **P. 10125**, 5; **P. 10191**, I, 6; **P. 10260**, I, x + 8; II, x + 16; III, x + 12; **P. 10282**, 22; **P. 10283**, 6; **P. 10337**, 5; **P. 10718**, 7; **P. 71513A**, 6; **P. 71513B**, [4]
see under *inr n Mꜣꜥt*, index I, *ww Mꜣꜥt*, *wsḫt ww Mꜣꜥt*, *st Mꜣꜥt*, index II

Mꜣꜥty the two Maats
P. 9995, I, 7; **P. 10048**, II, 2; **P. 10115**, 8 (?), 11, 12; **P. 10260**, II, x + 2; **P. 10343**, 9
see under *wsḫt Mꜣꜥty*, index II

Mꜣꜥtyw the Just ones
P. 10091, II, 7; **P. 10314**, II, 6

Mnw Min
— *m Ipw*: **P. 10110 + 10111**, I, 29; **P. 10304**, 27

Mnḳt Menqet
P. 10110 + 10111, II, 17; **P. 10199**, 28; **P. 10304**, 47

Mnṯw Montu
— *nb Iwnw Šmꜥ*: **P. 10344**, 13
The four Montus
— *m-ḫnw niw(w)t.sn*: **P. 10110 + 10111**, I, 19; **P. 10116**, 17; **P. 10304**, 17

Mḥt-wrt Mehet-ouret (Methyer)
P. 10256, 6–7

Nwt Nut
P. 10048, I, 3; **P. 10191**, I, 47, 50, 52; II, 27
— *m Ḥwt šnw*: **P. 9977**, 7; **P. 10110 + 10111**, I, 11; **P. 10116**, 9; **P. 10125**, 25; **P. 10264**, 4; **P. 10282**, 8; **P. 10304**, 9; **P. 10331**, 5; **P. 71513A**, 29

Nwbt Nubet
— *mnḫt*: **P. 10256**, 5

Nwn Nun
P. 10048, VI, 10; **P. 10191**, I, 45; II, 25, 26; **P. 10338**, x + 14; **P. 10206C**, 5

Nb-r-ḏr Lord of All
P. 10191, I, 17; II, 23; **P. 71513A**, 21

Nb-Ḫmnw Lord of Hermopolis
P. 10110 + 10111, I, 3; **P. 10116**, 2; **P. 10304**, 2; **P. 71513D**, x + 3

Nb-Ḫr-ꜥḥꜣ Lord of Kher-Aha
P. 10338, x + 16
in the plural (*nbw Ḫr-ꜥḥꜣ*)
P. 10191, I, 47

Nb-šsp lord of light
P. 10191, I, 29; **P. 10199**, 15; **P. 10206A + B**, 4

Nb-ṯꜣw Lord of the winds
— *di n mr.f*: **P. 10048**, VI, 9

Nbi-ḥr Fiery-faced
— *pr m ḫtḫt*: **P. 10048**, V, 8

Nbt-ḥwt Nephthys
P. 9995, IV, 2; **P. 10091**, I, 3; **P. 10191**, I, 46; **P. 10338**, x + 15
— *m Iwnw*: **P. 9977**, 9; **P. 10110 + 10111**, I, 16; **P. 10116**, 14; **P. 10125**, 26; **P. 10264**, 6; **P. 10282**, 16; **P. 10304**, 14; **P. 10331**, 10; **P. 71513A**, 34
— *m Ḥwt šnw*: **P. 10124**, 7
— *m Dp*: **P. 10286**, 6
— *mnḫt*: **P. 10260**, I, x + 3
— *snt-nṯr*: **P. 10260**, I, x + 3

Npri Nepri
P. 10110 + 10111, II, 16; **P. 10304**, 47

Np(r)it Neprit
P. 10199, 28

Nfr-ḥtp Neferhotep
— *m Ḥwt sḫmw*: **P. 10110 + 10111**, I, 28; **P. 10304**, 26

Nfr-tm Nefertum
— *pr m Ḥwt-kꜣ-Ptḥ*: **P. 10048**, VI, 8
— *m-ḫnw Inb-ḥḏ*: **P. 10110 + 10111**, I, 37
— *m-ḫnw Mn-nfr*: **P. 10304**, 35

Nmty Nemty
— *m Wꜣḏ*: **P. 10110 + 10111**, I, 30; **P. 10304**, 28

Nnt Nenet (lower heaven)
P. 10048, I, 3; **P. 10191**, II, 26

Nhꜣ-ḥr Nehaher
— *pr m Rꜣ-sṯꜣw*: **P. 9995**, III, 6–7; **P. 10048**, V, 5; **P. 10260**, III, x + 8–9

Nḥbkꜣ Nehebka
P. 10191, I, 42; **P. 10338**, x + 12
— *ḫnty Wꜣst*: **P. 10048**, VII, 1

Nḥḥ — Neheh (eternity divinized)
P. 10114, 13

Nḫbt — Nekhbet
P. 9995, I, 4; **P. 10048**, I, 8
— *m Nḫb*: **P. 10110 + 10111**, I, 23; **P. 10304**, 21

Nḥḥ — Aged One
— *pr m Ḥkꜣ-ꜥnḏ*: **P. 10048**, VI, 6

Nt — Neith
— *nbt Sꜣw*: **P. 10191**, I, 46; **P. 10338**, x + [16]

Rꜥ — Re
P. 9995, I, 8, 9, 12, 17, 21 (*pꜣ* —); II, 1, 11, 19, 25; III, 1; **P. 10048**, I, 2; II, 3, 4, 7; III, 2, 3, 4 (*pꜣ* —), 6, 7; IV, 3, 4, 6, 11, 12; **P. 10108**, 1, 15; **P. 10109**, 1, 14; **P. 10110 + 10111**, I, 2; II, 6, 14; **P. 10112**, 22; **P. 10114**, 1, 2; **P. 10115**, 2, 4, 5; **P. 10116**, 2; **P. 10125**, 2; **P. 10191**, I, 1, 8, 44, 45, 51; II, 7, 14, 25, 27, 34; **P. 10194**, 5; **P. 10199**, 2, 27; **P. 10206C**, 3, 4, 11; **P. 10256**, 4; **P. 10260**, I, x + 7; II, x + 3, 4, 6, 11, 15 (*pꜣ* —); III, x + 6; **P. 10264A**, x + <3> (?); **P. 10282**, 26; **P. 10283**, 1, 9; **P. 10303**, 2; **P. 10304**, 2, 40, 46; **P. 10314**, I, 2; II, 3; **P. 10337**, 1, 8; **P. 10338**, x + 13, 14; **P. 10340**, 5, 6; **P. 10343**, [2], 9; **P. 71513A**, 2, 9; **P. 71513B**, [1], 5; **P. 71513C**, [8]; **P. 71513D**, x + 1; **frag. 2**, [1]; **frag. 3**, 1
see under *Ỉrt Rꜥ* and *pr Rꜥ*, index II

Rꜥ-Ỉtm — Re-Atum
P. 10191, II, 6

Rꜥ-Ḥr-ꜣḫty — Re-Horakhty
P. 10108, 14; **P. 10110 + 10111**, II, 5; **P. 10116**, 2; **P. 10191**, I, 7; II, 1; **P. 10283**, 4, 9; **P. 10304**, 3, 39; **P. 10337**, 6; **P. 71513A**, 7; **P. 71513B**, [4]; **frag. 4**, 3

Rwty — Ruty
P. 10191, II, 6
— *pr m pt*: **P. 9995**, III, 8; **P. 10048**, V, 6; **P. 10260**, III, x + 9

Hkr — Haker festival
P. 10109, 12; **P. 10344**, 12

Ḥꜣyty — the two mourners
P. 10314, II, 1

Ḥꜥpy — Hapy
P. 9995, II, 3; **P. 10091**, II, 2; **P. 10109**, 14; **P. 10110 + 10111**, II, 16; **P. 10125**, 28; **P. 10191**, II, 21, 22, 32, 34; **P. 10199**, 25; **P. 10282**, 27; **P. 10283**, 10; **P. 10304**, 47; **P. 10340**, 7
— *wr*: **P. 10048**, III, 8; **P. 10191**, II, 19, 21; **P. 10206C**, 1
— *wr n pt*: **P. 10191**, II, 14
— *bꜣ tpy n Wsir*: **P. 10191**, II, 24

Ḥwt-Ḥr — Hathor
1) as designation of the goddess
P. 10091, I, 3; **P. 10191**, I, 45; **P. 10314**, I, 1–[2]
— *wrt*: **P. 10201**, I, 3
— *m Ỉk*: **P. 10110 + 10111**, I, 27; **P. 10304**, 25
— *m Ḥbnw*: **P. 10304**, 31
— *m Ḳws*: **P. 10110 + 10111**, I, 32; **P. 10304**, [30]
— *ḥnwt Ỉmntt*: **P. 9997**, 1; **P. 10109**, 6; **P. 10125**, 5; **P. 10191**, I, <5>; **P. 10199**, 6; **P. 10256**, 1; **P. 10282**, 18; **P. 10283**, 5; **P. 10303** vs.; **P. 10337**, 5; **P. 71513A**, 6; **P. 71513B**,[4]; **frag. 4**, [4]
— *ḥnwt ndbw(t)*: **P. 10286**, 2
— *ḥkꜣt* (?) *Ṯꜣmt*: **P. 9977, 1**
2) as designation of the female deceased
P. 9977, 12; vs.; **P. 10108**, 1; **P. 10109**, 1; vs.; **P. 10112**, 1; **P. 10114**, 1; **P. 10115**, 1; **P. 10116**, 1; **P. 10123**, 5, 10; **P. 10124**, 3, 6; **P. 10199**, 1; vs.; **P. 10201**, I, 1; II, 4, 9; **P. 10254**, 1; **P. 10285**, 1; **P. 10286**, 1; **P. 10340**, 1; **P. 10343**, 1; **P. 10344**, 6, 14 (written ); **P. 10718**, 8; vs.; **frag. 6**, 1

Ḥpy — Hapy
P. 10116, 29

Ḥnw — see under *ḥb Ḥnw*, *grḥ n ḥb Ḥ[nw]*, index I, and *pr Ḥnw*, index II

Ḥnwt ndb(w)t — mistress of the foundations of the earth
P. 10112, 10; vs.; **P. 10125** vs.; **P. 10194** vs.; **P. 10282** vs.; **P. 10285** vs.; **P. 10290**, x + 3; vs.
see under *Ḥwt-Ḥr*

Ḥr — Horus
P. 10091, I, 3; **P. 10109**, 13; **P. 10125**, 21; **P. 10191**, I, 8, 21, 22, 31; **P. 10194**, 4; **P. 10206A + B**, 6; **P. 10304**, 30 (?); **P. 10337**, 8; **P. 10705**, 4; **P. 71513A**, 9; **P. 71513B**, 5; **frag. 16**, 2
— *iwꜥ n Rꜥ*: **P. 10191**, I, 51
— *ꜥꜣ*: **P. 10048**, III, 11
— *ꜥꜣ ibw*: **P. 9995**, II, 7–8
— *m Ḥbnw*: **P. 10110 + 10111**, I, 33
— *m (n) P*: **P. 10110 + 10111**, I, 14; **P. 10116**, 12; **P. 10124**, 6; **P. 10264**, 5 (?); **P. 10282**, 14; **P. 10286**, 6; **P. 10304**, 12; **P. 10331**, 8; **P. 71513A**, 32
— *m Ḥwt nsw*: **P. 10125**, 27
— *nb pr iit*: **P. 10191**, I, 9; **P. 71513B**, [6]
— *nb Ḫm*: **P. 10191**, I, 9; **P. 71513B**, [6]
— *nb ḥnw*: **P. 9995**, II, 13
— *nfr n nwb*: **P. 10110 + 10111**, II, 8; **P. 10304**, 42
— *ḥkꜣ nst.f n tꜣ nb*: **P. 10191**, I, 50
— *ḫnty ḥḥ n ḥb-sd*: **P. 10191**, I, 50
— *sꜣ Ỉst sꜣ Wsir*: **P. 10191**, I, 7; **P. 10282**, 20; **P. 10283**, 4; **P. 10337**, 7; **P. 71513A**, 8; **P. 71513B**, [5]; **P. 71513C**, 7
see under *irt Ḥr*, index I, and *Rꜥ-Ḥr-ꜣḫty*

Ḥr-ꜣḫty — Horakhty
P. 10110 + 10111, I, 4

Ḥr-wr — Haroeris
— *m Nwbt*: **P. 10110 + 10111**, I, 21; **P. 10304**, 19
— *m-ḫnw Gsy*: **P. 10110 + 10111**, I, 25; **P. 10304**, 23
— *nb Šmꜥ*: **P. 10191**, I, 8; **P. 10110 + 10111**, I, 25
— *nb Tꜣ šmꜥ*: **P. 10282**, 12; **P. 10283**, 5; **P. 10337**, 7; **P. 71513A**, 8–[9]; **P. 71513B**, [5]
— *nb pr ii*: **P. 10283**, 5
— *swnw*: **P. 10194**, 5

Ḥr Bḥdty — Horus of Behedet
P. 9995, II, 8; **P. 10048**, III, 6, 11
— *m Ḏbꜣt*: **P. 10110 + 10111**, I, 22; **P. 10304**, 20

Ḥr-mrty — Hor-merty
P. 9995, II, 8; **P. 10048**, IV, 1
— *nb rꜣ-ꜥ-ḫt*: **P. 10191**, I, 8–9; **P. 10337**, 8; **P. 71513A**, 9–[10]; **P. 71513B**, [6]

Ḥr-nḏ-it.f — Harendotes
P. 9995, I, 24

Ḥr-šfy — Heryshef
— *m Ḥwt nn-nsw*: **P. 10110 + 10111**, I, 35; **P. 10304**, 33

Ḥr-Šdty — Horus of Shedet
P. 9995, II, 8

Ḥsꜣ-ḥr — Savage-faced
— *pr m Bꜣst*: **P. 10048**, V, 10

Ḥk(ꜣ) (?) — the Ruler (?)
P. 10201, II, 12

Ḥḏ-ḥtp — Hedjhotep
P. 10314, II, 4

Ḫpri — Kheperi
P. 10191, II, 23–4; **P. 10206C**, 3

Ḫmnw (nꜣ —) — the Ogdoad
— *ꜥꜣw wrw n pꜣwty tpy*
P. 10116, 32

Ḫnsw-Šw — Khonsu-Shu
— *wr m Wꜣst*: **P. 10108**, 13; **P. 10112**, 21

Ḫnty-Ỉmntt — Khentymenty
P. 9995, II, 14; **P. 10091**, I, 4–5

Ḫnty-nmt — Foremost of the bed
P. 10115, 7

Ḫnty-Ḫm — Khenty-Khem
P. 10191, I, 45; **P. 10338**, x + 15
see under *Ḥr*

Ḫnmw — Khnum
— *m ꜣbw*: **P. 10110 + 10111**, I, 20; **P. 10304**, 18

Sꜣw-n.sn — Sauensen-deities
P. 10115, 7

Sꜣḥ — Orion
P. 10048, I, 3

Sbk — Sobek
— *m Mr-wr*: **P. 10110 + 10111**, I, 36; **P. 10304**, 34

Smꜣ-wr — Semawer
— *snn n Rꜥ*: **P. 10115**, 5

snsnty — the two Sisters
P. 10260, I, x + 9

Srḳt — Serqet
P. 10191, I, 46; **P. 10338**, x + 15

sḫm wr ḥry nṯrw nbw — Great Image foremost of all the Gods
P. 10108, 14.

Sḫmt — Sekhmet
P. 9995, II, 7; **P. 10048**, III, 11; **P. 10108**, 9; **P. 10191**, I, 33, 47; II, 16, 27; **P. 10338**, x + 16
— *m-ḫnw Ỉnb-ḥḏ*: **P. 10110 + 10111**, I, 37
— *m-ḫnw Mn-nfr*: **P. 10304**, 35

Sḫd<-ḥr> — He <whose head> is reversed
— *pr m Tnw*: **P. 10048**, VI, 7

Skr — Sokar
P. 9995, IV, 1; **P. 10108**, 6, 11; **P. 10112**, 13; **P. 10125**, 10
— *psḏ m ḥnw*: **P. 10108**, 11
in Sokar-Osiris
P. 10191, I, 32; **P. 10206A + B**, 7

Sd-ḳsw — Breaker of Bones
— *pr m Ḫm*: **P. 10048**, V, 9

Šw — Shu
P. 10091, II, 3; **P. 10110 + 10111**, II, 12; **P. 10114**, 5; **P. 10116**, 27; **P. 10125**, 28; **P. 10191**, I, 51; **P. 10304**, 44
— *m (n) Mnst ḥrt m Ỉwnw*: **P. 9977**, 4; **P. 10110 + 10111**, I, 8; **P. 10116**, 6; **P. 10125**, 23–4; **P. 10264**, 2; **P. 10304**, 6; **P. 10331**, 2; **P. 71513A**, 26
— *m st ḥrt m Ỉwnw*: **P. 10124**, 2; **P. 10275**, [7]-8; **P. 10282**, 6
— *sꜣ Rꜥ*: **P. 10048**, IV, 4
see under *Bꜣ n Šw*, *Ḫnsw-Šw*

Šd-ḫrw — Strong of voice
— *pr m wryt*: **P. 10048**, VI, 5

Ḳbḥ-snw.f — Qebehsenuf
P. 10116, 30

Kꜣ-ḥtp — the satisfied bull
P. 10109, 9

Gb — Geb
P. 10108, 2; **P. 10112**, 4; **P. 10114**, 3; **P. 10191**, I, 50, 51; II, 9, 31; **P. 10199**, 24; **P. 10206C**, 9; **P. 10260**, I, x + 8; **P. 10262 + 10263**, 3; **P. 10275**, [10]
— *m (n) bw šmꜣw*: **P. 9977**, 6; **P. 10110 + 10111**, I, 10; **P. 10116**, 8; **P. 10124**, 2–3; **P. 10125**, 24; **P. 10282**, 7; **P. 10304**, 8; **P. 10331**, 4; **P. 71513A**, 28
see under *wsḫt Gb*, *pr Gb*, index II

Tꜣ-nn — Tanen
P. 10116, 21;
— *wr*: **P. 10191**, I, 38; **P. 10338**, x + 8

Tp.f-ḥꜣ.f — He whose head is behind him
— *pr m Ṯpḥt-Ḏꜣt*: **P. 10048**, VI, 2

Tpy-ḏw.f — He-who-is-on-his-hill
P. 9995, IV, 1; **P. 10718**, 4

Tfnwt — Tefnut
P. 10191, I, 51
— *m (n) Mnst ḥrt m Ỉwnw*: **P. 9977**, 5; **P. 10110 + 10111**, I, 9; **P. 10116**, 7; **P. 10125**, 24; **P. 10304**, 7; **P. 10331**, 3; **P. 71513A**, 27 (?)
— *m (n) st ḥrt m Ỉwnw*: **P. 10124**, 2; **P. 10275**, [9]; **P. 10282**, 9

Dwꜣ-mwt.f — Duamutef
P. 10116, 29

Dr-ꜥhꜣ — Repeller of the fighter
— *pr m Wnw*: **P. 10048**, VI, 1

Dr-ḫrwy — Strong of voice
P. 10048, VI, 5

Ḏrty — the two kites
P. 10314, II, 1

Ḏḥwty — Thoth
P. 10191, I, 17, 20, 27; **P. 10304**, 50
see under *Ỉ*

Personal Names

ꜣpwltyty (Apollodote)
Daughter of Arsinoe: **P. 10285** and **P. 10286**

ꜣplwynyds (Apollonides)
Son of *Ḳndꜣwgy* (Candace): **P. 10331**

ꜣrwꜣsyny (Arsinoe)
Mother of *ꜣpwltyty* (Apollodote): **P. 10285** and **P. 10286**

Ỉst-wrt (Esoeris)
Daughter of *Tꜣ-ḥrt-(nt-)Mnw* (Tchormenis ?): **P. 10199**

Ỉst-wrt (Esoeris)
Name of her mother lost: **P. 10264**

Ỉst-wrt (Esoeris)
Mother of *Tȝ-šrit-(n-)p(ȝ)*[...] **P. 10275**

Wrš-nfr (Orsenouphis and var.)
Son of *Tȝ-ḫy-biȝ* (Chibois): **P.** BM EA **10261**

Pȝ-ỉi-n-Ḥr (or *Pȝ-ỉw-n-Ḥr*) (Pinuris)
Son of *Tȝ-ḫy-biȝ* (Chibois): **P. 10048**

Pȝ-wr-ỉȝbt(t) (Poregebthis)
Son of *Tȝ-(nt-)nȝ-mʿȝw* (?): **P. 10194**

P(ȝ)-fdw-Mnṯw: see under *Fdw-Mnṯw*

P(ȝ)-krr
Father (?) of *Swtr* (Soter): **P. 10282** and **P. 10283**

Pȝ-di-wr-ỉȝbt(t) (Peteporegebthis)
Son of *Tȝ-šrit-hry* (Senerieus): **P. 10191** and **P. 10304**

Pȝ-di-Ḫnsw (Petechon)
Son of *Tȝ-* ...: **P. 10337**

Pȝ-di-Ḫnsw-pȝ-ḫrd (Petechenpocrates)
P. 10262 + 10263

P(ȝ)y-Tm (Patemis)
Husband of *Tȝ-šri(t)-(n-)p(ȝ)-šri-Mnṯw* (Senpsemonthes), and father of *Fdw-Mnṯw* (Phtomontes): **P. 10091**

P(ȝ)y.f-ṯȝw-ʿwy-Mnṯw
Son of *Ns-wrt* (Esoeris): **P. 10110 + 10111**

Pylt (Philous)
Mother of *S(ȝ)wtr*: **P. 10282** and **P. 10283**

Fdw-Mnṯw, alias *P(ȝ)-fdw-Mnṯw* (Phtomontes)
Son of *P(ȝ)y-Tm* and of *Tȝ-šri(t)-(n-)p(ȝ)-šri-Mnṯw*: **P. 10091**

Ns-wrt (Esoeris)
Mother of *P(ȝ)y.f-ṯȝw-ʿwy-Mnṯw*: **P. 10110 + 10111**

Hȝyrn
Mother of *Tȝ-šrit-Gpryn*: **P. 10343**

Ḫȝʿ.s(.t)-n-Ỉst
Mother of a man whose name is lost: **P. 10125**

S(ȝ)wtr (Soter)
Son of *Pylt* (Philous): **P. 10282** and **P. 10283**

Srpy (Sarapous)
Mother of *Tȝ-ḥfȝt*: **P. 10256**

Ḳndȝwgy, Ḳn[dg]ȝy, Ḳndgy (Candace)
Mother of *ȝplwnyds* (Apollonides): **P. 10331**
Daughter of *Ṯȝpȝr* I (Sapaulis): **P. 9977**

Krʿšr (Kalasiris)
Son of *Tȝ-snt-snty* (Tsonesontis): **P. 9995**

Gȝprn (Kephalon)
Son of *Tȝ-nt-kȝw*: **P. 10260**

Gȝrwptrʿ, Grȝiwptr (Cleopatra)
Daughter of *Ḳnt*[...] (Candace): **P. 10114** and **P. 10115**

Tȝ-(nt-)Ỉmn-Ỉpt (Tamennopis)
Mother of *Tȝ-(nt)-Ỉst* (Taesis): **P. 10201**

Tȝ-(nt-)Ỉst (Taesis)
Daughter of *Tȝ-(nt)-Ỉmn-Ỉpt* (Tamennopis): **P. 10201**

Tȝ-(nt-)pȝ-ỉhȝy
Mother of a [...]-*Mnṯw*: **P. 10314**

Tȝ-(nt-)nȝ-mʿȝw (?)
Mother of *Pȝ-wr-ỉȝbt(t)* (Poregebthis): **P. 10194**

Tȝ-nt-nwb
Mother of *Tȝ-šrit-pȝ-wr-ỉȝbt(t)* (Senporegebthis): **P. 10112**

Tȝ-rmṯ-n-ip-ib (?)
Mother of *Tȝ-(nt-)Ḫnsw*: **P. 10344**

Tȝ-ḥfȝt (Tphous)
Daughter of *Srpy* (Sarapous): **P. 10256**

Tȝ-ḥtrt... (?)
Mother of *Tȝ-ḥtrt-nnt*: **P. 10254**

Tȝ-ḥtrt-nnt
Daughter of *Tȝ-ḥtrt...* (?): **P. 10254**

Tȝ-ḫy-biȝ (Chibois)
Mother of *Pȝ-ỉi-n-Ḥr* (Pinuris): **P. 10048**

Tȝ-ḫy-biȝ (Chibois)
Mother of *Wrš-nfr*: **P. 10261**

Tȝ-(nt-)Ḫnsw (Tachonsis)
Daughter of *Tȝ-rmṯ-n-ip-ib* (?): **P. 10344**

Tȝ-ḫrt-(nt-)Mnw (Tchormenis ?)
Mother of *Ỉst-wrt*: **P. 10199**

T(ȝ)-ḫrd(t)-Mnw (?)
P. 10192

Tȝ-snt-snty (Tsonesontis)
Mother of *Krʿšr* (Kalasiris): **P. 9995**

Tȝ-špst
Mother of *Tȝ-šrit-Ỉnpw*: **P. 10340**

Tȝ-šrit-Ỉnpw (Senanoupis)
Daughter of *Tȝ-špst*: **P. 10340**

Tȝ-šrit-pȝ-wr-ỉȝbt(t) (Senporegebthis)
Daughter of *Tȝ-nt-nwb*: **P. 10112**

Tȝ-šri(t)-(n-)p(ȝ)-šri-Mnṯw (Senpsemonthes)
Wife of *P(ȝ)y-Tm* (Patemis) and mother of *Fdw-Mnṯw* (Phtomontes): **P. 10091**

Tȝ-šrit-pȝ-di-Ḫnsw-pȝ-ḫrd (Senpetechespochrates)
Mother of *Tȝ-šrit-Ns-Mnw* (Senesminis): **P. 10116**

Tɜ-šrit-Ns-Mnw (Senesminis)
Daughter of *Tɜ-šrit-pɜ-di-Ḫnsw-pɜ-ẖrd* (Senpetechespochrates): **P. 10116**

Tɜ-šrit-hry (Senerieus)
Mother of *Pɜ-di-wr-iɜbt(t)* (Peteporegebthis): **P. 10191** and **P. 10304**

Tɜ-šrit-Ḫnsw (Senchonsis) also called *Ṯɜp(w)r* (Sapaulis)
Daughter of *Tɜḳḏɜ* (Tkauthi): **P. 10123** and **P. 10124**

Tɜ-šrit-Gpryn
Daughter of *Hɜyrn*: **P. 10343**

Tɜ-(nt-)kɜ (?)
Mother of *Tɜ-nt-Ḏɜm*: **P. 10108** and **P. 10109**

Tɜ-nt-kɜw
Mother of *G(ɜ)prn*: **P. 10260**

Tɜḳḏɜ (Tkhauthi)
Mother of *Tɜ-šrit-Ḫnsw* (Senchonsis) also called *Ḏɜp(w)r* (Sapaulis): **P. 10123** and **P. 10124**

Tɜ-nt-Ḏɜm (Tasemis)
Daughter of *Tɜ-(nt)-kɜ* (?) (Tikos): **P. 10108** and **P. 10109**

Ṯɜpɜr I (Sapaulis):
Mother of *Ḳn[dg]ɜy, Ḳndgy* (Candace): **P. 9977**

Ṯɜp(w)r II (Sapaulis). See under *Tɜ-šrit-Ḫnsw*

Truncated or unreadable personal names

Pɜ-di-p[...]
Son of *Tɜ*[...]*yn*: **P. 71513A**

Nfr (?)...
Mother of a person whose name is unreadable: **P. 10718**

Tɜ [...]
Mother of *Pɜ-di-Ḫnsw*: **P. 10337**

Tɜ-[...]*yn*
Mother of *Pɜ-di-p*[...]. **P. 71513A**

Tɜ-šrit-(n)-p(ɜ)[...]
Daughter of *Ỉst-wrt*. **P. 10275**

[...]*-wrt*
Mother of *Tɜ-šrit-(n)-p(ɜ)*[...]: **P. 10275**

[...]*-p(ɜ)-Mnṯw*
Mother (?) of a person whose name is lost: **P. 71513D**

[...]*pwr*... (?)
Son of a person whose name is lost: **frag. 4**, 1

[...]*-Mnṯw*
Son of *Tɜ(nt)-pɜ-ihɜy*: **P. 10314**

[...]*-ḥtp*
P. 71513C

[...]*-šrit-Mnṯw*
Mother of a person whose name is lost: **frag. 11**, 3

[...]*-tɜ-šrit*, or read *Tɜ-šrit* (?)
Mother of a man whose name is lost: **P. 10303**

Titles

it-nṯr ḥm-nṯr n Ỉmn-Rᶜ nsw nṯrw, 'god's father and prophet of Amun-Re king of the gods': **P. 10048**
iry-ᶜɜ n pr-nwb n Ỉmn, 'doorkeeper of the treasury of Amun': **P. 10125**
nbt-pr, 'housewife': **P. 10091**
rpᶜ-ḥɜt-p-ᶜ, 'nomarch': **P. 9995**
rḫ ḫyt wr m h[...] (dem.), 'great scholar in [...] (?)': **P. 10110 + 10111** vs.
ḥm-nṯr n ḥwt-nwb Ỉmn, 'Prophet of the Mansion of Gold of Amun': **P. 10110 + 10111**
ḥry mnḫt n pr Ỉmn-Rᶜ nsw nṯrw, 'head of clothing of the estate of Amun-Re king of the gods': **P. 10125**
ḫt-ᶜḥ (?) *n Ỉɜt Ḏɜm r tɜ ḏsr m Wɜst*, '*ḫt-ᶜḥ* (?) of the Mound of Djeme and of the sacred land in Thebes': **P. 10091**
sɜwty pr-ḥḏ n pr Ỉmn, 'guardian of the Treasury of the House of Amun': **P. 10110 + 10111**. Var. (dem.): *swɜt* [*pr-ḥḏ*] *n pr Ỉmn irm nɜy=f rpy.w*, 'guardian of the Treasury of the House of Amun and of his temples': **P. 10110 + 10111** vs.

List of Manuscripts Cited

The following list includes all manuscripts belonging to the category of the Books of Breathing used in this catalogue to deduce parallel versions and variants. Apart from the First Book, the Second Book, and the Book of Breathing made by Isis, original texts, most related to the Book of Breathing (either explicitly by their title or by their contents), are also mentioned, as well as some ritual compositions without direct connection with our texts, but quoted here and there in the commentary. All are of Ptolemaic or Roman Period, which is specified when known. Generally, these documents come from the Theban area.

P. Beck. Original text. E. Drioton, 'Un chapitre inédit du rituel égyptien de l'embaumement', in *Mémoires de la Société d'agriculture, commerce, sciences et arts de la Marne* 72 (1957), p. 19–23; cf. Goyon, *Rituels funéraires*, pp. 283–4)
Owner: *Tȝ-ḫm-ꜥȝw* (?)
Mother of the owner: *Tȝ-šrit*.

P. Berlin 3028. First Book of Breathing. U. Kaplony-Heckel, *Ägyptische Handschriften* III (Stuttgart 1986), p. 23.
Owner: name in lacuna.
Titles:
— *it-nṯr ḥm-nṯr n Imn-Rꜥ nsw nṯrw*, 'god's father and prophet of Amun-Re king of the gods';
— *smȝty n Kȝ-mwt.f*, '*smȝty*-priest of Kamutef';
— *smȝty n Kȝ-fȝy-ꜥ*, '*smȝty*-priest of *Kȝ-fȝy-ꜥ*';
— *ḥm-nṯr n Ḫnsw-p(ȝ)-ir-sḫrw-m-Wȝst*, 'prophet of Khonsu-who-governs-in-Thebes';
— *ḥm-nṯr n Mwt ḥnwt nfrw*, 'prophet of Mut mistress of perfection'.
Mother of the owner: *Tȝ-ḥy-biȝ* (Chibois).

P. Berlin 3030. First (and Second ?) Book of Breathing, and original text. Kaplony-Heckel, op. cit., p. 23; col. VIII: Möller, *Pal.* III, pl. X; cols VI–IX: F.R. Herbin, *BIFAO* 84 (1984), p. 251 with pls XLIX–L. Date: AD 125 (cf. O. Neugebauer and R.A. Parker, *Egyptian Astronomical Texts* III [Providence 1969] p. 93).
Owner: *Ḥtr.*[1]
Titles:
— *it-nṯr ḥm-nṯr n Imn-Rꜥ nsw nṯrw*, 'god's father and prophet of Amun-Re king of the gods';
— *ḥm-nṯr 2.nw ḥm-nṯr 3.nw ḥm-nṯr 4.nw*, 'Second prophet, third prophet, fourth prophet';
— *stm ꜥȝ wꜥb n Imn*, 'great *stm*-priest, *wꜥb*-priest of Amun';
— *ḥm-nṯr n Imn-Ipt n Ḏȝm nṯr ꜥȝ ꜥnḫ ḥry nṯrw ḥnꜥ nȝ nty m-sȝ.f* (?), 'prophet of Amenipet of Djeme, the great living god, overseer of the gods with those who are behind him (?)';
— *ḥm-nṯr n Mwt wrt nbt Išrw*, 'prophet of Mut the great, lady of Icheru';
— *ḥm-nṯr ꜥȝ-pr n Ḫnsw-m-Wȝst-Nfr-ḥtp*, 'prophet and majordomo of Khonsu-in-Thebes-Neferhotep';
— *mr wꜥb Sḫmt*, 'overseer of the web-priests of Sekhmet'.
Father of the owner: *Ḥr-sȝ-Ist* (Harsiesis).
Titles:
— *ḥry sštȝ*, 'overseer of the mystery';
— *ꜥb-nṯr n pr Imn-Rꜥ nsw nṯrw*, 'purifier of the god of the House of Amun-Re king of the gods';
Mother of the owner: *Tȝy-ḥr* (Tiuris).

P. Berlin 3044. Book of Traversing Eternity. Kaplony-Heckel, op. cit., pp. 26–7; *LPE*, pp. 10–11 with pl. XVII.
Owner: *Hry* (Erieus).
Titles:
— *it-nṯr ḥm-nṯr n Imn-Rꜥ nsw nṯrw*, 'god's father and prophet of Amun-Re king of the gods'.
His father: *Ḥr-sȝ-Ist* (Harsiesis).
Titles:
— *ḥry sštȝ*, 'overseer of the mystery';
— *ꜥb-nṯr*, 'purifier of the god'.
Mother of the owner: *Mwt-mwt(.i)*.
Title:
— *iḥyt n Imn-Rꜥ*, 'sistrum-player of Amun-Re'.

P. Berlin 3052. First and Second Book of Breathing. Kaplony-Heckel, op. cit., p. 29; LD VI, pl. 122.
Owner: *Hryw* (I, 1)[2] (Erieus) or (*Wsir*)-*wr* (IV, 9) (Osoroeris).
Father of the owner*: Ii-m-ḥtp* (Imouthes).
Mother of the owner: *Mwt-Mnw* (?)

P. Berlin 3068 and **3069**. Manuscripts of unknown contents, now lost, discovered in the coffin of *Tȝ-šrt-Ḏd-Ḥr* (Sensaos) and her sister *Tȝ-kȝw-ḏȝ*

1. To the same owner belong P. Cairo CG 58018 (Second Book of Breathing) and P. Boulaq 3 (Ritual of Embalming), as well as a coffin formerly in the Vienna Museum and lost now (PM I/2, p. 647; Neugebauer and Parker, op. cit.).

2. The name of the mother was written in the space above the line, now in a lacuna. The names of the owner and of his mother, both revised, are found again in col. IV, 16–17.

(Tkauthi), both daughters of the archon Soter and Cleopatra Candace (cf. *supra*, p. 12, nos 13 and 14). Kaplony-Heckel, op. cit., p. 33.

P. Berlin 3135. Book of Breathing made by Isis. Kaplony-Heckel, op. cit., p. 39. Col. I is published in facsimile in G. Möller, *Hieratische Lesestücke* (1910), pl. 32; col. III, in his *Hier. Pal.* III, pl. 11. For a dating to the end of the Ptolemaic Period, cf. J. Quaegebeur, in Bierbrier (ed.), *Portraits and Masks*, p. 73.
Owner: *Pꜣ-Mnṯw-ryn-ẖm* (Pamonthes-Plenis).
Titles:
— *ḥnk-nwn ḫr(y)-ḥb ḥr-tp m Ỉwnw šmꜥ*, 'ḥnk-nwn-priest, lector and chief[3] in Karnak', with the following variants:
— *ḥnk-nwn nb Šmꜥ ḫr(y)-ḥb ḥr-tp*, 'ḥnk-nwn-priest, lord of the South, lector and chief';
— *ḫr(y)-ḥb tp n Mnṯw nb Šmꜥ*, 'lector and chief of Montu lord of Upper Egypt';
— *ḥnk Nwn m Ỉwnw šmꜥ*, 'ḥnk-nwn-priest in Karnak';
— *ḥnk Nwn*, 'ḥnk-nwn-priest';
— *ḫr(y)-ḥb tp*, 'lector and chief';
— *mr ḥmw-nṯrw m spꜣt ḥꜣt n Rꜥ*, 'overseer of the prophets in the first nome of Re',[4] var.:
— *mr ḥmw-nṯrw m Ỉrt Rꜥ*, 'overseer of the prophets in the Eye of Re'.[5]
Father of the owner: *Ḥr-Ḥr*.[6]
Titles:
— *mi nn* (priest of the same rank as the son);[7]
— *ḥꜣty-ꜥ m-ḫt*, 'ḥꜣty-ꜥ-priest, second in command'.[8]
Mother of the owner: *ꜥrtymytwrꜣ* (Artemidora).

P. Berlin 3154. Book of Breathing made by Isis. Partly published. H. Brugsch, *Sai an sinsin sive liber mempsychosis* (Berolini 1851), pp. 13–24; Kaplony-Heckel, op. cit., p. 42, who dates it to the second to third century AD
Owner: *Ḥr-sꜣ-Ỉst* (Harsiesis).
Titles:
— *it-nṯr ḥm-nṯr Ỉmn-Rꜥ nsw nṯrw*, 'god's father and prophet of Amun-Re king of the gods';
— *ḥm nṯrw*, 'prophet of the gods';
Father of the owner: *Ḥr-Ššnḳ*.
Titles:
— *it-nṯr ḥm-nṯr n Ỉmn-Rꜥ nsw nṯrw*, 'god's father and prophet of Amun-Re king of the gods';
— *ḥm nṯrw*, 'servant of the gods'.
Mother of the owner: *Tꜣ-nt-Bꜣstt* (Tobastis).
Titles:
— *nbt pr*, 'housewife';
— *iḥyt n Ỉmn-Rꜥ*, 'sistrum player of Amun-Re'.

P. Berlin 3155. Book of Traversing Eternity. Kaplony-Heckel, op. cit., pp. 42–3; *LPE*, pp. 12–13 with pls XIX–XX.
Owner: *Tꜣ-šri(t)-(n-)tꜣ-iht* (Sentaes).
Titles:
— *iḥyt n Ỉmn-Rꜥ*, 'sistrum-player of Amun-Re'.
Mother of the owner: *Tꜣ-šri(t)-(n-)tꜣ-iht* (Sentaes).

P. Berlin 3162. Invocations to Osiris. Kaplony-Heckel, op. cit., p. 45; Frank-Kamenetzky, *OLZ* 17 (1914), pp. 145–53 with pls I–II.
Owner: *Ḏḥwty-iw*.
Mother of the owner: *Mwt-mn.ti* (*RPN* II, 288, 28).

P. Berlin 3164 + Moscow 4661. Original text related to the Book of Breathing. Kaplony-Heckel, op. cit., p. 45. For the Russian part, see B.A. Touraiev, in *Mémoires du Musée des Beaux-Arts de l'Empereur Alexandre III à Moscou* (1912–13), pp. 27–8 (in Russian).
Owner: *Pꜣy.f-kꜣ*.
Title:
— *sꜣwty pr-ḥḏ n pr Ỉmn*, 'guardian of the Treasury of the House of Amun'.
Mother of the owner: *Ỉst-wrt* (Esoeris).

P. Berlin 8351 (dem.). Smith, *Liturgy*, pp. 2–4 with pls 5–6. Parallel text in P. Bodl. MS. Egypt. c. 9 + P. Louvre E 10605 (dem.), and P. Louvre E 10607 (dem.), which both offer an abridged version of the text.
Owner: *Ḥr-* ... (?).
Father of the owner: *Mḏꜣ*.

P. BM EA 10209. Text entitled 'Extract from the Book of the Valley Festival'. Haikal, *Two Hier. Fun. Pap.* Date: 312–311 BC;[9] Quirke, *Owners*, p. 49, no. 139.
Owner: *Ns-Mnw* (Esminis, Sminis).[10]
Titles:
— *it-nṯr ḥm-nṯr n Ỉmn-Rꜥ nsw nṯrw*, 'god's father, prophet of Amun-Re king of the gods';
— *ḥm-nṯr n Ỉmn spd ꜥbwy*, 'prophet of Amun sharp of horns';
— *idnw n Ỉmn n sꜣ 2.nw sꜣ 4.nw*, 'deputy of Amun of the second and fourth phyle';
— *sš sḏꜣwty-nṯr n Ỉmn ḥr sꜣ 2.nw*, 'scribe and god's treasurer of Amun in the second phyle';
— *ḥm-nṯr n Ḫnsw ḥr(y)-ib Bnnt*, 'prophet of Khonsu dwelling in the Benenet';
— *ḥm-nṯr n Wsir wp išd*, 'prophet of Osiris who opens the *išd*-tree';
— *ḥm-nṯr n Wsir ḥr(y)-ib Ỉšrw*, 'prophet of Osiris dwelling in Icheru';
— *wꜥb n pꜣ Rꜥ tp ḥwt n pr Ỉmn ḥr sꜣ 2.nw*, 'wꜥb-priest of Pre on the roof of the temple of Amun in the second phyle';
— *ḥm-nṯr n Ỉmn ḳꜣ šwty ḥr(y)-ib Ỉpt-swt*, 'prophet of Amun tall of plumes who dwells in *Ỉpt-swt* (Karnak)';
— *sš n Ỉmn n sꜣ 3.nw*, 'scribe of Amun of the third phyle';
— *ḥm-nṯr n Nfr-ḥtp pꜣ nṯr ꜥꜣ*, 'prophet of Neferhotep the great god';
— *ḥm-nṯr n Wsir Ḥr Ỉst Nbt-ḥwt n ḥwt n Ḥwt*, 'prophet of Osiris, Isis, Nephthys of the Mansion of Hou';
— *ḥm-nṯr n Nfr-ḥtp pꜣ sꜣ n pꜣ ꜥnḫ*, 'prophet of Neferhotep the son of *Pꜣ-ꜥnḫ* (?)';
— *ḥm-nṯr n Mnw*, 'prophet of Min';
— *ḥm-nṯr n Ḥwt-Ḥr ḥr(yt)-ib Ḥwt sḫmw*, 'prophet of Hathor dwelling in *Ḥwt sḫmw* (Diospolis Parva)';
— *ḥm-nṯr n Mḥyt*, 'prophet of Mehyt';
— *ḥm-nṯr Ỉtm ḥr(y)-ib Ḥwt sḫmw*, 'prophet of Atum dwelling in *Ḥwt sḫmw* (Diospolis Parva)';
— *ḥm-nṯr tpy n Nfr-ḥtp*, 'First prophet of Neferhotep';

3. On this translation, see J. Quaegebeur, in *Form und Mass. Beiträge zur Literatur, Sprache und Kunst des alten Ägypten* (Fs. für Gerhard Fecht), ÄAT 12, 1987, pp. 368 ff.
4. Probable designation of Thebes. For the construction, cf. *GDG* V, p. 30: *ḥꜣt spꜣt n Ḥr*.
5. Designation of Thebes. Cf. *GDG* I, p. 99; R.A. Caminos, *The Chronicle of Prince Osorkon* (Rome 1958), p. 50 § 67, n. d.
6. The name, written 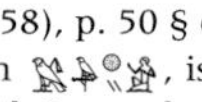, is wrongly read *Ḥr-ḥy* by Kaplony-Heckel, op. cit., p. 39. On this man, cf. Quaegebeur, in Bierbrier (ed.), *Portraits and Masks*, p. 73.
7. For this translation of the expression *mi nn*, see J. Quaegebeur, in *Aspekte spätägyptischer Kultur* (Fs. Erich Winter), *AegTrev* 7, 1994, p. 214.
8. Quaegebeur, op. cit., p. 215 and n. 35.
9. The date 'year 12 of Alexander the Fourth' is read in the colophon of P. BM EA 10188, belonging to the same Nesmin; see R.O. Faulkner, *The Papyrus Bremner-Rhind* (*BiAe* 3, 1933), p. 32.
10. P. BM EA 10208 and 10188 (cf. n. 9) also belong to this owner.

— *idnw n Nfr-ḥtp n pꜣ 4 sꜣw*, 'deputy of Neferhotep of the four phylae';
— *ḥm-nṯr nꜣ nṯrw n Ḥwt*, 'prophet of the gods of Hu'.
Father of the owner: *Pꜣ-di-ʾImn-nb-nswt-tꜣwy* (Petemostous).
Title:
— *mi nn* (priest of the same rank as the son).
Mother of the owner: *ʾIrt-ir-w* alias *Tꜣ-šrit-(n-)tꜣ-iḥt* (Sentaes).
Title:
— *nbt-pr*, 'housewife';
— *iḥyt n ʾImn-Rꜥ*, 'sistrum-player of Amun-Re'.

P. BM EA 10507 (dem.). Smith, *Mortuary Texts*. Contains three compositions: 1) 'The book which Isis made for Osiris, foremost in the West'; 2) 'The book which was made in exact accordance with his desire for Horemheb the son of Petemin to cause it to be recited as an opening of the mouth document in his presence on the night of his burial feast'; 3) 'The chapters of awakening the ba which are recited on the night of mummification for a god's servant, a wab-priest, a magistrate, a scribe, and the rest of the men who are great and before whom it is fitting to recite them'. Provenance: Akhmim. Date: First half of the first century AD
Owner: *Ḥr-m-ḥb* (Harmais).
Father of the owner: *Pꜣ-ti-mn* (Petemin).

P. BN 149 (dem.). Book of Traversing Eternity, short version, followed by a version of the Book of the Dead. M.A. Stadler, *Der Totenpayrus des Pa-Month (P. Bib. nat. 149)*, Wiesbaden 2003; *LPE*, p. 31 with pl. XXXV. Date: AD 63–4
Owner: *Pꜣ-Mnṯ* (Pamonthes).
Father of the owner: *Pꜣ-Mnṯ* (Pamonthes).

P. BN 151. First Book of Breathing. Unpublished. Cf. *LPE*, p. 7. Date: AD 65[11]
Owner: *Ḥr-sꜣ-ʾIst* (Harsiesis).
Titles:
— *it-nṯr ḥm-nṯr n ʾImn-Rꜥ nsw nṯrw*, 'god's father and prophet of Amun-Re king of the gods';
— *ḥm-nṯr n Ḫnsw pꜣ-ir-sḫrw-m-Wꜣst*, 'prophet of Khonsu-who-governs-in-Thebes';
— *ḥm-nṯr n Bꜣstt ḥr(t)-ib Wꜣst*, 'prophet of Bastet dwelling in Thebes';
— *ḥry sštꜣ*, 'overseer of the mystery';
— *ꜥb-nṯr*, 'purifier of the god';
— *rḫ ḥwt wr m Wꜣst*, 'great scholar in Thebes';
— *smꜣwy rnw nsww ḥr sꜣt*, 'he who renews the names of the kings on the wall'.[12]
Mother of the owner: *Ḳꜣyḳꜣy*.
Titles:
— *nbt pr*, 'housewife';
— *iḥyt n ʾImn-Rꜥ*, 'sistrum-player of Amun-Re'.

P. BN 152. First Book of Breathing. Unpublished. Date: AD 116. See *supra*, p. 11, no. **6**.
Owner: *Pꜣ-di-ʾImn-ʾIpt* (Petamenophis).
Mother of the owner: *Gꜣrwꜣptr* (Cleopatra), also called *Ḳntꜣgy* (Candace).

P. BN 179–81. Book of Breathing made by Isis. Unpublished.

Owner: *ꜥnḫ-pꜣ-ḫrd* (Chapocrates).
Titles:
— *it-nṯr ḥm-nṯr n ʾImn m ʾIpt-swt*, 'god's father and prophet of Amun-Re in Karnak';
— *it-nṯr*, 'god's father';
— *ḥry mnḫt*[13] *n ʾImn*, 'head of clothing of Amun-Re';
— *ḥm-nṯr n Wsir ḥḳꜣ ḏt*, 'prophet of Osiris ruler of eternity'.
His father: *Wr* (?)
Titles:
— *mi nn* (priest of the same rank as the son).
His mother: *ʾIpt-wrt* (Epoeris).
Titles:
— *nbt pr*, 'housewife';
— *iḥyt n ʾImn-Rꜥ*, 'sistrum-player of Amun-Re'.

P. BN 239. Original text. Unpublished. The verso is occupied by accounts written in demotic.
Owner: *Tꜣ-šrit-p(ꜣ)-di-Ḫnsw-pꜣ-ḫrd* (Senpetechespochrates).
Mother of the owner: *Tꜣ-šrit-p(ꜣ)-šri-ʾImn* (Senpsenamounis).

P. Bodl. MS. Egypt.c.9 + P. Louvre E 10605 (dem.). See under **P. Berlin 8351** (dem.).
Owner: *Gm=w-Ḥp* (Komoapis).
Father of the owner: *Pꜣ-šr-ʾImn* (Psenamounis).

P. Brussels E 5298. First Book of Breathing and original text. L. Speleers, *RT* 39 (1921), pp. 25–43, with pls I–II.
Owner: name lost.
Mother of the owner: *ʾIsgrt* (?)

P. Brussels E. 8258 (dem.). Text related to the Book of Breathing. J. Quaegebeur, in *Studies in Egyptology presented to Miriam Lichtheim* II (Jerusalem 1990), pp. 776–95.
Owner: *Tꜣ-šr.t-pꜣ-ḥtr* (?) (Senphatres).
Mother (or father) of the owner: name lost.

P. Cairo CG 31172 (dem.). Text related to the Book of Breathing. W. Spiegelberg, *Die demotischen Denkmäler* II. *Die demotischen Papyrus (CGC)*, Strassburg 1906–8, p. 282 with pl. CXII; Quaegebeur, op. cit., pp. 782–3.
Owner: *Tiwns* (Dionus).
Mother of the owner: *ꜣgꜥthe* (Agathe).

P. Cairo CG 58007. First and Second Book of Breathing. Golenischeff, *Pap. hiérat.* I, pp. 23–35 with pls V–VII.
Owner: *Ḥꜣr* .
Mother of the owner: *Tꜣwꜣ* (Tages).

P. Cairo CG 58008. First Book of Breathing. Golenischeff, *Pap. hiérat.* I, pp. 36–44 with pl. VIII.
Owner: name uncertain.
Mother of the owner: *Tꜣ-šrit-wꜣw* (?)

P. Cairo CG 58009. First and Second Book of Breathing, and original text.[14]
Golenischeff, *Pap. hiérat.* I, pp. 44–54 with pls IX–X.
Owner: *ꜥnḫ-Ḥsꜣt* .

---

11. According to P. Leiden T 32, belonging to the same owner (*LPE*, p. 5, n. 1).
12. Title attested in this papyrus only, and to be compared with *spḫr sꜣwt m gsw-prw*, 'he who inscribes the temple walls (*Wb*. IV, 14, 14; P. Louvre N 3157, 2 and 3291, 4).
13. On this title: *ProsPtol* IX, p. xvii.
14. See *supra*, p. 3, nn. 42 and 46.

Titles:
— *it-nṯr*, 'god's father';
— *smꜣty wr*, 'great *smꜣty*-priest'.
Father of the owner: *Ns-Ptḥ* (Esptais).
Mother of the owner: *Tꜣ-nt-Ḥwt-Ḥr*.

P. Cairo CG 58010. Original text related to the Book of Breathing. Golenischeff, *Pap. hiérat.* I, pp. 54–7 with pl. XI.
Owner: *Tꜣ-šrit-Ḥr-sꜣ-Ꜣst* (Tsenharsiesis).
Mother of the owner: *Tꜣsynyry*.

P. Cairo CG 58011. First Book of Breathing. Golenischeff, *Pap. hiérat.* I, pp. 57–8 with pl. XII.
Owner: Name lost.

P. Cairo CG 58012. Text related to the Book of Breathing. Golenischeff, *Pap. hiérat.* I, pp. 59–63 with pl. XII.
Owner: *Ns-pꜣwty-tꜣwy* (Spotous).
Titles:
— *it-nṯr ḥm-nṯr n Ꞽmn-Rꜥ nsw nṯrw*, 'god's father and prophet of Amun-Re king of the gods';
— *ḥm-nṯr n Ḫnsw p(ꜣ)-ir-sḫrw-m-Wꜣst*, 'prophet of Khonsu-who-governs-in-Thebes'.
Father of the owner: *Ḥr-sꜣ-Ꜣst* (Harsiesis).
Mother of the owner: *Tꜣ-ꜥr*.

P. Cairo CG 58013. Second Book of Breathing. Golenischeff, *Pap. hiérat.* I, pp. 63–5 with pl. XIII.
Owner: *Ꞽpr* (?)
Mother of the owner: *Tꜣ-šrit* (or *Tꜣ-ẖrdt* = Tachratis ?), daughter of *Wr*.

P. Cairo CG 58014. First Book of Breathing. Golenischeff, *Pap. hiérat.*, pp. 66–8 with pl. XIV. Same owner as P. **Cairo CG 58013**.

P. Cairo CG 58015. First Book of Breathing. Golenischeff, *Pap. hiérat.*, pp. 68–70 with pl. XV.
Owner: *Tꜣ-šrit-Ꞽnpw* (Senanoupis).
Father of the owner: *Ꞽs-wr* (?)

P. Cairo CG 58016. First Book of Breathing. Golenischeff, *Pap. hiérat.*, pp. 70–1 with pl. XV. Same owner as P. **Cairo CG 58015**.

P. Cairo CG 58017. Second Book of Breathing. Golenischeff, *Pap. hiérat.*, pp. 72–4 with pl. XVI.
Owner: [...]*npy*... (?)
Mother of the owner: *Tꜣ-Ꞽmn-rwꜣ* (?) (R*PN* I, 358, 7).

P. Cairo CG 58018. Second Book of Breathing. Golenischeff, *Pap. hiérat.*, pp. 74–80 with pl. XVII. See under P. **Berlin 3030**.
Owner: *Ḥtr*.
Titles:
— *it-nṯr ḥm-nṯr n Ꞽmn-Rꜥ nsw nṯrw*, 'god's father and prophet of Amun-Re king of the gods';
— *mr wꜥb Sḫmt*, 'overseer of the *wꜥb*-priests of Sekhmet'.
Father of the owner: *Ḥr-sꜣ-Ꜣst* (Harsiesis).
Title:
— *it-nṯr*, 'god's father'.
Mother of the owner: *Tꜣy-ḥr* (Tiuris).

P. Cairo CG 58019. First Book of Breathing. Golenischeff, *Pap. hiérat.*, pp. 80–3 with pl. XVIII.
Owner: *ꜥꜣ-pḥ(ty)* (Apathes) (R*PN* I, 57, 14 and 15).
Mother of the owner: *Tꜣ-šrit-hb* (R*PN* I, 369, 11).

P. Cairo CG 58020. Original text, then Second Book of Breathing. Golenischeff, *Pap. hiérat.*, pp. 83–7 with pl. XIX.
Owner: Name lost.

P. Cairo CG 58021. First Book of Breathing. Golenischeff, *Pap. hiérat.*, pp. 87–90 with pls XX-XXI.
Owner: Name lost.

P. Cairo CG 58022. Second Book of Breathing. Golenischeff, *Pap. hiérat.*, pp. 90–2.
Owner: *Fḫ-Mnṯw*.
Mother of the owner: *ꜥrtm*[...] (Artemis ?).

P. Cairo CG 58023. First Book of Breathing. Golenischeff, *Pap. hiérat.*, pp. 92–9.
Owner: *Tꜣ-rpyt* or [...]-*tꜣ-rpyt*.

P. Cairo CG 58027. Book for the protection of the king during the night. Golenischeff, *Pap. hiérat.*, pp. 114–31. Facsimile in A. Mariette, *Les papyrus égyptiens du Musée de Boulaq* I (Paris 1871), pls 36–7.

P. Denon. Book of Breathing made by Isis. M. Coenen in Quaegebeur, *De Papyrus Denon in het Museum Meermanno-Westreenianum, Den Haag* (Leuven 1995). For the titles, see J. Quaegebeur, in *Aspekte spätägyptischer Kultur* (Fs. Erich Winter), *AegTrev* 7, 1994), pp. 213–25. End of the Ptolemaic Period.
Owner: *Ns-pꜣwty-tꜣwy* (Spotous).
Titles:
— *it-nṯr ḥm-nṯr n Ꞽmn-Rꜥ nsw nṯrw*, 'god's father and prophet of Amun-Re king of the gods';
— *ḥm Ḥḏt*, 'servant of the White';
— *ḥm Ḥr*, 'servant of Horus';
— *wr wꜣḏty*, 'great of the two diadems';
— *ḥry sštꜣ*, 'overseer of the mystery';
— *ꜥb-nṯr*, 'purifier of the god'.
Father of the owner: *Ḥr-m-ḥb* (Harmais).
Titles:
— *mi nn*, (priest of the same rank as the son);
— *pr m ꜣḫt ḫf imy.s*, 'he who comes forth from the horizon and sees what is in it';
— *wn ꜥꜣwy pt m Ꞽpt-swt*, 'he who opens the doors of the sky in Karnak';
— *ḥꜣty-(p)-ꜥ m-ḫt*, '*ḥꜣty-(p)-ꜥ*-priest, second in command'.[15]
Mother of the owner: *Twꜣyt*.

P. Florence 3662. First Book of Breathing. A. Pellegrini, *Bessarione* 8/2 (1904), pp. 48–57, 147–58 with pl.
Owner: *ꜣrswynyꜣt* (Arsinoe).
Mother of the owner: *Tꜣ-šrit-twt* (Sentotoes).

P. Florence 3665 + P. Vienna 3850. Book of Breathing made by Isis. A. Pellegrini, in *Rendiconti della Reale Accademia dei Lincei* (Rome 1904), pp. 87–104 with pl. The lower part of the document (P. Vienna 3850) is unpublished.

15. See n. 8.

Owner: *Mwt-mwt.i.*[16]
Title:
— *iḥyt n Ỉmn-Rʿ*, 'sistrum-player of Amun-Re'.
Father of the owner: *P(ꜣ)-di-Nfr-ḥtp* (Petenephotes).
Title:
— *it-nṯr*, 'god's father'.

P. Florence 3669. Original text and Second Book of Breathing. A. Pellegrini, *Sphinx* 8 (1902), pp. 216–17 with pl.; W. Spiegelberg, *Sphinx* 9 (1906), p. 21; G. Möller, *Hieratische Lesestücke* III (Leipzig 1910), pl. 31, no. 5.
Owner: *Kšꜣrys*, translated in Greek [Ch]aris on the verso.
Mother of the owner: unknown woman (*bw rḫ.w.s*).

P. Florence 3670. A. Pellegrini, *Sphinx* 8 (1902), p. 217 with pl. (verso only). Same owner as P. Florence 3669, and text almost identical.[17]

P. Florence 3676 (dem.). Text related to the Book of Breathing. G. Botti, *Testi demotici* I (Florence 1941), pp. 32–5 with pl. 6.
Owner: *Gʿꜣ* (Kaies).
Father of the owner: [*Pꜣ*]-*šr-(n)-tꜣ-šr.t-(n)-pꜣ-4-Mnw* (Psensenphthouminis).[18]

P. Joseph Smith I, X and XI (formerly P. MMA 47.102.8–9, 11). Book of Breathing made by Isis. Belonging now to the Mormon Church. K. Baer, *Dialogue: A Journal of Mormon Thought* 3/3 (1968), pp. 109–34; J. Quaegebeur, in Bierbrier (ed.), *Portraits and Masks*, p. 74; M. Coenen, *RdE* 49 (1998), p. 38 with n. 11. For the sake of convenience, this text is cited as P. Joseph Smith.[19]
Owner: *Ḥr* (Horos).
Titles:
— *it-nṯr ḥm-nṯr n Ỉmn-Rʿ nsw nṯrw*, 'god's father and prophet of Amun-Re king of the gods';
— *ḥm Mnw smꜣ rkyw.f* (?), 'prophet of Min who destroys his enemy';[20]
— [*ḥm-nṯr*] *Ḫnsw pꜣ-ir-sḫrw* [...], '[prophet] of Khonsu-who-governs-in-Thebes' [...].
Father of the owner: *Wsir-wr* (Osoroeris).
Titles:
— *mi nn* (priest of the same rank as the son);
— *ḥry sštꜣ*, 'overseer of the mystery';
— *ʿb-nṯr*, 'purifier of the god';
Mother of the owner: *Tꜣ-ḫy-biꜣ* (Chibois).

P. Lausanne 3391. Book of Breathing made by Isis. M. Vallogia, in: *Hommages à Serge Sauneron* I (*BdE* 81, 1979), pp. 285–304, with pls XLV–VII.
Owner: *Tꜣ-wgš*[21] (Tekusis).
Title:
— *iḥy(t) n Ỉmn-Rʿ*, 'sistrum-player of Amun-Re'.
Father of the owner: *Mnṯw-m-ḥꜣt* (Mentemes).
Titles:
— *ḥꜣty-ʿ wr m Wꜣst*, 'great *ḥꜣty-ʿ*-priest in Thebes';[22]
— *it-nṯr*, 'god's father'.
Mother of the owner: *Tꜣ-šri(t-nt)-Ỉmn-ḥtp* (Senamenothes).

P. Leiden T 11. Original funerary formulae with vignette of *BD* ch. 100. M. Coenen, *OMRO* 79 (1999), p. 67 and pl. 1.
Owner: *Mwt-Mnw.*
Mother of the owner: *Tꜣ-ḫy* (Tachois).

P. Leiden T 22. Book of Traversing Eternity, short fragmentary version. M. Coenen, *OMRO* 79 (1999), pp. 69–71 with pl. 2.

P. Leiden T 32. Book of Traversing Eternity, long version. *LPE*, pp. 5–7 with pls I–VIII. Date: AD 65
Owner: *Ḥr-sꜣ-Ỉst* (Harsiesis).
Titles:
— *it-nṯr ḥm-nṯr n Ỉmn-Rʿ nsw nṯrw*, 'god's father and prophet of Amun-Re king of the gods';
— *ḥm-nṯr n Ḫnsw-p(ꜣ)-ir-sḫrw-m-Wꜣst*, 'prophet of Khonsu-who-governs-in-Thebes';
— *ḥry sštꜣ* 'overseer of the mystery';
— *rḫ ḫt*, 'scholar';
— *rḫ st-rꜣ.f*, 'he who knows his affair'.
Father of the owner: *Ḥr* (Horos).
Mother of the owner: *Ḳꜣyḳꜣy.*
Titles:
— *nbt pr*, 'housewife';
— *iḥyt n Ỉmn-Rʿ*, 'sistrum-player of Amun-Re'.

P. Leiden T 33. First Book of Breathing. B.H. Stricker, *OMRO* 23 (1942), pp. 30–47 with pl. Date: AD 109. See *supra*, p. 6, no. **8**.
Owner: *Tꜣ-šrit-Ḏd-ḥr* (Sensaos).
Mother of the owner: *Gꜣrwꜣptrʿ* (Cleopatra) also called *Ḳndgy* (Candace).

P. Lieblein. Original text and Second Book of Breathing. Lieblein, *Que mon nom fleurisse*, p. lxx with pl.
Owner: [...]*wꜣpʿt.*
Mother of the owner: *Tꜣ-šrit-pyrmʿy* (?)

P. Louvre E 3452 (dem.). G. Legrain, *Le livre des transformations* (Paris 1890); M. Smith, *The Demotic Mortuary Papyrus Louvre E 3452* (1979, unpublished dissertation). Date: 56 BC
Owner: *Ỉi-m-ḥtp* (Imouthes).
Titles:
— *ʿꜣ n sꜣ*, 'phylarch';
— *ʿꜣ n sꜣ n Ḏm*, 'phylarch of Djeme';
— *ḥry wn.w n Ỉmn n Ḏm*, 'chief of pastophores of Amun of Djeme';
— *ḥm-nṯr n Ỉi-m-ḥtp*, 'prophet of Imhotep';
— *wʿb n Ḥ.t-Ḥr ḥnw.t Ỉmnṯ n Ḏm*, '*wʿb*-priest of Hathor mistress of the West of Djeme';
— *ḥr-tb ḥt n tꜣy=f ḥm*, 'magician pre-eminent in his craft'.
Father of the owner: *Pa-nꜣ-ḫty.w* (Panekhates).
Mother of the owner: *Tꜣ-šr.t-Bꜣs.t* (Senobastis).

16. Another (?) *Mwt-mwt.i*, bearing the same title, is owner of P. Berlin 3044; see *LPE*, p. 11, n. 19.
17. This differs from P. Florence 3669 only in some minor orthographic variations and in the depiction on the verso of two feet (and no longer a head) showing the place where the manuscript was to be deposited.
18. On this name, see J. Quaegebeur, in *Religion und Philosophie im Alten Ägypten* (Festgabe für Philippe Derchain) (*OLA* 39), 1991, p. 253.
19. Correspondences are following: P. Joseph Smith I = P. MMA 47.102.11: vignette with hieroglyphic text; P. Joseph Smith XI = P. MMA 47.102.9: cols I–II; P. Joseph Smith X = P. MMA 47.102, 8: cols III–IV. P. MMA 47.102.10 has no relationship to the Book of Breathing of Isis; it shows only the vignette of ch. 110 of the Book of the Dead.
20. On this title: M. Coenen, in *Egyptian Religion the Last Thousand Years (Studies Dedicated to the Memory of Jan Quaegebeur)*, (*OLA* 85, 1998), pp. 1103–15.
21. She bears both qualifications of 'Osiris' and 'Hathor'; see Smith, *Mortuary Texts*, p. 129–31 (XII, 24, a).
22. Cf. the titles borne by the owner of P. Louvre N 3278: *ḥꜣt p-ʿ mr ḥmw-nṯr m Wꜣst*. On the title *ḥꜣty-p-ʿ wr*: J. Quaegebeur, in: *Aspekte spätägyptischer Kultur* (Fs. Erich Winter), *AegTrev* 7, 1994, p. 215 with n. 36.

P. Louvre E 3865. First and Second Book of Breathing. Devéria, *Catalogue*, p. 151 (V, 16).
Owner: *Ỉi-m-ḥtp* (Imouthes).[23]
Titles:
— *it-nṯr ḥm-nṯr n Ỉmn-Rꜥ nsw nṯrw*, 'god's father and prophet of Amun-Re king of the gods';
— *smꜣty wr m Gbtyw-tꜣwy*, 'great *smꜣty*-priest of Coptos of the two lands';
— *ḥm-nṯr n Ỉst wrt nṯrt ꜥꜣt ḥr(t)-ib Gbtyw*, 'prophet of Isis the great, the great goddess dwelling in Coptos';
— *ḥm-nṯr 2.nw n Ỉmn*, 'second prophet of Amun';
— *ḥm-nṯr 4.nw n Ỉmn*, 'fourth prophet of Amun';
— *ḥm-nṯr n Mwt wrt nbt Ỉšrw*, 'prophet of Mut the great, lady of Icheru';
— *ꜥꜣ-pr n Ḫnsw-m-Wꜣst-Nfr-ḥtp*, 'majordomo of Khonsu-in-Thebes-Neferhotep';
— *ḥm-nṯr n Mnw-Ỉmn*, 'prophet of Min-Amun';
— *ḥm-nṯr n Wsir ḫt Mnw*, 'prophet of Osiris of the terrace of Min';
Father of the owner: *ꜥnḫ-Ḥsꜣt*.
Mother of the owner: *Tꜣ-nt-ri*.
Titles:
— *nbt pr*, 'housewife';
— *iḥyt n imn-Rꜥ*, 'sistrum-player of Amun-Re king of the gods';
— *ibht n Mnw*, 'dancer of Min'.

P. Louvre E 10263. Fragmentary text related to the Book of Breathing. Unpublished.
Owner: name lost.

P. Louvre E 10264. Fragmentary text related to the Book of Breathing. Unpublished.
Owner: *Tisgꜣhꜣy* (or *Misgꜣhꜣy*).
Mother of the owner: [...]*r*.

P. Louvre E 10284. First Book of Breathing. Unpublished.
Owner: name lost.

P. Louvre E 10605 (dem.). See under **P. Bodl. MS. Egypt. c. 9 + P. Louvre E 10605** (dem.) and **P. Berlin 8351** (dem.).

P. Louvre E 10607 (dem.). See under **P. Berlin 8351** (dem.).
Owner: *Tꜣ-tꜣ-rpy.t* (Tatriphis).
Mother of the owner: *Klwḏ* (Kollouthes).

P. Louvre E 11079. Book of Breathing made by Isis. Unpublished.
Owner: *Ỉst-wrt* (Esoeris).
Mother of the owner: *Tꜣ-šrit-Ḏḥwty* (Senthotes).
Father of the owner: *Ḥr-nḏ-it.f* (Harendotes).

P. Louvre N 2420 c (dem.). Text for a deceased woman. Chauveau, *RdE* 41 (1990), pp. 3–8 with pl. 1.
Owner: not mentioned.

P. Louvre N 3083. Book of Breathing made by Isis. Devéria, *Catalogue*, p. 74 (III, 31); F.R. Herbin, *RdE* 50 (1999), pp. 155–7 with pls XIX–XXI. It comprises a copy of the Book of the Dead (I, 1–V, 1), followed by an original version of the Book of Breathing made by Isis. The first column is fragmentary.
Owner: *Ỉst-ršti* (Eserecht)
Mother of the owner: *Tꜣ-ḫy-biꜣ* (Chibois).

P. Louvre N 3121. Book of Breathing made by Isis. Devéria, *Catalogue*, p. 117 (IV, 9); Herbin, *RdE* 50 (1999), pp. 150–4 with pls XV–XIX.
Owner: *Tꜣ-šrit-Mnw* (Semminis, R*PN* I, 369, 3).
Title:
— *iḥyt n Ỉmn-Rꜥ*, 'sistrum-player of Amun-Re'.
Mother of the owner: *Tꜣ-šrit-(nt-)ꜥšꜣ-ḥwt* (Senasuchis, R*PN* I, 368, 13).
Father of the owner: *Ḏd-Ḥr* (Teos) son of *Ỉi-m-ḥtp* (Imouthes).
Titles:
— *it-nṯr ḥm-nṯr Ỉmn-Rꜥ* ... (?), 'god's father and prophet of Amun-Re ... (?);
— *ḥm Wsir wp išd*, 'prophet of Osiris who inaugurated the *išd* tree;[24]
— *ḥm Mnw smꜣ* (?) *ḫrwyw.f*, 'prophet of Min who destroys his enemies';
— *ḥꜣt-p-ꜥ wr*, 'great *ḥꜣt-p-ꜥ*-priest';[25]
— *mr ḥmw-nṯr m Wꜣst*, 'chief of prophets in Thebes';
— *ḥm 2.nw Ỉmn*, 'second prophet of Amun'.

P. Louvre N 3126. Book of Breathing made by Isis. Devéria, *Catalogue*, p. 136 (IV, 6). Unpublished.
Owner: *Pꜣ-šri-ꜥšꜣ-ḥt* (Senasuchis).
Titles:
— *it-nṯr ḥm-nṯr n Ỉmn-Rꜥ nsw nṯrw*, 'god's father and prophet of Amun-Re king of the gods'.
Father of the owner: *Wsir-wr* (Osoroeris).
Title:
— *mi nn* (priest of the same rank as the son).
Mother of the owner: *Tꜣ-ḫy-biꜣ* (Chibois).

P. Louvre N 3147. Book of Traversing Eternity. Devéria, *Catalogue*, p. 150 (V, 14); *LPE*, p. 23 with pls XXVII–VIII.
Owner: *P(ꜣ)y-kꜣ* (Pikos).
Titles:
—*smn* ... (?)
— ... (?) *wr n Wꜣst-nḫt*, '... (?) great of Thebes victorious.[26]
— *ḫw* ... (?) *Ỉpt-swt* ... (?) ... (?), 'who protects ... (?) Karnak ... (?)'
Father of the owner: *Pꜣ-šri-Ỉmn* (Psenamounis).
Title:
— *mi nn* (priest of the same rank as the son).
Mother of the owner: *Tꜣ-šrit-Mwt* (Senmouthes).
Title:
— *nbt pr*, 'housewife'.

P. Louvre N 3148. First and Second Book of Breathing, and original texts. Devéria, *Catalogue*, p. 147 (V, 12). Partly published.[27] Pierret, *Etudes égyptologiques*, pp. 42–79; Goyon, *Rituels funéraires*, pp. 233–4; col. VII: F.R. Herbin, *BIFAO* 84 (1984), p. 252 with pl. 51.
Owner: *ꜥnḫ.f-n-Ḫnsw* (Chapochonsis).
Title:
— *it-nṯr ḥm-nṯr n Ỉmn-Rꜥ nsw nṯrw*, 'god's father and prophet of Amun-Re king of the gods'.
Mother of the owner: *Tꜣ-šrit-Mnṯw* (Senmonthes).

P. Louvre N 3154. Book of Breathing made by Isis. Devéria, *Catalogue*, p. 132 (IV, 3). Unpublished.
Owner: *Ḥr* (Horos).

23. There is a coffin fragment of *Ỉi-m-ḥtp* son of *ꜥnḫ-Ḥsꜣt* kept in the museum of Marseilles; see G. Maspero, *RT* 37 (1915), p. 2.
24. The reading *wp šꜥt (tꜣwy)* (*RdE* 50, p. 150, n. 8) must be emended (L. Coulon, pers. comm.).
25. See n. 22.
26. Title perhaps linked to the former.
27. Other fragments of this manuscript have been found in the Louvre Museum (P. Louvre N 3220 A), and the document as a whole is in course of reconstruction.

Titles:
— *it-nṯr ḥm-nṯr n Ỉmn-Rˁ nsw nṯrw*, 'god's father and prophet of Amun-Re king of the gods';
— *smȝty*, '*smȝty*-priest';
— *ḥnk-Nwn*, '*ḥnk-Nwn*-priest';
— *sš mḏȝt nṯr n Ỉmn*,[28] 'scribe of the divine book of Amun'.
His mother: *Tȝbḥt*.

P. Louvre N 3156. Original text and part of the Second Book of Breathing. *Naissance de l'écriture*, exh. cat., Galeries Nationales du Grand Palais (Paris 1982), p. 161 with pl. Date: reign of Trajan or Hadrian. See *supra*, p. 6, no. **21**.
Owner: *Swtr* (Soter).
Mother of the owner: *Ḏȝpwr* (Sapaulis).

P. Louvre N 3157. Second Book of Breathing. Devéria, *Catalogue*, pp. 152–3 (V, 20). Unpublished. P. BN 151, P. Leiden T 32, P. Louvre N 3285 and N 3291, belong to the same owner.
Owner: *Ḥr-sȝ-Ỉst* (Harsiesis).
Titles:
— *it-nṯr ḥm-nṯr n Ỉmn-Rˁ nsw nṯrw*, 'god's father and prophet of Amun-Re king of the gods';
— *ḥm-nṯr n Ḫnsw-pȝ-ir-sḫrw-m-Wȝst*, 'prophet of Khonsu-who-governs-in-Thebes';
— *ḥm-nṯr n Bȝstt ḫr(t)-ib Wȝst*, 'prophet of Bastet dwelling in Thebes';
— *ḥry sštȝ*, 'overseer of the mystery';
— *ˁb-nṯr*, 'purifier of the god';
— *sp̱ḫr sȝww m gsw-prw*, 'he who inscribes the temple walls';
— *rḫ ḫt*, 'scholar';
— *rḫ st-rȝ.f*, 'he who knows his affair'.
Mother of the owner: *Ḳȝyḳȝy*.

P. Louvre N 3158. Book of Breathing made by Isis. Devéria, *Catalogue*, p. 136 (IV, 8). Unpublished. Col. I is lost. Date: end of the Ptolemaic Period or beginning of the Roman Period.
Owner: *Tȝ-šrit-pȝwty-tȝwy*[29] (*Senpotous)
Mother of the owner: *Šˁḥpry* (Sachperis, *RPN* I, 324, 21).

P. Louvre N 3159 + 3194. First and Second Book of Breathing, and original texts. Unpublished. *LPE*, pp. 26–7, n. 75. Date: ± 113 BC
Owner: *Ns-pȝwty-tȝwy* (Spotous).
Titles:
— *it-nṯr*, 'god's father';
— *ḥm-nṯr n Ỉmn-Rˁ nsw nṯrw*, 'prophet of Amun-Re king of the gods';
— *ḥm-nṯr n Mnw-Ỉmn*, 'prophet of Min-Amun';
— *ḥȝty-ˁ wr m Wȝst*, 'great *ḥȝty-ˁ*-priest in Thebes'.[30]
Father of the owner: *Wsir-wr* (Osoroeris).
Titles:
— *it-nṯr*, 'god's father';
— *ḥm-nṯr n Ỉmn-Rˁ nsw nṯrw*, 'prophet of Amun-Re king of the gods';
— [*ḥm-nṯr n Mnw-Ỉmn-Rˁ kȝ*] *mwt.f ḥry st.f wrt*, '[prophet of Min-Amun-Re bull] of his mother, who is upon his great seat'.
Mother of the owner: *Tȝ-nwb*.
Titles:
— *nbt pr*, 'housewife';
— *iḥyt n Ỉmn-Rˁ nsw nṯrw*, 'sistrum-player of Amun-Re king of the gods'.

P. Louvre N 3161. Second Book of Breathing. Devéria, *Catalogue*, p. 152 (V, 18). Unpublished. Date: reign of Trajan or Hadrian. See *supra*, p. 6, no. **24**.
Owner: *Pˁtrˁny* (Petronius).
Mother of the owner: *Ḳndˁgys* (Candace).

P. Louvre N 3162. Second Book of Breathing. Devéria, *Catalogue*, p. 153 (V, 21). Unpublished.
Owner: *P(ȝ)-šri-Ỉst-wrt* (Psenesoeris).
Mother of the owner: *Ỉst* (Isis).

P. Louvre N 3166. Book of Breathing made by Isis. Devéria, *Catalogue*, p. 135 (IV, 5); *LPE*, pp. 18–19 and pls XXI–XXII; Herbin, *RdE* 50 (1999), pp. 158–60 with pl. XXII.
Owner: *Wsir-wr* (Osoroeris).
Mother of the owner: *Tȝ-ḫy-biȝ* (Chibois).

P. Louvre N 3167 + 3222. Book of Breathing made by Isis. Devéria, *Catalogue*, p. 136 (IV, 7); Quaegebeur, in Bierbrier (ed.), *Portraits and Masks*, p. 74.
Owner: *Tȝ-wgš* (Techosis).[31]
Title:
— *iḥy(t) n Ỉmn-Rˁ*, 'sistrum-player of Amun-Re'.
Father of the owner: *Ḥr-sȝ-Ỉst* (Harsiesis).
Title:
— *it-nṯr ḥm-nṯr n Ỉmn-Rˁ nsw nṯrw*, 'god's father and prophet of Amun-Re king of the gods'.
Her mother: *Ns-(tȝ)-nṯrt-tn*.

P. Louvre N 3174. Second Book of Breathing and original text. Devéria, *Catalogue*, pp. 154–5 (V, 25). Unpublished.
Owner: *P(ȝ)-šri-(n)-tȝ-iḥt* (Psentaes).[32]
Titles:
— *it-nṯr*, 'god's father' (before many titles);
— *imy pr n Ḫnsw-m-Wȝst-Nfr-ḥtp*, 'steward of Khonsu-in-Thebes-Nefer-hotep';
— *idnw n pr-ḥḏ n Ỉmn*, 'deputy of the Treasure of Amun'
— *ˁ-pr n Ḫnsw-m-Wȝst-Nfr-ḥtp*, 'majordomo of Khonsu-in-Thebes-Nefer-hotep';
— *wˁb ȝḫ*, '*wˁb-ȝḫ* (?)-priest;
— *wˁb iḥy*, '*wˁb-iḥy*-priest';[33]
— *wˁb n itn wr*, '*wˁb*-priest of the great disk';
— *wˁb n … (?)*, '*wˁb*-priest of … (?)';
— *wˁb ˁȝ n nṯr niwt (?)*, 'great *wˁb*-priest of the god of the town (?)';
— *wˁb ˁȝ n Ḥwt Ỉpt*, 'great *wˁb*-priest of the Mansion of Ipet';
— *wˁb wr m Wȝst-nḫt*, 'great *wˁb*-priest in Thebes the victorious';
— *wn ˁȝwy pt n Ỉmn ḥnˁ Psḏt*, 'he who opens the doors of the sky of Amun with the Ennead';
— *wn <ˁwy> pt m swḥt-ms-nṯrw*, 'he who opens <the doors> of the sky in the Egg which gave birth to the gods';[34]
— *wn rȝ n imḥt m Ỉȝt Ḏȝm*, 'he who opens the door of the tomb (?) in the Mound of Djeme';[35]
— *rḫ iḫwt wr m-ḫnw Wȝst-nḫt*, 'great scholar in Thebes the victorious';
— *ḥm-nṯr n Ỉmn-Rˁ nsw nṯrw*, 'prophet of Amun-Re king of the gods';
— *ḥm-nṯr n ḥry nṯrw*, 'prophet of the overseer of the gods';

---

28. *sš mḏȝt-nṯr n Ỉmn*, also attested in P. Louvre SN 173, I, 5.
29. Name unknown elsewhere. For the masculine counterpart: *Demot. Nb.*, 243.
30. See n. 22.
31. On this *Tȝ-wgš*: *ProsPtol* IX, 7245 c.
32. P. Louvre N 3176 N probably belongs to the same owner.

33. On this title: *LPE*, p. 145 (II, 31–III, 1).
34. A designation of Thebes: *GDG* V, p. 19.
35. For the title *wn rȝ n imḥt* and the different meanings of the word *imḥt*, see L. Coulon, *RdE* 57 (2006), pp. 6–7, (I).

— *ḥm-nṯr n snty wr m pr Ỉmn*, 'prophet of the great foundation[36] in the House of Amun';
— *ḥm-nṯr wʿb ʿ3 m Ỉwnw*, 'prophet and great *wʿb*-priest in (South) Heliopolis;
— *ḥm-nṯr tpy m Ỉrt Rʿ rḫ ḫwt wr m-ẖnw sp3wt.f*, 'First prophet in the Eye of Re, great scholar in his nomes';
— *ḥm-nṯr tpy n Ỉmn-Rʿ nsw nṯrw*, 'First prophet of Amun-Re king of the gods';
— *ḥm-nṯr tpy n mniw* 'First prophet of the shepherd' (Amun);
— *ḥm-nṯr tpy n niwt ms niwwt*, 'First prophet of the town which gave birth to the towns';
— *ḥm-nṯr tpy n nsw nṯrw*, 'First prophet of the king of the gods';
— *ḥm-nṯr tpy n nṯr ir ṯ3w*, 'First prophet of the god who makes breath';
— *ḥm-nṯr tpy n ḏnḥw wʿ*, 'First prophet of ... (?)';
— *ḥry ḫ3wt*, 'overseer of the altar';
— *ḥry sšt3 ʿb-nṯr m Ỉpt rsyt*, 'overseer of the mystery, purifier of the god in Luxor';
— *sb3 ʿ3 n pt*, 'great star of the sky';
— *sš n Ỉmn iw.f ipy*, 'scribe of Amun who makes reckoning';[37]
— *ḳbḥ m Bnbn*, 'libationer in Benben';
— ... (?) *m Psḏt W3st*, '... in the Ennead of Thebes';
— ... (?) *n ḥwt* ... (?), '... (?) of the Mansion ...'.
Mother of the owner: *Y3ʿ*, *Ỉryʿ(ʿ)* .

P. Louvre N 3176 A. First Book of Breathing. Devéria, *Catalogue*, pp. 159–60 (V, 44). Unpublished.
Owner: *T3-ẖnmty*.
Mother of the owner: *T3-ḫy-bi3* (Chibois).

P. Louvre N 3176 D. First Book of Breathing. Devéria, *Catalogue*, p. 153 (V, 43). Unpublished.
Owner: name lost.
Mother of the owner: [...]-(?) *T3-šrit-Ḫnsw* ([...]-(?) Senchonsis).

P. Louvre N 3176 E. First Book of Breathing. Devéria, *Catalogue*, p. 159 (V, 42). Unpublished.
Owner: name in lacuna.
Mother of the owner: *T3-(nt-)Ḫnsw* (Tachonsis).

P. Louvre N 3176 F. First Book of Breathing. Unpublished. Devéria, *Catalogue*, p. 154 (V, 23).
Owner: *P3-di-nfr-ḥtp* (Petenephotes).
His mother: *T3-rmṯ-n-Ḏʿm* (?).

P. Louvre N 3176 G. First Book of Breathing. Devéria, *Catalogue*, pp. 158–9 (V, 40). Unpublished.
Owner: *3rtymy* (Artemis).
Mother of the owner: name unreadable.

P. Louvre N 3176 J. Second Book of Breathing. Devéria, *Catalogue*, p. 158 (V, 39). Unpublished.
Owner: *T3-(nt-)fdw-Mnw* (Taphthouminis).
Mother of the owner: *T3-šrit-Ỉmn-Ỉpt* (Senamenophis).

P. Louvre N 3176 M. Fragmentary text related to the Book of Breathing. Devéria, *Catalogue*, p. 155 (V, 29). Unpublished.
Owner: [...] *wr*.
Mother of the owner: name in lacuna.

P. Louvre N 3177 A. Second Book of Breathing. Devéria, *Catalogue*, p. 157 (V, 34). Unpublished.
Owner: *T3-šrit-Twtw* (Sentotoes).
Mother of the owner: *T3-šrit*-[...].

P. Louvre N 3194. See under P. Louvre N 3159 + 3194.

P. Louvre N 3220 A. See under P. Louvre N 3148.

P. Louvre N 3236. Text related to the Book of Breathing. F.R. Herbin, *BIFAO* 84 (1984), pp. 253–4, with pls LII–LIV.[38]
Owner: *T3-šrit-(nt-)p3-wr* (Senpoeris).

P. Louvre N 3258 (dem.). Some formulae related to the Book of Breathing. Devéria, *Catalogue*, p. 155 (V, 26).
Owner: *T3-šrit-p3-di-Ḫnsw* (Senpetechonsis).
Mother of the owner: *T3-šrit-(nt-)t3-wrt* (Senteuris)

P. Louvre N 3279. First Book of Breathing. J.C. Goyon, *Le papyrus du Louvre N. 3279* (*BdE* 42, 1966).
Owner: *T3w3* (Thaues).[39]
Title:
— *iḥyt n Ỉmn-Rʿ*, 'Sistrum-player of Amun-Re'.
Mother of the owner: *Ỉpt-wrt* (Epoeris).

P. Louvre N 3284. Book of Breathing made by Isis. Devéria, *Catalogue*, pp. 132–5 (IV, 4); Horrack, *Le Livre des Respirations*, pls I–IV; *LPE*, pp. 25–7 with pls XXIX–XXXI. On the owner and his family, see J. Quaegebeur, in *Aspekte spätägyptischer Kultur* (Fs. Erich Winter), *AegTrev* 7, 1994, pp. 215–18; id., in Bierbrier (ed.), *Portraits and Masks*, p. 74.
Owner: *Wsir-wr* (Osoroeris).
Titles:
— *it-nṯr ḥm-nṯr n Ỉmn-Rʿ nsw nṯrw*, 'god's father and prophet of Amun-Re king of the gods';
— *ḥm-nṯr n Mnw-Ỉmn-Rʿ k3 mwt.f ḥry st.f wrt*, 'prophet of Min-Amun-Re, bull of his mother, who is upon his great seat';
Father of the owner: *Ns-p3wtyw-t3wy* (Spotous).
Titles:
— *mi nn* (priest of the same rank as the son).
Mother of the owner: *Ns-Ḥr-p3-Rʿ* (Esarpres).

P. Louvre N 3285. Book of Breathing made by Isis. Devéria, *Catalogue*, p. 131 (IV, 1). Unpublished.
Owner: *Ḥr-s3-Ỉst* (Harsiesis).
Titles:
— *it-nṯr ḥm-nṯr n Ỉmn-Rʿ nsw nṯrw*, 'god's father and prophet of Amun-Re king of the gods';
— *ḥm-nṯr n Ḫnsw p(3) ir sḫrw m W3st*, 'prophet of Khonsu-who-governs-in-Thebes'.
Father of the owner: *Ḥr* (Horos).
Title:
— *mi nn* (priest of the same rank as the son).
Mother of the owner: *T3-wgš* (Techosis).

36. Other attestations of the title in *Dendara* X, 14; R.A. Parker, J. Leclant and J.C. Goyon, *The Edifice of Taharqa by the Sacred Lake of Karnak* (Providence 1979), p. 68, with n. 39.
37. Same title in P. Louvre N 3175: Devéria, *Catalogue*, p. 69 (III, 20).
38. Since this publication appeared, other fragments of the manuscript have been found in the Louvre Museum.
39. H. de Meulenaere, *CdE* 84 (1967), p. 338.

P. Louvre N 3289. Original text and part of the Second Book of Breathing. Devéria, *Catalogue*, pp. 163–4 (V, 48). Unpublished. Found with P. Louvre N 3156. See *supra*, p. 6, no. **21**.
Owner: *Swtr* (Soter).
Mother of the owner: *Ḏ3pwr* (Sapaulis).

P. Louvre N 3290. First Book of Breathing. Devéria, *Catalogue*, p. 163 (V, 47). J.F. Champollion, in F. Cailliaud, *Voyage à Méroé* IV, pp. 26–7 with pl. 1. Unpublished. Date: reign of Trajan or Hadrian. See *supra*, p. 6, no. **2**.
Owner: *Ḳ3rnyr* (Cornelius).
Mother of the owner: *Ỉst-wrt* (Esoeris).

P. Louvre N 3291. Book of Breathing made by Isis. Devéria, *Catalogue*, pp. 131–2, IV, 2. Horrack, *Le Livre des Respirations*, pls VI–VII. On the owner, see *LPE*, pp. 5–7.
Owner: *Ḥr-s3-Ỉst* (Harsiesis).
Titles:
— *it-nṯr ḥm-nṯr n Ỉmn-Rʿ nsw nṯrw*, 'god's father and prophet of Amun-Re king of the gods';
— *ḥm-nṯr n Ḫnsw p3 ir sḫrw m W3st*, 'prophet of Khonsu-who-governs-in-Thebes';
— *ḥm-nṯr n B3stt ḥr(yt)-ib W3st*, 'prophet of Bastet dwelling in Thebes';
— *rḫ ḫt wr m W3st*, 'great scholar in Thebes';
— *rḫ st-r3.f m mdw-nṯr*, 'he who knows his affair in hieroglyhics';
— *wʿb ʿ3*, 'great *wʿb*-priest';
— *wḥm irw.f*, 'he who repeats his form' (?);
— *sphr s3ww m gsw-prw*, 'he who inscribes the temple walls';
— *ḥry sšt3*, 'overseer of the mystery';
— *ʿb-nṯr*, 'purifier of the god';
— *ʿḳ bw ḏsr n nṯr ʿ3*, 'he who enters the sacred place of the great god';
— *rḫ irw n k3t rḥty*[40], 'he who knows the form of the work of the two Damsels'.
Mother of the owner: *Ḳ3yḳ3y*.

P. Louvre SN. First Book of Breathing. Unpublished.
Owner: *P3-di-Ḫnsw-p3-ḫrd* (Petechenpokrates).
Mother of the owner: [...] (?)-*t3-ḫrd*.

P. MMA 35.9.21. Several ritual texts. J.C. Goyon, *Le papyrus d'Imouthès fils de Psintaês au Metropolitan Museum of Art de New York* (New York, 1999). Provenance: Meir. Date: Ptolemaic Period.
Owner: *Ỉi-m-ḥtp* (Imouthes).[41]
Titles:
— *Ḥr ḏsr-ḥʿw*, 'Horus sacred of body (?);
— *ḥm ʿḥ3 sw*, 'priest (?) of he who fight him'.
Mother of the owner: *Ṯḥnt*.
Her titles:
— *nbt-pr*, 'housewife';
— *iḥyt n Ḥwt-Ḥr nbt Kws*, 'sistrum-player of Hathor lady of Cusae'.
Father of the owner: *P3-šri-n-t3-iḥt* (Psentaes).
Title:
— *mi nn* (priest of the same rank as the son).

P. MMA 47.102.8–11. See under **P. Joseph Smith I, X and XI.**

P. Moscow 4661. See under **P. Berlin 3164 + Moscow 4661**.

P.(?) Moscow, no. unknown = MSS Golenischeff 517–18, 520. Maybe linen and papyrus. Texts related to the Book of Breathing. F.R. Herbin, *BIFAO* 84 (1984), pp. 254–6 with pls LV–LVII.
Owner: *Bs*.[42]
Title:
— *ḥm-wn*, '*ḥm-wn*-priest'.
Mother of the owner: *T3-di-nbt-hw*.

P. Munich 834 a (dem.). Some formulae related to the Book of Breathing. Brunsch, in *Studien zur Sprache und Religion Ägyptens* I (Fs. Westendorff), 1984, pp. 455–6, with pl. 1.
Owner: *T3-šr.t-p3-šj* (Senpsais).
Father of the owner: *P3-ḥtr* (Patres).
Mother of the owner: *T3-Ỉmn* (Tamounis).

P. Munich 834 b (dem.). Some formulae related to the Book of Breathing. Brunsch, op. cit., pp. 457–60, with pl. 2.
Owner: *Ỉmn-i.ir-dj-s* (Amyrtaios)
Mother of the owner: *T3-šr.t-p3j-k3* (Senpikos).

P. OIC 25389. Various funerary texts. *LPE*, pp. 15–18. Provenance: Esna.
Owner: *Šmʿ-nfr*.
Titles:
— *ḥm-nṯr n ʿnḫ wrh ir mi ḥʿw*, 'prophet of the Living one, the dancer who does as the body';
— *ḥm-nṯr n wrh ir mi ḥʿw*, 'prophet of the dancer who does as the body'
— *ḥm-nṯr n Ḫmnw*, 'prophet of Khnum'
— *ḥm-nṯr n Wsir ḫnty Ỉmntt nb ʿb3*, 'prophet of Osiris foremost of the West, the lord of Aba (Esna);
— *ḥm-nṯr n Bstt*, 'prophet of Bastet';
— *ḥm-nṯr n Ỉst Nbt-ḥwt*, 'prophet of Isis and Nephthys';
— *ʿb-nṯr*, 'purifier of the god';
— *rḫ ḫt*, 'scholar';
— *sš mḏ3t nṯr*, 'scribe of the divine book';
— *mr wʿb Sḫmt*, 'overseer of the *wʿb*-priests of Sekhmet';
— *ḥry sšt3*, 'overseer of the mystery'.
Father of the owner: *Ḥk3-t(3y).f-nḫt* (Aketephnachthes).
Title:
— *ḥm-nṯr*, 'prophet'.
Mother of the owner: *T3-bikt* (Tbekis).
— *nbt-pr*, 'housewife';
— *iḥyt (n) Nt*, 'sistrum-player of Neith'.

P. Oxford Bod. MS Egypt. a. 3 (P). Papyrus bearing texts written in hieratic and demotic: a new version of the Ritual of Bringing Sokaris out of the Shrine (hier.), and various liturgies (dem.). Unpublished; M. Smith, in *Sesto Congresso Internazionale di Egittologia. Atti*, II (Turin 1993), pp. 491–5.

P. Parma 183. Original text related to the Book of Breathing. G. Botti, in *Atti della 'Societa Colombaria Fiorentina'* (Florence 1939), pp. 1–12 with pls I–II.
Owner: *P(3)ih3y*.[43]
Mother of the owner: *T3-šrit-Ỉmn-ḥtp* (Senamenothes).

40. Fairman, *ASAE* 44 (1944), pp. 266–7.
41. *ProsPtol* III, 6121. He is also the owner of a copy of the Book of the Dead (P. MMA 35.9.20). His coffin is published by A. Kamal, *ASAE* 15 (1915), pp. 199–202.
42. To *Bs* son of *T3-di-nbt-hw* also belongs the mummy-board BM EA 36502 published by G. Vittmann, in *Zwischen den beiden Ewigkeiten* (Fs. Gertrud Thausing), 1994, pp. 222–75.
43. Spiegelberg, *ZÄS* 53 (1917), p. 25.

P. Rhind I. G. Möller, *Die beiden Totenpapyrus Rhind* [*DemSt. 6*] (Leipzig, 1913), pp. 15–52 and pls I–XI. Date: 9 BC
Owner: *Mnṯ(-m)-sꜣ.f* (Menthesouphis).[44]
Titles:
— *ḥm*, 'craftsman'.
His father: *Mn-kꜣ-Rꜥ* (Menkeres).[45]
Titles:
— *wr n niwt.f Ỉwnw šmꜥ*, 'great of his town, Karnak';
— *mr n niwt.f*, 'mayor of his town';
— *mr n Ỉwnw šmꜥ*, 'mayor of Karnak';
— *ḥm-nṯr n Mnṯw-Rꜥ nb Ỉwnw šmꜥ*, 'prophet of Montu-Re lord of Karnak';
— *wr mnft m Ỉwnw šmꜥ*, 'great of soldiery in Karnak';
— *rpꜥ-ḥꜣty-ꜥ*, 'prince and governor';
— *rwḏ nsw*, 'king's agent'.
Mother of the owner: *Tꜣ-šrit-(n-)p(ꜣ)-Mnṯw* (Senpamonthes).

P. Rhind II. It succeeds the preceding text, of which it is a kind of shorter version. Möller, op. cit., pp. 52–70 and pls XII–XX.
Owner: *Tꜣ(-nt)-Ỉwnyt*.[46]
Father of the owner: *Gr-šr* (Kalasiris).[47]
Titles:
— *rpꜥ-ḥꜣty-ꜥ*, 'prince and governor'.
— *ḥm-nṯr n Mnṯw-Rꜥ nb Ỉwnw šmꜥ*, 'prophet of Montu-Re, lord of Karnak';
— *sr ꜥꜣ m-ḥꜣt rḫyt*, 'great prince chief of mankind';
— *bwꜣ m Ỉwnw šmꜥ*, 'magistrate in Karnak';
— *rwḏ nsw n Ỉwnw Mnṯw*, 'king's agent in Heliopolis of Montu' (Karnak);
Mother of the owner: *Ḥwt-Ḥr-ỉỉ.ti*.

P. Toulouse 49–220. Original text related to the Book of Breathing. P. Ramond, *Notes sur le papyrus 49–220* (Toulouse 1978).
Owner: *ḥr* [...]
Mother of the owner: *Tꜣ-nt-Ỉst* (Taisis).

P. Tübingen 2001. Book of Traversing Eternity, and short version of the Second Book of Breathing. *Hieroglyphenschrift und Totenbuch. Die Papyri der ägyptischen Sammlung der Universität Tübingen* (Tübingen 1985), pp. 75–6 with ill; *LPE*, pp. 580–1.
Owner: *Tꜣ-(nt-)ỉỉ-m-ḥtp* (Taimouthes).
Title: *ỉḥyt n Ỉmn-Rꜥ*, 'sistrum-player of Amun-Re'.
Mother of the owner: name lost.

P. Tübingen 2012. Book of the Dead, preceded by a column of original text related to the Book of Breathing. E. Brunner-Traut and H. Brunner, *Die ägyptische Sammlung der Universität Tübingen* (Mainz 1981), pls 151–2.
Owner: *Mnṯw-m-ḥꜣt* (Mentemes).
Title:
— *ỉt-nṯr ḥm-nṯr n Ỉmn-Rꜥ nsw nṯrw*, 'god's father, prophet of Amun-Re king of the gods'.
Father of the owner: *Ḥr* (Horos) son of *Ḥr* son of *Wsir-wr* (Osoroeris) son of *ꜥnḫ.f-n-Ḫnsw* (Chapochonsis);[48]
Title:
— *sꜣ mi nn* (priest of the same rank as the son).

P. Tübingen 2016. Book of Breathing made by Isis. Brunner-Traut und Brunner, op. cit., p. 296 and pls 13, 150; J. Quaegebeur, in Bierbrier (ed.), *Portraits and Masks*, p. 74. The version of the Book of Breathing made by Isis to her brother Osiris is preceded of a sixteen-line text entitled 'Book of Breathing and Book of coming forth by day of the Osiris N' (*tꜣ šꜥt n snsn ḥnꜥ tꜣ pr m hrw n Wsir N*).
Owner: *Ḏd-Ḫnsw-iw.f-ꜥnḫ* (Techenphonuchos).
Titles:
— *ỉt-nṯr ḥm-nṯr n Ỉmn-Rꜥ nsw nṯrw*, 'god's father and prophet of Amun-Re king of the gods';
— *ḥm n Ḫnsw pꜣ ỉr sḫrw m Wꜣst*, 'prophet of Khonsu-who-governs-in-Thebes'.
Father of the owner: *Ḥr* (Horos).[49]
Titles:
— *mi nn* (priest of the same rank as the son);
— *ḥry sštꜣ*, 'overseer of the mystery';
— *ꜥb-nṯr*, 'purifier of the god'.
Mother of the owner: *Tꜣ-šrit-Ḫnsw* (Senchonsis).

P. Turin 766 (dem.). Original text related to the Book of Breathing. M.A. Stadler, *Enchoria* 25 (1999), pp. 76–110, and 26 (2000), pp. 110–24.
Owner: *Pa-Rmwt* (Patermuthis).
Mother of the owner: *Tꜣ-šr.t-(n)-Ḫnsw* (Senchonsis).

P. Turin 1848. Various original texts. Unpublished. A. Fabretti, F. Rossi and R.V. Lanzone, *Regio Museo di Torino. Antichità egizie*, I (Turin 1882), p. 231.
Owner: *Pꜣ-Mnṯw* (Pamonthes).

P. Turin 1861 B (=14964). Second Book of Breathing. Unpublished. Date: AD 123. See *supra*, p. 6, no. **18**.
Owner: [*Pꜣ-di-*]*Ỉmn-Ỉpt* (Petemenophis).
Mother of the owner: *Tꜣ-kꜣ-ꜥꜣ-ṯꜣ* (Tkauthi).

P. Turin 1861 C (= 14965). First Book of Breathing. Unpublished. Found with P. Turin 1861 B. See *supra*, p. 6, no. **18**.
Owner: *Pꜣ-di-Ỉmn-Ỉpt* (Petemenophis).
Mother of the owner: *Tꜣ*-[...] (Tkauthi).

P. Turin 1989. Text related to the Book of Breathing. E. Pleyte and F. Rossi, *Papyrus de Turin* (Leide 1869–76), pp. 199–200 with pls CXLI–CXLII.
Owner: *Tꜣ-šrit-pꜣ-di-Ỉmn-Ỉpt* (Senpetemenophis).
Mother of the owner: *Tꜣ-šrit-Ỉmn-Ỉpt* (Senamenophis).

P. Turin 1990. First Book of Breathing and original text. Pleyte and Rossi, op. cit., p. 201 with pl. CXLIII; Goyon, *Rituels funéraires*, pp. 313–14.
Owner: *Pꜣ-šri-ꜥꜣ-pḥty* (Psenapathes).
Mother of the owner: *Tꜣ-šrit-pꜣ-šri-Mnṯw* (Senpsenmonthes).

P. Varsovie 147822 (= P. Bytomski). Glorifications of Osiris. Michalowski, *Sztuka Strozytna* (1955), p. 19, fig. 6; B. Kokot, *Przeglad Orientalistyczny* 1 (21), 1957, pp. 83–8, with 1 pl.
Owner: *Pꜣ-(n-)tꜣ-st-ꜥꜣt* (Patseus).
Mother of the owner: *Tꜣ-šrit-Mnw* (Semminis).

44. *ProsPtol* VII, p. 210. A canopy in Edinburgh belongs to the same owner; cf. A.H. Rhind, *Thebes, its Tombs and their Tenants Ancient and Present* (London 1862), frontispiece.
45. *ProsPtol* III, 5640. On the family, see H.J. Thissen, *ZPE* 27 (1977), pp. 181–91.
46. She is the wife of *Mnṯ(-m)-sꜣ.f* in P. Rhind I.
47. He is the son of *Mn-kꜣ-Rꜥ*. On *Gr-šr*, see *supra*, p. 37.
48. For the genealogy, see M. Coenen, in *Egyptian Religion the Last Thousand Years (Studies Dedicated to the Memory of Jan Quaegebeur)*, OLA 85, 1998, pp. 1106–11.
49. Col. I contains a long genealogy of the family going back to five generations before the parents of *Ḏd-Ḫnsw-iw.f-ꜥnḫ* are mentioned.

P. Vatican Inv. 38570 (formerly no. 55). Book of Traversing Eternity. *LPE*, pp. 7–8 with pls IX–XIV; A. Gasse, *Les papyrus hiératiques et hiéroglyphiques du museo gregoriano egizio* (Vatican City 1993), pp. 74–5, no. 67, with pls L–LIII.
Owner: *Ḥr* (Horos).
Titles:
— *it-nṯr ḥm-nṯr*, 'god's father and prophet';
— *it-nṯr ḥm-nṯr n Imn-Rꜥ nsw nṯrw*, 'god's father and prophet of Amun-Re king of the gods';
— *šn* (?) *nṯrw*, '... (?) of the gods';
— *šn* (?) *n Wsir*, '... (?) of Osiris';
— *šn* (?) *n Mnw-Imn*, '... (?) of Min-Amun';
— *rḫ ḫt wr m Wꜣst*, 'great scholar in Thebes';
Father of the owner: *P(ꜣ)-fdw-Mnṯw* (Phtomonthes).
Titles:
— *ḥry sštꜣ*, 'overseer of the mystery';
— *ꜥb-nṯr*, 'purifier of the god'.
Mother of the owner: *Tꜣi-rwḏt*.
Titles:
— *nbt-pr*, 'housewife';
— *iḥyt n Imn-Rꜥ*, 'sistrum-player of Amun-Re'
— *gmḥt ꜥꜣt m Gbtyw-tꜣwy*, 'great widow in Coptos of the two Lands'.

P. Vatican Inv. 38596. Glorifications of Osiris. Gasse, op. cit., pp. 66–7, no. 55 with pl. XLV.
Owner: *Irt-Ḥr-ir.w* (Inaros).
Father of the owner: ... (?)-*Imn-Ipt*.
Mother of the owner: (*Tꜣ*)-*dit-Ḥr-wr* (Tetearoeris).
Title:
— *nbt-pr*, 'housewife'.

P. Vatican Inv. 38599. First Book of Breathing. Gasse, op. cit., pp. 78–9, no. 76 with pl. LV.
Owner: *Pꜣ-Mnw* (Paminis).
Mother of the owner: *Tꜣ-šrit-p(ꜣ)-Mnṯw* (Senpamonthès).

P. Vatican Inv. 38580. Book of Traversing Eternity. Gasse, op. cit., pp. 77–8.
Owner: *Tꜣ-ḥy-biꜣ* (Chibois).
Mother of the owner: [...]-*Twtw*.

P. Vatican Inv. 38608. Extracts of various rituals. Gasse, op. cit., pp. 73–4 with pl. XLIX; F.R. Herbin, *RdE* 54 (2003), pp. 67–127 with pl. IX.
Owner: *Ḫnsw-Ḏḥwty* (Chensthotes).
Father of the owner: *P(ꜣ)-di-Wsir* (Petosiris).
Mother of the owner: *T(ꜣ)-šrit-n-Ḫnsw* (Senchonsis).

P. Vienna 3850. Book of Breathing made by Isis. Unpublished. See under **P. Florence 3665**.

P. Vienna 3863. Book of Breathing made by Isis. Unpublished. H. Satzinger, *GM* 75 (1984), p. 33.
Owner: *Ḥr* (Horos).
Titles:
— *it-nṯr ḥm-nṯr n Imn-Rꜥ nsw nṯrw*, 'god's father and prophet of Amun-Re king of the gods';
— *ḥry sštꜣ*, 'overseer of the mystery';
— *ꜥb-nṯr*, 'purifier of the god';
— *ḥm n Ḫnsw pꜣ ir sḫrw m Wꜣst*, 'prophet of Khonsu-who-governs-in-Thebes'.
Father of the owner: *Ḥr-sꜣ-Ist* (Harsiesis).
Title:
— *mi nn* (priest of the same rank as the son).
Mother of the owner: *Tꜣ-šrit-Mnṯw* (Senmontes).

P. Vienna 3865. Liturgy of rites performed each decade in Djeme. Herbin, *RdE* 35 (1984), pp. 105–6 with pl. 9.

P. Vienna 3870. First Book of Breathing. Satzinger, *GM* 75 (1984), p. 33. Unpublished.
Owner: *Ii-m-ḥtp* (Imouthes).
Father of the owner: *Pꜣ-fdw-Mnṯw* (Phtomonthes).
Mother of the owner: *Tꜣ-* ... .

P. Vienna 3875. Book of Traversing Eternity. E. von Bergmann, *Das Buch vom Durchwandeln der Ewigkeit* (1877); *LPE*, pp. 9–10 with pls XV–XVI.
Owner: *Ns-pꜣwty-tꜣwy* (Spotous).
Titles:
— *it-nṯr ḥm-nṯr n Imn-Rꜥ nsw nṯrw*, 'god's father and prophet of Amun-Re king of the gods';
— *ḥm n Bꜣstt ḥr(yt)-ib Wꜣst*, 'prophet of Bastet dwelling in Thebes';
— *ḥm-nṯr n Ḫnsw-p(ꜣ)-ir-sḫrw-m-Wꜣst*, 'prophet of Khonsu-who-governs-in-Thebes';
— *ꜥꜣ-pr n Ḫnsw-m-Wꜣst-nfr-ḥtp*, 'majordomo of Khonsu-in-Thebes-Neferhotep';
— *ḥm-nṯr 4-nw n Imn*, 'fourth prophet of Amun';
— *ḥry sštꜣ*, 'overseer of the mystery';
— *ꜥb-nṯr*, 'purifier of the god'.
Father of the owner: *P(ꜣ)-šri-(n-)ꜥšꜣ-ḫwt* (Psenasuchis).
Title:
— *it-nṯr n Imn-Rꜥ nsw nṯrw*, 'god's father of Amun king of the gods'.
Mother of the owner: *Ṯꜣtw*.
Titles:
— *nbt-pr*, 'housewife';
— *iḥyt n Imn-Rꜥ*, 'sistrum-player of Amun-Re'

P. Vienna 3931. Book of Breathing made by Isis. Unpublished. H. Satzinger, *GM* 75 (1984), p. 34 (incorrect reading of the name).
Owner: *Gg*.
Title:
— *iḥyt n Imn-Rꜥ*, 'sistrum-player of Amun-Re'.
Father of the owner: *Irt-Ḥr-ir.w* (Inaros).
Title: reading uncertain.

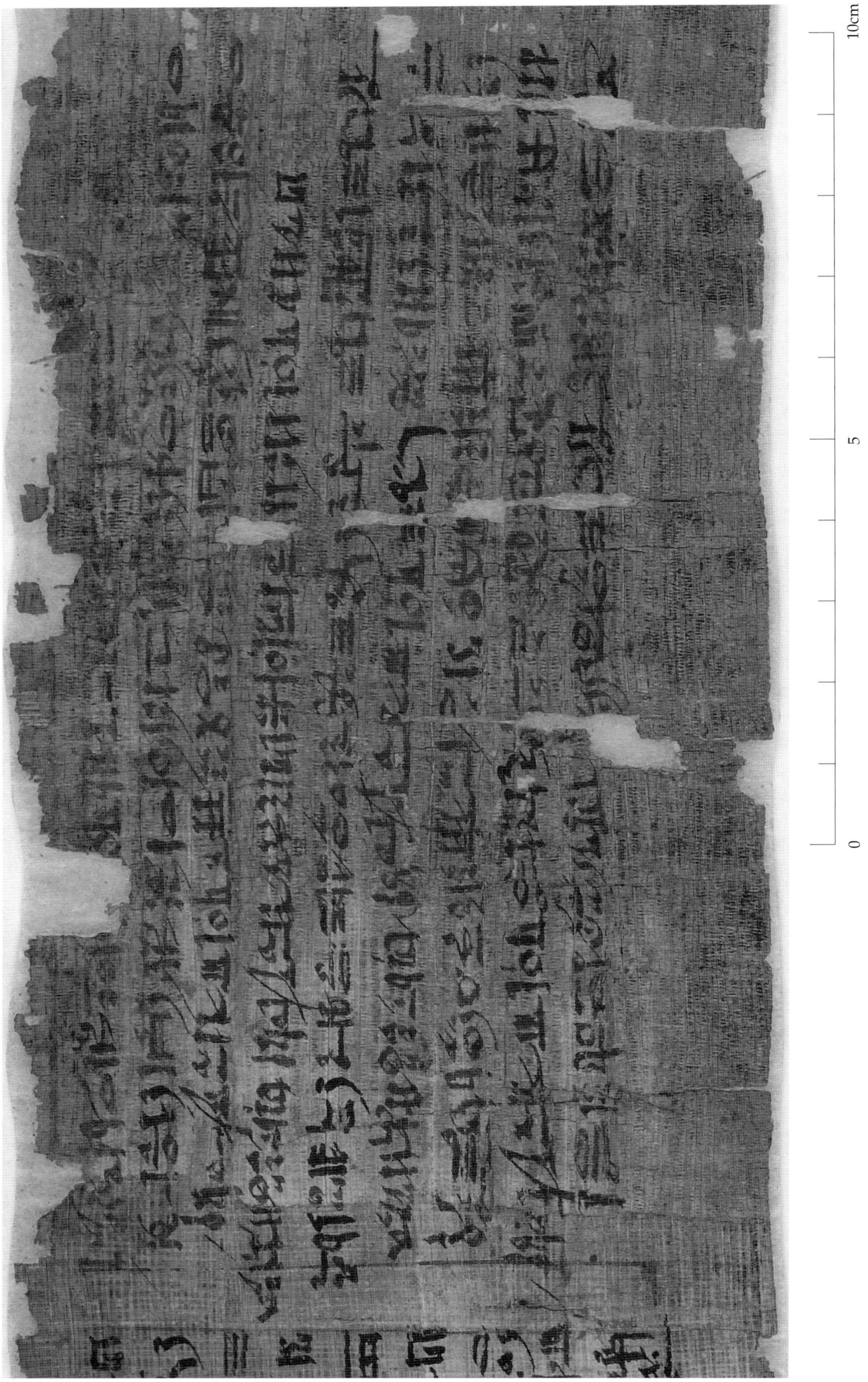

P. BM EA 10048, column I

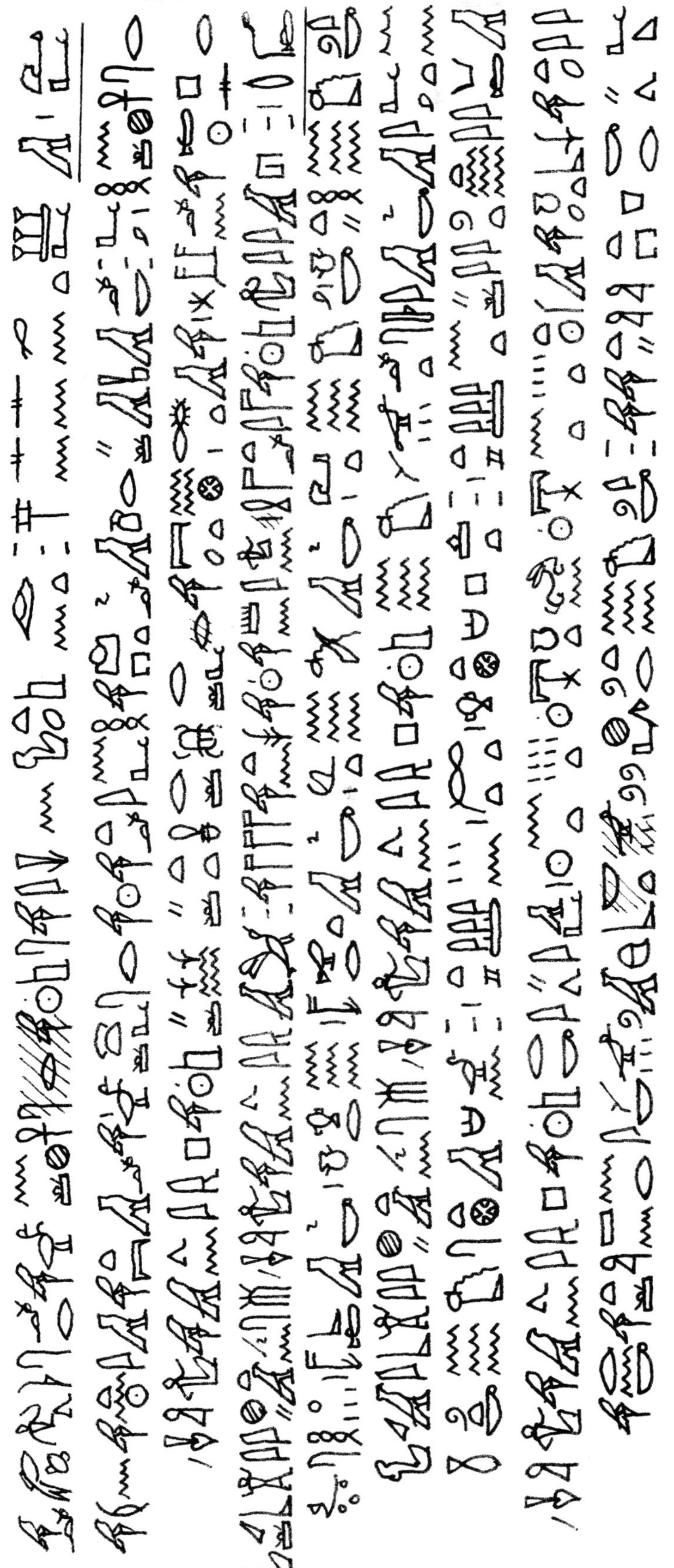

P. BM EA 10048, column I

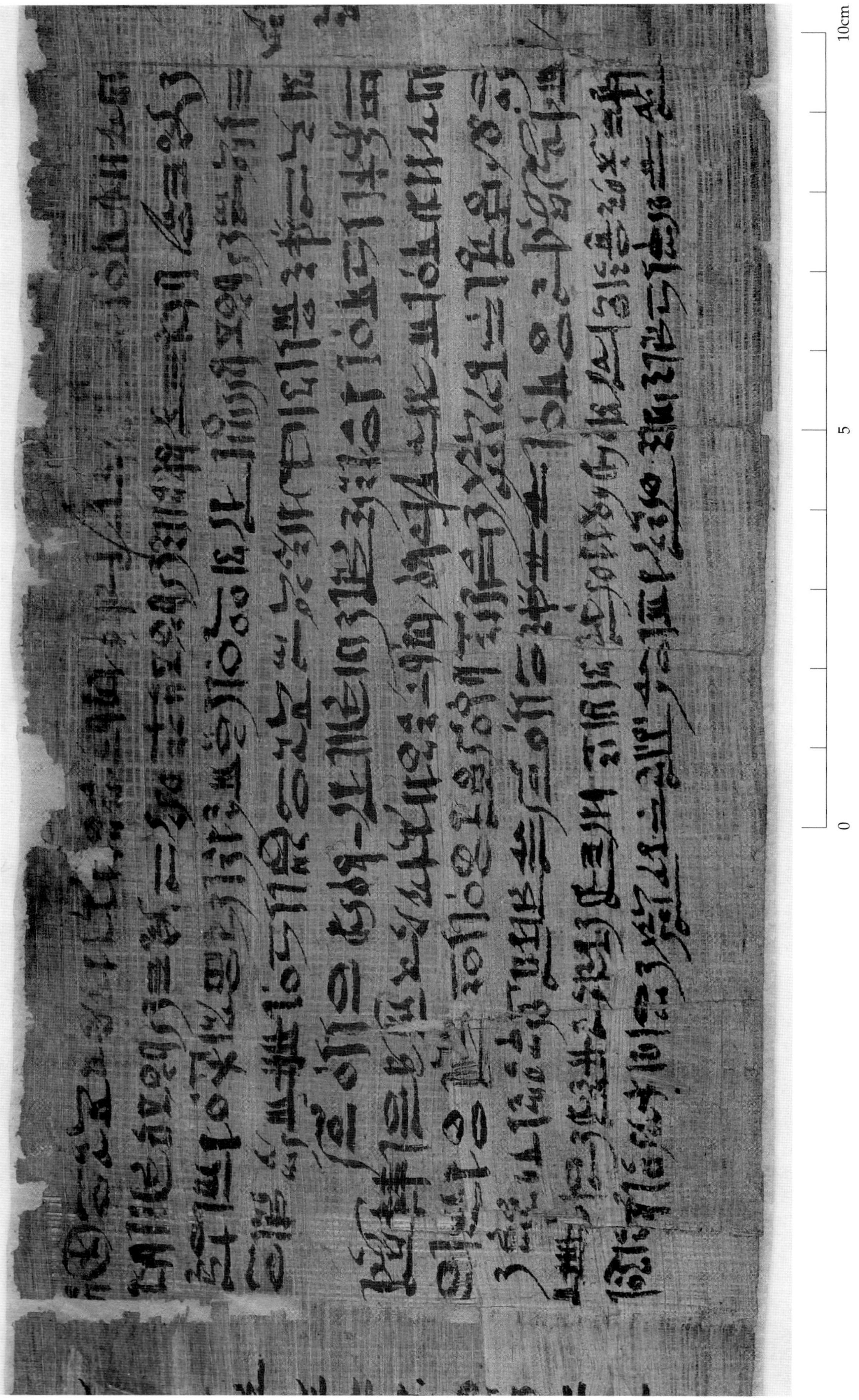

P. BM EA 10048, column II

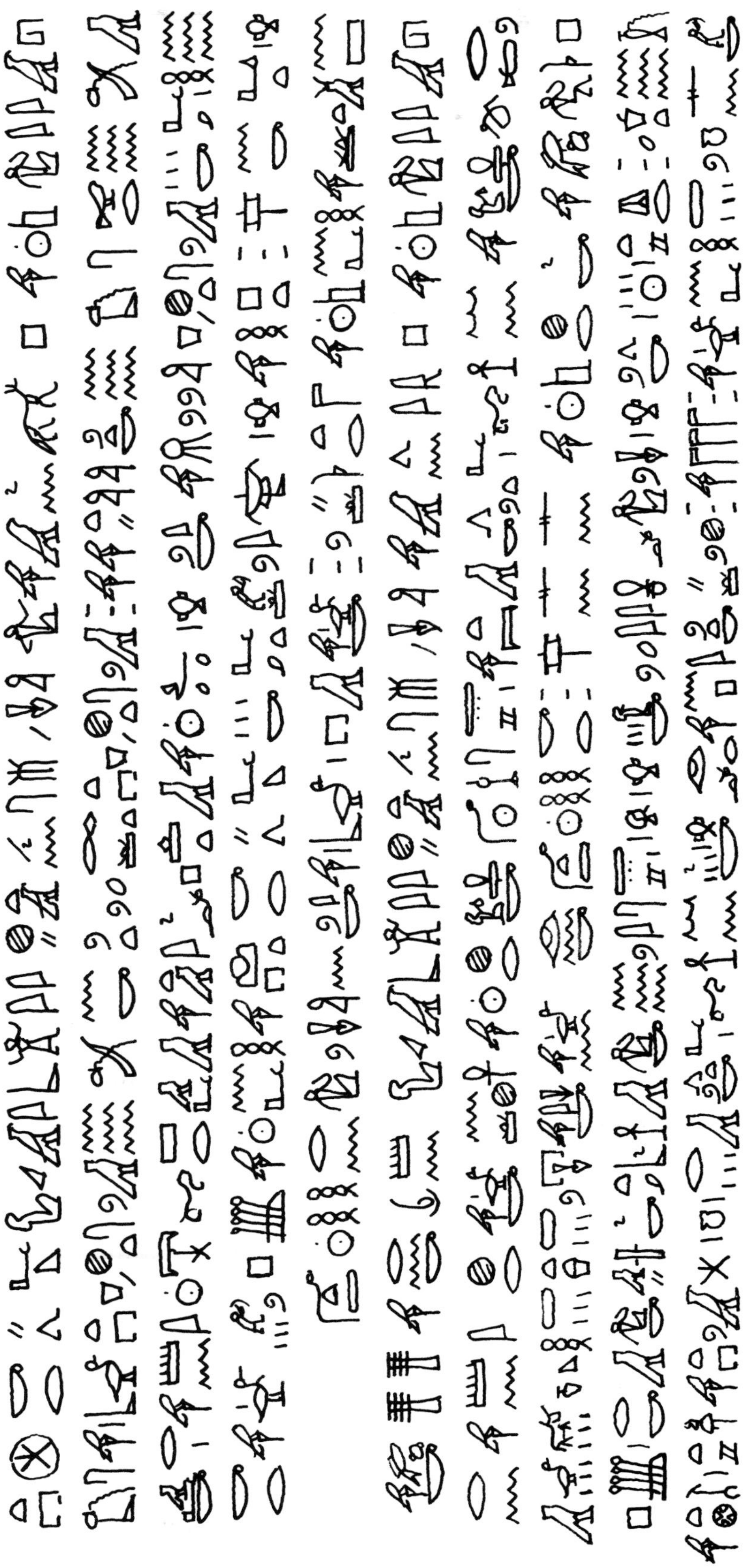

P. BM EA 10048, column II

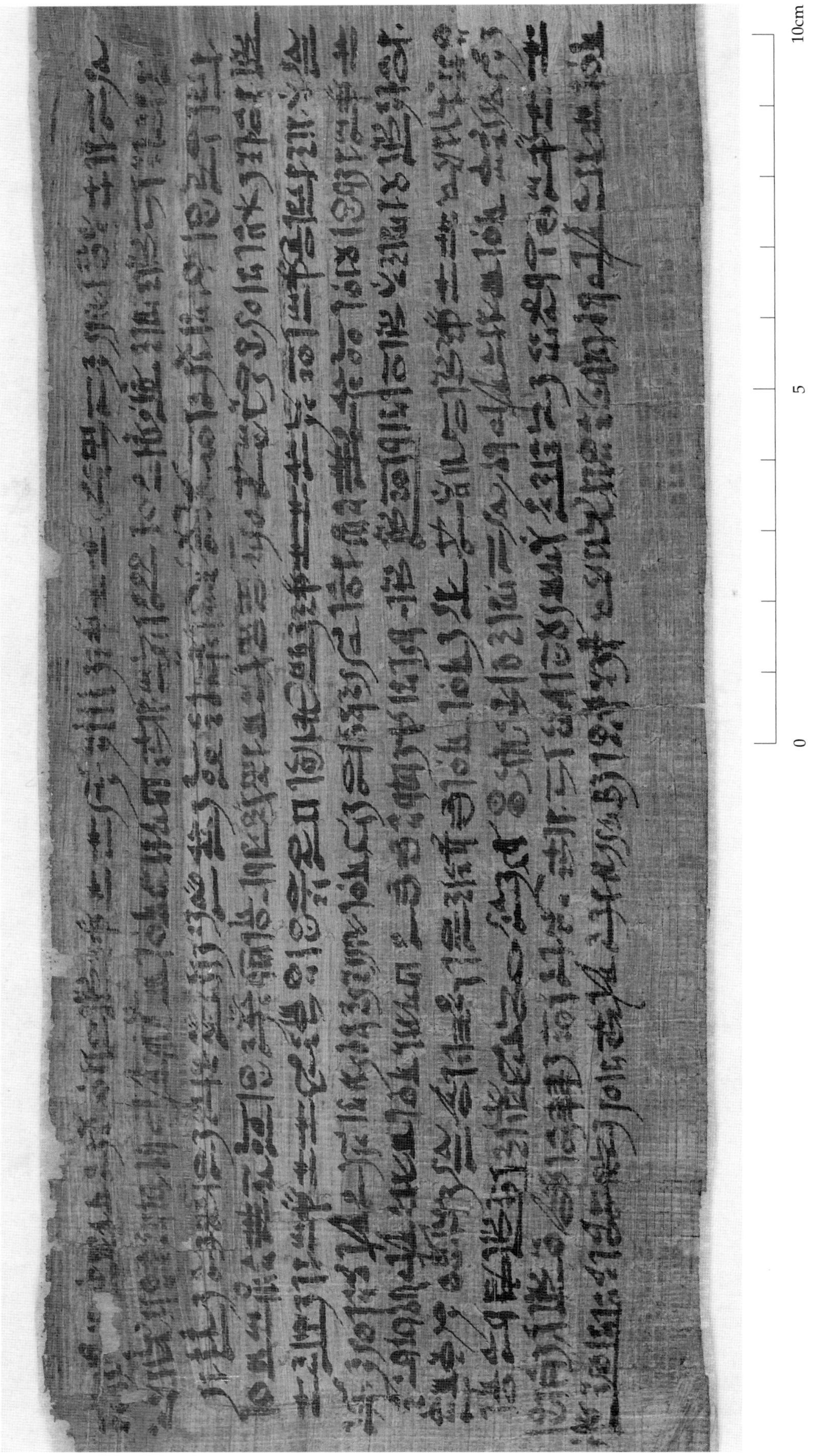

P. BM EA 10048, column III

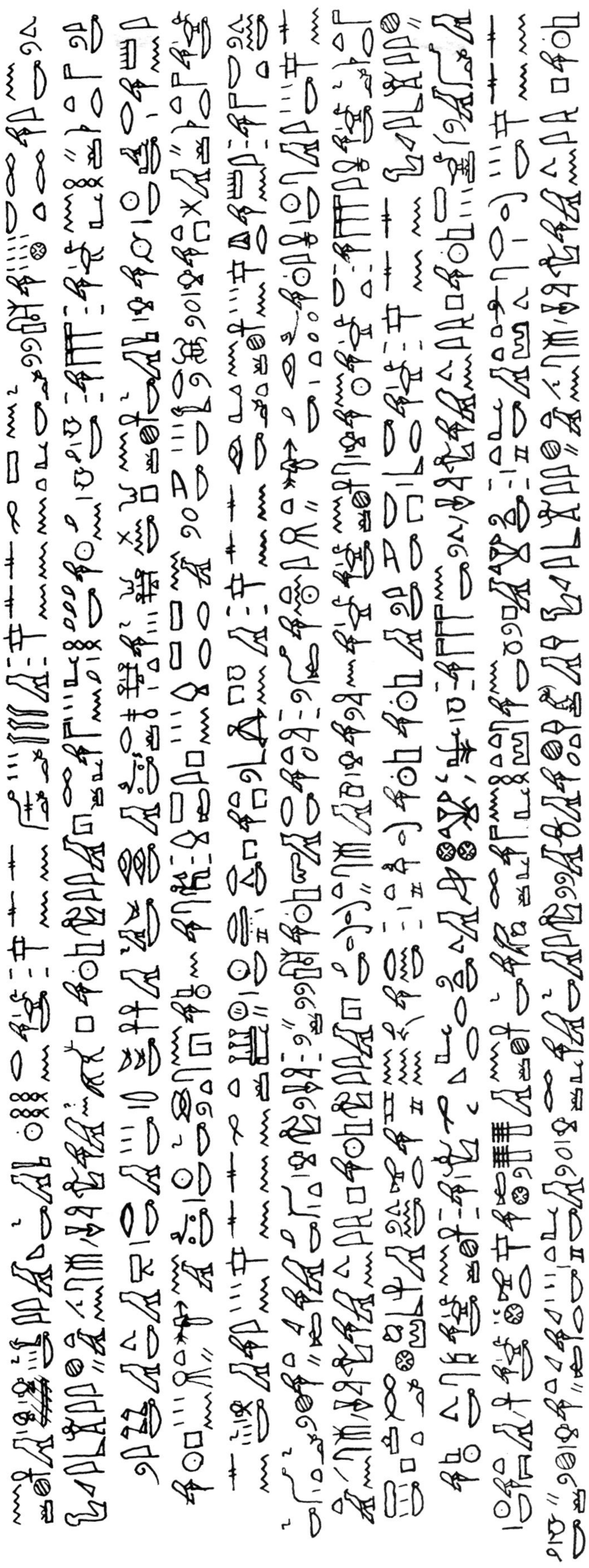

P. BM EA 10048, column III

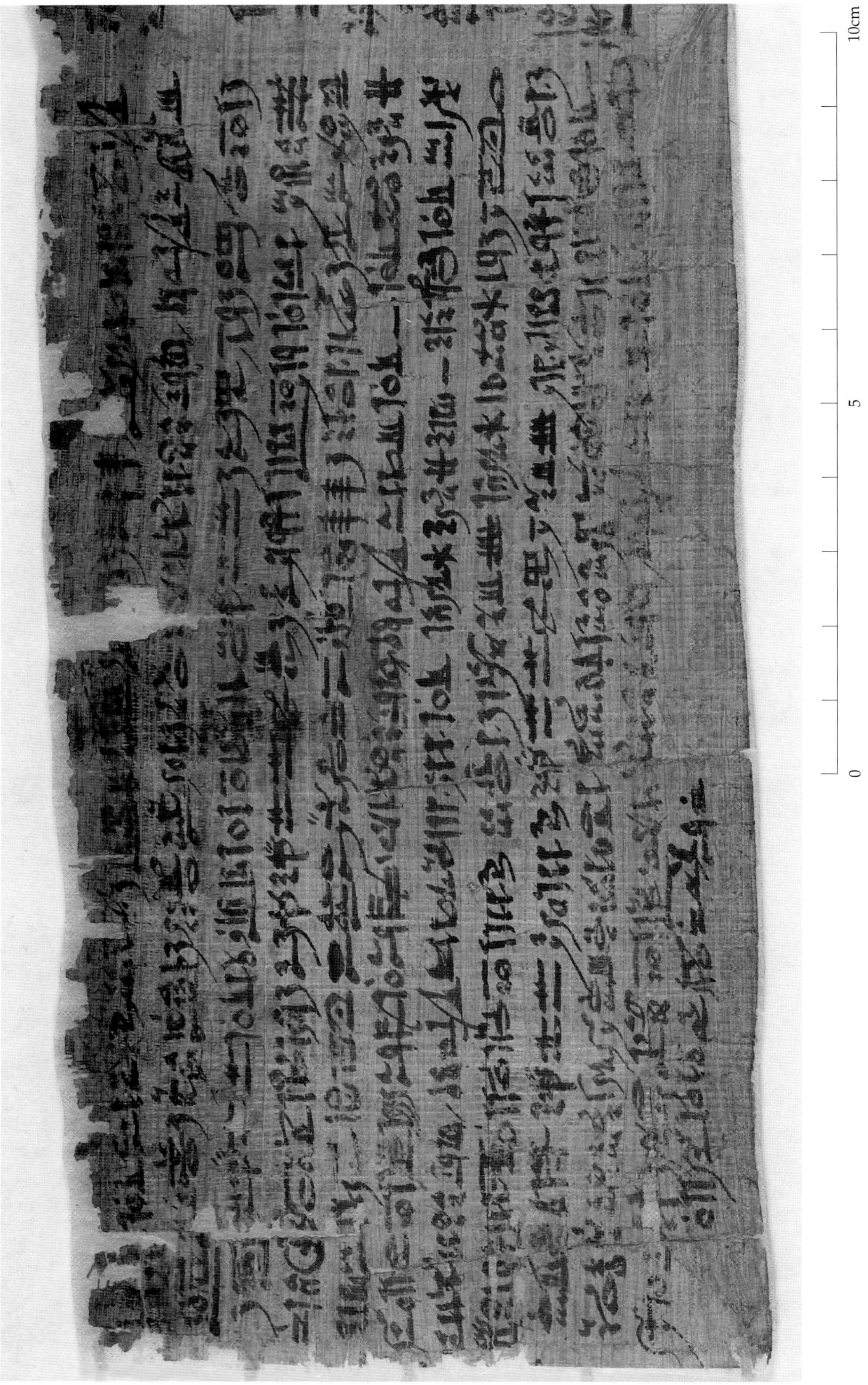

P. BM EA 10048, column IV

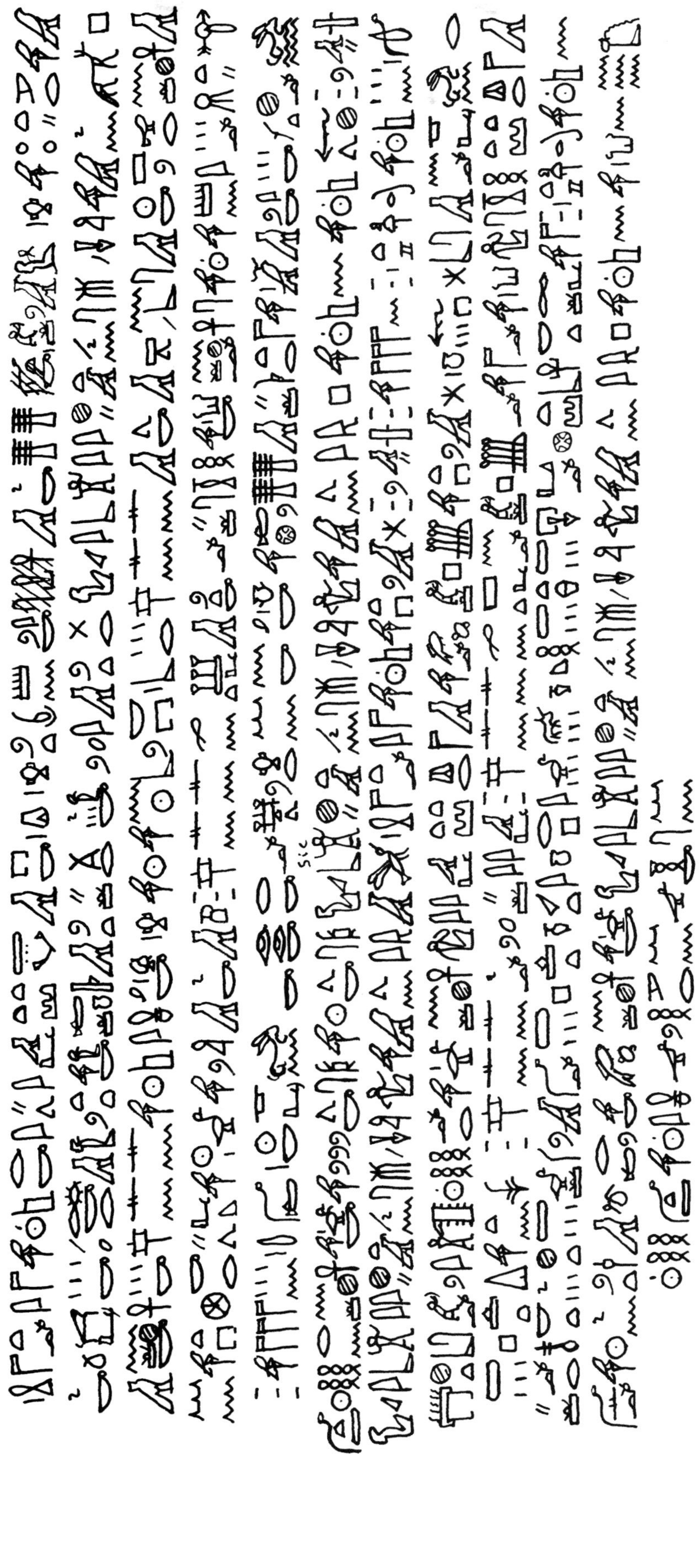

P. BM EA 10048, column IV

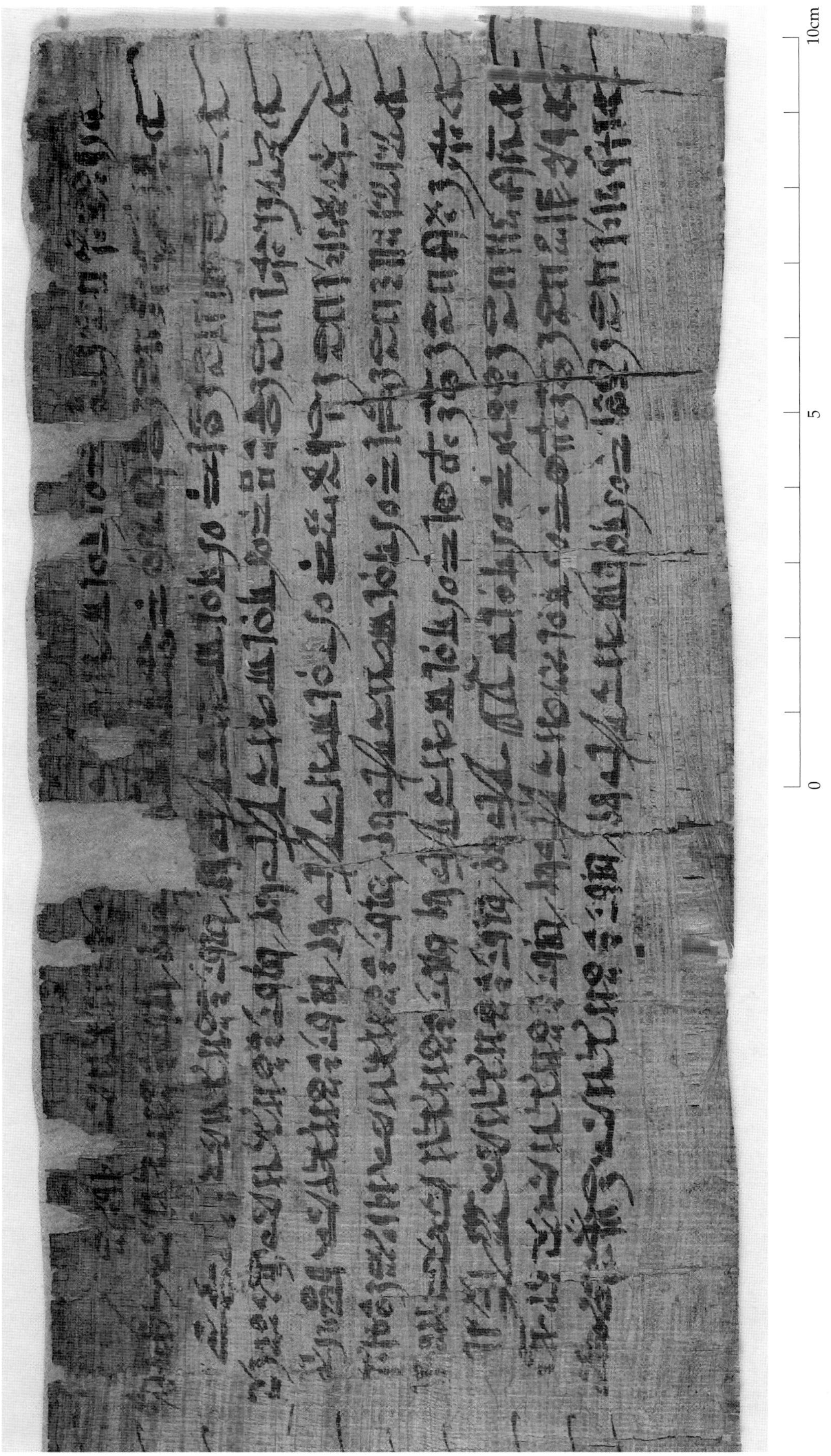

P. BM EA 10048, column V

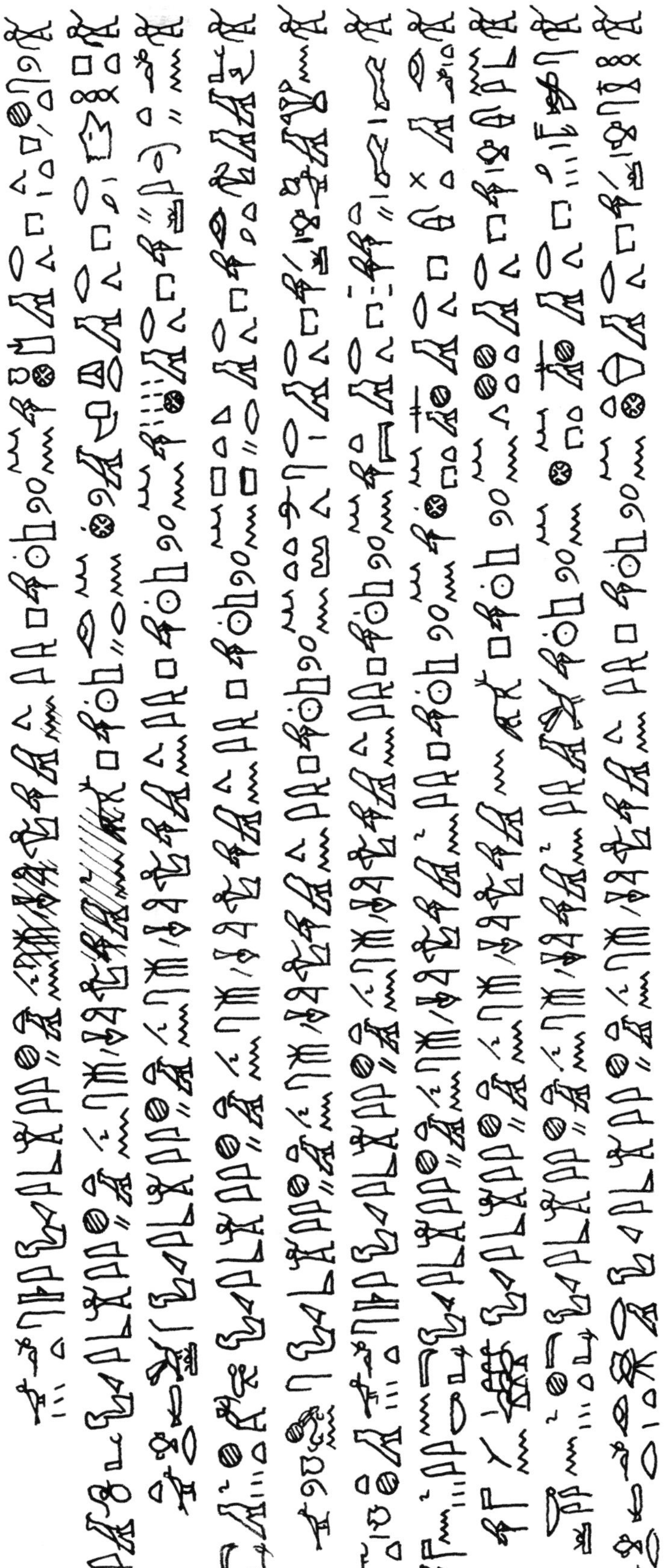

P. BM EA 10048, column V

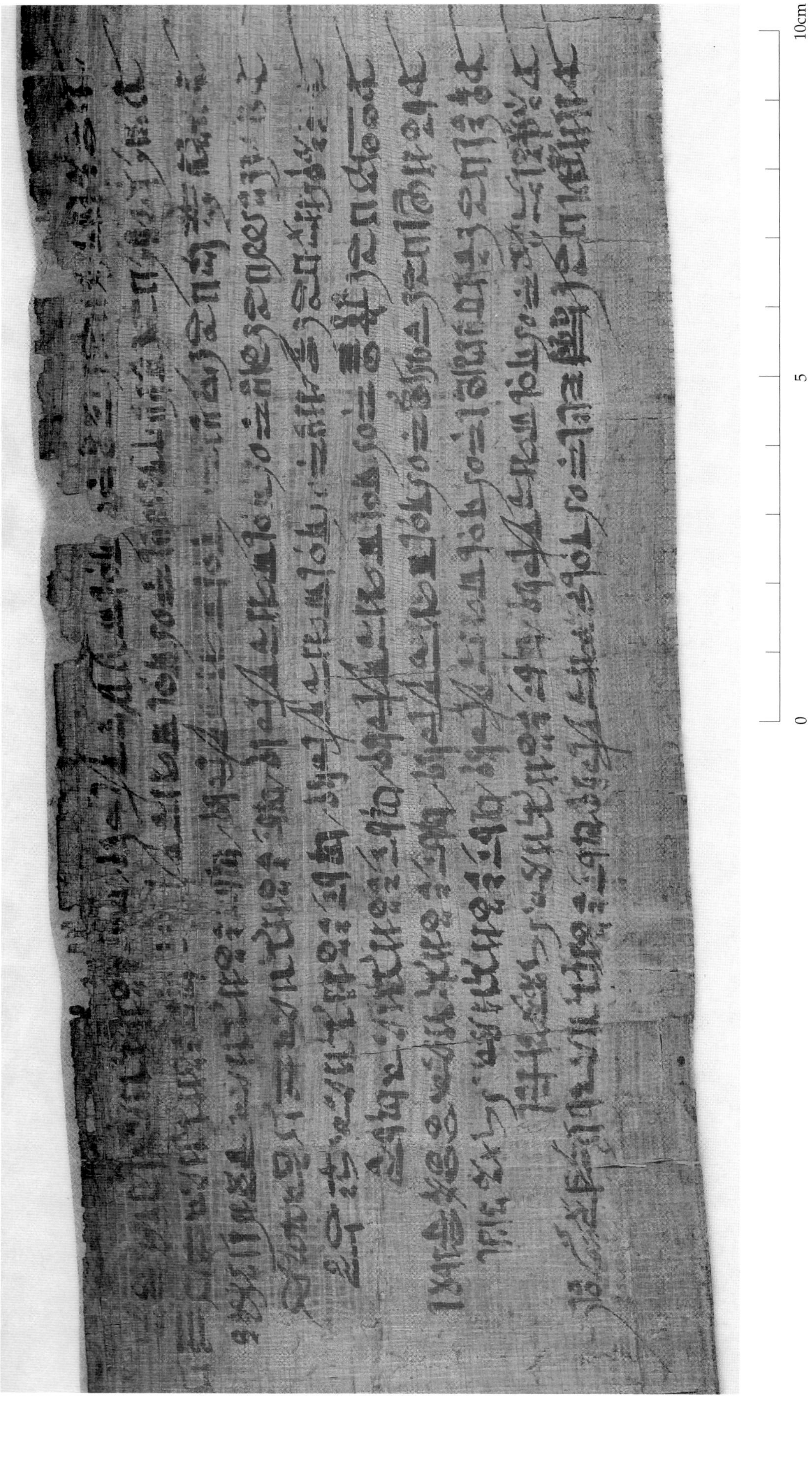

P. BM EA 10048, column VI

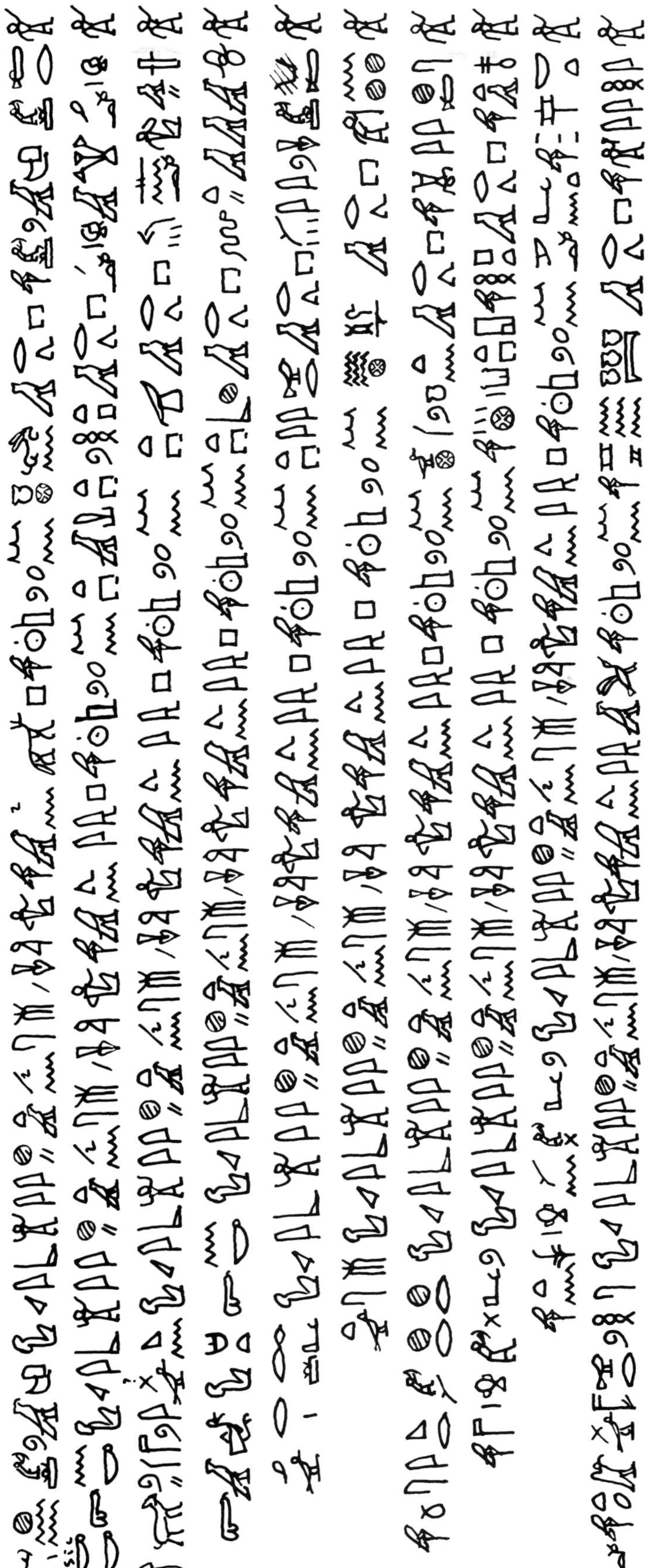

P. BM EA 10048, column VI

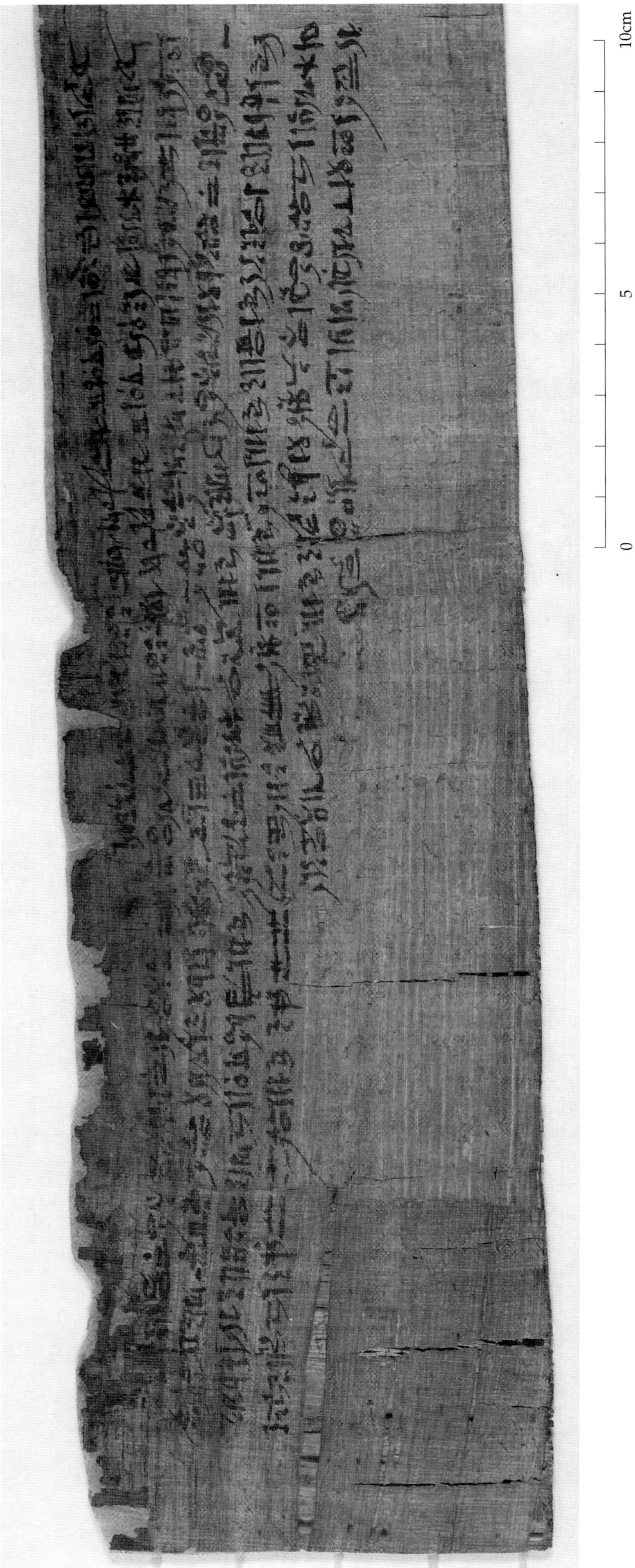

P. BM EA 10048, column VII

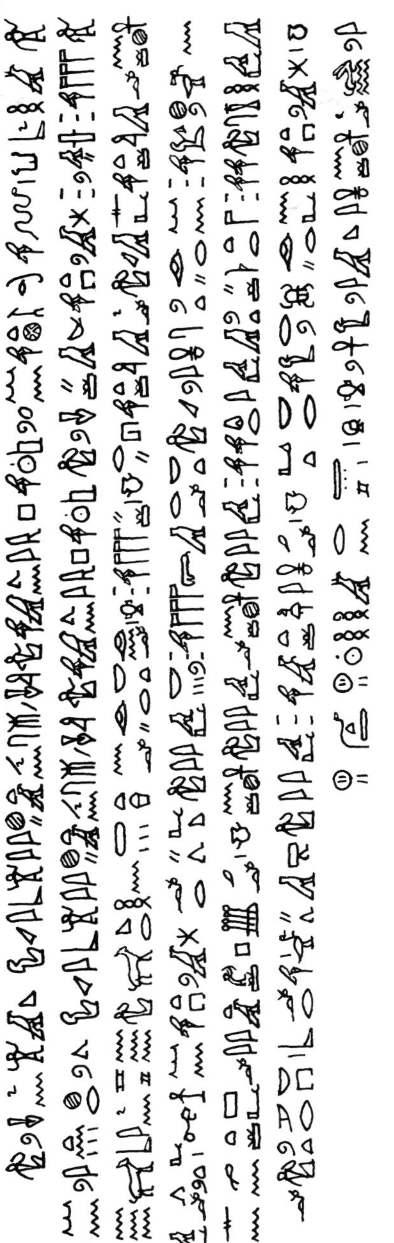

P. BM EA 10048, column VII

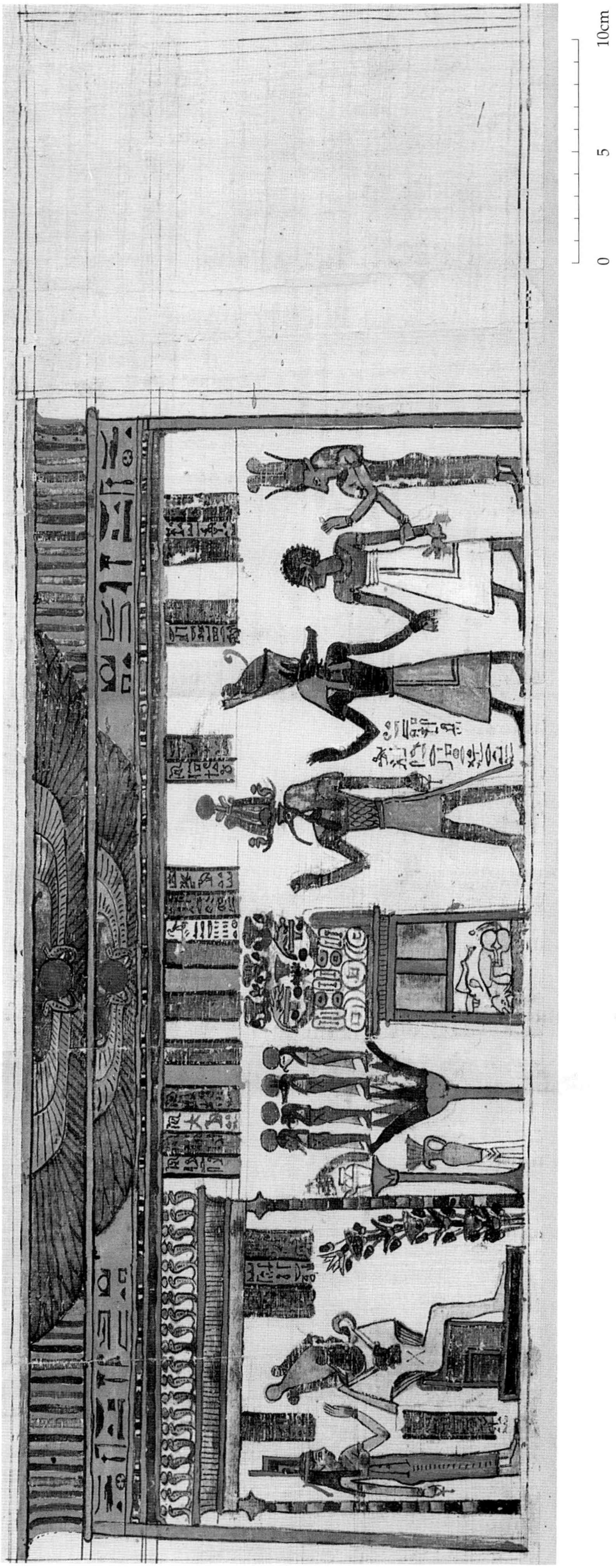

P. BM EA 9995, initial vignette

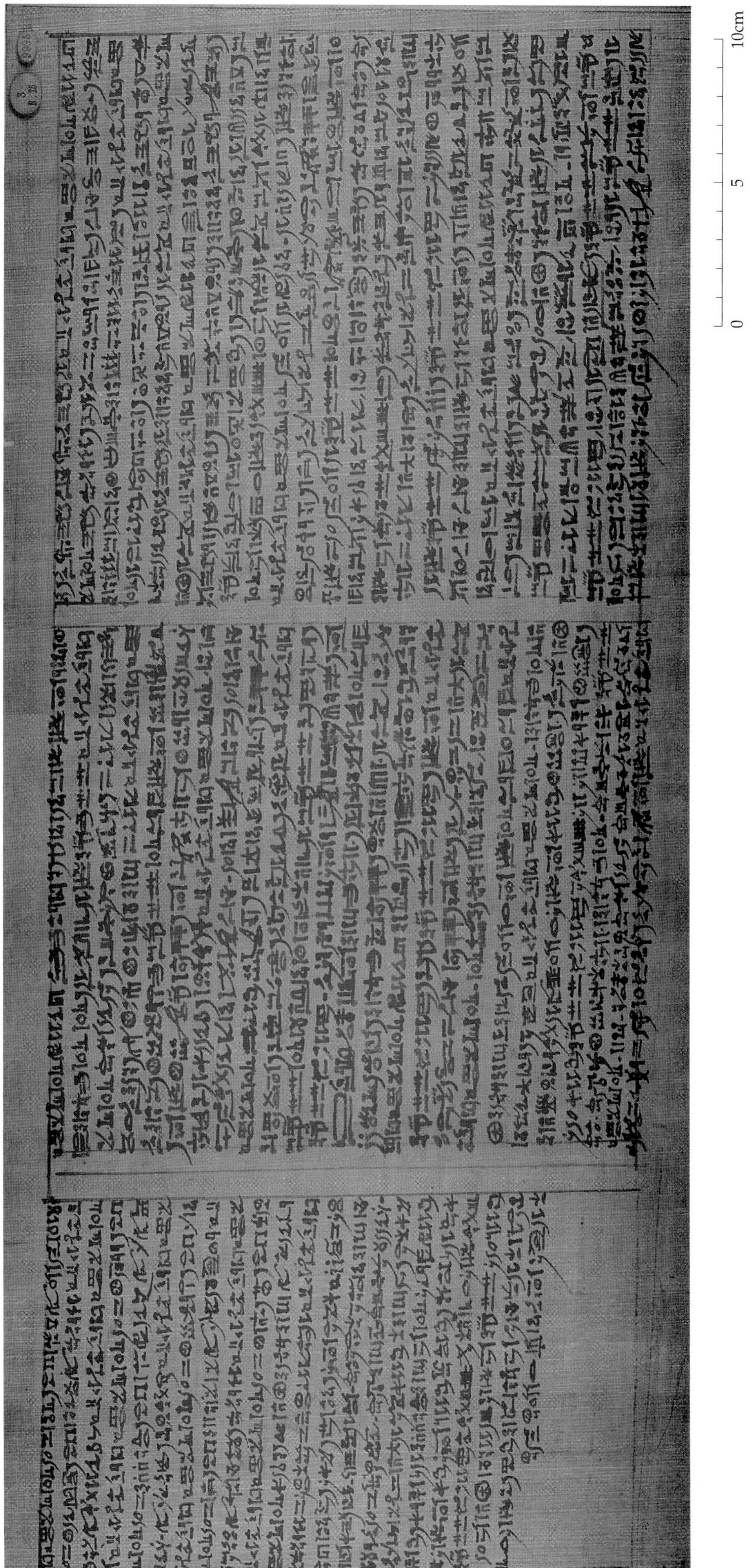

P. BM EA 9995, columns I–III

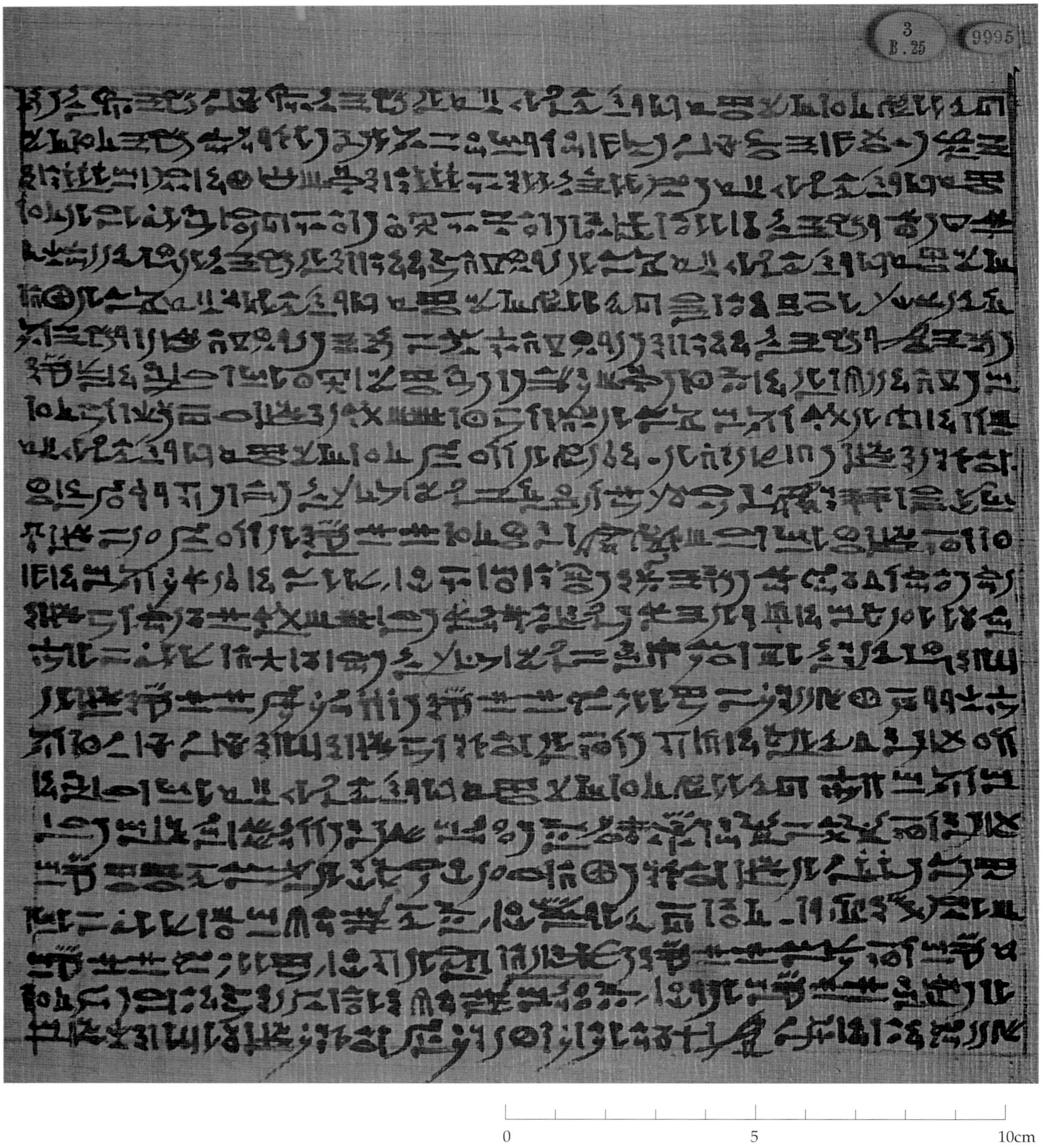

P. BM EA 9995, column I

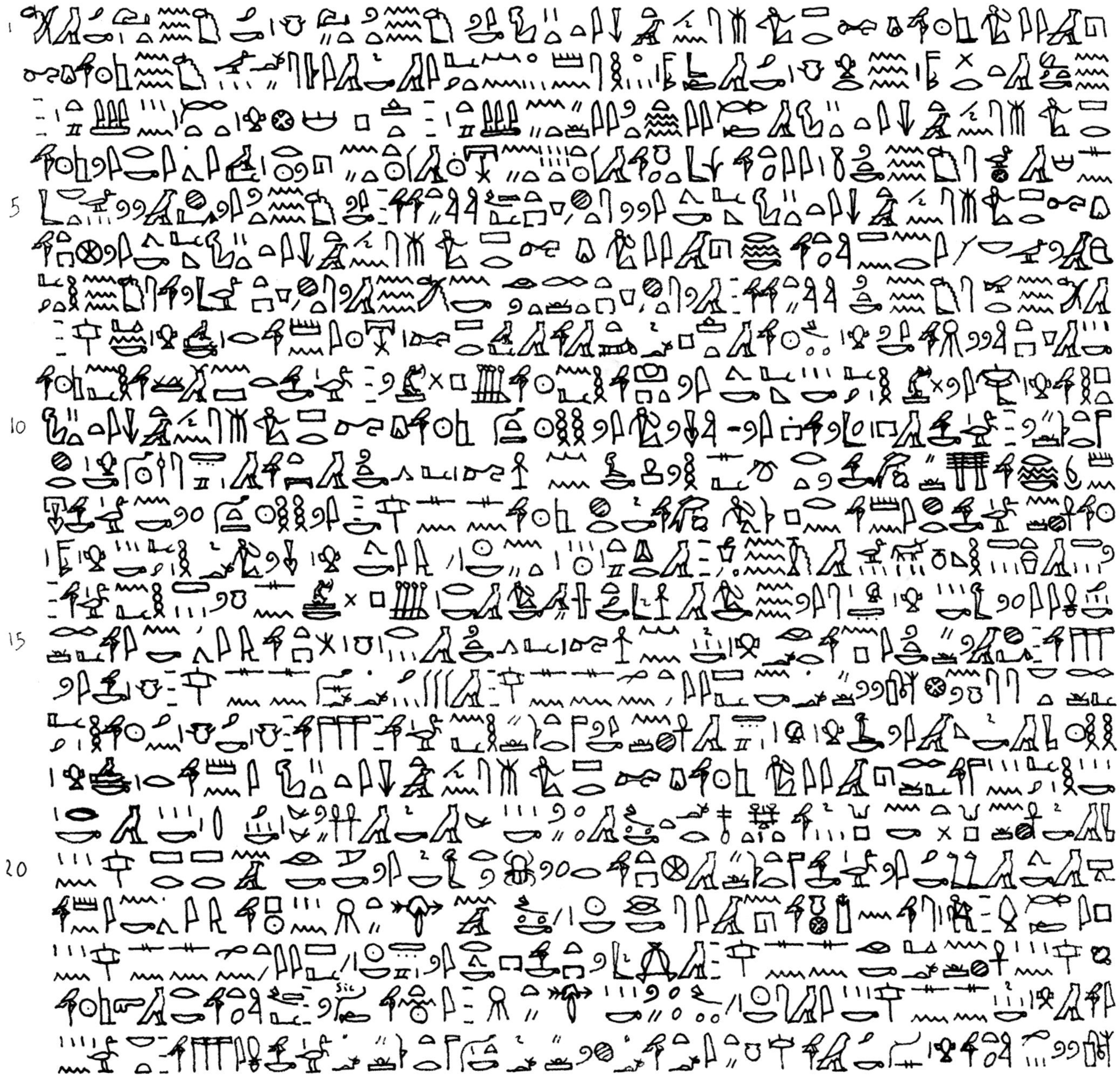

P. BM EA 9995, column I

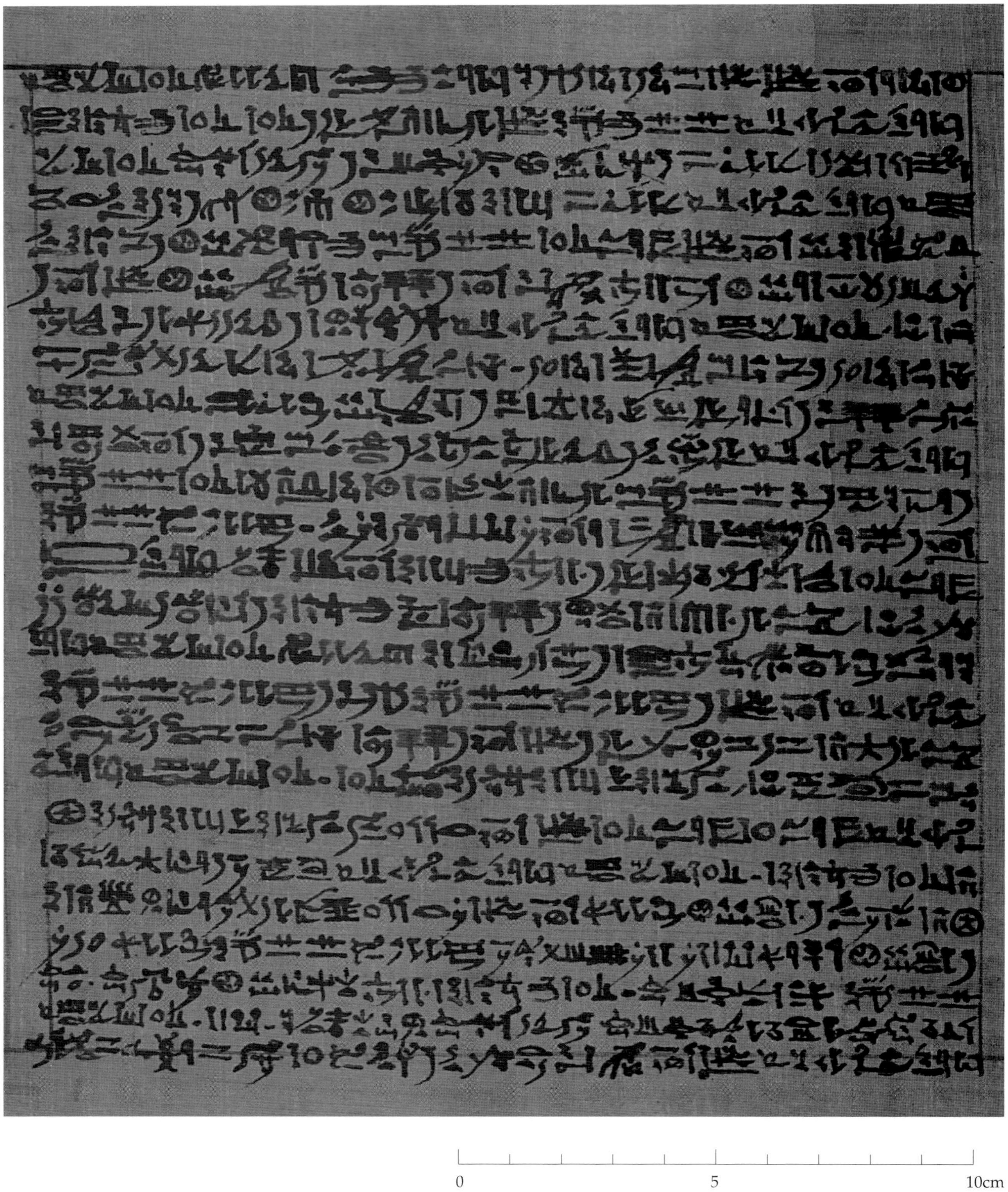

P. BM EA 9995, column II

P. BM EA 9995, column II

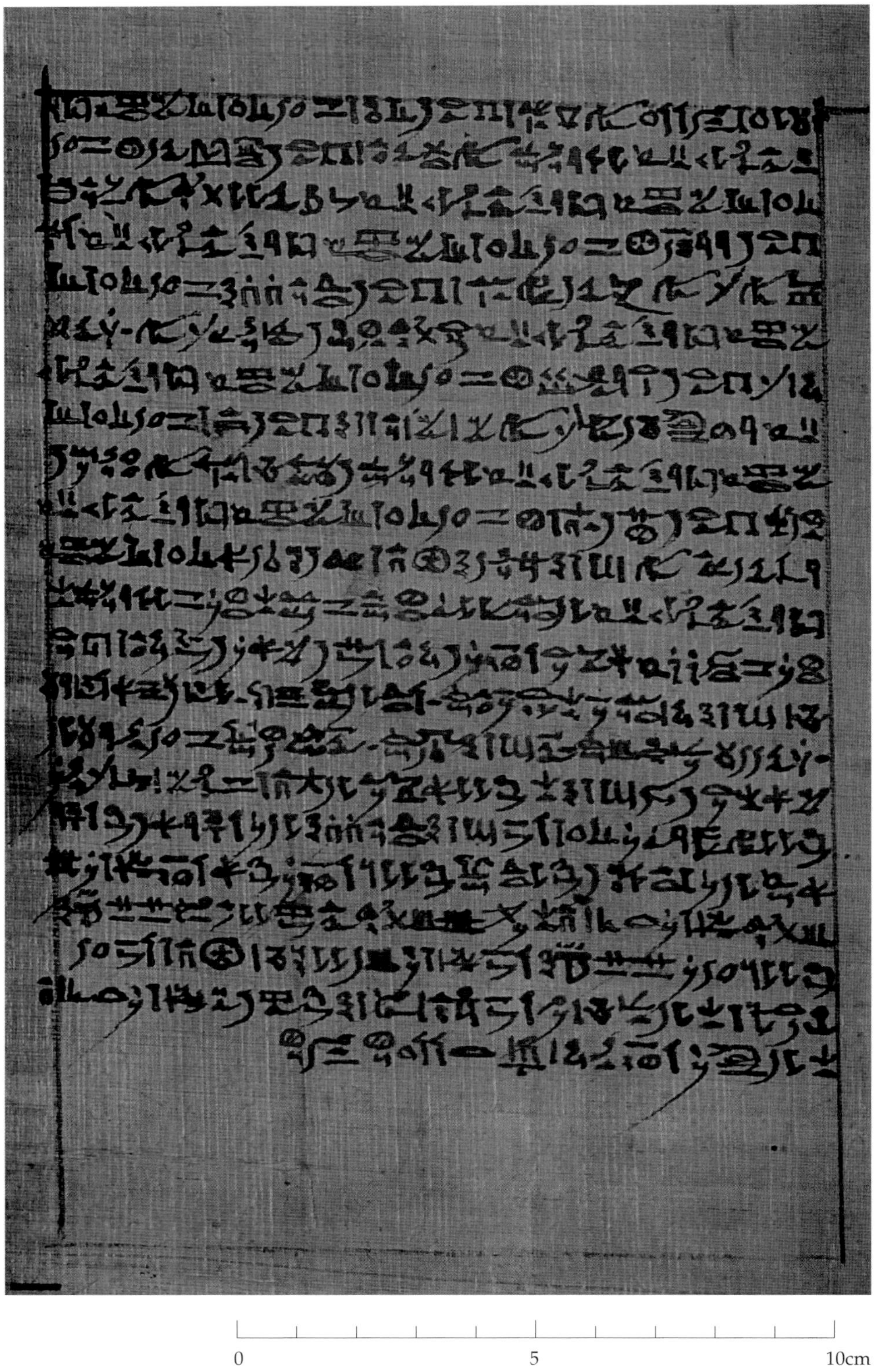

P. BM EA 9995, column III

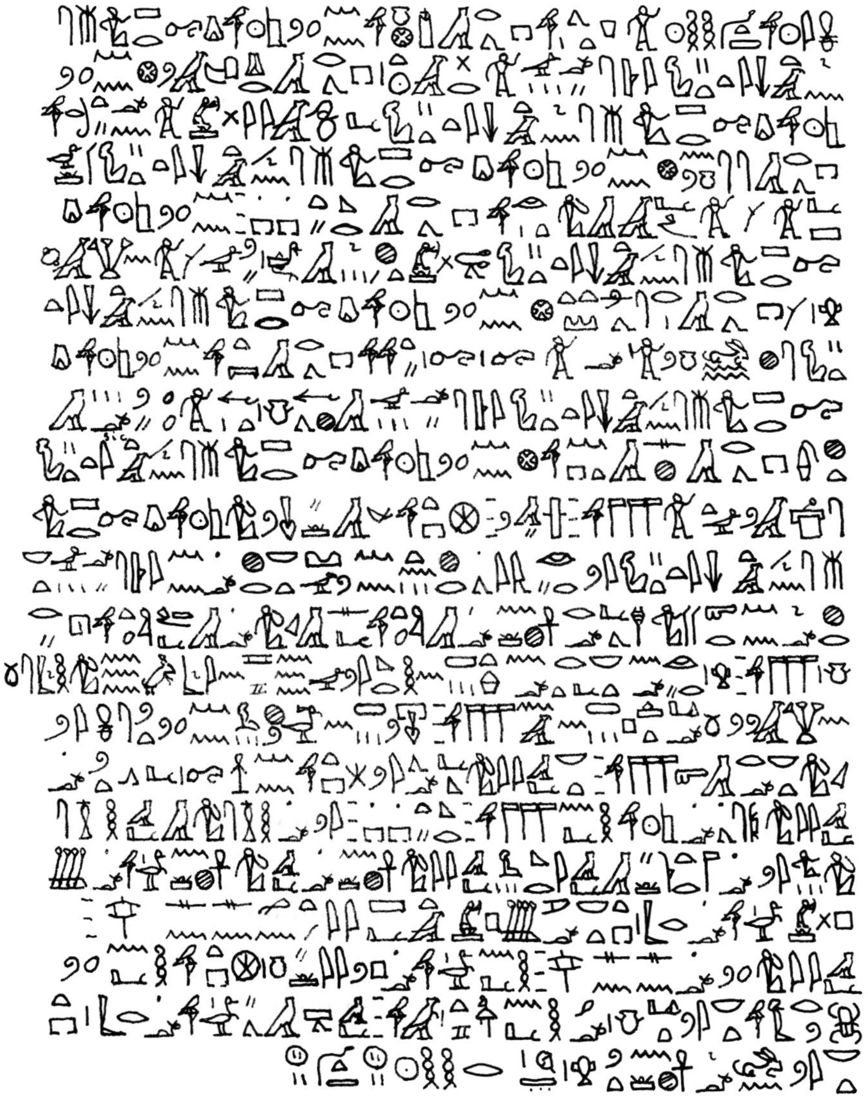

P. BM EA 9995, column III

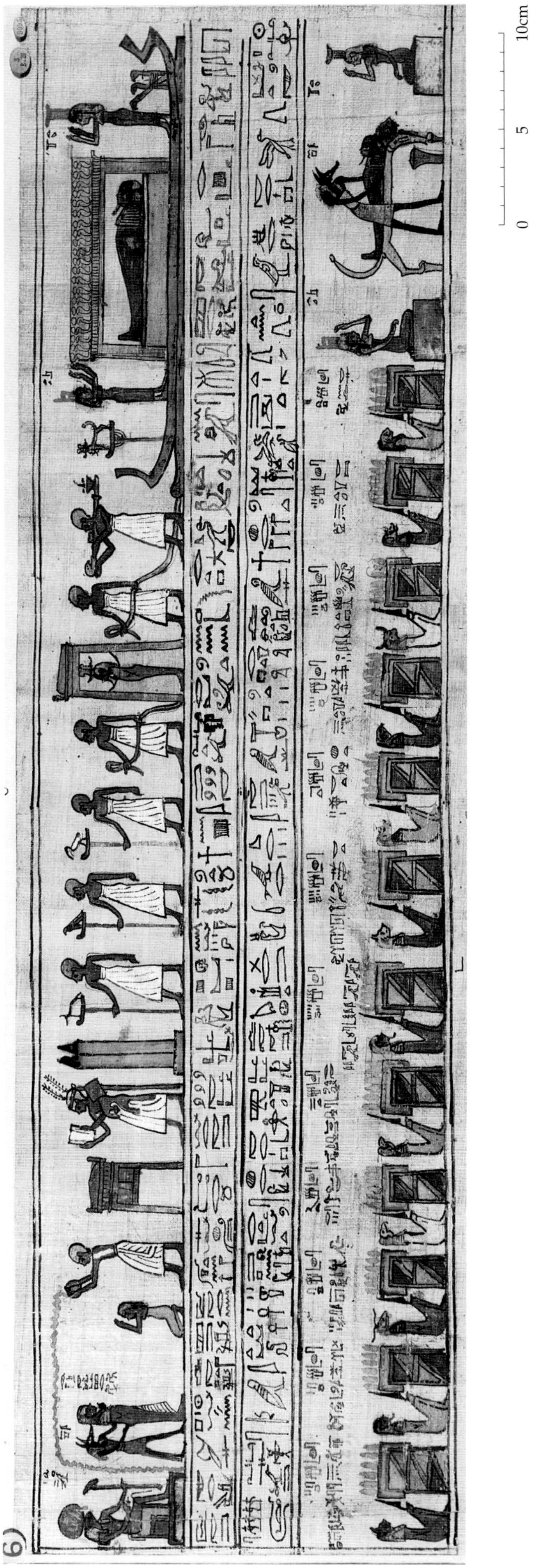

P. BM EA 9995, vignette

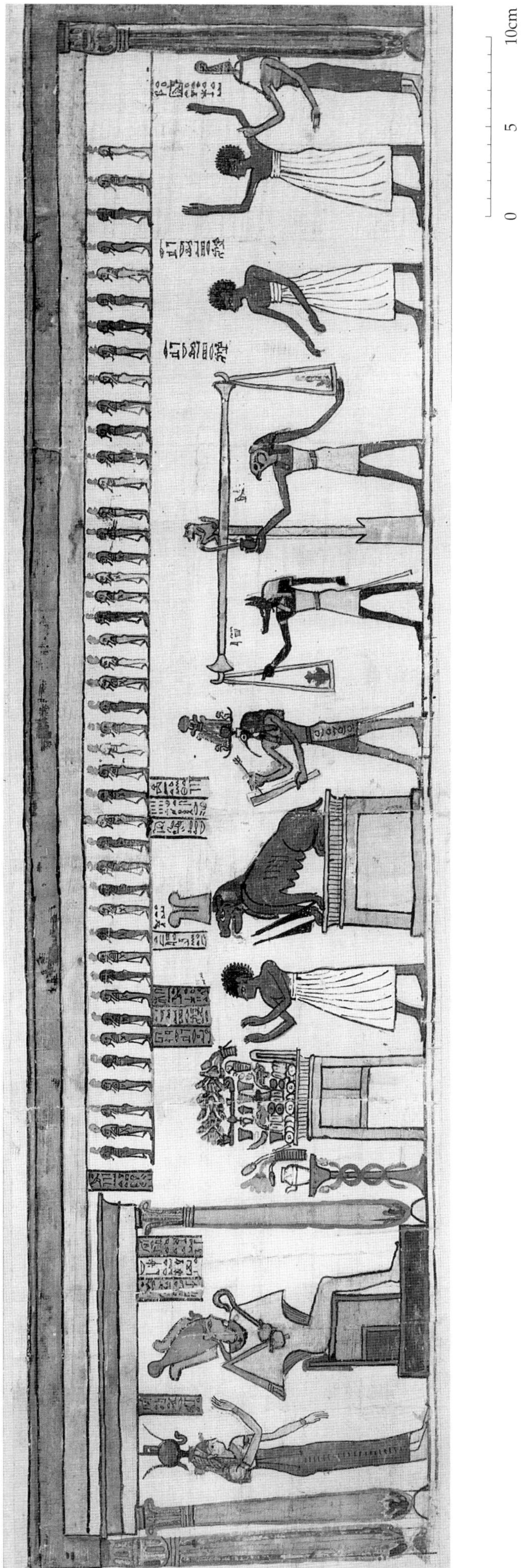

P. BM EA 9995, final vignette

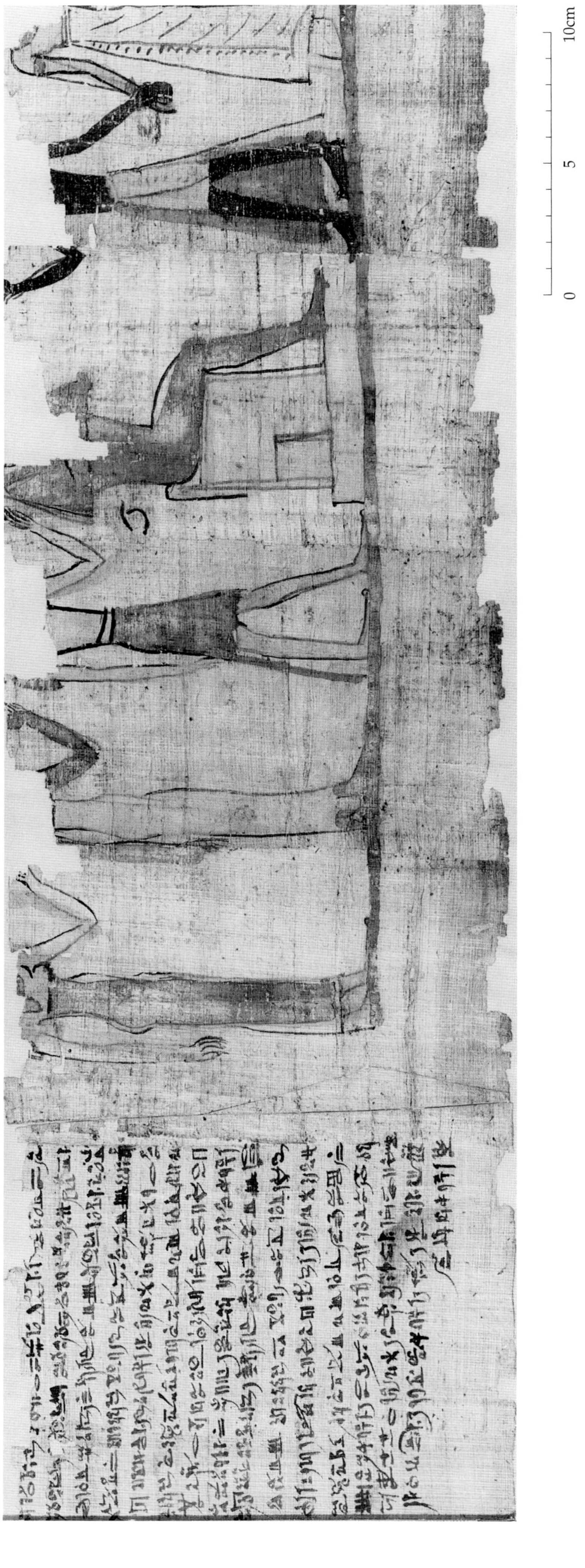

P. BM EA 10260, initial vignette and column I

P. BM EA 10260, column I

Plate 27

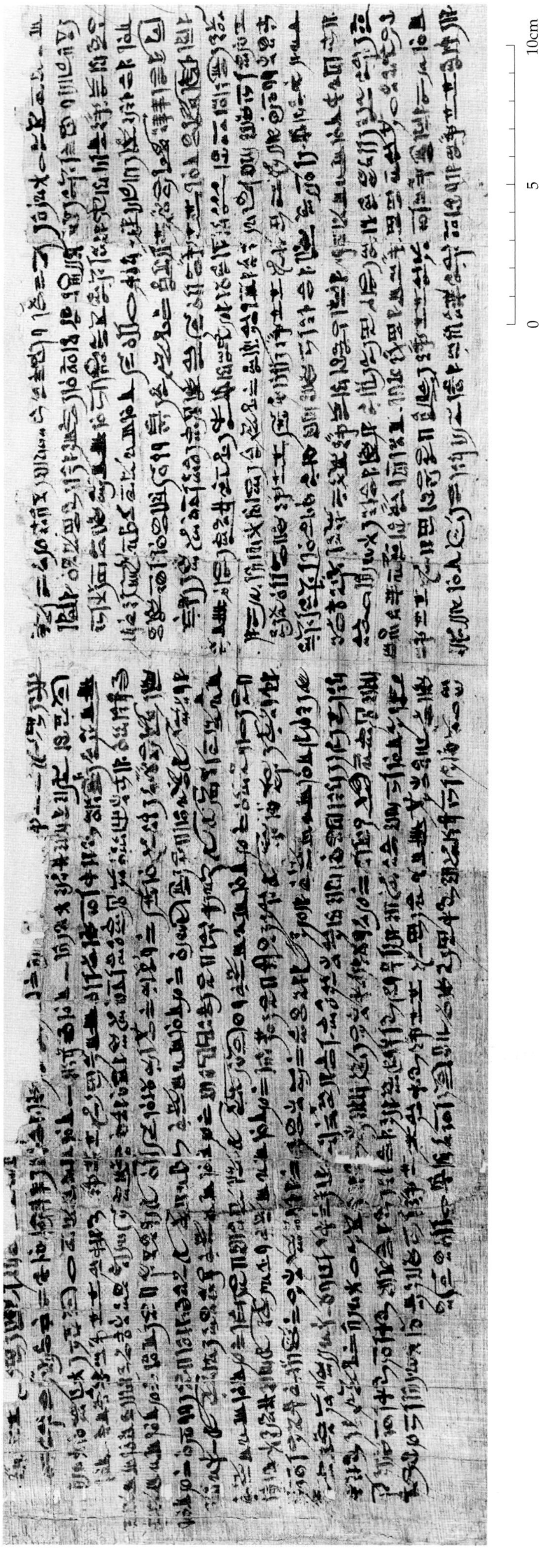

P. BM EA 10260, columns II–III

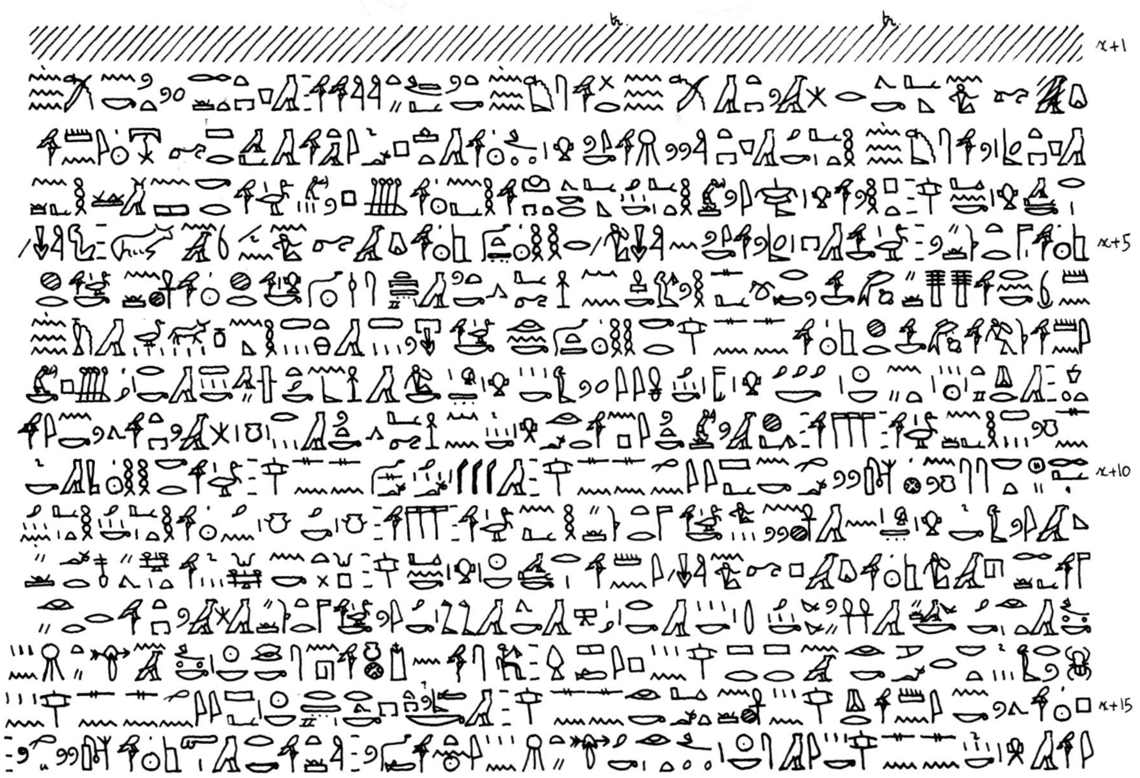

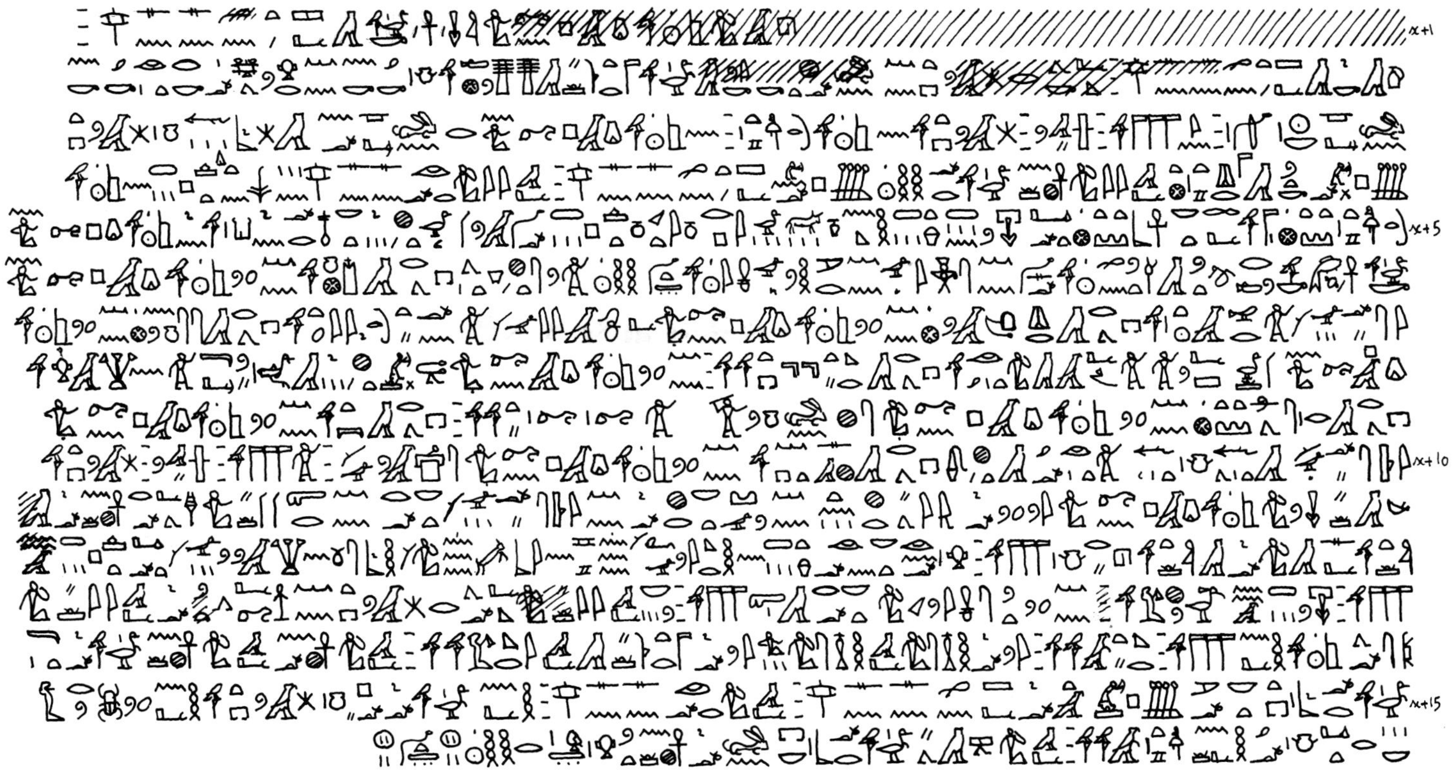

P. BM EA 10260, columns II–III

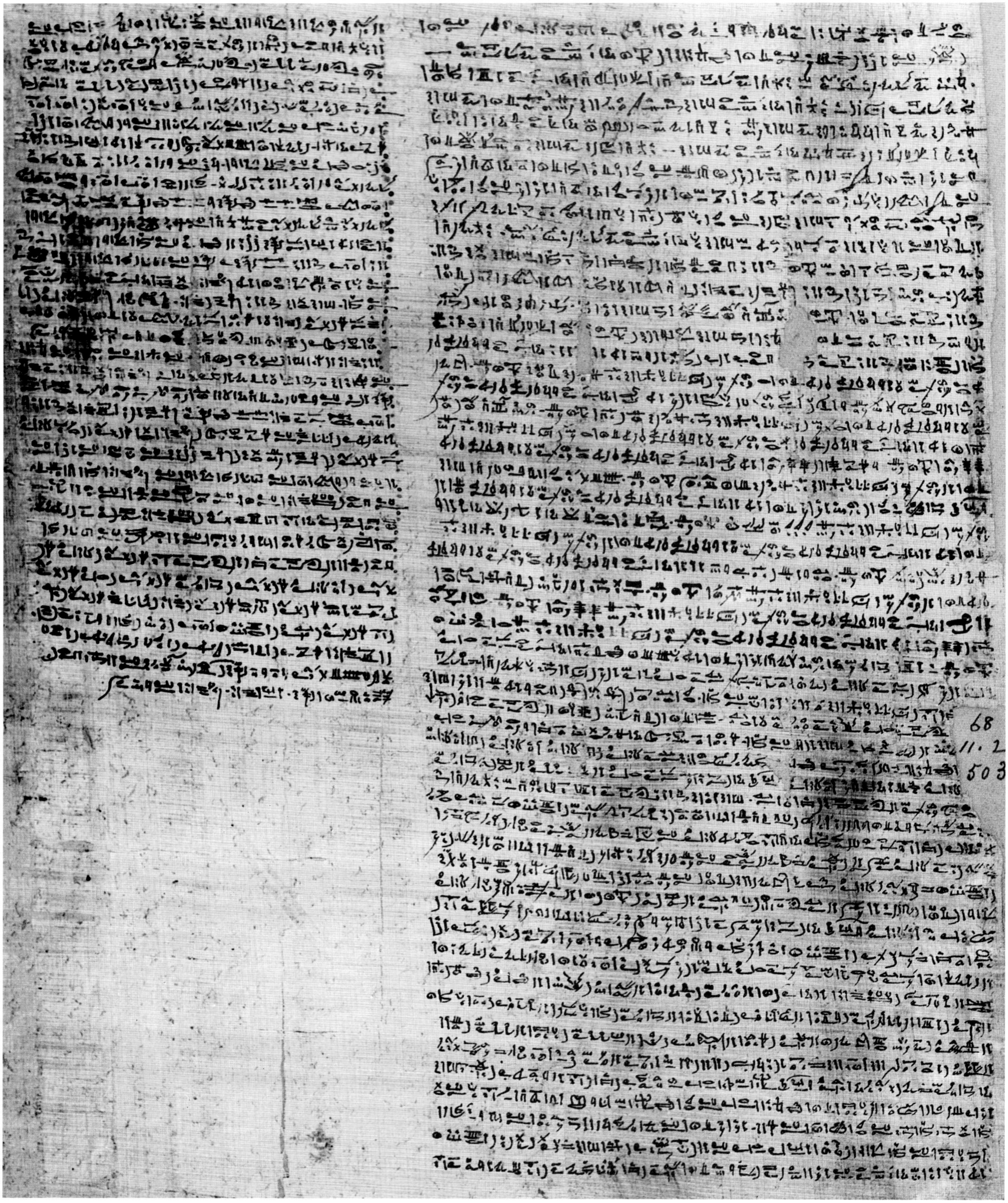

P. BM EA 10191 recto

0 5 10cm

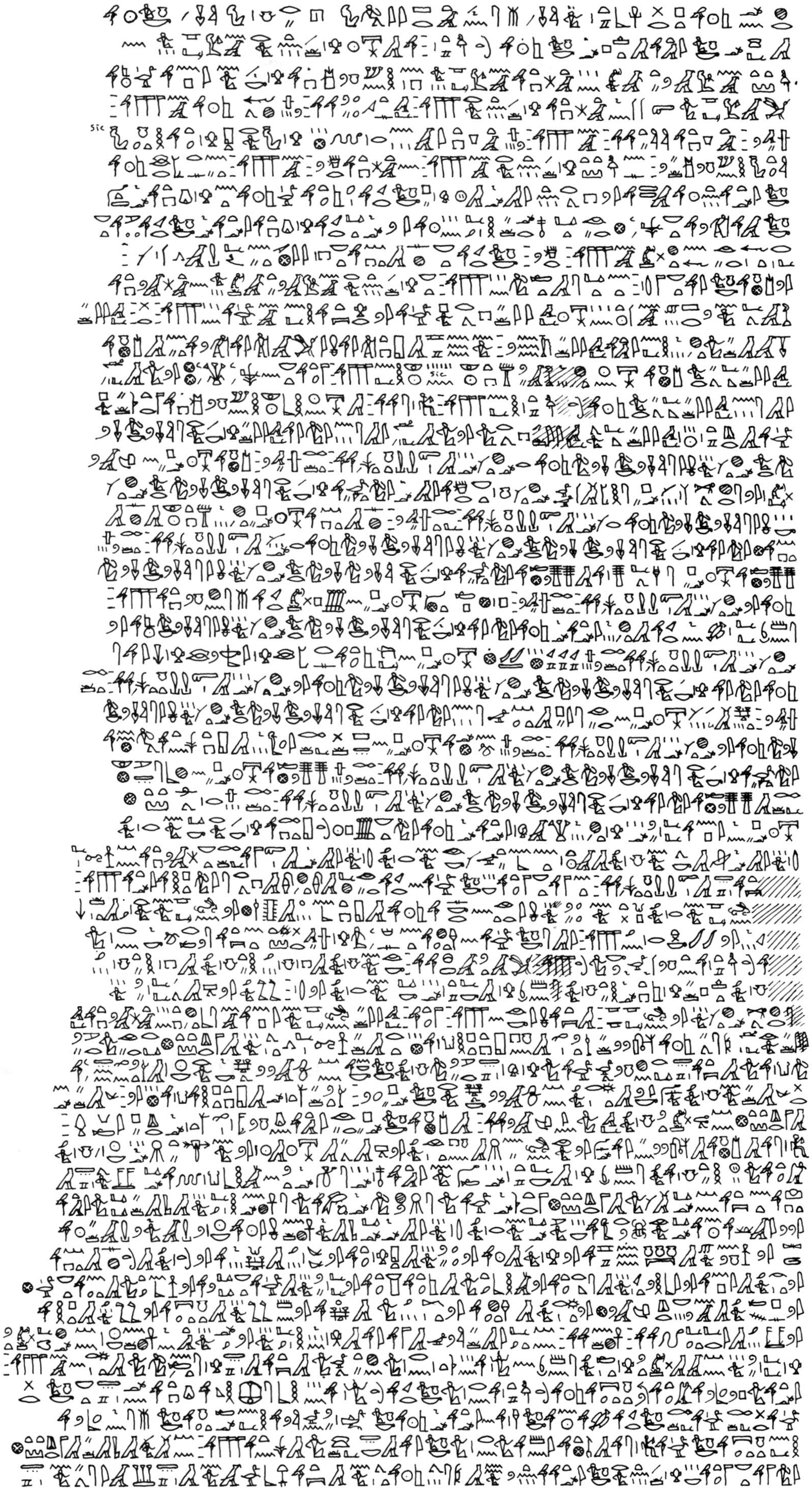

P. BM EA 10191 recto, column I

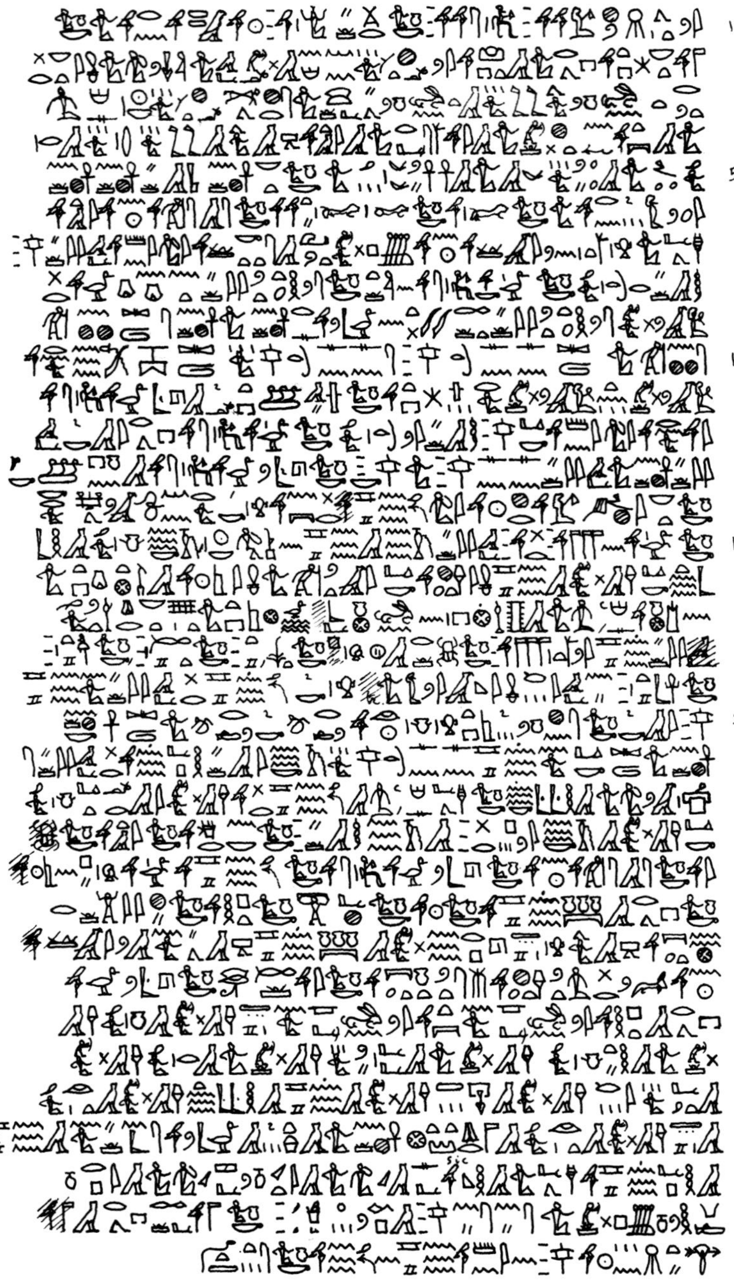

P. BM EA 10191 recto, column II

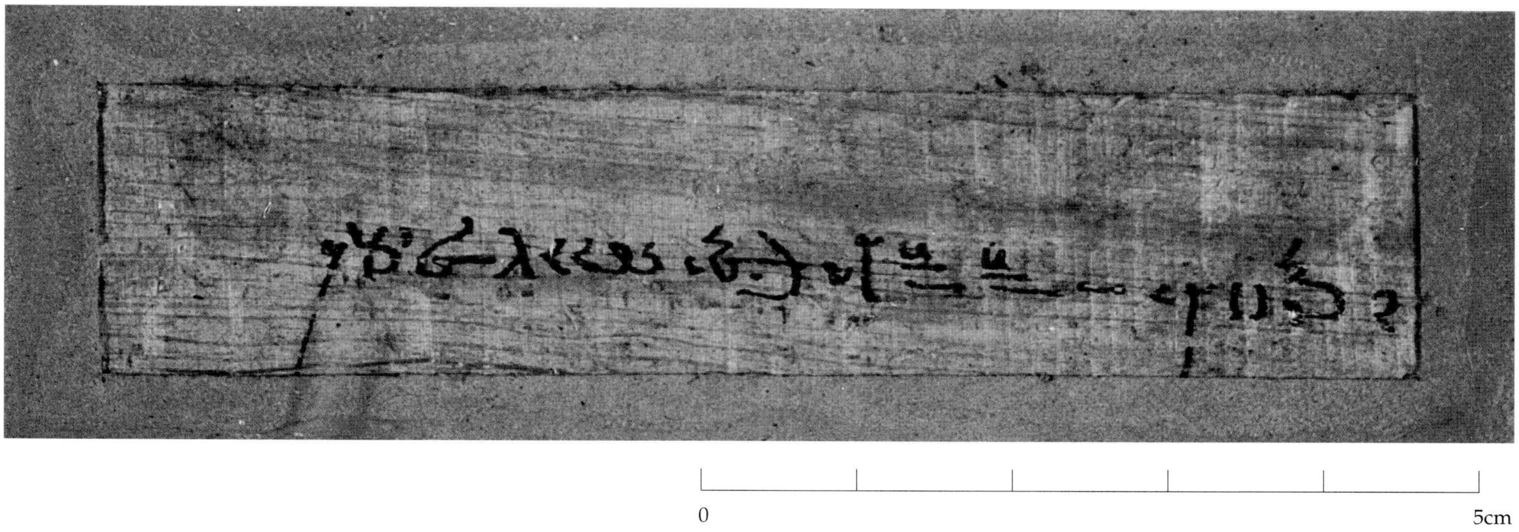

(dem.) t3 šꜥ.t n snsn nty šm ḫr ḏ3 ḏ3=f

P. BM EA 10191 verso

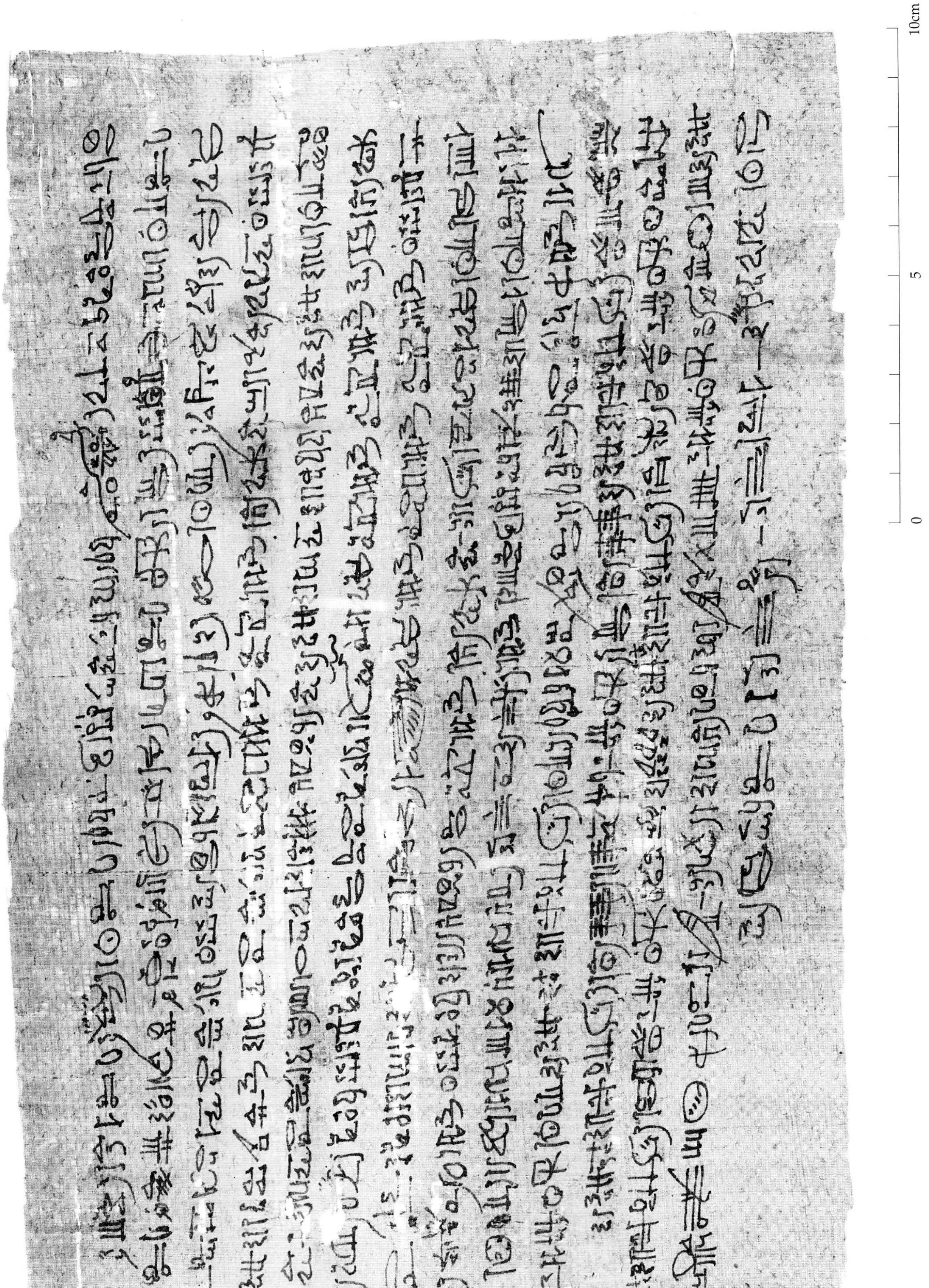

P. BM EA 10109 recto

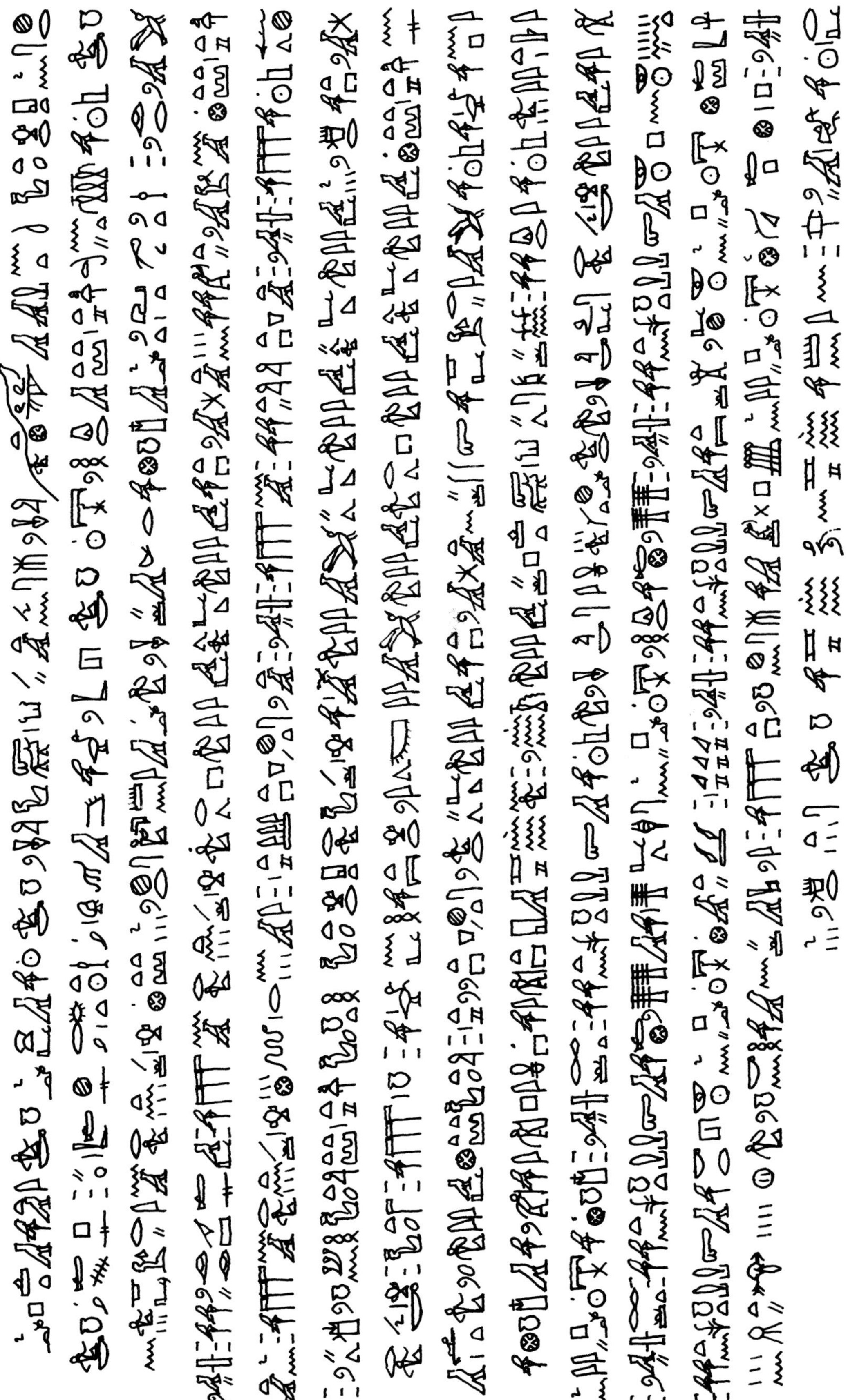

P. BM EA 10109 recto

P. BM EA 10109 verso

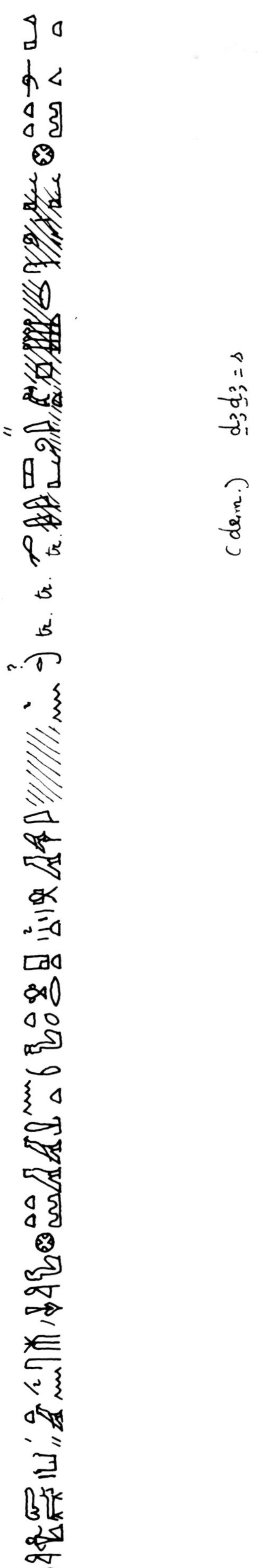

P. BM EA 10109 verso

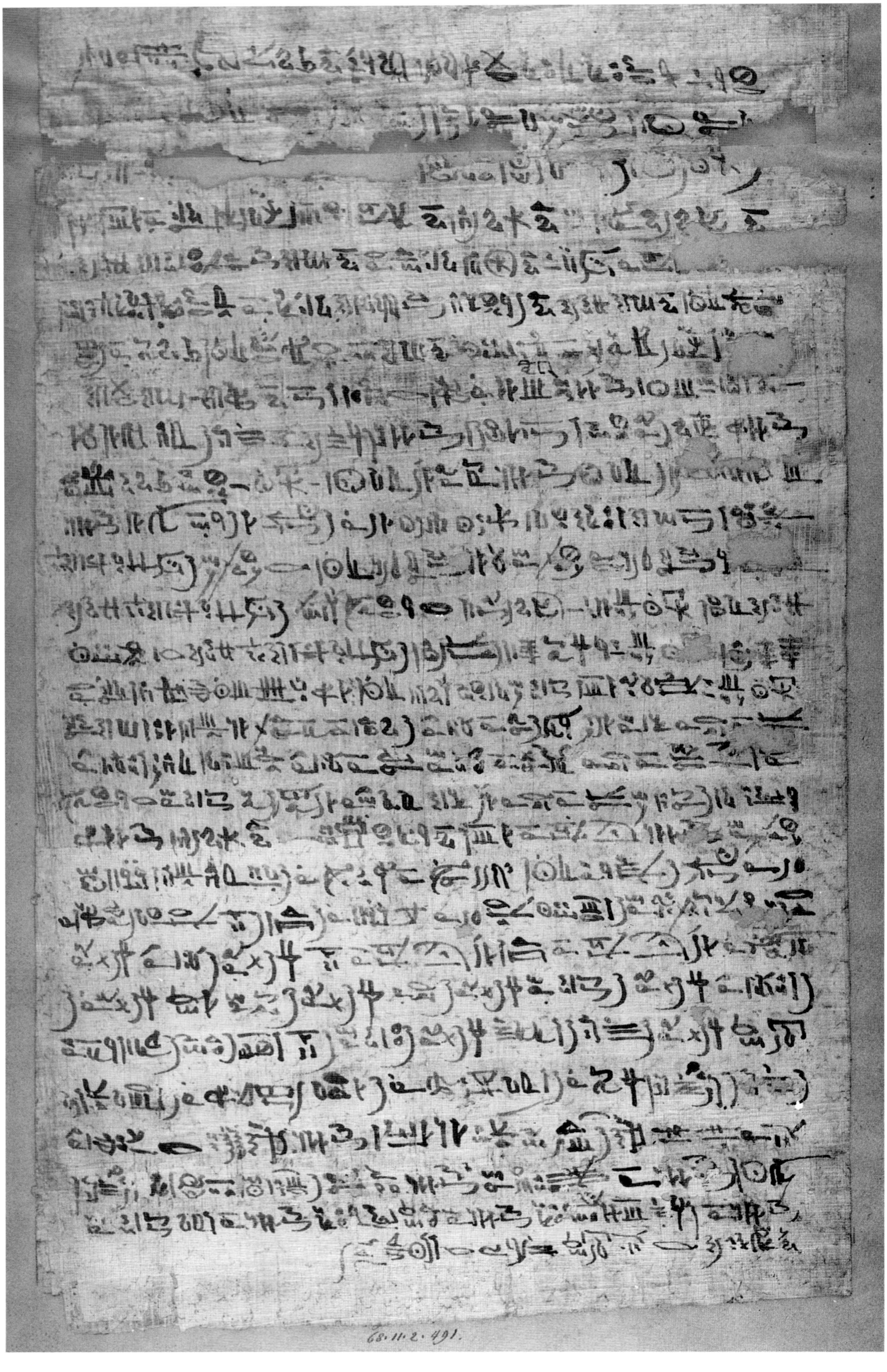

P. BM EA 10199 recto

0 5 10cm

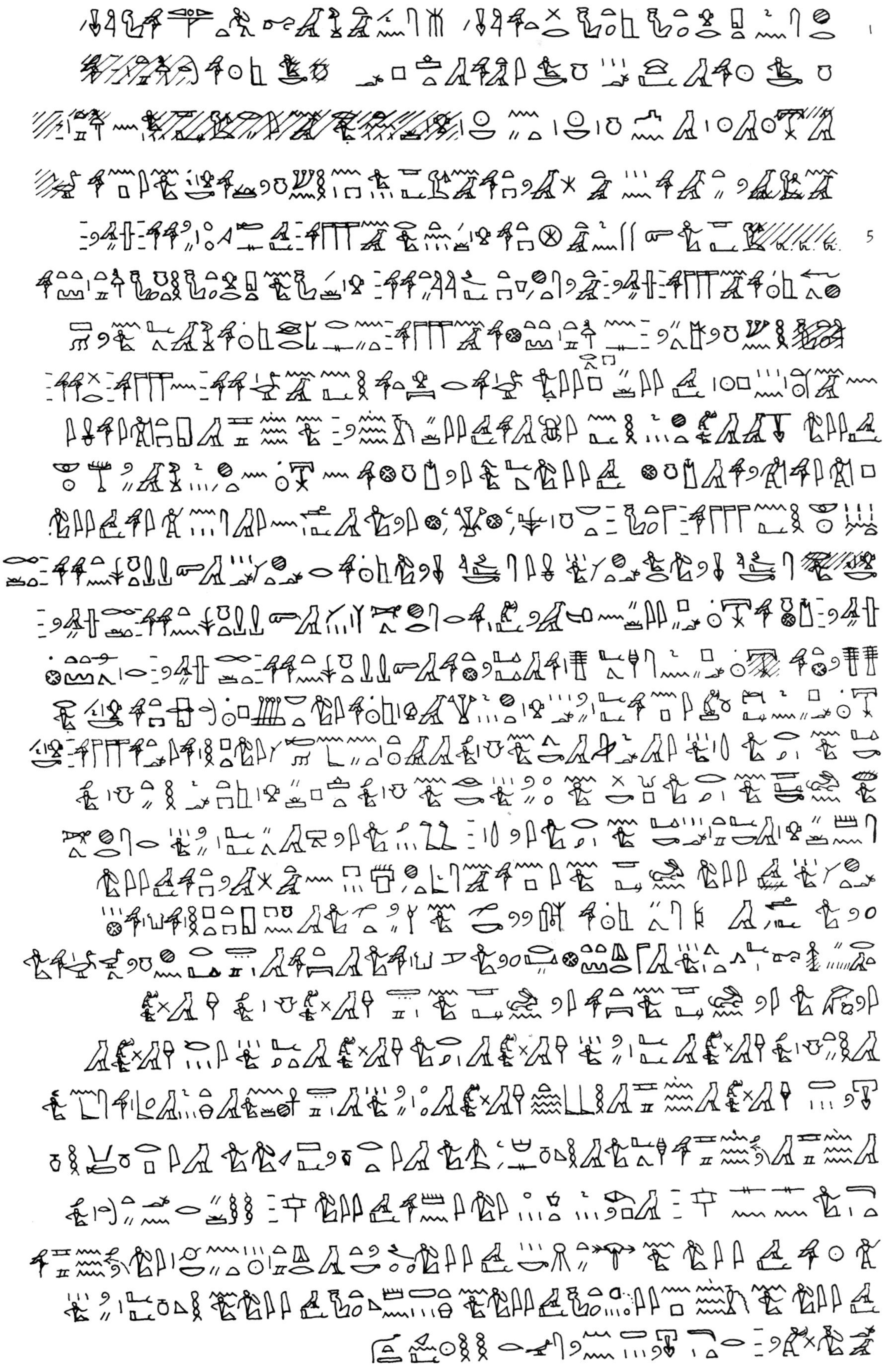

P. BM EA 10199 recto

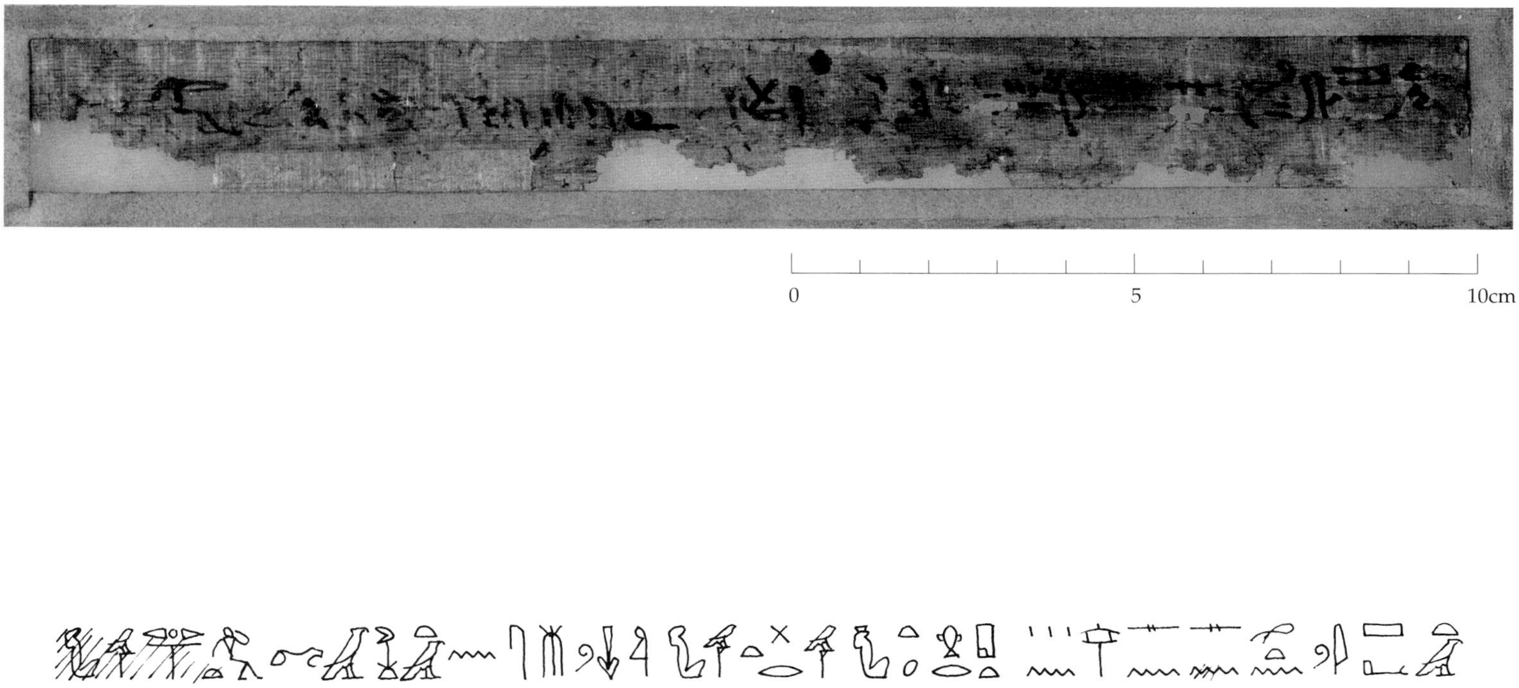

P. BM EA 10199 verso

A + B

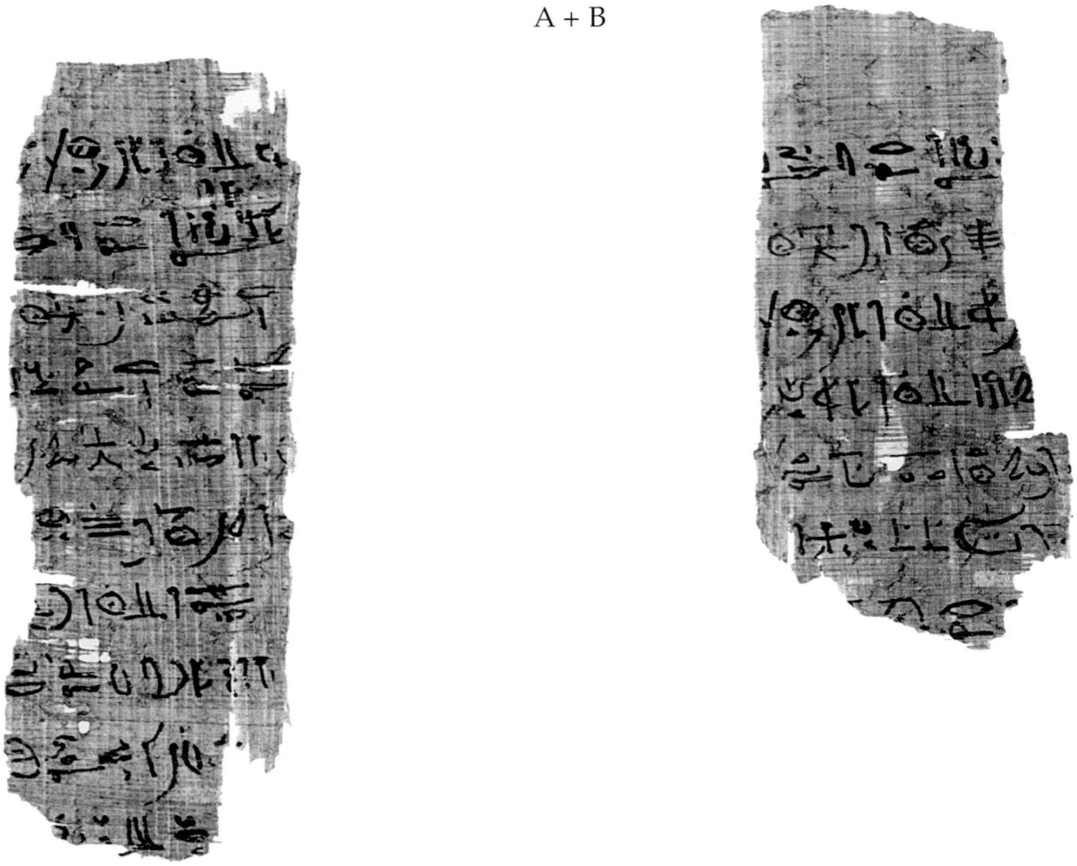

C

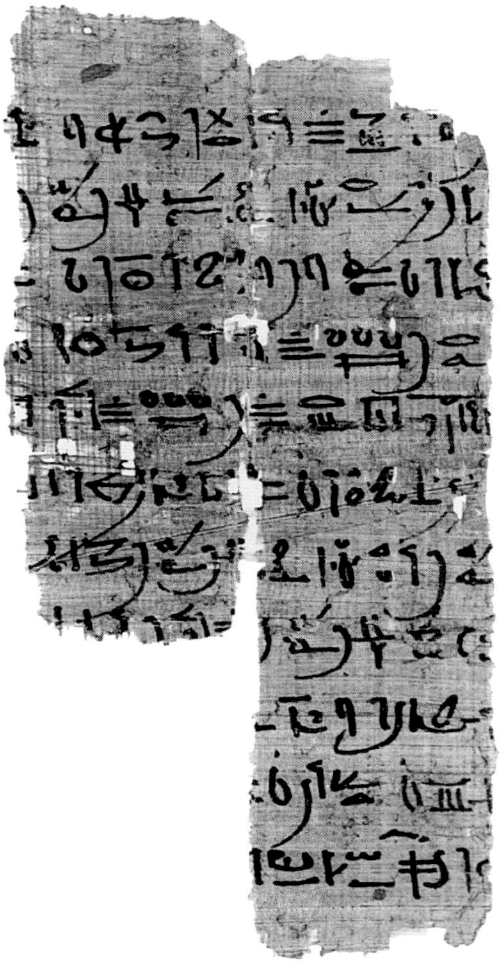

P. BM EA 10206, A–C

A + B

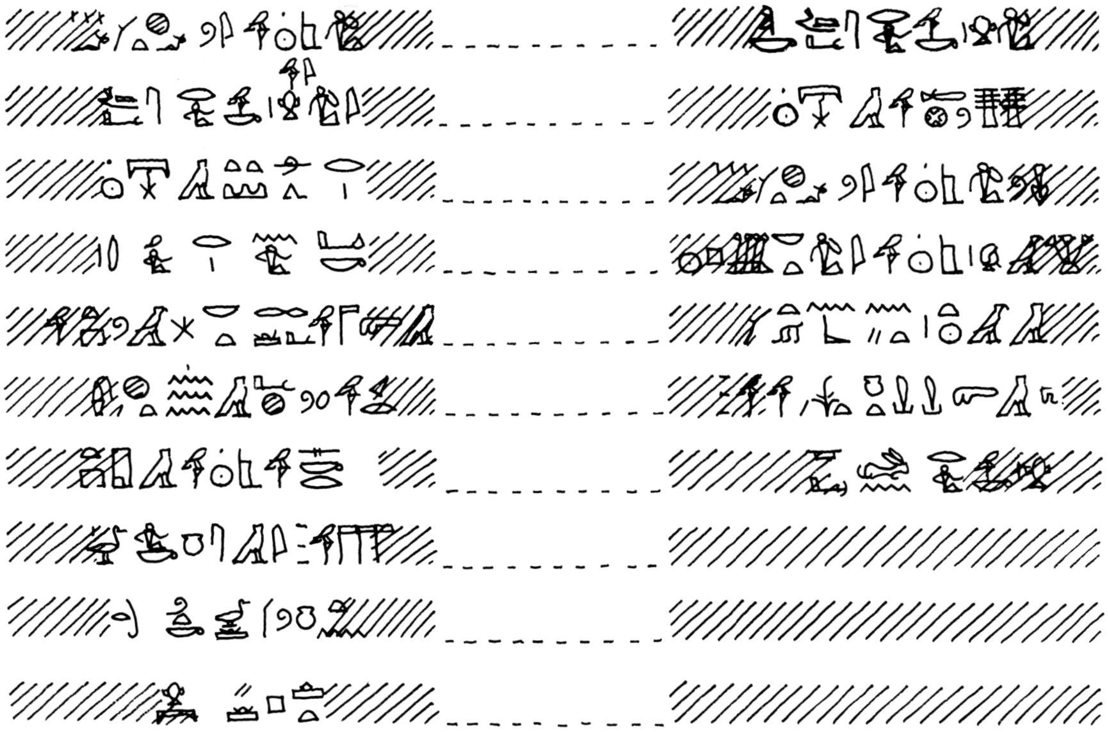

C

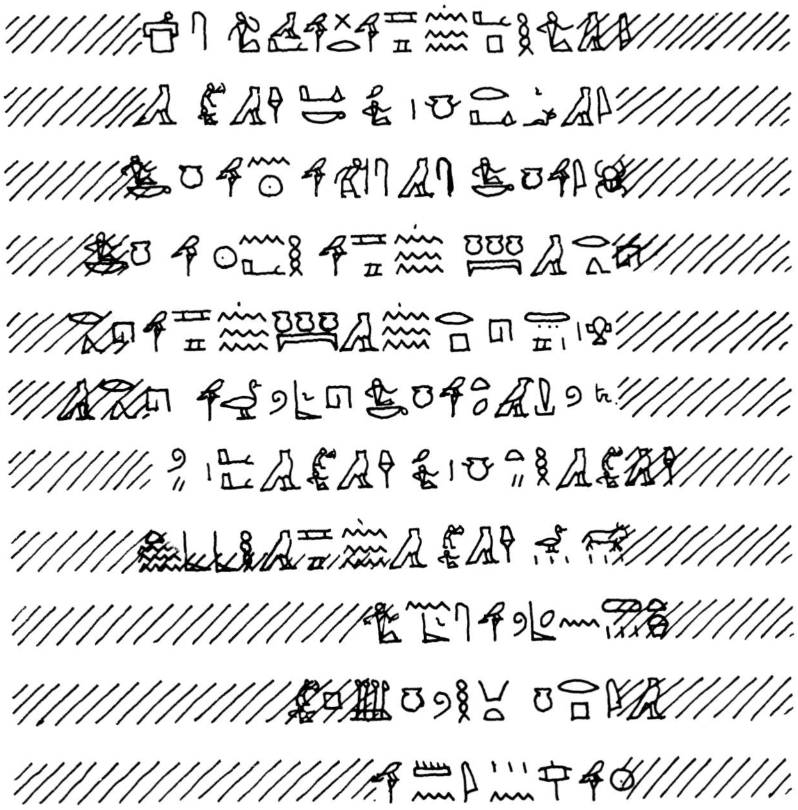

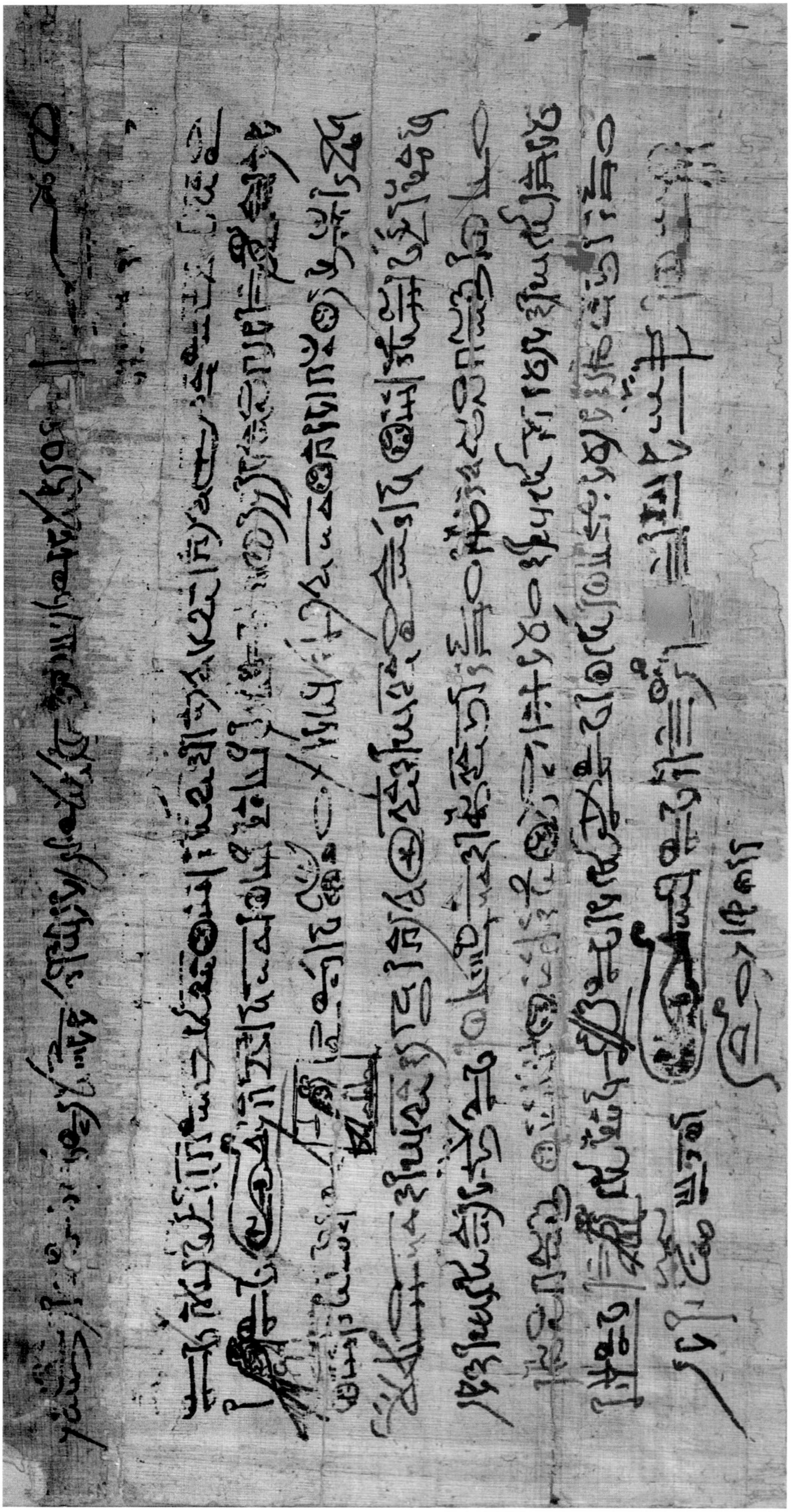

0 5 10cm

P. BM EA 10283 recto

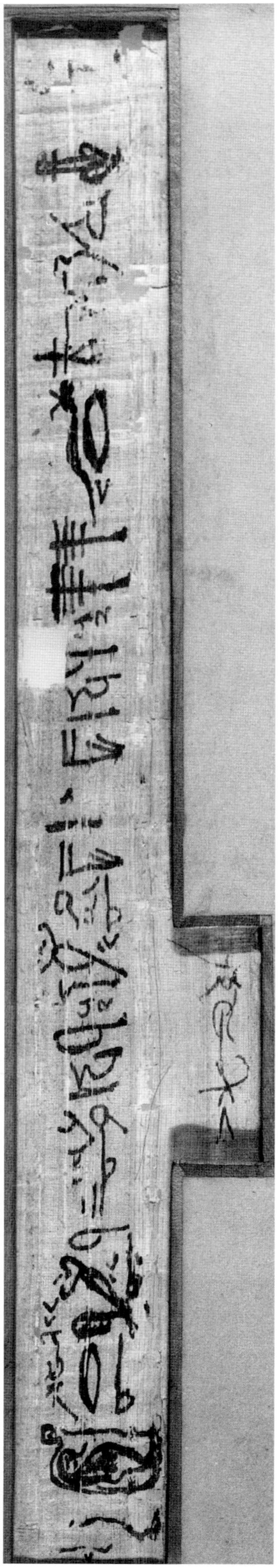

P. BM EA 10283 verso

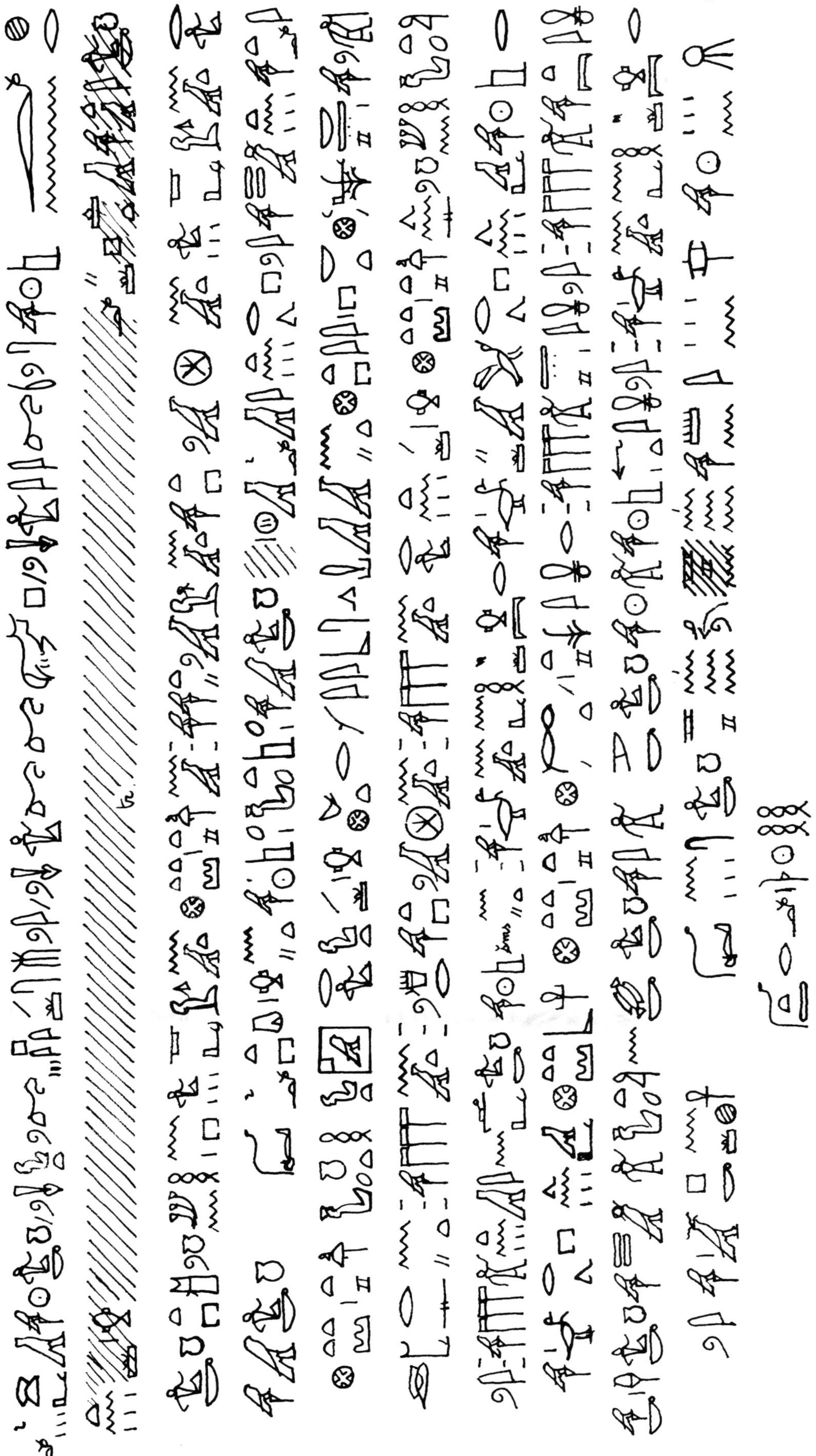

P. BM EA 10283 verso

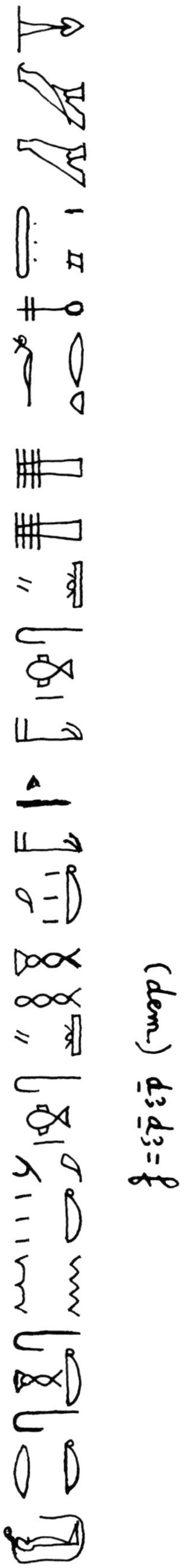

P. BM EA 10283 verso

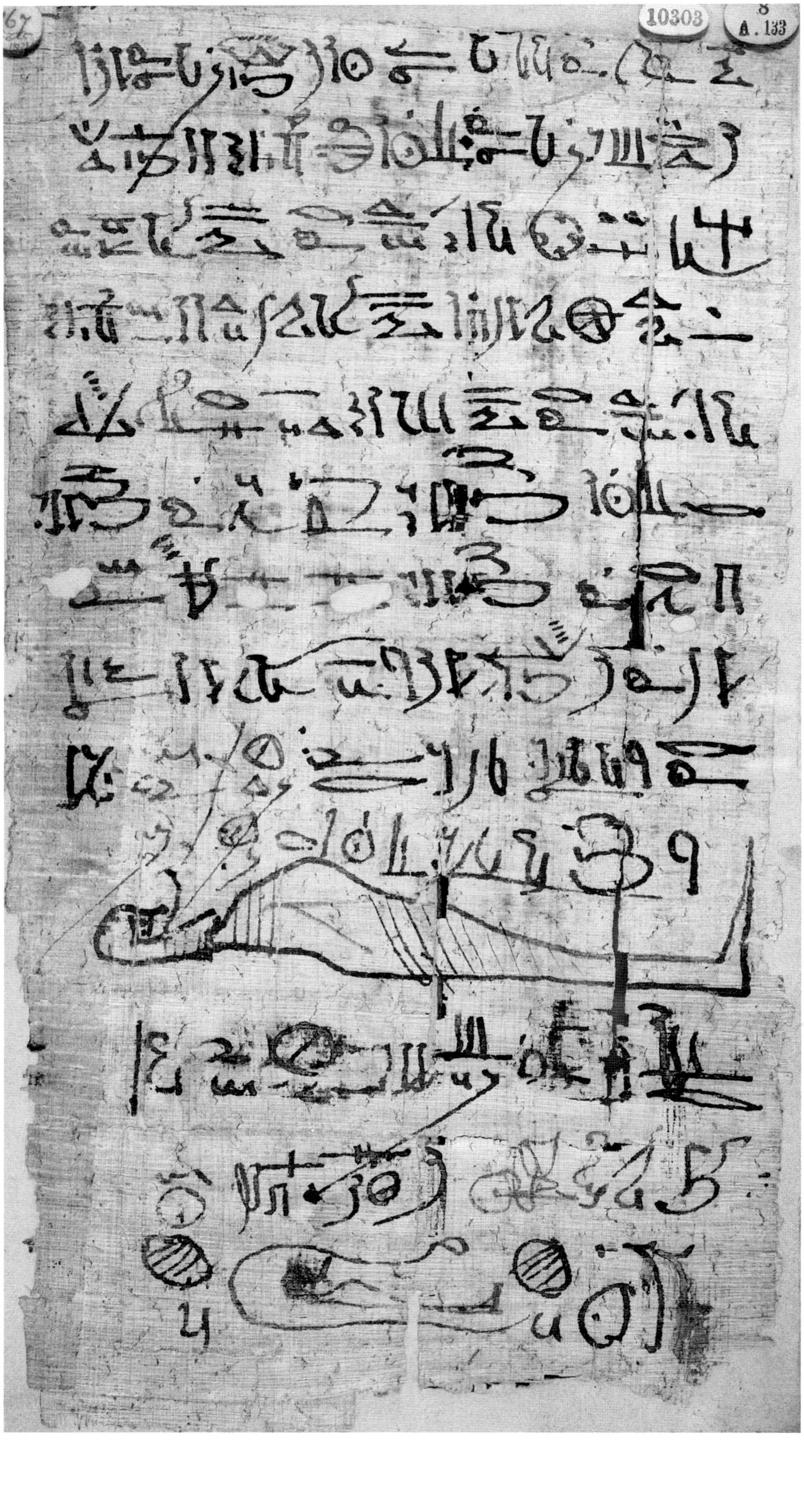

P. BM EA 10303 recto

P. BM EA 10303 verso

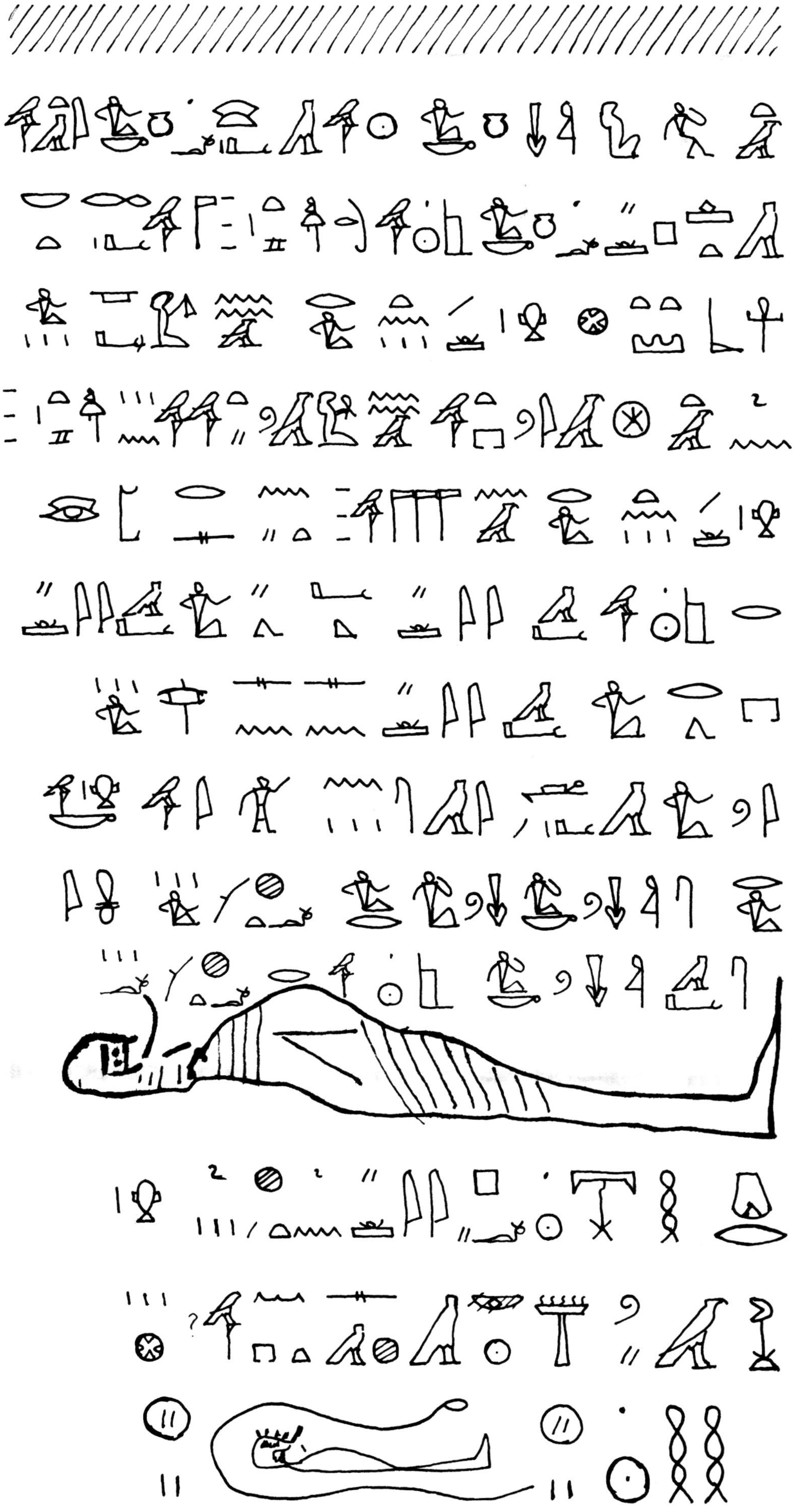

P. BM EA 10303 recto

P. BM EA 10303 verso

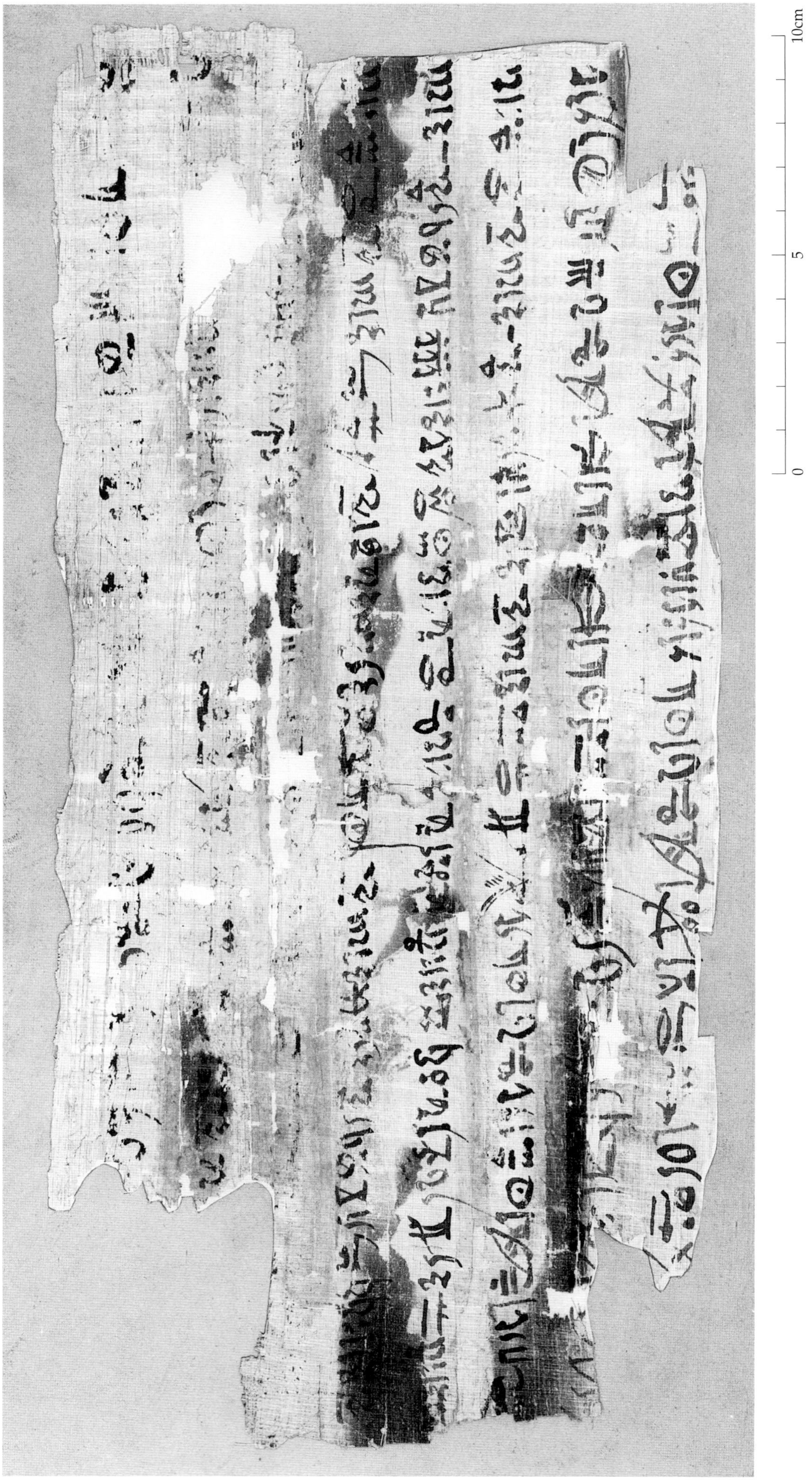

P. BM EA 10337 recto

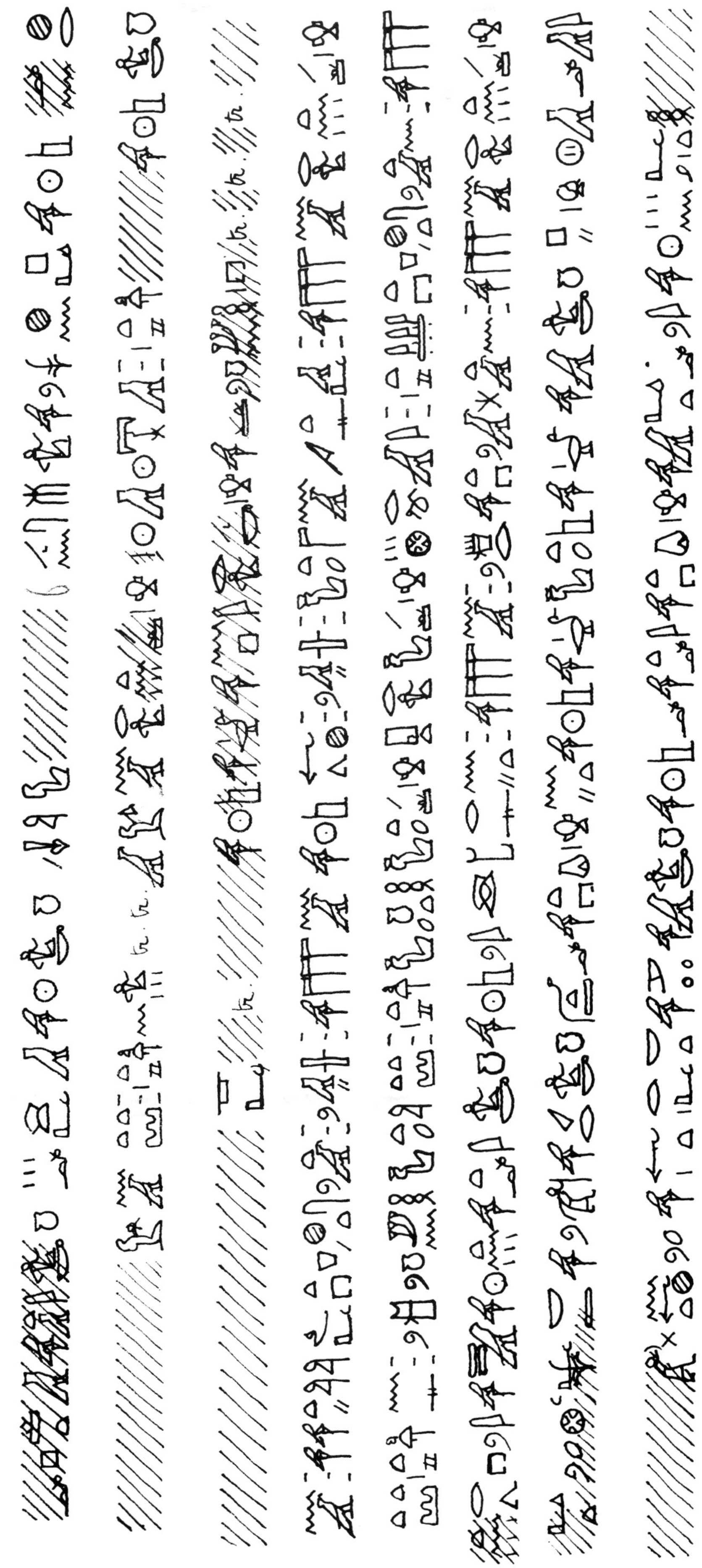

P. BM EA 10337 recto

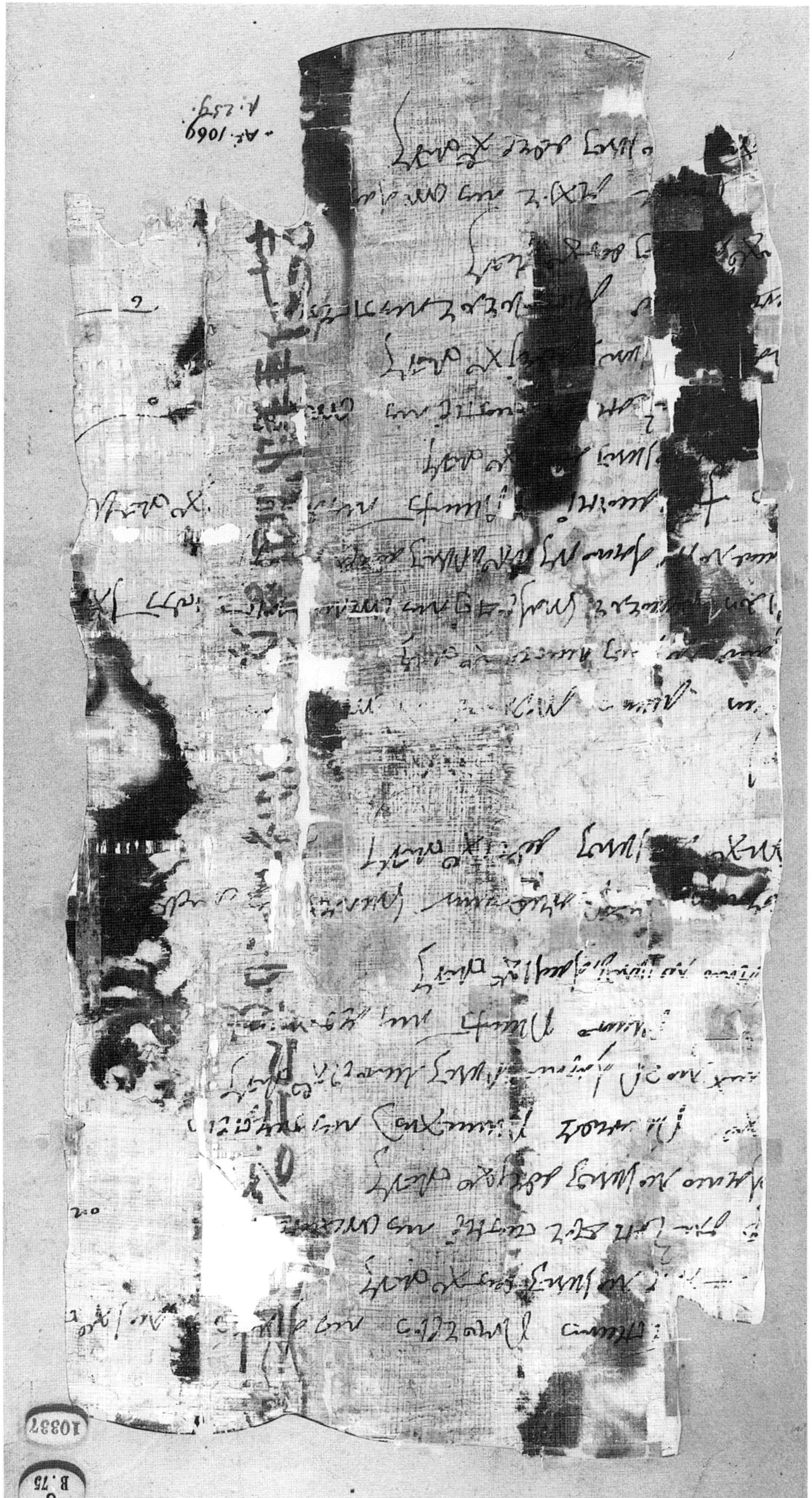

P. BM EA 10337 verso

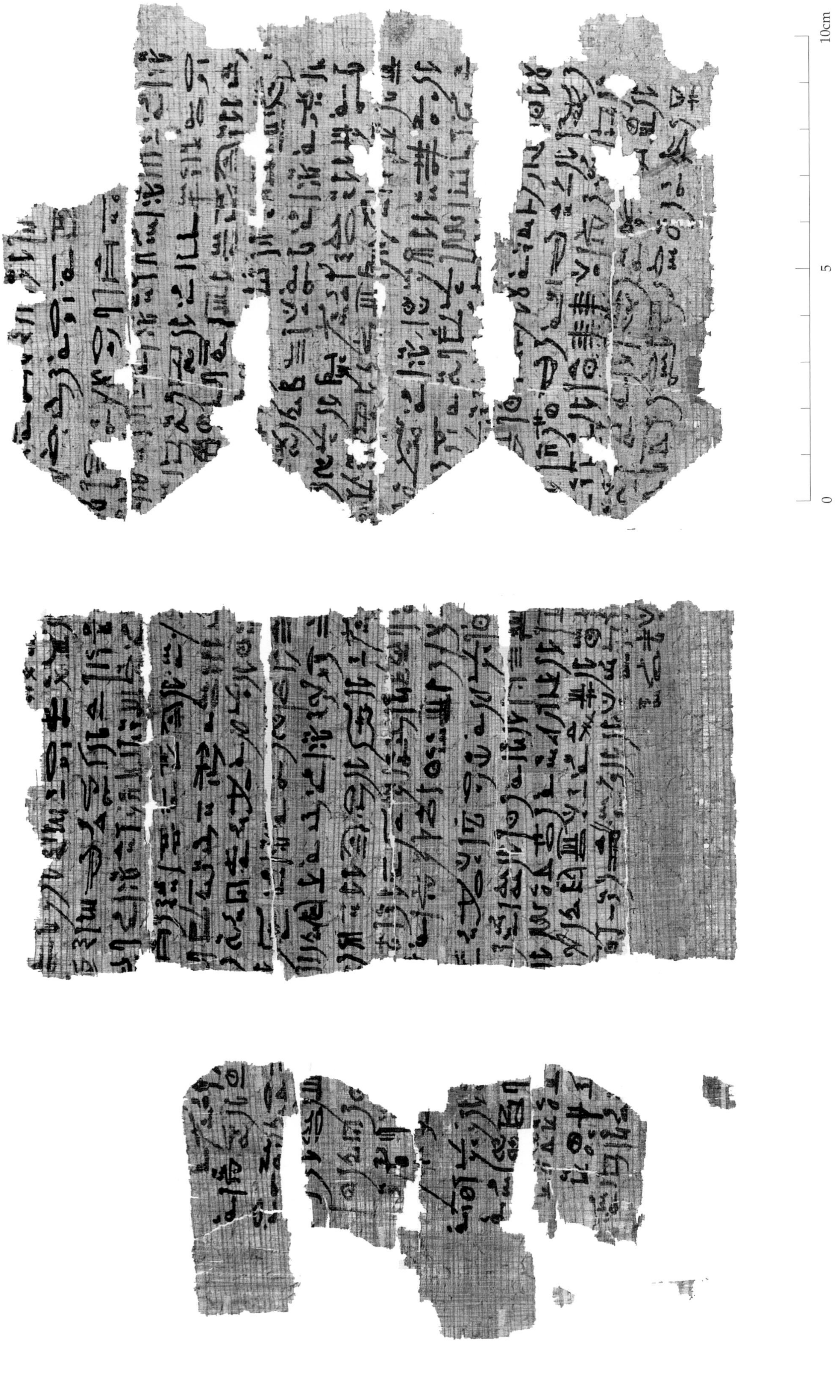

P. BM EA 10338

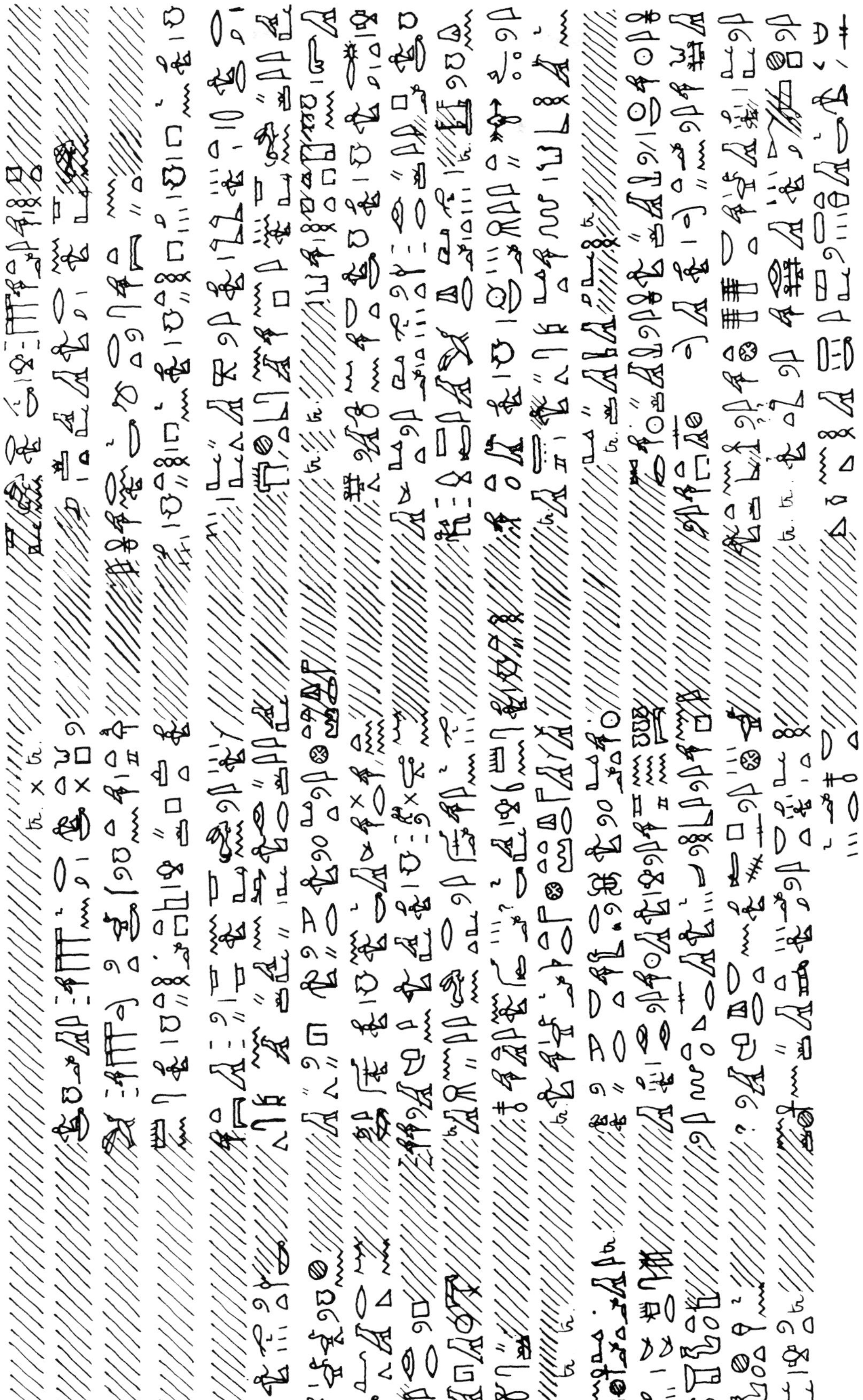

P. BM EA 10338

P. BM EA 10705

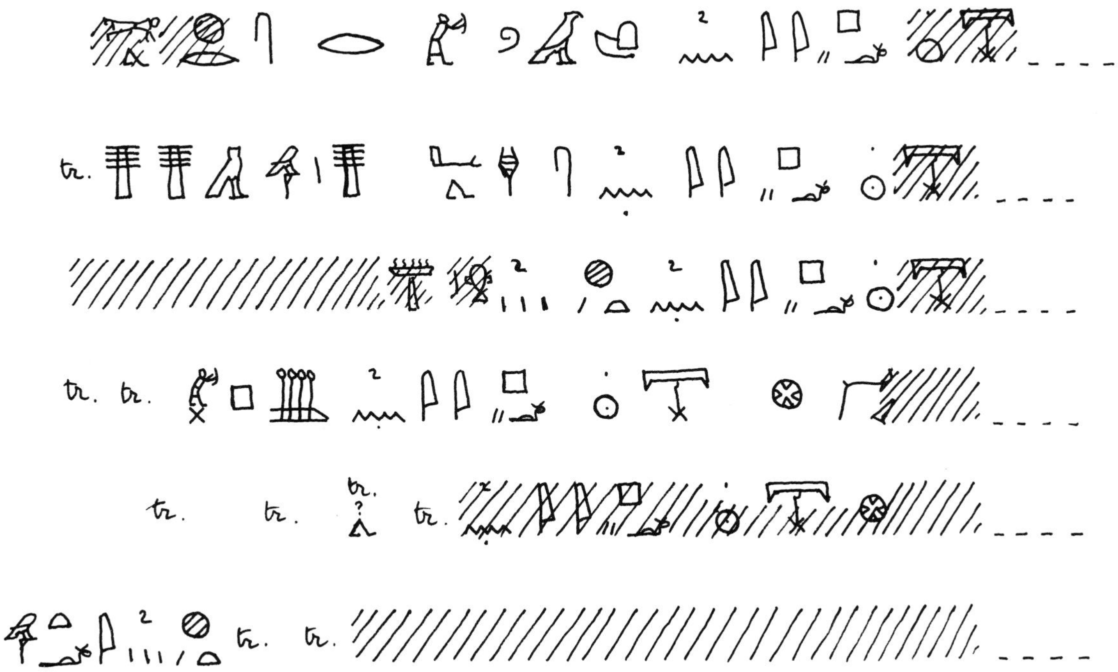

P. BM EA 10705

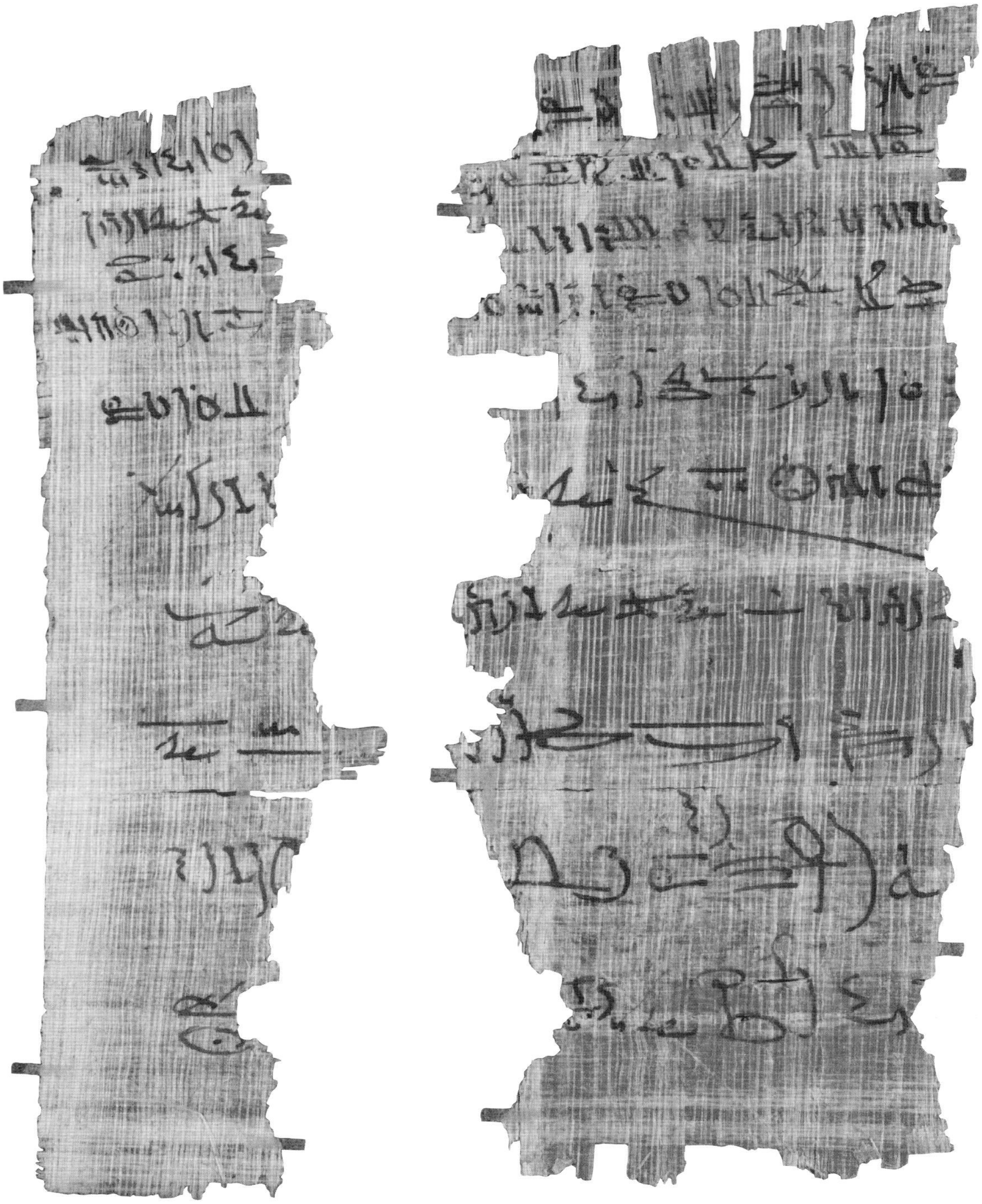

P. BM EA 71513B recto

P. BM EA 71513B verso

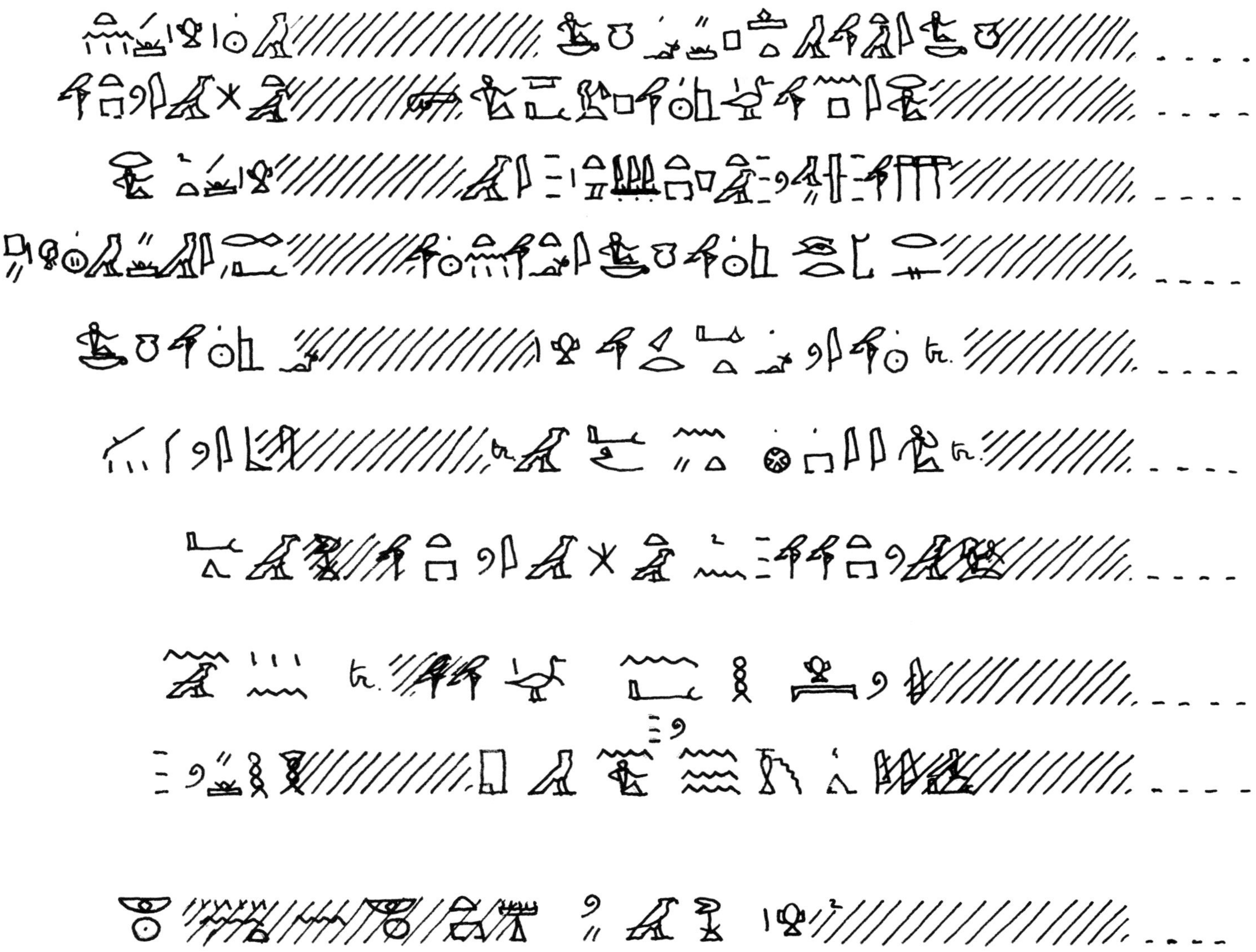

P. BM EA 71513B recto

P. BM EA 71513B verso

P. BM EA 71513C recto

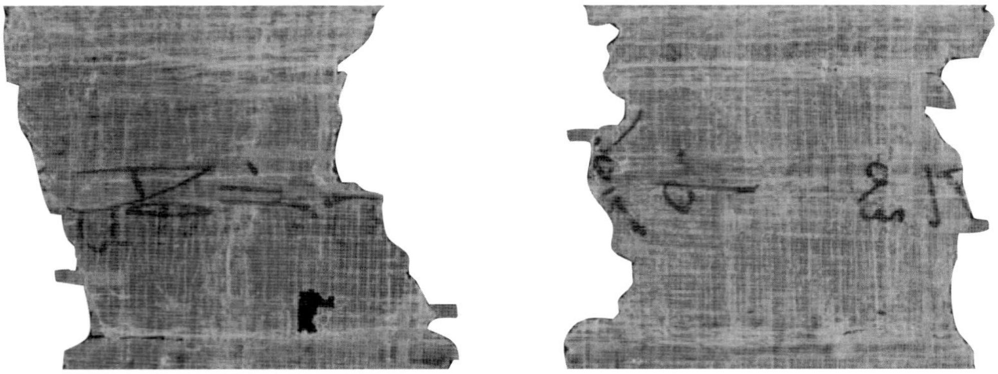

P. BM EA 71513C verso

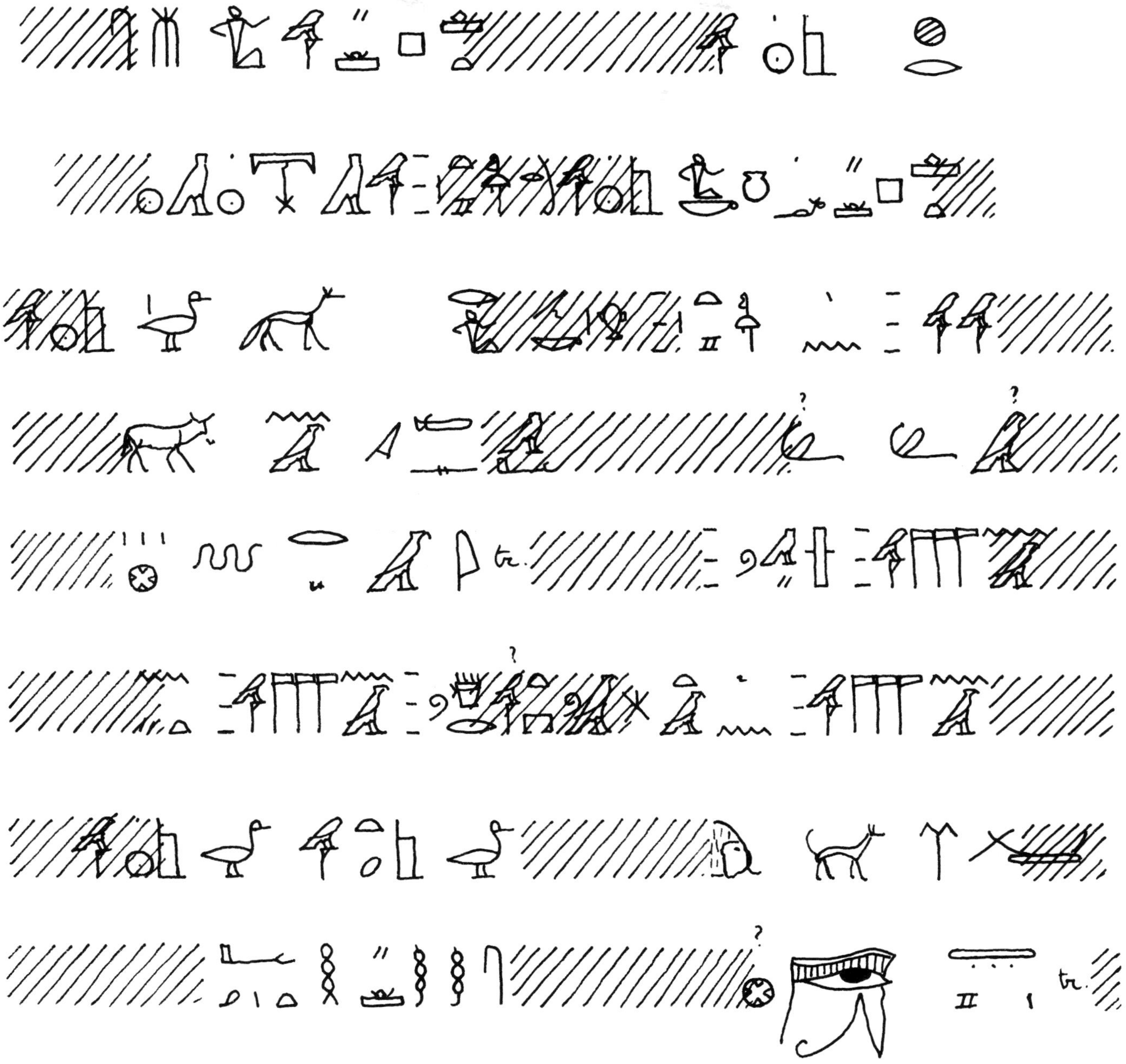

P. BM EA 71513C recto

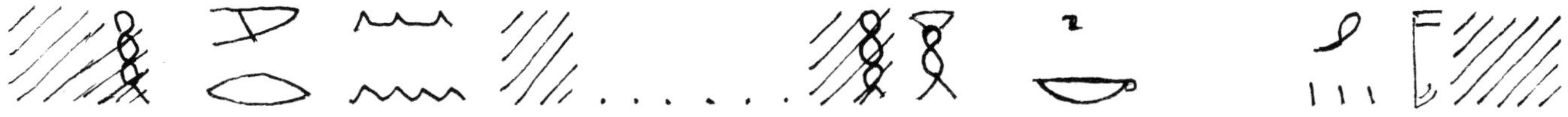

P. BM EA 71513C verso

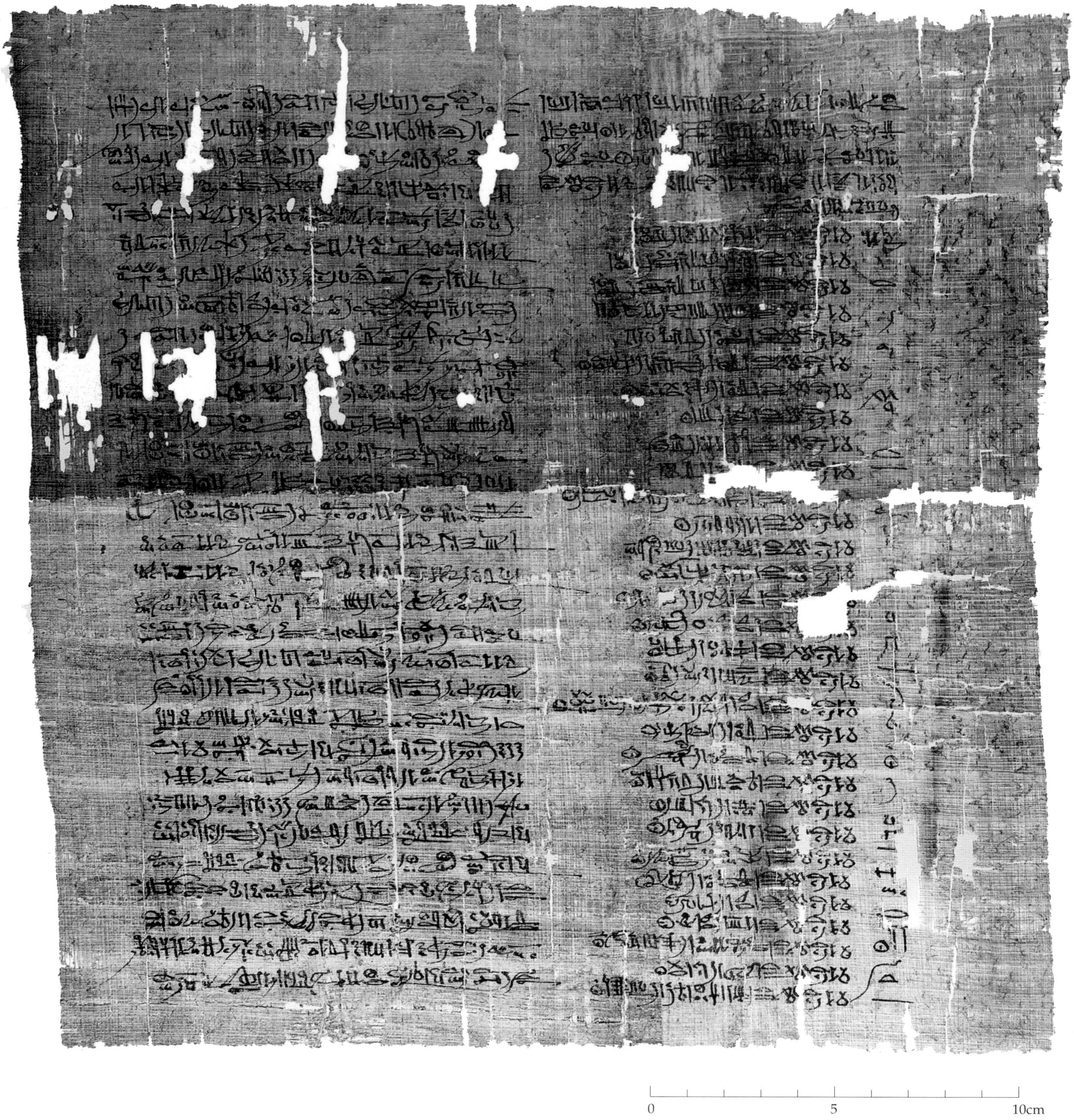

P. BM EA 10110 + 10111 recto

P. BM EA 10110 + 10111 recto

0 5 10cm

(dem.): t3 š'.t n snsn mḥ 2.t nty iw=w r ꜥḥꜥ=s i.ir rd.wy.ṯ Wsir s3w.t(y) [pr-ḥḏ] n pr Imn irm n3y=f rpy.w rḫ ḥwt wr

P. BM EA 10110 + 10111 verso

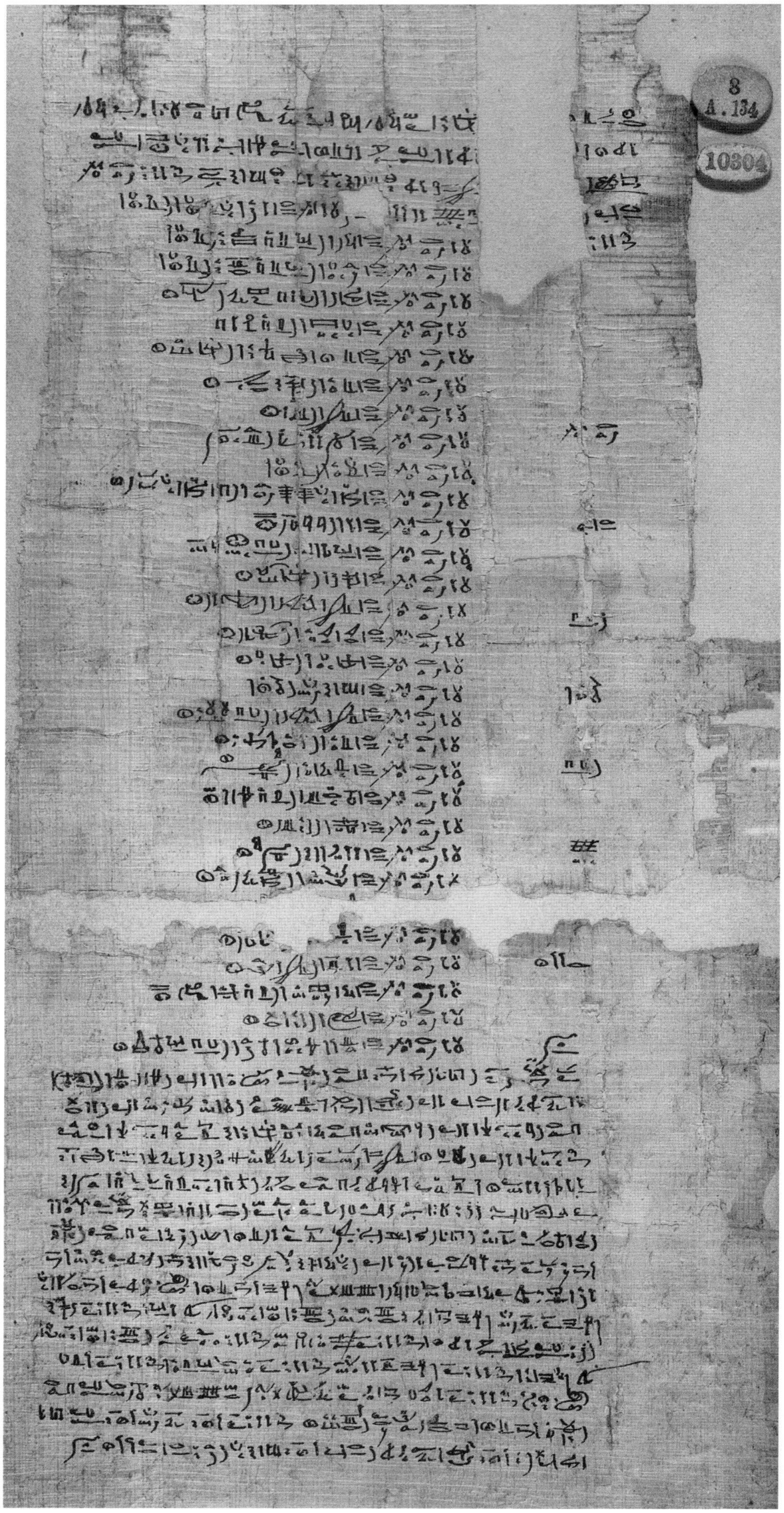

0 5 10cm

P. BM EA 10304 recto

P. BM EA 10304 verso

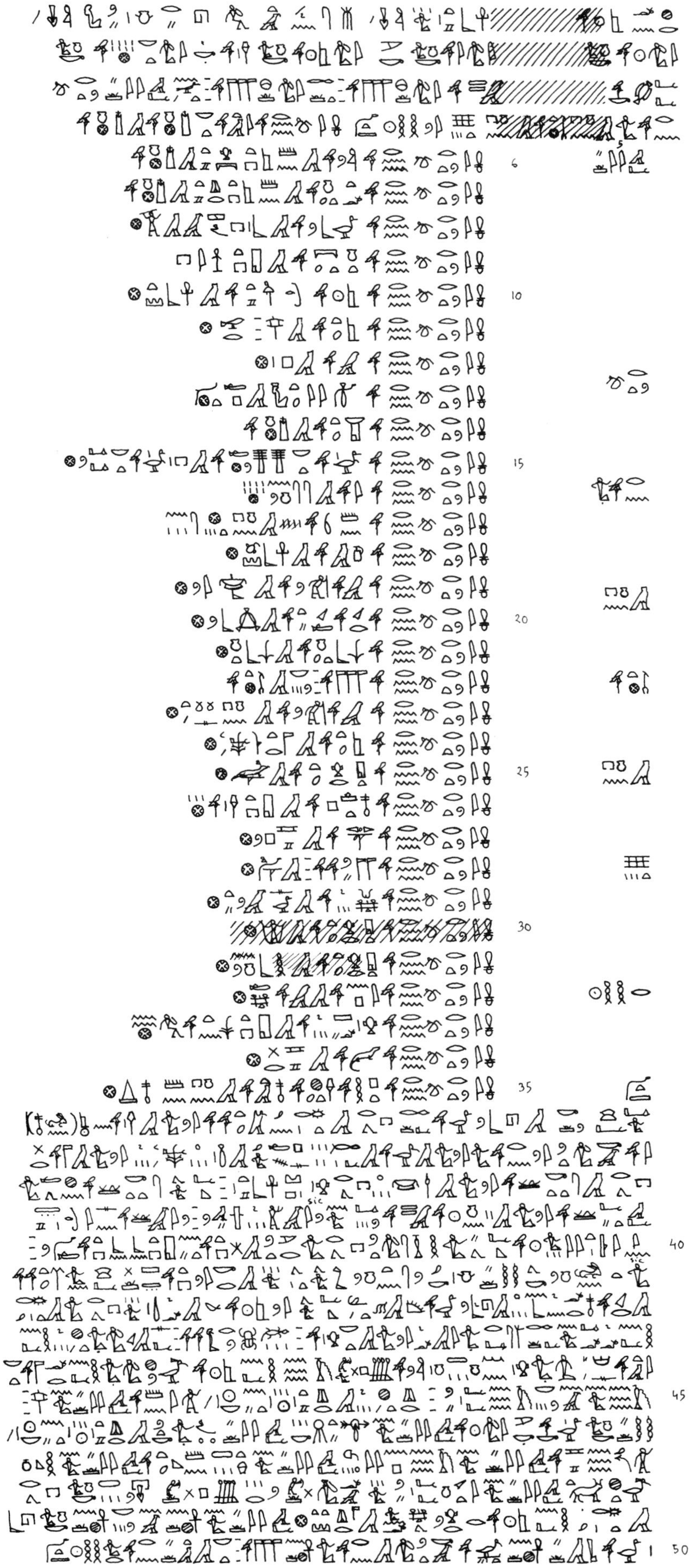

P. BM EA 10304 recto

(dem.) t3 š˓.t n snsn nty šm ḫr rd.wy=f

P. BM EA 10304 verso

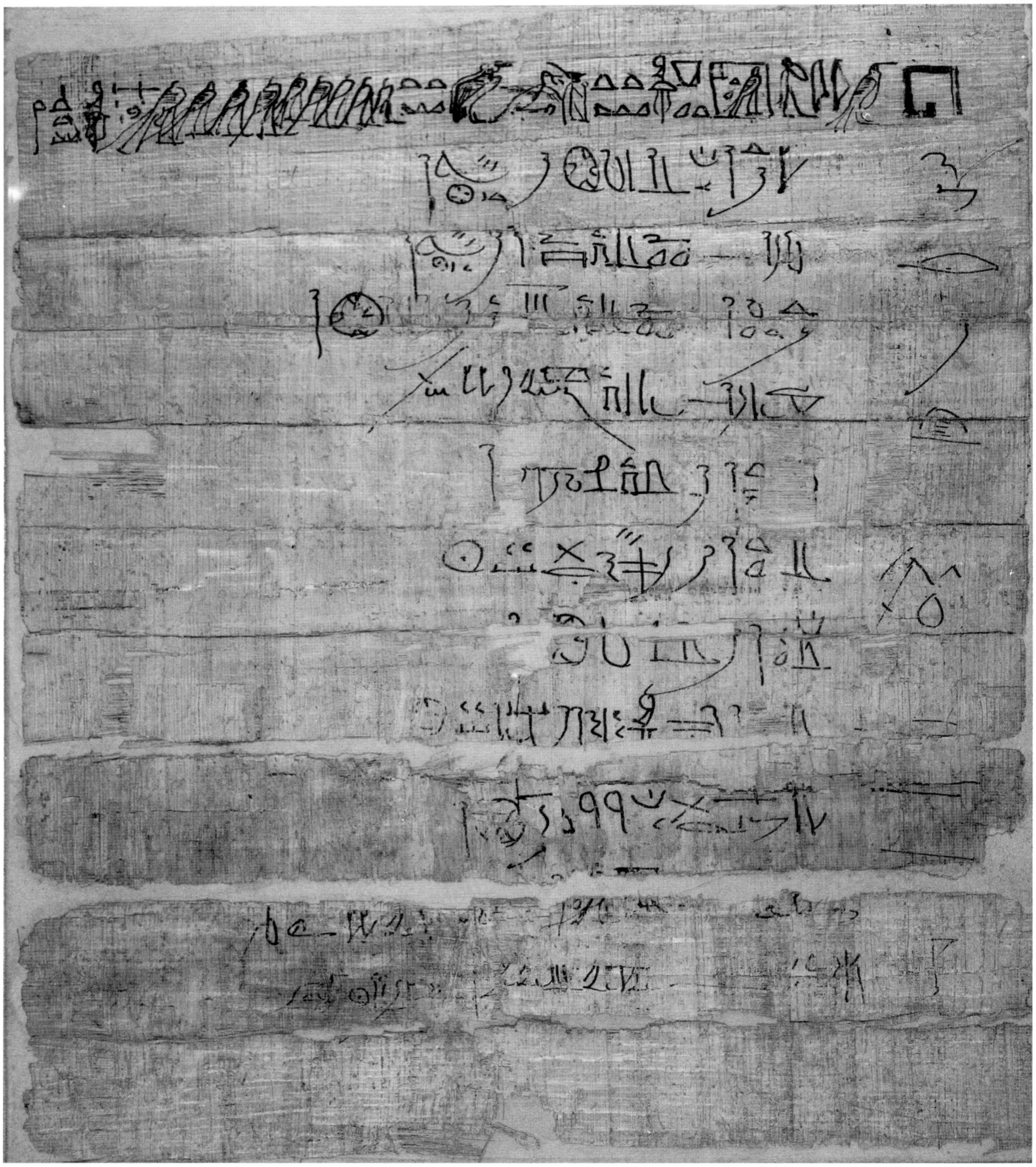

P. BM EA 9977 recto

0 5 10cm

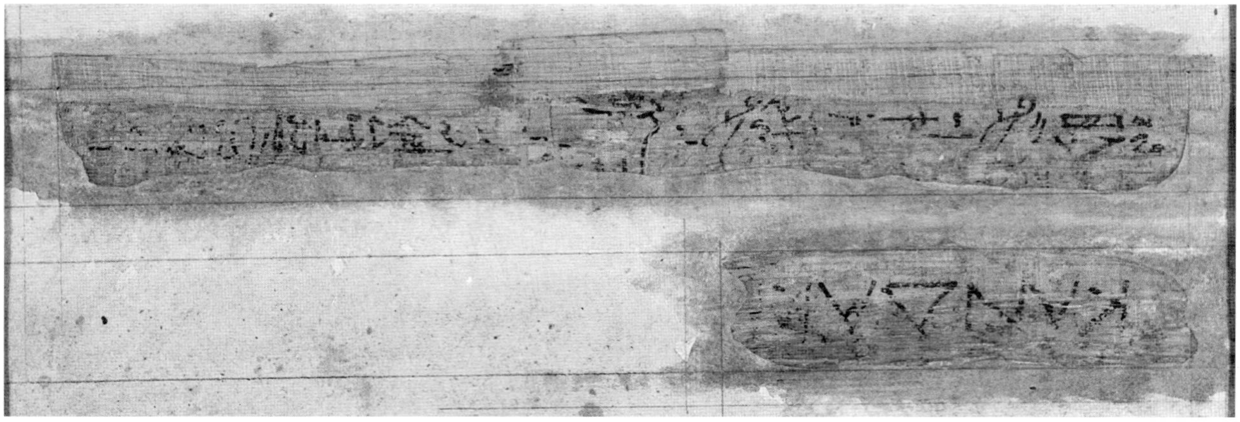

P. BM EA 9977 verso

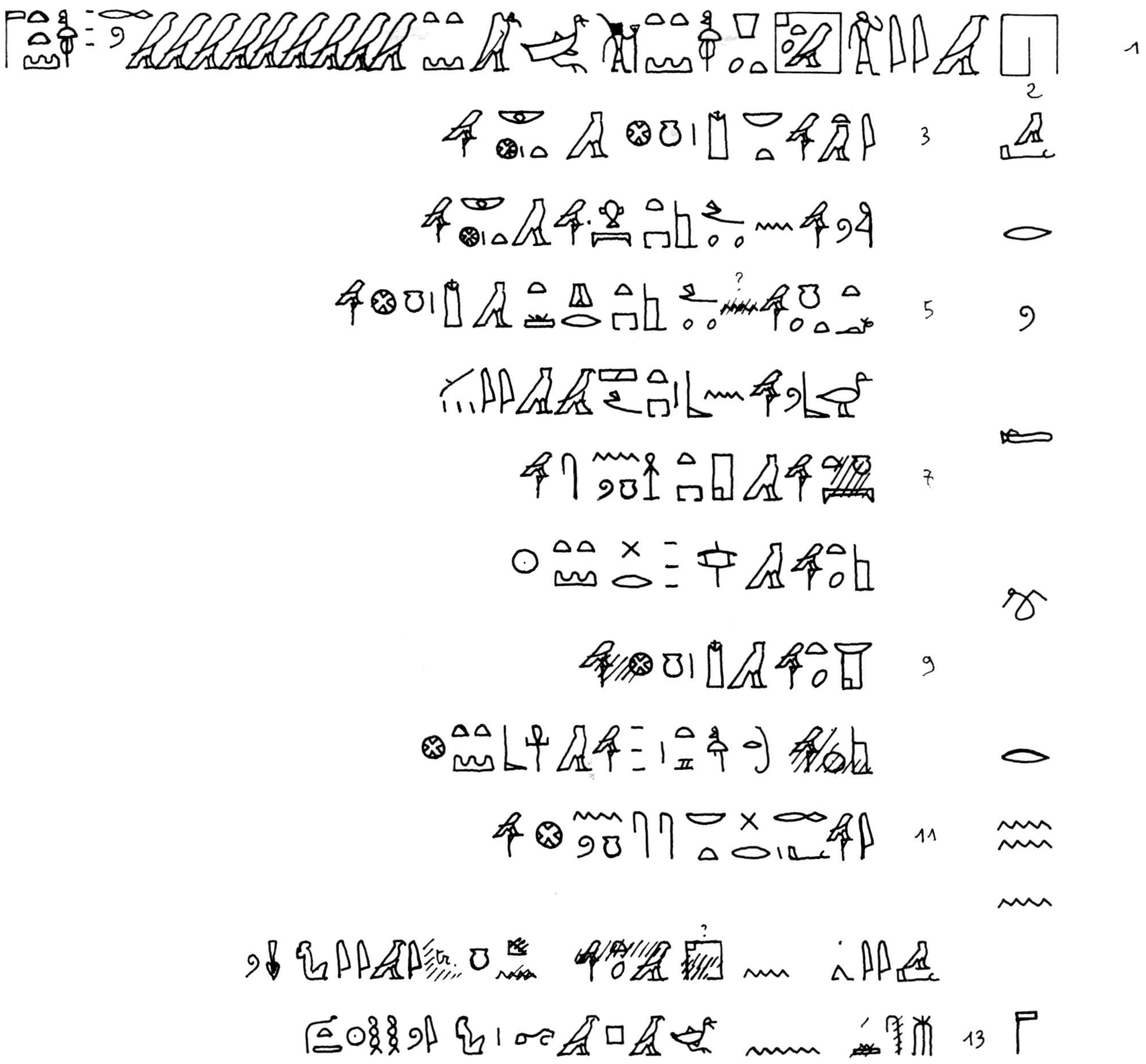

P. BM EA 9977 recto

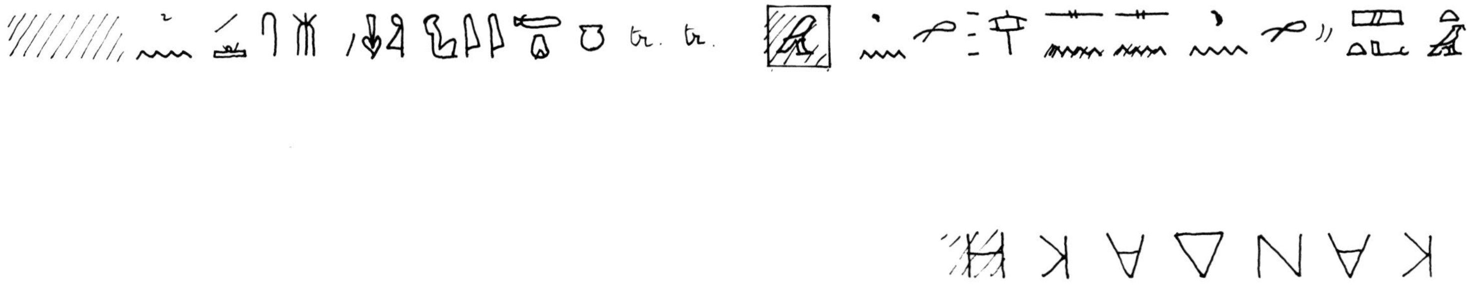

P. BM EA 9977 verso

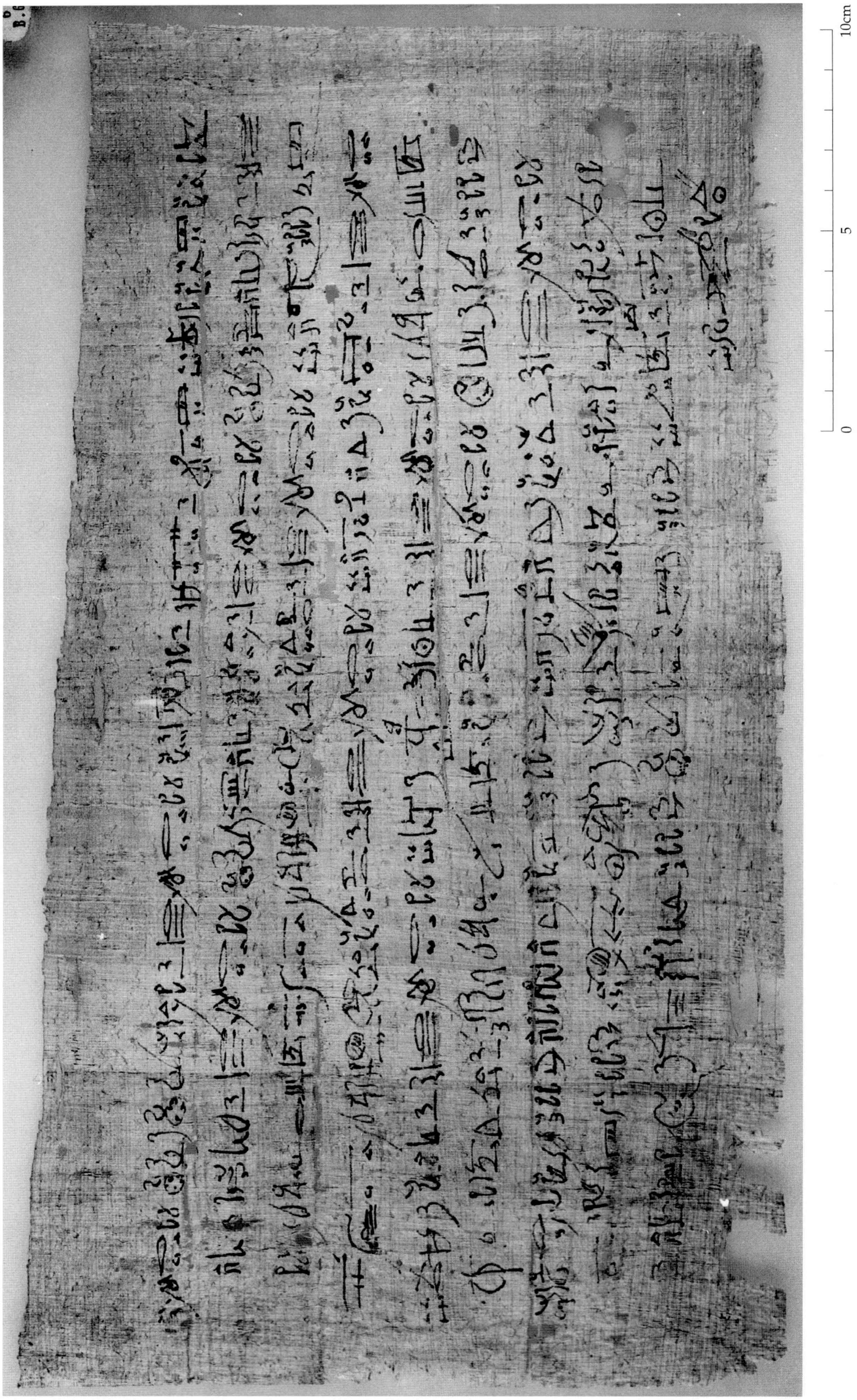

P. BM EA 10124 recto

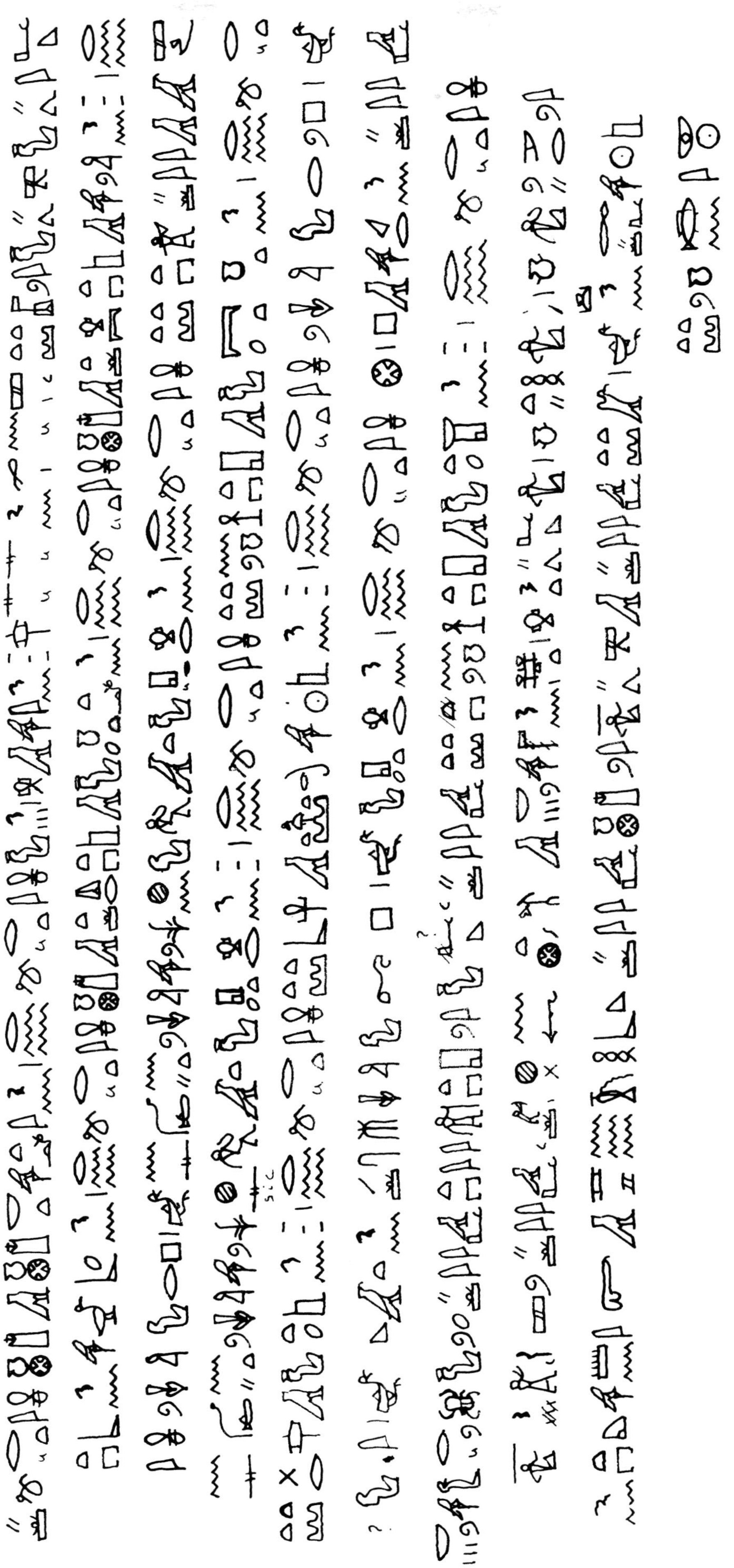

P. BM EA 10124 recto

P. BM EA 10124 verso

P. BM EA 10124 verso

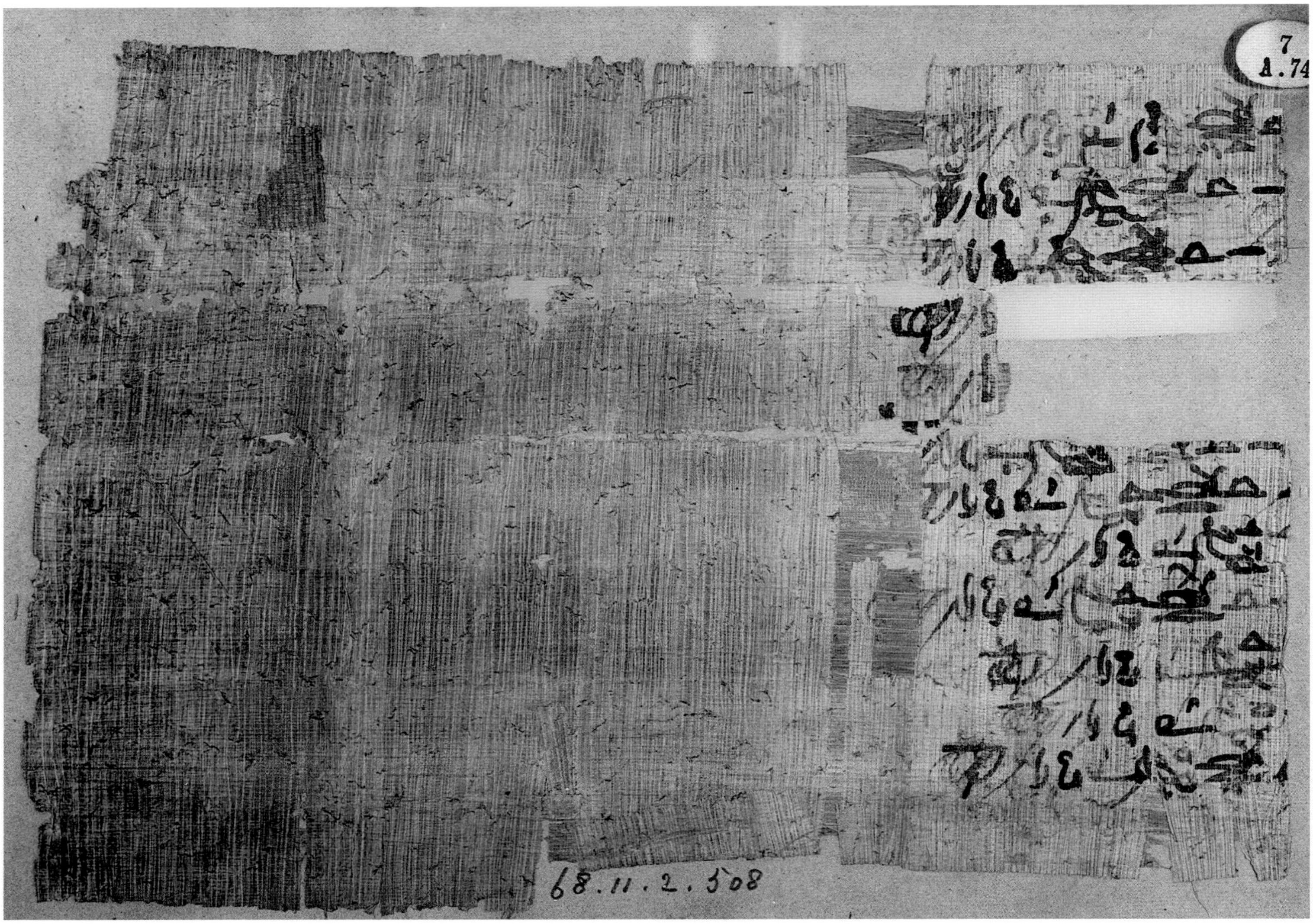

P. BM EA 10192 recto

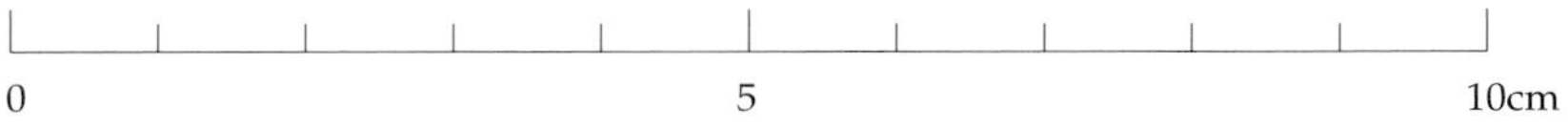

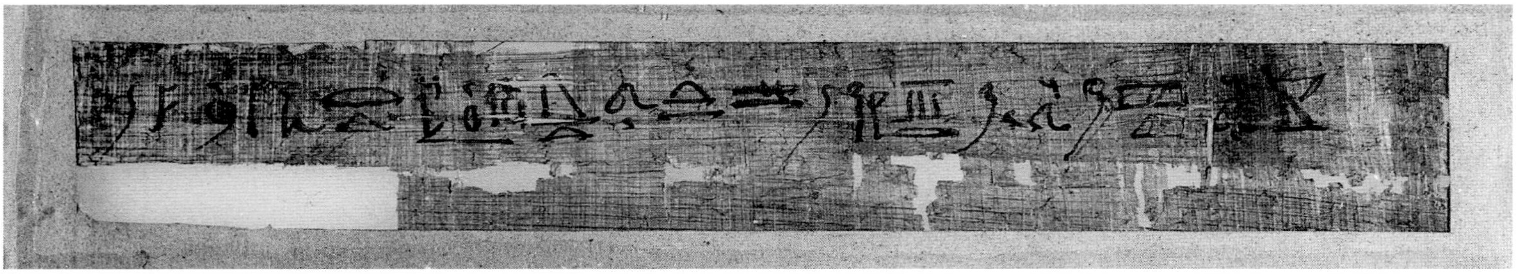

P. BM EA 10192 verso

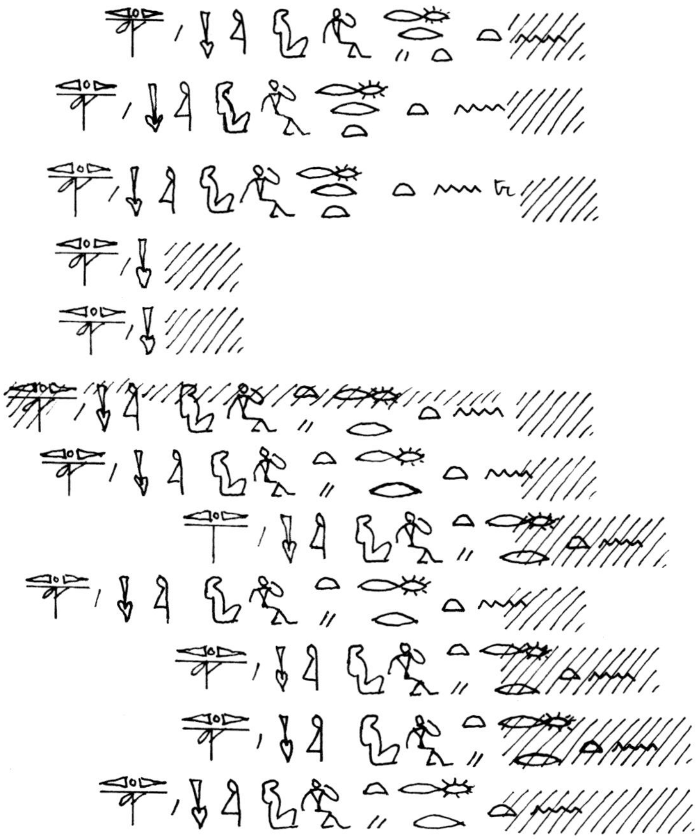

P. BM EA 10192 recto

P. BM EA 10192 verso

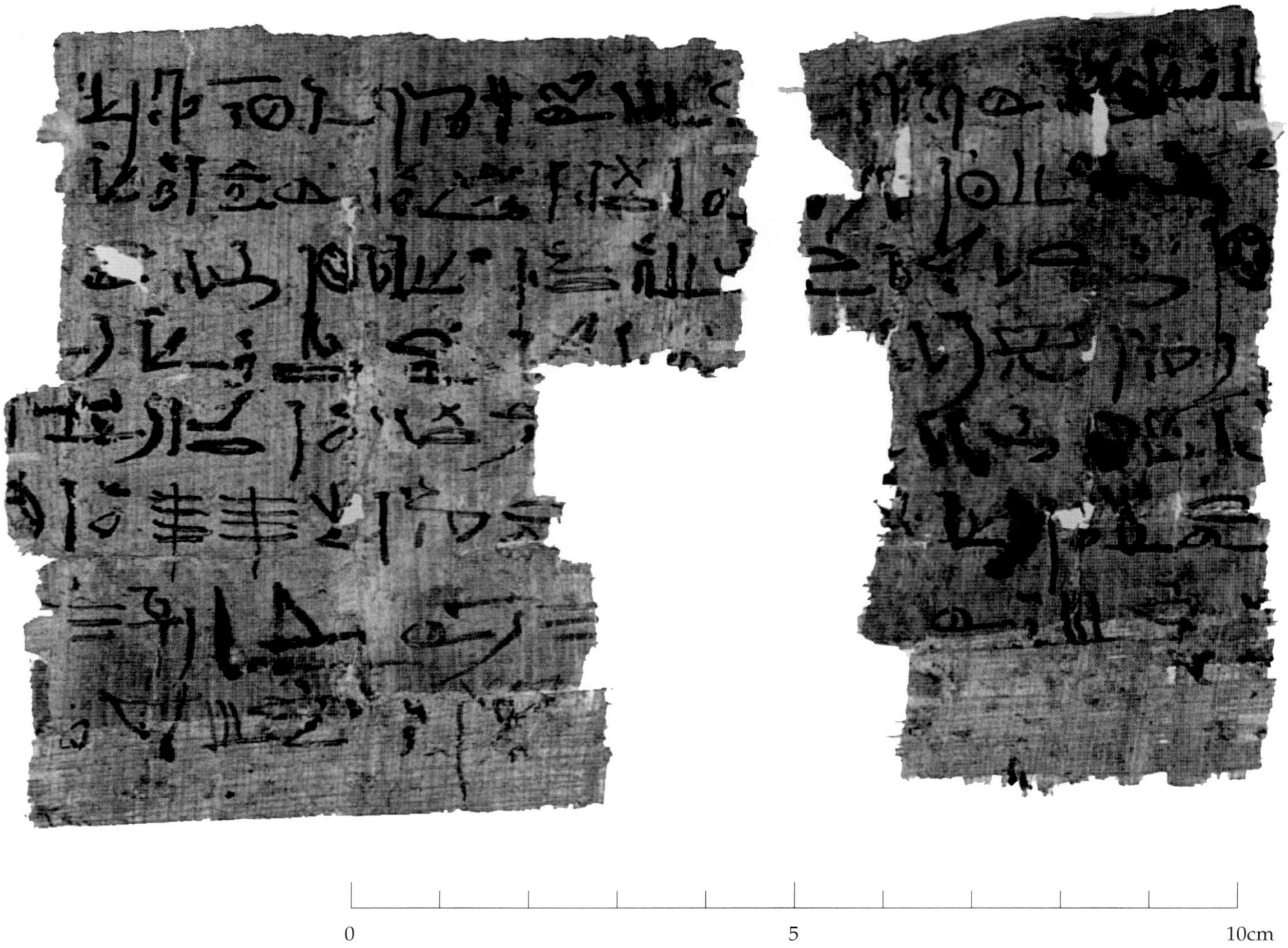

P. BM EA 10264

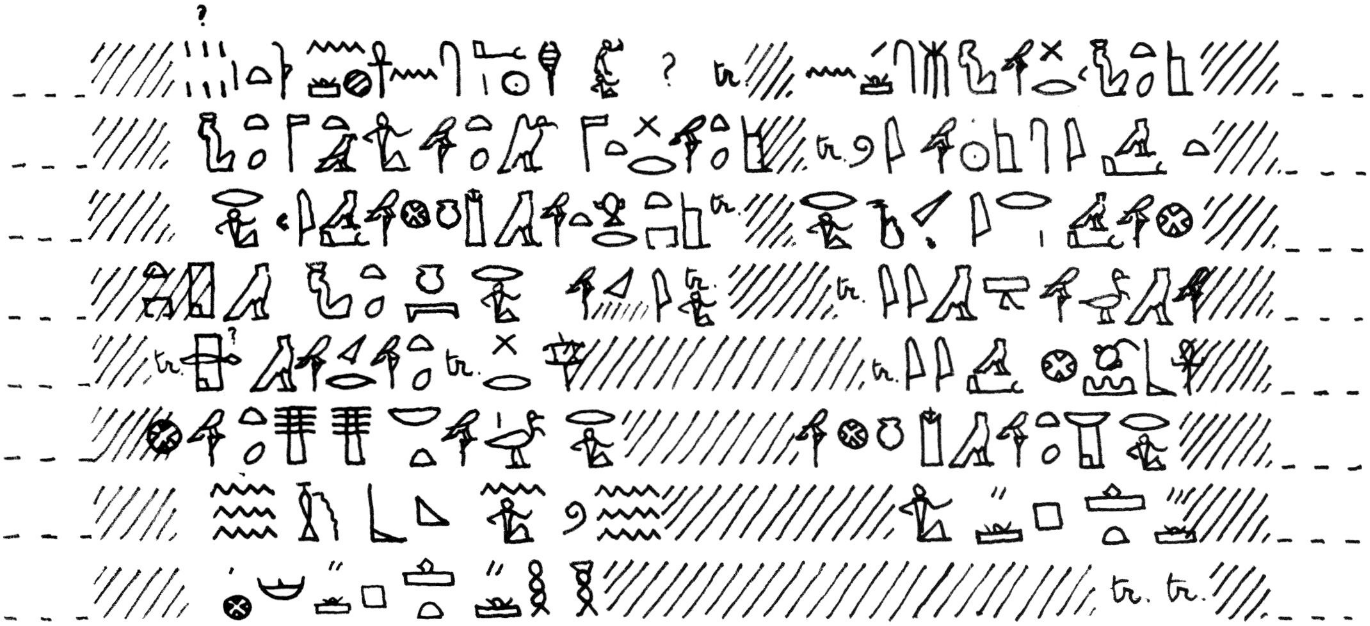

P. BM EA 10264

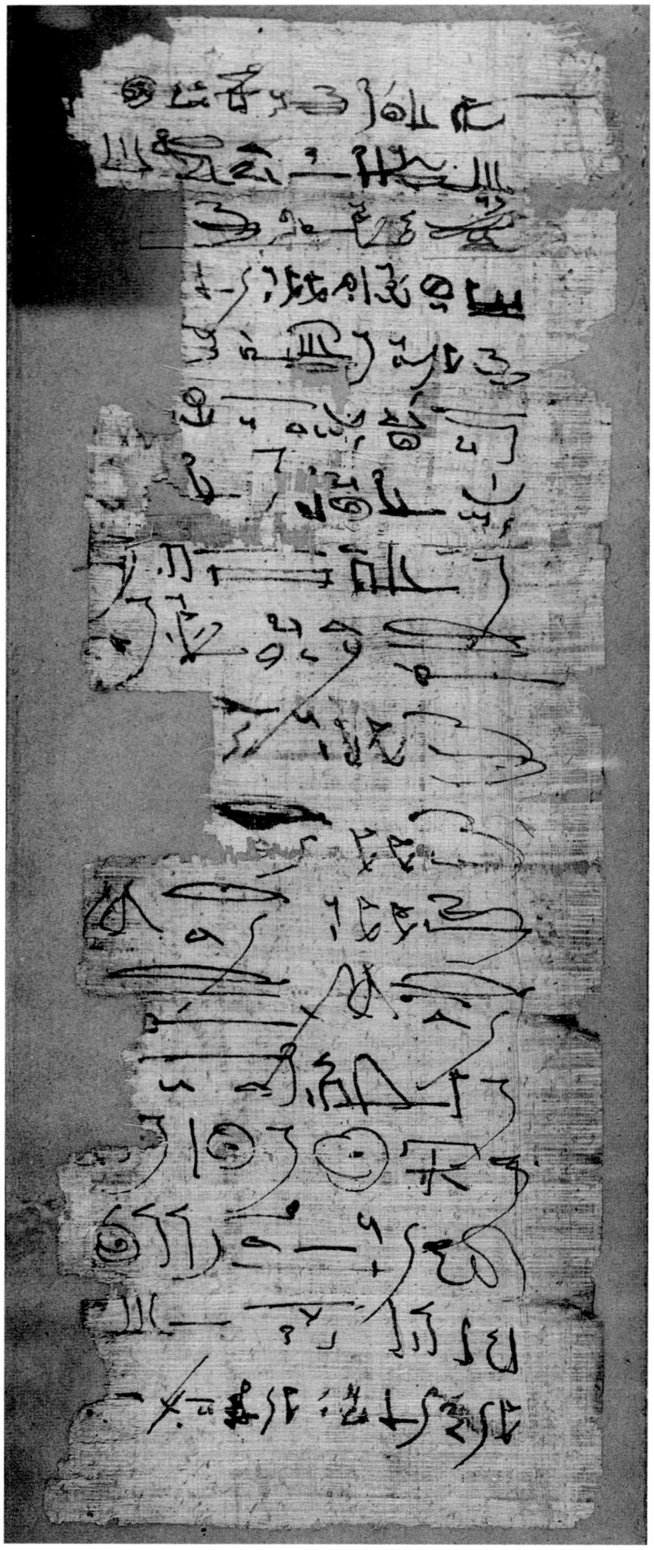

P. BM EA 10275 recto

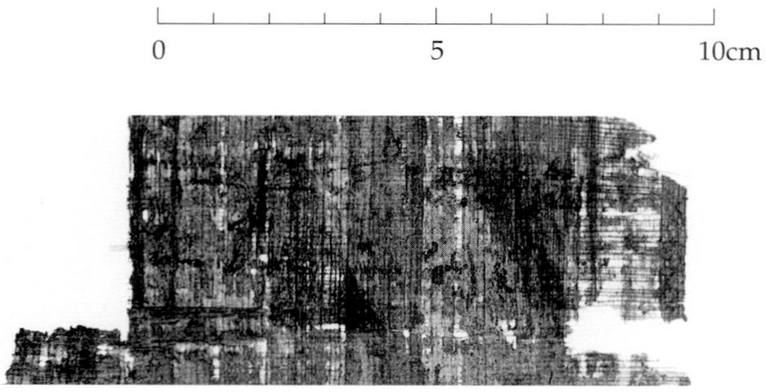

P. BM EA 10275 verso

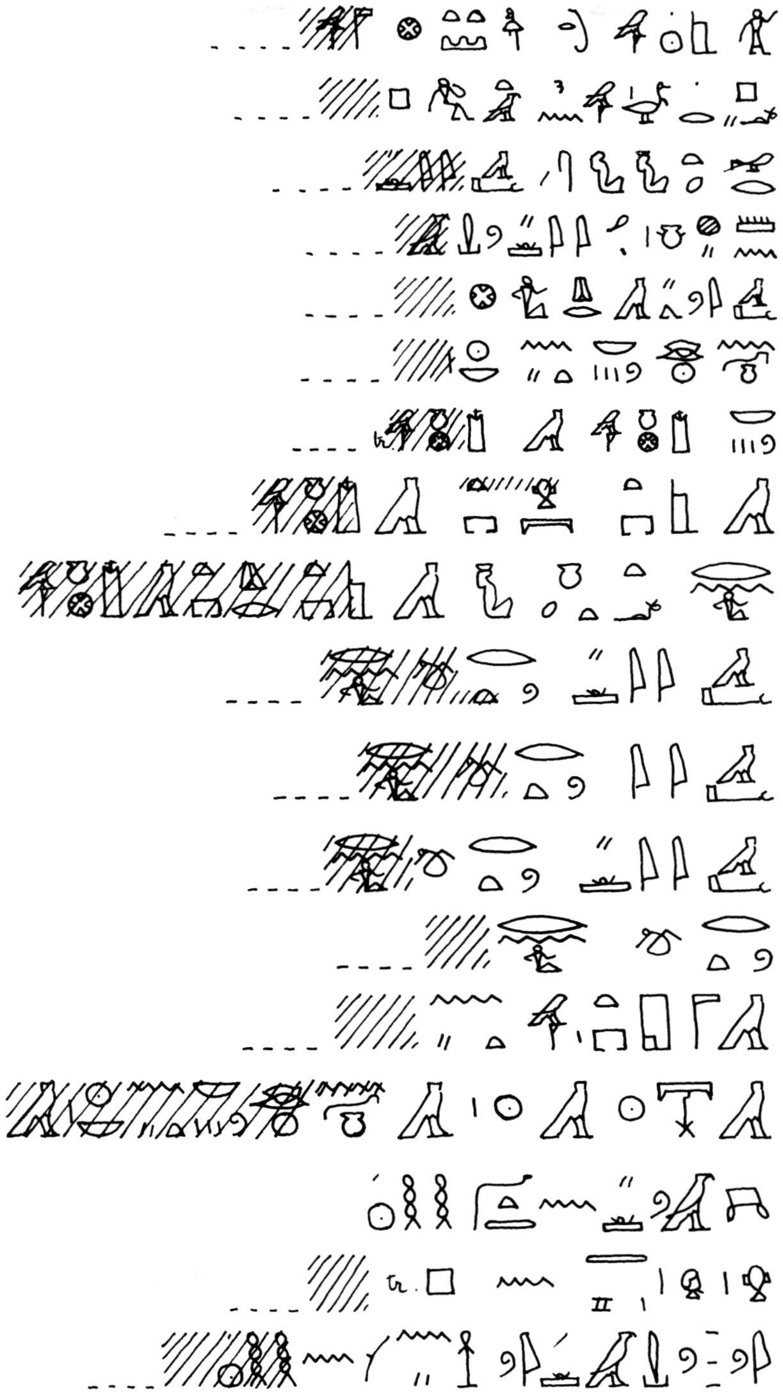

P. BM EA 10275 recto

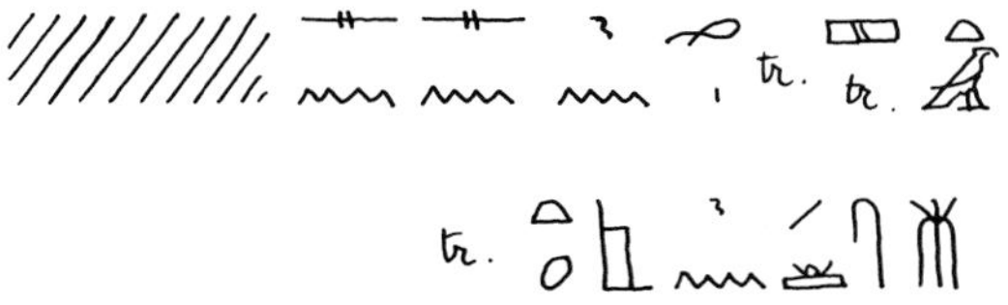

P. BM EA 10275 verso

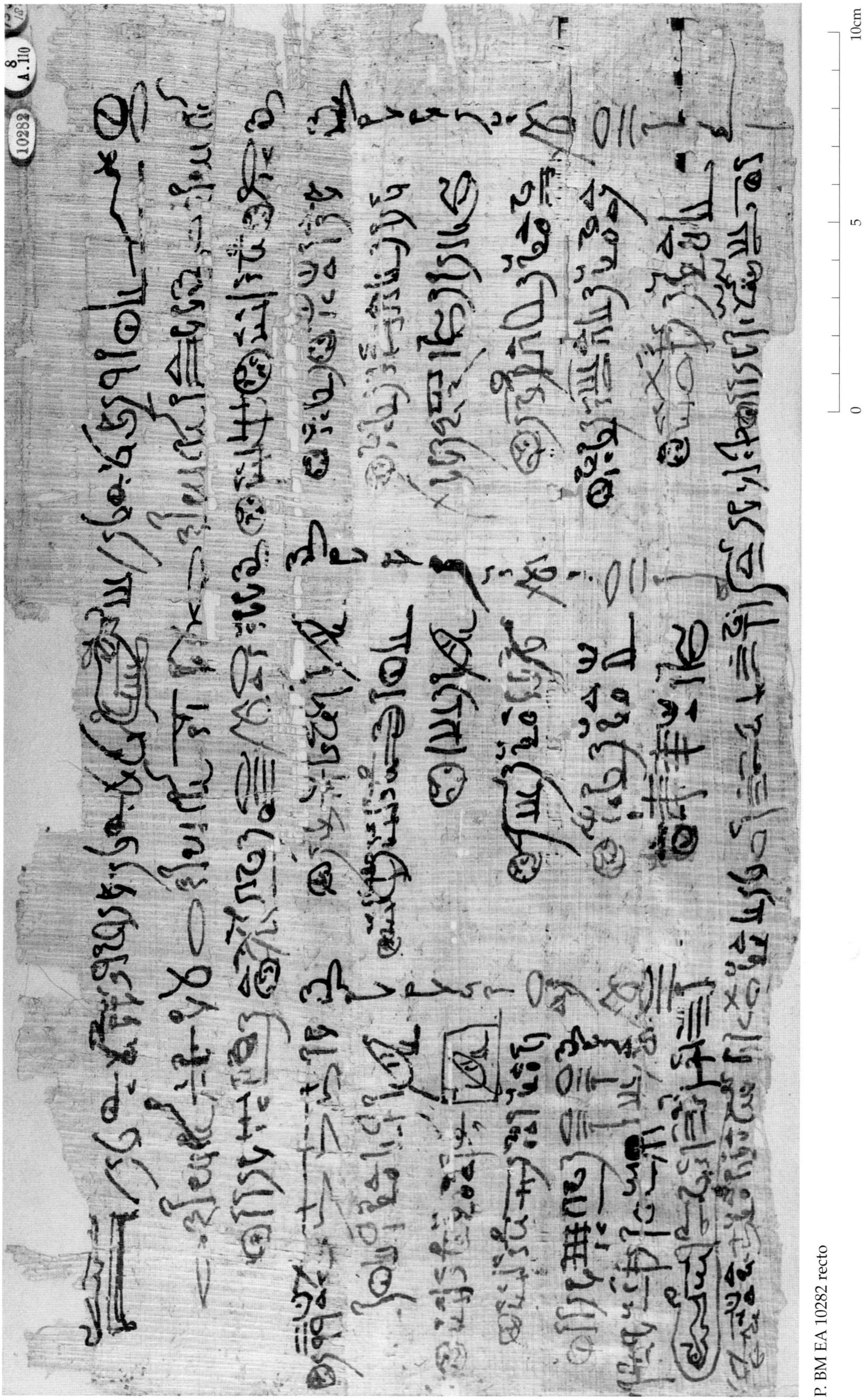

P. BM EA 10282 recto

P. BM EA 10282 verso

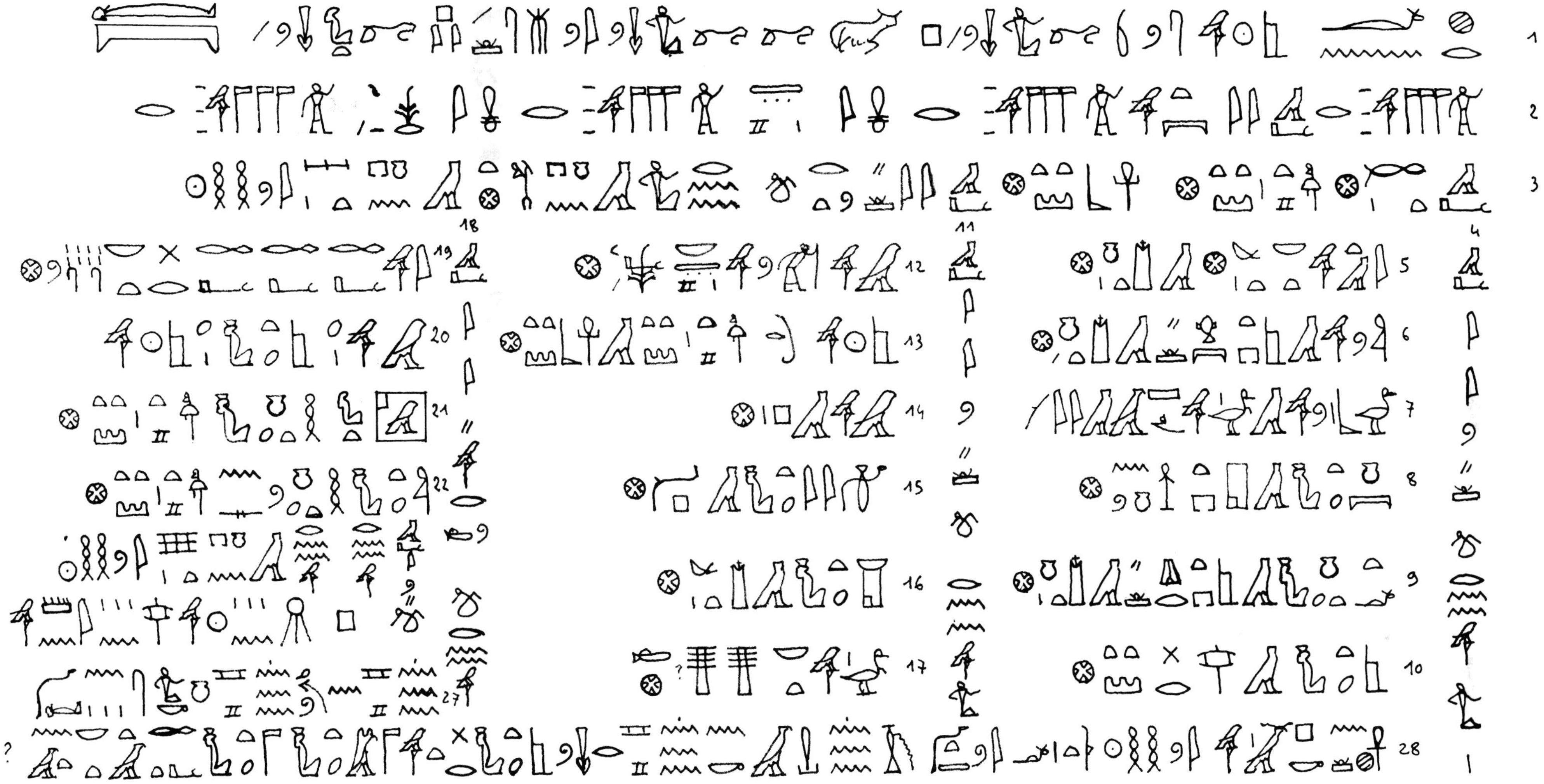

P. BM EA 10282 recto

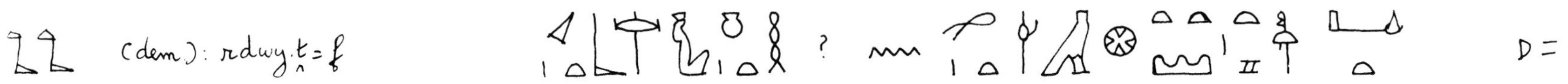

P. BM EA 10282 verso

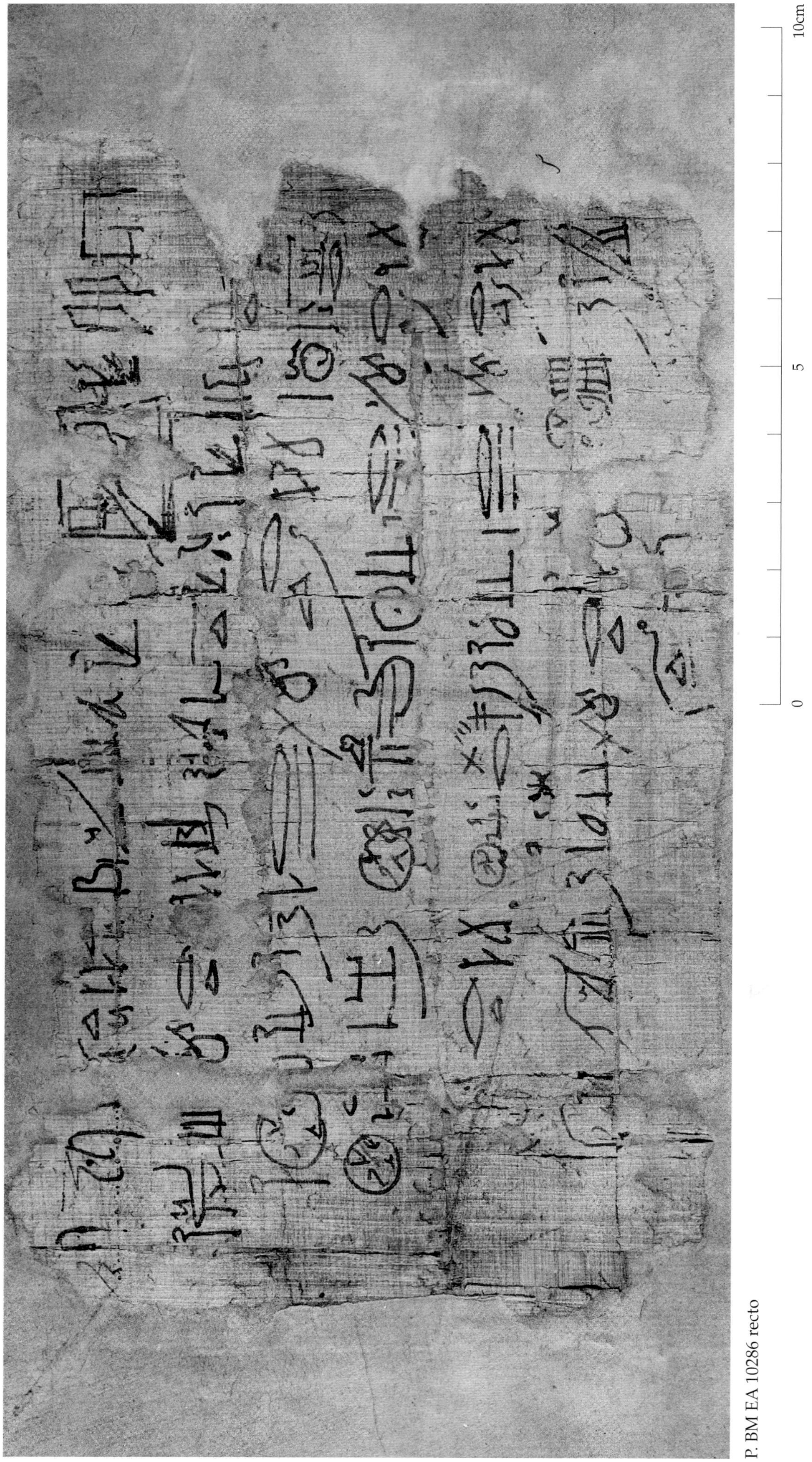

P. BM EA 10286 recto

P. BM EA 10286 verso

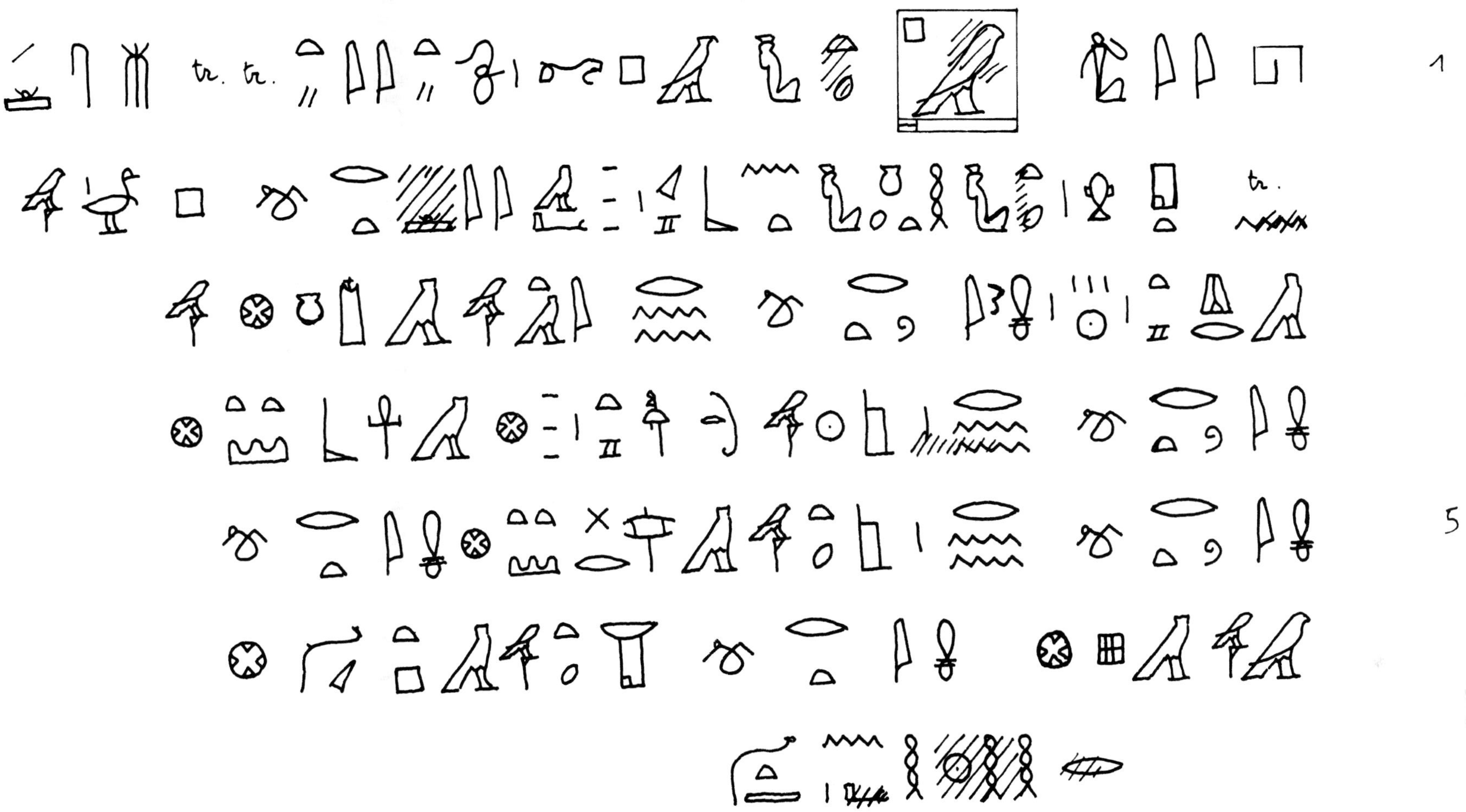

P. BM EA 10286 recto

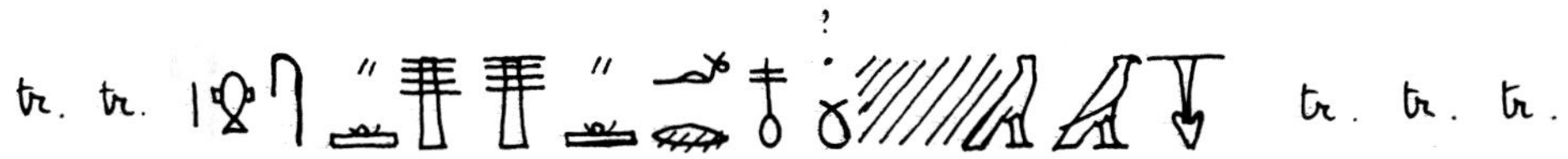

P. BM EA 10286 verso

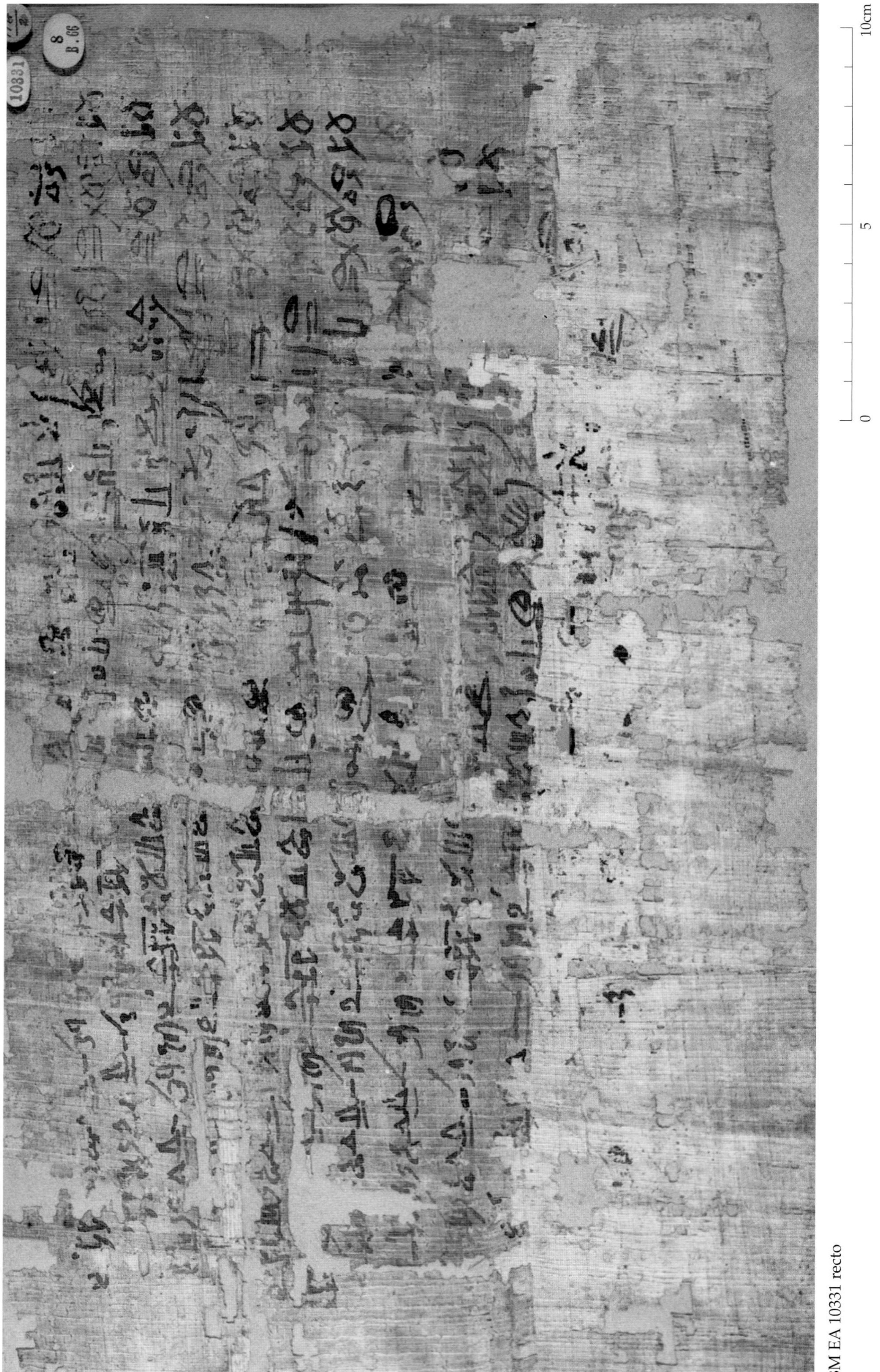

P. BM EA 10331 recto

P. BM EA 10331 verso

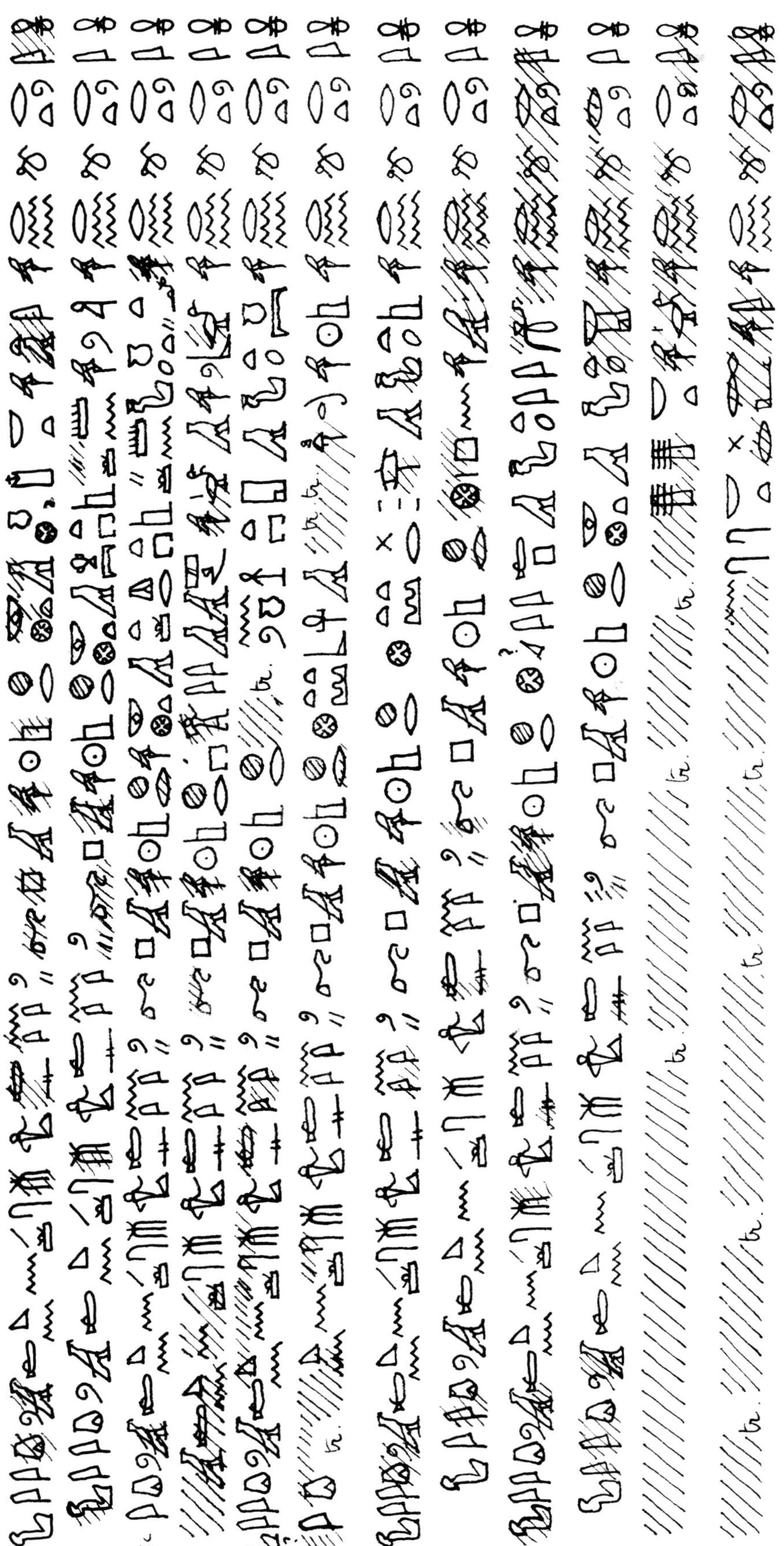

P. BM EA 10331 recto

P. BM EA 10331 verso

P. BM EA 71513D recto

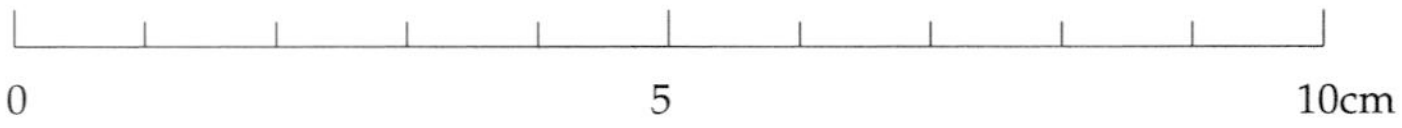

P. BM EA 71513D verso

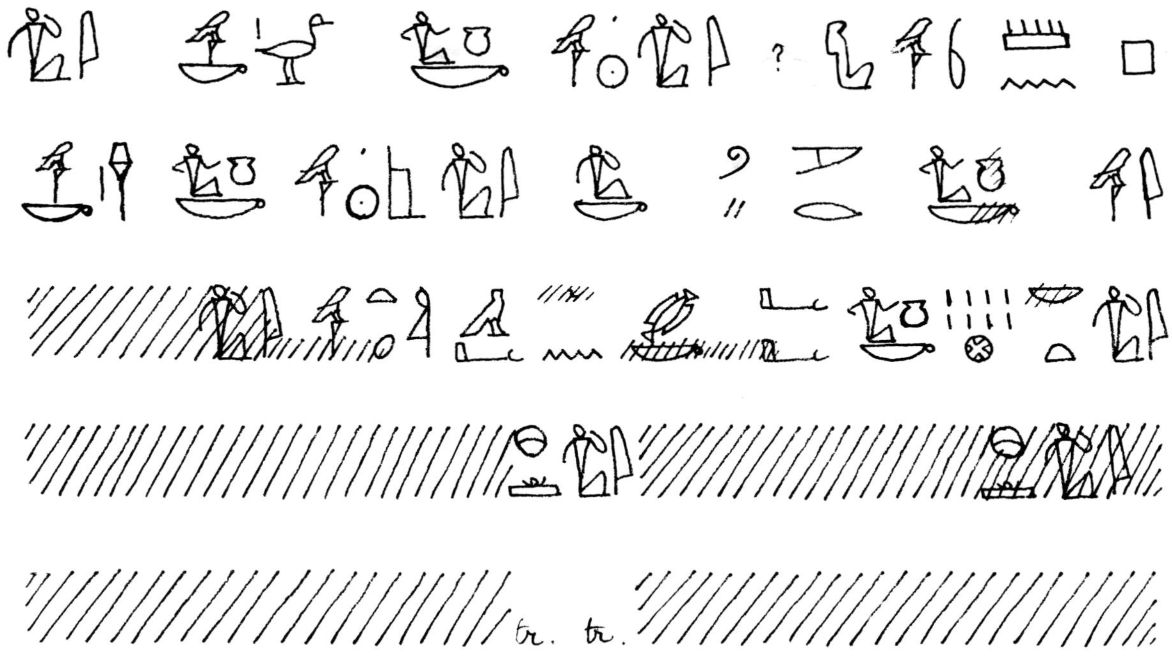

x + 1

x + 5

P. BM EA 71513D recto

P. BM EA 71513D verso

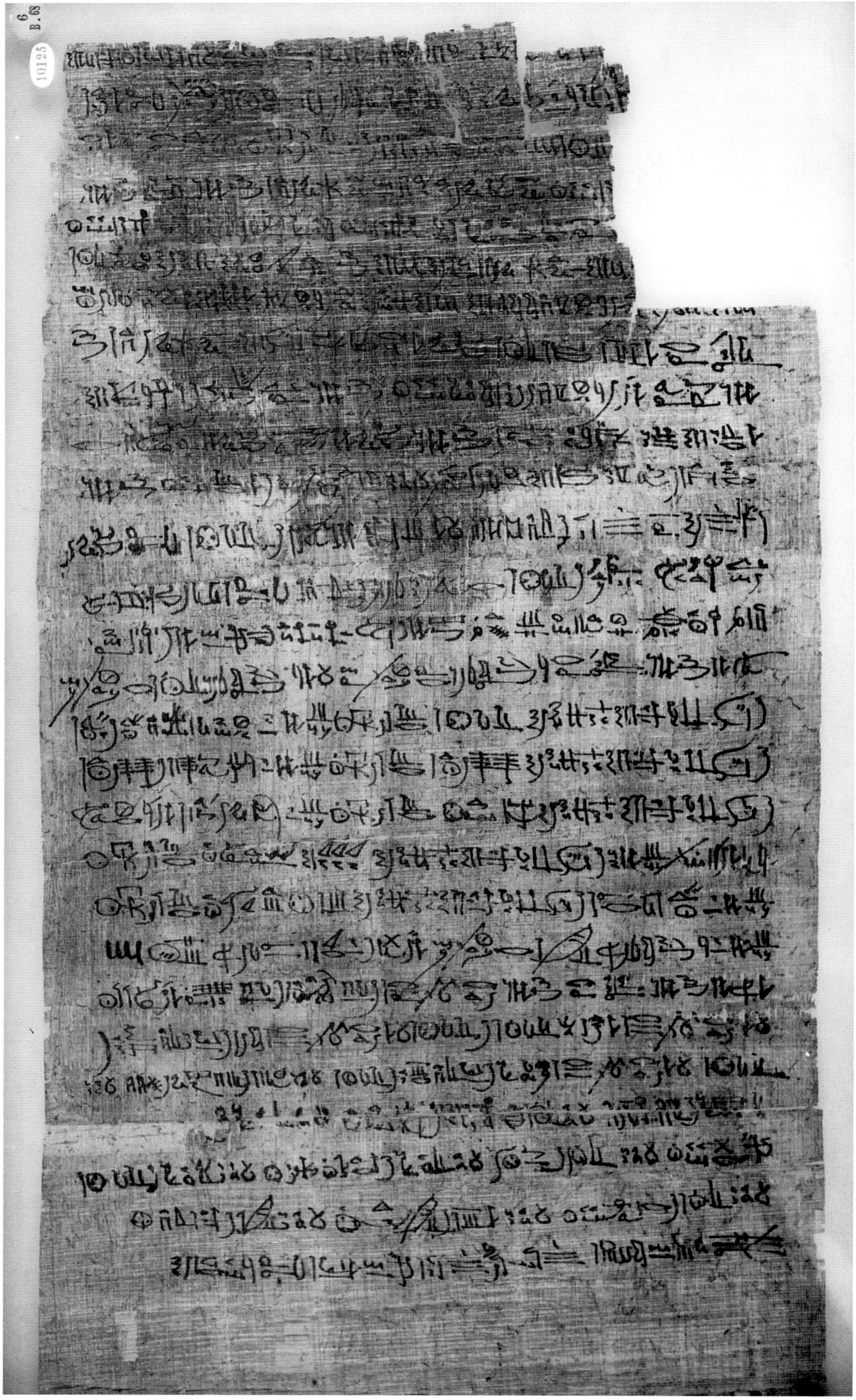

P. BM EA 10125 recto

0 5 10cm

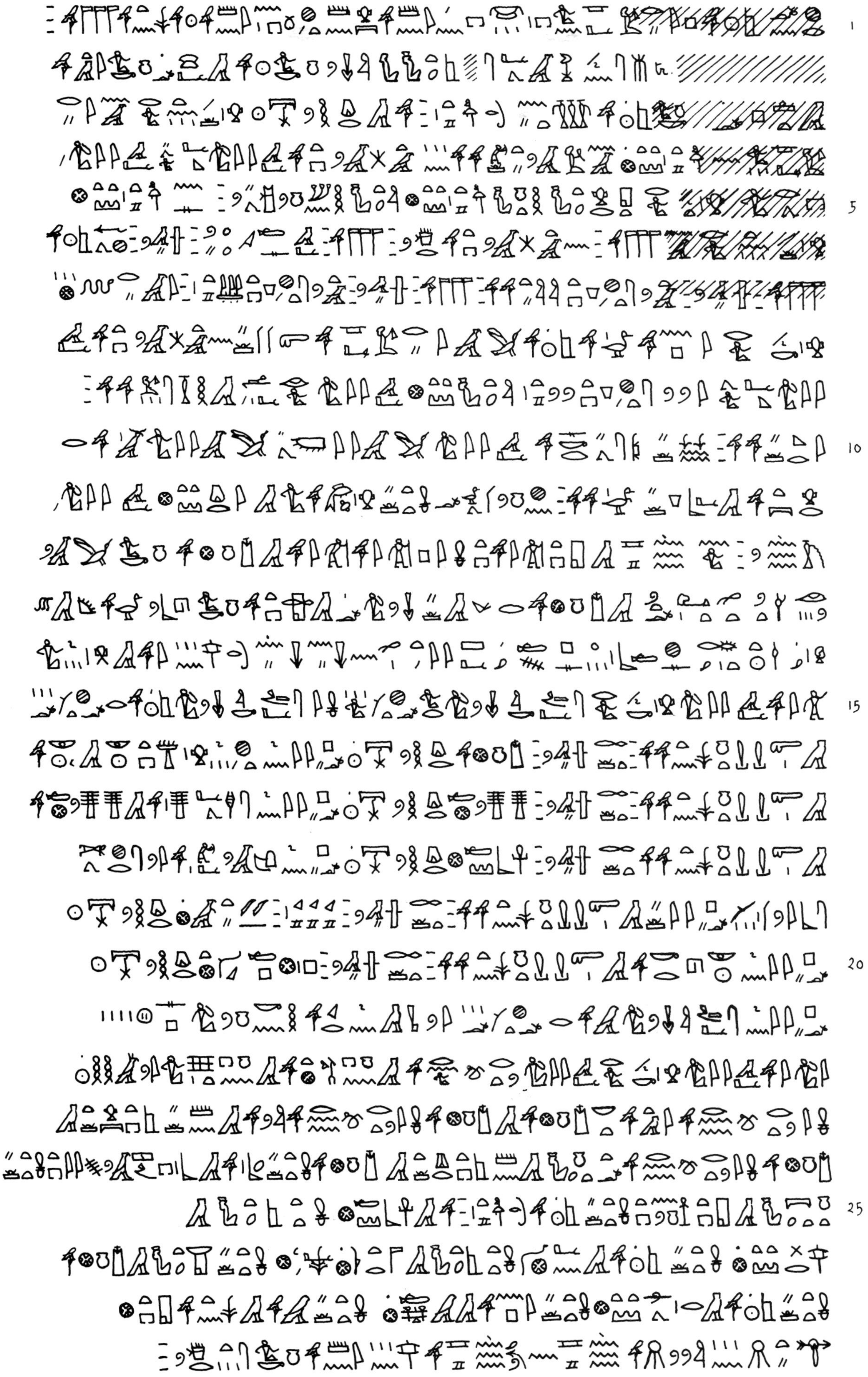

P. BM EA 10125 recto

P. BM EA 10125 verso

P. BM EA 10125 verso

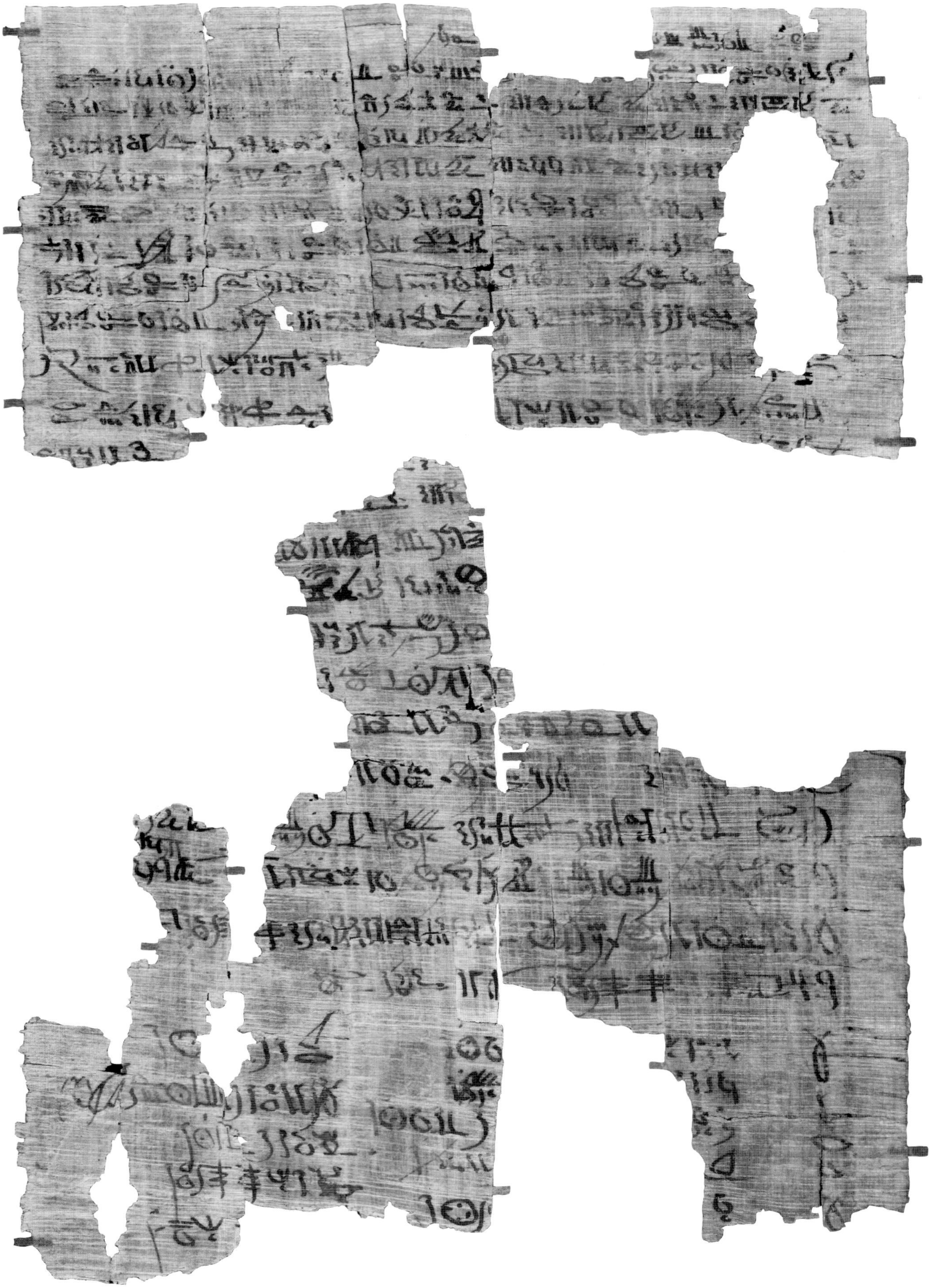

P. BM EA 71513A recto

0 5 10cm

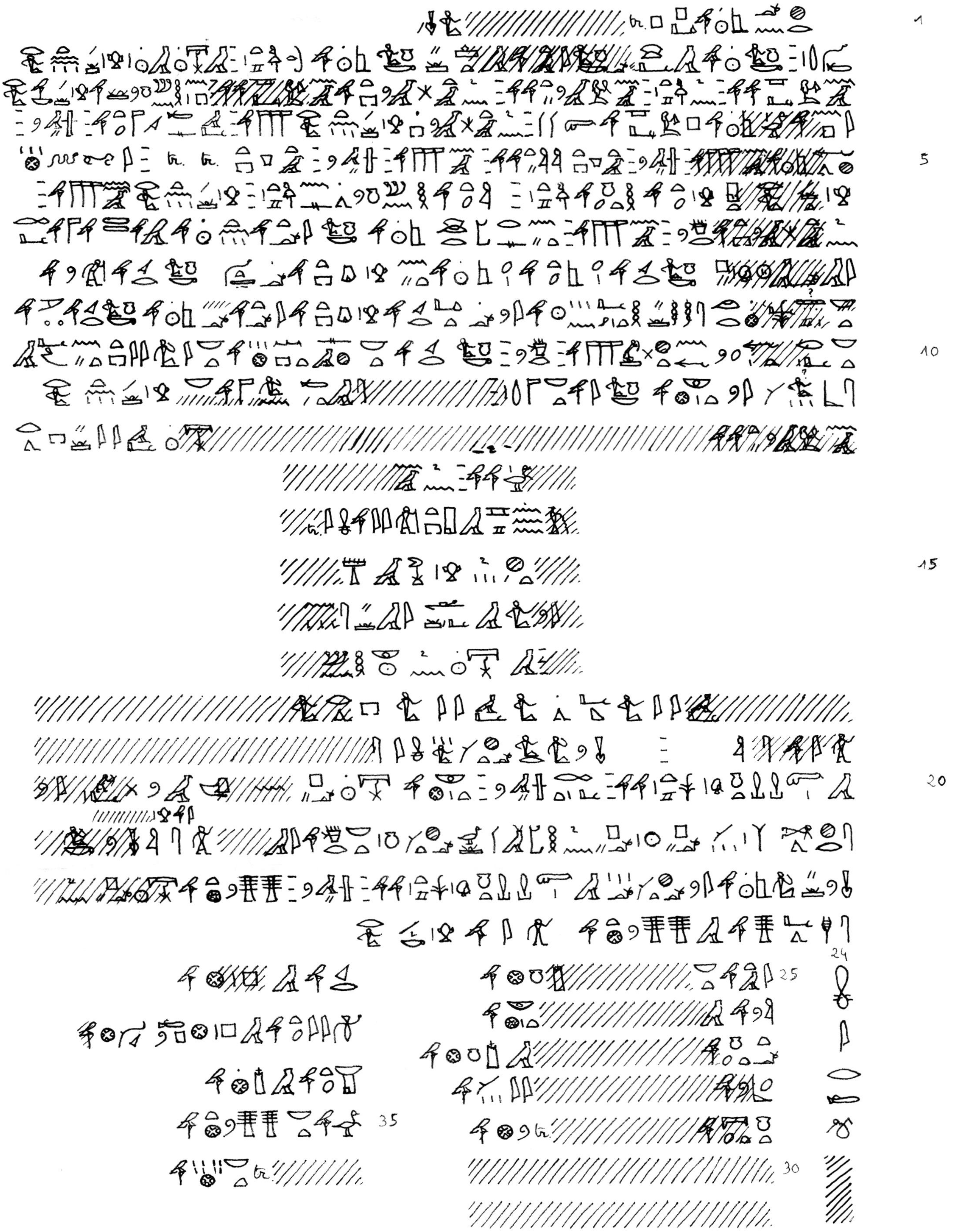

P. BM EA 71513A recto

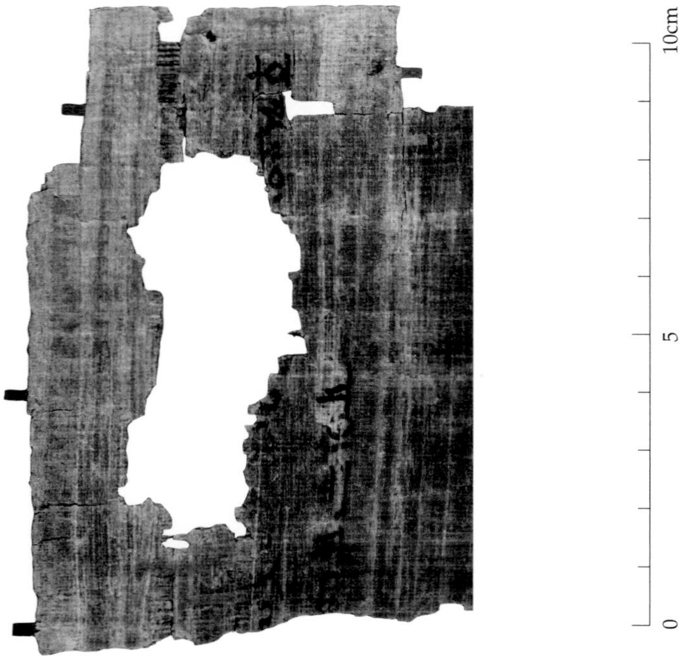

P. BM EA 71513A verso

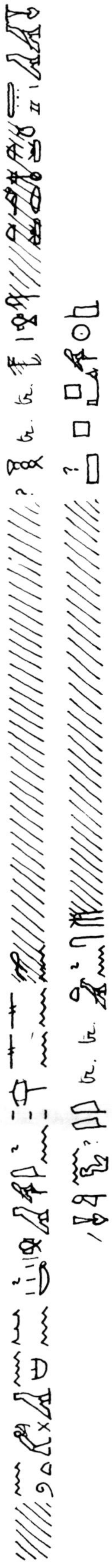

P. BM EA 71513A verso

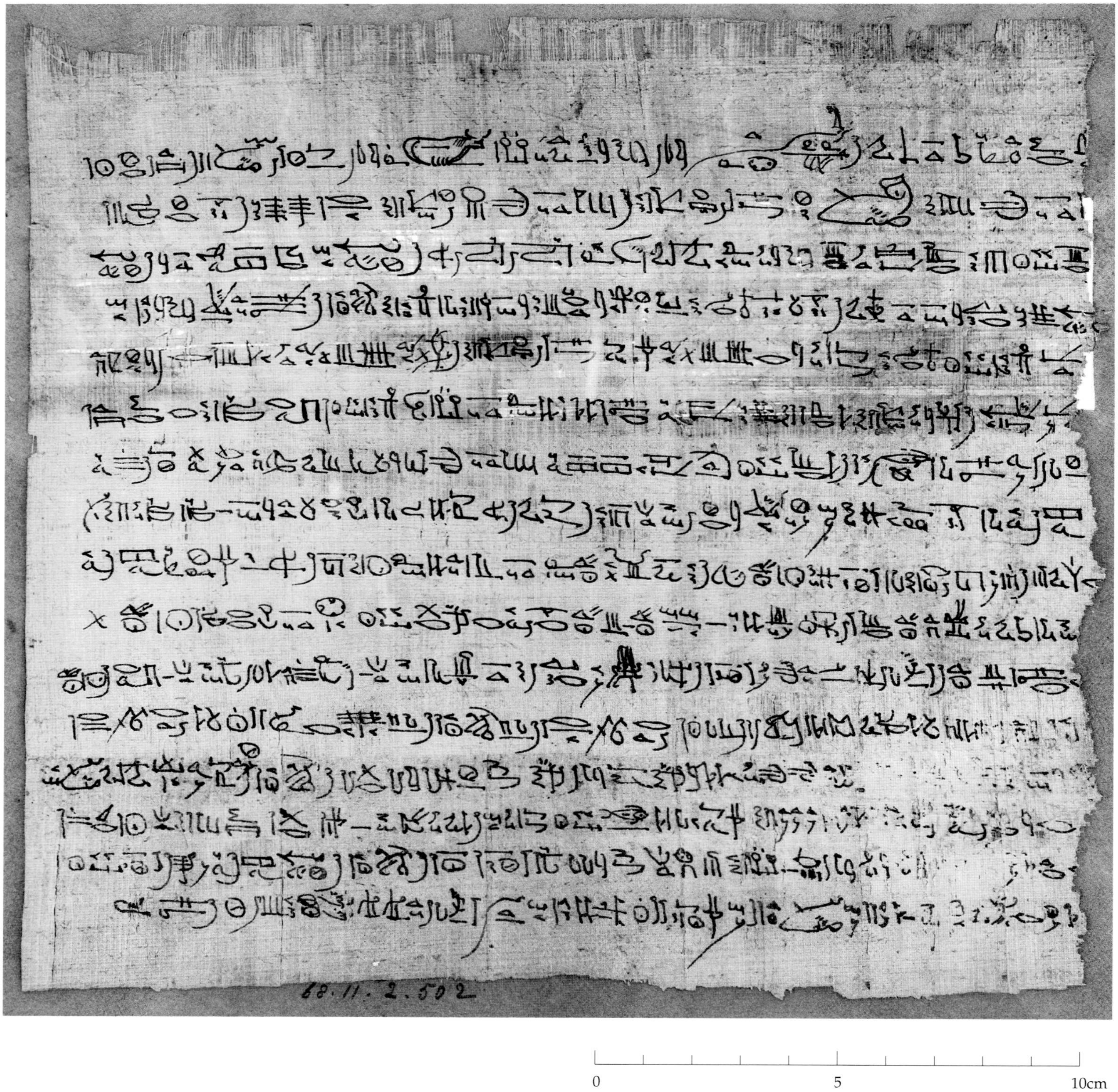

P. BM EA 10108 recto

P. BM EA 10108 recto

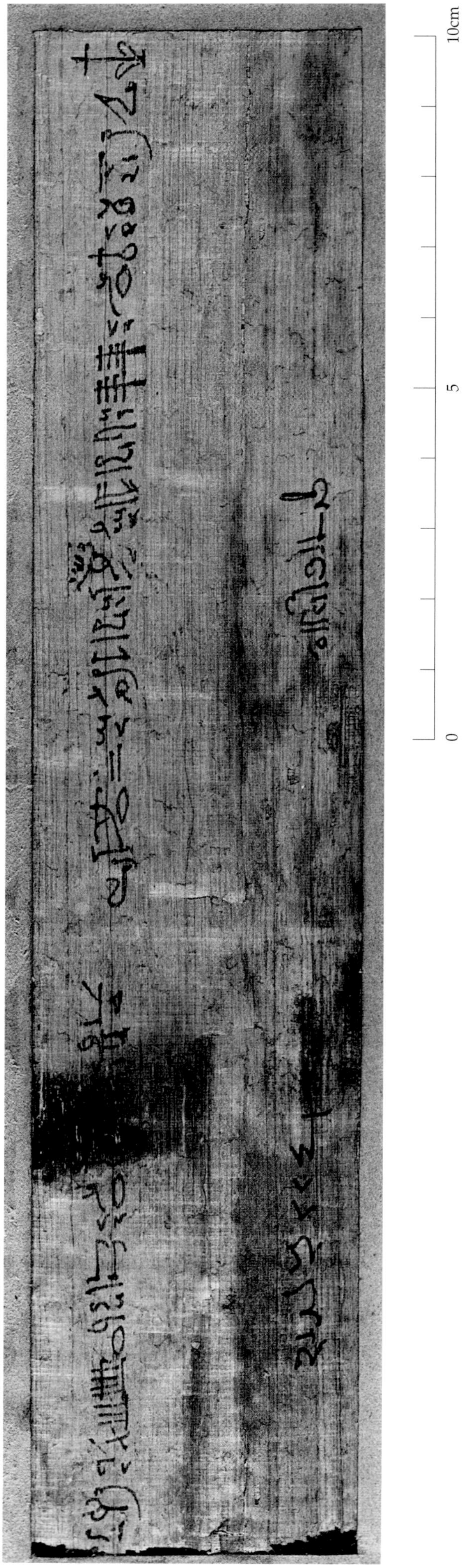

P. BM EA 10108 verso

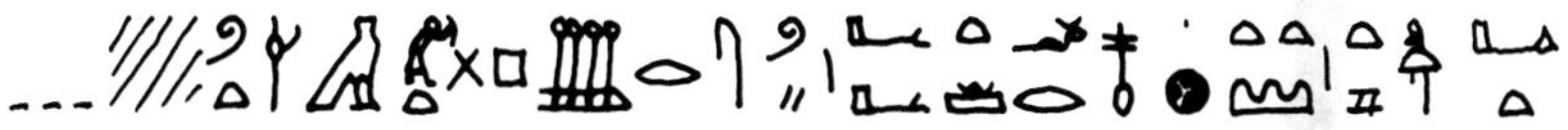

(dem.): rd.wy.ṯ=s

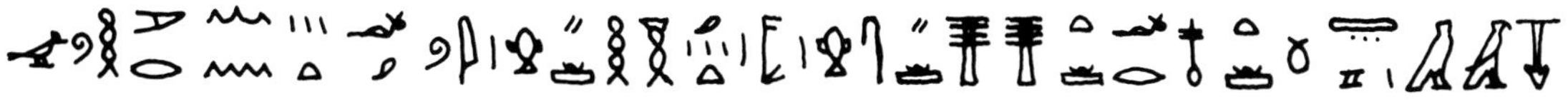

(dem.): Ta(-n.t)-Ḏm3ʿ

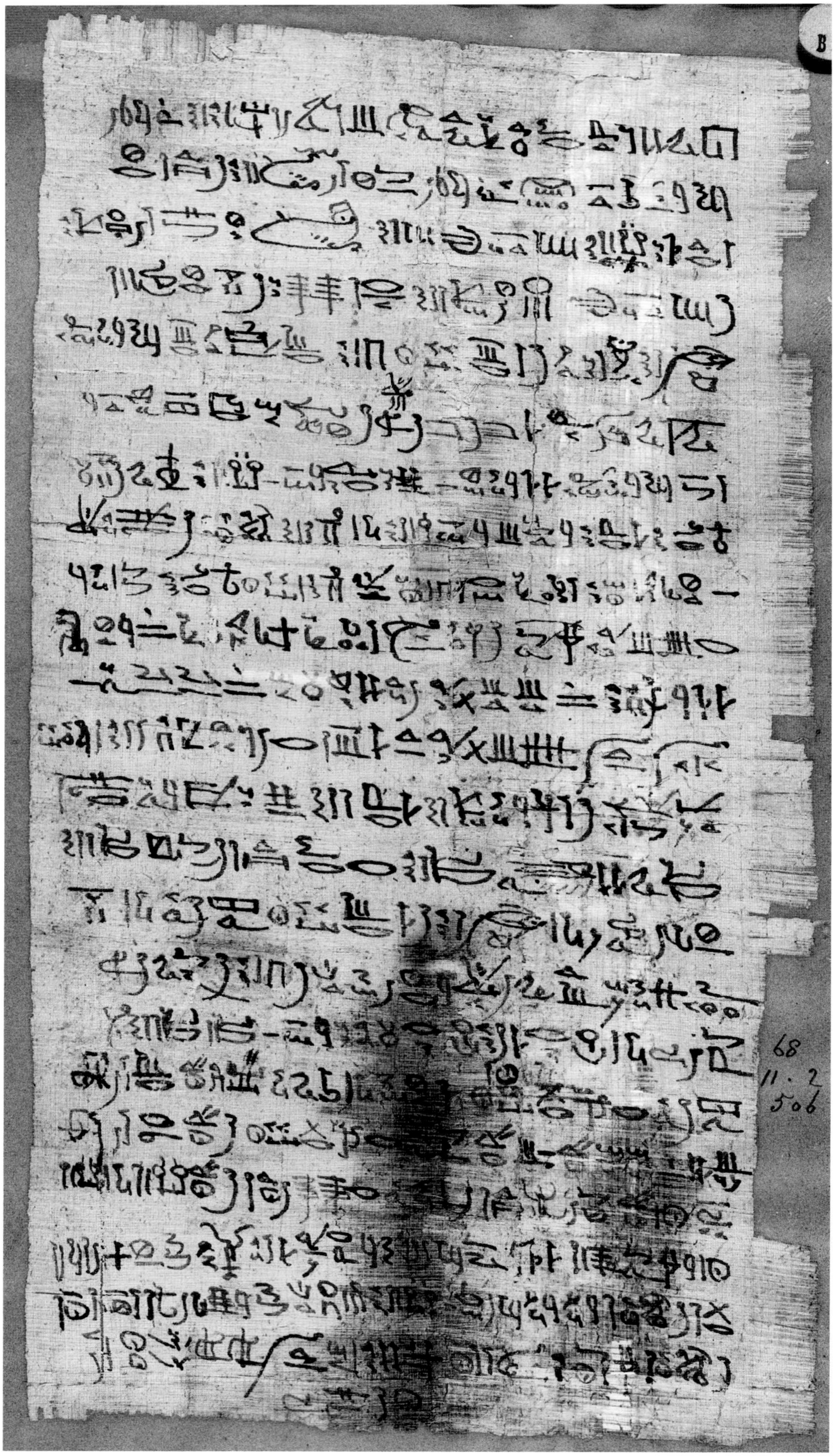

0 5 10cm

P. BM EA 10112 recto

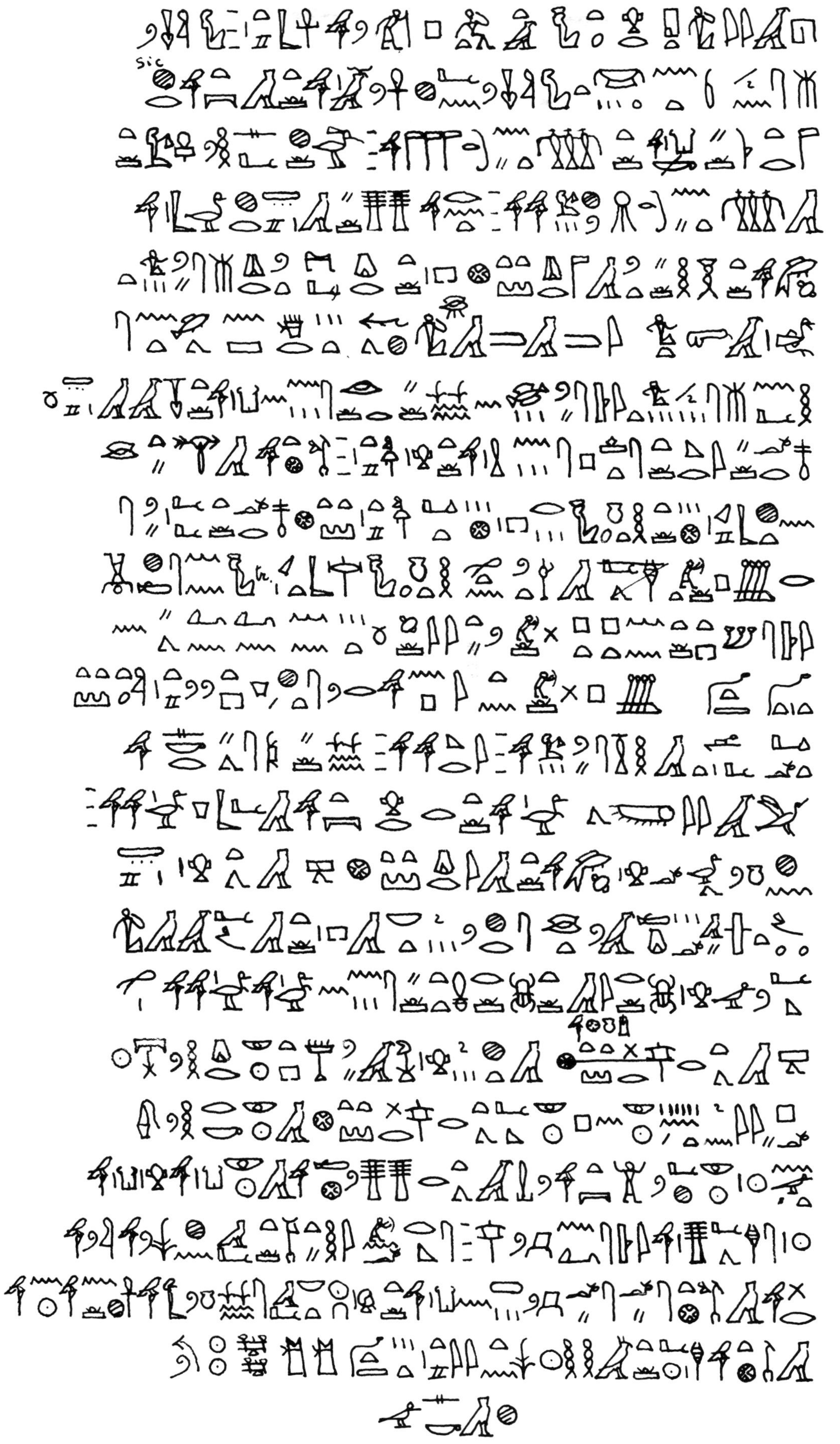

P. BM EA 10112 recto

P. BM EA 10112 verso

P. BM EA 10112 verso

P. BM EA 10115 recto

0 5 10cm

P. BM EA 10115 verso

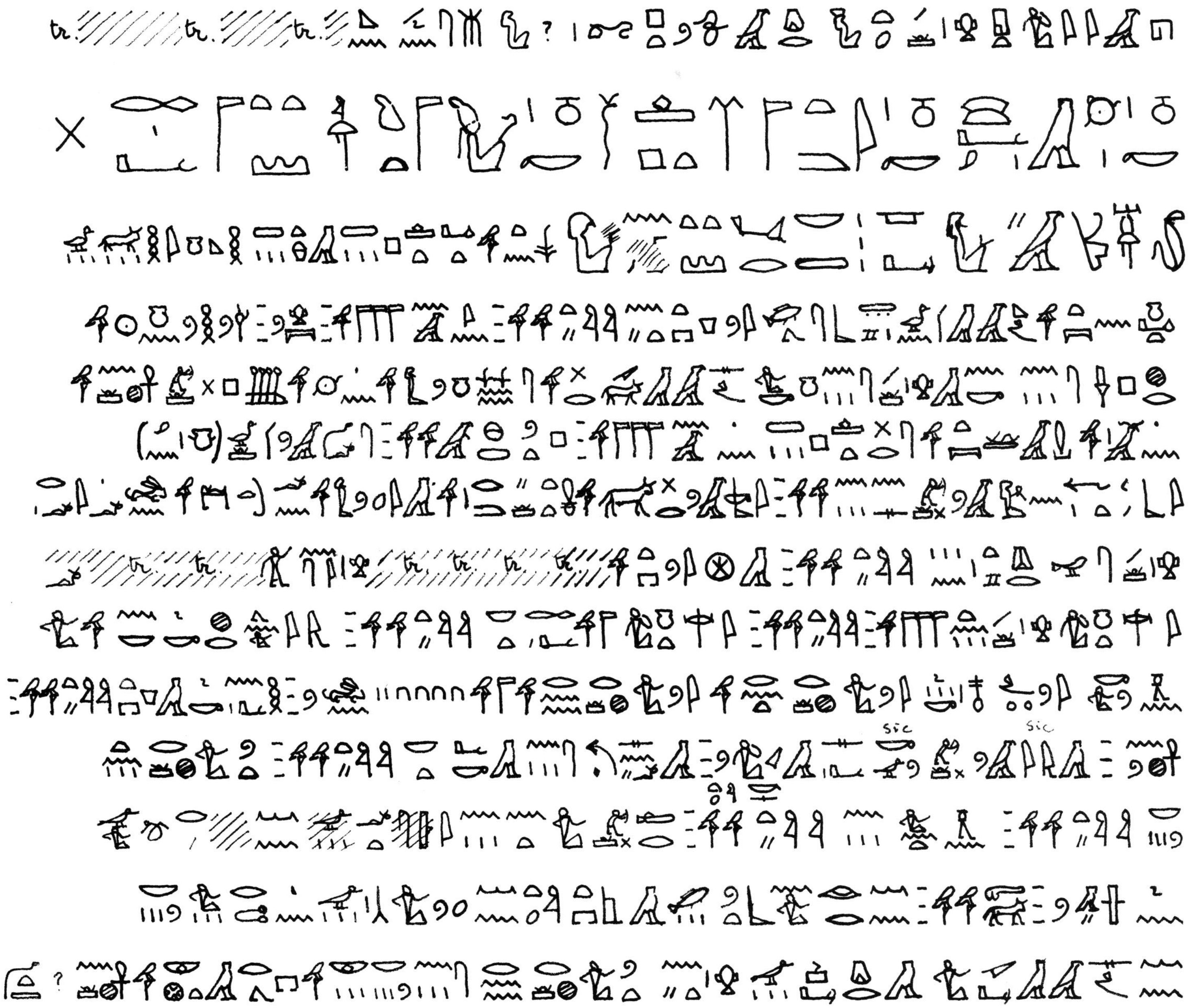

P. BM EA 10115 recto

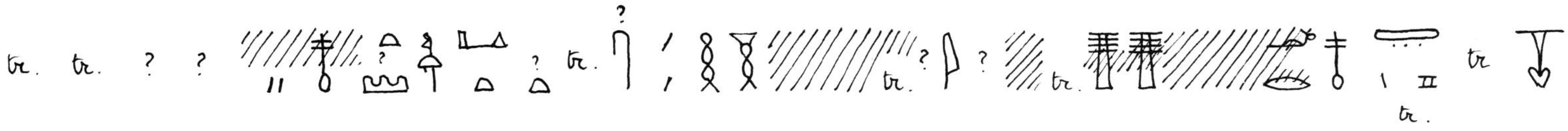

P. BM EA 10115 verso

P. BM EA 10116 recto

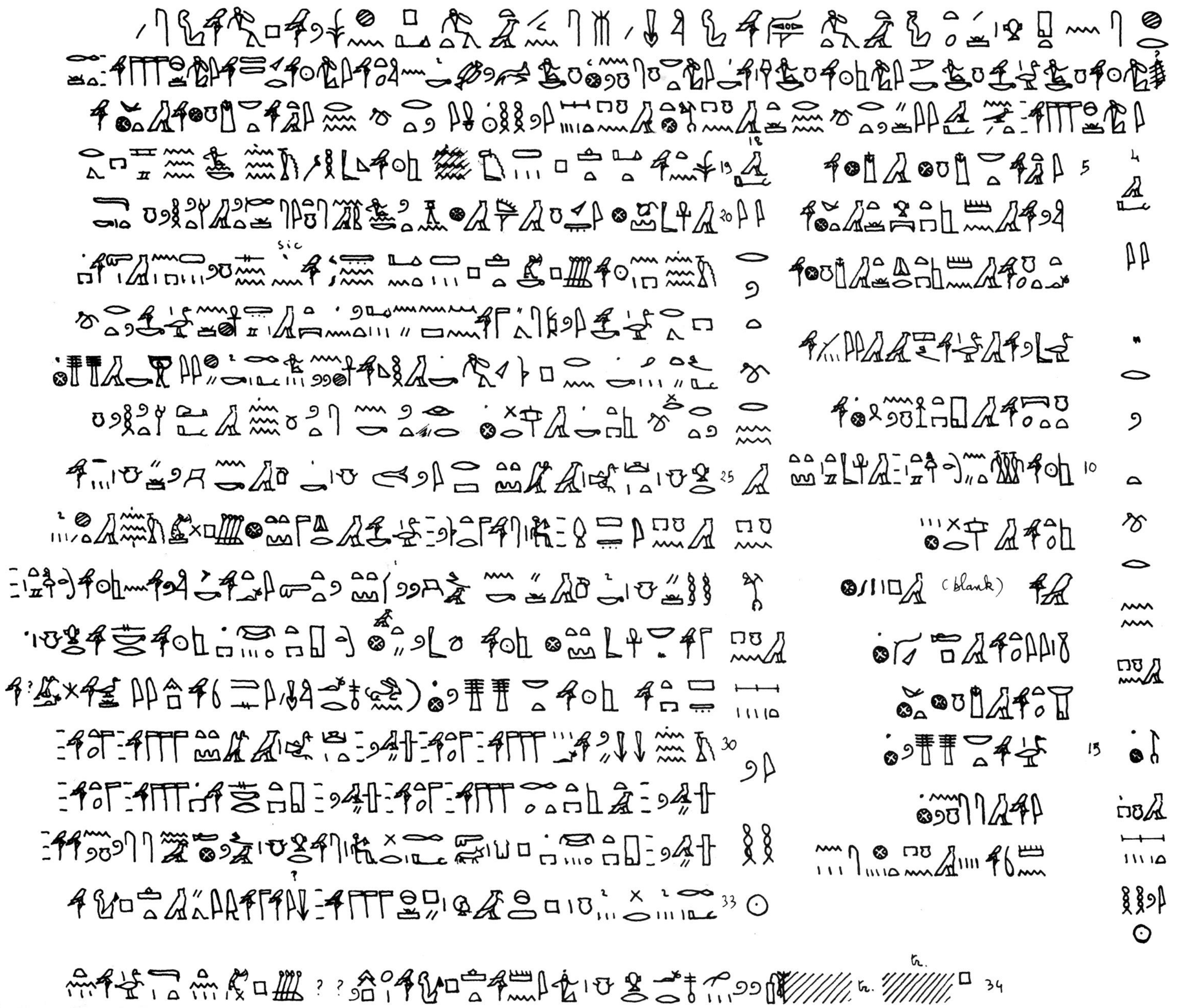

P. BM EA 10116 recto

P. BM EA 10116 verso

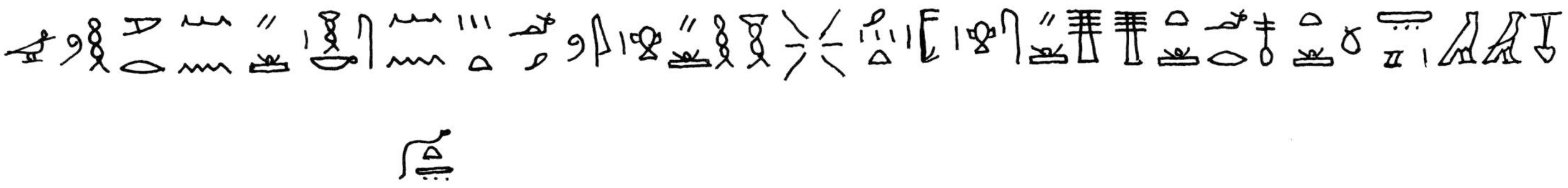

(dem) rd.wy.ṯ=s

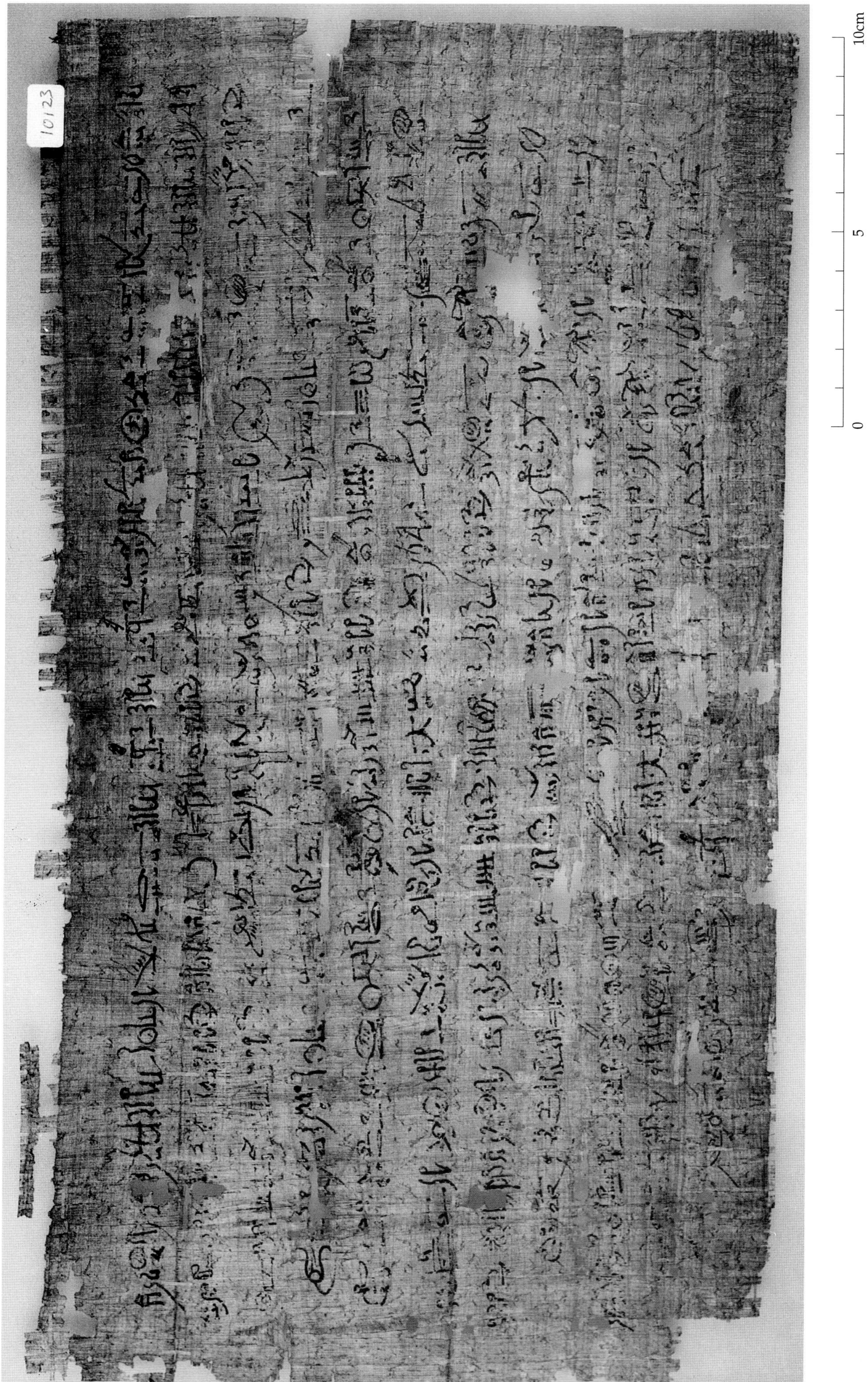

P. BM EA 10123 recto

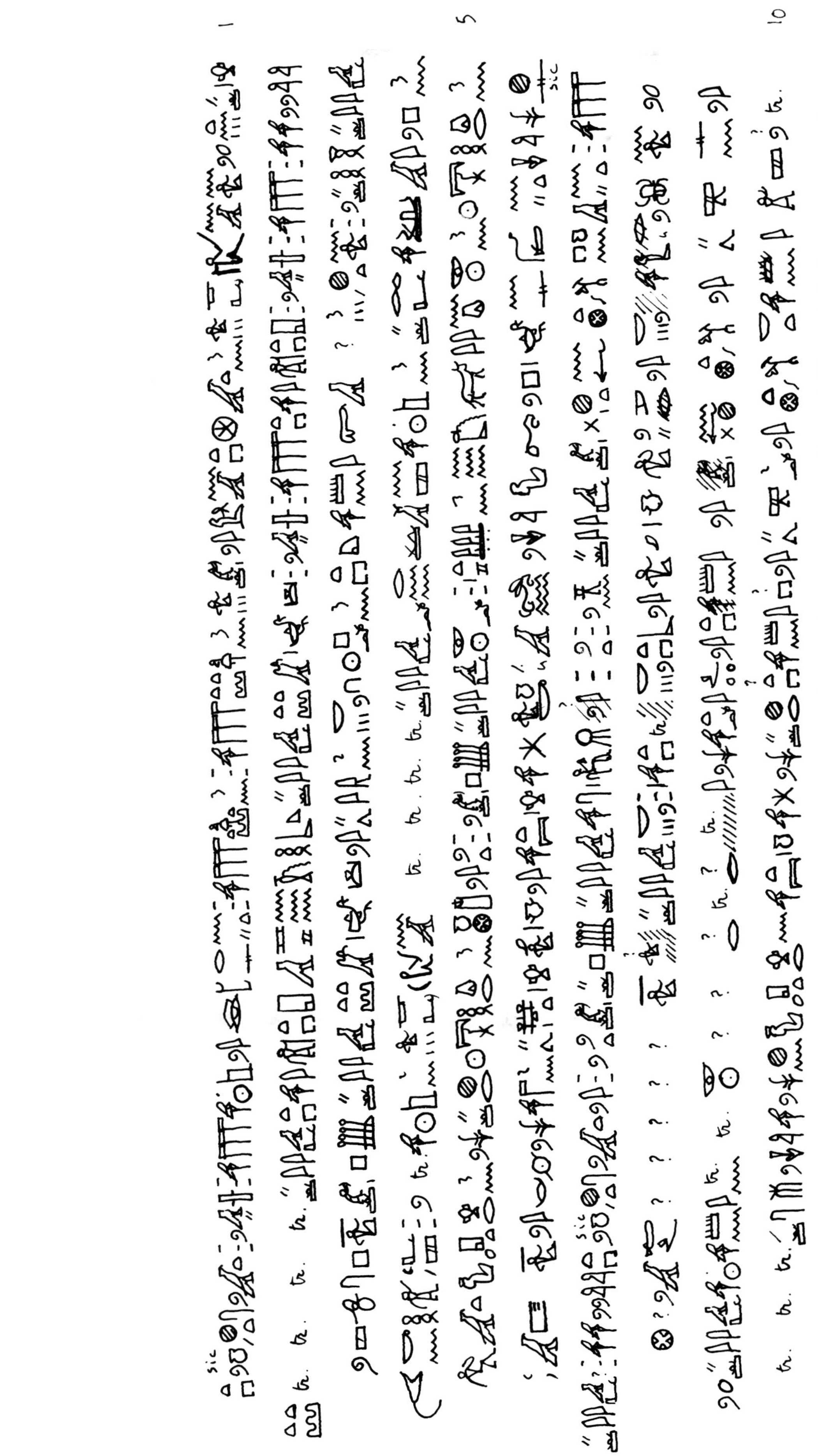

P. BM EA 10123 recto

P. BM EA 10123 verso

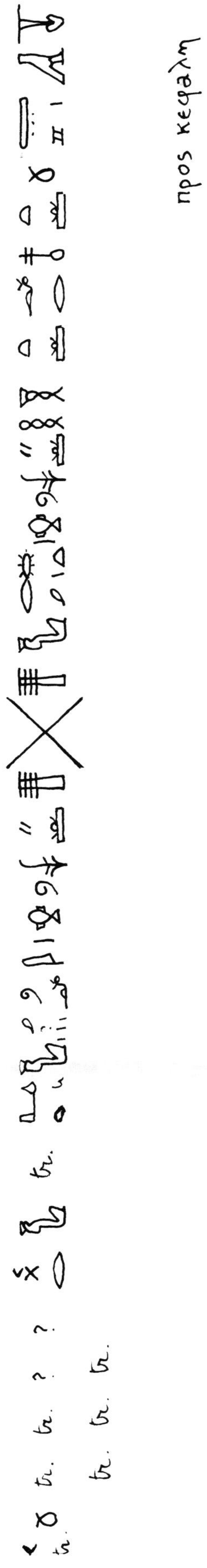

P. BM EA 10123 verso

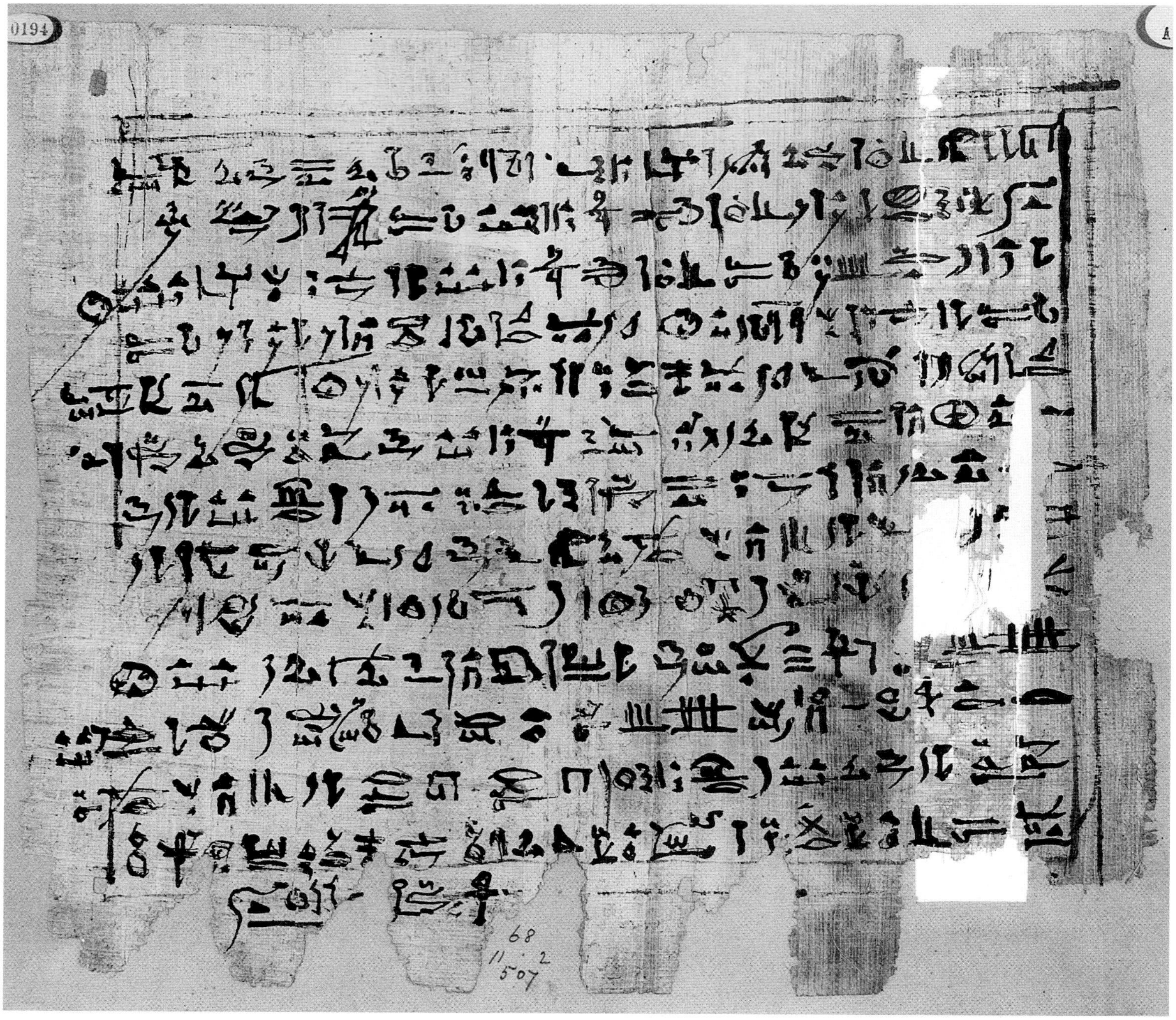

P. BM EA 10194 recto

0 5 10cm

P. BM EA 10194 verso

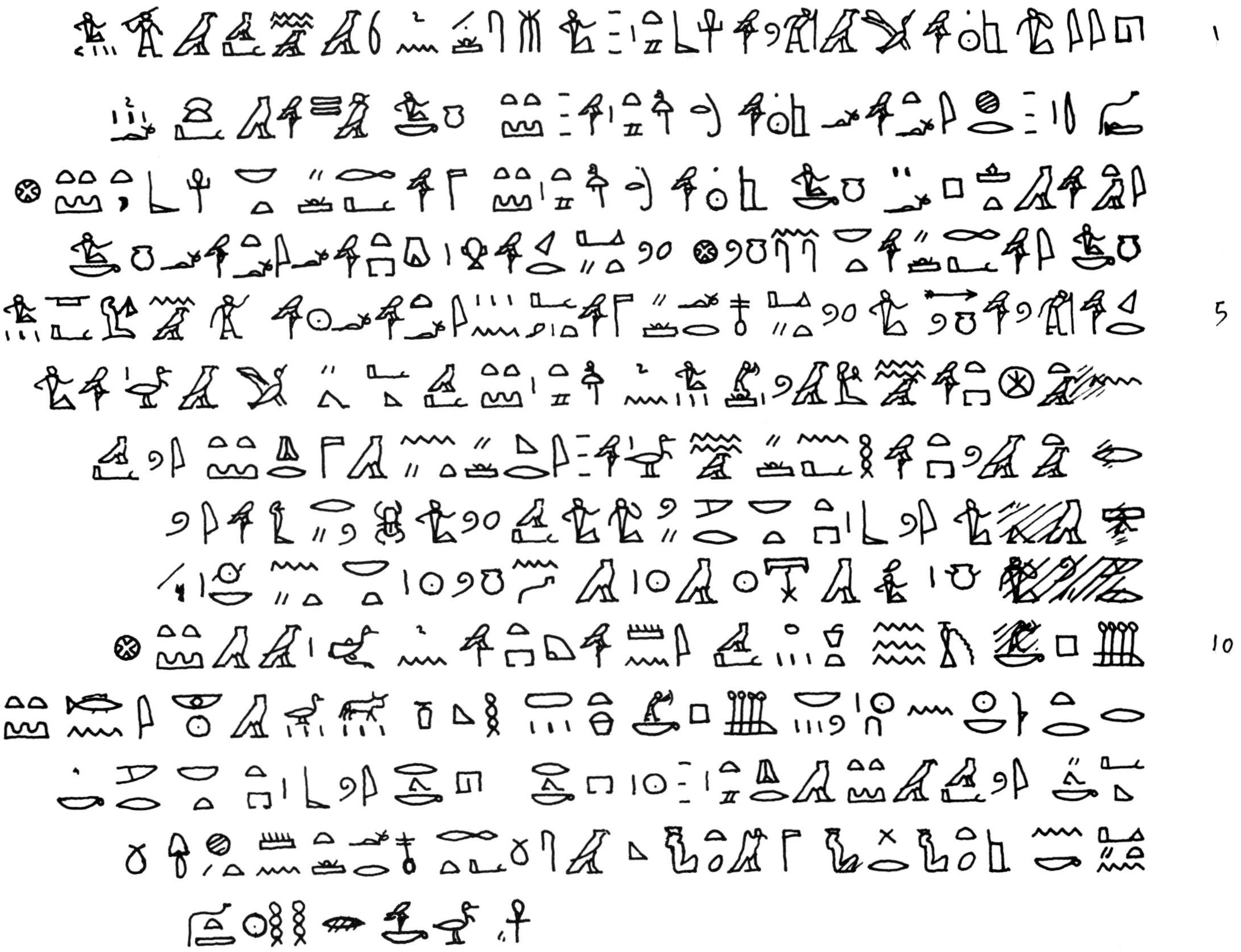

P. BM EA 10194 recto

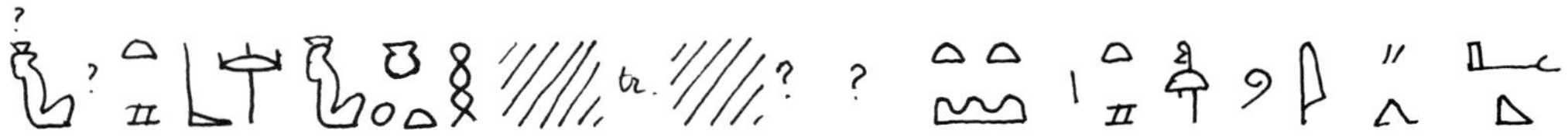

P. BM EA 10194 verso

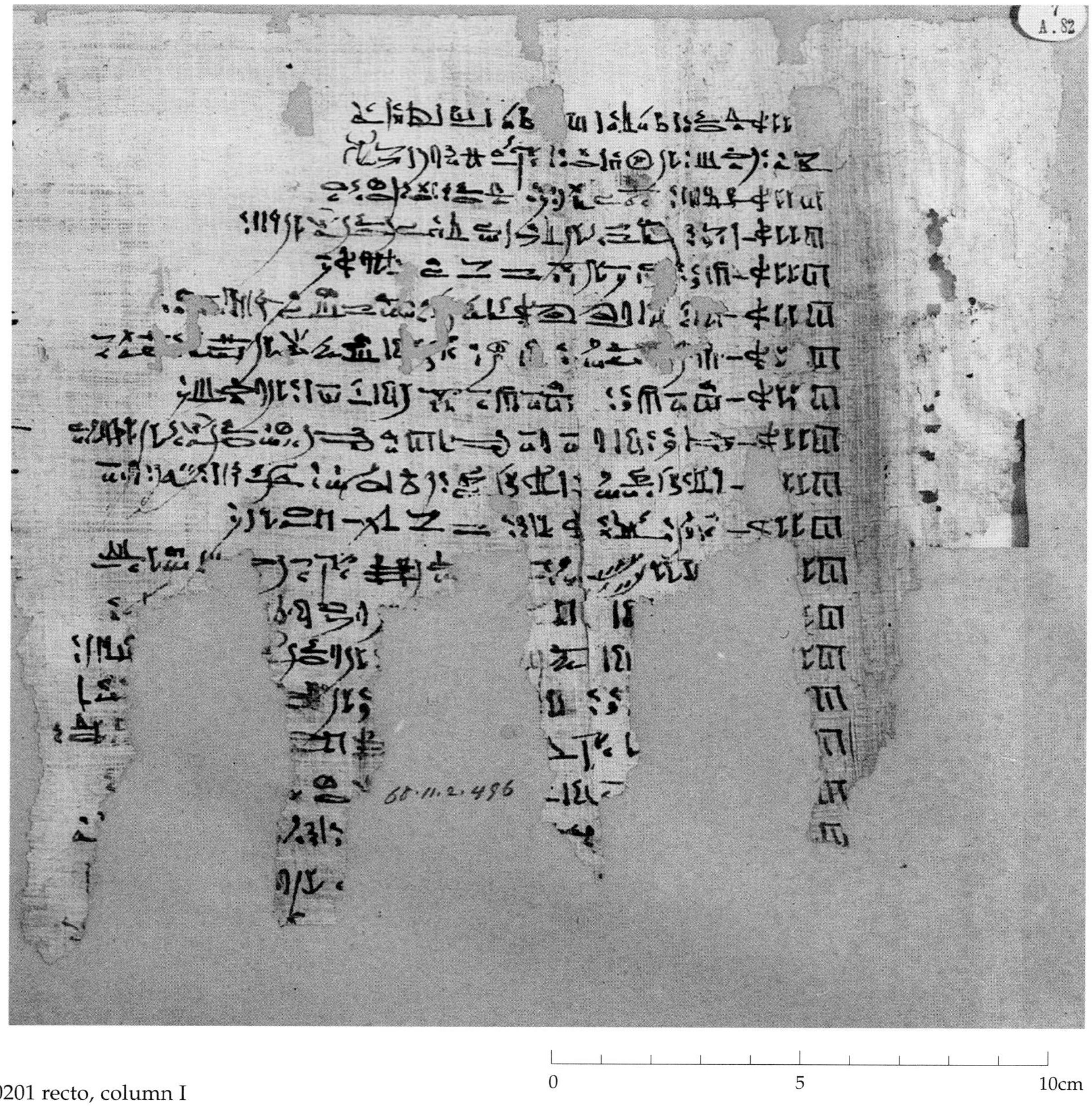

P. BM EA 10201 recto, column I

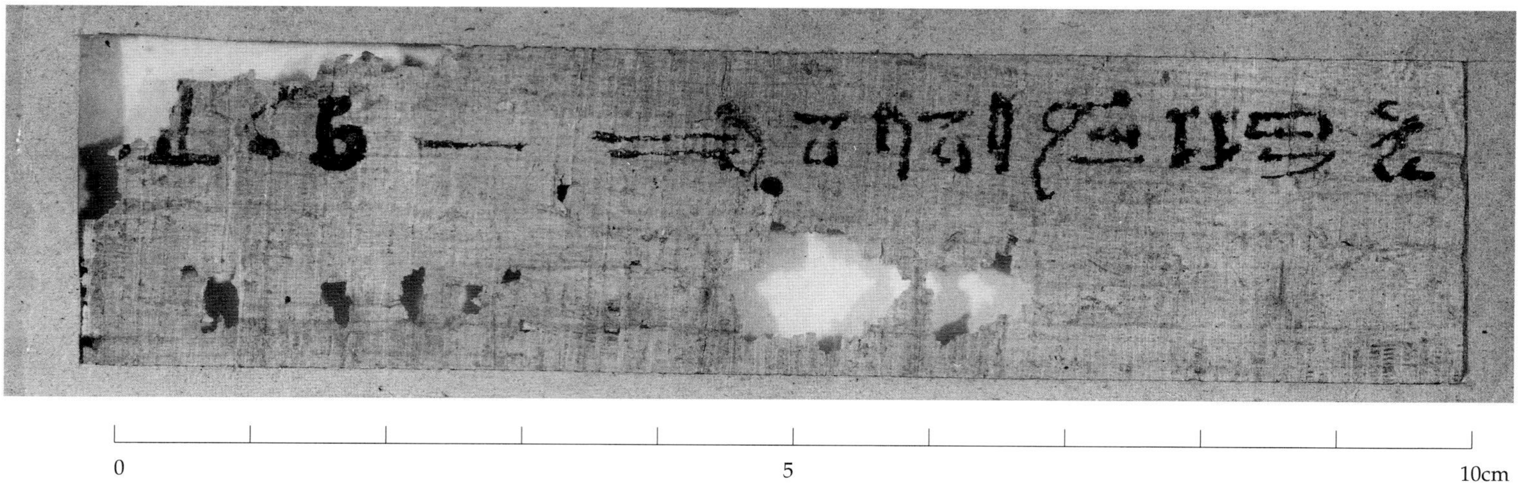

P. BM EA 10201 verso

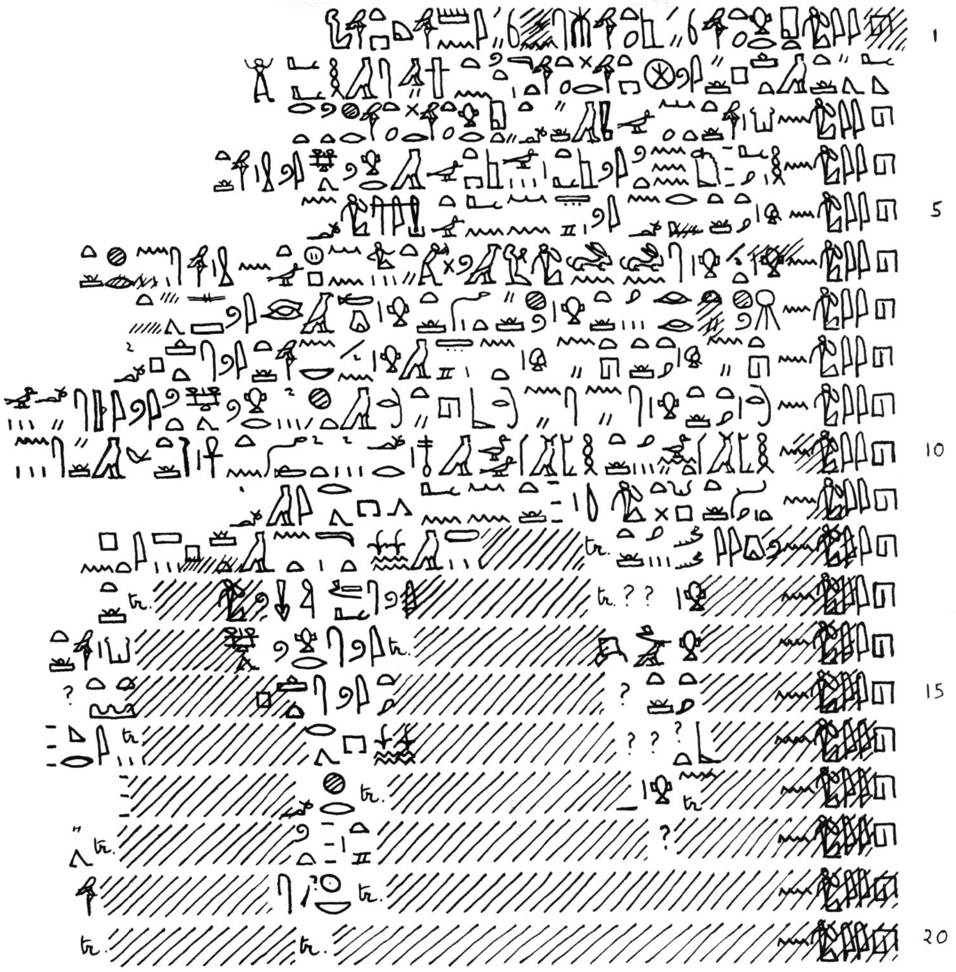

P. BM EA 10201 recto, column I

P. BM EA 10201 verso

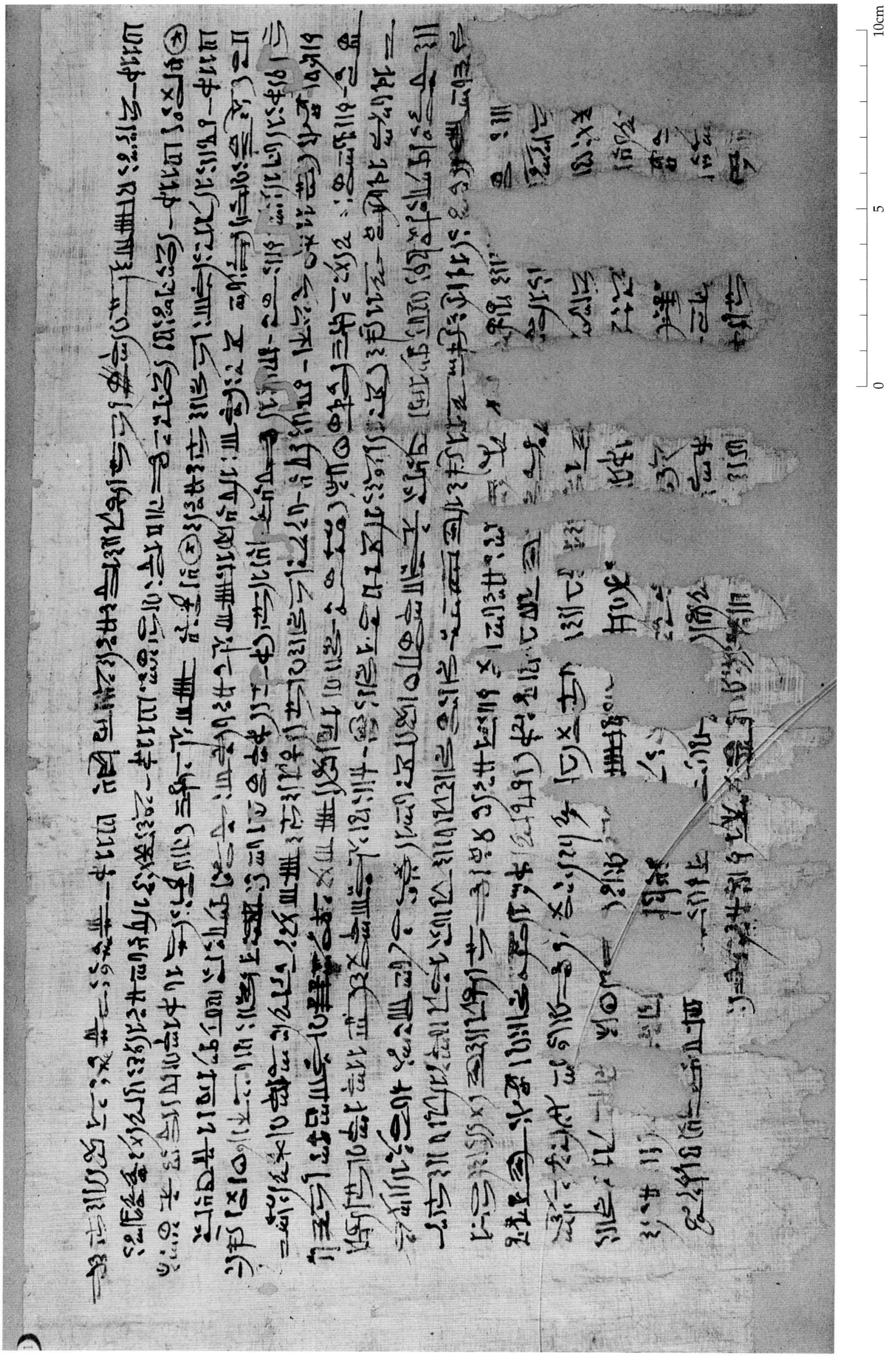

P. BM EA 10201 recto, column II

P. BM EA 10201 recto, column II

P. BM EA 10254 recto

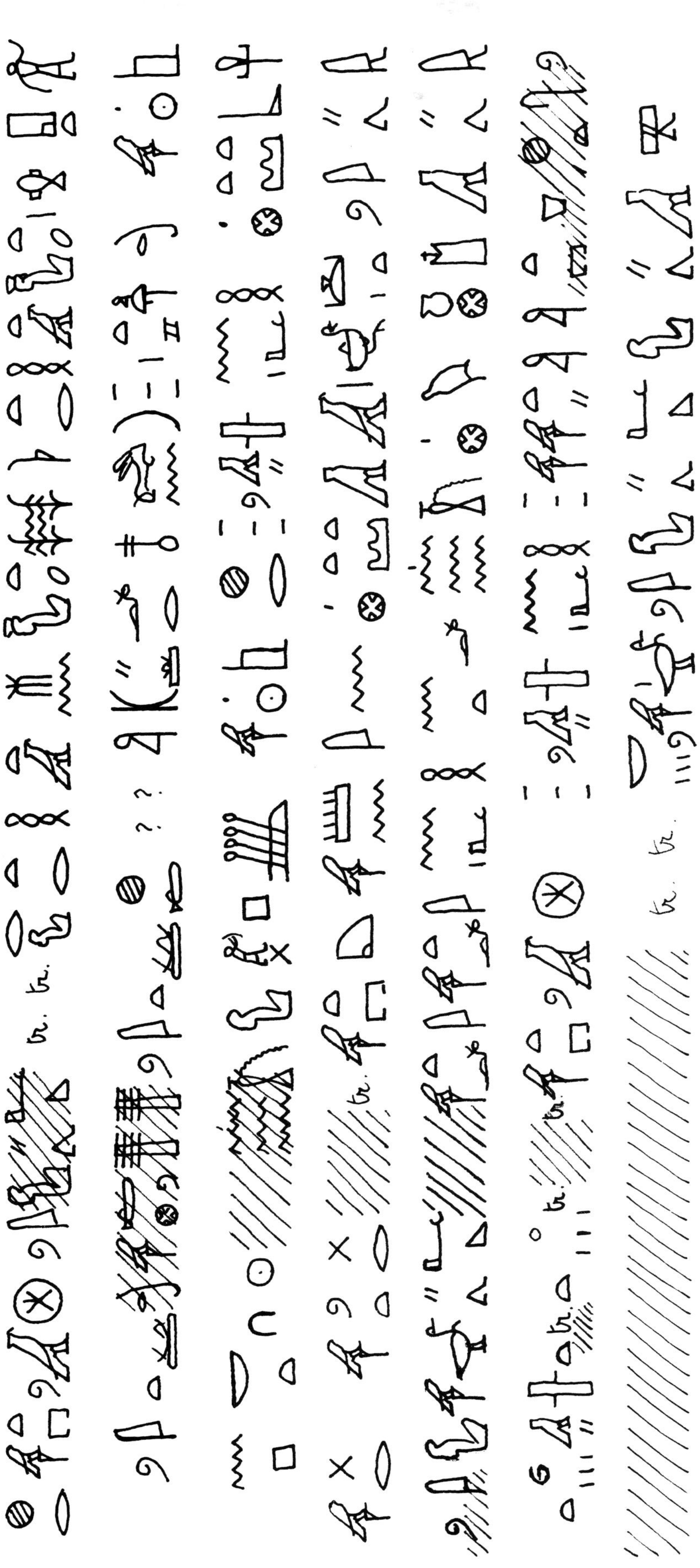

P. BM EA 10254 recto

Plate 116

P. BM EA 10254 verso

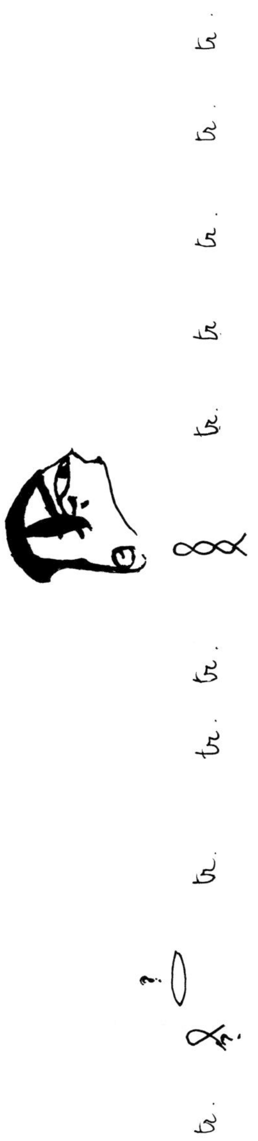

P. BM EA 10254 verso

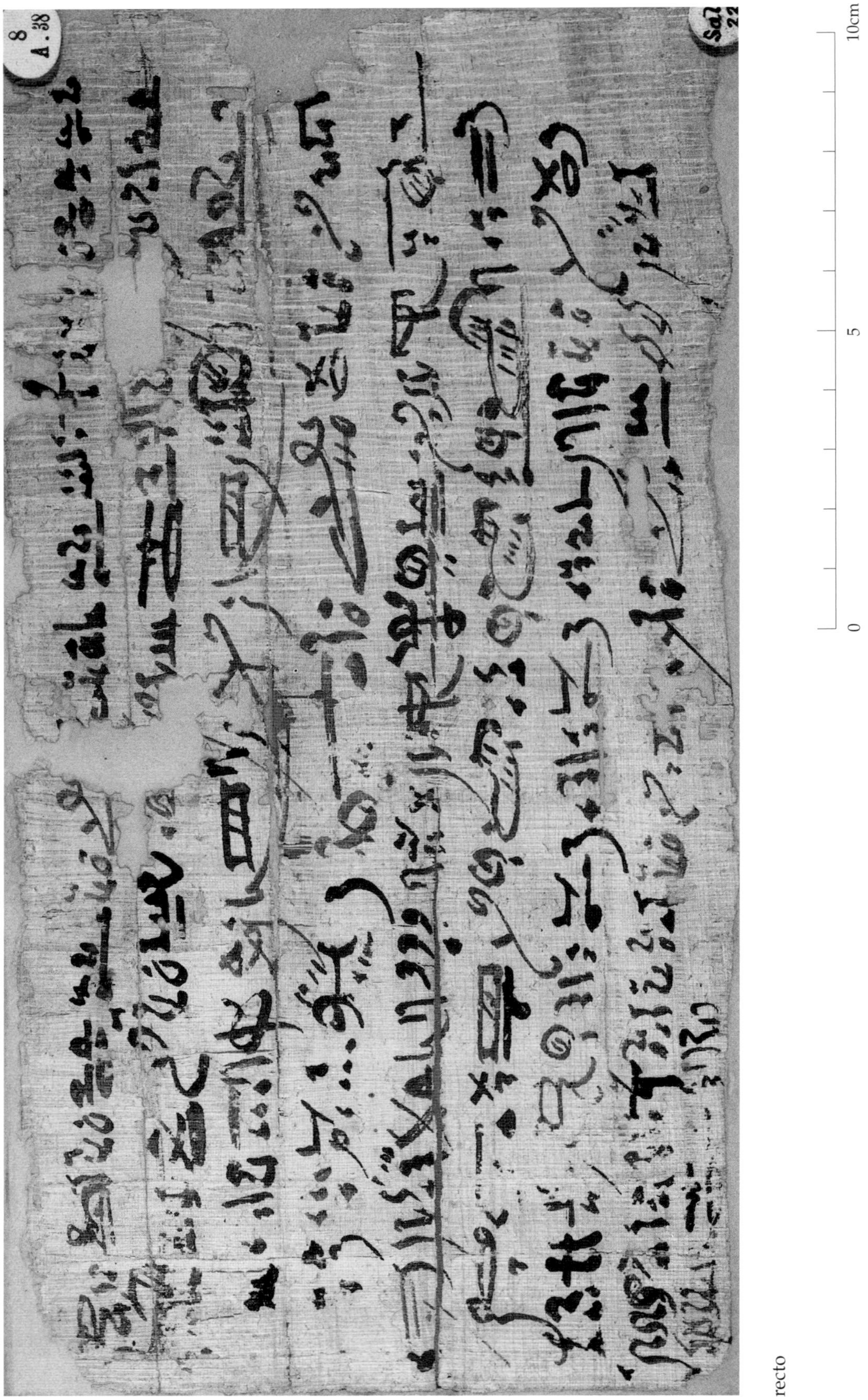

P. BM EA 10256 recto

P. BM EA 10256 verso

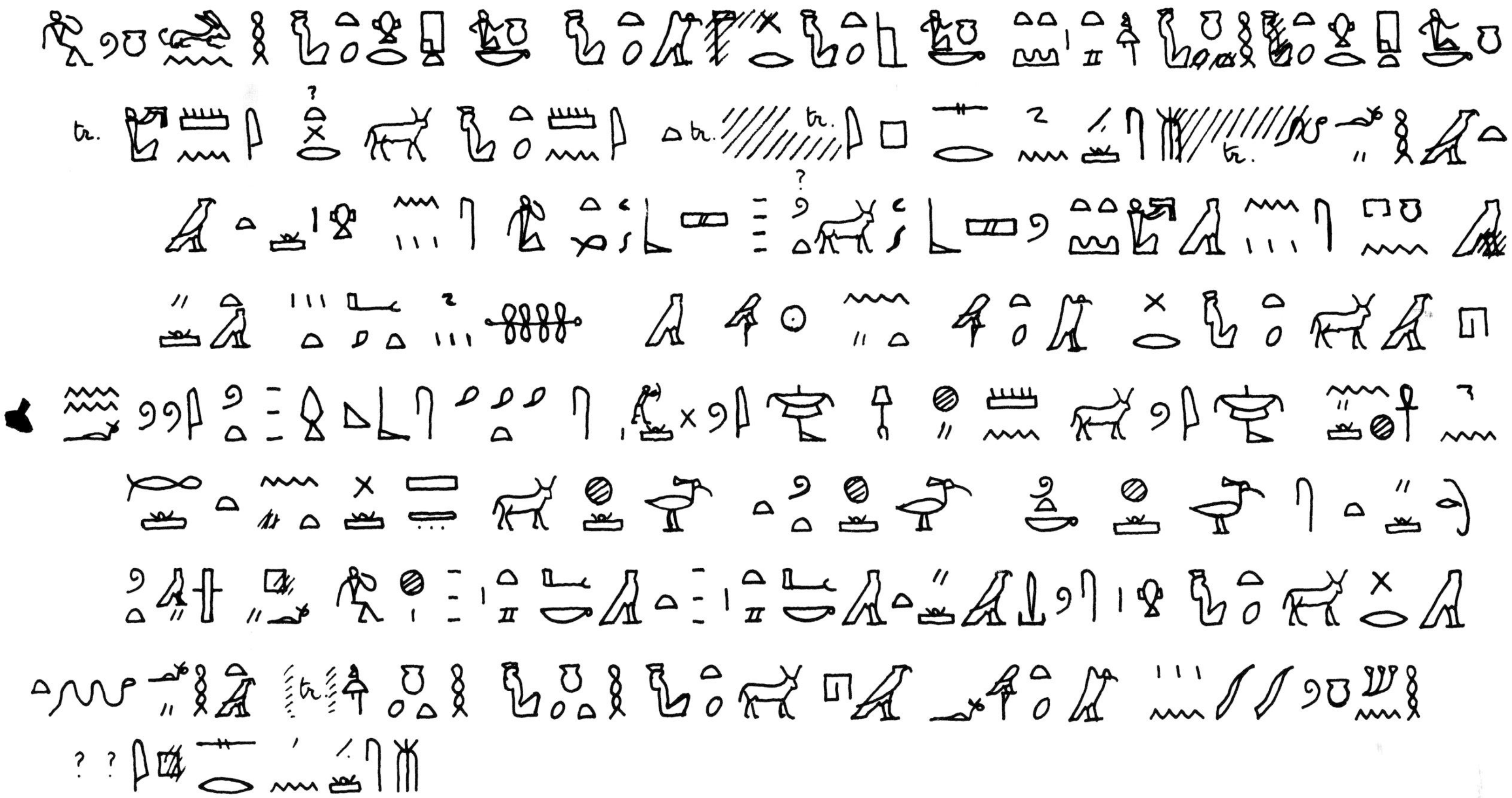

P. BM EA 10256 recto

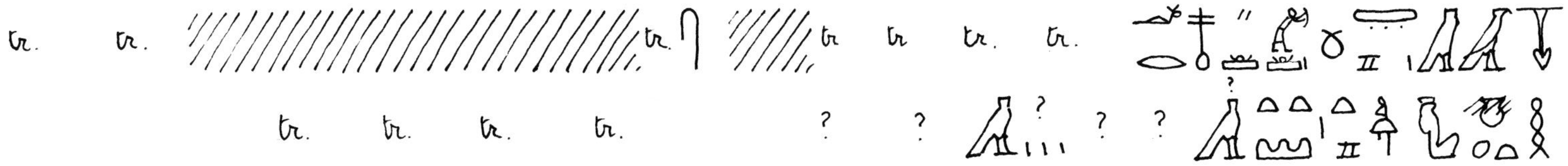

P. BM EA 10256 verso

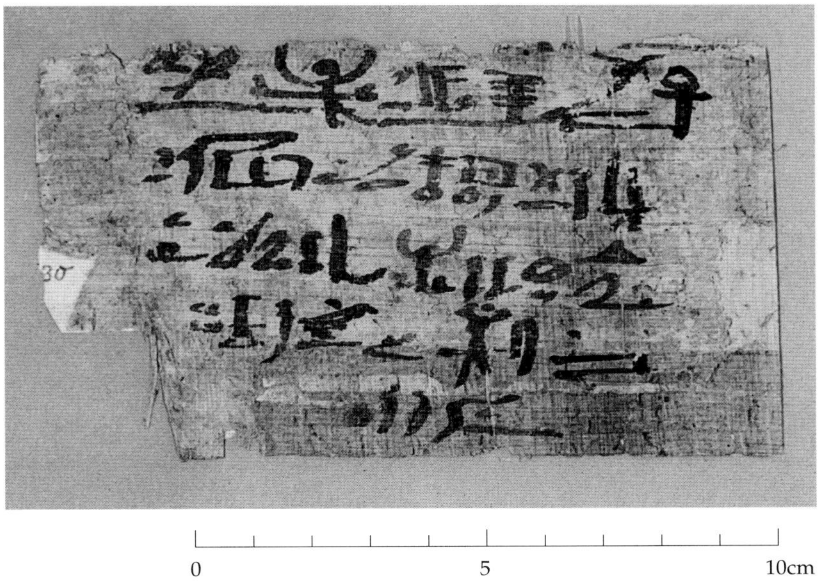

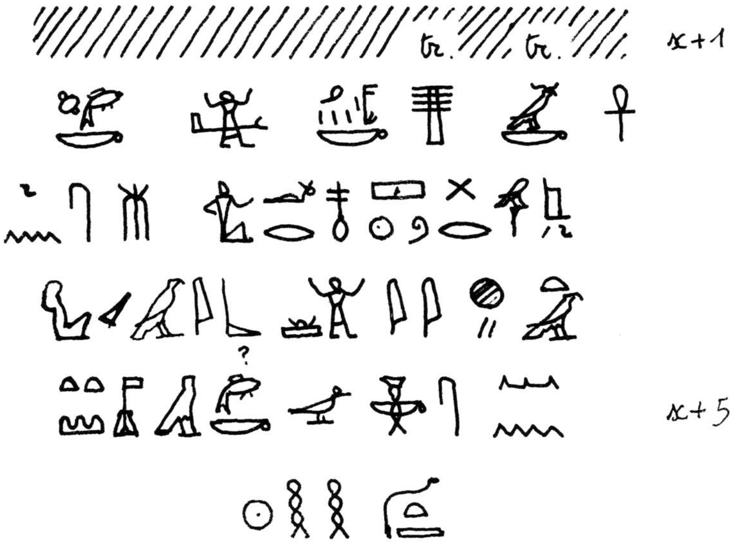

P. BM EA 10261

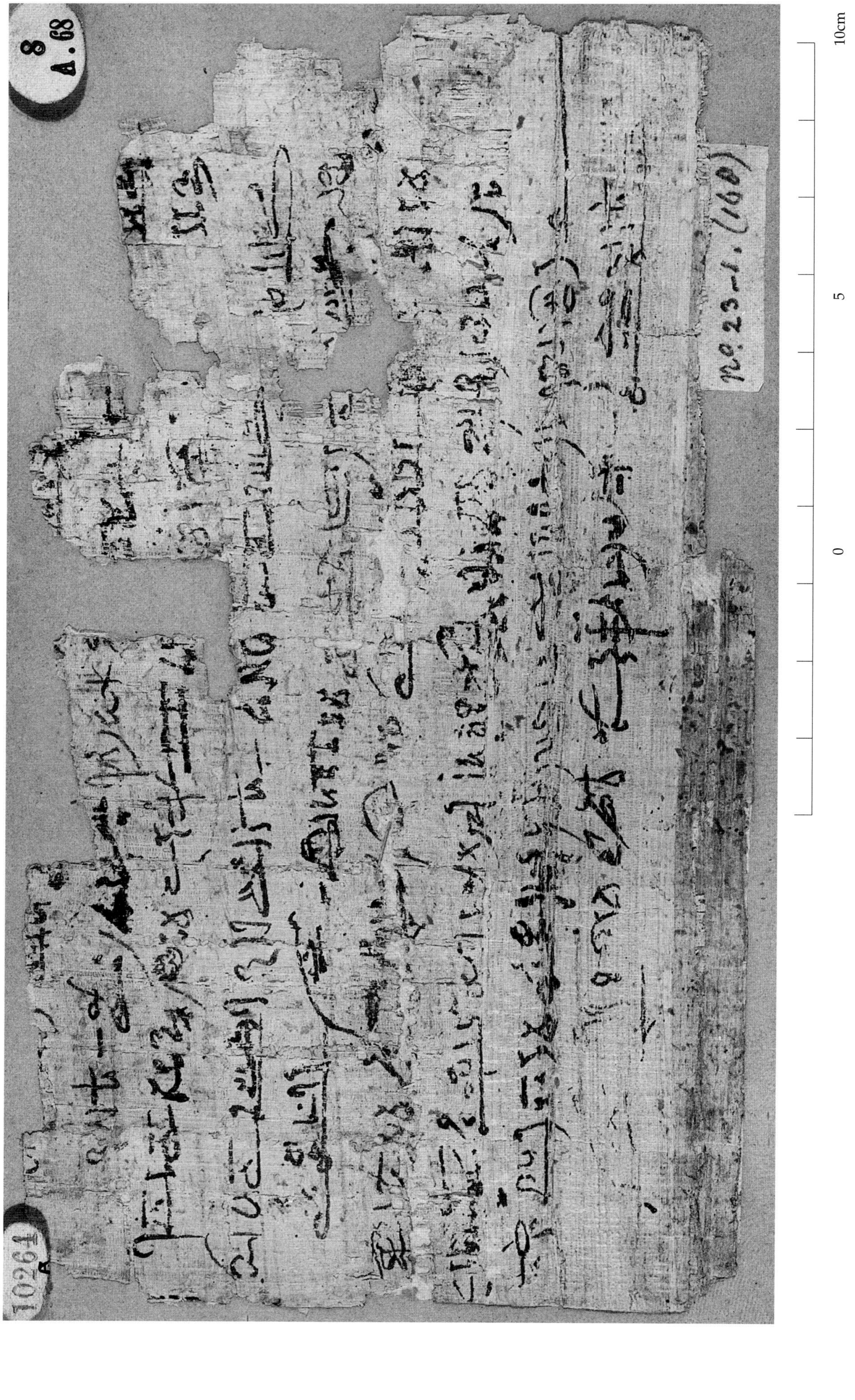

P. BM EA 10264A

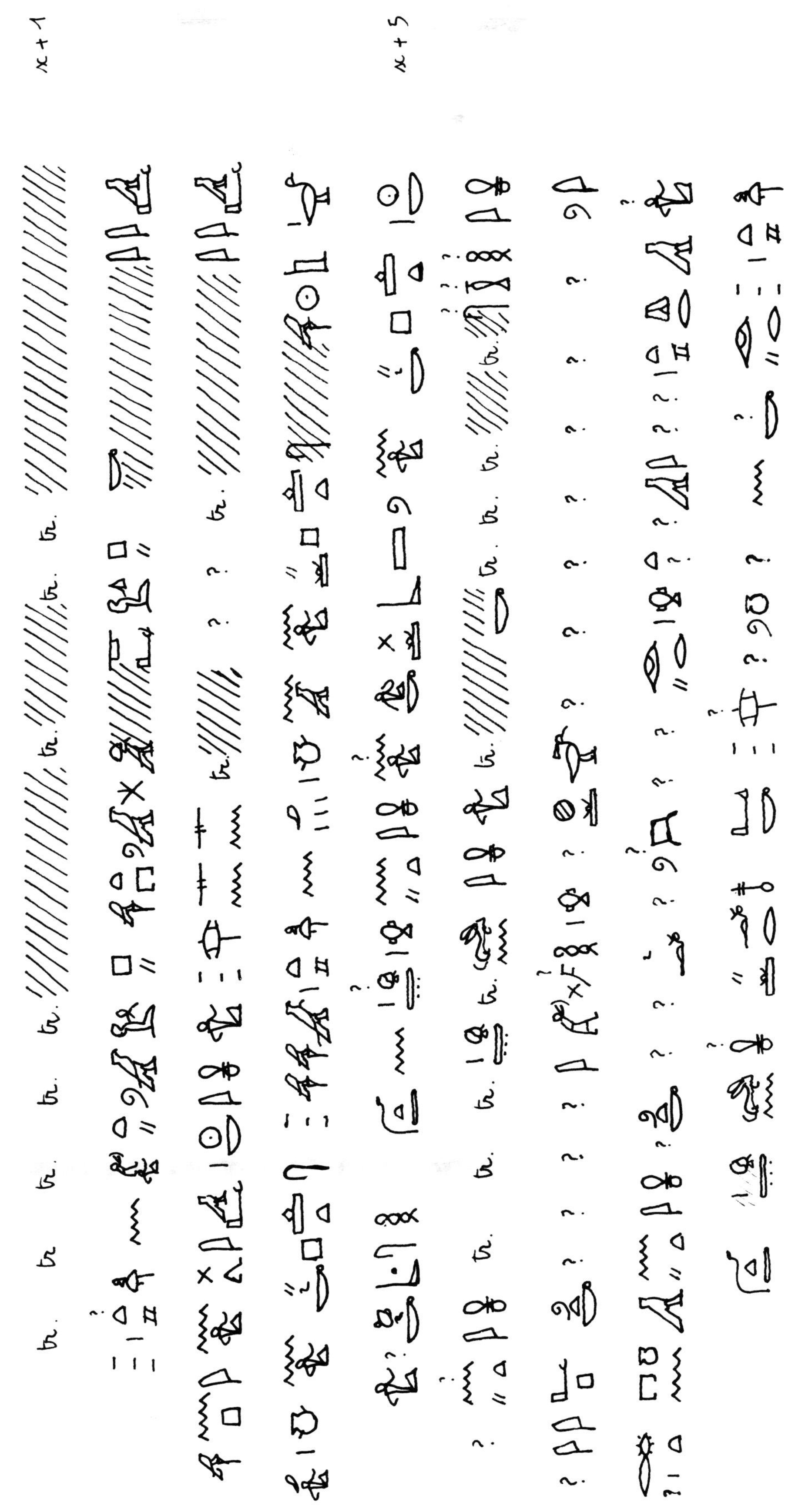

P. BM EA 10264A

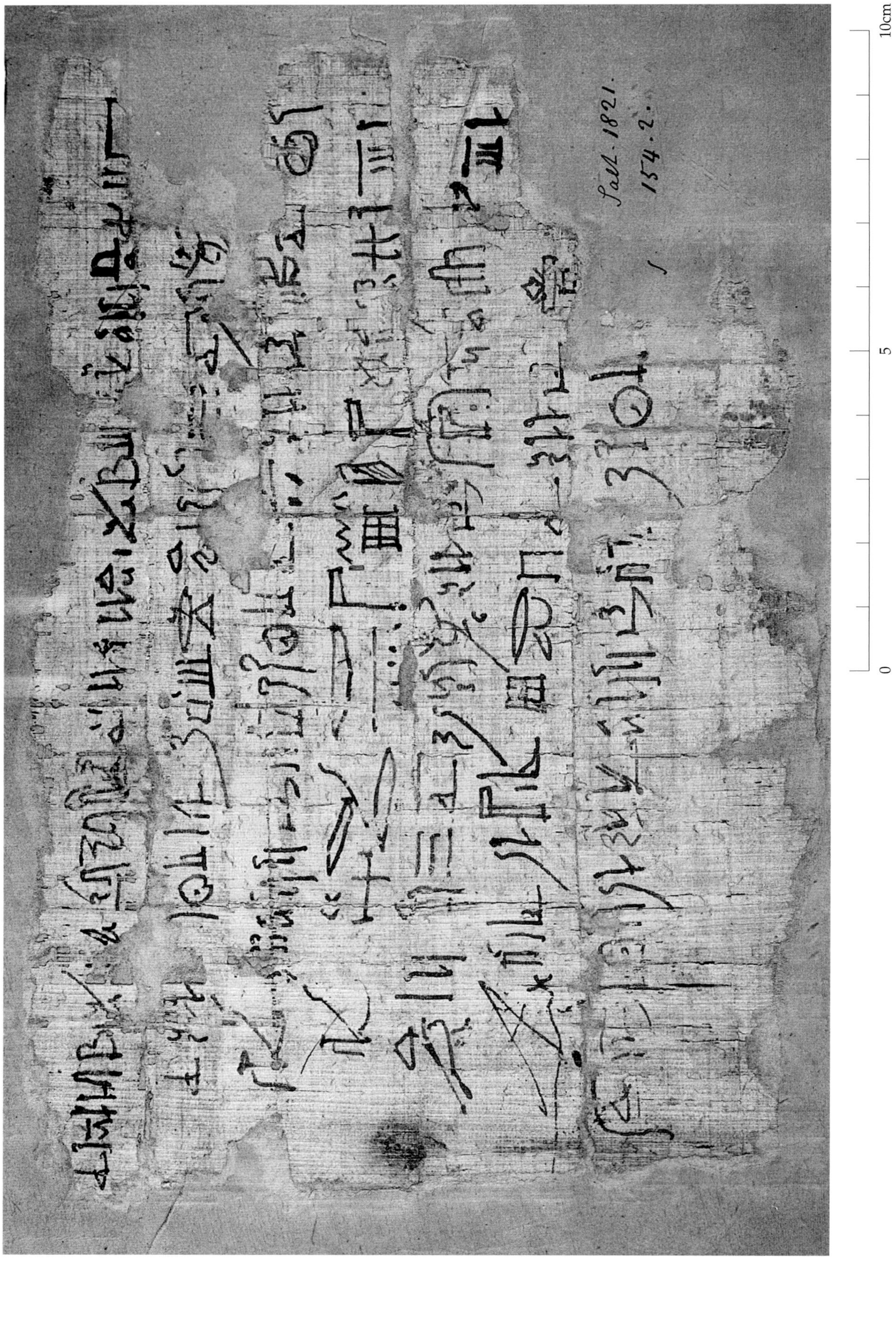

P. BM EA 10285 recto

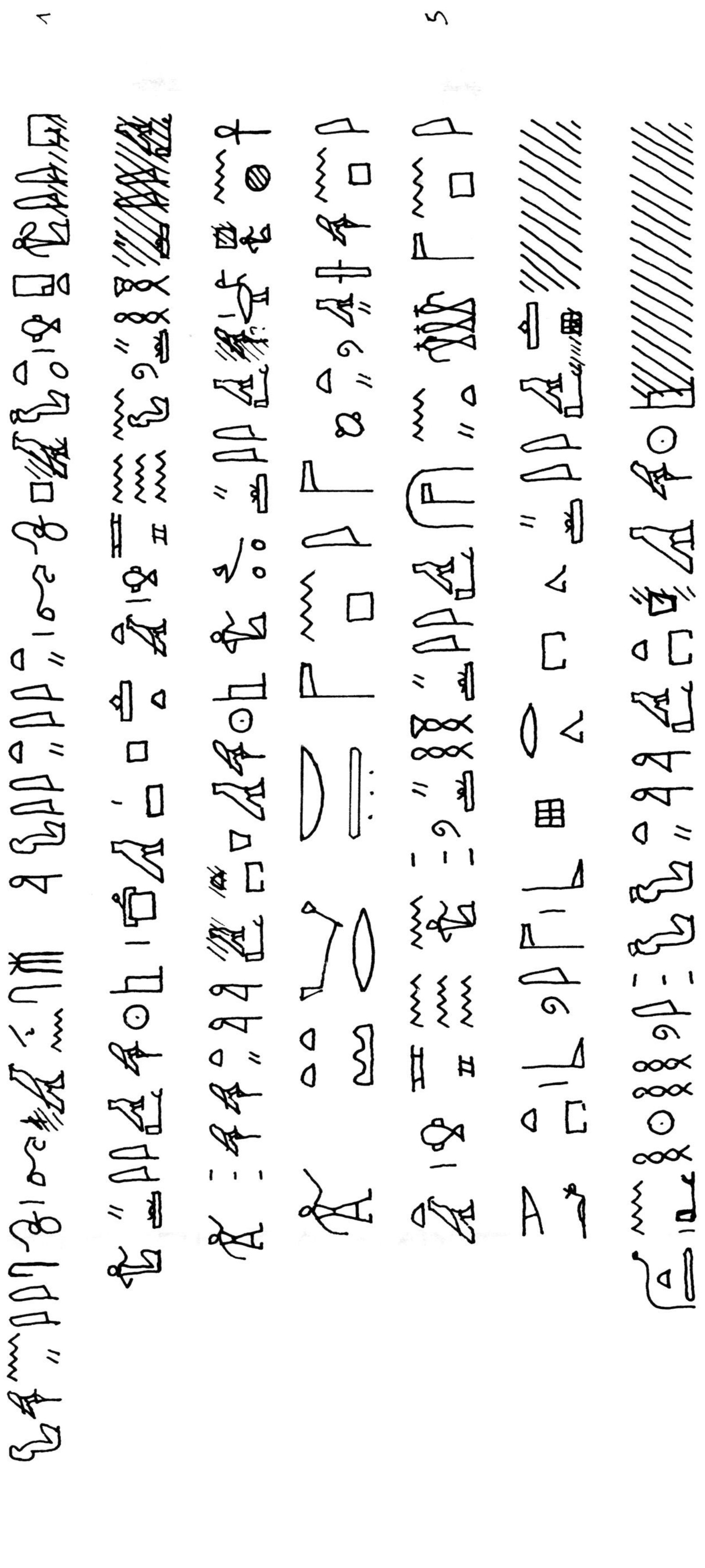

P. BM EA 10285 recto

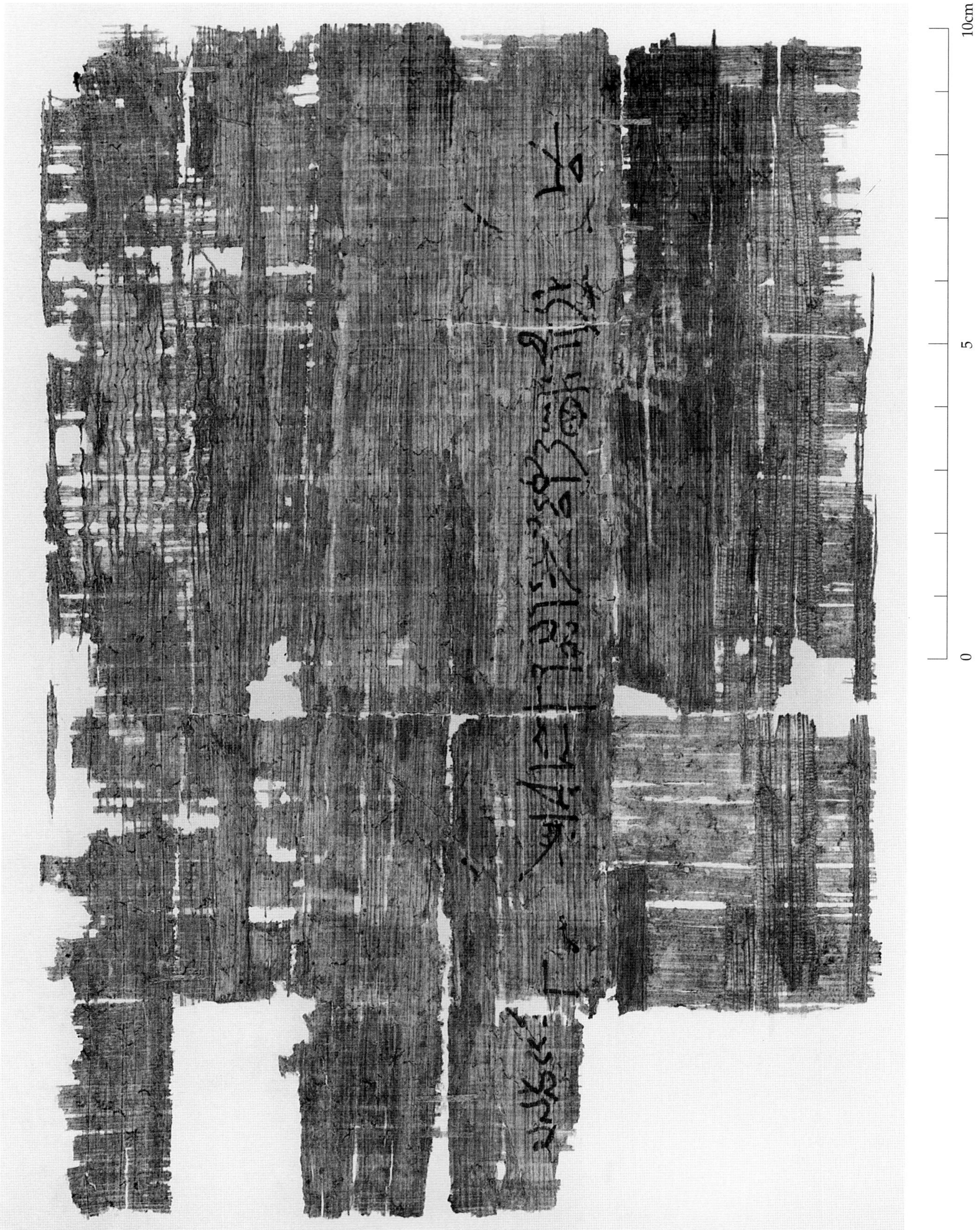

P. BM EA 10285 verso

(dem) rd.wy.t=s

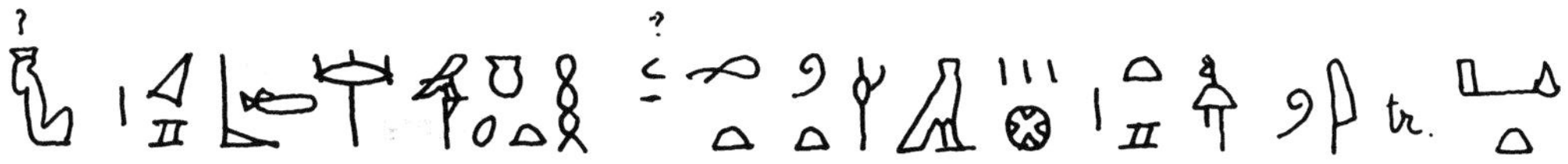

P. BM EA 10285 verso

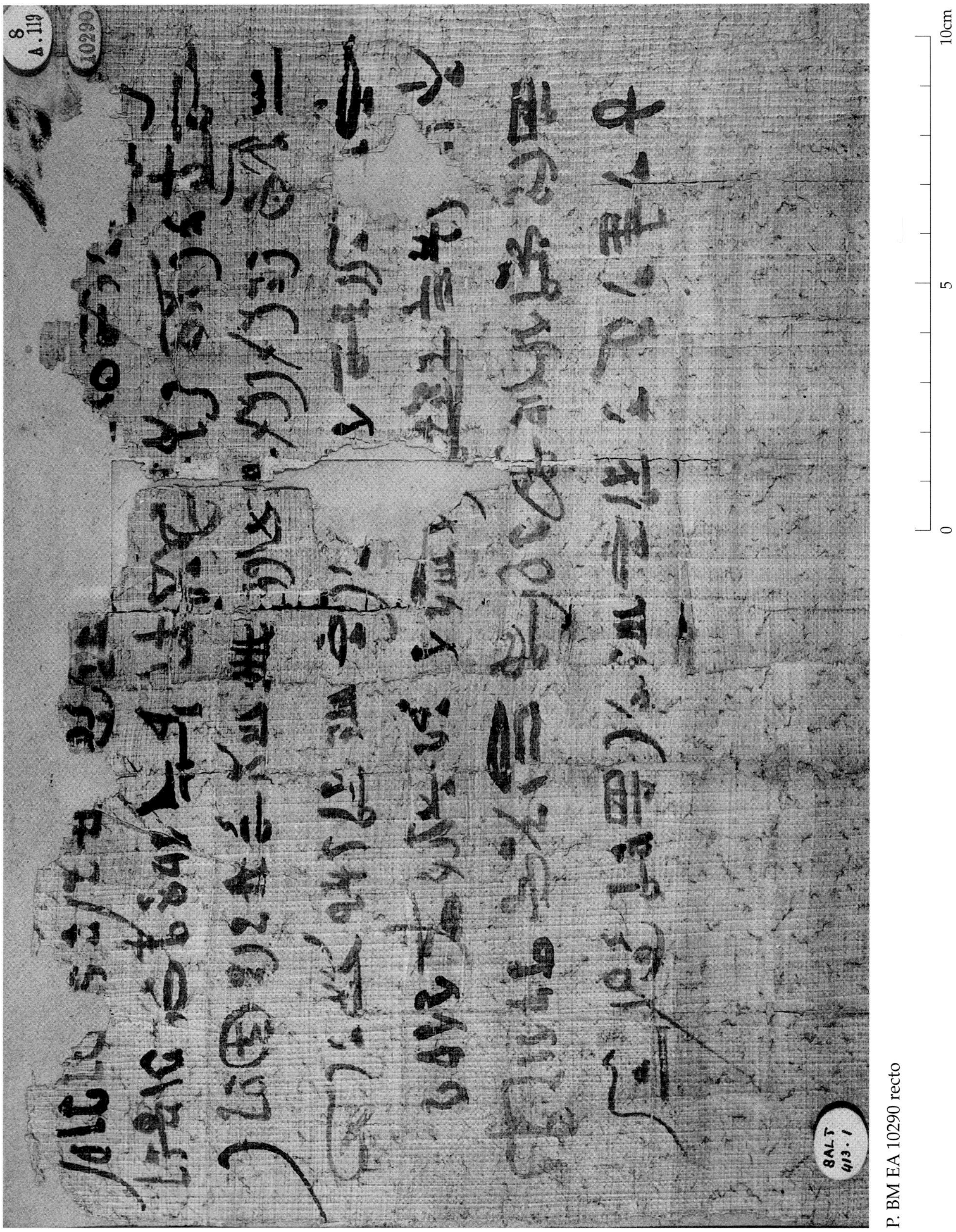

P. BM EA 10290 recto

P. BM EA 10290 verso

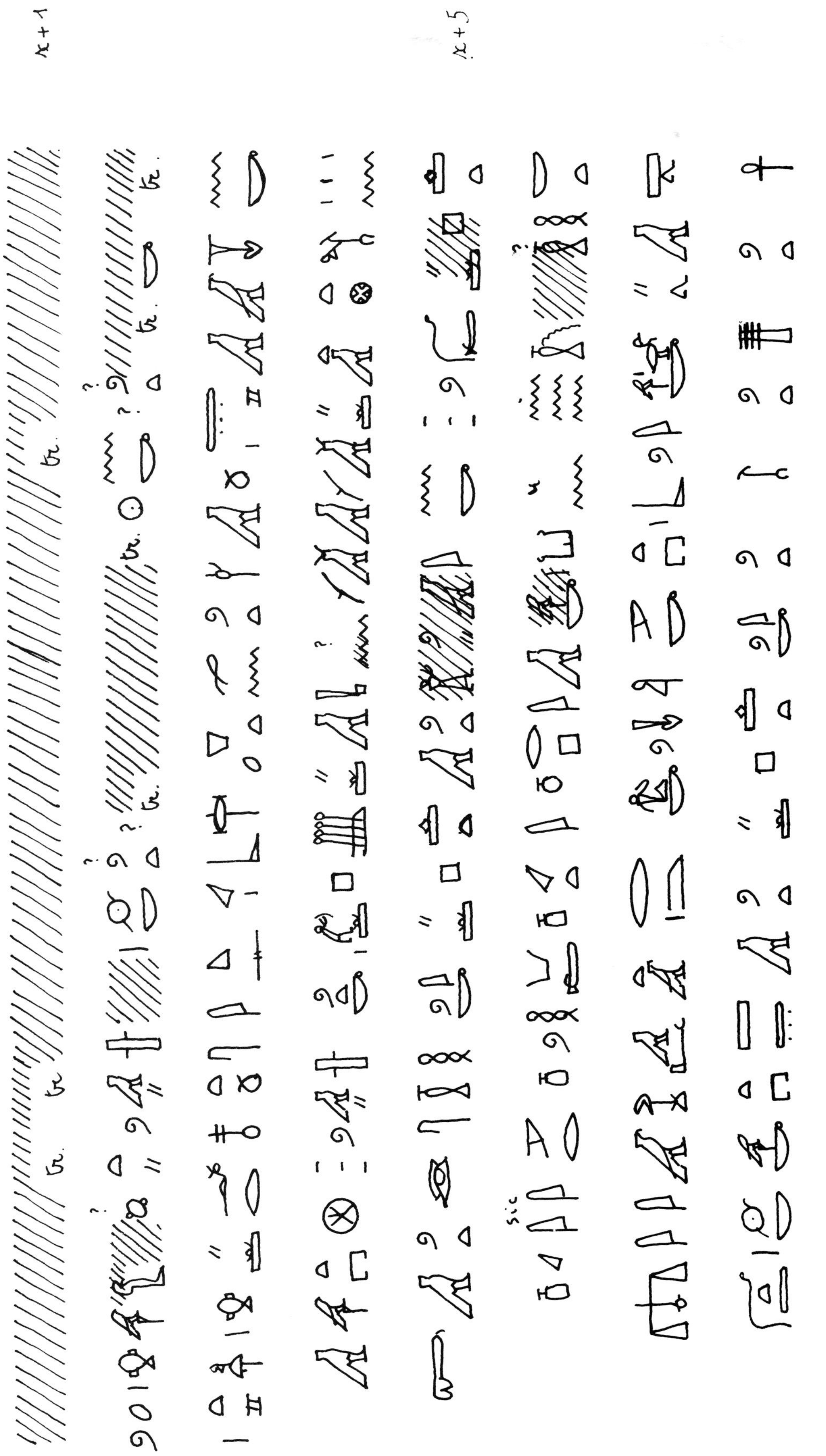

P. BM EA 10290 recto

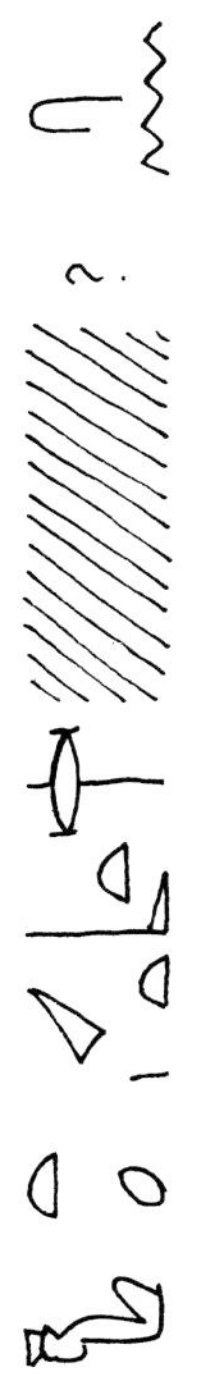

P. BM EA 10290 verso

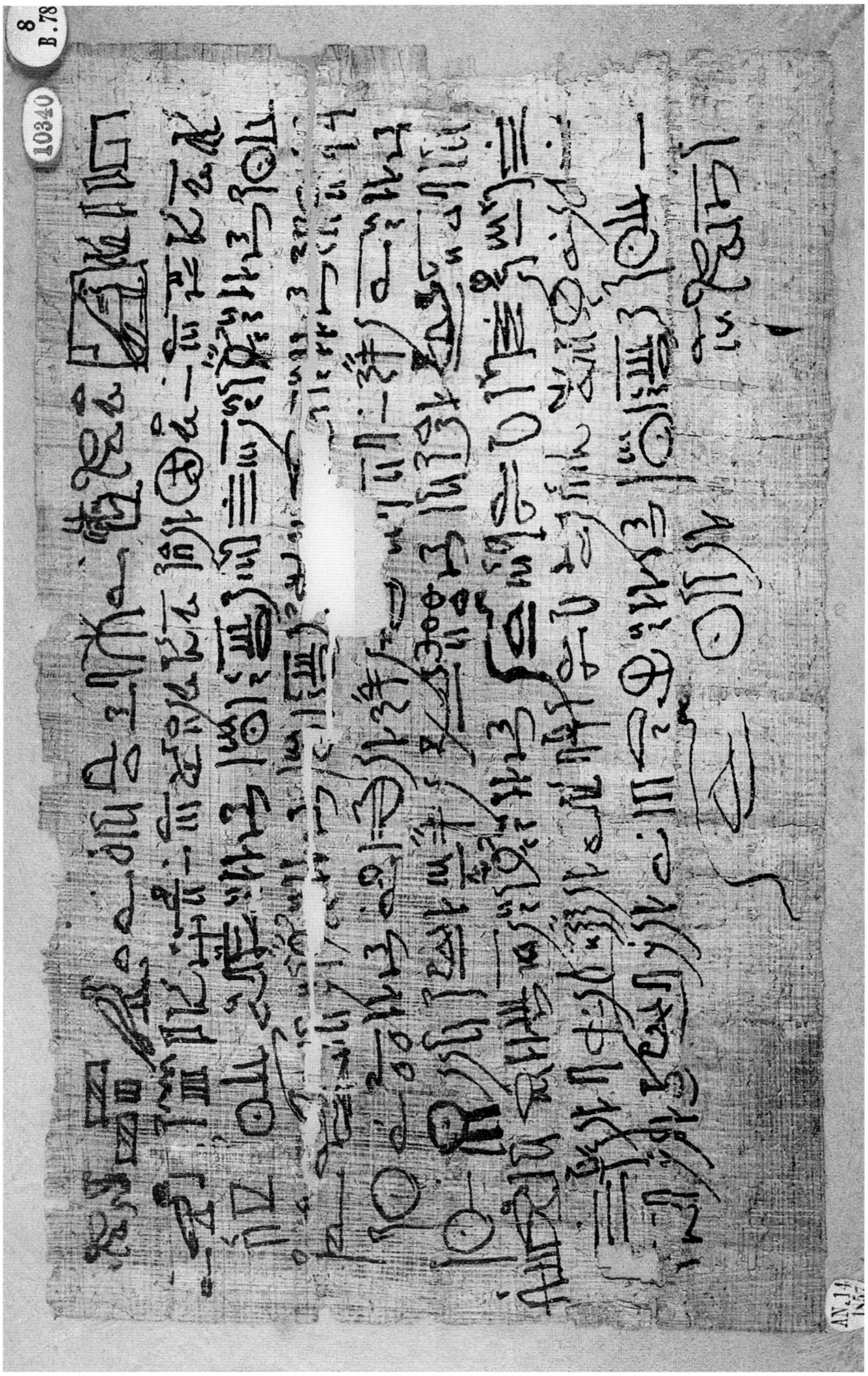

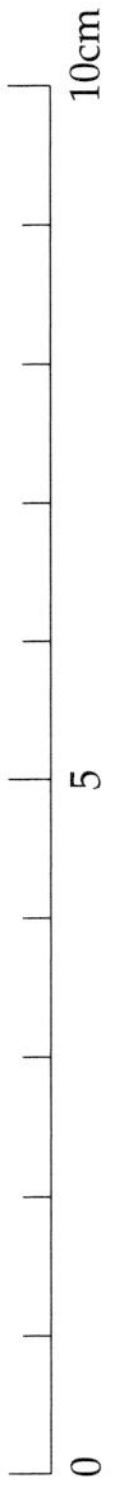

P. BM EA 10340 recto

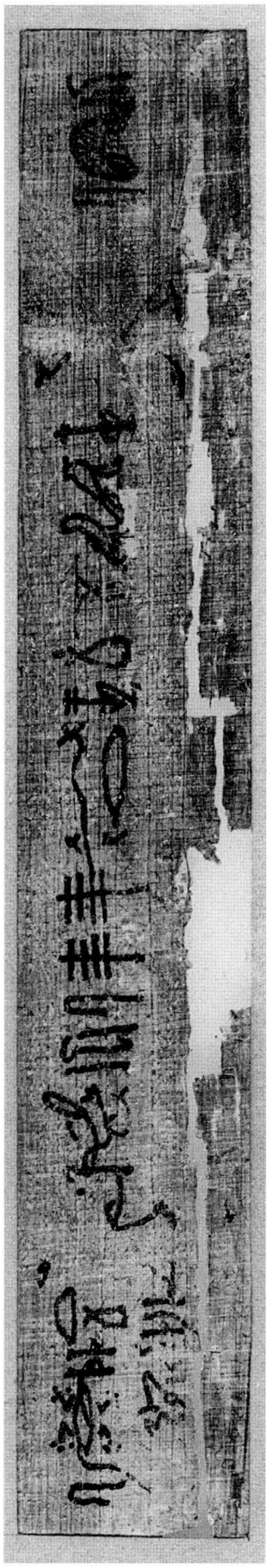

P. BM EA 10340 verso

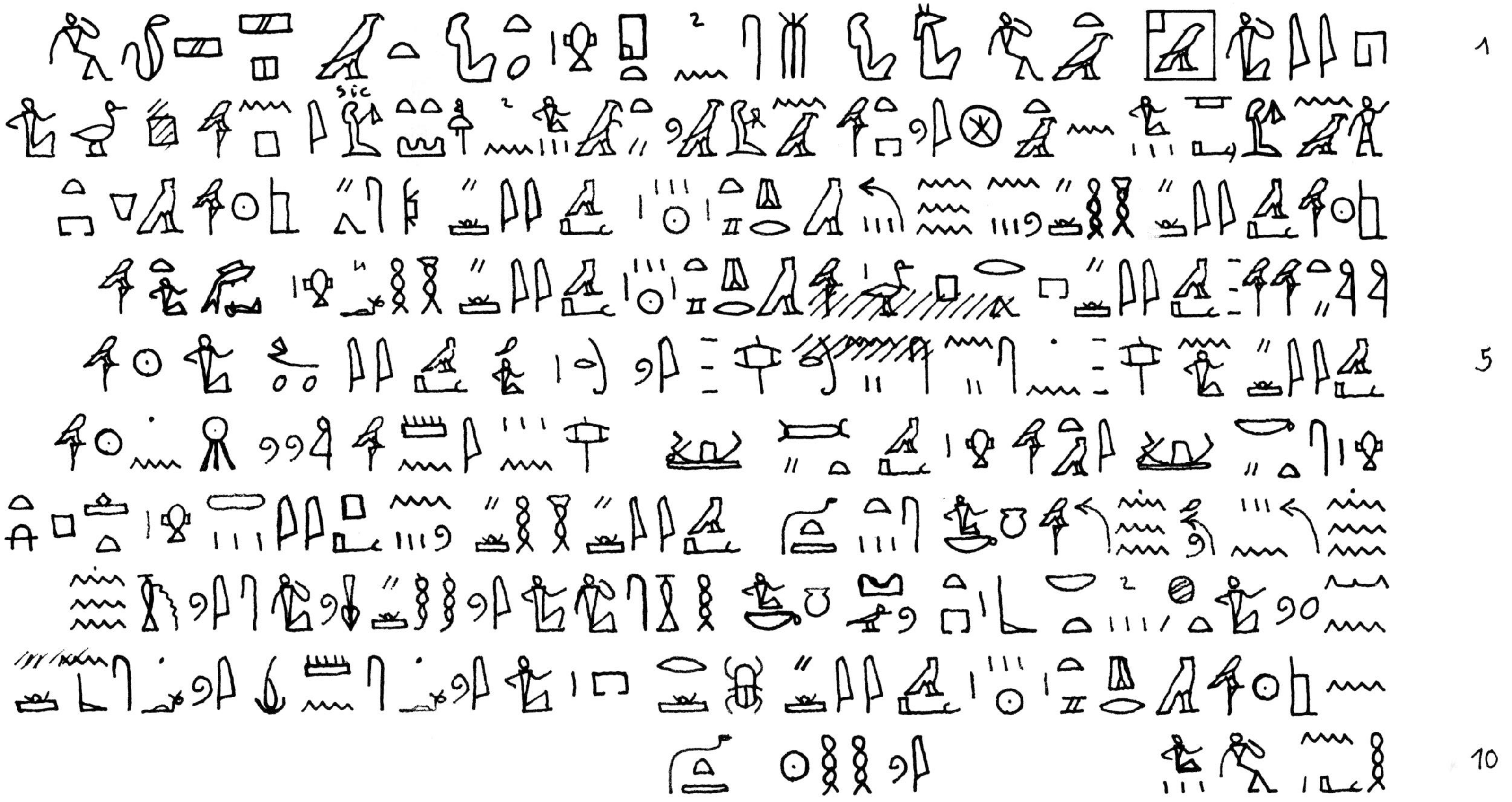

P. BM EA 10340 recto

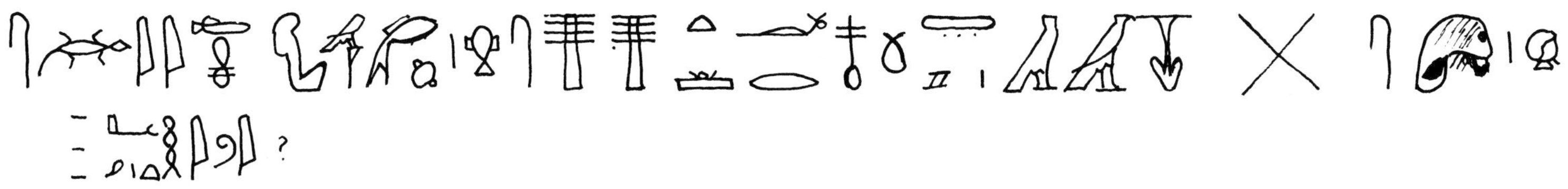

P. BM EA 10340 verso

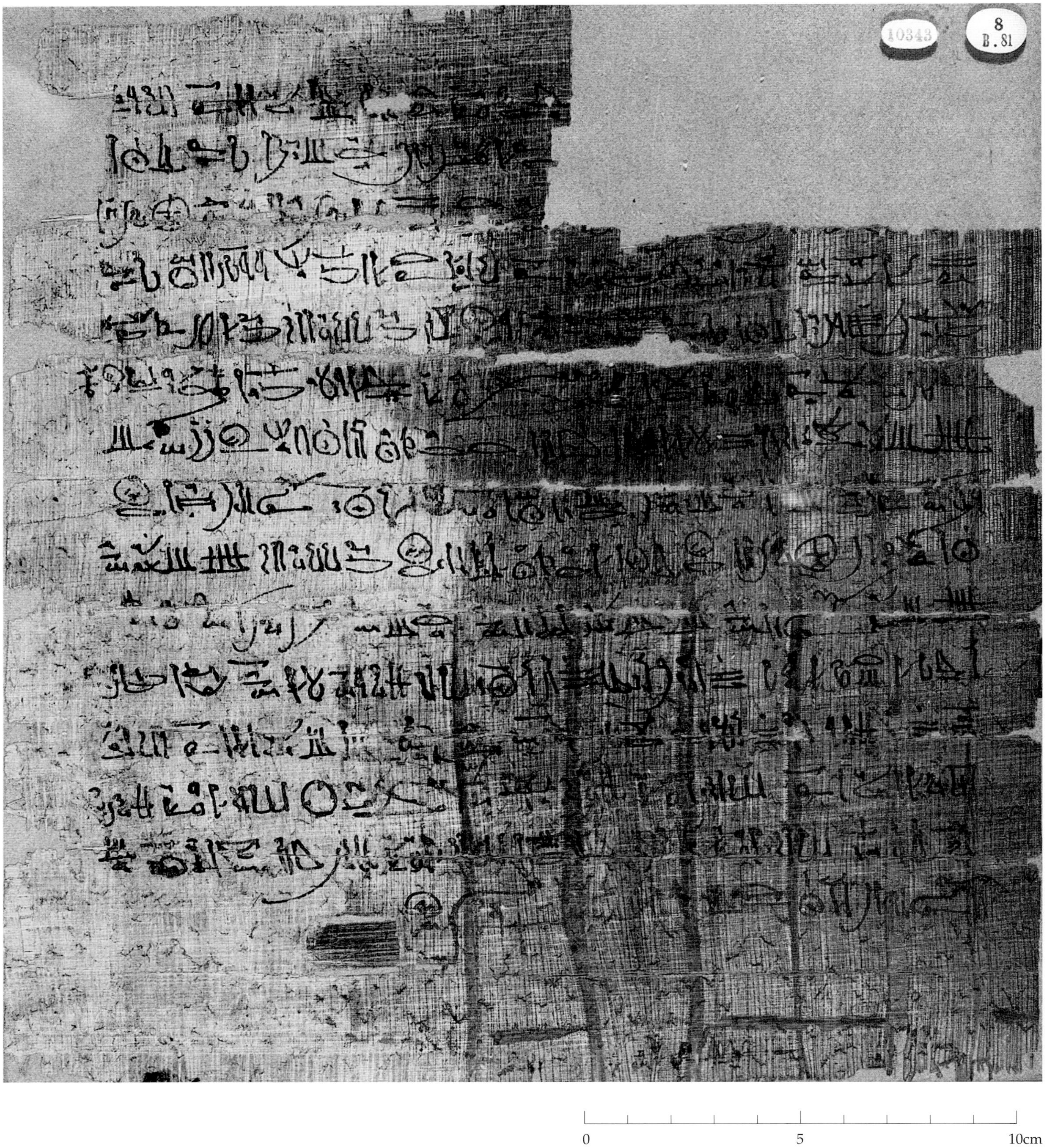

P. BM EA 10343 recto

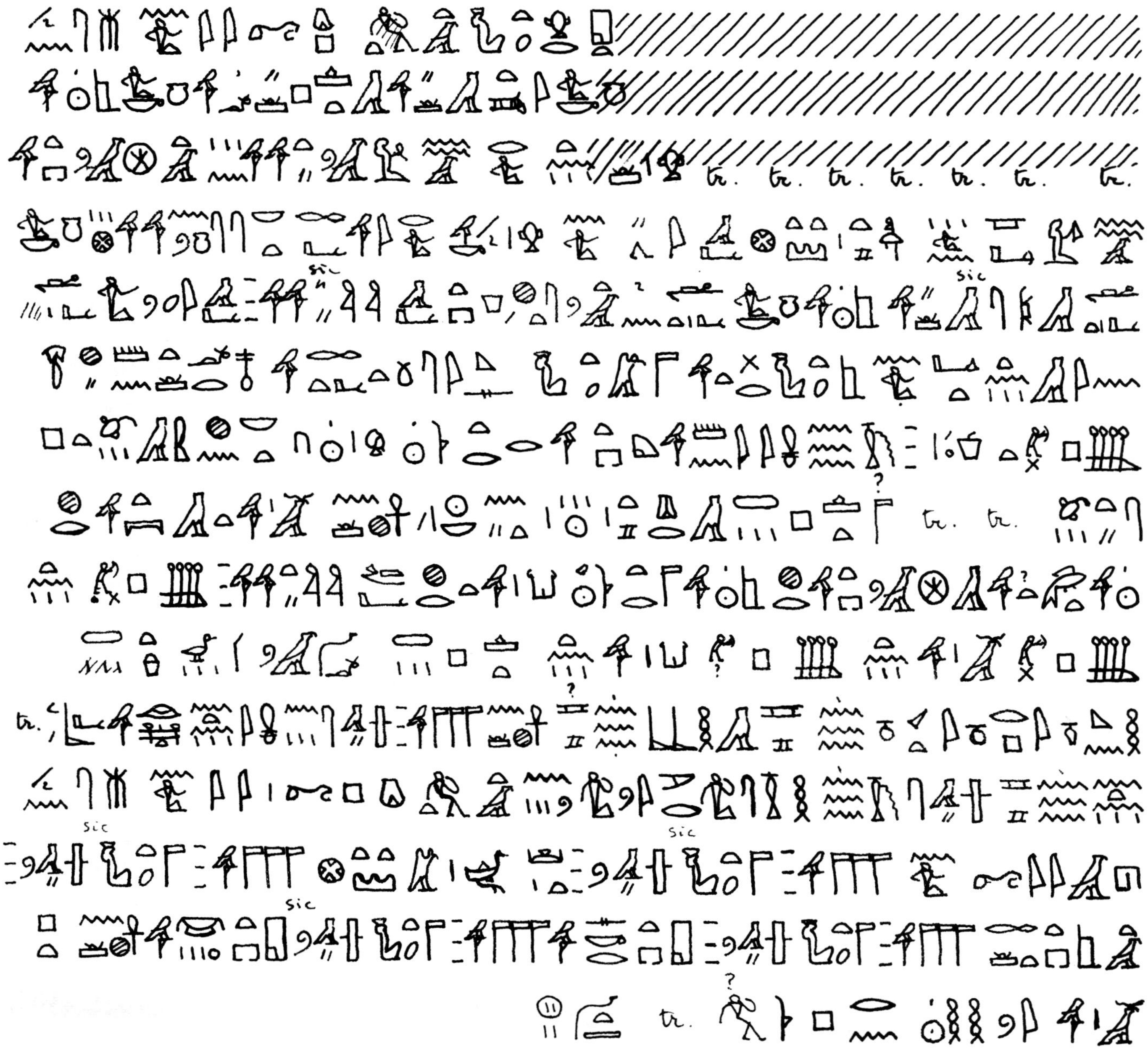

P. BM EA 10343 recto

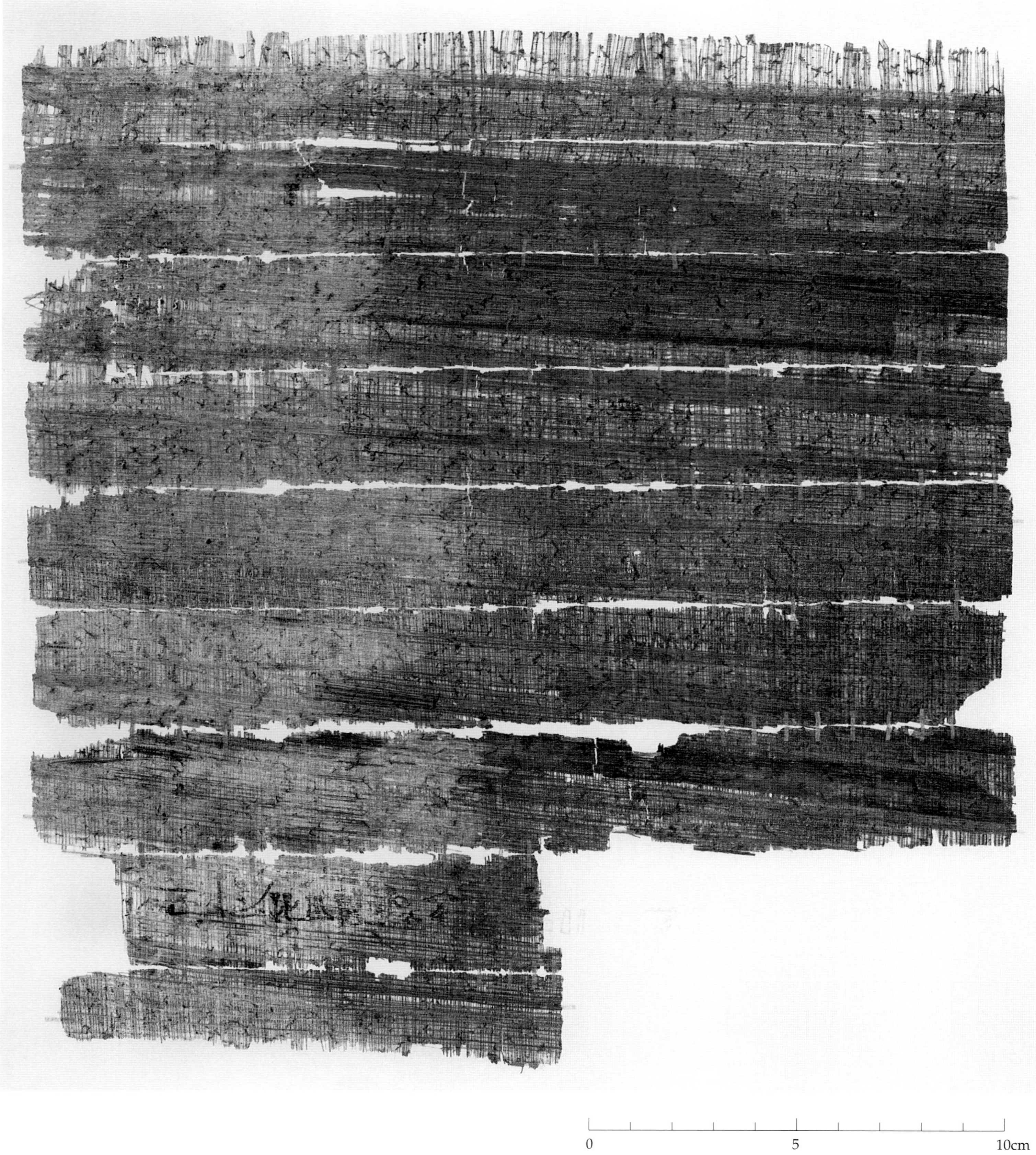

P. BM EA 10343 verso

P. BM EA 10343 verso

P. BM EA 10344 recto

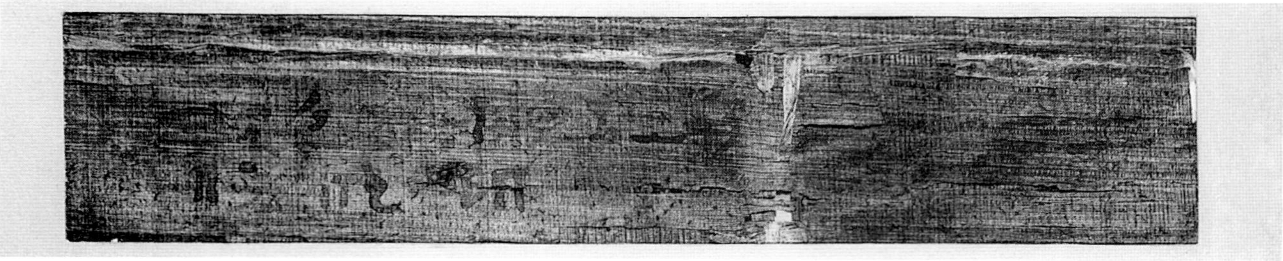

P. BM EA 10344 verso

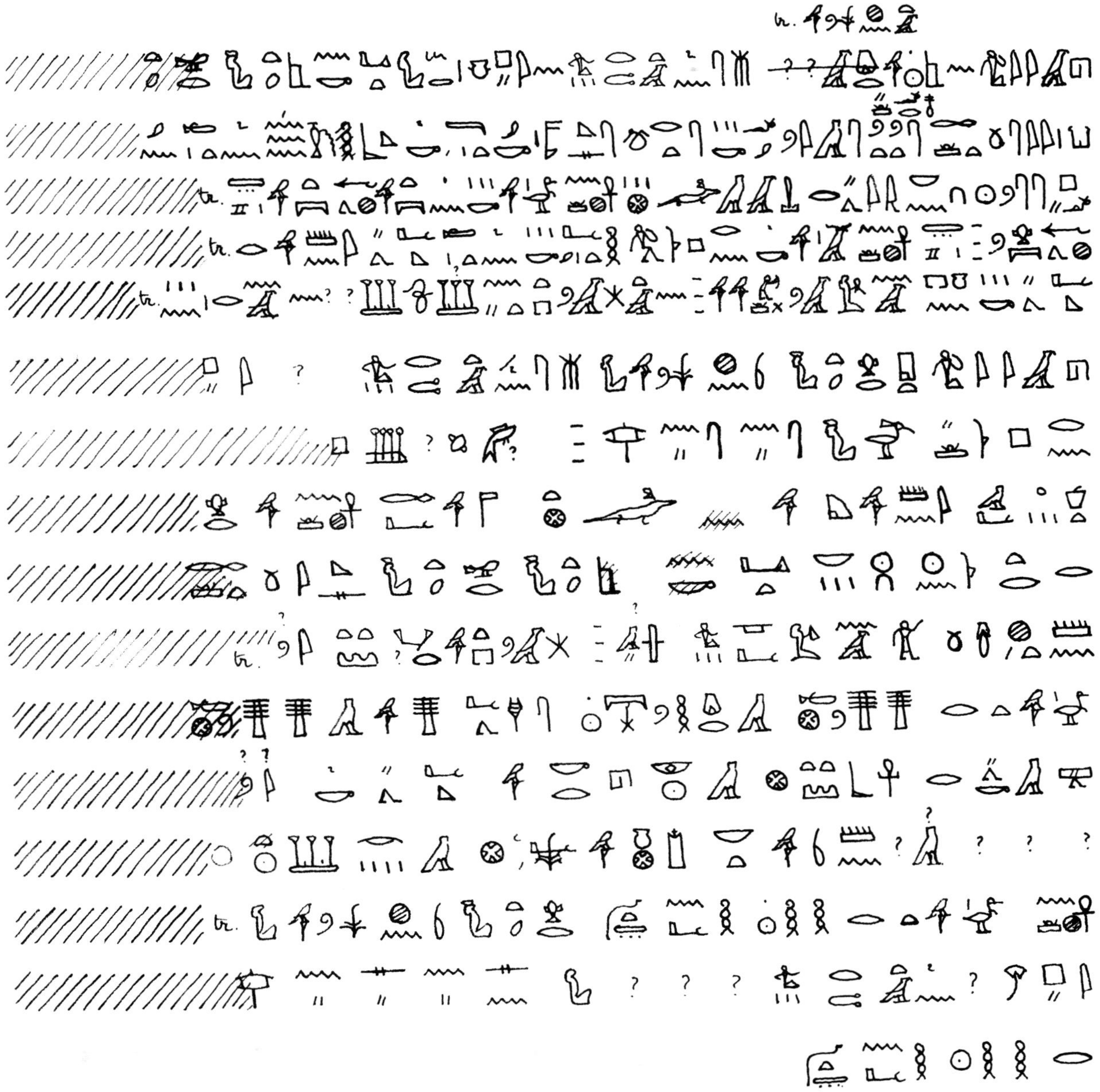

P. BM EA 10344 recto

P. BM EA 10344 verso

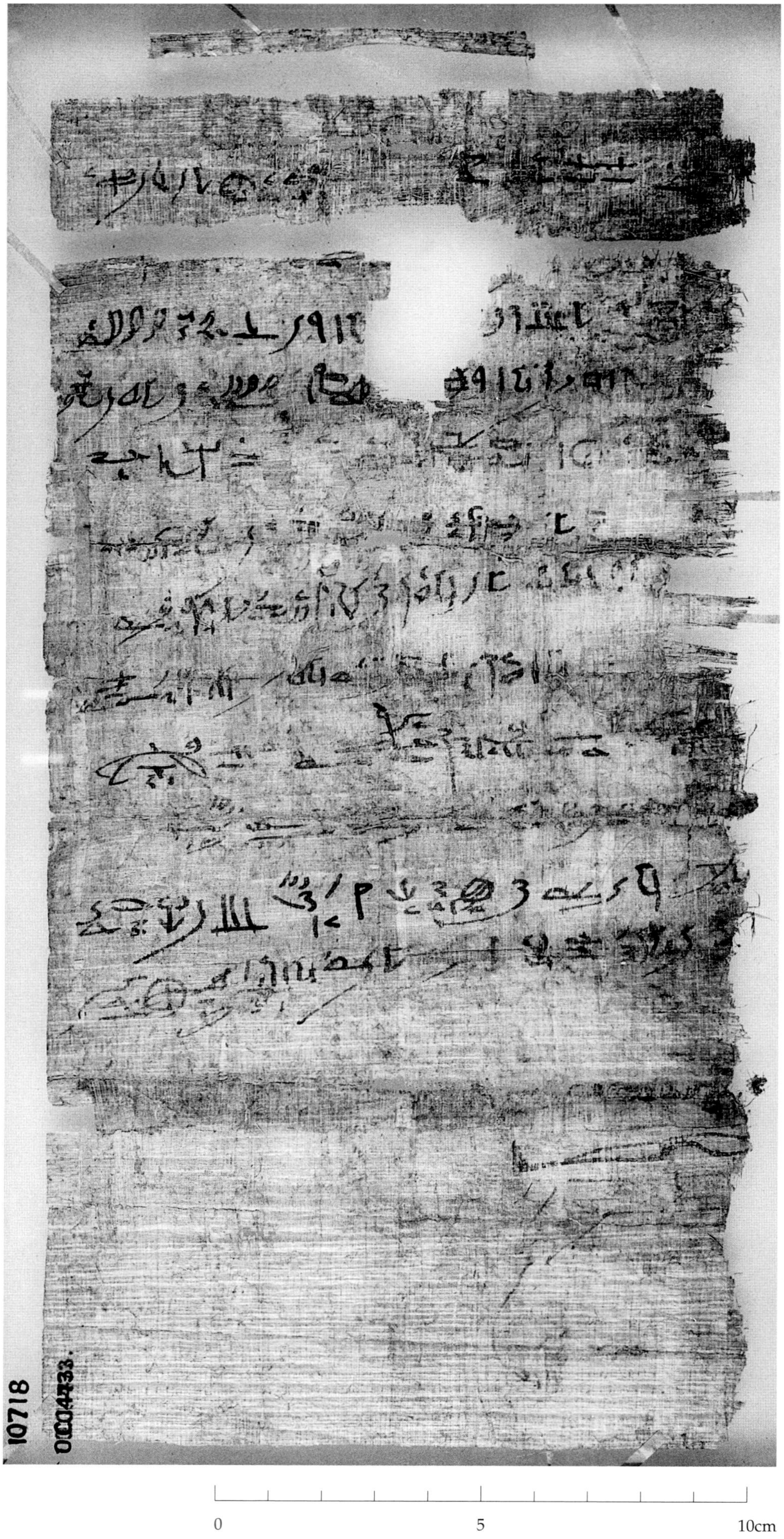

P. BM EA 10718 recto

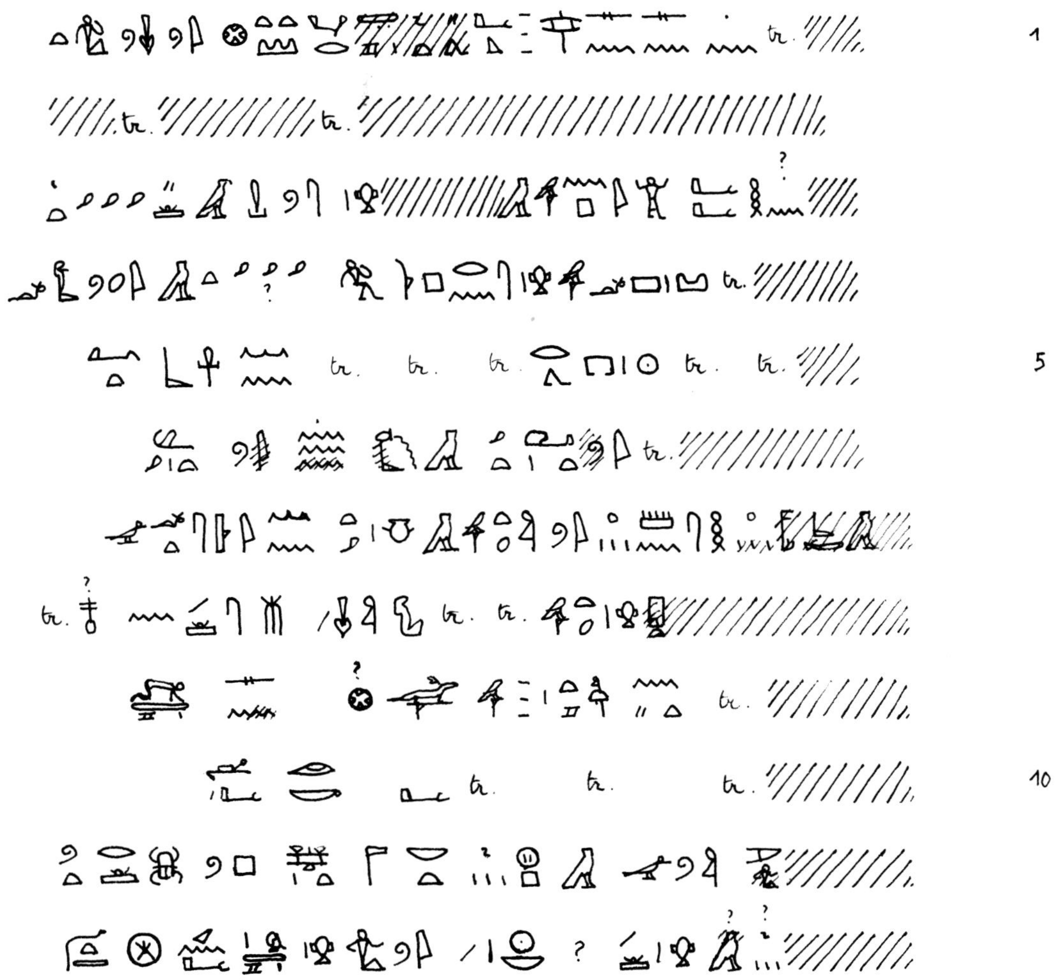

P. BM EA 10718 recto

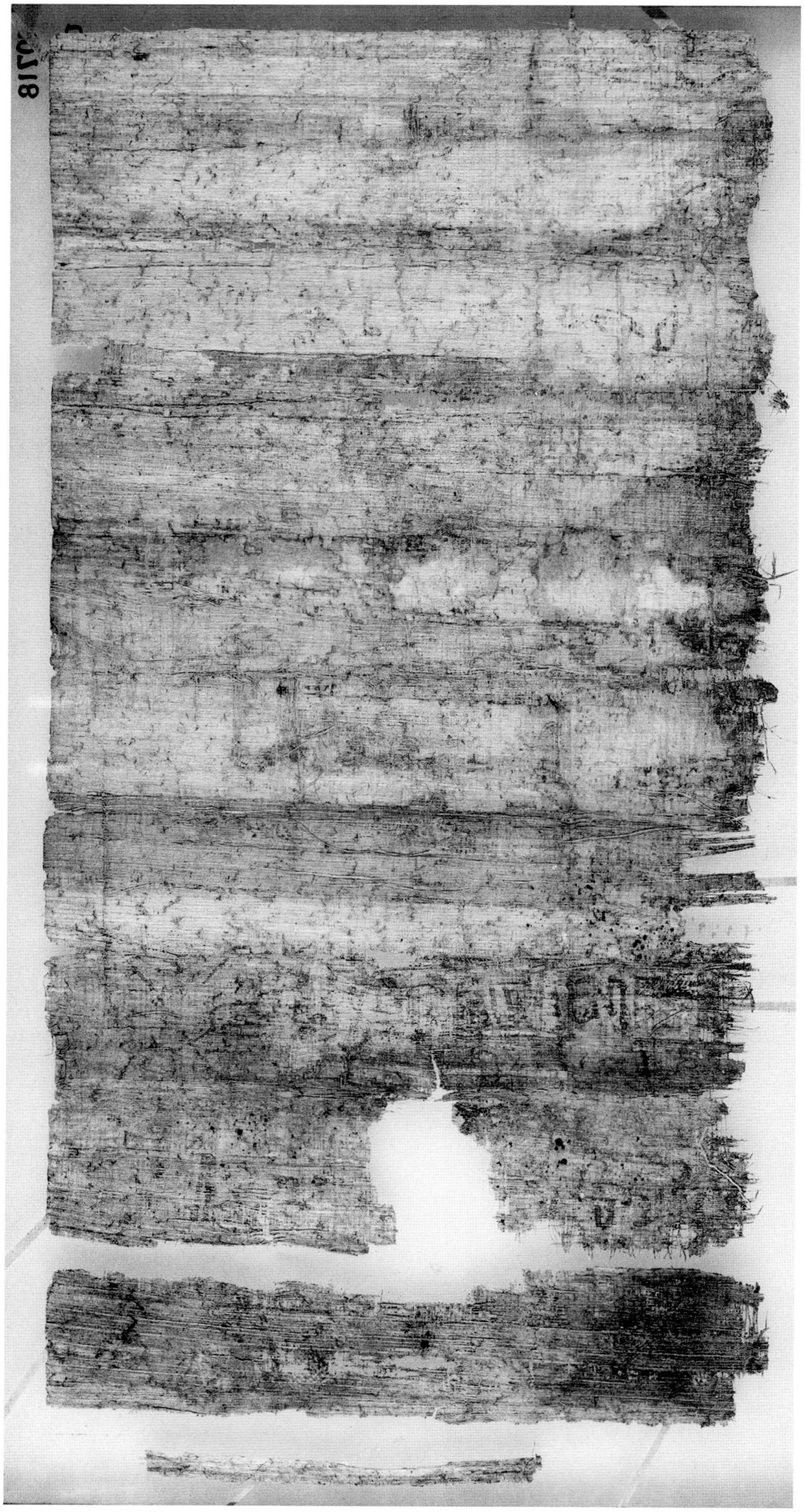

0 5 10cm

P. BM EA 10718 verso

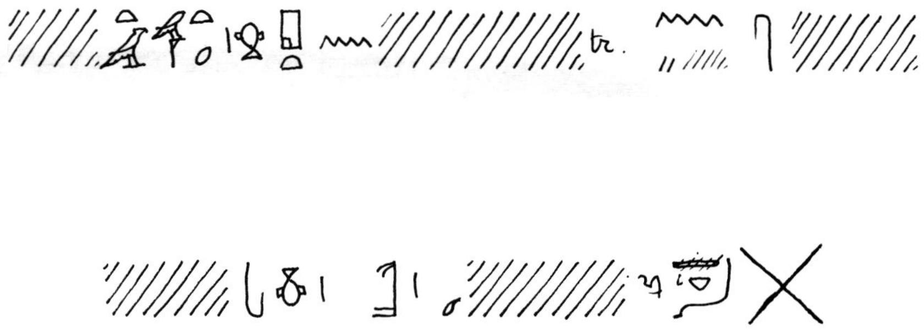

P. BM EA 10718 verso

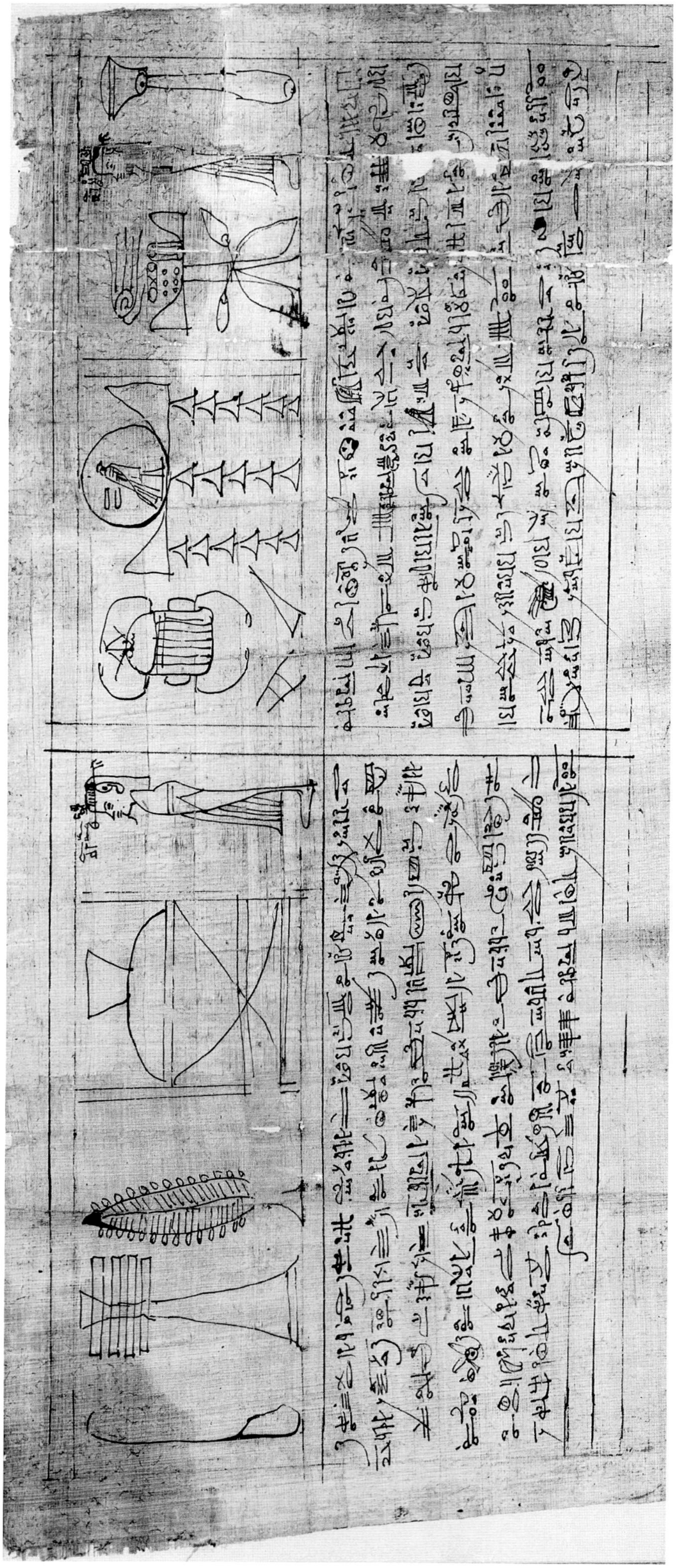

P. BM EA 10091 recto

P. BM EA 10091 verso

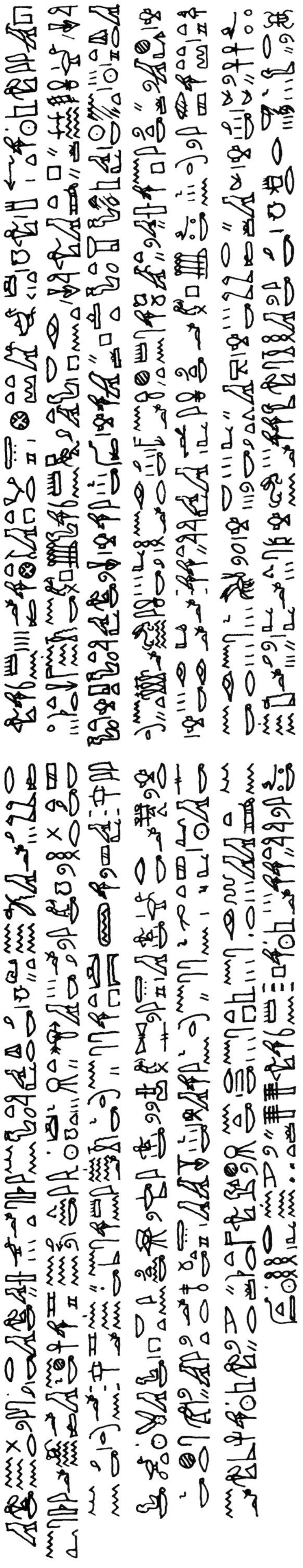

P. BM EA 10091 recto

P. BM EA 10091 verso

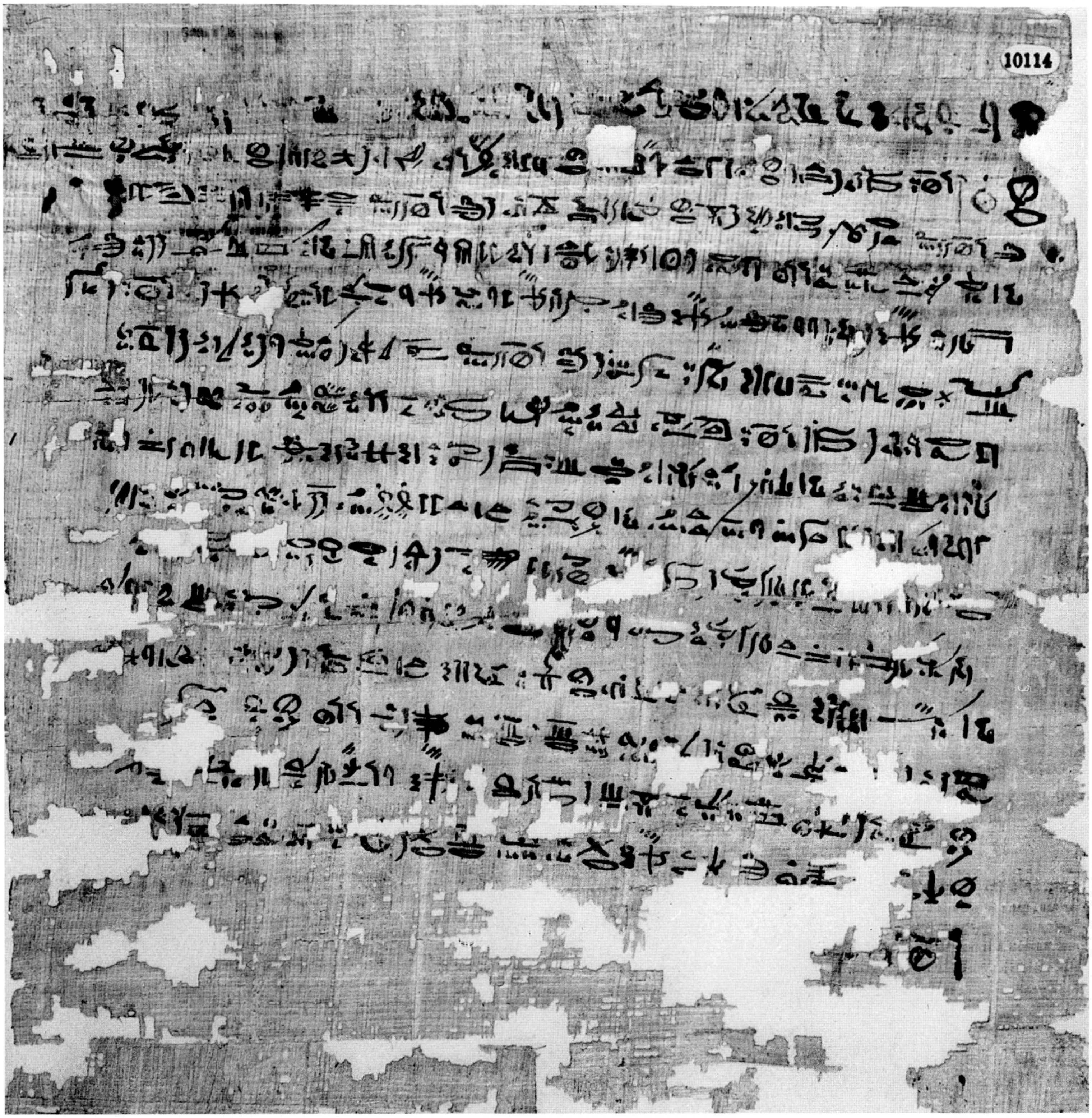

P. BM EA 10114 recto

0 5 10cm

P. BM EA 10114 verso

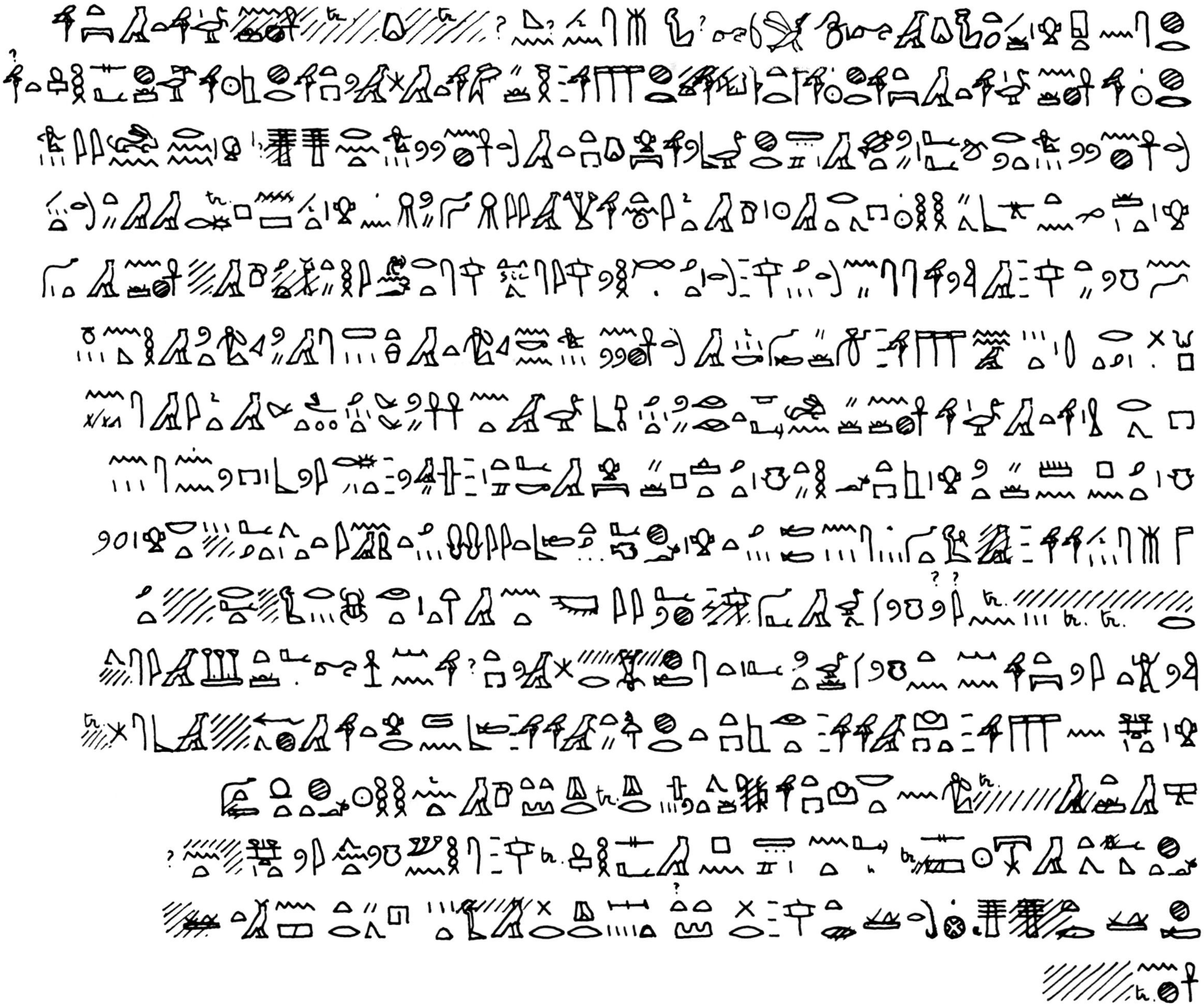

P. BM EA 10114 recto

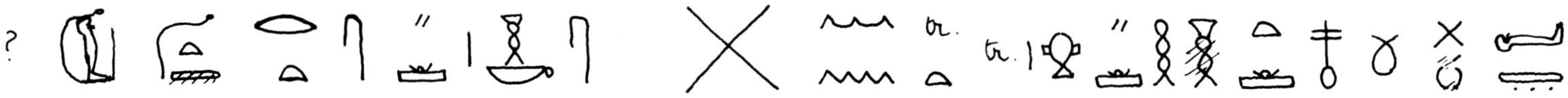

P. BM EA 10114 verso

P. BM EA 10262 + 10263 recto

0 5 10cm

P. BM EA 10262 + 10263 verso

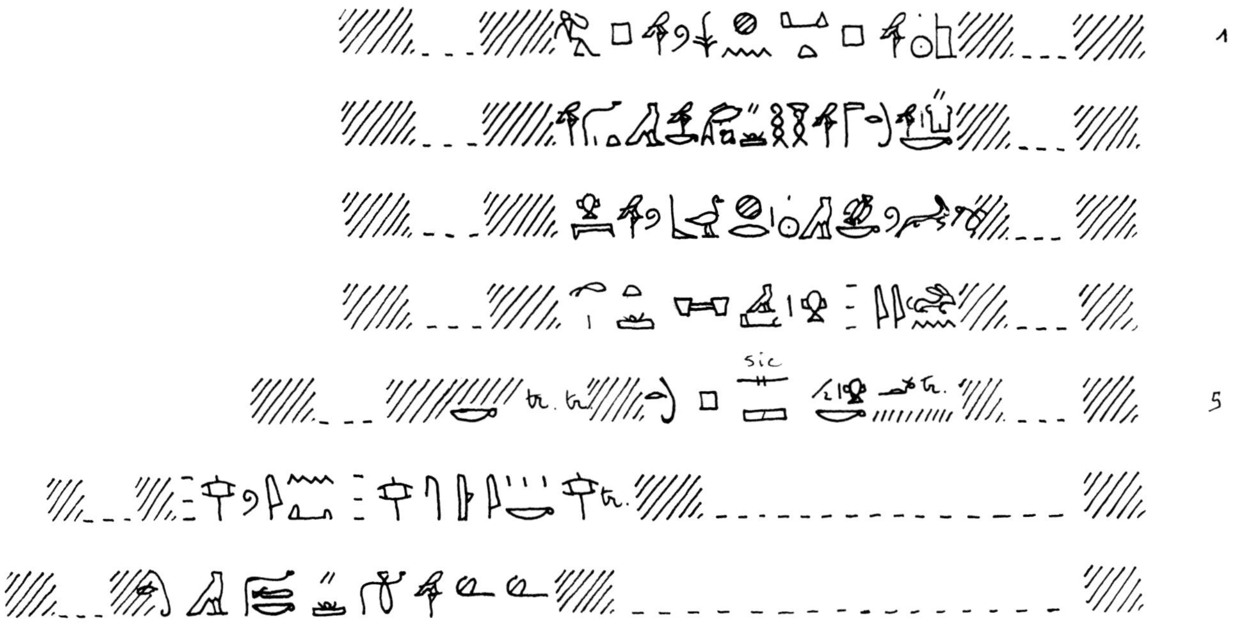

P. BM EA 10262 + 10263 recto

P. BM EA 10262 + 10263 verso

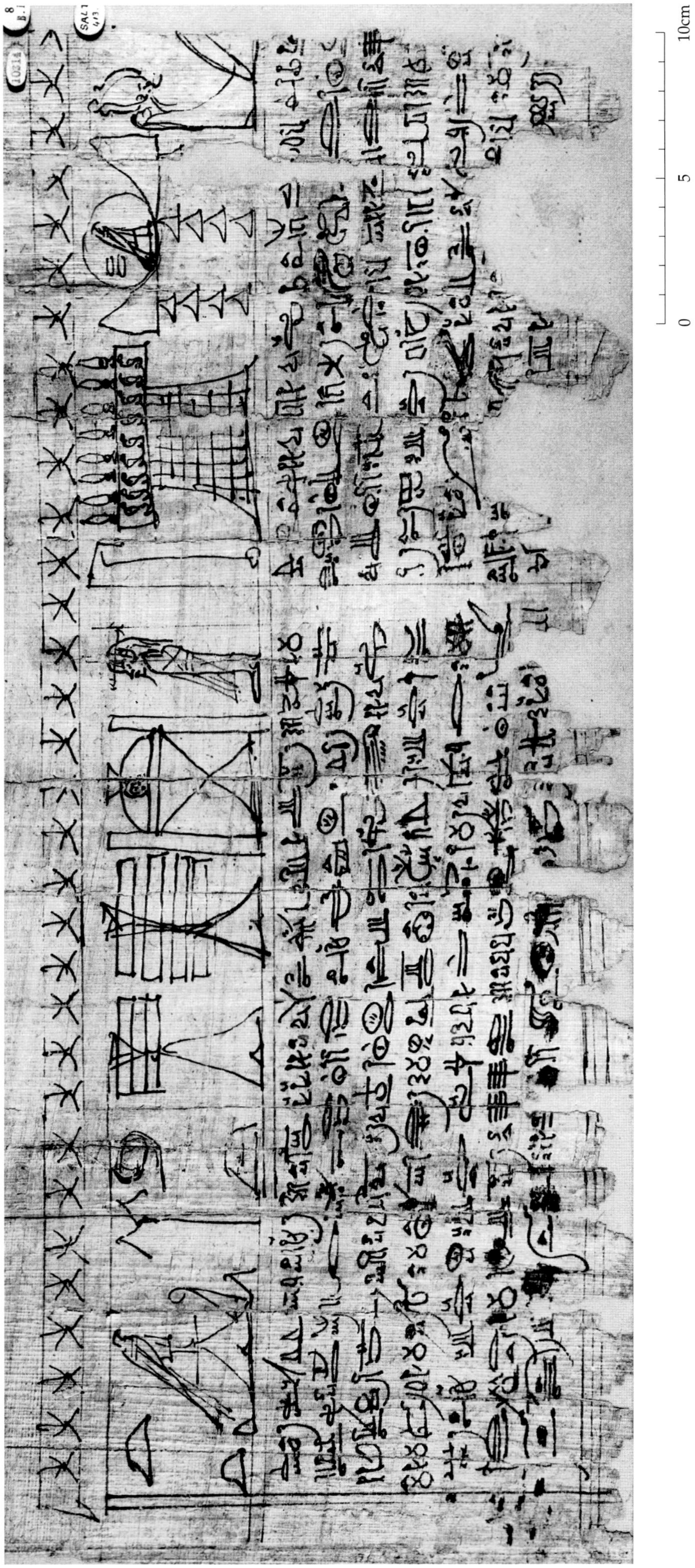

P. BM EA 10314 recto

P. BM EA 10314 recto

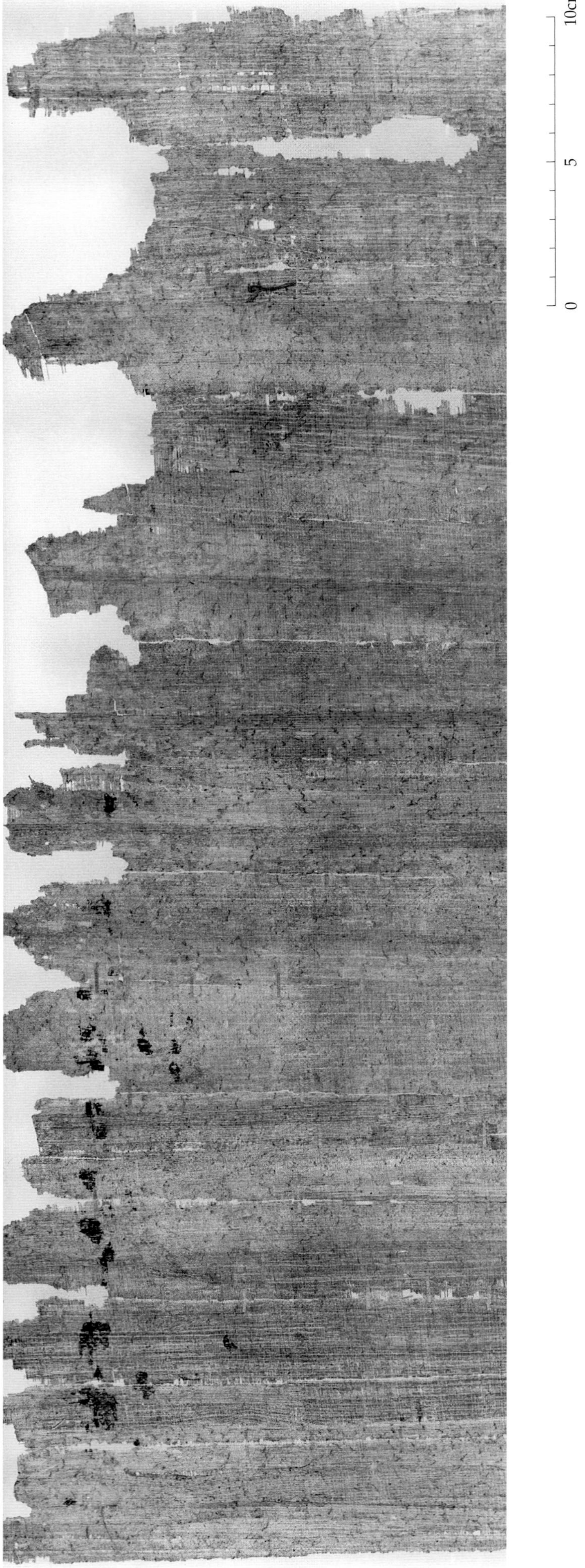

P. BM EA 10314 verso

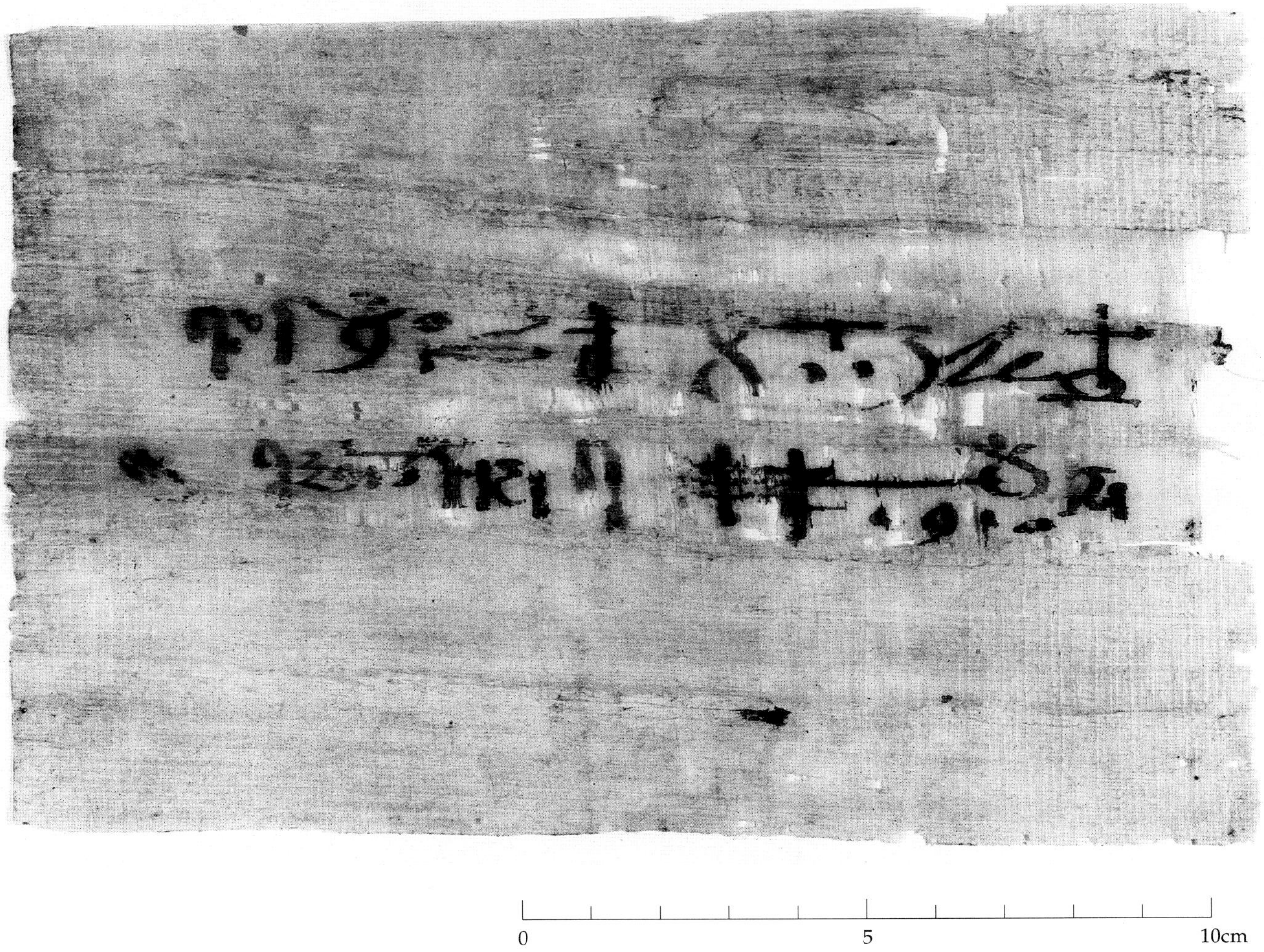

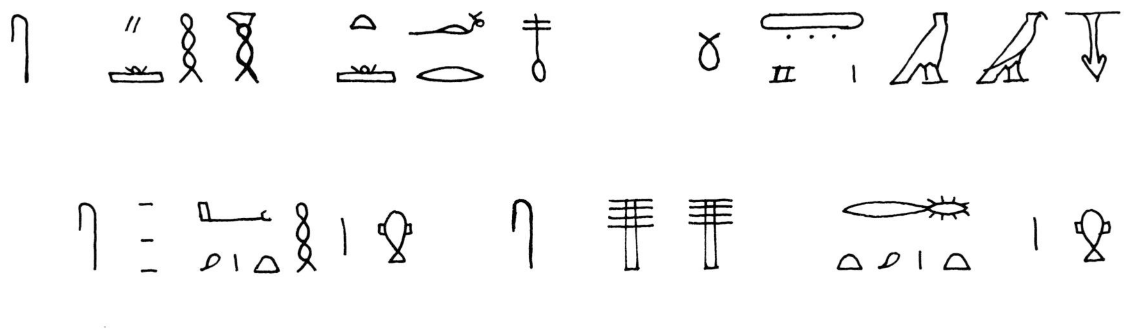

Fragment 1 = P. BM EA 10291 verso

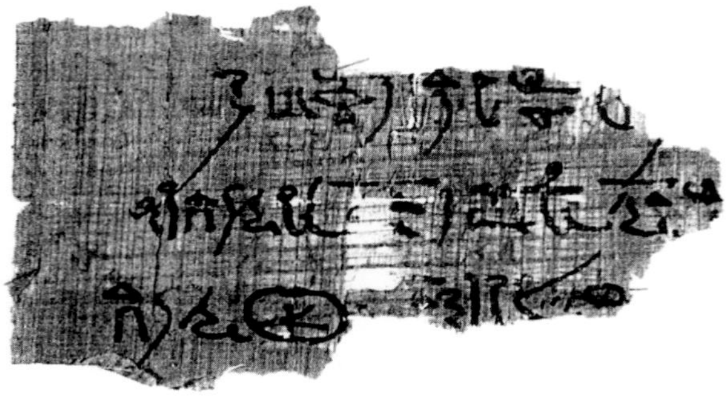

Fragment 2

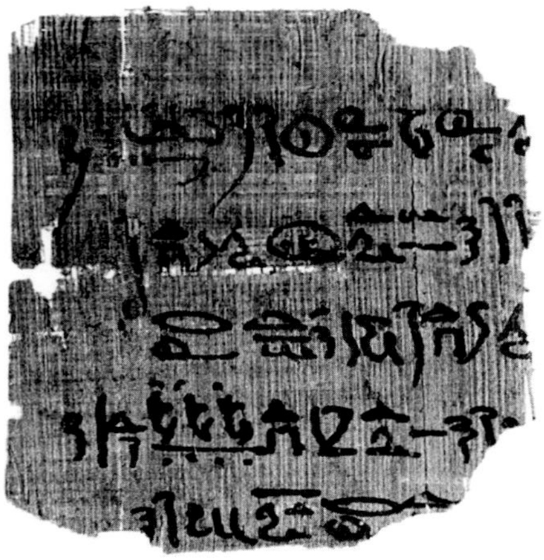

Fragment 3

0 5cm

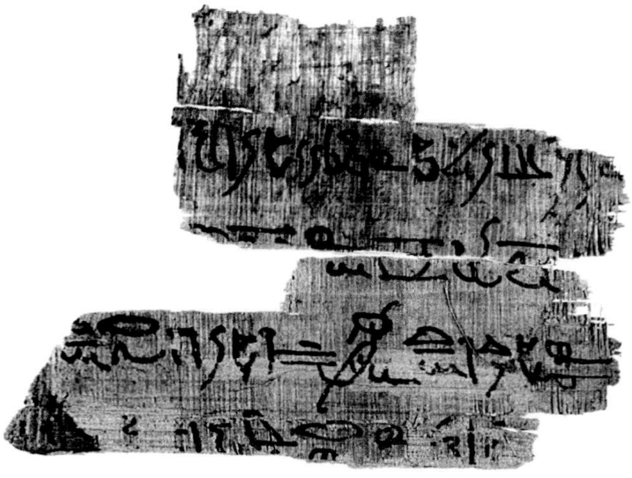

Fragment 4

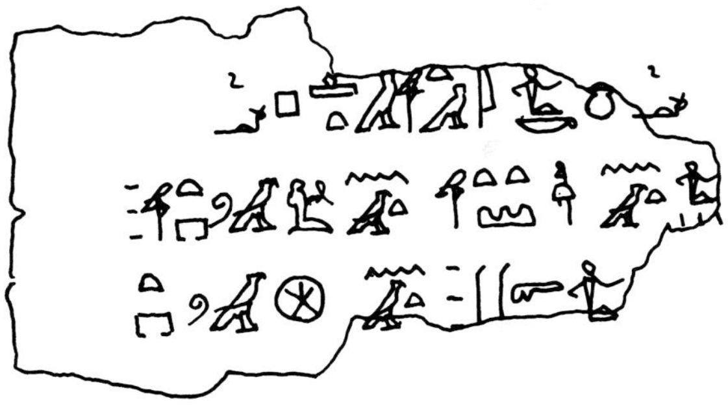

Fragment 2

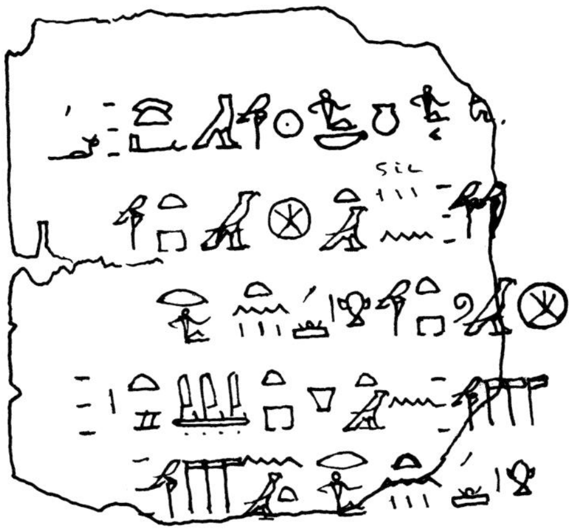

Fragment 3

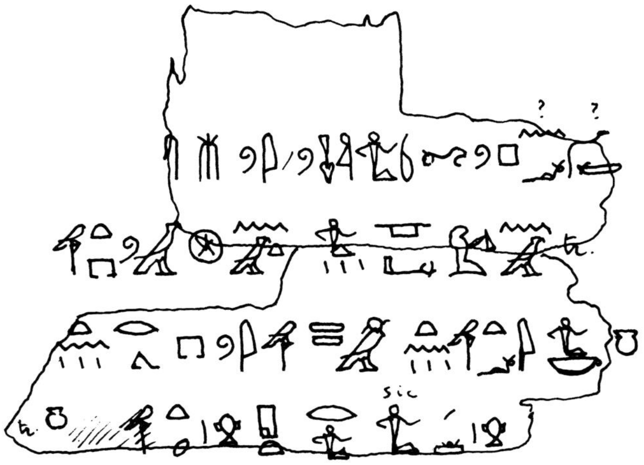

Fragment 4

Fragment 5

0 3cm

Fragment 6

0 3cm

Fragment 7

0 3cm

Fragment 8

0 3cm

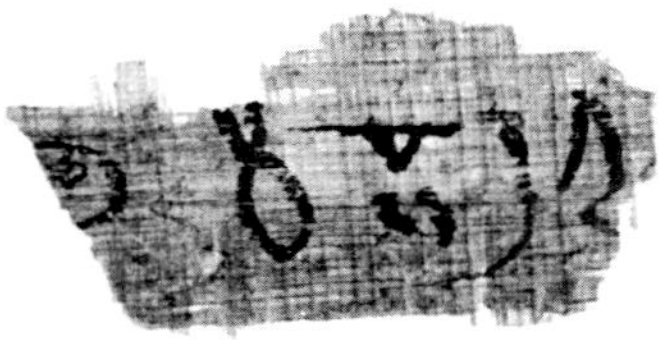

Fragment 9

0 3cm

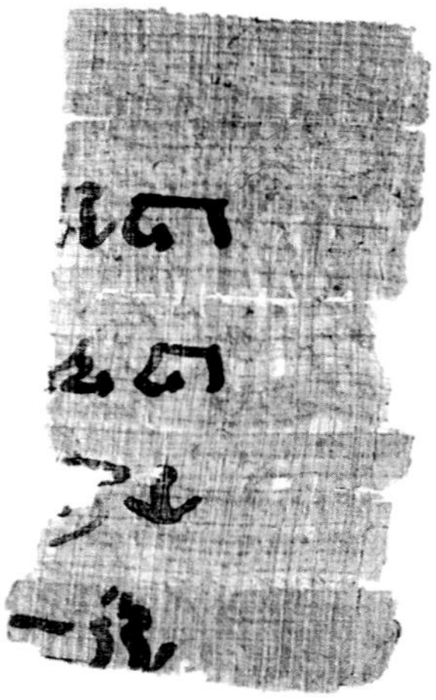

Fragment 10

Fragment 11

0 5 10cm

Fragments 5–11

Fragment 5

Fragment 6

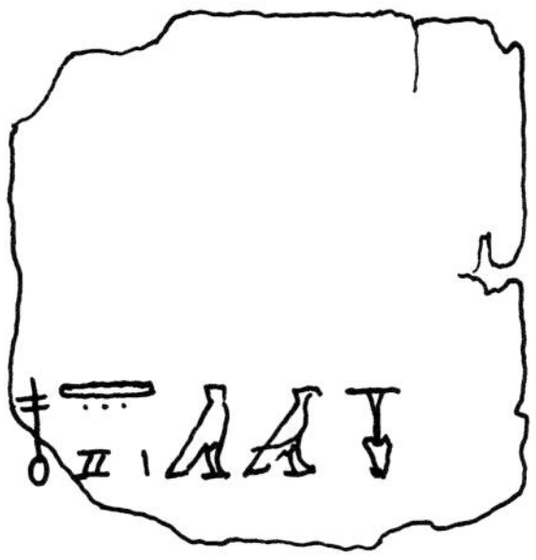

Fragment 7

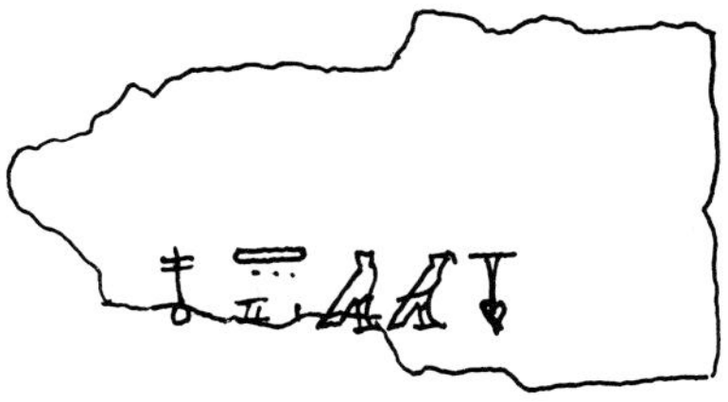

Fragment 8

Fragment 9

Fragment 10

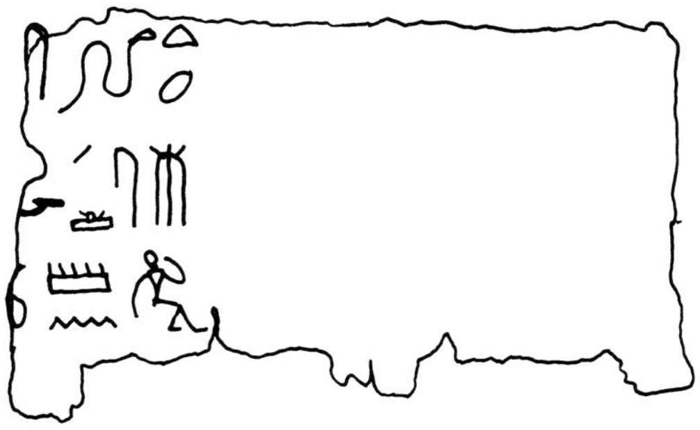

Fragment 11

Fragment 12

0 1cm

Fragment 13

0 3cm

Fragment 14

0 3cm

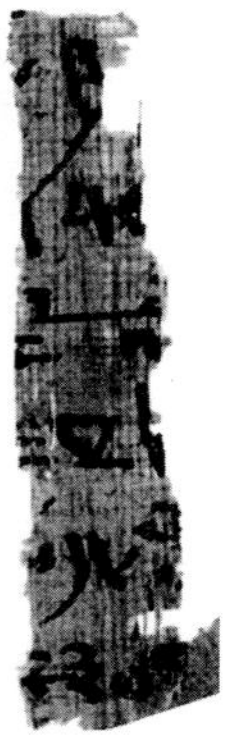

Fragment 15

Fragment 16

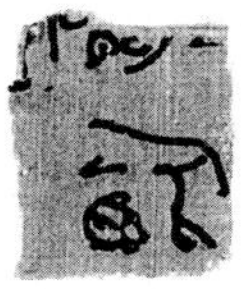

Fragment 17

0 1cm

0 5 10cm

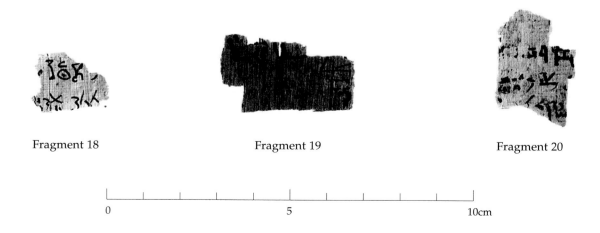

Fragment 18

Fragment 19

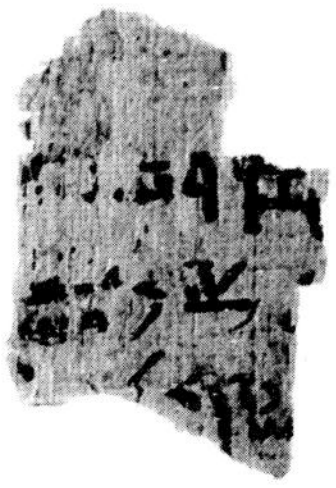

Fragment 20

0 5 10cm

Fragment 12

Fragment 13

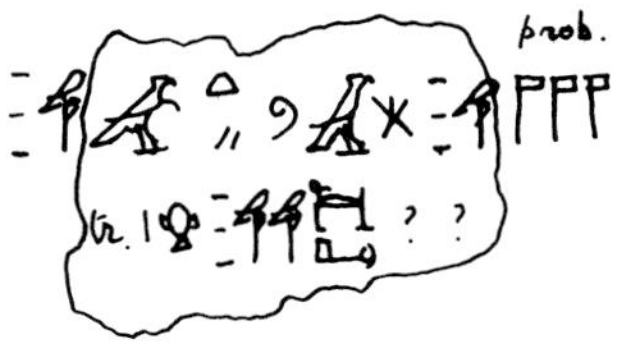

Fragment 14

Fragment 15

Fragment 16

Fragment 17

Fragment 18

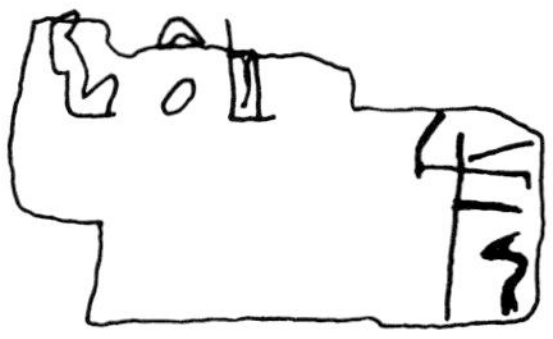

Fragment 19

Fragment 20